ton
Hull
127
rimsby
118 119
Skegness
Boston
104 105
King's
Lynn
Cromer
106 107
orough
90 91
Thetford
Norwich
92 93
Cambridge
76 77
d
78 79
Ipswich
60 61
helmsford
62 63
NDON
4 45
46 47
Maidstone
Sevenoaks
32 33
34 35
Dover
Folkestone
Hastings
nton
9 20 21

# Mileage chart

The mileage chart shows distances in miles between two towns along AA-recommended routes. Using motorways and other main roads this is normally the fastest route, though not necessarily the shortest.

The journey times, shown in hours and minutes, are average off-peak driving times along AA-recommended routes. These times should be used as a guide only and do not allow for unforeseen traffic delays, rest breaks or fuel stops.

For example, the 378 miles (608 km) journey between Glasgow and Norwich should take approximately 7 hours 28 minutes.

## Journey time

| | Aberystwyth | Barnstaple | Birmingham | Brighton | Bristol | Cambridge | Cardiff | Carlisle | Carmarthen | Dorchester | Dover | Edinburgh | Exeter | Fort William | Glasgow | Gloucester | Guildford | Hereford | Holyhead | Hull | Inverness | Kendal | Leeds | Lincoln | Liverpool | Maidstone | Manchester | Middlesbrough | Newcastle | Northampton | Norwich | Nottingham | Oxford | Penzance | Perth | Peterborough | Plymouth | Portsmouth | Preston | Salisbury | Sheffield | Shrewsbury | Southampton | Stoke-on-Trent | Stranraer | Taunton | Wick | York | LONDON |
|---|---|---|---|---|---|---|---|---|---|---|---|---|---|---|---|---|---|---|---|---|---|---|---|---|---|---|---|---|---|---|---|---|---|---|---|---|---|---|---|---|---|---|---|---|---|---|---|---|---|
| Aberdeen | 906 | 1052 | 750 | 1051 | 913 | 907 | 936 | 426 | 1020 | 1047 | 1108 | 236 | 1027 | 357 | 301 | 836 | 1007 | 850 | 843 | 735 | 240 | 517 | 655 | 753 | 636 | 1029 | 632 | 545 | 510 | 840 | 1007 | 757 | 907 | 1246 | 151 | 837 | 1114 | 1039 | 558 | 1009 | 721 | 747 | 1024 | 703 | 505 | 950 | 513 | 643 | [illegible] |
| Aberystwyth | | 436 | 249 | 538 | 301 | 431 | 229 | 444 | 115 | 432 | 612 | 647 | 412 | 901 | 624 | 251 | 443 | 158 | 234 | 436 | 959 | 359 | 345 | 430 | 244 | 533 | 304 | 456 | 527 | 340 | 554 | 339 | 354 | 631 | 720 | 419 | 459 | 455 | 317 | 412 | 350 | 154 | 439 | 252 | 713 | 335 | 1231 | 410 | [illegible] |
| Barnstaple | | | 326 | 423 | 200 | 501 | 234 | 629 | 335 | 206 | 513 | 832 | 115 | 1047 | 810 | 227 | 339 | 303 | 636 | 547 | 1144 | 544 | 529 | 507 | 456 | 434 | 448 | 628 | 700 | 409 | 624 | 422 | 319 | 233 | 906 | 452 | 145 | 324 | 503 | 232 | 500 | 403 | 307 | 400 | 858 | 109 | 1417 | 543 | [illegible] |
| Birmingham | | | | 310 | 147 | 154 | 210 | 327 | 311 | 321 | 334 | 530 | 301 | 745 | 507 | 110 | 226 | 125 | 334 | 233 | 842 | 242 | 216 | 157 | 153 | 255 | 146 | 315 | 346 | 102 | 316 | 108 | 126 | 520 | 604 | 142 | 348 | 258 | 200 | 243 | 146 | 101 | 243 | 058 | 556 | 224 | 1115 | 229 | [illegible] |
| Brighton | | | | | 301 | 213 | 336 | 628 | 436 | 232 | 154 | 831 | 351 | 1045 | 808 | 301 | 102 | 348 | 635 | 451 | 1143 | 543 | 436 | 353 | 454 | 116 | 447 | 535 | 606 | 223 | 320 | 329 | 200 | 610 | 905 | 248 | 438 | 109 | 501 | 151 | 406 | 402 | 127 | 359 | 857 | 319 | 1416 | 449 | [illegible] |
| Bristol | | | | | | 315 | 059 | 451 | 159 | 144 | 337 | 654 | 134 | 908 | 631 | 048 | 206 | 124 | 457 | 408 | 1005 | 405 | 351 | 328 | 317 | 258 | 310 | 450 | 521 | 224 | 439 | 243 | 134 | 353 | 727 | 313 | 221 | 217 | 324 | 128 | 321 | 224 | 202 | 221 | 720 | 057 | 1238 | 404 | [illegible] |
| Cambridge | | | | | | | 347 | 448 | 448 | 345 | 210 | 637 | 438 | 906 | 628 | 247 | 200 | 302 | 516 | 248 | 1003 | 422 | 242 | 149 | 336 | 131 | 319 | 335 | 407 | 112 | 135 | 144 | 201 | 657 | 721 | 044 | 525 | 252 | 342 | 254 | 221 | 243 | 244 | 240 | 717 | 401 | 1236 | 250 | [illegible] |
| Cardiff | | | | | | | | 514 | 116 | 230 | 413 | 717 | 210 | 931 | 654 | 117 | 241 | 117 | 455 | 431 | 1029 | 429 | 414 | 351 | 340 | 334 | 333 | 513 | 544 | 257 | 511 | 307 | 210 | 429 | 751 | 337 | 257 | 253 | 347 | 210 | 345 | 239 | 237 | 245 | 743 | 133 | 1302 | 428 | [illegible] |
| Carlisle | | | | | | | | | 558 | 625 | 649 | 207 | 605 | 422 | 145 | 414 | 545 | 429 | 421 | 316 | 519 | 056 | 237 | 334 | 214 | 610 | 210 | 200 | 125 | 418 | 549 | 338 | 445 | 824 | 241 | 418 | 652 | 618 | 136 | 547 | 300 | 326 | 602 | 241 | 233 | 528 | 752 | 225 | [illegible] |
| Carmarthen | | | | | | | | | | 330 | 513 | 756 | 310 | 1011 | 734 | 217 | 341 | 200 | 349 | 531 | 1108 | 508 | 454 | 451 | 359 | 434 | 414 | 605 | 637 | 357 | 611 | 407 | 310 | 529 | 830 | 436 | 357 | 353 | 427 | 310 | 444 | 249 | 337 | 344 | 822 | 233 | 1341 | 520 | [illegible] |
| Dorchester | | | | | | | | | | | 345 | 828 | 123 | 1042 | 805 | 222 | 208 | 258 | 631 | 542 | 1139 | 539 | 525 | 454 | 451 | 306 | 444 | 624 | 655 | 315 | 503 | 417 | 222 | 342 | 901 | 356 | 210 | 135 | 458 | 102 | 455 | 358 | 118 | 355 | 854 | 104 | 1412 | 538 | [illegible] |
| Dover | | | | | | | | | | | | 838 | 445 | 1106 | 829 | 337 | 145 | 424 | 656 | 449 | 1204 | 604 | 442 | 350 | 515 | 046 | 508 | 536 | 607 | 241 | 318 | 345 | 236 | 704 | 922 | 245 | 532 | 238 | 522 | 254 | 422 | 423 | 244 | 420 | 918 | 411 | 1436 | 450 | [illegible] |
| Edinburgh | | | | | | | | | | | | | 807 | 311 | 057 | 616 | 747 | 630 | 623 | 505 | 332 | 257 | 426 | 523 | 416 | 759 | 412 | 315 | 240 | 620 | 738 | 527 | 647 | 1026 | 049 | 607 | 854 | 819 | 338 | 749 | 455 | 527 | 804 | 442 | 301 | 730 | 605 | 414 | [illegible] |
| Exeter | | | | | | | | | | | | | | 1022 | 745 | 202 | 311 | 238 | 611 | 522 | 1119 | 519 | 504 | 442 | 431 | 406 | 423 | 603 | 635 | 344 | 559 | 357 | 254 | 225 | 841 | 427 | 057 | 254 | 438 | 203 | 435 | 338 | 237 | 335 | 833 | 044 | 1352 | 518 | [illegible] |
| Fort William | | | | | | | | | | | | | | | 242 | 831 | 1002 | 845 | 838 | 733 | 140 | 512 | 653 | 751 | 631 | 1027 | 627 | 615 | 541 | 835 | 1005 | 754 | 902 | 1241 | 234 | 835 | 1109 | 1034 | 552 | 1004 | 716 | 742 | 1019 | 657 | 441 | 945 | 413 | 641 | [illegible] |
| Glasgow | | | | | | | | | | | | | | | | 554 | 725 | 609 | 601 | 456 | 353 | 235 | 417 | 514 | 354 | 750 | 350 | 340 | 305 | 558 | 728 | 518 | 625 | 1004 | 115 | 558 | 832 | 757 | 316 | 727 | 440 | 506 | 742 | 421 | 207 | 708 | 625 | 404 | [illegible] |
| Gloucester | | | | | | | | | | | | | | | | | 208 | 053 | 420 | 331 | 928 | 328 | 314 | 251 | 240 | 258 | 232 | 413 | 444 | 155 | 410 | 206 | 110 | 421 | 650 | 236 | 249 | 219 | 247 | 147 | 244 | 147 | 204 | 144 | 643 | 125 | 1201 | 327 | [illegible] |
| Guildford | | | | | | | | | | | | | | | | | | 254 | 551 | 410 | 1059 | 459 | 352 | 314 | 410 | 106 | 403 | 451 | 523 | 139 | 310 | 245 | 116 | 530 | 821 | 210 | 358 | 058 | 418 | 120 | 323 | 318 | 106 | 315 | 813 | 238 | 1332 | 406 | [illegible] |
| Hereford | | | | | | | | | | | | | | | | | | | 353 | 345 | 943 | 343 | 328 | 305 | 254 | 345 | 247 | 427 | 458 | 211 | 425 | 221 | 156 | 457 | 704 | 251 | 325 | 306 | 301 | 233 | 258 | 122 | 250 | 159 | 657 | 201 | 1215 | 341 | [illegible] |
| Holyhead | | | | | | | | | | | | | | | | | | | | 412 | 935 | 335 | 321 | 426 | 221 | 617 | 241 | 432 | 503 | 424 | 638 | 351 | 451 | 830 | 657 | 457 | 658 | 623 | 254 | 553 | 327 | 239 | 608 | 247 | 649 | 534 | 1208 | 347 | [illegible] |
| Hull | | | | | | | | | | | | | | | | | | | | | 831 | 249 | 109 | 105 | 217 | 410 | 148 | 200 | 234 | 239 | 332 | 143 | 326 | 740 | 549 | 219 | 608 | 458 | 209 | 447 | 115 | 312 | 443 | 229 | 545 | 444 | 1103 | 058 | [illegible] |
| Inverness | | | | | | | | | | | | | | | | | | | | | | 609 | 751 | 848 | 728 | 1124 | 724 | 642 | 607 | 932 | 1102 | 852 | 959 | 1338 | 243 | 932 | 1206 | 1131 | 650 | 1101 | 814 | 840 | 1116 | 755 | 556 | 1042 | 237 | 738 | [illegible] |
| Kendal | | | | | | | | | | | | | | | | | | | | | | | 158 | 308 | 129 | 526 | 125 | 149 | 205 | 333 | 522 | 300 | 400 | 739 | 332 | 352 | 607 | 532 | 050 | 502 | 214 | 240 | 517 | 155 | 324 | 443 | 843 | 209 | [illegible] |
| Leeds | | | | | | | | | | | | | | | | | | | | | | | | 129 | 124 | 405 | 054 | 124 | 155 | 223 | 343 | 127 | 310 | 722 | 510 | 213 | 550 | 442 | 116 | 431 | 048 | 224 | 427 | 139 | 506 | 426 | 1024 | 040 | [illegible] |
| Lincoln | | | | | | | | | | | | | | | | | | | | | | | | | 236 | 311 | 205 | 221 | 253 | 151 | 227 | 057 | 238 | 701 | 607 | 117 | 529 | 407 | 228 | 359 | 108 | 242 | 355 | 200 | 603 | 405 | 1122 | 136 | [illegible] |
| Liverpool | | | | | | | | | | | | | | | | | | | | | | | | | | 437 | 046 | 237 | 308 | 244 | 450 | 211 | 311 | 650 | 450 | 317 | 518 | 444 | 047 | 413 | 142 | 137 | 428 | 107 | 443 | 354 | 1001 | 152 | [illegible] |
| Maidstone | | | | | | | | | | | | | | | | | | | | | | | | | | | 429 | 457 | 528 | 201 | 239 | 306 | 157 | 625 | 843 | 206 | 453 | 159 | 443 | 215 | 343 | 343 | 205 | 341 | 839 | 332 | 1357 | 411 | [illegible] |
| Manchester | | | | | | | | | | | | | | | | | | | | | | | | | | | | 208 | 239 | 236 | 419 | 146 | 304 | 642 | 446 | 249 | 510 | 436 | 045 | 405 | 106 | 144 | 420 | 059 | 439 | 346 | 957 | 122 | [illegible] |
| Middlesbrough | | | | | | | | | | | | | | | | | | | | | | | | | | | | | 048 | 321 | 436 | 225 | 408 | 822 | 359 | 306 | 650 | 540 | 226 | 529 | 153 | 338 | 525 | 253 | 429 | 526 | 914 | 109 | [illegible] |
| Newcastle | | | | | | | | | | | | | | | | | | | | | | | | | | | | | | 351 | 506 | 256 | 438 | 853 | 324 | 336 | 721 | 611 | 244 | 559 | 223 | 408 | 555 | 323 | 354 | 557 | 839 | 142 | [illegible] |
| Northampton | | | | | | | | | | | | | | | | | | | | | | | | | | | | | | | 234 | 114 | 058 | 604 | 653 | 100 | 432 | 231 | 250 | 219 | 152 | 150 | 215 | 147 | 646 | 308 | 1204 | 235 | [illegible] |
| Norwich | | | | | | | | | | | | | | | | | | | | | | | | | | | | | | | | 253 | 324 | 820 | 823 | 154 | 648 | 400 | 444 | 413 | 324 | 406 | 403 | 355 | 820 | 524 | 1338 | 352 | [illegible] |
| Nottingham | | | | | | | | | | | | | | | | | | | | | | | | | | | | | | | | | 201 | 615 | 611 | 115 | 443 | 333 | 218 | 322 | 056 | 151 | 318 | 108 | 607 | 319 | 1125 | 139 | [illegible] |
| Oxford | | | | | | | | | | | | | | | | | | | | | | | | | | | | | | | | | | 514 | 721 | 152 | 342 | 136 | 318 | 125 | 238 | 218 | 120 | 215 | 714 | 217 | 1232 | 321 | [illegible] |
| Penzance | | | | | | | | | | | | | | | | | | | | | | | | | | | | | | | | | | | 1100 | 646 | 148 | 514 | 657 | 423 | 654 | 557 | 457 | 554 | 1053 | 303 | 1611 | 737 | [illegible] |
| Perth | | | | | | | | | | | | | | | | | | | | | | | | | | | | | | | | | | | | 652 | 928 | 853 | 412 | 823 | 535 | 601 | 838 | 517 | 318 | 804 | 516 | 458 | 809 |
| Peterborough | | | | | | | | | | | | | | | | | | | | | | | | | | | | | | | | | | | | | 514 | 303 | 313 | 306 | 152 | 232 | 255 | 214 | 648 | 350 | 1206 | 221 | [illegible] |
| Plymouth | | | | | | | | | | | | | | | | | | | | | | | | | | | | | | | | | | | | | | 341 | 525 | 250 | 522 | 425 | 324 | 422 | 920 | 131 | 1439 | 605 | 425 |
| Portsmouth | | | | | | | | | | | | | | | | | | | | | | | | | | | | | | | | | | | | | | | 450 | 054 | 410 | 350 | 030 | 347 | 846 | 222 | 1404 | 453 | 145 |
| Preston | | | | | | | | | | | | | | | | | | | | | | | | | | | | | | | | | | | | | | | | 420 | 134 | 159 | 435 | 114 | 405 | 401 | 923 | 144 | 406 |
| Salisbury | | | | | | | | | | | | | | | | | | | | | | | | | | | | | | | | | | | | | | | | | 359 | 320 | 037 | 317 | 816 | 130 | 1334 | 442 | 150 |
| Sheffield | | | | | | | | | | | | | | | | | | | | | | | | | | | | | | | | | | | | | | | | | | 224 | 356 | 124 | 529 | 357 | 1047 | 107 | 307 |
| Shrewsbury | | | | | | | | | | | | | | | | | | | | | | | | | | | | | | | | | | | | | | | | | | | 335 | 102 | 554 | 301 | 1112 | 251 | 306 |
| Southampton | | | | | | | | | | | | | | | | | | | | | | | | | | | | | | | | | | | | | | | | | | | | 332 | 830 | 205 | 1349 | 437 | 140 |
| Stoke-on-Trent | | | | | | | | | | | | | | | | | | | | | | | | | | | | | | | | | | | | | | | | | | | | | 509 | 258 | 1028 | 206 | 302 |
| Stranraer | | | | | | | | | | | | | | | | | | | | | | | | | | | | | | | | | | | | | | | | | | | | | | 757 | 829 | 453 | 802 |
| Taunton | | | | | | | | | | | | | | | | | | | | | | | | | | | | | | | | | | | | | | | | | | | | | | | 1315 | 441 | 301 |
| Wick | | | | | | | | | | | | | | | | | | | | | | | | | | | | | | | | | | | | | | | | | | | | | | | | 1011 | 1320 |
| York | | | | | | | | | | | | | | | | | | | | | | | | | | | | | | | | | | | | | | | | | | | | | | | | | 352 |

| | Aberdeen | Aberystwyth | Barnstaple | Birmingham | Brighton | Bristol | Cambridge | Cardiff | Carlisle | Carmarthen | Dorchester | Dover | Edinburgh | Exeter | Fort William | Glasgow | Gloucester | Guildford | Hereford | Holyhead | Hull | Inverness | Kendal | Leeds | Lincoln | Liverpool | Maidstone | Manchester | Middlesbrough | Newcastle | Northampton | Norwich | Nottingham | Oxford | Penzance | Perth | Peterborough | Plymouth | Portsmouth | Preston | Salisbury | Sheffield | Shrewsbury | Southampton | Stoke-on-Trent | Stranraer | Taunton | Wick | York |
|---|---|---|---|---|---|---|---|---|---|---|---|---|---|---|---|---|---|---|---|---|---|---|---|---|---|---|---|---|---|---|---|---|---|---|---|---|---|---|---|---|---|---|---|---|---|---|---|---|---|
| Aberystwyth | 472 |
| Barnstaple | 608 | 214 |
| Birmingham | 436 | 124 | 180 |
| Brighton | 613 | 288 | 210 | 171 |
| Bristol | 518 | 130 | 100 | 90 | 169 |
| Cambridge | 463 | 215 | 267 | 97 | 120 | 170 |
| Cardiff | 537 | 111 | 128 | 109 | 202 | 44 | 203 |
| Carlisle | 236 | 236 | 371 | 199 | 376 | 281 | 256 | 300 |
| Carmarthen | 520 | 48 | 190 | 172 | 264 | 107 | 266 | 68 | 284 |
| Dorchester | 600 | 206 | 94 | 172 | 119 | 62 | 184 | 120 | 364 | 182 |
| Dover | 587 | 326 | 272 | 208 | 82 | 205 | 124 | 239 | 381 | 301 | 200 |
| Edinburgh | 126 | 336 | 471 | 299 | 476 | 381 | 333 | 400 | 100 | 386 | 463 | 458 |
| Exeter | 593 | 198 | 44 | 165 | 178 | 84 | 259 | 113 | 356 | 175 | 57 | 248 | 455 |
| Fort William | 156 | 435 | 570 | 398 | 576 | 480 | 456 | 499 | 199 | 485 | 562 | 580 | 137 | 554 |
| Glasgow | 150 | 332 | 467 | 295 | 472 | 377 | 353 | 396 | 96 | 382 | 459 | 477 | 47 | 451 | 102 |
| Gloucester | 484 | 113 | 126 | 56 | 155 | 36 | 150 | 63 | 248 | 125 | 118 | 192 | 346 | 110 | 445 | 343 |
| Guildford | 571 | 224 | 175 | 128 | 44 | 106 | 96 | 139 | 335 | 201 | 97 | 97 | 433 | 150 | 532 | 430 | 99 |
| Hereford | 487 | 79 | 144 | 59 | 189 | 54 | 153 | 59 | 250 | 85 | 136 | 225 | 349 | 129 | 448 | 346 | 34 | 133 |
| Holyhead | 464 | 102 | 339 | 167 | 345 | 249 | 259 | 202 | 228 | 150 | 331 | 369 | 326 | 323 | 425 | 323 | 215 | 302 | 156 |
| Hull | 376 | 227 | 320 | 139 | 258 | 230 | 138 | 250 | 170 | 311 | 312 | 262 | 247 | 304 | 367 | 266 | 196 | 239 | 198 | 218 |
| Inverness | 106 | 496 | 631 | 459 | 637 | 541 | 517 | 561 | 260 | 546 | 623 | 641 | 157 | 616 | 66 | 176 | 507 | 595 | 510 | 488 | 430 |
| Kendal | 283 | 189 | 324 | 153 | 330 | 234 | 251 | 254 | 47 | 240 | 316 | 354 | 145 | 309 | 245 | 143 | 200 | 288 | 203 | 181 | 164 | 307 |
| Leeds | 329 | 173 | 301 | 120 | 262 | 211 | 146 | 230 | 123 | 224 | 293 | 271 | 200 | 285 | 321 | 219 | 177 | 220 | 179 | 165 | 59 | 383 | 110 |
| Lincoln | 388 | 199 | 275 | 98 | 216 | 185 | 95 | 205 | 182 | 267 | 246 | 220 | 258 | 260 | 379 | 277 | 151 | 173 | 154 | 204 | 44 | 441 | 176 | 74 |
| Liverpool | 362 | 110 | 272 | 101 | 278 | 182 | 193 | 202 | 126 | 158 | 264 | 302 | 224 | 257 | 324 | 222 | 148 | 236 | 151 | 102 | 128 | 386 | 79 | 74 | 139 |
| Maidstone | 545 | 284 | 234 | 166 | 50 | 167 | 82 | 200 | 339 | 262 | 161 | 41 | 416 | 209 | 537 | 435 | 153 | 58 | 186 | 327 | 220 | 599 | 313 | 231 | 178 | 261 |
| Manchester | 357 | 134 | 261 | 89 | 266 | 171 | 160 | 190 | 120 | 184 | 253 | 290 | 219 | 245 | 318 | 216 | 136 | 224 | 139 | 125 | 97 | 380 | 74 | 44 | 85 | 34 | 248 |
| Middlesbrough | 276 | 244 | 357 | 176 | 318 | 267 | 197 | 286 | 95 | 294 | 349 | 322 | 146 | 341 | 283 | 190 | 232 | 276 | 235 | 235 | 89 | 308 | 84 | 64 | 122 | 145 | 280 | 114 |
| Newcastle | 235 | 275 | 388 | 207 | 349 | 298 | 229 | 317 | 60 | 325 | 380 | 353 | 106 | 372 | 242 | 153 | 264 | 307 | 266 | 266 | 142 | 267 | 102 | 95 | 154 | 176 | 311 | 145 | 39 |
| Northampton | 486 | 174 | 212 | 56 | 133 | 115 | 56 | 162 | 249 | 224 | 159 | 155 | 348 | 196 | 447 | 345 | 79 | 90 | 111 | 217 | 152 | 509 | 203 | 136 | 94 | 151 | 113 | 139 | 189 | 220 |
| Norwich | 488 | 278 | 329 | 160 | 168 | 233 | 63 | 266 | 282 | 328 | 241 | 172 | 359 | 313 | 480 | 378 | 212 | 160 | 215 | 321 | 147 | 542 | 276 | 174 | 103 | 240 | 130 | 185 | 223 | 254 | 118 |
| Nottingham | 395 | 162 | 232 | 51 | 193 | 142 | 86 | 161 | 189 | 223 | 224 | 210 | 266 | 216 | 387 | 285 | 107 | 151 | 110 | 178 | 93 | 449 | 164 | 77 | 39 | 112 | 168 | 71 | 130 | 161 | 64 | 119 |
| Oxford | 510 | 160 | 170 | 68 | 109 | 73 | 82 | 107 | 274 | 169 | 115 | 146 | 373 | 154 | 472 | 370 | 48 | 67 | 81 | 242 | 190 | 534 | 228 | 174 | 132 | 176 | 107 | 164 | 227 | 258 | 44 | 146 | 102 |
| Penzance | 702 | 308 | 108 | 274 | 287 | 193 | 368 | 222 | 466 | 284 | 167 | 357 | 564 | 109 | 663 | 562 | 220 | 259 | 238 | 434 | 415 | 726 | 419 | 403 | 370 | 367 | 318 | 356 | 451 | 482 | 326 | 433 | 326 | 265 |
| Perth | 86 | 388 | 523 | 351 | 529 | 433 | 378 | 453 | 152 | 438 | 515 | 503 | 42 | 507 | 102 | 64 | 399 | 486 | 401 | 379 | 291 | 114 | 199 | 245 | 303 | 278 | 461 | 275 | 192 | 150 | 400 | 404 | 310 | 426 | 617 |
| Peterborough | 435 | 204 | 263 | 86 | 158 | 173 | 37 | 193 | 229 | 255 | 204 | 162 | 306 | 248 | 427 | 325 | 139 | 115 | 142 | 225 | 110 | 489 | 223 | 121 | 51 | 159 | 120 | 132 | 170 | 201 | 45 | 78 | 58 | 86 | 357 | 351 |
| Plymouth | 633 | 239 | 62 | 205 | 218 | 124 | 299 | 153 | 397 | 215 | 98 | 288 | 495 | 44 | 594 | 493 | 151 | 190 | 169 | 365 | 346 | 657 | 350 | 334 | 301 | 298 | 249 | 287 | 382 | 413 | 257 | 364 | 257 | 196 | 78 | 544 | 288 |
| Portsmouth | 596 | 244 | 162 | 154 | 53 | 125 | 137 | 158 | 360 | 220 | 73 | 141 | 458 | 132 | 558 | 456 | 118 | 45 | 152 | 328 | 276 | 620 | 314 | 260 | 215 | 262 | 102 | 250 | 313 | 344 | 130 | 204 | 188 | 85 | 241 | 508 | 157 | 172 |
| Preston | 326 | 146 | 281 | 110 | 287 | 191 | 209 | 211 | 89 | 197 | 273 | 311 | 188 | 266 | 287 | 185 | 157 | 245 | 160 | 138 | 122 | 349 | 43 | 69 | 134 | 36 | 269 | 35 | 103 | 139 | 159 | 235 | 121 | 184 | 375 | 237 | 180 | 306 | 270 |
| Salisbury | 549 | 184 | 118 | 121 | 90 | 52 | 145 | 98 | 313 | 160 | 39 | 160 | 411 | 93 | 511 | 409 | 72 | 62 | 105 | 281 | 261 | 573 | 267 | 244 | 202 | 215 | 121 | 203 | 298 | 329 | 115 | 212 | 173 | 70 | 203 | 461 | 165 | 134 | 44 | 223 |
| Sheffield | 397 | 166 | 272 | 91 | 233 | 182 | 122 | 201 | 161 | 263 | 264 | 247 | 236 | 256 | 359 | 257 | 148 | 191 | 150 | 157 | 66 | 421 | 115 | 38 | 47 | 79 | 205 | 39 | 100 | 131 | 104 | 148 | 45 | 142 | 366 | 309 | 93 | 297 | 228 | 73 | 212 |
| Shrewsbury | 417 | 75 | 220 | 48 | 226 | 130 | 140 | 111 | 181 | 110 | 212 | 250 | 279 | 205 | 379 | 277 | 96 | 184 | 52 | 105 | 162 | 441 | 135 | 119 | 124 | 65 | 208 | 71 | 190 | 221 | 98 | 203 | 87 | 123 | 314 | 329 | 129 | 245 | 209 | 92 | 161 | 88 |
| Southampton | 578 | 225 | 142 | 135 | 66 | 106 | 136 | 140 | 342 | 201 | 53 | 152 | 440 | 111 | 539 | 437 | 100 | 49 | 133 | 309 | 258 | 601 | 295 | 241 | 199 | 243 | 113 | 232 | 294 | 325 | 111 | 204 | 169 | 67 | 221 | 489 | 157 | 152 | 20 | 252 | 23 | 209 | 191 |
| Stoke-on-Trent | 392 | 112 | 220 | 48 | 226 | 130 | 140 | 150 | 156 | 211 | 212 | 250 | 254 | 205 | 353 | 251 | 96 | 184 | 99 | 123 | 129 | 415 | 109 | 93 | 91 | 57 | 208 | 46 | 164 | 195 | 98 | 172 | 54 | 123 | 314 | 303 | 99 | 245 | 209 | 66 | 161 | 50 | 38 | 191 |
| Stranraer | 235 | 342 | 477 | 305 | 482 | 387 | 363 | 406 | 106 | 392 | 469 | 487 | 132 | 461 | 181 | 86 | 352 | 440 | 355 | 333 | 276 | 261 | 153 | 229 | 288 | 232 | 445 | 229 | 201 | 163 | 354 | 388 | 295 | 380 | 571 | 149 | 333 | 502 | 466 | 195 | 418 | 267 | 287 | 447 | 261 |
| Taunton | 560 | 165 | 50 | 132 | 160 | 51 | 226 | 80 | 323 | 142 | 45 | 224 | 422 | 34 | 521 | 419 | 77 | 126 | 96 | 291 | 272 | 583 | 277 | 261 | 228 | 225 | 185 | 213 | 309 | 340 | 183 | 291 | 184 | 123 | 144 | 471 | 215 | 75 | 114 | 234 | 70 | 224 | 172 | 94 | 172 | 429 |
| Wick | 207 | 597 | 732 | 560 | 738 | 642 | 618 | 662 | 361 | 647 | 724 | 742 | 258 | 716 | 166 | 277 | 608 | 695 | 610 | 588 | 531 | 104 | 408 | 484 | 543 | 487 | 700 | 484 | 409 | 367 | 609 | 644 | 550 | 635 | 826 | 215 | 589 | 757 | 721 | 451 | 673 | 523 | 542 | 702 | 516 | 362 | 684 |
| York | 323 | 201 | 314 | 133 | 275 | 224 | 154 | 243 | 116 | 251 | 306 | 279 | 193 | 298 | 314 | 212 | 189 | 233 | 192 | 192 | 38 | 376 | 91 | 24 | 79 | 102 | 237 | 71 | 51 | 89 | 146 | 180 | 87 | 184 | 408 | 239 | 125 | 339 | 269 | 96 | 254 | 57 | 146 | 251 | 120 | 223 | 265 | 477 |
| LONDON | 550 | 239 | 216 | 121 | 54 | 120 | 59 | 153 | 314 | 215 | 125 | 78 | 413 | 200 | 512 | 410 | 102 | 31 | 136 | 282 | 186 | 574 | 268 | 201 | 143 | 216 | 39 | 204 | 254 | 285 | 68 | 118 | 129 | 56 | 310 | 462 | 86 | 241 | 75 | 225 | 85 | 169 | 163 | 77 | 161 | 420 | 167 | 675 | 211 |

Distances in miles (one mile equals 1.6093 km)

# DRIVER'S ATLAS
# BRITAIN

## Contents

| Map pages south | inside front cover |
|---|---|
| Mileage chart and journey times | endpaper |
| Route planner | *II–VII* |
| Motorways | *VIII–X* |
| Restricted junctions | *VIII–IX* |
| Smart motorways | *X* |
| Atlas symbols | 1 |
| Road maps 1:250,000 scale | 2–237 |
| Channel Islands 1:150,000 scale | 236 |
| Isle of Man 1:317,000 scale | 237 |
| Orkney Islands 1:636,000 scale | 234 |
| Shetland Islands 1:636,000 scale | 235 |
| Western Isles 1:700,000 scale | 232–233 |
| Index to place names | 238–318 |
| County, administrative area map | 238–239 |
| Place name index | 240–318 |
| Ireland | endpaper |
| Map pages north | inside back cover |

Scale 1:250,000
or 3.95 miles to 1 inch

**17th edition June 2018**

**Cartography:** All cartography in this atlas edited, designed and produced by the Mapping Services Department of AA Publishing (A05621).

**Publisher's notes:** Published by AA Publishing (a trading name of AA Media Limited, whose registered office is Fanum House, Basing View, Basingstoke, Hampshire RG21 4EA, UK. Registered number 06112600).

**ISBN:** 978 0 7495 7952 4 (flexibound)

A CIP catalogue record for this book is available from The British Library.

The publishers would welcome information to correct any errors or omissions and to keep this atlas up to date. Please write to the Atlas Editor, AA Publishing, The Automobile Association, Fanum House, Basing View, Basingstoke, Hampshire RG21 4EA, UK.
**E-mail:** *roadatlasfeedback@theaa.com*

**Acknowledgements:** AA Publishing would like to thank the following for information used in the creation of this atlas: Cadw, English Heritage, Forestry Commission, Historic Scotland, National Trust and National Trust for Scotland, RSPB, The Wildlife Trust, Scottish Natural Heritage, Natural England, The Countryside Council for Wales. Award winning beaches from 'Blue Flag' and 'Keep Scotland Beautiful' (summer 2017 data): for latest information visit *www.blueflag.org* and *www.keepscotlandbeautiful.org*

Ireland mapping: Republic of Ireland census 2011 © Central Statistics Office and Northern Ireland census 2011 © NISRA (population data); Logainm.ie (placenames); Roads Service and Transport Infrastructure Ireland

**Printer:** Oriental Press, Dubai.

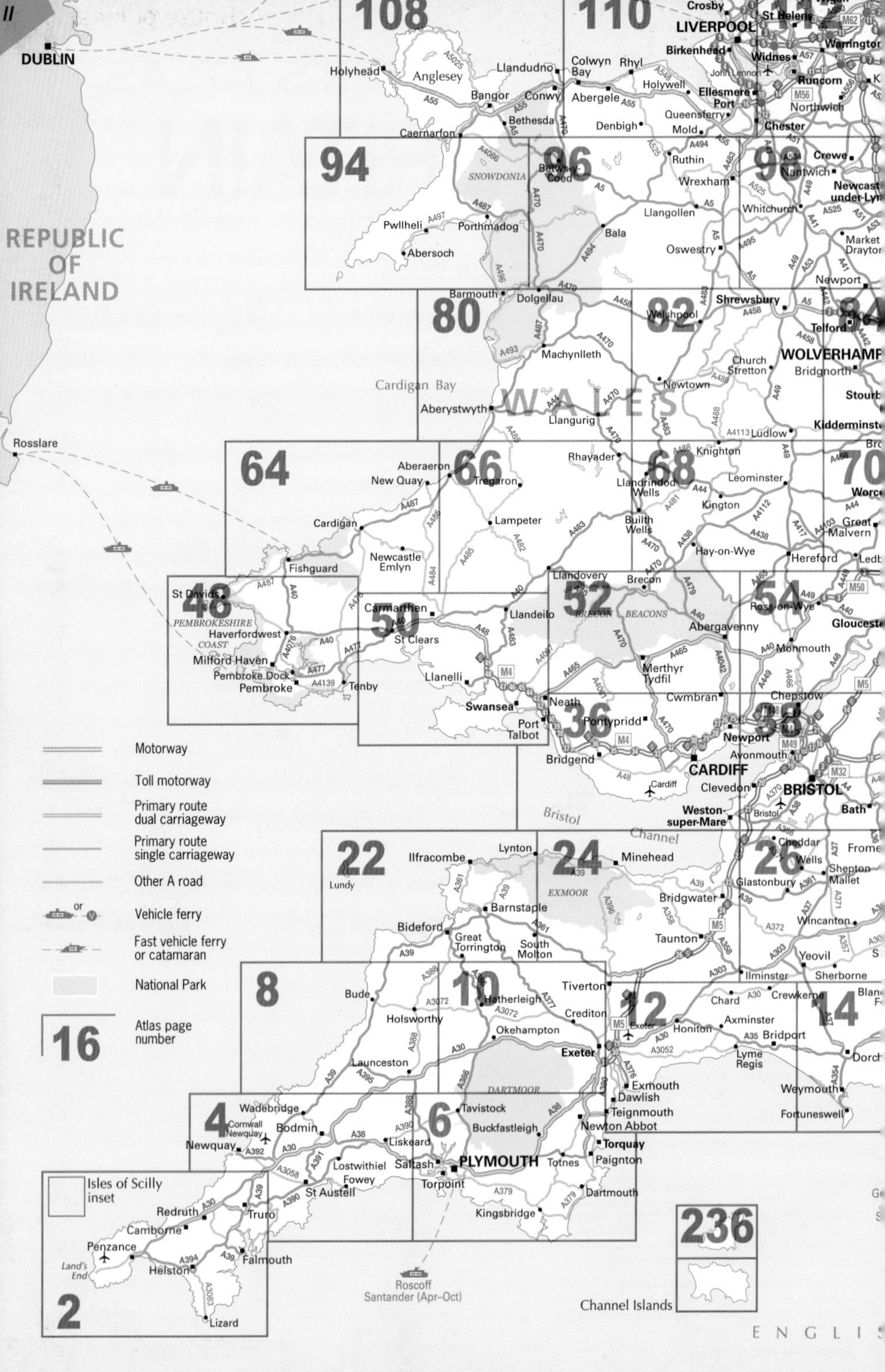
REPUBLIC OF IRELAND
DUBLIN
Rosslare
WALES
Cardigan Bay
Bristol Channel
108
110
94
96
98
80
82
64
66
68
70
46
50
52
54
36
58
22
24
26
8
10
12
14
4
6
2
236
LIVERPOOL
Holyhead
Anglesey
Llandudno
Bangor
Conwy
Caernarfon
Colwyn Bay
Rhyl
Abergele
Denbigh
Chester
Wrexham
Pwllheli
Abersoch
Porthmadog
SNOWDONIA
Bala
Llangollen
Oswestry
Barmouth
Dolgellau
Shrewsbury
Welshpool
Machynlleth
Aberystwyth
Newtown
Llangurig
WOLVERHAMPTON
Aberaeron
New Quay
Tregaron
Cardigan
Lampeter
Fishguard
Newcastle Emlyn
St Davids
PEMBROKESHIRE COAST
Haverfordwest
Milford Haven
Pembroke Dock
Pembroke
Tenby
Carmarthen
St Clears
Llandeilo
Llanelli
Swansea
Neath
Port Talbot
Llandovery
Brecon
BRECON BEACONS
Abergavenny
Merthyr Tydfil
Pontypridd
Cwmbran
Newport
CARDIFF
Bridgend
BRISTOL
Clevedon
Weston-super-Mare
Ilfracombe
Lynton
Minehead
EXMOOR
Lundy
Barnstaple
Bideford
Bridgwater
Taunton
Bude
Holsworthy
Okehampton
Exeter
Tiverton
Launceston
DARTMOOR
Tavistock
PLYMOUTH
Torquay
Paignton
Newquay
Bodmin
St Austell
Truro
Falmouth
Penzance
Helston
Lizard
Land's End
Roscoff
Santander (Apr–Oct)
Channel Islands
Isles of Scilly inset
Motorway
Toll motorway
Primary route dual carriageway
Primary route single carriageway
Other A road
or
Vehicle ferry
Fast vehicle ferry or catamaran
National Park
16
Atlas page number
E N G L I S

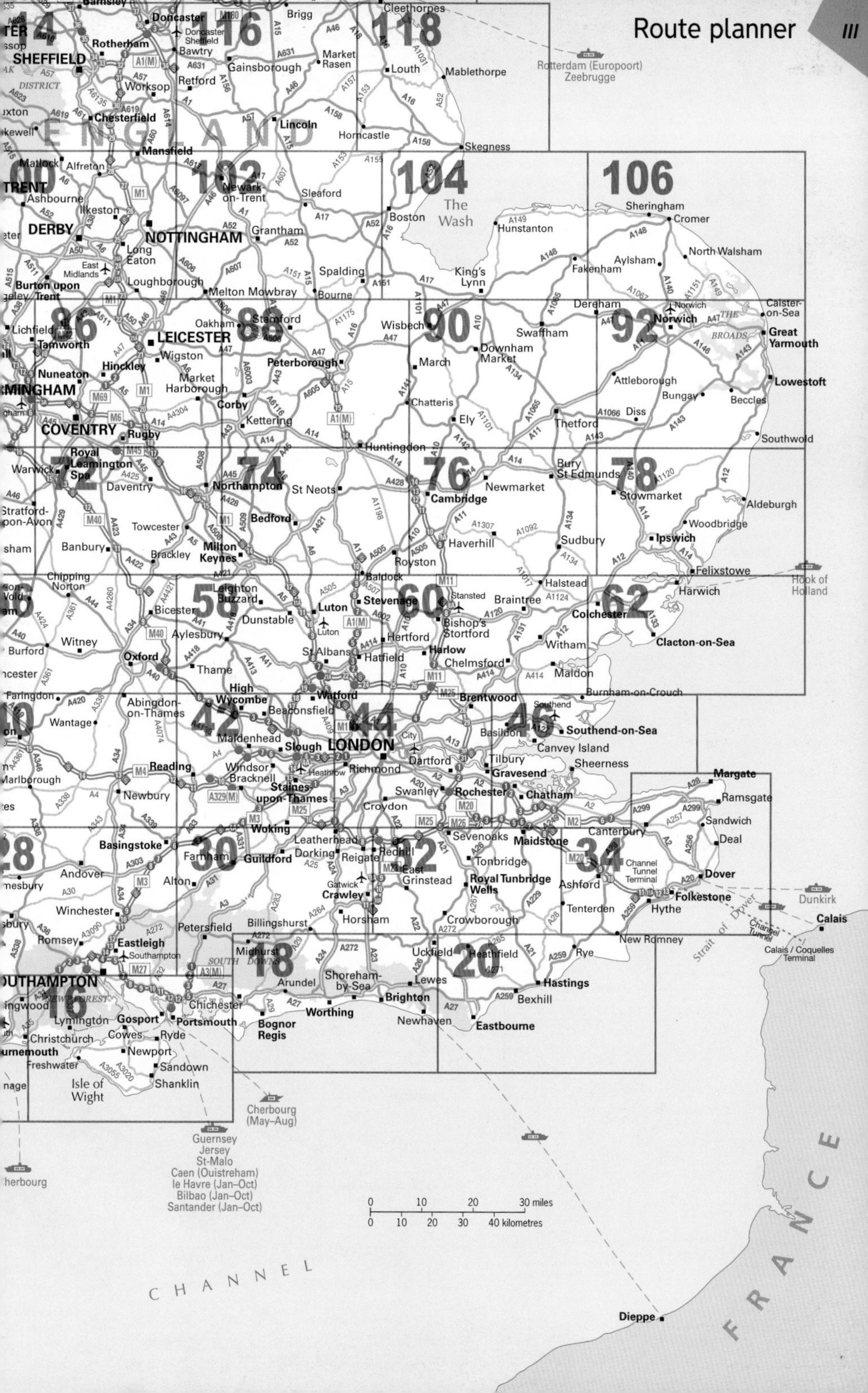

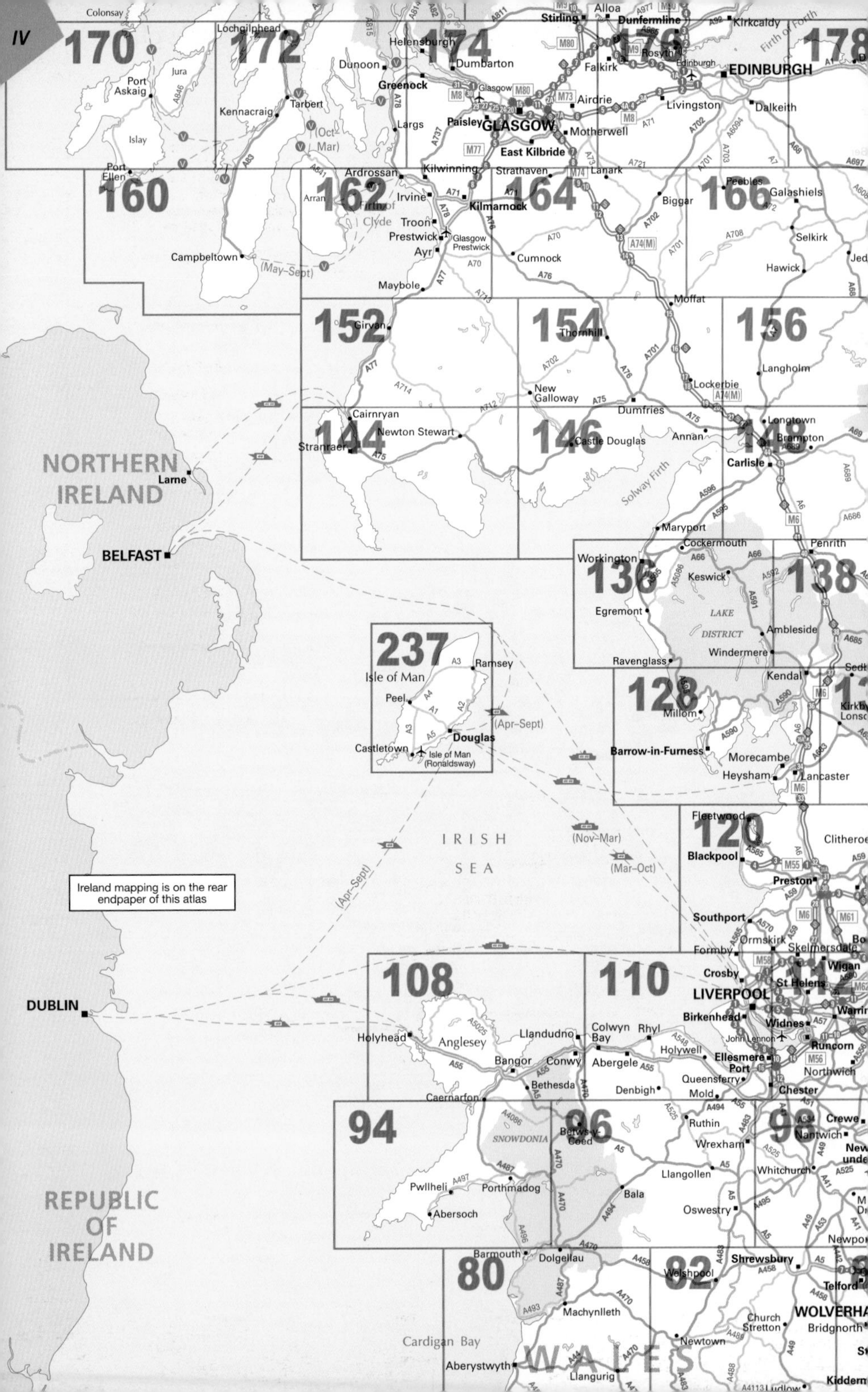
IV
170
172
174
176
178
160
162
164
166
152
154
156
144
146
148
136
138
128
120
237
108
110
94
96
98
80
82
Colonsay
Lochgilphead
Helensburgh
Dumbarton
Stirling
Alloa
Dunfermline
Kirkcaldy
Firth of Forth
Rosyth
Falkirk
Edinburgh
EDINBURGH
Port Askaig
Jura
Tarbert
Kennacraig
Islay
(Oct–Mar)
Dunoon
Greenock
Glasgow
GLASGOW
Paisley
Largs
Airdrie
Motherwell
East Kilbride
Livingston
Dalkeith
Port Ellen
Campbeltown
(May–Sept)
Ardrossan
Arran
Firth of Clyde
Irvine
Kilwinning
Kilmarnock
Troon
Prestwick
Glasgow Prestwick
Ayr
Maybole
Strathaven
Lanark
Biggar
Peebles
Galashiels
Selkirk
Hawick
Cumnock
Moffat
Girvan
Thornhill
Langholm
Lockerbie
New Galloway
Dumfries
Cairnryan
Newton Stewart
Stranraer
Castle Douglas
Annan
Longtown
Brampton
Carlisle
Solway Firth
Maryport
Cockermouth
Penrith
Workington
Keswick
Egremont
LAKE DISTRICT
Ambleside
Windermere
Ravenglass
Kendal
Millom
Barrow-in-Furness
Morecambe
Heysham
Lancaster
Fleetwood
Blackpool
Preston
Clitheroe
Southport
Formby
Ormskirk
Skelmersdale
Wigan
Crosby
St Helens
LIVERPOOL
Birkenhead
Widnes
Warrington
John Lennon
Runcorn
Ellesmere Port
Northwich
Chester
NORTHERN IRELAND
Larne
BELFAST
Isle of Man
Ramsey
Peel
Douglas
Castletown
Isle of Man (Ronaldsway)
(Apr–Sept)
(Nov–Mar)
(Mar–Oct)
IRISH SEA
Ireland mapping is on the rear endpaper of this atlas
DUBLIN
Holyhead
Anglesey
Llandudno
Colwyn Bay
Rhyl
Holywell
Bangor
Conwy
Abergele
Denbigh
Queensferry
Mold
Bethesda
Caernarfon
SNOWDONIA
Betws-y-Coed
Ruthin
Wrexham
Crewe
Nantwich
Whitchurch
Llangollen
Pwllheli
Porthmadog
Abersoch
Bala
Oswestry
Barmouth
Dolgellau
Welshpool
Shrewsbury
Telford
Machynlleth
WOLVERHAMPTON
Church Stretton
Bridgnorth
Cardigan Bay
Newtown
Aberystwyth
WALES
Llangurig
Ludlow
Kidderminster
REPUBLIC OF IRELAND

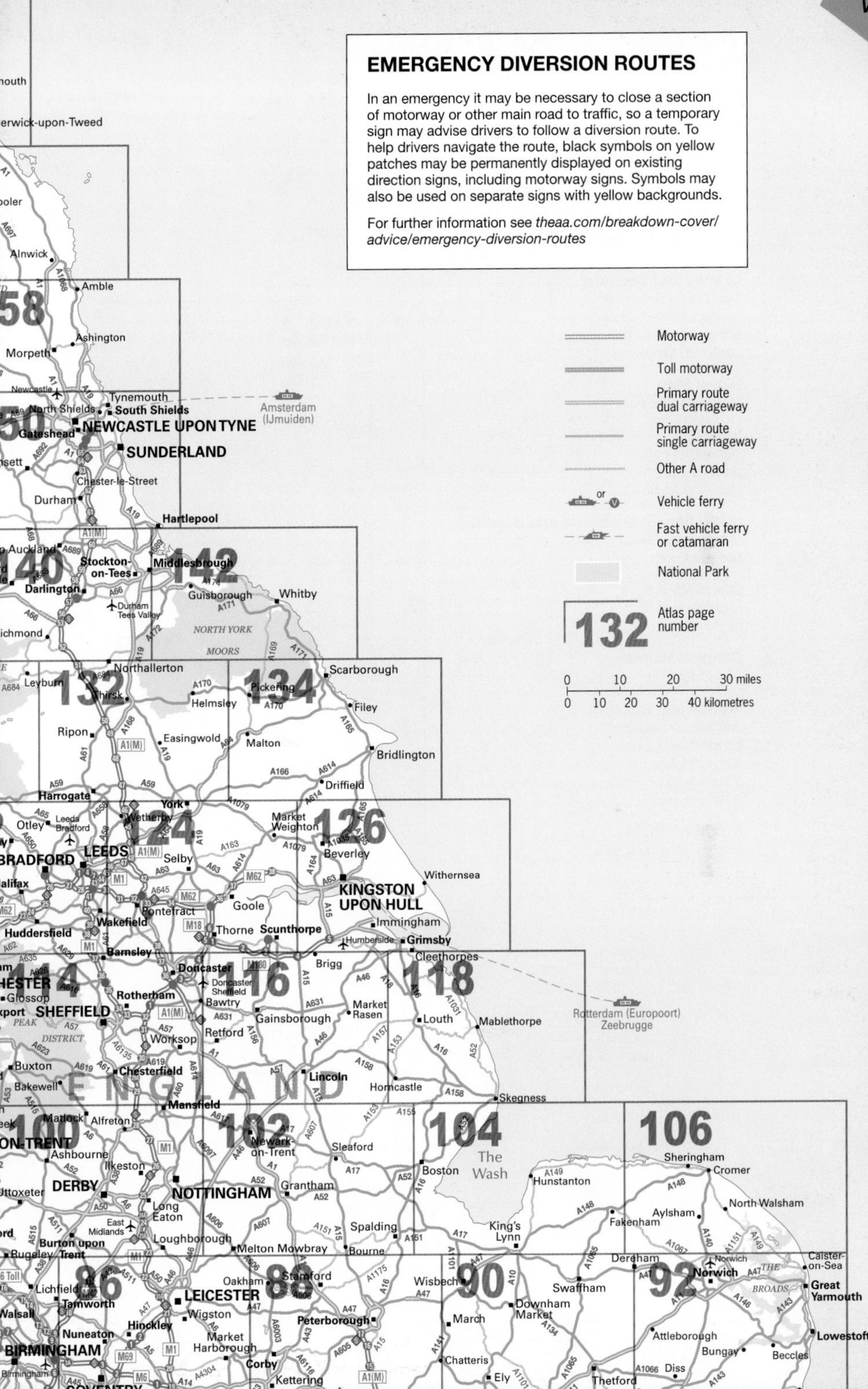
EMERGENCY DIVERSION ROUTES
In an emergency it may be necessary to close a section of motorway or other main road to traffic, so a temporary sign may advise drivers to follow a diversion route. To help drivers navigate the route, black symbols on yellow patches may be permanently displayed on existing direction signs, including motorway signs. Symbols may also be used on separate signs with yellow backgrounds.
For further information see theaa.com/breakdown-cover/advice/emergency-diversion-routes
Motorway
Toll motorway
Primary route dual carriageway
Primary route single carriageway
Other A road
Vehicle ferry
Fast vehicle ferry or catamaran
National Park
132
Atlas page number
0 10 20 30 miles
0 10 20 30 40 kilometres
Berwick-upon-Tweed
Alnwick
Amble
58
Ashington
Morpeth
Tynemouth
North Shields
South Shields
Amsterdam (IJmuiden)
NEWCASTLE UPON TYNE
Gateshead
SUNDERLAND
Chester-le-Street
Durham
Hartlepool
Stockton-on-Tees
Middlesbrough
140
142
Darlington
Guisborough
Whitby
Durham Tees Valley
Richmond
NORTH YORK MOORS
Northallerton
Scarborough
Leyburn
132
Thirsk
Helmsley
134
Pickering
Filey
Ripon
Easingwold
Malton
Bridlington
Driffield
Harrogate
York
Wetherby
124
Market Weighton
126
Otley
Leeds Bradford
LEEDS
BRADFORD
Selby
Beverley
Withernsea
Halifax
KINGSTON UPON HULL
Pontefract
Goole
Huddersfield
Wakefield
Thorne
Scunthorpe
Immingham
Humberside
Grimsby
Barnsley
Cleethorpes
Doncaster
Brigg
114
116
118
Doncaster Sheffield
Rotherham
Bawtry
Market Rasen
Glossop
SHEFFIELD
Gainsborough
Louth
Mablethorpe
Rotterdam (Europoort)
Zeebrugge
PEAK DISTRICT
Retford
Worksop
Buxton
Chesterfield
Lincoln
Horncastle
Bakewell
ENGLAND
Skegness
Mansfield
Matlock
Alfreton
100
102
104
106
Newark-on-Trent
Sleaford
Ashbourne
Ilkeston
Boston
The Wash
Sheringham
Cromer
Hunstanton
DERBY
NOTTINGHAM
Grantham
Uttoxeter
North Walsham
Long Eaton
Aylsham
Fakenham
East Midlands
Loughborough
Spalding
King's Lynn
Burton upon Trent
Melton Mowbray
Bourne
Rugeley
Dereham
Norwich
Caister-on-Sea
86
88
90
92
Lichfield
Stamford
Oakham
Wisbech
Swaffham
THE BROADS
Great Yarmouth
Tamworth
LEICESTER
Downham Market
Walsall
Wigston
Peterborough
Nuneaton
Hinckley
Market Harborough
March
Attleborough
Lowestoft
BIRMINGHAM
Bungay
Beccles
Corby
Chatteris
Birmingham
Kettering
Ely
Diss
Thetford
COVENTRY

## FERRY OPERATORS

**Hebrides and west coast Scotland**
*calmac.co.uk*
*skyeferry.co.uk*
*western-ferries.co.uk*

**Orkney and Shetland**
*northlinkferries.co.uk*
*pentlandferries.co.uk*
*orkneyferries.co.uk*
*shetland.gov.uk/ferries*

**Isle of Man**
*steam-packet.com*

**Ireland**
*irishferries.com*
*poferries.com*
*stenaline.co.uk*

**North Sea (Scandinavia and Benelux)**
*dfdsseaways.co.uk*
*poferries.com*

**Isle of Wight**
*wightlink.co.uk*
*redfunnel.co.uk*

**Channel Islands**
*condorferries.co.uk*

**France and Belgium**
*brittany-ferries.co.uk*
*condorferries.co.uk*
*eurotunnel.com*
*dfdsseaways.co.uk*
*poferries.com*

**Northern Spain**
*brittany-ferries.co.uk*

Motorway
Toll motorway
Primary route dual carriageway
Primary route single carriageway
Other A road
Vehicle ferry (or V)
Fast vehicle ferry or catamaran
National Park
192 Atlas page number

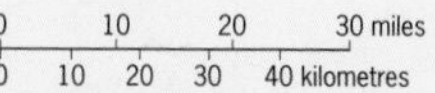


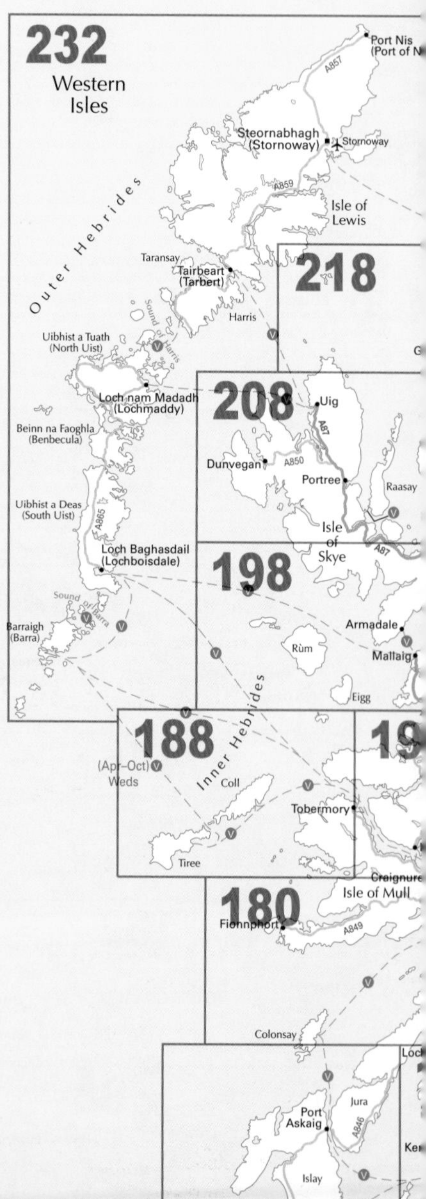

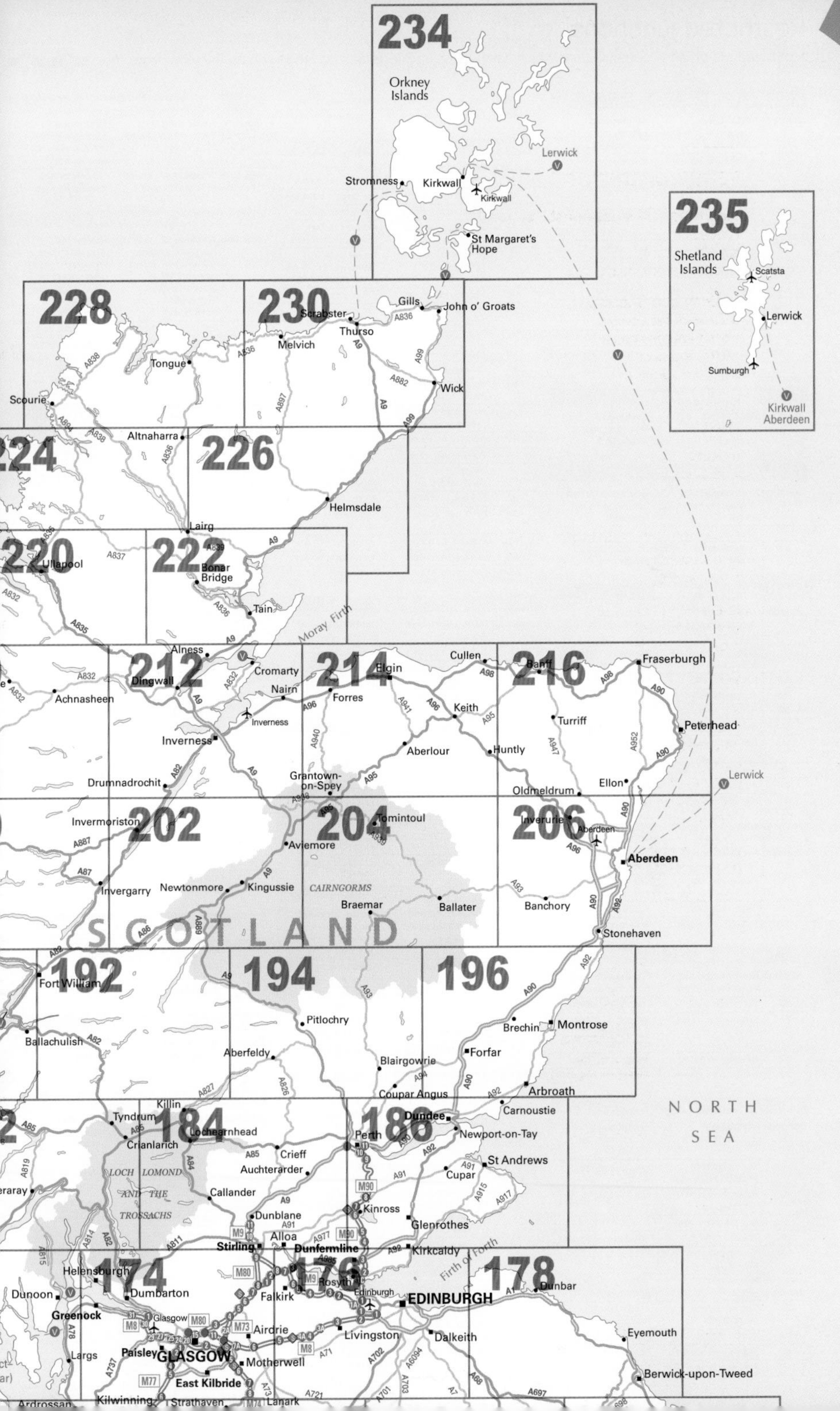
234
Orkney Islands
Lerwick
Stromness
Kirkwall
Kirkwall
St Margaret's Hope
235
Shetland Islands
Scatsta
Lerwick
Sumburgh
Kirkwall
Aberdeen
228
230
Scrabster
Gills
John o' Groats
Thurso
Melvich
Tongue
Wick
Scourie
Altnaharra
224
226
Helmsdale
Lairg
220
222
Ullapool
Bonar Bridge
Tain
Moray Firth
Alness
212
214
216
Cullen
Banff
Fraserburgh
Dingwall
Cromarty
Elgin
Nairn
Forres
Achnasheen
Inverness
Keith
Turriff
Peterhead
Inverness
Aberlour
Huntly
Drumnadrochit
Grantown-on-Spey
Oldmeldrum
Ellon
Lerwick
202
204
206
Invermoriston
Tomintoul
Inverurie
Aberdeen
Aviemore
Aberdeen
Invergarry
Newtonmore
Kingussie
CAIRNGORMS
Braemar
Ballater
Banchory
SCOTLAND
Stonehaven
192
194
196
Fort William
Pitlochry
Brechin
Montrose
Ballachulish
Aberfeldy
Forfar
Blairgowrie
Coupar Angus
Arbroath
184
186
Killin
Tyndrum
Lochearnhead
Dundee
Carnoustie
NORTH SEA
Crianlarich
Perth
Newport-on-Tay
Crieff
St Andrews
Auchterarder
Cupar
LOCH LOMOND AND THE TROSSACHS
Callander
Kinross
Dunblane
Glenrothes
Alloa
Stirling
Dunfermline
Kirkcaldy
Firth of Forth
174
176
178
Helensburgh
Rosyth
Dunbar
Dunoon
Dumbarton
Falkirk
Edinburgh
EDINBURGH
Greenock
Glasgow
Airdrie
Livingston
Dalkeith
Eyemouth
Paisley
GLASGOW
Largs
Motherwell
Berwick-upon-Tweed
East Kilbride
Ardrossan
Kilwinning
Strathaven
Lanark

# Restricted junctions

Motorway and primary route junctions which have access or exit restrictions are shown on the map pages thus: 

## M1 London - Leeds

| Junction | Northbound | Southbound |
|---|---|---|
| 2 | Access only from A1 *(northbound)* | Exit only to A1 *(southbound)* |
| 4 | Access only from A41 *(northbound)* | Exit only to A41 *(southbound)* |
| 6A | Access only from M25 (no link from A405) | Exit only to M25 (no link from A405) |
| 7 | Access only from A414 | Exit only to A414 |
| 17 | Exit only to M45 | Access only from M45 |
| 19 | Exit only to M6 *(northbound)* | Exit only to A14 *(southbound)* |
| 21A | Exit only, no access | Access only, no exit |
| 23A | Access only from A42 | No restriction |
| 24A | Access only, no exit | Exit only, no access |
| 35A | Exit only, no access | Access only, no exit |
| 43 | Exit only to M621 | Access only from M621 |
| 48 | Exit only to A1(M) *(northbound)* | Access only from A1(M) *(southbound)* |

## M2 Rochester - Faversham

| Junction | Westbound | Eastbound |
|---|---|---|
| 1 | No exit to A2 *(eastbound)* | No access from A2 *(westbound)* |

## M3 Sunbury - Southampton

| Junction | Northeastbound | Southwestbound |
|---|---|---|
| 8 | Access only from A303, no exit | Exit only to A303, no access |
| 10 | Exit only, no access | Access only, no exit |
| 14 | Access from M27 only, no exit | No access to M27 *(westbound)* |

## M4 London - South Wales

| Junction | Westbound | Eastbound |
|---|---|---|
| 1 | Access only from A4 *(westbound)* | Exit only to A4 *(eastbound)* |
| 2 | Access only from A4 *(westbound)* | Access only from A4 *(eastbound)* |
| 21 | Exit only to M48 | Access only from M48 |
| 23 | Access only from M48 | Exit only to M48 |
| 25 | Exit only, no access | Access only, no exit |
| 25A | Exit only, no access | Access only, no exit |
| 29 | Exit only to A48(M) | Access only from A48(M) |
| 38 | Exit only, no access | No restriction |
| 39 | Access only, no exit | No access or exit |
| 42 | Exit only to A483 | Access only from A483 |

## M5 Birmingham - Exeter

| Junction | Northeastbound | Southwestbound |
|---|---|---|
| 10 | Access only, no exit | Exit only, no access |
| 11A | Access only from A417 *(westbound)* | Exit only to A417 *(eastbound)* |
| 18A | Exit only to M49 | Access only from M49 |
| 18 | Exit only, no access | Access only, no exit |

## M6 Toll Motorway

| Junction | Northwestbound | Southeastbound |
|---|---|---|
| T1 | Access only, no exit | No access or exit |
| T2 | No access or exit | Exit only, no access |
| T5 | Access only, no exit | Exit only to A5148 *(northbound)*, no access |
| T7 | Exit only, no access | Access only, no exit |
| T8 | Exit only, no access | Access only, no exit |

## M6 Rugby - Carlisle

| Junction | Northbound | Southbound |
|---|---|---|
| 3A | Exit only to M6 Toll | Access only from M6 Toll |
| 4 | Exit only to M42 *(southbound)* & A446 | Exit only to A446 |
| 4A | Access only from M42 *(southbound)* | Exit only to M42 |
| 5 | Exit only, no access | Access only, no exit |
| 10A | Exit only to M54 | Access only from M54 |
| 11A | Access only from M6 Toll | Exit only to M6 Toll |
| with M56 (jct 20A) | No restriction | Access only from M56 *(eastbound)* |
| 20 | Exit only to M56 *(westbound)* | Access only from M56 *(eastbound)* |
| 24 | Access only, no exit | Exit only, no access |
| 25 | Exit only, no access | Access only, no exit |
| 30 | Access only from M61 | Exit only to M61 |
| 31A | Exit only, no access | Access only, no exit |
| 45 | Exit only, no access | Access only, no exit |

## M8 Edinburgh - Bishopton

| Junction | Westbound | Eastbound |
|---|---|---|
| 6 | Exit only, no access | Access only, no exit |
| 6A | Access only, no exit | Exit only, no access |
| 7 | Access only, no exit | Exit only, no access |
| 7A | Exit only, no access | Access only from A725 *(northbound)*, no exit |
| 8 | No access from M73 *(southbound)* or from A8 *(eastbound)* & A89 | No exit to M73 *(northbound)* or to A8 *(westbound)* & A89 |
| 9 | Access only, no exit | Exit only, no access |
| 13 | Access only from M80 *(southbound)* | Exit only to M80 *(northbound)* |
| 14 | Access only, no exit | Exit only, no access |
| 16 | Exit only to A804 | Access only from A879 |
| 17 | Exit only to A82 | No restriction |
| 18 | Access only from A82 *(eastbound)* | Exit only to A814 |
| 19 | No access from A814 *(westbound)* | Exit only to A814 *(westbound)* |
| 20 | Exit only, no access | Access only, no exit |
| 21 | Access only, no exit | Exit only to A8 |
| 22 | Exit only to M77 *(southbound)* | Access only from M77 *(northbound)* |
| 23 | Exit only to B768 | Access only from B768 |
| 25 | No access or exit from or to A8 | No access or exit from or to A8 |
| 25A | Exit only, no access | Access only, no exit |
| 28 | Exit only, no access | Access only, no exit |
| 28A | Exit only to A737 | Access only from A737 |

## M9 Edinburgh - Dunblane

| Junction | Northwestbound | Southeastbound |
|---|---|---|
| 2 | Access only, no exit | Exit only, no access |
| 3 | Exit only, no access | Access only, no exit |
| 6 | Access only, no exit | Exit only to A905 |
| 8 | Exit only to M876 *(southwestbound)* | Access only from M876 *(northeastbound)* |

## M11 London - Cambridge

| Junction | Northbound | Southbound |
|---|---|---|
| 4 | Access only from A406 *(eastbound)* | Exit only to A406 |
| 5 | Exit only, no access | Access only, no exit |
| 8A | Exit only, no access | No direct access, use jct 8 |
| 9 | Exit only to A11 | Access only from A11 |
| 13 | Exit only, no access | Access only, no exit |
| 14 | Exit only, no access | Access only, no exit |

## M20 Swanley - Folkestone

| Junction | Northwestbound | Southeastbound |
|---|---|---|
| 2 | Staggered junction; follow signs - access only | Staggered junction; follow signs - exit only |
| 3 | Exit only to M26 *(westbound)* | Access only from M26 *(eastbound)* |
| 5 | Access only from A20 | For access follow signs - exit only to A20 |
| 6 | No restriction | For exit follow signs |
| 11A | Access only, no exit | Exit only, no access |

## M23 Hooley - Crawley

| Junction | Northbound | Southbound |
|---|---|---|
| 7 | Exit only to A23 *(northbound)* | Access only from A23 *(southbound)* |
| 10A | Access only, no exit | Exit only, no access |

## M25 London Orbital Motorway

| Junction | Clockwise | Anticlockwise |
|---|---|---|
| 1B | No direct access, use slip road to jct 2 Exit only | Access only, no exit |
| 5 | No exit to M26 *(eastbound)* | No access from M26 |
| 19 | Exit only, no access | Access only, no exit |
| 21 | Access only from M1 *(southbound)* Exit only to M1 *(northbound)* | Access only from M1 *(southbound)* Exit only to M1 *(northbound)* |
| 31 | No exit (use slip road via jct 30), access only | No access (use slip road via jct 30), exit only |

## M26 Sevenoaks - Wrotham

| Junction | Westbound | Eastbound |
|---|---|---|
| with M25 (jct 5) | Exit only to clockwise M25 *(westbound)* | Access only from anticlockwise M25 *(eastbound)* |
| with M20 (jct 3) | Access only from M20 *(northwestbound)* | Exit only to M20 *(southeastbound)* |

## M27 Cadnam - Portsmouth

| Junction | Westbound | Eastbound |
|---|---|---|
| 4 | Staggered junction; follow signs - access only from M3 *(southbound)*. Exit only to M3 *(northbound)* | Staggered junction; follow signs - access only from M3 *(southbound)*. Exit only to M3 *(northbound)* |
| 10 | Exit only, no access | Access only, no exit |
| 12 | Staggered junction; follow signs - exit only to M275 *(southbound)* | Staggered junction; follow signs - access only from M275 *(northbound)* |

## M40 London - Birmingham

| Junction | Northwestbound | Southeastbound |
|---|---|---|
| 3 | Exit only, no access | Access only, no exit |
| 7 | Exit only, no access | Access only, no exit |
| 8 | Exit only to M40/A40 | Access only from M40/A40 |
| 13 | Exit only, no access | Access only, no exit |
| 14 | Access only, no exit | Exit only, no access |
| 16 | Access only, no exit | Exit only, no access |

## M42 Bromsgrove - Measham

| Junction | Northeastbound | Southwestbound |
|---|---|---|
| 1 | Access only, no exit | Exit only, no access |
| 7 | Exit only to M6 *(northwestbound)* | Access only from M6 *(northwestbound)* |
| 7A | Exit only to M6 *(southeastbound)* | No access or exit |
| 8 | Access only from M6 *(southeastbound)* | Exit only to M6 *(northwestbound)* |

## M45 Coventry - M1

| Junction | Westbound | Eastbound |
|---|---|---|
| Dunchurch (unnumbered) | Access only from A45 | Exit only, no access |
| with M1 (jct 17) | Access only from M1 *(northbound)* | Exit only to M1 *(southbound)* |

## M48 Chepstow

| Junction | Westbound | Eastbound |
|---|---|---|
| 21 | Access only from M4 *(westbound)* | Exit only to M4 *(eastbound)* |
| 23 | No exit to M4 *(eastbound)* | No Access from M4 *(westbound)* |

## M53 Mersey Tunnel - Chester

| Junction | Northbound | Southbound |
|---|---|---|
| 11 | Access only from M56 *(westbound)* Exit only to M56 *(eastbound)* | Access only from M56 *(westbound)* Exit only to M56 *(eastbound)* |

## M54 Telford - Birmingham

| Junction | Westbound | Eastbound |
|---|---|---|
| with M6 (jct 10A) | Access only from M6 *(northbound)* | Exit only to M6 *(southbound)* |

## M56 Chester - Manchester

| Junction | Westbound | Eastbound |
|---|---|---|
| 1 | Access only from M60 *(westbound)* | Exit only to M60 *(eastbound)* & A34 *(northbound)* |
| 2 | Exit only, no access | Access only, no exit |
| 3 | Access only, no exit | Exit only, no access |
| 4 | Exit only, no access | Access only, no exit |
| 7 | Exit only, no access | No restriction |
| 8 | Access only, no exit | No access or exit |
| 9 | No exit to M6 *(southbound)* | No access from M6 *(northbound)* |
| 15 | Exit only to M53 | Access only from M53 |
| 16 | No access or exit | No restriction |

## M57 Liverpool Outer Ring Road

| Junction | Northwestbound | Southeastbound |
|---|---|---|
| 3 | Access only, no exit | Exit only, no access |
| 5 | Access only from A580 *(westbound)* | Exit only, no access |

## M58 Liverpool - Wigan

| Junction | Westbound | Eastbound |
|---|---|---|
| 1 | Exit only, no access | Access only, no exit |

## M60 Manchester Orbital

| Junction | Clockwise | Anticlockwise |
|---|---|---|
| 2 | Access only, no exit | Exit only, no access |
| 3 | No access from M56 | Access only from A34 *(northbound)* |
| 4 | Access only from A34 *(northbound)*. Exit only to M56 | Access only from M56 *(eastbound)*. Exit only to A34 *(southbound)* |
| 5 | Access and exit only from and to A5103 *(northbound)* | Access and exit only from and to A5103 *(southbound)* |
| 7 | No direct access, use slip road to jct 8. Exit only to A56 | Access only from A56. No exit, use jct 8 |
| 14 | Access from A580 *(eastbound)* | Exit only to A580 *(westbound)* |
| 16 | Access only, no exit | Exit only, no access |
| 20 | Exit only, no access | Access only, no exit |
| 22 | No restriction | Exit only, no access |
| 25 | Exit only, no access | No restriction |
| 26 | No restriction | Exit only, no access |
| 27 | Access only, no exit | Exit only, no access |

## M61 Manchester - Preston

| Junction | Northwestbound | Southeastbound |
|---|---|---|
| 3 | No access or exit | Exit only, no access |
| with M6 (jct 30) | Exit only to M6 *(northbound)* | Access only from M6 *(southbound)* |

## M62 Liverpool - Kingston upon Hull

| Junction | Westbound | Eastbound |
|---|---|---|
| 23 | Access only, no exit | Exit only, no access |
| 32A | No access to A1(M) *(southbound)* | No restriction |

## M65 Preston - Colne

| Junction | Northeastbound | Southwestbound |
|---|---|---|
| 9 | Exit only, no access | Access only, no exit |
| 11 | Access only, no exit | Exit only, no access |

## M66 Bury

| Junction | Northbound | Southbound |
|---|---|---|
| with A56 | Exit only to A56 *(northbound)* | Access only from A56 *(southbound)* |
| 1 | Exit only, no access | Access only, no exit |

## M67 Hyde Bypass

| Junction | Westbound | Eastbound |
|---|---|---|
| 1 | Access only, no exit | Exit only, no access |
| 2 | Exit only, no access | Access only, no exit |
| 3 | Exit only, no access | No restriction |

## M69 Coventry - Leicester

| Junction | Northbound | Southbound |
|---|---|---|
| 2 | Access only, no exit | Exit only, no access |

## M73 East of Glasgow

| Junction | Northbound | Southbound |
|---|---|---|
| 1 | No exit to A74 & A721 | No exit to A74 & A721 |
| 2 | No access from or exit to A89. No access from *(eastbound)* | No access from or exit to A89. No exit to M8 *(westbound)* |

## M74 and A74(M) Glasgow - Gretna

| Junction | Northbound | Southbound |
|---|---|---|
| 3 | Exit only, no access | Access only, no exit |
| 3A | Access only, no exit | Exit only, no access |
| 4 | No access from A74 & A721 | Access only, no exit to A74 & A721 |
| 7 | Access only, no exit | Exit only, no access |
| 9 | No access or exit | Exit only, no access |
| 10 | No restriction | Access only, no exit |
| 11 | Access only, no exit | Exit only, no access |
| 12 | Exit only, no access | Access only, no exit |
| 18 | Exit only, no access | Access only, no exit |

## M77 Glasgow - Kilmarnock

| Junction | Northbound | Southbound |
|---|---|---|
| with M8 (jct 22) | No exit to M8 *(westbound)* | No access from M8 *(eastbound)* |
| 4 | Access only, no exit | Exit only, no access |
| 6 | Access only, no exit | Exit only, no access |
| 7 | Access only, no exit | No restriction |
| 8 | Exit only, no access | Exit only, no access |

## M80 Glasgow - Stirling

| Junction | Northbound | Southbound |
|---|---|---|
| 4A | Exit only, no access | Access only, no exit |
| 6A | Access only, no exit | Exit only, no access |
| 8 | Exit only to M876 *(northeastbound)* | Access only from M876 *(southwestbound)* |

## M90 Edinburgh - Perth

| Junction | Northbound | Southbound |
|---|---|---|
| 1 | No exit, access only | Exit only to A90 *(eastbound)* |
| 2A | Exit only to A92 *(eastbound)* | Access only from A92 *(westbound)* |
| 7 | Access only, no exit | Exit only, no access |
| 8 | Exit only, no access | Access only, no exit |
| 10 | No access from A912. No exit to A912 *(southbound)* | No access from A912 *(northbound)* No exit to A912 |

## M180 Doncaster - Grimsby

| Junction | Westbound | Eastbound |
|---|---|---|
| 1 | Access only, no exit | Exit only, no access |

## M606 Bradford Spur

| Junction | Northbound | Southbound |
|---|---|---|
| 2 | Exit only, no access | No restriction |

## M621 Leeds - M1

| Junction | Clockwise | Anticlockwise |
|---|---|---|
| 2A | Access only, no exit | Exit only, no access |
| 4 | No exit or access | No restriction |
| 5 | Access only, no exit | Exit only, no access |
| 6 | Exit only, no access | Access only, no exit |
| with M1 (jct 43) | Exit only to M1 *(southbound)* | Access only from M1 *(northbound)* |

## M876 Bonnybridge - Kincardine Bridge

| Junction | Northeastbound | Southwestbound |
|---|---|---|
| with M80 (jct 5) | Access only from M80 *(northeastbound)* | Exit only to M80 *(southwestbound)* |
| with M9 (jct 8) | Exit only to M9 *(eastbound)* | Access only from M9 *(westbound)* |

## A1(M) South Mimms - Baldock

| Junction | Northbound | Southbound |
|---|---|---|
| 2 | Exit only, no access | Access only, no exit |
| 3 | No restriction | Exit only, no access |
| 5 | Access only, no exit | No access or exit |

## A1(M) Pontefract - Bedale

| Junction | Northbound | Southbound |
|---|---|---|
| 41 | No access to M62 *(eastbound)* | No restriction |
| 43 | Access only from M1 *(northbound)* | Exit only to M1 *(southbound)* |

## A1(M) Scotch Corner - Newcastle upon Tyne

| Junction | Northbound | Southbound |
|---|---|---|
| 57 | Exit only to A66(M) *(eastbound)* | Access only from A66(M) *(westbound)* |
| 65 | No access Exit only to A194(M) & A1 *(northbound)* | No exit Access only from A194(M) & A1 *(southbound)* |

## A3(M) Horndean - Havant

| Junction | Northbound | Southbound |
|---|---|---|
| 1 | Access only from A3 | Exit only to A3 |
| 4 | Exit only, no access | Access only, no exit |

## A38(M) Birmingham, Victoria Road (Park Circus)

| Junction | Northbound | Southbound |
|---|---|---|
| with B4132 | No exit | No access |

## A48(M) Cardiff Spur

| Junction | Westbound | Eastbound |
|---|---|---|
| 29 | Access only from M4 *(westbound)* | Exit only to M4 *(eastbound)* |
| 29A | Exit only to A48 *(westbound)* | Access only from A48 *(eastbound)* |

## A57(M) Manchester, Brook Street (A34)

| Junction | Westbound | Eastbound |
|---|---|---|
| with A34 | No exit | No access |

## A58(M) Leeds, Park Lane and Westgate

| Junction | Northbound | Southbound |
|---|---|---|
| with A58 | No restriction | No access |

## A64(M) Leeds, Clay Pit Lane (A58)

| Junction | Westbound | Eastbound |
|---|---|---|
| with A58 | No exit (to Clay Pit Lane) | No access (from Clay Pit Lane) |

## A66(M) Darlington Spur

| Junction | Westbound | Eastbound |
|---|---|---|
| with A1(M) (jct 57) | Exit only to A1(M) *(southbound)* | Access only from A1(M) *(northbound)* |

## A74(M) Gretna - Abington

| Junction | Northbound | Southbound |
|---|---|---|
| 18 | Exit only, no access | No exit |

## A194(M) Newcastle upon Tyne

| Junction | Northbound | Southbound |
|---|---|---|
| with A1(M) (jct 65) | Access only from A1(M) *(northbound)* | Exit only to A1(M) *(southbound)* |

## A12 M25 - Ipswich

| Junction | Northeastbound | Southwestbound |
|---|---|---|
| 13 | Access only, no exit | No restriction |
| 14 | Exit only, no access | Access only, no exit |
| 20A | Exit only, no access | Access only, no exit |
| 20B | Access only, no exit | Exit only, no access |
| 21 | No restriction | Access only, no exit |
| 23 | Exit only, no access | Access only, no exit |
| 24 | Access only, no exit | Exit only, no access |
| 27 | Exit only, no access | Access only, no exit |
| Dedham & Stratford St Mary (unnumbered) | Exit only | Access only |

## A14 M1 - Felixstowe

| Junction | Westbound | Eastbound |
|---|---|---|
| with M1/M6 (jct19) | Exit only to M6 and M1 *(northbound)* | Access only from M6 and M1 *(southbound)* |
| 4 | Exit only, no access | Access only, no exit |
| 31 | Exit only to M11 *(for London)* | Access only, no exit |
| 31A | Exit only to A14 *(northbound)* | Access only, no exit |
| 34 | Access only, no exit | Exit only, no access |
| 36 | Exit only to A11, access only from A1303 | Access only from A11 |
| 38 | Access only from A11 | Exit only to A11 |
| 39 | Exit only, no access | Access only, no exit |
| 61 | Access only, no exit | Exit only, no access |

## A55 Holyhead - Chester

| Junction | Westbound | Eastbound |
|---|---|---|
| 8A | Exit only, no access | Access only, no exit |
| 23A | Access only, no exit | Exit only, no access |
| 24A | Exit only, no access | No access or exit |
| 27A | No restriction | No access or exit |
| 33A | Exit only, no access | No access or exit |
| 33B | Exit only, no access | Access only, no exit |
| 36A | Exit only to A5104 | Access only from A5104 |

# Smart motorways

Since Britain's first motorway (the Preston Bypass) opened in 1958, motorways have changed significantly. A vast increase in car journeys over the last 60 years has meant that motorways quickly filled to capacity. To combat this, the recent development of **smart motorways** uses technology to monitor and actively manage traffic flow and congestion.

**Various active traffic management methods are used:**

- Traffic flow is monitored using CCTV
- Speed limits are changed to smooth traffic flow and reduce stop-start driving
- Capacity of the motorway can be increased by either temporarily or permanently opening the hard shoulder to traffic
- Warning signs and messages alert drivers to hazards and traffic jams ahead
- Lanes can be closed in the case of an accident or emergency by displaying a red X sign
- Emergency refuge areas are located regularly along the motorway where there is no hard shoulder available

**Smart motorways can be classified into three different types as shown below. The table lists smart motorways operating by 2019 and the colour-coded text indicates the type of smart motorway.**

| | |
|---|---|
| CONTROLLED MOTORWAY | Variable speed limits without hard shoulder (the hard shoulder is used in emergencies only) |
| HARD SHOULDER RUNNING | Variable speed limits with part-time hard shoulder (the hard shoulder is open to traffic at busy times when signs permit) |
| ALL LANE RUNNING | Variable speed limits with hard shoulder as permanent running lane (there is no hard shoulder); this is standard for all new smart motorway schemes since 2013 |

| SMART MOTORWAY SECTIONS | |
|---|---|
| M1 | J6A–10, J10–13, J16–19, J23A–25, J25–28, J28–31, J31–32, J32–35A, J39–42 |
| M3 | J2–4A |
| M4 | J19–20, J24–28 |
| M5 | J4A–6, J15–17 |
| M6 | J4–10A, J10A–13 |
| M9 | J1–1A |
| M20 | J4–7 |
| M25 | J2–3, J5–6, J6–23, J23–27, J27–30 |
| M42 | J3A–7, J7–9 |
| M60 | J8–18 |
| M62 | J18–20, J25–26, J26–28, J28–29, J29–30 |
| M90 | M9 J1A–M90 J3 |

## Quick tips

- Never drive in a lane closed by a red X
- Keep to the speed limit shown on the gantries
- A solid white line indicates the hard shoulder – do not drive in it unless directed
- A broken white line indicates a normal running lane
- Exit the smart motorway where possible if your vehicle is in difficulty. In an emergency, move onto the hard shoulder where there is one, or the nearest emergency refuge area
- Put on your hazard lights if you break down

|  |  |
|---|---|
| M4 | Motorway with number |
| Toll T4 Toll | Toll motorway with toll station |
| 5 | Restricted motorway junctions |
| Fleet S R | Motorway service area, rest area |
| | Motorway and junction under construction |
| A3 | Primary route single/dual carriageway |
| 11 | Primary route junction with and without number |
| 3 | Restricted primary route junctions |
| S | Primary route service area |
| BATH | Primary route destination |
| A1123 | Other A road single/dual carriageway |
| B2070 | B road single/dual carriageway |
| | Minor road, more than 4 metres wide, less than 4 metres wide |
| | Roundabout |
| | Interchange/junction |
| | Narrow primary/other A/B road with passing places (Scotland) |
| | Road under construction |
| | Road tunnel |
| Toll | Road toll, steep gradient (arrows point downhill) |
| 5 | Distance in miles between symbols |
| | Railway line, in tunnel |
| | Railway/tram station, level crossing |
| | Tourist railway |
| 628 637 Lecht Summit | Height in metres, mountain pass |
| | Snow gates (on main routes) |
| or V | Vehicle ferry |
| | Fast vehicle ferry or catamaran |
| H | Airport (major/minor), heliport |
| F | International freight terminal |

|  |  |
|---|---|
| H | 24-hour Accident & Emergency hospital |
| C | Crematorium |
| P+R | Park and Ride (at least 6 days per week) |
| | City, town, village or other built-up area |
| | National boundary, county or administrative boundary |
| | Scenic route |
| i | Tourist Information Centre (all year/seasonal) |
| V | Visitor or heritage centre |
| | Caravan site (AA inspected) |
| | Camping site (AA inspected) |
| | Caravan & camping site (AA inspected) |
| | Abbey, cathedral or priory |
| | Ruined abbey, cathedral or priory |
| | Castle, historic house or building |
| M | Museum or art gallery |
| | Industrial interest |
| | Aqueduct or viaduct |
| | Garden, arboretum |
| | Vineyard, brewery or distillery |
| | Country park, theme park |
| | Agricultural showground |
| | Farm or animal centre |
| | Zoological or wildlife collection |
| | Bird collection, aquarium |
| RSPB | RSPB site |
| | National Nature Reserve (England, Scotland, Wales) |
| | Local nature reserve, Wildlife Trust reserve |
| | Forest drive |
| | National trail |

|  |  |
|---|---|
| | Picnic site |
| | Waterfall |
| | Viewpoint |
| | Hill-fort |
| | Prehistoric monument, Roman antiquity |
| 1066 | Battle site with year |
| | Steam railway centre |
| | Cave or cavern |
| | Windmill, monument |
| | Beach (award winning) |
| | Lighthouse |
| | Golf course (AA listed) |
| | Football stadium |
| | County cricket ground |
| | Rugby Union national stadium |
| | International athletics stadium |
| | Horse racing, show jumping |
| | Air show venue, motor-racing circuit |
| | Ski slope (natural, artificial) |
| | National Trust site (England & Wales, Scotland) |
| | English Heritage site |
| | Historic Scotland site |
| | Cadw (Welsh heritage) site |
| | Major shopping centre, other place of interest |
| | Attraction within urban area |
| | World Heritage Site (UNESCO) |
| | National Park and National Scenic Area (Scotland) |
| | Forest Park |
| | Heritage coast |

Isles of Scilly
White Island
King Charles's Castle
ST MARTIN'S
BRYHER
Old Grimsby
Cromwell's Castle
St Martin's Head
Old Blockhouse
Higher Town
Isles of Scilly Heritage Coast
New Lizard Point
Grimsby
Great Ganilly
Tresco Abbey
TRESCO
Eastern Isles
Samson
Innisidgen Tomb
Great Arthur
North West Passage
Bant's Carn Burial
Crow Sound
ST MARY'S
Harry's Walls
Higher & Lower Moors
Deep Point
Hugh Town
Porth Hellick Down Tombs
Garrison Walls
Isles of Scilly (St Mary's)
Old Town
Middle Town
Peninnis Head
Annet
St Mary's Sound
Broad Sound
Gugh
Smith Sound
ST AGNES
Horse Point
Western Rocks
3 miles
5 kilometres
Carn Naun Point
The Island or St Ives Head
Porthmeor
St Ives
Porthminster
Zennor Head
Gurnards Head
Zennor
South West Coast Path
Halsetown
Carbis Bay
Towednack
Lelant
Pendeen Watch
Carn Galver Mine
Chysauster Ancient Village
Penwith Heritage Coast
Pendeen
Morvah
Men-An-Tol
Mulfra Quoit
Bakers Pit
Canonstown
Geevor Tin Mine
New Mill
Levant Mine & Beam Engine
Pendeen
Lanyon Quoit
Crowlas
Botallack
St Just Mining District
Ludgvan
St Just
Trengwainton Garden
Madron
Gulval
Cape Cornwall
Newbridge
Longrock
Ballowall Barrow
Heamoor
Chyandour
Marazion
Penzance
Perranuthnoe
Kelynack
Carn Euny Ancient Village
Tereife
Sancreed
St Michael's Mount
Whitesand Bay
Land's End
Drift
Newlyn
Kerris
Paul
Crows-an-Wra
Cudden Point
Sennen Cove
Mousehole
St Buryan
LAND'S END
Sennen
MOUNT'S B
The Merry Maidens
Trevescan
Lamorna
Trethewey
Lamorna Cove
Porthcurno
Treen
Telegraph
Merthen Point
Porthgwarra
Minack Open Air Theatre
Cribba Head
Gwennap Head
St Levan
A30
A3071
A3074
A3110
B3306
B3311
B3309
B3318
B3283
B3315
4 miles
5 kilometres

Land's End & the Lizard
3
G
H
4
J
Ligger or Perran Bay
K
L
M
St Newlyn East
Lappa Valley
Enodoc
A30
Summercourt
1
Scarcewater
A3076
Rose
A3075
Fiddlers Green
Mitchell
Perranzabuloe
Perranporth
B3285
Goonhavern
Cligga Point
Bolingey
B3285
St Agnes Heritage Coast
Trevellas Downs
Perranzabuloe
Zelah
St Allen
A39
Trispen
Ladock
ST AGNES HEAD
St Agnes
Penhallow
Callestick
Wheal Coates
Mithian
Barkla Shop
2
B3275
St Erme
Goonvrea
Goonbell
St Agnes Mining District
Probus
Mount Hawke
B3277
B3284
Idless
Porthtowan
Shortlanesend
P+R
Tresillian
South West Coast Path
Mawla
Kenwyn
Godrevy-Portreath Heritage Coast
Portreath
Cambrose
Wheal Peevor
Blackwater
A390
Threemilestone
Truro
B3300
Chacewater
Navax Point
Illogan
A30
Scorrier
Gwennap Mining District
Higher Town
St Clement
Tehidy
Mount Ambrose
Malpas
3
South Tehidy
St Day
Kea
St Michael Penkevil
Ruan Lanihorne
A3078
East Pool Mine
Twelveheads
Reskadinnick
Redruth
4
Playing Place
Lamorran
Tuckingmill
Pool
Carn Brea
Carharrack
Bissoe
Carnon Downs
Trelissick Garden
Kehelland
B3298
Philleigh
Camborne
Carnkie
Gwennap
Devoran
Lanner
A393
Perranwell
Penponds
Connor Downs
B3329
Perranarworthal
A39
Devoran & Perran
Feock
B3289
Gwithian
Trewithian
Veryan
Gwinear
Barripper
Four Lanes
Penhalvean
Kennall Vale
Carnhell Green
B3303
Troon
Ponsanooth
Gerrans Bay
4
Nare Head
Mylor Bridge
St Just-in-Roseland
Stithians
Portscatho
Praze-an-Beeble
B3280
B3297
Mylor
Carrick Roads
Gerrans
B3280
Carnkie
Longdowns
Penryn
P+R
Flushing
Percuil River
Leedstown
Crowan
Porkellis
Rame
Mabe Burnthouse
A39
Pendennis Castle
Castle
Greeb Point
Godolphin House
Budock Water
St Mawes
Wendron Mining District
Argal & College Water Park
Pendennis Point
A394
Godolphin Cross
Trenear
Poldark Mine
Falmouth
Bohortha
B3302
Treverva
South West Coast Path
Prospidnick
Sewrgan
ZONE POINT
Wendron
5
Crowntown
Penjerrick
Helston Heritage Railway
Carleen
Coverack Bridges
Brill
Falmouth Bay
Sithney
Ashton
Breage
Constantine
Mawnan Smith
Trebah
Carwinion
ROSEMULLION HEAD
A394
Helston
Gweek
Porth Navas
Glendurgan Garden
Helford Passage
Durgan
Mawnan
Trewavas Head
B3304
Flambards
Seal Sanctuary
Helford River
Helford
St Anthony-in-Meneage
Porthleven
A3083
Mawgan
Manaccan
Nare Point
Garras
Halliggye Fogou
St Martin
6
Gunwalloe
Porthallow
White Cross
Porthoustock
Manacle Point
B3293
Cury
B3293
St Keverne
The Lizard
Poldhu Point
Marconi Memorial
GOONHILLY DOWNS
Lowland Point
B3296
B3294
Mullion Cove
Mullion
Mullion Island
Coverack
7
Ruan Major
Kuggar
Predannack Head
South West Coast Path
Black Head
Ruan Minor
Vellan Head
Cadgwith
The Lizard
Devil's Frying Pan
The Lizard Heritage Coast
A3083
Lizard Head
Kynance Cove
Church Cove
Lizard
8
LIZARD POINT
Bass Point
Lizard Lighthouse & Heritage Centre
G
H
J
K
L
M

Padstow Bay
Stepper Point
Polzeath
Trebetherick
St Minver
Rock
Padstow
Trevose Head Heritage Coast
TREVOSE HEAD
Harlyn
Trevone
Windmill
Constantine Bay
St Merryn
Porthcothan
St Issey
Wadebridge
Little Petherick
Trenance
Penrose
St Ervan
Rumford
Park Head
Bedruthan Steps
St Jidgey
St Eval
Trenance
Mawgan Porth
St Mawgan
Talskiddy
Trevarrian
Watergate Bay
Newquay
St Columb Major
St Columb Minor
Colan
Mountjoy
Crantock
Quintrell Downs
St Columb Road
Indian Queens
Fraddon
Holywell
Cubert
St Newlyn East
Perranporth
Goonhavern
Mitchell
Summercourt
St Agnes
Ladock
St Stephen
St Allen
Trispen
St Erme
Probus
Grampound
Shortlanesend
Tresillian
Threemilestone
Truro
Tregony
Redruth
St Day
Malpas
St Michael Penkevil
Ruan Lanihorne
Veryan
Philleigh
Portloe
Perranarworthal
Feock
Devoran
Mylor Bridge
St Just-in-Roseland
Penryn
St Mawes
Falmouth
0 1 2 3 4 miles
0 1 2 3 4 5 kilometres

BODMIN MOOR
Bodmin
Lostwithiel
Liskeard
Looe
Fowey
Callington
Altarnun
Trewint
Bolventor
Jamaica Inn
Colliford Lake
Temple
Blisland
Helland
Cardinham
Warleggan
St Neot
Mount
Dobwalls
Moorswater
Trevelmond
St Pinnock
East Taphouse
West Taphouse
Herodsfoot
St Keyne
Duloe
Widegates
Sandplace
St Martin
Pelynt
Lanreath
Lerryn
Muchlarnick
St Veep
Penpoll
Golant
Lanteglos Highway
Bodinnick
Polruan
Polperro
Lansallos
Crumplehorn
Porthallow
Talland Bay
Looe Bay
Looe or St George's Island
Seaton
Downderry
Portwrinkle
Hessenford
Polbathic
Sheviock
Trerulefoot
St Erney
Budge's Shop
Tideford
Menheniot
Quethiock
Pillaton
St Ive
Merrymeet
Tremar
St Cleer
Darite
Common Moor
Minions
Pensilva
Upton
Henwood
Rilla Mill
Linkinhorne
South Hill
Golberdon
Frogwell
Stoke Climsland
Bray Shop
Treburley
Bathpool
Coad's Green
North Hill
Middlewood
Illand
Trebullett
Lezant
St Breward
Churchtown
Michaelstow
Treveighan
Helstone
St Teath
St Tudy
Lanivet
Sweetshouse
Lanlivery
Luxulyan
St Blazey
Tywardreath
Par
Polkerris
Gribbin Head
St Austell Bay
Lantic Bay
Lantivet Bay
Pencarrow Head
Black Head
A30
A38
A390
A387
A3082
A388
A39
B3266
B3268
B3269
B3359
B3254
B3252
B3251
B3253
B3257
B3247
B3249
Gribbin Head - Polperro Heritage Coast
South West Coast Path
Bodmin & Wenford Railway
Lanhydrock
Restormel Castle
Helman Tor
Eden Project
Porfell Wildlife Park
Carnglaze
Golitha Falls
King Doniert's Stone
Trethevy Quoit
Cheesewring
The Hurlers Stone Circles
Siblyback Lake
Sterts Open-Air Theatre
Caradon Mining District
Monkey Sanctuary
Seaton Valley
Model Village
St Catherine's Castle
Wesley Cottage
Brown Willy
SMALLACOMBE DOWNS
BROWNGELLY DOWNS
G
H
J
K
L
M
1
2
3
4
5
6
7
8
9

6
9
10
5
Lawhitton
Meadwell
Kelly
Bradstone
Milton Abbot
Chillaton
North Brentor
Horndon
DARTMO
FOREST
Lezant
Trekenner
Dunterton
Chaddlehanger
Mary Tavy
Cudliptown
Rezare
Treburley
Bealsmill
Lamerton
Peter Tavy
Kingston
Bray Shop
Horsebridge
Sydenham Damerel
Tavistock
Stoke Climsland
Oldmill
Luckett
Downgate
Latchley
Chilsworthy
South Hill
Gulworthy
Gunnislake
Whitchurch
St Ann's Chapel
Golberdon
Harrowbarrow
Callington
Frogwell
Metherell
St Dominick
Albaston
Calstock
Horrabridge
Walkhampton
Dousland
Yelverton
Sheepstor
Buckland Monachorum
Bere Alston
Milton Combe
Meavy
Sowton
Clearbrook
St Mellion
Quethiock
Pillaton
Cotts
Weir Quay
Maristow
Bere Ferrers
Cargreen
Hatt
Landulph
Tamerton Foliot
Roborough
Bickleigh
Shaugh Prior
Botusfleming
Carkeel
Tideford
Landrake
Trematon
Saltash
St Erney
Trerulefoot
St Germans
Trehan
Polbathic
Crownhill
St Budeaux
Eggbuckland
PLYMOUTH
Hemerdon
Lutton
Cornwood
Sparkwell
Venton
Ivybridge
Plympton
Lee Mill
Sheviock
Antony
Crafthole
Torpoint
St John
Devonport
Stonehouse
Cremyll
Portwrinkle
Plymstock
Elburton
Brixton
Westlake
Worston
Freathy
Millbrook
Kingsand
Cawsand
Rame
RAME HEAD
Penlee Point
The Sound
Hooe
Down Thomas
Spriddlestone
Yealmpton
Dunstone
Staddiscombe
Heybrook Bay
Wembury
Newton Ferrers
Holbeton
Bridgend
Noss Mayo
Mothecombe
Gara Point
Stoke Point
Beacon Point
Bigbury-on-Sea
Burgh Island
Roscoff
Santander (Apr-Oct)
Whitsand Bay
Princetown
Sampford Spiney
A388
A38
A386
A390
A374
A379
0 1 2 3 4 miles
0 1 2 3 4 5 kilometres

South Devon
7
Grimspound
529
Manaton
Lustleigh
Water
Becky Falls
Hennock
Harcombe
11
Southcott
Chudleigh
Ashcombe
Cockwood
Model Railway
Hound Tor Medieval Village
HAYTOR 454
Bovey Tracey
Chudleigh Knighton
Ugbrooke Park
Ideford
Luton
12
Dawlish Warren
Dawlish
Widecombe in the Moor
Haytor Vale
Brimley
The Church House
Dunstone
477 RIPPON TOR
Ilsington
Liverton
Coldeast
Stover
Sandygate
Preston
Ponsworthy
Halford
Bishopsteignton
Holcombe
Buckland in the Moor
Teigngrace
Kingsteignton
Coombe
Teignmouth
Bickington
Coombe Cellars
R Teign
Lower Town
Highweek
Netherton
Shaldon
Ringmore
Combeinteignhead
Stokeinteignhead
Newton Abbot
Bradley Manor
Decoy
Middle Rocombe
Lower Gabwell
Higher Gabwell
Ashburton
West Ogwell
East Ogwell
Abbotskerswell
Holne
River Dart
Hembury Castle
Woodland
Denbury
Wildlife Hospital
Coffinswell
Maidencombe
Daccombe
Kingskerswell
Buckfast
Forder Green
Barton
Coombe
Pafford
Model Village
Babbacombe Bay
Torbryan
Ipplepen
Buckfastleigh
Oddicombe
St Marychurch
Babbacombe
Ellacombe
Woolston Green
Broadhempston
Shiphay
Butterfly Farm & Otter Sanctuary
Compton Castle
TORQUAY
Deancombe
Dean
Staverton
Combe Fishacre
South Devon Railway
Compton
Cockington
Dean Prior
Marldon
Pennywell Farm
Dartington
R Dart
Littlehempston
Hollicombe
Preston
Rockend
Meadfoot
Hopes Nose
Berry Pomeroy Castle
Westerland
Rattery
Cott
Berry Pomeroy
Lutton
Tigley
Totnes Castle
Blagdon
Paignton
Totnes
Longcombe
Collaton St Mary
Tor Bay
Belsford
Harberton
Aish
Yalberton
Goodrington
Sharpham
Broadsands
Brixham
Avonwick
Diptford
Luscombe
Ashprington
Stoke Gabriel
Waddeton
Breakwater
Galmpton
BERRY HEAD
North Huish
Tuckenhay
Cornworthy
Dittisham
Harbertonford
Washbourne
East Cornworthy
Greenway
Churston Ferrers
St Mary's Bay
Higher Brixham
Sharkham Point
Curtisknowle
Allaleigh
Capton
Paignton & Dartmouth Railway
Halwell
Moreleigh
Woodlands
Dartmouth
Coleton Fishacre
Scabbacombe Head
Blackawton
Kingswear
Bayard's Cove Fort
Dartmouth Castle
Warfleet
Loddiswell
Woodleigh
Stoke Fleming
East Allington
Aveton Gifford
Blackpool
Blackpool Sands
Churchstow
Goveton
Strete
Buckland-Tout-Saints
Harleston
Slapton
South Devon Heritage Coast
Kingsbridge
Sherford
Frittiscombe
Upton
East Charleton
Chillington
Stokenham
West Alvington
West Charleton
Frogmore
Torcross
Start Bay
Sutton
Kingsbridge Estuary
South Pool
Beeson
Beesands
Malborough
Salcombe
Chivelstone
Kellaton
Collaton
East Portlemouth
South Allington
South West Coast Path
Overbeck's
Rickham
Start Point
East Prawle
Bolt Head
Prawle Point
A38
A380
A381
A383
A384
A385
A379
A3022
A3122
B3387
B3344
B3193
B3192
B3196
B3205
B3060
G
H
J
K
L
M
1
2
3
4
5
6
7
8

A
B
C
D
E
F
1
2
3
4
5
6
7
8
Dizzard Point
St Gennys
Crackington Haven
Cambeak
Sweets
Witchcraft & Magic
Pentire Point - Widemouth Heritage Coast
Boscastle
Tresparrett
Lesnewth
Trevalga
Castle
TINTAGEL HEAD
Tintagel
Trethevey
Bossiney
B3263
B3266
Old Post Office
Davidstow
Penhallic Point
Trewarmett
Treknow
B3314
B3266
South West Coast Path
Delabole
Pengelly
Camelford
Port Isaac Bay
Westdowns
Lanteglos
Trewalder
Helstone
Rumps Point
Port Quin Bay
Kellan Head
Varley Head
Pentire Point
Padstow Bay
Port Quin
Port Isaac
Port Gaverne
B3314
B3267
St Teath
Long Cross
Bee Centre
Hayle Bay
Trelights
Pendoggett
Treveighan
Stepper Point
Polzeath
Michaelstow
4
B3314
St Endellion
A39
St Minver
Churchtown
Trevose Heritage Coast
TREVOSE HEAD
Dinas Head
Trevone
Trequite
St Tudy
St Kew
St Kew Highway
St Breward
De Lank River
0 1 2 3 4 miles
0 1 2 3 4 5 kilometres
Highe
Lowe
Trema
Ma

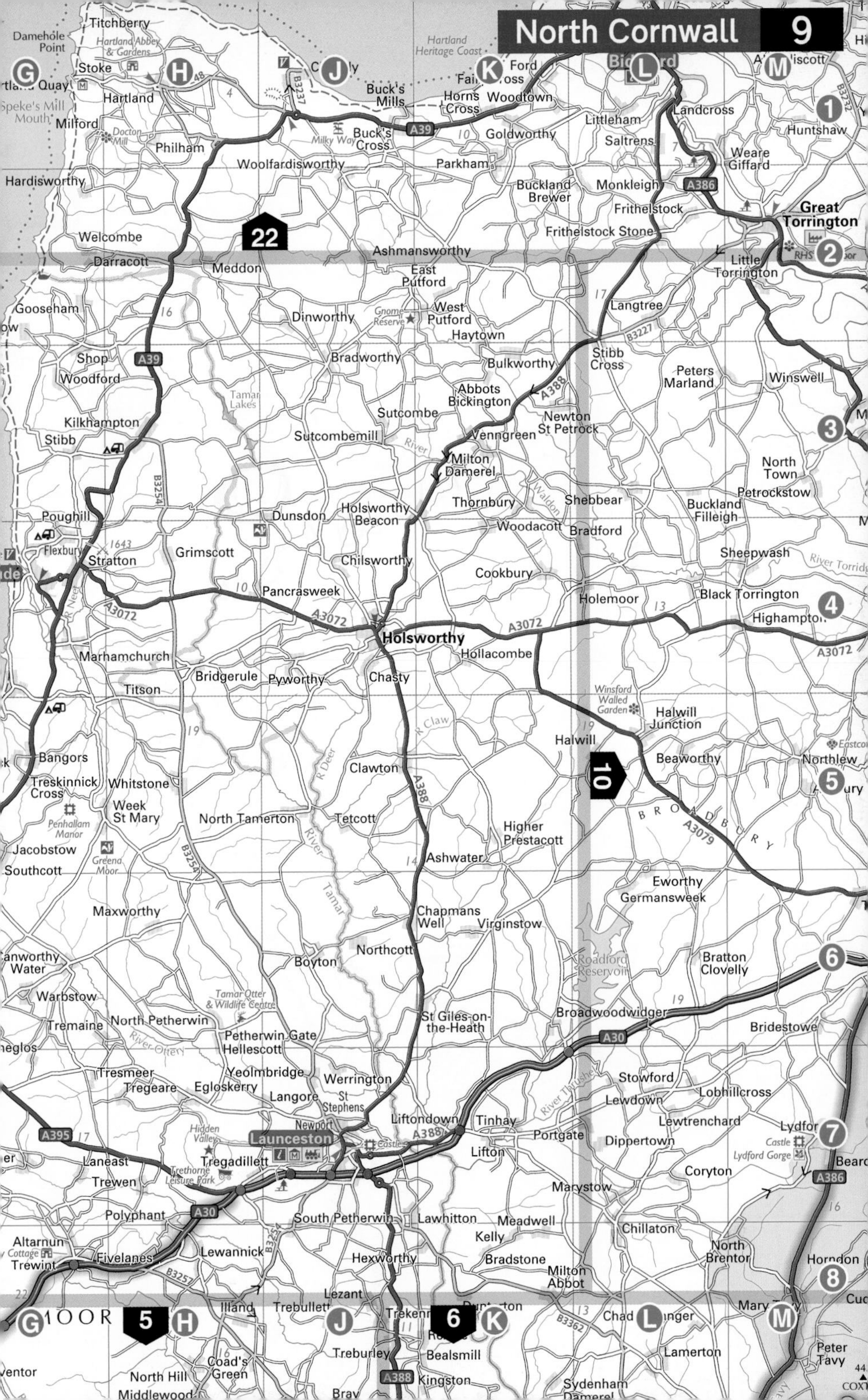
Titchberry
Damehole Point
Hartland Abbey & Gardens
Hartland Heritage Coast
Stoke
Hartland Quay
Speke's Mill Mouth
Hartland
Milford
Docton Mill
Philham
B3237
Buck's Mills
Horns Cross
Woodtown
Fairy Cross
Ford
Bideford
Abbotsham
Landcross
Littleham
Saltrens
Huntshaw
Weare Giffard
A39
Milky Way
Buck's Cross
Goldworthy
Parkham
Woolfardisworthy
Hardisworthy
Buckland Brewer
Monkleigh
A386
Frithelstock
Great Torrington
Frithelstock Stone
Welcombe
22
Ashmansworthy
Darracott
Meddon
East Putford
Little Torrington
RHS
Gooseham
Dinworthy
Gnome Reserve
West Putford
Haytown
Langtree
B3227
B3232
Shop
Woodford
Bradworthy
Bulkworthy
Stibb Cross
Peters Marland
Winswell
Tamar Lakes
Abbots Bickington
A388
Sutcombe
Newton St Petrock
Kilkhampton
Stibb
Sutcombemill
Venngreen
Milton Damerel
North Town
B3254
Thornbury
Waldon
Shebbear
Petrockstow
Poughill
Flexbury
1643
Stratton
Dunsdon
Holsworthy Beacon
Woodacott
Bradford
Buckland Filleigh
Grimscott
Chilsworthy
Sheepwash
River Torridge
Cookbury
Pancrasweek
Holemoor
Black Torrington
A3072
Holsworthy
Highampton
Marhamchurch
Hollacombe
R Neet
Titson
Bridgerule
Pyworthy
Chasty
Winsford Walled Garden
Halwill Junction
R Claw
Halwill
Bangors
Beaworthy
Northlew
10
Treskinnick Cross
Whitstone
Clawton
R Deer
Week St Mary
Penhallam Manor
North Tamerton
Tetcott
Higher Prestacott
BROADBURY
A3079
Jacobstow
Greena Moor
Ashwater
Southcott
River Tamar
Eworthy
Germansweek
Maxworthy
Chapmans Well
Virginstow
Boyton
Northcott
Roadford Reservoir
Bratton Clovelly
Warbstow
Tamar Otter & Wildlife Centre
St Giles-on-the-Heath
Broadwoodwidger
Tremaine
North Petherwin
Petherwin Gate
A30
Bridestowe
River Ottery
Hellescott
Tresmeer
Yeolmbridge
Werrington
Stowford
River Thrushel
Tregeare
Egloskerry
Langore
St Stephens
Lewdown
Lobhillcross
Hidden Valley
Newport
Liftondown
Tinhay
Lewtrenchard
A395
Launceston
Castle
Portgate
Dippertown
Lydford
Laneast
Tregadillett
Lifton
Lydford Gorge
Trewen
Trethorne Leisure Park
Coryton
Marystow
Polyphant
South Petherwin
Lawhitton
Meadwell
Chillaton
Altarnun
Cottage
Lewannick
Kelly
Trewint
Fivelanes
Hexworthy
Bradstone
North Brentor
Horndon
B3257
Milton Abbot
Lezant
Illand
Trebullett
Trekenner
Chadlinger
B3362
5
6
Treburley
Bealsmill
Lamerton
Peter Tavy
Coad's Green
North Hill
Middlewood
Kingston
Sydenham Damerel
Bray

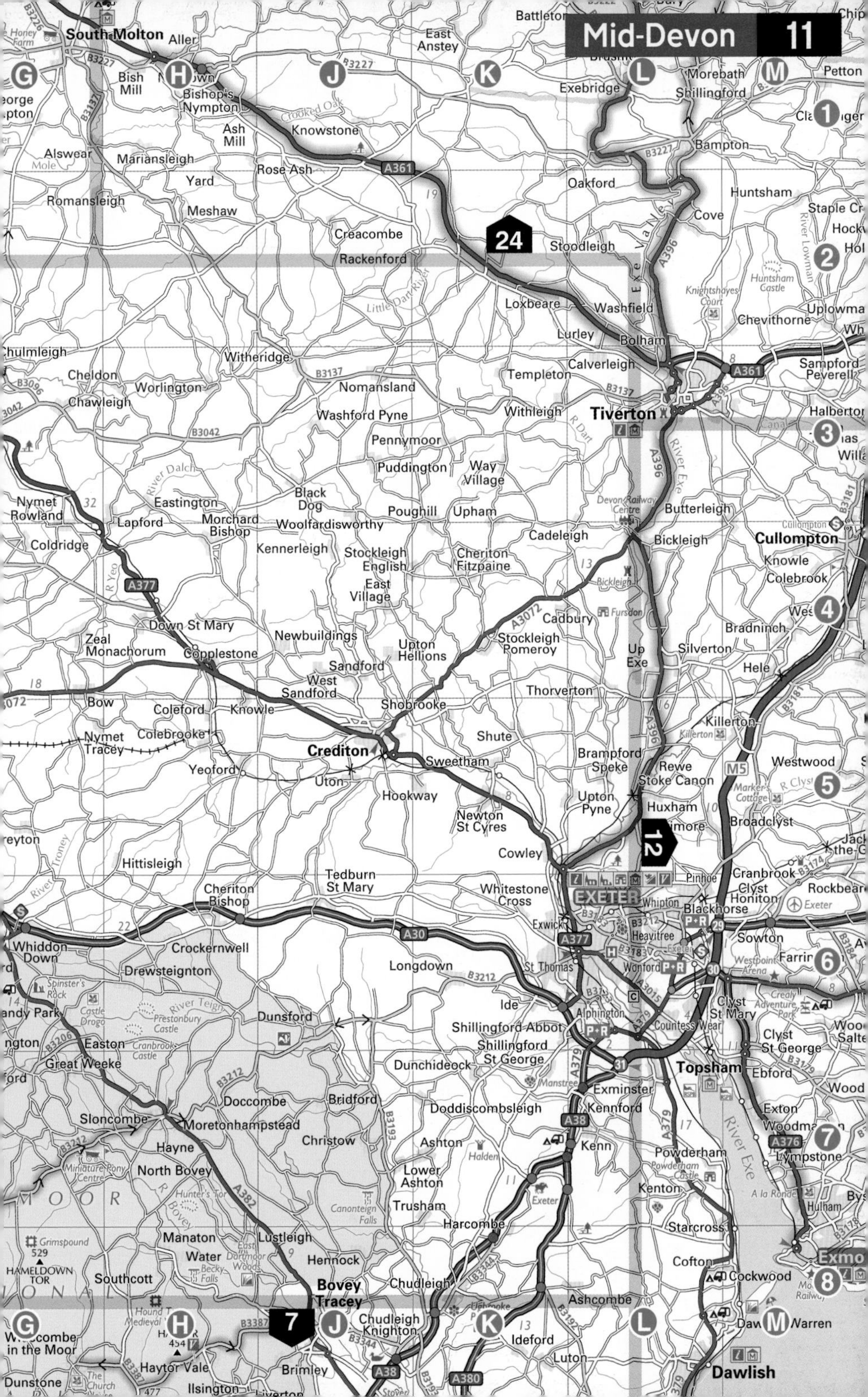
South Molton
Bishop's Nympton
Knowstone
Rose Ash
Creacombe
Rackenford
Stoodleigh
Exebridge
Morebath
Shillingford
Bampton
Oakford
Huntsham
Cove
Loxbeare
Washfield
Bolham
Calverleigh
Templeton
Tiverton
Withleigh
Witheridge
Nomansland
Washford Pyne
Pennymoor
Puddington
Way Village
Black Dog
Poughill
Upham
Woolfardisworthy
Morchard Bishop
Lapford
Eastington
Nymet Rowland
Coldridge
Chulmleigh
Cheldon
Chawleigh
Worlington
Kennerleigh
Stockleigh English
Cheriton Fitzpaine
Cadeleigh
Bickleigh
Butterleigh
Cullompton
Sampford Peverell
Halberton
Chevithorne
Uplowman
Knowle
Colebrook
Bradninch
Silverton
Hele
Killerton
Westwood
Broadclyst
Up Exe
Thorverton
Cadbury
Stockleigh Pomeroy
Upton Hellions
Newbuildings
Sandford
West Sandford
Shobrooke
Crediton
Down St Mary
Zeal Monachorum
Copplestone
Bow
Coleford
Knowle
Colebrooke
Nymet Tracey
Yeoford
Uton
Sweetham
Hookway
Shute
Brampford Speke
Rewe
Stoke Canon
Huxham
Upton Pyne
Newton St Cyres
Cowley
Hittisleigh
Tedburn St Mary
Cheriton Bishop
Whitestone Cross
Exeter
Exwick
Whipton
Heavitree
Pinhoe
Cranbrook
Clyst Honiton
Blackhorse
Sowton
Rockbeare
St Thomas
Wonford
Alphington
Countess Wear
Clyst St Mary
Clyst St George
Ide
Shillingford Abbot
Shillingford St George
Longdown
Crockernwell
Whiddon Down
Drewsteignton
Dunsford
Easton
Great Weeke
Dunchideock
Exminster
Kennford
Kenn
Topsham
Ebford
Exton
Woodmanton
Lympstone
Doddiscombsleigh
Doccombe
Bridford
Moretonhampstead
Sloncombe
Christow
Ashton
Hayne
North Bovey
Lower Ashton
Trusham
Powderham
Kenton
Starcross
Cofton
Cockwood
Harcombe
Manaton
Lustleigh
Water
Hennock
Southcott
Bovey Tracey
Chudleigh
Chudleigh Knighton
Ashcombe
Ideford
Luton
Haytor Vale
Brimley
Ilsington
Dunstone
Widecombe in the Moor
Dawlish
Warren
Exmouth
A361
A396
A377
A3072
A30
A38
A379
A376
A382
A380
B3137
B3227
B3042
B3212
B3193
B3344
M5
24
12
7

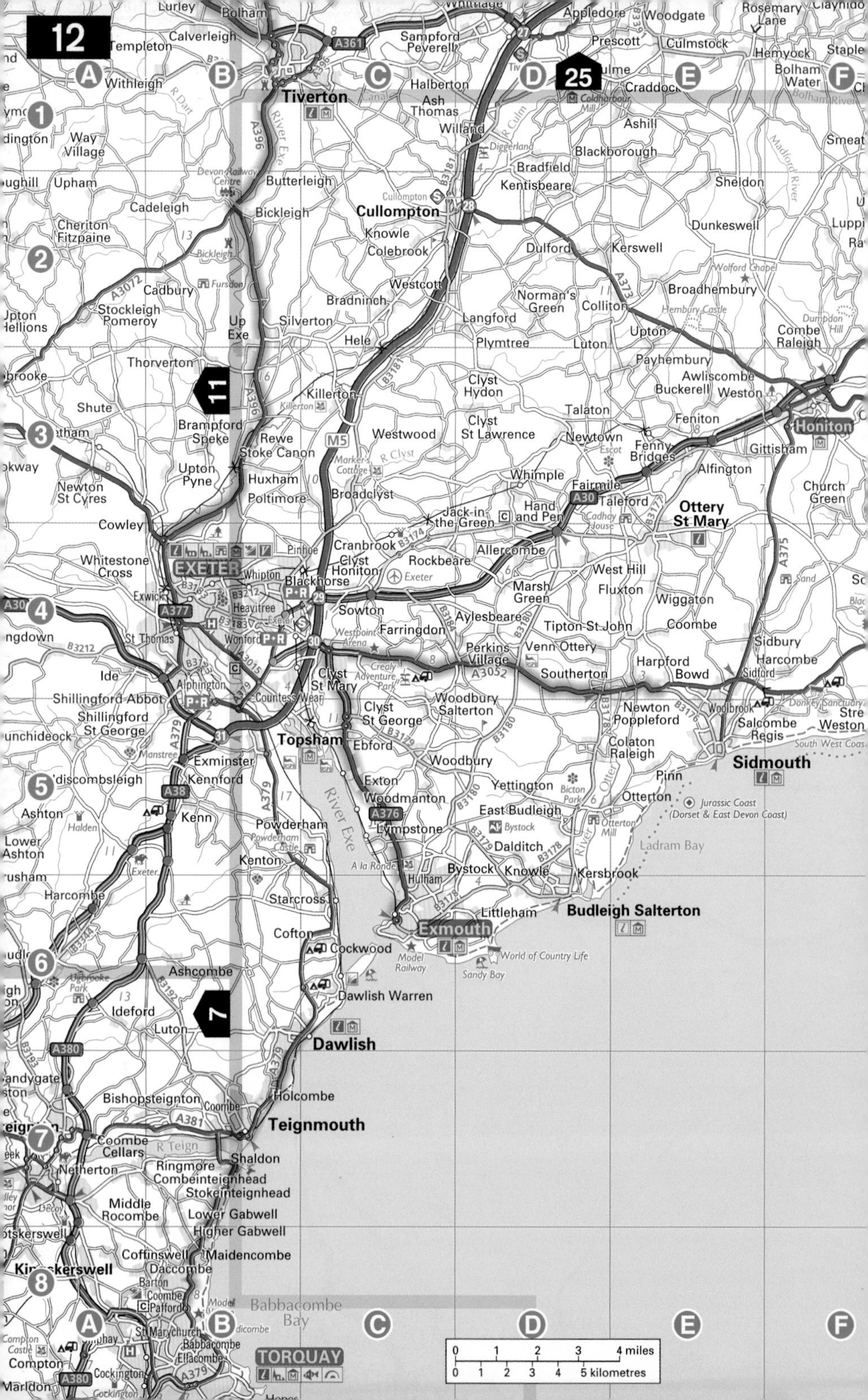
12
Tiverton
Cullompton
Exeter
Exmouth
Topsham
Dawlish
Teignmouth
Sidmouth
Budleigh Salterton
Ottery St Mary
Honiton
Torquay
Dawlish Warren
Crediton
Broadclyst
Cranbrook
Woodbury
East Budleigh
Otterton
Newton Poppleford
Kenton
Starcross
Cockwood
Lympstone
Exminster
Kenn
Kennford
Shaldon
Maidencombe
Babbacombe Bay
Sandy Bay
Ladram Bay
Jurassic Coast (Dorset & East Devon Coast)
South West Coast Path
River Exe
River Otter
M5
A30
A38
A380
A379
A376
A3052
A373
A375
A396
A377
A381
25
11
7
0 1 2 3 4 miles
0 1 2 3 4 5 kilometres

Horton
Buckland St Mary
Birch Wood
Donyatt
Ilminster
Kingston
25
26
14
Beetham
Combe St Nicholas
Knowle St Giles
Dowlish Wake
Ludney
Hinton St George
Merriott
Hardington Mandeville
East Coker
Northay
Wadeford
Chardleigh Green
Cudworth
Chillington
Higher Chillington
Haselbury Plucknett
Pendomer
Whitestaunton
Higher Wambrook
Chaffcombe
Purtington
Roundham
Crewkerne
North Perrott
Hardington Marsh
Closworth
Howley
Cricket St Thomas
Hewish
BIRTS HILL
Halstock
Yarcombe
Chard
Forton
Woolminstone
Misterton
South Perrott
Wambrook
Whatley
Wayford
Clapton
Burridge
Tatworth
Winsham
Seaborough
Mosterton
Netherhay
River Axe
Corscombe
East Chelborough
Stockland
Forde Abbey
Drimpton
Chedington
Furley
Chard Junction
Laymore
Chardstock
Membury
Hewood
Blackdown
Alston
Tytherleigh
Thorncombe
Burstock
Broadwindsor
Benville
Holditch
Ham
Churchill
Pilsdon Pen
Higher Wraxhall
Birdsmoorgate
Stoke Abbott
Beaminster
Dalwood
Loughwood Meeting House
Smallridge
Hawkchurch
Hooke
Bettiscombe
Mapperton
Weycroft
Marshwood
Pilsdon
Axminster
Netherbury
Lambert's Castle
Melplash
North Poorton
South Poorton
Shute
Kilmington
Waytown
Powerstock Common
Monkton Wyld
Coney's Castle
Broadoak
Salway Ash
West Milton
Shute Barton
Wootton Fitzpaine
Marshwood Vale
Whitchurch Canonicorum
Powerstock
Nettlecombe
Whitford
Musbury
Maidenhayne
Harcombe Bottom
Catherston Leweston
Ryall
North Chideock
Bradpole
Colyton
Pymore
Loders
Musbury Castle
Symondsbury
Uploders
Uplyme
Charmouth
Morcombelake
Allington
St Andrews Well
Spyway
Colyford
Chideock
Bridport
Walditch
Askerswell
GOLDEN CAP
Bothenhampton
Seaton
Axmouth
Lyme Regis
Seatown
Eype
Watton
Shipton Gorge
Rousdon
Chilcombe
Seaton Tramway
West Bay
Litton Cheney
Jurassic Coast (Dorset & East Devon Coast)
Beer
Axmouth to Lyme Regis Undercliffs
Burton Bradstock
Puncknowle
Swyre
Abbotsbury Castle
West Bexington
Coast Path
LYME BAY
A30
A358
A356
A3066
A35
A3052
A303
B3162
B3165
B3167
B3172
B3261
B3164
B3163
B3157
River Axe
R Yarty
R Brit
R Bride
G H J K L M
1 2 3 4 5 6 7 8

14
26
13
A
B
C
D
E
F
1
2
3
4
5
6
7
8
Barwick
Bradford Abbas
North Wootton
Allweston
Bishop's Caundle
Caundle Marsh
Lydlinch
Bagber
Sturminster Newton
Hammoon
Harding Moor
East Coker
Stoford
Folke
Fiddleford
Beer Hackett
Knighton
Holwell
Crouch Hill
Fifehead Neville
Sturminster Common
Okeford Fitzpaine
Shilling
Hardington Marsh
Pendomer
Closworth
Ryme Intrinseca
Yetminster
King's Stag
Kingston
Hazelbury Bryan
Fifehead St Quintin
Belchalwell
BIRTS HILL
Halstock
Hamlet
Leigh
Glanvilles Wootton
Pulham
Melbury Osmond
Chetnole
Stockwood
Hermitage
Middlemarsh
Wonston
Droop
Ibberton
Woolland
Bulbarrow Hill
East Chelborough
Melbury Bubb
Lyon's Gate
Duntish
Buckland Newton
Mappowder
Winterborne Houghton
Batcombe
Evershot
Holywell
Minterne Magna
Minterne House
Henley
Higher Ansty
Lower Ansty
Melcombe Bingham
Hilton
Benville
Uphall
Rampisham
Frome St Quintin
Alton Pancras
Cerne Giant
Plush
Milton Abbey
Milton Abbas
Lower Wraxhall
Higher Wraxhall
Hooke
Cerne Abbas
Cerne Abbey
Mapperton
Cattistock
Sydling St Nicholas
Piddletrenthide
Cheselbourne
Bingham
North Poorton
South Poorton
Chilfrome
Toller Porcorum
Maiden Newton
Nether Cerne
White Lackington
PUDDLETON DOWN
Dewlish
Milborne St Andrew
Toller Fratrum
Hog Cliff
Godmanstone
Piddlehinton
Powerstock
Nettlecombe
West Compton Abbas
Wynford Eagle
Frampton
Higher Waterston
Athelhampton
Tolpuddle
EGGARDON HILL
Southover
Grimstone
Stratton
Charlton Down
Puddletown
YELLOWHAM HILL
Burleston
Affpuddle
Uploders
Compton Valence
Spyway
Askerswell
Bradford Peverell
Charminster
Hardy's Cottage
Briantspuddle
Higher Bockhampton
Tincleton
Pallington
Kingston Russell
Winterbourne Abbas
Dorchester
Stinsford
Woodsford
Chilcombe
R Bride
Barrows
Long Bredy
The Nine Stones
Poundbury
Kingston Maurward
West Stafford
Clouds Hill
Litton Cheney
Winterbourne Steepleton
Martinstown
Winterborne Came
Whitcombe
Moreton
Littlebredy
Maiden Castle
River Frome
Puncknowle
Valley of Stones
Hardy Monument
Winterborne Monkton
West Knighton
Crossways
Winfrith
Swyre
Abbotsbury Castle
Kingston Russell
West Bexington
WHITE HILL
Portesham
Broadmayne
Warmwell
Tadnoll
Abbotsbury
Abbey Remains
Owermoigne
South West Coast Path
Bincombe
White Horse
Poxwell
East Knighton
Jurassic Coast (Dorset & East Devon Coast)
St Catherine's Chapel
Swannery
Rodden
Winfrith Newburgh
Osmington
Langton Herring
Buckland Ripers
Overcombe
Preston
Jordan Hill
Upton
West Chaldon
East Chaldon / Chaldon Herring
Osmington Mills
CHALDON DOWN
P+R
Lodmoor
Chickerell
Weymouth Bay
Ringstead Bay
West Lulworth
Lulworth Cove
Chesil Beach
The Fleet
Fleet
Water Gardens
Chesil Bank & The Fleet
Westham
Weymouth
Jurassic Skyline
Durdle Door
Nothe Fort
Wyke Regis
Sandsfoot
Portland Harbour
Chesil Beach
Portland Castle
West Bay
Fortuneswell
PORTLAND
Easton
Portland
Portland Bill
PORTLAND BILL
A37
A35
A352
A354
A356
A3030
A357
A353
B3146
B3143
B3142
B3150
B3147
B3159
B3157
B3156
B3155
B3163
B3390
B3070
0 1 2 3 4 miles
0 1 2 3 4 5 kilometres

27
28
16
G H J K L M
1 2 3 4 5 6 7 8
Tarrant Gunville
Chettle
Gussage St Andrew
Cranborne
Alderholt
Gussage St Michael
Tarrant Hinton
North Gorley
South Gorley
Edmondsham
Long Crichel
Gussage All Saints
Romford
Verwood
Ibsley
Tarrant Launceston
Pimperne
Tarrant Monkton
Moor Crichel
Woodlands
Horton
Royal Signals
Manswood
Tarrant Rawston
Witchampton
Mannington
Three Legged Cross
Ringwood
Poulner
Hinton Martell
Tarrant Rushton
Charlton Marshall
Tarrant Keyneston
Holt
St Leonards
Tarrant Crawford
Badbury Rings
Honeybrook
West Moors
Spetisbury
Shapwick
Kingston Lacy
Abbott Street
Hillbutts
Colehill
Ferndown
FOXBURY HILL
Bisterne
Sandford
Sturminster Marshall
Pamphill
Wimborne Minster
Leigh Park
Hampreston
Knoll
Avon
Ripley
Bransgore
Longham
Dudsbury
West Parley
Bournemouth Aviation
Hurn
Sopley
Winterborne Zelston
Merley
Kinson
Corfe Mullen
Bearwood
West Howe
Cudnell
Ensbury
Red Hill
Adventure Wonderland
West Morden
Morden
East Howe
Throop
Broadstone
Upton Heath
Moordown
Burton
East Morden
Lytchett Matravers
Canford Heath
Wallisdown
Talbot Village
Winton
Iford
Somerford
Christchurch
Upton
Newtown
Branksome
Pokesdown
Tuckton
Mudeford
Wick
Morden Bog
Organford
Lytchett Minster
Hamworthy
Lower Hamworthy
Parkstone
Westbourne
Branksome Park
Boscombe
Southbourne
Christchurch Bay
Hengistbury Head
HENGISTBURY
Lilliput
BOURNEMOUTH
POOLE
Canford Cliffs
Sandford
Northport
Arne
Poole Harbour
Brownsea Island
Sandbanks
POOLE BAY
Wareham
Stoborough
Ridge
Stoborough Heath
East Holme
Toll
Purbeck Heritage Coast
Studland Bay
Studland Beach
Hartland Moor
The Blue Pool
ISLE OF PURBECK
Studland
THE FORELAND
Corfe Castle
Swanage Railway
Cherbourg
Church Knowle
Harman's Cross
Ulwell
Ballard Point
Swanage Bay
Kingston
Swanage
Purbeck Marine
Kimmeridge
Kimmeridge Bay
South West Coast Path
Langton Matravers
Durlston
DURLSTON HEAD
Guernsey Jersey St-Malo
Jurassic Coast (Dorset & East Devon Coast)
Chapman's Pool
Worth Matravers
Anvil Point
ST ALDHELM'S OR ST ALBAN'S HEAD
A354
A350
A31
A35
A351
A338
A341
A348
A347
A349
A3049
A3060
B3078
B3081
B3072
B3082
B3075
B3074
B3068
B3061
B3073
B3065
B3369
B3351
B3069
B3347
Liberty's Owl, Raptor & Reptile Centre
Kingston Great Common
Ibsley Common
Rockford Common
Holt Heath
Moors Valley
Avon Heath
Dorset Heavy Horse Farm Park
Church & Earthworks

28
15
NEW FOREST NATIONAL PARK
SOUTHAMPTON
Lyndhurst
Brockenhurst
Lymington
New Milton
Christchurch
Yarmouth
Freshwater
Hythe
Fawley
Netley
Beaulieu
Sway
Hordle
Milford on Sea
Barton-on-Sea
Bransgore
Totland
THE NEEDLES
Christchurch Bay
Brighstone Bay
Southampton Water
0 1 2 3 4 miles
0 1 2 3 4 5 kilometres

29
30
18
G
H
J
K
L
M
1
2
3
4
5
6
7
8
Wickham
Shedfield
Curdridge
Shirrell Heath
Soberton Heath
Newtown
Hambledon
Catherington
Blendworth
Forestside
Stoughton
Bow Hill
Walderton
Curbridge
Whiteley
North Boarhunt
Worlds End
Soake
Cowplain
Rowland's Castle
Stansted Park
Kingley Vale
WATERLOOVILLE
Southwick
Purbrook
Stakes
Leigh Park
Westbourne
Woodend
West Stoke
Funtington
Mid Lavant
Boarhunt
Royal Armouries Fort Nelson
Portsdown
HAVANT
Woodmancote
West Ashling
East Ashling
Titchfield Abbey
Wallington
Catisfield
Bedhampton
Hambrook
Southbourne
Broadbridge
Cosham
Drayton
Farlington
Brockhampton
Langstone
Emsworth
Nutbourne
Walton
Fishbourne
Titchfield
FAREHAM
Portchester
Castle
Portsmouth Harbour
Hilsea
Northney
Chidham
Bosham
Dell Quay
Apuldram
Stubbington
Hill Head
Bridgemary
Whale Island
Continental Ferry Terminal
North End
North Hayling
THORNEY ISLAND
West Thorney
Donnington
Elson
Fort Brockhurst
Stoke
HAYLING ISLAND
Langstone Harbour
Rowner
Hardway
Portsmouth Dockyard
West Itchenor
Birdham
GOSPORT
Portsea
Fratton
Chichester Harbour
Lee-on-the-Solent
Spinnaker Tower
Southsea
West Town
South Hayling
Shipton Green
Isle of Wight Ferry Terminal
East Head
West Wittering
Somerley
Stokes Bay
Alverstoke
Eastney
Fort Cumberland
Hayling Bay
PORTSMOUTH
Gilkicker Point
East Wittering
Earnley
Bracklesham
Osborne
Cowes
Osborne Bay
Spitbank Fort
SPITHEAD
Bracklesham Bay
Whippingham
Wootton Bridge
Fishbourne
Ryde
Puckpool Point
Nettlestone Point
Seaview
Binstead
Rosemary
Havenstreet
Little Whitefield
Nettlestone
St Helens
Isle of Wight Steam Railway
Robin Hill
The Duver
East Ashey
Bembridge
Bembridge Windmill
Lifeboat Station
FORELAND
Nunwell
Brading
Guernsey
Jersey
St-Malo
Caen (Ouistreham)
le Havre (Jan-Oct)
Bilbao (Jan-Oct)
Santander (Jan-Oct)
Cherbourg (May-Aug)
WIGHT
Newchurch
Alverstone
Whitecliff Bay
Bembridge Down
Bembridge & Culver Downs
Queen's Bower
Dinosaur Isle
Yaverland
Culver Cliff
Winford
Lake
Sandown
Branstone
Sandown Bay
Apse Heath
Sandford
Whiteley Bank
Shanklin
Old Smithy & Gardens
Shanklin Chine
Luccombe Village
Luccombe Chine
Appuldurcombe House
Wroxall
Ventnor Downs
DUNNOSE
Ventnor
Botanic Garden
St Lawrence
The Undercliff
M27
M275
A3(M)
A27
A259
A32
A334
A3
A3023
A2030
A288
A286
A3054
A3055
A3056
A3020
B2177
B2150
B2149
B2148
B2146
B2147
B2178
B3385
B3334
B3333
B3330
B3395
B3327
B2179
B2198
B2201
B2145

18
Linchmere
Kingsley Green
Black Down
280
BLACKDOWN HILL
Plaistow
Northchapel
Hollycombe Steam
Fernhurst
Lurgashall
Milland
Woodmansgreen
Ebernoe Common
Kirdford
Five Oaks
Barns Green
Redford
Henley
Lickfold
Lurgashall
Balls Cross
Wisborough Green
Fishers
Billingshurst
Fyning
SOUTH DOWNS
Chithurst
Iping
Woolbeding
Lodsworth
River
Upperton
Coneyhurst Common
Trotton
Stedham
Easebourne
Petworth House
Adversane
Nyewood
Iping & Stedham Common
Midhurst
Petworth
Byworth
Broadford Bridge
Coolham
Harting
NATIONAL PARK
Tillington
Little Bognor
Codmore Hill
30
Minsted
Selham
Elsted
Cocking Causeway
West Lavington
South Ambersham
East Harting
Didling
Fittleworth
Stopham
Nutbourne
Treyford
Harting Beacon
249
Bepton
Cocking
Upper Norwood
Duncton
Coates
Pulborough
Marehill
West Chiltington
Thakeham
LINCH DOWN
Heyshott
Burton & Chingford Ponds
Hardham
South Downs Way
Graffham
Duncton Hill
Coldwaltham
Abingworth
East Lavington
Barlavington
Greatham
Ashington
Roman Villa
255
DUNCTON HILL
Sutton
Waterfield
Chilgrove
LEVIN DOWN
170
East Marden
Singleton
Bignor
Rackham
Parham
West Dean
225
BIGNOR HILL
Storrington
Upwaltham
Charlton
East Dean
Bury
Amberley
212
KITHURST HILL
Washington
Stoughton
Weald & Downland Open Air
Goodwood
Houghton
Amberley Museum
Bow Hill
The Trundle
206
THE TRUNDLE
South Downs Way
Kingley Vale
Halnaker Hill
North Stoke
144
NORE HILL
South Stoke
West Stoke
Eartham
167
HARROW HILL
East Lavant
Offham
Burpham
Mid Lavant
Waterbeach
Slindon
Wepham
Findon
Goodwood
Strettington
Halnaker
Arundel
East Ashling
Priory
Fontwell
Arundel Wetland Centre
Summersdale
Goodwood
Boxgrove
Warningcamp
Clapham
Broadbridge
Tangmere
Norton
Fontwell Park
Binsted
Poling Corner
Patching
High Salvington
Roman Palace
Westhampnett
Nyton
Walberton
Walton
Aldingbourne
Eastergate
Tortington
Poling
Durrington
Fishbourne
Chichester
Oving
Westergate
North End
Lyminster
Angmering
HIGHDOWN HILL
Salvington
Bosham
Woodgate
Barnham
Wick
Dell Quay
Apuldram
Colworth
Ford
West Tarring
Merston
Shripney
Yapton
Climping
Rustington
Ferring
Donnington
Runcton
Bilsham
East Preston
Goring-by-Sea
Hunston
North Mundham
Flansham
Littlehampton
Birdham
South Mundham
Ancton
Bersted
Elmer
Middleton-on-Sea
Street End
Sidlesham
Rose Green
Felpham
Highleigh
Nyetimber
Aldwick
BOGNOR REGIS
17
Earnley
Pagham Harbour
Pagham
Church Norton
Selsey
SELSEY BILL
A272
A286
A283
A29
A264
A285
A284
A27
A259
A280
A24
A2032
B2070
B2133
B2139
B2138
B2141
B2146
B2178
B2201
B2166
B2145
B2179
B2198
B2233
B2132
B2259
B2187
B2140
A B C D E F
1 2 3 4 5 6 7 8
0 1 2 3 4 miles
0 1 2 3 4 5 kilometres

Horsham
Balcombe
Handcross
Staplefield
Slaugham
Lower Beeding
Warninglid
Nuthurst
Maplehurst
Crabtree
Cuckfield
Haywards Heath
Lindfield
Horsted Keynes
Danehill
Nutley
Fairwarp
Maresfield
Five Ash Down
Buxted
Sheffield Park
Splayne's Green
Fletching
Scayne's Hill
Piltdown
Uckfield
Newick
North Chailey
Bolney
Ansty
Bolnore
Cowfold
Hickstead
Twineham
Sayers Common
Worlds End
Wivelsfield
Burgess Hill
Wivelsfield Green
Chailey
Town Littleworth
South Chailey
Isfield
Little Horsted
Halland
Ridgewood
New Town
Henfield
Blackstone
Albourne
Hurstpierpoint
Hassocks
Keymer
Plumpton Green
Ditchling
East Chiltington
Barcombe
Barcombe Cross
Upper Wellingham
Shortgate
Woodmancote
Clayton
Westmeston
Streat
Plumpton
Pyecombe
Ditchling Beacon
Small Dole
Poynings
Edburton
Upper Beeding
Fulking
Pangdean
Saddlescombe
South Downs National Park
Mount Harry
Offham
Hamsey
Ringmer
Laughton
South Malling
Lewes
Wallands Park
Stanmer
Truleigh Hill
Devil's Dyke
Patcham
Coldean
Withdean
Hollingbury
Moulsecoomb
Falmer
Kingston near Lewes
Iford
Beddingham
Glynde
Firle
Mount Caburn
Mile Oak
Hangleton
West Blatchington
Portslade
Preston
Newmarket Hill
Rodmell
Southease
Tarring Neville
Old Shoreham
Southwick
Shoreham-by-Sea
Portslade-by-Sea
HOVE
BRIGHTON
Kemp Town
Woodingdean
Ovingdean
Telscombe
South Heighton
Denton
Newhaven
Norton
Bishopstone
East Blatchington
Rottingdean
Saltdean
Piddinghoe
Peacehaven
Newhaven Fort
Seaford Bay
Seaford
Sutton
Seaford Head
Firle Beacon
Dieppe
A23
A27
A259
A270
A272
A273
A275
A26
A22
A281
A283
A2037
A2300
20
31
32

Tidebrook
Rotherfield
Ticehurst
Hawkhurst
Sweethaws
Fairwarp
Stonegate
Mayfield
Witherenden Hill
Etchingham
Hurst Green
Five Ash Down
Pound Green
Hadlow Down
Five Ashes
Burwash
Bodiam
Salehurst
Buxted
Broad Oak
Robertsbridge
Cross in Hand
Heathfield
Burwash Common
Burwash Weald
Staplecross
Uckfield
Blackboys
Framfield
Cade Street
Three Cups Corner
Brightling
Mountfield
New Town
Ridgewood
Waldron
Little London
Punnett's Town
Wood's Corner
Maynard's Green
Dallington
Netherfield
Whatlington
Little Horsted
Rushlake Green
Warbleton
Horam
Vines Cross
Battle
Halland
East Hoathly
Gun Hill
Shortgate
Chiddingly
Cowbeech
Bodle Street Green
Whitesmith
Muddles Green
Catsfield
Crowhurst
Laughton
Hellingly
Herstmonceux
Ringmer
Windmill Hill
Ninfield
Henley's Down
Lower Dicker
Horsebridge
Magham Down
Boreham Street
Lunsford's Cross
Ripe
Upper Dicker
Leap Cross
Hailsham
Hooe
Chalvington
Wartling
Little Common
Pebsham
Selmeston
Pevensey Levels
Firle
Arlington
Cooden
Bexhill
Charleston
Alciston
Polegate
Berwick
Westham
Pevensey
Tarring Neville
Wilmington
South Heighton
Folkington
Lower Willingdon
Pevensey Bay
Alfriston
Willingdon
Hampden Park
Langney
Sovereign Harbour
Ratton Village
Norton
Litlington
Jevington
Bishopstone
East Blatchington
St Anthony's Hill
Roselands
Langney Point
Westdean
Old Town
Sutton
Friston
Seaford
EASTBOURNE
East Dean
Seaford Head
Cuckmere Haven
Beachy Head Countryside Centre
BEACHY HEAD
Sussex Heritage Coast
Dieppe
South Downs Way
The Long Man of Wilmington
Michelham Priory
Arlington Reservoir
Herstmonceux Castle
Observatory Science Centre
Darwell Reservoir
Bateman's
Pashley Manor
Merriments
Wilderness Wood
FIRLE BEACON
Seven Sisters
Drusillas
Clergy House
Lullington Heath
Miniature
Castle
0 1 2 3 4 miles
0 1 2 3 4 5 kilometres

Rolvenden
Rolvenden Layne
Kent & East Sussex Railway
Newenden
Wittersham
Small Hythe
Chapel Down
Smallhythe Place
ISLE OF OXNEY
Stone in Oxney
The Stocks
Appledore
Horne's Place Chapel
34
Snargate
Brenzett
Ivychurch
Aeronautical
Romney Marsh
Romney Warren
St Mary in the Marsh
Martello
St Mary's Bay
Old Romney
Brookland
A259
B2080
B2082
B2088
B2165
B2089
B2071
B2075
A268
Royal Military Canal
River Rother
Rother Levels
Northiam
Beckley
Clayhill
Peasmarsh
Rye Foreign
Iden
Playden
Rye
Houghton Green
East Guldeford
WALLAND MARSH
Littlestone-on-Sea
New Romney
Greatstone-on-Sea
Lydd
Broad Oak
R Tillingham
Cock Marling
Broadland Row
Udimore
Brede
River Brede
Camber
Camber Castle
Dungeness
Dungeness Power Station
The Old Lighthouse
DUNGENESS
Rye Bay
Broad Street
Winchelsea
Icklesham
Guestling Thorn
Guestling Green
Pett
Cliff End
Fairlight
Ore
Hastings

A
B
C
D
E
F
1
2
3
4
5
6
7
8
North West Point
Lundy Heritage Coast
LUNDY
142
Marine Reserve
Marisco
Shutter Point
Surf Point
BARNSTAPLE
OR
BIDEFORD BAY
West
HARTLAND POINT
Shipload Bay
Titchberry
Damehole Point
Hartland Abbey & Gardens
Stoke
Hartland Quay
Hartland
B3248
Clovelly
B3237
Hartland Heritage Coast
Abb
For
Fairy Cross
Horns Cross
Woodto
Buck's Mills
Speke's Mill Mouth
Milford
Docton Mill
Philham
Milky Way
Buck's Cross
A39
10
Goldwo
Woolfardisworthy
Parkham
Hardisworthy
Welcombe
Ashmansworthy
Darracott
Meddon
9
East Putford
Gooseham
16
Dinworthy
Gnome Reserve
West Putford
Morwenstow
Haytown
Higher Sharpnose Point
Shop
A39
Bradworthy
Bulkwo
South West Coast Path
Woodford
Tamar Lakes
Abbots Bickington
Lower Sharpnose Point
Sutcombe
Kilkhampton
Steeple Point
Sutcombemill
River
Milton Damerel
0 1 2 3 4 miles
0 1 2 3 4 5 kilometres
B3254
Northcott
Poughill
Dunsdon
Holsworthy Beacon
Thornbury

Ilfracombe
Lynton
Lynmouth
Countisbury
Combe Martin
Berrynarbor
Kentisbury
Parracombe
Martinhoe
Trentishoe
Barbrook
Rockford
Mortehoe
Lee
Slade
Hele
Trimstone
West Down
Bittadon
Clifton
Arlington
Loxhore
Milltown
Muddiford
Shirwell
Braunton
Wrafton
Chivenor
Heanton Punchardon
Ashford
Pilton
Barnstaple
Goodleigh
Fremington
Bickington
Roundswell
Landkey
Swimbridge
Instow
Westleigh
Horwood
Tawstock
Bishop's Tawton
Chittlehampton
Umberleigh
Atherington
Great Torrington
Little Torrington
St Giles in the Wood
Kingscott
Roborough
Burrington
Beaford
South Molton
North Molton
Filleigh
Chulmleigh
Eggesford
Dolton
Merton
Huish
EXMOOR FOREST
Challacombe
Barton Town
Bratton Fleming
Brayford
Charles
Heasley Mill
Upcott
Kings Nympton
Romansleigh
Chittlehamholt
Satterleigh
George Nympton
Ashreigney
Riddlecombe
Wembworthy
Dowland
Petrockstow
Buckland
Peters Marland
Winswell
Yarnscombe
Huntshaw
Weare Giffard
Landcross
Alverdiscott
Hiscott
Eastleigh
Newton Tracey
Harracott
Cobbaton
Chapelton
Hannaford
East Stowford
Gunn
Stoodleigh
West Buckland
East Buckland
Stoke Rivers
High Bray
Bentwichen
Bish Mill
Alswear
Mariansleigh
Meshaw
Cheldon
Chawleigh
Worlington
Hollocombe
Ashley
Nymet Rowland
Eastington
A39
A361
A399
A377
A386
A3124
A3123
B3227
B3226
B3232
B3233
B3230
B3229
B3343
B3358
B3042
B3096
B3217
B3221
24
10

Lynton
Lynmouth
Countisbury
Foreland Point
Lynmouth Bay
Countisbury Cove
Brendon
Malmsmead
Rockford
Watersmeet
Oare
Porlock Weir
Porlock Bay
West Porlock
Porlock
Horner
Hurlstone Point
Bossington
Selworthy Beacon
Allerford
Holnicote
Selworthy
Woodcombe
Minehead
Alcombe
Dunster
Exmoor Heritage Coast
South West Coast Path
Dean
Barbrook
Hoaroak Hill 474
Exmoor Forest
Exmoor National Park
Hawkcombe Woods
Dunkery & Horner Woods
Luccombe
Huntscott
Wootton Courtenay
Ranscombe
Knowle
Timberscombe
Burrow
Dunkery Beacon
Dunkery Hill
Dry Hill
Challacombe
Barton Town
Simonsbath
Newland
Edgcott
Exford
Wheddon Cross
Cutcombe
Luckwell Bridge
Luxborough
Brendon
Withypool
Winsford
Winsford Hill
Span Head
Kinsford Water
River Barle
River Exe
High Bray
Bentwichen
Charles
Heasley Mill
North Molton
Tarr Steps Woodland
Liscombe
Hawkridge
Exton
Bridgetown
Withiel Florey
Brompton Regis
Wimbleball Lake
Twitchen
Upcott
Molland
West Anstey
Dulverton
Battleton
Bury
Skilgate
South Molton
Quince Honey Farm
Aller
East Anstey
Brushford
Exebridge
Morebath
Shillingford
Bampton
Bish Mill
Newtown
Bishop's Nympton
George Nympton
Ash Mill
Knowstone
Crooked Oak
Alswear
Mariansleigh
Rose Ash
Yard
Romansleigh
Meshaw
Kings Nympton
Oakford
Huntsham
Cove
Creacombe
Rackenford
Stoodleigh
Exe Valley
Loxbeare
Washfield
Knightshayes Court
Huntsham Castle
Chevithorne
Lurley
Bolham
Chulmleigh
Witheridge
Cheldon
Worlington
Chawleigh
Nomansland
Templeton
Calverleigh
Tiverton
Washford Pyne
Withleigh
Pennymoor
Puddington
Way Village
Black Dog
Poughill
Upham
Devon Railway Centre
Butterleigh
Nymet Rowland
Little Dart River
0 1 2 3 4 miles
0 1 2 3 4 5 kilometres

23
11
12

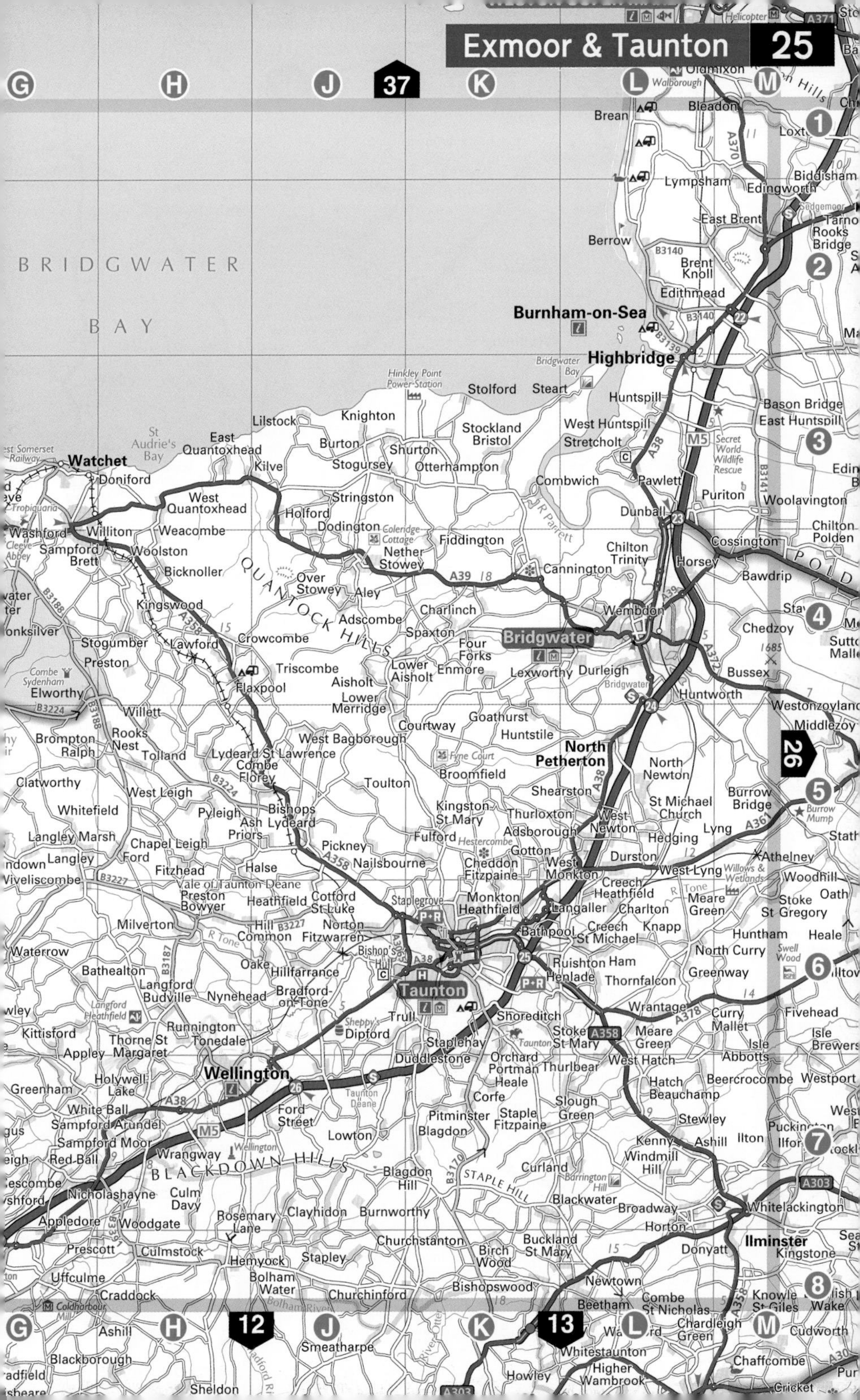
37
26
12
13
G
H
J
K
L
M
1
2
3
4
5
6
7
8
BRIDGWATER
BAY
Helicopter
Uphill
Oldmixon
Walborough
Bleadon
Brean
Loxton
A370
Lympsham
Biddisham
Edingworth
Sadgemoor
East Brent
Rooks Bridge
Berrow
B3140
Brent Knoll
Edithmead
Burnham-on-Sea
B3139
Highbridge
Bridgwater Bay
Hinkley Point Power Station
Stolford
Steart
Huntspill
Bason Bridge
East Huntspill
Knighton
Lilstock
Stockland Bristol
West Huntspill
Stretcholt
Secret World Wildlife Rescue
M5
B3141
St Audrie's Bay
East Quantoxhead
Burton
Shurton
Stogursey
Otterhampton
Kilve
West Somerset Railway
Watchet
Doniford
Combwich
Pawlett
Puriton
Woolavington
West Quantoxhead
Stringston
Holford
Dodington
Coleridge Cottage
Dunball
Chilton Polden
Tropiquaria
Washford
Cleeve Abbey
Williton
Weacombe
Fiddington
R Parrett
Nether Stowey
Cossington
Chilton Trinity
Sampford Brett
Woolston
Bicknoller
QUANTOCK HILLS
Over Stowey
A39
Cannington
Horsey
Bawdrip
POLDEN
B3188
Kingswood
Aley
Charlinch
Wembdon
Monksilver
A358
Adscombe
Spaxton
Bridgwater
Chedzoy
Stogumber
Lawford
Crowcombe
Four Forks
1685
Preston
Triscombe
Lower Aisholt
Enmore
Lexworthy
Durleigh
Bussex
Combe Sydenham
Flaxpool
Aisholt
Lower Merridge
Elworthy
B3224
Willett
Huntworth
Westonzoyland
Middlezoy
Goathurst
Courtway
Huntstile
Brompton Ralph
Rooks Nest
Tolland
West Bagborough
Lydeard St Lawrence
Combe Florey
North Petherton
Fyne Court
North Newton
Clatworthy
Toulton
Broomfield
Shearston
Burrow Bridge
Burrow Mump
West Leigh
Pyleigh
Bishops Lydeard
Kingston St Mary
Thurloxton
St Michael Church
Whitefield
Ash Priors
West Newton
Adsborough
Hedging
Lyng
A361
Langley Marsh
Chapel Leigh
Fulford
Hestercombe
Athelney
Langley
Ford
Pickney
Gotton
Durston
Wiveliscombe
Fitzhead
Halse
Nailsbourne
Cheddon Fitzpaine
West Monkton
West Lyng
Willows & Wetlands
Woodhill
B3227
Vale of Taunton Deane
Creech Heathfield
Preston Bowyer
Heathfield
Cotford St Luke
Monkton Heathfield
Staplegrove
Langaller
Charlton
Meare Green
Stoke St Gregory
Oath
Milverton
Hill Common
Norton Fitzwarren
Creech St Michael
Knapp
Huntham
Heale
R Tone
Bathpool
Waterrow
B3187
Bishop's Hull
Oake
North Curry
Swell Wood
Bathealton
Hillfarrance
A38
Ruishton
Ham
Henlade
Greenway
Taunton
Langford Budville
Nynehead
Bradford-on-Tone
Thornfalcon
Langford Heathfield
Wrantage
A378
Curry Mallet
Fivehead
Trull
Shoreditch
Sheppy's
Dipford
Runnington
Stoke St Mary
A358
Meare Green
Isle Brewers
Kittisford
Thorne St Margaret
Tonedale
Staplehay
Orchard Portman
Thurlbear
Isle Abbotts
Appley
Duddlestone
West Hatch
Wellington
Heale
Hatch Beauchamp
Beercrocombe
Westport
Greenham
Holywell Lake
Taunton Deane
Corfe
White Ball
Ford Street
Slough Green
Sampford Arundel
Pitminster
Staple Fitzpaine
Stewley
Blagdon
Sampford Moor
Lowton
Kenny
Ashill
Ilton
Puckington
Ilford
Wrangway
Wellington
Red Ball
Windmill Hill
BLACKDOWN HILLS
Curland
Blagdon Hill
STAPLE HILL
B3170
Barrington Hill
A303
Nicholashayne
Culm Davy
Blackwater
Broadway
Whitelackington
Appledore
Woodgate
Rosemary Lane
Clayhidon
Burnworthy
Horton
B3391
Churchstanton
Buckland St Mary
Ilminster
Prescott
Culmstock
Birch Wood
Hemyock
Stapley
Donyatt
Kingstone
Uffculme
Bolham Water
Newtown
Craddock
Churchinford
Bishopswood
Combe St Nicholas
Knowle St Giles
Coldharbour Mill
Bolham River
Beetham
Wake
Ashill
Smeatharpe
River Otter
Wadeford
Chardleigh Green
Cudworth
Whitestaunton
Blackborough
Chaffcombe
Higher Wambrook
Howley
Sheldon
Cricket
A303

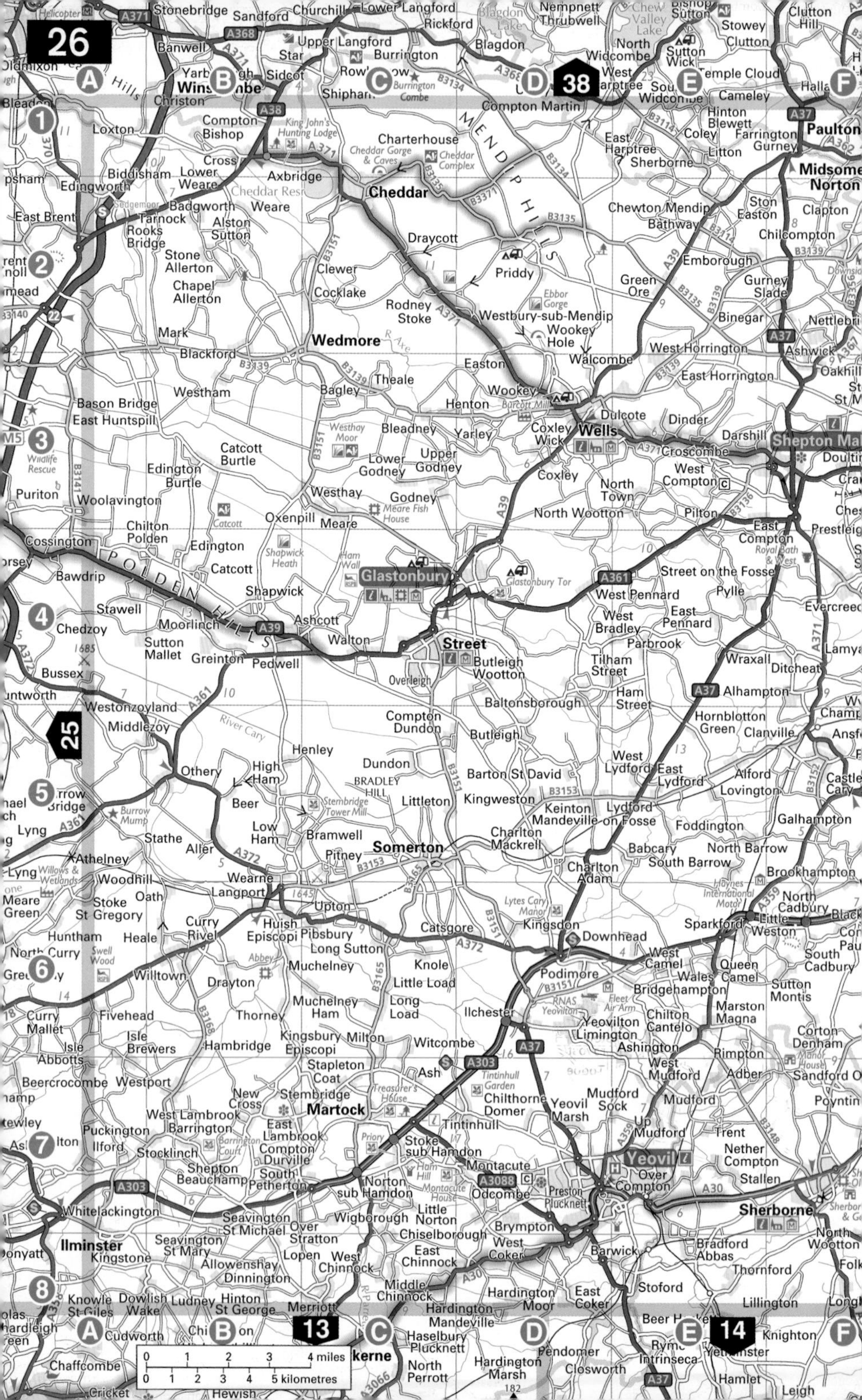

26
Stonebridge
Sandford
Churchill
Lower Langford
Rickford
Blagdon Lake
Nempnett Thrubwell
Chew Valley Lake
Bishop Sutton
Stowey
Clutton Hill
Clutton
Banwell
A371
A368
Upper Langford
Burrington
Blagdon
North Widcombe
Sutton Wick
Oldmixon
Star
Winscombe
Sidcot
Rowberrow
Burrington Combe
West Harptree
Temple Cloud
Christon
Shipham
Compton Martin
South Widcombe
Cameley
Hallatrow
38
Bleadon
Compton Bishop
King John's Hunting Lodge
Charterhouse
East Harptree
Hinton Blewett
Coley
Farrington Gurney
Paulton
Loxton
A38
Cheddar Gorge & Caves
Cheddar Complex
MENDIP HILLS
Litton
Midsomer Norton
Lympsham
Edingworth
Biddisham
Cross
Lower Weare
Axbridge
Cheddar Resr
Cheddar
Sherborne
Sedgemoor
Badgworth
Weare
Chewton Mendip
Ston Easton
Clapton
East Brent
Tarnock
Rooks Bridge
Alston Sutton
Bathway
Chilcompton
Draycott
Brent Knoll
Stone Allerton
Clewer
Priddy
Emborough
Chapel Allerton
Cocklake
Green Ore
Gurney Slade
Rodney Stoke
Ebbor Gorge
Westbury-sub-Mendip
Binegar
Nettlebridge
Mark
Wedmore
R Axe
Wookey Hole
Blackford
West Horrington
Ashwick
Oakhill
Walcombe
Easton
East Horrington
Westham
Theale
Bagley
Wookey
Bason Bridge
Henton
Burcott Mill
Dulcote
Dinder
East Huntspill
Westhay Moor
Bleadney
Yarley
Coxley Wick
Wells
Darshill
Shepton Mallet
Wildlife Rescue
Catcott Burtle
Croscombe
Doulting
Lower Godney
Upper Godney
Coxley
West Compton
Edington Burtle
Puriton
Woolavington
Westhay
Godney
North Town
Meare Fish House
Chilton Polden
Catcott
Oxenpill
Meare
North Wootton
Pilton
East Compton
Prestleigh
Cossington
Edington
Shapwick Heath
Ham Wall
Royal Bath & West
POLDEN HILLS
Bawdrip
Catcott
Glastonbury
Glastonbury Tor
A361
Street on the Fosse
Shapwick
West Pennard
Pylle
Evercreech
Stawell
Ashcott
West Bradley
East Pennard
Chedzoy
Moorlinch
A39
Walton
Parbrook
Sutton Mallet
Street
Lamyatt
Greinton
Pedwell
Butleigh Wootton
Tilham Street
Wraxall
Ditcheat
Bussex
1685
Overleigh
A37
Alhampton
Weston Zoyland
Ham Street
Baltonsborough
25
Middlezoy
River Cary
Compton Dundon
Butleigh
Hornblotton Green
Clanville
Ansford
Henley
West Lydford
East Lydford
Othery
High Ham
Dundon
Barton St David
Alford
Castle Cary
Burrow Bridge
BRADLEY HILL
Lovington
Beer
Stembridge Tower Mill
Littleton
Kingweston
Lydford
Burrow Mump
Keinton Mandeville
Lydford on Fosse
Galhampton
Lyng
Low Ham
Bramwell
Foddington
Stathe
Charlton Mackrell
Aller
Somerton
Babcary
North Barrow
Athelney
A372
Pitney
South Barrow
Willows & Wetlands
Woodhill
Wearne
B3153
Charlton Adam
Brookhampton
Oath
Langport
1645
Haynes International Motor Museum
Stoke St Gregory
Upton
Lytes Cary Manor
North Cadbury
Curry Rivel
Huish Episcopi
Pibsbury
Catsgore
Kingsdon
Sparkford
Little Weston
Hunthan
Heale
Long Sutton
Downhead
North Curry
Swell Wood
Abbey
West Camel
South Cadbury
Knole
Queen Camel
Willtown
Drayton
Muchelney
Podimore
Wales
Little Load
Bridgehampton
Sutton Montis
Muchelney Ham
Long Load
Fleet Air Arm
RNAS Yeovilton
Chilton Cantelo
Marston Magna
Curry Mallet
Fivehead
Thorney
Ilchester
Yeovilton
Limington
Isle Brewers
Hambridge
Kingsbury Episcopi
Milton
Witcombe
Ashington
Corton Denham
Isle Abbotts
Stapleton
Rimpton
Beercrocombe
Westport
Coat
Ash
A303
Tintinhull Garden
West Mudford
Adber
Sandford Orcas
New Cross
Stembridge
Treasurer's House
Chilthorne Domer
Yeovil Marsh
Mudford Sock
Mudford
Poyntington
West Lambrook
Martock
Tintinhull
Puckington
Barrington
East Lambrook
Up Mudford
Trent
Ilton
Ilford
Barrington Court
Priory
Stoke sub Hamdon
Yeovil
Nether Compton
Stocklinch
Compton Durville
Montacute
Shepton Beauchamp
South Petherton
Ham Hill
A3088
Over Compton
Stallen
Whitelackington
Norton sub Hamdon
Montacute House
Odcombe
Preston Plucknett
A30
Sherborne
Seavington St Michael
Over Stratton
Wigborough
Little Norton
Ilminster
Seavington St Mary
Chiselborough
Brympton
North Wootton
Donyatt
Kingstone
Lopen
West Chinnock
East Chinnock
West Coker
Barwick
Bradford Abbas
Allowenshay
Dinnington
Thornford
Knowle St Giles
Dowlish Wake
Ludney
Hinton St George
Middle Chinnock
Hardington Moor
East Coker
Stoford
Merriott
Hardington Mandeville
Lillington
Cudworth
Chillington
13
Haselbury Plucknett
Beer Hackett
14
Knighton
Chaffcombe
Crewkerne
North Perrott
Pendomer
Hardington Marsh
Closworth
Ryme Intrinseca
Yetminster
Cricket
Hewish
182
Hamlet
Leigh
0 1 2 3 4 miles
0 1 2 3 4 5 kilometres

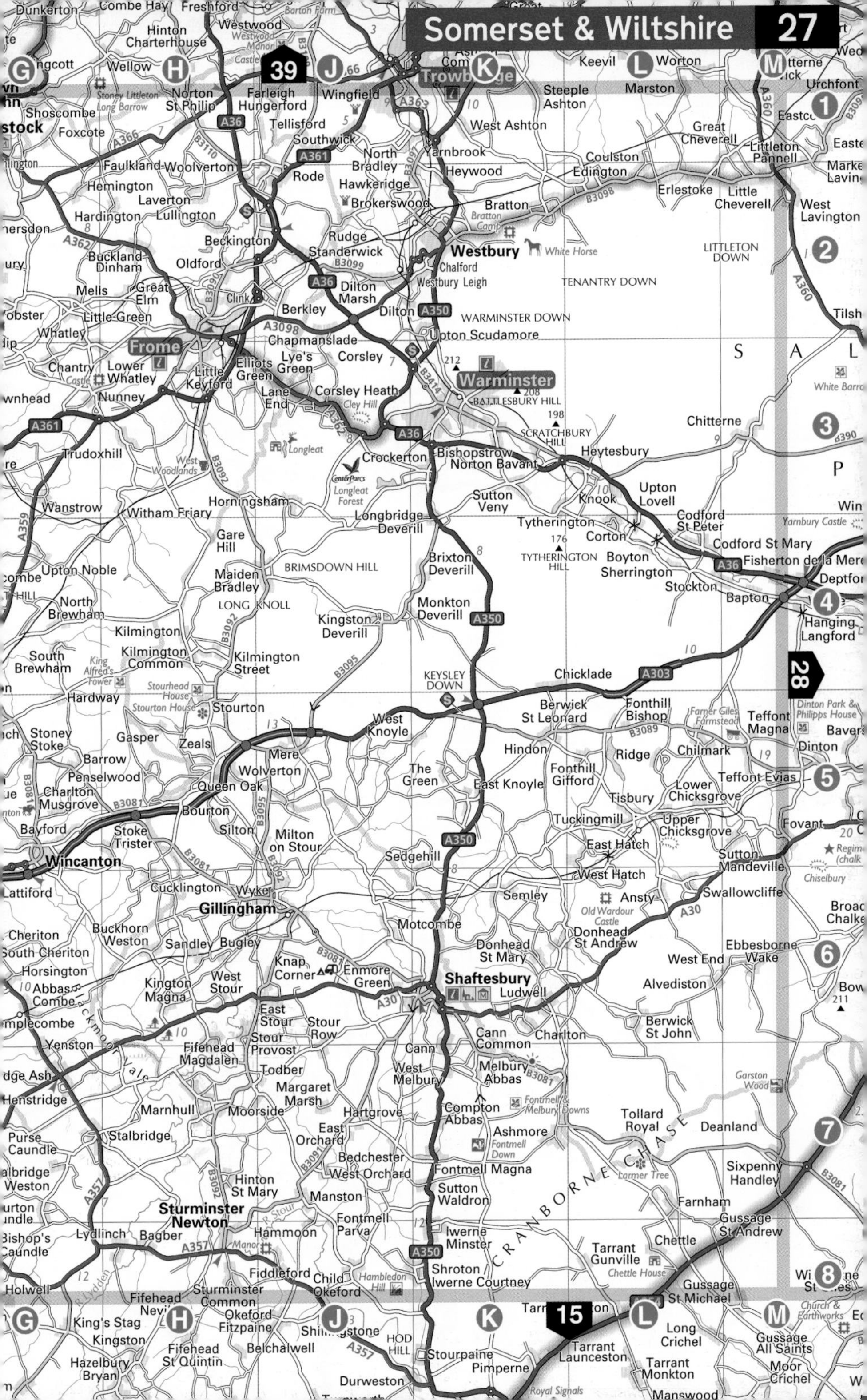

Frome
Trowbridge
Westbury
Warminster
Wincanton
Gillingham
Shaftesbury
Sturminster Newton
Mere
Longleat
Heytesbury
Tisbury
CRANBORNE CHASE
39
28
15

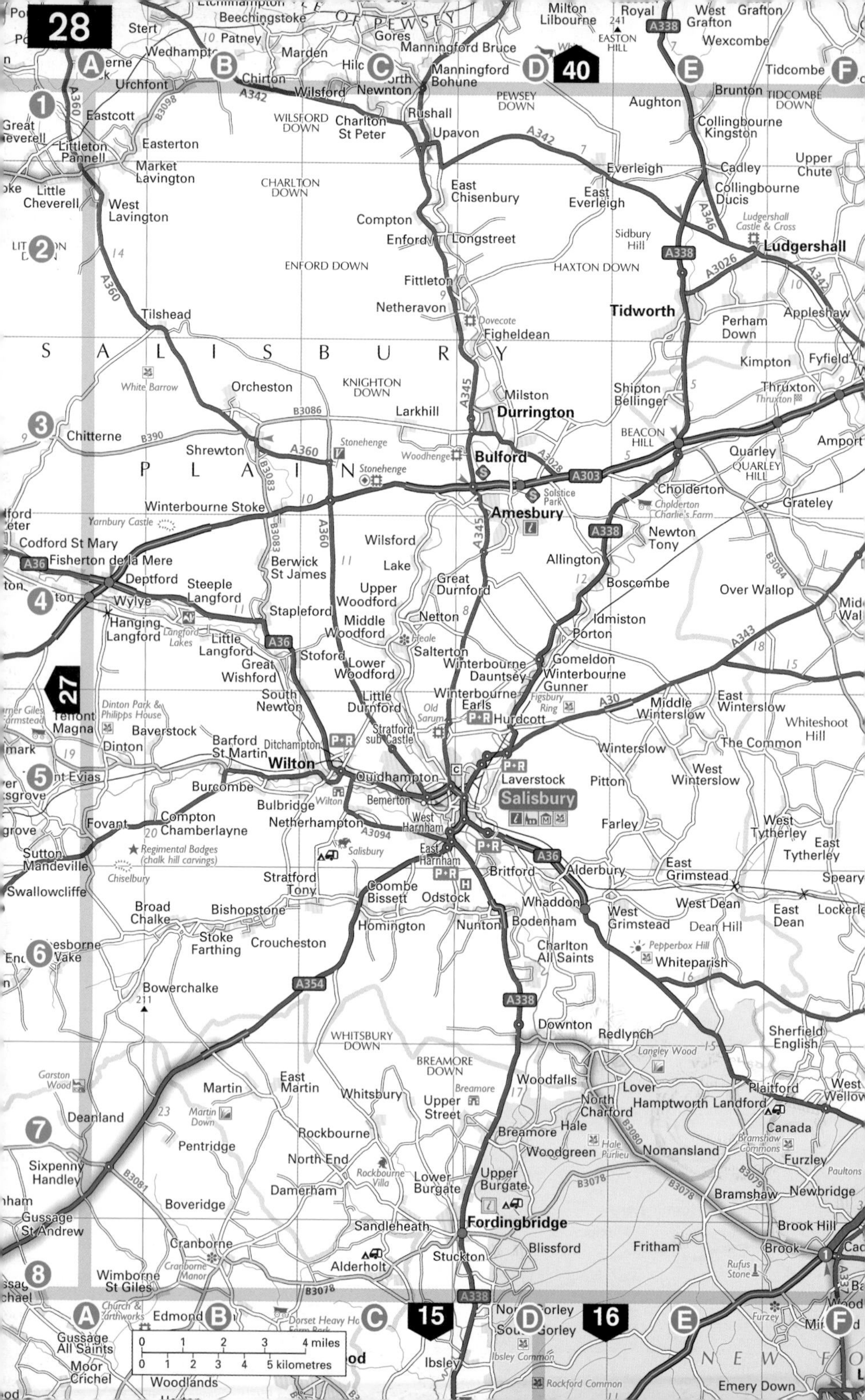
Beechingstoke
Stert
Patney
Wedhampton
Marden
Gores
Manningford Bruce
Milton Lilbourne
Royal
West Grafton
Grafton
Easton Hill
Wexcombe
Chirton
Urchfont
Wilsford
Newnton
Manningford Bohune
40
Tidcombe
Brunton
Tidcombe Down
Pewsey Down
Aughton
Eastcott
Rushall
Wilsford Down
Charlton St Peter
Upavon
Collingbourne Kingston
Great Cheverell
Littleton Pannell
Easterton
Market Lavington
Charlton Down
Everleigh
Cadley
Upper Chute
Little Cheverell
West Lavington
East Chisenbury
East Everleigh
Collingbourne Ducis
Compton
Enford
Longstreet
Sidbury Hill
Ludgershall Castle & Cross
Ludgershall
Enford Down
Haxton Down
Fittleton
Netheravon
Dovecote
Figheldean
Tidworth
Perham Down
Appleshaw
Tilshead
SALISBURY
PLAIN
Kimpton
Fyfield
White Barrow
Orcheston
Knighton Down
Milston
Shipton Bellinger
Thruxton
Larkhill
Durrington
Chitterne
Beacon Hill
Amport
Shrewton
Stonehenge
Woodhenge
Bulford
Quarley
Quarley Hill
Winterbourne Stoke
Solstice Park
Cholderton
Grateley
Amesbury
Cholderton Charlie's Farm
Yarnbury Castle
Codford St Mary
Fisherton de la Mere
Wilsford
Newton Tony
Lake
Allington
Deptford
Steeple Langford
Berwick St James
Great Durnford
Boscombe
Over Wallop
Wylye
Upper Woodford
Stapleford
Netton
Idmiston
Hanging Langford
Langford Lakes
Little Langford
Middle Woodford
Heale
Porton
Salterton
Stoford
Great Wishford
Lower Woodford
Winterbourne Dauntsey
Gomeldon
Winterbourne Gunner
South Newton
Little Durnford
Winterbourne Earls
Figsbury Ring
Middle Winterslow
East Winterslow
Teffont Magna
Dinton Park & Philipps House
Baverstock
Barford St Martin
Ditchampton
Old Sarum
Stratford sub Castle
Hurdcott
Whiteshoot Hill
Winterslow
The Common
Dinton
Wilton
Quidhampton
Laverstock
Pitton
West Winterslow
Burcombe
Bulbridge
Bemerton
Salisbury
Fovant
Compton Chamberlayne
Netherhampton
West Harnham
Farley
West Tytherley
East Tytherley
Sutton Mandeville
Regimental Badges (chalk hill carvings)
East Harnham
Alderbury
East Grimstead
Chiselbury
Stratford Tony
Coombe Bissett
Odstock
Britford
Spearywell
Swallowcliffe
Whaddon
West Dean
Broad Chalke
Bishopstone
Homington
Nunton
Bodenham
West Grimstead
Dean Hill
East Dean
Lockerley
Stoke Farthing
Croucheston
Charlton All Saints
Pepperbox Hill
Whiteparish
Bowerchalke
Downton
Whitsbury Down
Redlynch
Sherfield English
Breamore Down
Langley Wood
Garston Wood
Martin
East Martin
Whitsbury
Woodfalls
Lover
Plaitford
West Wellow
Breamore
Upper Street
North Charford
Hamptworth
Landford
Martin Down
Deanland
Canada
Rockbourne
Breamore
Hale
Pentridge
Woodgreen
Hale Purlieu
Nomansland
Bramshaw Commons
Furzley
Sixpenny Handley
North End
Rockbourne Villa
Lower Burgate
Upper Burgate
Paultons
Damerham
Bramshaw
Newbridge
Boveridge
Gussage St Andrew
Sandleheath
Fordingbridge
Brook Hill
Cranborne
Blissford
Fritham
Brook
Stuckton
Cranborne Manor
Alderholt
Rufus Stone
Wimborne St Giles
Church & Earthworks
Edmondsham
Dorset Heavy Horse Farm Park
15
North Gorley
South Gorley
16
Furzey
Minstead
Gussage All Saints
Moor Crichel
Ibsley
Ibsley Common
NEW FOREST
Woodlands
Rockford Common
Emery Down
0 1 2 3 4 miles
0 1 2 3 4 5 kilometres
27

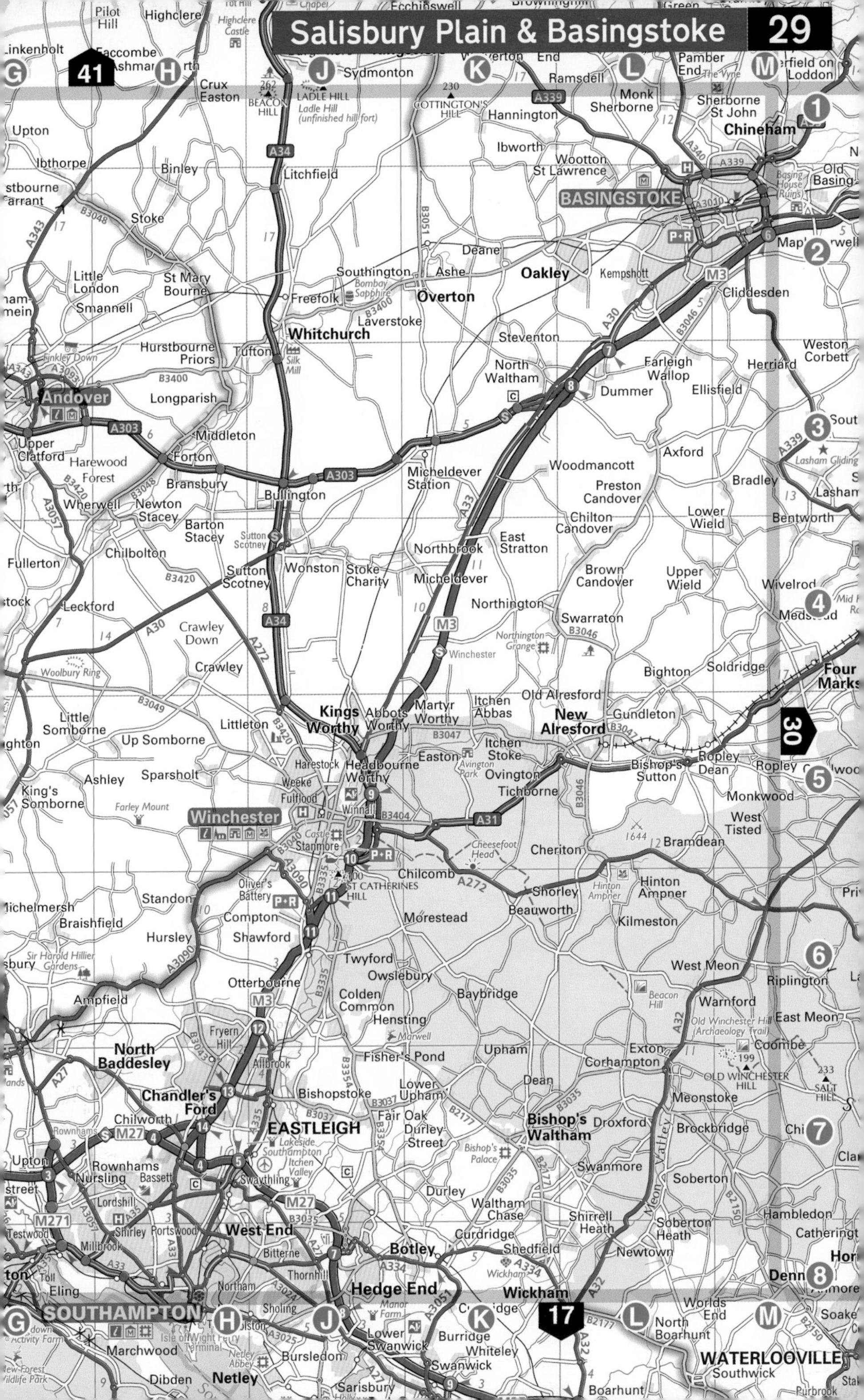

41
30
17
Andover
Whitchurch
Overton
Oakley
BASINGSTOKE
Chineham
Winchester
Kings Worthy
New Alresford
EASTLEIGH
SOUTHAMPTON
West End
Botley
Hedge End
Wickham
Bishop's Waltham
Chandler's Ford
North Baddesley
WATERLOOVILLE
Netley
Bursledon
Marchwood
Dibden
Highclere
Sydmonton
Litchfield
Freefolk
Laverstoke
Tufton
Longparish
Middleton
Forton
Bullington
Barton Stacey
Sutton Scotney
Wonston
Micheldever
Micheldever Station
Northington
Swarraton
Old Alresford
Itchen Abbas
Itchen Stoke
Ovington
Tichborne
Cheriton
Bramdean
Hinton Ampner
Kilmeston
West Meon
Warnford
East Meon
Exton
Corhampton
Meonstoke
Droxford
Swanmore
Soberton
Shedfield
Curdridge
Durley
Twyford
Owslebury
Colden Common
Otterbourne
Compton
Shawford
Hursley
Ampfield
Braishfield
Stockbridge
Leckford
Chilbolton
Wherwell
Harewood Forest
Fullerton
Upper Clatford
Smannell
Hurstbourne Priors
St Mary Bourne
Stoke
Binley
Ibthorpe
Upton
Crux Easton
Faccombe
Hannington
Ibworth
Wootton St Lawrence
Ramsdell
Monk Sherborne
Sherborne St John
Old Basing
Cliddesden
Farleigh Wallop
Dummer
Ellisfield
Herriard
Axford
Preston Candover
Chilton Candover
Brown Candover
Upper Wield
Lower Wield
Bradley
Bentworth
Medstead
Four Marks
Ropley
Bishop's Sutton
Monkwood
West Tisted
Steventon
North Waltham
Deane
Ashe
Southington
Kempshott
Dean
Upham
Fisher's Pond
Hensting
Bishopstoke
Fair Oak
Durley Street
Lower Upham
Waltham Chase
Shirrell Heath
Newtown
Soberton Heath
Hambledon
Denmead
Worlds End
North Boarhunt
Southwick
Burridge
Whiteley
Swanwick
Lower Swanwick
Sarisbury
Rownhams
Nursling
Bassett
Chilworth
Swaythling
Bitterne
Thornhill
Sholing
Woolston
Northam
Portswood
Shirley
Millbrook
Lordshill
Eling
Testwood
Totton
A34
A303
A30
A343
A339
M3
A33
A31
A272
A32
A27
M27
M271
A3090
A335
A3057
A334
A3024
A3025
B3400
B3420
B3048
B3049
B3051
B3046
B3047
B3404
B3335
B3354
B3037
B2177
B3035
B2150

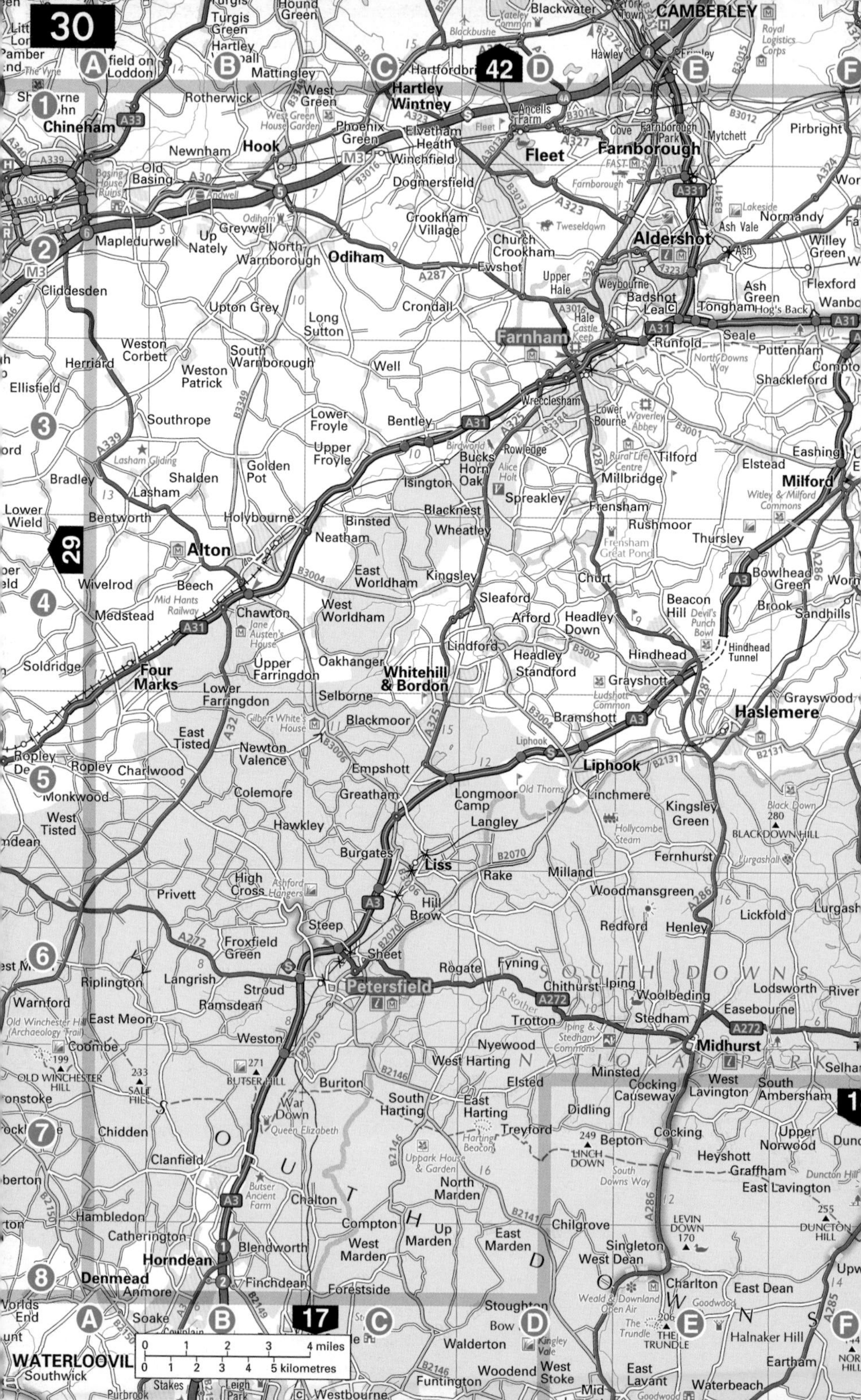

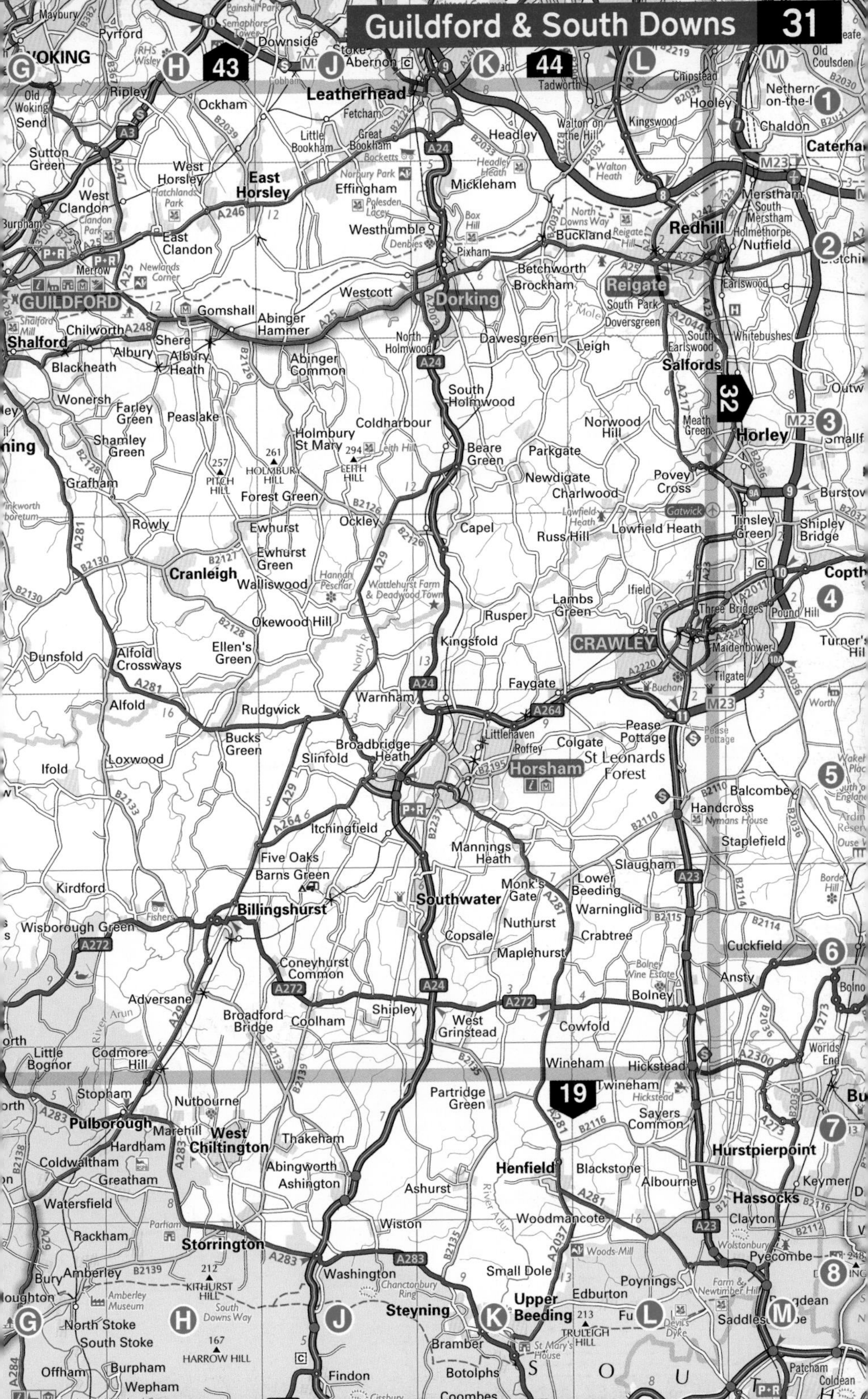

43
44
32
19
WOKING
Maybury
Pyrford
RHS Wisley
Painshill Park
Semaphore Tower
Downside
Stoke D'Abernon
Cobham
Leatherhead
Fetcham
Tadworth
Chipstead
Old Coulsden
Netherne-on-the-Hill
Hooley
Chaldon
Caterham
Old Woking
Send
Ripley
Ockham
Little Bookham
Great Bookham
Bocketts
Headley
Walton on the Hill
Kingswood
Walton Heath
Headley Heath
Sutton Green
West Horsley
Hatchlands Park
East Horsley
Norbury Park
Effingham
Mickleham
Polesden Lacey
Box Hill
North Downs Way
West Clandon
Clandon Park
Burpham
East Clandon
Merrow
Westhumble
Denbies
Buckland
Reigate Hill
Redhill
Merstham
South Merstham
Holmethorpe
Nutfield
Newlands Corner
GUILDFORD
Gomshall
Westcott
Dorking
Pixham
Betchworth
Brockham
Reigate
South Park
Doversgreen
Earlswood
Whitebushes
Shalford Mill
Shalford
Chilworth
Shere
Albury
Albury Heath
Abinger Hammer
Abinger Common
North Holmwood
Dawesgreen
Leigh
South Earlswood
Salfords
Blackheath
Wonersh
Farley Green
Peaslake
South Holmwood
Coldharbour
Holmbury St Mary
Leith Hill
Norwood Hill
Meath Green
Horley
Outwood
Smallfield
Shamley Green
Beare Green
Parkgate
Newdigate
Charlwood
Povey Cross
Burstow
257
PITCH HILL
261
HOLMBURY HILL
294
LEITH HILL
Grafham
Forest Green
Ockley
Gatwick
Lowfield Heath
Winkworth Arboretum
Rowly
Ewhurst
Capel
Russ Hill
Tinsley Green
Shipley Bridge
Ewhurst Green
Cranleigh
Walliswood
Hannah Peschar
Wattlehurst Farm & Deadwood Town
Ifield
Lambs Green
Rusper
Three Bridges
Pound Hill
Copthorne
Okewood Hill
Kingsfold
CRAWLEY
Maidenbower
Turner's Hill
Ellen's Green
Dunsfold
Alfold Crossways
Tilgate
Buchan
Faygate
Worth
Alfold
Rudgwick
Warnham
Littlehaven
Roffey
Colgate
Pease Pottage
Bucks Green
Broadbridge Heath
Slinfold
Horsham
St Leonards Forest
Ifold
Loxwood
Wakehurst Place
Balcombe
Handcross
Nymans House
Staplefield
Itchingfield
Mannings Heath
Slaugham
Five Oaks
Barns Green
Monk's Gate
Lower Beeding
Kirdford
Southwater
Borde Hill
Warninglid
Billingshurst
Fishers
Nuthurst
Wisborough Green
Copsale
Crabtree
Cuckfield
Maplehurst
Coneyhurst Common
Bolney Wine Estate
Ansty
Bolney
Adversane
Shipley
Broadford Bridge
Coolham
West Grinstead
Cowfold
River Arun
Little Bognor
Codmore Hill
Wineham
Hickstead
Worlds End
Stopham
Nutbourne
Partridge Green
Twineham
Pulborough
Marehill
West Chiltington
Sayers Common
Hardham
Thakeham
Coldwaltham
Abingworth
Henfield
Blackstone
Hurstpierpoint
Greatham
Ashington
Albourne
Keymer
Waltersfield
Ashurst
River Adur
Hassocks
Woodmancote
Clayton
Rackham
Parham
Wiston
Storrington
Wolstonbury
Pyecombe
Washington
Woods Mill
Small Dole
Bury
Amberley
212
KITHURST HILL
Chanctonbury Ring
Poynings
Farm & Newtimber Hill
Houghton
Amberley Museum
Steyning
Upper Beeding
Edburton
213
TRULEIGH HILL
Fulking
Devil's Dyke
Saddlescombe
Ditchling
South Downs Way
North Stoke
South Stoke
167
HARROW HILL
Bramber
St Mary's House
Offham
Burpham
Findon
Botolphs
Wepham
Cissbury
Coombes
Patcham
Coldean
S O U T H

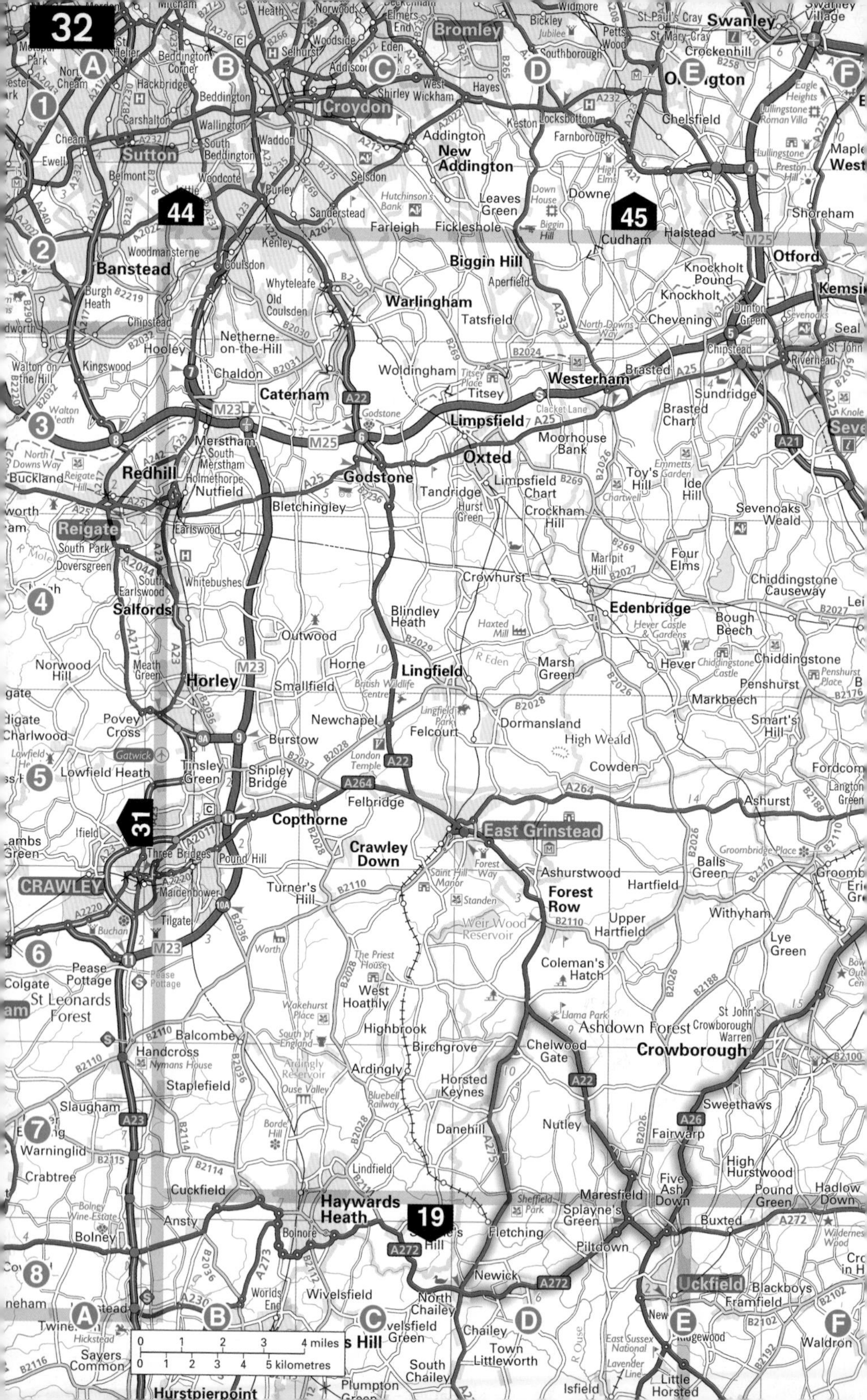

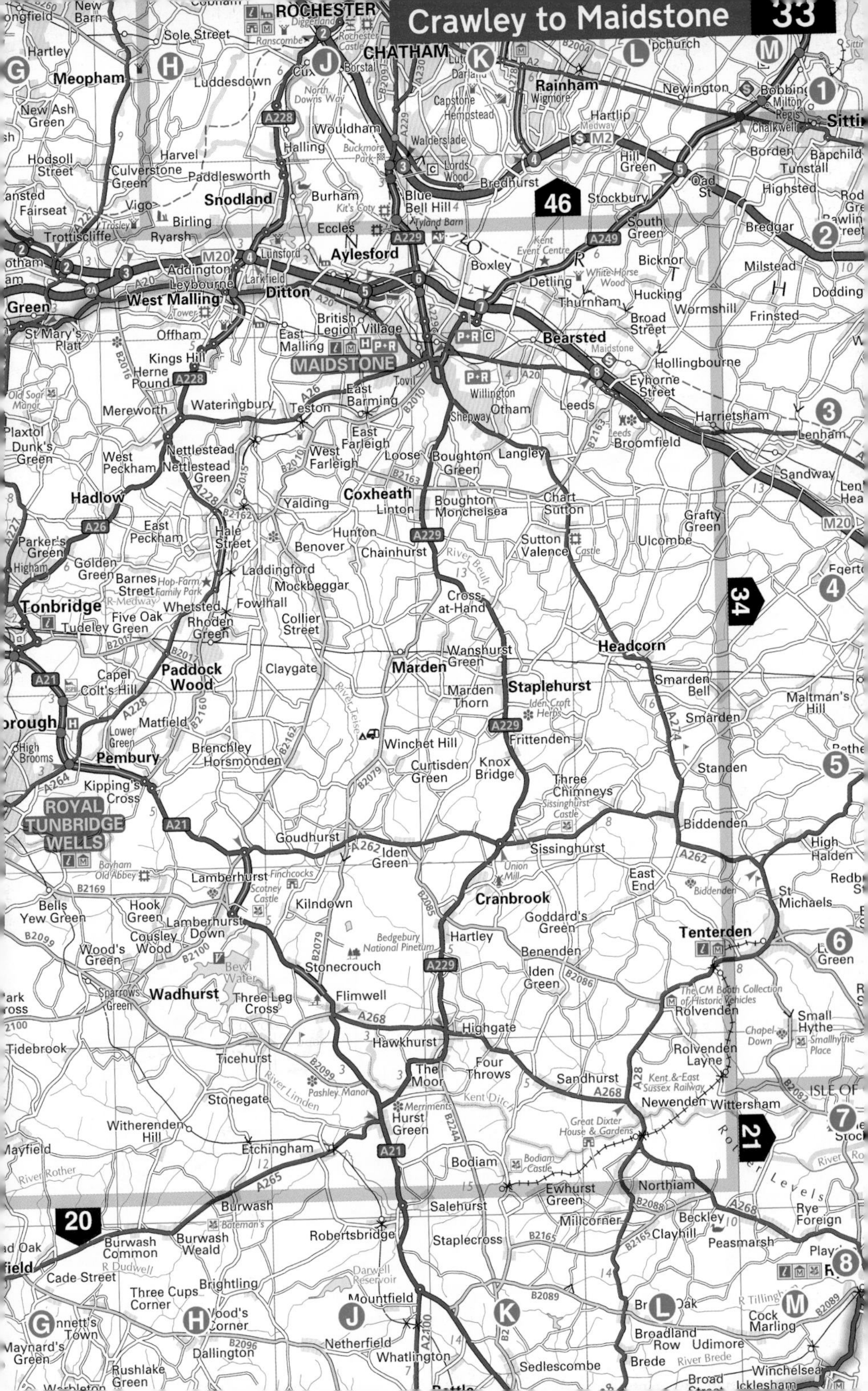

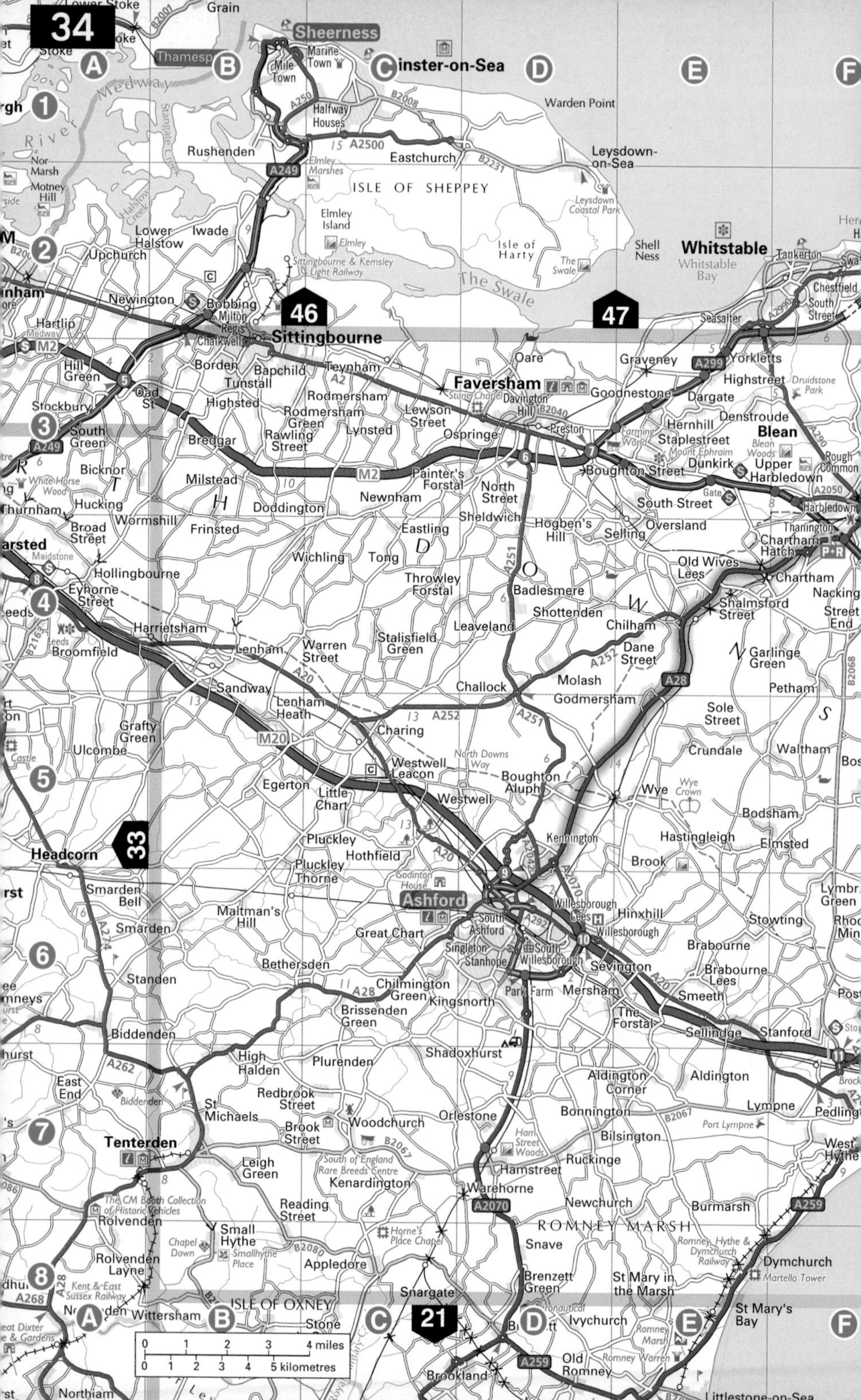

34
Sheerness
Minster-on-Sea
Warden Point
Eastchurch
Leysdown-on-Sea
Rushenden
ISLE OF SHEPPEY
Elmley Island
Isle of Harty
Lower Halstow
Iwade
Upchurch
Shell Ness
Whitstable
Whitstable Bay
Tankerton
The Swale
Newington
Bobbing
Milton Regis
Sittingbourne
46
47
Hartlip
Seasalter
Chestfield
Graveney
Yorkletts
Borden
Bapchild
Teynham
Tunstall
Oare
Faversham
Goodnestone
Highstreet
Dargate
Rodmersham
Rodmersham Green
Stockbury
Highsted
Lewson Street
Davington Hill
Preston
Hernhill
Denstroude
Blean
South Green
Bredgar
Rawling Street
Lynsted
Ospringe
Staplestreet
Dunkirk
Upper Harbledown
Rough Common
Bicknor
Milstead
Painter's Forstal
North Street
Boughton Street
Harbledown
Hucking
Newnham
South Street
Thurnham
Broad Street
Wormshill
Doddington
Sheldwich
Hogben's Hill
Selling
Oversland
Thanington
Frinsted
Eastling
Chartham Hatch
Hollingbourne
Wichling
Tong
Old Wives Lees
Chartham
Eyhorne Street
Throwley Forstal
Badlesmere
Shalmsford Street
Nackington
Shottenden
Leeds
Harrietsham
Leaveland
Chilham
Street End
Broomfield
Lenham
Warren Street
Stalisfield Green
Dane Street
Garlinge Green
Sandway
Molash
Challock
Godmersham
Petham
Lenham Heath
Charing
Sole Street
Grafty Green
Ulcombe
Crundale
Waltham
Westwell Leacon
North Downs Way
Boughton Aluph
Egerton
Little Chart
Westwell
Wye
Bodsham
33
Headcorn
Pluckley
Hothfield
Kennington
Hastingleigh
Elmsted
Pluckley Thorne
Brook
Smarden Bell
Ashford
Godinton House
Willesborough Lees
Hinxhill
Maltman's Hill
South Ashford
Willesborough
Stowting
Smarden
Great Chart
Singleton
Stanhope
South Willesborough
Brabourne
Bethersden
Sevington
Brabourne Lees
Standen
Chilmington Green
Kingsnorth
Park Farm
Mersham
Smeeth
Brissenden Green
The Forstal
Biddenden
Sellindge
Stanford
Shadoxhurst
High Halden
Plurenden
East End
Aldington Corner
Aldington
Redbrook Street
Lympne
Pedling
St Michaels
Brook Street
Woodchurch
Orlestone
Bonnington
Port Lympne
Tenterden
Bilsington
Leigh Green
Ham Street Woods
Ruckinge
West Hythe
Kenardington
Hamstreet
South of England Rare Breeds Centre
The CM Booth Collection of Historic Vehicles
Warehorne
Reading Street
Newchurch
Burmarsh
Rolvenden
Small Hythe
Smallhythe Place
Chapel Down
Horne's Place Chapel
ROMNEY MARSH
Snave
Romney, Hythe & Dymchurch Railway
Rolvenden Layne
Appledore
Dymchurch
Martello Tower
Kent & East Sussex Railway
Brenzett Green
St Mary in the Marsh
Snargate
ISLE OF OXNEY
Wittersham
Stone
21
Ivychurch
St Mary's Bay
Romney Marsh
Great Dixter
Old Romney
Romney Warren
Brookland
Littlestone-on-Sea
Northiam
0 1 2 3 4 miles
0 1 2 3 4 5 kilometres

Foreness Point
MARGATE
Botany Bay
Cliftonville
Kingsgate
St Mildred's Bay
Westgate-on-Sea
Westbrook
Northdown
NORTH FORELAND
Joss Bay
North Foreland
Minnis Bay
Reculver Towers & Roman Fort
Reculver
Bishopstone
Birchington
Garlinge
Reading Street
Hornby
St Peter's
Stone Bay
ISLE OF THANET
Lydden
Westwood
Broadstairs
A299
A28
St Nicholas-at-Wade
Acol
RAF Manston
Dumpton
Boyden Gate
Sarre
Manston
Hereson
A253
Monkton
St Lawrence
Ramsgate
Chislet
Durlock
Minster
St Augustine's Cross
Viking Ship 'Hugin'
Pegwell
Hoath
Upstreet
West Stourmouth
R Stour
Pegwell Bay
East Stourmouth
Westmarsh
A256
Richborough Roman Fort
Westbere
Preston
Elmstone
Cop Street
Sandwich Bay
Hoaden
Wickhambreaux
Wingham
Seaton
Ash
Sandwich
Ickham
A257
Royal St George's
Durlock
Wingham
Marshborough
Stone Cross
Toll
Bramling
Woodnesborough
Staple
Bekesbourne
Statenborough
Worth
Goodnestone
Eastry
Patrixbourne
Ham
Hacklinge
Adisham
Ratling
Chillenden
Finglesham
B2046
The Downs
Fowlmead
Aylesham
Nonington
Sholden
North Downs Way
Betteshanger
Northbourne
Deal
Great Mongeham
Upper Deal
Tilmanstone
Womenswold
Elvington
Ripple
Lower Eythorne
Walmer Castle
Barfrestone
Eythorne
Sutton
Woolage Green
East Studdal
East Kent Railway
Ringwould
Shepherdswell
Ashley
Sutton Downs
Kingsdown
North Downs Way
West Langdon
Martin
A258
Denton
Lydden Hill
Coldred
Wootton
Lydden
A2
Whitfield
East Langdon
St John's Commandery
St Margaret's at Cliffe
Selsted
Lydden Temple Ewell
Guston
St Margaret's Bay
Ewell Minnis
Kearsney
West Cliffe
The Pines
SOUTH FORELAND
Swingfield Minnis
Swingfield Street
River
Lighthouse
South Foreland Heritage Coast
A260
Buckland
Castle
The White Cliffs of Dover
Alkham
St Radigunds
Densole
South Alkham
Maxton
Upper Standen
Drellingore
B2011
Calais
Dunkirk
Hawkinge
Lower Standen
West Hougham
DOVER
A20
Capel-le-Ferne
Battle of Britain
East Cliff & Warren
Samphire Hoe
Dover - Folkestone Heritage Coast
Channel Tunnel (Rail)
Cheriton
East Wear Bay
Morehall
FOLKESTONE
Sandgate
A259
STRAIT OF DOVER

Craig Llangiwg
Cilybebyll
Gellinudd
Alltwen
Crynant
Vale of Neath
Blaengwrach
Rhigos
Hirwaun
Penywaun
Cwmdare
Aberdare (Aberdâr)
Resolven
RESOLVEN MOUNTAIN
CRAIG-Y-LLYN
Melin Cwrt
Cefn Coed Colliery
River Dulais
River Neath
Glais
Cilfrew
Cadoxton Juxta-Neath
Clyne
Aberdulais
Tin Works & Waterfall
Bryn-côch
Birchgrove
Llansamlet
Winshwen
MOEL-YR HYRDDAD
Mynydd Ystradffernol
Blaenrhondda
Cwmaman
Maerdy
Tonna
Cefn Mawr
Glyncorrwg
Treherbert
Neath (Castell-nedd)
Cefn Morfydd
Afan Forest Park
Cymer
Blaengwynfi
Abergwynfi
Treorchy
Pentre
Ystrad
Rhondda Valley
Cwmparc
Crymlyn Bog
Pentre-chwyth
Port Tennant
Cimla
Tonmawr
Abercregan
Duffryn
Cynonville
Croeserw
Caerau
Efail-fach
Pont-rhyd-y-fen
South Wales Miners
Briton Ferry
FOEL MYNYDDAU
MOEL TRAWSNANT
MYNYDD CAERAU
WERFA
Nant-y-moel
Clydach Vale
Baglan
Pwll-y-glaw
Blaengarw
Cwmafan
Bryn
Pontycymer
Mynydd Llangeinwyr
Cricklepit Mill
Tonypandy
Penygraig
Maesteg
Glanllynfi
Aberavon
Port Talbot
Mynydd Margam
Cwmfelin
Ogmore Vale
Gilfach Goch
Taibach
Llangynwyd
Stones Museum
Margam
MOEL TON-MAWR
Llangeinor
Betws
Lewistown
Blackmill
Coytrahen
Bryngarw
Brynmenyn
Mynydd Maen
Tondu
Heol-y-Cyw
Afon Kenfig
Bedford Park
Cefn Cribwr
Aberkenfig
Brynna Woods
Brynna
Pyle (Y Pîl)
Sarn Park
Pant-ffrwyth
Mawdlam
Litchard
Pencoed
North Cornelly
Kenfig
Bridgend (Pen-y-bont-ar-Ogwr)
Castle
Coity
Llanilid
Llanharry
South Cornelly
Laleston
Brackla
Coychurch
Rest Bay
NEWTON DOWN
Nottage
Tythegston
Merthyr Mawr
Candleston
Ogmore Castle
Priory
Treoes
Llangan
Corntown
Newton
Porthcawl
Porthcawl Point
Trecco Bay
Ogmore
Ewenny
Penllyn
St Bride's Major
Colwinston
Pentre Meyrick
St Quentin's Castle
Ogmore-by-Sea
Llysworney
Cowbridge
Southerndown
Llandow
Llanblethian
Llandough
Wick
Sigingstone
Broughton
Monknash
Marcross
Llanmaes
St Donats
Nash Point
Nash Point & Visitor Centre
Llantwit Major (Llanilltud Fawr)
St Athan
Glamorgan Heritage Coast
Cwn Colhuw
Gileston
Limpert Bay
A465
A4067
A474
A48
A483
A4107
B4287
B4286
B4282
A4241
B4283
A4063
A4064
A4061
A4093
B4281
A473
B4280
A4229
A4106
B4265
B4524
B4268
B4270
B4181
A4233
A4059
B4223
A4119
B4564
B4278
B4434
B4291
B4290
M4
51
52
A B C D E F
1 2 3 4 5 6 7 8
0 1 2 3 4 miles
0 1 2 3 4 5 kilometres

Abertillery
(Abertyleri)
Pontypool
(Pont-y-Pŵl)
Usk
(Brynbuga)
Bargoed
(Bargod)
Oakdale
Crumlin
Treharris
Pengam
Penmaen
Blackwood
Newbridge
Gelligaer
Pontllanfraith
Abercynon
Abercarn
Cwmbran
(Cwmbrân)
Caerleon
Crosskeys
Risca
Llanbradach
Bedwas
Rogerstone
Caerphilly
(Caerffili)
NEWPORT
(CASNEWYDD-AR-WYSG)
Church Village
Llantrisant
Tongwynlais
Radyr
CARDIFF
(CAERDYDD)
Penarth
Barry
(Y Barri)
SEVERN ESTUARY
Flat Holm
Steep Holm
WESTON-SUPER-MARE
Kewstoke
Uphill
Oldmixon
Bleadon
Lympsham
Edingworth
Biddisham
Loxton
Locking
Hutton
Sand Bay
Woodspring Bay
Wick St Lawrence
Sand Point
Lavernock
Lavernock Point
Sully
Sully Island
Barry Island
Cold Knap Point
Porthkerry
Rhoose
Penmark
Moulton
Wenvoe
Dinas Powys
Cogan
Llandough
Michaelston-le-Pit
Penarth Head
Lower Penarth
Cosmeston Lakes & Medieval Village
St Andrews Major
Cadoxton
St Nicholas
Bonvilston
St Lythans
Dyffryn Gardens
Burial Chamber
Tinkinswood
Welsh Hawking Centre
St Fagans
St Brides-super-Ely
Peterston-super-Ely
St George's
Fairwater
Ely
Caerau
Canton
Llandaff
Whitchurch
Rhiwbina
Llanishen
Birchgrove
Roath
Splottlands
Pengam
Rumney
Llanrumney
St Mellons
Llanedeyrn
Lisvane
Cardiff Gate
Castleton
Marshfield
St Brides Wentlooge
Peterstone Wentlooge
Michaelstone-y-Fedw
Tredegar House
Nash
Goldcliff
Newport Wetlands
Llanwern
Liswerry
Christchurch
Maindee
Pillgwenlly
Transporter Bridge
Bassaleg
Rhiwderyn
Draethen
Rudry
Lower Machen
Machen
Wattsville
Cwmfelinfach
Ynysddu
Senghenydd
Abertridwr
Groes-Wen
Pentyrch
Creigiau
Taff's Well
Castell Coch
Efail Isaf
Tyn-y-nant
Llantwit Fardre
Trefforest
Cilfynydd
Ystrad Mynach
Hengoed
Nelson
Maesycwmmer
Pentwynmawr
Merthyr Vale
Aberfan
Bedlinog
Troedyrhiw
Pentrebach
Tirphil
New Tredegar
Manmoel
Markham
Bedwellty
Argoed
Llanhilleth
Griffithstown
New Inn
Monkswood
Llandegfedd Reservoir
Llanbadoc
Coed-y-paen
Llangybi
Llandegveth
Tredunnock
Llanfrechfa
Llanhennock
Ponthir
Llantarnam
Croesyceiliog
Pontnewydd
Forge Hammer
Henllys
Bettws
Malpas
Cefn
Mynydd Maen
Greenmeadow Community Farm
Cwmcarn Forest Drive
Pontywaun
Cwmcarn
Mynydd Eglwysilan
Mynydd Lan
Wales Millennium Centre
Principality
National History
Bream Down
Tropical Bird Garden
Brean
M4
A48(M)
A470
A4232
38
53
25

38
A
B
C
D
E
F
1
2
3
4
5
6
7
8
54
37
26
Kemeys Commander
Llandenny
Harold's Stones
St Briavels
Bream
Allaston
Lydney
Llanishen
Llansoy
Llandogo
Hewelsfield
Aylburton
Alvington
Usk (Brynbuga)
Usk Rural Life
Gwernesney
Pentre
Tintern
Tintern Abbey
Brockweir
Woolaston Common
Llanbadoc
Llangwm
Wolvesnewton
Offa's Dyke Path
Netherend
Woolaston
Llanllowell
Springdale Farm
Coed-y-paen
Kilgwrrwg Common
Devauden
Wye Valley
River Wye
River Severn
Newchurch
Stroat
Llangybi
Gaerllwyd
Itton Common
St Arvans
Llantrisant
Chepstow Racecourse
National Diving Centre
Woodcroft
Tidenham
Itton
Mynydd-bach
Tutshill
Sedbury
Tredunnock
Llanfrechfa
Llanhennock
Shirenewton
Llanvair Discoed
Mounton
Port Wall
Chepstow (Cas-gwent)
Oldbury-on-Severn
Rockhampton
Lower Morton
Parc Seymour
Llanmelin
Runston Chapel
Pwllmeyric
Newton Green
Bulwarks Camp
Caerleon
Llanvaches
Penhow
Caerwent
Cowhill
Kington
Thornbury
Llanbeder
Llandevaud
Roman Town
Caldicot (Cil-y-coed)
St Pierre
Mathern
Severn Bridge westbound only
Toll westbound only
Littleton-on-Severn
Severn View
Elberton
Alveston
Celtic Manor
Christchurch
Llanmartin
Magor
Dewstow
Llanfihangel Rogiet
Portskewett
Tolls to cease end of 2018
Aust
Bishton
Llanwern
Ifton
Rogiet
Sudbrook
Ingst
Olveston
Liswerry
Transporter Bridge
Newport (Casnewydd-ar-Wysg)
Llandevenny
Magor Marsh
Undy
Toll westbound only
Second Severn Crossing
Redwick
Tockington
Rudgeway
Severn Beach
Pilning
Almondsbury
Nash
Goldcliff
Whitson
Redwick
Newport Wetlands
Severn Estuary
Easter Compton
Compton Greenfield
Wild Place
Patchway
Bradley Stoke
Great Stoke
Cribbs Causeway
Hallen
Filton
Winterbourne
Stoke Gifford
Battery Point
Avonmouth
Kings Weston
Blaise Hamlet
Henbury
Shirehampton
Westbury-on-Trym
Horfield
Frenchay
Portishead
Gordano
Bristol
Redland
Fishponds
Eastville
Weston-in-Gordano
Clapton-in-Gordano
Portbury
Easton-in-Gordano
Abbots Leigh
Walton-in-Gordano
Gordano Valley
Oakham Treasures
Leigh Woods
Clifton
Walton Park
Clevedon Court
Noah's Ark
Lower Failand
Failand
Kingswood
Hanham
Cadbury Camp
Tyntesfield
Ashton Court
SS Great Britain
Bedminster
Clevedon
Tickenham
Wraxall
Nailsea
Long Ashton
Ashton Vale
Knowle
Brislington
Flax Bourton
Bedminster Down
R Kenn
Kenn
West End
Chelvey
Farleigh
Backwell
Bishopsworth
Stockwood
Woodspring Bay
Kingston Seymour
West Town
Barrow Gurney
Withywood
Keynsham
Queen Charlton
Wick St Lawrence
Claverham
Brockley
Dundry
East Dundry
Whitchurch
Maes Knoll
Chewton Keynsham
Cleeve
Lulsgate Bottom
Upper Town
Maiden Head
Norton Malreward
Yatton
Felton
Bristol Airport
Winford
Norton Hawkfield
R Yeo
Congresbury
Belluton
Publow
St Georges
Worle
West Hewish
Puxton
Redhill
Chew Magna
Pensford
Wrington
Regil
Butcombe
Stone Circle
Stanton Drew
Chelwood
Stanton Wick
Stock
Blackmoor
Cowslip Green
Chew Stoke
Havyatt
Chew Valley Lake
Helicopter Museum
Locking
Hutton
Stonebridge
Sandford
Churchill
Lower Langford
Rickford
Blagdon Lake
Nempnett Thrubwell
Bishop Sutton
Clutton Hill
Stowey
Clutton
Upper Langford
Burrington
Blagdon
North Widcombe
Sutton Wick
Banwell
Star
Oldmixon
Bleadon Hills
Yarborough
Sidcot
Rowberrow
Temple Cloud
Winscombe
Burrington Combe
West Harptree
South Widcombe
Hallatrow
Bleadon
Christon
Shipham
Ubley
Cameley
Compton Martin
Hinton Blewett
King John's Hunting Lodge
Charterhouse
Cheddar Gorge & Caves
Cheddar Complex
East Harptree
Farrington Gurney
Litton
Sherborne
Midsomer Norton
Edingworth
Weare
Cheddar Reservoir
Cheddar
0 1 2 3 4 miles
0 1 2 3 4 5 kilometres
M4
M48
M49
M5
M32
A48
A449
A466
A403
A4
A369
A38
A370
A371
A368
A37
A4174
A4810
A420
A431
A432
A4018
A4162
A4055
B4598
B4293
B4235
B4245
B4228
B4461
B4055
B4056
B4057
B4058
B4427
B3124
B3128
B3129
B3130
B3133
B3134
B3114
B3440
B3135

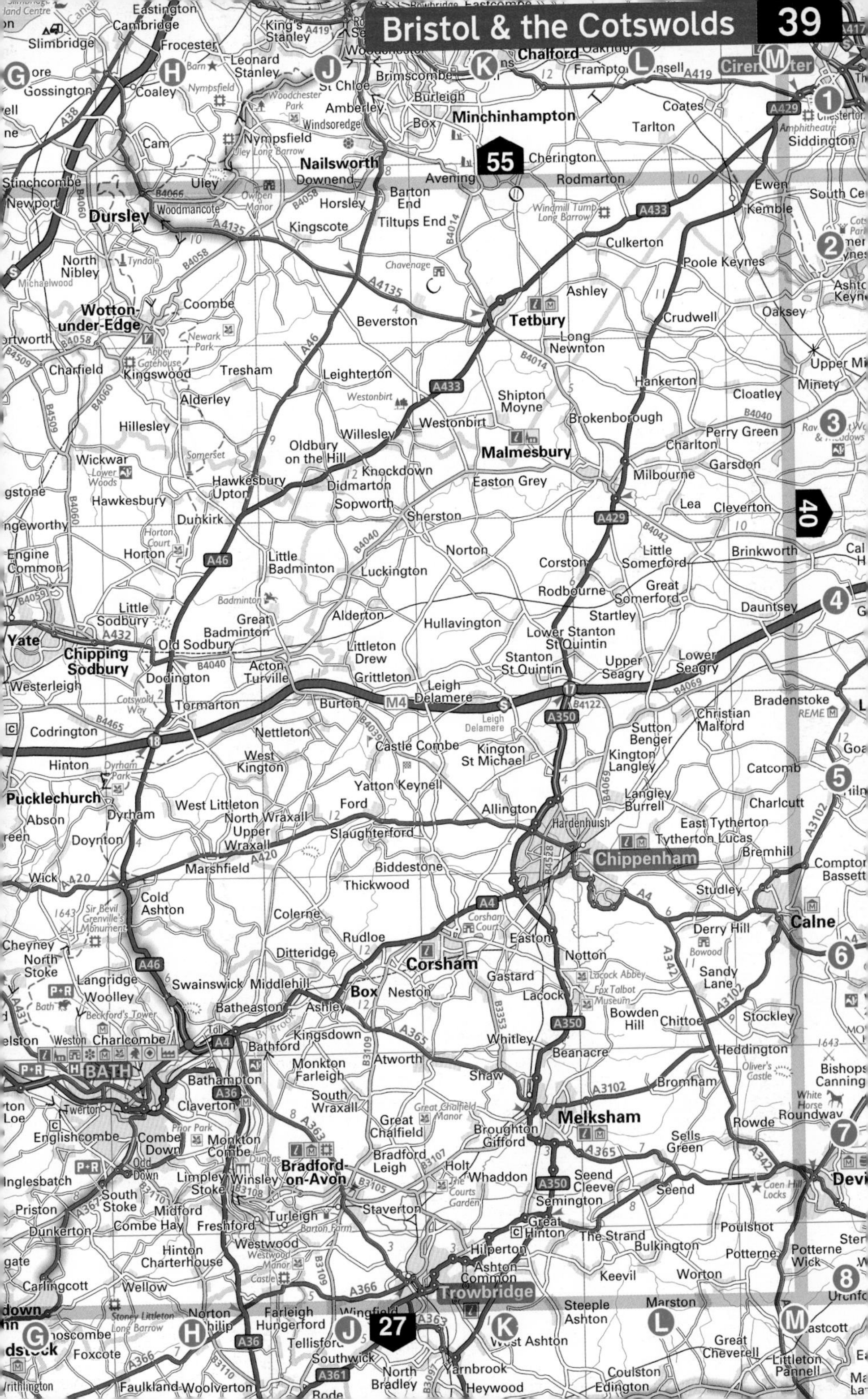
Dursley
Wotton-under-Edge
Nailsworth
Minchinhampton
Tetbury
Malmesbury
Chipping Sodbury
Yate
Chippenham
Corsham
Calne
Melksham
Bradford-on-Avon
Trowbridge
BATH
Box
Chalford
Cherington
Rodmarton
Kemble
Siddington
Beverston
Leighterton
Westonbirt
Sherston
Luckington
Hullavington
Castle Combe
Marshfield
Lacock
Hilperton
Keevil
Wickwar
Hawkesbury
Dyrham
Pucklechurch
Great Badminton
Little Badminton
Old Sodbury
Acton Turville
Tormarton
Codrington
Nettleton
Biddestone
Colerne
Batheaston
Bathampton
Claverton
Monkton Combe
Freshford
Westwood
Staverton
Semington
Seend
Bromham
Heddington
Bishops Cannington
Devizes
55
40
27

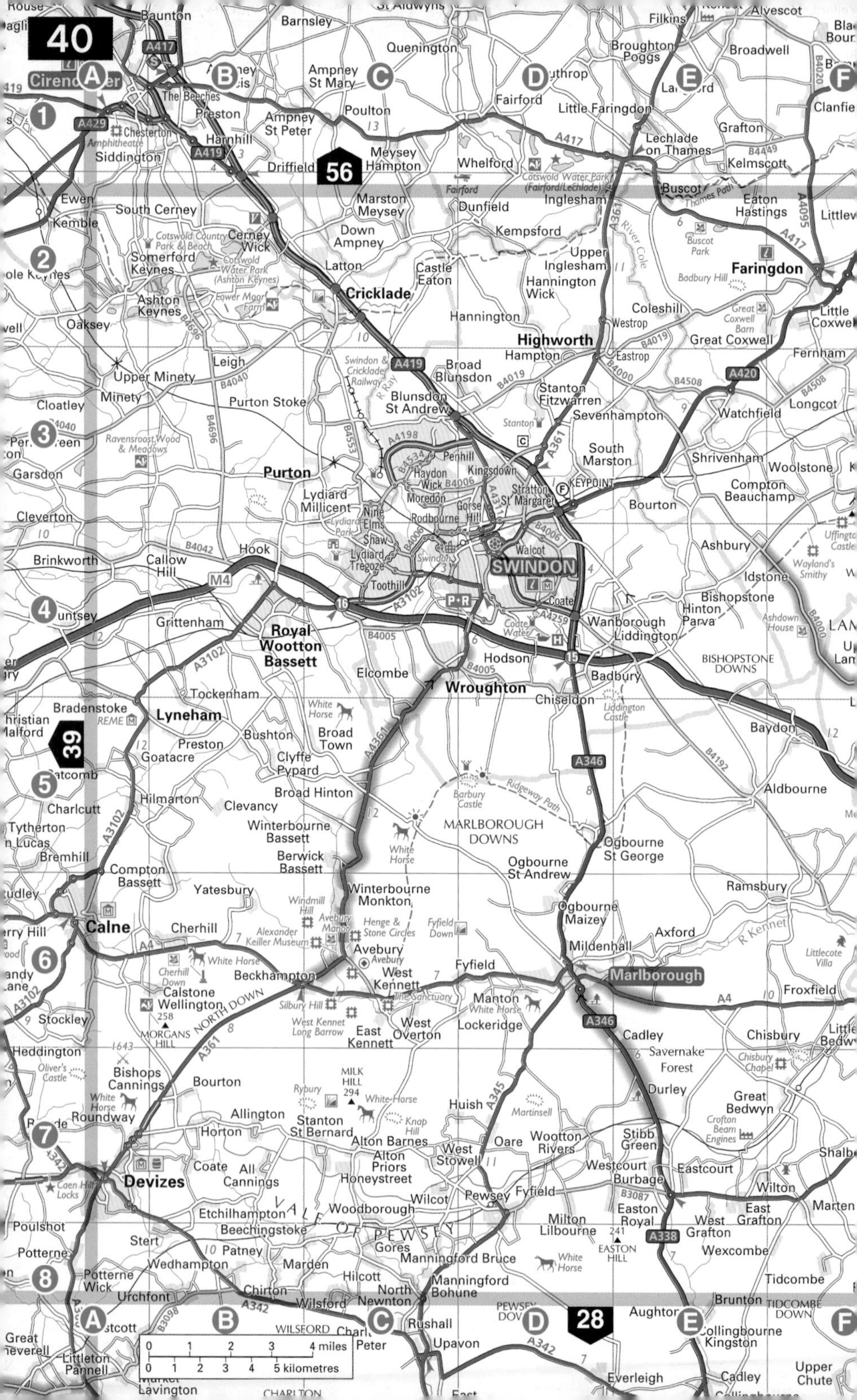

40
Baunton
Barnsley
Quenington
Filkins
Alvescot
Broughton Poggs
Broadwell
A417
Ampney St Mary
Cirencester
The Beeches
Preston
Poulton
Ampney St Peter
Fairford
Little Faringdon
Langford
Clanfield
B4020
A419
A429
Chesterton
Amphitheatre
Siddington
Harnhill
Driffield
56
Meysey Hampton
Whelford
Cotswold Water Park (Fairford/Lechlade)
Lechlade on Thames
Grafton
Kelmscott
B4449
Fairford
Buscot
Thames Path
Ewen
Kemble
South Cerney
Marston Meysey
Dunfield
Inglesham
Eaton Hastings
A4095
Littleworth
Cotswold Country Park & Beach
Cerney Wick
Down Ampney
Kempsford
A361
River Cole
Buscot Park
A417
Somerford Keynes
Cotswold Water Park (Ashton Keynes)
Latton
Castle Eaton
Upper Inglesham
Faringdon
Badbury Hill
Ashton Keynes
Lower Moor Farm
Cricklade
Hannington Wick
Hannington
Coleshill
Great Coxwell Barn
Little Coxwell
Oaksey
B4696
Westrop
Highworth
Great Coxwell
Hampton
Eastrop
B4019
Fernham
Swindon & Cricklade Railway
R Ray
A419
Broad Blunsdon
Leigh
Upper Minety
B4040
Minety
Purton Stoke
Blunsdon St Andrew
B4019
Stanton Fitzwarren
B4000
B4508
A420
Longcot
Cloatley
Sevenhampton
Watchfield
Ravensroost Wood & Meadows
B4696
B4553
A4198
Stanton
A361
South Marston
Shrivenham
Garsdon
Purton
B4534
Penhill
Haydon Wick
Kingsdown
Woolstone
Lydiard Millicent
Moredon
B4006
Stratton St Margaret
KEYPOINT
Compton Beauchamp
Nine Elms
Rodbourne
Gorse Hill
Bourton
Cleverton
Lydiard Park
Shaw
Lydiard Tregoze
B4006
Walcot
Ashbury
Uffington Castle
Brinkworth
Callow Hill
B4042
Hook
SWINDON
Wayland's Smithy
Idstone
M4
Toothill
A3102
P+R
Coate
Bishopstone
Hinton Parva
Grittenham
Royal Wootton Bassett
B4005
Coate Water
A4259
Wanborough
Liddington
Ashdown House
B4000
A3102
Hodson
B4005
BISHOPSTONE DOWNS
Elcombe
Wroughton
Badbury
Tockenham
Chiseldon
Liddington Castle
Christian Malford
Bradenstoke
REME
Lyneham
White Horse
Broad Town
A4361
Baydon
39
Preston
Goatacre
Bushton
Clyffe Pypard
A346
B4192
Catcomb
Broad Hinton
Barbury Castle
Ridgeway Path
Aldbourne
Charlcutt
Hilmarton
Clevancy
Tytherton Lucas
A3102
Winterbourne Bassett
MARLBOROUGH DOWNS
Ogbourne St George
White Horse
Bremhill
Berwick Bassett
Ogbourne St Andrew
Compton Bassett
Yatesbury
Winterbourne Monkton
Ramsbury
Windmill Hill
Avebury Manor
Henge & Stone Circles
Fyfield Down
Ogbourne Maizey
Calne
Cherhill
Alexander Keiller Museum
Avebury
Axford
R Kennet
Mildenhall
Littlecote Villa
A4
White Horse
Cherhill Down
West Kennett
Fyfield
Marlborough
Beckhampton
The Sanctuary
Calstone Wellington
Silbury Hill
Manton
White Horse
A4
Froxfield
Stockley
MORGANS HILL
NORTH DOWN
West Kennet Long Barrow
East Kennett
West Overton
Lockeridge
A346
Cadley
Chisbury
Little Bedwyn
Heddington
Savernake Forest
Chisbury Chapel
Oliver's Castle
A361
MILK HILL
Bishops Cannings
Bourton
Rybury
White Horse
Durley
White Horse
Roundway
Huish
A345
Martinsell
Great Bedwyn
Allington
Stanton St Bernard
Knap Hill
Crofton Beam Engines
Horton
Alton Barnes
Oare
Wootton Rivers
Stibb Green
Shalbourne
A342
Alton Priors
West Stowell
Caen Hill Locks
Coate
All Cannings
Honeystreet
Westcourt
Burbage
Eastcourt
Devizes
Pewsey
Fyfield
B3087
Wilton
Poulshot
Etchilhampton
Woodborough
Wilcot
East Grafton
Marten
VALE OF PEWSEY
Milton Lilbourne
Easton Royal
West Grafton
Beechingstoke
A338
Stert
EASTON HILL
Potterne
Patney
Gores
Manningford Bruce
White Horse
Wexcombe
Wedhampton
Marden
Potterne Wick
Hilcott
Manningford Bohune
Tidcombe
Chirton
North Newnton
Urchfont
Wilsford
A342
Brunton
TIDCOMBE DOWN
PEWSEY DOWN
28
Aughton
Eastcott
B3098
WILSFORD
Charlton
Rushall
Collingbourne Kingston
Great Cheverell
Upavon
Littleton Pannell
A342
Everleigh
Cadley
Upper Chute
Market Lavington
CHARLTON
0 1 2 3 4 miles
0 1 2 3 4 5 kilometres

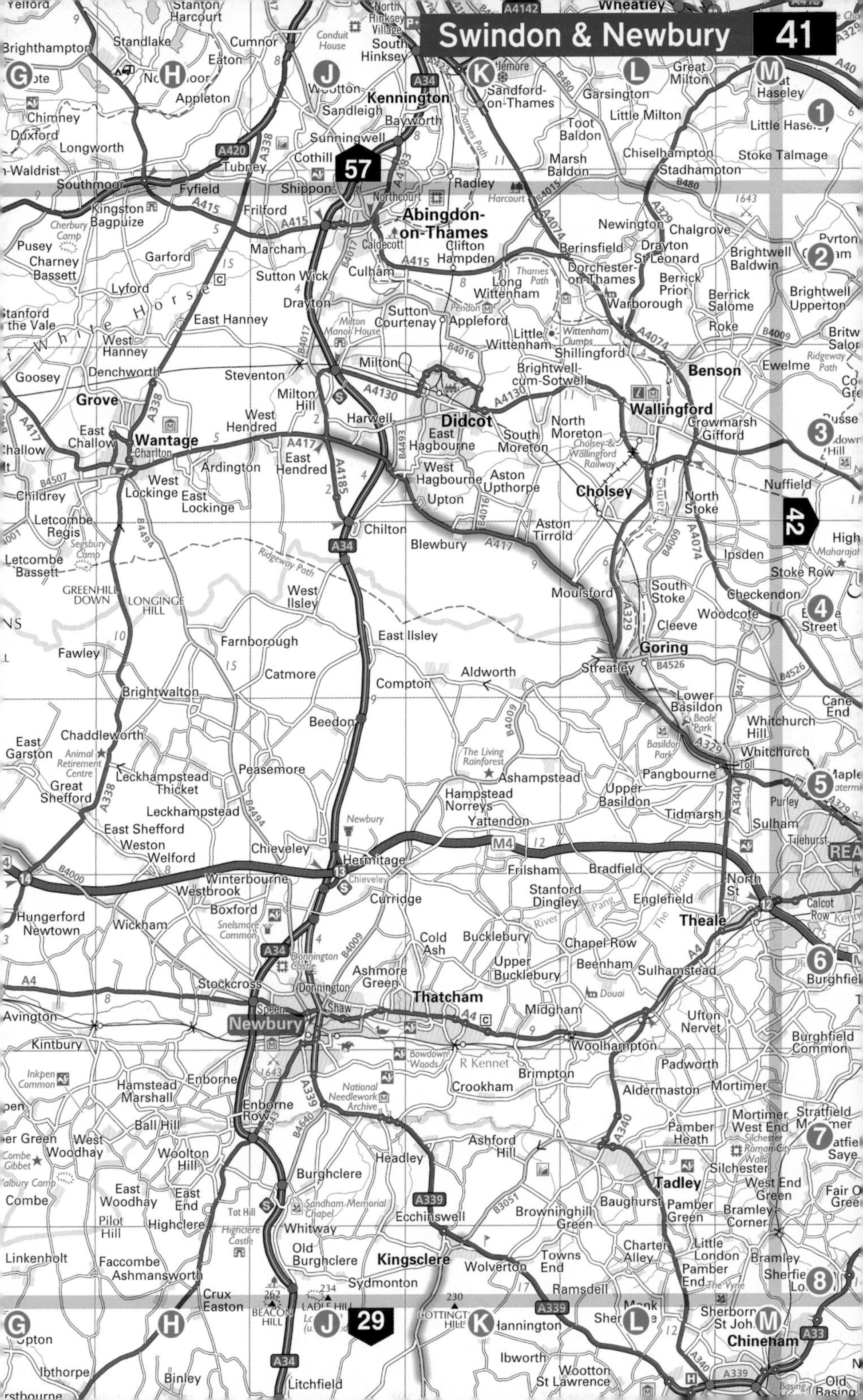
Swindon & Newbury
41
57
42
29
Abingdon-on-Thames
Didcot
Wantage
Grove
Wallingford
Newbury
Thatcham
Kingsclere
Tadley
Theale
Goring
Cholsey
Kennington
Chineham

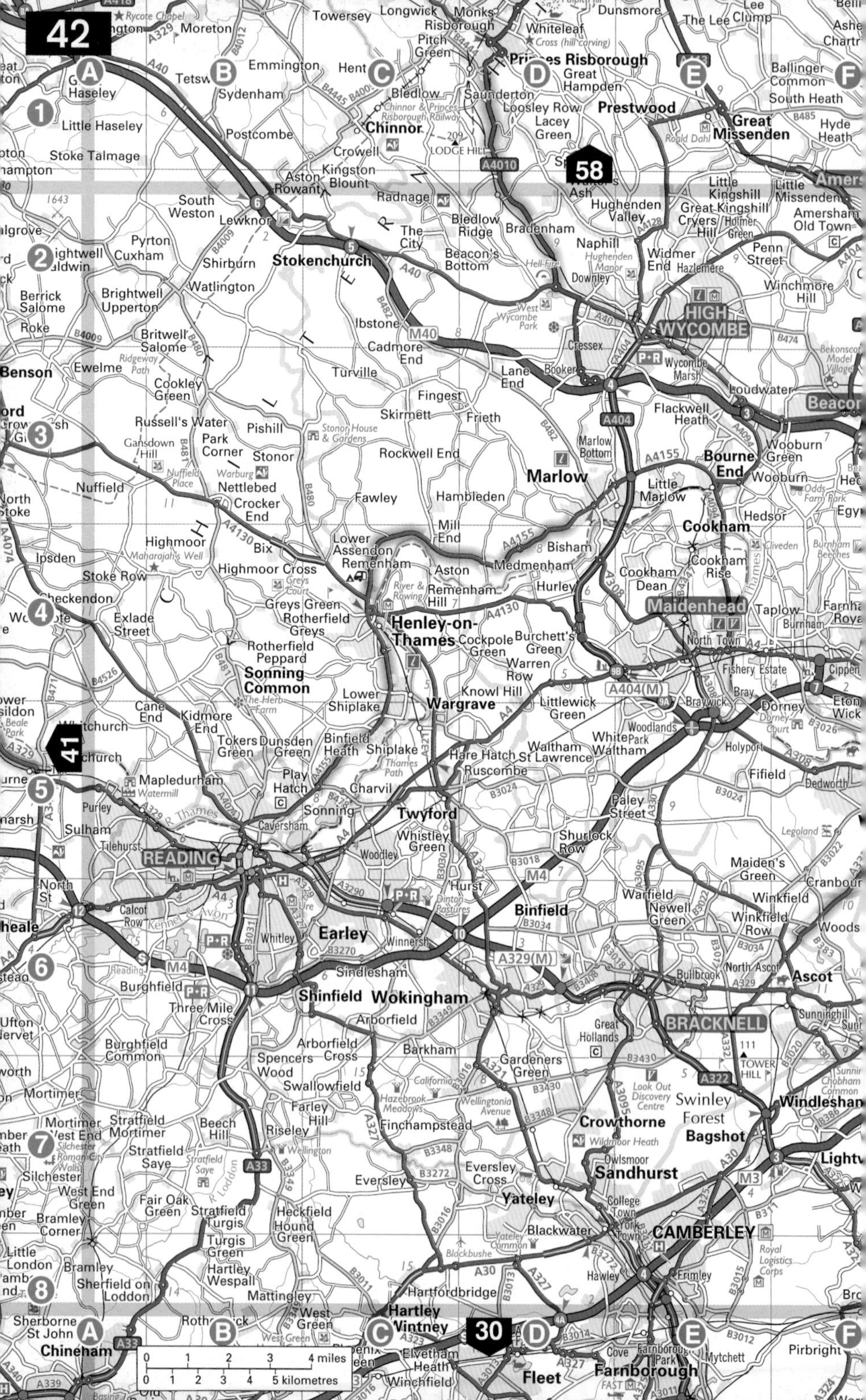

Rycote Chapel
Moreton
Towersey
Longwick
Monks Risborough
Whiteleaf
Cross (hill carving)
Dunsmore
Lee
The Lee
Clump
Pitch Green
Princes Risborough
Great Hampden
Ballinger Common
South Heath
Emmington
Hent
Tetsworth
Sydenham
Bledlow
Chinnor & Princes Risborough Railway
Saunderton
Loosley Row
Lacey Green
Prestwood
Great Missenden
Roald Dahl
Hyde Heath
Great Haseley
Little Haseley
Postcombe
Chinnor
209
LODGE HILL
Stoke Talmage
Crowell
Kingston Blount
Aston Rowant
Radnage
Walters Ash
Hughenden Valley
Little Kingshill
Great Kingshill
Little Missenden
Amersham
Amersham Old Town
1643
South Weston
Lewknor
Bledlow Ridge
Bradenham
Cryers Hill
Holmer Green
Pyrton
Cuxham
Brightwell Baldwin
Shirburn
Stokenchurch
The City
Beacon's Bottom
Naphill
Hughenden Manor
Widmer End
Hazlemere
Penn Street
Downley
Hell-Fire
Winchmore Hill
Berrick Salome
Brightwell Upperton
Watlington
West Wycombe Park
HIGH WYCOMBE
Roke
Britwell Salome
Ibstone
Cadmore End
Cressex
Wycombe Marsh
Beaconsfield Model Village
Ridgeway Path
Benson
Ewelme
Turville
Lane End
Booker
Loudwater
Cookley Green
Fingest
Skirmett
Frieth
Flackwell Heath
Russell's Water
Pishill
Stonor House & Gardens
Wooburn Green
Park Corner
Stonor
Rockwell End
Marlow Bottom
Bourne End
Gangsdown Hill
Nuffield Place
Warburg
Marlow
Wooburn
Nuffield
Nettlebed
Crocker End
Fawley
Hambleden
Little Marlow
Odds Farm Park
North Stoke
Hedsor
Cookham
Mill End
Highmoor
Maharajah's Well
Bix
Lower Assendon
Remenham
Bisham
Medmenham
Cliveden
Burnham Beeches
Ipsden
Stoke Row
Highmoor Cross
Greys Court
Aston
Cookham Dean
Cookham Rise
Checkendon
Greys Green
Rotherfield Greys
River & Rowing
Remenham Hill
Hurley
Maidenhead
Taplow
Burnham
Woodcote
Exlade Street
Henley-on-Thames
Cockpole Green
Burchett's Green
North Town
Rotherfield Peppard
Warren Row
Fishery Estate
Sonning Common
Lower Shiplake
Knowl Hill
Littlewick Green
Bray
Braywick
Dorney
Dorney Court
Eton Wick
Cane End
Kidmore End
The Herb Farm
Wargrave
Woodlands Park
Whitchurch
Beale Park
Tokers Green
Dunsden Green
Binfield Heath
Shiplake
Thames Path
Hare Hatch
Waltham St Lawrence
White Waltham
Holyport
Pangbourne
Whitchurch
Mapledurham
Watermill
Ruscombe
Fifield
Dedworth
Purley
Play Hatch
Charvil
Sonning
Paley Street
Sulham
R. Thames
Caversham
Twyford
Tilehurst
READING
Whistley Green
Woodley
Shurlock Row
Legoland
North St
Calcot Row
Kennet & Avon
Hurst
Dinton Pastures
Maiden's Green
Cranbourne
Warfield
Winkfield
Newell Green
Winkfield Row
Theale
Whitley
Earley
Winnersh
Binfield
Reading
Sindlesham
North Ascot
Ascot
Burghfield
Three Mile Cross
Shinfield
Wokingham
Bullbrook
Ufton Nervet
Arborfield
BRACKNELL
Sunninghill
Burghfield Common
Arborfield Cross
Barkham
Great Hollands
111
TOWER HILL
Spencers Wood
Swallowfield
California
Gardeners Green
Look Out Discovery Centre
Swinley Forest
Windlesham
Mortimer
Hazebrook Meadows
Wellingtonia Avenue
Farley Hill
Finchampstead
Crowthorne
Bagshot
Mortimer West End
Stratfield Mortimer
Beech Hill
Riseley
Wellington
Wildmoor Heath
Owlsmoor
Silchester Roman City
Stratfield Saye
Silchester
Eversley
Eversley Cross
Sandhurst
Lightwater
West End Green
Fair Oak Green
Yateley
College Town
Bramley Corner
Stratfield Turgis
Heckfield
Hound Green
Blackwater
York Town
CAMBERLEY
Turgis Green
Yateley Common
Blackbushe
Royal Logistics Corps
Little London
Bramley
Hartley Wespall
Hawley
Frimley
Sherfield on Loddon
Mattingley
Hartfordbridge
Sherborne St John
West Green
Hartley Wintney
Chineham
Elvetham Heath
Cove
Farnborough Park
Mytchett
Pirbright
Winchfield
Fleet
Farnborough
FAST
Old Basing
M40
M4
A404(M)
A329(M)
M3
A40
A4010
A4128
A404
A4155
A4094
A4130
A308
A4
A4074
A329
A33
A327
A30
A322
A3095
A321
A3290
B4009
B480
B481
B482
B4526
B471
B3024
B3018
B3030
B3034
B3270
B3349
B3348
B3016
B3272
B3011
B3013
B3430
B3022
B3026
B3014
B3015
B311
B3012
B485
B474
0 1 2 3 4 miles
0 1 2 3 4 5 kilometres


58
41
30

Bovingdon
Kings Langley
Potters Bar
Radlett
Shenley
South Mimms
Chorleywood
Rickmansworth
WATFORD
Bushey
Borehamwood
Barnet
Elstree
Harefield
Chalfont St Peter
Northwood
Harrow
Stanmore
Edgware
Hendon
Finchley
Wembley
Uxbridge
Northolt
Ealing
Acton
Camden Town
Hammersmith
Chiswick
Hounslow
Richmond
Wimbledon
Brixton
Staines-upon-Thames
Sunbury-on-Thames
Kingston upon Thames
Walton-on-Thames
Chertsey
Addlestone
Weybridge
Esher
Byfleet
Cobham
Epsom
Sutton
Banstead
WOKING
Leatherhead
59
44
31

Langley
M25
How Wood
De Havilland Aircraft Heritage Centre
A1(M)
Northaw
Potters Bar
Belsize
Chipperfield
Abbots Langley
Bricket Wood
South Mimms
Ridge
Radlett
Warner Bros Studio Tour
Flaunden
Sarratt
Latimer
Amersham on the Hill
Chenies
Chandler's Cross
Aldenham
Green Street
Letchmore Heath
Botany Bay
Hadley Wood
Amersham Common
Little Chalfont
Chorleywood
WATFORD
Monken Hadley
Trent
Cockfosters
Borehamwood
Croxley Green
Bushey
Barnet
New Barnet
Rickmansworth
Elstree
Arkley
East Barnet
Chiltern Open Air
Batchworth
Oxhey
Merry Hill
Bushey Heath
London Gateway
Totteridge Fields
Totteridge
Southgate
Chalfont St Giles
Seer Green
Chalfont Common
Eastbury
Highwood Hill
Mill Hill
Friern Barnet
Chalfont St Peter
Bishop's Wood
Stanmore
Edgware
Northwood
Hatch End
Harrow Weald
Harefield
Ruislip Woods
Pinner Green
Pinner
Wealdstone
Hendon
Church End
Finchley
Muswell Hill
Gerrards Cross
Denham Green
Bayhurst Wood
Eastcote
Harrow
Kenton
Kingsbury
Brent Resr
Golders Green
Highgate
Ruislip
Harrow on the Hill
Fryent
Brent Cross
Kenwood House
Denham
Ickenham
Neasden
Hampstead
Farnham Common
Fulmer
New Denham
Northolt
Sudbury
Wembley
Wembley Complex
Cricklewood
Fenton House
Uxbridge
North Hillingdon
Northolt
Willesden
Camden Town
Stoke Poges
Black Park
Iver Heath
Gutteridge Wood
Yeading Brook
Alperton
Harlesden
Kilburn
St John's Wood
Lord's
Perivale
Cowley
Hayes End
Yeading
Greenford
Park Royal
George Green
Iver
Wood End
Ealing
Marylebone
Paddington
Yiewsley
Hayes
Lake Farm
Acton
Shepherd's Bush
Upton
West Drayton
Minet
Hanwell
Kensington Palace
Southall
Norwood Green
Hammersmith
Olympia
Kensington
Westminster
Langley
Harlington
Heston
Chiswick
Chelsea
Datchet
Colnbrook
Poyle
Cranford
Brentford
Osterley
Kew
Syon
Chiswick House
London Wetland Centre
Carlyle's House
Battersea
Frogmore House
Heathrow
Kew Palace
Barnes
Fulham
Windsor
Old Windsor
Horton
Hounslow
Mortlake
East Sheen
Clapham
Stanwell
West Bedfont
Hatton
Isleworth
Twickenham
Richmond
Putney
Wandsworth
Wraysbury
East Bedfont
Marble Hill
Roehampton
Runnymede
Hythe End
Bedfont Lakes
Feltham
Twickenham
Petersham
Ham House
Richmond Park
Earlsfield
Balham
Great Park
Egham
Ashford
Lower Feltham
Ham
All England Tennis
Tooting Bec
Savill
Englefield Green
Thorpe Lea
Staines-upon-Thames
Queen Mary Resr
Felthamhill
Hanworth
Kempton Park
Teddington
Kingston upon Thames
Wimbledon
Tooting
Merton
Valley
Thorpe
Hampton
Sunbury-on-Thames
Hampton Wick
Norbiton
Morden
Mitcham
Virginia Water
Thorpe Park
Littleton
Upper Halliford
Hampton Court Palace
Surbiton
New Malden
Raynes Park
Lower Halliford
West Molesey
East Molesey
Thames Ditton
Motspur Park
St Helier
Beddington Corner
Lyne
Chertsey
Shepperton
Walton-on-Thames
Long Ditton
Tolworth
Worcester Park
North Cheam
Hackbridge
Great Cockcrow
Thames Path
Sandown Park
Hinchley Wood
Addlestone
Weybridge
Oatlands Park
Esher
Hook
Carshalton
Wallington
Ottershaw
Hersham
West End
Chessington
Cheam
Sutton
Burrowhill
Chobham
New Haw
Claremont Landscape Garden
Claygate
Ewell
Belmont
Woodham
Chessington World of Adventures
Little Woodcote
West Byfleet
Byfleet
Fairmile
Sheerwater
Cobham
Oxshott
Epsom
Horsell
Maybury
Painshill Park
Ashtead Common
Woodmansterne
Banstead
Pyrford
Semaphore Tower
Downside
Epsom Downs
WOKING
RHS Wisley
Stoke D'Abernon
Burgh Heath
Knaphill
Goldsworth Park
St Johns
Ripley
Cobham
Leatherhead
Ashtead
Tadworth
Chipstead
Mayford
Old Woking
Send
Ockham
Fetcham
Headley
Walton on the Hill
Kingswood
Hooley
Little Bookham
Great Bookham
Bocketts
Sutton Green
West
Norbury Park
Headley Heath
Effingham
Polesden Lacey
Mickleham
Burpham
Westhumble
Box Hill
North Downs Way
Redhill
43
59
31
0 1 2 3 4 miles
0 1 2 3 4 5 kilometres

Epping
Cheshunt
Waltham Abbey
Theydon Bois
60
Navestock
Kelvedon Hatch
Doddinghurst
Ingatestone
Mountnessing
Loughton
Chigwell
Abridge
BRENTWOOD
Shenfield
Romford
Chingford
Walthamstow
Wanstead
Ilford
Barking
Hornchurch
Upminster
Dagenham
Rainham
Stratford
Hackney
Woolwich
Greenwich
Lewisham
Thamesmead
Erith
Purfleet
Aveley
South Ockendon
Grays
Tilbury
Dartford
Dartford Crossing (Electronic Toll)
Northfleet
GRAVESEND
Bexleyheath
Sidcup
Chislehurst
Swanley
Orpington
Bromley
Eynsford
West Kingsdown
Meopham
46
Biggin Hill
32
Otford
Kemsing
Borough Green
33
West Malling
Westerham
Sevenoaks
Limpsfield
Oxted
River Thames

Margaretting
Ingatestone
West Hanningfield
South Hanningfield
Billericay
Wickford
Rayleigh
Rochford
BASILDON
Hadleigh
South Benfleet
Canvey Island
SOUTHEND-ON-SEA
Stanford le Hope
THAMES ESTUARY
HOO PENINSULA
Tilbury
GRAVESEND
Hoo St Werburgh
ROCHESTER
CHATHAM
GILLINGHAM
Rainham
Sittingbourne
Snodland
Aylesford
West Malling
MAIDSTONE
Bearsted
South Woodham Ferrers
Hullbridge
Hockley
Hawkwell
Ashingdon
River Medway
0 1 2 3 4 miles
0 1 2 3 4 5 kilometres

61
45
33

Holliwell Point
Foulness Point
Courtsend
Churchend
Sea
Warden Point
Leysdown-on-Sea
Leysdown Coastal Park
Isle of Harty
Shell Ness
Whitstable
Whitstable Bay
Tankerton
Herne Bay
Hampton
Swalecliffe
Chestfield
South Street
Greenhill
Beltinge
Broomfield
Herne
East Blean
Bishopstone
Reculver
Reculver Towers & Roman Fort
Minnis Bay
Westgate-on-Sea
St Mildred's Bay
Birchington
Acol
St Nicholas-at-Wade
Boyden Gate
Sarre
Monkton
Durlock
Minster
Chislet
Hoath
Upstreet
West Stourmouth
East Stourmouth
Westmarsh
Seasalter
Yorkletts
Highstreet
Druidstone Park
Dargate
Goodnestone
Davington Hill
Preston
Hernhill
Staplestreet
Mount Ephraim
Farming World
Denstroude
Blean
Blean Woods
Dunkirk
Upper Harbledown
Rough Common
Wildwood
Broad Oak
Tyler Hill
Hales Place
Sturry
Westbere
Stodmarsh
Fordwich
Town Hall
Preston
Elmstone
Cop Street
Hoaden
Wickhambreaux
Wingham
Littlebourne
Seaton
Ickham
Canterbury
Howletts
Boughton Street
North Street
South Street
Oversland
Harbledown
Thanington
Sheldwich
Hogben's Hill
Selling
Chartham Hatch
Chartham
Old Wives Lees
Shalmsford Street
Badlesmere
Shottenden
Chilham
Dane Street
Garlinge Green
Street End
Bridge
Lower Hardres
Bishopsbourne
Bekesbourne
Patrixbourne
Bramling
Adisham
Aylesham
North Downs Way
Nonington
Goodnestone
Chillenden
Staple
Statenborough
Eastry
Durlock
Wingham
Marshborough
Ash
Betteshang
Tilmanstone
A299
A28
A253
A291
A2050
A257
A2
A251
A252
B2040
B2205
B2231
B2190
B2046
62
34
35

A
B
C
D
E
F
1
2
3
4
5
6
7
8
Pen Brush
Garn Fawr
Trefasser
Pembrokeshire Coast Path
St Nicholas
Manorowen
Ynys Daullyn
Granston
Carreg Sampson
Porthgain
Trefin
Mathry
64
Abereiddy
Llanrhian
A487
Llangloffan Fen
B4331
Berea
Croes-goch
Treleddyd-fawr
Treglemais
ST DAVID'S HEAD
Rhodiad-y-brenin
River Solva
Llandeloy
B4330
Whitesands Bay
Caer Farchell
B4583
Bishop's Palace
Whitchurch
Treffgarne Owen
RAMSEY ISLAND
St Davids (Tyddewi)
Hayscastle
Ramsey Sound
Solva
Penycwn
178
DUDWELL MT
Newgale
St David's Peninsula Heritage Coast
Roch
Wolfsdale
PEMBROKESHIRE COAST NATIONAL PARK
Simpson Cross
Rickets Head
Keeston
Nolton Haven
Nolton
St Brides Bay
St Brides Bay Heritage Coast
Druidston
Haroldston West
Portfield Gate
B4341
Broad Haven
Broadway
B4327
Little Haven
Walton West
Pembrokeshire Coast Path
Talbenny
Tiers Cross
Walwyn's Castle
SKOMER ISLAND
Wooltack Point
Marloes
B4327
St Ishmael's
Herbrandston
Broad Sound
Hubberston
Marloes & Dale Heritage Coast
Dale
Hakin
SKOKHOLM ISLAND
Westdale Bay
Great Castle Head
Dale Point
Milford Haven
Milford Haven (Aberdaugleddau)
Angle
Angle Bay
St Ann's Head
Rhoscrowther
B4320
Rosslare
Castlemartin Brook
Freshwater West
B4319
Castlemartin
Linney Head
PEMBROKESHIRE NATIONAL
Pembrokeshire Coast Path
0 1 2 3 4 miles
0 1 2 3 4 5 kilometres

Newport
Dinas
Felindre Farchog
Castell Henllys
Crosswell
Brynberian
Crymych
Blaenffos
Bwlch-y-groes
Star
Tegryn
Hermon
Llanfyrnach
Trelech
Mynydd Melyn
Llanychaer
Pontfaen
MYNYDD PRESELI
PEMBROKESHIRE COAST
NATIONAL PARK
Foel Drygarn
Foel Eryr
FOEL CWMCERWYN
Mynachlog ddu
FOEL DRYCH
Rosebush
Puncheston
Castlebythe
Tufton
Maenclochog
Llandre Isaf
Glandwr
Hebron
Blaenwaun
Henry's Moat (Castell Hendre)
Llangolman
Llanglydwen
Cefn-y-pant
Cwmbach
Llanwinio
Ambleston
Llys-y-frân Resr
New Moat
Llanycefn
Efailwen
Login
Llanboidy
Gellywen
Llys-y-frân
Walton East
Pen-ffordd
Llandissilio
Clarbeston
Clarbeston Road
Bletherston
Llanfallteg
Clunderwen
Llanfallteg West
Cwmfelin Boeth
Llangynin
Meidrim
Whitland Abbey
Wiston
Bethesda
Llawhaden
Robeston Wathen
Llanddewi Velfrey
Whitland
Pwll-trap
St Clears (Sanclêr)
Haverfordwest (Hwlffordd)
Narberth (Arberth)
Crinow
Lampeter Velfrey
Llanddowror
Picton Castle
Bluestone
Oakwood
Templeton
Tavernspite
Red Roses
Martletwy
Ludchurch
Llanteg
Crunwear
Llansadurnen
Cwm Deri
Llanmiloe
Loveston
Reynalton
Folly Farm
Colby Woodland Garden
Pendine
Museum of Speed
Begelly
Stepaside
Amroth
Lawrenny
West Williamston
Cresswell
Jeffreyston
Kilgetty
Summerhill
Cresselly
Broadmoor
Coppet Hall
Wiseman's Bridge
Burton
West Williamston
Carew Newton
Redberth
East Williamston
Saundersfoot
Waterloo
Tidal Mill
Milton
Carew
Cosheston
Sageston
Monkstone Point
New Hedges
Carew Cheriton
St Florence
Gumfreston
Bishop's Palace
Lamphey
Manorbier Newton
Medieval House
Tenby (Dinbych-y-pysgod)
CARMARTHEN BAY
Penally
Hodgeston
Jameston
Lydstep
Giltar Point
Trewent Point
Manorbier
Lydstep Point
CALDEY ISLAND
Stackpole Elidor / Cheriton
South Pembrokeshire Heritage Coast
Stackpole
Stackpole Head
St Govan's Head
A487 A40 A477 A478 A4075 A4115 A4066 A4139 B4313 B4329 B4314 B4315 B4328 B4318 B4586 B4584 B4585 B4319 B4299
65 50
G H J K L M
1 2 3 4 5 6 7 8

65
49
Trelech
Llanpumsaint
Glandwr
Hebron
Blaenwaun
Blaen-y-coed
Cynwyl Elfed
Llanglydwen
Cefn-y-pant
Cwmbach
Llanwinio
Rhydargaeau
Efailwen
Talog
Gwili Railway
Login
Llanboidy
Gellywen
Abernant
Bronwydd
Meidrim
Carmarthen
(Caerfyrddin)
Abergwili
Llangunnor
Tre-gynwr
Johnstown
Llanllwch
United Counties
Llanfallteg West
Cwmfelin Boeth
Whitland Abbey
Llangynin
Bancyfelin
Whitland
Llanddewi Velfrey
Pwll-trap
St Clears
(Sanclêr)
Cwmffrwd
Croesyceiliog
Lampeter Velfrey
Llanddowror
Llangynog
Idole
Bancycapel
Tavernspite
Pontantwn
Red Roses
Laugharne
Llanybri
Llansteffan
Tin Shed
Dylan Thomas' Boathouse
Castle
Llandyfaelog
Llanteg
Crunwear
Llansadurnen
Ferryside
Llanmiloe
Four Roads
Wharley Point
Pendine
Amroth
Colby Woodland Garden
Museum of Speed
Ginst Point
Pontyates
Llansaint
Mynyddgarreg
Summerhill
Coppet Hall
Wiseman's Bridge
Kidwelly
(Cydweli)
Ffos Las
Saundersfoot
Trimsaran
Pembrey Forest
Monkstone Point
Ffrwd Farm Mire
Pembrey
Cefn Sidan
Tenby
(Dinbych-y-pysgod)
Burry Port
(Porth Tywyn)
CARMARTHEN BAY
CALDEY ISLAND
Burry Inlet
Whiteford Burrows
Broughton Bay
Llanmadoc
Burry Holms
Llangennith
Cheriton
Burry Green
Rhossili Bay
Rhossili Down
Reynoldston
Llanddewi
Rhossili
Visitor Centre
WORMS HEAD
Middleton
Gower Coast
Paviland
Port Eynon
Overton
Culver Hole
Port Eynon Point
River Towy
R Gwendraeth
River Tâf
Afon Cywyn
Afon Cynin
Afon Gronw
River Gwili
A40
A477
A4066
A484
B4298
B4299
B4312
B4314
B4328
B4300
B4306
B4309
B4317
B4308
B4311
B4301
B4247
A4118
0 1 2 3 4 miles
0 1 2 3 4 5 kilometres

66
52
36
Llandeilo
Ammanford
(Rhydaman)
Gwaun-Cae-Gurwen
Ystradgynlais
Ystalyfera
Pontardawe
Pontarddulais
Clydach
Gorseinon
Birchgrove
Neath
(Castell-nedd)
Gowerton
Dunvant
(Dyfnant)
SWANSEA
(ABERTAWE)
Swansea Bay
Port Talbot
Briton Ferry
Baglan
Cwmafan
Maesteg
Pyle
(Y Pil)
BLACK MOUNTAIN
Vale of Neath
Llangennech
Llanelli Wetland Centre
National Botanic Garden of Wales
National Showcaves Centre for Wales
The Mumbles
Mumbles Head
Oxwich Bay
Gower Heritage Coast

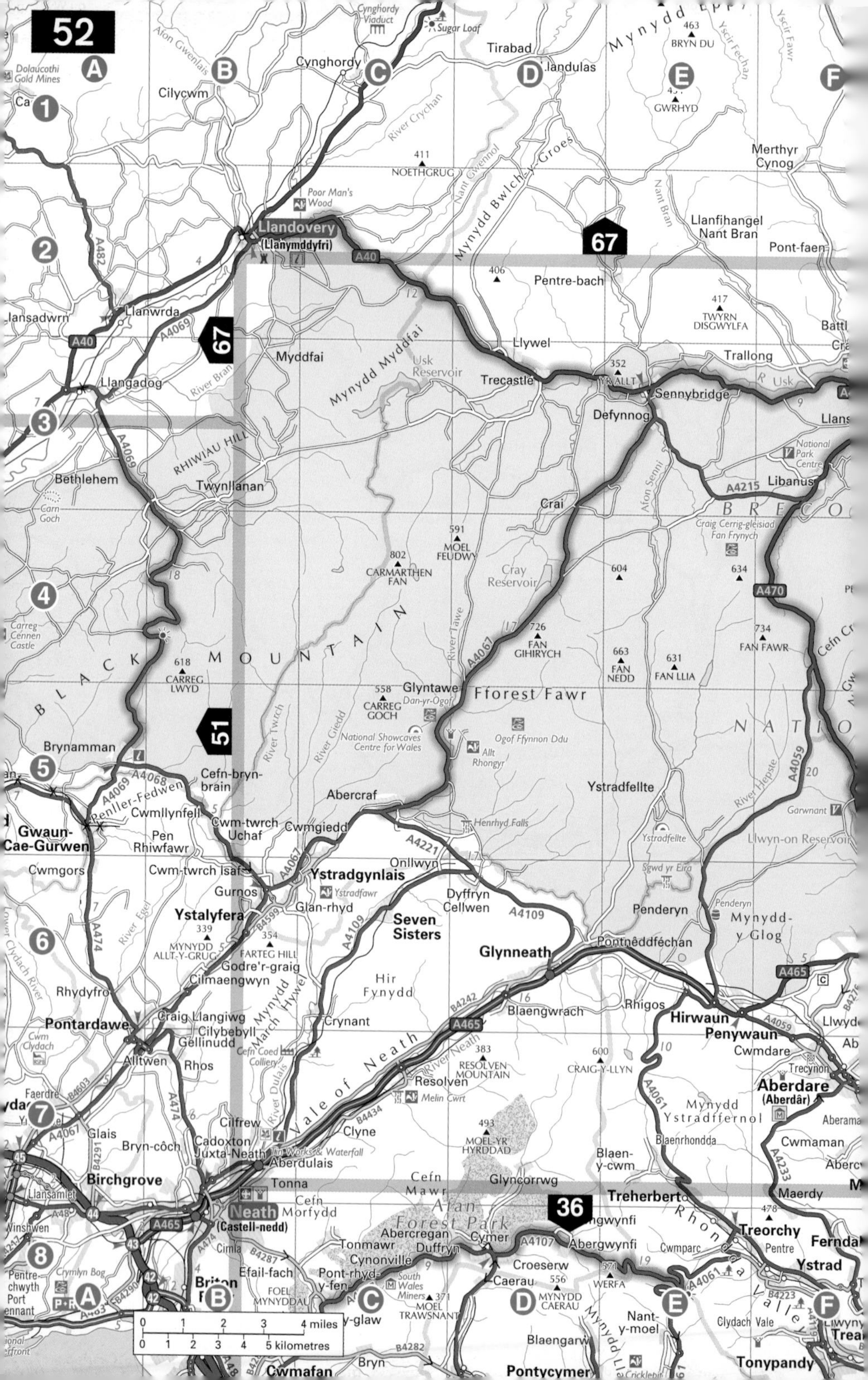
Llandovery
(Llanymddyfri)
Cynghordy
Cynghordy Viaduct
Sugar Loaf
Tirabad
Llandulas
Mynydd Epynt
Cilycwm
Dolaucothi Gold Mines
Llansadwrn
Llanwrda
Llangadog
Myddfai
Mynydd Myddfai
Usk Reservoir
Trecastle
Sennybridge
Defynnog
Trallong
Llywel
Pentre-bach
Merthyr Cynog
Llanfihangel Nant Bran
Pont-faen
Poor Man's Wood
NOETHGRUG
Mynydd Bwlch-y-Groes
BRYN DU
GWRHYD
TWYRN DISGWYLFA
RHIWIAU HILL
Twynllanan
Bethlehem
Carn Goch
Carreg Cennen Castle
BLACK MOUNTAIN
CARREG LWYD
CARMARTHEN FAN
MOEL FEUDWY
Cray Reservoir
Crai
FAN GIHIRYCH
FAN NEDD
FAN LLIA
FAN FAWR
Craig Cerrig-gleisiad Fan Frynych
Libanus
National Park Centre
BRECON
NATIONAL
Glyntawe
Dan-yr-Ogof
CARREG GOCH
National Showcaves Centre for Wales
Fforest Fawr
Ogof Ffynnon Ddu
Allt Rhongyr
Brynamman
Cefn-bryn-brain
Abercraf
Ystradfellte
Henrhyd Falls
Garwnant
Llwyn-on Reservoir
Gwaun-Cae-Gurwen
Penller-Fedwen
Cwmllynfell
Cwm-twrch Uchaf
Cwmgiedd
Pen Rhiwfawr
Cwmgors
Cwm-twrch Isaf
Gurnos
Ystradgynlais
Ystradfawr
Onllwyn
Dyffryn Cellwen
Sgwd yr Eira
Penderyn
Mynydd-y Glog
Ystalyfera
Glan-rhyd
Seven Sisters
MYNYDD ALLT-Y-GRUG
FARTEG HILL
Godre'r-graig
Cilmaengwyn
Glynneath
Pontnêddféchan
Hir Fynydd
Mynydd March Hywel
Rhydyfro
Pontardawe
Craig Llangiwg
Cilybebyll
Gellinudd
Crynant
Alltwen
Rhos
Cwm Clydach
Cefn Coed Colliery
Blaengwrach
Rhigos
Hirwaun
Penywaun
Cwmdare
Trecynon
Aberdare
(Aberdâr)
Vale of Neath
RESOLVEN MOUNTAIN
Resolven
Melin Cwrt
CRAIG-Y-LLYN
Mynydd Ystradffernol
Blaenrhondda
Faerdre
Glais
Cilfrew
Clyne
MOEL-YR-HYRDDAD
Bryn-côch
Cadoxton Juxta-Neath
Aberdulais
Tin Works & Waterfall
Blaen-y-cwm
Cwmaman
Birchgrove
Llansamlet
Tonna
Cefn Mawr
Glyncorrwg
Treherbert
Maerdy
Neath
(Castell-nedd)
Cefn Morfydd
Afan Forest Park
Winshwen
Abercregan
Cymer
Duffryn
Abergwynfi
Cwmparc
Treorchy
Pentre
Ystrad
Rhondda Valley
Cimla
Tonmawr
Cynonville
Croeserw
Caerau
Crymlyn Bog
Efail-fach
Pont-rhyd-y-fen
South Wales Miners
MOEL TRAWSNANT
MYNYDD CAERAU
WERFA
Nant-y-moel
Clydach Vale
Pentre-chwyth
Port Tennant
Briton Ferry
FOEL MYNYDDAU
Blaengarw
Bryn
Cwmafan
Pontycymer
Tonypandy
0 1 2 3 4 miles
0 1 2 3 4 5 kilometres
67
51
36

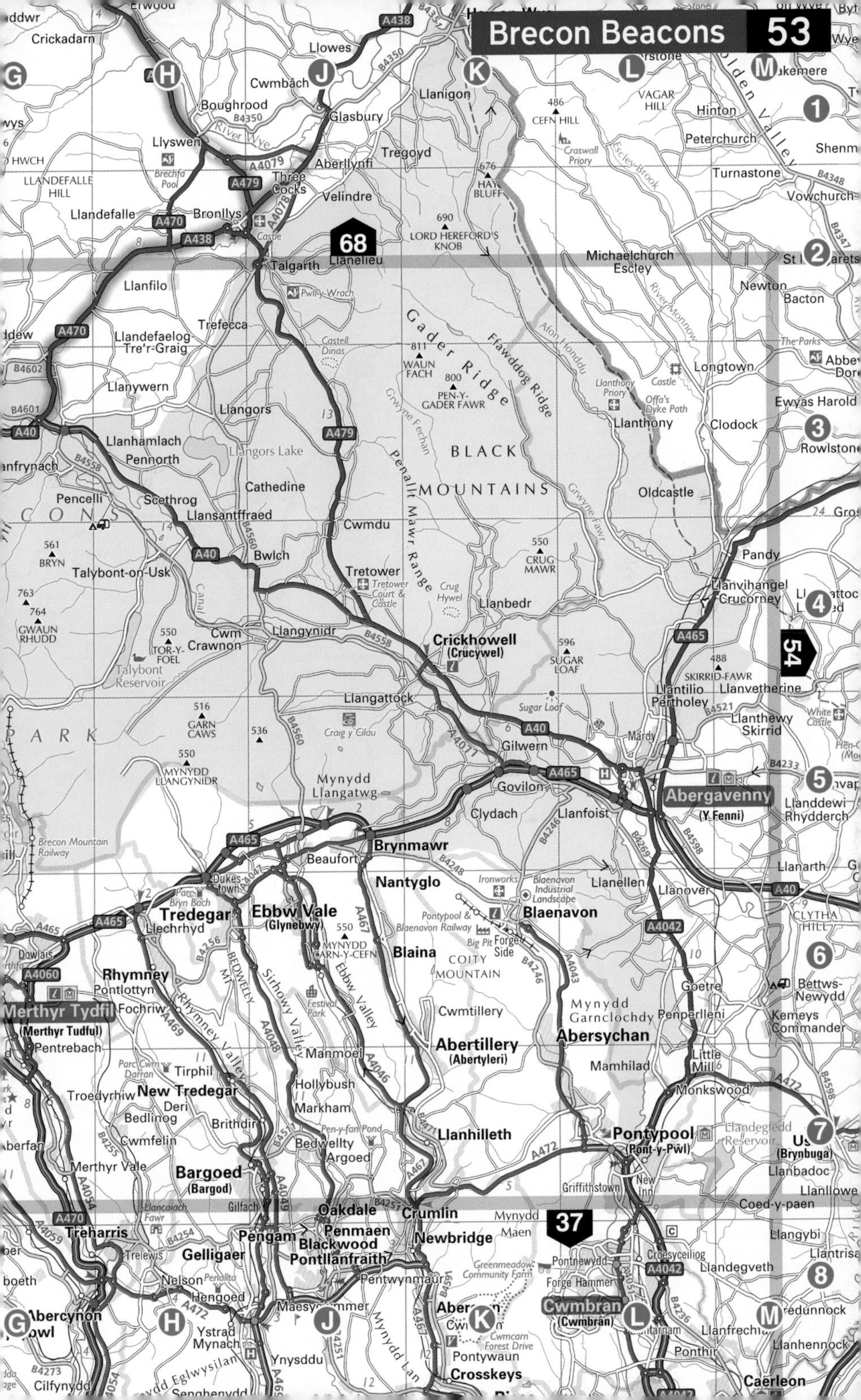

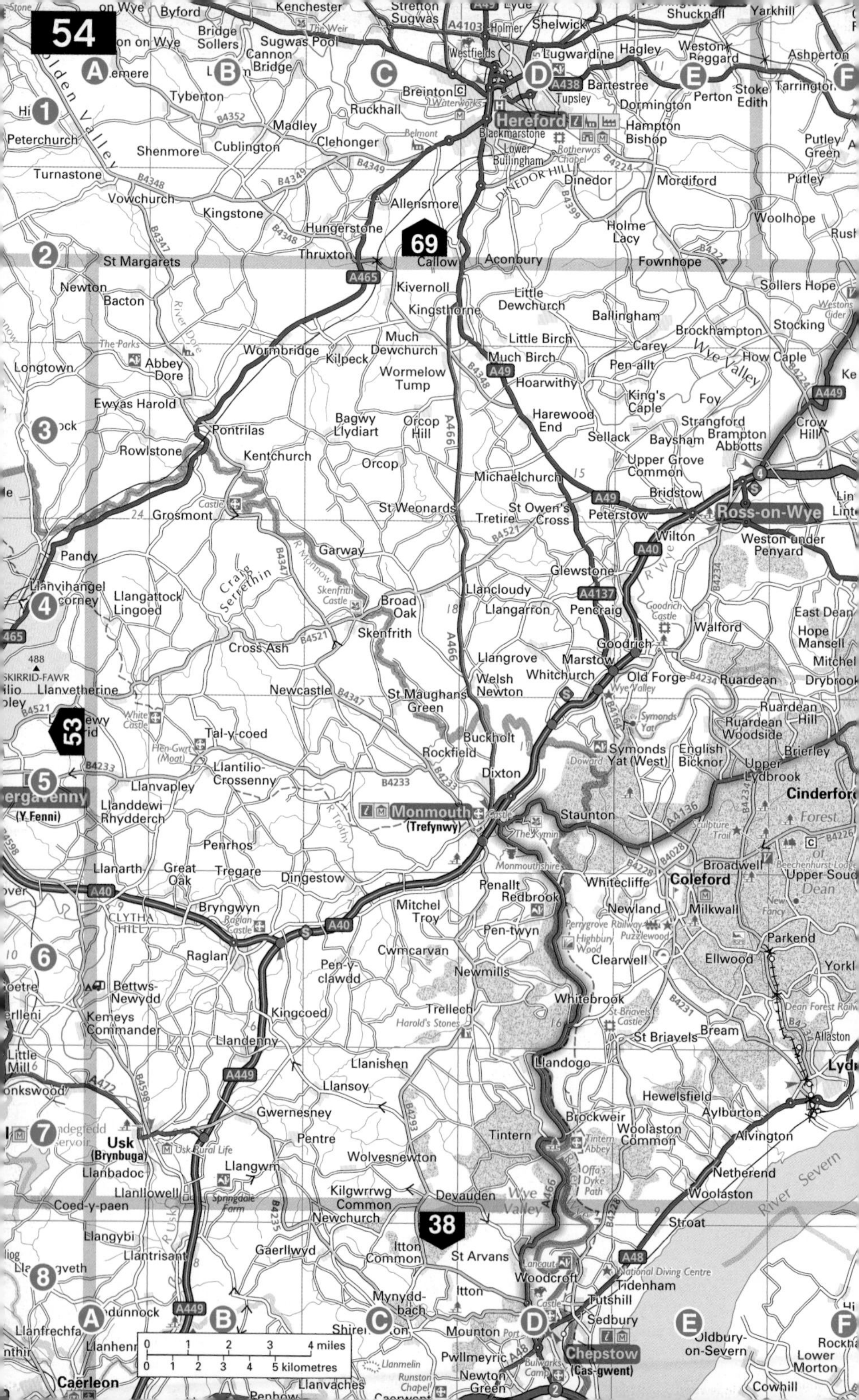
Hereford
Ross-on-Wye
Monmouth
(Trefynwy)
Chepstow
(Cas-gwent)
Usk
(Brynbuga)
Coleford
Caerleon
Golden Valley
Wye Valley
River Severn
Forest of Dean
69
53
38
Peterchurch
Madley
Kingstone
Pontrilas
Grosmont
Skenfrith
Raglan
Tintern
St Briavels
Symonds Yat (West)
Goodrich
Ewyas Harold
Abbey Dore
Kilpeck
Much Birch
Fownhope
Lydbrook
Parkend
Lydney
Tidenham
Woolaston
0 1 2 3 4 miles
0 1 2 3 4 5 kilometres

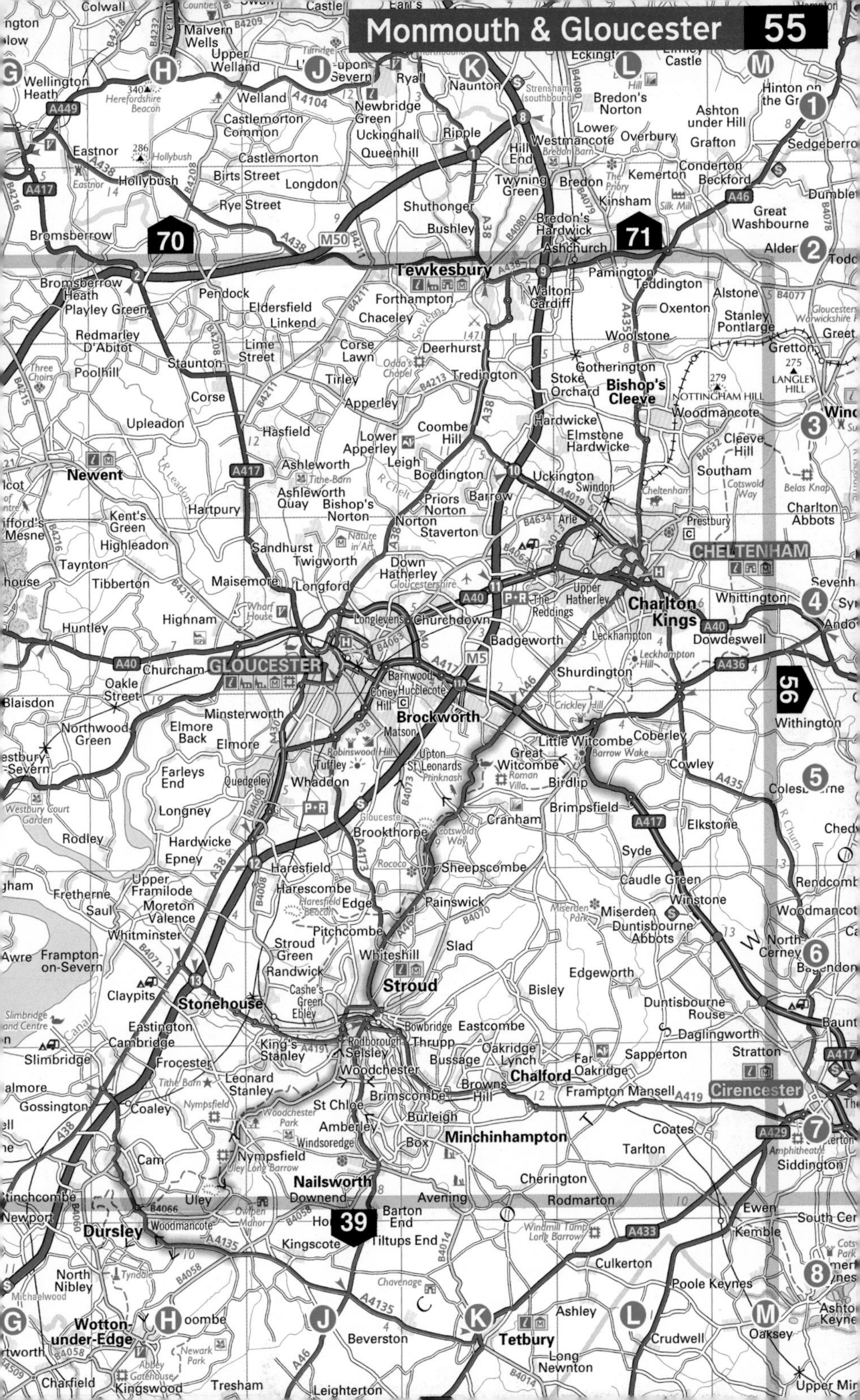
Tewkesbury
GLOUCESTER
CHELTENHAM
Bishop's Cleeve
Charlton Kings
Brockworth
Stroud
Stonehouse
Nailsworth
Minchinhampton
Chalford
Cirencester
Dursley
Wotton-under-Edge
Tetbury
Newent
Malvern Wells
Upton-upon-Severn
70
71
56
39

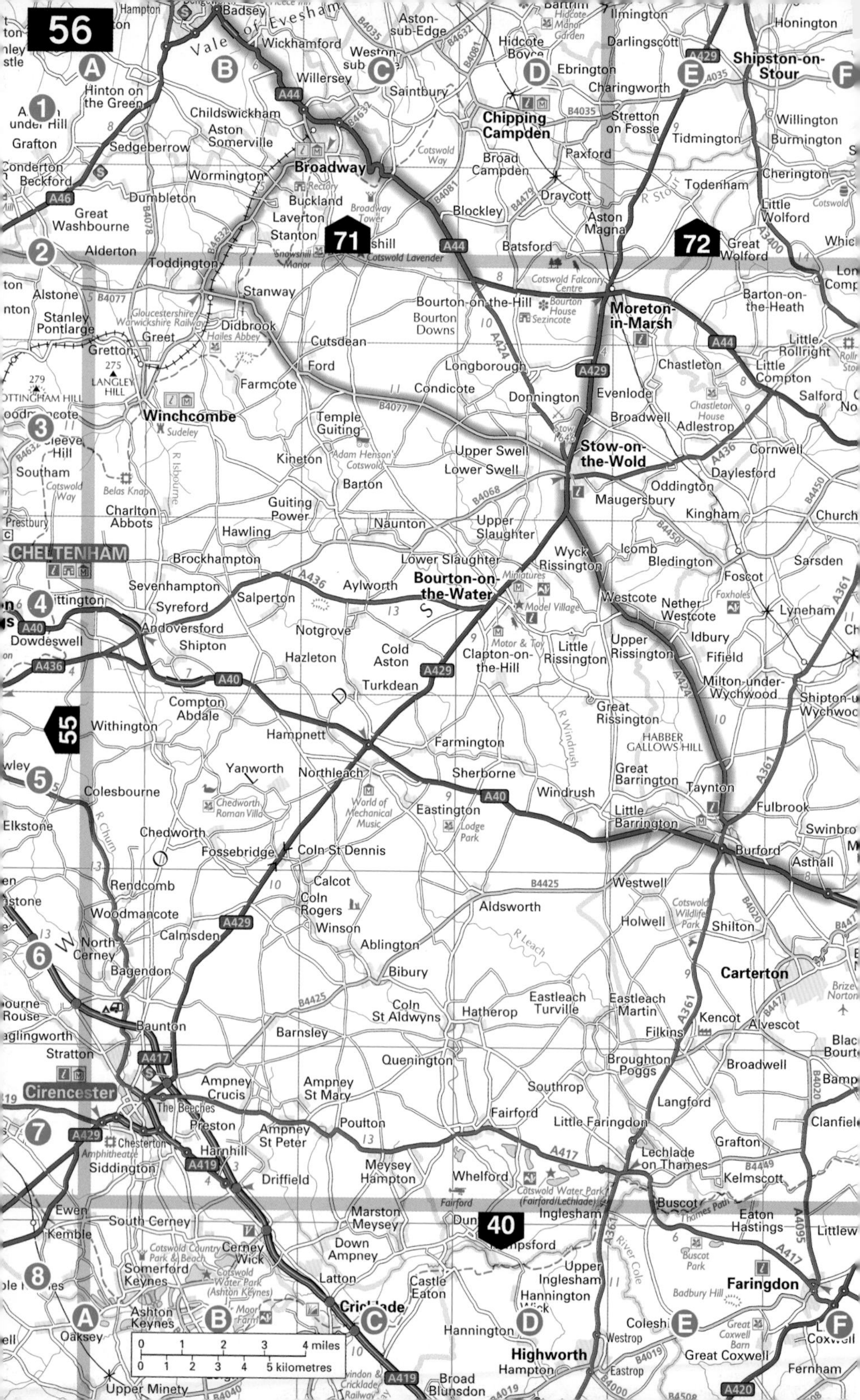
Badsey
Vale of Evesham
Wickhamford
Aston-sub-Edge
Weston sub Edge
Hinton on the Green
Willersey
Saintbury
Hidcote Boyce
Hidcote Manor Garden
Ebrington
Ilmington
Darlingscott
Honington
Shipston-on-Stour
Charingworth
Childswickham
Aston Somerville
Sedgeberrow
Grafton
Conderton
Beckford
Broadway
Chipping Campden
Stretton on Fosse
Tidmington
Willington
Burmington
Cotswold Way
Broad Campden
Paxford
Cherington
Wormington
Dumbleton
Buckland
Broadway Tower
Draycott
Todenham
Little Wolford
Great Washbourne
Laverton
Stanton
Blockley
Aston Magna
Alderton
Snowshill
Snowshill Manor
Cotswold Lavender
Batsford
Great Wolford
Toddington
Alstone
Stanway
Bourton-on-the-Hill
Cotswold Falconry Centre
Bourton House
Sezincote
Bourton Downs
Moreton-in-Marsh
Barton-on-the-Heath
Stanley Pontlarge
Gloucestershire Warwickshire Railway
Didbrook
Greet
Hailes Abbey
Gretton
Cutsdean
Ford
Longborough
Chastleton
Little Rollright
Little Compton
Langley Hill
Farmcote
Condicote
Donnington
Evenlode
Salford
Winchcombe
Sudeley
Temple Guiting
Broadwell
Chastleton House
Adlestrop
Cleeve Hill
Southam
Kineton
Adam Henson's Cotswold
Upper Swell
Lower Swell
Stow-on-the-Wold
Cornwell
Daylesford
Belas Knap
Barton
Oddington
Maugersbury
Prestbury
Charlton Abbots
Guiting Power
Naunton
Upper Slaughter
Kingham
Hawling
Cheltenham
Brockhampton
Lower Slaughter
Wyck Rissington
Icomb
Bledington
Sarsden
Sevenhampton
Aylworth
Bourton-on-the-Water
Miniatures
Model Village
Foscot
Foxholes
Syreford
Salperton
Westcote
Nether Westcote
Lyneham
Andoversford
Dowdeswell
Notgrove
Shipton
Motor & Toy
Idbury
Upper Rissington
Little Rissington
Clapton-on-the-Hill
Hazleton
Cold Aston
Fifield
Milton-under-Wychwood
Turkdean
Compton Abdale
Great Rissington
Withington
Hampnett
Farmington
Habber Gallows Hill
R Windrush
Yanworth
Northleach
Sherborne
Great Barrington
Taynton
Colesbourne
World of Mechanical Music
Eastington
Windrush
Little Barrington
Fulbrook
Chedworth Roman Villa
Lodge Park
Elkstone
Chedworth
Fossebridge
Coln St Dennis
Burford
Asthall
Rendcomb
Calcot
Coln Rogers
Westwell
Woodmancote
Winson
Aldsworth
Cotswold Wildlife Park
Holwell
Shilton
Calmsden
Ablington
North Cerney
Bagendon
Bibury
Carterton
Coln St Aldwyns
Hatherop
Eastleach Turville
Eastleach Martin
Kencot
Alvescot
Baunton
Barnsley
Filkins
Stratton
Quenington
Broughton Poggs
Broadwell
Cirencester
Ampney Crucis
Ampney St Mary
Southrop
Langford
The Beeches
Preston
Ampney St Peter
Poulton
Fairford
Little Faringdon
Grafton
Chesterton
Amphitheatre
Harnhill
Siddington
Driffield
Meysey Hampton
Whelford
Cotswold Water Park (Fairford/Lechlade)
Lechlade on Thames
Kelmscott
Ewen
South Cerney
Marston Meysey
Inglesham
Buscot
Thames Path
Eaton Hastings
Kemble
Cotswold Country Park & Beach
Cerney Wick
Down Ampney
Kempsford
Buscot Park
Somerford Keynes
Cotswold Water Park (Ashton Keynes)
Latton
Upper Inglesham
Castle Eaton
Faringdon
Ashton Keynes
Cricklade
Hannington Wick
Badbury Hill
Oaksey
Hannington
Coleshill
Great Coxwell Barn
Coxwell
Westrop
Highworth
Great Coxwell
Upper Minety
Swindon & Cricklade Railway
Broad Blunsdon
Hampton
Eastrop
Fernham
0 1 2 3 4 miles
0 1 2 3 4 5 kilometres
55
71
72
40

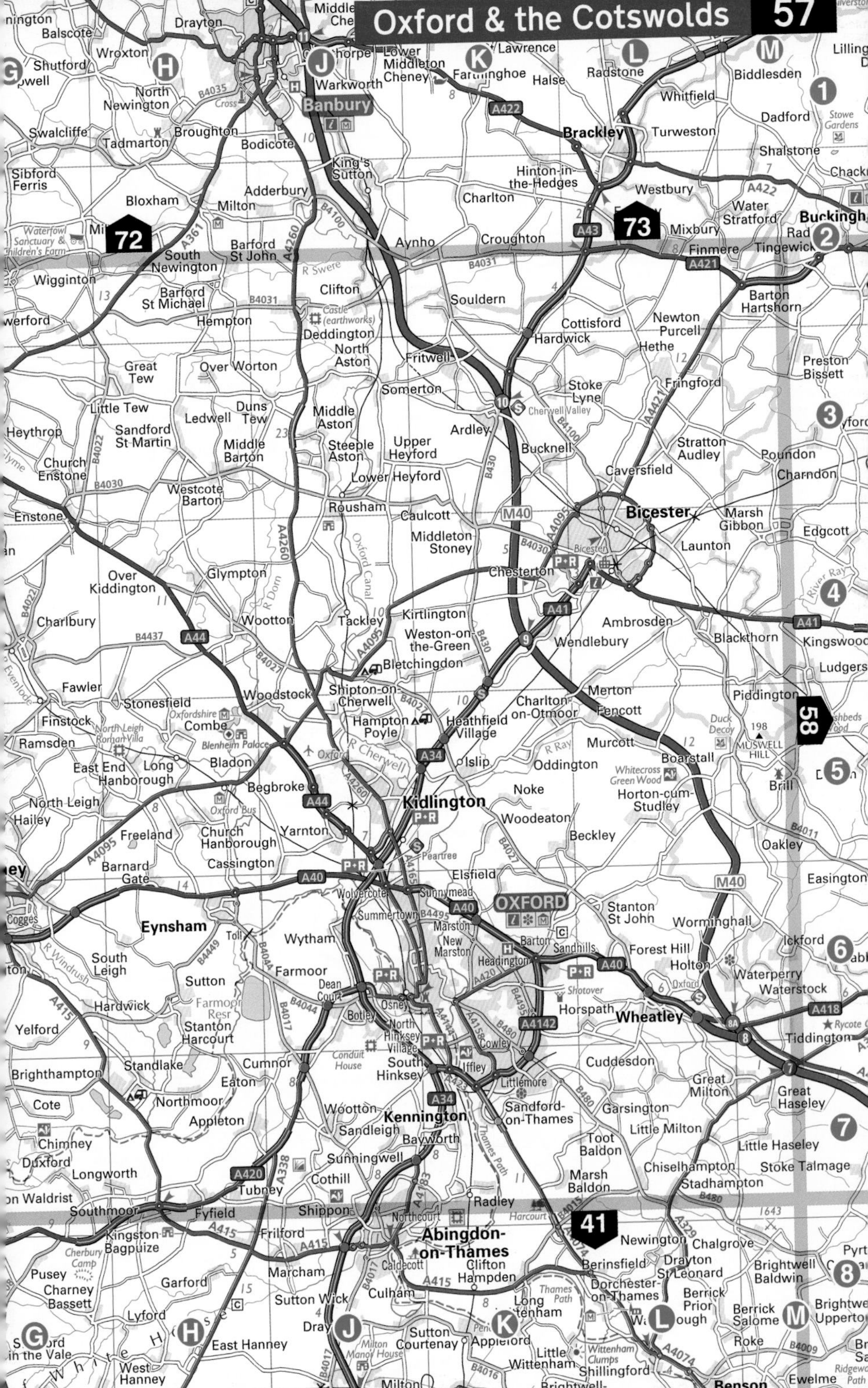
Banbury
Brackley
Bicester
Kidlington
OXFORD
Eynsham
Wheatley
Abingdon-on-Thames
Kennington
Woodstock
Deddington
Chipping Norton
Bloxham
Adderbury
Aynho
Croughton
Souldern
Fritwell
Somerton
Ardley
Bucknell
Caversfield
Launton
Chesterton
Wendlebury
Ambrosden
Blackthorn
Charlbury
Enstone
Great Tew
Steeple Aston
Upper Heyford
Lower Heyford
Rousham
Middleton Stoney
Kirtlington
Tackley
Bletchingdon
Islip
Noke
Beckley
Woodeaton
Elsfield
Cassington
Yarnton
Begbroke
Bladon
Combe
Stonesfield
Finstock
Ramsden
Freeland
Hanborough
Wolvercote
Summertown
Headington
Cowley
Iffley
Littlemore
Botley
Cumnor
Wytham
Farmoor
Stanton Harcourt
Standlake
Appleton
Tubney
Fyfield
Marcham
Culham
Radley
Sandford-on-Thames
Garsington
Cuddesdon
Horspath
Forest Hill
Holton
Stanton St John
Worminghall
Brill
Oakley
Boarstall
Murcott
Charlton-on-Otmoor
Merton
Piddington
Dorchester-on-Thames
Berinsfield
Clifton Hampden
Long Wittenham
Little Wittenham
Sutton Courtenay
Drayton
Steventon
Benson
Chalgrove
Stadhampton
Great Milton
Little Milton
Tiddington
Thame
M40
A34
A40
A44
A41
A43
A420
A415
A4260
A4095
A4142
A421
A422
A418
A4074
A329
72
73
58
41

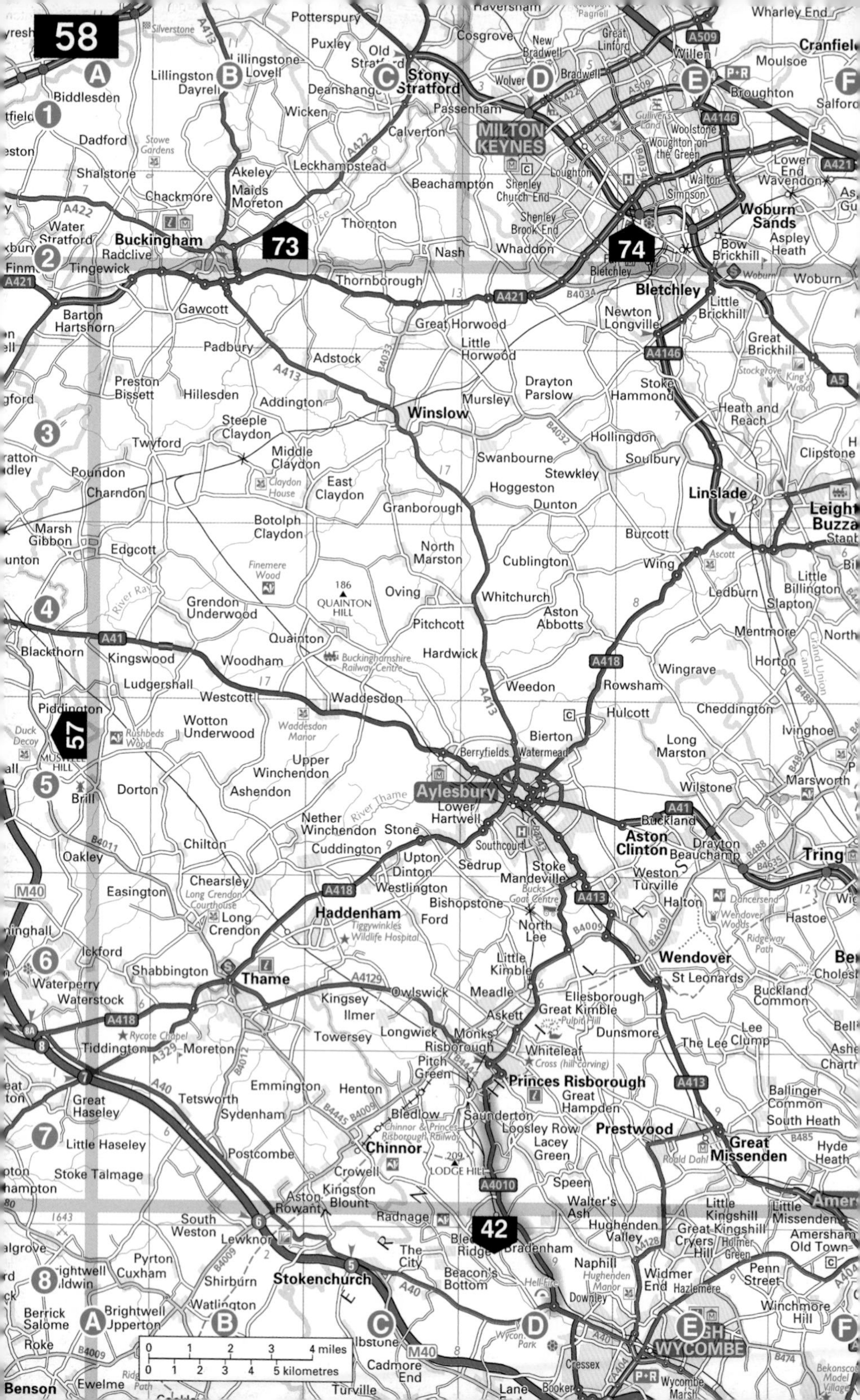
Silverstone
Potterspury
Haversham
Wharley End
Pagnell
Cranfield
Great Linford
Puxley
Cosgrove
New Bradwell
A509
Moulsoe
Lillingstone Lovell
Lillingstone Dayrell
Old Stratford
Stony Stratford
Wolverton
Bradwell
Willen
Broughton
Salford
Biddlesden
Deanshanger
Wicken
Passenham
MILTON KEYNES
A4146
Woolstone
Woughton on the Green
Dadford
Stowe Gardens
Calverton
Xscape
Gulliver's Land
Shalstone
Akeley
Leckhampstead
Loughton
Lower End
A421
Wavendon
Maids Moreton
Beachampton
Shenley Church End
B4034
Walton
Chackmore
A422
Water Stratford
Buckingham
Thornton
Shenley Brook End
Simpson
Woburn Sands
Aspley Heath
Radclive
73
Nash
Whaddon
74
Bow Brickhill
Tingewick
Bletchley
Woburn
A421
Thornborough
Barton Hartshorn
Gawcott
Great Horwood
B4034
Newton Longville
Little Brickhill
Padbury
Adstock
Little Horwood
Great Brickhill
B4033
A4146
Stockgrove
King's Wood
A5
Preston Bissett
Hillesden
A413
Addington
Drayton Parslow
Stoke Hammond
Winslow
Mursley
Heath and Reach
Steeple Claydon
Twyford
B4032
Hollingdon
Middle Claydon
Swanbourne
Soulbury
Clipstone
Poundon
Claydon House
Stewkley
East Claydon
Hoggeston
Charndon
Linslade
Granborough
Dunton
Leighton Buzzard
Marsh Gibbon
Botolph Claydon
Burcott
North Marston
Edgcott
Cublington
Wing
Ascott
Finemere Wood
Little Billington
186 QUAINTON HILL
Oving
Grendon Underwood
Ledburn
Whitchurch
River Ray
Slapton
Aston Abbotts
Pitchcott
Blackthorn
A41
Quainton
Mentmore
Kingswood
Hardwick
Buckinghamshire Railway Centre
Horton
Woodham
A418
Wingrave
Ludgershall
Rowsham
Westcott
Weedon
Waddesdon
Grand Union Canal
Piddington
Wotton Underwood
Waddesdon Manor
Hulcott
Cheddington
Duck Decoy
Rushbeds Wood
57
Bierton
Ivinghoe
Muswell Hill
Upper Winchendon
Berryfields
Watermead
Long Marston
Brill
Dorton
Ashendon
B489
Aylesbury
Marsworth
River Thame
Wilstone
Lower Hartwell
Nether Winchendon
Stone
Buckland
A41
B4011
Chilton
Cuddington
Southcourt
B4443
Aston Clinton
Drayton Beauchamp
Tring
Oakley
Upton
Dinton
Sedrup
Stoke Mandeville
Weston Turville
B488
B4635
Chearsley
Westlington
Bishopstone
Bucks Goat Centre
A413
M40
Easington
Long Crendon Courthouse
Long Crendon
Haddenham
Ford
Halton
Dancersend
Wendover Woods
Hastoe
Tiggywinkles Wildlife Hospital
North Lee
B4009
Ridgeway Path
Ickford
Little Kimble
Wendover
Shabbington
Thame
A4129
St Leonards
Cholesbury
Waterperry
Kingsey
Owlswick
Meadle
Ellesborough
Buckland Common
Waterstock
A418
Great Kimble
Pulpit Hill
Ilmer
Askett
Dunsmore
Rycote Chapel
Towersey
Longwick
Monks Risborough
The Lee
Lee Clump
Tiddington
A329
Moreton
Whiteleaf Cross (hill carving)
B4012
Pitch Green
Princes Risborough
Chartridge
Great Haseley
A40
Emmington
Henton
Great Hampden
Ballinger Common
Tetsworth
Sydenham
B4445
B4009
Bledlow
Chinnor & Princes Risborough Railway
Saunderton
Loosley Row
Prestwood
South Heath
Little Haseley
Lacey Green
Great Missenden
B485
Hyde Heath
Chinnor
209 LODGE HILL
Roald Dahl
Postcombe
Crowell
Speen
Stoke Talmage
A4010
Kingston Blount
Aston Rowant
Walter's Ash
Little Kingshill
Little Missenden
South Weston
Radnage
Hughenden Valley
Great Kingshill
Amersham Old Town
Lewknor
Bledlow Ridge
42
Bradenham
Cryers Hill
Holmer Green
Pyrton
The City
Naphill
Hughenden Manor
Widmer End
Penn Street
Cuxham
A4128
Hazlemere
Shirburn
Stokenchurch
Beacon's Bottom
Hell-Fire
Downley
Winchmore Hill
Berrick Salome
Brightwell Upperton
Watlington
Wycombe Park
Roke
B4009
Ibstone
M40
HIGH WYCOMBE
Cadmore End
Cressex
B474
Benson
Ewelme
Ridgeway Path
Turville
Lane End
Booker
Wycombe Marsh
Bekonscot Model Village
P+R
0 1 2 3 4 miles
0 1 2 3 4 5 kilometres

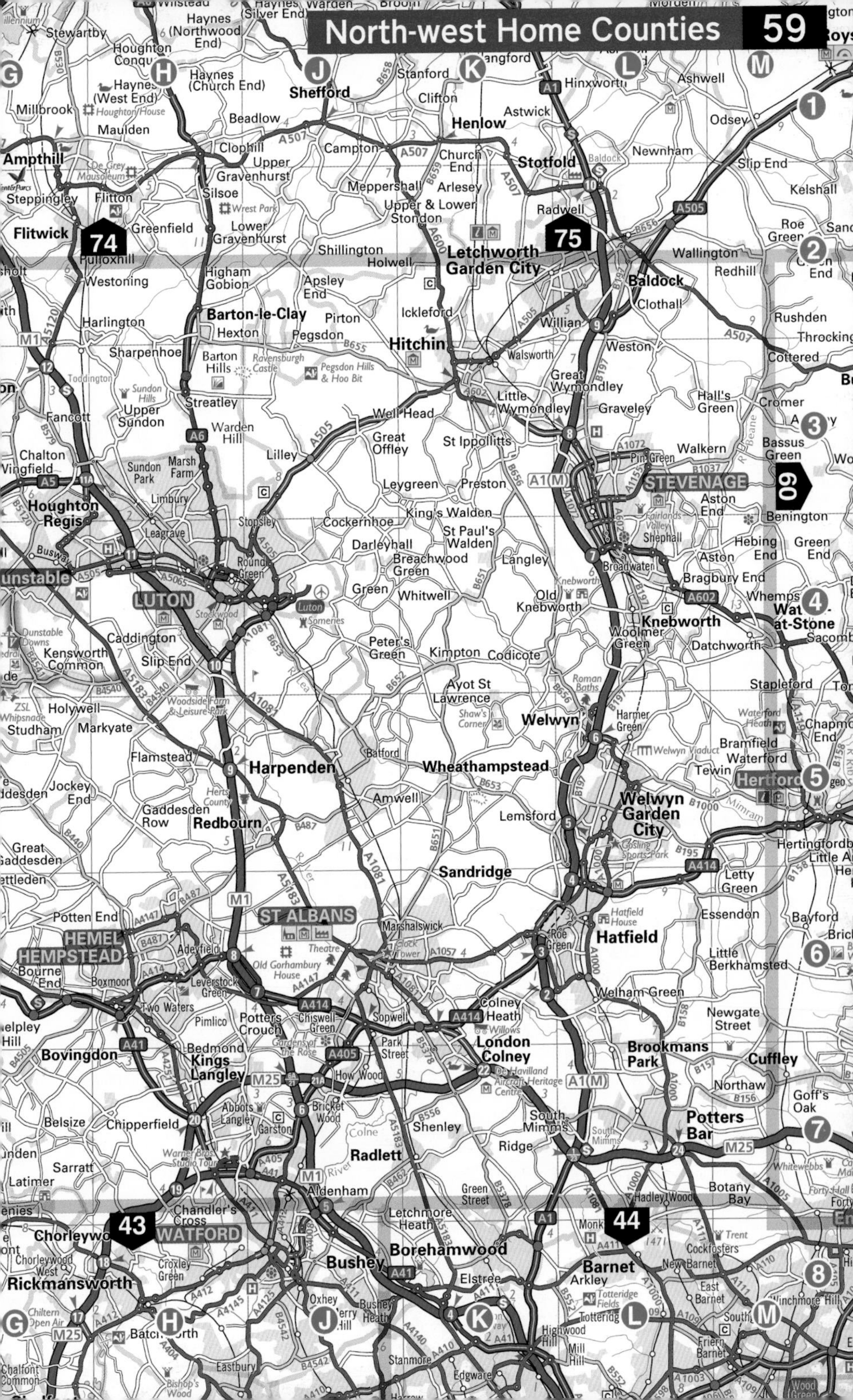
Shefford
Henlow
Stotfold
Ampthill
Flitwick
Letchworth Garden City
Baldock
Hitchin
Barton-le-Clay
Houghton Regis
LUTON
Dunstable
STEVENAGE
Knebworth
Welwyn
Welwyn Garden City
Harpenden
Wheathampstead
Redbourn
ST ALBANS
HEMEL HEMPSTEAD
Hatfield
London Colney
Kings Langley
Radlett
Potters Bar
Brookmans Park
Cuffley
WATFORD
Rickmansworth
Bushey
Borehamwood
Barnet
Hertford
Sandridge
74
75
60
43
44

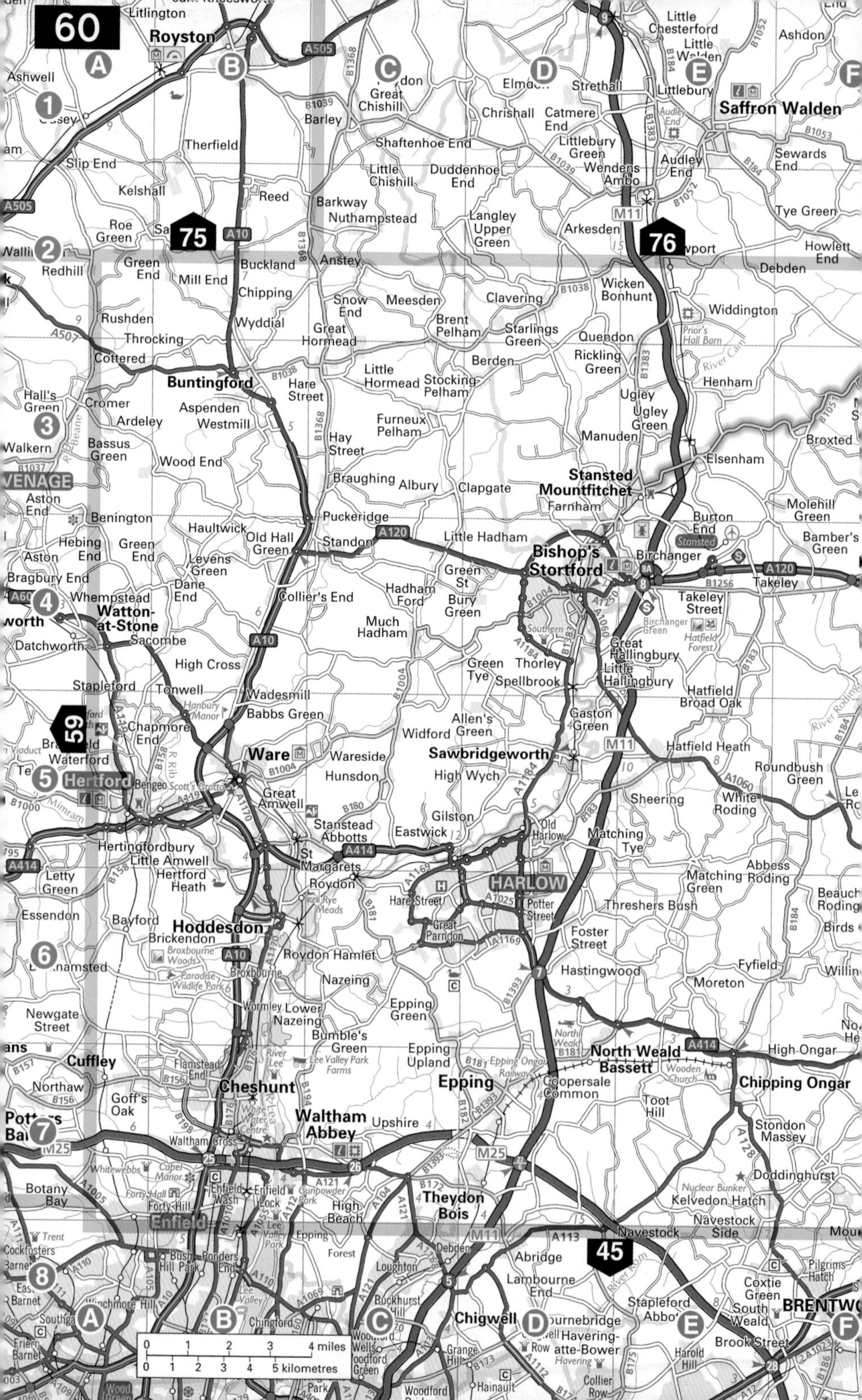
60
Royston
Saffron Walden
Buntingford
Stansted Mountfitchet
Bishop's Stortford
Watton-at-Stone
Ware
Sawbridgeworth
Hertford
HARLOW
Hoddesdon
Cheshunt
Waltham Abbey
Epping
North Weald Bassett
Chipping Ongar
Theydon Bois
Chigwell
Cuffley
Enfield
BRENTWOOD
Stansted
75
76
59
45
0 1 2 3 4 miles
0 1 2 3 4 5 kilometres

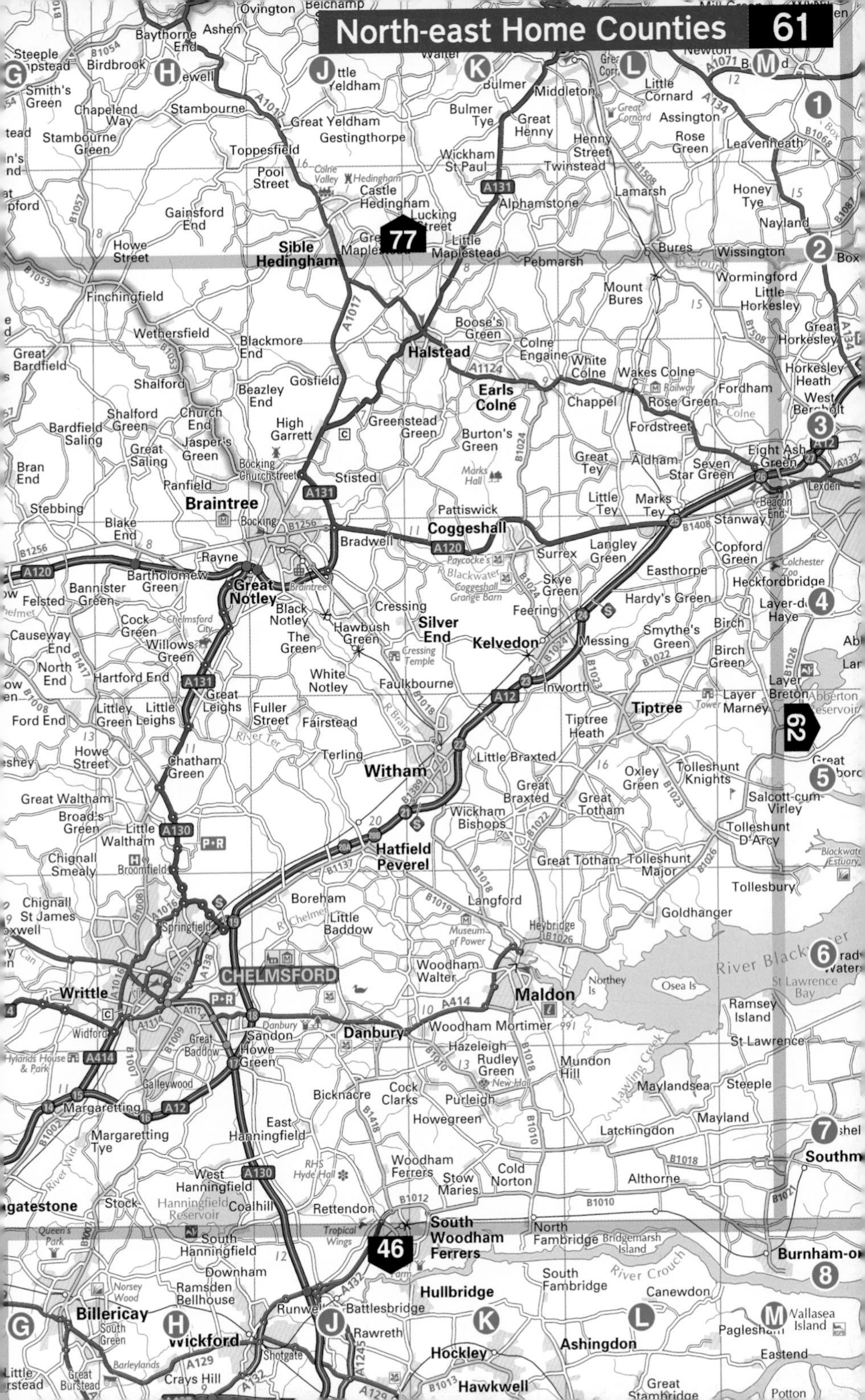

Ovington
Belchamp
Ashen
Baythorne End
Steeple Bumpstead
Birdbrook
Smith's Green
Chapelend Way
Stambourne
Stambourne Green
Toppesfield
Great Yeldham
Gestingthorpe
Bulmer
Bulmer Tye
Middleton
Little Cornard
Great Cornard
Assington
Great Henny
Henny Street
Rose Green
Leavenheath
Wickham St Paul
Twinstead
Lamarsh
Honey Tye
Nayland
Pool Street
Colne Valley
Hedingham
Castle Hedingham
Lucking Street
Alphamstone
Gainsford End
Howe Street
Sible Hedingham
Little Maplestead
Pebmarsh
Bures
Wissington
R Stour
Wormingford
Mount Bures
Little Horkesley
Great Horkesley
Horkesley Heath
Finchingfield
Wethersfield
Blackmore End
Boose's Green
Halstead
Colne Engaine
White Colne
Wakes Colne
Railway
Great Bardfield
Shalford
Gosfield
Beazley End
Earls Colne
Chappel
Rose Green
Fordham
West Bergholt
R Colne
Shalford Green
Church End
High Garrett
Greenstead Green
Burton's Green
Fordstreet
Bardfield Saling
Great Saling
Jasper's Green
Eight Ash Green
Bran End
Bocking Churchstreet
Stisted
Marks Hall
Great Tey
Aldham
Seven Star Green
Lexden
Panfield
Braintree
Pattiswick
Little Tey
Marks Tey
Beacon End
Stebbing
Blake End
Bocking
Coggeshall
Stanway
Bradwell
Copford Green
Rayne
Bartholomew Green
Paycocke's
R Blackwater
Surrex
Langley Green
Colchester Zoo
Easthorpe
Bannister Green
Felsted
Great Notley
Braintree
Coggeshall Grange Barn
Skye Green
Heckfordbridge
Hardy's Green
Layer-de-la-Haye
Cock Green
Chelmsford City
Black Notley
Cressing
Feering
Causeway End
Willows Green
Hawbush Green
Silver End
Kelvedon
Messing
Smythe's Green
Birch
North End
The Green
Cressing Temple
Birch Green
Hartford End
White Notley
Faulkbourne
Inworth
Layer Breton
Littley Green
Little Leighs
Great Leighs
Fuller Street
Fairstead
R Brain
Tiptree
Layer Marney
Tower
Abberton Reservoir
Ford End
Tiptree Heath
Howe Street
River Ter
Terling
Little Braxted
Chatham Green
Witham
Oxley Green
Tolleshunt Knights
Great Braxted
Great Totham
Salcott-cum-Virley
Great Waltham
Broad's Green
Little Waltham
Wickham Bishops
Tolleshunt D'Arcy
Chignall Smealy
Broomfield
Hatfield Peverel
Great Totham
Tolleshunt Major
Blackwater Estuary
Tollesbury
Chignall St James
Boreham
Langford
Springfield
Little Baddow
R Chelmer
Museum of Power
Heybridge
Goldhanger
CHELMSFORD
Woodham Walter
Maldon
Northey Is
Osea Is
River Blackwater
St Lawrence Bay
Writtle
Danbury
Woodham Mortimer
Ramsey Island
Widford
Sandon
Great Baddow
Howe Green
Hazeleigh
Rudley Green
Mundon Hill
St Lawrence
Hylands House & Park
Galleywood
New Hall
Lawling Creek
Maylandsea
Steeple
Margaretting
Bicknacre
Cock Clarks
Purleigh
Mayland
Howegreen
East Hanningfield
Margaretting Tye
Latchingdon
Southminster
RHS Hyde Hall
Woodham Ferrers
Cold Norton
Stow Maries
Althorne
River Wid
West Hanningfield
Hanningfield Reservoir
Stock
Coalhill
Rettendon
Ingatestone
Queen's Park
Tropical Wings
South Woodham Ferrers
North Fambridge
Bridgemarsh Island
South Hanningfield
Burnham-on-Crouch
Downham
Ramsden Bellhouse
Norsey Wood
River Crouch
South Fambridge
Hullbridge
Canewdon
Billericay
South Green
Runwell
Battlesbridge
Wallasea Island
Paglesham
Rawreth
Wickford
Shotgate
Barleylands
Hockley
Ashingdon
Eastend
Little Burstead
Great Burstead
Crays Hill
Hawkwell
Great Stambridge
Potton
A1017
A131
A134
A1071
A120
A1124
A12
A130
A414
A132
A129
A1245
A1016
A138
A1114
B1054
B1057
B1053
B1058
B1068
B1087
B1508
B1256
B1024
B1408
B1022
B1023
B1026
B1018
B1389
B1137
B1019
B1008
B1417
B1009
B1007
B1002
B1010
B1418
B1012
B1021
B1013
77
62
46

Hadleigh
COLCHESTER
Manningtree
Wivenhoe
Brightlingsea
West Mersea
MERSEA ISLAND
CLACTON-ON-SEA
Jaywick
St Osyth
Southminster
Burnham-on-Crouch
Bradwell-on-Sea
Tollesbury
River Blackwater
River Stour
River Orwell
Holbrook Bay
Colne Point
Dengie
Tillingham
77
78
61
47
4 miles
5 kilometres

Hollesley Bay
Alderton
Bawdsey
Old Felixstowe
Felixstowe
79
ook of Holland

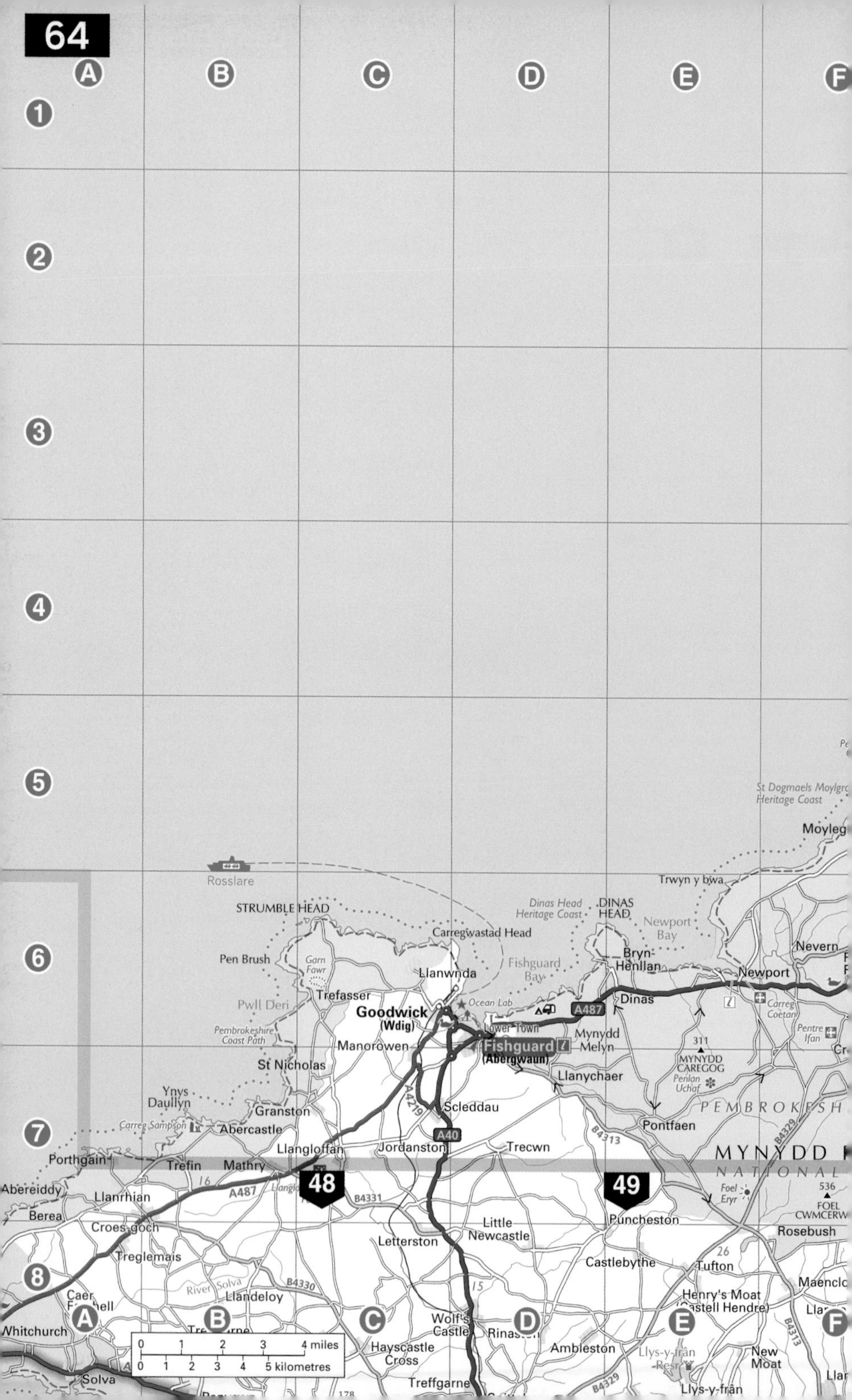
A
B
C
D
E
F
1
2
3
4
5
6
7
8
St Dogmaels Moylgrove Heritage Coast
Moylegrove
Rosslare
Trwyn y bwa
STRUMBLE HEAD
Dinas Head Heritage Coast
DINAS HEAD
Newport Bay
Carregwastad Head
Nevern
Pen Brush
Garn Fawr
Fishguard Bay
Bryn-Henllan
Llanwnda
Newport
Pwll Deri
Trefasser
Ocean Lab
Dinas
Goodwick
(Wdig)
A487
Carreg Coetan
Pembrokeshire Coast Path
Lower Town
Mynydd Melyn
Pentre Ifan
Manorowen
Fishguard
(Abergwaun)
311
MYNYDD CAREGOG
St Nicholas
Llanychaer
Penlan Uchaf
Ynys Daullyn
A4219
Granston
Scleddau
PEMBROKESH
Carreg Sampson
Abercastle
B4313
Pontfaen
B4329
A40
MYNYDD
Porthgain
Llangloffan
Jordanston
Trecwn
NATIONAL
Trefin
Mathry
48
49
Abereiddy
16
A487
Foel Eryr
536
Llanrhian
B4331
FOEL CWMCERWYN
Berea
Little Newcastle
Puncheston
Croes-goch
Rosebush
Letterston
Treglemais
26
Castlebythe
Tufton
8
Maenclochog
River Solva
B4330
15
Caerfarchell
Llandeloy
Henry's Moat
(Castell Hendre)
Whitchurch
Wolf's Castle
Rinaston
B4313
0 1 2 3 4 miles
0 1 2 3 4 5 kilometres
Hayscastle Cross
Ambleston
Llys-y-frân Resr
New Moat
Solva
Treffgarne
178
B4329
Llys-y-frân

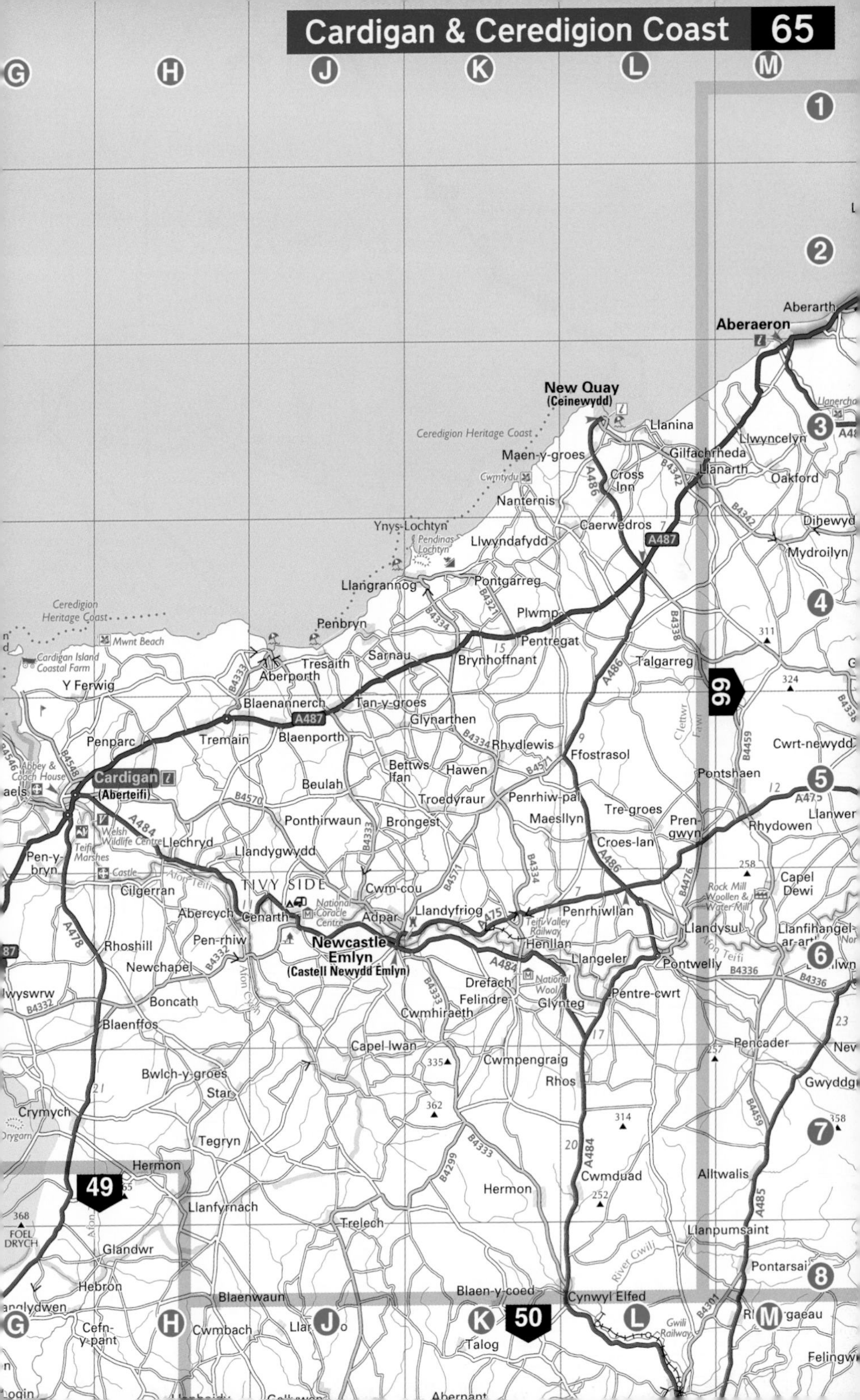
Aberarth
Aberaeron
New Quay
(Ceinewydd)
Llanina
Ceredigion Heritage Coast
Llwyncelyn
Maen-y-groes
Gilfachrheda
Cross Inn
Llanarth
Oakford
Cwmtydu
Nanternis
Dihewyd
Ynys-Lochtyn
Pendinas Lochtyn
Caerwedros
Llwyndafydd
Mydroilyn
Llangrannog
Pontgarreg
Plwmp
Penbryn
Pentregat
Mwnt Beach
Cardigan Island Coastal Farm
Tresaith
Sarnau
Brynhoffnant
Talgarreg
Aberporth
Y Ferwig
Blaenannerch
Tan-y-groes
Glynarthen
Penparc
Tremain
Blaenporth
Rhydlewis
Ffostrasol
Cwrt-newydd
Abbey & Coach House
Cardigan
(Aberteifi)
Bettws Ifan
Hawen
Pontshaen
Beulah
Troedyraur
Penrhiw-pal
Tre-groes
Llanwer
Welsh Wildlife Centre
Teifi Marshes
Llechryd
Ponthirwaun
Brongest
Maesllyn
Pren-gwyn
Rhydowen
Pen-y-bryn
Llandygwydd
Croes-lan
Castle
Afon Teifi
Capel Dewi
Rock Mill Woollen & Water Mill
Cilgerran
TIVY SIDE
Cwm-cou
Abercych
Cenarth
National Coracle Centre
Adpar
Llandyfriog
Penrhiwllan
Llandysul
Llanfihangel-ar-arth
Teifi Valley Railway
Rhoshill
Pen-rhiw
Newcastle Emlyn
(Castell Newydd Emlyn)
Henllan
Llangeler
Pontwelly
Newchapel
Drefach
National Wool
Felindre
Glynteg
Pentre-cwrt
Boncath
Cwmhiraeth
Blaenffos
Capel-Iwan
Pencader
Cwmpengraig
Bwlch-y-groes
Rhos
Star
Crymych
Drygarn
Tegryn
Cwmduad
Alltwalis
Hermon
Llanfyrnach
FOEL DRYCH
Glandwr
Trelech
Llanpumsaint
River Gwili
Hebron
Pontarsai
Blaenwaun
Blaen-y-coed
Cynwyl Elfed
Cwmbach
Cefn-y-pant
Talog
Gwili Railway
Felingw
Afon Cych
Afon Cleddau
Clettwr Fawr
A487
A484
A486
A475
A478
A484
A485
B4333
B4334
B4321
B4342
B4338
B4548
B4546
B4570
B4571
B4476
B4459
B4336
B4332
B4299
B4301
49
50
99
311
324
258
257
335
362
314
252
358
368
G
H
J
K
L
M
1
2
3
4
5
6
7
8

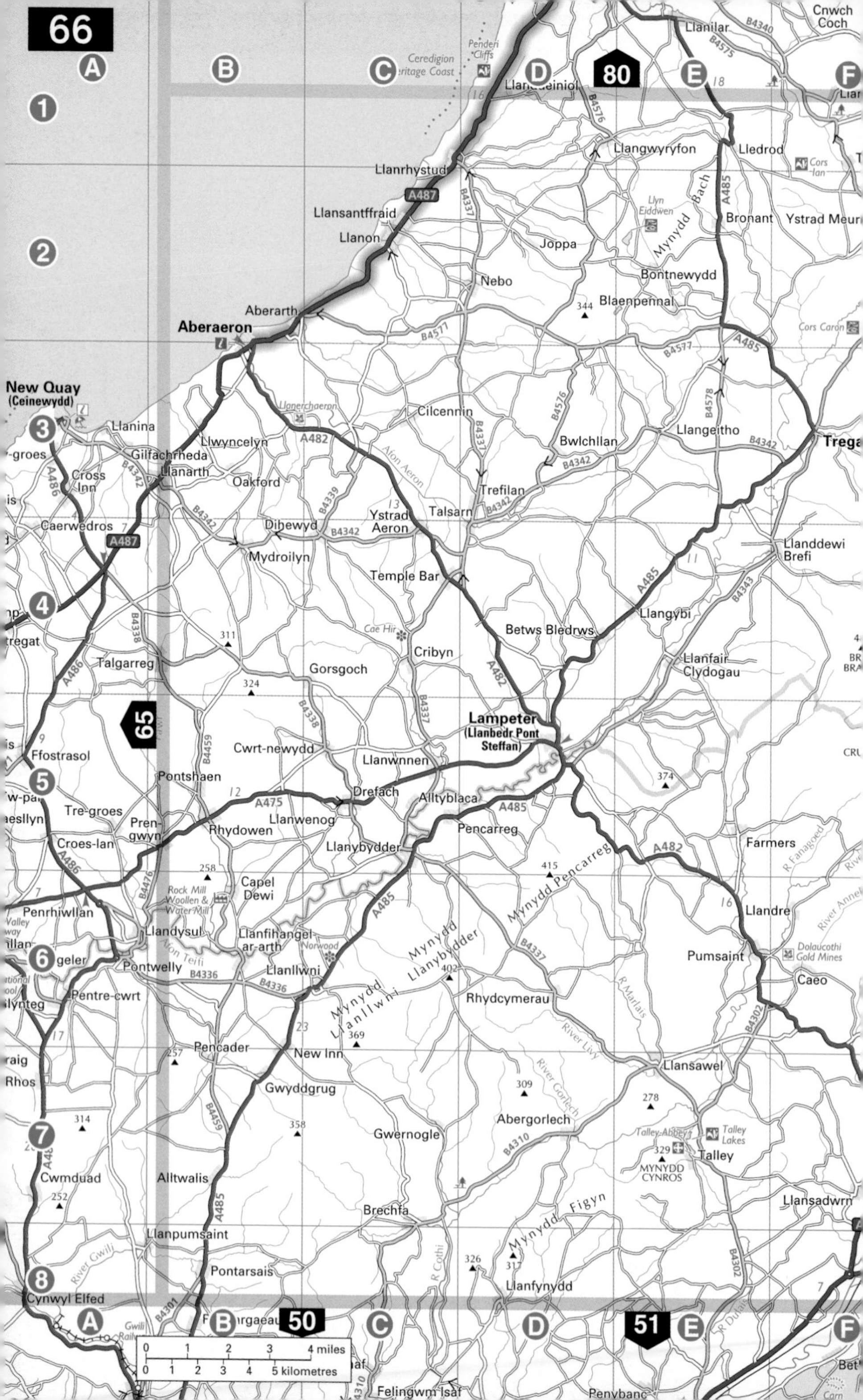

66
A
B
C
D
E
F
1
2
3
4
5
6
7
8
80
65
50
51
Ceredigion Heritage Coast
Penderi Cliffs
Llanddeiniol
Llanilar
Cnwch Coch
B4340
B4575
B4576
Llangwyryfon
Lledrod
Cors Ian
Llanrhystud
A487
B4337
Llyn Eiddwen
Mynydd Bach
A485
Llansantffraid
Llanon
Bronant
Ystrad Meurig
Joppa
Nebo
Bontnewydd
Blaenpennal
344
Aberarth
Aberaeron
B4577
Cors Caron
New Quay
(Ceinewydd)
Llanerchaeron
Cilcennin
B4576
B4578
Llanina
Llwyncelyn
A482
Bwlchllan
Llangeitho
B4342
Tregaron
Gilfachrheda
Llanarth
Cross Inn
A486
Oakford
Afon Aeron
Trefilan
Caerwedros
B4339
Ystrad Aeron
Talsarn
Dihewyd
Mydroilyn
Temple Bar
Llanddewi Brefi
B4343
B4338
311
Cae Hir
Cribyn
Betws Bledrws
Llangybi
Talgarreg
Gorsgoch
Llanfair Clydogau
324
Lampeter
(Llanbedr Pont Steffan)
B4459
Cwrt-newydd
Ffostrasol
Llanwnnen
374
Pontshaen
Drefach
A475
Alltyblaca
Tre-groes
Llanwenog
Pren-gwyn
Rhydowen
Pencarreg
Croes-lan
Llanybydder
Farmers
258
415
Mynydd Pencarreg
Capel Dewi
Rock Mill Woollen & Water Mill
B4476
Penrhiwllan
Llandysul
Llanfihangel-ar-arth
Norwood
Afon Teifi
Mynydd Llanybydder
Llandre
Dolaucothi Gold Mines
Pumsaint
Pontwelly
B4336
Llanllwni
402
Mynydd Llanllwni
Rhydcymerau
Caeo
Pentre-cwrt
R Marlais
369
B4302
River Livy
Pencader
New Inn
257
River Gorlech
Llansawel
Gwyddgrug
309
278
314
358
Abergorlech
Talley Abbey
Talley Lakes
Gwernogle
B4310
329
Talley
MYNYDD CYNROS
Cwmduad
Alltwalis
252
Llansadwrn
Brechfa
Mynydd Figyn
Llanpumsaint
River Gwili
R Cothi
326
317
Pontarsais
Llanfynydd
Cynwyl Elfed
B4301
Bargaeau
Gwili Railway
R Dulais
0 1 2 3 4 miles
0 1 2 3 4 5 kilometres
Felingwm Isaf
Penybanc

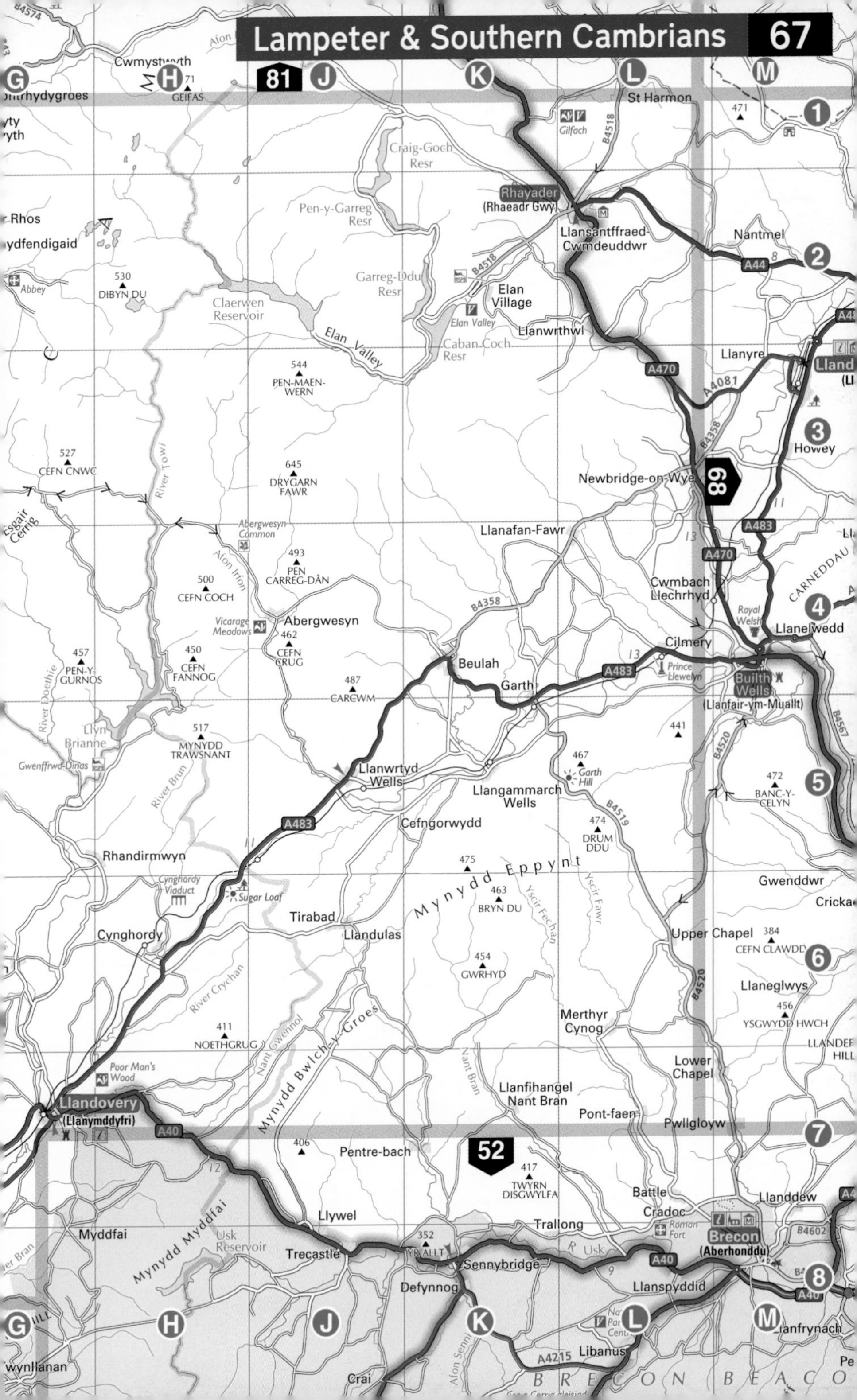
Cwmystwyth
GEIFAS
St Harmon
Gilfach
B4518
Craig-Goch Resr
Pen-y-Garreg Resr
Rhayader
(Rhaeadr Gwy)
Llansantffraed-Cwmdeuddwr
Nantmel
A44
Garreg-Ddu Resr
Claerwen Reservoir
Elan Village
Elan Valley
Llanwrthwl
Caban Coch Resr
DIBYN DU
Abbey
A470
Llanyre
A4081
PEN-MAEN-WERN
B4358
Howey
CEFN CNWC
DRYGARN FAWR
River Towi
Newbridge-on-Wye
A483
Abergwesyn Common
Llanafan-Fawr
PEN CARREG-DÂN
CEFN COCH
Cwmbach Llechrhyd
CARNEDDAU
Abergwesyn
Vicarage Meadows
Royal Welsh
Llanelwedd
CEFN CRUG
Cilmery
PEN-Y-GURNOS
CEFN FANNOG
Beulah
Prince Llewelyn
Builth Wells
(Llanfair-ym-Muallt)
Garth
CARCWM
River Doethie
Llyn Brianne
MYNYDD TRAWSNANT
Gwenffrwd-Dinas
B4520
Garth Hill
River Brun
Llanwrtyd Wells
Llangammarch Wells
BANC-Y-CELYN
B4519
DRUM DDU
Cefngorwydd
Rhandirmwyn
Mynydd Eppynt
Cynghordy Viaduct
Sugar Loaf
BRYN DU
Gwenddwr
Tirabad
Llandulas
Ysgir Fechan
Ysgir Fawr
Cynghordy
Upper Chapel
CEFN CLAWDD
GWRHYD
Llaneglwys
River Crychan
Merthyr Cynog
YSGWYDD HWCH
NOETHGRUG
Nant Gwennol
Mynydd Bwlch-y-Groes
Nant Bran
Lower Chapel
Poor Man's Wood
Llanfihangel Nant Bran
Llandovery
(Llanymddyfri)
Pont-faen
Pwllgloyw
A40
Pentre-bach
TWYRN DISGWYLFA
Battle
Llanddew
Mynydd Myddfai
Llywel
Cradoc
Roman Fort
Myddfai
Usk Reservoir
Trallong
Brecon
(Aberhonddu)
B4602
Trecastle
YR ALLT
R Usk
Sennybridge
Defynnog
Llanspyddid
A4215
Libanus
Llanfrynach
Afon Senni
Crai
BRECON BEACO
81
52
68
1 2 3 4 5 6 7 8
G H J K L M

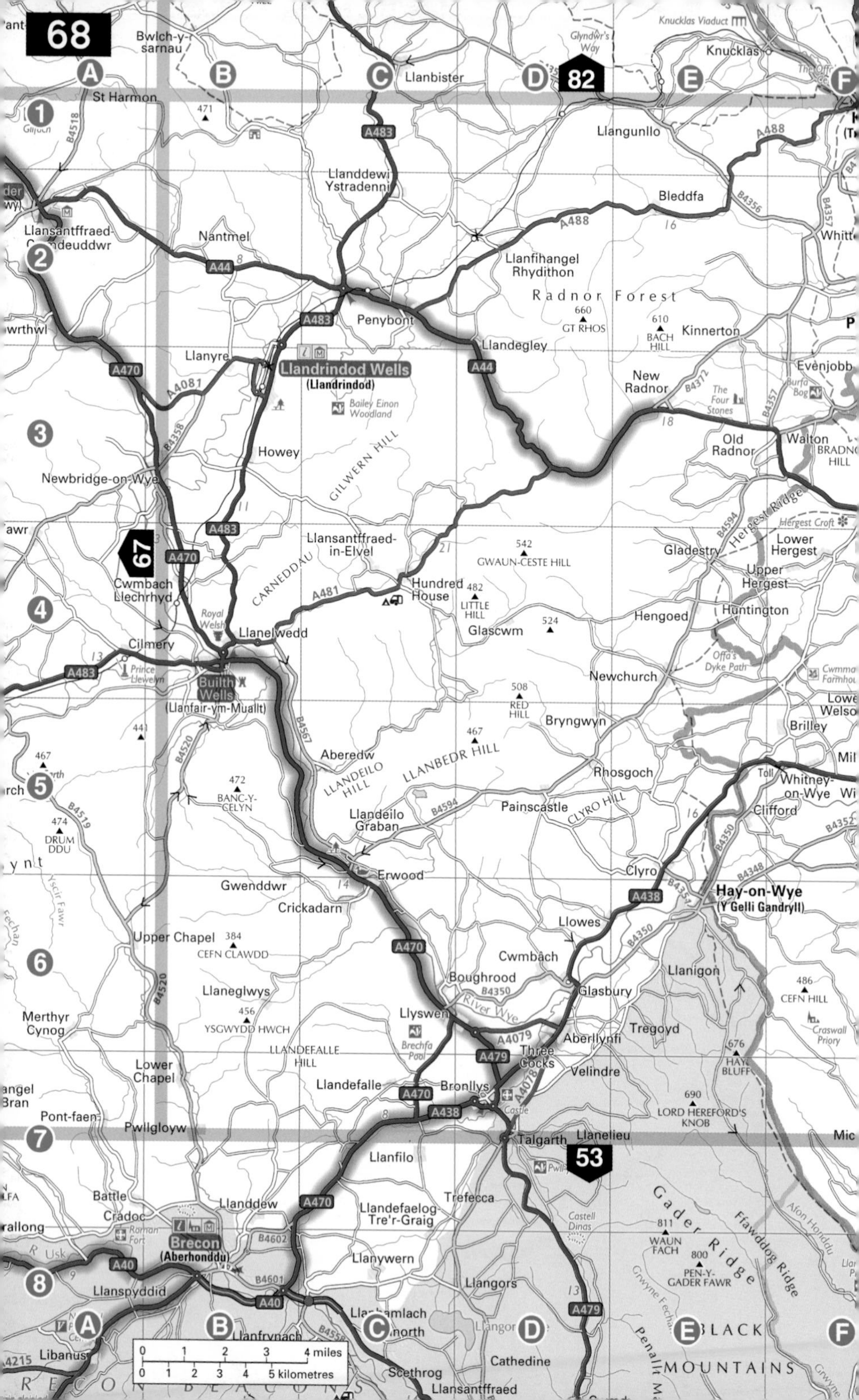
St Harmon
Bwlch-y-sarnau
Llanbister
Knucklas Viaduct
Knucklas
Glyndŵr's Way
82
Llangunllo
Llanddewi Ystradenni
Bleddfa
Llansantffraed-Cwmdeuddwr
Nantmel
Llanfihangel Rhydithon
Radnor Forest
Penybont
660 GT RHOS
610 BACH HILL
Kinnerton
Llandegley
Llanyre
Llandrindod Wells
(Llandrindod)
Bailey Einon Woodland
New Radnor
The Four Stones
Evenjobb
Burfa Bog
Walton
Old Radnor
BRADNOR HILL
Howey
GILWERN HILL
Newbridge-on-Wye
Hergest Ridge
Hergest Croft
67
Llansantffraed-in-Elvel
542 GWAUN-CESTE HILL
Gladestry
Lower Hergest
Upper Hergest
CARNEDDAU
Hundred House
482 LITTLE HILL
Cwmbach Llechrhyd
Hengoed
Huntington
Royal Welsh
Llanelwedd
Glascwm
524
Cilmery
Prince Llewelyn
Builth Wells
(Llanfair-ym-Muallt)
Offa's Dyke Path
Newchurch
Cwmmau Farmhouse
508 RED HILL
441
Bryngwyn
Brilley
467
LLANBEDR HILL
Aberedw
LLANDEILO HILL
Rhosgoch
472 BANC-Y-CELYN
Whitney-on-Wye
Toll
Painscastle
CLYRO HILL
Clifford
474 DRUM DDU
Llandeilo Graban
Erwood
Clyro
Gwenddwr
Crickadarn
Hay-on-Wye
(Y Gelli Gandryll)
Llowes
Upper Chapel
384 CEFN CLAWDD
Cwmbâch
Llanigon
Boughrood
486 CEFN HILL
Llaneglwys
Glasbury
River Wye
Merthyr Cynog
Llyswen
456 YSGWYDD HWCH
Tregoyd
Craswall Priory
Brechfa Pool
Aberllynfi
LLANDEFALLE HILL
Three Cocks
676 HAY BLUFF
Lower Chapel
Velindre
Llandefalle
Bronllys
Castle
690 LORD HEREFORD'S KNOB
Pont-faen
Pwllgloyw
Talgarth
Llanelieu
53
Llanfilo
Pwll
Battle
Llanddew
Trefecca
Gader Ridge
Ffawddog Ridge
Afon Honddu
Cradoc
Llandefaelog-Tre'r-Graig
Castell Dinas
Roman Fort
Brecon
(Aberhonddu)
811 WAUN FACH
800 PEN-Y-GADER FAWR
Usk
Llanywern
Llanspyddid
Llangors
Grwyne Fechan
Llanhamlach
Llanfrynach
Llangors
BLACK MOUNTAINS
Libanus
Scethrog
Cathedine
Penallt
Llansantffraed
0 1 2 3 4 miles
0 1 2 3 4 5 kilometres
A470
A483
A44
A488
A481
A4081
A438
A479
A4079
A40
B4518
B4358
B4567
B4520
B4519
B4594
B4350
B4351
B4348
B4356
B4357
B4372
B4602
B4601
B4558
B4352

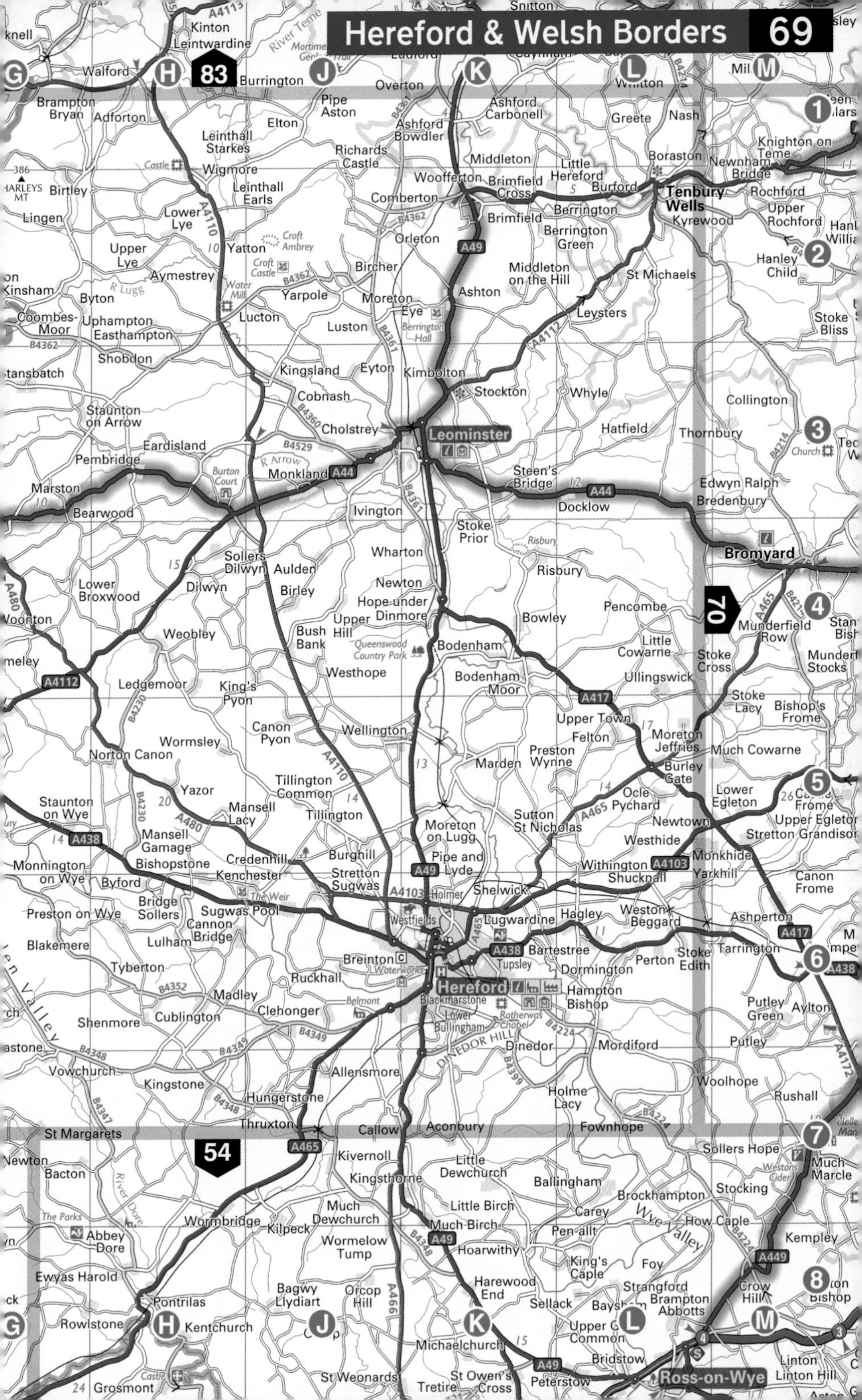
Kinton
Leintwardine
Walford
83
Burrington
Overton
Brampton Bryan
Adforton
Pipe Aston
Elton
Ashford Bowdler
Ashford Carbonell
Greete
Nash
Leinthall Starkes
Richards Castle
Wigmore
Middleton
Little Hereford
Boraston
Knighton on Teme
Newnham Bridge
Birtley
Leinthall Earls
Woofferton
Brimfield Cross
Burford
Tenbury Wells
Rochford
Lingen
Lower Lye
Comberton
Brimfield
Berrington
Kyrewood
Upper Rochford
Upper Lye
Yatton
Croft Ambrey
Orleton
Berrington Green
Hanley Child
Croft Castle
Bircher
Middleton on the Hill
St Michaels
Aymestrey
Kinsham
Byton
Yarpole
Moreton
Eye
Ashton
Coombes-Moor
Uphampton
Easthampton
Luston
Lucton
Berrington Hall
Leysters
Stoke Bliss
Shobdon
Kingsland
Eyton
Kimbolton
Cobnash
Stockton
Whyle
Collington
Staunton on Arrow
Cholstrey
Leominster
Hatfield
Thornbury
Eardisland
Pembridge
Monkland
Burton Court
Steen's Bridge
Edwyn Ralph
Bredenbury
Marston
Bearwood
Docklow
Ivington
Stoke Prior
Risbury
Wharton
Bromyard
Sollers Dilwyn
Aulden
Lower Broxwood
Dilwyn
Birley
Newton
Hope under Dinmore
Pencombe
70
Munderfield Row
Upper Hill
Bowley
Weobley
Bush Bank
Queenswood Country Park
Bodenham
Little Cowarne
Stoke Cross
Munderfield Stocks
Westhope
Ledgemoor
King's Pyon
Bodenham Moor
Ullingswick
Stoke Lacy
Bishop's Frome
Canon Pyon
Upper Town
Wellington
Moreton Jeffries
Much Cowarne
Wormsley
Felton
Norton Canon
Preston Wynne
Marden
Burley Gate
Tillington Common
Yazor
Ocle Pychard
Lower Egleton
Staunton on Wye
Mansell Lacy
Tillington
Sutton St Nicholas
Newtown
Upper Egleton
Stretton Grandison
Mansell Gamage
Moreton on Lugg
Westhide
Monnington on Wye
Bishopstone
Credenhill
Burghill
Pipe and Lyde
Withington
Monkhide
Kenchester
Stretton Sugwas
Shucknall
Yarkhill
Canon Frome
Byford
Holmer
Shelwick
Bridge Sollers
Sugwas Pool
The Weir
Westfields
Lugwardine
Hagley
Weston Beggard
Ashperton
Preston on Wye
Cannon Bridge
Blakemere
Lulham
Bartestree
Tarrington
Breinton
Tupsley
Perton
Stoke Edith
Tyberton
Dormington
Ruckhall
Hereford
Hampton Bishop
Madley
Belmont
Blackmarstone
Putley Green
Aylton
Shenmore
Cublington
Clehonger
Lower Bullingham
Rotherwas Chapel
Dinedor Hill
Dinedor
Mordiford
Putley
Vowchurch
Allensmore
Kingstone
Woolhope
Hungerstone
Holme Lacy
Rushall
Thruxton
St Margarets
Callow
Aconbury
Fownhope
54
Kivernoll
Sollers Hope
Much Marcle
Newton
Bacton
Little Dewchurch
Kingsthorne
Ballingham
Westons Cider
Brockhampton
Stocking
The Parks
Much Dewchurch
Little Birch
Carey
Wormbridge
Kilpeck
Much Birch
How Caple
Abbey Dore
Wormelow Tump
Pen-allt
Kempley
Hoarwithy
Wye Valley
Ewyas Harold
King's Caple
Foy
Bagwy Llydiart
Orcop Hill
Harewood End
Strangford
Crow Hill
Pontrilas
Sellack
Brampton Abbotts
Rowlstone
Kentchurch
Upper Common
Michaelchurch
Bridstow
Linton
Linton Hill
Grosmont
St Weonards
Tretire
St Owen's Cross
Peterstow
Ross-on-Wye
River Teme
R Lugg
R Arrow
River Dore
A4113
A49
A4110
B4362
A4112
B4361
B4360
B4529
A44
B4214
A465
A417
A480
B4230
A438
A4103
B4352
B4349
B4348
B4347
B4224
B4399
A466
A449
A4172

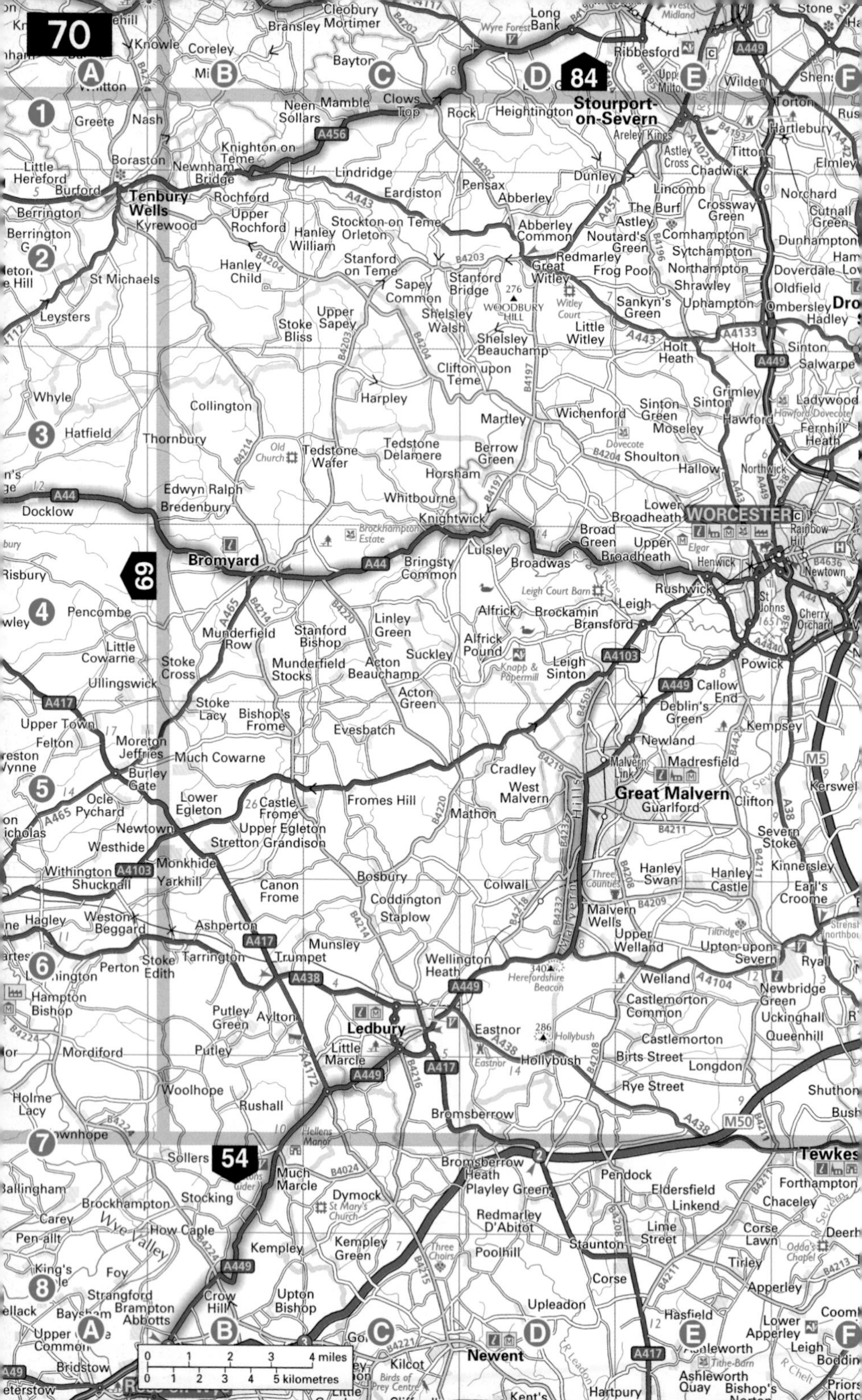

70
84
69
54
Cleobury Mortimer
Bransley
Knowle
Coreley
Baytor
Long Bank
Wyre Forest
Ribbesford
Upper Milton
Wilden
Stone
Whitton
Greete
Nash
Neen Sollars
Mamble
Clows Top
Rock
Heightington
Stourport-on-Severn
Areley Kings
Hartlebury
Torton
Boraston
Knighton on Teme
Newnham Bridge
Lindridge
Astley Cross
Titton
Chadwick
Elmley
Little Hereford
Burford
Tenbury Wells
Rochford
Eardiston
Pensax
Abberley
Dunley
Lincomb
Norchard
Berrington
Kyrewood
Upper Rochford
Hanley William
Stockton-on Teme
Orleton
Abberley Common
The Burf
Astley
Noutard's Green
Crossway Green
Comhampton
Cutnall Green
Dunhampton
Sytchampton
Northampton
Doverdale
Shrawley
Oldfield
Uphampton
Ombersley
Hadley
Berrington Green
Hanley Child
Stanford on Teme
Sapey Common
Stanford Bridge
Great Witley
Redmarley
Frog Pool
Sankyn's Green
St Michaels
Leysters
Upper Sapey
Stoke Bliss
Shelsley Walsh
Woodbury Hill
Witley Court
Little Witley
Shelsley Beauchamp
Holt Heath
Holt
Sinton
Salwarpe
Clifton upon Teme
Whyle
Collington
Harpley
Martley
Wichenford
Sinton Green
Grimley
Ladywood
Hawford
Hawford Dovecote
Moseley
Fernhill Heath
Hatfield
Thornbury
Old Church
Tedstone Wafer
Tedstone Delamere
Berrow Green
Dovecote
Shoulton
Hallow
Northwick
Horsham
Edwyn Ralph
Bredenbury
Docklow
Whitbourne
Knightwick
Lower Broadheath
WORCESTER
Rainbow Hill
Brockhampton Estate
Lulsley
Broad Green
Upper Broadheath
Elgar
Henwick
Newtown
Bromyard
Bringsty Common
Broadwas
Risbury
Leigh Court Barn
Rushwick
Leigh
St Johns
Cherry Orchard
Pencombe
Munderfield Row
Stanford Bishop
Linley Green
Alfrick
Brockamin
Bransford
Alfrick Pound
Little Cowarne
Suckley
Powick
Stoke Cross
Munderfield Stocks
Acton Beauchamp
Knapp & Papermill
Leigh Sinton
Ullingswick
Callow End
Acton Green
Deblin's Green
Stoke Lacy
Bishop's Frome
Kempsey
Upper Town
Evesbatch
Newland
Felton
Moreton Jeffries
Much Cowarne
Malvern Link
Madresfield
Cradley
Burley Gate
West Malvern
Great Malvern
Guarlford
Kerswell
Ocle Pychard
Lower Egleton
Castle Frome
Fromes Hill
Clifton
Newtown
Upper Egleton
Mathon
Westhide
Stretton Grandison
Malvern Hills
Severn Stoke
Withington
Monkhide
Hanley Swan
Hanley Castle
Kinnersley
Shucknall
Yarkhill
Canon Frome
Bosbury
Three Counties
Colwall
Earl's Croome
Hagley
Weston Beggard
Coddington
Malvern Wells
Ashperton
Staplow
Upper Welland
Upton-upon-Severn
Tiltridge
Ryall
Munsley
Trumpet
Tarrington
Stoke Edith
Perton
Wellington Heath
Herefordshire Beacon
Welland
Newbridge Green
Hampton Bishop
Castlemorton Common
Putley Green
Aylton
Ledbury
Eastnor
Hollybush
Uckinghall
Queenhill
Castlemorton
Mordiford
Putley
Little Marcle
Birts Street
Longdon
Woolhope
Rye Street
Shuthonger
Holme Lacy
Rushall
Bromsberrow
Bushley
Fownhope
Hellens Manor
Sollers
Much Marcle
Bromsberrow Heath
Pendock
Tewkesbury
Forthampton
Ballingham
Dymock
Playley Green
Eldersfield
Linkend
Chaceley
Brockhampton
Stocking
St Mary's Church
Redmarley D'Abitot
Carey
Wye Valley
How Caple
Lime Street
Corse Lawn
Deerhurst
Pen-allt
Kempley
Kempley Green
Three Choirs
Poolhill
Staunton
Odda's Chapel
Tirley
Foy
Corse
King's Caple
Strangford
Brampton Abbotts
Crow Hill
Upton Bishop
Apperley
Upleadon
Hasfield
Baysham
Lower Apperley
Upper Common
Gorsley
Newent
Leigh
Ashleworth
Bridstow
Kilcot
Birds of Prey Centre
Ashleworth Quay
Tithe Barn
Hartpury
Bishop's Norton
Peterstow
Kent's Green
Clifford's Mesne
R Leadon
R Chelt
R Severn
R Teme
0 1 2 3 4 miles
0 1 2 3 4 5 kilometres
A456
A443
A451
A4025
A449
A4133
A44
A465
A417
A4103
A438
A4172
A4104
M5
M50
A38
A4440
B4202
B4204
B4203
B4197
B4214
B4220
B4219
B4232
B4211
B4208
B4209
B4224
B4216
B4215
B4221
B4024
B4213

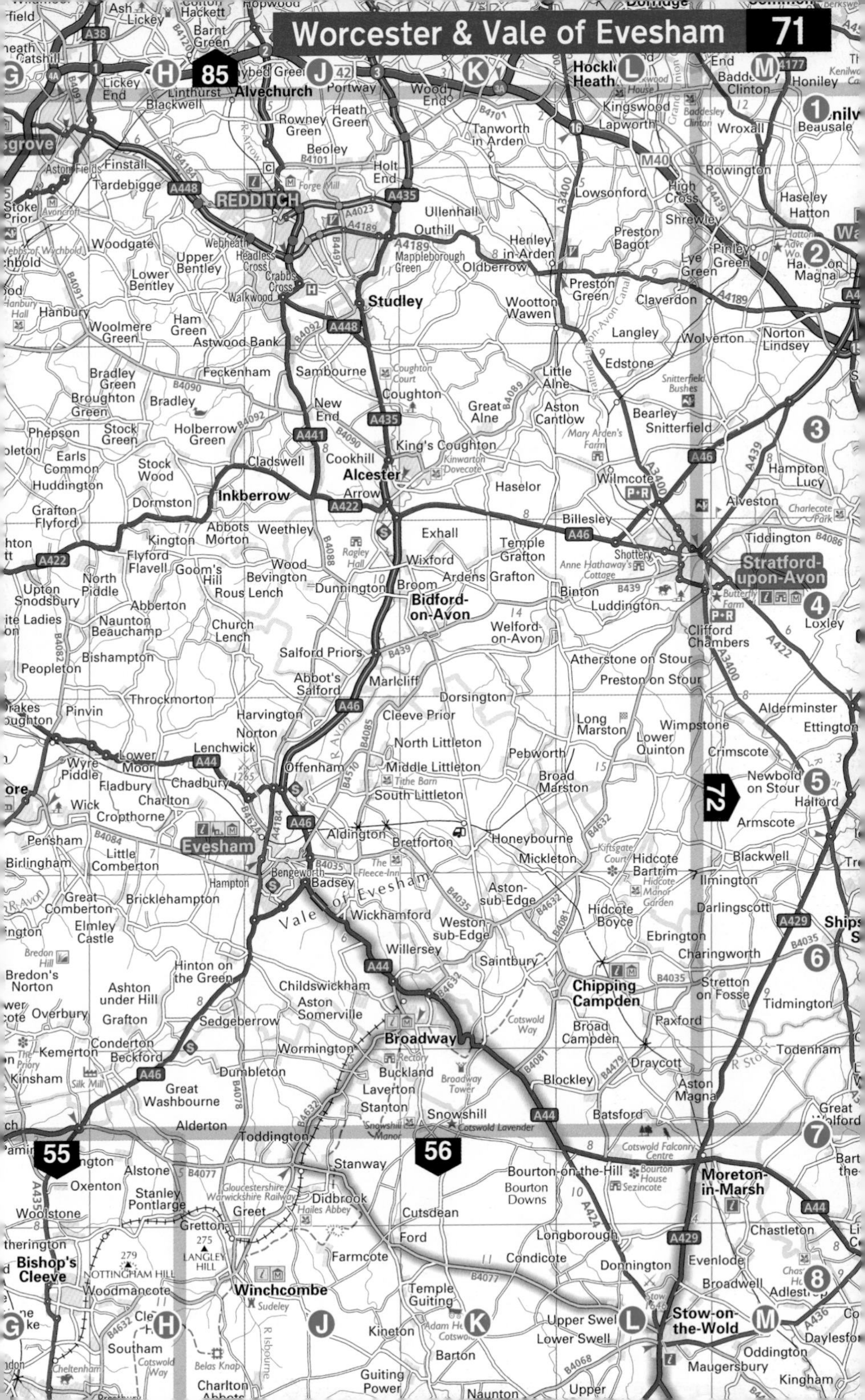
REDDITCH
Alvechurch
Studley
Alcester
Inkberrow
Bidford-on-Avon
Evesham
Broadway
Chipping Campden
Stratford-upon-Avon
Moreton-in-Marsh
Stow-on-the-Wold
Winchcombe
Bishop's Cleeve
Henley-in-Arden
Vale of Evesham
85
72
55
56

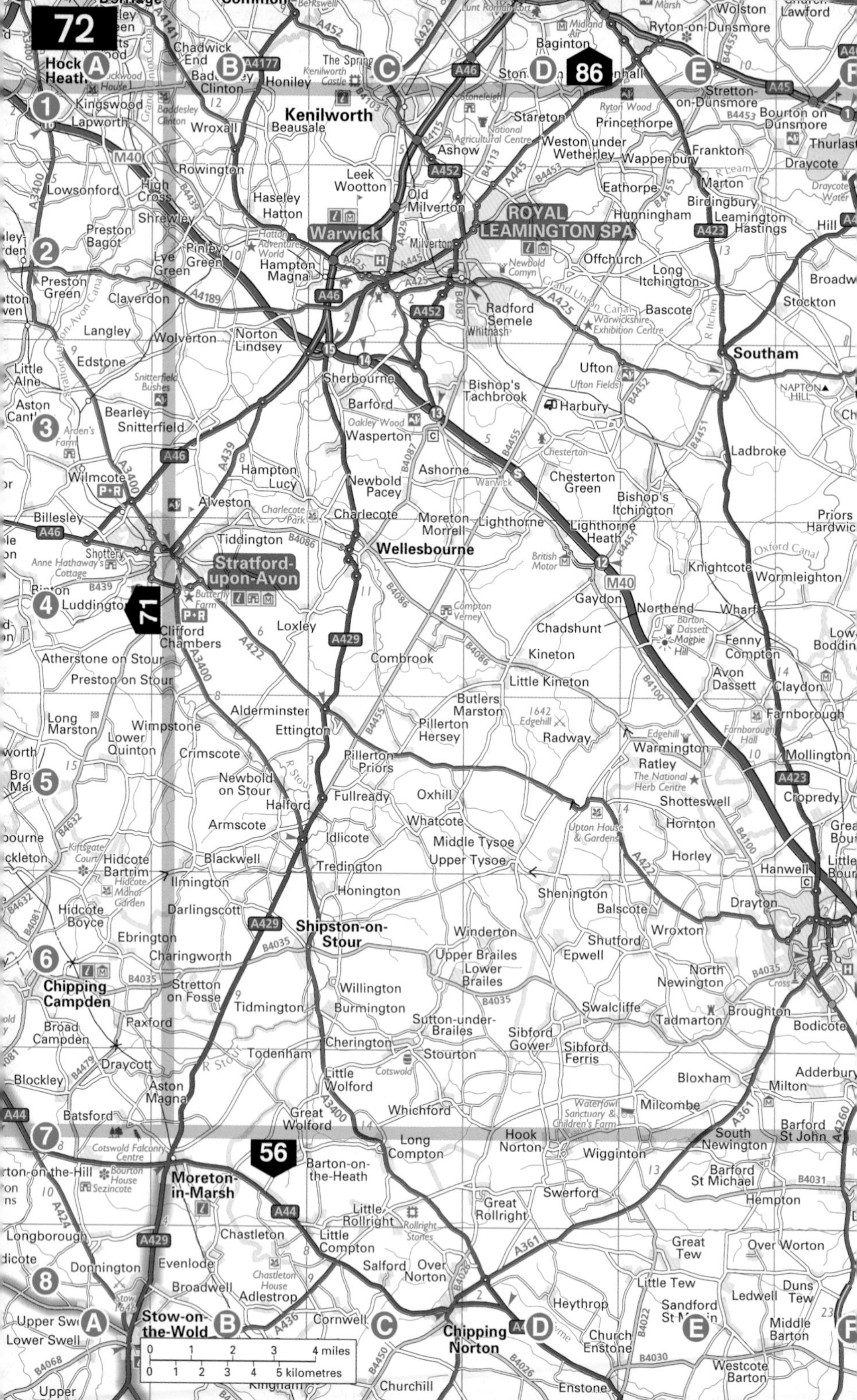
72
A
B
C
D
E
86
Hockley Heath
Chadwick End
Baddesley Clinton
Honiley
The Spring
Kenilworth Castle
Stoneleigh
Baginton
Midland Air Museum
Lunt Roman Fort
Berkswell
Wolston
Ryton-on-Dunsmore
Church Lawford
Marsh
Stretton-on-Dunsmore
Bourton on Dunsmore
Kingswood
Lapworth
Wroxall
Kenilworth
Beausale
Stareton
National Agricultural Centre
Ryton Wood
Princethorpe
Weston under Wetherley
Wappenbury
Frankton
Thurlaston
Draycote
Draycote Water
Ashow
Rowington
Lowsonford
High Cross
Shrewley
Haseley
Hatton
Leek Wootton
Old Milverton
Eathorpe
Hunningham
Marton
Birdingbury
Leamington Hastings
Warwick
ROYAL LEAMINGTON SPA
Milverton
Preston Bagot
Hatton Adventure World
Pinley Green
Lye Green
Hampton Magna
Newbold Comyn
Offchurch
Long Itchington
Hill
Broadwell
Preston Green
Claverdon
Grand Union Canal
Radford Semele
Whitnash
Warwickshire Exhibition Centre
Bascote
Stockton
Langley
Wolverton
Norton Lindsey
Southam
Little Alne
Edstone
Sherbourne
Ufton
Ufton Fields
Napton Hill
Snitterfield Bushes
Bishop's Tachbrook
Harbury
Aston Cantlow
Arden's Farm
Bearley
Snitterfield
Barford
Oakley Wood
Wasperton
Ladbroke
Chesterton
Chesterton Green
Wilmcote
Hampton Lucy
Newbold Pacey
Ashorne
Bishop's Itchington
Alveston
Charlecote Park
Charlecote
Moreton Morrell
Lighthorne
Lighthorne Heath
Priors Hardwick
Billesley
Tiddington
Wellesbourne
British Motor Museum
Oxford Canal
Shottery
Anne Hathaway's Cottage
Stratford-upon-Avon
Knightcote
Wormleighton
Binton
Luddington
71
Butterfly Farm
Gaydon
Northend
Wharf
Compton Verney
Chadshunt
Burton Dassett
Magpie Hill
Fenny Compton
Clifford Chambers
Loxley
Atherstone on Stour
Combrook
Kineton
Avon Dassett
Claydon
Preston on Stour
Little Kineton
Farnborough
Farnborough Hall
Long Marston
Wimpstone
Alderminster
Ettington
Butlers Marston
Pillerton Hersey
1642 Edgehill
Radway
Edgehill
Warmington
Ratley
The National Herb Centre
Mollington
Lower Quinton
Crimscote
Pillerton Priors
Cropredy
Newbold on Stour
Fullready
Oxhill
Shotteswell
Halford
Upton House & Gardens
Hornton
Armscote
Whatcote
Idlicote
Middle Tysoe
Upper Tysoe
Horley
Kiftsgate Court
Hidcote Bartrim
Blackwell
Tredington
Hanwell
Hidcote Manor Garden
Ilmington
Honington
Shenington
Hidcote Boyce
Darlingscott
Balscote
Drayton
Shipston-on-Stour
Winderton
Shutford
Wroxton
Ebrington
Charingworth
Upper Brailes
Lower Brailes
Epwell
North Newington
Chipping Campden
Stretton on Fosse
Willington
Tidmington
Burmington
Swalcliffe
Tadmarton
Broughton
Bodicote
Paxford
Broad Campden
Sutton-under-Brailes
Sibford Gower
Sibford Ferris
Cherington
Stourton
Todenham
Draycott
Little Wolford
Cotswold
Bloxham
Adderbury
Milton
Blockley
Aston Magna
Batsford
Great Wolford
Whichford
Waterfowl Sanctuary & Children's Farm
Milcombe
South Newington
Barford St John
Cotswold Falconry Centre
Long Compton
Hook Norton
Wigginton
56
Barton-on-the-Heath
Bourton-on-the-Hill
Bourton House
Sezincote
Moreton-in-Marsh
Swerford
Barford St Michael
Hempton
Little Rollright
Rollright Stones
Great Rollright
Longborough
Chastleton
Little Compton
Great Tew
Over Worton
Donnington
Evenlode
Salford
Over Norton
Chastleton House
Broadwell
Adlestrop
Little Tew
Ledwell
Duns Tew
Heythrop
Sandford St Martin
Middle Barton
Upper Swell
Lower Swell
Stow-on-the-Wold
Cornwell
Chipping Norton
Church Enstone
Westcote Barton
Churchill
Kingham
Enstone
Upper
0 1 2 3 4 miles
0 1 2 3 4 5 kilometres

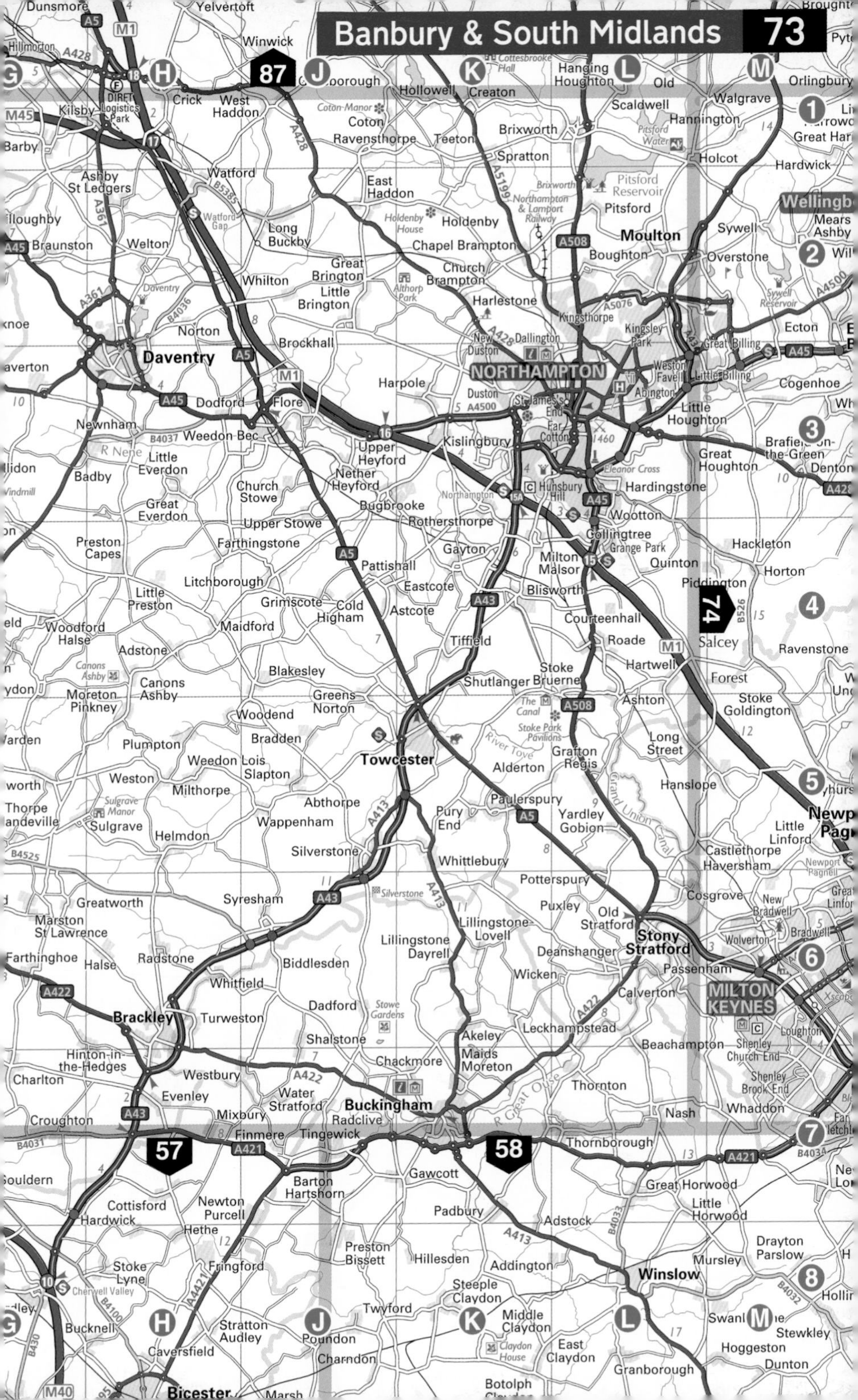
Northampton
Daventry
Towcester
Brackley
Buckingham
Stony Stratford
Milton Keynes
Winslow
Bicester
Moulton
Pitsford Reservoir
Silverstone
Stowe Gardens
Salcey Forest
Newport Pagnell
87
74
57
58

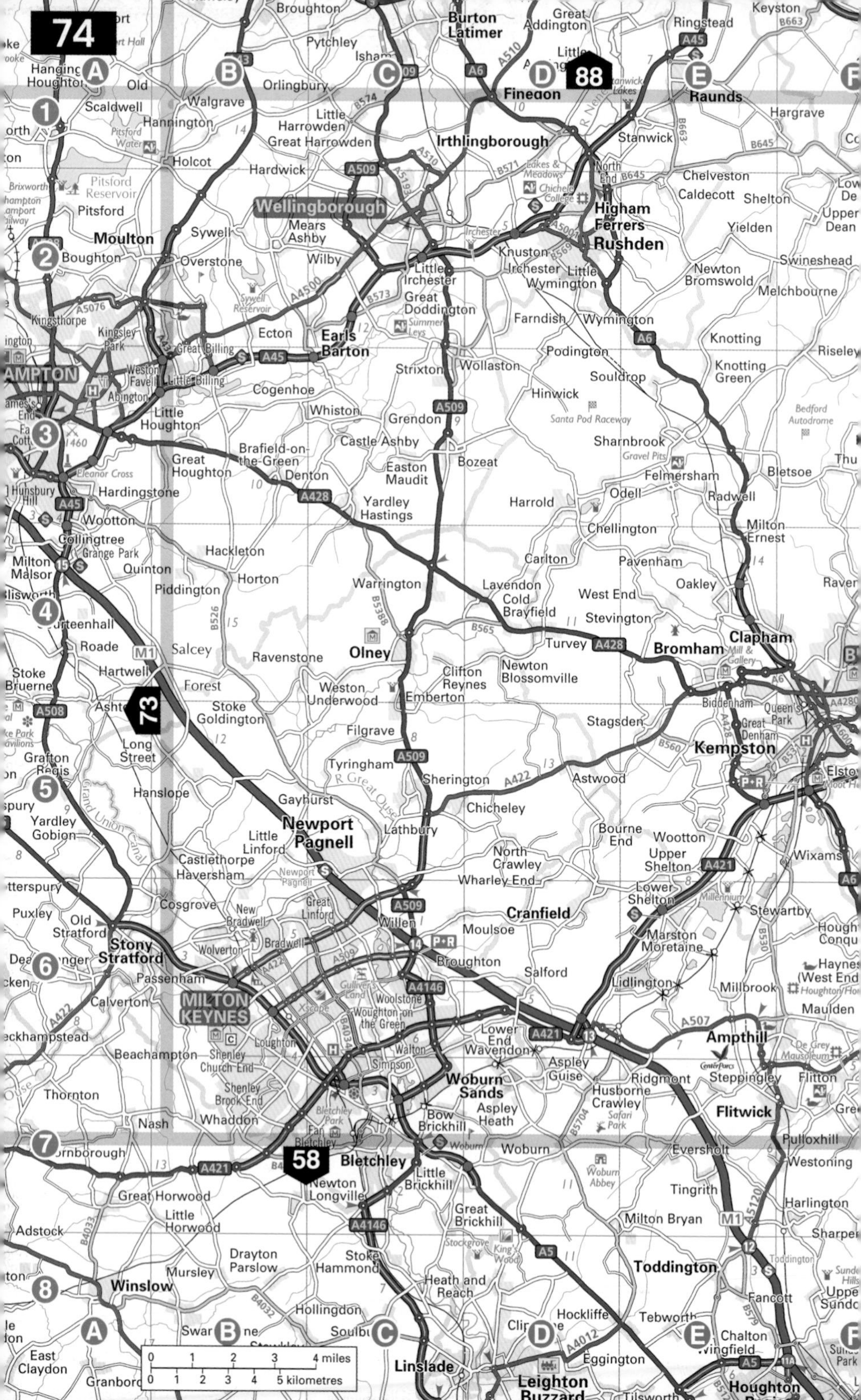
A
B
C
D
E
F
88
73
58
Broughton
Burton Latimer
Great Addington
Ringstead
Keyston
Pytchley
Isham
Little Addington
Hanging Houghton
Old
Orlingbury
Finedon
Raunds
Scaldwell
Walgrave
Hannington
Little Harrowden
Great Harrowden
Irthlingborough
Stanwick
Hargrave
Pitsford Water
Holcot
Hardwick
Chelveston
Caldecott
Shelton
Pitsford Reservoir
Pitsford
Wellingborough
Higham Ferrers
Rushden
Moulton
Mears Ashby
Sywell
Yielden
Upper Dean
Boughton
Overstone
Wilby
Knuston
Irchester
Little Irchester
Swineshead
Newton Bromswold
Melchbourne
Little Wymington
Great Doddington
Farndish
Wymington
Kingsthorpe
Kingsley Park
Sywell Reservoir
Ecton
Earls Barton
Knotting
Riseley
Great Billing
Summer Leys
Podington
Weston Favell
Little Billing
Strixton
Wollaston
Souldrop
Knotting Green
Abington
Cogenhoe
Hinwick
Little Houghton
Whiston
Grendon
Santa Pod Raceway
Bedford Autodrome
Castle Ashby
Sharnbrook
Great Houghton
Brafield-on-the-Green
Denton
Easton Maudit
Bozeat
Gravel Pits
Felmersham
Bletsoe
Eleanor Cross
Hardingstone
Hunsbury Hill
Yardley Hastings
Harrold
Odell
Radwell
Wootton
Collingtree
Grange Park
Chellington
Milton Ernest
Hackleton
Milton Malsor
Quinton
Carlton
Pavenham
Horton
Piddington
Warrington
Lavendon
Oakley
Cold Brayfield
West End
Stevington
Roade
Salcey Forest
Ravenstone
Olney
Turvey
Bromham
Clapham
Stoke Bruerne
Hartwell
Clifton Reynes
Newton Blossomville
Weston Underwood
Emberton
Biddenham
Queen's Park
Stoke Goldington
Stagsden
Great Denham
Long Street
Filgrave
Kempston
Grafton Regis
Tyringham
Sherington
Astwood
Hanslope
Gayhurst
Chicheley
Yardley Gobion
Grand Union Canal
R Great Ouse
Little Linford
Newport Pagnell
Lathbury
Bourne End
Wootton
Castlethorpe
Haversham
North Crawley
Upper Shelton
Wixams
Wharley End
Lower Shelton
Cosgrove
Puxley
Old Stratford
New Bradwell
Great Linford
Willen
Cranfield
Stewartby
Stony Stratford
Bradwell
Moulsoe
Marston Moretaine
Wolverton
Broughton
Passenham
Salford
Haynes (West End)
Lidlington
Millbrook
Calverton
Milton Keynes
Gulliver's Land
Woolstone
Woughton on the Green
Maulden
Lower End
Wavendon
Ampthill
Beachampton
Shenley Church End
Loughton
Walton
Aspley Guise
Simpson
Woburn Sands
Husborne Crawley
Ridgmont
Steppingley
Flitton
Thornton
Shenley Brook End
Bletchley Park
Aspley Heath
Flitwick
Bow Brickhill
Safari Park
Nash
Whaddon
Fenny Stratford
Bletchley
Woburn
Eversholt
Pulloxhill
Westoning
Woburn Abbey
Little Brickhill
Newton Longville
Tingrith
Great Horwood
Great Brickhill
Little Horwood
Milton Bryan
Harlington
Adstock
Stockgrove
King's Wood
Drayton Parslow
Stoke Hammond
Toddington
Mursley
Winslow
Heath and Reach
Fancott
Hollingdon
Hockliffe
Tebworth
Soulbury
Chalton
Wingfield
East Claydon
Eggington
Linslade
Leighton Buzzard
Tilsworth
Houghton Regis
0 1 2 3 4 miles
0 1 2 3 4 5 kilometres
M1
A45
A6
A509
A428
A422
A421
A4146
A5
A508
A507
A4012
A500
A4500
A5076
A510
A5193
B574
B571
B573
B645
B663
B565
B5388
B526
B560
B4034
B4033
B4032
B5704
B530
A5120
B5120

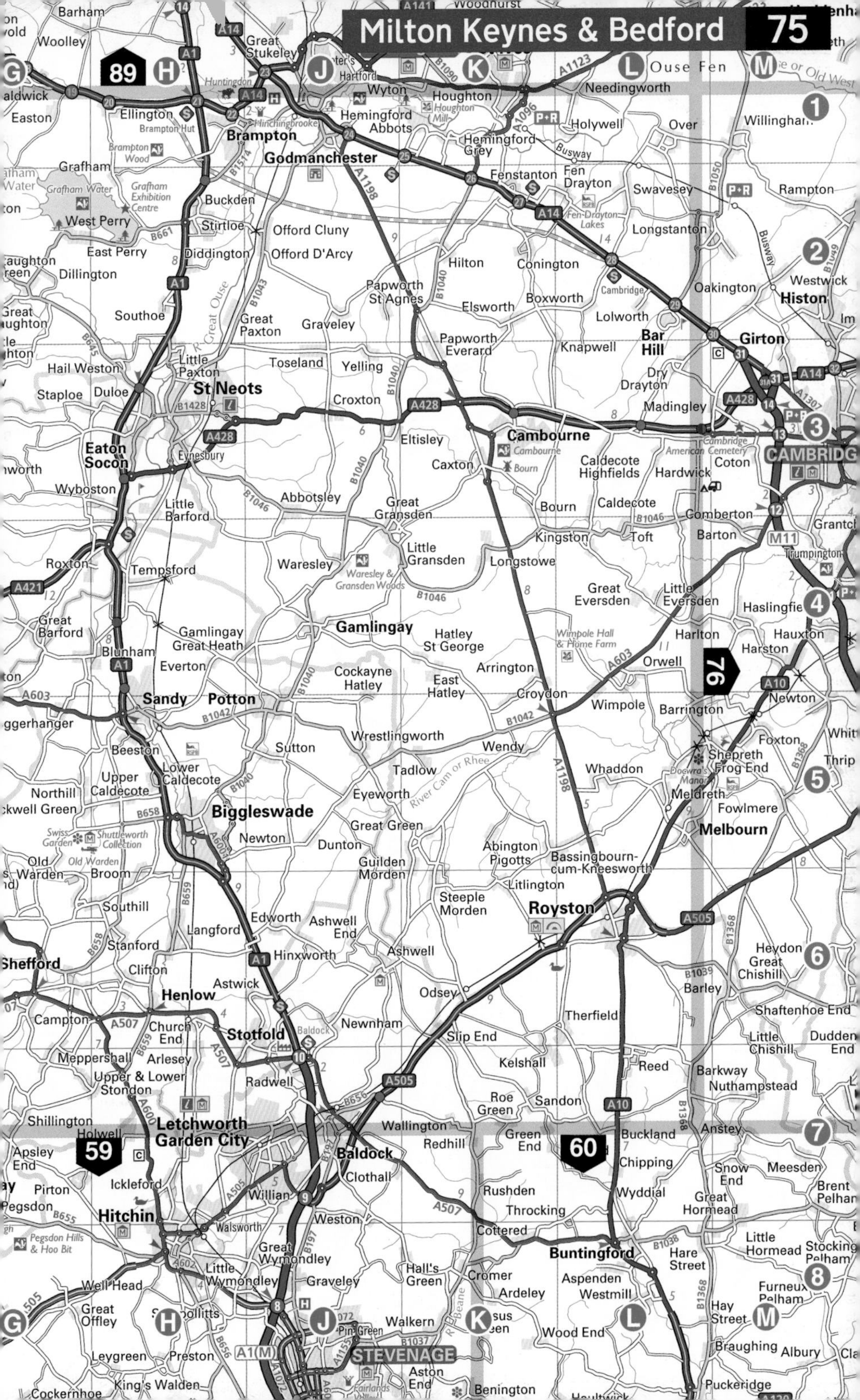
89
76
59
60

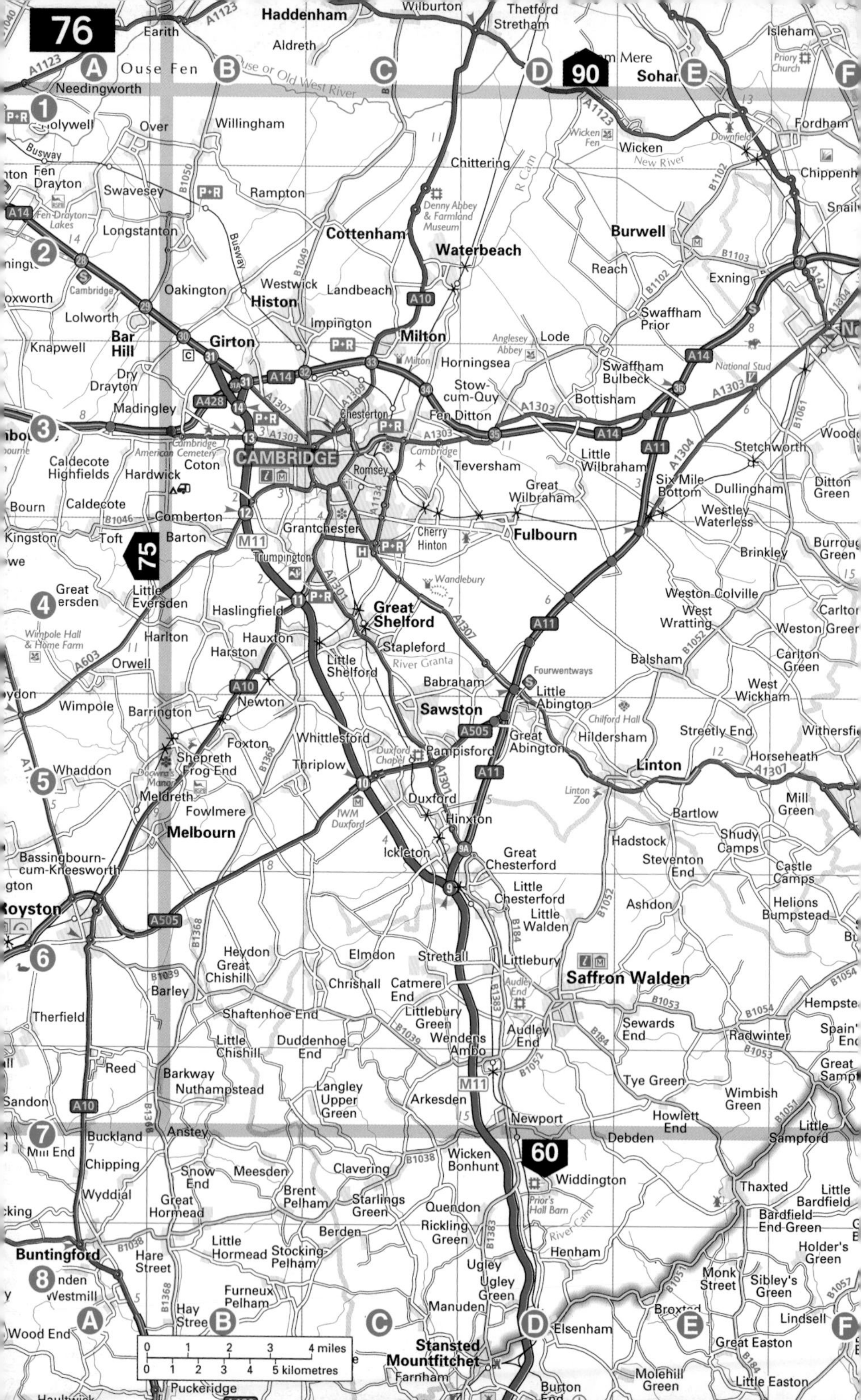
Haddenham
Wilburton
Thetford
Stretham
Earith
A1123
Aldreth
Ouse Fen
Ouse or Old West River
90
Soham
Isleham
Priory Church
Needingworth
Holywell
Over
Willingham
A1123
Wicken Fen
Wicken
New River
Fordham
Downfield
Busway
Fen Drayton
Swavesey
B1050
Rampton
Chittering
R Cam
Chippenham
Snailwell
Fen Drayton Lakes
A14
Longstanton
Busway
Denny Abbey & Farmland Museum
Cottenham
Waterbeach
Burwell
B1102
B1103
Reach
Exning
Cambridge
Oakington
Westwick
Histon
Landbeach
B1049
A10
B1102
Swaffham Prior
Lolworth
Bar Hill
Impington
Knapwell
Girton
Milton
Anglesey Abbey
Lode
A142
Dry Drayton
A14
Chesterton
Horningsea
Swaffham Bulbeck
A14
National Stud
Madingley
A428
A1307
Stow-cum-Quy
Bottisham
A1303
A1309
Fen Ditton
A1303
B1061
A1303
Cambridge American Cemetery
CAMBRIDGE
Cambridge
A14
A11
Stetchworth
Caldecote Highfields
Hardwick
Coton
Romsey
Teversham
Little Wilbraham
A1304
Six Mile Bottom
Dullingham
Ditton Green
Bourn
Caldecote
B1046
Comberton
Great Wilbraham
A1134
Westley Waterless
Kingston
Toft
Barton
M11
Grantchester
Cherry Hinton
Fulbourn
Burrough Green
75
Trumpington
Brinkley
Great Eversden
Little Eversden
Wandlebury
Haslingfield
A1301
Great Shelford
A1307
Weston Colville
West Wratting
Carlton
Wimpole Hall & Home Farm
Harlton
Hauxton
Harston
Stapleford
A11
B1052
Weston Green
A603
Orwell
Little Shelford
River Granta
Balsham
Carlton Green
Fourwentways
Babraham
Little Abington
West Wickham
A10
Newton
Wimpole
Barrington
Sawston
Chilford Hall
A505
Great Abington
Hildersham
Streetly End
Withersfield
Foxton
Whittlesford
Duxford Chapel
Pampisford
B1368
Shepreth
Frog End
Thriplow
Linton
Horseheath
A1307
Whaddon
A11
Meldreth
Docwra's Manor
Fowlmere
A1301
Duxford
Linton Zoo
Bartlow
Mill Green
Melbourn
IWM Duxford
Hinxton
Hadstock
Shudy Camps
Bassingbourn-cum-Kneesworth
Ickleton
Great Chesterford
Steventon End
Castle Camps
Little Chesterford
Royston
A505
B1368
Ashdon
Helions Bumpstead
Little Walden
B1184
B1052
Heydon
Great Chishill
Elmdon
Strethall
Littlebury
B1039
Barley
Chrishall
Catmere End
Saffron Walden
B1054
B1383
Audley End
Therfield
Shaftenhoe End
Littlebury Green
B1053
Hempstead
Sewards End
B1054
Radwinter
Spain's End
Little Chishill
Duddenhoe End
Wendens Ambo
B1039
Audley End
B184
Reed
B1053
Great Sampford
Barkway
Nuthampstead
B1052
M11
Tye Green
Sandon
Langley Upper Green
Arkesden
Wimbish Green
A10
B1368
Howlett End
B1051
Newport
Buckland
Anstey
Debden
Little Sampford
Mill End
60
Chipping
Snow End
Meesden
Clavering
B1038
Wicken Bonhunt
Widdington
Wyddial
Great Hormead
Brent Pelham
Starlings Green
Quendon
Prior's Hall Barn
Thaxted
Little Bardfield
River Cam
Bardfield End Green
Rickling Green
B1383
Berden
Buntingford
B1038
Hare Street
Little Hormead
Stocking Pelham
Henham
Holder's Green
Ugley
Ugley Green
Monk Street
Sibley's Green
B1057
Westmill
Furneux Pelham
B1051
Hay Street
B1368
Manuden
Broxted
Lindsell
Wood End
Elsenham
Great Easton
Stansted Mountfitchet
B184
0 1 2 3 4 miles
0 1 2 3 4 5 kilometres
Farnham
Molehill Green
Little Easton
Puckeridge
Burton End

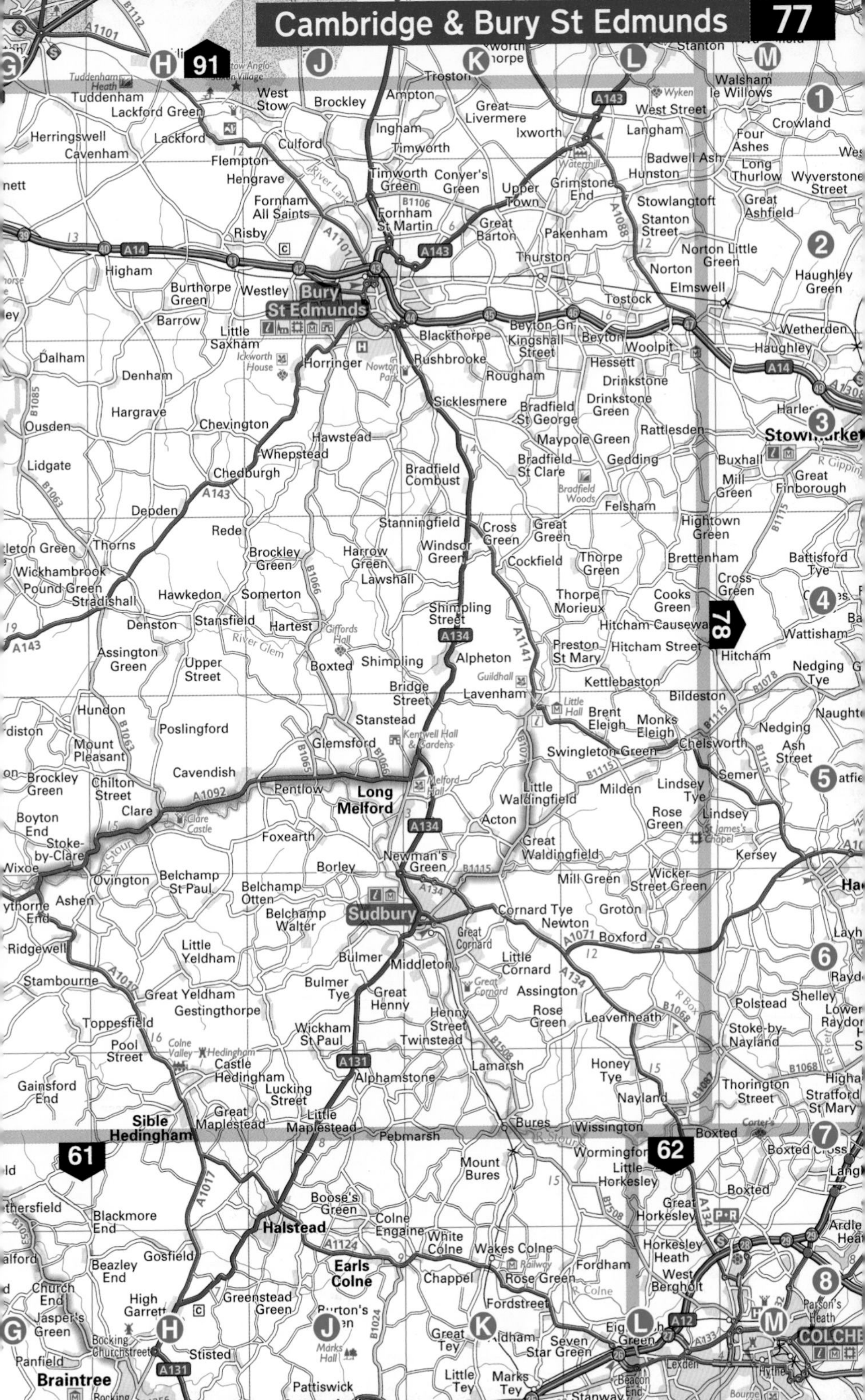
91
Tuddenham Heath
Tuddenham
Lackford Green
Herringswell
Cavenham
Lackford
West Stow
Brockley
Ampton
Troston
Great Livermere
Ixworth
Stanton
Walsham le Willows
Wyken
West Street
Langham
Crowland
Four Ashes
Culford
Ingham
Timworth
Flempton
Hengrave
Fornham All Saints
Timworth Green
Conyer's Green
Upper Town
Grimstone End
Watermill
Badwell Ash
Hunston
Long Thurlow
Wyverstone Street
Fornham St Martin
Great Barton
Pakenham
Stowlangtoft
Stanton Street
Great Ashfield
Risby
Thurston
Norton Little Green
Norton
Elmswell
Haughley Green
Higham
Burthorpe Green
Westley
Bury St Edmunds
Tostock
Barrow
Little Saxham
Blackthorpe
Beyton Green
Kingshall Street
Beyton
Woolpit
Wetherden
Haughley
Dalham
Denham
Ickworth House
Horringer
Nowton Park
Rushbrooke
Rougham
Hessett
Drinkstone
Drinkstone Green
Stowmarket
Ousden
Hargrave
Chevington
Sicklesmere
Bradfield St George
Rattlesden
Maypole Green
Lidgate
Hawstead
Whepstead
Bradfield St Clare
Gedding
Buxhall
Mill Green
Great Finborough
Chedburgh
Bradfield Combust
Bradfield Woods
Felsham
Depden
Rede
Stanningfield
Cross Green
Great Green
Hightown Green
Thorns
Brockley Green
Harrow Green
Windsor Green
Cockfield
Thorpe Green
Brettenham
Battisford Tye
Wickhambrook
Pound Green
Stradishall
Lawshall
Cross Green
Hawkedon
Somerton
Thorpe Morieux
Cooks Green
Denston
Stansfield
Hartest
Shimpling Street
Hitcham Causeway
Gifford's Hall
Wattisham
River Glem
Assington Green
Upper Street
Boxted
Shimpling
Alpheton
Preston St Mary
Hitcham Street
Hitcham
Guildhall
Nedging Tye
Bridge Street
Lavenham
Kettlebaston
Bildeston
Hundon
Stanstead
Little Hall
Brent Eleigh
Monks Eleigh
Naughton
Poslingford
Kentwell Hall & Gardens
Nedging
Mount Pleasant
Glemsford
Swingleton Green
Chelsworth
Ash Street
Cavendish
Brockley Green
Chilton Street
Pentlow
Long Melford
Melford Hall
Little Waldingfield
Milden
Lindsey Tye
Semer
Clare
Clare Castle
Acton
Rose Green
Lindsey
Boyton End
Stoke-by-Clare
Foxearth
Great Waldingfield
St James's Chapel
Kersey
Wixoe
River Stour
Borley
Newman's Green
Ovington
Belchamp St Paul
Mill Green
Wicker Street Green
Ashen
Belchamp Otten
Sudbury
Cornard Tye
Groton
Belchamp Walter
Newton
Great Cornard
Boxford
Ridgewell
Little Yeldham
Bulmer
Middleton
Little Cornard
Stambourne
Great Yeldham
Bulmer Tye
Great Henny
Great Cornard
Assington
Polstead
Shelley
Gestingthorpe
Rose Green
Leavenheath
Toppesfield
Henny Street
R Box
Stoke-by-Nayland
Pool Street
Wickham St Paul
Twinstead
Colne Valley
Hedingham Castle
Castle Hedingham
Lamarsh
Honey Tye
Gainsford End
Alphamstone
Thorington Street
Lucking Street
Nayland
Stratford St Mary
Sible Hedingham
Great Maplestead
Little Maplestead
Pebmarsh
Bures
Wissington
Boxted
Carter's
Boxted Cross
61
Mount Bures
Wormingford
62
Little Horkesley
Blackmore End
Boose's Green
Great Horkesley
Boxted
Halstead
Colne Engaine
White Colne
Wakes Colne
Railway
Horkesley Heath
Gosfield
Beazley End
Earls Colne
Chappel
Fordham
Rose Green
West Bergholt
Church End
High Garrett
Greenstead Green
Burton's Green
Fordstreet
Eight Ash Green
Jasper's Green
Bocking Churchstreet
Stisted
Marks Hall
Great Tey
Aldham
Seven Star Green
Panfield
Braintree
Bocking
Little Tey
Marks Tey
Stanway
Beacon End
Lexden
Hythe
Colchester
Parson's Heath
Pattiswick
Coggeshall
78
A14
A143
A1101
A1088
A134
A1141
A1092
A131
A1017
A1124
A12
A133
A1071
B1106
B1115
B1066
B1065
B1063
B1085
B1071
B1068
B1508
B1087
B1024
B1256
B1408
B1078
B1112

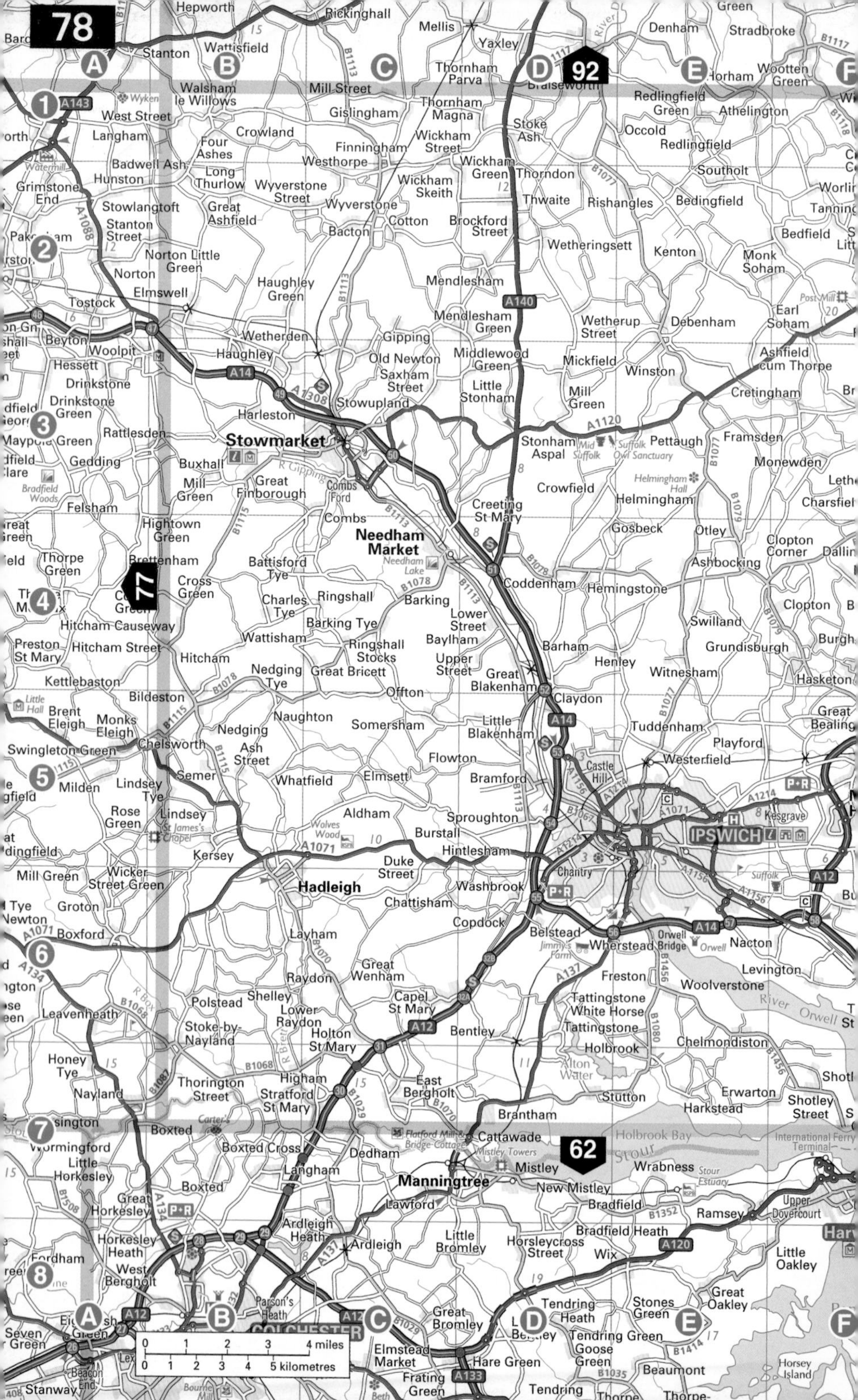

78
Hepworth
Rickinghall
Mellis
Yaxley
Denham
Stradbroke
Stanton
Wattisfield
Thornham Parva
92
Horham
Wootten Green
Walsham le Willows
Mill Street
Braiseworth
Redlingfield Green
Athelington
Wyken
West Street
Gislingham
Thornham Magna
Stoke Ash
Occold
Redlingfield
Langham
Crowland
Wickham Street
Four Ashes
Finningham
Watermill
Badwell Ash
Westhorpe
Wickham Green
Thorndon
Southolt
Hunston
Long Thurlow
Wyverstone Street
Wickham Skeith
Grimstone End
Wyverstone
Thwaite
Rishangles
Bedingfield
Stowlangtoft
Great Ashfield
Cotton
Stanton Street
Bacton
Brockford Street
Bedfield
Wetheringsett
Kenton
Monk Soham
Norton Little Green
Norton
Elmswell
Haughley Green
Mendlesham
Tostock
Post Mill
Earl Soham
Mendlesham Green
Wetherup Street
Debenham
Beyton
Woolpit
Wetherden
Gipping
Hessett
Haughley
Old Newton
Middlewood Green
Mickfield
Ashfield cum Thorpe
Saxham Street
Winston
Drinkstone
Little Stonham
Drinkstone Green
Stowupland
Mill Green
Cretingham
Harleston
Rattlesden
Stowmarket
Stonham Aspal
Mid Suffolk
Suffolk Owl Sanctuary
Pettaugh
Framsden
Maypole Green
Gedding
Buxhall
Monewden
R Gipping
Bradfield Woods
Mill Green
Great Finborough
Combs Ford
Helmingham Hall
Creeting St Mary
Crowfield
Helmingham
Charsfield
Felsham
Combs
Hightown Green
Needham Market
Gosbeck
Otley
Clopton Corner
Thorpe Green
Brettenham
Battisford Tye
Needham Lake
Coddenham
Ashbocking
77
Cross Green
Hemingstone
Charles Tye
Ringshall
Barking
Clopton
Lower Street
Swilland
Hitcham Causeway
Barking Tye
Baylham
Preston St Mary
Hitcham Street
Wattisham
Ringshall Stocks
Barham
Grundisburgh
Burgh
Hitcham
Upper Street
Henley
Nedging Tye
Great Bricett
Great Blakenham
Witnesham
Kettlebaston
Offton
Claydon
Hasketon
Little Hall
Bildeston
Brent Eleigh
Monks Eleigh
Naughton
Somersham
Little Blakenham
Tuddenham
Great Bealings
Nedging
Chelsworth
Ash Street
Swingleton Green
Flowton
Castle Hill
Playford
Westerfield
Semer
Milden
Lindsey Tye
Whatfield
Elmsett
Bramford
Rose Green
Lindsey
St James's Chapel
Aldham
Wolves Wood
Sproughton
Kesgrave
IPSWICH
Burstall
Kersey
Hintlesham
Duke Street
Chantry
Mill Green
Wicker Street Green
Hadleigh
Washbrook
Suffolk
Groton
Chattisham
Newton
Boxford
Copdock
Layham
Belstead
Orwell Bridge
Nacton
Jimmy's Farm
Wherstead
Orwell
Great Wenham
Freston
Levington
Raydon
Woolverstone
Polstead
Shelley
Capel St Mary
River Orwell
Leavenheath
Lower Raydon
Tattingstone White Horse
R Box
Stoke-by-Nayland
Holton St Mary
Bentley
Tattingstone
Holbrook
Chelmondiston
Honey Tye
Alton Water
Higham
Nayland
Thorington Street
Stratford St Mary
East Bergholt
Stutton
Erwarton
Shotley Street
Carter's
Brantham
Harkstead
Boxted
Flatford Mill & Bridge Cottage
Cattawade
Holbrook Bay
Mistley Towers
International Ferry Terminal
Wormingford
Boxted Cross
Dedham
Mistley
62
Stour
Wrabness
Stour Estuary
Little Horkesley
Langham
Manningtree
New Mistley
Boxted
Great Horkesley
Lawford
Bradfield
Ramsey
Upper Dovercourt
Ardleigh Heath
Bradfield Heath
Horkesley Heath
Ardleigh
Little Bromley
Horsleycross Street
Wix
Little Oakley
Fordham
West Bergholt
Parson's Heath
Tendring Heath
Stones Green
Great Oakley
Great Bromley
Eight Ash Green
COLCHESTER
Little Bentley
Tendring Green
Seven Green
Elmstead Market
Goose Green
Beacon End
Hare Green
Beaumont
Horsey Island
Stanway
Frating Green
Tendring
Bourne Mill
Beth
Thorpe
0 1 2 3 4 miles
0 1 2 3 4 5 kilometres

93
Huntingfield
Walpole
Blackheath
Thorington
Walberswick
Bramfield
Heveningham
Ubbeston Green
Dunwich Forest
Suffolk Coast
Darsham
Westleton Heath
Dunwich
Sibton
Peasenhall
Yoxford
Westleton
Badingham
Middleton
Minsmere
Dunwich Heath
Middleton Moor
Bruisyard
Bruisyard Street
Theberton
Eastbridge
Carlton Meres
Cransford
Rendham
Kelsale
Leiston Abbey
Power Station
Carlton
Saxmundham
Swefling
Knodishall
Great Glemham
Benhall Street
Benhall Green
Sternfield
Leiston
Aldringham
Thorpe Ness
Stratford St Andrew
Friday Street
Friston
Knodishall Common
Thorpeness
Farnham
Snape
Hacheston
North Warren
Snape Street
Little Glemham
Snape Maltings
Aldeburgh
Blaxhall
Snape
Campsea Ash
Tunstall
Aldeburgh Bay
River Alde
Rendlesham
Sudbourne
Chillesford
Eyke
Bromeswell
Butley
Orford
Castle
Orford Ness
Capel St Andrew
Boyton
Orfordness-Havergate
River Ore
Suffolk Heritage Coast
Sutton
Shottisham
Hollesley
North Weir Point
Hollesley Bay
Alderton
Bawdsey
Deben
Old Felixstowe
Felixstowe
Hook of Holland
A12
A144
A1120
A1094
A1152
B1117
B1387
B1125
B1122
B1119
B1121
B1353
B1069
B1078
B1084
B1083
G
H
J
K
L
M
2
3
4
5
6
7
8

Suffolk
79
95
66
Barmouth
Barmouth Bridge
Afon Mawddach
Barmouth Bay
Fairbourne Steam Railway
Fairbourne
Penmaenpool
Mawddach Valley
SNOWDONIA NATIONAL PARK
Llwyngwril
Llangelynin
Castell y Bere
Afon Dysynni
Rhoslefain
Llanegryn
Bryncrug
Talyllyn Railway
Dolgoch Falls
TAREN HENDRE
Aber Dysynni
Tywyn
Pennal
Aberdovey
Aberdyfi
Afon Dyfi (River Dovey)
Ynys-hir
Dyfi Furnace
CARDIGAN BAY
Tre Taliesin
Cwm Clettwr
Borth
Tal-y-bont
Ceredigion Heritage Coast
Llandre
Rhyd-y-pennau
Bow Street
Salem
Clarach Bay
Cliff Railway & Camera Obscura
Penrhyn-coch
Capel Dewi
Waunfawr
Aberystwyth
Llanbadarn Fawr
Capel Bangor
Goginan
Rheidol Power Station
Capel Seion
Coed Penglanowen
Llanfarian
Afon Ystwyth
Llanfihangel-y-Creuddyn
Blaenplwyf
Cnwch Coch
Llanilar
Penderi Cliffs
Llanddeiniol
Llangwyryfon
Lledrod
Cors Caron
Llanrhystud
0 1 2 3 4 miles
0 1 2 3 4 5 kilometres

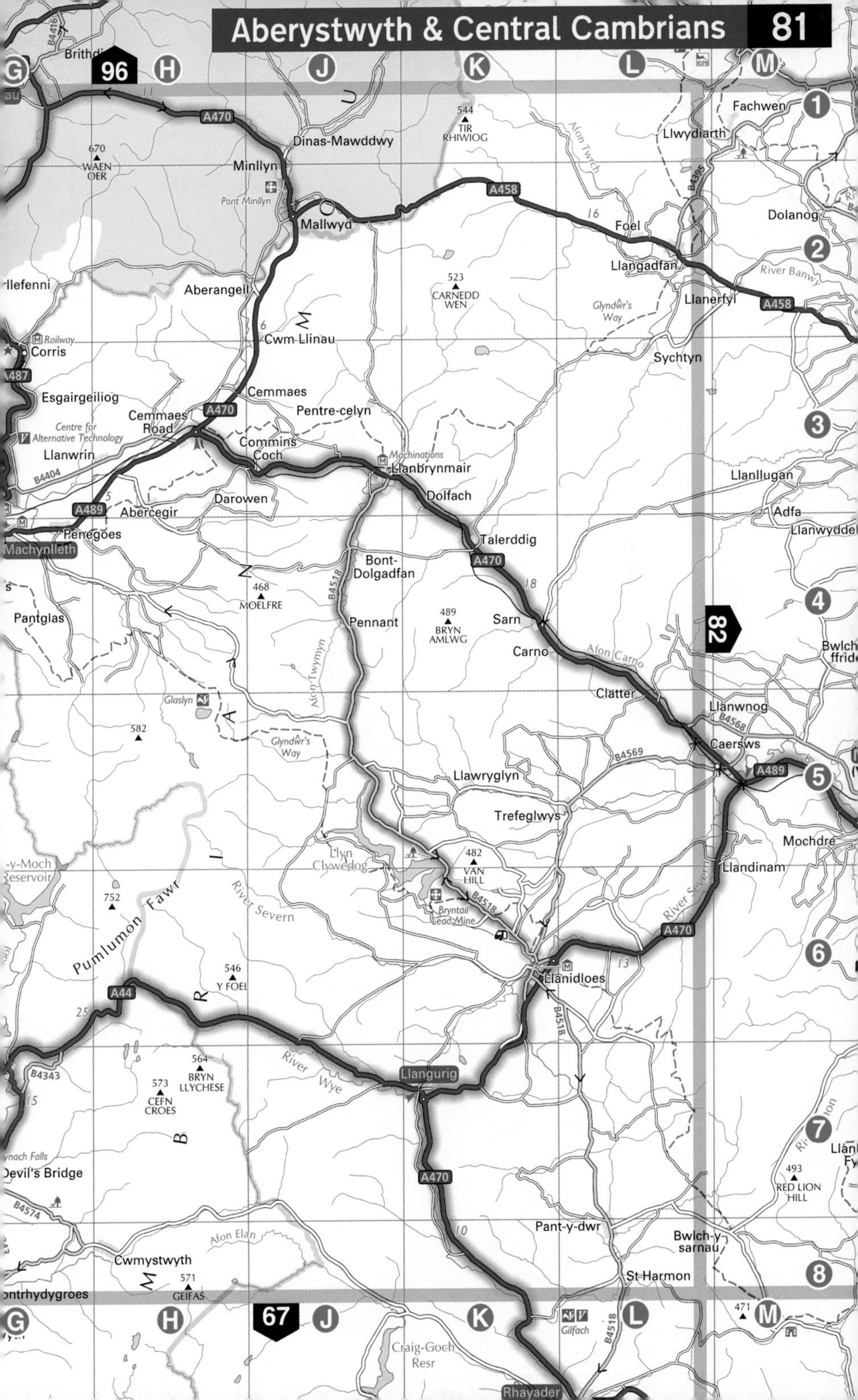
Dinas-Mawddwy
Minllyn
Mallwyd
Aberangell
Cwm Llinau
Corris
Esgairgeiliog
Cemmaes
Cemmaes Road
Pentre-celyn
Commins Coch
Llanwrin
Llanbrynmair
Dolfach
Darowen
Abercegir
Penegoes
Machynlleth
Talerddig
Bont-Dolgadfan
Pennant
Sarn
Carno
Clatter
Llanwnog
Caersws
Llawryglyn
Trefeglwys
Llyn Clywedog
Llanidloes
Llangurig
Pumlumon Fawr
River Severn
River Wye
Devil's Bridge
Cwmystwyth
Pant-y-dwr
Bwlch-y-sarnau
St Harmon
Craig-Goch Resr
Rhayader
Foel
Llangadfan
Llanerfyl
Sychtyn
Fachwen
Llwydiarth
Dolanog
Llanllugan
Adfa
Mochdre
Llandinam
Glyndŵr's Way
Centre for Alternative Technology
Bryntail Lead Mine
Gilfach
A470
A458
A489
A44
B4518
B4569
B4568
B4343
B4574
B4404
B4395
96
82
67

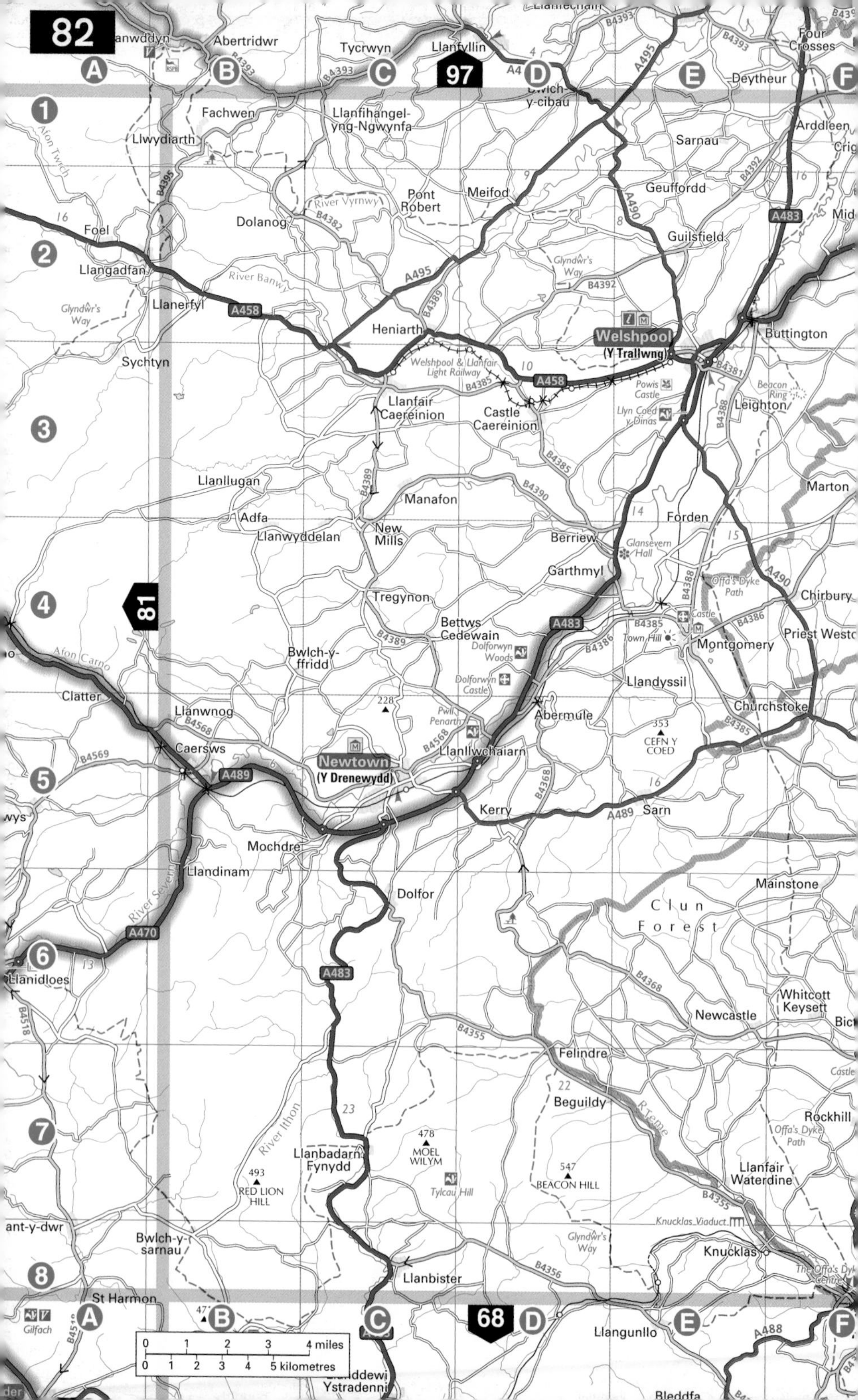

Abertridwr
Tycrwyn
Llanfyllin
97
Four Crosses
Deytheur
Bwlch-y-cibau
Fachwen
Llanfihangel-yng-Ngwynfa
Arddleen
Llwydiarth
Sarnau
Afon Twrch
Geufforddd
Pont Robert
Meifod
River Vyrnwy
Dolanog
Foel
Guilsfield
Llangadfan
River Banwy
Glyndŵr's Way
Llanerfyl
Heniarth
Welshpool
(Y Trallwng)
Buttington
Sychtyn
Welshpool & Llanfair Light Railway
Powis Castle
Beacon Ring
Llanfair Caereinion
Castle Caereinion
Llyn Coed y Dinas
Leighton
Llanllugan
Manafon
Marton
Adfa
Forden
Llanwyddelan
New Mills
Berriew
Glansevern Hall
Garthmyl
Offa's Dyke Path
Tregynon
Chirbury
81
Bettws Cedewain
Castle
Town Hill
Montgomery
Priest Weston
Afon Carno
Bwlch-y-ffridd
Dolforwyn Woods
Dolforwyn Castle
Llandyssil
Clatter
228
Pwll Penarth
Abermule
Churchstoke
Llanwnog
353
CEFN Y COED
Caersws
Newtown
(Y Drenewydd)
Llanllwchaiarn
Kerry
Sarn
Mochdre
Llandinam
River Severn
Dolfor
Mainstone
Clun Forest
Llanidloes
Whitcott Keysett
Newcastle
Felindre
Beguildy
Rockhill
R Teme
River Ithon
478
MOEL WILYM
Llanbadarn Fynydd
493
RED LION HILL
Tylcau Hill
547
BEACON HILL
Llanfair Waterdine
Knucklas Viaduct
Knucklas
The Offa's Dyke Centre
Bwlch-y-sarnau
Llanbister
St Harmon
Gilfach
68
Llangunllo
Llanddewi Ystradenni
Bleddfa
0 1 2 3 4 miles
0 1 2 3 4 5 kilometres
A458
A495
A490
A483
A489
A470
A488
B4393
B4395
B4382
B4392
B4389
B4385
B4390
B4388
B4381
B4386
B4568
B4569
B4368
B4518
B4355
B4356

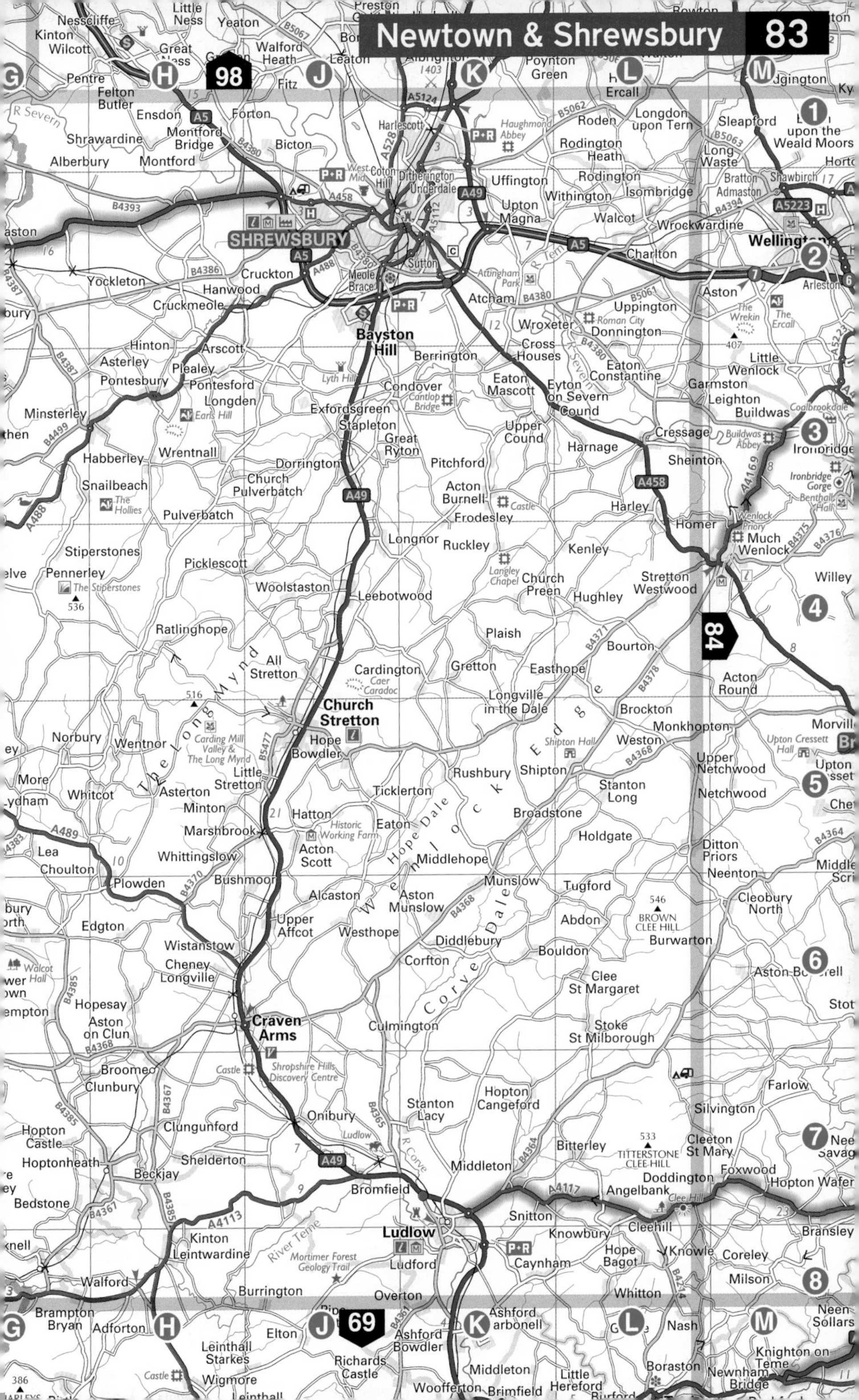
SHREWSBURY
Bayston Hill
Church Stretton
Craven Arms
Ludlow
Wellington
Much Wenlock
Nesscliffe
Kinton
Wilcott
Pentre
Felton Butler
Ensdon
Shrawardine
Alberbury
Montford Bridge
Montford
Forton
Bicton
Yeaton
Walford Heath
Leaton
Fitz
Harlescott
Haughmond Abbey
Ditherington
Underdale
Coton Hill
Uffington
Upton Magna
Withington
Roden
Rodington Heath
Rodington
Isombridge
Walcot
Wrockwardine
Charlton
Longdon upon Tern
Sleapford
Long Waste
Bratton
Admaston
Shawbirch
Yockleton
Cruckton
Hanwood
Cruckmeole
Meole Brace
Sutton
Atcham
Attingham Park
Wroxeter
Roman City
Uppington
Donnington
Aston
The Wrekin
The Ercall
Arleston
Hinton
Arscott
Asterley
Pontesbury
Plealey
Pontesford
Longden
Earls Hill
Minsterley
Lyth Hill
Berrington
Condover
Cantlop Bridge
Exfordsgreen
Stapleton
Great Ryton
Eaton Mascott
Cross Houses
Eaton Constantine
Eyton on Severn
Cound
Upper Cound
Garmston
Leighton
Little Wenlock
Buildwas
Buildwas Abbey
Coalbrookdale
Ironbridge
Ironbridge Gorge
Benthall Hall
Cressage
Sheinton
Harnage
Habberley
Wrentnall
Dorrington
Church Pulverbatch
Pitchford
Snailbeach
The Hollies
Pulverbatch
Acton Burnell
Castle
Frodesley
Harley
Homer
Wenlock Priory
Stiperstones
Pennerley
The Stiperstones
536
Picklescott
Longnor
Ruckley
Kenley
Langley Chapel
Church Preen
Hughley
Stretton Westwood
Willey
Woolstaston
Leebotwood
Ratlinghope
Plaish
Bourton
All Stretton
Cardington
Caer Caradoc
Gretton
Easthope
Acton Round
Longville in the Dale
Brockton
Monkhopton
The Long Mynd
516
Norbury
Wentnor
Carding Mill Valley & The Long Mynd
Hope Bowdler
Shipton Hall
Weston
Upton Cressett Hall
Rushbury
Shipton
Upper Netchwood
Netchwood
More
Whitcot
Asterton
Little Stretton
Minton
Ticklerton
Stanton Long
Broadstone
Wenlock Edge
Hope Dale
Hatton
Historic Working Farm
Eaton
Marshbrook
Holdgate
Ditton Priors
Neenton
Lea
Choulton
Whittingslow
Acton Scott
Middlehope
Plowden
Bushmoor
Munslow
Tugford
Cleobury North
Alcaston
Aston Munslow
546
BROWN CLEE HILL
Burwarton
Edgton
Upper Affcot
Westhope
Abdon
Corve Dale
Diddlebury
Bouldon
Wistanstow
Cheney Longville
Corfton
Clee St Margaret
Walcot Hall
Hopesay
Aston on Clun
Culmington
Stoke St Milborough
Broome
Clunbury
Castle
Shropshire Hills Discovery Centre
Farlow
Hopton Cangeford
Stanton Lacy
Silvington
Onibury
Hopton Castle
Clungunford
Hoptonheath
Shelderton
Beckjay
533
TITTERSTONE CLEE HILL
Bitterley
Cleeton St Mary
Middleton
Doddington
Foxwood
Hopton Wafers
Angelbank
Clee Hill
Bromfield
Bedstone
Snitton
Cleehill
Knowbury
Bransley
Kinton
Leintwardine
River Teme
Mortimer Forest Geology Trail
Caynham
Hope Bagot
Knowle
Coreley
Ludford
Milson
Walford
Burrington
Overton
Whitton
Brampton Bryan
Adforton
Elton
Ashford Carbonell
Ashford Bowdler
Nash
Neen Sollars
Leinthall Starkes
Richards Castle
Middleton
Little Hereford
Boraston
Knighton on Teme
Newnham Bridge
Wigmore
Woofferton
Brimfield
386
98
69
84
A5
A49
A458
A5124
A528
A5112
A488
A489
A4113
A4117
A4169
A5223
B4380
B4386
B4387
B4393
B4499
B4370
B4371
B4368
B4378
B4385
B4367
B4365
B4364
B4368
B4364
B4214
B4361
B4375
B4376
B4394
B5061
B5062
B5063
B5067
B5477
R Severn
R Tern
R Corve

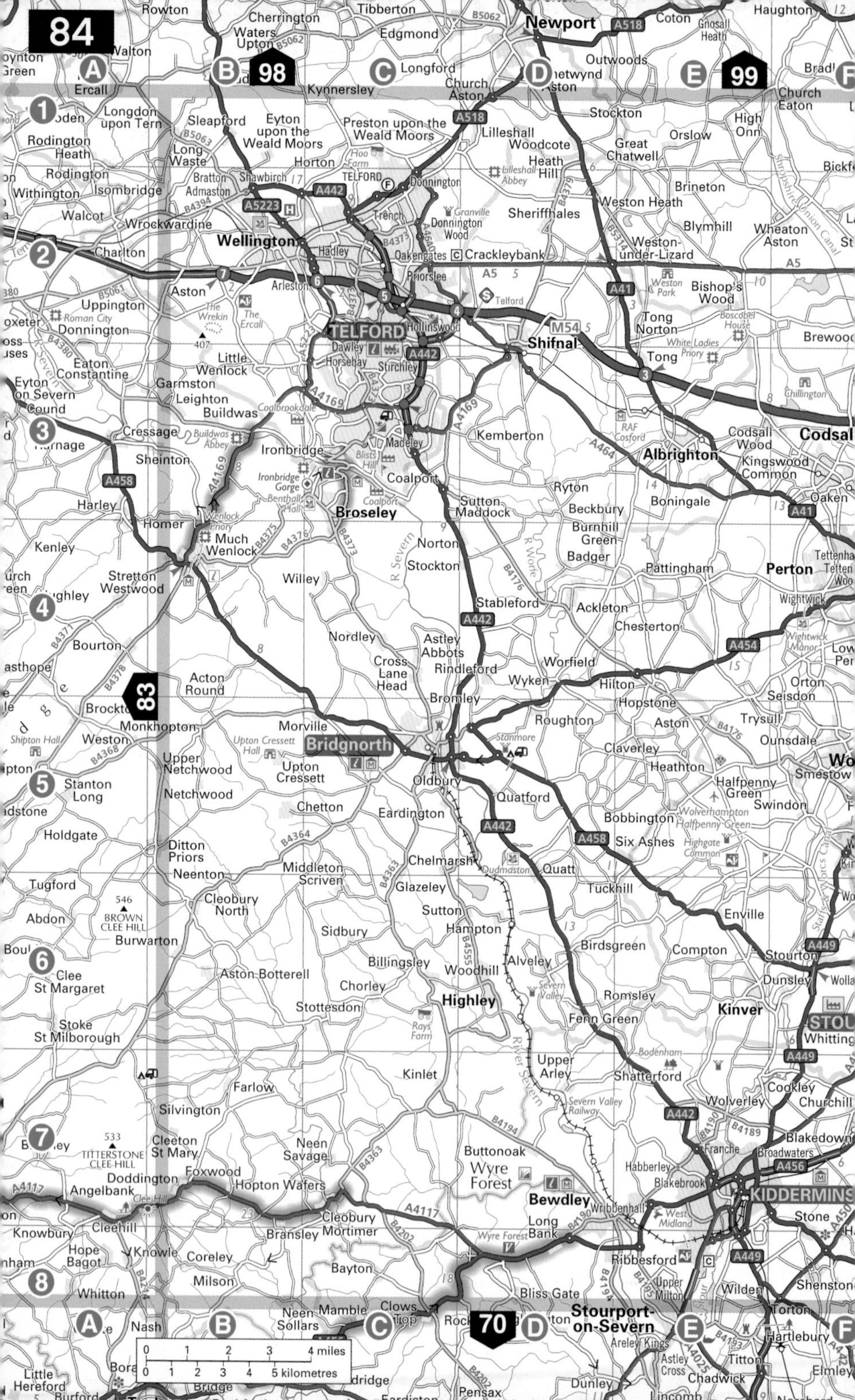

84
98
99
83
70
Rowton
Cherrington
Tibberton
Edgmond
Waters Upton
Walton
Ercall
Newport
Coton
Gnosall Heath
Haughton
Longford
Kynnersley
Church Aston
Chetwynd Aston
Outwoods
Church Eaton
Longdon upon Tern
Rodington Heath
Rodington
Withington
Isombridge
Walcot
Wrockwardine
Sleapford
Eyton upon the Weald Moors
Long Waste
Preston upon the Weald Moors
Horton
Bratton
Admaston
Shawbirch
Hoo Farm
TELFORD
Donnington
Trench
Lilleshall
Woodcote
Lilleshall Abbey
Stockton
Great Chatwell
Orslow
High Onn
Heath Hill
Granville
Donnington Wood
Sheriffhales
Brineton
Weston Heath
Blymhill
Wheaton Aston
Weston-under-Lizard
Shropshire Union Canal
Wellington
Charlton
Hadley
Oakengates
Crackleybank
Priorslee
Aston
Arleston
Uppington
Roman City
Donnington
The Wrekin
407
The Ercall
Telford
Weston Park
Bishop's Wood
Tong Norton
Boscobel House
White Ladies Priory
Tong
Brewood
Shifnal
Hollinswood
Dawley
Horsehay
Stirchley
Eaton Constantine
Eyton on Severn
Little Wenlock
Garmston
Leighton
Buildwas
Coalbrookdale
Cressage
Buildwas Abbey
Sheinton
Ironbridge
Ironbridge Gorge
Madeley
Blists Hill
Coalport
Benthall Hall
Broseley
Kemberton
RAF Cosford
Albrighton
Chillington
Codsall Wood
Codsall
Kingswood Common
Oaken
Ryton
Boningale
Beckbury
Burnhill Green
Badger
Sutton Maddock
Norton
Stockton
R Severn
R Worfe
Pattingham
Perton
Harley
Homer
Wenlock Priory
Much Wenlock
Kenley
Stretton Westwood
Willey
Stableford
Ackleton
Chesterton
Wightwick
Wightwick Manor
Bourton
Nordley
Astley Abbots
Cross Lane Head
Rindleford
Worfield
Wyken
Hilton
Orton
Seisdon
Acton Round
Brockton
Monkhopton
Morville
Bromley
Hopstone
Roughton
Aston
Trysull
Ounsdale
Shipton Hall
Weston
Upton Cressett Hall
Bridgnorth
Stanmore
Claverley
Heathton
Halfpenny Green
Smestow
Upper Netchwood
Netchwood
Upton Cressett
Oldbury
Quatford
Swindon
Stanton Long
Chetton
Eardington
Bobbington
Wolverhampton Halfpenny Green
Holdgate
Six Ashes
Highgate Common
Ditton Priors
Neenton
Middleton Scriven
Chelmarsh
Dudmaston
Quatt
Tuckhill
Tugford
546
BROWN CLEE HILL
Cleobury North
Glazeley
Abdon
Burwarton
Sidbury
Sutton
Hampton
Enville
Birdsgreen
Compton
Stourton
Clee St Margaret
Aston Botterell
Billingsley
Woodhill
Alveley
Severn Valley
Dunsley
Chorley
Highley
Romsley
Kinver
Stottesdon
Rays Farm
Fenn Green
Stoke St Milborough
Whittington
Bodenham
River Severn
Upper Arley
Shatterford
Kinlet
Farlow
Wolverley
Cookley
Churchill
Silvington
Severn Valley Railway
533
TITTERSTONE CLEE HILL
Cleeton St Mary
Neen Savage
Buttonoak
Franche
Blakedown
Wyre Forest
Habberley
Broadwaters
Doddington
Foxwood
Hopton Wafers
Blakebrook
Angelbank
Clee Hill
Bewdley
KIDDERMINSTER
Cleehill
Cleobury Mortimer
Wribbenhall
West Midland
Long Bank
Stone
Knowbury
Hope Bagot
Bransley
Wyre Forest
Knowle
Coreley
Ribbesford
Bayton
Milson
Bliss Gate
Upper Milton
Wilden
Shenstone
Whitton
Clows Top
Stourport-on-Severn
Torton
Nash
Neen Sollars
Mamble
Rock
Hartlebury
Areley Kings
Titton
Astley Cross
Chadwick
Elmley
Little Hereford
Dunley
Pensax
Burford
Lincomb
A518
B5062
A442
A5223
A5
M54
A41
A4169
A458
A464
A454
B4176
B4373
B4375
B4376
B4378
B4371
B4368
B4364
B4363
B4555
B4194
B4190
B4189
A449
A456
A4117
B4202
B4214
B4195
A4025
A450
B5063
B4394
B5061
B4380
B4379
B5314
0 1 2 3 4 miles
0 1 2 3 4 5 kilometres

Rugeley
Lichfield
Hednesford
Heath Hayes & Wimblebury
Cannock
Burntwood
Norton Canes
Great Wyrley
Cheslyn Hay
Brownhills
Pelsall
Aldridge
Walsall
Wednesbury
Royal Sutton Coldfield
West Bromwich
Smethwick
Birmingham
Halesowen
Solihull
Tamworth
Fazeley
Kingsbury
Coleshill
Knowle
Dorridge
Hockley Heath
Alvechurch
Romsley
Balsall Common
Whittington
Streethay
Elford
Shenstone
Hopwas
Edingale
Harlaston
Haunton
Wigginton
Seckington
Drayton Bassett
Middleton
Water Orton
Castle Bromwich
Meriden
Hampton-in-Arden
Shirley
Wythall
Hopwood
Northfield
Edgbaston
Harborne
Oldbury
Tipton
Bilston
Darlaston
Essington
Huntington
Armitage
Longdon
Fradley
Alrewas
Wychnor
Rosliston
Coton in the Elms
Lullington
Clifton Campville
Thorpe Constantine
Comberford
Shuttington
Amington
Kettlebrook
Glascote
Whateley
Marston
Nether Whitacre
Over Whitacre
Shustoke
Maxstoke
Little Packington
Stonebridge
Bickenhill
Elmdon
Eastcote
Barston
Chadwick End
Baddesley Clinton
Wroxall
Rowington
Lapworth
Tanworth in Arden
Beoley
Holt End
Earlswood
Tanner's Green
Portway
Wood End
Lickey End
Barnt Green
Cofton Hackett
Lydiate Ash
Rubery
Longbridge
Frankley
Illey
Hasbury
Wednesfield
Willenhall
Bloxwich
Stonnall
Little Hay
Weeford
Hints
Maney
Wylde Green
Walmley
Curdworth
Wishaw
Erdington
Aston
Ladywood
Moseley
Sparkhill
Yardley
Sheldon
Acock's Green
Olton
Bournville
Selly Oak
Kings Norton
Cotteridge
Walker's Heath
Major's Green
Blackheath
Cradley
Rowley Regis
Coseley
Bradley
M6 Toll
M6
M5
M42
M40
A38(M)

100
85
72
Swadlincote
Ashby-de-la-Zouch
Coalville
Whitwick
Donisthorpe
Measham
Ibstock
TAMWORTH
Polesworth
Dordon
Fazeley
Atherstone
Kingsbury
Baddesley Ensor
Hartshill
NUNEATON
Hinckley
Bedworth
Coleshill
COVENTRY
Kenilworth
Knowle
Dorridge
Balsall Common
Barwell
Earl Shilton
Market Bosworth
0 1 2 3 4 miles
0 1 2 3 4 5 kilometres

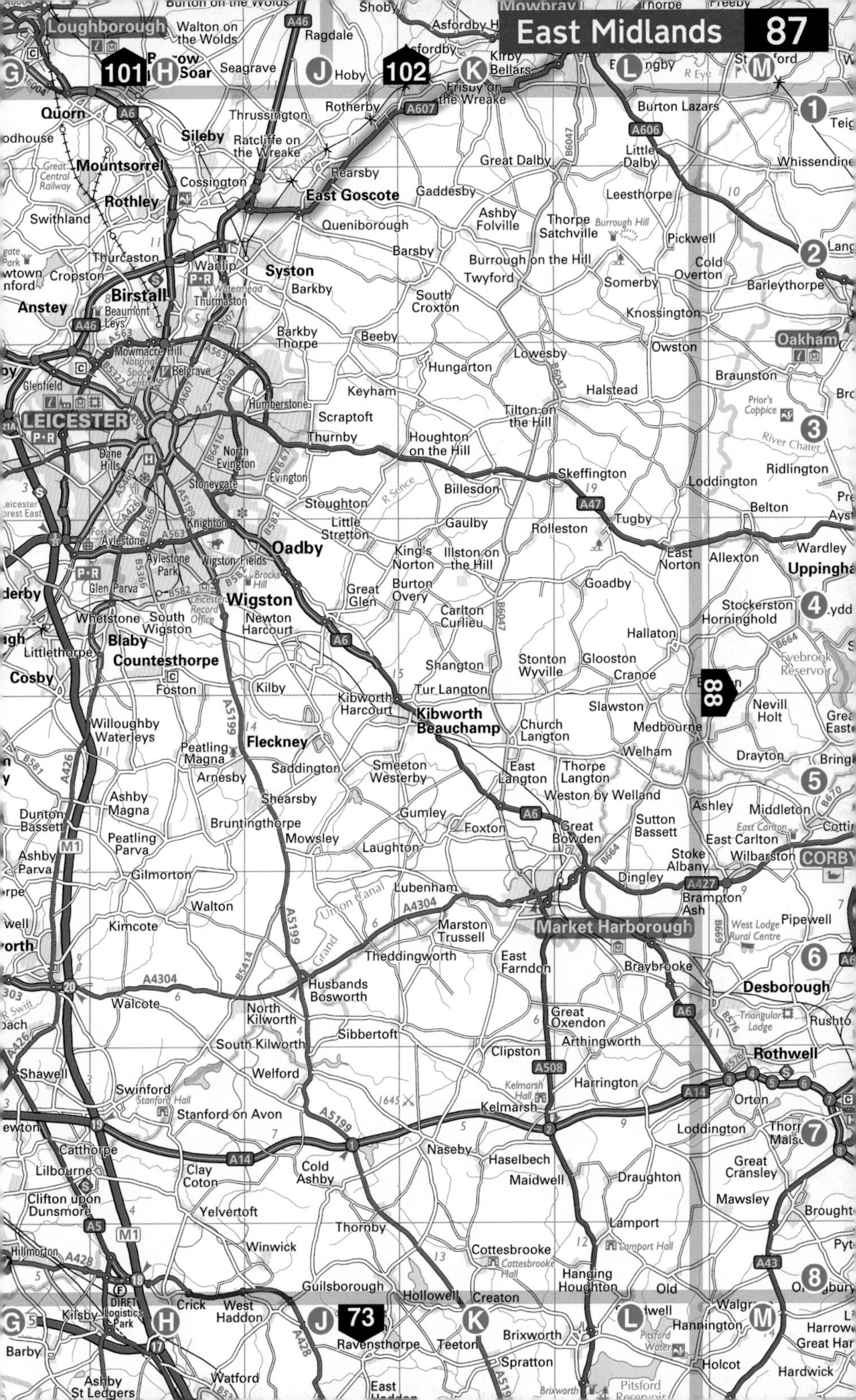
Loughborough
Walton on the Wolds
Ragdale
Shoby
Asfordby
Kirby Bellars
Frisby on the Wreake
101
102
88
73
Seagrave
Hoby
Quorn
Thrussington
Rotherby
Burton Lazars
Sileby
Ratcliffe on the Wreake
Mountsorrel
Great Central Railway
Cossington
Rearsby
East Goscote
Gaddesby
Great Dalby
Little Dalby
Whissendine
Rothley
Leesthorpe
Swithland
Queniborough
Ashby Folville
Thorpe Satchville
Burrough Hill
Pickwell
Thurcaston
Barsby
Burrough on the Hill
Cold Overton
Barleythorpe
Cropston
Wanlip
Syston
Twyford
Somerby
Birstall
Watermead
Thurmaston
Barkby
South Croxton
Knossington
Anstey
Beaumont Leys
Barkby Thorpe
Beeby
Owston
Oakham
Mowmacre Hill
National Space Centre
Belgrave
Lowesby
Hungarton
Braunston
Glenfield
Keyham
Halstead
LEICESTER
Humberstone
Scraptoft
Tilton on the Hill
Prior's Coppice
Thurnby
Houghton on the Hill
River Chater
Dane Hills
North Evington
Evington
Skeffington
Ridlington
Loddington
Stoneygate
Billesdon
R Sence
Stoughton
Little Stretton
Gaulby
Rolleston
Tugby
Belton
Knighton
Aylestone
Aylestone Park
Wigston Fields
Brocks Hill
Oadby
King's Norton
Illston on the Hill
East Norton
Allexton
Wardley
Uppingham
Glen Parva
Wigston
Great Glen
Burton Overy
Goadby
Leicester Record Office
Whetstone
South Wigston
Newton Harcourt
Carlton Curlieu
Stockerston
Horninghold
Blaby
Littlethorpe
Hallaton
Countesthorpe
Cosby
Foston
Kilby
Shangton
Stonton Wyville
Glooston
Cranoe
Eyebrook Reservoir
Kibworth Harcourt
Tur Langton
Kibworth Beauchamp
Slawston
Nevill Holt
Willoughby Waterleys
Church Langton
Medbourne
Peatling Magna
Fleckney
Welham
Drayton
Arnesby
Saddington
Smeeton Westerby
East Langton
Thorpe Langton
Weston by Welland
Ashby Magna
Shearsby
Ashley
Middleton
Dunton Bassett
Bruntingthorpe
Gumley
Foxton
Great Bowden
Sutton Bassett
East Carlton
Peatling Parva
Mowsley
Laughton
Stoke Albany
Wilbarston
CORBY
Ashby Parva
Gilmorton
Lubenham
Dingley
Brampton Ash
Union Canal
Walton
Marston Trussell
Market Harborough
West Lodge Rural Centre
Pipewell
Kimcote
Theddingworth
East Farndon
Braybrooke
Desborough
Walcote
Husbands Bosworth
Grand
North Kilworth
Great Oxendon
Triangular Lodge
Rushton
South Kilworth
Sibbertoft
Arthingworth
Clipston
Rothwell
Shawell
Welford
Harrington
Swinford
Stanford Hall
Kelmarsh Hall
Orton
Stanford on Avon
Kelmarsh
Loddington
Catthorpe
Naseby
Lilbourne
Clay Coton
Cold Ashby
Haselbech
Great Cransley
Clifton upon Dunsmore
Maidwell
Draughton
Yelvertoft
Mawsley
Thornby
Lamport
Winwick
Lamport Hall
Hillmorton
Cottesbrooke
Cottesbrooke Hall
DIRFT Logistics Park
Guilsborough
Hanging Houghton
Old
Crick
West Haddon
Hollowell
Creaton
Kilsby
Hannington
Harrowden
Brixworth
Pitsford Water
Great Harrowden
Barby
Ravensthorpe
Teeton
Spratton
Holcot
Hardwick
Ashby St Ledgers
Watford
East Haddon
Pitsford Reservoir

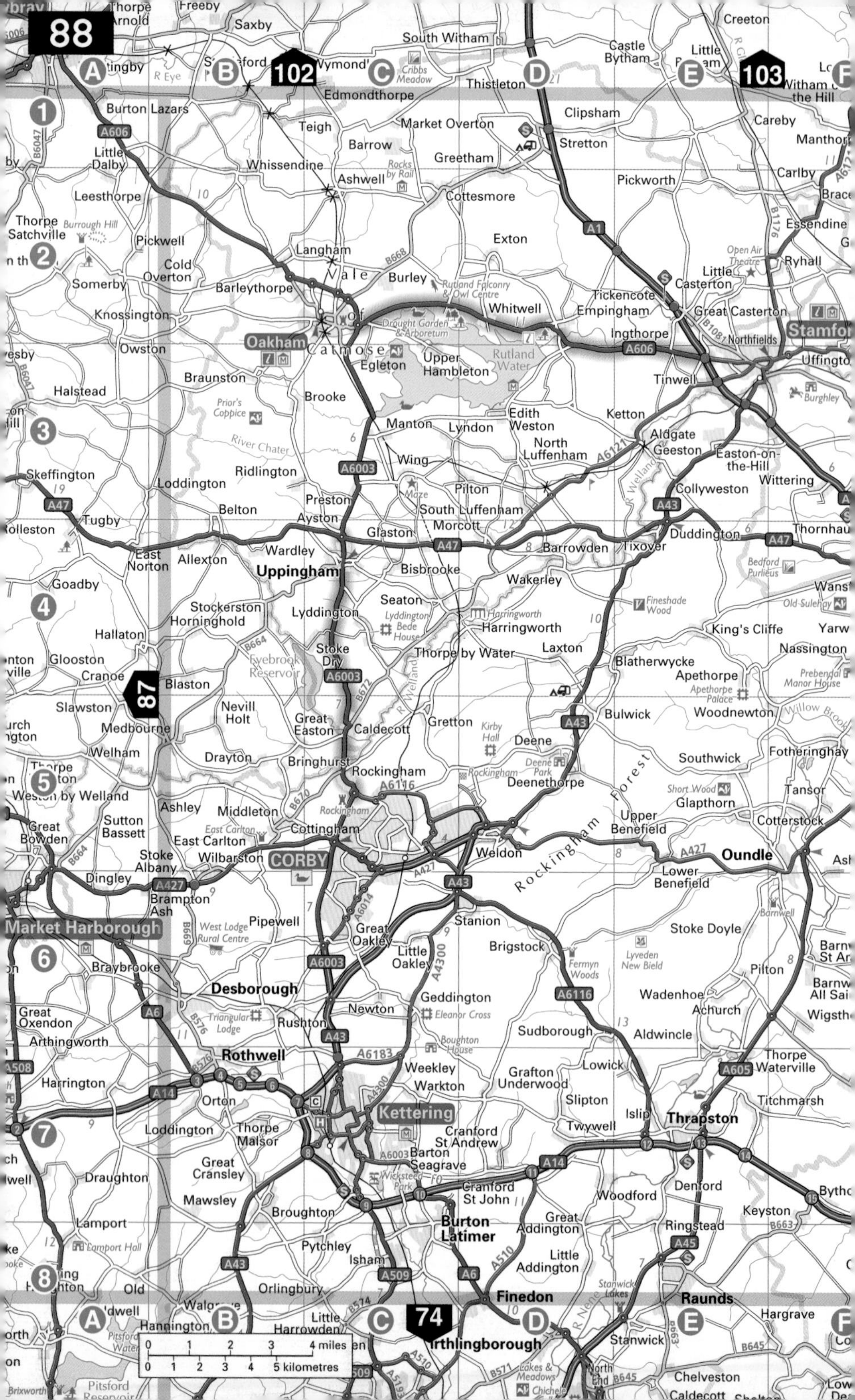
88
Thorpe Arnold
Freeby
Saxby
South Witham
Castle Bytham
Creeton
Little Bytham
Stapleford
102
Wymondham
Cribbs Meadow
103
Witham on the Hill
R Eye
Edmondthorpe
Thistleton
Burton Lazars
Clipsham
Careby
Teigh
Market Overton
Stretton
Manthorpe
A606
B6047
Barrow
Greetham
Little Dalby
Whissendine
Ashwell
Rocks by Rail
Pickworth
Carlby
Leesthorpe
Cottesmore
Braceborough
B1176
Thorpe Satchville
Burrough Hill
Essendine
A1
Exton
Pickwell
Langham
Open Air Theatre
Ryhall
Cold Overton
B668
Vale
Burley
Little Casterton
Somerby
Rutland Falconry & Owl Centre
Barleythorpe
Tickencote
Knossington
Whitwell
Empingham
Great Casterton
Drought Garden & Arboretum
B1081
Northfields
Stamford
Oakham
Catmose
Owston
Ingthorpe
A606
Uffington
Egleton
Upper Hambleton
Rutland Water
Braunston
Tinwell
Halstead
Burghley
Brooke
Prior's Coppice
Edith Weston
Ketton
Manton
Lyndon
Aldgate
River Chater
North Luffenham
A6121
Geeston
Easton-on-the-Hill
Skeffington
Wing
Ridlington
A6003
Wittering
R Welland
Loddington
Pilton
Collyweston
Maze
A47
Preston
South Luffenham
Tugby
Belton
A43
Thornhaugh
Rolleston
Ayston
Morcott
Glaston
Duddington
East Norton
Allexton
Wardley
A47
Barrowden
Tixover
Bedford Purlieus
Goadby
Uppingham
Bisbrooke
Wakerley
Wansford
Fineshade Wood
Old Sulehay
Seaton
Stockerston
Lyddington
Horninghold
Harringworth
Lyddington Bede House
King's Cliffe
Yarwell
Hallaton
B664
Thorpe by Water
Laxton
Nassington
Stoke Dry
Eyebrook Reservoir
Glooston
Blatherwycke
Cranoe
A6003
Apethorpe
Prebendal Manor House
87
Blaston
B672
Apethorpe Palace
Slawston
Nevill Holt
Great Easton
Gretton
Bulwick
Woodnewton
Willow Brook
Medbourne
Caldecott
A43
Kirby Hall
Welham
Deene
Drayton
Southwick
Fotheringhay
Thorpe Langton
Bringhurst
Rockingham
Deene Park
Rockingham
Weston by Welland
Deenethorpe
Short Wood
Tansor
A6116
Glapthorn
B670
Rockingham Forest
Ashley
Middleton
Upper Benefield
Cotterstock
Great Bowden
Sutton Bassett
East Carlton
Cottingham
East Carlton
A427
Oundle
Stoke Albany
Wilbarston
CORBY
Weldon
B664
Lower Benefield
Dingley
A427
A43
Brampton Ash
A6014
Stanion
Barnwell
Market Harborough
West Lodge Rural Centre
Pipewell
Great Oakley
Stoke Doyle
B669
Little Oakley
Brigstock
Barnwell St Andrew
Braybrooke
Lyveden New Bield
A6003
Fermyn Woods
Pilton
A4300
Barnwell All Saints
Desborough
Geddington
A6116
Wadenhoe
Great Oxendon
Newton
Achurch
Wigsthorpe
A6
Triangular Lodge
Eleanor Cross
B576
Rushton
Aldwincle
Arthingworth
Sudborough
A43
Boughton House
Thorpe Waterville
Rothwell
A6183
A508
Weekley
Lowick
Grafton Underwood
Harrington
Warkton
A605
A14
Orton
Slipton
Titchmarsh
Kettering
Islip
Thrapston
Loddington
Thorpe Malsor
Cranford St Andrew
Twywell
Barton Seagrave
A6003
Great Cransley
A14
Denford
Draughton
Wicksteed Park
Cranford St John
Woodford
Bythorn
Mawsley
Broughton
Keyston
Burton Latimer
Great Addington
Ringstead
B663
Lamport
Lamport Hall
Pytchley
A45
Little Addington
Isham
A43
A509
A6
A510
Old
Orlingbury
Finedon
Stanwick Lakes
Raunds
Walgrave
B574
74
Hargrave
Hannington
Little Harrowden
R Nene
Pitsford Water
Irthlingborough
Stanwick
B663
B645
A510
A509
B571
Lakes & Meadows
North End
B645
Chelveston
Pitsford Reservoir
Brixworth
Chichele
Caldecott
0 1 2 3 4 miles
0 1 2 3 4 5 kilometres
A B C D E F
1 2 3 4 5 6 7 8

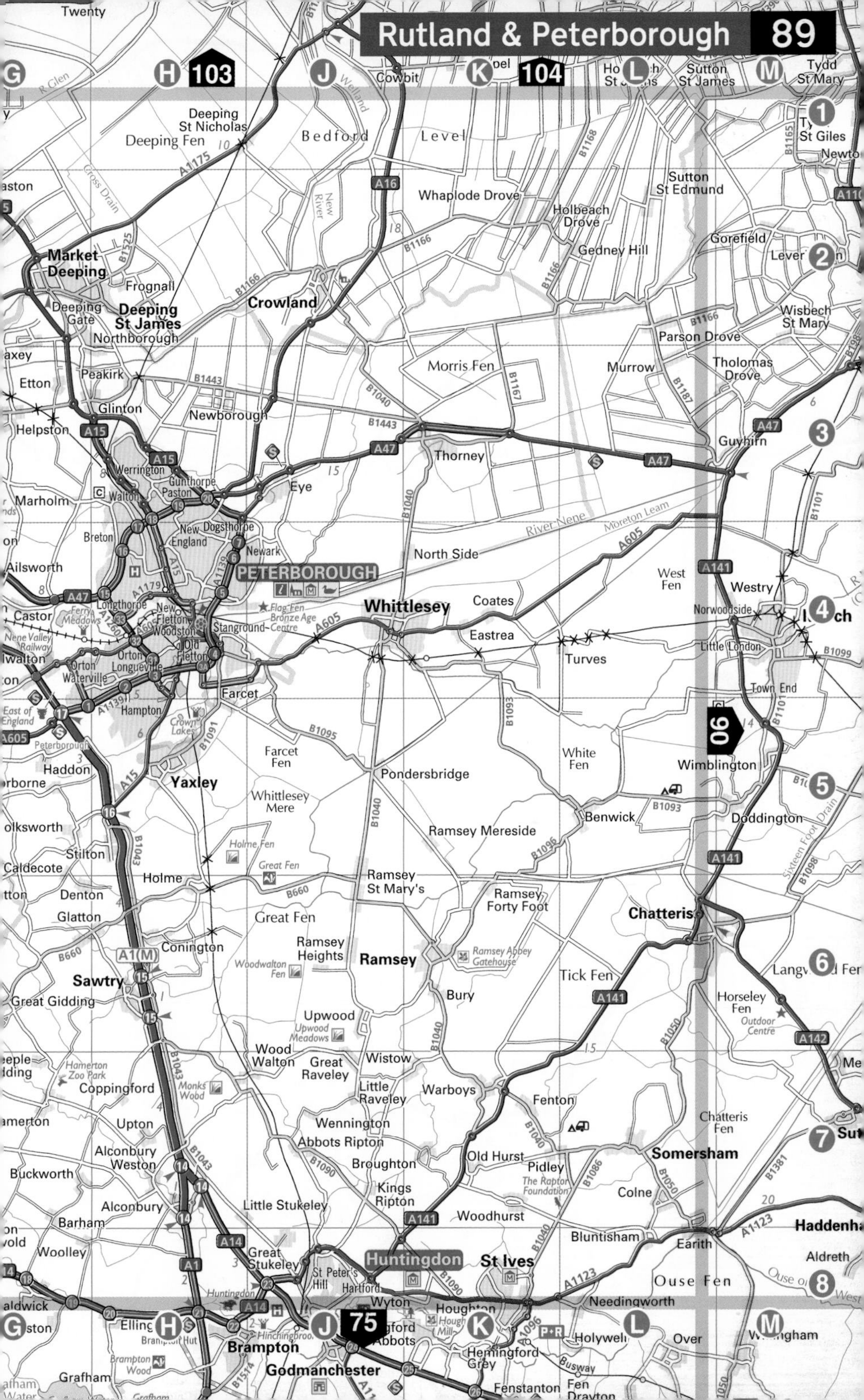
Market Deeping
Deeping St James
Crowland
Peterborough
Whittlesey
Yaxley
Sawtry
Ramsey
Chatteris
Somersham
Huntingdon
St Ives
Brampton
Godmanchester
Thorney
Eye
Wimblington
Doddington
Warboys
Haddenham

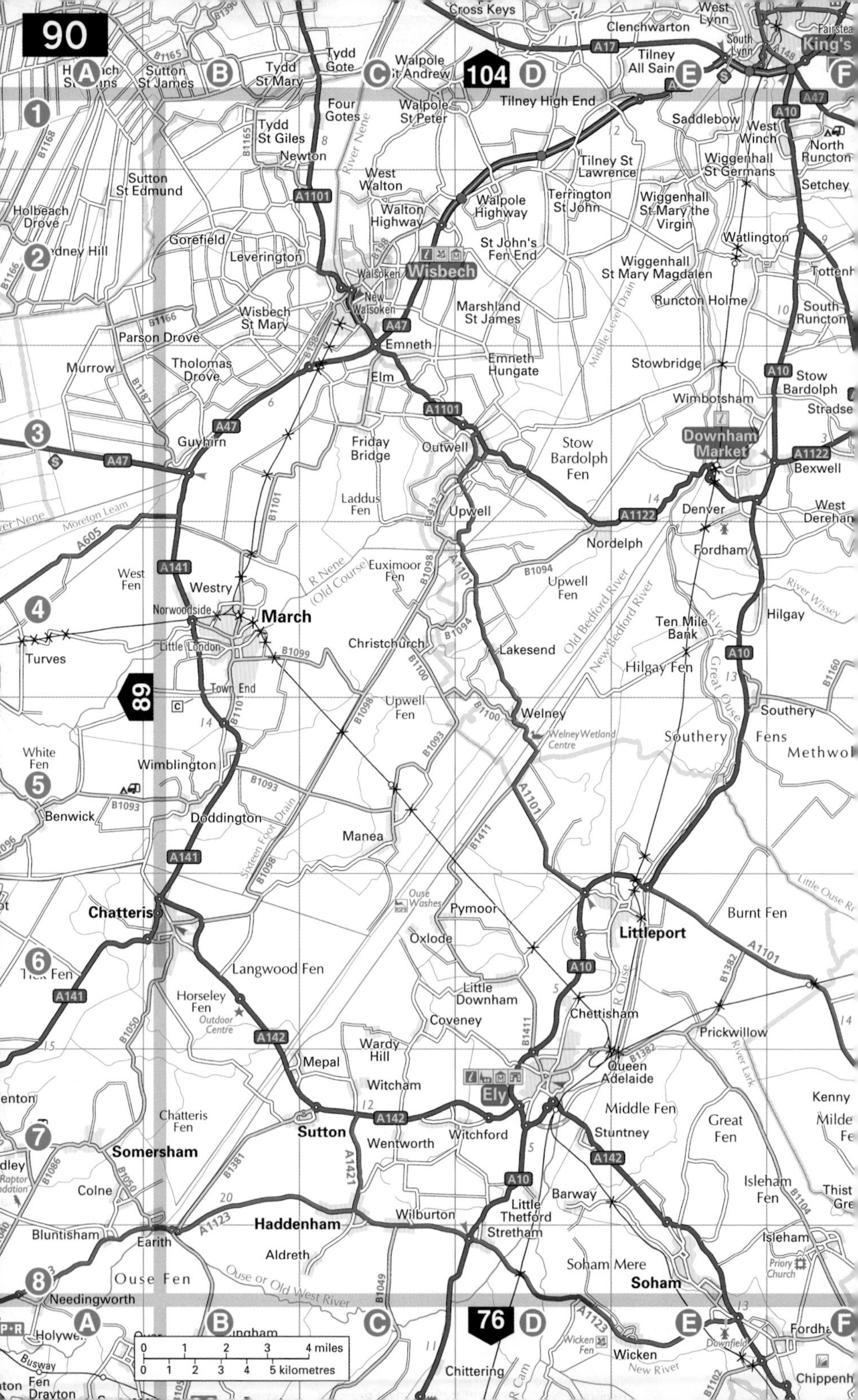

Cross Keys
West Lynn
Clenchwarton
King's
South Lynn
Tilney All Saints
Tydd Gote
Tydd St Mary
Walpole St Andrew
104
Sutton St James
Four Gotes
Walpole St Peter
Tilney High End
Saddlebow
West Winch
North Runcton
Tydd St Giles
Newton
Tilney St Lawrence
Wiggenhall St Germans
Setchey
Sutton St Edmund
West Walton
Walpole Highway
Terrington St John
Wiggenhall St Mary the Virgin
Holbeach Drove
Walton Highway
Watlington
Gorefield
Leverington
St John's Fen End
Wisbech
Wiggenhall St Mary Magdalen
Walsoken
New Walsoken
Runcton Holme
South Runcton
Wisbech St Mary
Marshland St James
Parson Drove
Emneth
Murrow
Tholomas Drove
Emneth Hungate
Stowbridge
Stow Bardolph
Elm
Wimbotsham
Guyhirn
Friday Bridge
Outwell
Stow Bardolph Fen
Downham Market
Bexwell
Laddus Fen
Upwell
Denver
West Dereham
Moreton Leam
Nordelph
Fordham
West Fen
Euximoor Fen
R Nene (Old Course)
Upwell Fen
Westry
Norwoodside
March
Hilgay
Ten Mile Bank
Turves
Little London
Christchurch
Lakesend
Old Bedford River
New Bedford River
Hilgay Fen
River Great Ouse
River Wissey
89
Town End
Upwell Fen
Welney
Southery
Welney Wetland Centre
Southery Fens
White Fen
Wimblington
Methwold
Benwick
Doddington
Manea
Sixteen Foot Drain
Ouse Washes
Pymoor
Chatteris
Littleport
Burnt Fen
Little Ouse River
Oxlode
Langwood Fen
Tick Fen
Little Downham
Horseley Fen
Outdoor Centre
Coveney
Chettisham
Prickwillow
River Lark
Wardy Hill
Mepal
Queen Adelaide
Witcham
Ely
Kenny
Middle Fen
Great Fen
Chatteris Fen
Sutton
Witchford
Stuntney
Somersham
Wentworth
Isleham Fen
Raptor Foundation
Colne
Barway
Haddenham
Wilburton
Little Thetford
Stretham
Bluntisham
Earith
Aldreth
Isleham
Priory Church
Soham Mere
Ouse Fen
Ouse or Old West River
Soham
Needingworth
76
Holywell
Downfield
Wicken Fen
Wicken
New River
Busway
Fen Drayton
Chittering
R Cam
Chippenham
A17 A47 A10 A1101 A148 A1122 A141 A605 A142 A1421 A1123
B1165 B1168 B1166 B1187 B198 B1101 B1098 B1094 B1099 B1100 B1093 B1411 B1050 B1381 B1086 B1049 B1382 B1104 B1102 B1160
0 1 2 3 4 miles
0 1 2 3 4 5 kilometres

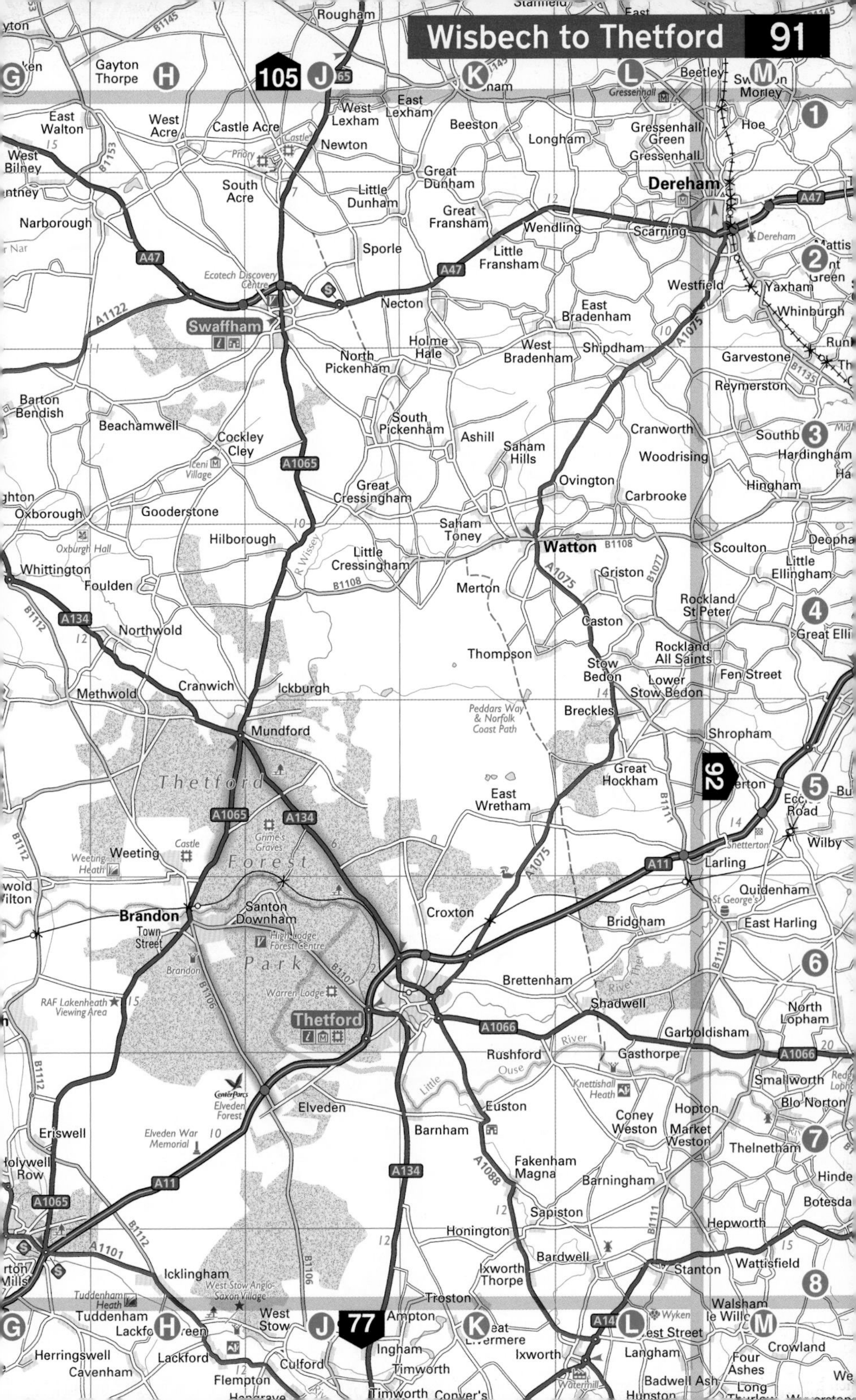
Rougham
Gayton Thorpe
East Walton
West Acre
Castle Acre
West Lexham
East Lexham
Newton
Beeston
Longham
Gressenhall Green
Gressenhall
Beetley
Hoe
West Bilney
Narborough
South Acre
Little Dunham
Great Dunham
Great Fransham
Dereham
Wendling
Scarning
Sporle
Little Fransham
Swaffham
Necton
Westfield
Yaxham
Whinburgh
East Bradenham
Holme Hale
West Bradenham
Shipdham
North Pickenham
Garvestone
Reymerston
Barton Bendish
Beachamwell
South Pickenham
Ashill
Cockley Cley
Saham Hills
Cranworth
Woodrising
Hardingham
Ovington
Hingham
Great Cressingham
Carbrooke
Oxborough
Gooderstone
Hilborough
Saham Toney
Watton
Scoulton
Little Cressingham
Whittington
Foulden
Merton
Griston
Little Ellingham
Rockland St Peter
Northwold
Caston
Thompson
Rockland All Saints
Methwold
Cranwich
Ickburgh
Stow Bedon
Lower Stow Bedon
Fen Street
Mundford
Breckles
Peddars Way & Norfolk Coast Path
Shropham
Thetford Forest Park
Great Hockham
East Wretham
Weeting
Grime's Graves
Larling
Wilby
Quidenham
Brandon
Santon Downham
Croxton
Bridgham
East Harling
Town Street
High Lodge Forest Centre
Brettenham
RAF Lakenheath Viewing Area
Warren Lodge
Shadwell
North Lopham
Thetford
Garboldisham
Rushford
Gasthorpe
Smallworth
Knettishall Heath
Blo Norton
Elveden
Euston
Hopton
Coney Weston
Market Weston
Thelnetham
Eriswell
Elveden War Memorial
Barnham
Fakenham Magna
Barningham
Sapiston
Botesdale
Honington
Hepworth
Bardwell
Icklingham
Ixworth Thorpe
Stanton
Wattisfield
West Stow Anglo-Saxon Village
Troston
Walsham
Tuddenham
West Stow
Ampton
Ixworth
Langham
Crowland
Herringswell
Lackford
Ingham
Four Ashes
Cavenham
Culford
Timworth
Badwell Ash
Flempton
A47
A1065
A134
A1075
A11
A1066
A1088
A1101
B1108
B1106
B1107
B1112
B1111
105
77
92

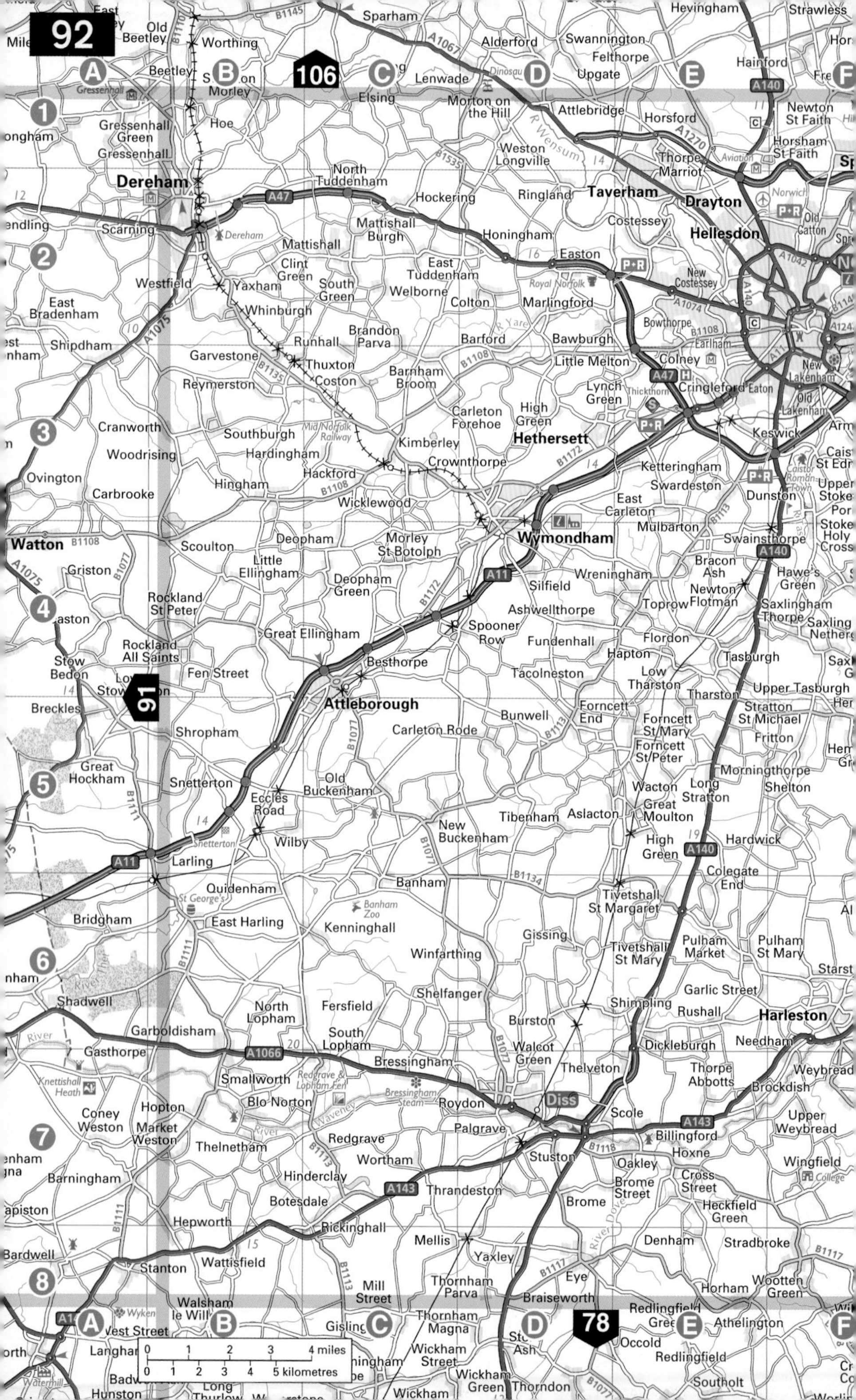
106
91
78
Dereham
Wymondham
Attleborough
Taverham
Drayton
Hellesdon
Hethersett
Watton
Harleston
Diss
Sparham
Alderford
Swannington
Felthorpe
Hevingham
Strawless
Hainford
Lenwade
Elsing
Morton on the Hill
Attlebridge
Horsford
Newton St Faith
Horsham St Faith
Worthing
Beetley
Old Beetley
Hoe
Gressenhall
Gressenhall Green
Scarning
Westfield
Yaxham
Whinburgh
Shipdham
East Bradenham
Garvestone
Reymerston
Thuxton
Runhall
Coston
Cranworth
Woodrising
Southburgh
Hardingham
Hackford
Hingham
Ovington
Carbrooke
Scoulton
Griston
North Tuddenham
Mattishall
Mattishall Burgh
Clint Green
South Green
East Tuddenham
Welborne
Brandon Parva
Barnham Broom
Hockering
Ringland
Weston Longville
Honingham
Easton
Costessey
New Costessey
Colton
Marlingford
Barford
Bawburgh
Little Melton
Colney
Cringleford
Eaton
Lynch Green
Carleton Forehoe
High Green
Kimberley
Crownthorpe
Wicklewood
Deopham
Morley St Botolph
Little Ellingham
Deopham Green
Rockland St Peter
Rockland All Saints
Great Ellingham
Besthorpe
Spooner Row
Silfield
Ashwellthorpe
Wreningham
Fundenhall
Tacolneston
Bunwell
Carleton Rode
Shropham
Snetterton
Eccles Road
Wilby
Old Buckenham
New Buckenham
Larling
Quidenham
East Harling
Bridgham
Banham
Kenninghall
Winfarthing
Shelfanger
North Lopham
South Lopham
Fersfield
Garboldisham
Gasthorpe
Shadwell
Great Hockham
Breckles
Stow Bedon
Smallworth
Blo Norton
Bressingham
Roydon
Palgrave
Redgrave
Wortham
Hinderclay
Thelnetham
Hopton
Coney Weston
Market Weston
Barningham
Hepworth
Botesdale
Rickinghall
Thrandeston
Mellis
Yaxley
Stanton
Wattisfield
Bardwell
Walsham le Willows
Mill Street
Thornham Parva
Thornham Magna
Wickham Street
Wickham Green
Thorndon
Gislingham
Braiseworth
Eye
Stuston
Scole
Billingford
Oakley
Hoxne
Brome
Brome Street
Cross Street
Heckfield Green
Denham
Stradbroke
Horham
Redlingfield
Redlingfield Green
Athelington
Occold
Southolt
Wingfield
Upper Weybread
Weybread
Brockdish
Thorpe Abbotts
Needham
Dickleburgh
Rushall
Shimpling
Burston
Walcot Green
Thelveton
Gissing
Tivetshall St Mary
Tivetshall St Margaret
Pulham Market
Pulham St Mary
Garlic Street
Colegate End
Hardwick
High Green
Great Moulton
Wacton
Aslacton
Tibenham
Long Stratton
Morningthorpe
Shelton
Fritton
Stratton St Michael
Upper Tasburgh
Tasburgh
Forncett End
Forncett St Mary
Forncett St Peter
Low Tharston
Tharston
Hapton
Flordon
Toprow
Newton Flotman
Bracon Ash
Mulbarton
East Carleton
Swardeston
Ketteringham
Keswick
Dunston
Swainsthorpe
Saxlingham Thorpe
Hawe's Green
A47
A11
A140
A1067
A1075
A1066
A143
A1270
A1074
B1145
B1110
B1135
B1108
B1172
B1113
B1077
B1111
B1134
B1118
B1117
R Wensum
R Yare
River Waveney
Mid Norfolk Railway
Banham Zoo
Bressingham Steam
Redgrave & Lopham Fen
Knettishall Heath
Snetterton
Royal Norfolk
Dinosaur
Norwich
P+R
0 1 2 3 4 miles
0 1 2 3 4 5 kilometres

107
79
Hemsby
Ormesby Broad
Ormesby St Michael
Scratby
California
Caister-on-Sea
Rollesby
Fleggburgh/Burgh St Margaret
Ormesby St Margaret
Filby
Mautby
Thrigby
West End
West Caister
Acle
Stokesby
Runham
Stracey Arms Windpump
Damgate
Tunstall
THE BROADS
River Yare
Elizabethan House
GREAT YARMOUTH
Southtown
Burgh Castle
Gorleston on Sea
East Port
Bradwell
Belton
Wickhampton
Berney Marshes
Berney Arms Windmill
Halvergate
Freethorpe
Freethorpe Common
Reedham
Pettitts Animal Adventure Park
Fritton
Fritton Lake
St Olave's Priory
St Olaves
Lound
Hopton on Sea
Corton
Herringfleet
Somerleyton Hall & Gardens
Blundeston
Somerleyton
Pleasurewood Hills
Oulton
Oulton Broad
Lowestoft Ness
LOWESTOFT
Kirkley
Pakefield
Carlton Colville
Gisleham
Kessingland
Black Street
Africa Alive!
Benacre
Benacre Ness
Wrentham
Covehithe
South Cove
Suffolk Heritage Coast
Sole Bay
Southwold
Walberswick
Wangford
Hen Reedbeds
Blythburgh
Wenhaston
Blyford
Holton
Halesworth
Beccles
Worlingham
North Cove
Barnby
Mutford
Rushmere
Hulver Street
Henstead
Sotterley
Shadingfield
Stoven
Brampton
Uggeshall
Westhall
Redisham
Ringsfield Corner
Ringsfield
Barsham
Ilketshall St Andrew
Ilketshall St Margaret
Mettingham
Shipmeadow
Geldeston
Broome
Gillingham
Aldeby
Wheatacre
Burgh St Peter
Toft Monks
River Waveney
Haddiscoe
Thurlton
Norton Subcourse
Hales
Raveningham
Maypole Green
Stockton
Kirby Cane
Ellingham
Bungay
Earsham
Ditchingham
Hedenham
Thwaite St Mary
Loddon
Chedgrave
Mundham
Seething
Thurton
Hardley Street
Langley Street
Carleton St Peter
Claxton
Cantley
Limpenhoe
Rockland St Mary
Hassingham
Buckenham
Strumpshaw
Brundall
Surlingham
Ashby St Mary
Bergh Apton
Lingwood
Blofield
Blofield Heath
Witton
Beighton
Moulton St Mary
South Burlingham
North Burlingham
Upton
South Walsham
Cargate Green
Pilson Green
Ranworth
Panxworth
Salhouse
Woodbastwick
Horning
Upper Street
Hoveton
Irstead
Ludham
Potter Heigham
Martham
Repps
Thurne
Clippesby
Billockby
Bure Marshes
Broads Wildlife Centre
Ranworth Broad
Fairhaven
BeWILDerwood
RAF Air Defence Radar
Flixton
St Margaret South Elmham
Stone Street
Rumburgh
St James South Elmham
Spexhall
Wissett
Chediston
Linstead Parva
Cookley
Cratfield
Huntingfield
Walpole
Blackheath
Thorington
Bramfield
Heveningham
Ubbeston Green
Darsham
Dunwich Forest
Dunwich
Westleton Heath
Westleton
Sibton
Peasenhall
Yoxford

Aberffraw Bay Heritage Coast
CAERNARFON BAY
Lleyn Heritage Coast
Trwyn y Grolech
Carreg Ddu
Porth Nefyn
Morfa Nefyn
Nefyn
Pistyll
B4417
Edern
Bodfuan
A497
Porth Ysgaden
Tudweiliog
LLEYN
Dinas
Carn Fadrun
371
B4415
Rhyd-y-clafdy
Porth Colman
Llaniestyn
Pen-y-graig
Llangwnnadl
Sarn Meyllteyrn
Bryn-mawr
Botwnnog
Llanbedrog
B4413
Bryncroes
Porthoer
Rhoshirwaun
Plas yn Rhiw
St Tudwal's Road
Llangian
Abersoch
Y Rhiw
Llanengan
Aberdaron
Llanfaelrhys
Porth Neigwl or Hell's Mouth
Porth Ysgo
Bwlchtocyn
Marchros
Aberdaron Bay
Bardsey Sound
Porth Geiriad
Lleyn Heritage Coast
St Mary's
Ynys Enlli
BARDSEY ISLAND
0 1 2 3 4 miles
0 1 2 3 4 5 kilometres

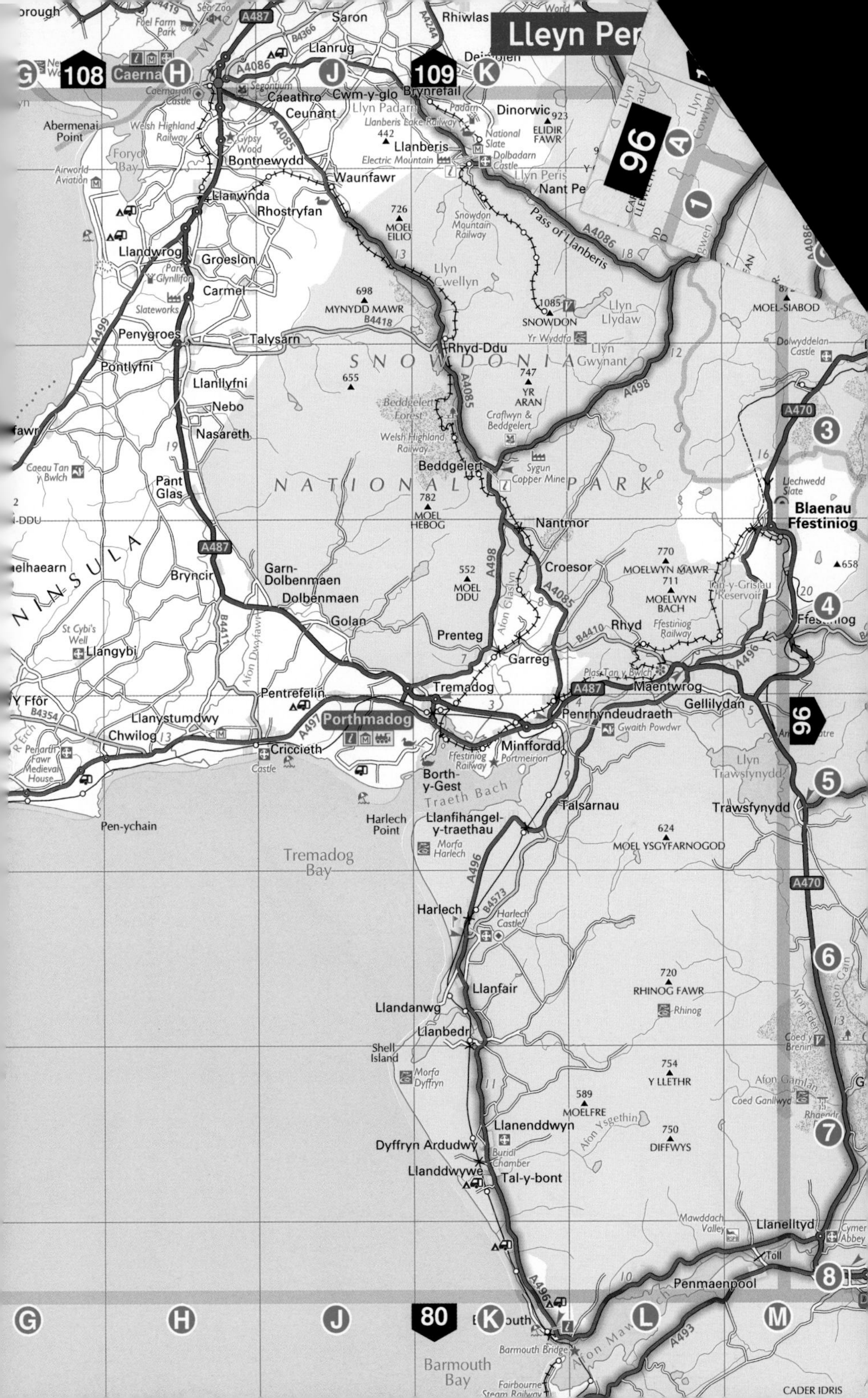

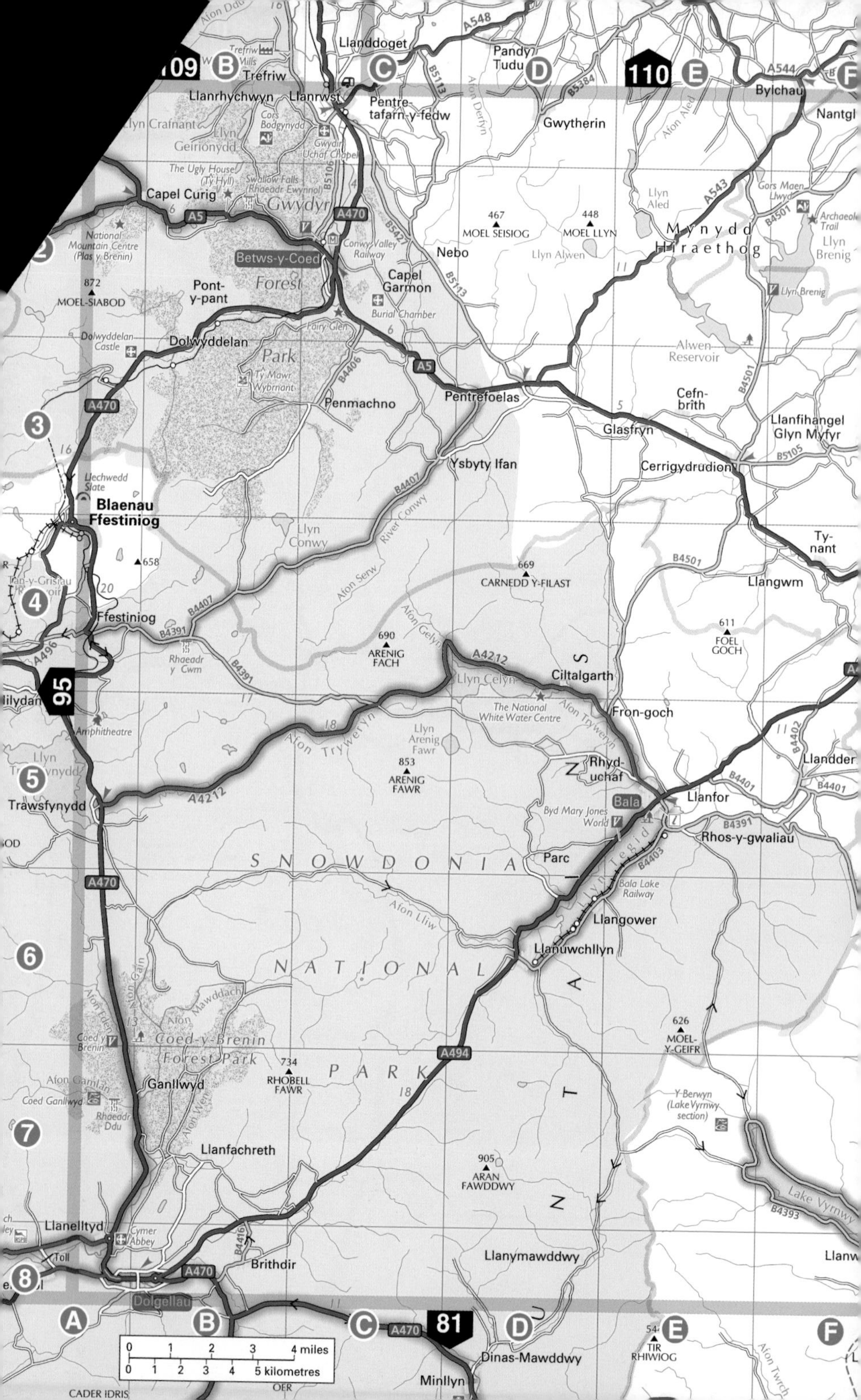

109
110
95
81
Llanddoget
Pandy Tudu
Trefriw
Llanrhychwyn
Llanrwst
Pentre-tafarn-y-fedw
Gwytherin
Bylchau
Llyn Crafnant
Llyn Geirionydd
Cors Bodgynydd
Gwydir Uchaf Chapel
The Ugly House (Ty Hyll)
Swallow Falls (Rhaeadr Ewynnol)
Capel Curig
Gwydyr
Forest
Park
National Mountain Centre (Plas y Brenin)
Betws-y-Coed
Conwy Valley Railway
Capel Garmon
Burial Chamber
Nebo
MOEL SEISIOG
MOEL LLYN
Llyn Alwen
Llyn Aled
Mynydd Hiraethog
Gors Maen Llwyd
Archaeological Trail
Llyn Brenig
MOEL-SIABOD
Pont-y-pant
Dolwyddelan
Dolwyddelan Castle
Fairy Glen
Ty Mawr Wybrnant
Penmachno
Pentrefoelas
Alwen Reservoir
Cefn-brîth
Glasfryn
Llanfihangel Glyn Myfyr
Cerrigydrudion
Ysbyty Ifan
Llechwedd Slate
Blaenau Ffestiniog
Llyn Conwy
River Conwy
Afon Serw
Tan-y-Grisiau Reservoir
Ffestiniog
Rhaeadr y Cwm
CARNEDD Y-FILAST
ARENIG FACH
Afon Gelyn
Ty-nant
Llangwm
FOEL GOCH
Llyn Celyn
Ciltalgarth
The National White Water Centre
Fron-goch
Afon Tryweryn
Llyn Arenig Fawr
ARENIG FAWR
Amphitheatre
Llyn Trawsfynydd
Trawsfynydd
Rhyd-uchaf
Bala
Llanfor
Llandderfel
Byd Mary Jones World
Rhos-y-gwaliau
Parc
SNOWDONIA NATIONAL PARK
Llyn Tegid
Bala Lake Railway
Afon Lliw
Llangower
Llanuwchllyn
Afon Gain
Afon Mawddach
Afon Eden
Coed y Brenin
Coed-y-Brenin Forest Park
MOEL-Y-GEIFR
RHOBELL FAWR
Ganllwyd
Afon Gamlan
Coed Ganllwyd
Rhaeadr Ddu
Afon Wen
Y-Berwyn (Lake Vyrnwy section)
Llanfachreth
ARAN FAWDDWY
Lake Vyrnwy
Llanelltyd
Cymer Abbey
Brithdir
Llanymawddwy
Toll
Dolgellau
TIR RHIWIOG
Afon Twrch
Dinas-Mawddwy
Minllyn
CADER IDRIS
0 1 2 3 4 miles
0 1 2 3 4 5 kilometres

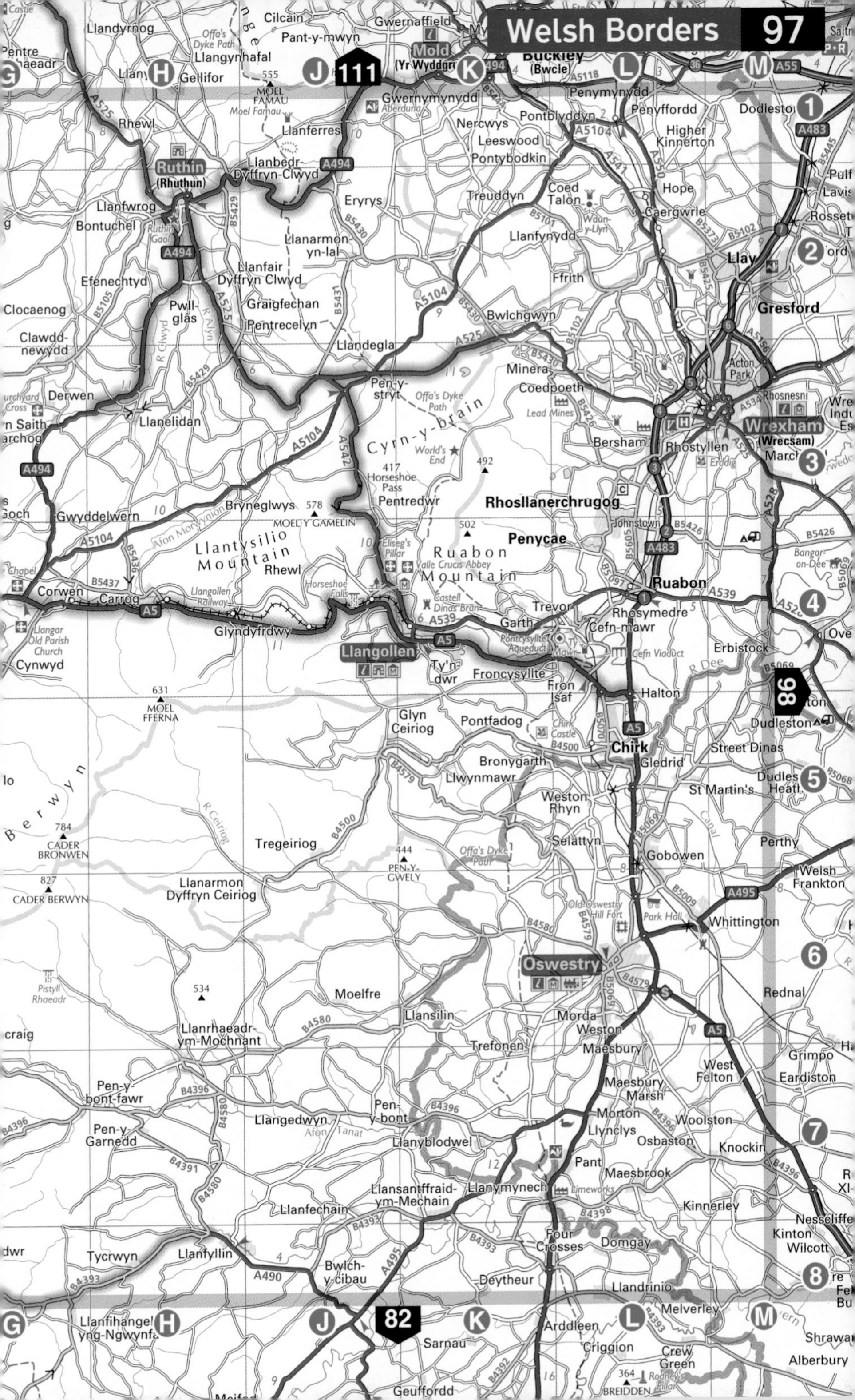
Llandyrnog
Cilcain
Gwernaffield
Pant-y-mwyn
Llangynhafal
Gellifor
Mold
(Yr Wyddgrug)
Buckley
(Bwcle)
Penymynydd
Dodleston
Gwernymynydd
Penyffordd
Rhewl
Nercwys
Pontblyddyn
Higher Kinnerton
Leeswood
Pontybodkin
Llanferres
Ruthin
(Rhuthun)
Llanbedr-Dyffryn-Clwyd
Hope
Coed Talon
Treuddyn
Eryrys
Caergwrle
Llanfwrog
Bontuchel
Llanarmon-yn-Ial
Llanfynydd
Llay
Llanfair Dyffryn Clwyd
Ffrith
Efenechtyd
Gresford
Clocaenog
Pwll-glâs
Graigfechan
Pentrecelyn
Bwlchgwyn
Clawdd-newydd
Llandegla
Minera
Coedpoeth
Pen-y-stryt
Derwen
Llanelidan
Cyrn-y-brain
Bersham
Rhostyllen
Wrexham
(Wrecsam)
Gwyddelwern
Bryneglwys
Horseshoe Pass
Pentredwr
Rhosllanerchrugog
Llantysilio Mountain
Rhewl
Ruabon Mountain
Penycae
Johnstown
Corwen
Carrog
Llangollen Railway
Valle Crucis Abbey
Ruabon
Glyndyfrdwy
Garth
Trevor
Rhosymedre
Cefn-mawr
Llangollen
Ty'n-dwr
Froncysyllte
Erbistock
Cynwyd
Fron Isaf
Halton
Dudleston
Glyn Ceiriog
Pontfadog
Chirk Castle
Chirk
Gledrid
Street Dinas
Bronygarth
Llwynmawr
Weston Rhyn
St Martin's
Dudleston Heath
Berwyn
Tregeiriog
Selattyn
Gobowen
Perthy
Llanarmon Dyffryn Ceiriog
Welsh Frankton
Whittington
Oswestry
Pistyll Rhaeadr
Moelfre
Rednal
Llansilin
Morda
Weston
Llanrhaeadr-ym-Mochnant
Trefonen
Maesbury
West Felton
Grimpo
Eardiston
Pen-y-bont-fawr
Maesbury Marsh
Llangedwyn
Pen-y-bont
Morton
Llynclys
Woolston
Pen-y-Garnedd
Osbaston
Knockin
Llanyblodwel
Pant
Maesbrook
Llansantffraid-ym-Mechain
Llanymynech
Kinnerley
Llanfechain
Four Crosses
Domgay
Nesscliffe
Kinton
Wilcott
Tycrwyn
Llanfyllin
Bwlch-y-cibau
Deytheur
Llandrinio
Melverley
Llanfihangel yng-Ngwynfa
Arddleen
Sarnau
Criggion
Crew Green
Shrawardine
Alberbury
Geufforddd
111
82
98

98
A
B
C
D
E
F
111
112
83
97
1
2
3
4
5
6
7
8
Saltney
Handbridge
Huntington
Little Budworth
Oulton Park
Utkinton
Duddon
Clotton
Burton
Eaton
Rowton
Eccleston
Saighton
Hargrave
Tarporley
Dodleston
Huxley
Wettenhall
Tilstone Fearnall
Tiverton
Alpraham
Aldford
Cheshire Farm
Newton
Castle
Beeston
Tattenhall
Pulford
Lavister
Milton Green
Calveley
Handley
Rossett
Trevalyn
Burwardsley
Spurstow
Bunbury
Wardle
Haughton
Marford
Churton
Worleston
Peckforton
Harthill
Farndon
Clutton
Bulkeley
Holt
Gresford
Barton
Burland
Watermill
Crewe-by-Farndon
Faddiley
Acton
Nantwich
Cholmondeley Castle
Acton Park
Rhosnesni
Wrexham Industrial Estate
Tilston
Chorley
Horton Green
Wrexham
(Wrecsam)
Shocklach
Ebnal
Hampton Heath
Marchwiel
Erddig
R Clywedog
Chorlton Lane
Bickley
No Man's Heath
Wrenbury
Malpas
Sound
Cuddington Heath
Bickley Hall Farm
Norbury
Bangor-on-Dee
Worthenbury
Marbury
Aston
Bangor-on-Dee
Newhall
Threapwood
Tallarn Green
Bell o' th' Hill
Higher Wych
Dodd's Green
Audlem
Wirswall
Grindley Brook
Overton
Whitchurch
Burleydam
Horseman's Green
Eglwys Cross
Erbistock
R Dee
Broughall
Wilkesley
Penley
Hanmer
Bronington
Redbrook
Knolton
Ash Magna
Dudleston
Ightfield
Tilstock
Street Dinas
Prees Heath
Calverhall
Fenn's, Whixall & Bettisfield Mosses
Dudleston Heath
Prees Higher Heath
Ellesmere
Welshampton
Canal
Bettisfield
Whixall
Moreton Say
Perthy
Prees
Bletchley
Welsh Frankton
Tetchill
Lyneal
Northwood
Fauls
Colemere
Newtown
Edstaston
Ternhill
Whittington
Hordley
Prees Green
English Frankton
Hawkstone
Wollerton
Weston-under-Redcastle
Marchamley
Hodnet
R Perry
Loppington
Rednal
Cockshutt
Noneley
Wem
Aston
Hodnet Hall
Bury Walls
Bagley
Lee Brockhurst
Stoke upon Tern
Grimpo
Haughton
West Felton
Burlton
Eardiston
Wykey
Preston Brockhurst
High Hatton
Ollerton
Weston Lullingfields
Clive
Myddle
Stanton upon Hine Heath
Peplow
Grinshill
Moreton Corbet
Castle
Ellerdine Heath
Eyton
Knockin
Harmer Hill
Ruyton-XI-Towns
Baschurch
Shawbury
Kinnerley
Little Ness
Yeaton
Preston Gubbals
Hadnall
Rowton
Nesscliffe
Bomere Heath
Kinton
Wilcott
Great Ness
Walford Heath
Astley
Waters Upton
Grafton
Leaton
Albrighton
Poynton Green
Walton
Pentre
Fitz
High Ercall
Crudgington
Felton Butler
Forton
Haughmond Abbey
Roden
Sleapford
Rodington Heath
Long Waste
Rodington
Uffington
Ditherington
Underdale
Coton Hill
Bratton
Shawbirch
0 1 2 3 4 miles
0 1 2 3 4 5 kilometres
A55
A483
A41
A49
A51
A534
A525
A528
A539
A495
A5
A53
A442
A5124
A530
B5130
B5102
B5445
B5069
B5395
B5426
B5068
B5063
B5476
B5065
B4397
B5067
B4396
B5062
B5341

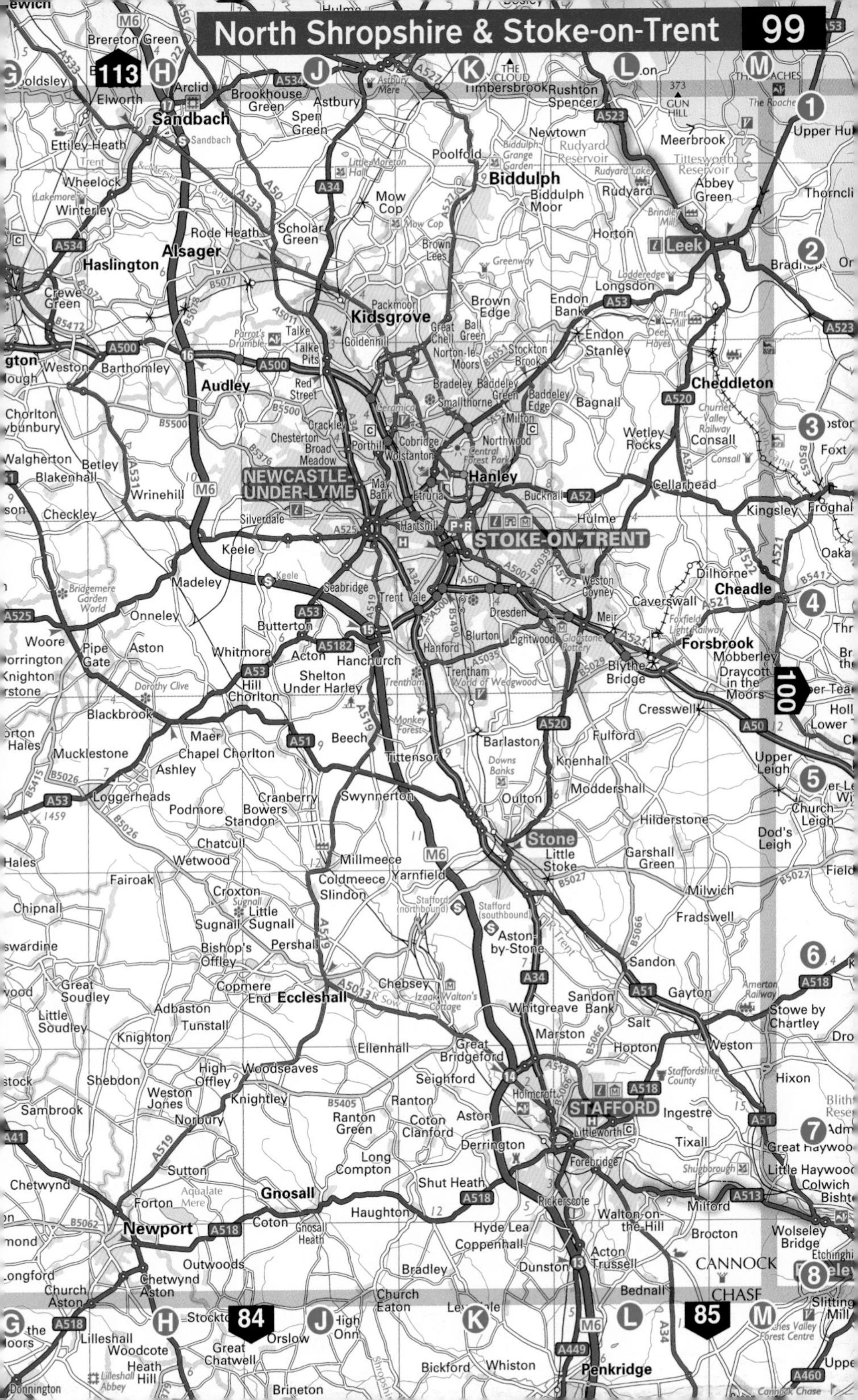
Sandbach
Alsager
Haslington
Kidsgrove
Audley
Biddulph
Leek
Cheddleton
NEWCASTLE-UNDER-LYME
Hanley
STOKE-ON-TRENT
Cheadle
Forsbrook
Stone
Eccleshall
STAFFORD
Newport
Gnosall
Penkridge
CANNOCK CHASE
113
84
85
100

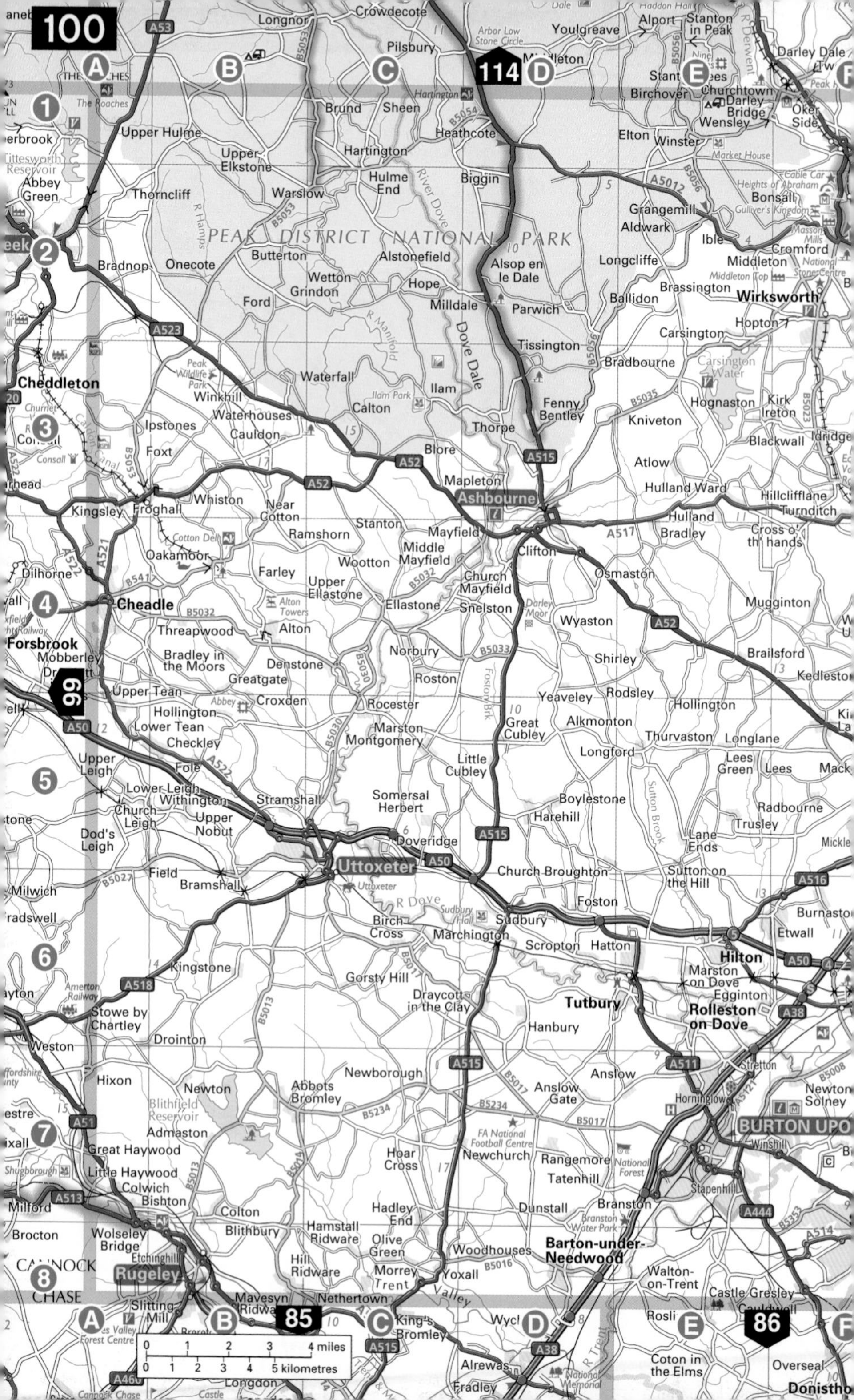
Longnor
Crowdecote
Pilsbury
Youlgreave
Alport
Stanton in Peak
Darley Dale
Middleton
114
The Roaches
Upper Hulme
Brund
Sheen
Hartington
Heathcote
Birchover
Churchtown
Darley Bridge
Wensley
Oker Side
Elton
Winster
Upper Elkstone
Hulme End
Biggin
Warslow
Abbey Green
Thorncliff
Grangemill
Aldwark
Bonsall
Ible
Cromford
PEAK DISTRICT NATIONAL PARK
Bradnop
Onecote
Butterton
Alstonefield
Alsop en le Dale
Longcliffe
Middleton
Wetton
Grindon
Hope
Ford
Milldale
Parwich
Ballidon
Brassington
Wirksworth
Dove Dale
Tissington
Carsington
Hopton
Cheddleton
Waterfall
Ilam
Bradbourne
Carsington Water
Winkhill
Waterhouses
Calton
Fenny Bentley
Hognaston
Kirk Ireton
Kniveton
Ipstones
Cauldon
Thorpe
Blackwall
Idridge
Consall
Foxt
Blore
Atlow
Mapleton
Ashbourne
Hulland Ward
Hillcliffane
Turnditch
Whiston
Kingsley
Froghall
Near Cotton
Stanton
Hulland
Ramshorn
Mayfield
Bradley
Cross o' th' hands
Clifton
Oakamoor
Middle Mayfield
Wootton
Dilhorne
Farley
Osmaston
Church Mayfield
Upper Ellastone
Cheadle
Ellastone
Snelston
Mugginton
Alton Towers
Wyaston
Threapwood
Alton
Forsbrook
Norbury
Brailsford
Mobberley
Bradley in the Moors
Shirley
Denstone
Kedleston
Greatgate
Roston
Upper Tean
Rodsley
Yeaveley
Croxden
Rocester
Hollington
Hollington
Lower Tean
Great Cubley
Alkmonton
Checkley
Marston Montgomery
Thurvaston
Longlane
Longford
Upper Leigh
Little Cubley
Lees Green
Lees
Fole
Lower Leigh
Withington
Stramshall
Somersal Herbert
Boylestone
Church Leigh
Radbourne
Upper Nobut
Harehill
Trusley
Dod's Leigh
Doveridge
Lane Ends
Uttoxeter
Church Broughton
Sutton on the Hill
Field
Milwich
Bramshall
R Dove
Foston
Birch Cross
Sudbury
Burnaston
Marchington
Etwall
Scropton
Hatton
Hilton
Kingstone
Gorsty Hill
Marston on Dove
Egginton
Draycott in the Clay
Tutbury
Rolleston on Dove
Stowe by Chartley
Hanbury
Weston
Drointon
Anslow
Hixon
Newton
Abbots Bromley
Newborough
Anslow Gate
Newton Solney
Blithfield Reservoir
Horninglow
Admaston
BURTON UPON
Great Haywood
FA National Football Centre
Newchurch
Hoar Cross
Rangemore
Winshill
Little Haywood
Colwich
Bishton
Tatenhill
Stapenhill
Milford
Colton
Hadley End
Dunstall
Branston
Brocton
Wolseley Bridge
Blithbury
Hamstall Ridware
Olive Green
Barton-under-Needwood
Woodhouses
CANNOCK CHASE
Rugeley
Hill Ridware
Morrey
Yoxall
Walton-on-Trent
Castle Gresley
Slitting Mill
Mavesyn Ridware
Nethertown
85
86
99
King's Bromley
Coton in the Elms
Overseal
Alrewas
Fradley
Longdon
0 1 2 3 4 miles
0 1 2 3 4 5 kilometres

North Wingfield
Clay Cross
Alfreton
South Normanton
Sutton-in-Ashfield
Kirkby-in-Ashfield
MANSFIELD
Rainworth
Blidworth
Ravenshead
Pinxton
Selston
Somercotes
Swanwick
Ripley
Codnor
Hucknall
Calverton
Heanor
Eastwood
Kimberley
Ilkeston
Arnold
Burton Joyce
NOTTINGHAM
DERBY
Stapleford
Beeston
West Bridgford
Radcliffe on Trent
Ockbrook
Borrowash
Breaston
Long Eaton
Clifton
Ruddington
Cotgrave
Keyworth
Castle Donington
Kegworth
East Leake
Melbourne
Shepshed
Loughborough
Barrow upon Soar
Sileby
Whitwick
Coalville
Mountsorrel
SHERWOOD FOREST

115
102
87

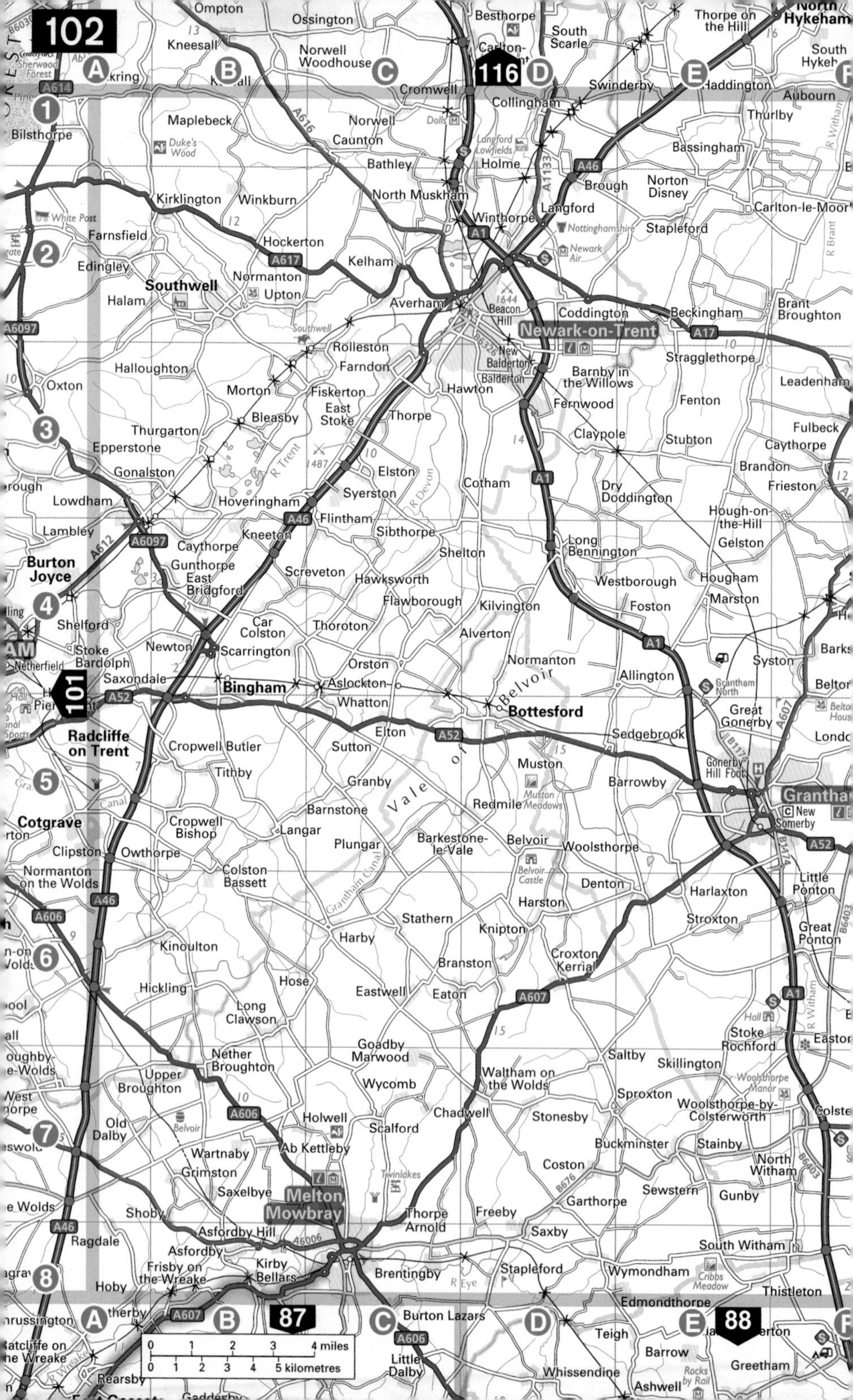
Ompton
Ossington
Besthorpe
South Scarle
Thorpe on the Hill
North Hykeham
Kneesall
Norwell Woodhouse
Carlton-on-Trent
South Hykeham
Sherwood Forest
A
B
C
116
D
E
A614
Cromwell
Swinderby
Haddington
Aubourn
1
Collingham
Thurlby
Maplebeck
Norwell
Dolls
Bilsthorpe
Duke's Wood
Caunton
Langford Lowfields
Bassingham
Bathley
Holme
A1133
A46
Kirklington
Winkburn
North Muskham
Brough
Norton Disney
White Post
Winthorpe
Langford
Carlton-le-Moorland
Farnsfield
Hockerton
A1
Nottinghamshire
Stapleford
2
Newark Air
R Brant
Edingley
A617
Kelham
Normanton
Southwell
Upton
Halam
Averham
1644
Beacon Hill
Coddington
Beckingham
Brant Broughton
A6097
Southwell
Newark-on-Trent
A17
Rolleston
B6326
New Balderton
Stragglethorpe
Halloughton
Farndon
Barnby in the Willows
Balderton
Leadenham
Oxton
Morton
Fiskerton
Hawton
Fernwood
East Stoke
Bleasby
Thorpe
Fenton
3
Thurgarton
Claypole
Stubton
Fulbeck
Caythorpe
Epperstone
R Trent
1487
Elston
Brandon
Gonalston
Cotham
Frieston
A1
R Devon
Syerston
Dry Doddington
Lowdham
Hoveringham
A46
Flintham
Hough-on-the-Hill
Lambley
A612
A6097
Kneeton
Sibthorpe
Gelston
Caythorpe
Long Bennington
Burton Joyce
Gunthorpe
Shelton
Screveton
Hawksworth
East Bridgford
Westborough
Hougham
4
Flawborough
Marston
Shelford
Car Colston
Kilvington
Foston
Thoroton
Netherfield
Stoke Bardolph
Newton
Scarrington
Alverton
A1
Barkston
Normanton
Syston
Orston
Saxondale
Vale of Belvoir
Allington
Belton
Bingham
Aslockton
Grantham North
101
A52
Whatton
Bottesford
Great Gonerby
Belton House
Radcliffe on Trent
A607
Elton
A52
Sedgebrook
Cropwell Butler
Sutton
Londonthorpe
B1174
Muston
Tithby
Gonerby Hill Foot
5
Granby
Barrowby
Grantham
Canal
Muston Meadows
Redmile
Barnstone
New Somerby
Cotgrave
Cropwell Bishop
Vale
Langar
Barkestone-le-Vale
Belvoir
Plungar
Woolsthorpe
A52
Clipston
Owthorpe
Belvoir Castle
B1174
Colston Bassett
Normanton on the Wolds
Denton
Harlaxton
Little Ponton
Grantham Canal
A46
Harston
A606
Stathern
Stroxton
Great Ponton
9
Knipton
B6403
Kinoulton
Harby
6
Croxton Kerrial
Branston
A1
Hickling
Hose
Eastwell
Eaton
A607
Long Clawson
R Witham
Hall
15
Stoke Rochford
Easton
Goadby Marwood
Saltby
Nether Broughton
Skillington
Waltham on the Wolds
Upper Broughton
Wycomb
Woolsthorpe Manor
Sproxton
10
A606
Woolsthorpe-by-Colsterworth
Colsterworth
Holwell
Chadwell
Stonesby
Old Dalby
Belvoir
Scalford
7
Buckminster
Stainby
Wartnaby
Ab Kettleby
Coston
North Witham
Twinlakes
Grimston
B676
B6403
Melton Mowbray
Saxelbye
Sewstern
Gunby
Garthorpe
Shoby
Thorpe Arnold
Freeby
A46
Asfordby Hill
Ragdale
A6006
Saxby
South Witham
Asfordby
Frisby on the Wreake
Kirby Bellars
8
Stapleford
Wymondham
Hoby
Brentingby
Cribbs Meadow
R Eye
Thistleton
Edmondthorpe
Thrussington
A607
87
Burton Lazars
88
F
Ratcliffe on the Wreake
R Wreake
A606
Teigh
Barrow
Greetham
0
1
2
3
4 miles
5 kilometres
Little Dalby
Rearsby
Whissendine
Rocks by Rail
Ashwell
Gaddesby

Nocton
Metheringham
Blankney
Martin
Scopwick
Kirkby Green
Timberland
Thorpe Tilney
Rowston
Walcott
Ashby de la Launde
Billinghay
Digby
Bloxholm
Dorrington
Ruskington
North Kyme
Cranwell
Anwick
Leasingham
South Kyme
Evedon
Holdingham
Ewerby
Kirkby la Thorpe
Howell
Sleaford
South Rauceby
Asgarby
Quarrington
Heckington
Great Hale
Little Hale
Silk Willoughby
Burton Pedwardine
Swarby
Scredington
Helpringham
Aswarby
Heydour
Aisby
Aunsby
Osbournby
Spanby
Swaton
Dembleby
Newton
Threekingham
Haceby
Walcot
Horbling
Billingborough
Pickworth
Folkingham
Humby
Laughton
Pointon
Aslackby
Lenton
Ingoldsby
Dowsby
Rippingale
Irnham
Kirkby Underwood
Dunsby
Hacconby
Hanthorpe
Morton
Elsthorpe
Grimsthorpe
Dyke
Swinstead
Edenham
Bourne
Twenty
Creeton
Lound
Witham on the Hill
Careby
Manthorpe
Carlby
Thurlby
Baston
Deeping Fen
Kirkstead
Woodhall Spa
Kirkby on Bain
Revesby
East Kirkby
Mareham le Fen
Tattershall Thorpe
Tumby
Tattershall
Coningsby
Tumby Woodside
New Bolingbroke
Tattershall Castle
Tattershall College
Battle of Britain Memorial Flight
Hawthorn Hill
New York
Dogdyke
Scrub Hill
Chapel Hill
West Fen
Holland Fen
Gipsey Bridge
Frithville
Langrick
Anton's Gowt
East Heckington
Holland Fen
Boston
Swineshead
Bicker
Kirton
Northorpe
Donington
Wigtoft
Sutterton
Algarkirk
Burtoft
Quadring Eaudike
Quadring
Westhorpe
Gosberton
Risegate
Surfleet
Pinchbeck
Weston
Moulton
Mill Green
Springfields
Spalding
Fulney
Moulton Seas End
Moulton Chapel
Cowbit
Bedford Level
Skeldyke
Fosdyke
R Witham
R Slea
R Welland
R Glen
South Forty Foot Drain
Timberland Delph
A15
A17
A52
A153
A155
A151
A16
A152
A1121
A1175
A6121
B1191
B1189
B1188
B1202
B1192
B1183
B1184
B1395
B1394
B1391
B1397
B1177
B1193
B1180
B1356
B1357
B1165
B1172
B1173
B1176
B1209
B1429
B1517
117
118
104
89

Old Bolingbroke
Bolingbroke Castle
Toynton All Saints
Holegate
Great Steeping
Bratoft
Burgh le Marsh
A158
Natureland Seal Sanctuary
Skeg
118
119
Northcote
B1195
Little Steeping
Firsby
in the Marsh
East Kirkby
Lincolnshire Aviation
Revesby
Mareham le Fen
Keal Cotes
Stickford
Croft
Fendike Corner
Thorpe St Peter
Wainfleet Haven
Wainfleet All Saints
Wainfleet St Mary
A52
Gibraltar Point
Tumby Woodside
New Bolingbroke
ARK
Stickney
New Leake
Eastville
Lincolnshire
Friskney
East Fen
A16
West Fen
B1183
Northlands
Leake Common Side
Sibsey Trader Windmill
Sibsey
Frithville
B1184
Fishtoft Drove
Wrangle
Old Leake
Hilldyke
Leverton
Anton's Gowt
Benington
Witham Way
Butterwick
Fen
Boston
A1121
A52
Freiston
Freiston Shore
Fishtoft
Scrane End
B1391
B1397
Wyberton East
Havenside
103
Frampton
The Haven
Frampton Marsh
Kirton
THE WASH
Skeldyke
Sutterton
Algarkirk
Fosdyke
Holbeach St Matthew
R Welland
Holbeach St Mark's
Holbeach Marsh
Gedney Drove End
B1359
B1357
A17
Moulton Seas End
Saracen's Head
Holbeach Bank
Holbeach Hurn
Gedney Dyke
Holbeach Clough
Lutton
The Wash
Weston
A151
Fleet Hargate
B1515
Moulton
Whaplode
Holbeach
Fleet
Gedney
Long Sutton
Gedney Broadgate
B1165
B1168
Sutton Bridge
Terrington St Clement
Walpole Cross Keys
B1390
Clenchwarton
B1357
Moulton Chapel
B1165
Tydd Gote
Walpole St Andrew
Tilney All Saints
Holbeach St Johns
Sutton St James
Tydd St Mary
A47
Four Gotes
Walpole St Peter
Tilney High End
89
90
Level
Tydd St Giles
River Nene
B1165
Newton
Tilney St Lawrence
West Walton
Sutton St Edmund
0 1 2 3 4 miles
0 1 2 3 4 5 kilometres
A B C D E F
1 2 3 4 5 6 7 8

G
H
J
K
L
M
1
2
3
4
5
6
7
8
North Norfolk Heritage Coast
Holkham Bay
Brancaster Bay
Scolt Head Island
Peddars Way & Norfolk Coast Path
Blakeney Poi
Holme Dunes
Holme next the Sea
Brancaster
Brancaster Staithe
Burnham Deepdale
Burnham Overy Staithe
Holkham
Wells-next-the-Sea
Stif
Old Hunstanton
Thornham
Titchwell
Branodunum Roman Fort
Burnham Norton
B1155
Holkham Hall
A149
Warham
Burnham Overy
Burnham Market
Burnham Thorpe
B1355
B1105
anton
Ringstead
A149
B1153
B1155
Wighton
106
Summerfield
Norfolk Lavender
Peddars Way & Norfolk Coast Path
North Creake
Creake Abbey
Wells & Walsingham Light Railway
The Shrine of Our Lady
Heacham
Docking
Stanhoe
Little Walsingham
Great Walsingham
Sedgeford
B1454
B1155
South Creake
North Barsham
Hindringham
Houghton St Giles
Fring
B1153
Bircham Newton
West Barsham
East Barsham
Great Snoring
Snettisham
Park
B1155
Thursford
Shernborne
Syderstone
R. Stiffkey
A148
goldisthorpe
Great Bircham
Bircham Tofts
Wicken Green Village
Little Snoring
Croxt
B1440
B1454
Sculthorpe
Kettlestone
ersingham
Dunton
Anmer
Tattersett
Coxford
Shereford
Fakenham
ersingham Bog
B1153
Houghton Hall
West Rudham
Hempton
Sandringham
West Newton
New Houghton
East Rudham
Tatterford
Little Ryburgh
A149
B1440
A148
Toftrees
B1146
Great Ryburgh
A1067
River
B1439
Flitcham
Helhoughton
East Raynham
Colkirk
River Wensum
Harpley
rising
Hillington
Little Massingham
West Raynham
Gateley
Castle
South Raynham
Congham
A148
Roydon
Grimston
Great Massingham
Weasenham St Peter
Whissonsett
Horningtoft
Roydon Common
Wellingham
Brisley
A149
Weasenham All Saints
Tittleshall
North Elmham
B1153
Stanfield
B1145
B1145
Gayton
Rougham
East Bilney
Old Beetley
Bawsey
s Lynn
Mileham
B1146
Ashwicken
Gayton Thorpe
B1145
A1065
Litcham
Beet
Fair Green
East Winch
West Lexham
East Lexham
Gressenhall
Middleton
East Walton
91
Castle Acre
Newton
Bee
Longham
Gressenhall Green
Blackborough End
West Bilney
B1153
Priory
South
Little
Great Dunham
Gressenhall
Pentney
Dereham

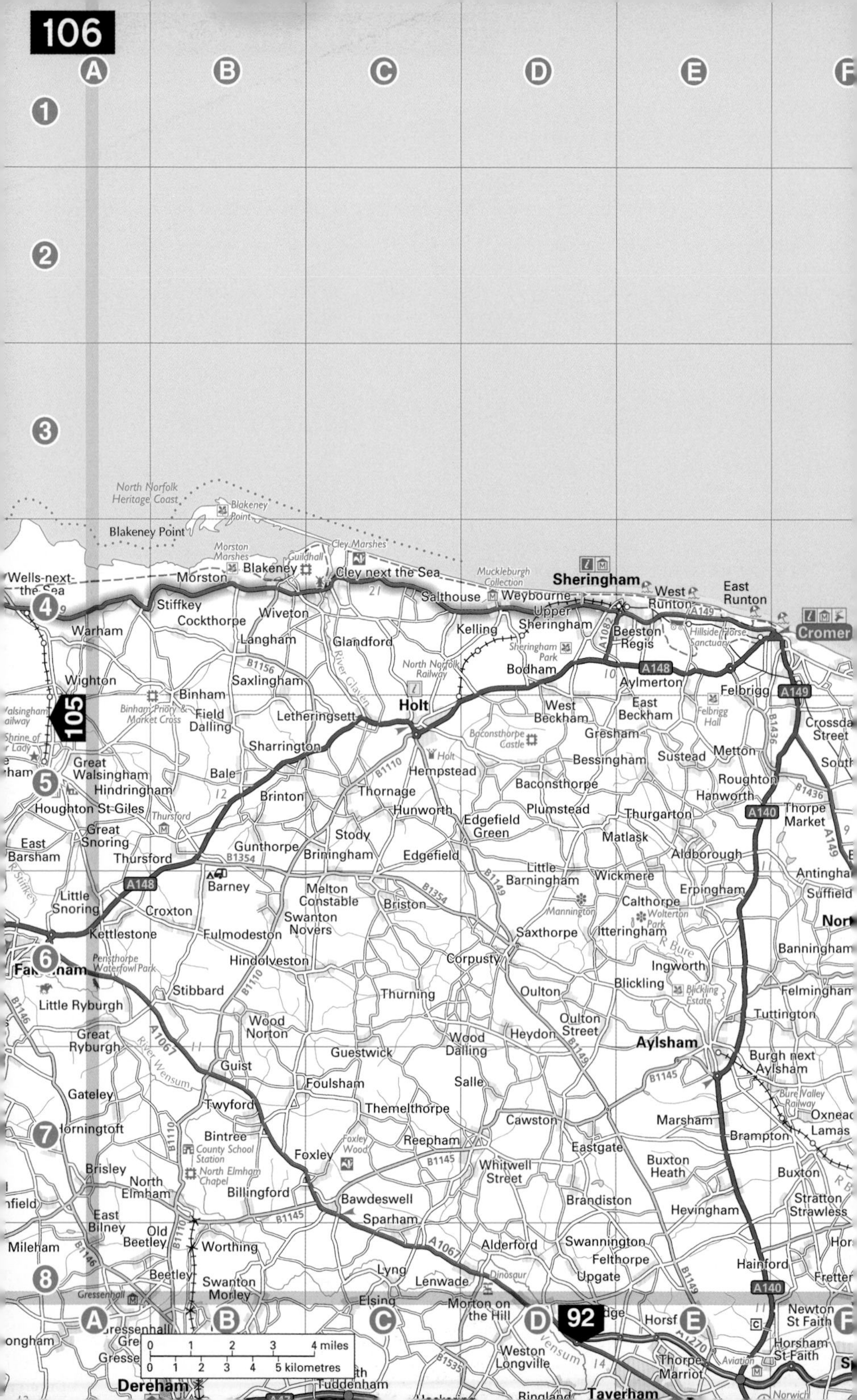

106
A
B
C
D
E
1
2
3
4
5
6
7
8
North Norfolk
Heritage Coast
Blakeney Point
Blakeney Point
Morston Marshes
Cley Marshes
Guildhall
Wells-next-the-Sea
Morston
Blakeney
Cley next the Sea
Muckleburgh Collection
Sheringham
West Runton
East Runton
Cromer
Salthouse
Weybourne
Upper Sheringham
Beeston Regis
Hillside Horse Sanctuary
Stiffkey
Cockthorpe
Wiveton
Warham
Langham
Glandford
Kelling
Sheringham Park
Bodham
A1082
A148
A149
B1156
Saxlingham
River Glaven
North Norfolk Railway
Aylmerton
Felbrigg
Wighton
Binham
Binham Priory & Market Cross
Field Dalling
Letheringsett
Holt
West Beckham
East Beckham
Felbrigg Hall
Crossdale Street
105
Walsingham
Shrine of Our Lady
Sharrington
Baconsthorpe Castle
Gresham
B1436
Great Walsingham
Bale
Hempstead
Bessingham
Sustead
Metton
Hindringham
B1110
Thornage
Baconsthorpe
Roughton
Houghton St Giles
Brinton
Hunworth
Plumstead
Hanworth
A140
Thorpe Market
Thursford
Edgefield Green
Thurgarton
Great Snoring
Stody
Matlask
East Barsham
Gunthorpe
Briningham
Edgefield
Aldborough
Thursford
B1354
Little Barningham
Wickmere
B1149
Barney
Antingham
Erpingham
Little Snoring
Melton Constable
Briston
Mannington
Calthorpe
Suffield
Croxton
Swanton Novers
Wolterton Park
Kettlestone
Fulmodeston
Saxthorpe
Itteringham
R Bure
Banningham
Fakenham
Pensthorpe Waterfowl Park
Hindolveston
Corpusty
Ingworth
Stibbard
Blickling
Blickling Estate
Felmingham
Little Ryburgh
Thurning
Oulton
B1146
Oulton Street
Tuttington
Great Ryburgh
A1067
Wood Norton
Wood Dalling
Heydon
Aylsham
Burgh next Aylsham
River Wensum
Guestwick
Guist
Foulsham
Salle
B1145
Gateley
Bure Valley Railway
Twyford
Themelthorpe
Cawston
Marsham
Oxnead
Horningtoft
Bintree
County School Station
Foxley Wood
Reepham
Lamas
Eastgate
Brampton
Foxley
Brisley
North Elmham Chapel
Whitwell Street
Buxton Heath
North Elmham
Billingford
Buxton
Bawdeswell
Brandiston
Stratton Strawless
East Bilney
Sparham
Hevingham
Old Beetley
Worthing
Alderford
Swannington
Mileham
Felthorpe
Hainford
Beetley
Lyng
Dinosaur
Swanton Morley
Lenwade
Upgate
Gressenhall
Elsing
Morton on the Hill
Newton St Faith
Horsham St Faith
92
Weston Longville
Vensum
A1270
B1535
Thorpe Marriot
Aviation
Dereham
Tuddenham
Taverham
Ringland
Norwich
0 1 2 3 4 miles
0 1 2 3 4 5 kilometres

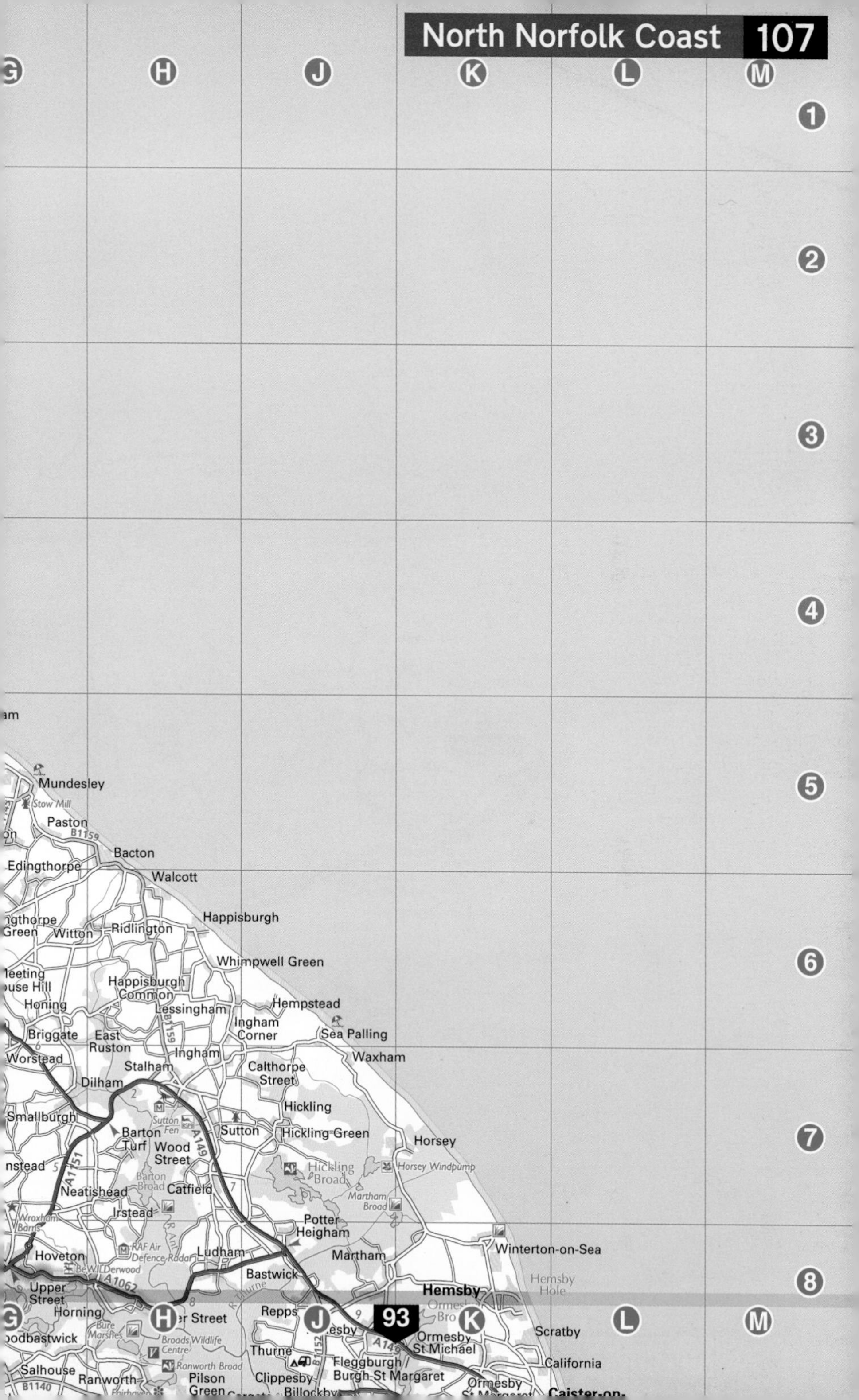

Mundesley
Stow Mill
Paston
Bacton
Edingthorpe
Walcott
Happisburgh
Witton
Ridlington
Whimpwell Green
Happisburgh Common
Honing
Lessingham
Hempstead
Briggate
East Ruston
Ingham Corner
Sea Palling
Worstead
Ingham
Waxham
Stalham
Calthorpe Street
Dilham
Hickling
Smallburgh
Sutton Fen
Barton Turf
Sutton
Hickling Green
Horsey
Wood Street
Hickling Broad
Horsey Windpump
Barton Broad
Neatishead
Catfield
Martham Broad
Irstead
Potter Heigham
Hoveton
RAF Air Defence Radar
Ludham
Martham
Winterton-on-Sea
BeWILDerwood
Bastwick
Hemsby
Hemsby Hole
Upper Street
Horning
Repps
Scratby
Bure Marshes
Broads Wildlife Centre
Thurne
Ormesby St Michael
Fleggburgh / Burgh St Margaret
California
Salhouse
Ranworth Broad
Ranworth
Pilson Green
Clippesby
Ormesby St Margaret
93

A
B
C
D
E
F
1
2
3
4
5
6
7
8
The Skerries
CARMEL HEAD
North Anglesey
Heritage Coast
Wylfa
Head
Cemaes
Bay
Porth
Wen
Bull
Bay
Cemlyn
Bay
Hen
Borth
Cemaes
A5025
Burwen
Tregele
Llanfairynghornwy
Llanfechell
Bodewryd
Penysarn
Swtan Folk
Dublin
Dublin
Holyhead
Bay
Church
Bay
Llanrhyddlad
Carreglefn
Rhosybol
Capel
Parc
Llanfaethlu
Llyn
Alaw
B5111
Porth
Tywynmawr
Llanddeusant
Llynnon Mill
Afon Alaw
Elim
North Stack
Breakwater
Llanfwrog
Llanerchymedd
Gogarth
Bay
Holyhead
(Caergybi)
Holyhead Mountain
Hut Circles
South Stack
Ellins
Tower
Penrhos Feliw
Kingsland
Llanfachraeth
B5112
Llyn
Llywenan
Holyhead Mountain
Heritage Coast
Llanynghenedl
ANGLESE
A5
Presaddfed
B5109
Penrhyn Mawr
Trefignath
A55
Valley
A5025
Bodedern
B5111
Trearddur Bay
B4545
Caergeiliog
B5112
Llynfaes
B5109
Llanfihangel
yn Nhowyn
Bryngwran
Cefni
Reserv
Oriel
Ynys Môn
HOLY ISLAND
Four Mile
Bridge
Bodffordd
Gwalchmai
Llanfair-yn-Neubwll
Valley
Anglesey
Rhoscolyn
Rhoscolyn
Head
A4080
A5
A55
Ty Newydd
Pencarnisiog
Cymyran
Bay
Llangristi
Rhosneigr
Llanfaelog
Din Dryfol
Pentre
A4080
Henblas
B4422
Barclodiad
y Gawres
Bethel
Porth Trecastell
Afon Cefni
Aberffraw
Llangadwaladr
Malltraeth
Anglesey
Circuit
Llangaffo
A4080
B4421
Aberffraw
Bay
Dwyran
Newborough
Aberffraw Bay
Heritage Coast
Malltraeth Bay
Newborough
Warren
Caern
Llanddwyn Island
95
Foryd
Bay
Airworld
Aviation
0
1
2
3
4 miles
0
1
2
3
4
5 kilometres

Anglesey
G
H
J
K
2
3
4
110
5
6
7
8
Seawatch Centre
Moelfre
Llanallgo
Great Orme Heritage Coast
GREAT ORMES HEAD
Toll
Great Orme Tramway
Little Ormes
Puffin Island
Benllech
Red Wharf Bay
Red Wharf Bay
Penmon Priory
Toll
Black Point
Llandudno
Conwy Bay
Deganwy
A470
Llanddona
Llangoed
Pentraeth
Hafoty Medieval House
B5109
A5025
Gaol
Beaumaris Castle
Beaumaris
Courthouse
Llansadwrn
Llandegfan
A545
Dwygyfylchi
Penmaenmawr
Conwy
Conwy Castle
Llandudno Junction
Capelulo
Llanfairfechan
Llansanffraid Glan Conwy
Henryd
A55
Menai Bridge (Porthaethwy)
Bangor
Penrhyn Castle
Spinnies Abergowen
SNOWDONIA
610 TAL-Y-FAN
Rowen
A470
Anglesey Column
Llandygai
Abergwyngregyn
Coedydd Aber
Ty'n-y-Groes
Bodnant
Graig
Tal-y-Cafn
Eglwysbach
Britannia Bridge
Plas Newydd
A4087
Tal-y-bont
Afon Anafon
Aber Falls
580 MOEL WINION
NATIONAL
Llanbedr-y-Cennin
A55
Glasinfryn
Llanllechid
Felinheli
GreenWood Forest Park
B4547
Rhyd-y-groes
Pentir
Tregarth
Rachub
Bethesda
757 Y DROSGL
942 FOEL-FRAS
Tal-y-Bont
Dolgarrog
Surf Snowdonia
Vale of Conwy
Seion
Bethel
Llanddeiniolen
B4409
Zip World
Afon Caseg
Afon Dulyn
PARK
Llyn Eigiau
Saron
Rhiwlas
A4244
B4366
Llanrug
Deiniolen
A5
1062 CARNEDD LLEWELYN
1044 CARNEDD DAFYDD
Afon Ddu
Trefriw Woollen Mills
Trefriw
Llanddoget
Llyn Cowlyd
Cwm-y-glo
Brynrefail
Llyn Padarn
95
923 ELIDIR FAWR
Llanberis Lake Railway
442
Llanberis
Electric Mountain
Dolbadarn Castle
Waunfawr
Llyn Peris
Nant Peris
946 Y GARN
917 Y TRYFAN
Llyn Ogwen
Llyn Crafnant
Llyn Geirionydd
96
Llanrwst
Gwydir Uchaf Chapel
Pentre-afarn-y-fedw
B5113
The Ugly House (Tŷ Hyll)
Swallow Falls
B5106

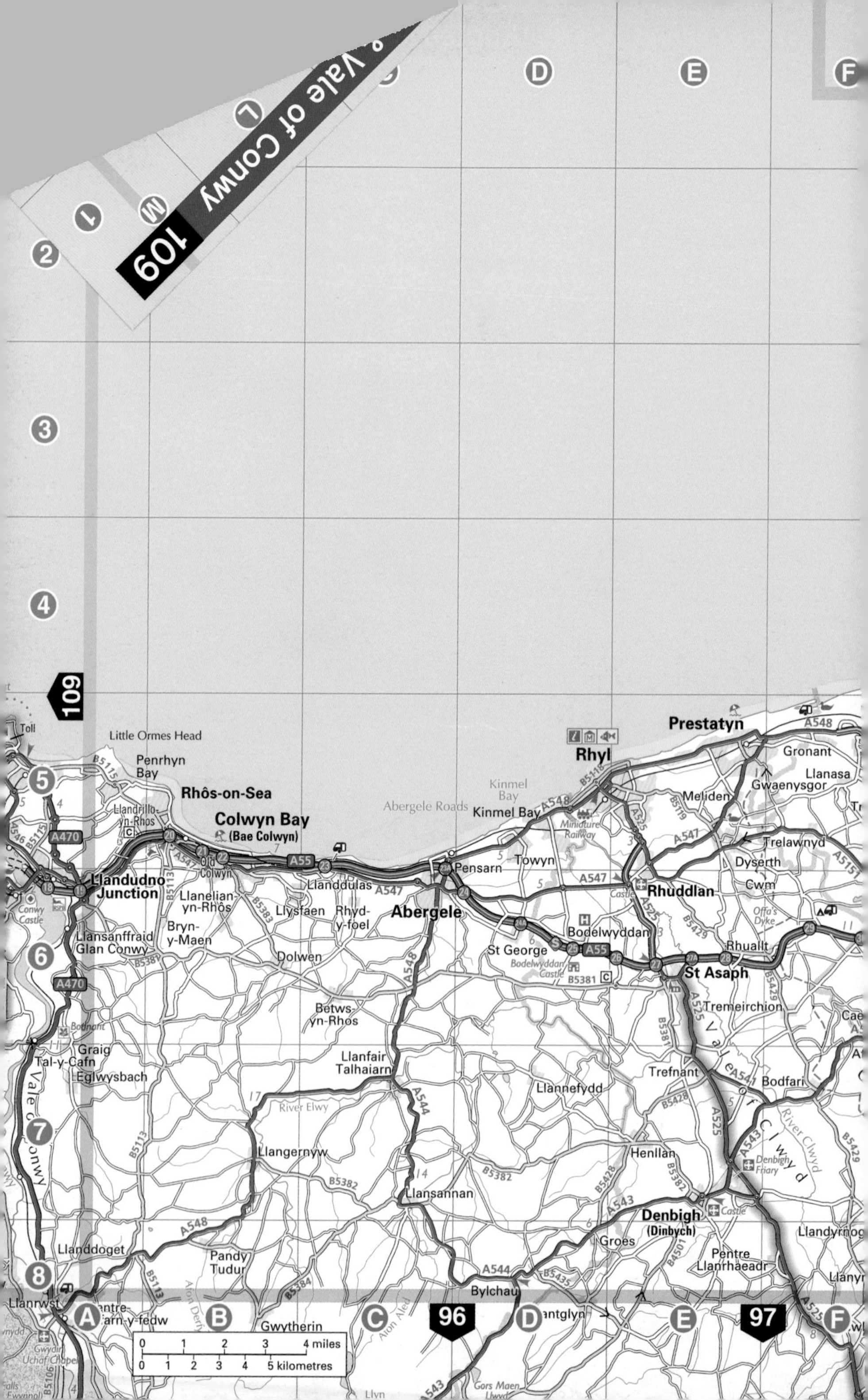

109
Vale of Conwy
Prestatyn
Rhyl
Gronant
Llanasa
Gwaenysgor
Meliden
Trelawnyd
Dyserth
Cwm
Offa's Dyke
Rhuddlan
Kinmel Bay
Abergele Roads
Kinmel Bay
Towyn
Pensarn
Abergele
Little Ormes Head
Penrhyn Bay
Rhôs-on-Sea
Colwyn Bay
(Bae Colwyn)
Old Colwyn
Llanddulas
Llandudno Junction
Llanelian-yn-Rhôs
Llysfaen
Rhyd-y-foel
Bryn-y-Maen
Llansanffraid Glan Conwy
Conwy Castle
Dolwen
Betws-yn-Rhos
St George
Bodelwyddan
Bodelwyddan Castle
St Asaph
Rhuallt
Tremeirchion
Graig
Tal-y-Cafn
Eglwysbach
Bodnant
Llanfair Talhaiarn
Trefnant
Llannefydd
Bodfari
River Elwy
River Clwyd
Vale of Clwyd
Llangernyw
Henllan
Denbigh Friary
Llansannan
Denbigh
(Dinbych)
Castle
Groes
Pentre Llanrhaeadr
Llandyrnog
Llanddoget
Pandy Tudur
Bylchau
Llanrwst
Gwytherin
Miniature Railway
Vale of Conwy
96
97
0 1 2 3 4 miles
0 1 2 3 4 5 kilometres
A55
A470
A547
A548
A525
A543
A544
A541
B5113
B5381
B5382
B5428
B5429

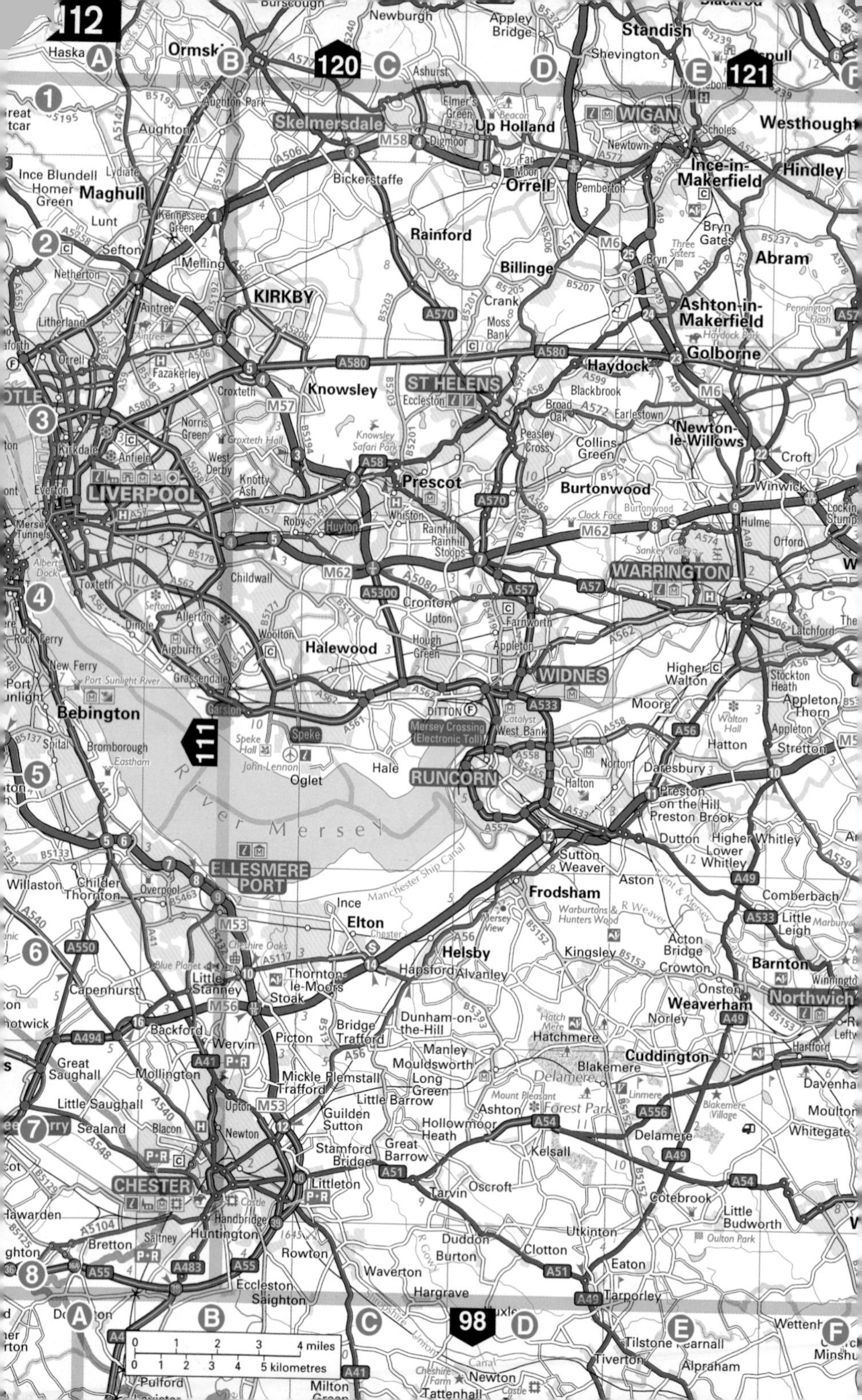

Burscough
Newburgh
Appley Bridge
Standish
Haskall
Ormskirk
120
Shevington
121
Aughton Park
Skelmersdale
Elmer's Green
Up Holland
WIGAN
Westhoughton
Aughton
Digmoor
Scholes
Newtown
Ince Blundell
Homer Green
Maghull
Bickerstaffe
Orrell
Pemberton
Ince-in-Makerfield
Hindley
Lunt
Kennessee Green
Sefton
Melling
Rainford
Bryn Gates
Three Sisters
Abram
Netherton
Billinge
Bryn
KIRKBY
Crank
Ashton-in-Makerfield
Litherland
Aintree
Moss Bank
Pennington Flash
Haydock Park
Orrell
Fazakerley
Haydock
Golborne
Croxteth
Knowsley
ST HELENS
Eccleston
Blackbrook
Norris Green
Croxteth Hall
Knowsley Safari Park
Broad Oak
Earlestown
Newton-le-Willows
Kirkdale
Anfield
West Derby
Peasley Cross
Collins Green
Croft
Everton
LIVERPOOL
Knotty Ash
Prescot
Burtonwood
Winwick
Mersey Tunnels
Roby
Huyton
Whiston
Rainhill
Rainhill Stoops
Clock Face
Sankey Valley
Hulme
Orford
Albert Dock
Childwall
M62
Toxteth
Cronton
WARRINGTON
Sefton Park
Allerton
Upton
Farnworth
Dingle
Woolton
Latchford
Rock Ferry
Aigburth
Halewood
Hough Green
Appleton
New Ferry
Port Sunlight River
Grassendale
WIDNES
Higher Walton
Stockton Heath
Bebington
Garston
DITTON
Catalyst
West Bank
Moore
Appleton Thorn
111
Speke
Mersey Crossing (Electronic Toll)
Walton Hall
Spital
Bromborough
Eastham
Speke Hall
John Lennon
Hale
Hatton
Stretton
Oglet
RUNCORN
Norton
Daresbury
Halton
Preston on the Hill
Preston Brook
River Mersey
Dutton
Higher Whitley
Lower Whitley
Sutton Weaver
Willaston
Childer Thornton
Overpool
ELLESMERE PORT
Manchester Ship Canal
Aston
Frodsham
Comberbach
Ince
Warburtons & Hunters Wood
R Weaver
Little Leigh
Elton
Mersey View
Trent & Mersey
Cheshire Oaks
Helsby
Acton Bridge
Kingsley
Crowton
Barnton
Blue Planet
Thornton-le-Moors
Capenhurst
Little Stanney
Hapsford
Alvanley
Onston
Winnington
Stoak
Weaverham
Northwich
Backford
Picton
Bridge Trafford
Dunham-on-the-Hill
Hatch Mere
Norley
Hatchmere
Wervin
Manley
Cuddington
Hartford
Great Saughall
Mollington
Mickle Trafford
Plemstall
Mouldsworth
Blakemere
Davenham
Delamere
Long Green
Little Saughall
Upton
Little Barrow
Mount Pleasant
Forest Park
Linmere
Blakemere Village
Sealand
Blacon
Guilden Sutton
Ashton
Moulton
Newton
Hollowmoor Heath
Whitegate
Stamford Bridge
Great Barrow
Kelsall
CHESTER
Littleton
Tarvin
Oscroft
Cotebrook
Little Budworth
Castle
Hawarden
Handbridge
Huntington
Utkinton
Oulton Park
Bretton
Saltney
Duddon
Clotton
Rowton
Burton
Eaton
Waverton
Eccleston
Saighton
Hargrave
Tarporley
Shropshire Union
98
Wettenhall
Tilstone Fearnall
Tiverton
Alpraham
Cheshire Farm
Newton
Pulford
Milton Green
Tattenhall
Castle
0 1 2 3 4 miles
0 1 2 3 4 5 kilometres

BOLTON
MANCHESTER
SALFORD
OLDHAM
STOCKPORT
Altrincham
Macclesfield
Congleton
MIDDLETON
Ashton-under-Lyne
Whitefield
Prestwich
Radcliffe
Chadderton
Royton
Walkden
Swinton
Pendlebury
Worsley
Eccles
Urmston
Stretford
Sale
Partington
Failsworth
Droylsden
Audenshaw
Denton
Hyde
Dukinfield
Stalybridge
Mossley
Romiley
Marple
Hazel Grove
Cheadle
Gatley
Bramhall
Poynton
Disley
High Lane
New Mills
Whaley Bridge
Wilmslow
Knutsford
Alderley Edge
Prestbury
Bollington
Holmes Chapel
Biddulph

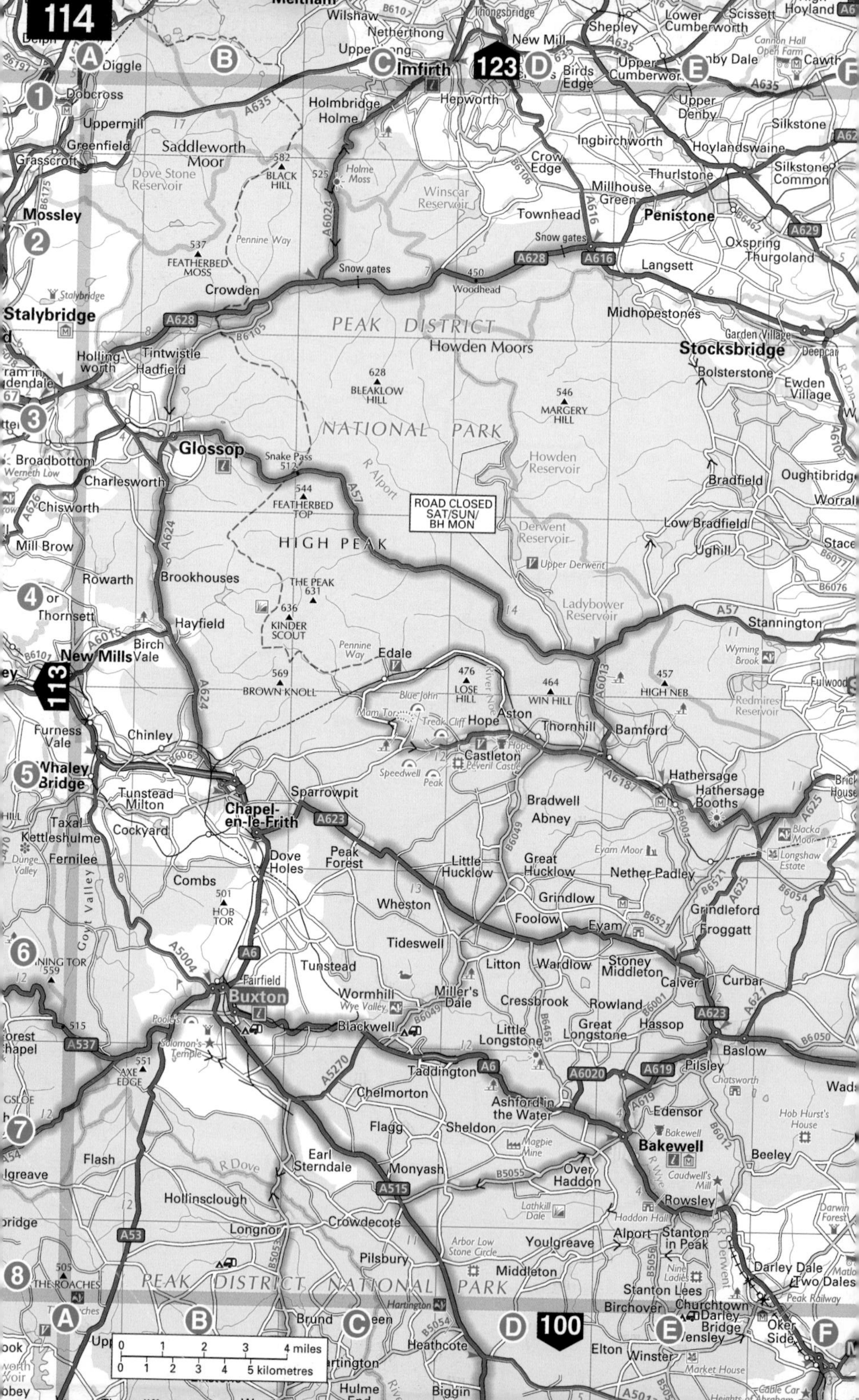
Diggle
Dobcross
Uppermill
Greenfield
Grasscroft
Saddleworth Moor
Dove Stone Reservoir
582 BLACK HILL
Wilshaw
Netherthong
Upperthong
Holmfirth
123
Thongsbridge
New Mill
Shepley
Lower Cumberworth
Scissett
Hoyland
Upper Cumberworth
Birds Edge
Upper Denby
Denby Dale
Cawthorne
Cannon Hall Open Farm
Hepworth
Holmbridge
Holme
Holme Moss
Winscar Reservoir
Ingbirchworth
Hoylandswaine
Silkstone
Silkstone Common
Crow Edge
Thurlstone
Millhouse Green
Penistone
Townhead
Oxspring
Thurgoland
Langsett
Snow gates
Mossley
537 FEATHERBED MOSS
Pennine Way
Crowden
450 Woodhead
Stalybridge
Midhopestones
PEAK DISTRICT
Howden Moors
Garden Village
Stocksbridge
Deepcar
Bolsterstone
Ewden Village
Hollingworth
Tintwistle
Hadfield
628 BLEAKLOW HILL
546 MARGERY HILL
NATIONAL PARK
Glossop
Broadbottom
Werneth Low
Snake Pass 512
Howden Reservoir
Bradfield
Oughtibridge
Charlesworth
544 FEATHERBED TOP
R Alport
ROAD CLOSED SAT/SUN/BH MON
Worrall
Chisworth
Derwent Reservoir
Low Bradfield
Mill Brow
HIGH PEAK
Ughill
Upper Derwent
Rowarth
Brookhouses
THE PEAK 631
636 KINDER SCOUT
Ladybower Reservoir
Stannington
Thornsett
Hayfield
Birch Vale
New Mills
113
Edale
569 BROWN KNOLL
476 LOSE HILL
464 WIN HILL
457 HIGH NEB
Wyming Brook
Fulwood
Redmires Reservoir
Blue John
Mam Tor
Treak Cliff
Hope
Aston
Thornhill
Bamford
Furness Vale
Chinley
Castleton
Peveril Castle
Speedwell
Peak
Whaley Bridge
Tunstead Milton
Sparrowpit
Chapel-en-le-Frith
Hathersage
Hathersage Booths
Bradwell
Abney
Taxal
Kettleshulme
Cockyard
Fernilee
Dunge Valley
Dove Holes
Peak Forest
Eyam Moor
Blacka Moor
Longshaw Estate
Little Hucklow
Great Hucklow
Nether Padley
Combs
501 HOB TOR
Wheston
Grindlow
Foolow
Eyam
Grindleford
Froggatt
Goyt Valley
Tideswell
Litton
Wardlow
Stoney Middleton
Calver
Curbar
559
Tunstead
Fairfield
Buxton
Wormhill
Miller's Dale
Cressbrook
Rowland
Hassop
Wye Valley
Poole's
Blackwell
Little Longstone
Great Longstone
Baslow
Solomon's Temple
551 AXE EDGE
Taddington
Pilsley
Chatsworth
Chelmorton
Ashford in the Water
Edensor
Hob Hurst's House
Flagg
Sheldon
Bakewell
Magpie Mine
Beeley
Flash
R Dove
Earl Sterndale
Monyash
Over Haddon
Caudwell's Mill
Hollinsclough
Rowsley
Lathkill Dale
Haddon Hall
Longnor
Crowdecote
Arbor Low Stone Circle
Youlgreave
Alport
Stanton in Peak
Darwin Forest
Pilsbury
Middleton
Nine Ladies
R Derwent
Darley Dale
Two Dales
505 THE ROACHES
PEAK DISTRICT NATIONAL PARK
Stanton Lees
Hartington
Birchover
Churchtown
Peak Railway
Darley Bridge
Brund
Wensley
Oker Side
100
Heathcote
Elton
Winster
Market House
Biggin
Hulme End
Cable Car
Heights of Abraham
0 1 2 3 4 miles
0 1 2 3 4 5 kilometres
A628
A616
A629
A57
A624
A6015
A6013
A6187
A623
A625
A621
A6
A5004
A537
A5270
A6020
A619
A515
A53
B6105
B6049
B6001
B6465
B5055
B5054
B5053
B5056
B6012
B6050
B6054
B6521
B6062
B6106
B6462
B6077
B6076
B6107
A635
A6024
A6102

124
116
101
DONCASTER
ROTHERHAM
CHESTERFIELD
MANSFIELD
BARNSLEY
Worksop
Cudworth
Thurnscoe
Bolton upon Dearne
Wombwell
Hoyland
Wath upon Dearne
Mexborough
Swinton
Conisbrough
Rawmarsh
Armthorpe
Bessacarr
New Rossington
Tickhill
Maltby
Bawtry
Bramley
Wickersley
Thurcroft
Dinnington
Aughton
Aston
Killamarsh
Mosborough
Eckington
Staveley
Brimington
Clowne
Bolsover
Shirebrook
Market Warsop
Edwinstowe
Ollerton
North Wingfield
Clay Cross
Sutton-in-Ashfield
Sherwood Forest
Clumber Park
DONCASTER RAILPORT
Doncaster Sheffield
Roche Abbey
Welbeck Abbey
Creswell Crags
Hardwick Hall
Bolsover Castle
Sutton Scarsdale Hall
Rufford Abbey
A1(M)
M1
M18
A1
A57
A60
A614
A616
A617
A619
A631
A634
A638
A630
A635

125
115
102
Epworth
Gainsborough
Retford
Bawtry
Ollerton
Saxilby
Skellingthorpe
North Hykeham
Kirton in Lindsey
Bottesford
Tuxford
Haxey
Misterton
Owston Ferry
Messingham
Scotter
Blyton
Corringham
Hemswell
Lea
Marton
Torksey
Dunham-on-Trent
Markham Moor
East Markham
Elkesley
Rampton
Clarborough
Mattersey
Everton
Finningley
Rossington
Doncaster Sheffield
Wroot
Misson
Harwell
Scaftworth
Scrooby
Drakeholes
Wiseton
Beckingham
Walkeringham
Gringley on the Hill
Saundby
Bole
North Wheatley
South Wheatley
Sturton le Steeple
North Leverton with Habblesthorpe
South Leverton
Littleborough
Cottam
Treswell
Grove
Welham
Babworth
Ranby
Ordsall
Eaton
Gamston
Upton
Askham
Headon
Rockley
West Drayton
Milton
Bothamsall
Walesby
Laxton
Egmanton
Kneesall
Eakring
Wellow
Ompton
Kersall
Ossington
Moorhouse
Weston
Sutton on Trent
Carlton-on-Trent
Cromwell
Girton
Besthorpe
South Scarle
North Scarle
Eagle
Swinderby
Thorpe on the Hill
Whisby
Doddington
Harby
Thorney
Wigsley
Spalford
Newton on Trent
Laughterton
Fenton
Kettlethorpe
Brampton
Sturton by Stow
Stow
Coates
Ingham
Fillingham
Glentworth
Kexby
Upton
Heapham
Springthorpe
Harpswell
Willingham by Stow
Gate Burton
Knaith
Pilham
Aisby
Blyborough
Grayingham
Northorpe
Laughton
Scotton
East Ferry
Wildsworth
Gunthorpe
West Stockwith
East Stockwith
Walkerith
Morton
East Lound
Graiselound
Westwoodside
Blaxton
Auckley
Branton
Belton
Beltoft
Westgate
Carrhouse
Sandtoft
West Butterwick
East Butterwick
Susworth
Scotterthorpe
Manton
Burringham
Althorpe
Brumby
Ashby
Yaddlethorpe
Hatfield Woodhouse
Dunsville
Low Burnham
Old Rectory
Ranskill
Torworth
Clayworth
Lound
Wetlands Animal Park
Sutton cum Lound
Hayton
Barnby Moor
Mattersey Abbey
Idle Valley
Nether Headon
Stokeham
Laneham
East Drayton
Ragnall
Darlton
North Clifton
South Clifton
Fledborough
High Marnham
Low Marnham
Skegby
Normanton on Trent
Grassthorpe
Sibthorpe
Bevercotes
West Markham
Kirton
Boughton
Perlethorpe
New Ollerton
National Holocaust Centre
Rufford Abbey
Norwell Woodhouse
Haddington
Aubourn
Thurlby
Bassingham
South Hykeham
Birchwood
Scofton
Bilsthorpe
Holme
Bathley
Langford Lowfields
Brough
Fossdyke Navigation
Burton Waters
North Carlton
South Carlton
Bransby
Scampton
Cammeringham
West Burton Power Station
Sundown Adventureland
River Idle
Chesterfield Canal
R Trent
R Till
R Eau
R Ryton
M18
M180
M181
A18
A1
A57
A614
A631
A638
A620
A634
A156
A159
A161
A1133
A1500
A6075
A46
B1396
B1403
B1205
B1241
B1190
B1398
B1400
B6420
B6079
B6387
B1164
0 1 2 3 4 miles
0 1 2 3 4 5 kilometres

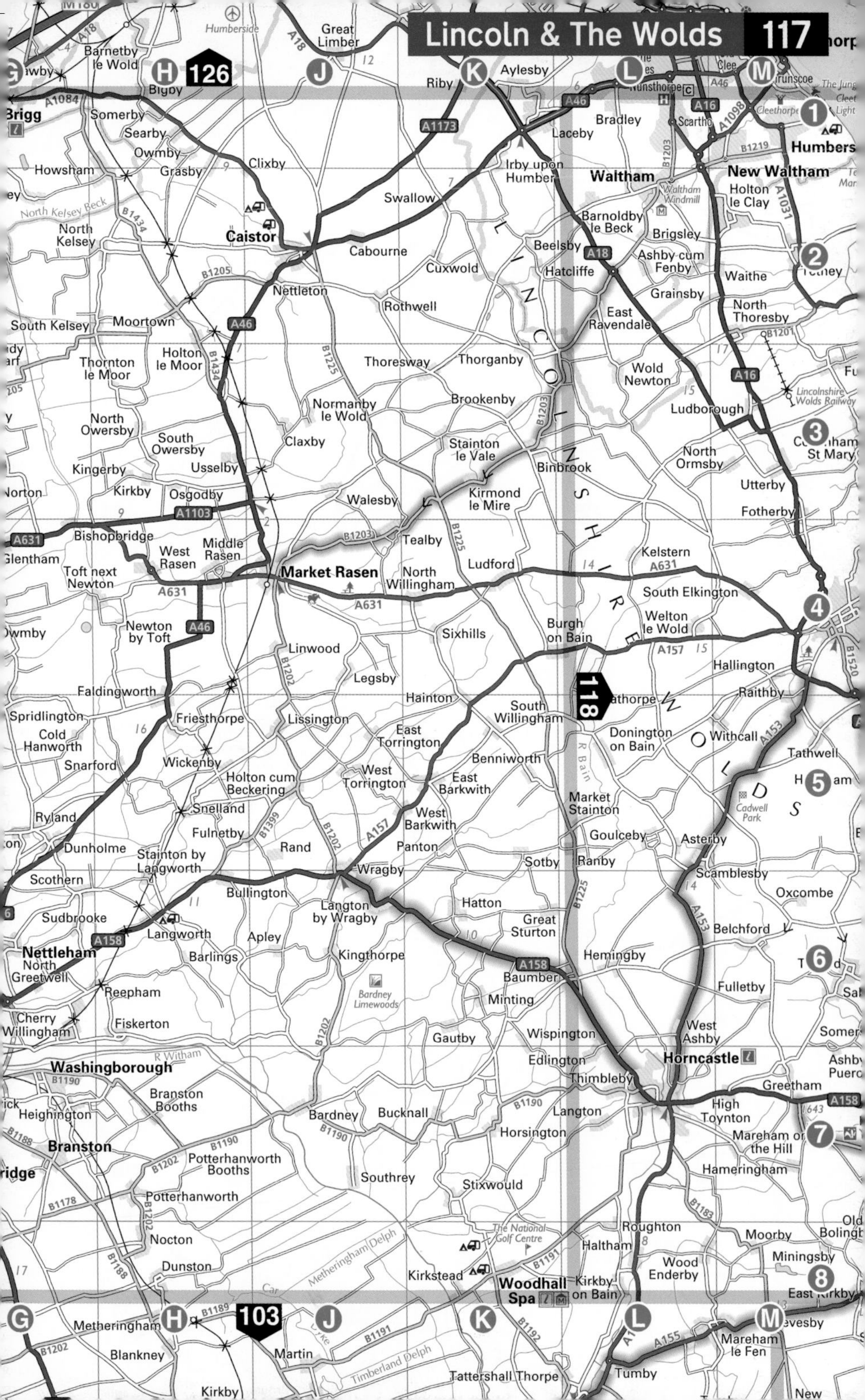

126
118
103
Humberside
Great Limber
Barnetby le Wold
Bigby
Riby
Aylesby
Nunsthorpe
Brigg
Somerby
Searby
Owmby
Grasby
Clixby
Howsham
North Kelsey
North Kelsey Beck
Caistor
Cabourne
Swallow
Irby upon Humber
Laceby
Bradley
Scartho
Waltham
Waltham Windmill
New Waltham
Holton le Clay
Humberston
Cleethorpes
Barnoldby le Beck
Beelsby
Brigsley
Ashby cum Fenby
Hatcliffe
Cuxwold
Nettleton
Rothwell
Waithe
Tetney
Grainsby
North Thoresby
East Ravendale
South Kelsey
Moortown
Holton le Moor
Thornton le Moor
Thoresway
Thorganby
Wold Newton
Lincolnshire Wolds Railway
Ludborough
Normanby le Wold
Brookenby
North Owersby
South Owersby
Claxby
Stainton le Vale
Binbrook
North Ormsby
Kingerby
Usselby
Kirkby
Osgodby
Walesby
Kirmond le Mire
Utterby
Fotherby
Bishopbridge
Glentham
West Rasen
Middle Rasen
Tealby
Toft next Newton
Market Rasen
North Willingham
Ludford
Kelstern
South Elkington
Welton le Wold
Newton by Toft
Sixhills
Burgh on Bain
Linwood
Legsby
Hallington
Faldingworth
Hainton
Raithby
South Willingham
Withcall
Spridlington
Friesthorpe
Lissington
East Torrington
Donington on Bain
Cold Hanworth
Snarford
Wickenby
Benniworth
Tathwell
Holton cum Beckering
West Torrington
East Barkwith
Market Stainton
Cadwell Park
Ryland
Snelland
West Barkwith
Goulceby
Asterby
Fulnetby
Dunholme
Stainton by Langworth
Rand
Panton
Sotby
Ranby
Scamblesby
Scothern
Wragby
Bullington
Oxcombe
Sudbrooke
Langton by Wragby
Hatton
Great Sturton
Langworth
Apley
Belchford
Nettleham
North Greetwell
Barlings
Kingthorpe
Baumber
Hemingby
Reepham
Bardney Limewoods
Minting
Fulletby
Cherry Willingham
Fiskerton
Gautby
Wispington
West Ashby
R Witham
Washingborough
Edlington
Horncastle
Thimbleby
Branston Booths
Greetham
Heighington
Bardney
Bucknall
Langton
High Toynton
Horsington
Branston
Mareham on the Hill
Potterhanworth Booths
Hameringham
Southrey
Potterhanworth
Stixwould
Nocton
The National Golf Centre
Roughton
Moorby
Haltham
Metheringham Delph
Dunston
Miningsby
Wood Enderby
Kirkstead
Woodhall Spa
Kirkby on Bain
East Kirkby
Metheringham
Revesby
Mareham le Fen
Blankney
Martin
Timberland Delph
Tattershall Thorpe
Tumby
Kirkby
New
LINCOLNSHIRE WOLDS

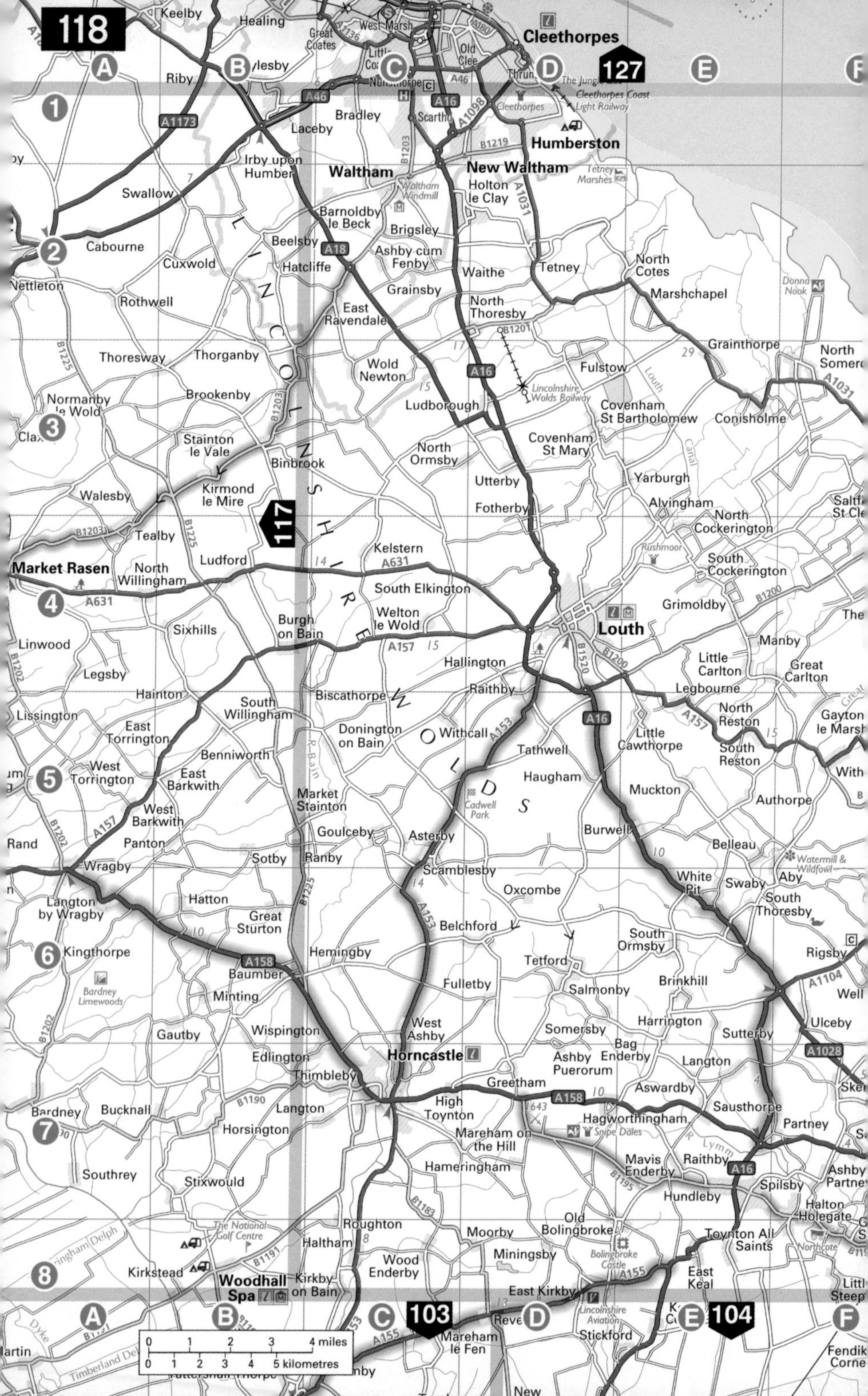
Keelby
Healing
Great Coates
West Marsh
Cleethorpes
127
Riby
Aylesby
Little Coates
Nunsthorpe
Old Clee
Thrunscoe
The Jungle
Cleethorpes Coast Light Railway
A1173
A46
Bradley
Scartho
A16
A1098
Laceby
Humberston
Irby upon Humber
B1203
B1219
Waltham
New Waltham
Tetney Marshes
Swallow
Waltham Windmill
Holton le Clay
A1031
Barnoldby le Beck
Brigsley
Beelsby
A18
Cabourne
Ashby cum Fenby
Cuxwold
Hatcliffe
Waithe
Tetney
North Cotes
Nettleton
Grainsby
Donna Nook
Rothwell
East Ravendale
North Thoresby
Marshchapel
B1201
B1225
Thoresway
Thorganby
Wold Newton
Grainthorpe
North Somercotes
Fulstow
Lincolnshire Wolds Railway
A1031
Normanby le Wold
Brookenby
Ludborough
Covenham St Bartholomew
Conisholme
Claxby
Stainton le Vale
Binbrook
North Ormsby
Covenham St Mary
Canal
Kirmond le Mire
Utterby
Yarburgh
Walesby
Alvingham
117
Fotherby
North Cockerington
Saltfleetby St Clement
B1203
Tealby
Rushmoor
Kelstern
South Cockerington
Market Rasen
North Willingham
Ludford
A631
South Elkington
Grimoldby
A631
Welton le Wold
B1200
Sixhills
Burgh on Bain
Louth
Manby
Linwood
A157
B1520
Legsby
Hallington
Little Carlton
Great Carlton
B1202
Hainton
Raithby
Legbourne
Biscathorpe
South Willingham
A16
North Reston
Lissington
East Torrington
Donington on Bain
Withcall
A153
Little Cawthorpe
Gayton le Marsh
Benniworth
Tathwell
South Reston
West Torrington
East Barkwith
Haugham
Market Stainton
Cadwell Park
Muckton
Authorpe
West Barkwith
Goulceby
Asterby
Burwell
Rand
A157
Panton
Sotby
Ranby
Belleau
Wragby
Scamblesby
Watermill & Wildfowl
Aby
Langton by Wragby
Hatton
Oxcombe
White Pit
Swaby
South Thoresby
Great Sturton
Belchford
South Ormsby
Kingthorpe
Hemingby
Tetford
Rigsby
A158
Baumber
Fulletby
Brinkhill
A1104
Bardney Limewoods
Minting
Salmonby
Well
West Ashby
Harrington
Ulceby
Gautby
Wispington
Somersby
Sutterby
Edlington
Horncastle
Ashby Puerorum
Bag Enderby
Langton
A1028
Thimbleby
Greetham
Aswardby
Bardney
Bucknall
B1190
Langton
High Toynton
A158
Hagworthingham
Sausthorpe
Partney
Horsington
Mareham on the Hill
Snipe Dales
R Lymn
Southrey
Mavis Enderby
Raithby
Stixwould
Hameringham
B1195
A16
Spilsby
Ashby by Partney
B1183
Hundleby
Halton Holegate
The National Golf Centre
Roughton
Old Bolingbroke
Haltham
Moorby
Toynton All Saints
Northcote
Bolingbroke Castle
Miningsby
B1191
Wood Enderby
Kirkstead
A155
East Keal
Woodhall Spa
Kirkby on Bain
East Kirkby
Little Steeping
103
Revesby
Lincolnshire Aviation
104
A155
Mareham le Fen
Stickford
Martin
Timberland Delph
Fendike Corner
New
0 1 2 3 4 miles
0 1 2 3 4 5 kilometres
A B C D E F
1 2 3 4 5 6 7 8

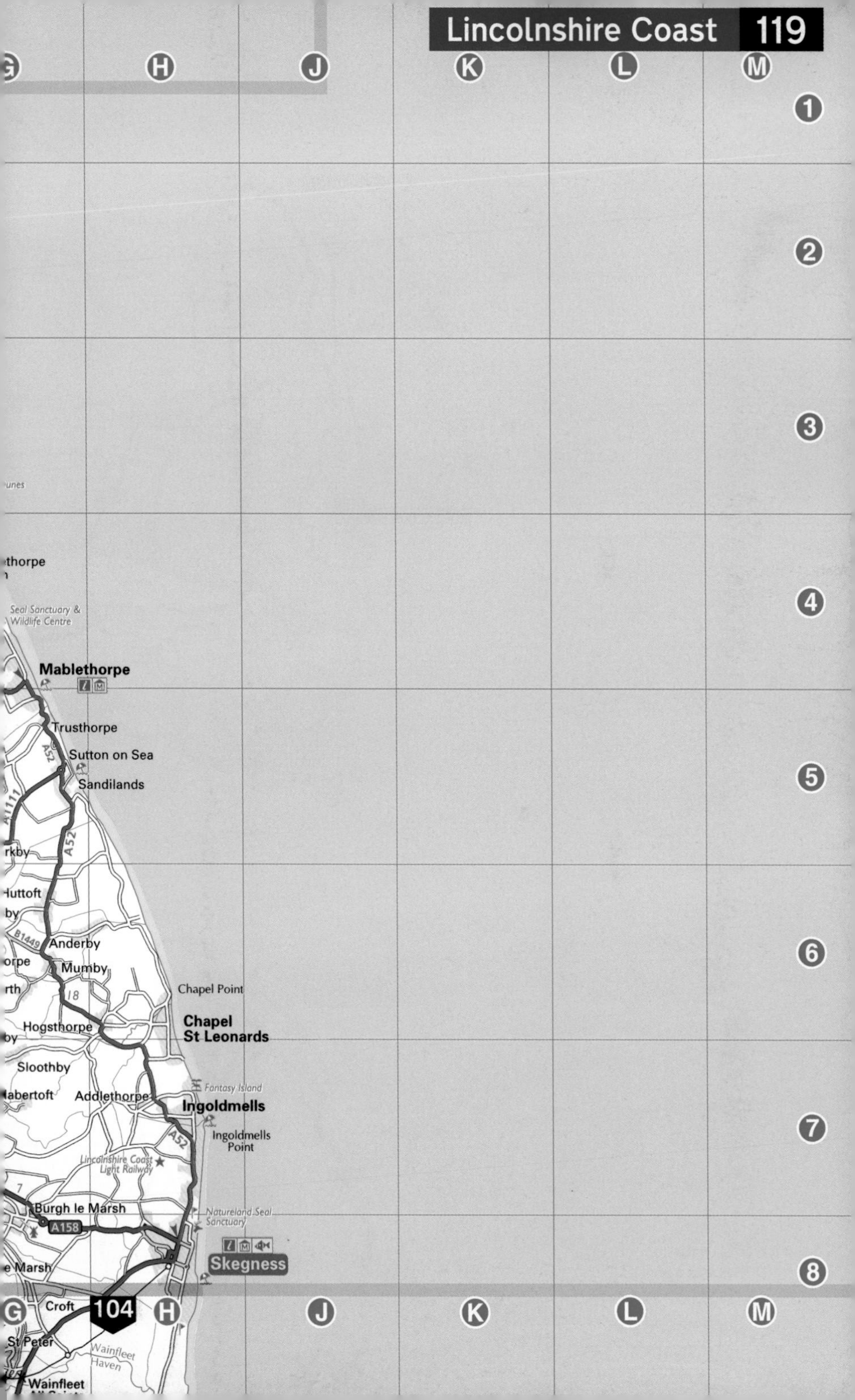

G
H
J
K
L
M
1
2
3
4
5
6
7
8
thorpe
Seal Sanctuary & Wildlife Centre
Mablethorpe
Trusthorpe
A52
Sutton on Sea
Sandilands
A1111
rkby
A52
Huttoft
B1449
Anderby
Mumby
Chapel Point
Hogsthorpe
Chapel St Leonards
Sloothby
Fantasy Island
Addlethorpe
Ingoldmells
A52
Ingoldmells Point
Lincolnshire Coast Light Railway
Burgh le Marsh
A158
Natureland Seal Sanctuary
Skegness
e Marsh
Croft
104
St Peter
Wainfleet Haven
Wainfleet

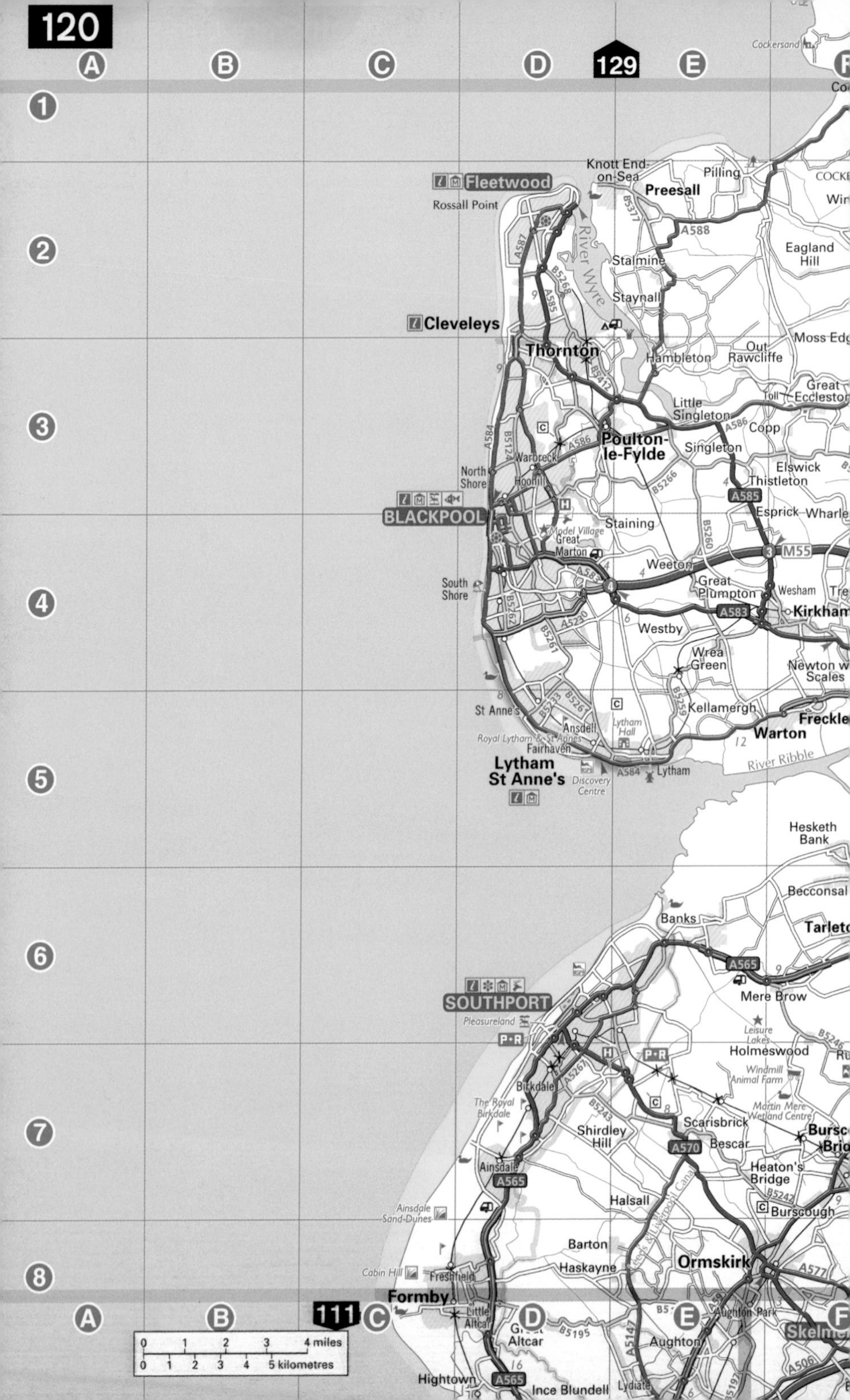

A
B
C
D
129
E
1
2
3
4
5
6
7
8
Cockersand
Knott End-on-Sea
Pilling
Preesall
Fleetwood
Rossall Point
B5377
A588
River Wyre
A587
B5268
A585
Stalmine
Staynall
Eagland Hill
Cleveleys
Thornton
Hambleton
Out Rawcliffe
Moss Edg
B5412
Great Eccleston
Toll
Little Singleton
A586
Copp
A584
B5124
Poulton-le-Fylde
Singleton
Warbreck
North Shore
Hoohill
B5266
Elswick
Thistleton
A585
BLACKPOOL
Staining
Esprick
Wharle
Model Village
Great Marton
B5260
M55
Weeton
South Shore
A583
Great Plumpton
Wesham
Kirkham
B5262
A5230
A583
Westby
B5261
Wrea Green
Newton w Scales
St Anne's
B5233
B5261
Ansdell
Lytham Hall
B5259
Kellamergh
Warton
Freckle
Royal Lytham & St Annes
Fairhaven
Lytham St Anne's
Discovery Centre
A584
Lytham
River Ribble
Hesketh Bank
Becconsal
Banks
Tarleto
A565
SOUTHPORT
Pleasureland
P+R
Mere Brow
Leisure Lakes
B5246
Holmeswood
H
Windmill Animal Farm
Birkdale
A5267
The Royal Birkdale
Martin Mere Wetland Centre
B5243
Scarisbrick
Shirdley Hill
Bescar
A570
Ainsdale
A565
Heaton's Bridge
Halsall
B5242
Burscough
Ainsdale Sand-Dunes
Leeds & Liverpool Canal
Barton
Cabin Hill
Freshfield
Haskayne
Ormskirk
A577
Formby
111
Little Altcar
Great Altcar
B5195
A5147
Aughton
Aughton Park
Skelme
0 1 2 3 4 miles
0 1 2 3 4 5 kilometres
Hightown
A565
Ince Blundell
Lydiate
A506

Forest of Bowland
Abbeystead
Dolphinholme
WHINS BROW
130
Slaidburn
HAWTHORNTHWAITE FELL
Newton-in-Bowland
Dunsop Bridge
Scorton
Calder Fell
TOTRIDGE FELL
BRADFORD FELL
Holden
Bolton-by-Bowland
Oakenclough
Sawley
FAIRSNAPE FELL
PARLICK
Calder Vale
Whitewell
Grindleton
Rimington
West Bradford
Downham
Waddington
Chatburn
Horrocksford
Worston
Bashall Eaves
Chipping
Claughton
Beacon Fell
Clitheroe
PENDLE HILL
Barley
White Chapel
Hesketh Lane
Longridge Fell
Pendleton
Inglewhite
Cromwell's Bridge
Bilsborrow
Knowle Green
Hurst Green
Barrow
Great Mitton
Longridge
Wiswell
Sabden
Fence
Goosnargh
Whalley
Higham
Old Langho
Chingle Hall
Broughton
Little Town
Ribchester
Copster Green
Billington
Read
Simonstone
Padiham
Gawthorpe Hall
Grimsargh
Langho
Higher Bartle
Sharoe Green
Fulwood
Balderstone
Great Harwood
Clayton-le-Moors
122
Osbaldeston
Wilpshire
Brockholes
Ribbleton
Samlesbury Hall
Mellor Brook
Mellor
Rishton
Church
Dill Hall
BLACKBURN
Witton
Higher Walton
Walton-le-Dale
Accrington
Oswaldtwistle
Hoghton
Pleasington
Baxenden
Hoghton Tower
Feniscliffe
Feniscowles
Riley Green
Lower Darwen
Goodshaw
Ewood
Earcroft
Bamber Bridge
Farington
Brindle
Belthorn
Reeds Holme
Haslingden
Wellybobs
Tockholes
Abbey Village
Blackburn with Darwen
Waterside
Leyland
Higher Wheelton
Sunnyhurst
Clough Head
Lane Side
East Lancashire Railway
Cuerden Valley
Clayton-le-Woods
Whittle-le-Woods
Withnell
Darwen
Roddlesworth
Hoddlesden
Helmshore
Textiles Museum
Buckshaw Village
Wheelton
Brinscall
Euxton
Leeds & Liverpool Canal
Chatterton
Stubbins
Edenfield
Chorley
Ramsbottom
Edgworth
Shuttleworth
Cowling
Charnock Richard
Turton Tower
Turton Bottoms
Chapeltown
Yarrow Valley
Belmont
WINTER HILL
Egerton
Nuttall
Summerseat
Rivington
Lever Park
Jumbles
Greenmount
Coppull
Grimeford Village
Mossy Lea
Adlington
Horwich
Bromley Cross
Tottington
Eagley
Smithills Hall
Astley Bridge
Chesham
BURY
Blackrod
Ainsworth
Halliwell
Breightmet
Appley Bridge
Standish
Shevington
Haigh Hall
Aspull
BOLTON
Deane
Daubhill
Moses Gate
Marylebone
Little Lever
Radcliffe
112
113
Holland
Scholes
Newtown
Orrell
Pemberton
Ince-in-Makerfield
Hindley
Kearsley
Atherton
Walkden
Prestwich
M6
M61
M65
M60
A59
A666
A671
A680
A677
A56
A6
A49
A675
A58
A673
A676
A5209
B6478
B6243
B6245
B5269
B6241
B6230
B6233
B6234
B6232
B6236
B6391
B6213
B6196
B6226
B6209
B5239
B5238
A5106
A579
A577

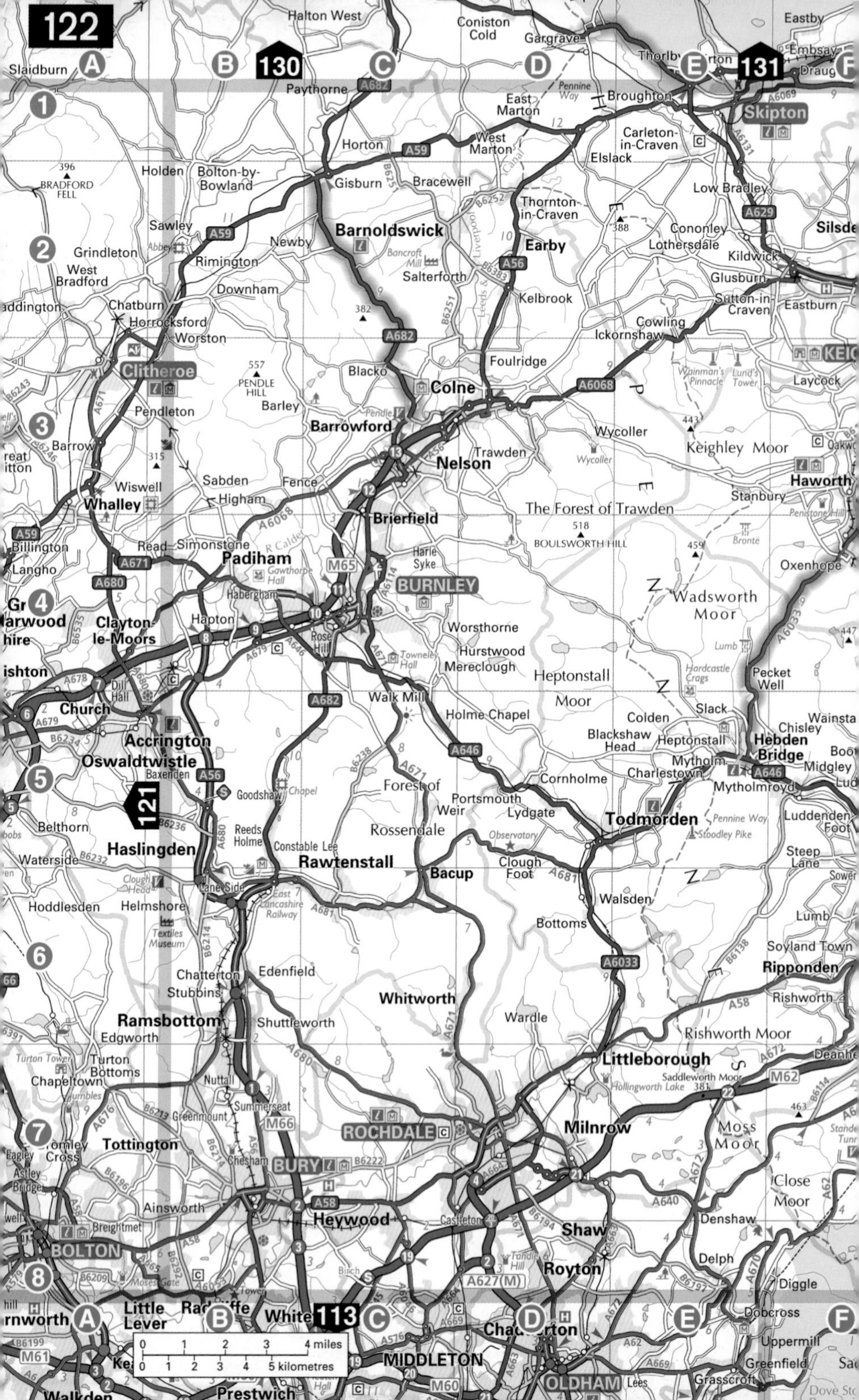

130
131
121
113
Slaidburn
Halton West
Coniston Cold
Gargrave
Eastby
Embsay
Paythorne
Broughton
Skipton
East Marton
Horton
West Marton
Carleton-in-Craven
Elslack
Holden
Bolton-by-Bowland
Gisburn
Bracewell
Low Bradley
BRADFORD FELL
Thornton-in-Craven
Sawley
Barnoldswick
Earby
Cononley
Lothersdale
Silsden
Grindleton
Newby
Rimington
Kildwick
West Bradford
Salterforth
Glusburn
Downham
Kelbrook
Sutton-in-Craven
Eastburn
Chatburn
Horrocksford
Worston
Cowling
Ickornshaw
Clitheroe
Blacko
Foulridge
Laycock
PENDLE HILL
Colne
Pendleton
Barley
Barrowford
Wycoller
Keighley Moor
Barrow
Nelson
Trawden
Haworth
Sabden
Fence
Wiswell
Whalley
Higham
Brierfield
The Forest of Trawden
Stanbury
BOULSWORTH HILL
Billington
Read
Simonstone
Padiham
Oxenhope
Langho
Harle Syke
BURNLEY
Wadsworth Moor
Habergham
Clayton-le-Moors
Hapton
Worsthorne
Rose Hill
Hurstwood
Mereclough
Heptonstall Moor
Pecket Well
Church
Dill Hall
Walk Mill
Colden
Slack
Accrington
Holme Chapel
Blackshaw Head
Heptonstall
Hebden Bridge
Oswaldtwistle
Mytholm
Charlestown
Midgley
Baxenden
Forest of Rossendale
Cornholme
Mytholmroyd
Goodshaw
Chapel
Portsmouth
Weir
Lydgate
Belthorn
Reeds Holme
Todmorden
Luddenden Foot
Haslingden
Constable Lee
Rawtenstall
Observatory
Stoodley Pike
Pennine Way
Waterside
Bacup
Clough Foot
Steep Lane
Lane Side
East Lancashire Railway
Walsden
Hoddlesden
Helmshore
Textiles Museum
Bottoms
Lumb
Soyland Town
Chatterton
Edenfield
Ripponden
Stubbins
Whitworth
Rishworth
Ramsbottom
Shuttleworth
Wardle
Edgworth
Rishworth Moor
Turton Tower
Turton Bottoms
Littleborough
Chapeltown
Nuttall
Saddleworth Moor
Hollingworth Lake
Summerseat
Greenmount
ROCHDALE
Milnrow
Moss Moor
Tottington
Bromley Cross
Eagley
Astley Bridge
Chesham
BURY
Close Moor
Ainsworth
Breightmet
Heywood
Castleton
Shaw
Denshaw
BOLTON
Delph
Royton
Diggle
Little Lever
Radcliffe
Whitefield
Chadderton
Dobcross
Uppermill
MIDDLETON
Greenfield
Walkden
Prestwich
OLDHAM
Lees
Grasscroft
0 1 2 3 4 miles
0 1 2 3 4 5 kilometres

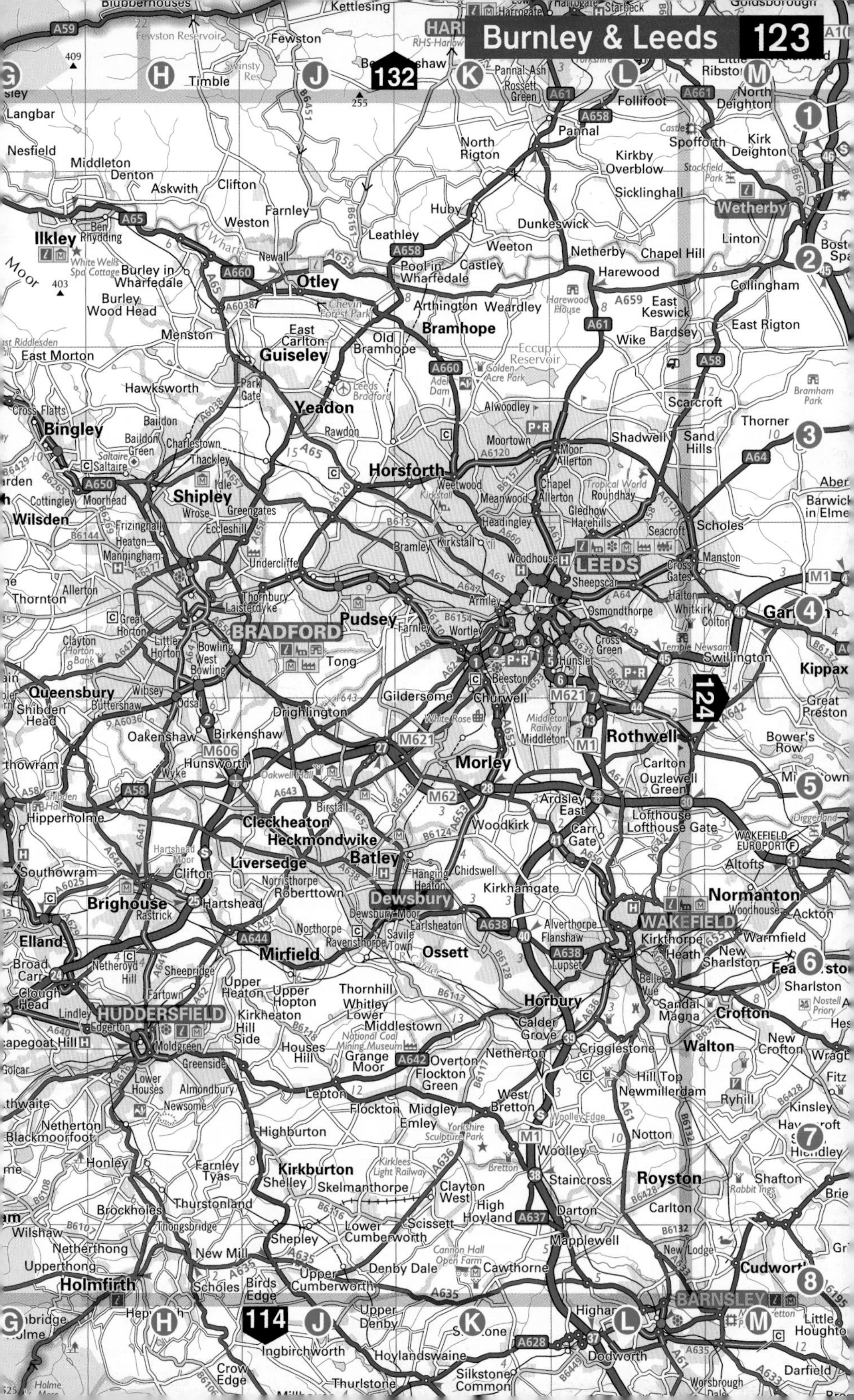
Blubberhouses
Kettlesing
Fewston Reservoir
Fewston
RHS Harlow
Timble
Swinsty Res
132
Pannal Ash
Rossett Green
Starbeck
Ribston
North Deighton
Follifoot
Pannal
Castle
Spofforth
Kirk Deighton
Langbar
Nesfield
Middleton
Denton
Askwith
Clifton
North Rigton
Kirkby Overblow
Sicklinghall
Stockfield Park
Wetherby
Farnley
Weston
Huby
Dunkeswick
Linton
Ben Rhydding
Ilkley
R. Wharfe
Leathley
Weeton
Netherby
Chapel Hill
Moor
White Wells Spa Cottage
Burley in Wharfedale
Newall
Otley
Pool in Wharfedale
Castley
Harewood
Collingham
Burley Wood Head
Chevin Forest Park
Arthington
Weardley
Harewood House
East Keswick
Bramhope
Menston
East Carlton
Old Bramhope
Wike
Bardsey
East Rigton
East Morton
Guiseley
Eccup Reservoir
Golden Acre Park
Hawksworth
Park Gate
Leeds Bradford
Adel Dam
Alwoodley
Scarcroft
Bramham Park
Cross Flatts
Bingley
Baildon
Yeadon
Rawdon
Baildon Green
Charlestown
Moortown
Shadwell
Sand Hills
Thorner
Saltaire
Thackley
Moor Allerton
Horsforth
Idle
Weetwood
Chapel Allerton
Tropical World
Roundhay
Aberford
Cottingley
Moorhead
Shipley
Kirkstall
Meanwood
Barwick in Elmet
Wilsden
Wrose
Greengates
Gledhow
Harehills
Scholes
Frizinghall
Eccleshill
Headingley
Seacroft
Heaton
Manningham
Bramley
Undercliffe
Woodhouse
LEEDS
Cross Gates
Manston
Thornton
Allerton
Thornbury
Laisterdyke
Sheepscar
Armley
Halton
Whitkirk
Colton
Osmondthorpe
Garforth
Great Horton
BRADFORD
Pudsey
Farnley
Wortley
Clayton
Horton Bank
Little Horton
Bowling
West Bowling
Tong
Hunslet
Beeston
Cross Green
Temple Newsam
Swillington
Kippax
Queensbury
Wibsey
Buttershaw
Odsal
Drighlington
Gildersome
Churwell
White Rose
Great Preston
Shibden Head
Middleton Railway
Middleton
124
Rothwell
Oakenshaw
Birkenshaw
Bower's Row
Southowram
Hunsworth
Wyke
Oakwell Hall
Morley
Carlton
Ouzlewell Green
Shibden Hall
Hipperholme
Birstall
Ardsley East
Lofthouse
Lofthouse Gate
Cleckheaton
Heckmondwike
Woodkirk
Carr Gate
Diggerland
WAKEFIELD EUROPORT
Hartshead Moor
Liversedge
Batley
Chidswell
Altofts
Clifton
Norristhorpe
Robertown
Hanging Heaton
Kirkhamgate
Normanton
Brighouse
Rastrick
Hartshead
Dewsbury
Dewsbury Moor
Earlsheaton
Alverthorpe
Flanshaw
WAKEFIELD
Woodhouse
Ackton
Elland
Northorpe
Savile Town
Kirkthorpe
Heath
Warmfield
Mirfield
Ravensthorpe
Ossett
Lupset
New Sharlston
Featherstone
Broad Carr
Netheroyd Hill
Sheepridge
R. Calder
Belle Vue
Sharlston
Clough Head
Fartown
Upper Heaton
Upper Hopton
Thornhill
Whitley Lower
Horbury
Sandal Magna
Nostell Priory
Crofton
Lindley
HUDDERSFIELD
Edgerton
Kirkheaton
Middlestown
Calder Grove
Hill Side
National Coal Mining Museum
Scapegoat Hill
Moldgreen
Houses Hill
Grange Moor
Overton
Netherton
Crigglestone
Walton
New Crofton
Golcar
Greenside
Flockton Green
Hill Top
Newmillerdam
Lower Houses
Almondbury
Lepton
West Bretton
Ryhill
Newsome
Flockton
Midgley
Woolley Edge
Kinsley
Netherton
Blackmoorfoot
Emley
Highburton
Yorkshire Sculpture Park
Notton
Havercroft
Hemsworth
Woolley
Honley
Farnley Tyas
Kirklees Light Railway
Bretton
Kirkburton
Shelley
Skelmanthorpe
Clayton West
Staincross
Royston
Shafton
Rabbit Ings
Thurstonland
High Hoyland
Brockholes
Carlton
Wilshaw
Thongsbridge
Lower Cumberworth
Scissett
Darton
Netherthong
Shepley
Mapplewell
New Lodge
New Mill
Cannon Hall Open Farm
Upperthong
Denby Dale
Cawthorne
Cudworth
Holmfirth
Scholes
Birds Edge
Upper Cumberworth
BARNSLEY
Hepworth
114
Upper Denby
Silkstone
Higham
Little Houghton
Ingbirchworth
Hoylandswaine
Dodworth
Crow Edge
Thurlstone
Silkstone Common
Worsbrough
Darfield
Holme Moss
A59
A65
A660
A658
A61
A661
A659
A58
A64
A6120
A650
A647
A6110
A62
A653
M621
M1
M606
M62
A643
A58
A641
A644
A6025
A629
A644
A638
A642
A636
A6117
A635
A637
A628
A633
B6451
B6161
B6157
B6154
B6481
B6123
B6124
B6128
B6117
B6118
B6116
B6108
B6107
B6106
B6449
B6132
B6428
B6378
B6164
B6144
B6265
B6429
B6269
A6038
A6036
A6037
A6177
A657
A616
A629
A640
A61
A6195
A6194

132
133
123
115
LEEDS
WAKEFIELD
BARNSLEY
DONCASTER
Wetherby
Tadcaster
Garforth
Castleford
Pontefract
Knottingley
Normanton
Featherstone
Rothwell
Hemsworth
Sherburn in Elmet
Kippax
Askern
Adwick le Street
South Elmsall
South Kirkby
Royston
Cudworth
Horbury
Crofton
Walton
Ackworth Moor Top
Thurnscoe
Bolton
0 1 2 3 4 miles
0 1 2 3 4 5 kilometres

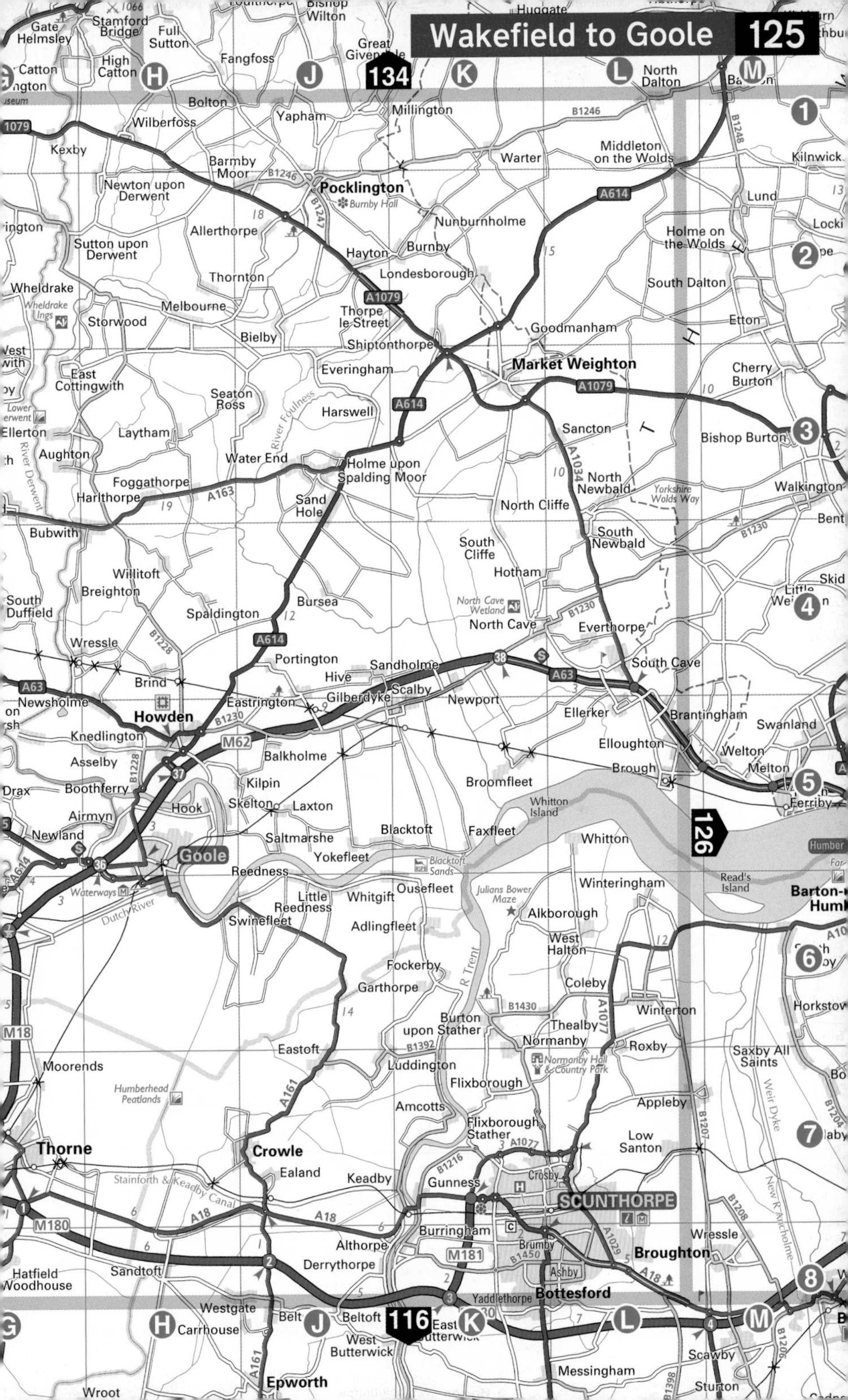

Pocklington
Market Weighton
Howden
Goole
Thorne
Crowle
Epworth
SCUNTHORPE
Bottesford
Broughton
Holme upon Spalding Moor
North Cave
South Cave
Brough
Gilberdyke
Stamford Bridge
Full Sutton
Fangfoss
Bolton
Wilberfoss
Yapham
Millington
Warter
Middleton on the Wolds
Kilnwick
Lund
Holme on the Wolds
South Dalton
Etton
Cherry Burton
Bishop Burton
Walkington
North Newbald
South Newbald
Sancton
Goodmanham
Londesborough
Nunburnholme
Burnby
Hayton
Shiptonthorpe
Everingham
Harswell
Seaton Ross
Bielby
Melbourne
Thornton
Allerthorpe
Barmby Moor
Newton upon Derwent
Kexby
Sutton upon Derwent
Wheldrake
Storwood
East Cottingwith
Laytham
Aughton
Foggathorpe
Harlthorpe
Bubwith
Willitoft
Breighton
South Duffield
Spaldington
Wressle
Bursea
Sand Hole
Water End
North Cliffe
South Cliffe
Hotham
Everthorpe
Sandholme
Portington
Hive
Eastrington
Scalby
Newport
Ellerker
Brantingham
Elloughton
Welton
Melton
Swanland
Broomfleet
Balkholme
Kilpin
Knedlington
Asselby
Boothferry
Skelton
Laxton
Hook
Airmyn
Newland
Saltmarshe
Blacktoft
Faxfleet
Yokefleet
Reedness
Whitton
Winteringham
Little Reedness
Whitgift
Ousefleet
Swinefleet
Adlingfleet
Alkborough
West Halton
Fockerby
Garthorpe
Coleby
Winterton
Thealby
Burton upon Stather
Normanby
Roxby
Eastoft
Luddington
Flixborough
Amcotts
Appleby
Flixborough Stather
Low Santon
Saxby All Saints
Horkstow
Moorends
Ealand
Keadby
Gunness
Crosby
Burringham
Althorpe
Derrythorpe
Brumby
Ashby
Yaddlethorpe
Wressle
Hatfield Woodhouse
Sandtoft
Westgate
Belt
Beltoft
Carrhouse
West Butterwick
East Butterwick
Messingham
Scawby
Sturton
Wroot
Newsholme
Brind
Drax
Humberhead Peatlands
Stainforth & Keadby Canal
Dutch River
Waterways
Blacktoft Sands
Julians Bower Maze
Whitton Island
Read's Island
Normanby Hall & Country Park
Burnby Hall
North Cave Wetland
Wheldrake Ings
Yorkshire Wolds Way
River Foulness
River Derwent
R Trent
Weir Dyke
New R Ancholme
A1079
A614
A163
A63
M62
A1034
A1077
A161
A18
M180
M181
A1029
M18
B1246
B1247
B1248
B1230
B1228
B1430
B1392
B1216
B1450
B1207
B1208
B1204
B1206
B1398
134
126
116

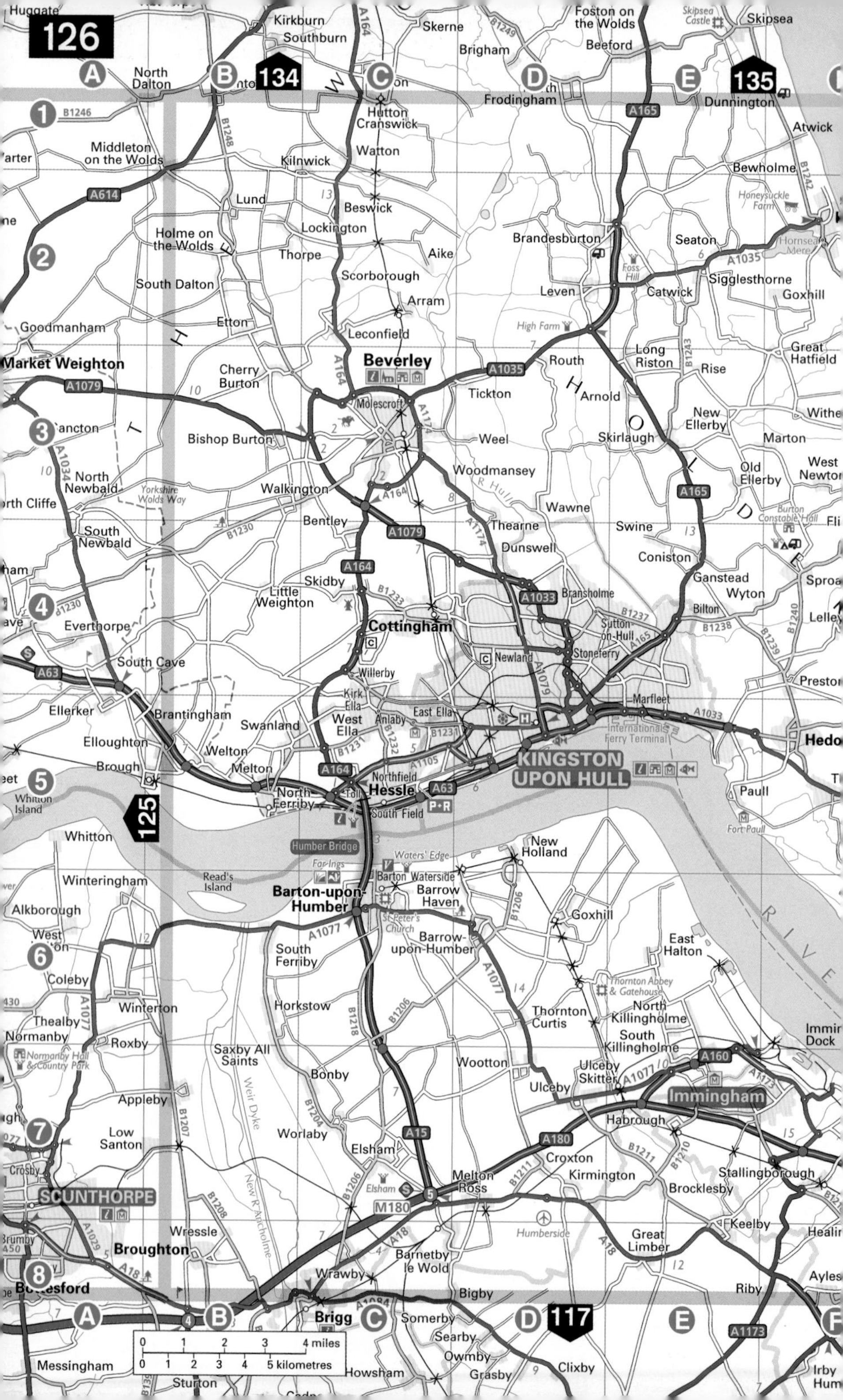
126
134
135
125
117
Huggate
Kirkburn
Southburn
Skerne
Foston on the Wolds
Skipsea Castle
Skipsea
North Dalton
Brigham
Beeford
Hutton Cranswick
Frodingham
Dunnington
Atwick
B1246
Middleton on the Wolds
Watton
Kilnwick
Bewholme
A614
Lund
Beswick
Honeysuckle Farm
Holme on the Wolds
Lockington
Brandesburton
Seaton
Hornsea Mere
Thorpe
Aike
Foss Hill
A1035
Sigglesthorne
South Dalton
Scorborough
Leven
Catwick
Goxhill
Arram
Goodmanham
Etton
Leconfield
High Farm
Long Riston
Great Hatfield
Market Weighton
Beverley
Routh
Rise
Cherry Burton
A1079
Tickton
Arnold
Molescroft
New Ellerby
Sancton
Bishop Burton
Weel
Skirlaugh
Marton
West Newton
North Newbald
Woodmansey
Old Ellerby
Walkington
Yorkshire Wolds Way
North Cliffe
A165
Wawne
Burton Constable Hall
Bentley
Thearne
Swine
South Newbald
B1230
A164
Dunswell
Coniston
A1174
Skidby
Ganstead
Sproatley
Little Weighton
A1033
Bransholme
Wyton
B1233
Bilton
Everthorpe
Cottingham
B1237
B1238
Lelley
Sutton-on-Hull
Newland
Stoneferry
B1240
South Cave
A1034
A63
Willerby
B1239
Preston
Kirk Ella
Ellerker
Brantingham
Swanland
West Ella
Anlaby
East Ella
Marfleet
Elloughton
B1231
B1232
A1105
International Ferry Terminal
Hedon
Welton
Kingston upon Hull
Brough
Melton
Northfield
Whitton Island
North Ferriby
Hessle
P+R
Paull
South Field
Whitton
Humber Bridge
Fort Paull
New Holland
Waters' Edge
Far Ings
Winteringham
Read's Island
Barton Waterside
Barton-upon-Humber
Barrow Haven
Goxhill
Alkborough
St Peter's Church
A1077
B1206
West Halton
South Ferriby
Barrow-upon-Humber
East Halton
Coleby
Thornton Abbey & Gatehouse
Horkstow
Winterton
Thornton Curtis
North Killingholme
Thealby
B1218
Normanby
Roxby
South Killingholme
Immingham Dock
Normanby Hall & Country Park
Saxby All Saints
Wootton
Ulceby Skitter
A160
A1173
Bonby
Ulceby
Immingham
Weir Dyke
Appleby
B1204
Habrough
Low Santon
Worlaby
A15
B1207
A180
Elsham
Croxton
B1211
B1210
Crosby
Kirmington
Stallingborough
Melton Ross
Brocklesby
Scunthorpe
New R. Ancholme
M180
B1208
Humberside
Keelby
Healing
Wressle
A1029
A18
Great Limber
Brumby
Broughton
Barnetby le Wold
Aylesby
Bottesford
Wrawby
Bigby
Riby
Brigg
Somerby
A1084
Searby
Owmby
Messingham
Grasby
Clixby
Howsham
Sturton
Irby upon Humber
RIVER
0 1 2 3 4 miles
0 1 2 3 4 5 kilometres
A B C D E F
1 2 3 4 5 6 7 8

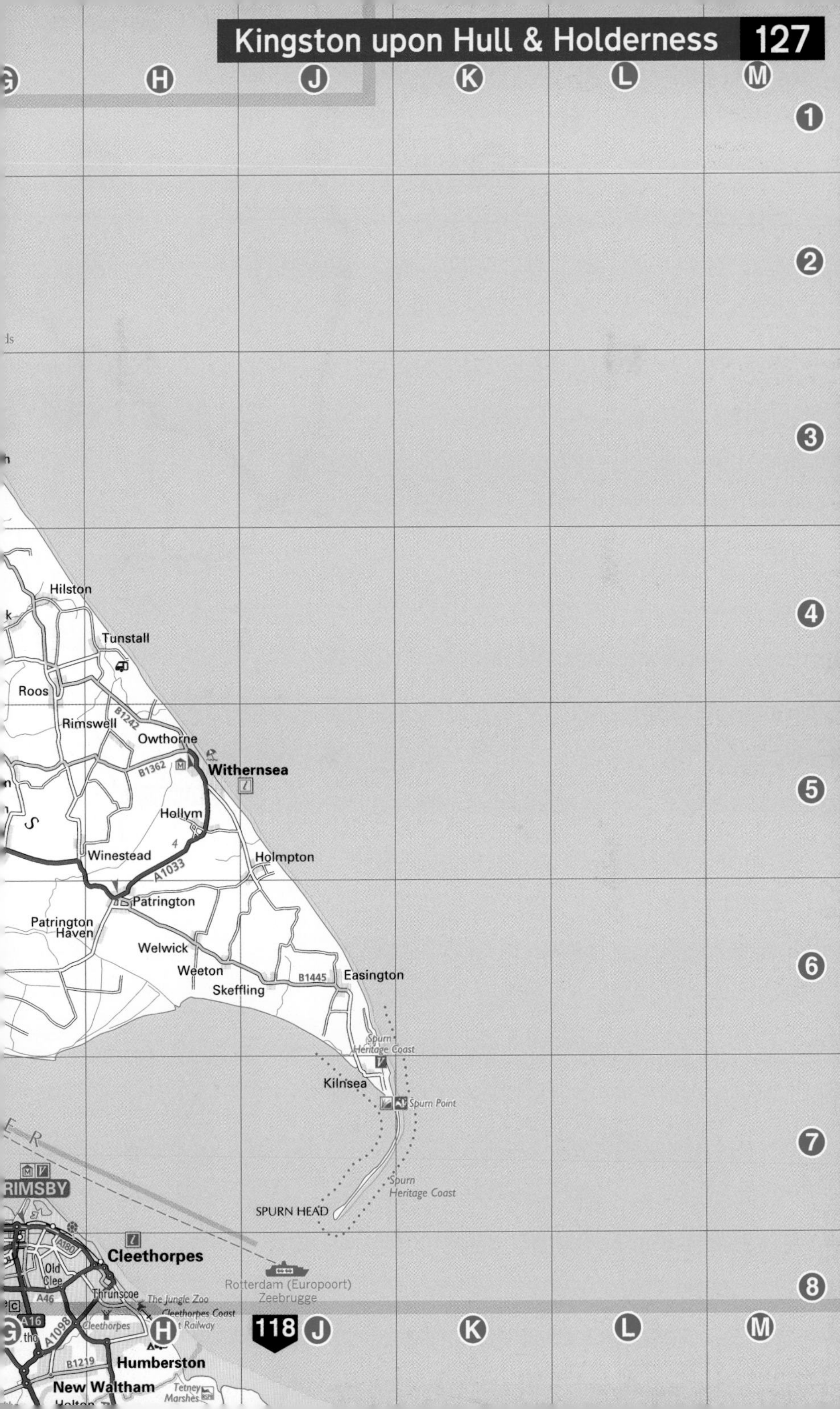
Hilston
Tunstall
Roos
Rimswell
B1242
Owthorne
B1362
Withernsea
Hollym
Winestead
A1033
Holmpton
Patrington
Patrington Haven
Welwick
Weeton
Skeffling
B1445
Easington
Spurn Heritage Coast
Kilnsea
Spurn Point
Spurn Heritage Coast
SPURN HEAD
GRIMSBY
A180
Cleethorpes
Old Clee
Thrunscoe
A46
The Jungle Zoo
Cleethorpes Coast Light Railway
A16
A1098
Humberston
B1219
New Waltham
Tetney Marshes
Rotterdam (Europoort)
Zeebrugge
118

Drigg
Holmrook
Hallsenna Moor
Muncaster Mill
Ravenglass & Eskdale Railway
Eskdale
652
HARTER FELL
River Esk
Devoke Water
Ravenglass
Roman Bath House
Muncaster
A595
Hall Dunnerdale
136
137
Waberthwaite
573
WHITFELL
Ulpha
LAKE DISTRICT
NATIONAL
PARK
Broughton Mills
Hycemoor
Selker Bay
Bootle
Swinside Stone Circle
A595
Lady Hall
Foxfield
600
BLACK COMBE
Whitbeck
The Green
Gutterby Spa
Whicham
The Hill
Silecroft
Kirksanton
A5093
Millom
Soutergate
A595
Hodbarrow
Haverigg
Haverigg Point
Askam in Furness
Sandscale Haws
South Lakes Safari Zoo
North Walney
BARROW-IN-FURNESS
Furness Abbey
Vickerstown
Barrow Island
A590
ISLE OF WALNEY
Sheep Island
Hilpsford Point
South Walney
A B C D E F
1 2 3 4 5 6 7 8
0 1 2 3 4 miles
0 1 2 3 4 5 kilometres

Hawkshead
Outgate
Bowness-on-Windermere
Kendal
Grange-over-Sands
Carnforth
Bolton-le-Sands
Morecambe
Heysham
Lancaster
MORECAMBE
BAY
Newby Bridge
Cartmel
Arnside
Silverdale
Milnthorpe
Levens
Oxenholme
Burneside
Crooklands
Burton-in-Kendal
Kirkby Lonsdale
Halton
Caton
Galgate
Glasson
Cockerham
Ellel
Scorton
Abbeystead
Dolphinholme
Hornby
Wray
Arkholme
Borwick
Warton
Yealand Conyers
Yealand Redmayne
Flookburgh
Allithwaite
Holker
Cark
Bardsea
Haverthwaite
Sunderland
Overton
Aldcliffe
Scorton
Pilling
Knott End-on-Sea
COCKERHAM MOSS
137
138
130
120
121

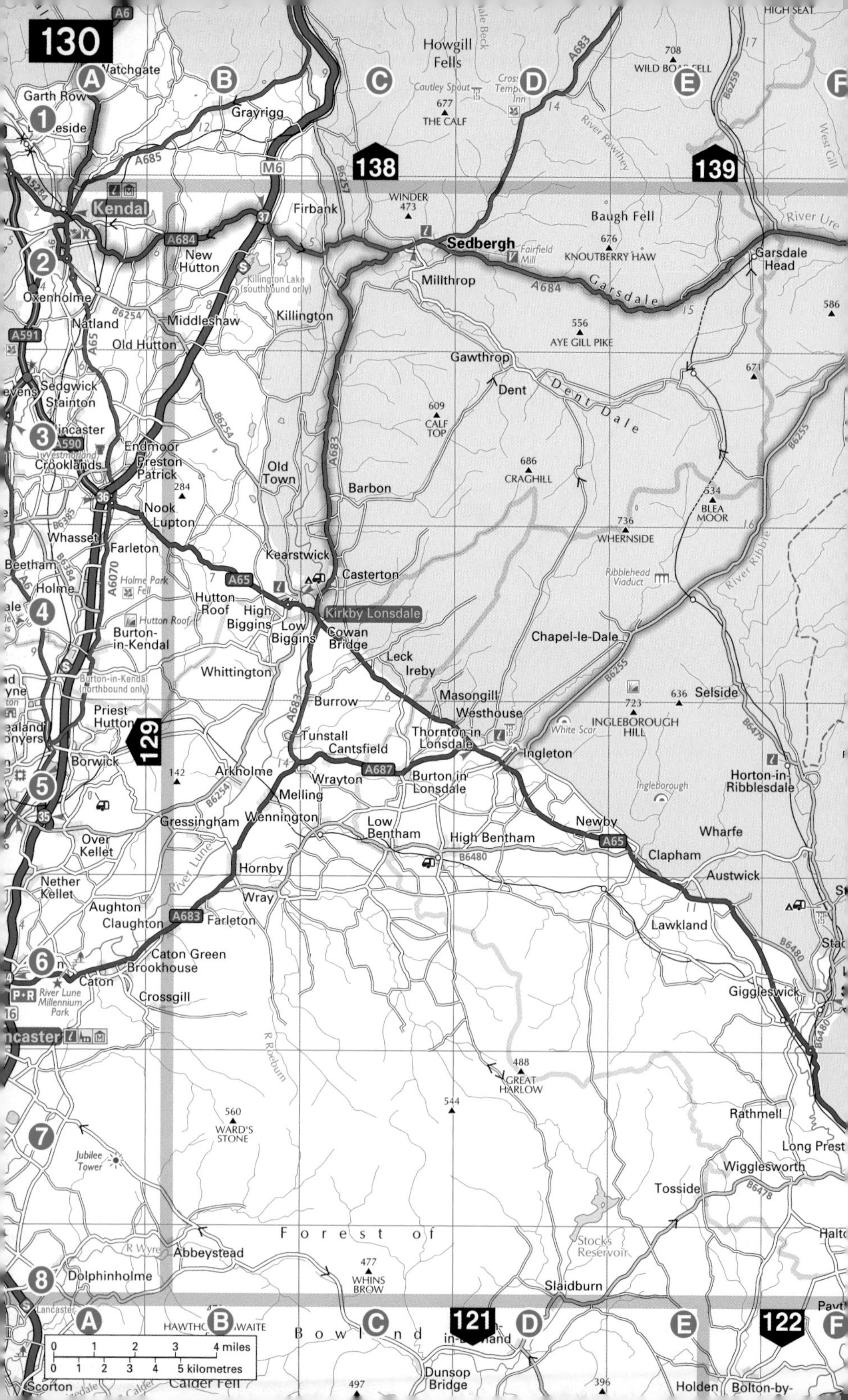

130
A
B
C
D
E
F
1
2
3
4
5
6
7
8
Watchgate
Garth Row
Grayrigg
Kendal
Oxenholme
Natland
Sedgwick
Stainton
Crooklands
Endmoor
Preston Patrick
Nook
Lupton
Whasset
Farleton
Beetham
Holme
Holme Park Fell
Hutton Roof
Burton-in-Kendal
Burton-in-Kendal (northbound only)
Priest Hutton
Borwick
Over Kellet
Nether Kellet
Aughton
Claughton
Caton Green
Brookhouse
Caton
River Lune Millennium Park
Crossgill
Jubilee Tower
Dolphinholme
Abbeystead
R Wyre
Scorton
Calder Fell
HAWTHORNTHWAITE
Howgill Fells
Cautley Spout
677
THE CALF
Cross Keys Temperance Inn
708
WILD BOAR FELL
HIGH SEAT
River Rawthey
West Gill
138
139
Firbank
WINDER
473
Sedbergh
Fairfield Mill
Baugh Fell
676
KNOUTBERRY HAW
Garsdale Head
Garsdale
River Ure
Milnthrop
New Hutton
Killington Lake (southbound only)
Killington
Middleshaw
Old Hutton
556
AYE GILL PIKE
586
Gawthrop
Dent
Dent Dale
609
CALF TOP
671
686
CRAGHILL
Old Town
Barbon
534
BLEA MOOR
736
WHERNSIDE
Ribblehead Viaduct
River Ribble
Kearstwick
Casterton
Kirkby Lonsdale
High Biggins
Low Biggins
Cowan Bridge
Leck
Ireby
Chapel-le-Dale
Whittington
Burrow
Masongill
Westhouse
723
INGLEBOROUGH HILL
636
Selside
White Scar
Thornton-in-Lonsdale
Ingleton
Tunstall
Cantsfield
129
142
Arkholme
Wrayton
Burton in Lonsdale
Melling
Ingleborough
Horton-in-Ribblesdale
Gressingham
Wennington
Low Bentham
High Bentham
Newby
Wharfe
Hornby
Clapham
Austwick
River Lune
Wray
Farleton
Lawkland
Giggleswick
R Roeburn
488
GREAT HARLOW
560
WARD'S STONE
544
Rathmell
Long Prest
Wigglesworth
Tosside
Forest of
Bowland
Stocks Reservoir
Halton
477
WHINS BROW
Slaidburn
121
122
Newton-in-Bowland
Dunsop Bridge
Holden
Bolton-by-
497
396
Lancaster
A6
A685
A684
A683
A65
A591
A590
A5284
A6070
A687
M6
B6254
B6257
B6259
B6255
B6385
B6384
B6480
B6479
B6478
Westmorland
36
35
37
0 1 2 3 4 miles
0 1 2 3 4 5 kilometres

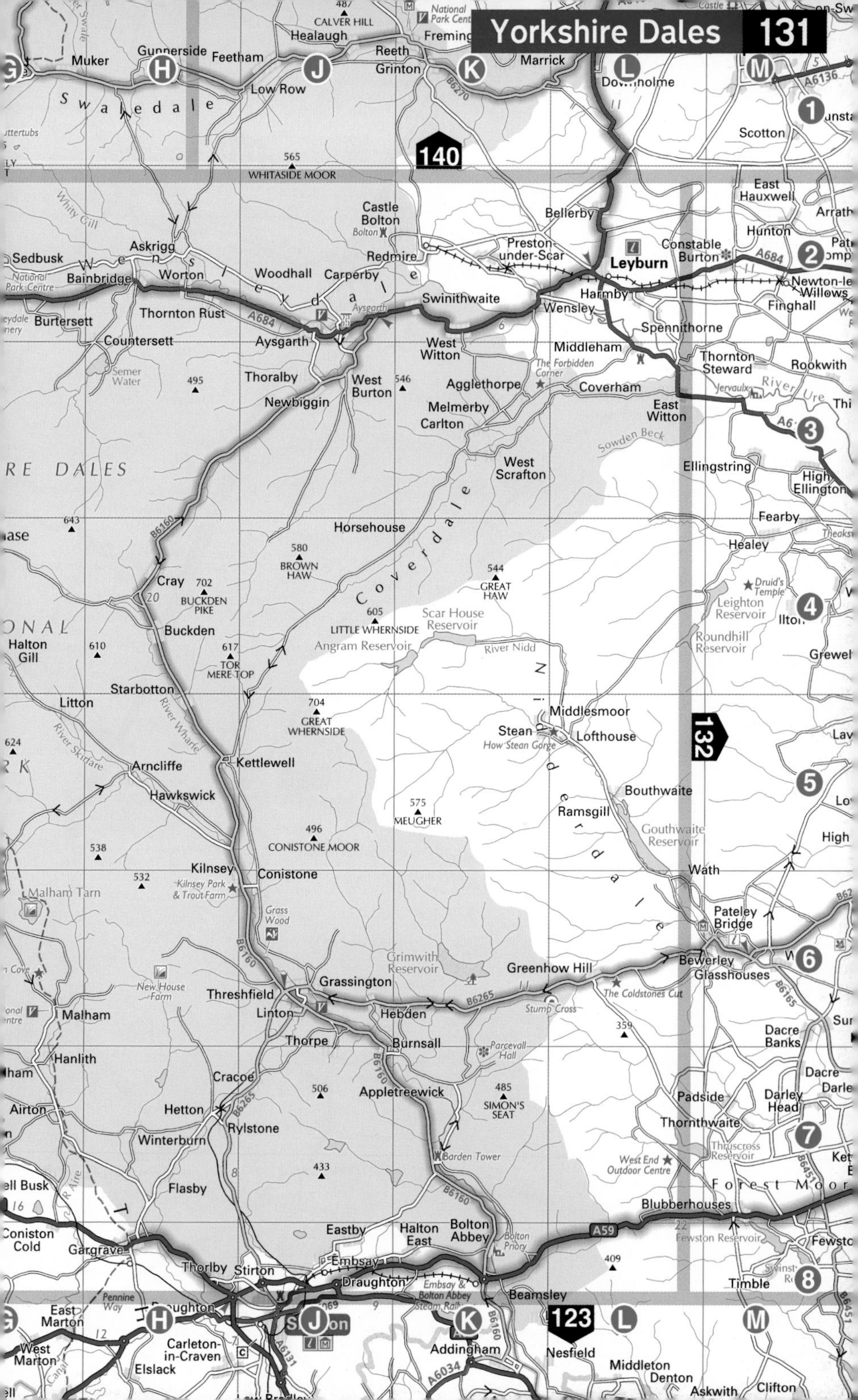

Muker
Gunnerside
Feetham
Healaugh
Reeth
Grinton
Low Row
Marrick
Downholme
Swaledale
Scotton
140
565
WHITASIDE MOOR
Castle Bolton
Bellerby
East Hauxwell
Hunton
Askrigg
Sedbusk
Bainbridge
Worton
Woodhall
Carperby
Redmire
Preston-under-Scar
Leyburn
Constable Burton
A684
Newton-le-Willows
Harmby
Wensley
Finghall
Swinithwaite
Thornton Rust
Burtersett
Countersett
Aysgarth
West Witton
Spennithorne
Middleham
Thornton Steward
Rookwith
The Forbidden Corner
Coverham
Agglethorpe
Semer Water
495
Thoralby
West Burton
546
Newbiggin
Melmerby
Carlton
East Witton
River Ure
Sowden Beck
West Scrafton
Ellingstring
High Ellington
643
B6160
Horsehouse
Fearby
Healey
580
BROWN HAW
544
GREAT HAW
Druid's Temple
Leighton Reservoir
Ilton
Cray
702
BUCKDEN PIKE
Buckden
605
LITTLE WHERNSIDE
Scar House Reservoir
Angram Reservoir
River Nidd
Roundhill Reservoir
Halton Gill
610
617
TOR MERE TOP
Coverdale
Starbotton
Litton
704
GREAT WHERNSIDE
Middlesmoor
Stean
How Stean Gorge
Lofthouse
132
River Wharfe
River Skirfare
Arncliffe
Kettlewell
Hawkswick
Bouthwaite
575
MEUGHER
Ramsgill
Nidderdale
496
CONISTONE MOOR
Gouthwaite Reservoir
538
Kilnsey
Conistone
Wath
532
Malham Tarn
Kilnsey Park & Trout Farm
Grass Wood
Pateley Bridge
Grimwith Reservoir
Greenhow Hill
Bewerley
Glasshouses
New House Farm
Threshfield
Grassington
Linton
Hebden
B6265
Stump Cross
The Coldstones Cut
B6165
Malham
359
Dacre Banks
Thorpe
Burnsall
Parcevall Hall
Hanlith
Cracoe
Dacre
Airton
Hetton
506
Appletreewick
485
SIMON'S SEAT
Padside
Darley Head
Rylstone
Thornthwaite
Winterburn
Barden Tower
Thruscross Reservoir
West End Outdoor Centre
B6451
433
Forest Moor
Flasby
Blubberhouses
Coniston Cold
Gargrave
Eastby
Halton East
Bolton Abbey
Bolton Priory
A59
Fewston Reservoir
Thorlby
Stirton
Embsay
Draughton
Embsay & Bolton Abbey Steam Railway
409
Timble
Beamsley
Pennine Way
East Marton
123
West Marton
Carleton-in-Craven
Elslack
A6131
Addingham
A6034
Nesfield
Middleton
Denton
Askwith
Clifton

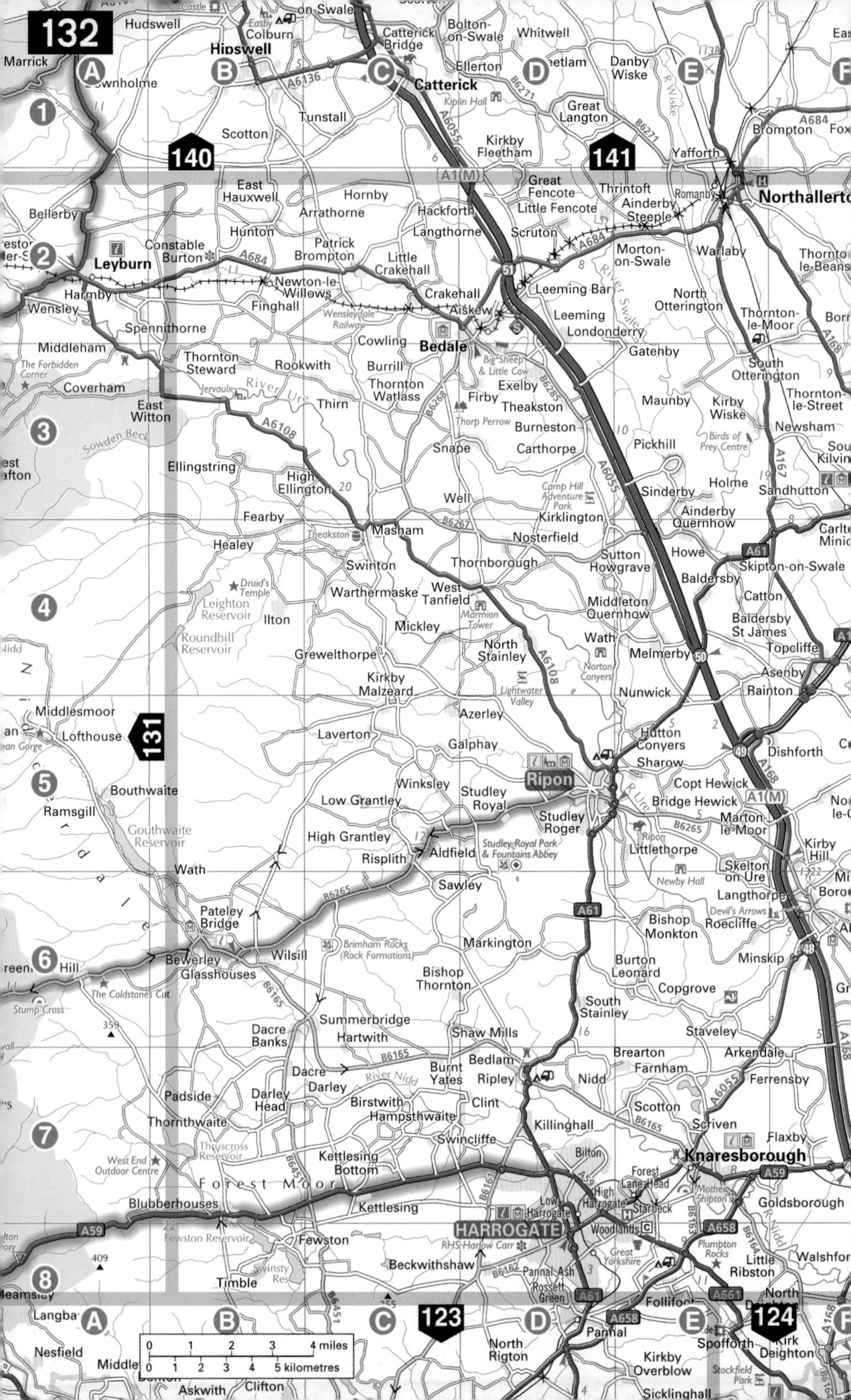


140 141 131 123 124

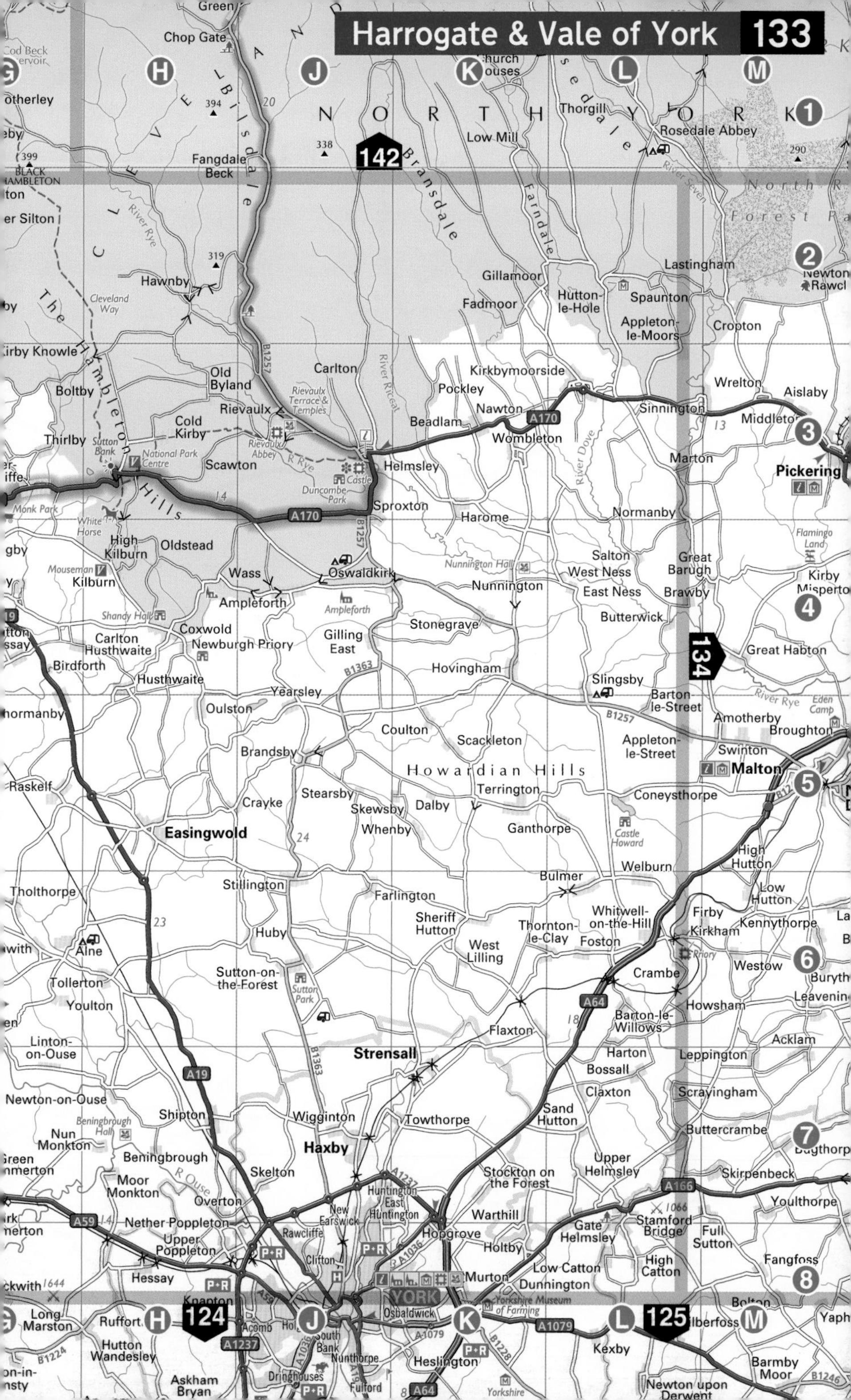
North York Moors
Cleveland Hills
Hambleton Hills
Howardian Hills
Helmsley
Kirkbymoorside
Pickering
Malton
Easingwold
Strensall
Haxby
York
142
134
124
125

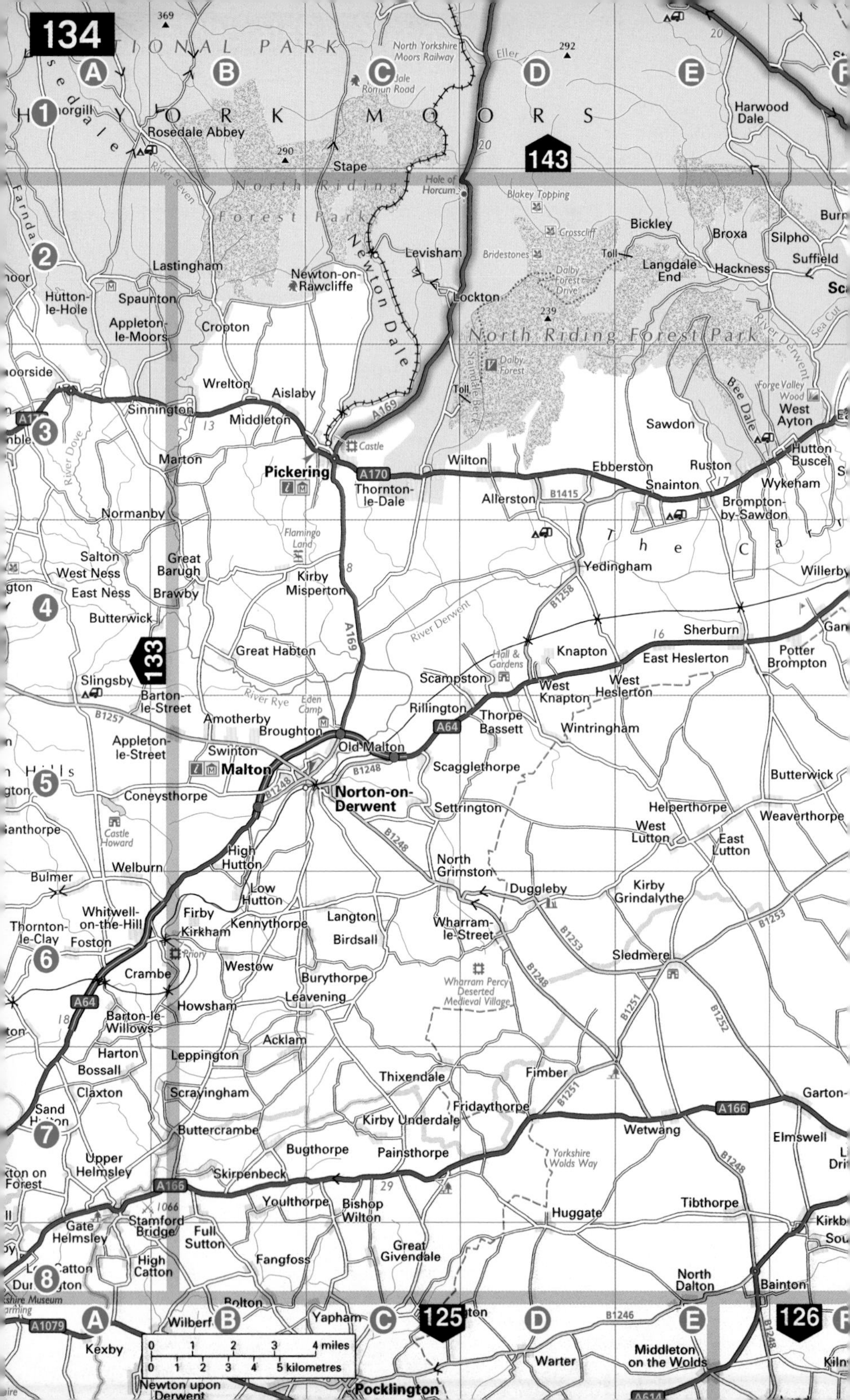
NORTH YORK MOORS NATIONAL PARK
North Yorkshire Moors Railway
Rosedale Abbey
River Seven
Stape
Hole of Horcum
Blakey Topping
Crosscliff
Bridestones
Dalby Forest Drive
North Riding Forest Park
Newton Dale
Levisham
Lockton
Lastingham
Newton-on-Rawcliffe
Hutton-le-Hole
Spaunton
Appleton-le-Moors
Cropton
Wrelton
Aislaby
Sinnington
Middleton
Marton
Pickering
Castle
Thornton-le-Dale
Wilton
Allerston
Ebberston
Snainton
Ruston
Sawdon
Bickley
Broxa
Langdale End
Hackness
Silpho
Suffield
Harwood Dale
West Ayton
Hutton Buscel
Wykeham
Brompton-by-Sawdon
Forge Valley Wood
Bee Dale
River Derwent
Dalby Forest
Staindale Beck
Normanby
Salton
West Ness
East Ness
Great Barugh
Brawby
Butterwick
Kirby Misperton
Flamingo Land
Great Habton
Yedingham
Knapton
Sherburn
East Heslerton
West Heslerton
West Knapton
Scampston
Hall & Gardens
Rillington
Thorpe Bassett
Wintringham
Potter Brompton
Willerby
Slingsby
Barton-le-Street
Appleton-le-Street
Amotherby
Broughton
Eden Camp
River Rye
Swinton
Malton
Old Malton
Norton-on-Derwent
Scagglethorpe
Settrington
Coneysthorpe
Castle Howard
Welburn
Bulmer
Whitwell-on-the-Hill
Thornton-le-Clay
Foston
High Hutton
Low Hutton
Firby
Kirkham
Priory
Kennythorpe
Langton
Birdsall
Westow
Crambe
Burythorpe
Leavening
Howsham
Barton-le-Willows
Harton
Bossall
Claxton
Acklam
Leppington
Scrayingham
Buttercrambe
Sand Hutton
Upper Helmsley
Gate Helmsley
Stamford Bridge
1066
Full Sutton
High Catton
Skirpenbeck
Bugthorpe
Youlthorpe
Bishop Wilton
Fangfoss
Great Givendale
Kirby Underdale
Painsthorpe
Thixendale
Fridaythorpe
Fimber
Wetwang
Huggate
Tibthorpe
North Dalton
Bainton
Middleton on the Wolds
Warter
Yapham
Pocklington
Kexby
Newton upon Derwent
Bolton
Wilberfoss
Helperthorpe
West Lutton
East Lutton
Weaverthorpe
Butterwick
North Grimston
Duggleby
Kirby Grindalythe
Wharram-le-Street
Wharram Percy Deserted Medieval Village
Sledmere
Yorkshire Wolds Way
Elmswell
Garton-
A169
A170
A64
A166
A1079
B1415
B1258
B1257
B1248
B1253
B1251
B1252
B1246
369
290
292
239
0 1 2 3 4 miles
0 1 2 3 4 5 kilometres
143
133
125
126

Scarborough
Osgodby
Cayton Bay
The Wyke
Filey Brigg
Gristhorpe
Filey
Muston
A1039
Filey Bay
Hunmanby
Flamborough Head Heritage Coast
Reighton
Speeton
Bempton Cliffs
Thornwick Bay
North Landing
Buckton
Bempton
Burton Fleming
Grindale
A165
Flamborough Cliffs
Selwicks Bay
FLAMBOROUGH HEAD
Flamborough
Sewerby
Bondville Miniature Village
Boynton
Rudston
Monolith
Bridlington
Bessingby
Hilderthorpe
BRIDLINGTON BAY
Carnaby
Haisthorpe
Kilham
Thornholme
Burton Agnes
Norman Manor House
Harpham
Lowthorpe
Fraisthorpe
Nafferton
Gransmoor
Great Kelk
Lissett
Barmston
Wansford
Gembling
Ulrome
Foston on the Wolds
Skipsea Castle
Skipsea
Brigham
Beeford
North Frodingham
Dunnington
126
Atwick
Bewholme
Honeysuckle

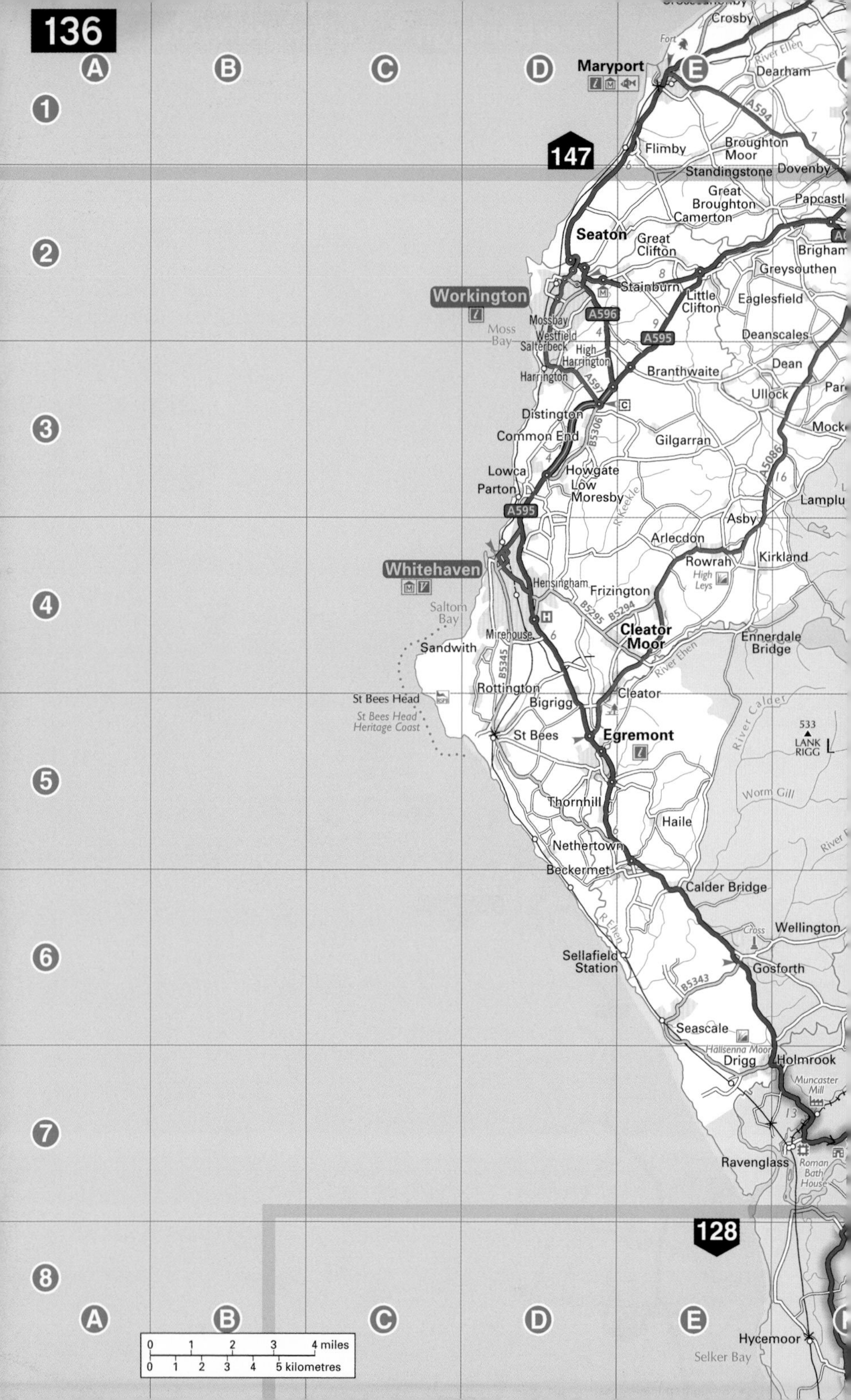

Crosby
Fort
Maryport
River Ellen
Dearham
A594
Flimby
Broughton Moor
147
Standingstone
Dovenby
Great Broughton
Camerton
Papcastl
Seaton
Great Clifton
Brigham
Greysouthen
Stainburn
Little Clifton
Eaglesfield
Workington
Mossbay
Westfield
Moss Bay
Salterbeck
A596
A595
Deanscales
High Harrington
Harrington
Branthwaite
Dean
A597
Ullock
Distington
B5306
Common End
Gilgarran
Lowca
Howgate
Parton
Low Moresby
R Keekle
A5086
Lamplu
A595
Asby
Arlecdon
Whitehaven
Rowrah
Kirkland
High Leys
Hensingham
Frizington
Saltom Bay
B5295
B5294
Cleator Moor
Ennerdale Bridge
Mirehouse
Sandwith
River Ehen
B5345
Rottington
St Bees Head
Cleator
Bigrigg
River Calder
St Bees Head Heritage Coast
St Bees
Egremont
533
LANK RIGG
Worm Gill
Thornhill
Haile
Nethertown
Beckermet
Calder Bridge
R Ehen
Cross
Wellington
Sellafield Station
Gosforth
B5343
Seascale
Hallsenna Moor
Drigg
Holmrook
Muncaster Mill
Ravenglass
Roman Bath House
128
Hycemoor
Selker Bay
0 1 2 3 4 miles
0 1 2 3 4 5 kilometres

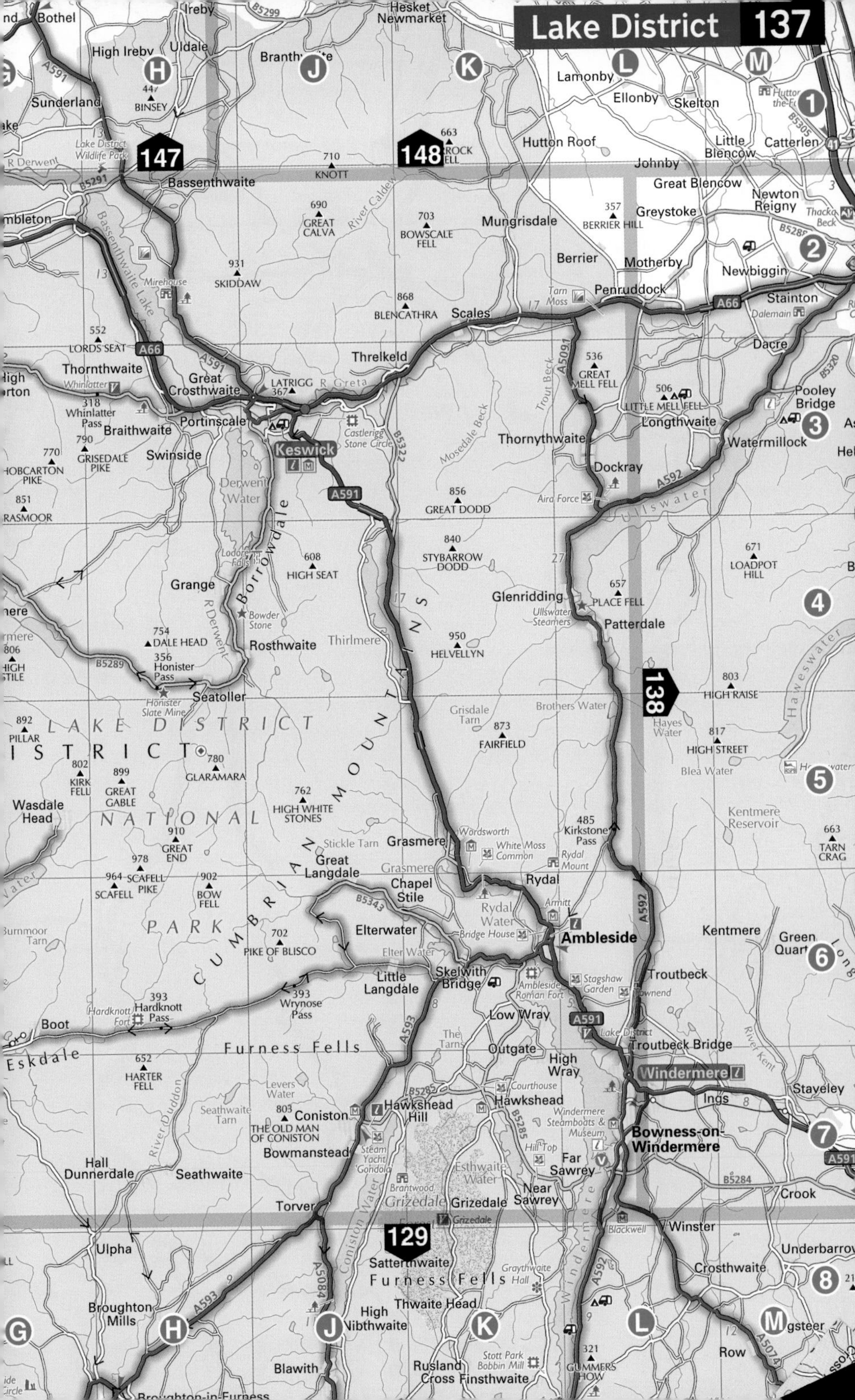
Bothel
Ireby
Hesket Newmarket
High Ireby
Uldale
Branthwaite
Lamonby
Ellonby
Skelton
Sunderland
Binsey
Hutton Roof
Little Blencow
Catterlen
Lake District Wildlife Park
147
Knott
148
Johnby
Bassenthwaite
Great Blencow
Newton Reigny
Great Calva
Bowscale Fell
Mungrisdale
Berrier Hill
Greystoke
Bassenthwaite Lake
Berrier
Motherby
Newbiggin
Skiddaw
Mirehouse
Tarn Moss
Penruddock
Stainton
Blencathra
Scales
Dalemain
Lords Seat
Dacre
Thornthwaite
Threlkeld
Great Mell Fell
Pooley Bridge
Great Crosthwaite
Latrigg
R Greta
Whinlatter
Whinlatter Pass
Little Mell Fell
Longthwaite
Braithwaite
Portinscale
Castlerigg Stone Circle
Watermillock
Grisedale Pike
Swinside
Keswick
Thornythwaite
Hobcarton Pike
Derwent Water
Dockray
Great Dodd
Aira Force
Ullswater
Stybarrow Dodd
Loadpot Hill
Lodore Falls
Borrowdale
High Seat
Grange
Place Fell
Glenridding
Ullswater Steamers
Patterdale
Bowder Stone
Dale Head
Rosthwaite
Thirlmere
Helvellyn
Honister Pass
Honister Slate Mine
Seatoller
138
High Raise
Haweswater
Pillar
Lake District
Grisdale Tarn
Brothers Water
Hayes Water
Fairfield
High Street
Glaramara
Kirk Fell
Great Gable
Blea Water
Wasdale Head
National
High White Stones
Kentmere Reservoir
Great End
Wordsworth
White Moss Common
Kirkstone Pass
Tarn Crag
Stickle Tarn
Grasmere
Great Langdale
Scafell Pike
Scafell
Bow Fell
Rydal Mount
Rydal
Chapel Stile
Rydal Water
Armitt
Park
Elterwater
Bridge House
Ambleside
Kentmere
Green Quarter
Pike of Blisco
Cumbrian Mountains
Elter Water
Burnmoor Tarn
Little Langdale
Skelwith Bridge
Troutbeck
Stagshaw Garden
Townend
Ambleside Roman Fort
Hardknott Pass
Wrynose Pass
Hardknott Fort
Low Wray
Boot
Furness Fells
The Tarns
Lake District
Outgate
Troutbeck Bridge
Eskdale
High Wray
Windermere
Harter Fell
Levers Water
Courthouse
Hawkshead
Staveley
Ings
Seathwaite Tarn
Coniston
Hawkshead Hill
Windermere Steamboats & Museum
Bowness-on-Windermere
River Duddon
The Old Man of Coniston
Bowmanstead
Steam Yacht Gondola
Hill Top
Far Sawrey
Hall Dunnerdale
Seathwaite
Brantwood
Esthwaite Water
Near Sawrey
Crook
Torver
Grizedale
Coniston Water
Blackwell
Winster
129
Ulpha
Satterthwaite
Underbarrow
Graythwaite Hall
Crosthwaite
Furness Fells
Broughton Mills
Thwaite Head
High Nibthwaite
Stott Park Bobbin Mill
Row
Blawith
Rusland
Cross
Finsthwaite
Gummers How
Broughton-in-Furness
A591
A66
A592
A5091
B5322
B5289
B5343
A593
B5285
B5284
A5084
A5074
B5291
B5299
B5305
B5288
B5320

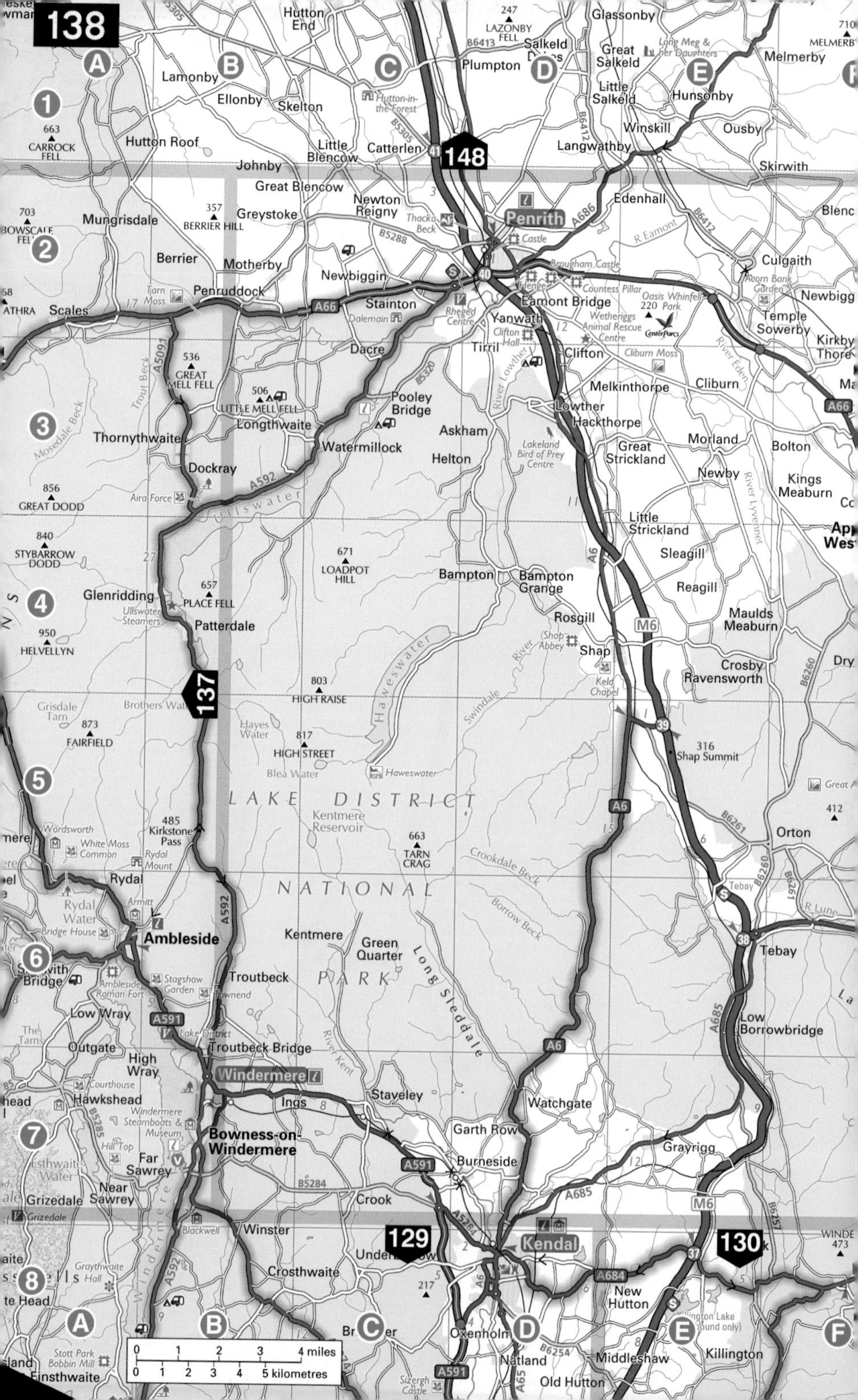

Hutton End
Lamonby
Ellonby
Skelton
Hutton-in-the-Forest
Plumpton
Salkeld Dykes
Glassonby
Great Salkeld
Long Meg & her Daughters
Little Salkeld
Hunsonby
Melmerby
Winskill
Ousby
Langwathby
Skirwith
663 CARROCK FELL
Hutton Roof
Little Blencow
Catterlen
148
Johnby
Great Blencow
Newton Reigny
Penrith
Edenhall
703 BOWSCALE FELL
Mungrisdale
357 BERRIER HILL
Greystoke
Thacka Beck
Castle
R Eamont
Berrier
Motherby
Newbiggin
Brougham Castle
Culgaith
Acorn Bank Garden
Penruddock
Tarn Moss
Scales
Stainton
Dalemain
Henge
Countess Pillar
Eamont Bridge
Oasis Whinfell 220 Park
Wetheriggs Animal Rescue Centre
Center Parcs
Rheged Centre
Yanwath
Clifton Hall
Tirril
Dacre
Clifton
Cliburn Moss
Temple Sowerby
Kirkby Thore
536 GREAT MELL FELL
506 LITTLE MELL FELL
Longthwaite
Pooley Bridge
River Lowther
Melkinthorpe
Cliburn
River Eden
Lowther
Hackthorpe
Askham
Thornythwaite
Watermillock
Helton
Lakeland Bird of Prey Centre
Great Strickland
Morland
Bolton
Dockray
Aira Force
Ullswater
856 GREAT DODD
Newby
Kings Meaburn
River Lyvennet
Little Strickland
840 STYBARROW DODD
671 LOADPOT HILL
Sleagill
Bampton
Bampton Grange
Reagill
657 PLACE FELL
Glenridding
Ullswater Steamers
Patterdale
Rosgill
Maulds Meaburn
950 HELVELLYN
Shap Abbey
Shap
River
Crosby Ravensworth
137
Keld Chapel
803 HIGH RAISE
Haweswater
Grisdale Tarn
Brothers Water
873 FAIRFIELD
Hayes Water
Swindale
817 HIGH STREET
316 Shap Summit
Blea Water
Haweswater
LAKE DISTRICT
Kentmere Reservoir
412
Orton
485 Kirkstone Pass
663 TARN CRAG
Wordsworth
White Moss Common
Rydal Mount
Crookdale Beck
Rydal
NATIONAL
Tebay
Rydal Water
Armitt
Borrow Beck
Bridge House
Ambleside
Kentmere
Green Quarter
Long Sleddale
Tebay
Skelwith Bridge
Ambleside Roman Fort
Stagshaw Garden
Troutbeck
Townend
PARK
Low Wray
The Tarns
Lake District
Low Borrowbridge
Outgate
Troutbeck Bridge
River Kent
High Wray
Windermere
Courthouse
Hawkshead
Ings
Staveley
Watchgate
Windermere Steamboats & Museum
Garth Row
Hill Top
Bowness-on-Windermere
Grayrigg
Esthwaite Water
Far Sawrey
Burneside
Near Sawrey
Grizedale
Crook
Blackwell
Winster
129
Underbarrow
Kendal
130
WINDER 473
Graythwaite Hall
Crosthwaite
New Hutton
217
Killington Lake (Southbound only)
Oxenholme
Brigsteer
Killington
Middleshaw
Stott Park Bobbin Mill
Natland
Sizergh Castle
Old Hutton
Finsthwaite
0 1 2 3 4 miles
0 1 2 3 4 5 kilometres

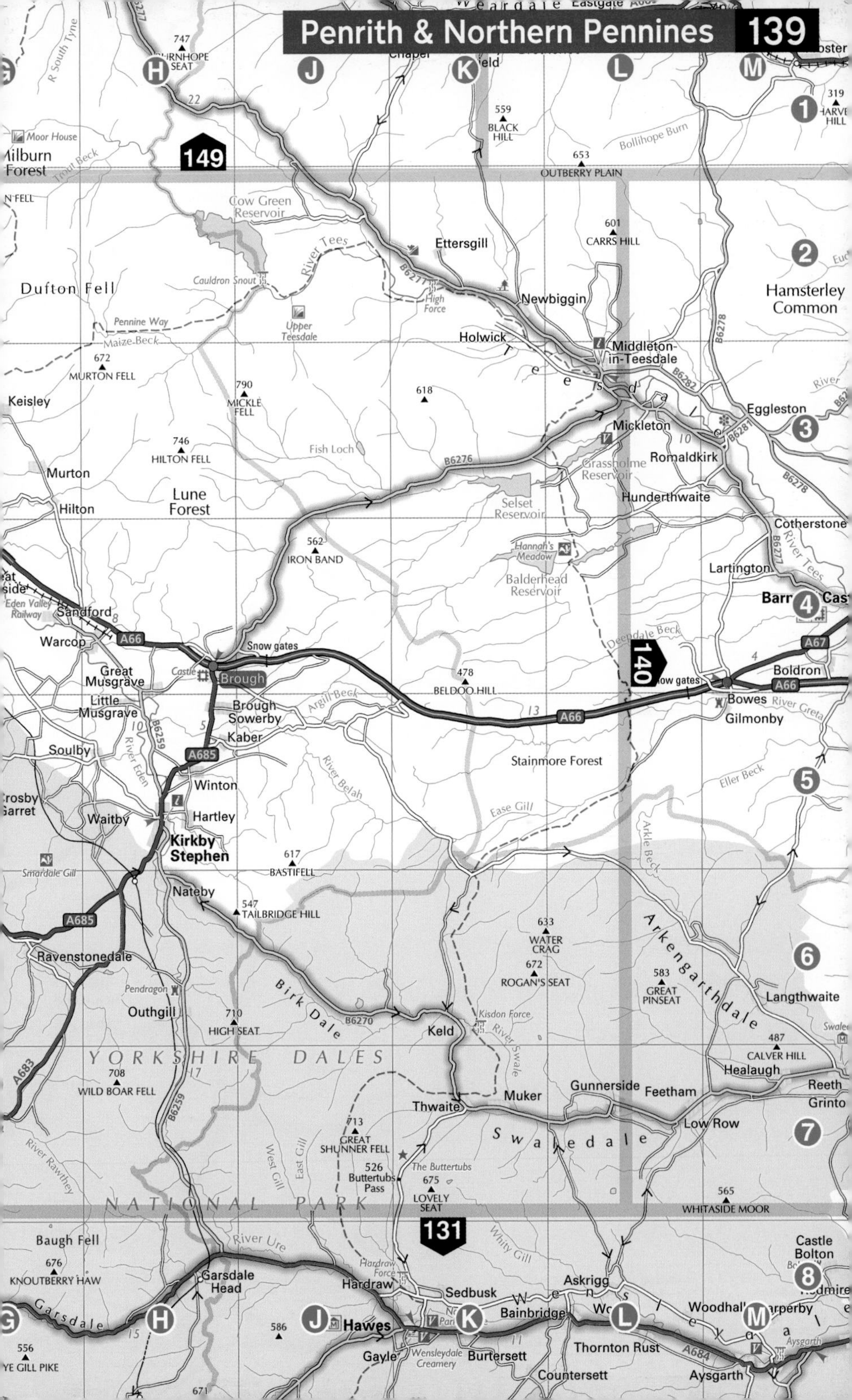

Milburn Forest
Moor House
Cow Green Reservoir
Cauldron Snout
Dufton Fell
Pennine Way
Upper Teesdale
Ettersgill
High Force
Newbiggin
Holwick
Middleton-in-Teesdale
Hamsterley Common
Eggleston
Mickleton
Romaldkirk
Grassholme Reservoir
Selset Reservoir
Hunderthwaite
Cotherstone
Lartington
Hannah's Meadow
Balderhead Reservoir
Keisley
Murton
Hilton
Lune Forest
IRON BAND
Sandford
Warcop
Snow gates
Great Musgrave
Brough
Little Musgrave
Brough Sowerby
Kaber
Soulby
Winton
Hartley
Waitby
Kirkby Stephen
Smardale Gill
Nateby
Stainmore Forest
Bowes
Gilmonby
Boldron
BELDOO HILL
BASTIFELL
TAILBRIDGE HILL
Ravenstonedale
Pendragon
Outhgill
Birk Dale
Keld
Kisdon Force
WATER CRAG
ROGAN'S SEAT
GREAT PINSEAT
Arkengarthdale
Langthwaite
CALVER HILL
Healaugh
Reeth
YORKSHIRE DALES
WILD BOAR FELL
HIGH SEAT
Thwaite
Muker
Gunnerside
Feetham
Low Row
Swaledale
GREAT SHUNNER FELL
Buttertubs Pass
The Buttertubs
LOVELY SEAT
WHITASIDE MOOR
NATIONAL PARK
Baugh Fell
KNOUTBERRY HAW
Garsdale Head
Garsdale
Hardraw
Hardraw Force
Sedbusk
Askrigg
Hawes
Bainbridge
Woodhall
Carperby
Gayle
Wensleydale Creamery
Burtersett
Thornton Rust
Countersett
Aysgarth
Castle Bolton
Redmire
MURTON FELL
MICKLE FELL
HILTON FELL
CARRS HILL
OUTBERRY PLAIN
BLACK HILL
Fish Loch
149
140
131

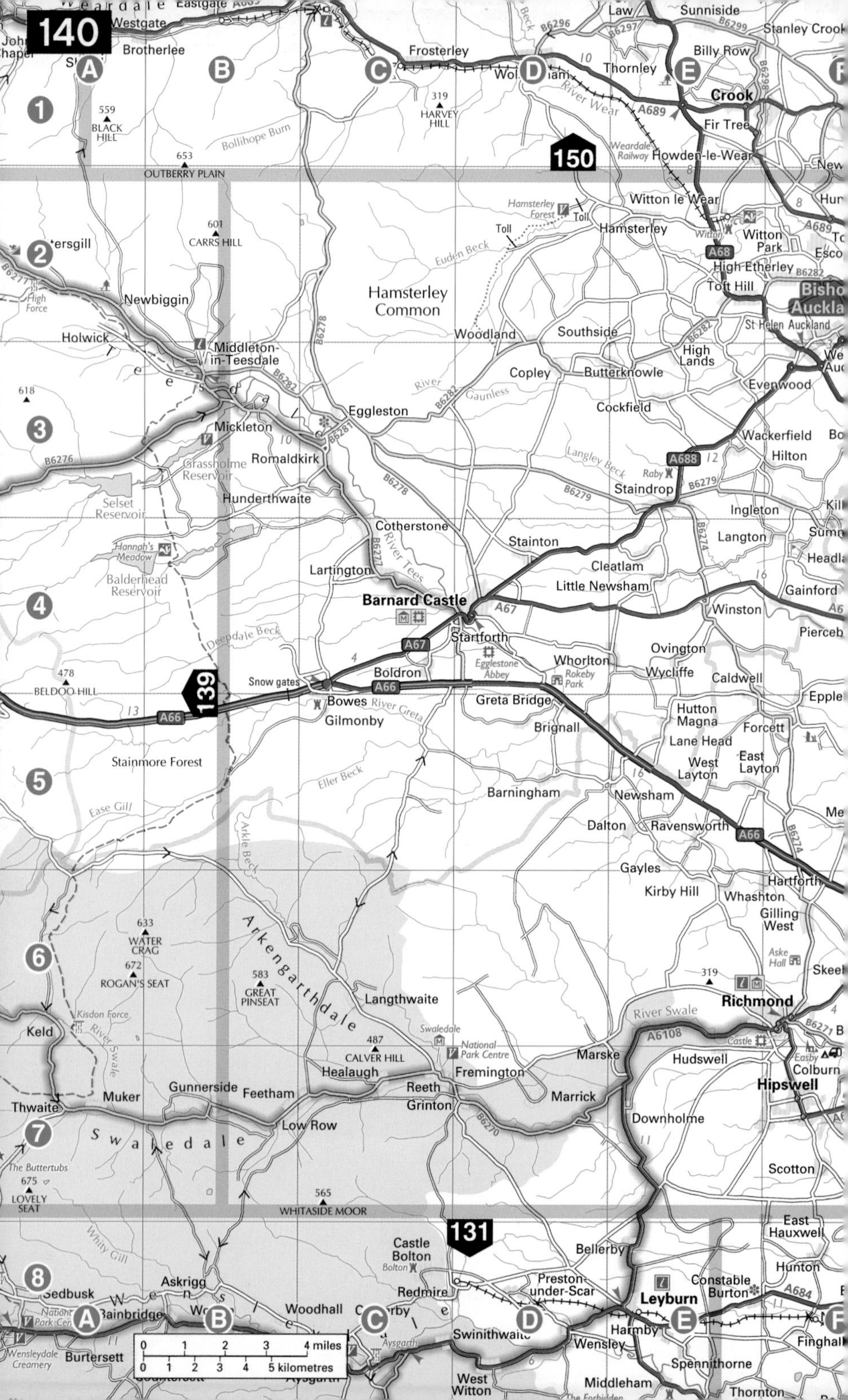
140
Westgate
Brotherlee
Frosterley
Wolsingham
Thornley
Sunniside
Billy Row
Stanley Crook
Crook
Fir Tree
Howden-le-Wear
Weardale Railway
A689
River Wear
B6296
B6297
B6299
B6298
559 BLACK HILL
653 OUTBERRY PLAIN
319 HARVEY HILL
Bollihope Burn
150
Witton le Wear
Hamsterley Forest
Toll
Hamsterley
Witton
Witton Park
A68
High Etherley
Toft Hill
St Helen Auckland
601 CARRS HILL
Newbiggin
High Force
Holwick
B6277
Middleton-in-Teesdale
Hamsterley Common
Euden Beck
Woodland
Southside
High Lands
B6282
Copley
Butterknowle
Evenwood
River Gaunless
Cockfield
Eggleston
B6278
B6281
618
Mickleton
Romaldkirk
Grassholme Reservoir
Selset Reservoir
B6276
Hunderthwaite
Wackerfield
Hilton
A688
Langley Beck
Raby
Staindrop
B6279
Ingleton
Langton
Cotherstone
Stainton
Hannah's Meadow
Balderhead Reservoir
Lartington
River Tees
Cleatlam
Little Newsham
Gainford
Barnard Castle
A67
Winston
Startforth
Egglestone Abbey
Whorlton
Ovington
Wycliffe
Caldwell
Rokeby Park
Deepdale Beck
478 BELDOO HILL
Snow gates
Boldron
Bowes
A66
River Greta
Gilmonby
Greta Bridge
Brignall
Hutton Magna
Forcett
Lane Head
West Layton
East Layton
139
Stainmore Forest
Ellerbeck
Ease Gill
Barningham
Newsham
Dalton
Ravensworth
B6274
Arkle Beck
Gayles
Kirby Hill
Hartforth
Whashton
Gilling West
633 WATER CRAG
672 ROGAN'S SEAT
583 GREAT PINSEAT
Arkengarthdale
Langthwaite
Aske Hall
319
Richmond
River Swale
A6108
Kisdon Force
Keld
Swaledale
National Park Centre
487 CALVER HILL
Healaugh
Fremington
Marske
Hudswell
Colburn
Easby
Castle
B6271
Hipswell
Gunnerside
Feetham
Reeth
Grinton
Muker
Thwaite
Marrick
Low Row
B6270
Downholme
Swaledale
The Buttertubs
675 LOVELY SEAT
565 WHITASIDE MOOR
Scotton
131
Whity Gill
Castle Bolton
Bolton
Bellerby
East Hauxwell
Hunton
Constable Burton
A684
Askrigg
Sedbusk
Redmire
Preston-under-Scar
Leyburn
National Park Centre
Bainbridge
Woodhall
Carperby
Harmby
Wensleydale Creamery
Burtersett
Aysgarth
Swinithwaite
Wensley
Finghall
Spennithorne
West Witton
Middleham
Thornton
0 1 2 3 4 miles
0 1 2 3 4 5 kilometres
A B C D E F
1 2 3 4 5 6 7 8

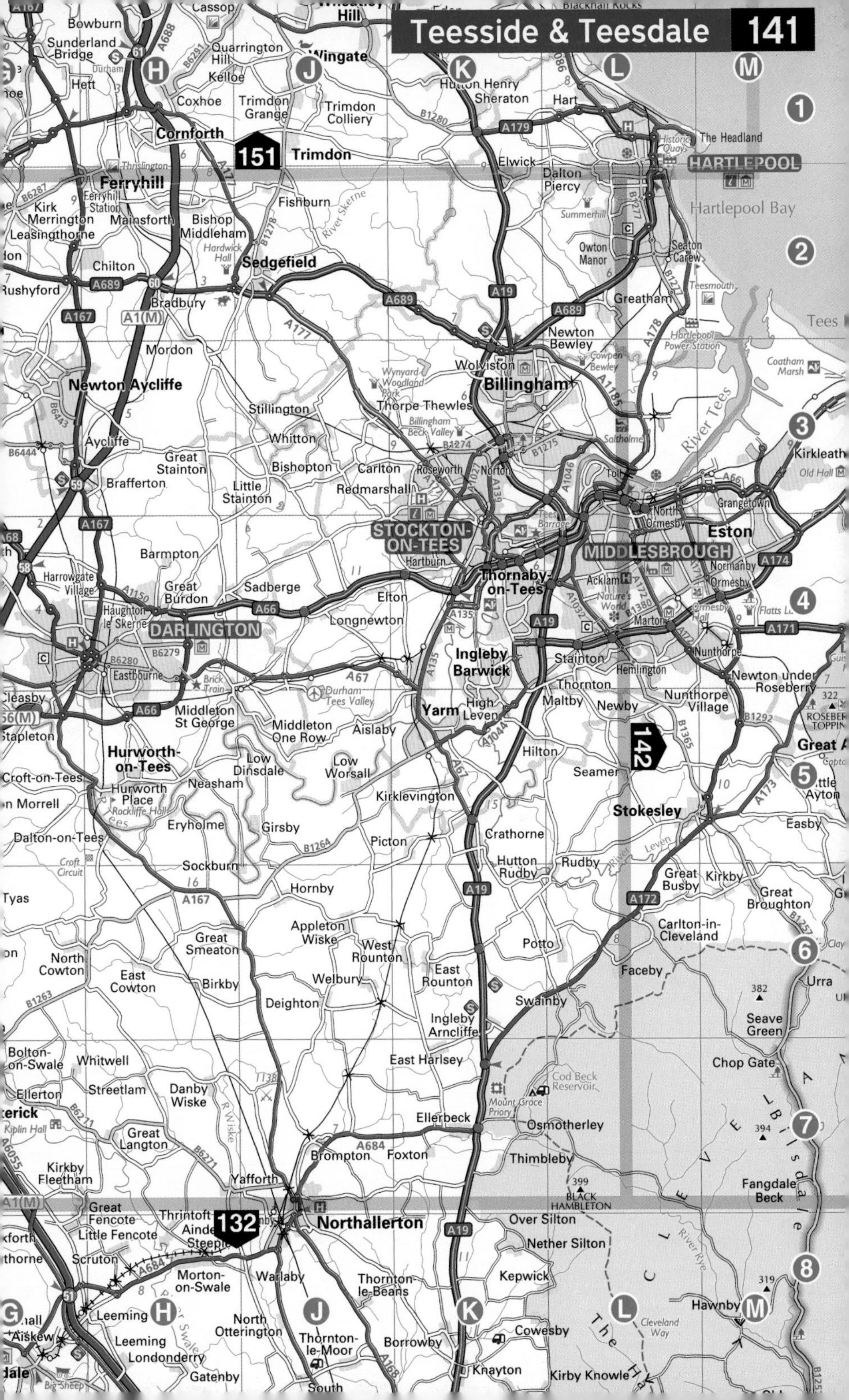
HARTLEPOOL
MIDDLESBROUGH
STOCKTON-ON-TEES
DARLINGTON
Billingham
Northallerton
Stokesley
Yarm
Sedgefield
Newton Aycliffe
Ferryhill
Cornforth
Trimdon
Wingate
Eston
Thornaby-on-Tees
Ingleby Barwick
Hurworth-on-Tees
Hartlepool Bay
River Tees
Osmotherley
Cleveland Way

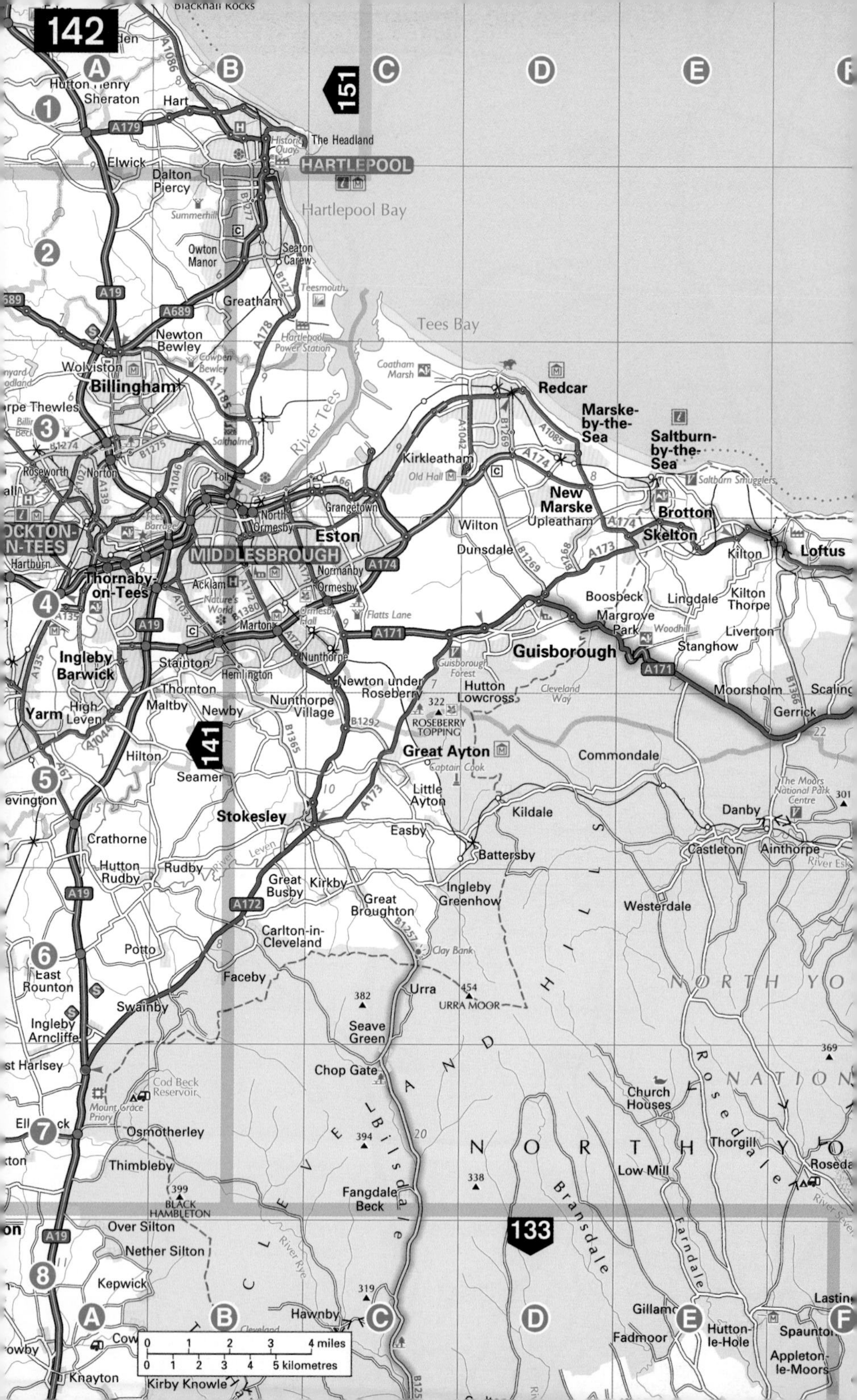

Hutton Henry
Sheraton
Hart
The Headland
HARTLEPOOL
Hartlepool Bay
Elwick
Dalton Piercy
Summerhill
Owton Manor
Seaton Carew
Teesmouth
Greatham
Tees Bay
Newton Bewley
Hartlepool Power Station
Cowpen Bewley
Wolviston
Billingham
Coatham Marsh
Redcar
Marske-by-the-Sea
Saltburn-by-the-Sea
Saltburn Smugglers
Saltholme
River Tees
Kirkleatham
Old Hall
Roseworth
Norton
Grangetown
North Ormesby
Eston
Wilton
New Marske
Upleatham
Brotton
Skelton
Loftus
Kilton
STOCKTON-ON-TEES
Tees Barrage
MIDDLESBROUGH
Dunsdale
Hartburn
Thornaby-on-Tees
Acklam
Normanby
Ormesby
Boosbeck
Lingdale
Kilton Thorpe
Nature's World
Flatts Lane
Margrove Park
Woodhill
Liverton
Marton
Ormesby Hall
Guisborough
Stanghow
Ingleby Barwick
Stainton
Nunthorpe
Guisborough Forest
Hemlington
Newton under Roseberry
Hutton Lowcross
Cleveland Way
Moorsholm
Scaling
Thornton
Yarm
High Leven
Maltby
Newby
Nunthorpe Village
ROSEBERRY TOPPING
Gerrick
Hilton
Great Ayton
Commondale
Seamer
Captain Cook
Little Ayton
The Moors National Park Centre
Danby
Kildale
Stokesley
Easby
Castleton
Ainthorpe
River Esk
Crathorne
Battersby
River Leven
Hutton Rudby
Rudby
Great Busby
Kirkby
Ingleby Greenhow
Westerdale
Great Broughton
Carlton-in-Cleveland
Clay Bank
Potto
East Rounton
Faceby
Urra
URRA MOOR
NORTH YO
Swainby
Ingleby Arncliffe
Seave Green
East Harlsey
Chop Gate
Cod Beck Reservoir
Church Houses
NATION
Mount Grace Priory
Osmotherley
Rosedale
Thorgill
Thimbleby
Bilsdale
NORTH YO
Low Mill
Rosedale
BLACK HAMBLETON
Fangdale Beck
Bransdale
CLEVELAND HILLS
133
Over Silton
Nether Silton
River Rye
Farndale
River Seven
Kepwick
Gillamoor
Lastingham
Hawnby
Fadmoor
Hutton-le-Hole
Spaunton
Appleton-le-Moors
Kirby Knowle
Knayton
0 1 2 3 4 miles
0 1 2 3 4 5 kilometres

G
H
J
K
L
M
1
2
3
4
5
6
7
8
Captain Cook
Staithes
Runswick Bay
North Yorkshire and Cleveland Heritage Coast
Runswick
Goldsborough
Ellerby
Overdale Wyke
A174
Lythe
Sandsend
Sandsend Wyke
East Barnby
West Barnby
Whitby
Abbey
Saltwick Bay
Dunsley
Newholm
A171
B1410
Ruswarp
Stainsacre
Aislaby
Briggswath
Sneaton
High Hawsker
Sleights
Ugglebarnby
B1447
Egton
Esk Dale
Iburndale
Ness Point or North Cheek
Grosmont
Robin Hood's Bay
A169
Fylingthorpe
Robin Hood's Bay
B1416
Old Peak or South Cheek
A171
Goathland
Ravenscar
North Yorkshire Moors Railway
292
Eller Beck
Staintondale
Shire Horse Centre
Wheeldale Roman Road
Hayburn Wyke
M O O R S
Harwood Dale
Cloughton Wyke
Stape
Cloughton
Hole of Horcum
Blakey Topping
134
Cromer Point
A165
Burniston
Bickley
Crosscliff
Broxa
Cleveland Way
Levisham
Bridestones
Toll
Silpho
Langdale End
Suffield
Hackness
Dalby Forest Drive
Scalby
Castle
Lock
239
North Riding Forest Park
River Derwent
Sea Cut
A171
Falsgrave
Scarborough
Newton Dale
Dalby

Belfast
Larne
A
B
C
D
E
F
1
2
3
4
5
6
7
8
321
CARLOCK HILL
387
ALTIMEG
305
BENBRAKE HILL
Southern Upland Way
Milleur Point
Corsewall Point
Glen App
Lady Bay
Barnhills
Portencalzie
Glenwhilly
Laggangairn Standing Stones
152
Main Water of Luce
Water of Luce
B738
Kirkcolm
Cairnryan
Penwhirn Reservoir
17
271
ARTFIELD FELL
Loch Connell
Ervie
B738
B798
A718
Low Barbeth
A77
Beoch Burn
Braid Fell
Low Salchrie
New Luce
Knocknain
Leswalt
Loch Ryan
B7043
Innermessan
A751
Castle of St John
Black Loch
Castle Kennedy
A77
White Loch
164
CRAIG FELL
Balgracie
Stranraer
Aird
Chlenry
Auchnotteroch
Castle Kennedy
Portslogan
Broadsea Bay
B738
A75
10
Glenwhan
Dunragit
Glenluce Abbey
Glenluce
THE RHINNS OF GALLOWAY
Lochans
Kildrochet House
Piltanton Burn
181
CAIRN PAT
8
B7084
Whitecrook
Black Head
Dunskey
14
B7077
Ringdoo Point
A747
Milton
A77
Portpatrick
A716
19
Stairhaven
Stoneykirk
B7084
North Milmain
18
Auchenmalg
B7042
Mull of Sinniness
Sandhead
Cairngarroch
Kirkmadrine Stones
Money Head
High Ardwell
Ardwell
Ardwell Bay
Ardwell House
Chapel Rossan
Drumbreddon
Balgowan
LUCE BA
Logan
Port Logan Bay
Port Logan
B7065
A716
Garrochtrie
Clanyard Bay
Kilstay
Laggantalluch Head
Kirkmaiden
Drummore
Barncorkrie
Cailiness Point
High Drummore
Damnaglaur
B7041
Maryport
Cardryne
Cardrain
West Cairngaan
MULL OF GALLOWAY
0 1 2 3 4 miles
0 1 2 3 4 5 kilometres

Creebank
Bargrennan
LAMACHAN HILL
GARLICK HILL
Wood of Cree
153
Galloway Deer Range
Murray's
ROUND FELL
FELL OF FLEET
Black Water of Dee
GALLOWAY
Loch Ochiltree
Knowe
Carseriggan
Challoch
Minnigaff
Newton Stewart
Creebridge
Barfad
Kirroughtree
Palnure
Shennanton
Kirkcowan
Baltersan
Causeway End
Loch Grannoch
Loch Fleet
AUCHENCLOY HILL
Skerrow
CAIRNSMORE OF FLEET
Big Water of Fleet
Cairnsmore of Fleet
WHITE TOP OF CULREACH
Upper Ruscoe
Carstramon Wood
Gem Rock
Creetown
Fleet Valley
146
Clugston
Torhouse Stone Circle
Fell Loch
Kirkmabreck
CAIRNHARROW
Anwoth
Gatehouse
Cardoness Castle
THE MACHARS
Wigtown
Bladnoch
Kirwaugh
Carsluith
Carsluith Castle
Cairnholy Chambered Cairns
Girthon
Braehead
Kirkinner
Orchardton Bay
Ravenshall Point
Mossyard
Fleet Bay
Lennox Plunton
Margrie
Whauphill
Barrachan
Little Airies
Culscadden
Islands of Fleet
Kirkandrews
Elrig
Wigtown Bay
Druchtag Motte
Sorbie
Garlieston
Mochrum
Pouton
Borness
Ringdoo Point
Drumtrodden Cup & Ring
Drumtrodden Standing Stones
Drummoddie
Broughton Mains
Galloway House
Cruggleton Bay
Port William
Big Balcraig
'Wren's Egg' Standing Stones
Priory
Barsalloch Fort
Monreith
Barsalloch Point
Whithorn Story
Point of Leg
Rispain Camp
Whithorn
Portyerrock
St Ninian's Cave
Kidsdale
Isle of Whithorn
St Ninian's Chapel (ruin)
Cutcloy
BURROW HEAD
G
H
J
K
L
M
1
2
3
4
5
6
7
8

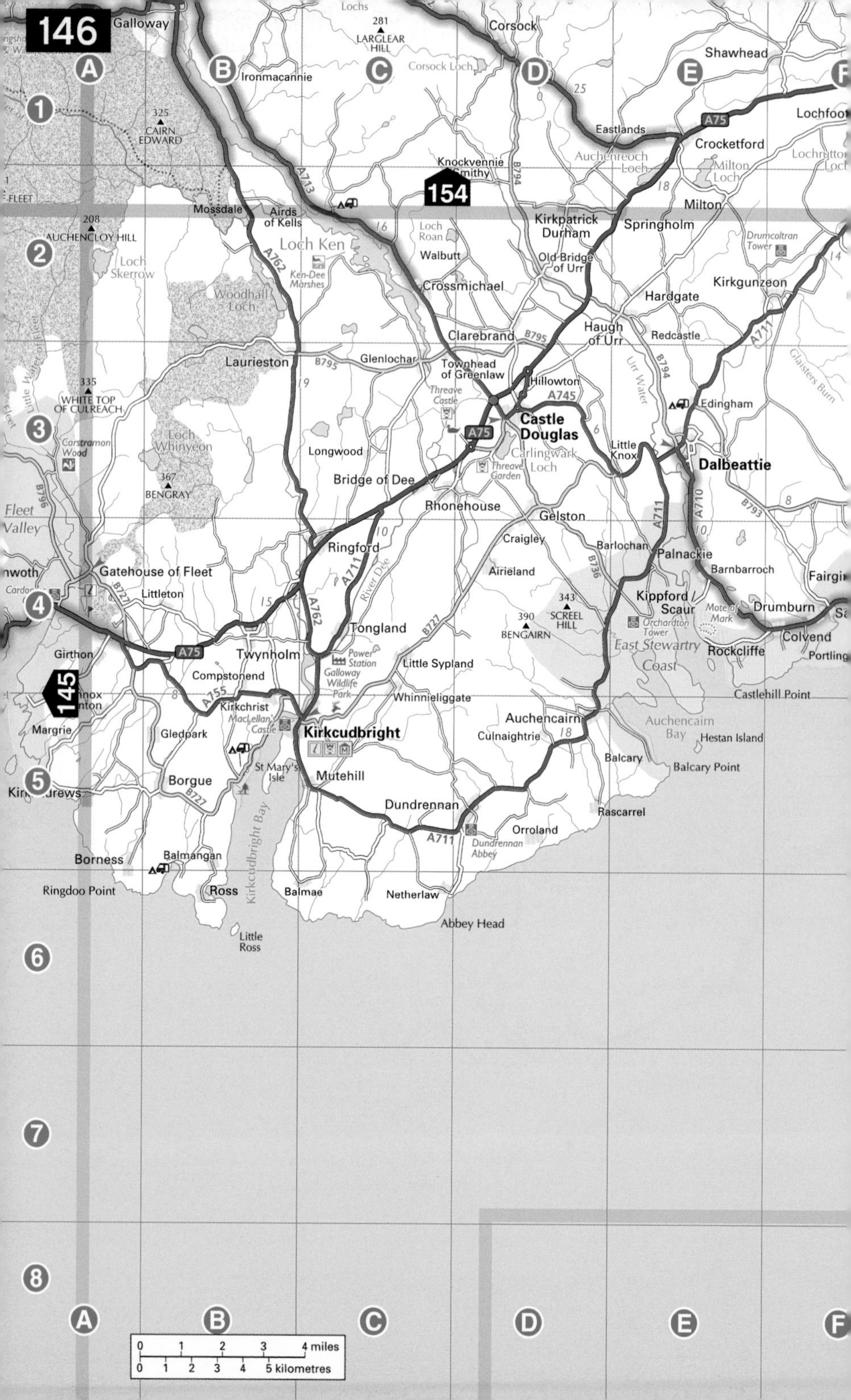

Galloway
Corsock
281
LARGLEAR HILL
Corsock Loch
Shawhead
Ironmacannie
Lochfoot
325
CAIRN EDWARD
A75
Eastlands
Crocketford
Knockvennie Smithy
154
Auchenreoch Loch
Milton Loch
Milton
FLEET
Mossdale
Airds of Kells
A713
B794
Kirkpatrick Durham
Springholm
208
AUCHENCLOY HILL
Loch Ken
Loch Roan
Walbutt
Drumcoltran Tower
Loch Skerrow
Ken-Dee Marshes
Old Bridge of Urr
Woodhall Loch
A762
Crossmichael
Kirkgunzeon
Hardgate
Haugh of Urr
Clarebrand
B795
Redcastle
Laurieston
Glenlochar
Townhead of Greenlaw
B794
A711
Glaisters Burn
335
WHITE TOP OF CULREACH
Hillowton
Threave Castle
A745
Urr Water
Edingham
Little Water of Fleet
Carstramon Wood
Loch Whinyeon
Castle Douglas
A75
Little Knox
Longwood
Carlingwark Loch
Dalbeattie
367
BENGRAY
Threave Garden
Bridge of Dee
B796
Fleet Valley
Rhonehouse
Gelston
A710
B793
Craigley
A711
Ringford
Barlochan
Palnackie
Gatehouse of Fleet
Airieland
B736
Barnbarroch
Fairgirth
B727
A711
River Dee
Littleton
343
SCREEL HILL
Kippford / Scaur
Drumburn
A762
Mote of Mark
390
BENGAIRN
Orchardton Tower
Tongland
B727
Colvend
Girthon
A75
Twynholm
Power Station
East Stewartry Coast
Rockcliffe
Portling
Little Sypland
Galloway Wildlife Park
Compstonend
145
Whinnieliggate
Castlehill Point
A755
Kirkchrist
Auchencairn
MacLellan's Castle
Margrie
Gledpark
Kirkcudbright
Culnaightrie
Auchencairn Bay
Hestan Island
St Mary's Isle
Balcary
Borgue
Mutehill
Balcary Point
B727
Kirkcudbright Bay
Dundrennan
Rascarrel
Orroland
A711
Dundrennan Abbey
Borness
Balmangan
Ringdoo Point
Ross
Balmae
Netherlaw
Abbey Head
Little Ross
0 1 2 3 4 miles
0 1 2 3 4 5 kilometres

Lincluden
Roucan
240
CARTHAT HILL
Kettleholm
Collin
Dumfries
Greenlea
Racks
Lochar Water
Kingholm Quay
Mouswald
Dalton
River Annan
Ecclefechan
Hoddom Cross
Thomas Carlyle's Birthplace
A74(M)
Eaglesfield
Kirtlebridge
Merkland Cross
Bonshaw Tower
Robgill Tower
Carrutherstown
Hoddom Mains
Brydekirk
155
Kelton
Kirkconnell Flow
Conheath
Kelhead
Creca
Hollee
Glencaple
Bankend
Clarencefield
Ruthwell Cross
Kirkconnell
Nith Estuary
Sweetheart Abbey
Shearington
Caerlaverock Castle
Ruthwell
Savings Banks
Cummertrees
Annan
Howes
Powfoot
Dornock
Eastriggs
Ingleston
Bowhouse
Blackshaw
Caerlaverock Wetlands Centre
Newbie
Loch Kindar
Torduff Point
569
CRIFFELL
Drumburn
Carse Bay
Bowness-on-Solway
Port Carlisle
Glasson
Campfield Marsh
Glasson Moss
Hadrian's Wall Path
Drumburgh
SOLWAY FIRTH
Kirkbean
Carsethorn
Bowness Common
Cardurnock
Drumburgh Moss
Borron Point
Arbigland
Grune Point
Anthorn
Moricambe Bay
Skinburness
Kirkbride
Gill Foot Bay
Southerness
Southerness Point
Newton Arlosh
Silloth
Seaville
South Solway Mosses
Biglands
148
Abbey Town
Holm Cultram
Kelsick
Dundraw
Oulton
Lessonhall
Beckfoot
R Waver
Waverbridge
Wigton
Newtown
Blencogo
Waverton
Holme St Cuthbert
Bromfield
Mawbray
Dubmill Point
Langrigg
Bolton Low Houses
Westnewton
Allonby
Allonby Bay
Fletchertown
Hayton
Aspatria
Blennerhasset
Boltongate
Prospect
Oughterside
Torpenhow
Allerby
Crosscanonby
Crosby
Plumbland
Bothel
Ireby
Fort
Gilcrux
High Ireby
Uldale
Maryport
River Ellen
Dearham
447
BINSEY
Sunderland
Tallentire
Blindcrake
Lake District Wildlife Park
R Derwent
Flimby
Broughton Moor
Bridekirk
Standingstone
Dovenby
Bassenthwaite
136
137
Great Broughton
Papcastle
Jennings
Camerton
Embleton
Seaton
Great Clifton
Cockermouth
Brigham
Bassenthwaite Lake
Greysouthen
Mirehouse
931
SKIDDAW
Workington
Stainburn
Little Clifton
Eaglesfield
Lorton
Mossbay
Westfield
Salterbeck
Moss Bay
High
Deanscales
552
LORDS SEAT
Low Lorton
A75
A780
A710
A74(M)
A596
A594
A595
A591
A66
B725
B724
B7020
B723
B722
B7076
B5307
B5302
B5300
B5301
B5299
B5291
B5292

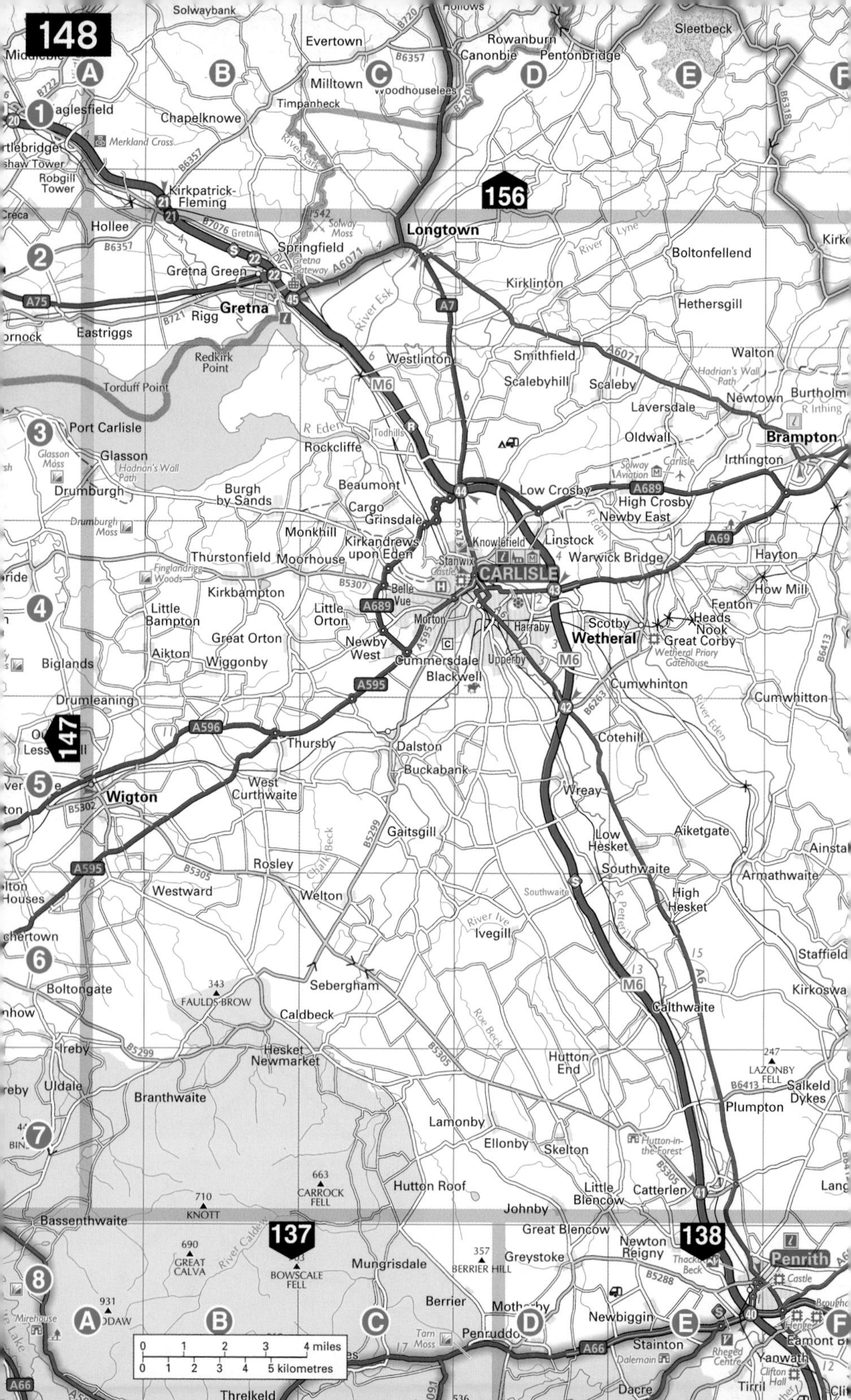

148
Solwaybank
Hollows
Evertown
B6357
B720
Rowanburn
Canonbie
Pentonbridge
Sleetbeck
A
B
C
D
E
F
B722
Milltown
Woodhouselees
Timpanheck
B7201
B6318
1
Eaglesfield
Chapelknowe
20
Merkland Cross
River Sark
B6357
shaw Tower
Robgill Tower
Kirkpatrick-Fleming
21
156
Creca
Hollee
B7076
Gretna
1542
Solway Moss
Longtown
River Lyne
2
B6357
Springfield
Gretna Gateway
A6071
Boltonfellend
Gretna Green
22
Kirklinton
A75
Gretna
Rigg
B721
45
A7
River Esk
Hethersgill
Eastriggs
Redkirk Point
Westlinton
Smithfield
A6071
Walton
Torduff Point
M6
Scalebyhill
Scaleby
Hadrian's Wall Path
Newtown
Burtholme
Laversdale
R Irthing
3
Port Carlisle
R Eden
Todhills
Oldwall
Brampton
Glasson Moss
Glasson
Rockcliffe
Solway Aviation
Carlisle
Irthington
Hadrian's Wall Path
Drumburgh
Burgh by Sands
Beaumont
44
Low Crosby
A689
High Crosby
Cargo
Grinsdale
R Eden
Newby East
Drumburgh Moss
Monkhill
Kirkandrews upon Eden
Knowlefield
Linstock
A69
Thurstonfield
Moorhouse
Stanwix
Warwick Bridge
Hayton
Finglandrigg Woods
Castle
CARLISLE
B5307
Belle Vue
43
How Mill
4
Kirkbampton
Fenton
Little Bampton
Little Orton
A689
Morton
Harraby
Scotby
Heads Nook
A595
A6
Great Orton
Newby West
Wetheral
Great Corby
Aikton
Biglands
Wiggonby
Cummersdale
Upperby
M6
Wetheral Priory Gatehouse
Blackwell
B6413
Drumleaning
A595
Cumwhinton
Cumwhitton
B6263
River Eden
42
147
A596
Thursby
Cotehill
Dalston
5
Wigton
B5302
West Curthwaite
Buckabank
Wreay
Low Hesket
Chalk Beck
Gaitsgill
Aiketgate
B5299
A595
Rosley
Southwaite
Armathwaite
Ainstable
B5305
Westward
Welton
Southwaite
High Hesket
R Petteril
River Ive
Ivegill
Houses
6
15
Staffield
Sebergham
13
A6
343
FAULDS BROW
M6
Boltongate
Calthwaite
Kirkoswald
Caldbeck
Roe Beck
Ireby
B5299
Hesket Newmarket
B5305
Hutton End
247
LAZONBY FELL
Uldale
B6413
Salkeld Dykes
Branthwaite
Plumpton
Lamonby
7
Ellonby
Skelton
Hutton-in-the-Forest
663
CARROCK FELL
710
KNOTT
Hutton Roof
Little Blencow
Catterlen
B5305
41
Lang
Johnby
Bassenthwaite
Great Blencow
137
138
690
GREAT CALVA
River Caldew
BOWSCALE FELL
Mungrisdale
357
BERRIER HILL
Greystoke
Newton Reigny
Thacka Beck
Penrith
Castle
8
B5288
931
Mirehouse
Berrier
Motherby
Newbiggin
40
Brougham Henge
0 1 2 3 4 miles
0 1 2 3 4 5 kilometres
Tarn Moss
Penruddock
A66
Stainton
Rheged Centre
Dalemain
Eamont Bridge
Yanwath
Clifton Hall
A66
Threlkeld
536
Dacre
Tirril

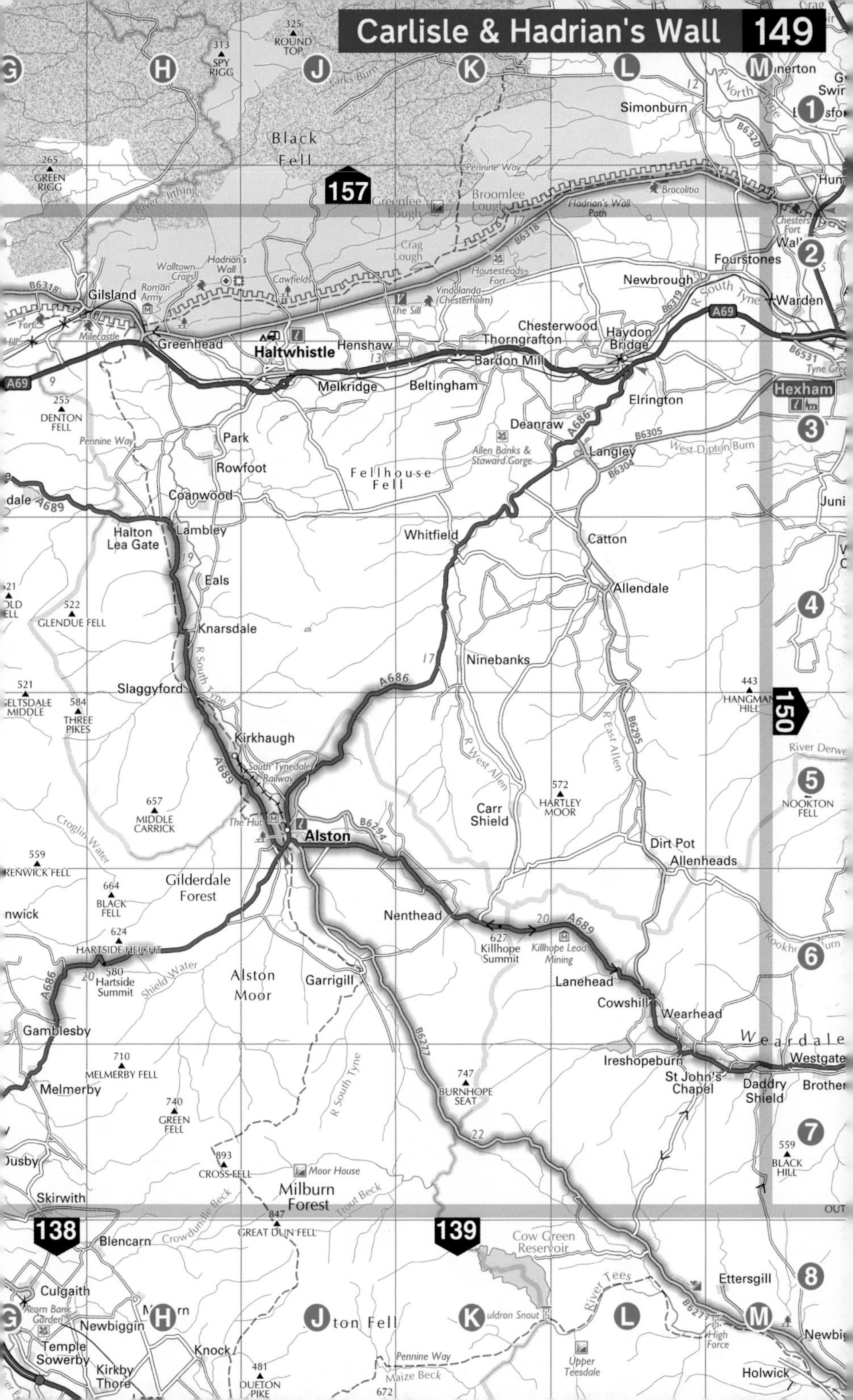
Simonburn
Black Fell
157
Greenlee Lough
Broomlee Lough
Brocolitia
Hadrian's Wall Path
Pennine Way
Crag Lough
Housesteads Fort
Vindolanda (Chesterholm)
The Sill
Walltown Crags
Hadrian's Wall
Roman Army
Cawfields
Fourstones
Newbrough
Warden
Gilsland
Greenhead
Haltwhistle
Henshaw
Chesterwood
Thorngrafton
Haydon Bridge
Bardon Mill
Melkridge
Beltingham
Elrington
Hexham
Deanraw
Allen Banks & Staward Gorge
Langley
West Dipton Burn
Park
Rowfoot
Fellhouse Fell
Coanwood
Halton Lea Gate
Lambley
Whitfield
Catton
Eals
Allendale
Knarsdale
Ninebanks
Slaggyford
Kirkhaugh
South Tynedale Railway
The Hub
Alston
Carr Shield
Dirt Pot
Allenheads
Gilderdale Forest
Nenthead
Killhope Summit
Killhope Lead Mining
Alston Moor
Garrigill
Lanehead
Cowshill
Wearhead
Weardale
Westgate
Ireshopeburn
St John's Chapel
Daddry Shield
Gamblesby
Melmerby
Milburn Forest
Moor House
Skirwith
138
139
Blencarn
Cow Green Reservoir
Culgaith
Newbiggin
Temple Sowerby
Kirkby Thore
Knock
Upper Teesdale
High Force
Ettersgill
Holwick
Pennine Way
Maize Beck
313 SPY RIGG
325 ROUND TOP
265 GREEN RIGG
255 DENTON FELL
522 GLENDUE FELL
584 THREE PIKES
657 MIDDLE CARRICK
559
664 BLACK FELL
624 HARTSIDE HEIGHT
580 Hartside Summit
710 MELMERBY FELL
740 GREEN FELL
893 CROSS FELL
847 GREAT DUN FELL
747 BURNHOPE SEAT
572 HARTLEY MOOR
443 HANGMAN HILL
150
NOOKTON FELL
559 BLACK HILL
481 DUFTON PIKE
A69
A686
A689
B6318
B6319
B6320
B6305
B6304
B6295
B6294
B6277
B6531
R South Tyne
R West Allen
R East Allen
River Tees
River Irthing
Croglin Water
Shield Water
Crowdundle Beck
Trout Beck

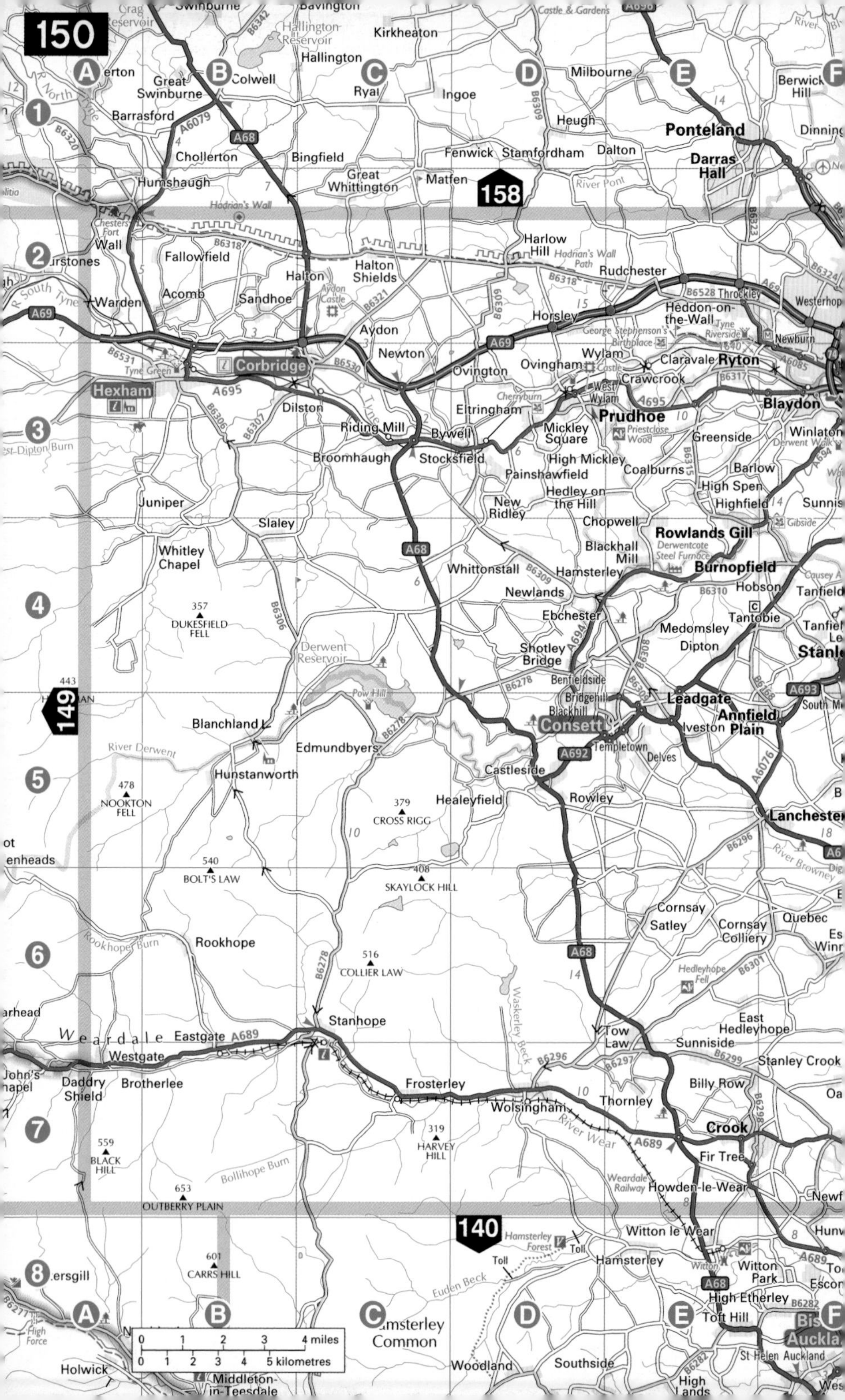
150
Crag Reservoir
Swinburne
Bavington
Hallington Reservoir
Kirkheaton
Castle & Gardens
A696
River Blyth
A
B
C
D
E
F
Great Swinburne
Colwell
Hallington
Ryal
Ingoe
Milbourne
Berwick Hill
1
R. North Tyne
Barrasford
A6079
B6342
B6320
B6309
Heugh
Ponteland
Dinnington
A68
Chollerton
Bingfield
Fenwick
Stamfordham
Dalton
Darras Hall
Humshaugh
Great Whittington
Matfen
158
River Pont
Hadrian's Wall
Chesters Fort
Wall
B6323
2
Fallowfield
B6318
Harlow Hill
Hadrian's Wall Path
Rudchester
B6324
Halton Shields
Halton
Aydon Castle
B6321
Throckley
Westerhope
R. South Tyne
Warden
Acomb
Sandhoe
Horsley
B6528
Heddon-on-the-Wall
A69
Aydon
George Stephenson's Birthplace
Tyne Riverside
Newburn
B6531
Tyne Green
Corbridge
Newton
B6530
Ovingham
Wylam
Claravale
Ryton
A6085
Hexham
A695
Dilston
Ovington
Castle
Crawcrook
B6317
R. Tyne
Cherryburn
West Wylam
Eltringham
Prudhoe
Blaydon
B6306
B6307
3
Riding Mill
Bywell
Mickley Square
Priestclose Wood
Greenside
Winlaton
Derwent Walk
West Dipton Burn
Broomhaugh
Stockfield
High Mickley
B6315
Barlow
A694
Painshawfield
Coalburns
Hedley on the Hill
High Spen
Juniper
New Ridley
Highfield
Sunniside
Chopwell
Gibside
Slaley
Rowlands Gill
Blackhall Mill
Derwentcote Steel Furnace
Whitley Chapel
Whittonstall
B6309
Hamsterley
Burnopfield
Causey Arch
B6310
Hobson
Tanfield
Newlands
4
357
DUKESFIELD FELL
Ebchester
Tantobie
Medomsley
Dipton
Derwent Reservoir
Shotley Bridge
B6308
Stanley
Benfieldside
B6278
443
149
Pow Hill
Bridgehill
Blackhill
Leadgate
A693
Annfield Plain
South Moor
Blanchland
Consett
Iveston
River Derwent
Edmundbyers
Templetown
A692
Delves
Hunstanworth
Castleside
A6076
5
478
NOOKTON FELL
379
CROSS RIGG
Healeyfield
Rowley
Lanchester
10
Allenheads
540
BOLT'S LAW
408
SKAYLOCK HILL
B6296
River Browney
Cornsay
Satley
Cornsay Colliery
Quebec
6
Rookhope Burn
Rookhope
516
COLLIER LAW
A68
Hedleyhope Fell
B6301
Waskerley Beck
Stanhope
East Hedleyhope
Tow Law
Weardale
Eastgate
A689
Westgate
Sunniside
B6299
Stanley Crook
Daddry Shield
Brotherlee
Frosterley
B6297
Billy Row
Wolsingham
Thornley
B6298
7
559
BLACK HILL
319
HARVEY HILL
River Wear
Crook
Fir Tree
Bollihope Burn
Weardale Railway
Howden-le-Wear
653
OUTBERRY PLAIN
140
Hamsterley Forest
Toll
Witton le Wear
601
CARRS HILL
Hamsterley
Witton
Witton Park
Escomb
8
Ettersgill
Eden Beck
High Etherley
B6282
B6277
High Force
Hamsterley Common
Toft Hill
Bishop Auckland
0 1 2 3 4 miles
0 1 2 3 4 5 kilometres
Holwick
Woodland
Southside
St Helen Auckland
Middleton-in-Teesdale
High Lands

New Hartley
Seaton
Seaton Sluice
Seaton Delaval
St Mary's
Earsdon
Monkseaton
Whitley Bay
Cullercoats
Killingworth
Shiremoor
Tynemouth
159
Forest Hall
New York
Tynemouth Priory & Castle
Amsterdam (IJmuiden)
Rising Sun
Longbenton
North Shields
Willington
SOUTH SHIELDS
Wallsend
Int. Ferry Terminal
Heaton
Jarrow
Tyne Tunnel
Westoe
Marsden Bay
Walker
Harton
Marsden
Byker
River Tyne
Hebburn
Souter Lighthouse & The Leas
Whitburn Coastal Park
Souter Point
Felling
Monkton
Cleadon
Whitburn
West Boldon
Wardley
GATESHEAD
East Boldon
Whitburn Bay
Seaburn
Low Fell
Wrekenton
Hylton Castle
Fulwell
Roker
Southwick
Bowes Railway
Monkwearmouth
Springwell
Usworth
Castletown
Wetland Centre
Birtley
South Hylton
SUNDERLAND
WASHINGTON
Pennywell
Hendon
Ouston
Washington
Penshaw Monument
High Newport
Grangetown
Fatfield
Penshaw
New Silksworth
Tunstall
Durham Heritage Coast
Herrington
Ryhope
River Wear
Shiney Row
Chester-le-Street
Bournmoor
Houghton-le-Spring
Seaham
Chester Moor
Great Lumley
Hetton-le-Hole
Parkside
Plawsworth
West Rainton
Hetton Lyons
Murton
Dalton-le-Dale
Finchale Priory
East Rainton
Dalton Park
Low Moorsley
South Hetton
Hawthorn
Pity Me
Adventure Valley
Pittington
Easington Lane
Easington Colliery
Hallgarth
Easington
Durham Heritage Coast
Crook Hall
Carrville
Littletown
Haswell
Little Thorpe
Gilesgate Moor
Sherburn
Haswell Plough
Durham
Shotton Colliery
Peterlee
Horden
Sherburn Hill
Ludworth
Shadforth
Shotton
Blackhall Colliery
Shincliffe
Thornley
Durham Coast
Castle Eden
Blackhall Rocks
Cassop
Wheatley Hill
Bowburn
Hesleden
Sunderland Bridge
Quarrington Hill
Wingate
Kelloe
Hett
Hutton Henry
Sheraton
Hart
Coxhoe
Trimdon Grange
Trimdon Colliery
Cornforth
The Headland
Historic Quays
Trimdon
HARTLEPOOL
Thrislington
Elwick
Dalton Piercy
Ferryhill
141
142
Ferryhill Station
Kirk Merrington
Mainsforth
Bishop Middleham
Summerhill
Leasingthorne
Hardwick Hall
River Skerne
Sedgefield
Owton Manor
Seaton Carew
Chilton
Bradbury
Greatham
Teesmouth
Newton Bewley
Hartlepool Power Station
Cowpen
Mordon
Tees

A
B
C
D
E
F
1
2
3
4
5
6
7
8
Culzean Bay
Maidenhead Bay
Maidens
A719
162
Turnberry
Turnberry Bay
Dipple
A77
Ailsa Craig
340
Old Dailly
Penkill
Girvan
B7035
Dounepark
Woodland
Pinminnoch
297
GREY HILL
Pinmore
13
Lendalfoot
A714
Balligmorr
A77
Bennane Head
Colmonell
B734
River Stinchar
Pinwherry
Muck Water
B734
Ballantrae
Heronsford
Water of Tig
Duisk River
Belfast
Currarie Port
437
BENERAIRD
321
CARLOCK HILL
387
ALTIMEG HILL
Larne
Glen App
305
BENBRAKE HILL
Milleur Point
Corsewall Point
Lady Bay
Southern Upland Way
Barnhills
Portencalzie
Laggangairn Standing Stones
Glenwhilly
B738
Kirkcolm
Cairnryan
144
Main Water of Luce
Cross Water of Luce
B738
Ervie
Loch Connell
A718
B798
Low Barbeth
271
ARTFIELD FELL
A77
Beoch Burn
Braid Fell
Low Salchrie
New
Knockna
0 1 2 3 4 miles
0 1 2 3 4 5 kilometres
Innermessan
A751
Castle of St John
Black Loch
A77

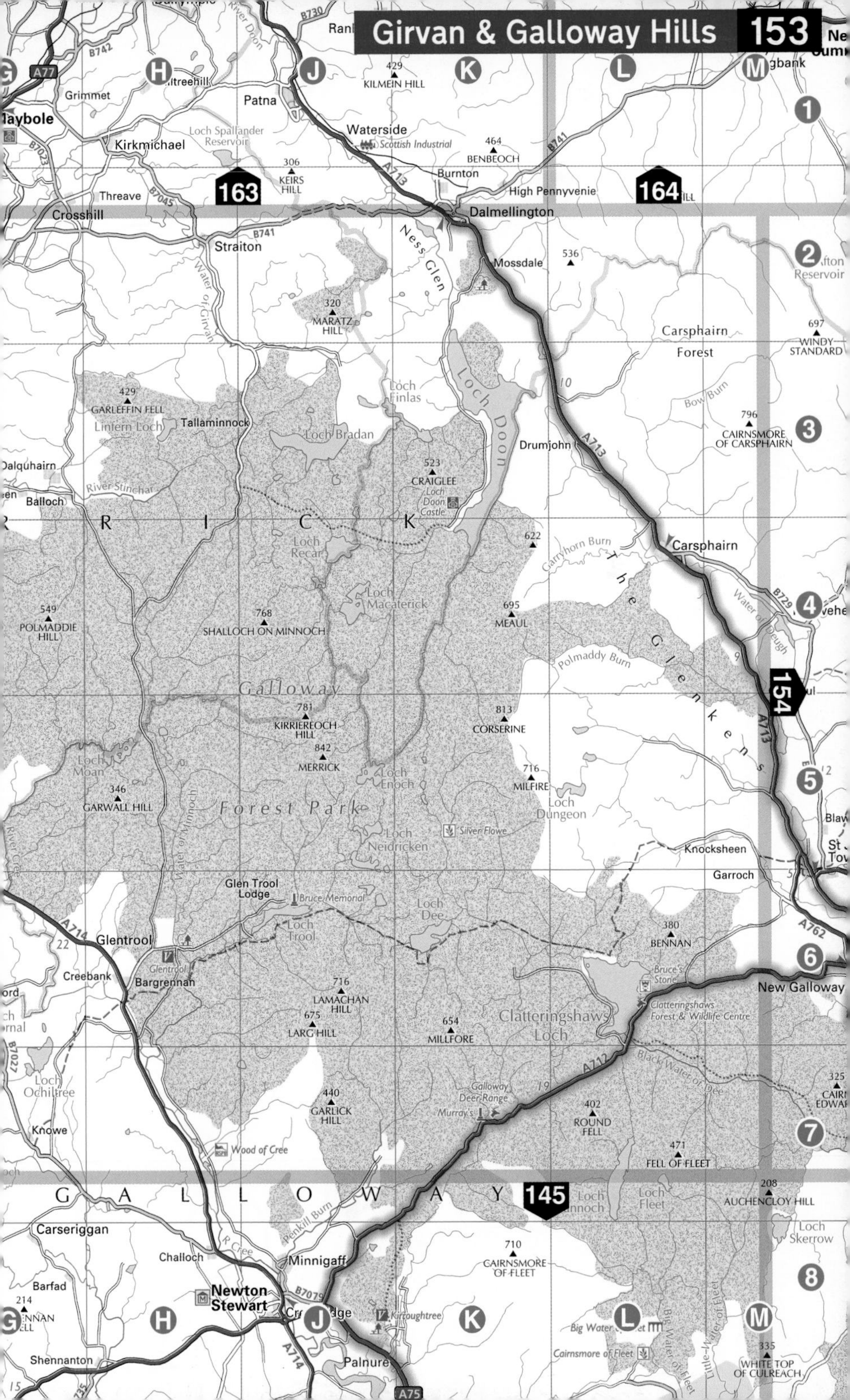

Girvan & Galloway Hills
153
H
J
K
L
M
G
1
2
3
4
5
6
7
8
B730
B742
A77
Grimmet
Patna
River Doon
429
KILMEIN HILL
Waterside
Scottish Industrial
Kirkmichael
Loch Spallander Reservoir
B7023
464
BENBEOCH
B741
306
KEIRS HILL
Burnton
A713
High Pennyvenie
163
164
Threave
B7045
Crosshill
Dalmellington
B741
Straiton
Ness Glen
Mossdale
536
Water of Girvan
320
MARATZ HILL
Carsphairn
Forest
697
WINDY STANDARD
Reservoir
Loch Finlas
Loch Doon
10
Bow Burn
429
GARLEFFIN FELL
Linfern Loch
Tallaminnock
Loch Bradan
796
CAIRNSMORE OF CARSPHAIRN
Drumjohn
A713
523
CRAIGLEE
Loch Doon Castle
River Stinchar
Balloch
R
I
C
K
622
Loch Recar
Garryhorn Burn
Carsphairn
The Glenkens
Loch Macaterick
695
MEAUL
B729
Water of Deugh
549
POLMADDIE HILL
768
SHALLOCH ON MINNOCH
Polmaddy Burn
9
154
Galloway
781
KIRRIEREOCH HILL
813
CORSERINE
A713
842
MERRICK
Loch Moan
Loch Enoch
346
GARWALL HILL
716
MILFIRE
Water of Minnoch
Forest Park
Loch Dungeon
River Cree
Loch Neidricken
Silver Flowe
Knocksheen
Garroch
Glen Trool Lodge
Bruce Memorial
Loch Dee
A714
Loch Trool
380
BENNAN
A762
22
Glentrool
Glentrool
Creebank
Bargrennan
Bruce's Stone
New Galloway
716
LAMACHAN HILL
Clatteringshaws Forest & Wildlife Centre
675
LARG HILL
654
MILLFORE
Clatteringshaws Loch
B7027
A712
Black Water of Dee
Loch Ochiltree
Galloway Deer Range
19
Murray's
325
402
ROUND FELL
440
GARLICK HILL
Knowe
Wood of Cree
471
FELL OF FLEET
G
A
L
L
O
W
A
Y
145
208
AUCHENCLOY HILL
Loch Fleet
Loch Skerrow
Carseriggan
Penkill Burn
R Cree
Challoch
Minnigaff
710
CAIRNSMORE OF FLEET
Barfad
Newton Stewart
B7079
214
Kirroughtree
Big Water
Big Water of Fleet
Little Water of Fleet
Cairnsmore of Fleet
335
WHITE TOP OF CULREACH
Shennanton
A714
Palnure
A75
15

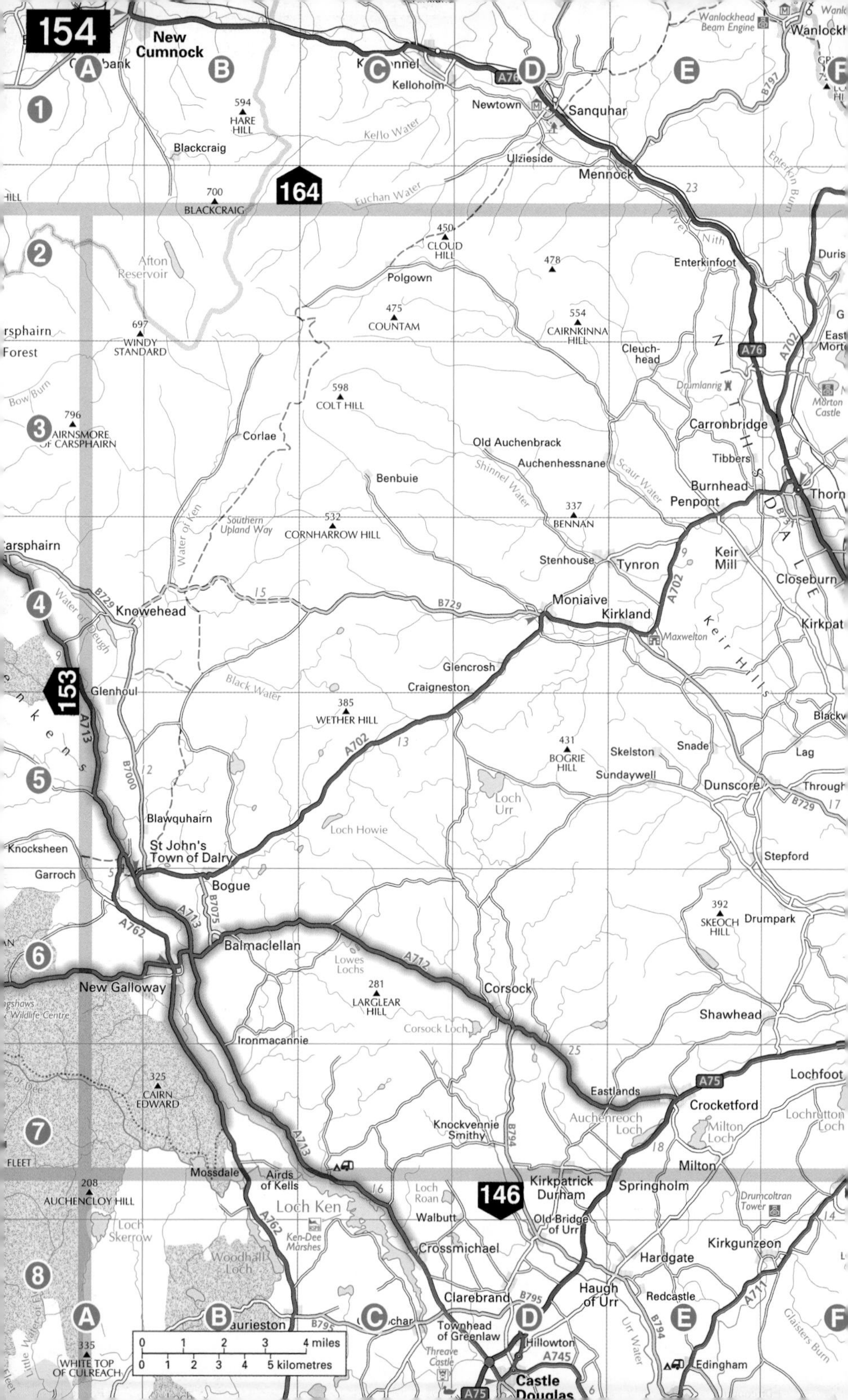

154
New Cumnock
Kirkconnel
Kelloholm
Newtown
Sanquhar
Wanlockhead Beam Engine
Wanlockhead
594 HARE HILL
Blackcraig
Kello Water
Ulzieside
Mennock
700 BLACKCRAIG
164
Euchan Water
450 CLOUD HILL
478
River Nith
Enterkinfoot
Enterkin Burn
Afton Reservoir
Polgown
475 COUNTAM
554 CAIRNKINNA HILL
697 WINDY STANDARD
Cleuchhead
Drumlanrig
Morton Castle
Bow Burn
796 CAIRNSMORE OF CARSPHAIRN
598 COLT HILL
Corlae
Carronbridge
Old Auchenbrack
Auchenhessnane
Tibbers
Shinnel Water
Scaur Water
Benbuie
Burnhead
Penpont
Thornhill
Nithsdale
337 BENNAN
Southern Upland Way
532 CORNHARROW HILL
Water of Ken
Carsphairn
Stenhouse
Tynron
Keir Mill
Closeburn
B729
Knowehead
Water of Deugh
Moniaive
Kirkland
Maxwelton
Keir Hills
Kirkpatrick
153
Glenhoul
Black Water
Glencrosh
Craigneston
385 WETHER HILL
A702
A713
B7000
Kenkens
431 BOGRIE HILL
Skelston
Snade
Sundaywell
Lag
Loch Urr
Dunscore
Blawquhairn
Loch Howie
Knocksheen
St John's Town of Dalry
Garroch
Bogue
B7075
Stepford
392 SKEOCH HILL
Drumpark
A762
Balmaclellan
Lowes Lochs
A712
281 LARGLEAR HILL
New Galloway
Corsock
Shawhead
Corsock Loch
Ironmacannie
325 CAIRN EDWARD
A75
Eastlands
Lochfoot
Auchenreoch Loch
Crocketford
Lochrutton Loch
Milton Loch
Knockvennie Smithy
B794
Mossdale
Airds of Kells
Milton
208 AUCHENCLOY HILL
Loch Ken
146
Kirkpatrick Durham
Springholm
Drumcoltran Tower
Loch Roan
Loch Skerrow
Ken-Dee Marshes
Walbutt
Old Bridge of Urr
Woodhall Loch
Crossmichael
Hardgate
Kirkgunzeon
Clarebrand
B795
Haugh of Urr
Redcastle
A711
Laurieston
Glaisters Burn
Townhead of Greenlaw
Hillowton
Urr Water
Threave Castle
A745
Little Water of Fleet
335 WHITE TOP OF CULREACH
Edingham
Castle Douglas
0 1 2 3 4 miles
0 1 2 3 4 5 kilometres

Moffat
Beattock
Lochmaben
Lockerbie
Locharbriggs
Dumfries
Annan
Eskdalemuir
Newton Wamphray
Johnstonebridge
Ecclefechan
Kirtlebridge
Eaglesfield
Middlebie
Waterbeck
Boreland
Corrie
Dalton
Ruthwell
Cummertrees
Powfoot
Dornock
Eastriggs
Glencaple
Kirkconnell
Carrutherstown
Mouswald
Torthorwald
Hightae
Templand
Forest of Ae
A74(M)
A701
A75
A709
B7076
B7020
B723
165
166
147
156

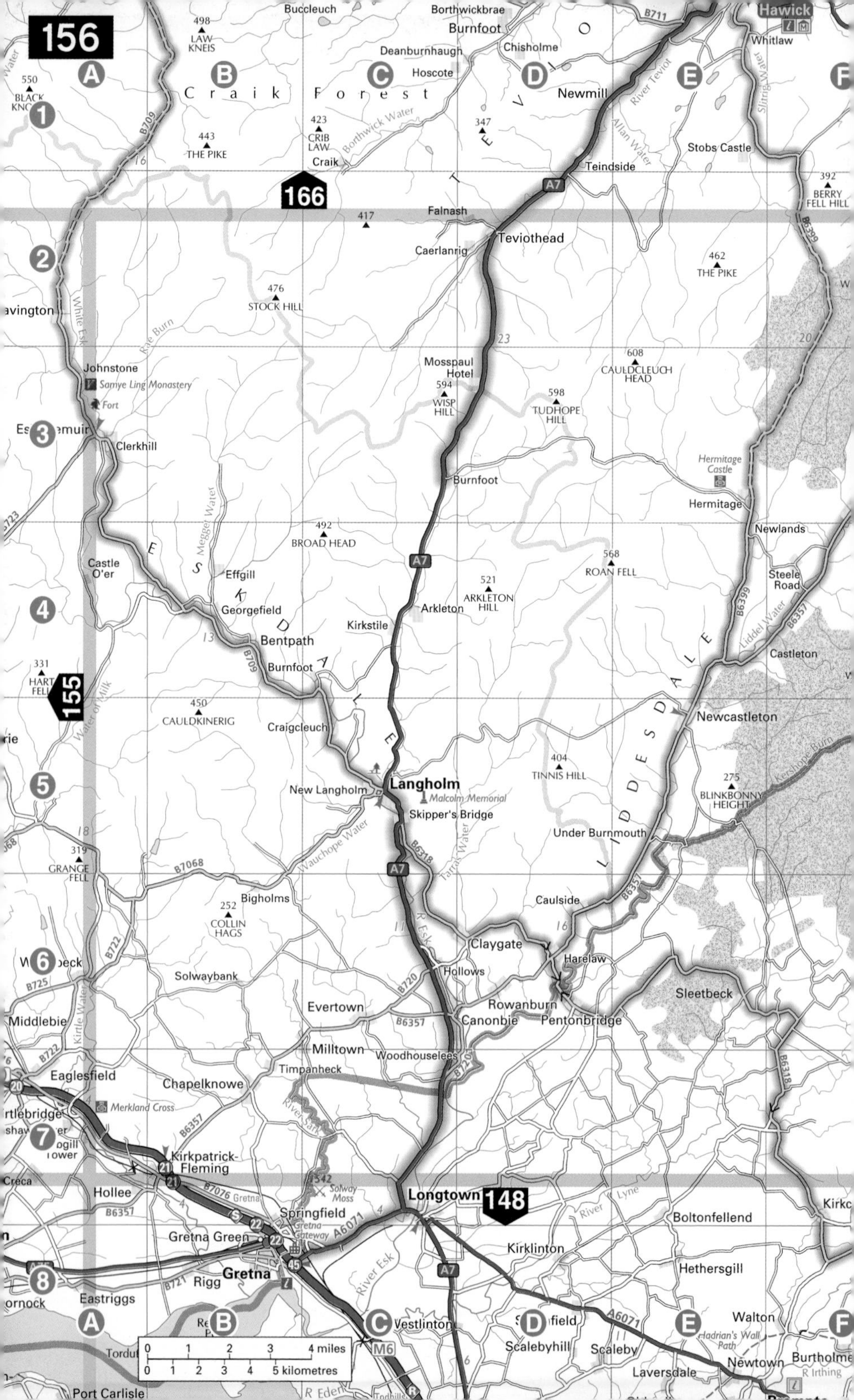
Buccleuch
Borthwickbrae
Burnfoot
Hawick
Whitlaw
Chisholme
Deanburnhaugh
Hoscote
Craik Forest
Newmill
550
BLACK KNOWE
498
LAW KNEIS
443
THE PIKE
423
CRIB LAW
Craik
Borthwick Water
347
TEVIOT
River Teviot
Allan Water
Slitrig Water
Stobs Castle
Teindside
392
BERRY FELL HILL
166
417
Falnash
Teviothead
Caerlanrig
462
THE PIKE
476
STOCK HILL
White Esk
Rae Burn
Johnstone
Samye Ling Monastery
Fort
Eskdalemuir
Clerkhill
Mosspaul Hotel
594
WISP HILL
598
TUDHOPE HILL
608
CAULDCLEUCH HEAD
Hermitage Castle
Hermitage
Burnfoot
Newlands
Megget Water
492
BROAD HEAD
568
ROAN FELL
Castle O'er
Effgill
ESKDALE
Georgefield
521
ARKLETON HILL
Arkleton
Steele Road
Kirkstile
Bentpath
Liddel Water
Castleton
Burnfoot
331
HART FELL
155
Water of Milk
450
CAULDKINERIG
Craigcleuch
Newcastleton
LIDDESDALE
404
TINNIS HILL
275
BLINKBONNY HEIGHT
Kershope Burn
New Langholm
Langholm
Malcolm Memorial
Skipper's Bridge
Under Burnmouth
Wauchope Water
Tarras Water
319
GRANGE FELL
252
COLLIN HAGS
Bigholms
Caulside
R Esk
Claygate
Harelaw
Hollows
Solwaybank
Evertown
Rowanburn
Sleetbeck
Canonbie
Pentonbridge
Middlebie
Kirtle Water
Milltown
Woodhouselees
Eaglesfield
Chapelknowe
Timpanheck
Merkland Cross
River Sark
Kirkpatrick-Fleming
Solway Moss
Hollee
Springfield
Longtown
148
River Lyne
Gretna Gateway
Boltonfellend
Gretna Green
Kirklinton
Gretna
Rigg
River Esk
Hethersgill
Eastriggs
Westlinton
Walton
Hadrian's Wall Path
Scaleby
Scalebyhill
Newtown
Burtholme
R Irthing
Laversdale
Port Carlisle
R Eden
A7
B709
B711
B6399
B6357
B6318
B7068
B722
B725
B720
B7076
B6357
B721
A6071
M6
0 1 2 3 4 miles
0 1 2 3 4 5 kilometres

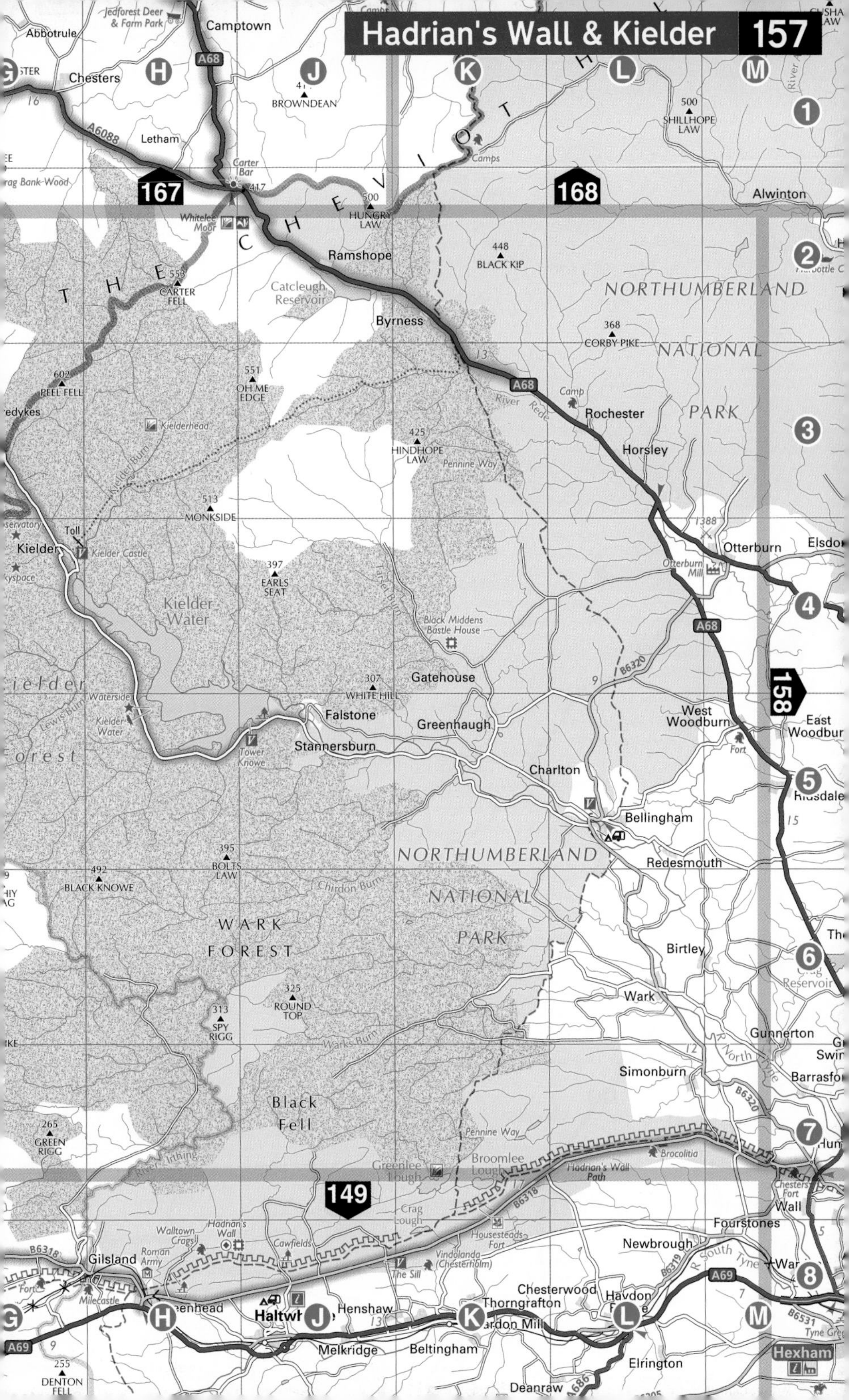

Jedforest Deer & Farm Park
Abbotrule
Camptown
A68
Chesters
A6088
Letham
BROWNDEAN
Carter Bar
417
167
168
THE CHEVIOT HILLS
500
SHILLHOPE LAW
Alwinton
500
HUNGRY LAW
Camps
Whitelee Moor
Ramshope
448
BLACK KIP
553
CARTER FELL
Catcleugh Reservoir
Byrness
NORTHUMBERLAND NATIONAL PARK
368
CORBY PIKE
602
PEEL FELL
551
OH ME EDGE
Kielderhead
Kielder Burn
River Rede
Camp
Rochester
Horsley
425
HINDHOPE LAW
Pennine Way
513
MONKSIDE
1388
Otterburn
Otterburn Mill
Elsdon
Toll
Kielder
Kielder Castle
397
EARLS SEAT
Kielder Water
Tarset Burn
Black Middens Bastle House
A68
307
WHITE HILL
Gatehouse
B6320
158
Waterside
Kielder Water
Lewis Burn
Kielder Forest
Falstone
Greenhaugh
West Woodburn
East Woodburn
Stannersburn
Tower Knowe
Fort
Charlton
Risdale
Bellingham
NORTHUMBERLAND NATIONAL PARK
Redesmouth
395
BOLTS LAW
492
BLACK KNOWE
Chirdon Burn
WARK FOREST
Birtley
Wark
325
ROUND TOP
313
SPY RIGG
Warks Burn
Gunnerton
Simonburn
R North Tyne
Barrasford
B6320
Black Fell
265
GREEN RIGG
River Irthing
Pennine Way
Broomlee Lough
Brocolitia
Greenlee Lough
149
Hadrian's Wall Path
Crag Lough
B6318
Chesters Fort
Wall
Fourstones
Hadrian's Wall
Walltown Crags
Roman Army
Cawfields
Housesteads Fort
Newbrough
B6318
Gilsland
Vindolanda (Chesterholm)
The Sill
B6319
R South Tyne
Fort
Milecastle
Chesterwood
Haydon Bridge
A69
Greenhead
Haltwhistle
Henshaw
Thorngrafton
Bardon Mill
A69
B6531
Tyne Green
Melkridge
Beltingham
Hexham
Elrington
255
DENTON FELL
Deanraw
A686

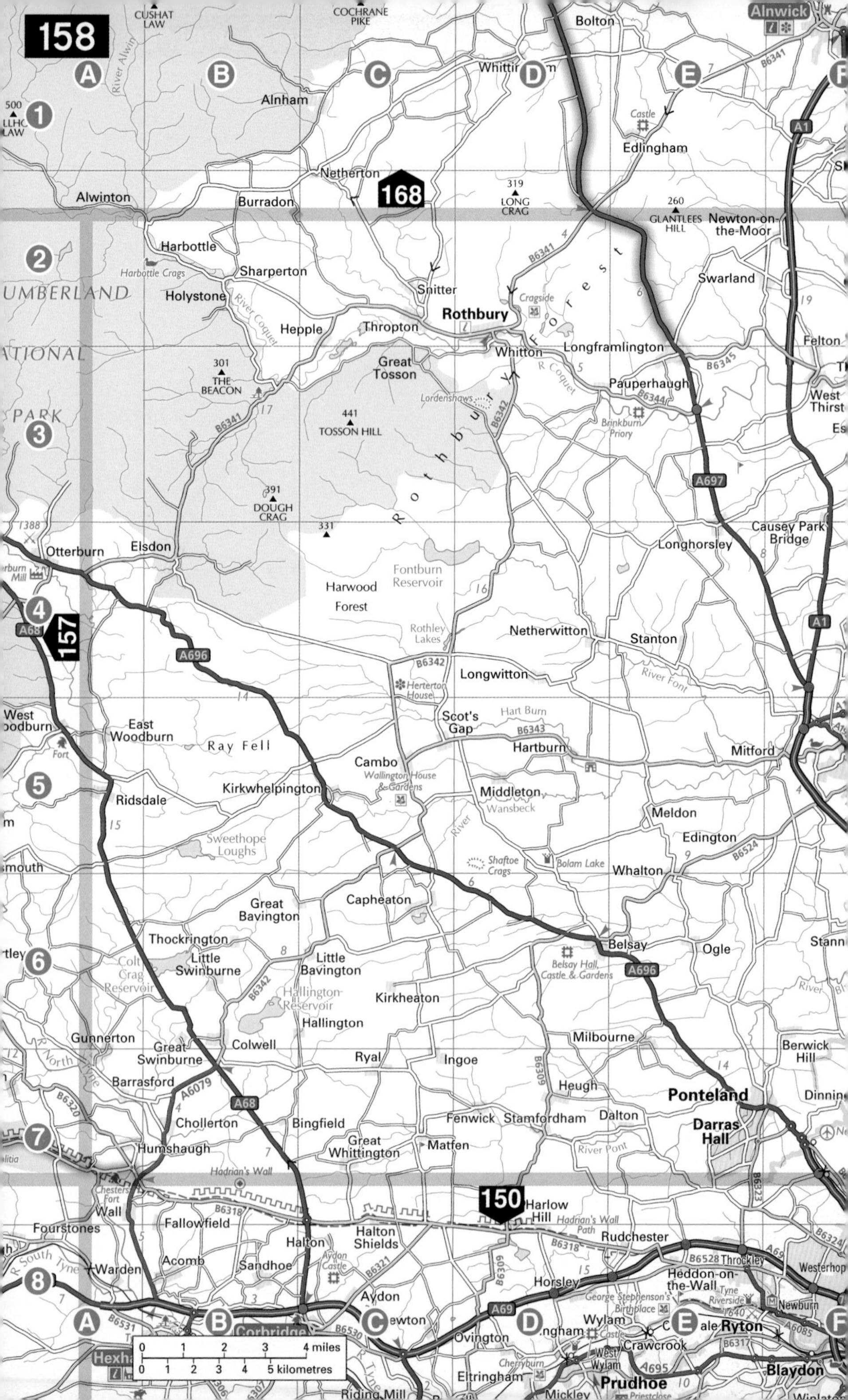
158
CUSHAT LAW
COCHRANE PIKE
Alnwick
Bolton
A
B
C
D
E
F
River Alwin
Alnham
Whittingham
B6341
500
1
Castle
Edlingham
A1
Netherton
168
319
LONG CRAG
260
GLANTLEES HILL
Newton-on-the-Moor
Alwinton
Burradon
Harbottle
2
Harbottle Crags
Sharperton
B6341
Swarland
NORTHUMBERLAND
Holystone
Snitter
Rothbury
Cragside
NATIONAL
River Coquet
Hepple
Thropton
Whitton
Longframlington
Felton
Great Tosson
R Coquet
B6345
301
THE BEACON
Lordenshaws
Pauperhaugh
B6344
West Thirston
PARK
3
B6341
441
TOSSON HILL
B6342
Brinkburn Priory
Rothbury Forest
A697
391
DOUGH CRAG
1388
331
Causey Park Bridge
Otterburn
Elsdon
Longhorsley
Otterburn Mill
Fontburn Reservoir
Harwood Forest
4
A68
157
Rothley Lakes
Netherwitton
Stanton
A1
A696
B6342
Longwitton
Herterton House
River Font
West Woodburn
East Woodburn
Scot's Gap
Hart Burn
B6343
Fort
Ray Fell
Hartburn
Cambo
Mitford
5
Wallington House & Gardens
Kirkwhelpington
Ridsdale
Middleton
Wansbeck
Meldon
River
Sweethope Loughs
Edington
Shaftoe Crags
Bolam Lake
B6524
Whalton
Capheaton
Great Bavington
Thockrington
Belsay
Ogle
6
Colt Crag Reservoir
Little Swinburne
Little Bavington
Belsay Hall, Castle & Gardens
A696
B6342
Hallington Reservoir
Kirkheaton
Hallington
Gunnerton
Milbourne
Berwick Hill
Great Swinburne
Colwell
Ryal
Ingoe
R North Tyne
B6309
Barrasford
Heugh
A6079
Ponteland
B6320
A68
Chollerton
Bingfield
Fenwick
Stamfordham
Dalton
Darras Hall
7
Humshaugh
Great Whittington
Matfen
River Pont
Hadrian's Wall
Chesters Fort
150
Harlow Hill
Wall
B6318
Hadrian's Wall Path
B6323
Fourstones
Fallowfield
Halton
Halton Shields
Rudchester
B6324
R South Tyne
Warden
Acomb
Sandhoe
Aydon Castle
B6321
B6309
B6318
B6528
Throckley
Heddon-on-the-Wall
Tyne Riverside
Westerhope
8
Horsley
A69
Aydon
George Stephenson's Birthplace
Newburn
A
B
C
D
E
F
B6531
Corbridge
B6530
Newton
Ovington
Wylam
Ryton
Castle
A6085
Hexham
Crawcrook
B6317
West Wylam
Eltringham
Cherryburn
A695
Prudhoe
Blaydon
Riding Mill
Mickley
0 1 2 3 4 miles
0 1 2 3 4 5 kilometres

Seaton Point
Alnmouth Bay
169
Warkworth
Amble
Coquet Island
High Hauxley
Druridge Bay
Druridge Bay
Widdrington
North Northumberland Heritage Coast
Cresswell
A1068
Ellington
Lynemouth
A189
Woodhorn
Beacon Point
QE2
Newbiggin-by-the-Sea
Wansbeck Riverside
B1334
A1147
A193
Blyth
Cowpen
B1331
A189
Newsham
B1505
A192
A1061
New Hartley
Seaton
Seaton Sluice
Seaton Hall
B1326
A190
Seaton Delaval
St Mary's
B1322
A192
B1325
A1148
Earsdon
Monkseaton
Whitley Bay
Cullercoats
A1056
Killingworth
Shiremoor
A191
A193
Tynemouth
Forest Hall
New York
Rising Sun
151
Tynemouth Priory & Castle
Amsterdam (IJmuiden)
North Shields
Longbenton
A1058
Willington
SOUTH SHIELDS
Wallsend
Int. Ferry Terminal
Heaton
A187
Jarrow
Tyne Tunnel
Westoe
A183
Marsden Bay
Walker
B1313
River Tyne
Hebburn
A185
A1300
Marsden
Souter Lighthouse & The Leas
Byker
Whitburn Coastal Park
Souter Point
Felling
Monkton
A194
A19
B1298
A183
Cleadon
A184
Wardley
West Boldon
Whitburn

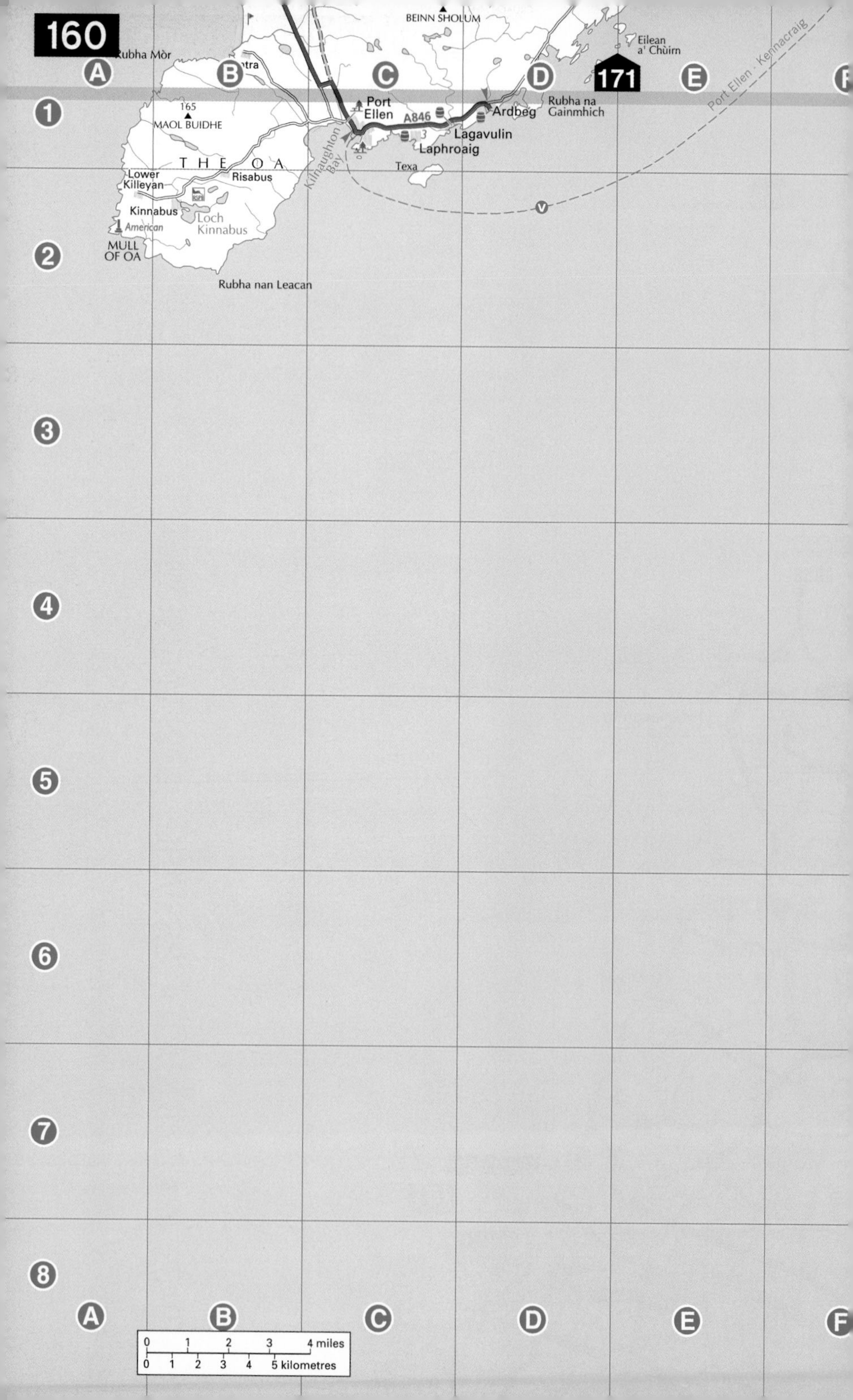

Rubha Mòr
BEINN SHOLUM
Eilean a' Chùirn
171
Port Ellen - Kennacraig
165
MAOL BUIDHE
Port Ellen
A846
Ardbeg
Rubha na Gainmhich
Lagavulin
Laphroaig
THE OA
Kilnaughton Bay
Texa
Lower Killeyan
Risabus
Kinnabus
Loch Kinnabus
American
MULL OF OA
Rubha nan Leacan
A B C D E F
1 2 3 4 5 6 7 8
0 1 2 3 4 miles
0 1 2 3 4 5 kilometres

Rhunahaorine Point
Ardminish
Achamore
Tayinloan
Rhunahaorine
172
Cara
A83
Muasdale
Glenacardoch Point
Belloch
Barr Water
Glenbarr
Clan MacAlister
Cleongart
Bellochantuy Bay
Bellochantuy
Tangy Loch
Lussa Loch
Kilkenzie
Kilmichael
Campbeltown
Campbeltown Loch
Stewarton
Drumlemble
B843
B842
Kilkerran
Kildalloig
Island Davaar
BEINN GHUILEAN
Achinhoan
THE STATE
Ru Stafnish
Dalsmeran
Glen Breakevie
Conie Glen
Glen Kerran
Strone Glen
Cattadale
Southend
Machariooch
Polliwilline Bay
Carskey
Dunaverty
Carskey Bay
Sanda Sound
Sheep Island
Sanda Island
Borgadalemore Point
CRUACH NAN GABHAR
BEINN AN TUIRC
BORD MOR
SCREADAN HILL
Glen Lussa
Peninver
Ardnacross Bay
Ugadale
Saddell
Saddell Bay
Saddell Water
Torrisdale
Carradale Bay
Carradale Point
Waterfoot
Dippen
Bridgend
Carradale House
Port Righ
Carradale
B879
Carradale Water
Grogport
Barmollack
KILBRANNAN SOUND
Campbeltown-Ardrossan (May-Sept)
Pirnmill
Penrioch
North Arran
Loch Tanna
BEINN BHARRAIN
Whitefarland
Imachar
Balliekine
Glen Iorsa
Iorsa Water
162
ARRAN
Auchagallon Stone Circle
Machrie
Machrie Bay
Machrie Moor Stone Circles
Tormore
Moss Farm Road Stone Circle
Balmichael
Shiskine
Torbeg
Drumadoon Point
Drumadoon Bay
Blackwaterfoot
Kilpatrick
Kilpatrick Dun
Brown Head
Corriecravie
Torr a' Chaisteal Fort
Slidderv

Catacol
Isle of Arran
Glen Chalmadale
A841
173
Portencross
Farland Head
A
B
C
D
E
F
1
2
3
4
5
6
7
8
Glen Catacol
Sannox
Pirnmill
Penrioch
North Arran
834
CAISTEAL ABHAIL
Loch Tanna
Corrie
715
BEINN BHARRAIN
874
GOATFELL
Glen Iorsa
machar
Balliekine
792
BEINN NUIS
Glen Rosa
Merkland Point
Brodick Castle, Garden & Country Park
Iorsa Water
Brodick Bay
FIRTH
OF
CLYDE
ARRAN
Brodick
Strathwhillan
Auchagallon Stone Circle
Machrie
Machrie Bay
Corriegills
512
A'CHRUACH
B880
A841
Clauchlands Point
Tormore
Machrie Moor Stone Circles
Moss Farm Road Stone Circle
503
BEINN BHREAC
Margnaheglish
Lamlash
Balmichael
Lamlash Bay
Holy Island
Cordon
Torbeg
Shiskine
Drumadoon Point
Blackwaterfoot
Campbeltown-Brodick (May-Sept, Sat only)
Campbeltown-Ardrossan (May-Sept)
Glen Scorrodale
Auchencairn
Kingscross
Knockenkelly
Drumadoon Bay
Kilpatrick
Kilpatrick Dun
Carn Ban
Whiting Bay
Brown Head
Whiting Bay
Glenashdale
Corriecravie
Largymore
Torr a' Chaisteal Fort
Sliddery
Kilmory Water
Largybeg
Dippen
Dippen Head
Kilmory
161
Lagg
Torrylin Cairn
Bennan
Kildonan
Bennan Head
Pladda
152
Ailsa Craig
340
0 1 2 3 4 miles
0 1 2 3 4 5 kilometres

Arran & Ayrshire Coast
163
174
164
153
Dalry
Munnoch
Burnhouse
Auchentiber
Dalgarven
Dalgarven Mill
Kilwinning
Crossgates
High Cross
Stewarton
Torranyard
Fergushill
Benslie
Fenwick
Waterside
Laigh Fenwick
Eglinton
Stevenston
Ardeer
Cunninghamhead
Kilmaurs
Girdle Toll
Perceton
Moscow
Polbaith Burn
Irvine
Maritime
Springside
Knockentiber
Knockinlaw
Dean Castle
KILMARNOCK
Dreghorn
Fullarton
Crosshouse
Newmilns
Crookedholm
Hurlford
Greenholm
Galston
Irvine Bay
Gatehead
Drybridge
Earlston
Riccarton
Shortlees
Gailes
Dundonald
Castle
Middleyard
Barassie
Symington
Bogend
Craigie
Carnell
Crosshands
Loans
Helenton
Troon
Royal Troon
Lady Isle
Wallace Monument
Auchmillan
Monkton
Bachelors' Club
Mauchline
Tarbolton
Failford
Glasgow Prestwick
Prestwick
Mossblown
Haugh
Catrine
Ayr Gorge Woodlands
New Prestwick
St Quivox
Ayr Bay
Whitletts
Annbank
Stair
Wallacetown
Gadgirth
Trabboch
Trabbochburn
Auchinleck
Dumfries House
Ayr
River Ayr
Ochiltree
Lugar Water
Belmont
Joppa
Coylton
Palmerston
Heads of Ayr
Doonfoot
Burns Cottage
Alloway
Drongan
Garrallan
Fisherton
Robert Burns Birthplace
Barbieston
Skares
Martnaham Loch
Sinclairston
Hollybush
Culroy
Drumshang
Minishant
Dalrymple
River Doon
CARSGAILOCH HILL
Croy Brae (Electric Brae)
Knoweside
Rankinston
Dalgig
Guiltreehill
KILMEIN HILL
Pennyglen
Grimmet
Patna
Whitefaulds
Maybole
Waterside
Scottish Industrial
Loch Spallander Reservoir
Kirkmichael
Crossraguel Abbey
KEIRS HILL
BENBEOCH
Kirkoswald
Souter Johnnie's Cottage
Burnton
High Pennyvenie
Threave
ENOCH
Crosshill
Dalmellington
Straiton
Roan of Craigoch
Ness Glen
Mossdale
Water of Girvan
Wallacetown
Kilgrammie
MARATZ HILL
Dailly
GARLEFFIN FELL
Loch Finlas
Linfern Loch
Tallaminnock

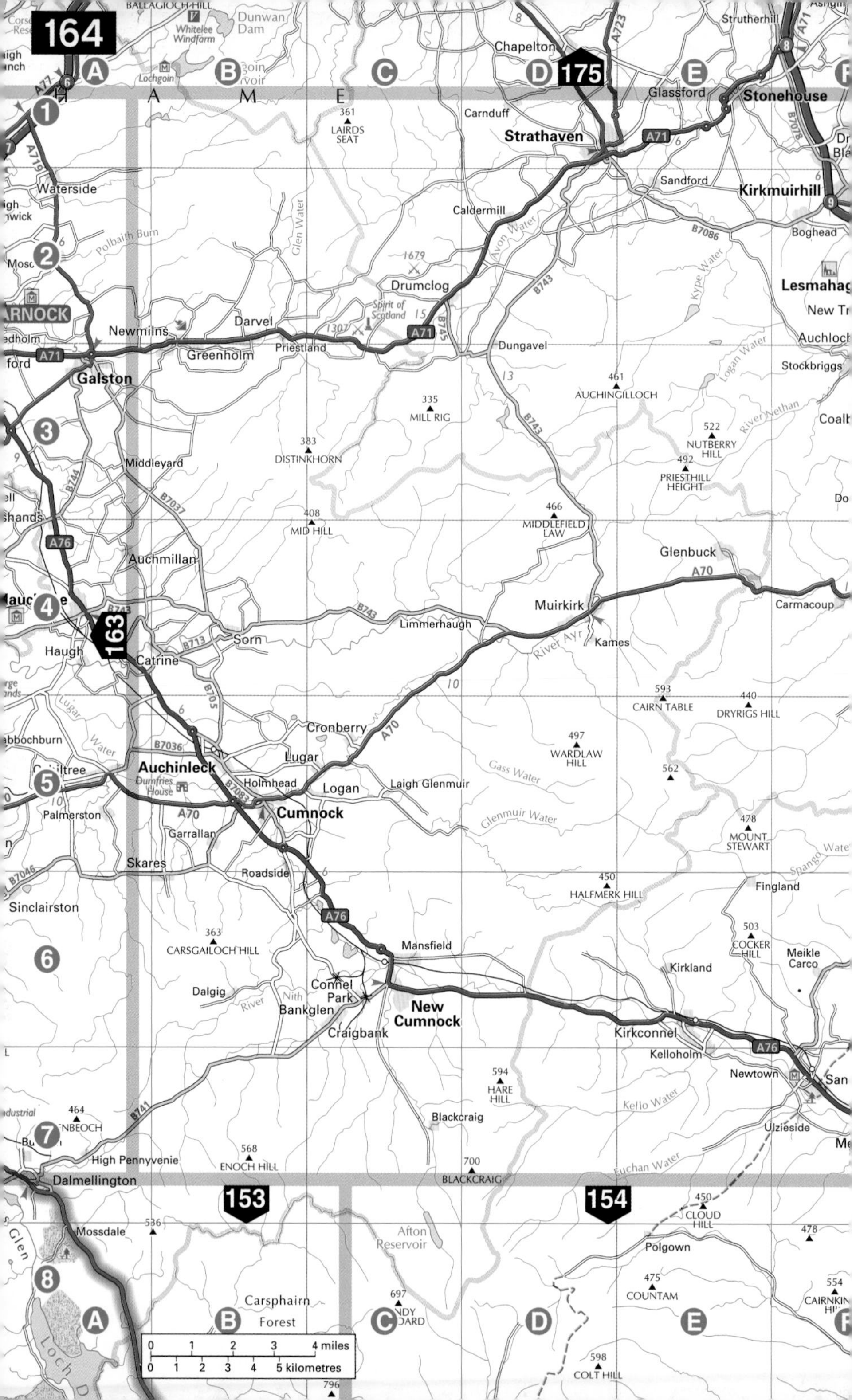
Whitelee Windfarm
Dunwan Dam
Lochgoin
Chapelton
175
Strutherhill
A723
A71
A77
Glassford
Stonehouse
H A M E
361
LAIRDS SEAT
Carnduff
Strathaven
A71
Sandford
Kirkmuirhill
A719
Waterside
Caldermill
Polbaith Burn
Glen Water
Avon Water
B7086
Boghead
1679
B743
Kype Water
Drumclog
Lesmahagow
Spirit of Scotland
Darvel
Newmilns
1307
A71
B745
New Trows
Auchlochan
Priestland
Greenholm
Dungavel
Logan Water
A71
Galston
13
Stockbriggs
461
AUCHINGILLOCH
335
MILL RIG
River Nethan
Coalburn
383
DISTINKHORN
522
NUTBERRY HILL
492
PRIESTHILL HEIGHT
Middleyard
B743
B744
B7037
408
MID HILL
466
MIDDLEFIELD LAW
A76
Glenbuck
A70
Auchmillan
Muirkirk
Carmacoup
B743
B743
Limmerhaugh
163
River Ayr
Kames
Haugh
B713
Sorn
Catrine
B705
10
593
CAIRN TABLE
440
DRYRIGS HILL
Lugar Water
Cronberry
A70
497
WARDLAW HILL
B7036
Lugar
Gass Water
Auchinleck
Dumfries House
562
Holmhead
Logan
Laigh Glenmuir
B7083
Palmerston
A70
Cumnock
Glenmuir Water
478
MOUNT STEWART
Garrallan
Spango Water
B7046
Skares
Roadside
450
HALFMERK HILL
Fingland
Sinclairston
A76
503
COCKER HILL
363
CARSGAILOCH HILL
Mansfield
Meikle Carco
Kirkland
Connel Park
Dalgig
River Nith
Bankglen
New Cumnock
Craigbank
Kirkconnel
A76
Kelloholm
594
HARE HILL
Newtown
Kello Water
B741
464
Blackcraig
Ulzieside
High Pennyvenie
568
ENOCH HILL
700
BLACKCRAIG
Euchan Water
Dalmellington
153
154
450
CLOUD HILL
536
Mossdale
Afton Reservoir
478
Polgown
Glen
475
COUNTAM
554
697
Carsphairn Forest
0 1 2 3 4 miles
0 1 2 3 4 5 kilometres
598
COLT HILL
796
Loch

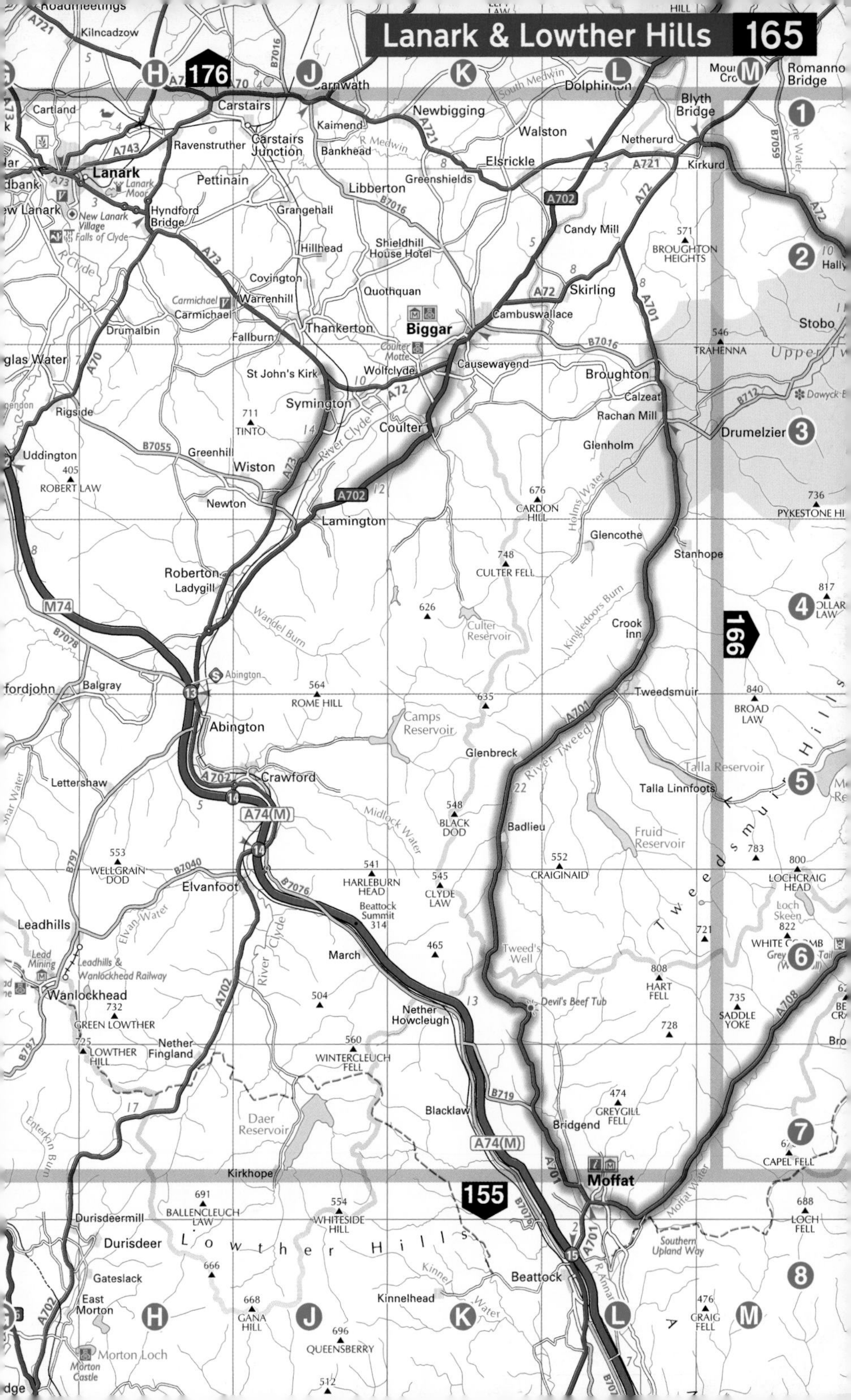
Kilncadzow
Carnwath
Carstairs
Cartland
Ravenstruther
Carstairs Junction
Kaimend
Bankhead
Newbigging
Walston
Dolphinton
Blyth Bridge
Romanno Bridge
Netherurd
Kirkurd
Elsrickle
Lanark
Pettinain
New Lanark
Hyndford Bridge
Grangehall
Libberton
Greenshields
Candy Mill
BROUGHTON HEIGHTS
Hillhead
Shieldhill House Hotel
Covington
Quothquan
Skirling
Carmichael
Warrenhill
Biggar
Cambuswallace
Stobo
Drumalbin
Fallburn
Thankerton
TRAHENNA
St John's Kirk
Wolfclyde
Causewayend
Broughton
Symington
Coulter
Rachan Mill
Drumelzier
Rigside
TINTO
Glenholm
Uddington
Greenhill
Wiston
ROBERT LAW
CARDON HILL
Newton
Lamington
PYKESTONE HILL
Glencothe
Stanhope
Roberton
Ladygill
CULTER FELL
Crook Inn
Culter Reservoir
Abington
Balgray
ROME HILL
Tweedsmuir
BROAD LAW
Camps Reservoir
Glenbreck
Crawford
Lettershaw
Talla Reservoir
Talla Linnfoots
BLACK DOD
Badlieu
Fruid Reservoir
WELLGRAIN DOD
Elvanfoot
HARLEBURN HEAD
CLYDE LAW
CRAIGINAID
LOCHCRAIG HEAD
Beattock Summit
Leadhills
Loch Skeen
March
Tweed's Well
WHITE COOMB
Wanlockhead
Devil's Beef Tub
HART FELL
Nether Howcleugh
GREEN LOWTHER
SADDLE YOKE
LOWTHER HILL
Nether Fingland
WINTERCLEUCH FELL
Blacklaw
GREYGILL FELL
Daer Reservoir
Bridgend
CAPEL FELL
Moffat
Kirkhope
BALLENCLEUCH LAW
WHITESIDE HILL
LOCH FELL
Durisdeermill
Durisdeer
Lowther Hills
Southern Upland Way
Beattock
Gateslack
East Morton
GANA HILL
Kinnelhead
CRAIG FELL
QUEENSBERRY
Morton Loch
Morton Castle
Tweedsmuir Hills
M74
A74(M)
A702
A701
A72
A73
A721
A70
A708
B7016
B7055
B7078
B7040
B7076
B719
B797
176
166
155

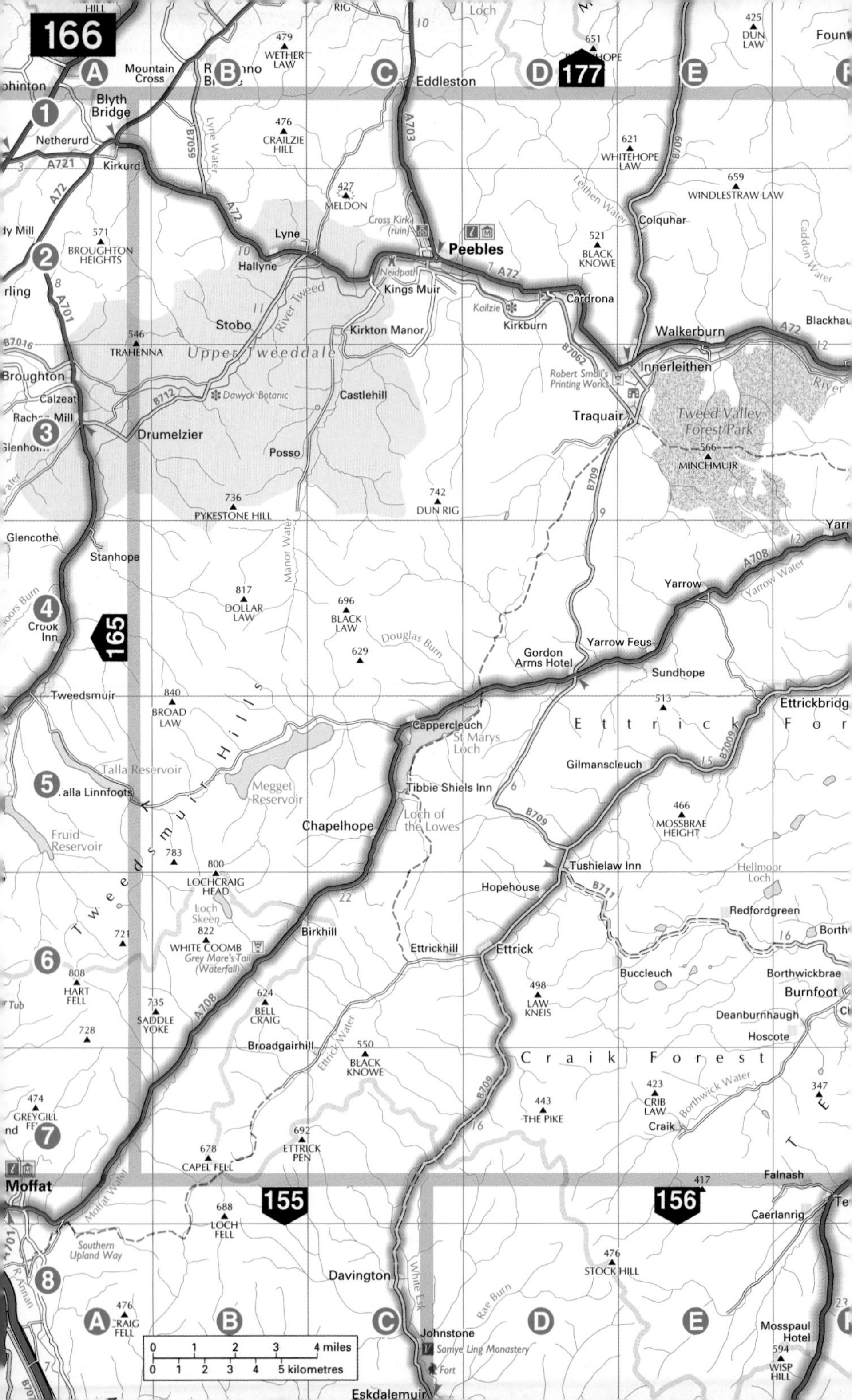

166
177
165
155
156
Peebles
Eddleston
Lyne
Hallyne
Kings Muir
Stobo
Kirkton Manor
Upper Tweeddale
Broughton
Drumelzier
Castlehill
Posso
Cardrona
Kirkburn
Walkerburn
Innerleithen
Traquair
Tweed Valley Forest Park
Blyth Bridge
Netherurd
Kirkurd
Mountain Cross
Colquhar
Yarrow
Yarrow Feus
Gordon Arms Hotel
Sundhope
Cappercleuch
St Marys Loch
Tibbie Shiels Inn
Loch of the Lowes
Chapelhope
Gilmanscleuch
Tushielaw Inn
Hopehouse
Ettrick
Ettrickhill
Birkhill
Tweedsmuir
Talla Reservoir
Megget Reservoir
Fruid Reservoir
Tweedsmuir Hills
Ettrick Forest
Craik Forest
Moffat
Davington
Johnstone
Samye Ling Monastery
Eskdalemuir
Southern Upland Way
Buccleuch
Redfordgreen
Borthwickbrae
Burnfoot
Deanburnhaugh
Hoscote
Craik
Falnash
Caerlanrig
Mosspaul Hotel
Broadgairhill
Glencothe
Stanhope
Crook Inn
Calzeat
Rachan Mill
Ettrickbridge
Blackhaugh
Robert Smail's Printing Works
Dawyck Botanic
Kailzie
Neidpath
Cross Kirk (ruin)
Grey Mare's Tail (Waterfall)
River Tweed
Manor Water
Leithen Water
Yarrow Water
Ettrick Water
Moffat Water
White Esk
Douglas Burn
Borthwick Water
Rae Burn
Lyne Water
Caddon Water
Loch Skeen
Hellmoor Loch
479 WETHER LAW
476 CRAILZIE HILL
427 MELDON
571 BROUGHTON HEIGHTS
546 TRAHENNA
736 PYKESTONE HILL
742 DUN RIG
621 WHITEHOPE LAW
659 WINDLESTRAW LAW
521 BLACK KNOWE
566 MINCHMUIR
425 DUN LAW
817 DOLLAR LAW
696 BLACK LAW
629
840 BROAD LAW
513
466 MOSSBRAE HEIGHT
783
800 LOCHCRAIG HEAD
822 WHITE COOMB
721
808 HART FELL
735 SADDLE YOKE
728
624 BELL CRAIG
550 BLACK KNOWE
498 LAW KNEIS
443 THE PIKE
423 CRIB LAW
347
474 GREYGILL FELL
692 ETTRICK PEN
678 CAPEL FELL
688 LOCH FELL
476 STOCK HILL
476 CRAIG FELL
594 WISP HILL
417
A72
A721
A701
A703
A708
B709
B7059
B712
B7016
B7062
B7009
B711
0 1 2 3 4 miles
0 1 2 3 4 5 kilometres

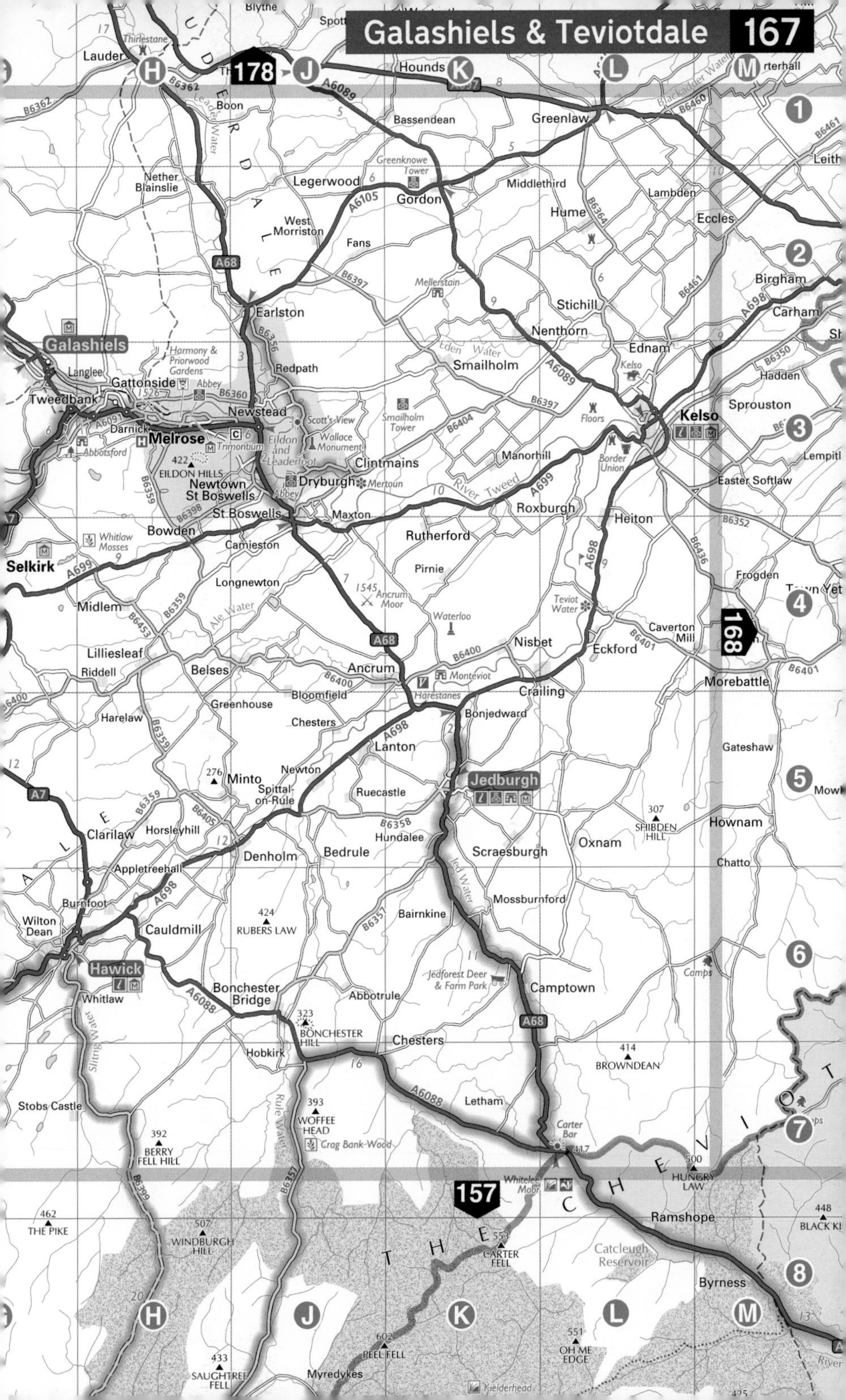

178
157
168
Lauder
Thirlestane
Blythe
Boon
Bassendean
Greenlaw
Hounds
Legerwood
Greenknowe Tower
Gordon
Middlethird
Hume
Lambden
Eccles
Leith
Nether Blainslie
West Morriston
Fans
Mellerstain
Stichill
Birgham
Carham
Earlston
Nenthorn
Ednam
Kelso
Galashiels
Harmony & Priorwood Gardens
Abbey
Redpath
Smailholm
Eden Water
Hadden
Langlee
Gattonside
Tweedbank
Newstead
Scott's View
Smailholm Tower
Sprouston
Darnick
Melrose
Trimontium
Eildon and Leaderfoot
Wallace Monument
Floors
Abbotsford
EILDON HILLS
Clintmains
Manorhill
Border Union
Lempitl
Newtown St Boswells
Dryburgh
Mertoun
Abbey
River Tweed
Easter Softlaw
St Boswells
Maxton
Roxburgh
Heiton
Bowden
Whitlaw Mosses
Rutherford
Camieston
Selkirk
Pirnie
Frogden
Longnewton
Ancrum Moor
Midlem
Teviot Water
Ale Water
Waterloo
Caverton Mill
Lilliesleaf
Nisbet
Eckford
Riddell
Belses
Ancrum
Monteviot
Morebattle
Bloomfield
Harestanes
Crailing
Greenhouse
Bonjedward
Harelaw
Chesters
Lanton
Gateshaw
Minto
Newton
Jedburgh
Spittal-on-Rule
Ruecastle
Clarilaw
Horsleyhill
Hundalee
SHIBDEN HILL
Hownam
Denholm
Bedrule
Scraesburgh
Oxnam
Appletreehall
Chatto
Jed Water
Burnfoot
Mossburnford
Wilton Dean
Cauldmill
RUBERS LAW
Bairnkine
Hawick
Camps
Whitlaw
Jedforest Deer & Farm Park
Camptown
Bonchester Bridge
Abbotrule
BONCHESTER HILL
Chesters
Hobkirk
BROWNDEAN
Slitrig Water
Rule Water
Stobs Castle
WOFFEE HEAD
Letham
Crag Bank Wood
Carter Bar
BERRY FELL HILL
HUNGRY LAW
Whitelee Moor
THE PIKE
Ramshope
BLACK KI
WINDBURGH HILL
CARTER FELL
Catcleugh Reservoir
Byrness
PEEL FELL
OH ME EDGE
SAUGHTREE FELL
Myredykes
Kielderhead
LAUDERDALE
THE CHEVIOTS

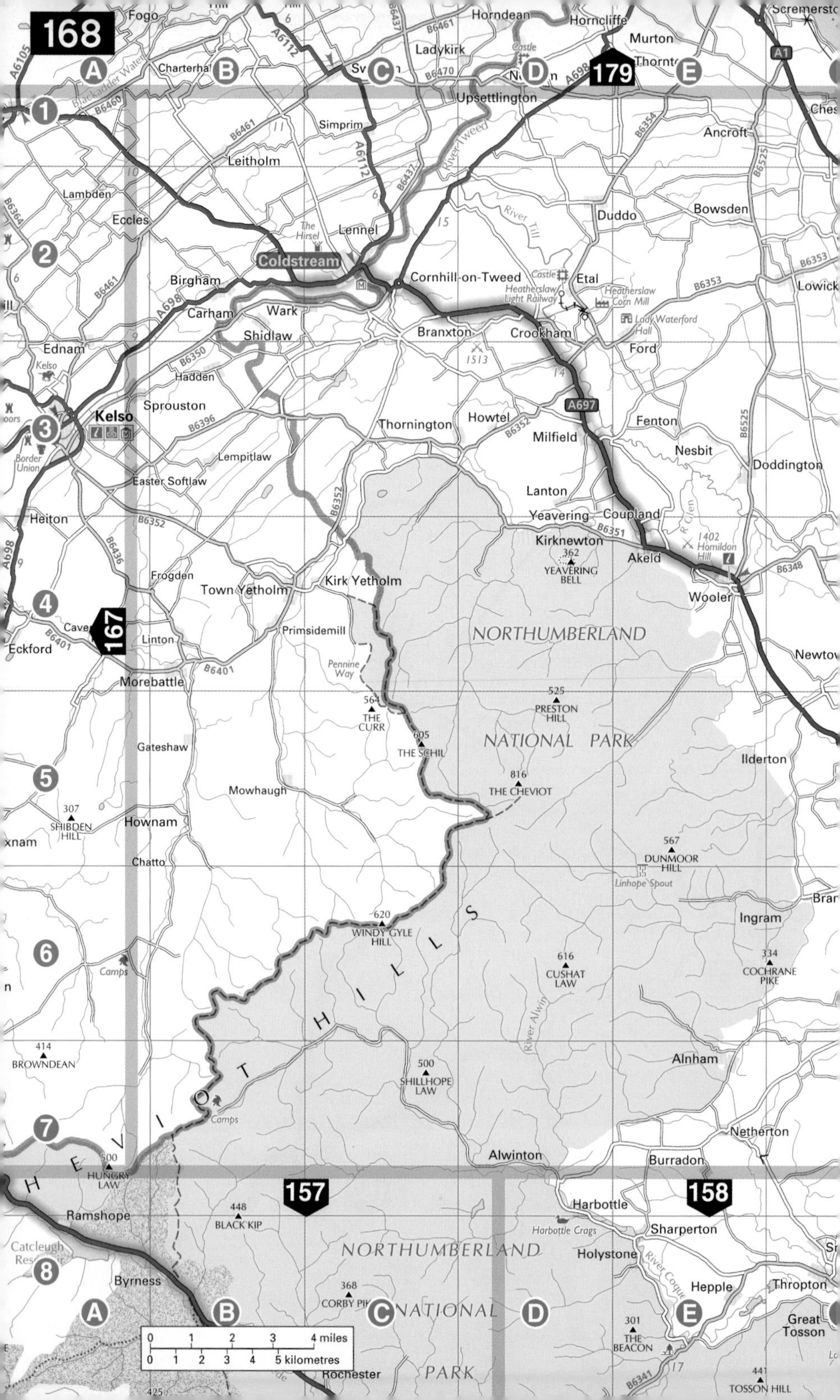

168
A
B
C
D
E
1
2
3
4
5
6
7
8
179
167
157
158
Fogo
Charterhall
Blackadder Water
Horndean
Horncliffe
Ladykirk
Murton
Upsettlington
Simprim
Leitholm
Lambden
Eccles
The Hirsel
Lennel
Coldstream
Cornhill-on-Tweed
River Tweed
River Till
Ancroft
Duddo
Bowsden
Lowick
Birgham
Carham
Wark
Shidlaw
Branxton
Crookham
Etal
Heatherslaw Light Railway
Heatherslaw Corn Mill
Lady Waterford Hall
Ford
1513
Ednam
Kelso
Hadden
Sprouston
Border Union
Thornington
Howtel
Milfield
Fenton
Nesbit
Doddington
Lempitlaw
Easter Softlaw
Lanton
Yeavering
Coupland
Kirknewton
Heiton
Akeld
R Glen
1402 Homildon Hill
Wooler
362 YEAVERING BELL
Frogden
Town Yetholm
Kirk Yetholm
Eckford
Linton
Primsidemill
Morebattle
Pennine Way
NORTHUMBERLAND
NATIONAL PARK
564 THE CURR
605 THE SCHIL
525 PRESTON HILL
816 THE CHEVIOT
Gateshaw
Mowhaugh
Ilderton
307 SHIBDEN HILL
Hownam
Chatto
567 DUNMOOR HILL
Linhope Spout
Ingram
620 WINDY GYLE HILL
CHEVIOT HILLS
616 CUSHAT LAW
334 COCHRANE PIKE
Camps
414 BROWNDEAN
River Alwin
500 SHILLHOPE LAW
Alnham
Netherton
Alwinton
Burradon
500 HUNGRY LAW
Ramshope
448 BLACK KIP
Harbottle
Harbottle Crags
Sharperton
Holystone
Catcleugh Reservoir
Byrness
368 CORBY PIKE
Hepple
River Coquet
Thropton
Great Tosson
301 THE BEACON
441 TOSSON HILL
Rochester
0 1 2 3 4 miles
0 1 2 3 4 5 kilometres
A1
A697
A698
A6112
A6105
A6364
B6460
B6461
B6437
B6470
B6354
B6525
B6353
B6350
B6396
B6352
B6351
B6348
B6436
B6401
B6341

CAUSEWAY FLOODED AT HIGH TIDE
HOLY ISLAND
Holy Island
Lindisfarne Castle
Lindisfarne Priory
Castle Point
Guile Point
Longstone
FARNE ISLANDS
Staple Sound
Inner Sound
North Northumberland Heritage Coast
Budle Bay
Bamburgh
Seahouses
North Sunderland
Lucker
Warenford
Beadnell
Swinhoe
Beadnell Bay
Chathill
Newstead
Tughall
Ellingham
Preston
Preston Pele Tower
Newton-by-the-Sea
Embleton & Newton Links
Christon Bank
Embleton
Embleton Bay
Dunstanburgh Castle
267
CATERAN HILL
North Charlton
Fallodon
South Charlton
Dunstan
Craster
Eglingham
Rock
Rennington
Stamford
Howick Hall
Howick
Cullernose Point
Longhoughton
Denwick
Boulmer
River Aln
Alnwick
Aln Valley Railway
Lesbury
Seaton Point
Alnmouth
Alnmouth Bay
Castle
Edlingham
Shilbottle
260
GLANTLEES HILL
Newton-on-the-Moor
Warkworth Castle & Hermitage
Warkworth
Amble
159
Coquet Island
Swarland
Gloster Hill
Guyzance
High Hauxley
Acklington
Togston
Felton
East Thirston
Broomhill
South Broomhill
Pauperhaugh
West Thirston
Red Row
Druridge Bay
Brinkburn Priory
Eshott
A1
A1068
B1342
B1340
B1341
B1339
B6347
B6341
B6346
B6344
B1330
H
J
K
L
M
1
2
3
4
5
6
7
8

A
B
C
D
E
1
2
3
4
5
6
7
8
Nave Island
Ardna
Point
Ton Mhòr
Kilnave
Sanaigmore
Eilean Mòr
Loch Gorr
Loch Gruinart
Rubha Lamanais
Lecht Gruinart
B8018
B8017
Saligo Bay
Loch Gorm
Gruinart
Coul Point
Sunderland
Kilchoman
Machir Bay
A847
Bruichladdich
Loch Indaal
Bowmor
Kilchiaran Bay
RHINNS OF ISLAY
Port Charlotte
231
BEINN TART A'MHILL
Lossit Bay
Nereabolls
Laggan Point
Rubha na Faing
Portnahaven
Port Wemyss
Orsay
RHINNS POINT
Laggan Bay
Rubha Mòr
160
165
MAOL BU
Lower Killeyan
0 1 2 3 4 miles
0 1 2 3 4 5 kilometres

181
JURA
Glen Grundale
Ardlussa
Lussa Point
Lussagiven
RAINBERG MÒR
Loch Righ Mòr
Rudh' ant-Sàilein
Loch Tarbert
Colonsay-Port Askaig
Rubha a' Mhàil
SCRINADLE
BEINN TARSUINN
Jura Forest
Paps of Jura
BEINN AN OIR
Jura
Knockrome
Ardfernal
GLASS BHEINN
Port Askaig
Feolin Ferry
Keills
Keils
Craighouse
Small Isles
Bunnahabhain
Ballygrant
Rubha na Caillich
BRAT BHEINN
Cabrach
Am Fraoch Eilean
Rubha na Tràille
Brosdale Island
McArthur's Head
Port Askaig - Kennacraig
Rubha Liath
Ardtalla
Claggain Bay
Kintour
Kildalton Cross
Ardmore Point
Eilean a' Chùirn
Port Ellen - Kennacraig
Tarbert
GIGHA
Ardminish
Achamore
Kinerara
Rhunahaorine Point
Tayinloan
Cara
Lagavulin
Laphroaig
Texa
160
172
A846
ISLAY

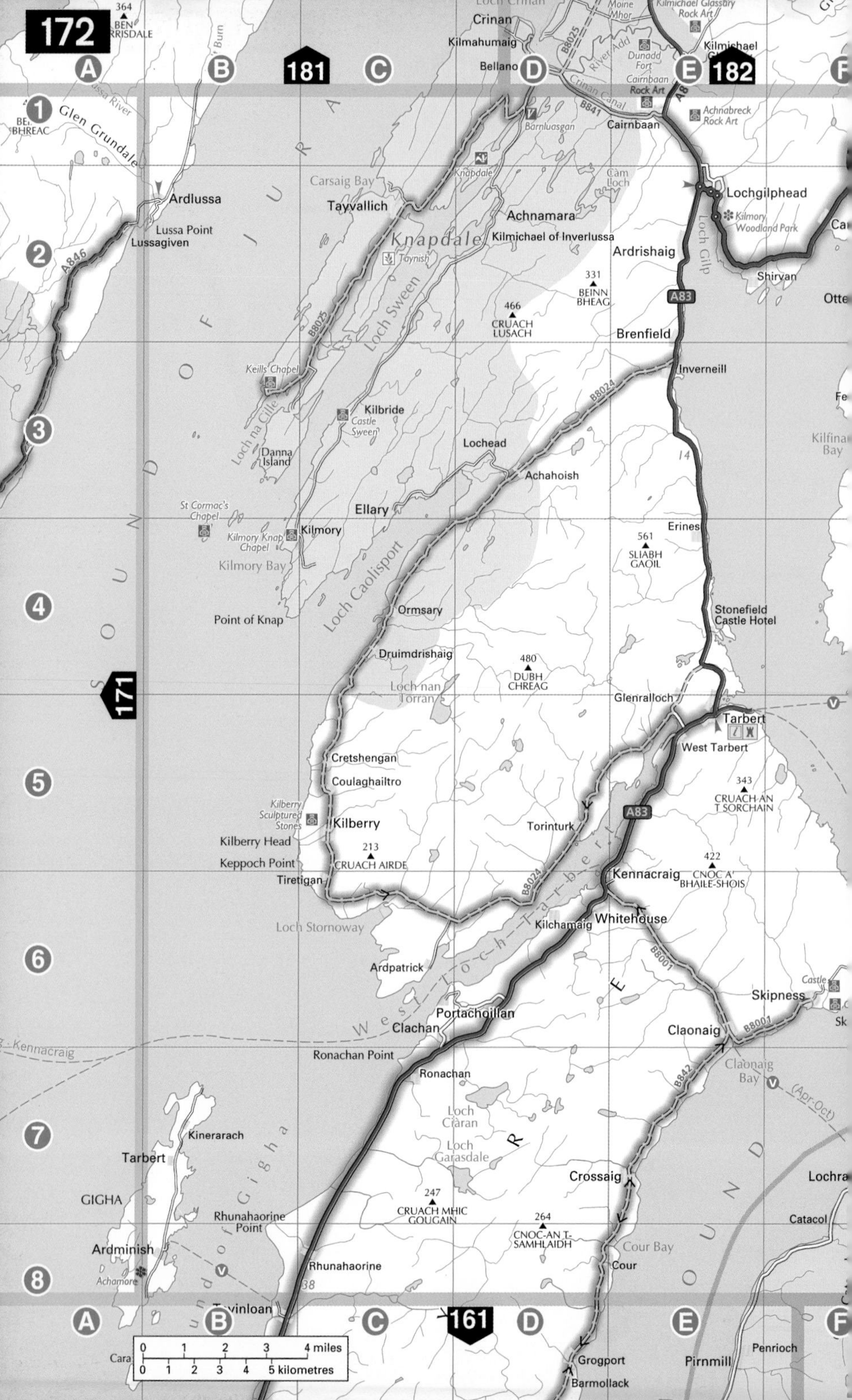
181
182
171
161
A
B
C
D
E
F
1
2
3
4
5
6
7
8
364
Glen Grundale
Ardlussa
Lussa Point
Lussagiven
A846
Carsaig Bay
Tayvallich
Knapdale
Taynish
Loch Sween
B8025
Keills Chapel
Loch na Cille
Danna Island
Kilbride
Castle Sween
St Cormac's Chapel
Kilmory Knap Chapel
Kilmory
Kilmory Bay
Point of Knap
Loch Caolisport
Ellary
Lochead
Achahoish
B8024
Ormsary
Druimdrishaig
Loch nan Torran
Cretshengan
Coulaghailtro
Kilberry Sculptured Stones
Kilberry
Kilberry Head
Keppoch Point
Tiretigan
213
CRUACH AIRDE
Loch Stornoway
Ardpatrick
Crinan
Kilmahumaig
Bellano
Moine Mhor
B8025
River Add
Dunadd Fort
Crinan Canal
B841
Barnluasgan
Knapdale
Cairnbaan
Cairnbaan Rock Art
Kilmichael Glassary Rock Art
Achnabreck Rock Art
Càm Loch
Lochgilphead
Kilmory Woodland Park
Achnamara
Kilmichael of Inverlussa
Ardrishaig
Loch Gilp
Shirvan
331
BEINN BHEAG
466
CRUACH LUSACH
A83
Brenfield
Inverneill
14
Erines
561
SLIABH GAOIL
Stonefield Castle Hotel
480
DUBH CHREAG
Glenralloch
Tarbert
West Tarbert
343
CRUACH-AN T SORCHAIN
Torinturk
A83
Kennacraig
422
CNOC A' BHAILE-SHOIS
Kilchamaig
Whitehouse
B8001
West Loch Tarbert
Portachoillan
Clachan
Ronachan Point
Ronachan
Kennacraig
Skipness
Castle
Claonaig
B8001
Claonaig Bay
(Apr-Oct)
B842
Loch Ciaran
Loch Garasdale
247
CRUACH MHIC GOUGAIN
264
CNOC-AN T-SAMHLAIDH
Crossaig
Cour Bay
Cour
Kinerarach
Tarbert
GIGHA
Ardminish
Achamore
Sound of Gigha
Rhunahaorine Point
Rhunahaorine
38
Grogport
Barmollack
Pirnmill
Penrioch
Catacol
Lochranza
Ottе
Kilfinan Bay
0 1 2 3 4 miles
0 1 2 3 4 5 kilometres

182
183
174
162
Barnacarry
CRUACH AN LOCHAIN
Dunans Castle
Argyll Forest Park
BEINN BHEAG
BEINN MHOR
CREACHAN MOR
Sligrachan
Garelochhead
Snow gates
Rockville
Greenfield
Glen Fruin
CLACH BHEINN
BEINN RUADH
Ardentinny
Glenmassen
Glen Massen
Coulport
Shandon
CRUACH UILCEACHAN
Benmore
STRONCHULLIN HILL
Loch Long
Gare Loch
Clynder
Rhu
CRUACH NAN CUILEAN
Loch Tarsan
SGORACH MÒR
Glendaruel
Rashfield
Ardbeg
Blairmore
Rosneath
Glen Lean
Kilmun
Cove
Stronafian
Clachaig
Holy Loch
Strone
Glenkin
Sandbank
Ardnadam
Hunter's Quay
Kilcreggan
CRUACH NAN CAPULL
Glenstriven
Loch Riddon
Gourock
BISHOP'S SEAT
Dunoon
Kirn
BEINN BHREAC
Kyles of Bute
Ashton
Lyle Hill
Cloch Point
Larkfield
Braeside
Chrisswell
Ardentraive
Colintraive
Port Driseach
Ardhallow
Lunderston Bay
Loch Thom
Loch Striven
Rhubodach
Altgaltraig
Ardgowan
Greenock Cut
Tighnabruaich
KILMARNOCK HILL
Ardyne Burn
Inverkip
Shielhill
BEINN RUADH
Dunan
Kames
Knockdow
Innellan
Garvock
Cairn
BUTE
Wemyss Bay
KAMES HILL
Ardmaleish
Kilbride
Ardyne Point
Upper Skelmorlie
Toward
Skelmorlie
St Colmac
Port Bannatyne
Toward Quay
Kildavanan
Ardbeg
Kildavaig
Ettrick Bay
Castle
Bogany Point
Rothesay
Ardlamont Point
St Mary's Chapel (ruin)
Ardencraig
Ascog
Knock Castle
Noddsdale Water
HILL OF STAKE
Ballanlay
Loch Ascog
Kerrycroy
Quarter
Routenburn
Meikle Kilmory
Loch Fad
Skelmorlie Aisle
Vikingar!
Midpark
Mount Stuart
Largs
IRISH LAW
Inchmarnock
Bruchag
GREAT CUMBRAE ISLAND
Kelburn Castle & Country Centre
Ardscalpsie Point
Kingarth
Camphill Reservoir
Stravanan Bay
Kilchattan Bay
Millport
Fairlie
Kilchattan
Sound of Bute
St Blane's Church
Fairlie Roads
COCK LAW
Garrochty
Hunterston Power Station
Garroch Head
Little Cumbrae Island
Drakemyre
Portencross
Dalry
Farland Head
Munnoch
West Kilbride
Seamill
Kilwinning
Sanno
Corrie
Ardrossan
A886
A815
A885
A880
A8003
A844
A78
A770
A760
A814
B836
B833
B872
B875
B878
B881
B896
B899
B7048
B781
B780
B714
B7047
B784
GREE
Kilbi
Glen

BEINN EICH
Edentaggart
Loch
Inchlonaig
Purdie's of Luss
Luss
Whistlefield
713
CHAPEL CROCH
183
655
BEINN THARSUINN
Garelochhead
Snow gates
Aldochlay
Loch Lomond
Balmaha
Milton of Buchanan
Highland Way
184
Rockville
Greenfield
Glen Fruin
Lomond
Buchanan Smithy
Drymen
A811
Coulport
Gare Loch
Snow gates
Shantron
A817
Inchmurrin
Gartocharn
Gartness
Shandon
Croftamie
Loch Long
Cross Keys
Arden
Loch Lomond Bird of Prey Centre
A811
Low Gartachorrans
Clynder
Rhu
Hill House
A818
Balloch Castle
Rosneath
Helensburgh
Dumgoyne
Cove
Balloch
Mill of Haldane
Archencarroch
Craigendoran
Jamestown
Strone
Kilcreggan
Queen's View
A814
Alexandria
Bonhill
John Muir Way
Carbeth Inn
Firth of Clyde
Ardmore
Cardross
Gourock
Geilston Garden
Renton
Kilpatrick Hills
Ashton
Lyle Hill
GREENOCK
Castlehill
Townend
Dumbarton
A770
Larkfield
Braeside
A78
Port Glasgow
Kirtonhill
Chrisswell
Newark Castle
Dumbarton Castle
Milton
Loch Thom
A8
Langbank
Faifley
Broadfield
Bowling
Old Kilpatrick
Duntocher
Greenock Cut
Gryffe Reservoir
Bardrainney
Finlaystone Country Estate
Hardgate
M8
Auchentoshan
Erskine Bridge
Parkhall
Shielhill
Bishopton
M898
Dalmuir
Garvock
Kilmacolm
Dargavel
Craigend
Erskine
Cairncurran
B788
CLYDEBANK
173
441
CREUCH HILL
Inchinnan
Upper Skelmorlie
Milton
Houston
Renfrew
B790
Quarrier's Village
A761
Craigends
Carruth House
Crosslee
Bridge of Weir
Ranfurly
Brookfield
Linwood
Weaver's Cottage
Hillington
Noddsdale Water
522
HILL OF STAKE
Muirshiel
Elderslie
Kilbarchan
PAISLEY
Johnstone
Routenburn
Milliken Park
A737
Foxbar
River Calder
Castle Semple
Castle Semple Loch
Skelmorlie Aisle
Howwood
Gleniffer Braes
Vikingar!
483
IRISH LAW
Largs
Lochwinnoch
Barrhead
Caplaw
Gateside
River Garnock
B775
A760
Newtown of Beltrees
Kelburn Castle & Country Centre
Barr Loch
Neilston
Barcraigs Reservoir
A736
Camphill Reservoir
Hall
Shillford
Fairlie
Kilbirnie
B776
Uplawmoor
Craigton
Kilbirnie Loch
Beith
B777
Dodside
371
COCK LAW
Gateside
Lugton
Glengarnock
A735
Long Loch
Halket
Barrmill
B784
B769
The Den
Drakemyre
B706
Gabroc Hill
Highfield
Burnhouse
Dalry
Fullwood
Corsehouse Reservoir
Munnoch
B780
B707
Dunlop
West Kilbride
B781
Kingsford
Laigh Clunch
Auchenmade
A737
Auchentiber
A77
A78
Dalgarven Mill
163
Stewarton
Annick Water
0 1 2 3 4 miles
0 1 2 3 4 5 kilometres
Torranyard
B778
A719
Fenwick
Ardrossan
B785
Waterside

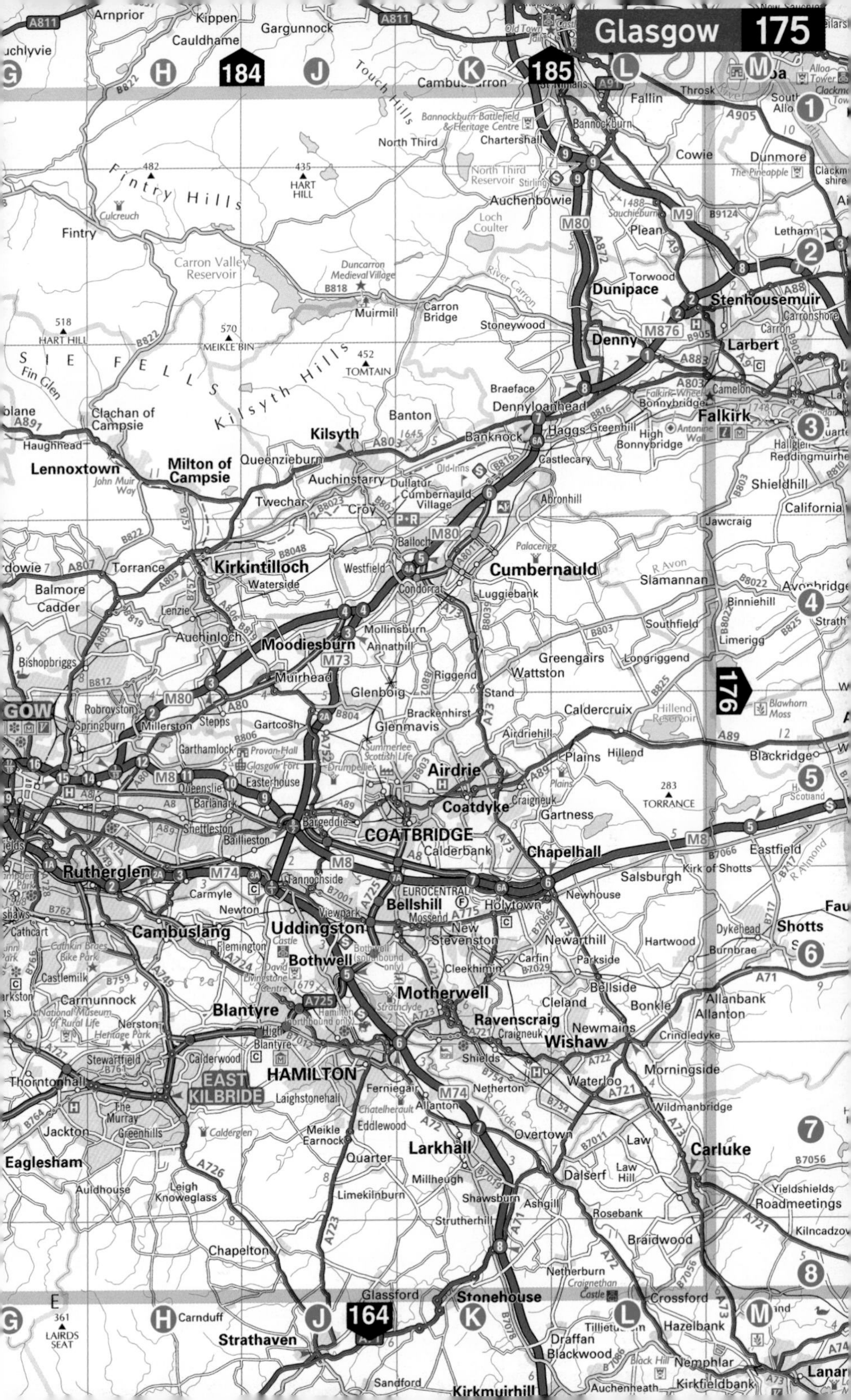

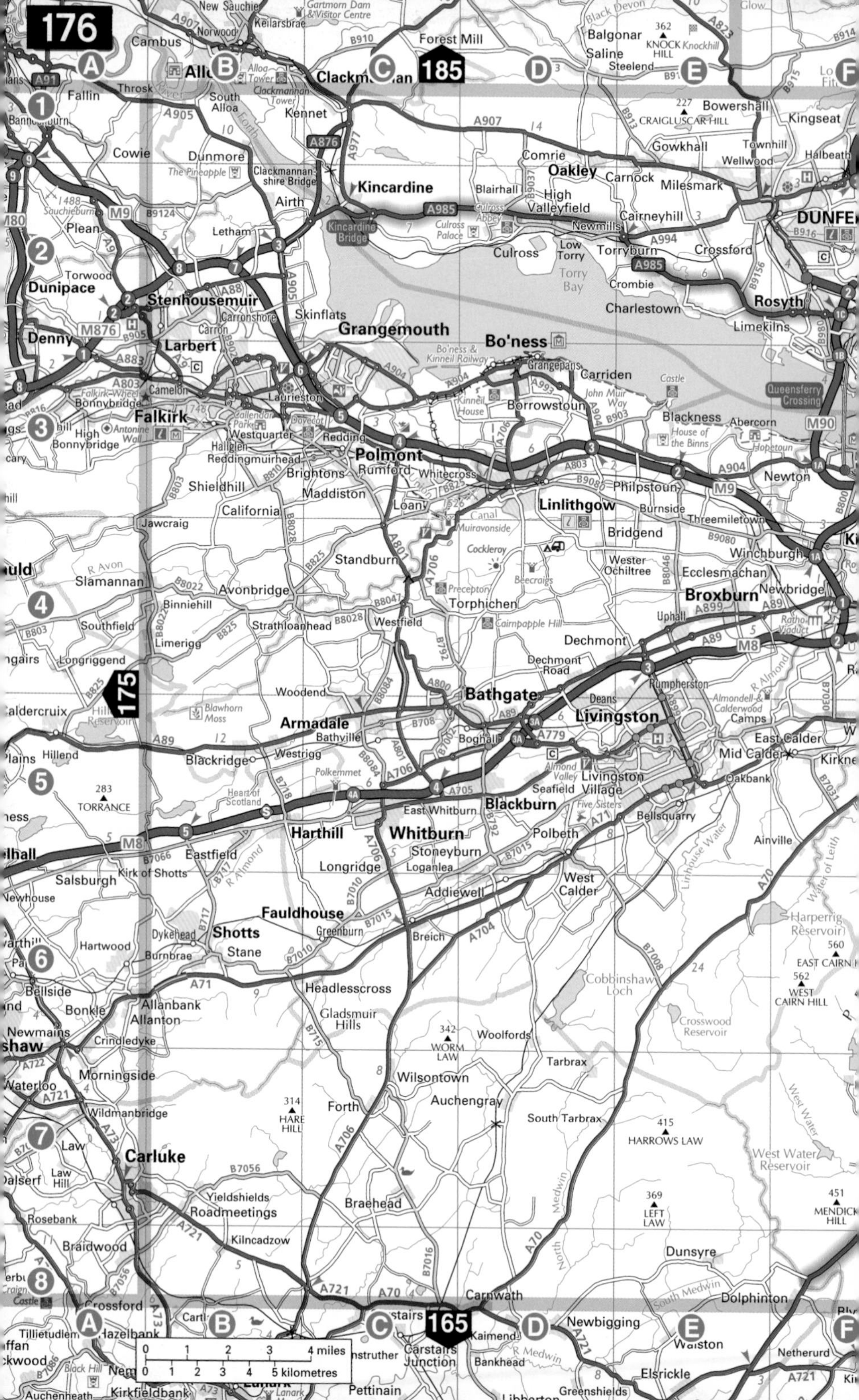

176
A
B
C
D
E
F
1
2
3
4
5
6
7
8
185
175
165
New Sauchie
Gartmorn Dam & Visitor Centre
Kellarsbrae
Norwood
Cambus
Forest Mill
Balgonar
Saline
Steelend
KNOCK HILL
Knockhill
Glow
Black Devon
Throsk
Alloa Tower
Clackmannan Tower
Clackmannan
Fallin
Bannockburn
South Alloa
Kennet
Bowershall
Kingseat
CRAIGLUSCAR HILL
Cowie
Dunmore
The Pineapple
Clackmannanshire Bridge
Kincardine
Comrie
Oakley
Carnock
Gowkhall
Townhill
Wellwood
Halbeath
Blairhall
High Valleyfield
Milesmark
Cairneyhill
Newmills
DUNFE
Airth
Plean
Sauchieburn
Letham
Kincardine Bridge
Culross Abbey
Culross Palace
Culross
Low Torry
Torryburn
Crossford
Torwood
Dunipace
Stenhousemuir
Carronshore
Carron
Skinflats
Grangemouth
Torry Bay
Crombie
Charlestown
Rosyth
Limekilns
Denny
Larbert
Bo'ness
Bo'ness & Kinneil Railway
Grangepans
Carriden
Castle
Queensferry Crossing
Falkirk Wheel
Bonnybridge
Camelon
Laurieston
Kinneil House
Borrowstoun
John Muir Way
Blackness
Abercorn
House of the Binns
Hopetoun
High Bonnybridge
Antonine Wall
Falkirk
Callendar Park
Westquarter
Dovecot
Redding
Hallglen
Reddingmuirhead
Polmont
Rumford
Brightons
Whitecross
Philpstoun
Newton
Shieldhill
Maddiston
Union Canal
Loany
Linlithgow
Burnside
Threemiletown
California
Jawcraig
Muiravonside
Bridgend
Cockleroy
Beecraigs
Standburn
Wester Ochiltree
Winchburgh
Ecclesmachan
R Avon
Slamannan
Avonbridge
Binniehill
Precepton
Torphichen
Broxburn
Newbridge
Southfield
Strathloanhead
Westfield
Cairnpapple Hill
Uphall
Ratho
Dechmont
Limerigg
Longriggend
Dechmont Road
Woodend
Bathgate
Pumpherston
R Almond
Almondell & Calderwood
Camps
Caldercruix
Hillend Reservoir
Blawhorn Moss
Armadale
Deans
Livingston
Bathville
Boghall
East Calder
Mid Calder
Kirkne
Hillend
Blackridge
Westrigg
Polkemmet
Almond Valley
Livingston Village
Oakbank
Heart of Scotland
Seafield
283 TORRANCE
East Whitburn
Blackburn
Five Sisters
Bellsquarry
Harthill
Whitburn
Polbeth
Ainville
Eastfield
Stoneyburn
Loganlea
Salsburgh
Kirk of Shotts
Longridge
West Calder
Linhouse Water
Water of Leith
Newhouse
Addiewell
Fauldhouse
Harperrig Reservoir
Dykehead
Shotts
Greenburn
Breich
Hartwood
Burnbrae
Stane
560 EAST CAIRN
Bellside
Headlesscross
Cobbinshaw Loch
562 WEST CAIRN HILL
Allanbank
Bonkle
Allanton
Gladsmuir Hills
Newmains
Crindledyke
342 WORM LAW
Woolfords
Crosswood Reservoir
Tarbrax
Morningside
Waterloo
Wilsontown
Wildmanbridge
314 HARE HILL
Forth
Auchengray
South Tarbrax
415 HARROWS LAW
West Water
Law
Carluke
West Water Reservoir
Dalserf
Law Hill
Yieldshields
Roadmeetings
Braehead
369 LEFT LAW
451 MENDICK HILL
Rosebank
Medwin
Kilncadzow
Braidwood
North Medwin
Dunsyre
Craignethan Castle
South Medwin
Crossford
Carnwath
Dolphinton
Carstairs
Newbigging
Tillietudlem
Hazelbank
Kaimend
Walston
Carstairs Junction
Netherurd
Bankhead
R Medwin
Elsrickle
Black Hill
Pettinain
Greenshields
Auchenheath
Kirkfieldbank
Lanark
Libberton
0 1 2 3 4 miles
0 1 2 3 4 5 kilometres

Cardenden
Gallatown
Chapel
186
Kirkcaldy
Pathhead
Linktown
Auchtertool
Balmule
Kinghorn
Aberdour
Pettycur
Pettycur Bay
Burntisland
Silversands Bay
Inchcolm Abbey
Inchkeith
FIRTH OF FORTH
Cramond Island
Eyebroughy
Dirleton
Gullane Bay
Gullane Point
Gullane
Muirfield
John Muir Way
Aberlady Bay
Craigelaw Point
Aberlady
Luffness
Drem
Myreton Motor
Ballencrieff
Gosford Bay
Spittal
Athelstaneford
Cockenzie and Port Seton
Seton Collegiate Church
Longniddry
Preston Market Cross
Prestonpans
Prestongrange Museum
Seton Mains
Huntington
Elvingston
Royal Yacht Britannia
EDINBURGH
Granton
Newhaven
Leith
Lauriston Castle
Cramond
Barnton
Davidson's Mains
Royal Botanic
Warriston
St Triduana's Chapel
Blackhall
Dovecot
Murrayfield
Castle
Dynamic Earth
ARTHUR'S SEAT 251
Portobello
Musselburgh
Joppa
Fisherrow
Tranent
Gladsmuir
Macmerry
Duddingston
Newcraighall
Craigmillar
Inveresk
Wallyford
New Winton
Corstorphine
Craiglockhart
Morningside
Craigmillar Castle
Elphinstone
Ormiston Market Cross
Samuelston
Boggs Holdings
Water of Leith
Royal Observatory
Blackford Hill
Newton
Whitecraig
Crossgatehall
Ormiston
Liberton
Millerhill
Danderhall
Pencaitland
178
Colinton
Gilmerton
Dalkeith Park
Cousland
East Saltoun
West Saltoun
Currie
Bonaly
Hillend
Butterfly Farm
Eskbank
Dalkeith
Glenkinchie
Kinleith
ALLERMUIR HILL 493
Straiton
Lasswade
Newbattle
Mayfield
Harlaw House
Boghall
Loanhead
Bilston
Bonnyrigg
Gilchriston
Woodhouselee
Castlelaw Hill Fort
Polton
Chesterhill
Pathhead
Newtongrange
Dewarton
Vogrie
Easter Howgate
Roslin
National Mining Museum
Humbie
Pentland Hills
Milton Bridge
Newtonloan
Newlandrig
Arniston
Crichton
Fala Dam
Blegbie
576 CARNETHY HILL
579 SCALD LAW
Rosewell
Crichton Castle
Fala
Auchendinny
Gorebridge
Penicuik
Carrington
Soutra Summit 363
Snow gates
Pomathorn
North Middleton
R North Esk
Howgate
Temple
394 DUN LAW
Mount Lothian
Gilston
380 TURF LAW
Leadburn
Rosebery Reservoir
Snow gates
Craigburn
Heriot
Oxton
Gladhouse Reservoir
Carfrae
Moorfoot Hills
Heriot Water
383 COLLIE LAW
Waterheads
324 WHITE RIG
Portmore Loch
425 DUN LAW
Fountainhall
479 WETHER LAW
651 BLACKHOPE SCAR
Torquhan
Eddleston
166
Killochyett
476 CRAILZIE HILL
621 WHITEHOPE LAW
Stow
659
427
A92
B981
A910
B925
B9157
A909
B923
A921
A198
B1345
A6137
B1348
A199
A1
B6414
B6363
B6355
B6371
A6093
B6471
A901
A902
B9085
B900
A90
A8
A900
A71
A70
A702
A720
A701
B701
A7
A6094
A6124
A6106
B6367
B6392
B7006
B7003
A703
B7026
A766
B6372
B6368
A68
B6458
B7007
B709
A702

A
B
C
D
E
F
1
2
3
4
5
6
7
8
Fidra
Craigleith
Bass Rock
North Berwick
Yellowcraig
Eyebroughy
Dirleton Castle & Gardens
Scottish Seabird
Tantallon Castle
Gullane Bay
Dirleton
Muirfield
A198
187
NORTH BERWICK LAW
Cleghornie
Gullane Point
Gullane
John Muir Way
Fenton Barns
Kingston
Whitekirk
St Baldred's Cradle
Aberlady Bay
Tyne Mouth
Belhaven Bay
Belhaven
Dunbar
Craigelaw Point
Aberlady
Luffness
Drem
Prora
B1377
East Fortune
Tyninghame
John Muir
Gosford Bay
Myreton Motor
Chesters Hill Fort
Museum of Flight
Markle
Preston Mill & Phantassie Doocot
B1407
A1087
West Barns
Broxburn
Spittal
Ballencrieff
B1343
East Linton
A199
Seton Collegiate Church
Athelstaneford
A6137
Longniddry
Hailes Castle
Spott
1296
Doonhill Homestead
A1
East Bar
Skatera
Seton Mains
Huntington
Haddington
Traprain
Pitcox
Elvingston
St Martin's Kirk (ruin)
Traprain Law
Luggate Burn
Dry Burn
Tranent
B6471
Stenton
The Brunt
Innerwick
Gladsmuir
Lauderdale Aisle St Mary's Church
Macmerry
B6363
B6368
Papple
A6093
319
COCKLAW HILL
New Winton
Lennoxlove
Morham
Garvald
B6355
Samuelston
B6369
B6370
Nunraw Abbey
397
BRANSLY HILL
Oldhamst
Boggs Holdings
Ormiston
B6371
Bolton
River Tyne
Pencaitland
Gifford
177
East Saltoun
Danskine
Monynut Water
West Saltoun
Glenkinchie
391
HEART LAW
Long Newton
Bothwell Water
463
SPARTLETON
Gilchriston
Longyester
LAMMERMUIR HILLS
St Agnes
Humbie
MEIKLE SAYS LAW
533
Whiteadder Reservoir
Fala Dam
528
LAMMER LAW
Blegbie
Cranshaws
Abbey S
A68
Fala
Ellemford
B6458
509
CRIB LAW
513
SEENES LAW
467
MEIKLE LAW
Soutra Summit 363
Whitchester
Snow gates
495
HUNT LAW
394
DUN LAW
Longformacus
Southern Upland Way
380
TURF LAW
Gilston
Soonhope Burn
448
HOGS LAW
Watch Water Reservoir
399
DIRRINGTON GREAT LAW
Snow gates
Wedderlie Burn
Oxton
Carfraemill
LAUDERDALE
383
COLLIE LAW
B6456
Polwar
Blythe
Westruther
Spottiswoode
A7
Fountainhall
Thornydykes
A6105
Thirlestane
Lauder
Houndslow
Torquhan
B6362
A6089
A697
Thirlestane
Killochyett
Boon
167
Bassendean
Greenlaw
Lugate Water
Leader Water
Greenknowe Tower
Nether Blainslie
Legerwood
Middlethird
0 1 2 3 4 miles
0 1 2 3 4 5 kilometres

Pease Bay
Siccar Point
Fast Castle Head
ST ABB'S HEAD
196 BROWN RIG
Coldingham Loch
Pease Dean
A1107
St Abbs
Coldingham Bay
Grantshouse
Coldingham
B6438
Houndwood
Heugh Head
Cairncross
Eyemouth
262 HORSELEY HILL
A1
B6355
Reston
Ayton
Burnmouth
B6438
Auchencrow
Marygold
Lintlaw
Lamberton
A6112
Preston
B6437
B6355
Chirnside
Marshall Meadows Bay
Cumledge
B6355
Edrom Church
Foulden
Chirnsidebridge
Edrom
Foulden Tithe Barn
1333
North Northumberland Heritage Coast
Manderston
Broadhaugh
Edington
Whiteadder Water
A6105
Berwick-upon-Tweed
A6105
Allanton
Hutton
Castle
Barracks & Main Guard
B6437
Paxton
Town Ramparts
Blackadder
B6460
B6461
Tweedmouth
B6460
Paxton
Spittal
Whitsome
Hilton
A1167
Huds Head
Sinclair's Hill
B6437
Horndean
Horncliffe
Scremerston
B6461
Murton
A6112
Ladykirk
Castle
A1
Thornton
Swinton
B6470
Norham
A698
Cheswick
Upsettlington
168
CAUSEWAY FLOODED AT HIGH TIDE
B6461
Simprim
B6354
Ancroft
River Tweed
A6112
Leitholm
B6437
B6525
Haggerston
Beal

Bac Mòr or Dutchman's Cap
eag
189
Little Colonsay
Staffa
Fingal's
Loch na Keal
Isle of Mull
Inchkenneth Cha (ruin)
491
Fossil Tree
IONA
Iona Abbey & Nunnery
Baile Mòr
MacLean's Cross
Sound of Iona
Rubha nan Cearc
Kintra
Loch na Làthaich
Fionnphort
Aridhglas
A849
St Columba Exhibition Centre
Bunessan
ROSS OF MULL
Soa Island
Erraid
Uisken
Ardchiavaig
Rubh' Ardalanish
Torran Rocks
Balnahard
Kiloran Bay
COLONSAY
Kiloran
Kilchattan
B8087
Scalasaig
B8086
Machrins
Colonsay
B8085
171
Oronsay
Rubha Bàn
Dubh Eilean
0 1 2 3 4 miles
0 1 2 3 4 5 kilometres

ISLE OF MULL
Craignure
Duart Point
Duart Bay
Torosay
Lochdonhead
Lochdon
Gorsten
Loch Don
Grass Point
Strathcoil
A849
Glen More
Aird of Kinloch
Pennyghael
Loch Fuaran
BEN MORE
CRUACHAN DEARG
BEN BUIE
BEN CREACH
BEINN NA CROISE
Lochbuie
Loch Uisg
Loch Spelve
Croggan
CARN BAN
Leidle Water
Carsaig
BEINN CHREAGACH
Rubha Dubh
Loch Buie
DRUIM FADA
MAOL BAN
FIRTH OF LORNE
Rubha Seanach
Insh Island
Clachan
Clachan-Seil
SEIL
Ellenabeich
Seafari
Easdale
Balvicar
Ardmaddy
B844
B8003
Colonsay - Oban
Cuan
Seil Sound
Cullipool
Torsa
Degnish
Loch Melfort
Garbh Eileach
Eilean Dubh Mòr
GARVELLACHS
Monastery & Beehive Cells
Eileach an Naoimh
LUNGA
LUING
Toberonochy
Sound of Luing
Shuna Sound
SHUNA
Scarba, Lunga and the Garvellachs
Arduaine Garden
Craobh Haven
Shuna Point
SCARBA
CRUACH SCARBA
Gulf of Corryvreckan
B8002
Aird
Loch Craignish
Craignish Point
Island Macaskin
Glengarrisdale Bay
CRUACH NA SEILCHEIG
Glendebadel Bay
BEN GARRISDALE
Lealt Burn
Loch Crinan
Crinan
Kilmahumaig
Bellanoch
B8025
Corpach Bay
JURA
Lussa River
Glen Grundale
Carsaig Bay
Barnluasgan
Knapdale
Shian
190
171
172
182

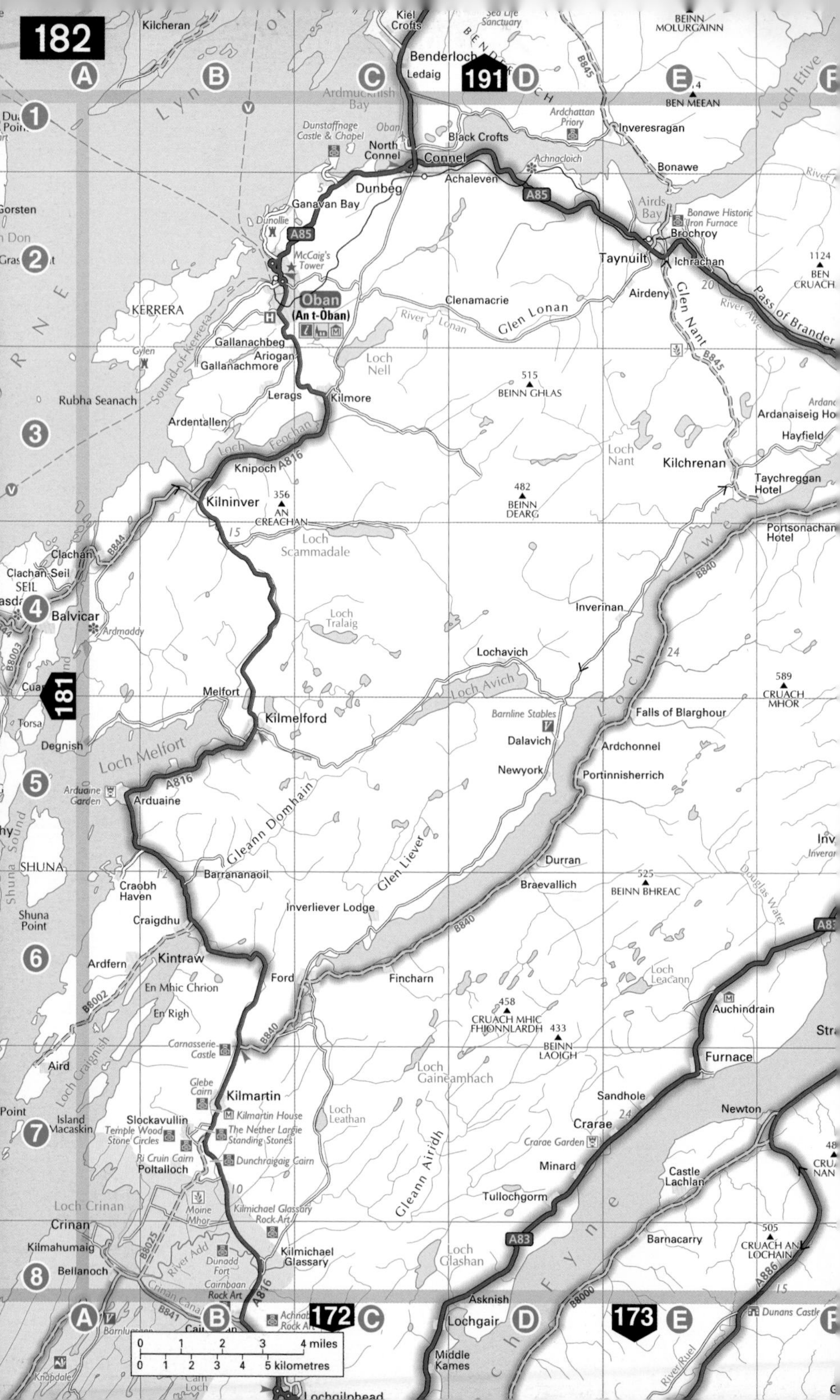
Kilcheran
Kiel Crofts
Sea Life Sanctuary
BEINN MOLURGAINN
Benderloch
Ledaig
191
Ardmucknish Bay
BEN MEEAN
Dunstaffnage Castle & Chapel
Oban
Ardchattan Priory
Inveresragan
North Connel
Black Crofts
Connel
Achnacloich
Achaleven
Bonawe
A85
Dunbeg
Ganavan Bay
Gorsten
Dunollie
Airds Bay
Bonawe Historic Iron Furnace
Brochroy
McCaig's Tower
Taynuilt
Ichrachan
1124
BEN CRUACH
Oban
(An t-Oban)
Airdeny
KERRERA
Clenamacrie
Glen Lonan
Glen Nant
River Awe
Pass of Brander
River Lonan
Gylen
Gallanachbeg
Ariogan
Gallanachmore
Sound of Kerrera
Loch Nell
B845
515
BEINN GHLAS
Rubha Seanach
Lerags
Kilmore
Ardentallen
Ardanaiseig Ho
Hayfield
Loch Feochan
Loch Nant
Knipoch
A816
Kilchrenan
482
BEINN DEARG
Taychreggan Hotel
Kilninver
356
AN CREACHAN
Portsonachan Hotel
Loch Scammadale
Clachan
Clachan Seil
SEIL
B844
Loch Awe
B840
Balvicar
Ardmaddy
Inverinan
Loch Tralaig
B8003
Lochavich
Loch Avich
589
CRUACH MHOR
Melfort
181
Barnline Stables
Falls of Blarghour
Torsa
Kilmelford
Dalavich
Degnish
Ardchonnel
Loch Melfort
Newyork
Portinnisherrich
Arduaine Garden
A816
Arduaine
Gleann Domhain
Glen Liever
Shuna Sound
SHUNA
Durran
Barrananaoil
525
BEINN BHREAC
Craobh Haven
Braevallich
Douglas Water
Shuna Point
Inverliever Lodge
Craigdhu
B840
Ardfern
Kintraw
Loch Leacann
Ford
Fincharn
En Mhic Chrion
B8002
En Righ
458
CRUACH MHIC FHIONNLARDH
Auchindrain
433
BEINN LAOIGH
Loch Craignish
Carnasserie Castle
Aird
Furnace
Loch Gaineamhach
Glebe Cairn
Kilmartin
Sandhole
Island Macaskin
Slockavullin
Kilmartin House
Loch Leathan
Newton
Temple Wood Stone Circles
The Nether Largie Standing Stones
Crarae
Crarae Garden
Ri Cruin Cairn
Dunchraigaig Cairn
Minard
Poltalloch
Gleann Airidh
Castle Lachlan
Loch Crinan
Moine Mhor
Kilmichael Glassary Rock Art
Tullochgorm
Crinan
A83
Barnacarry
505
CRUACH AN LOCHAIN
River Add
Kilmahumaig
Kilmichael Glassary
Loch Glashan
Dunadd Fort
Bellanoch
Cairnbaan Rock Art
B8025
Crinan Canal
A816
Asknish
B8000
A886
B841
Barnluasgan
Achnabreck Rock Art
172
Lochgair
173
Dunans Castle
Loch Fyne
Knapdale
Middle Kames
River Ruel
0 1 2 3 4 miles
0 1 2 3 4 5 kilometres
Lochgilphead

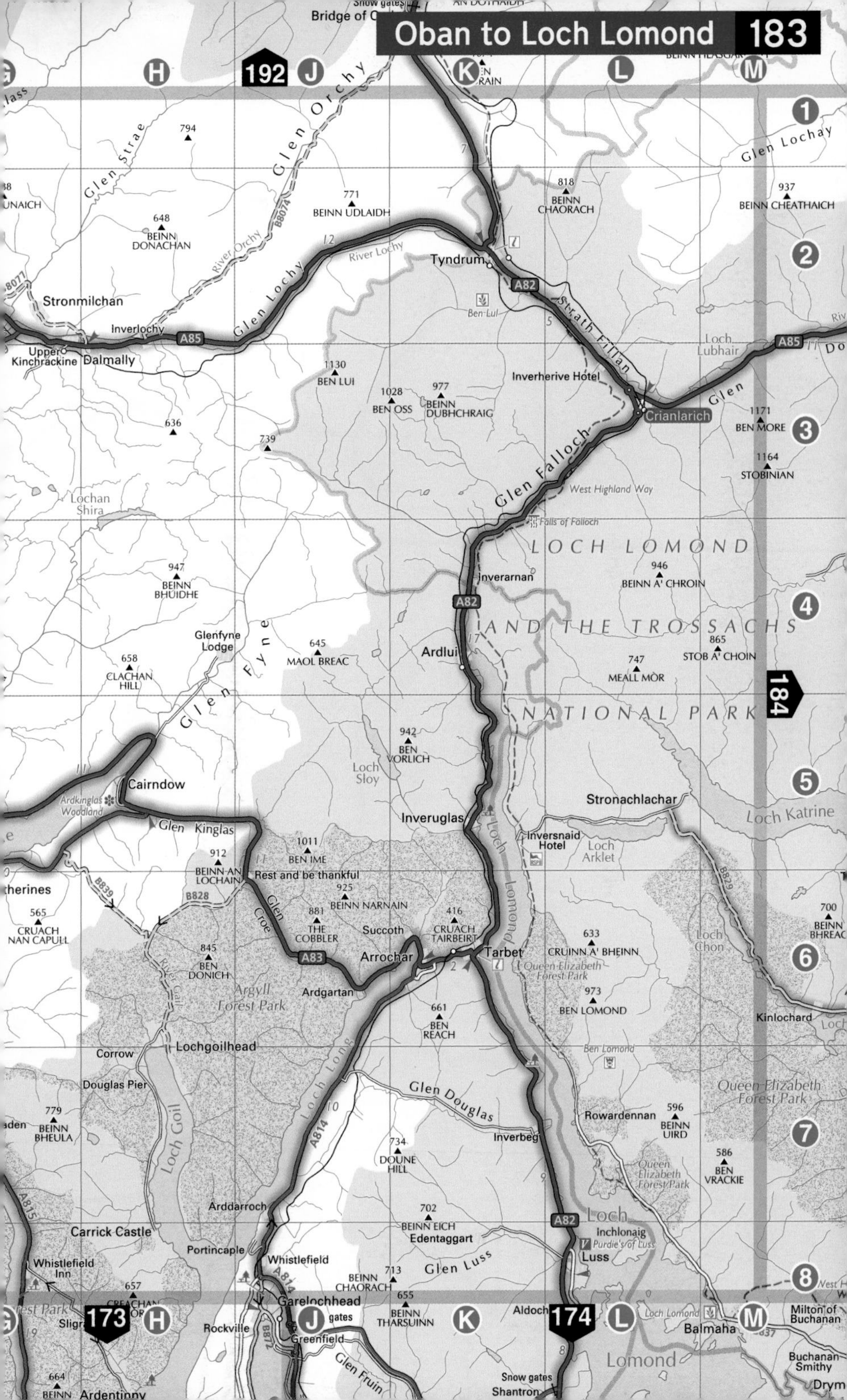
Bridge of Orchy
192
Glen Orchy
Glen Strae
794
771
BEINN UDLAIDH
648
BEINN DONACHAN
818
BEINN CHAORACH
937
BEINN CHEATHAICH
Glen Lochay
Tyndrum
River Lochy
River Orchy
B8074
Glen Lochy
A82
Strath Fillan
Ben Lui
Stronmilchan
Inverlochy
A85
Upper Kinchrackine
Dalmally
Loch Lubhair
A85
1130
BEN LUI
1028
BEN OSS
977
BEINN DUBHCHRAIG
Inverherive Hotel
Crianlarich
Glen
1171
BEN MORE
1164
STOBINIAN
636
739
Glen Falloch
West Highland Way
Lochan Shira
Falls of Falloch
LOCH LOMOND
AND THE TROSSACHS
NATIONAL PARK
947
BEINN BHUIDHE
Inverarnan
946
BEINN A' CHROIN
A82
Glenfyne Lodge
Glen Fyne
645
MAOL BREAC
Ardlui
865
STOB A' CHOIN
747
MEALL MÒR
658
CLACHAN HILL
184
942
BEN VORLICH
Loch Sloy
Cairndow
Ardkinglas Woodland
Glen Kinglas
Inveruglas
Stronachlachar
Loch Katrine
Inversnaid Hotel
Loch Arklet
1011
BEN IME
912
BEINN AN LOCHAIN
Rest and be thankful
B839
B828
Glen Croe
925
BEINN NARNAIN
881
THE COBBLER
Succoth
416
CRUACH TAIRBEIRT
Loch Lomond
B829
565
CRUACH NAN CAPULL
845
BEN DONICH
A83
Arrochar
Tarbet
633
CRUINN A' BHEINN
Queen Elizabeth Forest Park
Loch Chon
700
BEINN BHREAC
River Goil
Argyll Forest Park
Ardgartan
661
BEN REACH
973
BEN LOMOND
Kinlochard
Corrow
Lochgoilhead
Ben Lomond
Douglas Pier
Loch Long
Glen Douglas
Queen Elizabeth Forest Park
779
BEINN BHEULA
A814
734
DOUNE HILL
Inverbeg
Rowardennan
596
BEINN UIRD
Loch Goil
Queen Elizabeth Forest Park
586
BEN VRACKIE
A815
Arddarroch
702
BEINN EICH
A82
Loch
Carrick Castle
Edentaggart
Inchlonaig
Purdie's of Luss
Portincaple
Luss
Whistlefield Inn
Whistlefield
Glen Luss
713
BEINN CHAORACH
657
CREACHAN MOR
Garelochhead
655
BEINN THARSUINN
Aldoch
Milton of Buchanan
173
174
Rockville
Greenfield
B872
Balmaha
Loch Lomond
Buchanan Smithy
Glen Fruin
Lomond
664
Ardentinny
Snow gates
Shantron
Drym
G
H
J
K
L
M
1
2
3
4
5
6
7
8

193
183
174
175
Lawers
Ben Lawers
Milton Morenish
Morenish
Ardeonaig
Falls of Lochay
Moirlanich Longhouse
Glen Lochay
River Lochay
Finlarig
Killin
Falls of Dochart
Breadalbane Folklore Centre
937 BEINN CHEATHAICH
879 CREAG UCHDAG
682 RUADH MHEALL
BREADALBANE
Auchlyne
River Dochart
Loch Lubhair
Glen Dochart
A85
A827
Glen Ogle
Glen Beich
671 SRON MHOR
778 MEALL AN FHIODHAIN
1171 BEN MORE
1164 STOBINIAN
Dalveich
St Fillans
Lochearnhead
Loch Earn
Ardvorlich
Glen Vorlich
A84
Balquhidder
Auchtubh
Craigruie
Kingshouse Hotel
Loch Voil
Loch Doine
985 BEN VORLICH
975 STUC A' CHROIN
LOCH LOMOND AND THE TROSSACHS NATIONAL PARK
Ballimore
Strathyre
Dalchruin
865 STOB A' CHOIN
630 MEALL ODHAR
Ardchullarie More
818 BENVANE
Strathyre Forest
671 MEALL CALA
Queen Elizabeth Forest Park
Loch Lubnaig
Loch Katrine
876 BEN LEDI
Kilmahog Woollen Mill
The Trossachs
Glen Finglas Reservoir
Falls of Leny
Kilmahog
Callander (Calasraid)
SS Sir Walter Scott
Trossachs Pier
Brig o'Turk
Coilantogle
Upper Drumbane
Rob Roy & Trossachs
729 BEN VENUE
700 BEINN BHREAC
Loch Achray
Lendrick
A821
A81
B829
Loch Venachar
Loch Drunkie
Toll
Menteith Hills
427 BEINN DEARG
Drumvaich
Burn of Cambus
B822
B8032
Altskeith Hotel
Kinlochard
Loch Ard
Milton
Queen Elizabeth Forest Park
Aberfoyle
Port of Menteith
Ruskie
Deanston
Thornhill
B826
Goodie Water
Scottish Wool Centre
Inchmahome Priory
Lake of Menteith
A873
Duchray Water
208 ELRIG
Cunninghame Graham Memorial
Flanders Moss
Dykehead
B8031
B8075
Gartmore
River Forth
586 BEN VRACKIE
B8034
Dalmary
B8037
A811
Arnprior
Kippen
Gargunnock
B835
Buchlyvie
Cauldhame
B822
West Highland Way
Milton of Buchanan
Balmaha
Balfron
Drymen
482
435 HART
0 1 2 3 4 miles
0 1 2 3 4 5 kilometres

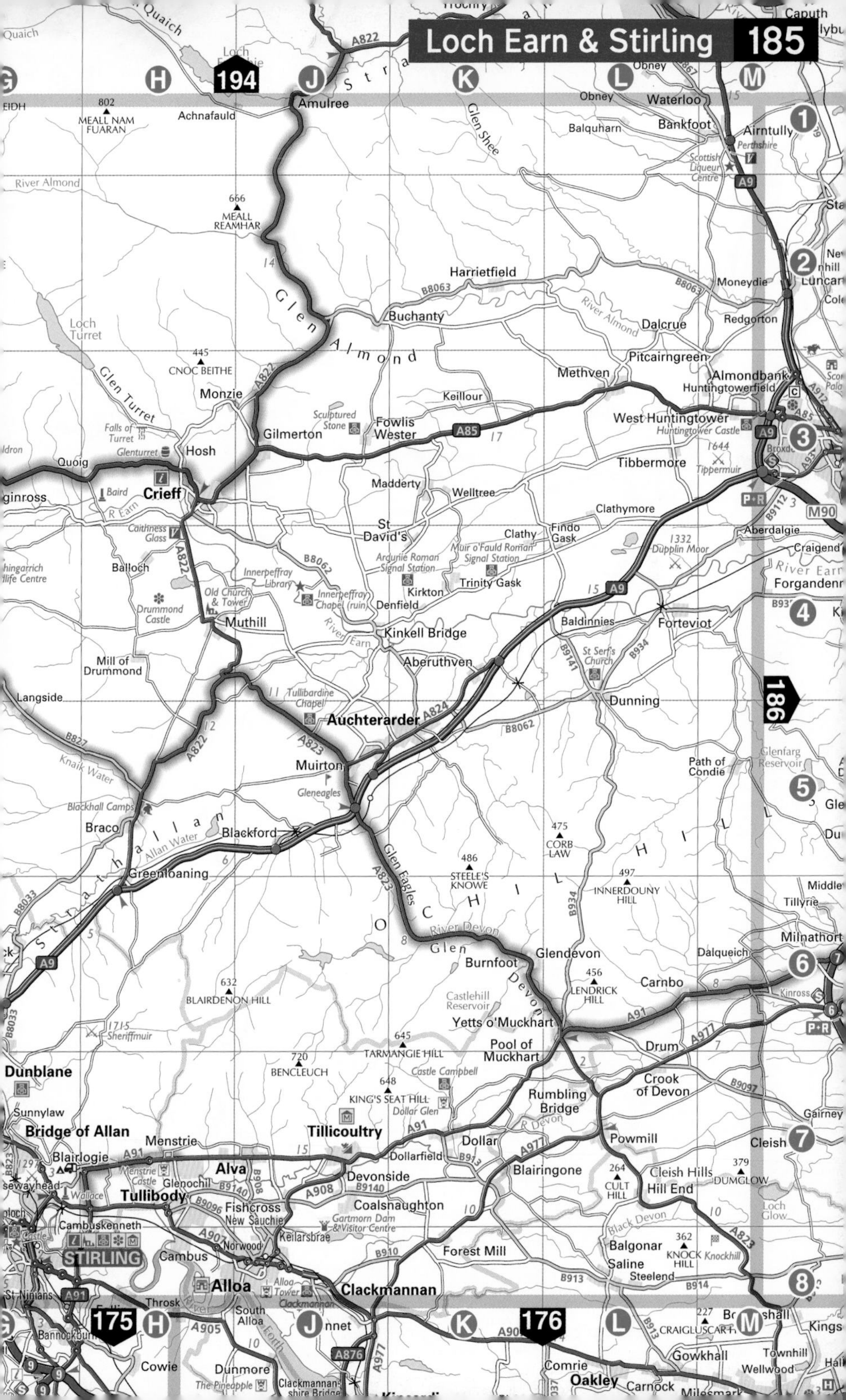
Amulree
Achnafauld
MEALL NAM FUARAN
River Almond
MEALL REAMHAR
Glen Almond
Loch Turret
CNOC BEITHE
Glen Turret
Monzie
Gilmerton
Hosh
Crieff
Muthill
Drummond Castle
Balloch
Mill of Drummond
Langside
Braco
Blackford
Greenloaning
Strathallan
Auchterarder
Muirton
Gleneagles
Aberuthven
Kinkell Bridge
Denfield
Kirkton
Trinity Gask
Madderty
St David's
Welltree
Fowlis Wester
Buchanty
Harrietfield
Keillour
Methven
Pitcairngreen
Dalcrue
Redgorton
Moneydie
Almondbank
Huntingtowerfield
West Huntingtower
Tibbermore
Clathymore
Clathy
Findo Gask
Aberdalgie
Forgandenny
Forteviot
Baldinnies
Dunning
Path of Condie
OCHIL HILLS
CORB LAW
STEELE'S KNOWE
INNERDOUNY HILL
Glen Eagles
Glendevon
Burnfoot
Yetts o'Muckhart
Pool of Muckhart
Carnbo
Drum
Crook of Devon
Rumbling Bridge
Powmill
Cleish
Milnathort
Dalqueich
Kinross
BLAIRDENON HILL
Sheriffmuir
TARMANGIE HILL
BENCLEUCH
KING'S SEAT HILL
Dunblane
Sunnylaw
Bridge of Allan
Menstrie
Blairlogie
Alva
Tillicoultry
Dollar
Dollarfield
Devonside
Blairingone
Tullibody
Fishcross
New Sauchie
Coalsnaughton
Cambuskenneth
STIRLING
Cambus
Norwood
Keilarsbrae
Forest Mill
Alloa
Clackmannan
Throsk
South Alloa
Balgonar
Saline
Steelend
Cleish Hills
Hill End
CULT HILL
DUMGLOW
KNOCK HILL
Knockhill
CRAIGLUSCAR HILL
Bannockburn
Cowie
Dunmore
Comrie
Oakley
Carnock
Gowkhall
Wellwood
Townhill
Obney
Waterloo
Bankfoot
Airntully
Balquharn
Glen Shee
Scottish Liqueur Centre
Huntingtower Castle
Tippermuir
Dupplin Moor
Glenfarg Reservoir
Castlehill Reservoir
Castle Campbell
Dollar Glen
Gartmorn Dam & Visitor Centre
Alloa Tower
Clackmannan Tower
Menstrie Castle
Glenochil
Wallace
St Ninians
A9
A822
A85
A823
A824
A91
A977
A908
A907
A905
B8062
B8063
B934
B9141
B827
B8033
B9140
B9096
B910
B913
B914
B9097
M90
194
186
175
176

186
Caputh
Gellyburn
Meikleour
Kinclaven
Meikleour Beech Hedge
Keithick
Coupar Angus
Kettins
195
Burrelton
Dys
Sidlaw Hills
Bonnyton
Kirkton of Auchterhouse
Auchterhouse
196
CRAIGOW
A
B
C
D
E
F
Cargill
Balholmie
Wood
Strelitz
Lundie
Dronley
1
Airntully
Perthshire
Scottish Liqueur Centre
A9
B9099
Gallowhill
Redstone
Wolfhill
Saucher
376
KINGS SEAT
Collace
Kirkton of Collace
B953
Muirhead
Birkhill
A923
Fowlis
Liff
Camperdown
Gourdie
Denhead of Gray
Lochee
Stanley
Guildtown
Kinrossie
A94
Abernyte
Benvie
2
Newmiln
Downhill
Luncarty
Moneydie
B8063
Redgorton
Colenden
St Martin's
Bandirran
Balbeggie
Ballindean
Baledgarno
Invergowrie
Mills Observatory
Longforgan
Kingoodie
Inchture
A85
Dundee
A93
Rait
A90
FIRTH OF TAY
Almondbank
Huntingtowerfield
Scone Palace
Scone
P+R
288
POLE HILL
Pitroddie
Kilspindie
Inchmichael
Grange
Balmerino Abbey
Balmerino
Kirkton
A912
A85
Perth
Bridgend
Huntingtower
3
A9
Broxden
Branklyn Garden
Kinnoull Tower
Tippermuir
Glendoick
Errol
Coultra
Kinfauns
Glencarse
11
Leetown
St Madoes
Inchyra
Creich
Hazelton Walls
M90
B9112
10
MONCREIFFE HILL
221
River Tay
Elcho Castle
Aberdalgie
Craigend
Rhynd
Fingask
332
285
NORMANS LAW
Brunton
Luthrie
A92
River Earn
Forgandenny
Bridge of Earn
Newburgh
Lindores
Glenduckie
Den of Lindores
4
B935
Kintillo
9
A912
A913
Dunbog
Lindores
Moonzie
Aberargie
Abernethy
Round Tower
Dron
Glenfoot
Grange of Lindores
B931
Fernie
185
B936
Monimail
Letham
Pleasance
Lochieheads
Collessie
Bow of Fife
Cupar Muir
A91
Path of Condie
Glenfarg Reservoir
M90
B996
Balvaird Castle
Auchtermuchty
Fife
Deer Centre
Springfield
5
Abbots Deuglie
Newton of Balcanquhal
Giffordtown
Glenfarg
Arngask
Dunshalt
Charlottetown
Ladybank
Scotstarvit Tower
A914
Struthers
A912
A91
Strathmiglo
River Eden
B9129
Duncrievie
Gateside
Pitlessie
Kingskettle
Drunzie
Burnside
Balmalcolm
Falkland Palace
A92
Lomond Hills
Middleton
522
WEST LOMOND
448
EAST LOMOND
Falkland
Freuchie
B936
Kettlebridge
248
CLATTO HILL
Tillyrie
8
Milnathort
Burleigh Castle
B919
Glenlomond
Ballo Reservoir
Muirhead
Langdyke
6
7
A922
A911
Holl Reservoir
Balfarg
Star
Baintown
Kinross
Kinnesswood
B969
Bonnybank
Kennoway
A977
6
P+R
Lochleven Castle
Loch Leven
Kinross House
Scotlandwell
Leslie
A911
Cadham
Markinch
Scottish Gliding Centre
Walkerton
A911
Windygates
A915
St Serf's Island
Auchmuirbridge
Glenrothes
Milton of Balgonie
Methilhill
B9097
B996
B920
Loch Leven
R Leven
Kinglassie
Pitteuchar
Coaltown of Balgonie
Gairneybridge
B9097
B921
7
Cleish
Ballingry
B9097
Thornton
5
Lochore Meadows
Lochore
B922
Dogton Stone
River Ore
A915
A955
East Wemyss
379
DUMGLOW
M90
B920
Crosshill
Auchterderran
B9130
Coaltown of Wemyss
B996
Loch Ore
B981
Cluny
Loch Glow
Kelty
Glencraig
Cardenden
B981
West Wemyss
A92
B987
Gallatown
362
KNOCK HILL
Knockhill
A823
B914
4
Lochgelly
Chapel
Dysart
B912
A909
B981
Ravenscraig Castle
8
B915
Loch Fitty
Lumphinnans
Loch Gelly
A910
B925
Pathhead
227
Bowhill
Kirkcaldy
Cowdenbeath
RAIGLUSCAR HILL
Kingseat
Hill of Beath
Linktown
177
B981
Auchtertool
Gowkhall
Townhill
Wellwood
B9157
Donibristle
Milesmark
0 1 2 3 4 miles
0 1 2 3 4 5 kilometres

196
G
H
J
K
L
M
1
2
3
4
5
6
7
8
Monikie
Kirkton of Monikie
Wellbank
Newbigging
Kellas
Murroes
Ardestie Earth-House
Carlungie Earth-House
Upper Victoria
Barry Mill
Barry
East Haven
Panbride
West Haven
Carnoustie
Baldovie
Claypotts Castle
Barnhill
Monifieth
Broughty Ferry
Broughty Castle
BUDDON NESS
Tayport
Tentsmuir Point
Morton Locks
Scottish National Golf Centre
Tentsmuir Forest & Beach
St Michaels
Leuchars
ST ANDREWS BAY
Guardbridge
River Eden
Kincaple
St Andrews
Castle
Brownhills
Boarhills
Botanic
Craigtoun
Blebocraigs
Denhead
Cameron Reservoir
Baldinnie
Dunino
Kingsbarns
Cambo
Balcomie Links
FIFE NESS
Peat Inn
Radernie
Kingsmuir
Scotland's Secret Bunker
Lathones
Lochty
Largoward
Carnbee
Crail
Easter Pitkierie
Kellie Castle
Arncroach
Wester Pitkierie
Kilrenny
Cellardyke
Colinsburgh
Newton of Balcormo
Fisheries
Anstruther
Drumeldrie
Kilconquhar
Pittenweem
St Monans
Earlsferry
Elie
Isle of May
A92
A930
A91
A917
A915
A919
B961
B962
B939
B940
B941
B942
B9131
B9171

A
B
C
D
E
F
1
2
3
4
5
6
7
8
Grishi
Clabhach
Hogh Bay
Ballyha
Totronald
Coll
Acha
Feall Bay
Arileod
Uig
Crossapol Bay
Loch Breachacha
Rubha Fàsacho
Calgary Point
Gunna
Bagh a Chaisteil (Castlebay)
(Apr-Oct, Weds only)
Rubha Dubh
Caoles
B8069
Ruaig
Gott Bay
Rubha Port Bhiosd
Clachan Mor
Balephetrish Bay
Loch Bhasapoll
B8068
Haugh Bay
Ballevullin
Cornoigmore
Kenovay
Tiree
Kilkenneth
Scarinish
B8065
Moss
Heylipoll
Middleton
Crossapol
TIREE
Barrapoll
Hynish Bay
Loch a' Phuill
B8067
Balemartine
Mannal
Rinn Thorbhais
Hynish
Balephuil Bay
0 1 2 3 4 miles
0 1 2 3 4 5 kilometres

198
MUCK
Port Mòr
Eilean nan Each
Eilean Chathastail
Sanna Point
Sanna
Sanna Bay
Portuairk
Achnaha
Kilmory
Branault
Ardnamurchan Point
Achosnich
B8007
436 MEALL NAN CON
342 BEINN NA SEILG
Ormsaigmore
Kilchoan
Mingary
527 BEN HIANT
Ardslignish
Loch Mudle
Bagh a Chaisteil (Castlebay)
Loch Baghasdail (Lochboisdale)
Eilean Mòr
Rubha Mòr
Rubha Sgor-innis
Bousd
Sorisdale
COLL
Coll - Oban
190
Ardmore Point
Sorne Point
Quinish Point
Glengorm Castle
Rubha nan Gall
Auliston Point
Tobermory
Calve Island
Caliach Point
292 'S AIRDE BEINN
Dervaig
Achnadrish House
Calgary
B8073
Calgary Bay
A848
444 SPEINNE MÒR
Loch Frisa
Treshnish Point
Ensay
342 CARN MÒR
Rudh' a' Chaoil
Burg
Glen Aros
390
Fanmore
CNOC AN DÀ CHINN
Glenaros House
Fladda
Loch Tuath
Ballygown
Eas Fors
333 BEINN NAN CÀRN
Killiechronan
B8035
Lunga
Gometra
ULVA
Oskamull
Gruline
Macquarie Mausoleum
TRESHNISH ISLES
Bac Mòr or Dutchman's Cap
Bac Beag
Eorsa
Loch na Keal
591
Little Colonsay
Staffa
Fingal's
Inchkenneth
180
Loch na Keal
Isle of Mull
Balnahard
966

199
200
189
181
A
B
C
D
E
F
1
2
3
4
5
6
7
8
Rubh' Arisaig
103
CRUACH DOIRE
Druimindarroch
Arisaig House
Cairn
Kinlochnanuagh
Loch nan Uamh
Ardnish
Sound of Arisaig
Rubha Choalais
Loch Ailort
Inverailort
A861
877
ROIS-BHEINN
712
Smearisary
Glenuig
Eilean Shona
Rubha Àird Druimnich
Loch Moidart
Tioram
Seven Men of Moidart
Kinlochmoidart
Glen Forsa
Brunery
Glen Moidart
239
BEINN BHREAC
Ardmolich
Ockle Point
Morar, Moidart and Ardnamurchan
MOIDART
Kilmory
Ockle
Ardtoe
Shielfoot
Langal
Mingarrypark
Branault
356
BEINN BHREAC
B8044
Kentra
Blain
Dalnabreck
Dalelia
Arevegaig
436
MEALL NAN CON
ARDNAMURCHAN
Acharacle
Claish Moss
B8007
Loch Mudle
437
846
BEINN RESIPOL
342
Kilchoan
Salen
Resipole Burn
Mingary
527
BEN HIANT
Natural History
Glenbeg
512
BEN LAGA
Loch Sunart
Glencripesdale
Ardslignish
Glenborrodale
Laga
339
GEÀRR CHREAG
Camasine
Camasach
Carna
Oronsay
Auliston Point
Liddesdale
Rubha nan Gall
A884
Tobermory
Calve Island
Loch Teacuis
571
BEINN LADAIN
522
MEALL A' CHOISE
292
'S AIRDE BEINN
Drimnin
Glen Dubh
437
BEINN BHUIDHE
Achnadrish House
A848
B849
550
SÌTHEAN NA RAPLAICH
Loch Arienas
Acharn
444
SPEINNE MÒR
Loch Frisa
Sound of Mull
Gleann Geal
Claggan
Larachbeg
339
MEALL DAMH
Rannoch River
Fuinary
Achranich
Loch Teàrnait
Glen Aros
Loch Aline
Aros
Lochaline
Glenaros House
464
GLAIS BHEINN
514
AN SLEAGHOCH
Salen
A849
Fishnish Point
Fishnish Pier
333
BEINN NAN CÀRN
Killiechronan
B8035
Glen Forsa
Oskamull
B8073
Gruline
408
BEINN NAN LUS
Macquarie Mausoleum
Scallastle Bay
Rubha an Ridire
Eorsa
Altcreich
Loch na Keal
Loch Bà
ISLE OF MULL
636
BEINN MHEADHON
591
BEINN A' GHRÀIG
Craignure
766
DÙN DA GHAOITHE
Duart Bay
Duart Point
Duart
Torosay
Balnahard
Lochdonhead
Lochdon
966
704
0 1 2 3 4 miles
0 1 2 3 4 5 kilometres

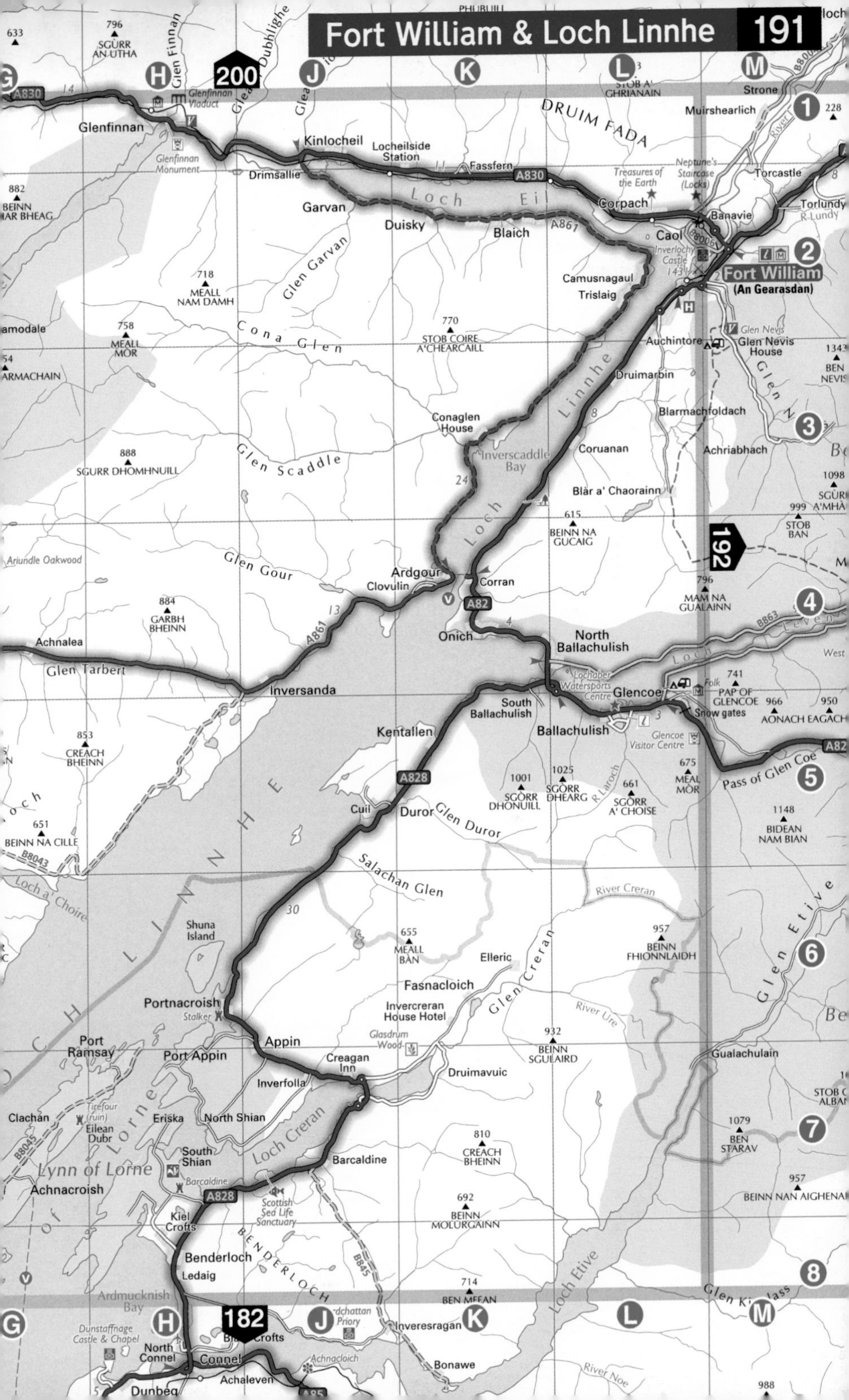
Glenfinnan
Glenfinnan Viaduct
Glenfinnan Monument
Kinlocheil
Locheilside Station
Drimsallie
Fassfern
DRUIM FADA
Loch Eil
Garvan
Duisky
Blaich
Corpach
Caol
Banavie
Strone
Muirshearlich
Torcastle
Torlundy
Treasures of the Earth
Neptune's Staircase (Locks)
Inverlochy Castle
Fort William
(An Gearasdan)
Camusnagaul
Trislaig
Glen Garvan
Cona Glen
718 MEALL NAM DAMH
758 MEALL MOR
770 STOB COIRE A'CHEARCAILL
Auchintore
Glen Nevis
Glen Nevis House
Druimarbin
Blarmachfoldach
Achriabhach
Conaglen House
Inverscaddle Bay
Coruanan
888 SGURR DHOMHNUILL
Glen Scaddle
Blàr a' Chaorainn
Loch Linnhe
615 BEINN NA GUCAIG
999 STOB BAN
1098 SGÙRR A'MHÀ
Ariundle Oakwood
Glen Gour
Ardgour
Clovulin
Corran
796 MAM NA GUALAINN
884 GARBH BHEINN
Onich
North Ballachulish
Achnalea
Glen Tarbert
Inversanda
Lochaber Watersports Centre
Glencoe
741 PAP OF GLENCOE
966 AONACH EAGACH
950
Snow gates
South Ballachulish
Ballachulish
Glencoe Visitor Centre
Kentallen
853 CREACH BHEINN
1001 SGORR DHONUILL
1025 SGORR DHEARG
661 SGORR A' CHOISE
675 MEALL MÒR
Pass of Glen Coe
Cuil
Duror
Glen Duror
1148 BIDEAN NAM BIAN
651 BEINN NA CILLE
Salachan Glen
River Creran
Loch a' Choire
Shuna Island
655 MEALL BÀN
Elleric
957 BEINN FHIONNLAIDH
Glen Etive
Fasnacloich
Invercreran House Hotel
Glen Creran
River Ure
Portnacroish
Stalker
Glasdrum Wood
932 BEINN SGULAIRD
Port Ramsay
Port Appin
Appin
Creagan Inn
Druimavuic
Gualachulain
Inverfolla
Clachan
Tirefour (ruin)
Eilean Dubr
Eriska
North Shian
Loch Creran
1079 BEN STARAV
South Shian
810 CREACH BHEINN
Lynn of Lorne
Barcaldine
Achnacroish
Scottish Sea Life Sanctuary
957 BEINN NAN AIGHENAN
692 BEINN MOLURGAINN
Kiel Crofts
Benderloch
BENDERLOCH
Ledaig
Loch Etive
714 BEN MEEAN
Glen Kinglass
Ardmucknish Bay
Dunstaffnage Castle & Chapel
Ardchattan Priory
Inveresragan
North Connel
Connel
Achnacloich
Bonawe
River Noe
Achaleven
Dunbeg
988
A830
A861
A82
A828
B8006
B863
B8043
B8045
B845
A85
200
192
182

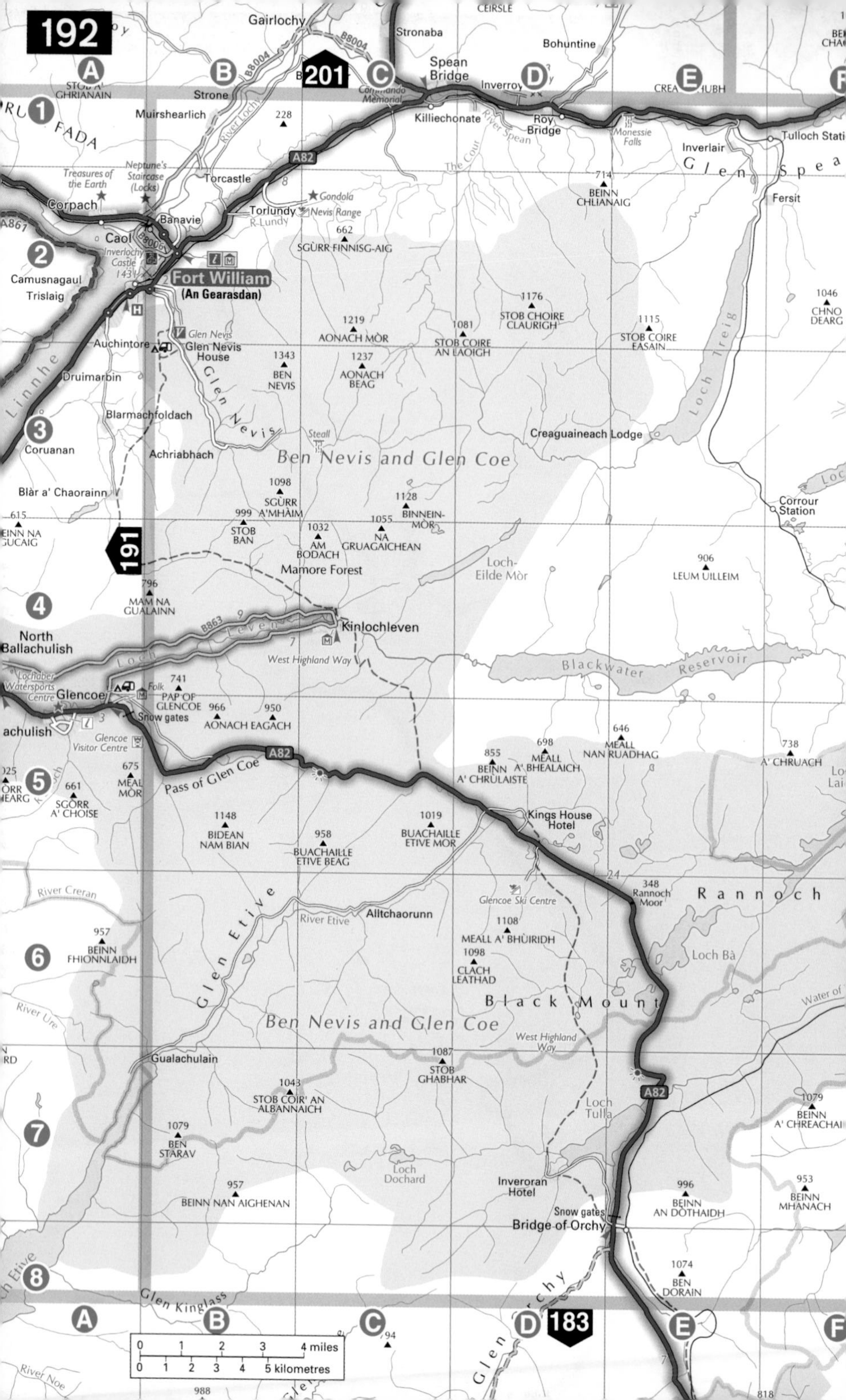

201
191
183
Gairlochy
Stronaba
Spean Bridge
Bohuntine
Commando Memorial
Inverroy
Strone
Muirshearlich
Killiechonate
Roy Bridge
Monessie Falls
Tulloch Station
Inverlair
Glen Spean
River Spean
The Cour
River Lochy
Treasures of the Earth
Neptune's Staircase (Locks)
Torcastle
Corpach
Banavie
Torlundy
Gondola
Nevis Range
R. Lundy
A82
B8004
B8006
A861
Caol
Inverlochy Castle
Fort William
(An Gearasdan)
Camusnagaul
Trislaig
Glen Nevis
Glen Nevis House
Auchintore
Druimarbin
Linnhe
Blarmachfoldach
Achriabhach
Coruanan
Blàr a' Chaoruinn
714 BEINN CHLIANAIG
Fersit
662 SGÙRR FINNISG-AIG
1176 STOB CHOIRE CLAURIGH
1219 AONACH MÒR
1081 STOB COIRE AN LAOIGH
1115 STOB COIRE EASAIN
1046 CHNO DEARG
1343 BEN NEVIS
1237 AONACH BEAG
Loch Treig
Steall
Creaguaineach Lodge
Ben Nevis and Glen Coe
1098 SGÙRR A'MHÀIM
1128 BINNEIN MÒR
Corrour Station
615 BEINN NA GUCAIG
999 STOB BAN
1032 AM BODACH
1055 NA GRUAGAICHEAN
Mamore Forest
Loch Eilde Mòr
906 LEUM UILLEIM
796 MAM NA GUALAINN
North Ballachulish
B863
Leven
Loch
Kinlochleven
West Highland Way
Blackwater Reservoir
Lochaber Watersports Centre
Glencoe
Folk
741 PAP OF GLENCOE
966 AONACH EAGACH
950
Snow gates
Ballachulish
Glencoe Visitor Centre
646 MEALL NAN RUADHAG
698 MEALL A' BHEALAICH
855 BEINN A' CHRULAISTE
738 A' CHRUACH
675 MEALL MÒR
661 SGORR A' CHOISE
Pass of Glen Coe
1148 BIDEAN NAM BIAN
958 BUACHAILLE ETIVE BEAG
1019 BUACHAILLE ETIVE MOR
Kings House Hotel
348 Rannoch Moor
Rannoch
River Creran
Glencoe Ski Centre
Alltchaorunn
River Etive
Glen Etive
1108 MEALL A' BHÙIRIDH
957 BEINN FHIONNLAIDH
Loch Bà
1098 CLACH LEATHAD
Black Mount
River Ure
Water of Tulla
Ben Nevis and Glen Coe
West Highland Way
Gualachulain
1087 STOB GHABHAR
1043 STOB COIR' AN ALBANNAICH
Loch Tulla
1079 BEINN A' CHREACHAIN
1079 BEN STARAV
Loch Dochard
957 BEINN NAN AIGHENAN
Inveroran Hotel
996 BEINN AN DOTHAIDH
953 BEINN MHANACH
Snow gates
Bridge of Orchy
1074 BEN DORAIN
Glen Orchy
Glen Kinglass
River Etive
River Noe
988
818
0 1 2 3 4 miles
0 1 2 3 4 5 kilometres
A B C D E F
1 2 3 4 5 6 7 8

202
194
184
Snow gates
CÀRN NA CAIM
GEAL CHÀRN
MEALL CRUAIDH
CREAGAN MÒR
Loch Pattack
BEINN A' CHLACHAIR
CÀRN DEARG
Loch Ericht
A' MHARCONAICH
Drumochter Summit
GLAS MHEALL MÒR
BEINN UDLAMAIN
SGAIRNEACH MHOR
Dalnaspidal
BEN ALDER
Loch Garry
Snow gates
Dalnacardoch
Glen Garry
Loch Con
Loch Errochty
SRON A CHLAONAIDH
BEINN MHOLACH
Trinafour
B847
TORR DUBH
BEINN A' CHUALLAICH
Tay Forest Park
R Ericht
B846
Bridge of Ericht
Killichonan
Loch Rannoch
Kinloch Rannoch
Drumchastle
Dunalastair
R Tummel
Tummel Bridge
Dunalastair Water
Dunan
Finnart
Inverhadden
Tempar
Bridge of Gaur
Carie
Camghouran
SCHIEHALLION
Tay Forest Park
Loch Rannoch and Glen Lyon
Glengoulandie Deer Park
MEALL A' MHUIC
CÀRN MAIRG
MEALL BUIDHE
CAM CHREAG
BEINN DEARG
CÀRN GORM
Glen Lyon
Bridge of Balgie
River Lyon
Fortingall
Loch an Daimh
Kenmore
Fearnan
The Crannog Centre
MEALL LUAIDHE
MEALL A' CHOIRE LEITH
MEALL GARBH
MEALL GREIGH
BEN LAWERS
BEINN NAN OIGHREAG
Lochan na Làirige
Leckbuie
BEINN BHREAC
MEALL GHAORDIE
Ben Lawers
Lawers
Loch Tay
A827
Milton Morenish
River Lochay
Falls of Lochay
Finlarig
Killin

Gaick Forest
TOABHAIN
gates
941
CÀRN NA CAIM
A
B
C
203
D
E
F
999
CÀRN
EALAR
1006
AN
SGARSOCH
R
1
Loch an Dùin
C A I R N G O R M S
Tarf Water
926
GLAS
MHEALL MÒR
2
814
SRON A'
CHLEIRICH
1007
BEINN
DEARG
N A T I O N A L   P A R K
River Tilt
897
BEINN
A' CHART
1119
CÀRN NAN
CABHAR
1068
20
Snow gates
Dalnacardoch
Glen Garry
A9
Bruar Water
491
CRAIG
BHAGAILTEACH
Glen Banvie
Glen Tilt
Glen Fender
973
CÀRN
LIATH
3
Loch
Con
Loch
Errochty
Clan
Donnachaidh
Bruar
Blair Castle
Middlebridge
Calvine
Struan
Old
Struan
B8079
Bridge of Tilt
Blair Atholl
Glen Girnaig
Aldclune
Trinafour
B847
470
TULACH HILL
1689
Killiecrankie
River Garry
14
Glen Errochty
511
TORR
DUBH
840
BEN
VRACKIE
4
892
BEINN
A' CHUALLAICH
Tay Forest Park
Killiecrankie
Tay
Forest
Park
Tressait
B8019
Moulin
Kinnaird
7
B846
R Tummel
Loch Tummel
Faskally Wayside
Centre
Drumchastle
Dunalastair
Tummel
Bridge
Frenich
13
Queen's
View
Dunalastair
Water
Foss
Tay Forest Park
Edradour
Pitlochry
(Baile Chloichridh)
verhadden
Tempar
193
Daloist
Loch Tummel
5
Tay Forest
Park
Dunfallandy
Stone
R Tummel
Dalc
1081
SCHIEHALLION
780
FARRAGON
HILL
780
MEALL
TAIRNEACHAN
Loch
Derculich
Strathtay
A9
A827
Glengoulandie
Deer Park
Loch
Glassie
Derculich
Grandtully
Logierait
1042
CÀRN
MAIRG
Edradynate
9
Balnaguard
B898
B846
14
St Mary's
Menzies
Weem
Dewar's
6
Camserney
Coshieville
Dull
Keltneyburn
Aberfeldy
Kincraigie
Tay Forest Park
River Tay
Dalguise
Fortingall
Tay
Forest
Park
Craftmoraig
Stone Circle
532
GRANDTULLY
HILL
Loch
Skiach
Kenmore
A827
9
Loch
Kennard
Fearnan
The Crannog
Centre
1000
MEALL
7
Acharn
A826
Ballinloan Burn
Loch Tay
616
MEALL DUBH
Leckbuie
713
BEINN
BHREAC
Glen Quaich
Trochry
Lawers
25
River Quaich
A822
8
Strathbraan
8
Loch
Freuchie
864
SRÒN A' CHAOINEIDH
802
MEALL NAM
FUARAN
185
Amulree
Ardeona
A
B
C
D
E
F
Glen Shee
0 1 2 3 4 miles
0 1 2 3 4 5 kilometres
River Almond

204
196
186
Glen Ey
Clunie
Glenshee
Baddoch Burn
BROAD CAIRN
CÀRN AN TUIRC
TOM BUIDHE
EASTERBALLOCH
LAIR OF ALDARARIE
Glen Doll
THE CAIRNWELL
GLAS MAOL
GLAS LAICHEAN
Corrie Fee
MAYAR
DRIESH
River Isla
Clova
CARN AIT
Glen Lochsie
BEN GULABIN
Snow gates
MEALL A' CHOIRE BHUIDHE
Spittal of Glenshee
MONAMEANOCH
CAIRN OF BAMS
Glen Clova
Glen Shee
MEALL UAINE
DUCHRAY HILL
BADENDUN HILL
CAIRN DAUNIE
Glen Damff
Runtaleave
Cormuir
Glen Prosen
Pitcarity
Presnerb
Glen Finlet
Straloch
Enochdhu
Clackavoid
MOUNT BLAIR
Folda
Bridge of Brewlands
Backwater Reservoir
Glenisla
Milton
River Ardle
Blacklunans
MEALL MOR
Kirkmichael
Bellaty
Balintore
Dykends
Braes of Coul
Strathardle
Loch of Lintrathen
Kirkton of Kingoldrum
Forest of Alyth
Ballintuim
Bridge of Craigisla
Bridgend of Lintrathen
CRAIG NAM MIAL
Alyth Burn
Dykehead
Reekie Linn Falls
Westmuir
BALDUFF HILL
Netherton
Tullymurdoch
Kirkton of Airlie
Gauldswell
Littleton
Loch Benachally
Bridge of Cally
HILL OF ALYTH
Airlie
Craigton of Airlie
Roundyhill
River Ericht
River Isla
Ruthven
Alyth
New Alyth
Dean Water
Eassie Sculptured Stone
Westfields of Rattray
Lornty
Balhary
Achalader
Blairgowrie
Kinloch
Rattray
Charleston
Loch of the Lowes
Concraigie
Rosemount
Longleys
Balkeerie
Kirkinch
Eassie and Nevay
Meigle
Sculptured Stone Museum
Clunie
Craigie
Muirton of Ardblair
Dunkeld
Newbigging
Lethendy
Ardler
KINPURNEY HILL
Nether Handwick
Spittalfield
Newtyle
Coupar Angus
Caputh
Gellyburn
Meikleour
River Tay
Meikleour Beech Hedge
Keithick
Kettins
Murthly
Kinclaven
Bonnyton
Kirkton of Auchterhouse
Woodside
Leys
Campmuir
Sidlaw Hills
Auchterhouse
Burrelton
Cargill
Strelitz
Balholmie
Waterloo
Dronley
Airntully
Perthshire
Scottish Liqueur Centre
Redstone
Muirhead
Birkhill
Wolfhill
Saucher
Fowlis
Camperdown

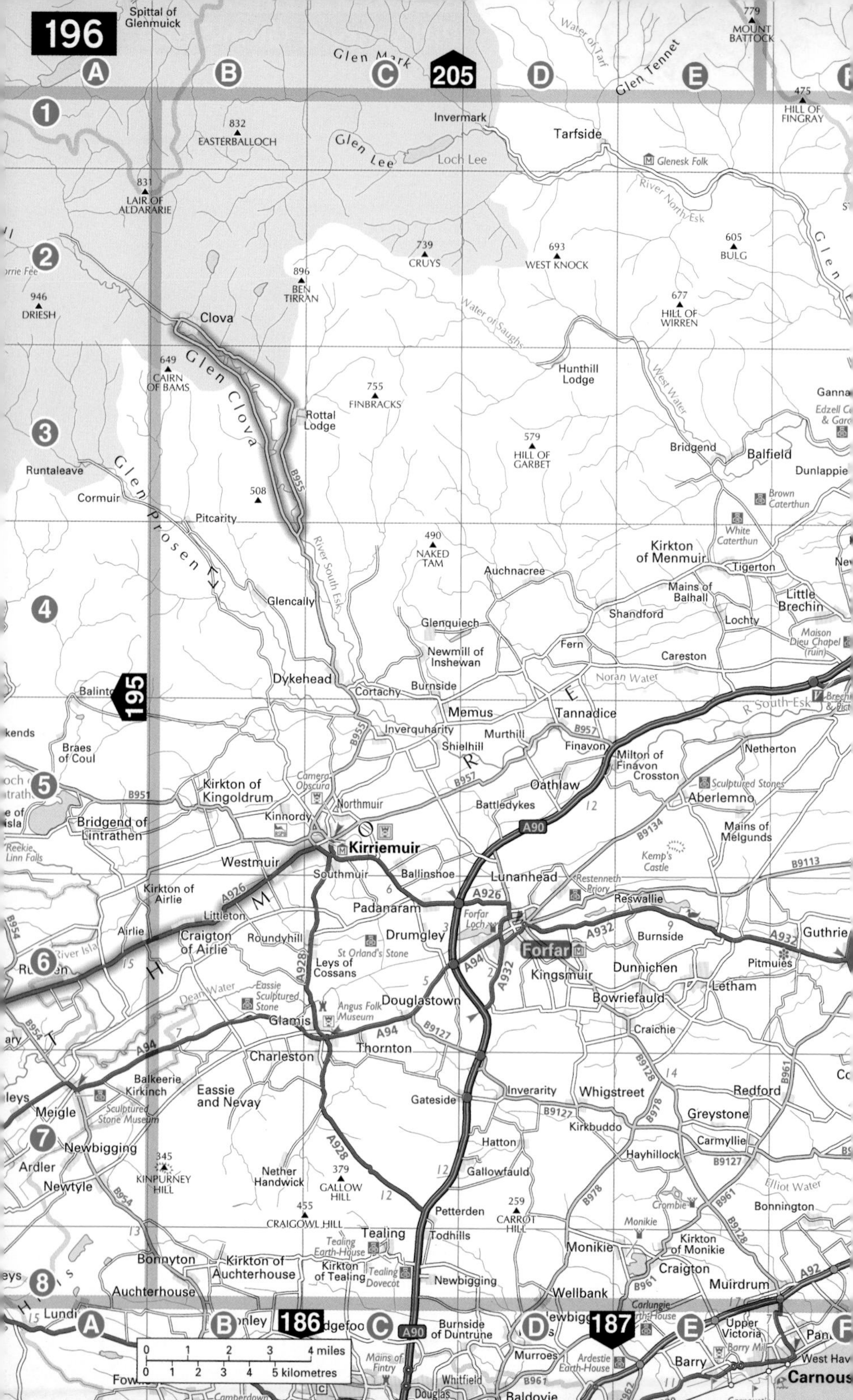
Spittal of Glenmuick
Glen Mark
205
Water of Tarf
779 MOUNT BATTOCK
Glen Tennet
475 HILL OF FINGRAY
Invermark
Tarfside
832 EASTERBALLOCH
Glen Lee
Loch Lee
Glenesk Folk
River North Esk
831 LAIR OF ALDARARIE
739 CRUYS
693 WEST KNOCK
605 BULG
896 BEN TIRRAN
946 DRIESH
677 HILL OF WIRREN
Water of Saughs
Clova
Glen Clova
649 CAIRN OF BAMS
755 FINBRACKS
Hunthill Lodge
West Water
Rottal Lodge
579 HILL OF GARBET
Runtaleave
Glen Prosen
Cormuir
508
B955
Pitcarity
Bridgend
Balfield
Dunlappie
Brown Caterthun
White Caterthun
490 NAKED TAM
River South Esk
Kirkton of Menmuir
Auchnacree
Tigerton
Mains of Balhall
Little Brechin
Shandford
Lochty
Glencally
Glenquiech
Maison Dieu Chapel (ruin)
Fern
Newmill of Inshewan
Careston
Noran Water
Dykehead
195
Cortachy
Burnside
R South Esk
Memus
Tannadice
Braes of Coul
Inverquharity
B957
Murthill
Shielhill
Finavon
Milton of Finavon
Netherton
Crosston
Camera Obscura
B957
Sculptured Stones
Kirkton of Kingoldrum
Oathlaw
Aberlemno
B951
Northmuir
Battledykes
Bridgend of Lintrathen
Kinnordy
B9134
Mains of Melgunds
A90
Kirriemuir
Reekie Linn Falls
Kemp's Castle
Westmuir
B9113
Southmuir
Ballinshoe
Lunanhead
Kirkton of Airlie
Restenneth Priory
A926
Reswallie
Padanaram
A926
Littleton
Forfar Loch
Airlie
Burnside
Craigton of Airlie
Roundyhill
Drumgley
A932
Guthrie
River Isla
St Orland's Stone
A932
Leys of Cossans
Forfar
Pitmuies
A928
A94
Dunnichen
Kingsmuir
Letham
Eassie Sculptured Stone
Dean Water
Douglastown
Bowriefauld
Angus Folk Museum
Glamis
B9127
Craichie
A94
B954
A94
Charleston
Thornton
B9128
Balkeerie
Kirkinch
Eassie and Nevay
Gateside
Inverarity
Whigstreet
Redford
B961
Meigle
Sculptured Stone Museum
B9127
Greystone
B978
Kirkbuddo
Newbigging
Hatton
Carmyllie
Ardler
345 KINPURNEY HILL
Hayhillock
B9127
A928
Nether Handwick
379 GALLOW HILL
Gallowfauld
Newtyle
B954
B978
Elliot Water
Crombie
B961
Bonnington
455 CRAIGOWL HILL
Petterden
259 CARROT HILL
Monikie
B9128
Tealing
Tealing Earth-House
Todhills
Monikie
Kirkton of Monikie
Bonnyton
Kirkton of Auchterhouse
Kirkton of Tealing
Tealing Dovecot
Craigton
Newbigging
A92
Auchterhouse
Wellbank
Muirdrum
B961
Carlungie Earth House
186
187
Burnside of Duntrune
Upper Victoria
Barry Mill
A90
Mains of Fintry
Murroes
Ardestie Earth-House
Barry
West Haven
Carnoustie
Whitfield
B961
Douglas
Baldovie
Camperdown
0 1 2 3 4 miles
0 1 2 3 4 5 kilometres

206
Goosecruives
Temple of Fiddes
Drumlithie
Glenbervie
Bervie Water
465 GOYLE HILL
Mondynes
414 Auchenblae
FINELLA HILL
Fowlsheugh
Crawton
Catterline
Kinneff
Todhead Point
B966
B967
Fordoun
Grassic Gibbon Centre
Pittarrow
Redmyre
Arbuthnott
A92
Mains of Haulkerton
B9120
Inverbervie
Laurencekirk
Bervie Bay
Gourdon
B974
B9120
Redford
Benholm
Dykelands
A90
A937
Johnshaven
Esk
Marykirk
Bush
Logie Pert
Craigo
Lochside
Milton Ness
St Cyrus
Logie
Morphie
Hillside
House of Dun
Dun
A935
Montrose Air Station
Montrose
Montrose Basin
Scurdie Ness
Barnhead
Ferryden
Maryton
A934
Craig
Usan
Westerton of Rossie
Boddin Point
Braehead
Lunan
Lunan Bay
Inverkeilor
Red Head
Marywell
Auchmithie
Carlingheugh Bay
The Deil's Head
Arbroath

208
189
A
B
C
D
E
1
2
3
4
5
6
7
8
Bay
Talisker
Minginish
Loch Eynort
447
BEINN BHREAC
434
AN CRUACHIN
Rubha an Dùnain
Loch Baghasdail
(Lochboisdale)
CANNA
210
CÀRN A' GHAILL
Garrisdale Point
A'Chill
Canna Harbour
Sanday
Sound of Canna
Kilmory Bay
Rubha Shamhnan
302
MULLACH MÒR
A' Bhrìdeanach
570
ORVAL
Oigh-sgeir
RÙM
810
ASKIVAL
Harris Bay
763
SGÙRR NAN GILLEAN
The Small Isles
Rubha nam Meirleach
Eilean nan Each
0 1 2 3 4 miles
0 1 2 3 4 5 kilometres

ISLE OF SKYE
The Cuillin Hills
Sligachan
Broadford
Corry
Broadford Bay
Waterloo
Lower Breakish
Breakish
Harrapool
Skulamus
Kyleakin
Skye Bridge
Pabay
Scalpay
Strollamus
Ard Dorch
Loch Ainort
BLAVEN
Torrin
Loch Coruisk
Loch na Crèitheach
Kirkibost
Loch Slapin
Heaste
BEINN NAN CARN
BEINN NA SEAMRAIG
Suisnish
Rubha Suisnish
Loch Eishort
Loch Scavaig
BEN MEABOST
Elgol
Glasnakille
SOAY
Strathaird Point
Drumfearn
Duisdalemore
Isleornsay
Loch na Dal
Ornsay
SGORACH BREAC
Tokavaig
Ord River
Tarskavaig
Tarskavaig Bay
Achnacloich
Loch nam Uamph
Teangue
Knock
Ferrindonald
Kilmore
Knock Bay
Kilbeg
Armadale Castle
Clan Donald
Ardvasar
Armadale
Calligarry
Aird of Sleat
Ard Thurinish
Point of Sleat
SOUND OF SLEAT
Rubh' Ard Slisneach
Inverguseran
Glen Guseran
Airor
DRUIM NA CLUAIN-AIRIDHE
Sandaig
Sandaig Bay
Inverie Bay
Rubha Raonuill
Sandaig Island
Rubha Buidhe
SGURR NA COINNICH
BEN ASLAK
Otter Haven
Courteachan
Mallaig
(Malaig)
Mallaigvaig
CÀRN A' GHOBHAIR
Glasnacardoch Bay
Loch an Nostaire
SGÙRR BHUIDHE
Beoraidbeg
Morar
Bracora
Bracorina
Tarbet
Swordland
Glenancross
Loch Morar
Lettermorar
CÀRN A' MHÀDAIDH-RUAIDH
Bunacaimb
Eilean Ighe
Back of Keppoch
Arisaig
Loch nan Ceall
Luinga Mhòr
SIDHEAN MOR
Prince Charlie's Cairn
Kinlochnanuagh
Rubh' Arisaig
CRUACH DOIRE
Druimindarroch
Arisaig House
Loch nan Uamh
Polnish
Lochailort
Ardnish
Inverailort
Rubha Choalais
Loch Ailort
Cleadale
AN CRUACHAN
Kildonnan
SGÙRR
Galmisdale
Eilean Chathastail
A87
A851
A830
A861
B8083
B8008
209
200
190

Kyle of Lochalsh
(Caol Loch Aillse)
Badicaul
Balmacara
Auchtertyre
Conchra
Loch Long
Camas Luinie
Glen Elchaig
Pabay
Skye Bridge
Kyleakin
Lochalsh Woodland Garden
Kirkton
Nostie
Ardelve
Carndu
Dornie
Eilean Donan
Loch Alsh
Keppoch
A87
Lower Breakish
Breakish
Letterfearn
Loch Duich
SGURR NA COINNICH
Otter Haven
Kyle Rhea
Bernera
Galltair
Kylerhea
(Apr-Oct)
Glenelg Bay
Glenelg
Eilanreach
BEN ASLAK
BEINN A'CHUIRN
SGÙRR AN AIRGID
Inverinate
Morvich
Carn-gorm
Ault a' chruinn
Inversheil
Shiel Bridge
Ratagan
Mam Ratagan
Moyle
BEINN A' CHAOINICH
Kintail
FIVE SISTERS
SGÙRR FHUARAN
Glen Shiel
Glenelg Brochs
Glean Beag
Balvraid
BEINN NA SEAMRAIG
Loch na Dal
Sandaig Island
Ornsay
Rubha Buidhe
SOUND OF SLEAT
BEINN SGRITHEAL
BEINN NAN CAORACH
THE SADDLE
SGURR NA-SGINE
Arnisdale
Loch Hourn
Glen Arnisdale
Corran
DRUM FADA
Rubh' Ard Slisneach
Inverguseran
BEINN NA CAILLICH
Barrisdale Bay
Kinloch Hourn
SGURR A MHAORAICH
Glen Guseran
LADHAR BHEINN
DRUIM NA CLUAIN-AIRIDHE
Sandaig
Knoydart
KNOYDART
LUINNE BHEINN
Inverie
Inverie Bay
Loch an Dubh-Lochain
MEALL BUIDHE
Rubha Raonuill
SGURR MOR
Mallaigvaig
CÀRN A' GHOBHAIR
BEINN BHUIDHE
SGURR NA CICHE
Loch an Nostaire
SGÙRR BHUIDHE
Loch Nevis
Glen Dessarry
Morar
Bracorina
Bracora
Kylesmorar
SGURR NAH-AIDE
Murlaggan
Tarbet
SGURR BREAC
Swordland
Loch Morar
Glen Pean
Lettermorar
CÀRN A' DAIDH-RUAIDH
AN STAC
Meoble
MEITH BHEINN
River Meoble
SGÙRR NAN COIREACHAN
SGÙRR THUILM
SIDHEAN MÒR
Prince Charlie's Cairn
Arisaig House
Kinlochnanuagh
Loch Beoraid
SGÙRR AN UTHA
Glen Finnan
Gleann Dubhlighe
Gleann Fionnlighe
Polnish
Lochailort
Loch Eilt
A830
Glenfinnan Viaduct
Glenfinnan Monument
Kinlocheil
Locheilside Station
Drimsallie
Rubha
0 1 2 3 4 miles
0 1 2 3 4 5 kilometres

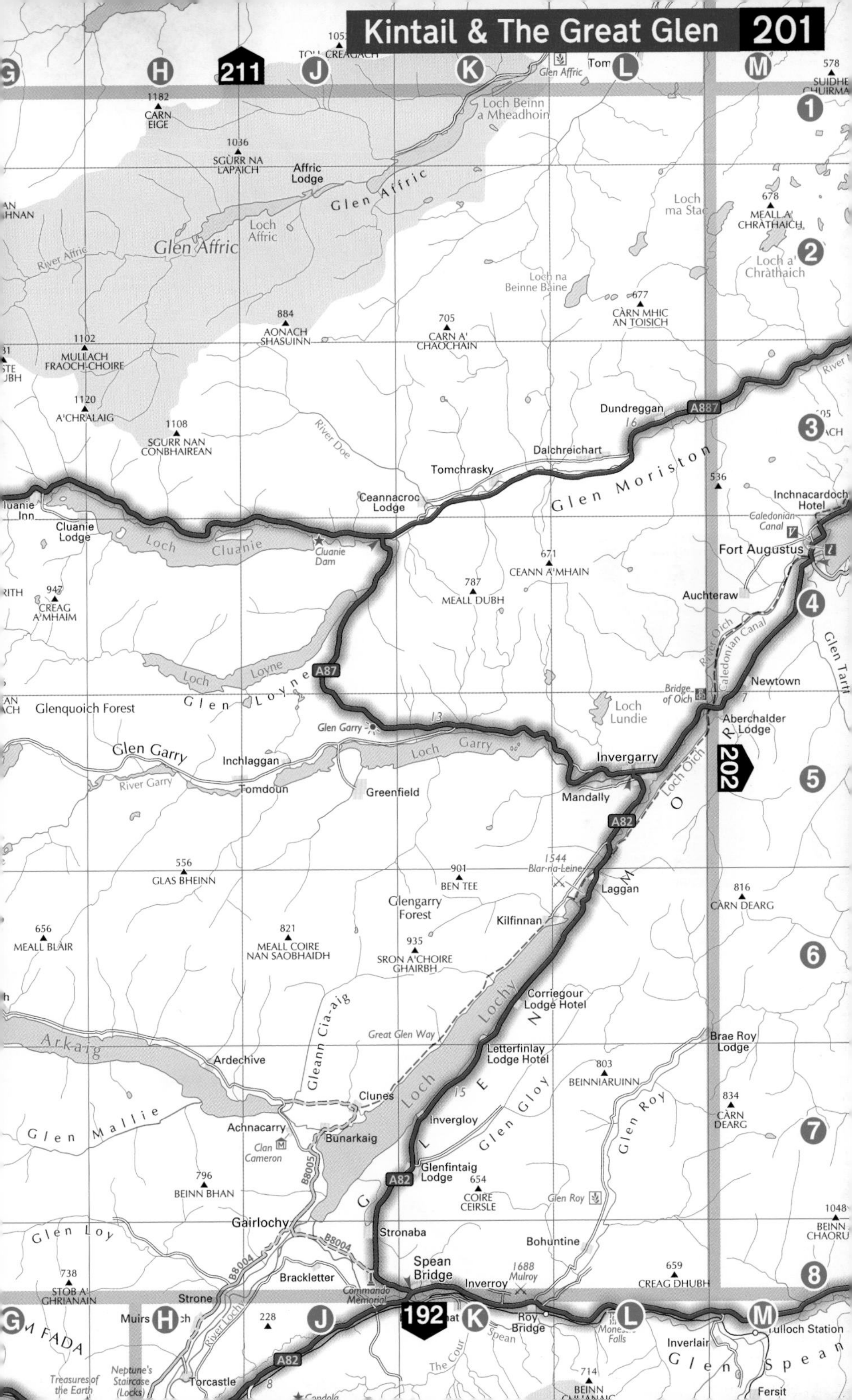

211
202
192
Carn Eige
Sgùrr na Lapaich
Affric Lodge
Glen Affric
Loch Affric
River Affric
Loch Beinn a Mheadhoin
Glen Affric
Loch ma Stac
Meall a' Chràthaich
Loch a' Chràthaich
Loch na Beinne Baine
Càrn Mhic an Toisich
Aonach Shasuinn
Carn a' Chaochain
Mullach Fraoch-Choire
A'Chralaig
Sgurr nan Conbhairean
River Doe
Dundreggan
A887
Dalchreichart
Tomchrasky
Glen Moriston
Ceannacroc Lodge
Cluanie Inn
Cluanie Lodge
Loch Cluanie
Cluanie Dam
Inchnacardoch Hotel
Caledonian Canal
Fort Augustus
Ceann a' Mhain
Meall Dubh
Creag a' Mhaim
Auchteraw
River Oich
Caledonian Canal
Glen Tarff
Loch Loyne
A87
Glen Loyne
Glenquoich Forest
Glen Garry
Loch Lundie
Bridge of Oich
Newtown
Aberchalder Lodge
Glen Garry
Inchlaggan
Loch Garry
Invergarry
River Garry
Tomdoun
Greenfield
Mandally
Loch Oich
A82
Glas Bheinn
Ben Tee
Blar-na-Leine
Laggan
Càrn Dearg
Glengarry Forest
Kilfinnan
Meall Blair
Meall Coire nan Saobhaidh
Sron a' Choire Ghairbh
Corriegour Lodge Hotel
Loch Lochy
Gleann Cia-aig
Great Glen Way
Brae Roy Lodge
Loch Arkaig
Ardechive
Letterfinlay Lodge Hotel
Beinniaruinn
Glen Gloy
Glen Roy
Clunes
Càrn Dearg
Glen Mallie
Achnacarry
Invergloy
Clan Cameron
Bunarkaig
B8005
Glenfintaig Lodge
Coire Ceirsle
Beinn Bhan
Glen Roy
Beinn Chaoru
Gairlochy
Glen Loy
B8004
Stronaba
Bohuntine
Spean Bridge
Brackletter
Mulroy
Creag Dhubh
Stob a' Ghrianain
Commando Memorial
Inverroy
Strone
Roy Bridge
Monessie Falls
Tulloch Station
Inverlair
Glen Spean
River Lochy
The Cour
Spean
Neptune's Staircase (Locks)
Treasures of the Earth
Torcastle
Beinn Chlianaig
Fersit
Great Glen

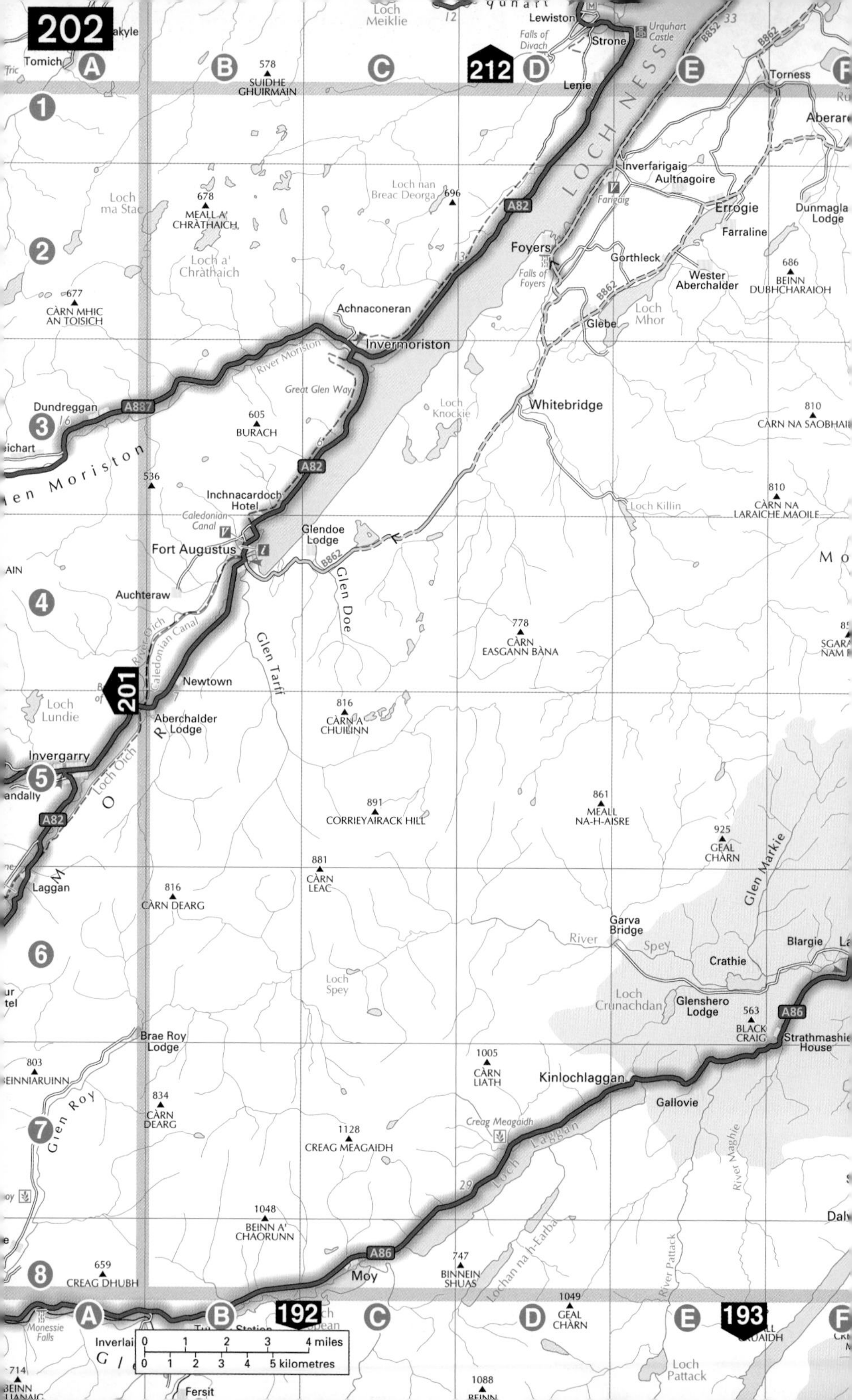
Tomich
Lewiston
Strone
Urquhart Castle
Falls of Divach
Lenie
Loch Meiklie
SUIDHE GHUIRMAIN
LOCH NESS
Torness
Aberarder
Loch ma Stac
MEALL A' CHRÀTHAICH
Loch a' Chràthaich
Loch nan Breac Deorga
Inverfarigaig
Aultnagoire
Farigaig
Errogie
Farraline
Dunmaglass Lodge
Foyers
Falls of Foyers
Gorthleck
Wester Aberchalder
BEINN DUBHCHARAIOH
CÀRN MHIC AN TOISICH
Achnaconeran
Invermoriston
Glebe
Loch Mhor
River Moriston
Great Glen Way
Dundreggan
Loch Knockie
Whitebridge
BURACH
CÀRN NA SAOBHAIDHE
Glen Moriston
Inchnacardoch Hotel
Loch Killin
CÀRN NA LARAICHE MAOILE
Caledonian Canal
Glendoe Lodge
Fort Augustus
Glen Doe
Auchteraw
River Oich
CÀRN EASGANN BÀNA
Newtown
Glen Tarff
Loch Lundie
Aberchalder Lodge
CÀRN A' CHUILINN
Invergarry
Loch Oich
CORRIEYAIRACK HILL
MEALL NA-H-AISRE
GEAL CHÀRN
CÀRN LEAC
Laggan
CÀRN DEARG
Glen Markie
Garva Bridge
River Spey
Blargie
Crathie
Loch Spey
Loch Crunachdan
Glenshero Lodge
BLACK CRAIG
Strathmashie House
Brae Roy Lodge
CÀRN LIATH
Kinlochlaggan
Gallovie
Glen Roy
CÀRN DEARG
CREAG MEAGAIDH
Creag Meagaidh
Loch Laggan
River Maghie
BEINN A' CHAORUNN
Lochan na h-Earba
River Pattack
BINNEIN SHUAS
CREAG DHUBH
Moy
GEAL CHÀRN
Monessie Falls
Inverlair
Fersit
Loch Pattack
0 1 2 3 4 miles
0 1 2 3 4 5 kilometres
212
201
192
193

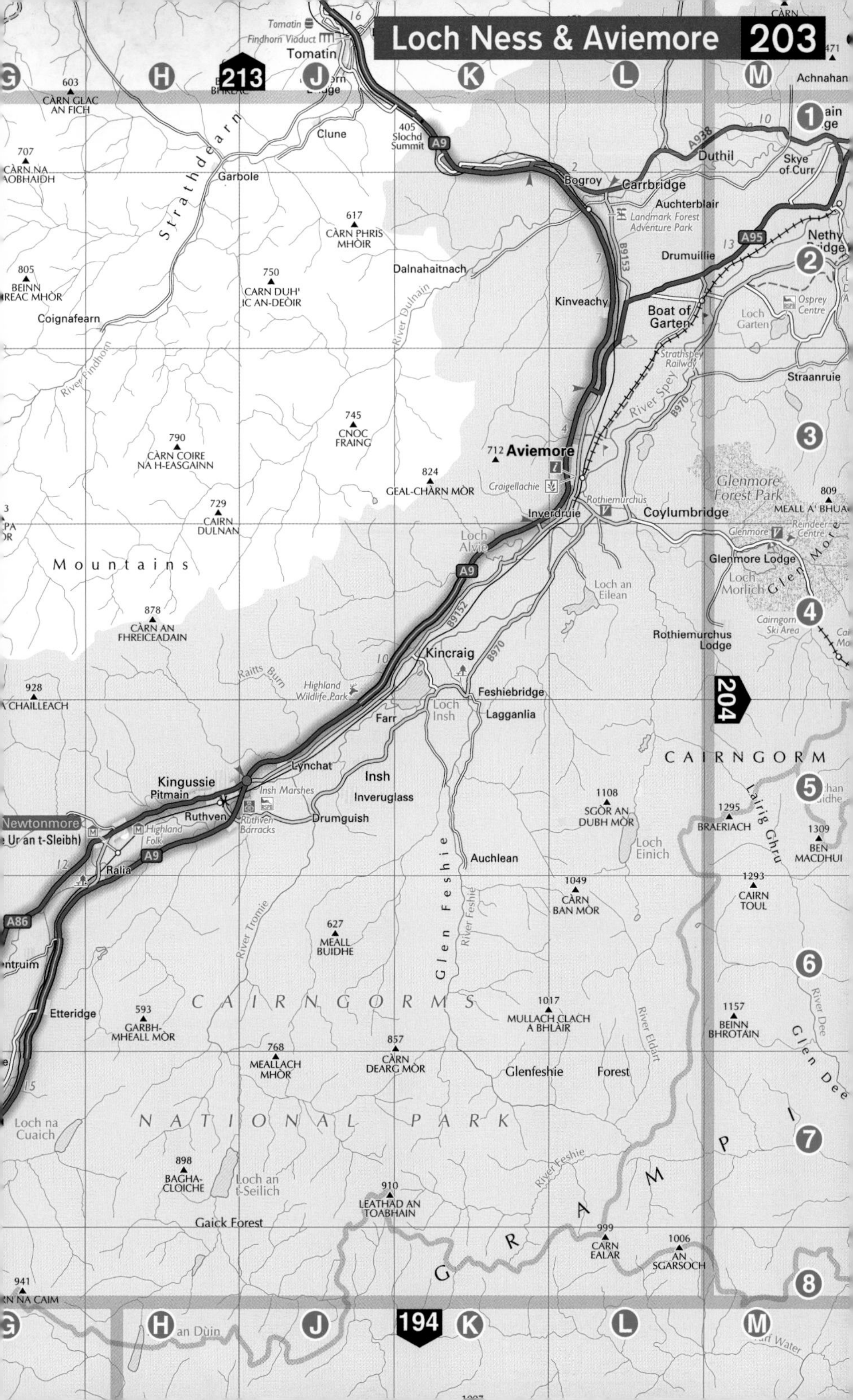
Tomatin
Findhorn Viaduct
Tomatin
213
603
CÀRN GLAC AN FICH
Strathdearn
Clune
405
Slochd Summit
A9
707
CÀRN NA
Garbole
Bogroy
Carrbridge
Duthil
A938
Skye of Curr
Auchterblair
Landmark Forest Adventure Park
617
CÀRN PHRIS MHÒIR
Nethy Bridge
A95
B9153
Drumuillie
805
750
CARN DUH'
Dalnahaitnach
River Dulnain
Kinveachy
Boat of Garten
Osprey Centre
Loch Garten
Coignafearn
River Findhorn
Strathspey Railway
River Spey
B970
Straanruie
745
CNOC FRAING
790
CÀRN COIRE NA H-EASGAINN
712
Aviemore
824
GEAL-CHÀRN MÒR
Craigellachie
Glenmore Forest Park
809
MEALL A' BHUA
729
CAIRN DULNAN
Rothiemurchus
Inverdruie
Coylumbridge
Loch Alvie
Glenmore
Reindeer Centre
Mountains
A9
Glenmore Lodge
Loch Morlich
Glen More
Loch an Eilean
878
CÀRN AN FHREICEADAIN
B9152
Cairngorm Ski Area
Rothiemurchus Lodge
Kincraig
B970
Raitts Burn
Highland Wildlife Park
928
Feshiebridge
204
Loch Insh
Lagganlia
Farr
CAIRNGORM
Lynchat
Kingussie
Pitmain
Insh
Insh Marshes
Inveruglass
1108
SGÒR AN DUBH MÒR
1295
BRAERIACH
Lairig Ghru
1309
BEN MACDHUI
Newtonmore
Ruthven
Ruthven Barracks
Highland Folk
Drumguish
A9
Ralia
Glen Feshie
Auchlean
Loch Einich
1049
CÀRN BAN MÒR
1293
CAIRN TOUL
A86
River Feshie
River Tromie
627
MEALL BUIDHE
Etteridge
593
GARBH-MHEALL MÒR
CAIRNGORMS
1017
MULLACH CLACH A BHLÀIR
River Eldart
1157
BEINN BHROTAIN
River Dee
Glen Dee
768
MEALLACH MHÒR
857
CÀRN DEARG MÒR
Glenfeshie
Forest
Loch na Cuaich
NATIONAL PARK
898
BAGHA-CLOICHE
Loch an t-Seilich
River Feshie
910
LEATHAD AN TOABHAIN
Gaick Forest
GRAMPI
999
CARN EALAR
1006
AN SGARSOCH
941
194
an Dùin

Grantown-on-Spey
Cromdale
Glenlivet
Hills of Cromdale
Achnahannet
Craggan
Dulnain Bridge
Speybridge
Tomnavoulin
Duthil
Skye of Curr
Carrbridge
Bogroy
Auchterblair
Landmark Forest Adventure Park
Speyside Way
Auchnarrow
Glen Lochy
Strath Avon
Nethy Bridge
CÀRN NA LOINNE
Bridge of Brown
Drumuillie
Lettoch
Tomintoul
Bridge of Avon
Milton
Dell Wood (Abernethy)
Osprey Centre
Boat of Garten
Loch Garten
Glen Brown
Dorback Lodge
Delnabo
Strathspey Railway
River Spey
Straanruie
River Nethy
CÀRN TUADHAM
Snow gates
GEAL CHÀRN
Glenmore Forest Park
MEALL A' BHUACHAILLE
CARN BHEADHAIR
CRAIG VEANN
Rothiemurchus
Coylumbridge
Glenmore
Reindeer Centre
Glenmore Lodge
Loch Morlich
Glen More
MAIM SUIM
Loch an Eilean
BIG GARVOUN
River Avon
CAIRNGORMS
Glen Avon
Cairngorm Ski Area
Cairngorm Mountain Funicular
Rothiemurchus Lodge
THE BRUACH
CAIRN GORM
Loch Builg
NATIONAL
CAIRNGORM
Loch Avon
BEN AVON
Lochan Buidhe
Loch Etchachan
BEINN A CHAORRUINN
NORTH TOP
SGÒR AN DUBH MÒR
BRAERIACH
Lairig Ghru
MOUNTAINS
River Gairn
BEN MACDHUI
CÀRN EÀS
CULARDOCH
Loch Einich
PARK
SOUTH TOP
CAIRN TOUL
BEINN BHREAC
Glen Derry
MOUNT
MEALL GORM
Quoich Water
Glen Lui
Linn of Dee
BEINN BHROTAIN
River Dee
Braemar
Keiloch
A93
Snow gates
Mar Lodge Estate
Allanaquoich
River Eidart
SGOR MOR
Glen Dee
Forest
Inverey
MORRONE HILL
GRAMPIAN
CARN LIATH
Clunie Water
Loch Callater
CAIRN TAGGART
CARN EALAR
AN SGARSOCH
CARN BHAC
Glen Ey
SGOR MOR
CÀRN AN TUIRC
Baddoch Burn
Glenshee
214
203
195
A95
A938
A939
B970
B9153
B9136
B9008
0 1 2 3 4 miles
0 1 2 3 4 5 kilometres

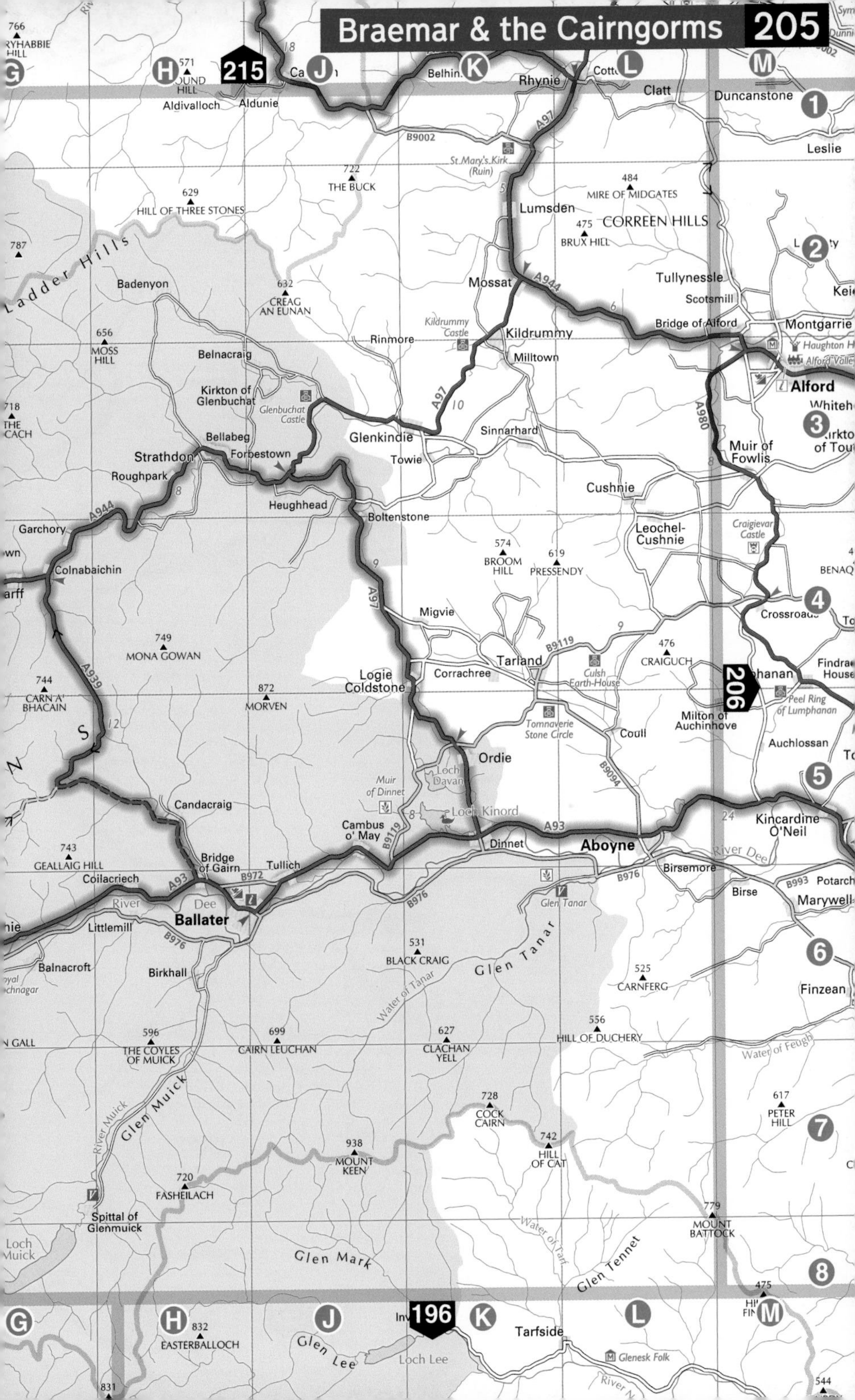
215
206
196
Rhynie
Clatt
Duncanstone
Leslie
B9002
St Mary's Kirk (Ruin)
722 THE BUCK
629 HILL OF THREE STONES
484 MIRE OF MIDGATES
Lumsden
475 BRUX HILL
CORREEN HILLS
Ladder Hills
Badenyon
632 CREAG AN EUNAN
Mossat
A944
Tullynessle
Scotsmill
Bridge of Alford
Montgarrie
Haughton
Alford Valley
Alford
Kildrummy Castle
Kildrummy
Milltown
Rinmore
656 MOSS HILL
Belnacraig
Kirkton of Glenbuchat
Glenbuchat Castle
A97
A980
Muir of Fowlis
Glenkindie
Towie
Sinnarhard
Bellabeg
Strathdon
Forbestown
Roughpark
Heughhead
Cushnie
Garchory
Boltenstone
Leochel-Cushnie
Craigievar Castle
Colnabaichin
574 BROOM HILL
619 PRESSENDY
BENAQ
Crossroads
749 MONA GOWAN
Migvie
B9119
Tarland
476 CRAIGUCH
Culsh Earth-House
Findrack House
744 CARN A' BHACAIN
A939
872 MORVEN
Logie Coldstone
Corrachree
Tomnaverie Stone Circle
Milton of Auchinhove
Peel Ring of Lumphanan
Coull
Auchlossan
Ordie
B9094
Loch Davan
Muir of Dinnet
Candacraig
Loch Kinord
A93
Cambus o' May
Dinnet
Aboyne
Kincardine O'Neil
River Dee
Birsemore
B976
743 GEALLAIG HILL
Bridge of Gairn
Tullich
B972
Coilacriech
Glen Tanar
Birse
B993
Potarch
Marywell
Ballater
Littlemill
531 BLACK CRAIG
Balnacroft
Birkhall
Water of Tanar
525 CARNFERG
Finzean
596 THE COYLES OF MUICK
699 CAIRN LEUCHAN
627 CLACHAN YELL
556 HILL OF DUCHERY
Water of Feugh
Glen Muick
River Muick
728 COCK CAIRN
617 PETER HILL
938 MOUNT KEEN
742 HILL OF CAT
720 FASHEILACH
Spittal of Glenmuick
Loch Muick
Water of Tarf
779 MOUNT BATTOCK
Glen Mark
Glen Tennet
475
832 EASTERBALLOCH
Tarfside
Glen Lee
Loch Lee
Glenesk Folk
831
544
766
571
Aldivalloch
Aldunie
787
718

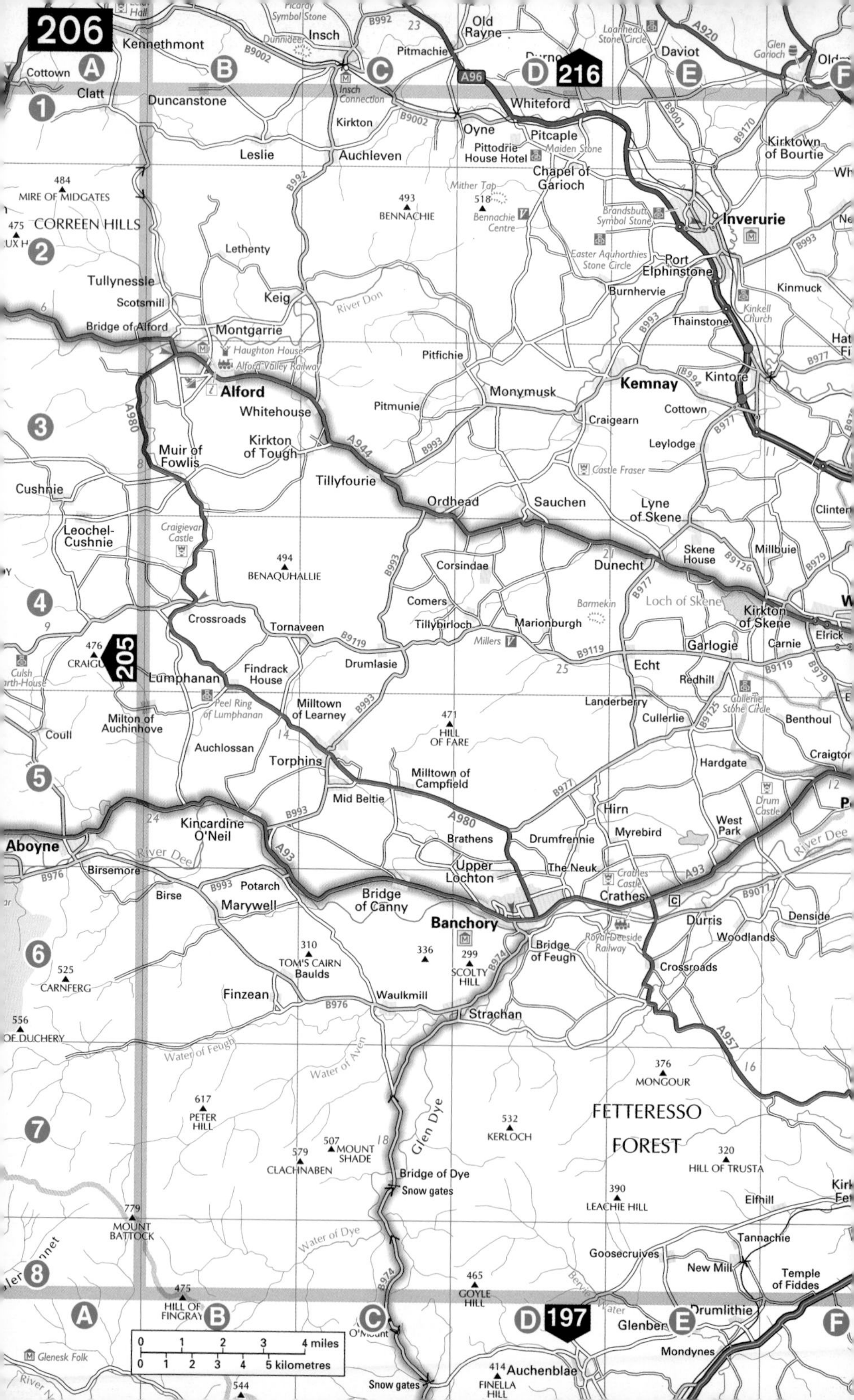
Kennethmont
Insch
Old Rayne
Pitmachie
Daviot
Cottown
Clatt
Duncanstone
Whiteford
Kirkton
Oyne
Pitcaple
Leslie
Auchleven
Pittodrie House Hotel
Maiden Stone
Chapel of Garioch
Kirktown of Bourtie
Inverurie
MIRE OF MIDGATES
CORREEN HILLS
BENNACHIE
Bennachie Centre
Mither Tap
Brandsbutt Symbol Stone
Easter Aquhorthies Stone Circle
Port Elphinstone
Lethenty
Tullynessle
Scotsmill
Keig
River Don
Burnhervie
Kinmuck
Thainstone
Kinkell Church
Bridge of Alford
Montgarrie
Haughton House
Alford Valley Railway
Pitfichie
Kintore
Alford
Whitehouse
Monymusk
Kemnay
Pitmunie
Craigearn
Cottown
Muir of Fowlis
Kirkton of Tough
Leylodge
Castle Fraser
Cushnie
Tillyfourie
Ordhead
Sauchen
Lyne of Skene
Leochel-Cushnie
Craigievar Castle
BENAQUHALLIE
Corsindae
Dunecht
Skene House
Millbuie
Comers
Tillybirloch
Marionburgh
Barmekin
Loch of Skene
Kirkton of Skene
Elrick
Crossroads
Tornaveen
Millers
Garlogie
Carnie
CRAIGIE
Lumphanan
Findrack House
Drumlasie
Echt
Redhill
Peel Ring of Lumphanan
Milltown of Learney
Landerberry
Cullerlie Stone Circle
Cullerlie
Benthoul
Milton of Auchinhove
Coull
Auchlossan
HILL OF FARE
Torphins
Milltown of Campfield
Hardgate
Craigton
Mid Beltie
Drum Castle
Kincardine O'Neil
Hirn
West Park
Aboyne
Brathens
Drumfrennie
Myrebird
River Dee
Upper Lochton
The Neuk
Crathes Castle
Birsemore
Potarch
Birse
Marywell
Bridge of Canny
Crathes
Durris
Banchory
Denside
Woodlands
Royal Deeside Railway
Bridge of Feugh
TOM'S CAIRN
Baulds
SCOLTY HILL
Crossroads
CARNFERG
Finzean
Waulkmill
Strachan
OF DUCHERY
Water of Feugh
Water of Aven
MONGOUR
PETER HILL
Glen Dye
FETTERESSO FOREST
KERLOCH
MOUNT SHADE
CLACHNABEN
HILL OF TRUSTA
Bridge of Dye
Snow gates
LEACHIE HILL
Elfhill
MOUNT BATTOCK
Water of Dye
Tannachie
Goosecruives
New Mill
Temple of Fiddes
GOYLE HILL
HILL OF FINGRAY
Bervie Water
Drumlithie
Glenbervie
Cairn O'Mount
Mondynes
Glenesk Folk
Auchenblae
FINELLA HILL
Snow gates
River N
0 1 2 3 4 miles
0 1 2 3 4 5 kilometres

Esslemont
Kirkton of Logie Buchan
Collieston
Pitmedden
Logierieve
217
Housieside
Udny Station
Newburgh
Pettymuk
Foveran
Cultercullen
Delfrigs
Causeyend
Kingseat
Balmedie
Whitecairns
Belhelvie
Potterton
Blackdog
Dyce
Middleton Park
Denmore
Stoneywood
Kirkwall Lerwick
Bankhead
Bridge of Don
Northfield
Old Aberdeen
Kittybrewster
Ruthrieston
Torry
Nigg Bay
Mannofield
Cults
Kincorth
Loirston
Nigg
Banchory-Devenick
Altens Haven
Cove Bay
Charlestown
Marywell
Hillside
Findon
Auchlee
Portlethen
Old Portlethen
Cammachmore Bay
Downies
Newtonhill
Skateraw
Muchalls
Doonie Point
Garron Point
Stonehaven Bay
Stonehaven
Dunnottar

Tairbeart (Tarbert)
Lùb Score
Borneskitaig
Kilmuir
Kilvax
Balgown
218
Loch nam Madadh (Lochmaddy)
Rubha Bhatairnis
Totscore
Idrigill
Ascrib Islands
Uig Bay
283 BEN GEARY
Geary
Trumpan
Loch Snizort
Earlish
Ardmore Point
Gillen
Hallin
Waternish
A87
DUNVEGAN HEAD
Isay
Mingay
Stein
Lusta
Loch Bay
214 BEN DIUBAIG
Loch Dunvegan
Claigan
Greshornish
Loch Greshornish
Loch Snizort
Boreraig
Bay
327 BEINN BHREAC
Treaslane
Uig
B886
Flashader
A850
Loch Pooltiel
Upperglen
Feriniquarrie
Totaig
Edinbane
Bernisdale
Oisgill Bay
Milovaig
Glendale
Colbost
Dunvegan
A850
Waterstein
Lephin
B884
Colbost Croft
Dunvegan
Skinidin
Giant Angus MacAskill
Kilmuir
Neist Point
Lonmore
265 BEN AKETIL
271 CRUACHAN BEINN A' CHEARCAILL
Caroy River
Moonen Bay
Duirinish
Roskhill
469 HEALAVAL MORE
Roag
Ramasaig
Orbost
Vatten
ISLE
Hoe Rape
488 HEALAVAL BHEAG
Harlosh
Loch Caroy
A863
Glen Ose
Ose
Hoe Point
Harlosh Island
Colbost Point
368 BEINN NA BOINEID
Dun Beag
Bracadale
Tarner Island
Struan
Coillore
Loch Bracadale
Ullinish Lodge Hotel
Wiay
Idrigill Point
Oronsay
Portnalong
Fiskavaig
Loch Harport
B8009
Rubha nan Clach
Fernilea
Talisker
369 ARNAVAL
Carbost
Merkadale
Talisker Bay
Talisker
Glen Eynort
Minginish
447 BEINN BHREAC
Grula
198
0 1 2 3 4 miles
0 1 2 3 4 5 kilometres
Loch Eynort

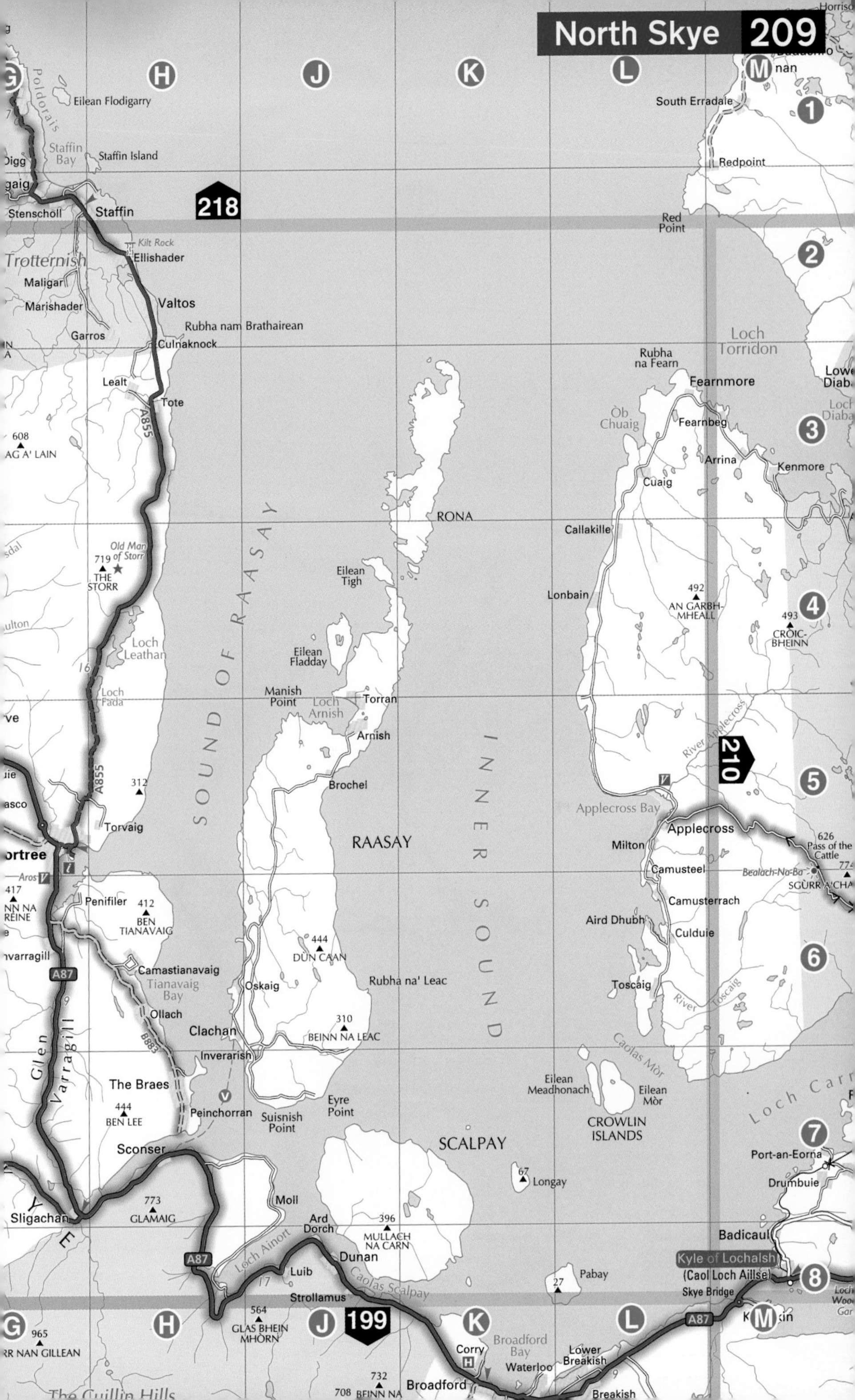

Eilean Flodigarry
Poldorais
Staffin Bay
Staffin Island
Digg
Staffin
Stenscholl
218
South Erradale
Redpoint
Red Point
Kilt Rock
Ellishader
Trotternish
Maligar
Marishader
Valtos
Rubha nam Brathairean
Garros
Culnaknock
Loch Torridon
Rubha na Fearn
Fearnmore
Lealt
Tote
A855
Òb Chuaig
Fearnbeg
Arrina
Kenmore
Cuaig
608
RONA
Callakille
Old Man of Storr
719
THE STORR
SOUND OF RAASAY
Eilean Tigh
Lonbain
492
AN GARBH-MHEALL
493
CROIC-BHEINN
Loch Leathan
Eilean Fladday
Loch Fada
Manish Point
Loch Arnish
Torran
Arnish
INNER SOUND
River Applecross
210
312
Brochel
Torvaig
Applecross Bay
Applecross
RAASAY
Milton
626
Pass of the Cattle
Aros
Camusteel
Bealach-Na-Ba
SGÙRR A' CHA
417
Penifiler
412
BEN TIANAVAIG
Camusterrach
Aird Dhubh
Culduie
444
DÙN CAAN
A87
Camastianavaig
Tianavaig Bay
Oskaig
Rubha na' Leac
Toscaig
River Toscaig
Ollach
310
BEINN NA LEAC
Clachan
B883
Glen Varragill
Caolas Mòr
Inverarish
The Braes
Eilean Meadhonach
Eilean Mòr
Loch Carron
444
BEN LEE
Peinchorran
Suisnish Point
Eyre Point
CROWLIN ISLANDS
SCALPAY
Sconser
Port-an-Eorna
67
Longay
Drumbuie
Moll
773
GLAMAIG
Sligachan
Ard Dorch
396
MULLACH NA CARN
Badicaul
Loch Ainort
Dunan
Kyle of Lochalsh
(Caol Loch Aillse)
Luib
Caolas Scalpay
Pabay
27
Skye Bridge
Strollamus
564
GLAS BHEIN MHÒRN
199
965
Broadford Bay
Corry
Lower Breakish
Waterloo
732
708
BEINN NA
Broadford
Breakish
The Cuillin Hills

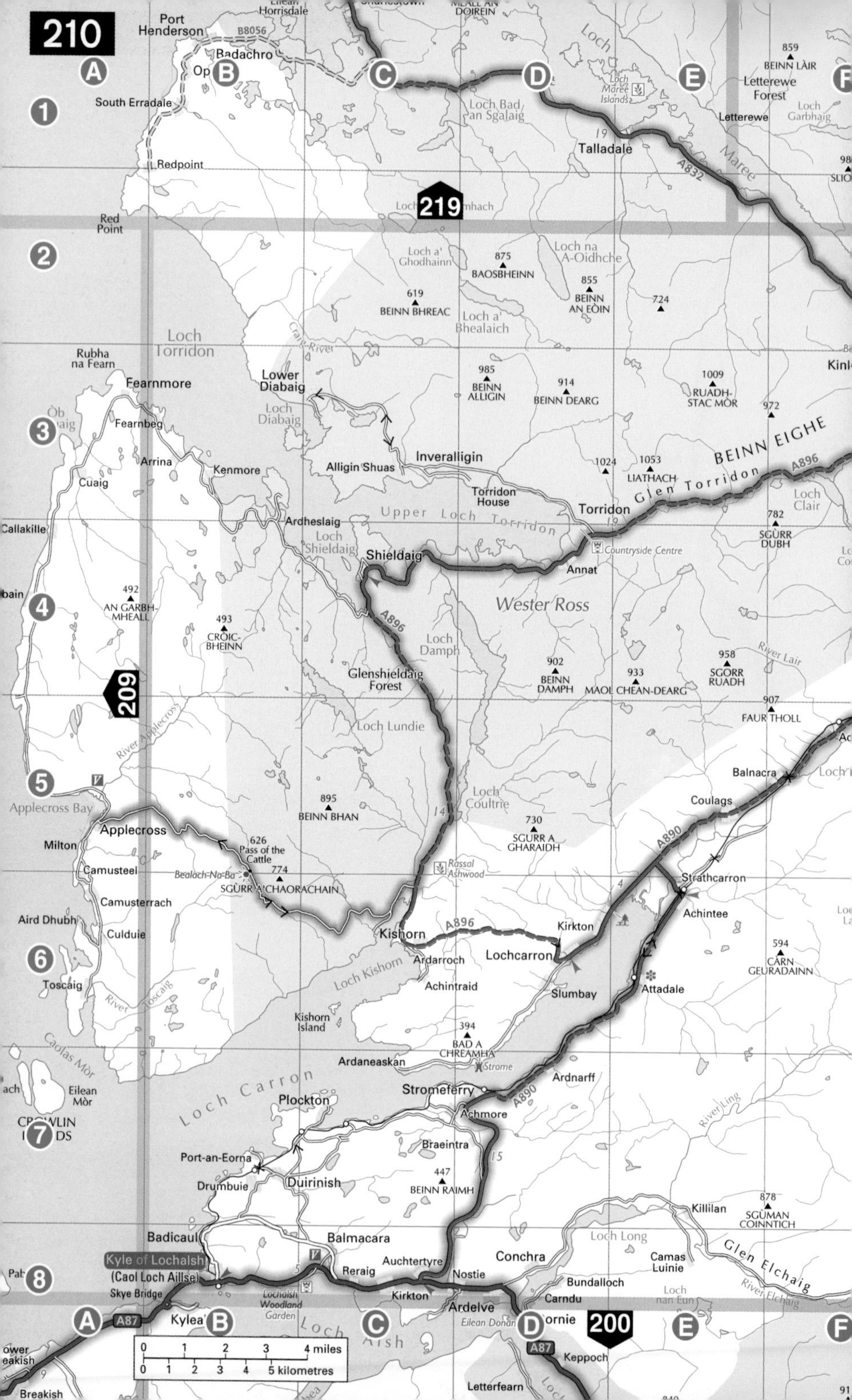

Port Henderson
B8056
Badachro
Opinan
South Erradale
Redpoint
Red Point
Loch Bad an Sgalaig
Loch Maree
Loch Maree Islands
Letterewe Forest
Letterewe
BEINN LÀIR
Talladale
A832
219
Loch a' Ghodhainn
BAOSBHEINN
Loch na A-Oidhche
BEINN AN EÒIN
BEINN BHREAC
Loch a' Bhealaich
Loch Torridon
Rubha na Fearn
Fearnmore
Fearnbeg
Arrina
Cuaig
Kenmore
Lower Diabaig
Loch Diabaig
Craig River
BEINN ALLIGIN
BEINN DEARG
RUADH-STAC MÒR
BEINN EIGHE
Inveralligin
Alligin Shuas
Torridon House
LIATHACH
Glen Torridon
A896
Loch Clair
Torridon
Upper Loch Torridon
Ardheslaig
Loch Shieldaig
Shieldaig
Countryside Centre
Annat
SGÙRR DUBH
Callakille
AN GARBH-MHEALL
CRÒIC-BHEINN
Wester Ross
Loch Damph
River Lair
BEINN DAMPH
MAOL CHEAN-DEARG
SGORR RUADH
FAUR THOLL
Glenshieldaig Forest
Loch Lundie
209
River Applecross
Balnacra
Coulags
Applecross Bay
Loch Coultrie
BEINN BHAN
Applecross
Milton
Pass of the Cattle
Bealach-Na-Ba
SGÙRR A'CHAORACHAIN
SGURR A GHARAIDH
Rassal Ashwood
A890
Strathcarron
Achintee
Camusteel
Camusterrach
Aird Dhubh
Culduie
Kishorn
Kirkton
Ardarroch
Lochcarron
CARN GEURADAINN
Toscaig
River Toscaig
Loch Kishorn
Achintraid
Slumbay
Attadale
Kishorn Island
BAD A CHREAMHA
Caolas Mòr
Ardaneaskan
Strome
Ardnarff
Eilean Mòr
Loch Carron
Plockton
Stromeferry
Achmore
River Ling
CROWLIN ISLANDS
Braeintra
Port-an-Eorna
Drumbuie
Duirinish
BEINN RAIMH
SGÙMAN COINNTICH
Killilan
Badicaul
Balmacara
Loch Long
Kyle of Lochalsh
(Caol Loch Aillse)
Auchtertyre
Reraig
Conchra
Camas Luinie
Glen Elchaig
River Elchaig
Skye Bridge
Nostie
Lochalsh Woodland Garden
Kirkton
Bundalloch
Carndu
Loch nan Eun
A87
Kyleakin
Ardelve
Eilean Donan
Dornie
200
Loch Alsh
Keppoch
Letterfearn
Breakish
0 1 2 3 4 miles
0 1 2 3 4 5 kilometres

Fannich Lodge
Loch Fannich
Corriemoille Forest
Kinlochewe Forest
BEINN NAN RAMH
A' CHAILLEACH
SGÙRR MÒR
BEINN LIATH BHEAG
Aultguish Inn
CÀRN NA DUBH CHOILLE
Corriemoille
Lochluichart
Loch Luichart
AN CABAR
Achanalt
A832
Loch Achanalt
Strath Bran
FIONN BHEINN
Achnasheen
Loch a' Chroisg
Loch Gowan
A890
Loch Sgamhain
SGÙRR MARCASAIDH
Little Scatwell
Loch Meig
SCUIR VUILLIN
CARN MHÀRTUIN
Strathconon Forest
MEALL NAN DAMH
CÀRN NACOINNICH
Loch Beannacharain
River Meig
MORUISG
BAC AN EICH
River Orrin
Glen Orrin
SGÙRR COIRE NAN EUN
Loch na Caoidhe
MAOILE LUNNDAIDH
SGÙRR A' CHAORRACHAIN
MEALLAN BUIDHE
CARN BÀM POLLON
SGÙRR A' CHOIRE GHLAIS
SGÙRR NA RUAIDHE
Loch Monar
Glen Strathfarrar
River Farrar
Loch Beannacharan
Inchvuilt
Loch an Tachdaidh
An Gead Loch
AN CRUACHAN
SGÒR NA DIOLLAID
CÀRN GORM
SGÙRR NA LAPAICH
Glencannich Forest
An-Riabhachan
River Cannich
River Glass
Cannich
Strath Glass
Chambered Cairn
Corrimony
Loch Mullardoch
Glen Cannich
Fasnakyle
TOLL CREAGACH
Glen Affric
Tomich
Loch Beinn Mheadhoin
Affric Lodge
220
221
212
201

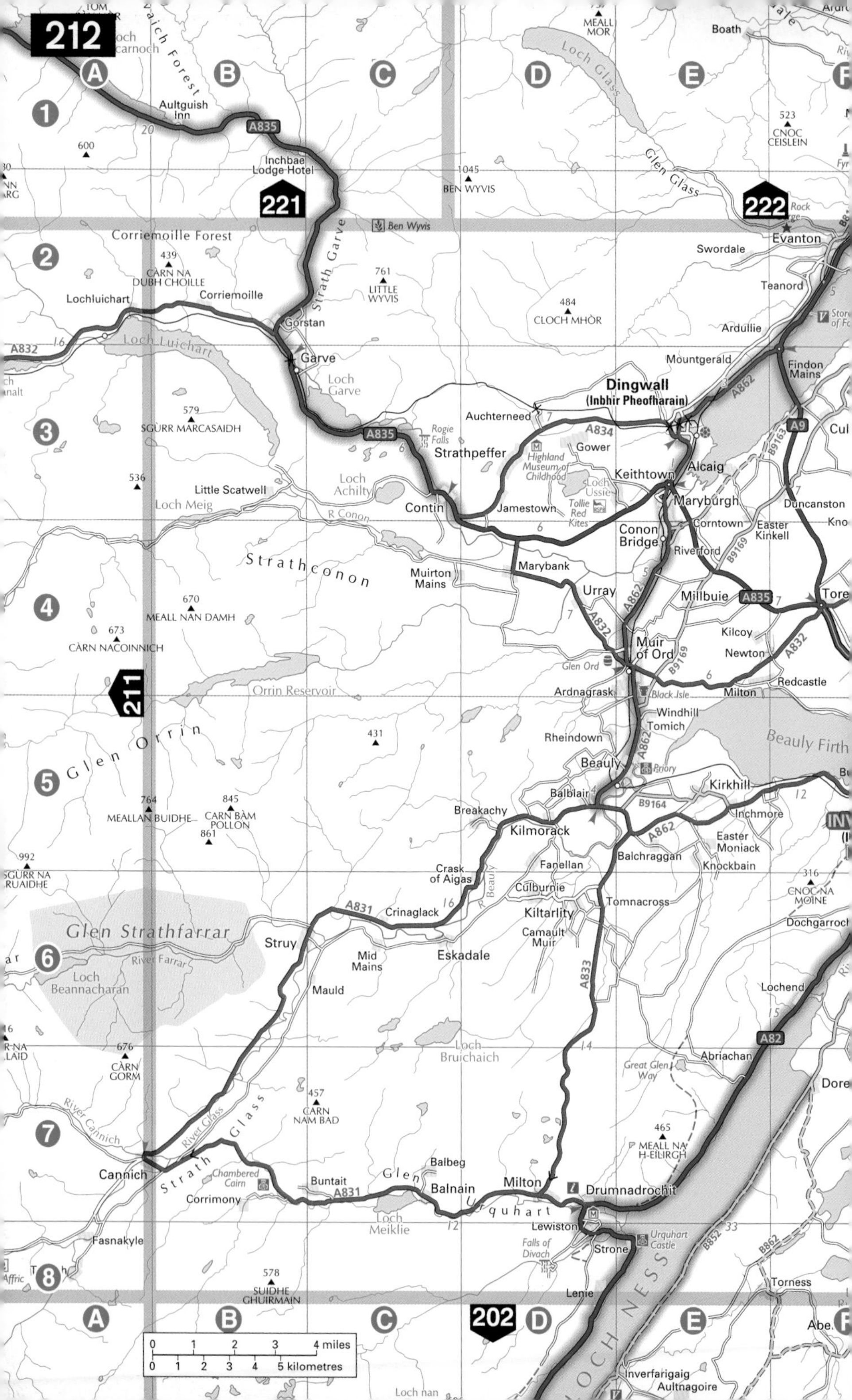

212
221
222
211
202
Aultguish Inn
Inchbae Lodge Hotel
Corriemoille Forest
Lochluichart
Corriemoille
Gorstan
Garve
Loch Luichart
Loch Garve
Strath Garve
BEN WYVIS
LITTLE WYVIS
CLOCH MHÒR
Loch Glass
Glen Glass
Boath
CNOC CEISLEIN
Evanton
Swordale
Teanord
Ardullie
Mountgerald
Findon Mains
Dingwall
(Inbhir Pheofharain)
Auchterneed
Rogie Falls
Strathpeffer
Highland Museum of Childhood
Gower
Loch Ussie
Tollie Red Kites
Keithtown
Alcaig
Maryburgh
Duncanston
Contin
Loch Achilty
Jamestown
Little Scatwell
Loch Meig
SGÙRR MARCASAIDH
CÀRN NA DUBH CHOILLE
R Conon
Strathconon
Muirton Mains
Marybank
Conon Bridge
Corntown
Easter Kinkell
Riverford
Urray
Millbuie
Tore
MEALL NAN DAMH
CÀRN NACOINNICH
Muir of Ord
Glen Ord
Kilcoy
Newton
Redcastle
Ardnagrask
Black Isle
Milton
Orrin Reservoir
Windhill
Tomich
Rheindown
Beauly Firth
Glen Orrin
Beauly
Priory
Kirkhill
Balblair
B9164
MEALLAN BUIDHE
CARN BÀM POLLON
Breakachy
Kilmorack
Inchmore
Balchraggan
Easter Moniack
Knockbain
SGÙRR NA RUAIDHE
Crask of Aigas
Fanellan
Culburnie
Kiltarlity
Tomnacross
CNOC NA MOINE
Dochgarroch
A831
Crinaglack
Camault Muir
Glen Strathfarrar
River Farrar
Loch Beannacharan
Struy
Mid Mains
Eskadale
Mauld
Lochend
Loch Bruichaich
Great Glen Way
Abriachan
CÀRN GORM
CÀRN NAM BAD
MEALL NA H-EILIRGH
River Cannich
River Glass
Strath Glass
Cannich
Chambered Cairn
Corrimony
Buntait
Glen Urquhart
Balbeg
Balnain
Milton
Drumnadrochit
Loch Meiklie
Lewiston
Falls of Divach
Strone
Urquhart Castle
Fasnakyle
SUIDHE GHUIRMAIN
Lenie
LOCH NESS
Torness
Inverfarigaig
Aultnagoire
Loch nan
A835
A832
A834
A862
A9
A82
A833
B9163
B9169
B852
B862
Ben Wyvis
0 1 2 3 4 miles
0 1 2 3 4 5 kilometres

Inverness & Black Isle
213
Kildary
Milton
Kilmuir
Barbaraville
Rhicullen
Tomich
Balintraid
Nigg Bay
Achnagarron
Saltburn
Invergordon
Pitcalnie
Nigg
Nigg Ferry
June-Sept
223
Cromarty
Sutors Stacks
Hugh Miller's Cottage
Balblair
Resolis
Udale Bay
Cromarty Bay
Newton
Jemimaville
Allerton
Navity
Upper Eathie
MORAY FIRTH
Culbin Forest
Kintessack
Raddery
Fairy Glen
Rosemarkie
Whiteness Head
Nairn
(Inbhir Nàrann)
Culbin Sands
Brodie Castle
Brodie
Cathedral
Groam House
Fort George & The Highlanders' Museum
Fortrose
Chanonry Point
Avoch
Tradespark
Ardersier
Boath Doocot
Househill
Auldearn
1645
Moss-side
Gollanfield
Foynesfield
Whitemire
Conicavel
Lochside
Inverness
Fisherton
MORAY FIRTH
Righoul
Clephanton
Cawdor
Piperhill
Fornighty
Littlemill
Logie Steading
Kilmuir
Castle Stuart
Easter Dalziel
Tornagrain
Culcharry
Alturlie Point
Croy
River Nairn
214
Relugas
Newton
Cantraywood
Balloch
Kirkton of Barevan
Clunas
Redburn
Culloden
Smithton
Culloden Viaduct
Ardclach Bell Tower
Ferness
Culcabock
Resaurie
Culloden Battlefield & Visitor Centre
Clava Cairns
323 CÀRN MAOL
401 CÀRN A' CHRASGIE
Drummossie Muir
Milton of Leys
Knagael Stone
Daviot House
548 BEINN BHUIDHE MHOR
Dulsie Bridge
Daviot
609 CÀRN NAN TRI-TIGHEARNAN
464
Lochindorb
Lochindorb Lodge
483
Loch Moy
Moy
Ruthven
River Findhorn
Farr
615 CÀRN NA H-EASGAINN
633 CÀRN AN T-SEAN-LIATHANAICH
Balvraid
485 CÀRN SGRIOB
Tomatin
Findhorn Viaduct
Raigbeg
617
659 CÀRN GLAS-CHOIRE
471
Tomatin
600 BEINN BHREAC
Findhorn Bridge
603 CÀRN GLAC AN FICH
203
405 Slochd Summit
Dulnain Bridge
Duthil
Skye of Curr
707 CÀRN NA AOBHAIDH
Garbole
Bogroy
Carrbridge

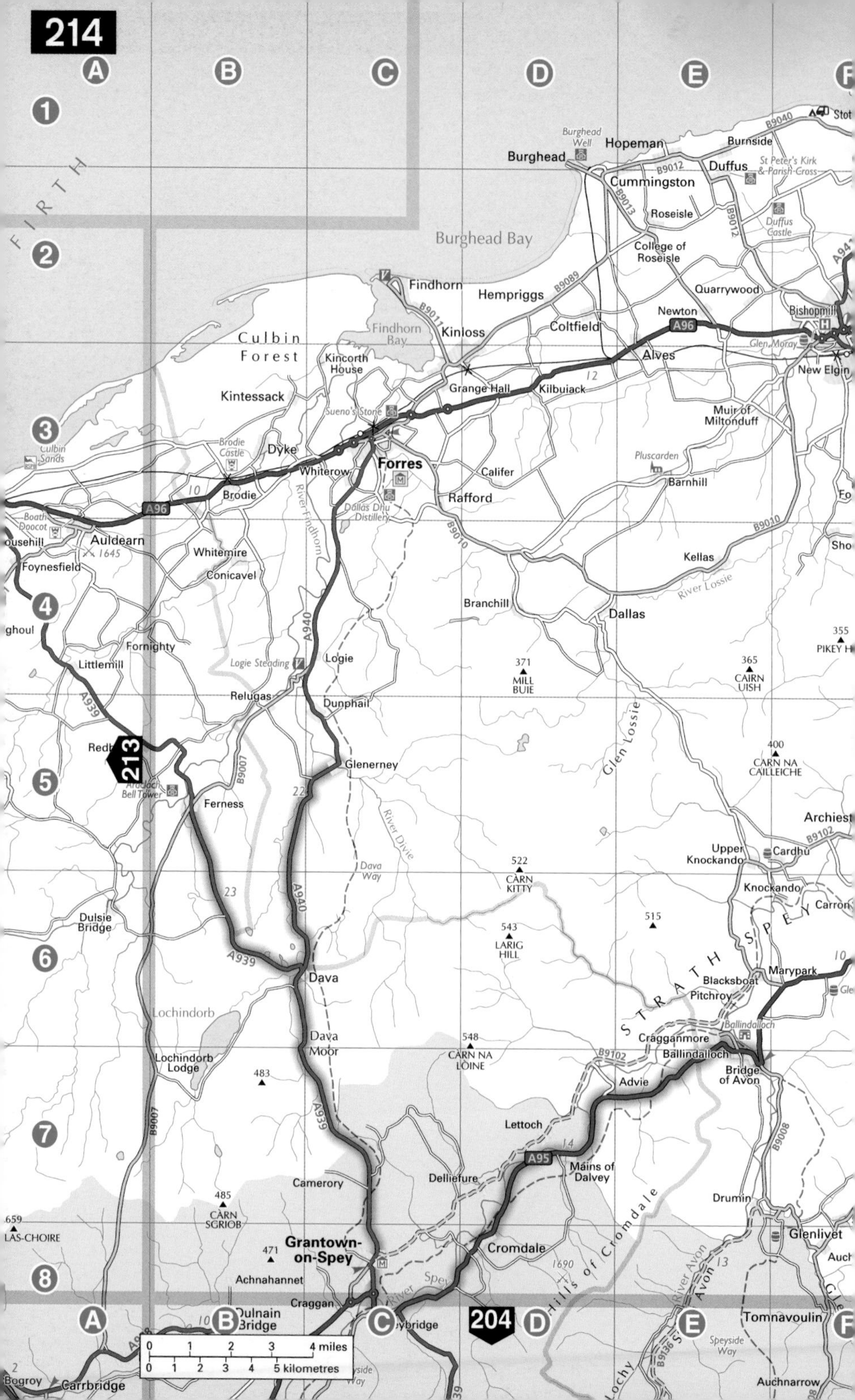
Burghead
Hopeman
Burghead Well
Burnside
Duffus
Cummingston
St Peter's Kirk & Parish Cross
Roseisle
Duffus Castle
Burghead Bay
College of Roseisle
Findhorn
Hempriggs
Quarrywood
Newton
Bishopmill
Coltfield
Kinloss
Findhorn Bay
Culbin Forest
Kincorth House
Alves
Glen Moray
New Elgin
Grange Hall
Kilbuiack
Kintessack
Sueno's Stone
Muir of Miltonduff
Culbin Sands
Brodie Castle
Dyke
Pluscarden
Forres
Whiterow
Califer
Barnhill
Brodie
Rafford
Dallas Dhu Distillery
Boath Doocot
Auldearn
1645
Whitemire
Kellas
Foynesfield
Conicavel
River Findhorn
River Lossie
Branchill
Dallas
Fornighty
Littlemill
Logie Steading
Logie
371 MILL BUIE
365 CAIRN UISH
355 PIKEY H
Relugas
Dunphail
Glen Lossie
400 CARN NA CAILLEICHE
Glenerney
Ardclach Bell Tower
Ferness
River Divie
Archiest
Upper Knockando
Cardhu
Dava Way
522 CARN KITTY
Knockando
Carron
515
543 LARIG HILL
Dulsie Bridge
Dava
Marypark
Blacksboat
Pitchroy
STRATH SPEY
Lochindorb
Ballindalloch
Cragganmore
548 CARN NA LOINE
Dava Moor
Lochindorb Lodge
483
Advie
Bridge of Avon
Lettoch
Mains of Dalvey
Dellefure
Camerory
Drumin
485 CARN SGRIOB
659 LAS-CHOIRE
Grantown-on-Spey
Cromdale
Glenlivet
471
Hills of Cromdale
River Avon
Achnahannet
River Spey
Craggan
Dulnain Bridge
Tomnavoulin
Speyside Way
Carrbridge
Bogroy
Auchnarrow
A96
A940
A939
A95
B9007
B9010
B9011
B9012
B9013
B9040
B9089
B9102
B9008
B9136
213
204
0 1 2 3 4 miles
0 1 2 3 4 5 kilometres

G
H
J
K
L
M
1
Portknockie
Bow Fiddle Rock
Findochty
Cullen Bay
Cullen
Findlater
Sandend Bay
Spey Bay
Scottish Dolphin Centre
Portessie
Buckie
Sandend
Portsoy
Stonewells
Kingston on Spey
Spey Bay
Moray Firth
Buckpool
Rathven
Lintmill
A98
Tochieneal
Birkenbog
2
Lochill
A942
field
Nether Dallachy
A98
321
BIN OF CULLEN
Innesmill
Garmouth
Upper Dallachy
A990
Portgordon
Milton
Fordyce
Bogmoor
B9015
B9104
Newton
Broadley
Drybridge
Deskford
Deskford Church
B9022
The Lochs
Stynie
Auchenhalrig
Bridge of Tynet
Berryhillock
Clochan
Windsole
A96
Baxters Visitor Centre
Mosstodloch
Crofts of Dipple
Fochabers
272
ADDIE HILL
Craibstone
3
B9103
B9016
B9018
Dipple
Braes of Enzie
Cornhill
264
WHITEASH HILL
301
MILLSTONE HILL
313
LURG HILL
Orbliston
Ordiequish
Gordonstown
A95
B9023
A96
Inchberry
429
KNOCK HILL
Glenbarry
250
THIEF'S HILL
Forgie
Grange Crossroads
Berryhillock
271
WETHER HILL
262
Sound Muir
Aultmore
Forgieside
Bracobrae
Lootcherbrae
Cairnty
Newmill
Davoch of Grange
Knock
4
Garbity
Rumbach
Drumnagorrach
Auchroisk
Upper Mulben
B9017
Farmtown
Bridge of Marnoch
B9015
B9103
Mulben
Strathisla
A95
B9117
Fife Keith
Keith
River Isla
Deanshaugh
Rosarie
365
MEIKLE BALLOCH
Milltown of Rothiemay
Rothes
Speyside Way
Tauchers
B9117
471
BEN AIGAN
A95
B9014
Keith & Dufftown Railway
338
HILL OF TOWIE
A96
B9118
Arndilly House
372
KNOCKAN
216
Ruthven
Dandaleith
Maggieknockater
Bognie
5
Craigellachie
Cairnie
A97
B9115
Drummuir
B9022
A941
Aberlour
Glenfiddich
B9014
River Deveron
Nordic Ski Centre
Castle
Affleck
Dufftown
Balvenie Castle
Milltown of Auchindoun
A920
Drumblade
Huntly
6
A96
Kirktown of Mortlach
Haugh of Glass
Auchindoun Castle
Strath Bogie
Thomastown
Bridgend
A941
Kirkstile
Hillhead
503
Glens of
Glen Fiddich
Culdrain
Achnastank
525
419
WICHACH HILL
466
7
Gartly
Kirkney
440
CRANSMILL HILL
Bridgend
A97
River Fiddich
Leith Hall
564
TAP O' NOTH
Mains of Lesmoir
766
A941
Kennethmont
B9002
8
571
ROUND HILL
Cabrach
Belhinnie
Rhynie
Cottown
Clatt
Aldunie
205
A97
B9002
St Mary's Kirk (Ruin)
Leslie
722
THE BUCK
484

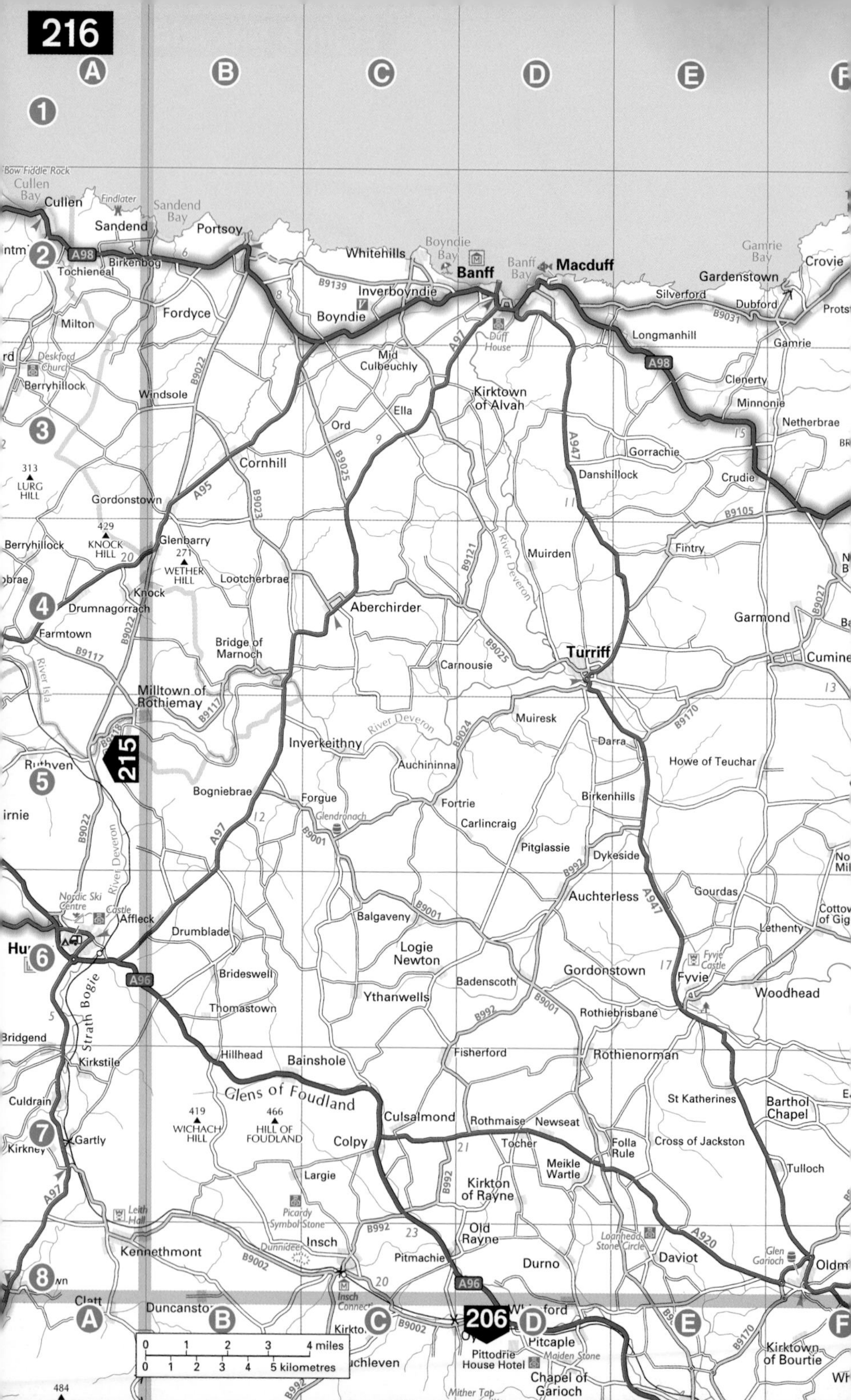
Bow Fiddle Rock
Cullen Bay
Cullen
Findlater
Sandend Bay
Sandend
Portsoy
Birkenbog
Tochieneal
A98
Whitehills
Boyndie Bay
Banff
Banff Bay
Macduff
Gamrie Bay
Crovie
Gardenstown
Silverford
Dubford
B9031
B9139
Inverboyndie
Boyndie
Fordyce
Milton
Deskford Church
Berryhillock
Windsole
B9022
Mid Culbeuchly
A97
Duff House
Longmanhill
Gamrie
Clenerty
Minnonie
Netherbrae
Kirktown of Alvah
Ella
Ord
Cornhill
A95
B9025
A947
Gorrachie
Danshillock
Crudie
313 LURG HILL
Gordonstown
429 KNOCK HILL
Glenbarry
271 WETHER HILL
B9023
B9105
Berryhillock
Muirden
Fintry
River Deveron
B9121
Lootcherbrae
Knock
Drumnagorrach
Aberchirder
Garmond
B9027
Farmtown
Bridge of Marnoch
B9117
River Isla
Carnousie
Turriff
Cumine
Milltown of Rothiemay
Muiresk
B9170
Inverkeithny
B9024
Darra
Howe of Teuchar
215
Ruthven
Auchininna
Bogniebrae
Forgue
Fortrie
Birkenhills
Glendronach
B9001
Carlincraig
Pitglassie
Dykeside
B992
Auchterless
Gourdas
Nordic Ski Centre
Castle
Affleck
Balgaveny
Lethenty
Drumblade
Logie Newton
Gordonstown
Fyvie Castle
Fyvie
Woodhead
A96
Brideswell
Badenscoth
Strath Bogie
Thomastown
Ythanwells
Rothiebrisbane
Bridgend
Fisherford
Hillhead
Bainshole
Rothienorman
Kirkstile
Glens of Foudland
St Katherines
Barthol Chapel
Culdrain
Culsalmond
Rothmaise
Newseat
419 WICHACH HILL
466 HILL OF FOUDLAND
Gartly
Colpy
Tocher
Folla Rule
Cross of Jackston
Kirkney
Largie
Meikle Wartle
Tulloch
Kirkton of Rayne
Leith Hall
Picardy Symbol Stone
Old Rayne
Loanhead Stone Circle
A920
Kennethmont
Dunnideer
Insch
Pitmachie
Durno
Daviot
Glen Garioch
B9002
Clatt
Duncanston
Insch Connect
206
Pitcaple
Maiden Stone
Pittodrie House Hotel
Chapel of Garioch
Mither Tap
Kirktown of Bourtie
B9170
0 1 2 3 4 miles
0 1 2 3 4 5 kilometres
484

Rosehearty
Sandhaven
Castle Lighthouse & Museum
Kinnaird Head
Fraserburgh
Pittulie
Peathill
Craigiefold
Fraserburgh Bay
Kirktown
Cairnbulg
Inverallochy
Percyhorner
Pitblae
Maggie's Hoosie
Whitelinks Bay
Coburby
Mid Ardlaw
Boyndlie
Memsie
St Combs
Tyrie
Memsie Cairn
Rathen
Crofts of Savoch
Newburgh
Lonmay
Rattray Head
Loch of Strathbeg
234
WAUGHTON HILL
Crimond
Blackhill
Strichen
New Leeds
Leys
Denhead
Backfolds
Kirktown
St Fergus
Fetterangus
Rora
Deer Abbey
Dunshillock
River Ugie
Maud
Aden
Mintlaw
Inverugie
Railway
Old Deer
Aberdeenshire Farming
Longside
Buchanhaven
Peterhead
Blackhill of Clackriach
Stuartfield
Inverquhomery
Peterhead Bay
Drymuir
Bulwark
Millbreck
Nether Kinmundy
Hillhead of Cocklaw
Invernettie
Nethermuir
Knaven
Clola
Boddam
Kinnadie
Blackhill
Stirling
Buchan Ness
Lendrum Terrace
Auchnagatt
Kinknockie
Longhaven
Inkhorn
Ardallie
Coldwells
Bullers of Buchan
Auchiries
Hatton
North Haven
Arthrath
Muirtack
Slains
Cruden Bay
Toll of Birness
Bogbrae
Chapel Hill
Bay of Cruden
Ythanbank
Birness
Whinnyfold
The Skares
Auchedly
Artrochie
Kinharrachie
Ythsie
Ellon
Esslemont
Kirkton of Logie Buchan
Kirktown of Slains
Collieston
Pitmedden
Logierieve
Forvie
Housieside
Udny Station
Newburgh
Pettymuk
Cultercullen
Foveran
A90
A98
A981
A952
A950
A948
A975
A920
A982
B9031
B9032
B9033
B9093
B9106
B9029
B9028
B9030
B9005
B9000
207
G
H
J
K
L
M
1
2
3
4
5
6
7
8

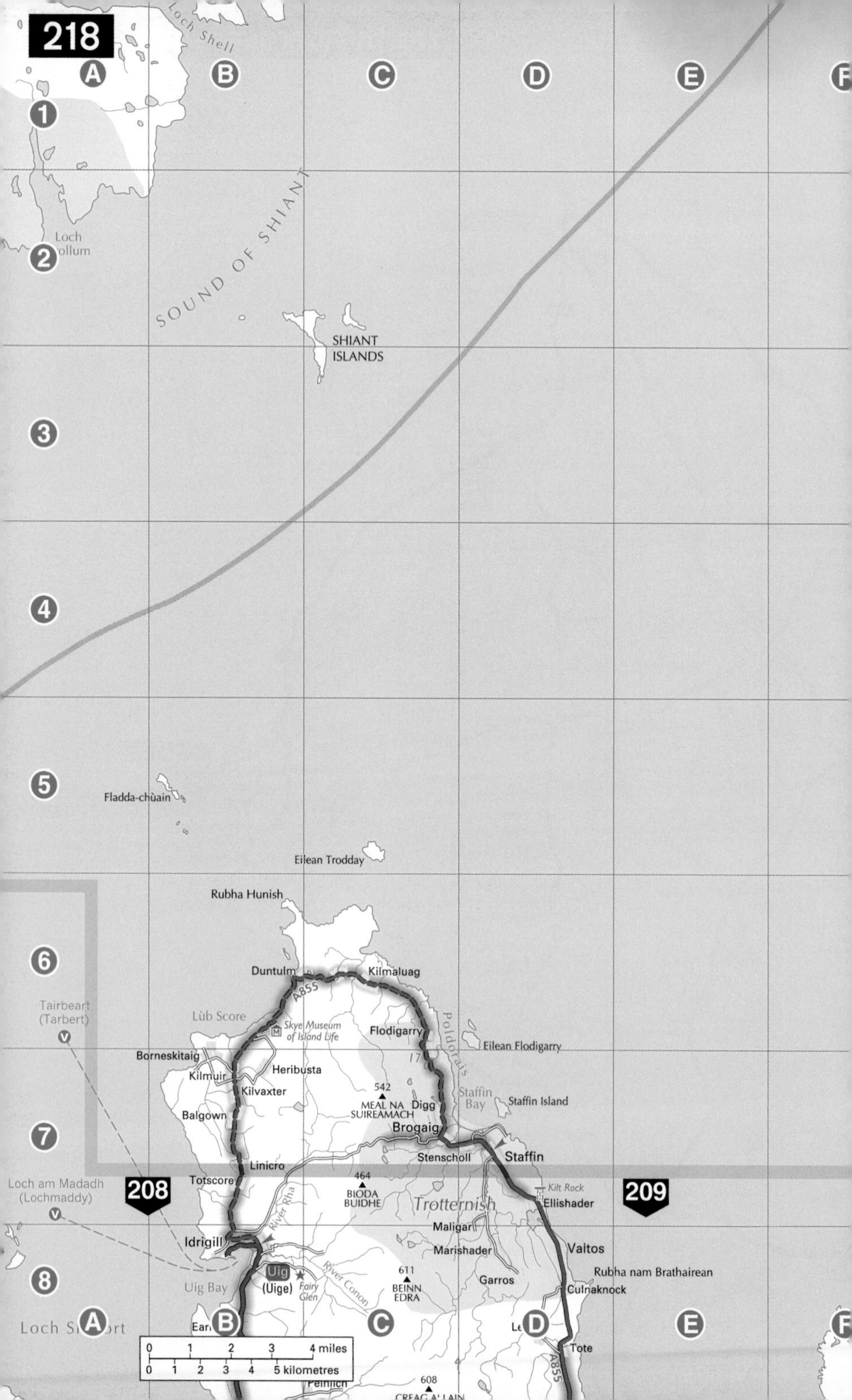
A
B
C
D
E
F
1
2
3
4
5
6
7
8
Loch Shell
Loch
SOUND OF SHIANT
SHIANT
ISLANDS
Fladda-chùain
Eilean Trodday
Rubha Hunish
Duntulm
Kilmaluag
A855
Lùb Score
Skye Museum of Island Life
Flodigarry
Eilean Flodigarry
Poldorais
Tairbeart
(Tarbert)
Borneskitaig
Kilmuir
Heribusta
Kilvaxter
542
MEAL NA
SUIREAMACH
Digg
Staffin
Bay
Staffin Island
Balgown
Brogaig
Stenscholl
Staffin
Linicro
Loch am Madadh
(Lochmaddy)
Totscore
208
464
BIODA
BUIDHE
Trotternish
Kilt Rock
Ellishader
209
River Rha
Maligar
Idrigill
Marishader
Valtos
Uig
(Uige)
Fairy
Glen
River Conon
611
BEINN
EDRA
Garros
Rubha nam Brathairean
Culnaknock
Uig Bay
Loch Sport
Tote
608
0
1
2
3
4 miles
0
1
2
3
4
5 kilometres

Steornabhagh (Stornoway)
Tanera Beg
Tanera Mòr
Glas-leac Beag
Eilean Dubh
Priest Island
Greenstone Point
Cailleach Head
Rubha Beag
Mellon Udrigle
Stattic Point
GRUINARD ISLAND
Badluarach
Gruinard Bay
Laide
Foura
Rubha Rèidh
Cove
Mellon Charles
Ormiscaig
Aultbea
Gruinard
296 AN CUAIDH
B8057
ISLE OF EWE
Little Gruinard River
Gruinard River
Melvaig
Aultgrishin
Loch Ewe
Loch Fada
347 CREAG-MHEAL BEAG
Inverasdale
293 CNOC BREAC
Naast
Inverewe Garden
220
681 BEINN A' CHAISGEIN BEAG
B8021
250 MEALL NA MEINE
North Erradale
Londubh
Poolewe
Big Sand
Wester Ross
Fionn Loch
Strath
A832
Smithstown
Lonemore
Auchtercairn
Heritage
Longa Island
Gairloch
Dubh Loch
791 BEINN AIRIDH CHARR
Loch Gairloch
421 MEALL AN DOIREIN
Charlestown
Eilean Horrisdale
Port Henderson
B8056
Badachro
Opinan
859 BEINN LÀIR
Letterewe Forest
Loch Maree
Loch Maree Islands
South Erradale
Loch Bad an Sgalaig
Letterewe
Loch Garbhaig
Talladale
Redpoint
981 SLIOCH
Loch Ghaineamhach
Red Point
210
875 BAOSBHEINN
Loch na h-Oidhche
855 BEINN AN EÒIN
724
619 BEINN BHREAC
Loch a' Bhealaich
Loch Torridon
Craig River
Rubha na Fearn
Lower Diabaig
914 BEINN DEARG
1009 RUADH-STAC MÒR
972
Kinloch
Loch Diabaig
Fearnbeg
Òb Chuaig
Inveralligin
BEINN EIGHE
1024
1053

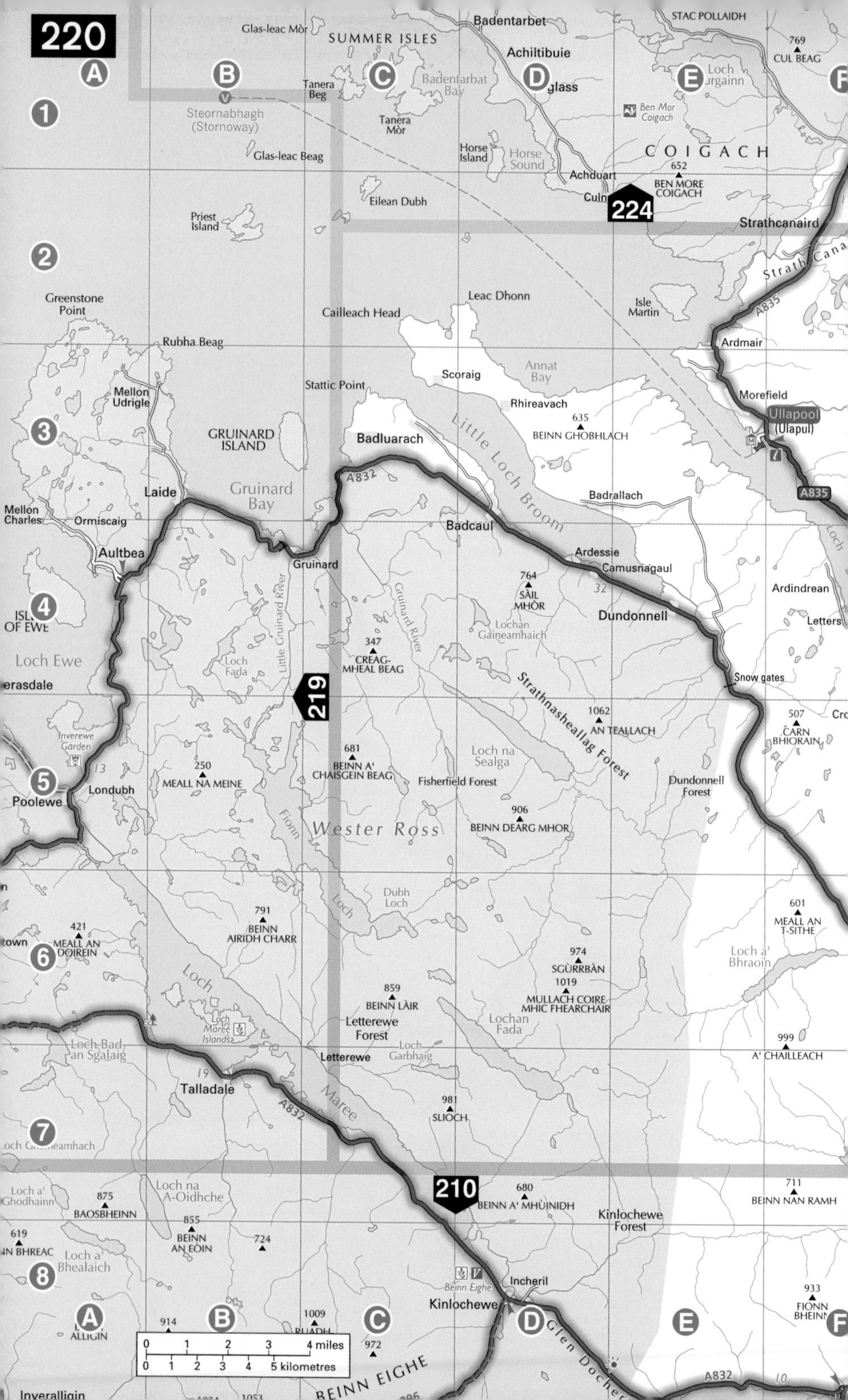

SUMMER ISLES
Glas-leac Mòr
Badentarbet
Achiltibuie
STAC POLLAIDH
769
CUL BEAG
Tanera Beg
Badentarbat Bay
Loch Lurgainn
Ben Mor Coigach
Steornabhagh (Stornoway)
Tanera Mòr
Glas-leac Beag
Horse Island
Horse Sound
COIGACH
Achduart
652
BEN MORE COIGACH
Culn
224
Eilean Dubh
Priest Island
Strathcanaird
Strath Canaird
A835
Greenstone Point
Leac Dhonn
Isle Martin
Cailleach Head
Rubha Beag
Ardmair
Scoraig
Annat Bay
Mellon Udrigle
Stattic Point
Morefield
Rhireavach
Ullapool (Ulapul)
635
BEINN GHOBHLACH
GRUINARD ISLAND
Badluarach
Little Loch Broom
Gruinard Bay
A832
Laide
Badrallach
Mellon Charles
Ormiscaig
Badcaul
Aultbea
Ardessie
Camusnagaul
Gruinard
764
SÀIL MHÒR
Ardindrean
ISLE OF EWE
Lochan Gaineamhaich
Dundonnell
Letters
Little Gruinard River
Gruinard River
347
CREAG-MHEAL BEAG
Loch Ewe
Loch Fada
Strathnasheallag Forest
Snow gates
219
1062
AN TEALLACH
507
CARN BHIORAIN
Inverewe Garden
681
BEINN A' CHAISGEIN BEAG
Loch na Sealga
Dundonnell Forest
250
MEALL NA MEINE
Fisherfield Forest
Poolewe
Londubh
906
BEINN DEARG MHOR
Fionn
Wester Ross
Dubh Loch
791
BEINN AIRIDH CHARR
601
MEALL AN T-SITHE
421
MEALL AN DOIREIN
Loch a' Bhraoin
974
SGÙRRBÀN
1019
MULLACH COIRE MHIC FHEARCHAIR
859
BEINN LÀIR
Loch Maree
Loch Maree Islands
Lochan Fada
Letterewe Forest
Loch Bad an Sgalaig
Loch Garbhaig
999
A' CHAILLEACH
Letterewe
Talladale
981
SLIOCH
210
Loch na A-Oidhche
680
BEINN A' MHÙINIDH
711
BEINN NAN RAMH
875
BAOSBHEINN
Kinlochewe Forest
855
BEINN AN EÒIN
724
619
Loch a' Bhealaich
Beinn Eighe
Incheril
Kinlochewe
933
1009
RUADH
914
972
Glen Docherty
BEINN EIGHE
A832
Inveralligin
0 1 2 3 4 miles
0 1 2 3 4 5 kilometres

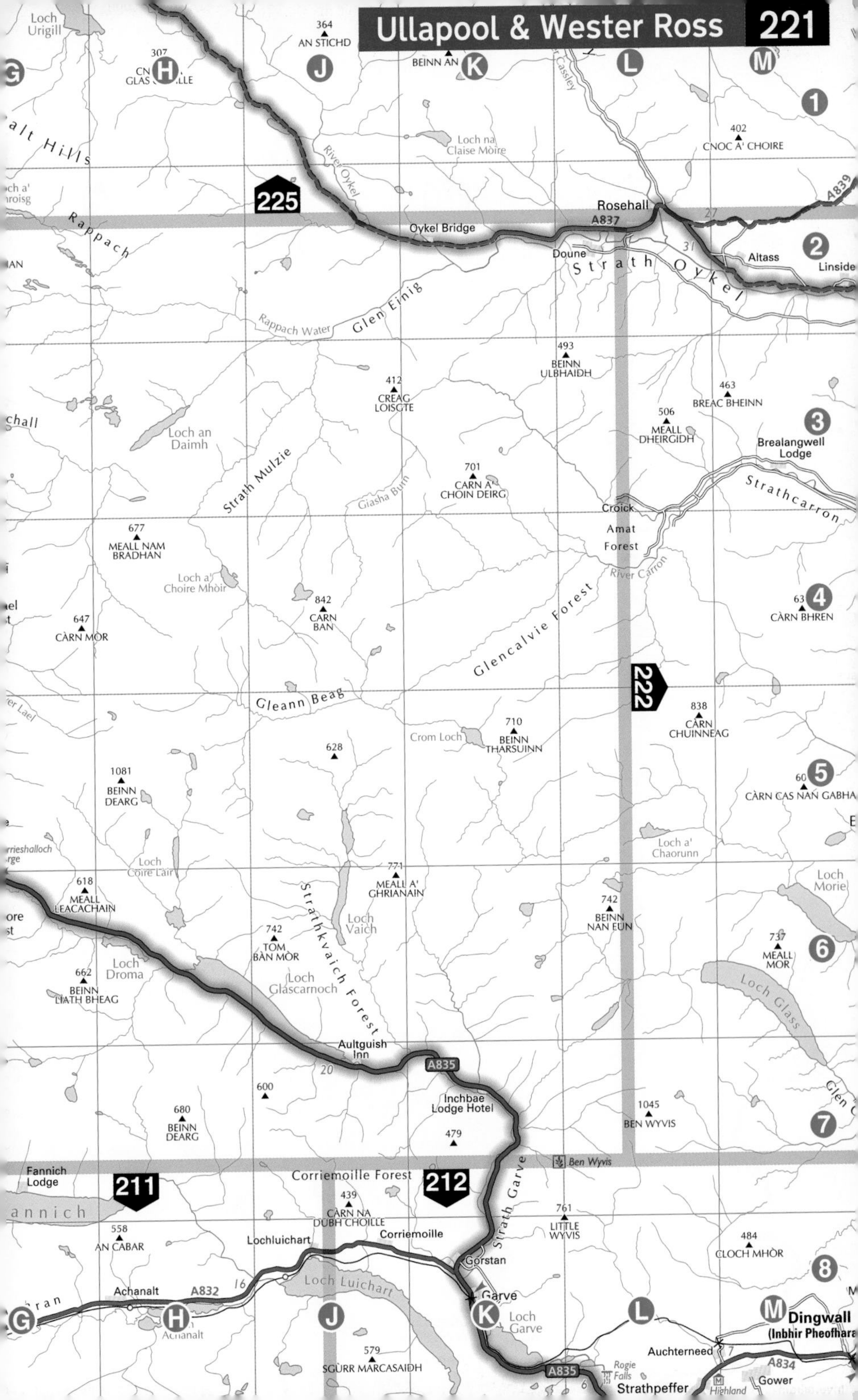
Loch Urigill
364
AN STICHD
307
BEINN AN
Cassley
402
CNOC A' CHOIRE
Loch na Claise Mòire
River Oykel
225
A839
Rosehall
A837
Rappach
Oykel Bridge
Doune
Strath Oykel
Altass
Linside
31
27
Rappach Water
Glen Einig
493
BEINN ULBHAIDH
412
CREAG LOISGTE
463
BREAC BHEINN
506
MEALL DHEIRGIDH
Loch an Daimh
Brealangwell Lodge
Strath Mulzie
701
CARN A' CHOIN DEIRG
Giasha Burn
Strathcarron
Croick
Amat Forest
677
MEALL NAM BRADHAN
Loch a' Choire Mhòir
River Carron
842
CARN BAN
Glencalvie Forest
647
CÀRN MÒR
CÀRN BHREN
222
Gleann Beag
838
CÀRN CHUINNEAG
710
BEINN THARSUINN
Crom Loch
628
1081
BEINN DEARG
CÀRN CAS NAN GABHAR
Loch a' Chaorunn
Loch Coire Lair
771
MEALL A' GHRIANAIN
Loch Morie
618
MEALL LEACACHAIN
742
BEINN NAN EUN
Strathkvaich Forest
Loch Vaich
742
TOM BÀN MÒR
737
MEALL MÒR
Loch Droma
662
BEINN LIATH BHEAG
Loch Glascarnoch
Loch Glass
Aultguish Inn
A835
20
600
Inchbae Lodge Hotel
680
BEINN DEARG
479
1045
BEN WYVIS
Ben Wyvis
Fannich Lodge
211
Corriemoille Forest
212
Strath Garve
439
CÀRN NA DUBH CHOILLE
761
LITTLE WYVIS
558
AN CABAR
Lochluichart
Corriemoille
484
CLOCH MHÒR
Gorstan
Achanalt
A832
16
Loch Luichart
Garve
Loch Garve
Dingwall
(Inbhir Pheofharan)
Auchterneed
A834
579
SGÙRR MARCASAIDH
A835
Rogie Falls
Strathpeffer
Highland
Gower

Ferrycroft
Lairg
Tomich
Torrobull
323 BEN DOULA
402 CNOC A' CHOIRE
Loch na Claise Mòire
River Cassley
225
226
Rosehall
Oykel Bridge
A837
A839
A836
Achany
313 CREAGAN GLAS
Doune
Strath Oykel
Altass
Linsidemore
Falls of Shin
333 MEALL EACHAINN
Loch Buidhe
Inveran
Invershin
Sleasdairidh
349 BEINN DONUILL
493 BEINN ULBHAIDH
463 BREAC BHEINN
506 MEALL DHEIRGIDH
Culrain
1650 Carbisdale
Kyle of Sutherland
701 CARN A CHOIN DEIRG
Brealangwell Lodge
Strathcarron
Croick
Amat Forest
River Carron
Lower Gledfield
Dounie
Bonar Bridge
Loch Migdale
A949
Ardgay
Kincardine
Upper Ardchronie
634 CÀRN BHREN
Glencalvie Forest
Struie Hill
221
838 CÀRN CHUINNEAG
710 BEINN THARSUINN
Crom Loch
477 BEINN CLACH AN FHEADAIN
Aultnamain Inn
602 CÀRN CAS NAN GABHAR
EASTER ROSS
692 BEINN THARSUINN
Loch a' Chaorunn
Loch Morie
Strath Rusdale
B9176
742 BEINN NAN EUN
737 MEALL MOR
Ardross
Boath
Loch Glass
River Alness
Achandunie
Rhicullen
Millcraig
Moultavie
523 CNOC CEISLEIN
A835
Inchbae Lodge Hotel
479
Glen Glass
Alness (Alanais)
Fyrish
Dalmore
1045 BEN WYVIS
Black Rock Gorge
B817
Cromarty Firth
Ben Wyvis
Evanton
212
Resolis
Strath Garve
761 LITTLE WYVIS
Teanord
B9163
484 CLOCH MHÒR
Storehouse of Foulis
Cullicudden
Gorstan
Ardullie
Brae
Garve
Mountgerald
Findon Mains
Dingwall (Inbhir Pheofharain)
B9169
BLACK ISLE
0 1 2 3 4 miles
0 1 2 3 4 5 kilometres
A834
A9
Culbokie
255 MOUNT EAGLE
Strathpeffer
Gower
Killen

River Brora
Dalreavoch
Loch Horn
520 BEN HORN
378 CAGAR FEOSAIG
Golspie Burn
Dalchalm
Clynelish
Brora
Doll
227
A9
Backies
446 BEN LUNDIE
383 BEN BHRAGGIE
Rhives
Dunrobin Castle
Carn Liath
Golspie
Loch Fleet
Platform
Skelbo
Skelbo Street
Fourpenny
Embo
Birichin
B9168
Embo Street
Pitgrudy
Evelix
A949
Royal Dornoch
Camore
Dornoch
Historylinks
Tarbat Ness
Cuthill
Dornoch Point
Dornoch Firth
Innis Mhor
Wilkhaven
Dornoch Firth Bridge
Portmahomack
Glenmorangie
Inver
Rockfield
B9165
Arboll
Tain
Toulvaddie
Lochslin
Loch Eye
Hill of Fearn
Rhynie
Balmuchy
B9165
Newfield
Hilton of Cadboll Chapel (ruin)
Fearn
Tullich
B9166
Hilton
Arabella
Balintore
Shandwick
Shandwick Bay
Ankerville
Milton
B9175
Kilmuir
Pitcalnie
Barbaraville
Nigg
Nigg Bay
Nigg Ferry
June-Sept
Cromarty
Sutors Stacks
Hugh Miller's Cottage
213
MORAY FIRTH
214
Burghead
Cromarty Bay
Newton
B9163
Navity
Findhorn
B9011
Findhorn Bay
Culbin Forest
Upper Eathie
Kincorth House
Kintessack
Grange
Sueno's Stone
Whiteness Head
Nairn
Culbin
Brodie Castle
Dyke

Scourie
Scourie More
Badcall
Badcall Bay
Loch a' Mhuilinn
386
BEN AUSKAIRD
Rubh' a' Mhucard
228
Point of Stoer
Old Man of Stoer
OLDANY ISLAND
Eddrachillis Bay
Culkein Drumbeg
Culkein
Clashnessie Bay
Oldany
Drumbeg
Achnacarnin
Nedd
Clashmore
Clashnessie
Loch Poll
Glen Leirg
Loch an Leothaid
776
SAIL GHORM
809
QUINAG
Stoer
Clachtoll
Bay of Clachtoll
Loch Beannach
Rhicarn
Achmelvich Bay
Achmelvich
A837
Loch Assynt
Baddidarrach
Lochinver
539
BEINN GHARBH
Soyea Island
Loch Inver
Strathan
Assynt - Coigach
Inverkirkaig
Loch na Gainimh
847
CANISP
Rubha Còigeach
River Kirkaig
Fionn Loch
732
SUILVEN
Eilean Mòr
Enard Bay
Rubha Mòr
Reiff
Achnahaird
Càm Loch
Altandhu
Loch Sionascaig
Loch Veyatie
Eilean Mullagrach
849
CUL MÒR
Isle Ristol
Loch Osgaig
Polbain
612
STAC POLLAIDH
Knockan
Elphin
Badentarbet
Glas-leac Mòr
SUMMER ISLES
769
CUL BEAG
Achiltibuie
Knockan Crag
Loch Lurgainn
Tanera Beg
Badentarbat Bay
Polglass
Cromalt H
Ben-Mor Coigach
Tanera Mòr
Glas-leac Beag
Horse Island
Horse Sound
COIGACH
Achduart
652
BEN MORE COIGACH
Drumrunie Lodge
Culnacraig
Eilean Dubh
Loch a' Chroisg
Strathcanaird
220
Strath Canaird
408
NA DROMANNAN
Leac Dhonn
Isle Martin
Cailleach Head
A835
Ardmair
Scoraig
Annat Bay
Stattic Point
Morefield
635
Ullapool (Ulapul)
Loch Achall
Glen Achall
GRUINARD ISLAND
Badluarach
0 1 2 3 4 miles
0 1 2 3 4 5 kilometres

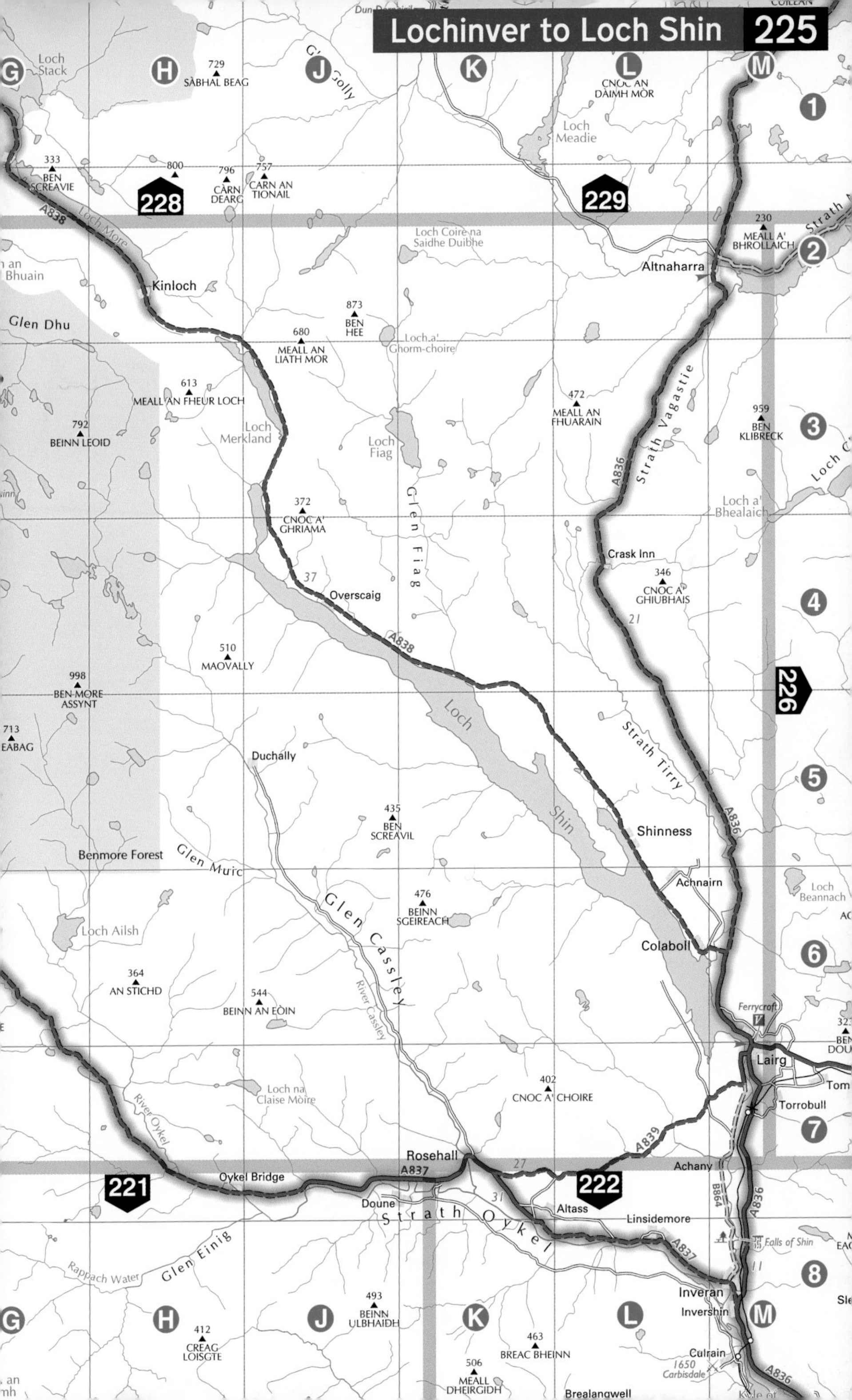
Loch Stack
729
SÀBHAL BEAG
G'Golly
CNOC AN DAIMH MÒR
Loch Meadie
333
BEN SCREAVIE
800
796
CÀRN DEARG
757
CARN AN TIONAIL
228
229
A838
Loch More
230
MEALL A' BHROLLAICH
Strath
Loch Coire na Saidhe Duibhe
Altnaharra
Kinloch
Glen Dhu
873
BEN HEE
680
MEALL AN LIATH MOR
Loch a' Ghorm-choire
613
MEALL AN FHEUR LOCH
472
MEALL AN FHUARAIN
Strath Vagastie
959
BEN KLIBRECK
792
BEINN LEOID
Loch Merkland
Loch Fiag
A836
Loch a' Bhealaich
372
CNOC A' GHRIAMA
Glen Fiag
Crask Inn
346
CNOC A' GHIUBHAIS
37
Overscaig
21
510
MAOVALLY
A838
998
BEN MORE ASSYNT
226
713
EABAG
Loch Shin
Strath Tirry
Duchally
435
BEN SCREAVIL
Shinness
A836
Benmore Forest
Glen Muic
Achnairn
Loch Beannach
476
BEINN SGEIREACH
Glen Cassley
Loch Ailsh
Colaboll
364
AN STICHD
544
BEINN AN EÒIN
River Cassley
Ferrycroft
Lairg
Loch na Claise Mòire
402
CNOC A' CHOIRE
Torrobull
River Oykel
A839
Rosehall
27
Achany
221
Oykel Bridge
A837
222
Doune
Strath Oykel
31
Altass
Linsidemore
B864
A836
Falls of Shin
A837
Rappach Water
Glen Einig
11
Inveran
Invershin
493
BEINN ULBHAIDH
412
CREAG LOISGTE
463
BREAC BHEINN
Culrain
1650
Carbisdale
506
MEALL DHEIRGIDH
Brealangwell
A836
G H J K L M
1 2 3 4 5 6 7 8

Syre
Loch Cròcach
CNOC A' BHREUN BHAID
345 CNOC NAM TRI-CHLACH
294 POLE HILL
404 BEINN MHADADH
588 BEN GRIAM BEG
259 BEINN ROSAIL
B871
Loch Druim a-Chliabhain
590 BEN GRIAM MOR
Strath Naver
B873
229
230
Loch an Ruathair
230 MEALL A' BHROLLAICH
270 BEADAIG
Loch Naver
River Mallart
Loch Rimsdale
Loch nan Clàr
Loch Badanloch
Badanloch
Loch Arichlinie
Loch an Alltan Fhearna
Loch Truderscaig
B871
River Helmsdale
Kinbrace
959 BEN KLIBRECK
Loch Choire Forest
694 CREAG N-IOLAIRE
434 CNOC AN LIATH-BHAID MHÒIR
202 CNOC DAIL-CHAIRN
713 CREAG MHÒR
Loch Choire
Loch a' Bhealaich
Strath Free
Borrobol Forest
Loch Ascaig
364 CNOC NA BREUN-CHOILLE
388 CREAG NAM FIADH
Learable Hill Cairns, Stone & Stone Circle
Gorm-loch Mòr
Ben Armine Forest
Strath Skinsdale
225
Glas-loch Mòr
337 CNOC NA H-INNSE MOIRE
462 MEALIAN LIATH MOR
421 CNOC NAN CRÙBAG
A836
Black Water
River Brora
Loch Beannach
317 SITHEAN ACHADH NAN EUN
293 CNOC LEAMHNACHD
Balnacoil
Strath Brora
River Brora
Loch Brora
Loch Craggie
Dalreavoch
Ferrycroft
323 BEN DOULA
Lairg
Tomich
Loch Horn
520 BEN HORN
Torrobull
A839
14
Golspie Burn
378 CAGAR FEOSAIG
Rogart
Backies
313 CREAGAN GLAS
446 BEN LUNDIE
223
383 BEN BHRAGGIE
Rhives
Dunrobin Castle
Carn Liath
Golspie
B864
A836
333 MEALL EACHAINN
Falls of Shin
Loch Buidhe
Torboll
Sleasdairidh
349 BEINN DONUILL
Loch Fleet
Badninish
Skelbo
Skelbo Street
Fourpenny
Achvaich
Culrain
A836
0 1 2 3 4 miles
0 1 2 3 4 5 kilometres

Altnabreac Station
Rumsdale Water
Strathmore W
Dalnawillan Lodge
Loch an Thulachan
Loch Sand
Achavanich
Loch Rangag
248
STEMSTER HILL
226
COIRE NA BEINN
230
348
BEN ALISKY
Glutt Water
Glutt Lodge
287
BEN-A-CHIELT
231
Upper Lybster
264
CNOCAN CONACHREAG
Houstry
Swiney
Invershore
Lybster
Waterlines
Lybster Bay
Forse
Land-hallow
Smerral
Latheron
Dunbeath Water
Latheronwheel
Janetstown
317
CNOC LOCH MHADADH
Berriedale Water
A9
Laidhay Croft
Braemore
Dunbeath
Snow gates
Dunbeath Bay
484
MAIDEN PAP
705
MORVEN
Knockally
518
CNOC AN EIREANNAICH
Ramscraigs
626
SCARABEN
Borgue
Langwell Forest
20
Newport
554
CREAG SCALABSDALE
Langwell House
Berriedale
401
CNOC NA MAOILE
Badbea Historic Village
A897
404
CREAG THORARAIDH
Torrish
River Helmsdale
Ord of Caithness
Navidale
Snow gates
Timespan
West Helmsdale
East Helmsdale
591
BEINN NA MEILICH
Helmsdale
Gartymore
Portgower
Glen Loth
Lothmore
G
H
J
K
L
M
1
2
3
4
5
6
7
8

CAPE WRATH
Kearvaig Bay
Cléit Dhubh
Faraid Head
371 SGRIBHIS-BHEINN
297 CNOC A GHIUBHAIS
300 MAOVALLY
Balnakeil Bay
Balnakeil
THE PARPH
Durness
Sangomore
457 FASHVEN
Sandwood Bay
Loch Airigh na Beinne
Keoldale
Kyle of Durness
Sandwood Loch
485 CREAG RIABACH
468 BEINN DEARG MHÒR
464 MEALL NA MÒINE
Rubh' an Fhir Lèithe
Strath Shinary
331 GHLAS-BHEINN
A838
Sheigra
Balchreick
Blairmore
Oldshoremore
521 FARVEALL
489 MEALL NA CRÀ
355 AN SOGACH
773 BEINN SPIONNAIDH
Kinlochbervie
Loch Clash
Badcall
801 CRANSTACKIE
B801
Loch Inchard
Achriesgill
Strath Dionard
Strath Beag
River Dionard
Rhiconich
Loch na Claise Càrnaich
Rubha Ruadh
908 FOINAVEN
Fanagmore
Skerricha
Loch Laxford
Tarbet
HANDA ISLAND
Foindle
A838
North-west Sutherland
Loch na Tuadh
Laxford Bridge
786 ARKLE
Scourie Bay
River Laxford
A894
Scourie
Scourie More
Loch Stack
729 SÀBHAL BEAG
721 BEN STACK
Badcall
Badcall Bay
Loch a' Mhuilinn
386 BEN AUSKAIRD
Strath Stack
Achfary
333 BEN SCREAVIE
800
796 CÀRN DEARG
757 CARN AN TIONAIL
Rubh' a' Mhucard
A838
Loch More
224
225
OLDANY ISLAND
Eddrachillis Bay
419 BEN STROME
Loch an Leathaid-Bhuain
Kinloch
Culkein Drumbeg
Loch a' Chàirn Bhàin
Kylestrome
Kylesku
Loch Glendhu
Glen Dhu
Drumbeg
Unapool
680 MEALL A LIATH
B869
Nedd
525 BEINN A DA LOCH
Loch Glencoul
613 MEALL AN FHEUR LOCH
Loch Poll
0 1 2 3 4 miles
0 1 2 3 4 5 kilometres
792 BEINN LEOID
QUINAG
Loch Merkland

Whiten Head
408 BEN HUTIG
Strathan
Talmine
Melness
Midtown
Rabbit Islands
Eilean Nan Ròn
Tongue Bay
Neave or Coomb Island
Skerray
Achtoty
Torrisdale
Torrisdale Bay
Farr Bay
Farr Point
Kirtomy Point
Ardmore Point
Farr
Kirtomy
Swordly
Armadale
Bettyhill
Strathnaver
Scullomie
Coldbackie
Invernaver
Achina
Borgie
Loch Meadie
A838
Kyle of Tongue
A836
262 DRUIM NAN CLIAR
Tongue
310 MEALL LEATHAD NA CRAOIBHE
River Borgie
Skelpick
Skelpick Burn
Strath Naver
318 CNOC CRAGGIE
Loch Craggie
Kinloch
Loch na Seilg
927 BEN HOPE
598 MEALLAN LIATH
763 BEN LOYAL
527 BEINN STUMANADH
213 CNOC MALPELLY
B871
Loch Loyal
Loch Loyal Lodge
Loch an Deerie
557 CNOC NAN CUILEAN
Loch Syre
Syre
River Naver
Loch Strathy
335 MEALL BAD NA CUAICHE
345 CNOC NA TRI-CHLAC
656 CNOC AN DÀIMH MÒR
Loch Meadie
294 POLE HILL
259 BEINN ROSAIL
404 BEINN MHADADH
B873
230 MEALL A' BHROLLAICH
270 BEADAIG
Loch Naver
Altnaharra
Loch Rimsdale
Loch nan Clàr
Loch Badanloch
Loch an Altan Fheàrna
Loch Truder
472 MEALL AN FHUARAIN
959 BEN KLIBRECK
Choire Forest
694
434
225
226
230

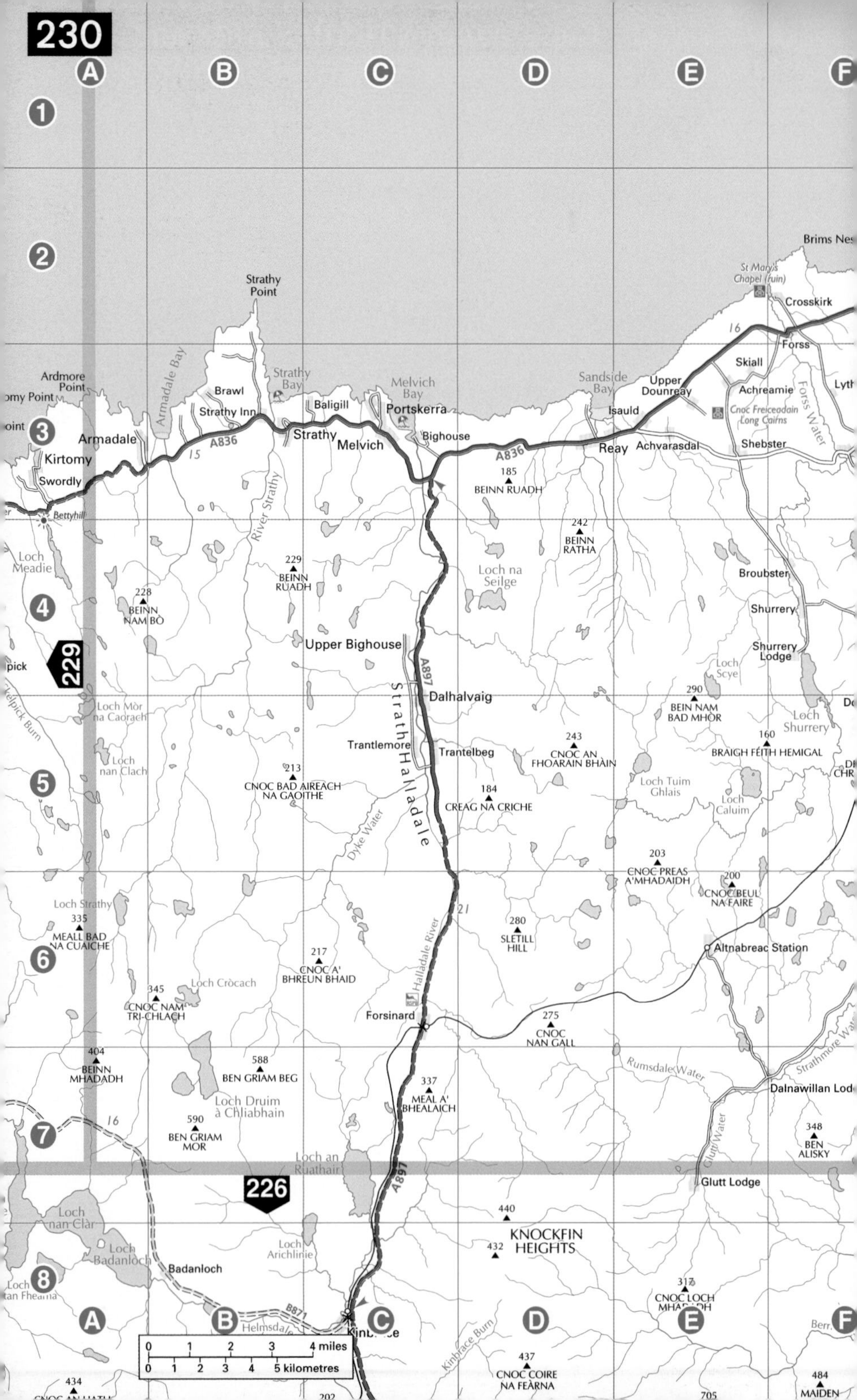

A
B
C
D
E
F
1
2
3
4
5
6
7
8
Brims Ness
St Mary's Chapel (ruin)
Crosskirk
Strathy Point
Forss
Skiall
Ardmore Point
Armadale Bay
Strathy Bay
Melvich Bay
Sandside Bay
Upper Dounreay
Achreamie
Lyth
Brawl
Baligill
Portskerra
Isauld
Cnoc Freiceadain Long Cairns
Forss Water
Strathy Inn
Bighouse
Armadale
Strathy
Melvich
A836
Reay
Achvarasdal
Shebster
Kirtomy
Swordly
Bettyhill
185 BEINN RUADH
242 BEINN RATHA
River Strathy
Loch Meadie
229 BEINN RUADH
Loch na Seilge
Broubster
228 BEINN NAM BÒ
Shurrery
Upper Bighouse
Shurrery Lodge
229
A897
Loch Scye
Strath Halladale
Dalhalvaig
290 BEIN NAM BAD MHOR
Loch Mòr na Caorach
Loch Shurrery
Trantlemore
Trantelbeg
243 CNOC AN FHOARAIN BHÀIN
160 BRAIGH FÉITH HEMIGAL
Loch nan Clach
213 CNOC BAD AIREACH NA GAOITHE
Loch Tuim Ghlais
Loch Caluim
184 CREAG NA CRICHE
Dyke Water
203 CNOC PREAS A'MHADAIDH
200 CNOC BEUL NA FAIRE
Loch Strathy
335 MEALL BAD NA CUAICHE
280 SLETILL HILL
Halladale River
Altnabreac Station
217 CNOC A' BHREUN BHAID
345 CNOC NAM TRI-CHLACH
Loch Cròcach
Forsinard
275 CNOC NAN GALL
404 BEINN MHADADH
588 BEN GRIAM BEG
Rumsdale Water
Strathmore Water
337 MEAL A' BHEALAICH
Dalnawillan Lodge
Loch Druim à Chliabhain
590 BEN GRIAM MOR
Glutt Water
348 BEN ALISKY
Loch an Ruathair
226
Glutt Lodge
Loch nan Clàr
440
KNOCKFIN HEIGHTS
432
Loch Arichlinie
Loch Badanloch
Badanloch
Loch nan Fheanna
317 CNOC LOCH MHADAIDH
B871
Helmsdale
Kinbrace
Kinbrace Burn
0 1 2 3 4 miles
0 1 2 3 4 5 kilometres
437 CNOC COIRE NA FEÀRNA
434
484 MAIDEN

234
227
PENTLAND FIRTH
ISLAND OF STROMA
Nethertown
Uppertown
Mell Head
St John's Point
Inner Sound
St Margaret's Hope
DUNNET HEAD
Briga Head
DUNNET HILL
Brough
Scarfskerry
Castle of Mey
Loch Mey
Mey
Rattar
St John's Loch
Gills Bay
Gills
Kirkstyle
Huna
DUNCANSBY HEAD
Muckle Stack
John o' Groats
Stacks of Duncansby
Canisbay
Stromness
West Dunnet
Barrock
Dunnet
Dunnet Bay
Clarden Head
Thurso
Murkle
Castlehill
Castletown
Inkstack
Brabstermire
Loch Heilen
Greenland
Skirza
Skirza Head
Gill Burn
Freswick
Freswick Bay
Ness Head
Slickly
Olrig House
Tain
Weydale
Hilliclay
Bowermadden
Kirk Burn
Caithness Broch
Auckengill
Nybster
Sortat
Lyth
Bower
Sordale
Howe
Brough Head
Burn of Lyth
Knockdee
Roadside
Loch Scarmclate
Halcro
Mireland
Keiss
Clayock
Gillock
Kirk
Loch of Wester
Sinclair's Bay
Georgemas Junction Station
Loch Watten
Killimster
Harpsdale
SPITTAL HILL
Castle Girnigoe & Sinclair
Noss Head
Reiss
Spittal
Watten
Winless
Wick River
Sibster
Ackergill
Wick John o' Groats
Staxigoe
Mybster
Bilbster
Loch of Toftingall
Papigoe
Westerdale
Janetstown
Haster
Milton
Wick
Wick Bay
Achairn Burn
Newton
Old Wick
South Head
Castle of Old Wick
Strath Beg
Badlipster
Whiterow
Loch Hempriggs
BEINN CHÀITEAG
Tannach
Thrumster
BALLHARN HILL
Grey Cairns of Camster
Loch Ruard
Loch Stemster
Loch of Yarrows
Sarclet
Achavanich
HILL OF YARROWS
STEMSTER HILL
Loch Rangag
Cairn o'Get
Ulbster
Whaligoe
COIRE NA BEINN
Whaligoe Steps
Roster
Bruan
Hill o'Many Stanes
Upper Lybster
BEN-A-CHIELT
Mid Clyth
Halberry Head
Swiney
Occumster
Clyth Ness
Houstry
Invershore
Lybster
Waterlines
Lybster Bay
Landhallow
Forse
Smerral
Latheron
Latheronwheel
Dunbeath Water
Janetstown
Laidhay Croft
Dunbeath
Knockally
Snow gates
A836
A9
B855
B876
B874
B870
A882
A99

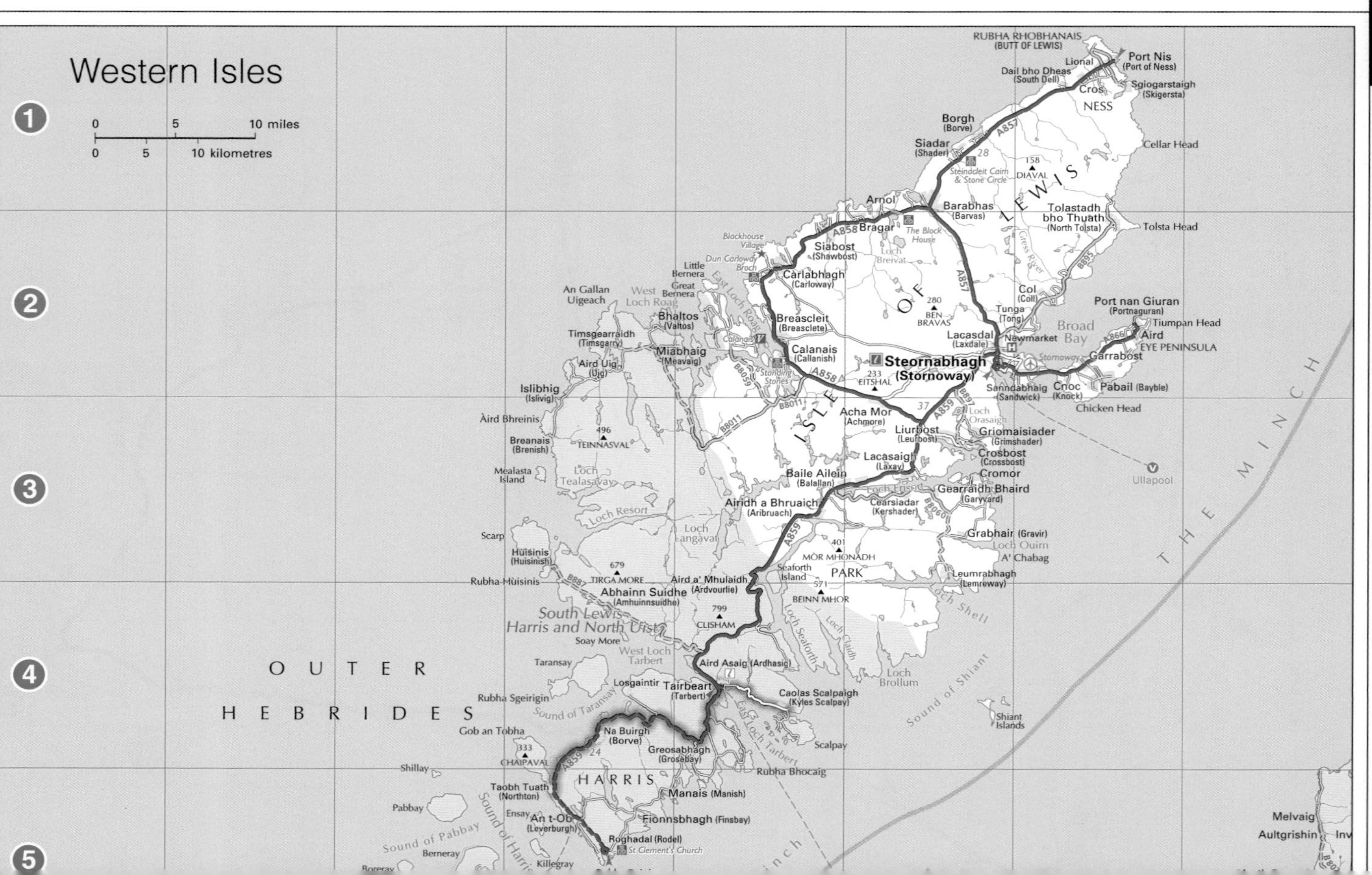
Western Isles
0 5 10 miles
0 5 10 kilometres
1
2
3
4
5
RUBHA RHOBHANAIS (BUTT OF LEWIS)
Port Nis (Port of Ness)
Lional
Dail bho Dheas (South Dell)
Cros
Sgiogarstaigh (Skigersta)
NESS
Borgh (Borve)
Siadar (Shader)
Cellar Head
Steinacleit Cairn & Stone Circle
158 DIAVAL
ISLE OF LEWIS
Arnol
Barabhas (Barvas)
Tolastadh bho Thuath (North Tolsta)
Tolsta Head
Bragar
The Block House
Blackhouse Village
Siabost (Shawbost)
Loch Breivat
Gress River
Dun Carloway Broch
Little Bernera
Great Bernera
Càrlabhagh (Carloway)
An Gallan Uigeach
West Loch Roag
East Loch Roag
280 BEN BRAVAS
Col (Coll)
Port nan Giuran (Portnaguran)
Tiumpan Head
Aird
EYE PENINSULA
Bhaltos (Valtos)
Breascleit (Breasclete)
Tunga (Tong)
Broad Bay
Timsgearraidh (Timsgarry)
Miabhaig (Meavaig)
Calanais (Callanish)
Lacasdal (Laxdale)
Newmarket
Aird Uig (Uig)
Standing Stones
Steornabhagh (Stornoway)
Stornoway
Garrabost
233 EITSHAL
Islibhig (Islivig)
Sanndabhaig (Sandwick)
Cnoc (Knock)
Pabail (Bayble)
Chicken Head
Àird Bhreinis
Acha Mor (Achmore)
Loch Orasaigh
496 TEINNASVAL
Liurbost (Leurbost)
Griomaisiader (Grimshader)
Breanais (Brenish)
Crosbost (Crossbost)
Lacasaigh (Laxay)
Mealasta Island
Loch Tealasavay
Cromor
Baile Ailein (Balallan)
Ullapool
Gearraidh Bhaird (Garyvard)
Cearsiadar (Kershader)
Airidh a Bhruaich (Aribruach)
Loch Resort
Scarp
Loch Langavat
Grabhair (Gravir)
Loch Ouirn
A' Chabag
401 MOR MHONADH
Hùisinis (Huisinish)
Seaforth Island
PARK
679 TIRGA MORE
Rubha Hùisinis
Aird a' Mhulaidh (Ardvourlie)
Leumrabhagh (Lemreway)
571 BEINN MHOR
Loch Shell
Abhainn Suidhe (Amhuinnsuidhe)
THE MINCH
South Lewis, Harris and North Uist
799 CLISHAM
Loch Seaforth
Loch Claidh
Soay More
West Loch Tarbert
Taransay
Loch Brollum
OUTER HEBRIDES
Aird Asaig (Ardhasig)
Sound of Shiant
Losgaintir
Tairbeart (Tarbert)
Rubha Sgeirigin
Caolas Scalpaigh (Kyles Scalpay)
Sound of Taransay
Shiant Islands
East Loch Tarbert
Gob an Tobha
Na Buirgh (Borve)
Scalpay
333 CHAIPAVAL
Greosabhagh (Grosebay)
Shillay
Rubha Bhocaig
HARRIS
Taobh Tuath (Northton)
Manais (Manish)
Pabbay
Ensay
An t-Ob (Leverburgh)
Fionnsbhagh (Finsbay)
Melvaig
Sound of Pabbay
Sound of Harris
Aultgrishin
Roghadal (Rodel)
St Clement's Church
Berneray
Killegray
A857
A858
A859
A866
B895
B897
B8011
B8059
B8060
B887

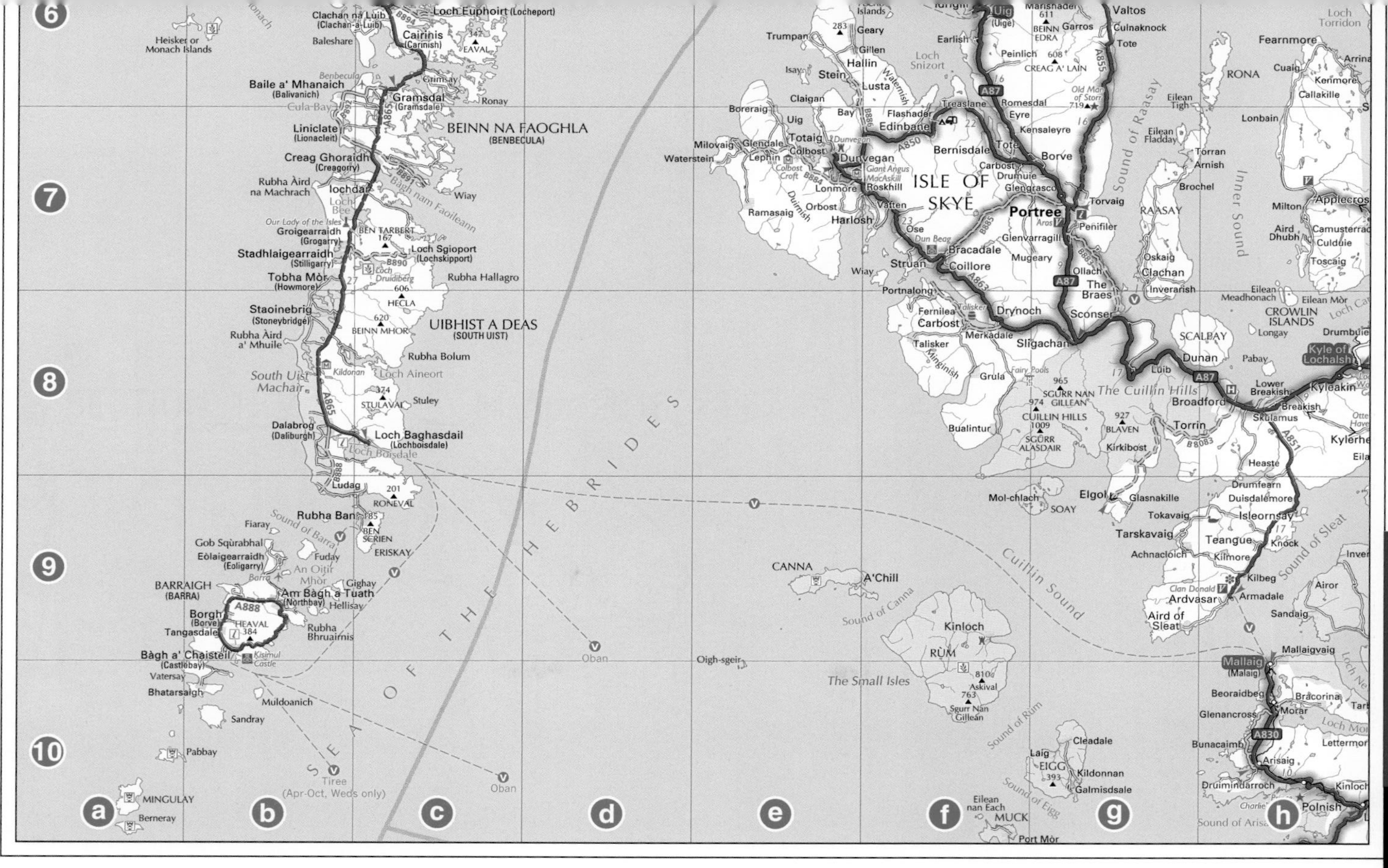
ISLE OF SKYE
Portree
Dunvegan
Uig
Broadford
Kyle of Lochalsh
Kyleakin
Armadale
Mallaig
RAASAY
SCALPAY
CROWLIN ISLANDS
RONA
Inner Sound
Sound of Raasay
Sound of Sleat
The Cuillin Hills
CUILLIN HILLS
Cuillin Sound
SOAY
Elgol
CANNA
A'Chill
Sound of Canna
RÙM
Kinloch
The Small Isles
Sound of Rùm
EIGG
MUCK
Sound of Eigg
Oigh-sgeir
SEA OF THE HEBRIDES
BEINN NA FAOGHLA
(BENBECULA)
UIBHIST A DEAS
(SOUTH UIST)
Loch Baghasdail
(Lochboisdale)
Baile a' Mhanaich
(Balivanich)
Loch Euphoirt (Locheport)
ERISKAY
BARRAIGH
(BARRA)
Bàgh a' Chaisteil
(Castlebay)
Sound of Barra
Vatersay
Sandray
Pabbay
MINGULAY
Berneray
Heisker or
Monach Islands
Oban
Tiree
(Apr-Oct, Weds only)
A87
A850
A863
A855
A851
A865
A888
A830
a
b
c
d
e
f
g
h
6
7
8
9
10

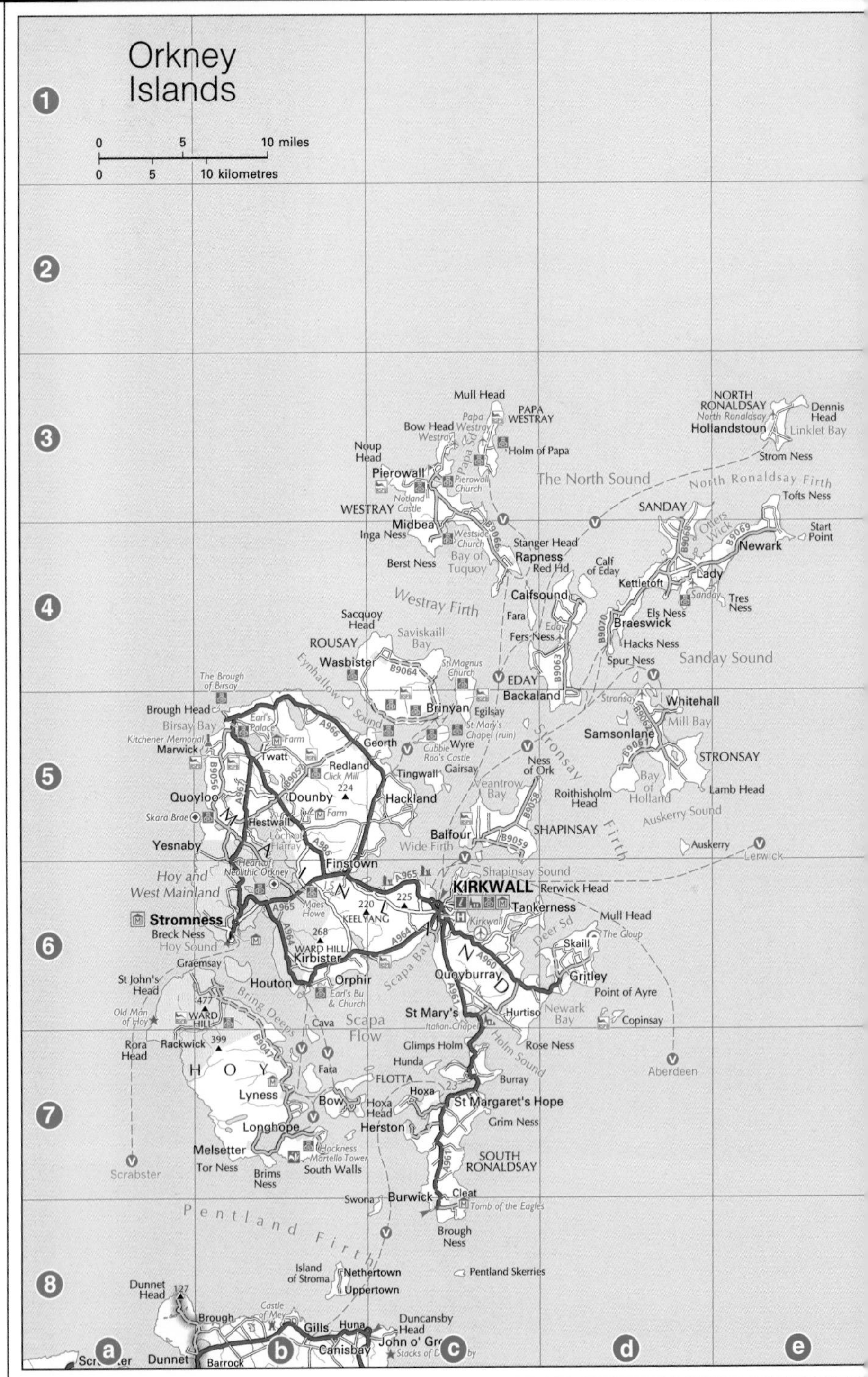
Orkney Islands
0 5 10 miles
0 5 10 kilometres
1
2
3
4
5
6
7
8
a
b
c
d
e
Mull Head
PAPA WESTRAY
Papa Westray
Holm of Papa
Bow Head
Noup Head
Pierowall
Pierowall Church
Noltland Castle
WESTRAY
Midbea
Inga Ness
Westside Church
Berst Ness
Bay of Tuquoy
Stanger Head
Rapness
Red Hd
Calf of Eday
The North Sound
North Ronaldsay Firth
NORTH RONALDSAY
North Ronaldsay
Hollandstoun
Dennis Head
Linklet Bay
Strom Ness
Tofts Ness
SANDAY
Otters Wick
Start Point
Newark
Lady
Kettletoft
Sanday
Tres Ness
Els Ness
Braeswick
Hacks Ness
Spur Ness
Sanday Sound
Westray Firth
Calfsound
Fara
Eday
Fers Ness
Sacquoy Head
ROUSAY
Saviskaill Bay
Wasbister
St Magnus Church
EDAY
Backaland
Eynhallow Sound
Brinyan
Egilsay
St Mary's Chapel (ruin)
Stronsay
Whitehall
Mill Bay
Samsonlane
STRONSAY
Bay of Holland
Lamb Head
Stronsay Firth
The Brough of Birsay
Brough Head
Birsay Bay
Earl's Palace
Farm
Kitchener Memorial
Marwick
Twatt
Georth
Cubbie Roo's Castle
Wyre
Gairsay
Ness of Ork
Redland
Click Mill
224
Tingwall
Veantrow Bay
Roithisholm Head
Auskerry Sound
Quoyloo
Dounby
Hackland
Skara Brae
Farm
Hestwall
Loch of Harray
SHAPINSAY
Yesnaby
Balfour
Wide Firth
Auskerry
Lerwick
Heart of Neolithic Orkney
Finstown
Shapinsay Sound
Hoy and West Mainland
KIRKWALL
Rerwick Head
Maes Howe
220
225
Tankerness
MAINLAND
Stromness
KEELYANG
Kirkwall
Mull Head
Breck Ness
Hoy Sound
268
WARD HILL
Kirbister
Deer Sd
The Gloup
Skaill
Graemsay
Scapa Bay
Quoyburray
Gritley
St John's Head
Houton
Orphir
Earl's Bu & Church
Point of Ayre
Bring Deeps
477
Old Man of Hoy
WARD HILL
Cava
Scapa Flow
St Mary's
Italian Chapel
Hurtiso
Newark Bay
Copinsay
Rora Head
Rackwick
399
Glimps Holm
Holm Sound
Rose Ness
HOY
Hunda
Fara
FLOTTA
Burray
Aberdeen
Lyness
Hoxa
Bow
Hoxa Head
St Margaret's Hope
Longhope
Herston
Grim Ness
Melsetter
Hackness Martello Tower
SOUTH RONALDSAY
Scrabster
Tor Ness
Brims Ness
South Walls
Swona
Burwick
Cleat
Tomb of the Eagles
Pentland Firth
Brough Ness
Island of Stroma
Nethertown
Uppertown
Pentland Skerries
Dunnet Head
127
Castle of Mey
Brough
Gills
Huna
Duncansby Head
Canisbay
Dunnet
Barrock
B9056
A967
A966
B9057
A986
A965
A964
A960
A961
B9066
B9064
B9063
B9070
B9068
B9069
B9062
B9067
B9058
B9059
B9047

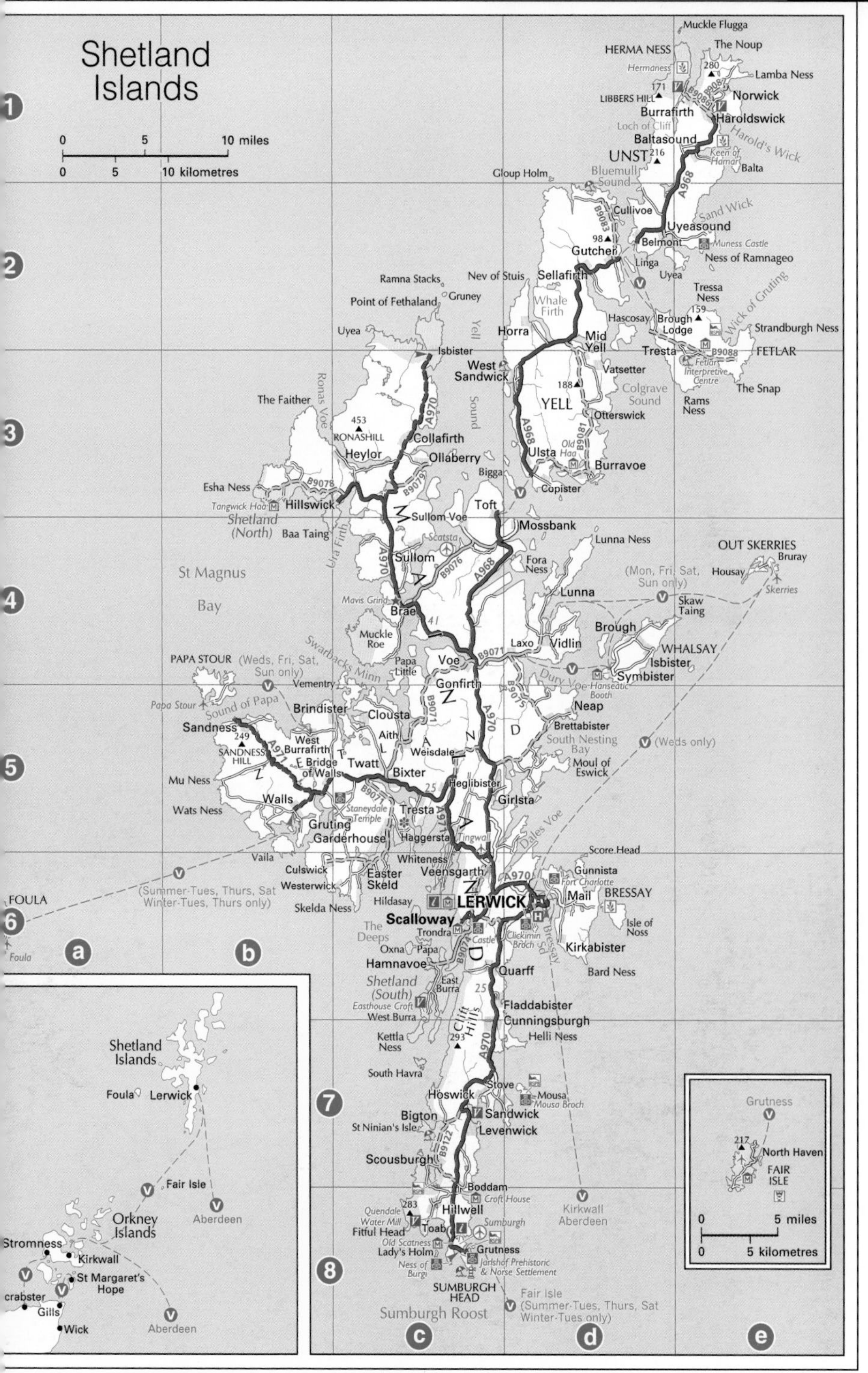

Shetland Islands
0
5
10 miles
0
5
10 kilometres
Muckle Flugga
HERMA NESS
The Noup
Hermaness
280
Lamba Ness
171
LIBBERS HILL
Norwick
Burrafirth
Haroldswick
Loch of Cliff
Baltasound
Harold's Wick
UNST
216
Keen of Hamar
Balta
Gloup Holm
Bluemull Sound
A968
B9083
Cullivoe
Sand Wick
Uyeasound
98
Belmont
Muness Castle
Gutcher
Ness of Ramnageo
Linga
Uyea
Ramna Stacks
Nev of Stuis
Sellafirth
Gruney
Tressa Ness
Point of Fethaland
Whale Firth
Wick of Gruting
Uyea
Yell Sound
Horra
Hascosay
Brough Lodge
159
Strandburgh Ness
Mid Yell
Tresta
B9088
FETLAR
Isbister
Fetlar Interpretive Centre
West Sandwick
Vatsetter
Ronas Voe
The Snap
188
Colgrave Sound
The Faither
YELL
Rams Ness
A970
453
RONASHILL
Otterswick
A968
Collafirth
B9081
Heylor
Old Haa
Ollaberry
Ulsta
Burravoe
B9079
Bigga
Esha Ness
B9078
Copister
Tangwick Haa
Hillswick
Toft
Shetland (North)
Sullom Voe
Baa Taing
Mossbank
Scatsta
Lunna Ness
Ura Firth
OUT SKERRIES
Bruray
St Magnus Bay
Sullom
B9076
Fora Ness
A968
(Mon, Fri, Sat, Sun only)
Housay
Skerries
A970
Lunna
Skaw Taing
Mavis Grind
Brae
Bay
Muckle Roe
Brough
41
WHALSAY
Laxo
Vidlin
Swarbacks Minn
PAPA STOUR
(Weds, Fri, Sat, Sun only)
B9071
Isbister
Voe
Papa Little
Dury Voe
Symbister
Vementry
Gonfirth
Hanseatic Booth
Papa Stour
B9071
B9075
Sound of Papa
Brindister
Neap
Clousta
Sandness
MAINLAND
A970
249
Aith
Brettabister
SANDNESS HILL
West Burrafirth
South Nesting Bay
A971
Weisdale
(Weds only)
Bridge of Walls
Twatt
Moul of Eswick
Mu Ness
Bixter
B9071
25
Heglibister
Walls
Girlsta
Staneydale Temple
A971
Wats Ness
Tresta
Gruting
Garderhouse
Haggersta
Tingwall
Dales Voe
Vaila
Whiteness
Score Head
Culswick
Veensgarth
A970
Gunnista
Easter Skeld
Fort Charlotte
(Summer-Tues, Thurs, Sat Winter-Tues, Thurs only)
Westerwick
Mail
BRESSAY
FOULA
Hildasay
LERWICK
Skelda Ness
Isle of Noss
Scalloway
The Deeps
Trondra
Castle
Clickimin Broch
Bressay Sd
Foula
Oxna
Papa
Kirkabister
Hamnavoe
B9074
Quarff
Bard Ness
Shetland (South)
East Burra
25
Easthouse Croft
Fladdabister
West Burra
Cunningsburgh
Kettla Ness
Cliff Hills
293
Helli Ness
A970
South Havra
Stove
Hoswick
Mousa
Mousa Broch
Bigton
Sandwick
St Ninian's Isle
Levenwick
B9122
Scousburgh
Boddam
Croft House
283
Quendale Water Mill
Hillwell
Kirkwall Aberdeen
Fitful Head
Toab
Sumburgh
Old Scatness
Lady's Holm
Grutness
Ness of Burgi
Jarlshof Prehistoric & Norse Settlement
SUMBURGH HEAD
Fair Isle
(Summer-Tues, Thurs, Sat Winter-Tues only)
Sumburgh Roost
Shetland Islands
Foula
Lerwick
Fair Isle
Orkney Islands
Aberdeen
Stromness
Kirkwall
St Margaret's Hope
crabster
Gills
Wick
Aberdeen
Grutness
217
North Haven
FAIR ISLE
0
5 miles
0
5 kilometres
1
2
3
4
5
6
7
8
a
b
c
d
e

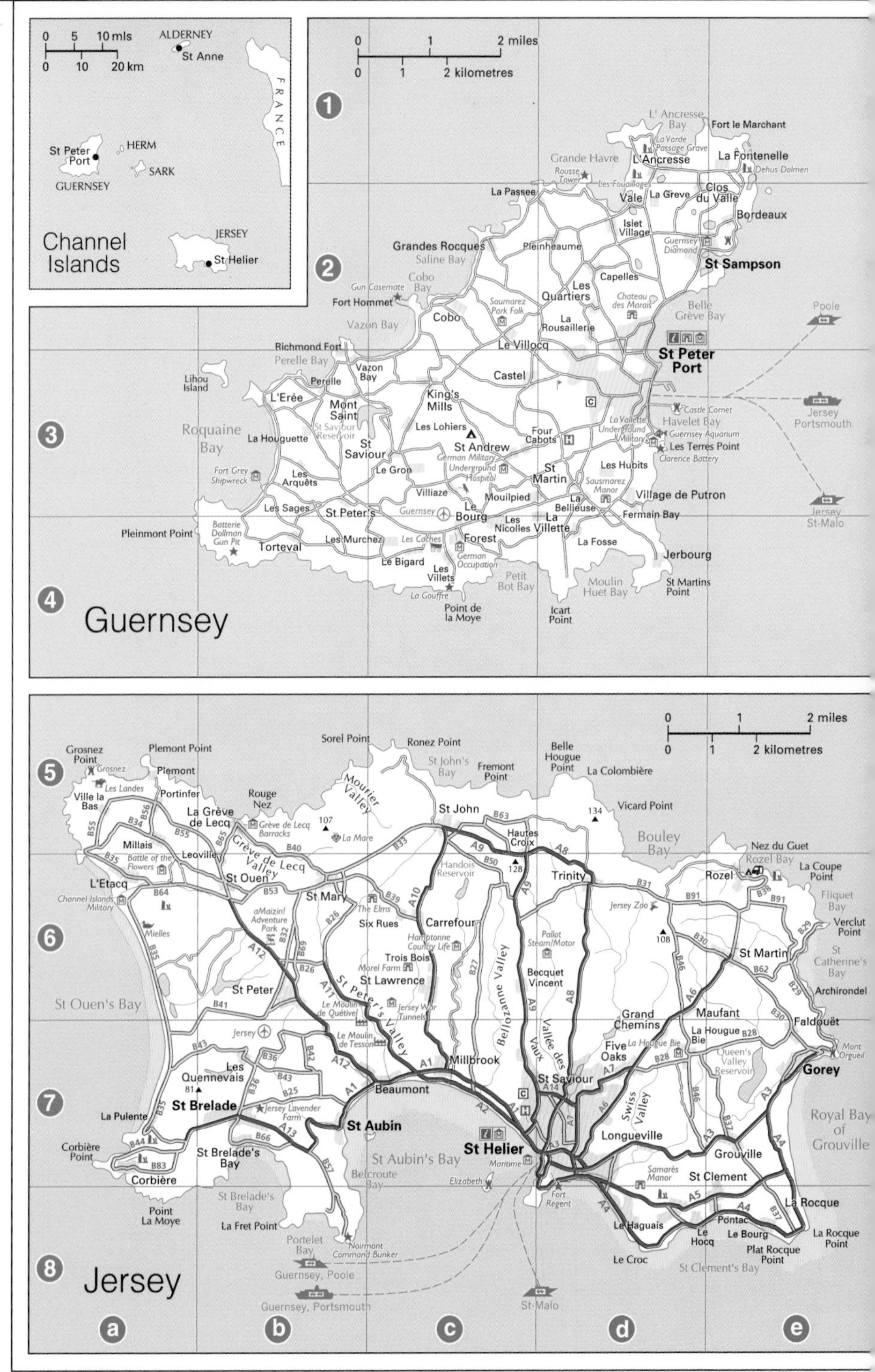

0 5 10 mls
0 10 20 km
ALDERNEY
St Anne
FRANCE
St Peter Port
HERM
SARK
GUERNSEY
JERSEY
St Helier
Channel Islands
0 1 2 miles
0 1 2 kilometres
1
2
3
4
L' Ancresse Bay
Fort le Marchant
La Varde Passage Grave
Grande Havre
L'Ancresse
La Fontenelle
Dehus Dolmen
Rousse Tower
Les Fouaillages
La Passee
Vale
La Greve
Clos du Valle
Bordeaux
Islet Village
Grandes Rocques
Saline Bay
Pleinheaume
Guernsey Diamond
St Sampson
Gun Casemate
Cobo Bay
Capelles
Fort Hommet
Les Quartiers
Chateau des Marais
Belle Grève Bay
Poole
Saumarez Park Folk
Vazon Bay
Cobo
La Rousaillerie
Le Villocq
St Peter Port
Richmond Fort
Perelle Bay
Castel
Vazon Bay
Lihou Island
Perelle
L'Erée
Mont Saint
King's Mills
Castle Cornet
Jersey
Portsmouth
Roquaine Bay
St Saviour Reservoir
Les Lohiers
La Vallette Underground Military
Havelet Bay
La Houguette
St Saviour
St Andrew
Four Cabots
Guernsey Aquarium
Les Terres Point
Clarence Battery
German Military Underground Hospital
Fort Grey Shipwreck
Les Arquêts
Le Gron
St Martin
Les Hubits
Sausmarez Manor
Villiaze
Moulpied
Village de Putron
Les Sages
St Peter's
Guernsey
Le Bourg
La Bellieuse
Jersey
St-Malo
Fermain Bay
Pleinmont Point
Batterie Dollman Gun Pit
Les Nicolles
La Villette
Torteval
Les Murchez
Les Caches
Forest
La Fosse
Le Bigard
German Occupation
Jerbourg
Les Villets
Petit Bot Bay
Moulin Huet Bay
St Martins Point
La Gouffre
Point de la Moye
Icart Point
Guernsey
0 1 2 miles
0 1 2 kilometres
Sorel Point
Ronez Point
Grosnez Point
Plemont Point
Belle Hougue Point
Grosnez
St John's Bay
Fremont Point
La Colombière
5
Plemont
Les Landes
Mourier Valley
Ville la Bas
Portinfer
Rouge Nez
St John
134
Vicard Point
La Grève de Lecq
Grève de Lecq Barracks
107
Hautes Croix
Bouley Bay
La Mare
Millais
Nez du Guet
Battle of the Flowers
Leoville
Grève de Lecq Valley
Handois Reservoir
128
Rozel Bay
La Coupe Point
L'Etacq
St Ouen
Trinity
Rozel
Channel Islands Military
St Mary
Jersey Zoo
Fliquet Bay
The Elms
aMaizin! Adventure Park
Verclut Point
6
Six Rues
Carrefour
Pallot Steam/Motor
108
Mielles
Hamptonne Country Life
St Martin
Trois Bois
St Catherine's Bay
Morel Farm
Becquet Vincent
St Lawrence
Bellozanne Valley
St Peter's Valley
Archirondel
St Peter
Le Moulin de Quétivel
Jersey War Tunnels
Vallée des Vaux
St Ouen's Bay
Grand Chemins
Maufant
Faldouët
Jersey
Le Moulin de Tesson
La Hougue Bie
Five Oaks
Mont Orgueil
Queen's Valley Reservoir
Les Quennevais
Millbrook
Gorey
81
St Saviour
Swiss Valley
7
Beaumont
Jersey Lavender Farm
St Brelade
La Pulente
St Aubin
Royal Bay of Grouville
Longueville
St Helier
St Aubin's Bay
Grouville
Corbière Point
St Brelade's Bay
Maritime
Belcroute Bay
Samarès Manor
St Clement
Corbière
Elizabeth
St Brelade's Bay
Fort Regent
La Rocque
Point La Moye
La Fret Point
Le Haguais
Pontac
Le Hocq
Le Bourg
La Rocque Point
Portelet Bay
Noirmont Command Bunker
Plat Rocque Point
Le Croc
St Clement's Bay
8
Jersey
Guernsey, Poole
Guernsey, Portsmouth
St-Malo
a
b
c
d
e

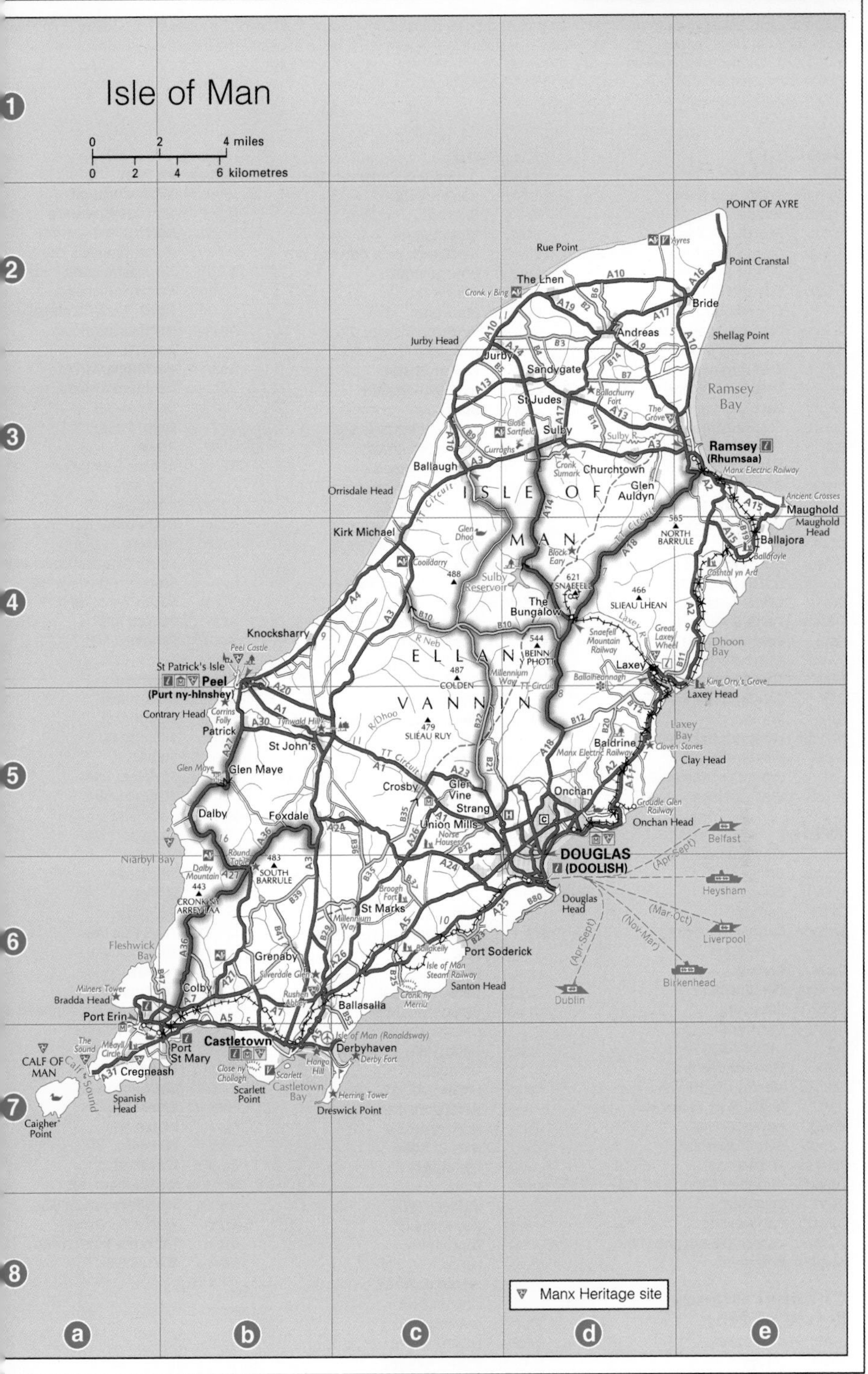
Isle of Man
0 2 4 miles
0 2 4 6 kilometres
POINT OF AYRE
Rue Point
Point Cranstal
The Lhen
Bride
Andreas
Jurby Head
Jurby
Shellag Point
Sandygate
Ramsey Bay
St Judes
Sulby
Ramsey
(Rhumsaa)
Ballaugh
Churchtown
Glen Auldyn
Orrisdale Head
ISLE OF MAN
Maughold
Maughold Head
Kirk Michael
NORTH BARRULE
Ballajora
Sulby Reservoir
SNAEFELL
The Bungalow
SLIEAU LHEAN
Knocksharry
ELLAN VANNIN
Dhoon Bay
Peel Castle
St Patrick's Isle
Peel
(Purt ny-hInshey)
BEINN Y PHOTT
COLDEN
Laxey
Laxey Head
Contrary Head
Corrins Folly
Patrick
Tynwald Hill
SLIEAU RUY
Laxey Bay
St John's
Baldrine
Clay Head
Glen Maye
Crosby
Glen Vine
Onchan
Dalby
Foxdale
Strang
Union Mills
Onchan Head
Belfast
Niarbyl Bay
SOUTH BARRULE
DOUGLAS
(DOOLISH)
Heysham
CRONK NY ARREY LAA
St Marks
Douglas Head
Liverpool
Fleshwick Bay
Grenaby
Port Soderick
Birkenhead
Colby
Santon Head
Bradda Head
Port Erin
Ballasalla
Dublin
Castletown
Derbyhaven
CALF OF MAN
Port St Mary
Cregneash
Calf Sound
Scarlett Point
Castletown Bay
Spanish Head
Dreswick Point
Caigher Point
Manx Heritage site

# Index to place names

This index lists places appearing in the main map section of the atlas in alphabetical order. The reference following each name gives the atlas page number and grid reference of the square in which the place appears. The map shows counties, unitary authorities and administrative areas, together with a list of the abbreviated name forms used in the index. The top 100 places of tourist interest are indexed in **red**, World Heritage sites in **green**, motorway service areas in **blue**, airports in blue *italic* an National Parks in green *italic*.

## Scotland

| | |
|---|---|
| Abers | **Aberdeenshire** |
| Ag & B | **Argyll and Bute** |
| Angus | **Angus** |
| Border | **Scottish Borders** |
| C Aber | **City of Aberdeen** |
| C Dund | **City of Dundee** |
| C Edin | **City of Edinburgh** |
| C Glas | **City of Glasgow** |
| Clacks | **Clackmannanshire (1)** |
| D & G | **Dumfries & Galloway** |
| E Ayrs | **East Ayrshire** |
| E Duns | **East Dunbartonshire (2)** |
| E Loth | **East Lothian** |
| E Rens | **East Renfrewshire (3)** |
| Falk | **Falkirk** |
| Fife | **Fife** |
| Highld | **Highland** |
| Inver | **Inverclyde (4)** |
| Mdloth | **Midlothian (5)** |
| Moray | **Moray** |
| N Ayrs | **North Ayrshire** |
| N Lans | **North Lanarkshire (6)** |
| Ork | **Orkney Islands** |
| P & K | **Perth & Kinross** |
| Rens | **Renfrewshire (7)** |
| S Ayrs | **South Ayrshire** |
| S Lans | **South Lanarkshire** |
| Shet | **Shetland Islands** |
| Stirlg | **Stirling** |
| W Duns | **West Dunbartonshire (8)** |
| W Isls | **Western Isles (Na h-Eileanan an Iar)** |
| W Loth | **West Lothian** |

## Wales

| | |
|---|---|
| Blae G | **Blaenau Gwent (9)** |
| Brdgnd | **Bridgend (10)** |
| Caerph | **Caerphilly (11)** |
| Cardif | **Cardiff** |
| Carmth | **Carmarthenshire** |
| Cerdgn | **Ceredigion** |
| Conwy | **Conwy** |
| Denbgs | **Denbighshire** |
| Flints | **Flintshire** |
| Gwynd | **Gwynedd** |
| IoA | **Isle of Anglesey** |
| Mons | **Monmouthshire** |
| Myr Td | **Merthyr Tydfil (12)** |
| Neath | **Neath Port Talbot (13)** |
| Newpt | **Newport (14)** |
| Pembks | **Pembrokeshire** |
| Powys | **Powys** |
| Rhondd | **Rhondda Cynon Taff (15)** |
| Swans | **Swansea** |
| Torfn | **Torfaen (16)** |
| V Glam | **Vale of Glamorgan (17)** |
| Wrexhm | **Wrexham** |

## Channel Islands & Isle of Man

| | |
|---|---|
| Guern | **Guernsey** |
| Jersey | **Jersey** |
| IoM | **Isle of Man** |

## England

| | |
|---|---|
| BaNES | **Bath & N E Somerset (18)** |
| Barns | **Barnsley (19)** |
| Bed | **Bedford** |
| Birm | **Birmingham** |
| Bl w D | **Blackburn with Darwen (20)** |
| Bmouth | **Bournemouth** |
| Bolton | **Bolton (21)** |
| Bpool | **Blackpool** |
| Br & H | **Brighton & Hove (22)** |
| Br For | **Bracknell Forest (23)** |
| Bristl | **City of Bristol** |
| Bucks | **Buckinghamshire** |
| Bury | **Bury (24)** |
| C Beds | **Central Bedfordshire** |
| C Brad | **City of Bradford** |
| C Derb | **City of Derby** |
| C KuH | **City of Kingston upon Hull** |
| C Leic | **City of Leicester** |
| C Nott | **City of Nottingham** |
| C Pete | **City of Peterborough** |
| C Plym | **City of Plymouth** |
| C Port | **City of Portsmouth** |
| C Sotn | **City of Southampton** |
| C Stke | **City of Stoke-on-Trent** |
| C York | **City of York** |
| Calder | **Calderdale (25)** |
| Cambs | **Cambridgeshire** |
| Ches E | **Cheshire East** |
| Ches W | **Cheshire West and Chester** |
| Cnwll | **Cornwall** |
| Covtry | **Coventry** |
| Cumb | **Cumbria** |
| Darltn | **Darlington (26)** |
| Derbys | **Derbyshire** |
| Devon | **Devon** |
| Donc | **Doncaster (27)** |
| Dorset | **Dorset** |
| Dudley | **Dudley (28)** |
| Dur | **Durham** |
| E R Yk | **East Riding of Yorkshire** |
| E Susx | **East Sussex** |
| Essex | **Essex** |
| Gatesd | **Gateshead (29)** |
| Gloucs | **Gloucestershire** |
| Gt Lon | **Greater London** |
| Halton | **Halton (30)** |
| Hants | **Hampshire** |
| Hartpl | **Hartlepool (31)** |
| Herefs | **Herefordshire** |
| Herts | **Hertfordshire** |
| IoS | **Isles of Scilly** |
| IoW | **Isle of Wight** |
| Kent | **Kent** |
| Kirk | **Kirklees (32)** |
| Knows | **Knowsley (33)** |
| Lancs | **Lancashire** |
| Leeds | **Leeds** |
| Leics | **Leicestershire** |
| Lincs | **Lincolnshire** |
| Lpool | **Liverpool** |
| Luton | **Luton** |
| M Keyn | **Milton Keynes** |
| Manch | **Manchester** |
| Medway | **Medway** |
| Middsb | **Middlesbrough** |
| N Linc | **North Lincolnshire** |
| N Som | **North Somerset (34)** |
| N Tyne | **North Tyneside (35)** |
| N u Ty | **Newcastle upon Tyne** |
| N York | **North Yorkshire** |
| NE Lin | **North East Lincolnshire** |
| Nhants | **Northamptonshire** |
| Norfk | **Norfolk** |
| Notts | **Nottinghamshire** |
| Nthumb | **Northumberland** |
| Oldham | **Oldham (36)** |
| Oxon | **Oxfordshire** |
| Poole | **Poole** |
| R & Cl | **Redcar & Cleveland** |
| Readg | **Reading** |
| Rochdl | **Rochdale (37)** |
| Rothm | **Rotherham (38)** |
| Rutlnd | **Rutland** |
| S Glos | **South Gloucestershire (3** |
| S on T | **Stockton-on-Tees (40)** |
| S Tyne | **South Tyneside (41)** |
| Salfd | **Salford (42)** |
| Sandw | **Sandwell (43)** |
| Sefton | **Sefton (44)** |
| Sheff | **Sheffield** |
| Shrops | **Shropshire** |
| Slough | **Slough (45)** |
| Solhll | **Solihull (46)** |
| Somset | **Somerset** |
| St Hel | **St Helens (47)** |
| Staffs | **Staffordshire** |
| Sthend | **Southend-on-Sea** |
| Stockp | **Stockport (48)** |
| Suffk | **Suffolk** |
| Sundld | **Sunderland** |
| Surrey | **Surrey** |
| Swindn | **Swindon** |
| Tamesd | **Tameside (49)** |
| Thurr | **Thurrock (50)** |
| Torbay | **Torbay** |
| Traffd | **Trafford (51)** |
| W & M | **Windsor & Maidenhead (5** |
| W Berk | **West Berkshire** |
| W Susx | **West Sussex** |
| Wakefd | **Wakefield (53)** |
| Warrtn | **Warrington (54)** |
| Warwks | **Warwickshire** |
| Wigan | **Wigan (55)** |
| Wilts | **Wiltshire** |
| Wirral | **Wirral (56)** |
| Wokham | **Wokingham (57)** |
| Wolves | **Wolverhampton (58)** |
| Worcs | **Worcestershire** |
| Wrekin | **Telford & Wrekin (59)** |
| Wsall | **Walsall (60)** |

ORKNEY ISLANDS
SHETLAND ISLANDS
WESTERN ISLES (Na h-Eileanan an Iar)
HIGHLAND
MORAY
SCOTLAND
ABERDEENSHIRE
Aberdeen
ANGUS
PERTH & KINROSS
Dundee
ARGYLL AND BUTE
STIRLING
FIFE
FALK
Edinburgh
E LOTH
W LOTH
Glasgow
NORTH AYRSHIRE
S LANS
SCOTTISH BORDERS
E AYRS
S AYRS
DUMFRIES & GALLOWAY
NORTHUMBERLAND
Newcastle upon Tyne
Sunderland
DURHAM
CUMBRIA
R & CL
Middlesbrough
IoM
NORTH YORKSHIRE
Blackpool
LANCASHIRE
Bradford
Leeds
York
EAST RIDING OF YORKSHIRE
Kingston upon Hull
N LINC
NE LIN
Liverpool
Manchester
Sheffield
IoA
CONWY
FLINTS
CHES W
CHES E
DERBYS
NOTTS
LINCOLNSHIRE
DENBGS
WREXHAM
Stoke-on-Trent
Nottingham
Derby
GWYNEDD
STAFFS
LEICS
RUTLAND
Leicester
Peterborough
NORFOLK
SHROPSHIRE
Birmingham
Coventry
POWYS
CAMBS
CERDGN
WORCS
WARWKS
NHANTS
SUFFOLK
Milton Keynes
BED
HEREFS
WALES
ENGLAND
PEMBKS
CARMTH
C BEDS
Luton
HERTS
ESSEX
MONS
GLOUCS
OXON
Swansea
Cardiff
BUCKS
Southend-on-Sea
Bristol
Swindon
Reading
GREATER LONDON
MEDWAY
W BERK
WILTSHIRE
SURREY
KENT
SOMERSET
HAMPSHIRE
W SUSX
E SUSX
DORSET
Southampton
DEVON
Bournemouth
Portsmouth
Poole
IoW
Guernsey
Jersey
CHANNEL ISLANDS
CORNWALL
Torbay
Plymouth
IoS

## A

**Abbas Combe** Somset 27 G6
**Abberley** Worcs 70 D2
**Abberley Common** Worcs 70 D2
**Abberton** Essex 62 B4
**Abberton** Worcs 71 H4
**Abbess Roding** Essex 60 F5
**Abbeydale** Sheff 114 F5
**Abbey Dore** Herefs 54 B3
**Abbey Green** Staffs 99 L2
**Abbey St Bathans** Border 178 F6
**Abbeystead** Lancs 130 B8
**Abbey Town** Cumb 147 L5
**Abbey Valley Crematorium** Derbys 101 H2
**Abbey Village** Lancs 121 J6
**Abbey Wood** Gt Lon 45 J4
**Abbotrule** Border 167 J6
**Abbots Bickington** Devon 9 K3
**Abbots Bromley** Staffs 100 B7
**Abbotsbury** Dorset 14 B5
**Abbots Deuglie** P & K 186 B5
**Abbotsham** Devon 22 F6
**Abbotskerswell** Devon 7 K3
**Abbots Langley** Herts 59 H7
**Abbots Leigh** N Som 38 D5
**Abbotsley** Cambs 75 J3
**Abbots Morton** Worcs 71 H4
**Abbots Ripton** Cambs 89 J7
**Abbot's Salford** Warwks 71 J4
**Abbots Worthy** Hants 29 J5
**Abbotts Ann** Hants 29 G3
**Abbott Street** Dorset 15 J3
**Abdon** Shrops 83 L6
**Aberaeron** Cerdgn 66 B3
**Aberaman** Rhondd 52 F7
**Aberangell** Gwynd 81 J2
**Aberarder** Highld 202 F1
**Aberargie** P & K 186 B4
**Aberarth** Cerdgn 66 B2
**Aberavon** Neath 51 L7
**Abercanaid** Myr Td 53 G7
**Abercarn** Caerph 37 K2
**Abercastle** Pembks 64 B7
**Abercegir** Powys 81 H3
**Aberchalder Lodge** Highld 202 B5
**Aberchirder** Abers 216 C4
**Abercorn** W Loth 176 E3
**Abercraf** Powys 52 C5
**Abercregan** Neath 36 D2
**Abercwmboi** Rhondd 52 F7
**Abercych** Pembks 65 H6
**Abercynon** Rhondd 37 G2
**Aberdalgie** P & K 185 M4
**Aberdare** Rhondd 52 F7
**Aberdaron** Gwynd 94 C7
**Aberdeen** C Aber 207 H4
*Aberdeen Airport* C Aber 207 G3
**Aberdeen Crematorium** C Aber 207 G4
**Aberdour** Fife 177 G2
**Aberdulais** Neath 52 B7
**Aberdyfi** Gwynd 80 E4
**Aberedw** Powys 68 C5
**Abereiddy** Pembks 48 D2
**Abererch** Gwynd 95 G5
**Aberfan** Myr Td 53 G7
**Aberfeldy** P & K 194 D6
**Aberffraw** IoA 108 D7
**Aberford** Leeds 124 C3
**Aberfoyle** Stirlg 184 C7
**Abergavenny** Mons 53 L5
**Abergele** Conwy 110 C6
**Abergorlech** Carmth 66 D7
**Abergwesyn** Powys 67 J4
**Abergwili** Carmth 50 F2
**Abergwynfi** Neath 36 D2
**Abergwyngregyn** Gwynd 109 J6
**Abergynolwyn** Gwynd 80 F3
**Aberkenfig** Brdgnd 36 D4
**Aberlady** E Loth 178 B3
**Aberlemno** Angus 196 E5
**Aberllefenni** Gwynd 81 G2
**Aberllynfi** Powys 68 D6
**Aberlour, Charlestown of** Moray 215 G5
**Abermule** Powys 82 D5
**Abernant** Carmth 50 D2
**Aber-nant** Rhondd 52 F7
**Abernethy** P & K 186 C4
**Abernyte** P & K 186 D2
**Aberporth** Cerdgn 65 J4
**Abersoch** Gwynd 94 E6
**Abersychan** Torfn 53 K7
**Aberthin** V Glam 36 F5
**Abertillery** Blae G 53 K7
**Abertridwr** Caerph 37 H3
**Abertridwr** Powys 97 G8
**Aberuthven** P & K 185 K4
**Aberystwyth** Cerdgn 80 D6
**Aberystwyth Crematorium** Cerdgn 80 E6
**Abingdon-on-Thames** Oxon 41 J2
**Abinger Common** Surrey 31 J3
**Abinger Hammer** Surrey 31 H2
**Abington** Nhants 73 L3
**Abington** S Lans 165 H5
**Abington Pigotts** Cambs 75 K5
*Abington Services* S Lans 165 H4
**Abingworth** W Susx 18 F3
**Ab Kettleby** Leics 102 B7
**Ablington** Gloucs 56 C6
**Abney** Derbys 114 D5
**Aboyne** Abers 205 L5
**Abhainn Suidhe** W Isls 232 d4
**Abram** Wigan 112 E2
**Abriachan** Highld 212 E7
**Abridge** Essex 45 J2
**Abronhill** N Lans 175 K3
**Abson** S Glos 39 G5
**Abthorpe** Nhants 73 J5
**Aby** Lincs 118 F5
**Acaster Malbis** C York 124 E2
**Acaster Selby** N York 124 E3
**Accrington** Lancs 121 L5
**Accrington Crematorium** Lancs 121 L5
**Acha** Ag & B 188 F5
**Achahoish** Ag & B 172 D3
**Achalader** P & K 195 H7
**Achaleven** Ag & B 182 D1
**Acha Mor** W Isls 232 f3
**Achanalt** Highld 211 K3
**Achandunie** Highld 222 E6
**Achany** Highld 222 D2
**Acharacle** Highld 190 D3
**Acharn** Highld 190 E6
**Acharn** P & K 194 B7
**Achavanich** Highld 231 H6
**Achduart** Highld 224 C7
**Achfary** Highld 228 D7
**A'Chill** Highld 198 D4
**Achiltibuie** Highld 224 C6
**Achina** Highld 229 L4
**Achinhoan** Ag & B 161 J6
**Achintee** Highld 210 E6
**Achintraid** Highld 210 C6
**Achmelvich** Highld 224 C4
**Achmore** Highld 210 D7
**Achmore** W Isls 232 f3
**Achnacarnin** Highld 224 C3
**Achnacarry** Highld 201 J7
**Achnacloich** Highld 199 J4
**Achnaconeran** Highld 202 C2
**Achnacroish** Ag & B 191 G7
**Achnadrish House** Ag & B 189 L6
**Achnafauld** P & K 185 J1
**Achnagarron** Highld 222 F7
**Achnaha** Highld 189 L3
**Achnahaird** Highld 224 B5
**Achnahannet** Highld 214 B8
**Achnairn** Highld 225 L6
**Achnalea** Highld 191 G4
**Achnamara** Ag & B 172 D2
**Achnasheen** Highld 211 J3
**Achnashellach** Highld 210 F5
**Achnastank** Moray 215 G7
**Achosnich** Highld 189 K3
**Achranich** Highld 190 E6
**Achreamie** Highld 230 E3
**Achriabhach** Highld 192 B3
**Achriesgill** Highld 228 C5
**Achtoty** Highld 229 K3
**Achurch** Nhants 88 E6
**Achvaich** Highld 222 F3
**Achvarasdal** Highld 230 E3
**Ackergill** Highld 231 L5
**Acklam** Middsb 141 L4
**Acklam** N York 134 B7
**Ackleton** Shrops 84 D4
**Acklington** Nthumb 159 G2
**Ackton** Wakefd 124 C6
**Ackworth Moor Top** Wakefd 124 C7
**Acle** Norfk 93 J2
**Acock's Green** Birm 85 K6
**Acol** Kent 35 J2
**Acomb** C York 124 E1
**Acomb** Nthumb 150 B2
**Aconbury** Herefs 54 D2
**Acton** Ches E 98 F2
**Acton** Gt Lon 44 D4
**Acton** Staffs 99 J4
**Acton** Suffk 77 K5
**Acton Beauchamp** Herefs 70 C4
**Acton Bridge** Ches W 112 E6
**Acton Burnell** Shrops 83 K3
**Acton Green** Herefs 70 C4
**Acton Park** Wrexhm 97 M3
**Acton Round** Shrops 84 B4
**Acton Scott** Shrops 83 J5
**Acton Trussell** Staffs 99 L8
**Acton Turville** S Glos 39 J4
**Adbaston** Staffs 99 H6
**Adber** Dorset 26 E7
**Adbolton** Notts 101 L5
**Adderbury** Oxon 72 F7
**Adderley** Shrops 98 F4
**Addiewell** W Loth 176 D5
**Addingham** C Brad 123 G1
**Addington** Bucks 58 C3
**Addington** Gt Lon 45 G7
**Addington** Kent 33 H2
**Addiscombe** Gt Lon 45 G6
**Addlestone** Surrey 43 H7
**Addlethorpe** Lincs 119 H7
**Adeyfield** Herts 59 H6
**Adfa** Powys 82 B4
**Adforton** Herefs 69 H1
**Adisham** Kent 35 G4
**Adlestrop** Gloucs 56 E3
**Adlingfleet** E R Yk 125 K6
**Adlington** Lancs 121 J7
**Admaston** Staffs 100 B7
**Admaston** Wrekin 84 B2
**Adpar** Cerdgn 65 J6
**Adsborough** Somset 25 L5
**Adscombe** Somset 25 J4
**Adstock** Bucks 58 C3
**Adstone** Nhants 73 H4
**Adversane** W Susx 31 H6
**Advie** Highld 214 D7
**Adwick le Street** Donc 124 E8
**Adwick upon Dearne** Donc 115 J2
**Ae** D & G 155 H4
**Ae Bridgend** D & G 155 H5
**Afan Forest Park** Neath 36 D2
**Affleck** Abers 216 B6
**Affpuddle** Dorset 14 F4
**Affric Lodge** Highld 201 J2
**Afon-wen** Flints 110 F6
**Afton** IoW 16 D5
**Agecroft Crematorium** Salfd 113 J2
**Agglethorpe** N York 131 K3
**Aigburth** Lpool 111 L4
**Aike** E R Yk 126 C2
**Aiketgate** Cumb 148 E5
**Aikton** Cumb 148 B4
**Ailsworth** C Pete 89 G4
**Ainderby Quernhow** N York 132 E4
**Ainderby Steeple** N York 132 E2
**Aingers Green** Essex 62 D4
**Ainsdale** Sefton 120 D7
**Ainstable** Cumb 148 F5
**Ainsworth** Bury 121 L8
**Ainthorpe** N York 142 E5
**Aintree** Sefton 111 L2
**Ainville** W Loth 176 F5
**Aird** Ag & B 181 M7
**Aird** D & G 144 D3
**Aird** W Isls 232 g2
**Àird a' Mhulaidh** W Isls 232 e3
**Aird Asaig** W Isls 232 e4
**Aird Dhubh** Highld 209 L6
**Airdeny** Ag & B 182 E2
**Aird of Kinloch** Ag & B 181 H2
**Aird of Sleat** Highld 199 J5
**Airdrie** N Lans 175 K5
**Airdriehill** N Lans 175 K5
**Airds of Kells** D & G 154 B7
**Aird Uig** W Isls 232 d2
**Airidh a bhruaich** W Isls 232 e3
**Airieland** D & G 146 D4
**Airlie** Angus 195 L6
**Airmyn** E R Yk 125 H5
**Airntully** P & K 186 A1
**Airor** Highld 199 L4
**Airth** Falk 176 B2
**Airton** N York 131 G7
**Aisby** Lincs 103 G5
**Aisby** Lincs 116 E3
**Aish** Devon 7 G4
**Aish** Devon 7 J4
**Aisholt** Somset 25 J4
**Aiskew** N York 132 D2
**Aislaby** N York 134 B3
**Aislaby** N York 143 H5
**Aislaby** S on T 141 J5
**Aisthorpe** Lincs 116 F5
**Aith** Shet 235 c5
**Akeld** Nthumb 168 E4
**Akeley** Bucks 73 K6
**Albaston** Cnwll 6 B2
**Alberbury** Shrops 83 G1
**Albourne** W Susx 19 H3
**Albrighton** Shrops 84 E3
**Albrighton** Shrops 98 C8
**Alburgh** Norfk 92 F6
**Albury** Herts 60 C3
**Albury** Surrey 31 H2
**Albury Heath** Surrey 31 H3
**Alcaig** Highld 212 E3
**Alcaston** Shrops 83 J6
**Alcester** Warwks 71 K3
**Alcester Lane End** Birm 85 J7
**Alciston** E Susx 20 B5
**Alcombe** Somset 24 F3
**Alconbury** Cambs 89 H7
**Alconbury Weston** Cambs 89 H7
**Aldborough** N York 132 F6
**Aldborough** Norfk 106 E5
**Aldbourne** Wilts 40 E5

**Aldbrough** E R Yk 127 G3
**Aldbrough St John** N York 140 F5
**Aldbury** Herts 58 F5
**Aldcliffe** Lancs 129 K7
**Aldclune** P & K 194 E4
**Aldeburgh** Suffk 79 K3
**Aldeby** Norfk 93 J5
**Aldenham** Herts 43 J2
**Alderbury** Wilts 28 D6
**Alderford** Norfk 106 D8
**Alderholt** Dorset 28 C8
**Alderley** Gloucs 39 H3
**Alderley Edge** Ches E 113 J5
**Aldermans Green** Covtry 86 D6
**Aldermaston** W Berk 41 L7
**Alderminster** Warwks 72 B5
**Aldershot** Hants 30 E2
**Alderton** Gloucs 56 A2
**Alderton** Nhants 73 K5
**Alderton** Suffk 79 H6
**Alderton** Wilts 39 J4
**Aldfield** N York 132 D5
**Aldford** Ches W 98 B2
**Aldgate** Rutlnd 88 E3
**Aldham** Essex 61 L3
**Aldham** Suffk 78 C5
**Aldingbourne** W Susx 18 C5
**Aldingham** Cumb 129 G5
**Aldington** Kent 34 E7
**Aldington** Worcs 71 J5
**Aldington Corner** Kent 34 E7
**Aldivalloch** Moray 205 H1
**Aldochlay** Ag & B 174 C1
**Aldreth** Cambs 90 C8
**Aldridge** Wsall 85 J4
**Aldringham** Suffk 79 J3
**Aldsworth** Gloucs 56 D6
**Aldunie** Moray 215 H8
**Aldwark** Derbys 100 E2
**Aldwark** N York 133 G6
**Aldwick** W Susx 18 C6
**Aldwincle** Nhants 88 E6
**Aldworth** W Berk 41 K4
**Alexandria** W Duns 174 D3
**Aley** Somset 25 J4
**Alfington** Devon 12 E3
**Alfold** Surrey 31 H5
**Alfold Crossways** Surrey 31 H4
**Alford** Abers 206 B3
**Alford** Lincs 118 F6
**Alford** Somset 26 E5
**Alford Crematorium** Lincs 118 F6
**Alfreton** Derbys 101 H2
**Alfrick** Worcs 70 D4
**Alfrick Pound** Worcs 70 D4
**Alfriston** E Susx 20 B5
**Algarkirk** Lincs 103 M5
**Alhampton** Somset 26 F4
**Alkborough** N Linc 125 K6
**Alkham** Kent 35 H6
**Alkmonton** Derbys 100 D5
**Allaleigh** Devon 7 J5
**Allanaquoich** Abers 204 D6
**Allanbank** N Lans 175 L6
**Allanton** Border 179 H7
**Allanton** N Lans 175 L6
**Allanton** S Lans 175 K7
**Allaston** Gloucs 54 F6
**Allbrook** Hants 29 J7
**All Cannings** Wilts 40 B7
**Allendale** Nthumb 149 L4
**Allen End** Warwks 85 L4
**Allenheads** Nthumb 149 L6
**Allen's Green** Herts 60 D5
**Allensmore** Herefs 69 J7
**Allenton** C Derb 101 G6
**Aller** Devon 24 B6
**Aller** Somset 26 B5
**Allerby** Cumb 147 J6
**Allercombe** Devon 12 D4
**Allerford** Somset 24 D3
**Allerston** N York 134 D3
**Allerthorpe** E R Yk 125 J2
**Allerton** C Brad 123 G4
**Allerton** Highld 213 H2
**Allerton** Lpool 111 L4
**Allerton Bywater** Leeds 124 C5
**Allerton Mauleverer** N York 132 F7
**Allesley** Covtry 86 C7
**Allestree** C Derb 101 G5
**Allexton** Leics 88 B4
**Allgreave** Ches E 113 L7
**Allhallows** Medway 46 D4
**Alligin Shuas** Highld 210 C3
**Allington** Dorset 13 L4
**Allington** Lincs 102 E4
**Allington** Wilts 28 D4
**Allington** Wilts 39 K5
**Allington** Wilts 40 B7
**Allithwaite** Cumb 129 J4
**Alloa** Clacks 185 J8
**Allonby** Cumb 147 J6
**Alloway** S Ayrs 163 J5
**Allowenshay** Somset 26 B8
**All Stretton** Shrops 83 J4
**Alltchaorunn** Highld 192 C6
**Alltwalis** Carmth 66 B7
**Alltwen** Neath 51 K5
**Alltyblaca** Cerdgn 66 C5
**Allweston** Dorset 26 F8
**Almeley** Herefs 69 G4
**Almington** Staffs 99 G5
**Almondbank** P & K 185 M3
**Almondbury** Kirk 123 H7
**Almondsbury** S Glos 38 E4
**Alne** N York 133 G6
**Alness** Highld 222 E7
**Alnham** Nthumb 168 E7
**Alnmouth** Nthumb 169 J7
**Alnwick** Nthumb 169 J6
**Alperton** Gt Lon 44 D4
**Alphamstone** Essex 77 K7
**Alpheton** Suffk 77 K4
**Alphington** Devon 11 L6
**Alport** Derbys 114 E8
**Alpraham** Ches E 98 E1
**Alresford** Essex 62 C4
**Alrewas** Staffs 85 L1
**Alsager** Ches E 99 H2
**Alsop en le Dale** Derbys 100 D2
**Alston** Cumb 149 J5
**Alston** Devon 13 H2
**Alstone** Gloucs 55 M2
**Alstonefield** Staffs 100 C2
**Alston Sutton** Somset 26 B2
**Alswear** Devon 23 L6
**Altandhu** Highld 224 B6
**Altarnun** Cnwll 9 G8
**Altass** Highld 222 C2
**Altcreich** Ag & B 190 D8
**Altgaltraig** Ag & B 173 H4
**Althorne** Essex 61 L7
**Althorpe** N Linc 125 K8
**Altnabreac Station** Highld 230 E6
**Altnaharra** Highld 225 M2
**Altofts** Wakefd 124 B5
**Alton** Derbys 115 G8
**Alton** Hants 30 B4
**Alton** Staffs 100 B4
**Alton Barnes** Wilts 40 C7
**Alton Pancras** Dorset 14 D3
**Alton Priors** Wilts 40 C7
**Alton Towers** Staffs 100 B4
**Altrincham** Traffd 113 H4
**Altrincham Crematorium** Traffd 113 G4
**Altskeith Hotel** Stirlg 184 B6
**Alva** Clacks 185 J7
**Alvanley** Ches W 112 D6
**Alvaston** C Derb 101 H5
**Alvechurch** Worcs 85 J8
**Alvecote** Warwks 86 B3
**Alvediston** Wilts 27 L6
**Alveley** Shrops 84 D6
**Alverdiscott** Devon 23 H6
**Alverstoke** Hants 17 H3
**Alverstone** IoW 17 H5
**Alverthorpe** Wakefd 123 L6
**Alverton** Notts 102 C4
**Alves** Moray 214 E3
**Alvescot** Oxon 56 F6
**Alveston** S Glos 38 F3
**Alveston** Warwks 72 B3
**Alvingham** Lincs 118 E4
**Alvington** Gloucs 54 E7
**Alwalton** C Pete 89 G4
**Alwinton** Nthumb 168 D7
**Alwoodley** Leeds 123 K3
**Alyth** P & K 195 K6
**Am Bàgh a Tuath** W Isls 233 b9
**Ambergate** Derbys 101 G3
**Amberley** Gloucs 55 J7
**Amberley** W Susx 18 D3
**Amble** Nthumb 159 G2
**Amblecote** Dudley 84 F6
**Ambler Thorn** C Brad 123 G5
**Ambleside** Cumb 137 K6
**Ambleston** Pembks 49 G3
**Ambrosden** Oxon 57 L4
**Amcotts** N Linc 125 K7
**Amersham** Bucks 42 F2
**Amersham Common** Bucks 42 F2
**Amersham Old Town** Bucks 42 F2
**Amersham on the Hill** Bucks 58 F7
**Amesbury** Wilts 28 D3
**Amhuinnsuidhe** W Isls 232 d4
**Amington** Staffs 86 B3
**Amisfield** D & G 155 H5
**Amlwch** IoA 108 F3
**Ammanford** Carmth 51 J3
**Amotherby** N York 134 B5
**Ampfield** Hants 29 H6
**Ampleforth** N York 133 J4
**Ampney Crucis** Gloucs 56 B7
**Ampney St Mary** Gloucs 56 C7
**Ampney St Peter** Gloucs 56 B7
**Amport** Hants 28 F3
**Ampthill** C Beds 74 F6
**Ampton** Suffk 77 J1
**Amroth** Pembks 49 K6
**Amulree** P & K 185 J1
**Amwell** Herts 59 K5
**Anaheilt** Highld 191 G4
**Ancaster** Lincs 103 G4
**Ancells Farm** Hants 30 D1
**Ancroft** Nthumb 168 E1
**Ancrum** Border 167 K4
**Ancton** W Susx 18 D5
**Anderby** Lincs 119 G6
**Andover** Hants 29 G3
**Andoversford** Gloucs 56 A4
**Andreas** IoM 237 d2
**Anerley** Gt Lon 45 G6
**Anfield** Lpool 111 K3
**Anfield Crematorium** Lpool 111 K3
**Angarrack** Cnwll 3 G4
**Angelbank** Shrops 83 L7
**Angle** Pembks 48 E6
**Anglesey** IoA 108 E5
**Anglesey Abbey** Cambs 76 D3
**Angmering** W Susx 18 E5
**Angram** N York 124 D2
**Ankerville** Highld 223 H6
**Anlaby** E R Yk 126 C5
**Anmer** Norfk 105 H6
**Anmore** Hants 17 J1
**Annan** D & G 147 L2
**Annandale Water Services** D & G 155 J4
**Annat** Highld 210 D4
**Annathill** N Lans 175 J4
**Anna Valley** Hants 29 G3
**Annbank** S Ayrs 163 K5
**Anne Hathaway's Cottage** Warwks 71 L4
**Annfield Plain** Dur 150 F5
**Anniesland** C Glas 174 F5
**Ansdell** Lancs 120 D5
**Ansford** Somset 26 F5
**Ansley** Warwks 86 C5
**Anslow** Staffs 100 E7
**Anslow Gate** Staffs 100 D7
**Anstey** Herts 60 C2
**Anstey** Leics 87 G2
**Anstruther** Fife 187 J6
**Ansty** W Susx 19 J2
**Ansty** Warwks 86 E6
**Ansty** Wilts 27 L6
**Anthorn** Cumb 147 L4
**Antingham** Norfk 106 F5
**An t-Ob** W Isls 232 d5
**Antonine Wall** 175 L3
**Anton's Gowt** Lincs 103 M3
**Antony** Cnwll 6 B5
**Antrobus** Ches W 112 F5
**Anwick** Lincs 103 J3
**Anwoth** D & G 145 M4
**Aperfield** Gt Lon 32 D2
**Apethorpe** Nhants 88 E4
**Apley** Lincs 117 J6
**Apperknowle** Derbys 115 G5
**Apperley** Gloucs 55 K3
**Appin** Ag & B 191 J6
**Appleby** N Linc 126 B7
**Appleby-in-Westmorland** Cumb 139 G3
**Appleby Magna** Leics 86 C2
**Appleby Parva** Leics 86 C2
**Applecross** Highld 209 L5
**Appledore** Devon 23 G5
**Appledore** Devon 25 G8
**Appledore** Kent 34 C8
**Appleford** Oxon 41 K2
**Applegarth Town** D & G 155 J5
**Appleshaw** Hants 28 F2
**Appleton** Halton 112 D4
**Appleton** Oxon 57 H7
**Appleton** Warrtn 112 F5
**Appleton-le-Moors** N York 133 L3
**Appleton-le-Street** N York 134 B5
**Appleton Roebuck** N York 124 E3
**Appleton Thorn** Warrtn 112 F5
**Appleton Wiske** N York 141 J6
**Appletreehall** Border 167 H6
**Appletreewick** N York 131 K7
**Appley** Somset 25 G6
**Appley Bridge** Lancs 121 G8
**Apse Heath** IoW 17 G5
**Apsley End** C Beds 59 J2
**Apuldram** W Susx 18 A5
**Arabella** Highld 223 H6
**Arbirlot** Angus 196 F7
**Arboll** Highld 223 J5
**Arborfield** Wokham 42 C6
**Arborfield Cross** Wokham 42 C6
**Arbourthorne** Sheff 115 G4
**Arbroath** Angus 197 G7
**Arbuthnott** Abers 197 K2
**Archddu** Carmth 50 F5
**Archdeacon Newton** Darltn 141 G4
**Archencarroch** W Duns 174 D3
**Archiestown** Moray 214 F5
**Archirondel** Jersey 236 e6
**Arclid** Ches E 99 H1
**Ardallie** Abers 217 J6
**Ardanaiseig Hotel** Ag & B 182 F3
**Ardaneaskan** Highld 210 C7
**Ardarroch** Highld 210 C6

**Ardbeg** Ag & B 160 D1
**Ardbeg** Ag & B 173 J5
**Ardbeg** Ag & B 173 K2
**Ardcharnich** Highld 220 F4
**Ardchiavaig** Ag & B 180 E4
**Ardchonnel** Ag & B 182 D5
**Ardchullarie More** Stirlg 184 D5
**Arddarroch** Ag & B 183 J7
**Arddleen** Powys 82 F1
**Ard Dorch** Highld 209 J8
**Ardechive** Highld 201 H7
**Ardeer** N Ayrs 163 H2
**Ardeley** Herts 60 A3
**Ardelve** Highld 210 D8
**Arden** Ag & B 174 C2
**Ardens Grafton** Warwks 71 K4
**Ardentallen** Ag & B 182 B3
**Ardentinny** Ag & B 173 L2
**Ardentraive** Ag & B 173 H4
**Ardeonaig** Stirlg 184 E1
**Ardersier** Highld 213 J4
**Ardessie** Highld 220 D4
**Ardfern** Ag & B 182 A6
**Ardfernal** Ag & B 171 K4
**Ardgartan** Ag & B 183 J6
**Ardgay** Highld 222 D4
**Ardgour** Highld 191 K4
**Ardgowan** Inver 173 L4
**Ardhallow** Ag & B 173 K4
**Ardhasig** W Isls 232 e4
**Ardheslaig** Highld 210 B3
**Ardindrean** Highld 220 F4
**Ardingly** W Susx 32 C7
**Ardington** Oxon 41 H3
**Ardlamont** Ag & B 173 G5
**Ardleigh** Essex 62 C3
**Ardleigh Heath** Essex 62 C2
**Ardler** P & K 195 L7
**Ardley** Oxon 57 K3
**Ardlui** Ag & B 183 K4
**Ardlussa** Ag & B 172 B2
**Ardmair** Highld 220 E2
**Ardmaleish** Ag & B 173 J5
**Ardminish** Ag & B 172 B8
**Ardmolich** Highld 190 E3
**Ardmore** Ag & B 174 C3
**Ardmore** Highld 222 F4
**Ardnadam** Ag & B 173 K3
**Ardnagrask** Highld 212 E4
**Ardnamurchan** Highld 190 B3
**Ardnarff** Highld 210 D7
**Ardnastang** Highld 190 F4
**Ardpatrick** Ag & B 172 C6
**Ardrishaig** Ag & B 172 E2
**Ardross** Highld 222 E6
**Ardrossan** N Ayrs 163 G2
**Ardsley East** Leeds 123 K5
**Ardslignish** Highld 190 B4
**Ardtalla** Ag & B 171 J7
**Ardtoe** Highld 190 C3
**Arduaine** Ag & B 182 A5
**Ardullie** Highld 212 E2
**Ardvasar** Highld 199 K5
**Ardvorlich** P & K 184 D3
**Ardvourlie** W Isls 232 e3
**Ardwell** D & G 144 D5
**Ardwick** Manch 113 J3
**Areley Kings** Worcs 70 E1
**Arevegaig** Highld 190 D3
**Arford** Hants 30 D4
**Argoed** Caerph 53 J7
**Argyll Forest Park** Ag & B 183 J6
**Aribruach** W Isls 232 e3
**Aridhglas** Ag & B 180 D3
**Arileod** Ag & B 188 F5
**Arinagour** Ag & B 189 G5
**Ariogan** Ag & B 182 C3
**Arisaig** Highld 199 K7
**Arisaig House** Highld 199 L7
**Arkendale** N York 132 F7
**Arkesden** Essex 76 C7
**Arkholme** Lancs 130 B5
**Arkleton** D & G 156 C4
**Arkley** Gt Lon 44 E2
**Arksey** Donc 115 L1
**Arkwright Town** Derbys 115 H7
**Arle** Gloucs 55 L4
**Arlecdon** Cumb 136 E4
**Arlesey** C Beds 75 H7
**Arleston** Wrekin 84 B2
**Arley** Ches E 112 F5
**Arley** Warwks 86 C5
**Arlingham** Gloucs 55 G6
**Arlington** Devon 23 K4
**Arlington** E Susx 20 B4
**Armadale** Highld 199 K5
**Armadale** Highld 230 A3
**Armadale** W Loth 176 C5
**Armathwaite** Cumb 148 E5
**Arminghall** Norfk 92 F3
**Armitage** Staffs 85 J1
**Armley** Leeds 123 K4
**Armscote** Warwks 72 B5
**Armthorpe** Donc 115 L1
**Arnabost** Ag & B 188 F4
**Arncliffe** N York 131 H5
**Arncroach** Fife 187 H6
**Arndilly House** Moray 215 G5
**Arne** Dorset 15 H5
**Arnesby** Leics 87 H5
**Arngask** P & K 186 B5
**Arnisdale** Highld 200 C3
**Arnish** Highld 209 J5
**Arniston** Mdloth 177 K6
**Arnol** W Isls 232 f1
**Arnold** E R Yk 126 E3
**Arnold** Notts 101 L4
**Arnprior** Stirlg 184 D7
**Arnside** Cumb 129 K4
**Aros** Ag & B 190 B7
**Arrad Foot** Cumb 129 G4
**Arram** E R Yk 126 C2
**Arran** N Ayrs 162 B3
**Arrathorne** N York 132 C2
**Arreton** IoW 17 G5
**Arrina** Highld 210 B3
**Arrington** Cambs 75 K4
**Arrochar** Ag & B 183 K6
**Arrow** Warwks 71 J3
**Arscott** Shrops 83 J2
**Artafallie** Highld 212 F4
**Arthington** Leeds 123 K2
**Arthingworth** Nhants 87 L7
**Arthrath** Abers 217 H6
**Artrochie** Abers 217 J7
**Arundel** W Susx 18 D4
**Asby** Cumb 136 E3
**Ascog** Ag & B 173 J5
**Ascot** W & M 42 F6
**Ascott-under-Wychwood** Oxon 56 F4
**Asenby** N York 132 F4
**Asfordby** Leics 102 B8
**Asfordby Hill** Leics 102 B8
**Asgarby** Lincs 103 J4
**Ash** Kent 35 H3
**Ash** Kent 45 L6
**Ash** Somset 26 C7
**Ash** Surrey 30 E2
**Ashampstead** W Berk 41 K5
**Ashbocking** Suffk 78 E4
**Ashbourne** Derbys 100 D3
**Ashbrittle** Somset 25 G6
**Ashburton** Devon 7 H2
**Ashbury** Devon 10 D5
**Ashbury** Oxon 40 E4
**Ashby** N Linc 125 L8
**Ashby by Partney** Lincs 118 F7
**Ashby cum Fenby** NE Lin 118 C2
**Ashby de la Launde** Lincs 103 H2
**Ashby-de-la-Zouch** Leics 86 D1
**Ashby Folville** Leics 87 K2
**Ashby Magna** Leics 87 H5
**Ashby Parva** Leics 87 G5
**Ashby Puerorum** Lincs 118 D7
**Ashby St Ledgers** Nhants 73 H2
**Ashby St Mary** Norfk 93 G3
**Ashchurch** Gloucs 55 L2
**Ashcombe** Devon 11 L8
**Ashcombe** N Som 37 M7
**Ashcott** Somset 26 C4
**Ashdon** Essex 76 E6
**Ashdown Forest** E Susx 32 E6
**Ashe** Hants 29 K2
**Asheldham** Essex 62 A7
**Ashen** Essex 77 H6
**Ashendon** Bucks 58 B5
**Asheridge** Bucks 58 F6
**Ashfield** Stirlg 185 G6
**Ashfield cum Thorpe** Suffk 78 E3
**Ashfield Green** Suffk 92 F8
**Ashford** Devon 7 G6
**Ashford** Devon 23 H4
**Ashford** Kent 34 D6
**Ashford** Surrey 43 H6
**Ashford Bowdler** Shrops 69 K1
**Ashford Carbonell** Shrops 69 K1
**Ashford Hill** Hants 41 K7
**Ashford in the Water** Derbys 114 D7
**Ashgill** S Lans 175 K7
**Ash Green** Surrey 30 E2
**Ash Green** Warwks 86 D6
**Ashill** Devon 12 E1
**Ashill** Norfk 91 K3
**Ashill** Somset 25 L7
**Ashingdon** Essex 46 E2
**Ashington** Nthumb 159 G5
**Ashington** Somset 26 E6
**Ashington** W Susx 18 F3
**Ashkirk** Border 167 G5
**Ashleworth** Gloucs 55 J3
**Ashleworth Quay** Gloucs 55 J3
**Ashley** Cambs 77 G3
**Ashley** Ches E 113 H5
**Ashley** Devon 10 F3
**Ashley** Gloucs 39 L2
**Ashley** Hants 16 B4
**Ashley** Hants 29 G5
**Ashley** Kent 35 J5
**Ashley** Nhants 87 L5
**Ashley** Staffs 99 H5
**Ashley** Wilts 39 J6
**Ashley Green** Bucks 58 F6
**Ash Magna** Shrops 98 E4
**Ashmansworth** Hants 41 H8
**Ashmansworthy** Devon 22 E7
**Ash Mill** Devon 24 C6
**Ashmore** Dorset 27 K7
**Ashmore Green** W Berk 41 J6
**Ashorne** Warwks 72 C3
**Ashover** Derbys 115 G8
**Ashow** Warwks 72 C1
**Ashperton** Herefs 70 B6
**Ashprington** Devon 7 J4
**Ash Priors** Somset 25 J5
**Ashreigney** Devon 10 F3
**Ash Street** Suffk 78 B5
**Ashtead** Surrey 44 D8
**Ash Thomas** Devon 12 C1
**Ashton** Ches W 112 D7
**Ashton** Cnwll 3 G5
**Ashton** Devon 11 K7
**Ashton** Herefs 69 K2
**Ashton** Inver 173 L3
**Ashton** Nhants 73 L5
**Ashton** Nhants 88 F5
**Ashton Common** Wilts 39 K8
**Ashton-in-Makerfield** Wigan 112 E2
**Ashton Keynes** Wilts 40 B2
**Ashton under Hill** Worcs 71 H6
**Ashton-under-Lyne** Tamesd 113 L2
**Ashton Vale** Bristl 38 E6
**Ashurst** Hants 16 D1
**Ashurst** Kent 32 F5
**Ashurst** Lancs 121 G8
**Ashurst** W Susx 19 G3
**Ashurstwood** W Susx 32 D6
**Ash Vale** Surrey 30 E2
**Ashwater** Devon 9 K5
**Ashwell** Herts 75 J6
**Ashwell** Rutlnd 88 C2
**Ashwell End** Herts 75 J6
**Ashwellthorpe** Norfk 92 D4
**Ashwick** Somset 26 F2
**Ashwicken** Norfk 105 H8
**Askam in Furness** Cumb 128 F4
**Askern** Donc 124 E7
**Askerswell** Dorset 14 A4
**Askett** Bucks 58 D6
**Askham** Cumb 138 D3
**Askham** Notts 116 C6
**Askham Bryan** C York 124 E2
**Askham Richard** C York 124 E2
**Asknish** Ag & B 172 F1
**Askrigg** N York 131 H2
**Askwith** N York 123 H2
**Aslackby** Lincs 103 H6
**Aslacton** Norfk 92 D5
**Aslockton** Notts 102 C4
**Aspatria** Cumb 147 K6
**Aspenden** Herts 60 B3
**Aspley Guise** C Beds 74 D7
**Aspley Heath** C Beds 74 D7
**Aspull** Wigan 121 J8
**Asselby** E R Yk 125 H5
**Assington** Suffk 77 L6
**Assington Green** Suffk 77 H4
**Astbury** Ches E 99 J1
**Astcote** Nhants 73 J4
**Asterby** Lincs 118 C5
**Asterley** Shrops 83 H3
**Asterton** Shrops 83 H5
**Asthall** Oxon 56 F5
**Asthall Leigh** Oxon 56 F5
**Astle** Highld 223 G3
**Astley** Shrops 98 D8
**Astley** Warwks 86 C5
**Astley** Wigan 113 G2
**Astley** Worcs 70 D2
**Astley Abbots** Shrops 84 C4
**Astley Bridge** Bolton 121 K7
**Astley Cross** Worcs 70 E1
**Aston** Birm 85 J5
**Aston** Ches E 98 E3
**Aston** Ches W 112 E5
**Aston** Derbys 114 D5
**Aston** Flints 111 J7
**Aston** Herts 59 L4
**Aston** Oxon 57 G7
**Aston** Rothm 115 J4
**Aston** Shrops 84 E5
**Aston** Shrops 98 D6
**Aston** Staffs 99 H4
**Aston** Staffs 99 K7
**Aston** Wokham 42 C4
**Aston** Wrekin 84 B2
**Aston Abbotts** Bucks 58 D4
**Aston Botterell** Shrops 84 B6
**Aston-by-Stone** Staffs 99 K6
**Aston Cantlow** Warwks 71 K3
**Aston Clinton** Bucks 58 E5
**Aston Crews** Herefs 54 F4
**Aston End** Herts 59 L3
**Aston Fields** Worcs 71 G1
**Aston Flamville** Leics 86 F5
**Aston Ingham** Herefs 55 G4
**Aston le Walls** Nhants 72 F4
**Aston Magna** Gloucs 71 L7

**Aston Munslow** Shrops 83 K6
**Aston on Clun** Shrops 83 H6
**Aston Pigott** Shrops 83 G3
**Aston Rogers** Shrops 83 G3
**Aston Rowant** Oxon 58 B7
**Aston Somerville** Worcs 71 J6
**Aston-sub-Edge** Gloucs 71 K6
**Aston Tirrold** Oxon 41 K3
**Aston-upon-Trent** Derbys 101 H6
**Aston Upthorpe** Oxon 41 K3
**Astwick** C Beds 75 J6
**Astwood** M Keyn 74 D5
**Astwood** Worcs 71 G2
**Astwood Bank** Worcs 71 J3
**Aswarby** Lincs 103 H4
**Aswardby** Lincs 118 E7
**Atcham** Shrops 83 K2
**Athelhampton** Dorset 14 E4
**Athelington** Suffk 78 E1
**Athelney** Somset 25 M5
**Athelstaneford** E Loth 178 C3
**Atherington** Devon 23 J6
**Atherstone** Warwks 86 C4
**Atherstone on Stour** Warwks 72 B4
**Atherton** Wigan 113 G2
**Atlow** Derbys 100 E3
**Attadale** Highld 210 E6
**Atterby** Lincs 117 G3
**Attercliffe** Sheff 115 G4
**Atterton** Leics 86 D4
**Attingham Park** Shrops 83 K2
**Attleborough** Norfk 92 C4
**Attleborough** Warwks 86 D5
**Attlebridge** Norfk 92 D1
**Attleton Green** Suffk 77 G4
**Atwick** E R Yk 126 F1
**Atworth** Wilts 39 J7
**Aubourn** Lincs 116 F8
**Auchbreck** Moray 214 F8
**Auchedly** Abers 217 G7
**Auchenblae** Abers 197 H1
**Auchenbowie** Stirlg 175 L2
**Auchencairn** D & G 146 D5
**Auchencairn** D & G 155 G5
**Auchencairn** N Ayrs 162 D4
**Auchencrow** Border 179 H6
**Auchendinny** Mdloth 177 H6
**Auchengray** S Lans 176 D7
**Auchenhalrig** Moray 215 J3
**Auchenheath** S Lans 164 F2
**Auchenhessnane** D & G 154 E3
**Auchenlochan** Ag & B 173 G4
**Auchenmade** N Ayrs 174 C8
**Auchenmalg** D & G 144 F4
**Auchentiber** N Ayrs 174 C8
**Auchindrain** Ag & B 182 E6
**Auchindrean** Highld 221 G5
**Auchininna** Abers 216 C5
**Auchinleck** E Ayrs 164 B5
**Auchinloch** N Lans 175 H4
**Auchinstarry** N Lans 175 J3
**Auchintore** Highld 191 L2
**Auchiries** Abers 217 K6
**Auchlean** Highld 203 K5
**Auchlee** Abers 207 G6
**Auchleven** Abers 206 C1
**Auchlochan** S Lans 164 F3
**Auchlossan** Abers 206 B5
**Auchlyne** Stirlg 184 B2
**Auchmillan** E Ayrs 164 A4
**Auchmithie** Angus 197 G7
**Auchmuirbridge** Fife 186 C6
**Auchnacree** Angus 196 D4
**Auchnagatt** Abers 217 H6
**Auchnarrow** Moray 204 F2
**Auchnotteroch** D & G 144 B3
**Auchroisk** Moray 215 H4
**Auchterarder** P & K 185 K5
**Auchteraw** Highld 202 B4
**Auchterblair** Highld 203 L2
**Auchtercairn** Highld 219 J6
**Auchterderran** Fife 186 C7
**Auchterhouse** Angus 196 B8
**Auchterless** Abers 216 D6
**Auchtermuchty** Fife 186 D5
**Auchterneed** Highld 212 D3
**Auchtertool** Fife 177 H1
**Auchtertyre** Highld 210 C8
**Auchtubh** Stirlg 184 C4
**Auckengill** Highld 231 L3
**Auckley** Donc 116 A2
**Audenshaw** Tamesd 113 K3
**Audlem** Ches E 98 F4
**Audley** Staffs 99 J3
**Audley End** Essex 76 D6
**Audley End House & Gardens** Essex 76 D6
**Audnam** Dudley 84 F6
**Aughton** E R Yk 125 G3
**Aughton** Lancs 111 L1
**Aughton** Lancs 129 L6
**Aughton** Rothm 115 J4
**Aughton** Wilts 28 E1
**Aughton Park** Lancs 112 B1
**Auldearn** Highld 213 L4
**Aulden** Herefs 69 J4
**Auldgirth** D & G 154 F5
**Auldhouse** S Lans 175 H7
**Ault a' chruinn** Highld 200 E2
**Aultbea** Highld 219 K4
**Aultgrishin** Highld 219 H4
**Aultguish Inn** Highld 221 J7
**Ault Hucknall** Derbys 115 J7
**Aultmore** Moray 215 J4
**Aultnagoire** Highld 202 E2
**Aultnamain Inn** Highld 222 F5
**Aunsby** Lincs 103 H5
**Aust** S Glos 38 E3
**Austerfield** Donc 115 M3
**Austrey** Warwks 86 C3
**Austwick** N York 130 E5
**Authorpe** Lincs 118 E5
**Avebury** Wilts 40 C6
**Avebury** Wilts 40 C6
**Aveley** Thurr 45 L4
**Avening** Gloucs 39 K2
**Averham** Notts 102 C2
**Aveton Gifford** Devon 7 G6
**Aviemore** Highld 203 L3
**Avington** W Berk 41 G6
**Avoch** Highld 213 G4
**Avon** Hants 15 L3
**Avonbridge** Falk 176 B4
**Avon Dassett** Warwks 72 E4
**Avonmouth** Bristl 38 D5
**Avonwick** Devon 7 G4
**Awbridge** Hants 28 F6
**Awliscombe** Devon 12 E3
**Awre** Gloucs 55 G6
**Awsworth** Notts 101 J4
**Axbridge** Somset 26 B1
**Axford** Hants 29 L3
**Axford** Wilts 40 E6
**Axminster** Devon 13 H3
**Axmouth** Devon 13 G4
**Aycliffe** Dur 141 G3
**Aydon** Nthumb 150 C2
**Aylburton** Gloucs 54 E7
**Aylesbeare** Devon 12 D4
**Aylesbury** Bucks 58 D5
**Aylesbury Crematorium** Bucks 58 D5
**Aylesby** NE Lin 126 F8
**Aylesford** Kent 33 J2
**Aylesham** Kent 35 H4
**Aylestone** C Leic 87 H4
**Aylestone Park** C Leic 87 H4
**Aylmerton** Norfk 106 E5
**Aylsham** Norfk 106 E6
**Aylton** Herefs 70 B6
**Aylworth** Gloucs 56 C4
**Aymestrey** Herefs 69 H2
**Aynho** Nhants 57 K2
**Ayot St Lawrence** Herts 59 K5
**Ayr** S Ayrs 163 J5
**Aysgarth** N York 131 J2
**Ayshford** Devon 25 G7
**Ayside** Cumb 129 J3
**Ayston** Rutlnd 88 C4
**Ayton** Border 179 J6
**Azerley** N York 132 C5

## B

**Babbacombe** Torbay 7 L3
**Babbs Green** Herts 60 C5
**Babcary** Somset 26 E5
**Babraham** Cambs 76 D4
**Babworth** Notts 116 B5
**Backaland** Ork 234 d4
**Backfolds** Abers 217 J4
**Backford** Ches W 111 L6
**Backies** Highld 223 H2
**Back of Keppoch** Highld 199 K7
**Backwell** N Som 38 C6
**Baconsthorpe** Norfk 106 D5
**Bacton** Herefs 54 A2
**Bacton** Norfk 107 H5
**Bacton** Suffk 78 C2
**Bacup** Lancs 122 C6
**Badachro** Highld 219 J6
**Badanloch** Highld 226 E2
**Badbury** Swindn 40 D4
**Badby** Nhants 73 H3
**Badcall** Highld 228 B7
**Badcall** Highld 228 C4
**Badcaul** Highld 220 D3
**Baddeley Edge** C Stke 99 K3
**Baddeley Green** C Stke 99 K3
**Baddesley Clinton** Warwks 86 B8
**Baddesley Ensor** Warwks 86 C4
**Baddidarrach** Highld 224 D4
**Baddinsgill** Border 176 F7
**Badenscoth** Abers 216 D6
**Badentarbet** Highld 224 B6
**Badenyon** Abers 205 H2
**Badger** Shrops 84 D4
**Badgeworth** Gloucs 55 K4
**Badgworth** Somset 26 B2
**Badicaul** Highld 210 B8
**Badingham** Suffk 79 G2
**Badlesmere** Kent 34 D4
**Badlieu** Border 165 K5
**Badlipster** Highld 231 J5
**Badluarach** Highld 220 C3
**Badninish** Highld 223 G3
**Badrallach** Highld 220 D3
**Badsey** Worcs 71 J5
**Badshot Lea** Surrey 30 E2
**Badsworth** Wakefd 124 C7
**Badwell Ash** Suffk 78 B2
**Bagber** Dorset 27 H8
**Bagby** N York 133 G4
**Bag Enderby** Lincs 118 E6
**Bagendon** Gloucs 56 A6
**Bàgh a' Chaisteil** W Isls 233 b9
**Bagillt** Flints 111 H6
**Baginton** Warwks 86 D8
**Baglan** Neath 51 L6
**Bagley** Shrops 98 B6
**Bagley** Somset 26 C3
**Bagnall** Staffs 99 L3
**Bagshot** Surrey 42 E7
**Bagstone** S Glos 39 G3
**Bagworth** Leics 86 F2
**Bagwy Llydiart** Herefs 54 C3
**Baildon** C Brad 123 H3
**Baildon Green** C Brad 123 H3
**Baile Ailein** W Isls 232 f3
**Baile a' Mhanaich** W Isls 233 b6
**Baile Mòr** Ag & B 180 D3
**Baillieston** C Glas 175 J5
**Bainbridge** N York 131 H2
**Bainshole** Abers 216 B7
**Bainton** C Pete 89 G3
**Bainton** E R Yk 134 E8
**Baintown** Fife 186 F6
**Bairnkine** Border 167 K6
**Bakewell** Derbys 114 E7
**Bala** Gwynd 96 E5
**Balallan** W Isls 232 f3
**Balbeg** Highld 212 C7
**Balbeggie** P & K 186 C2
**Balblair** Highld 212 D5
**Balblair** Highld 213 G2
**Balby** Donc 115 K2
**Balcary** D & G 146 E5
**Balchraggan** Highld 212 E5
**Balchreick** Highld 228 B4
**Balcombe** W Susx 32 B6
**Balcomie Links** Fife 187 K5
**Baldersby** N York 132 E4
**Baldersby St James** N York 132 E4
**Balderstone** Lancs 121 J4
**Balderton** Notts 102 D3
**Baldinnie** Fife 187 G5
**Baldinnies** P & K 185 L4
**Baldock** Herts 75 J7
**Baldock Services** Herts 75 J6
**Baldovie** C Dund 187 G2
**Baldrine** IoM 237 d5
**Baldslow** E Susx 20 F3
**Bale** Norfk 106 B5
**Baledgarno** P & K 186 D2
**Balemartine** Ag & B 188 C7
**Balerno** C Edin 177 G5
**Balfarg** Fife 186 D6
**Balfield** Angus 196 E3
**Balfour** Ork 234 c5
**Balfron** Stirlg 174 F1
**Balgaveny** Abers 216 C6
**Balgonar** Fife 185 L8
**Balgowan** D & G 144 D6
**Balgowan** Highld 202 F6
**Balgown** Highld 218 B7
**Balgracie** D & G 144 B3
**Balgray** S Lans 165 H5
**Balham** Gt Lon 44 F5
**Balhary** P & K 195 L6
**Balholmie** P & K 186 B1
**Baligill** Highld 230 C3
**Balintore** Angus 195 L5
**Balintore** Highld 223 J6
**Balintraid** Highld 223 G7
**Balivanich** W Isls 233 b6
**Balkeerie** Angus 196 B7
**Balkholme** E R Yk 125 J5
**Ballachulish** Highld 191 L5
**Ballajora** IoM 237 e4
**Ballanlay** Ag & B 173 H6
**Ballantrae** S Ayrs 152 C5
**Ballasalla** IoM 237 b6
**Ballater** Abers 205 J6
**Ballaugh** IoM 237 c3
**Ballchraggan** Highld 223 G6
**Ballencrieff** E Loth 178 B3
**Ballevullin** Ag & B 188 B6
**Ball Green** C Stke 99 K3
**Ball Hill** Hants 41 H7
**Ballidon** Derbys 100 D2
**Balliekine** N Ayrs 161 L2
**Balliemore** Ag & B 182 F7
**Balligmorrie** S Ayrs 152 F4
**Ballimore** Stirlg 184 C4
**Ballindalloch** Moray 214 E7
**Ballindean** P & K 186 D2
**Ballinger Common** Bucks 58 E7
**Ballingham** Herefs 54 E2
**Ballingry** Fife 186 C7
**Ballinluig** P & K 194 F6
**Ballinshoe** Angus 196 C5
**Ballintuim** P & K 195 H5
**Balloch** Highld 213 H5
**Balloch** N Lans 175 K4

Balloch P & K 185 H4
Balloch S Ayrs 153 G3
Balloch W Duns 174 D3
Balls Cross W Susx 31 G6
Balls Green E Susx 32 E6
Ballygown Ag & B 189 K7
Ballygrant Ag & B 171 G5
Ballyhaugh Ag & B 188 F5
Balmacara Highld 210 C8
Balmaclellan D & G 154 B6
Balmae D & G 146 C6
Balmaha Stirlg 174 D1
Balmalcolm Fife 186 E5
Balmangan D & G 146 B5
Balmedie Abers 207 H2
Balmerino Fife 186 F3
Balmichael N Ayrs 162 B3
Balmore E Duns 175 G4
Balmuchy Highld 223 J5
Balmule Fife 177 G2
Balmullo Fife 187 G4
Balnacoil Highld 226 E6
Balnacra Highld 210 F5
Balnacroft Abers 205 G6
Balnafoich Highld 213 G7
Balnaguard P & K 194 E6
Balnahard Ag & B 180 F1
Balnahard Ag & B 180 F7
Balnain Highld 212 C7
Balnakeil Highld 228 F2
Balne N York 124 F6
Balquharn P & K 185 L1
Balquhidder Stirlg 184 C3
Balsall Common Solhll 86 B7
Balsall Heath Birm 85 J6
Balscote Oxon 72 E6
Balsham Cambs 76 E4
Baltasound Shet 235 e1
Baltersan D & G 145 J3
Balthangie Abers 216 F4
Baltonsborough Somset 26 D4
Balvicar Ag & B 181 M4
Balvraid Highld 200 C3
Balvraid Highld 213 K7
Bamber Bridge Lancs 121 H5
Bamber's Green Essex 60 F4
Bamburgh Nthumb 169 H3
Bamburgh Castle Nthumb 169 H3
Bamford Derbys 114 E5
Bampton Cumb 138 D4
Bampton Devon 24 E6
Bampton Oxon 56 F7
Bampton Grange Cumb 138 D4
Banavie Highld 191 L2
Banbury Oxon 72 F6
Banbury Crematorium Oxon 72 F6
Bancffosfelen Carmth 50 F3
Banchory Abers 206 D6
Banchory-Devenick Abers 207 G5
Bancycapel Carmth 50 E3
Bancyfelin Carmth 50 D2
Bandirran P & K 186 C2
Banff Abers 216 D2
Bangor Gwynd 109 H6
Bangor Crematorium Gwynd 109 H6
Bangor-on-Dee Wrexhm 98 B4
Bangors Cnwll 9 G5
Banham Norfk 92 C6
Bank Hants 16 C2
Bankend D & G 147 H2
Bankfoot P & K 185 M1
Bankglen E Ayrs 164 C6
Bankhead C Aber 207 G4
Bankhead S Lans 165 J1
Banknock Falk 175 K3
Banks Lancs 120 E6
Bankshill D & G 155 L5
Banningham Norfk 106 F6
Bannister Green Essex 61 H4
Bannockburn Stirlg 175 L1
Banstead Surrey 44 E7
Bantham Devon 6 F6
Banton N Lans 175 K3
Banwell N Som 38 B8
Bapchild Kent 34 C3
Bapton Wilts 27 M4
Barabhas W Isls 232 f1
Barassie S Ayrs 163 J3
Barbaraville Highld 223 G6
Barbieston S Ayrs 163 K5
Barbon Cumb 130 C3
Barbrook Devon 23 L2
Barby Nhants 73 G1
Barcaldine Ag & B 191 J7
Barcombe E Susx 19 L3
Barcombe Cross E Susx 19 L3
Barden Park Kent 33 G4
Bardfield End Green Essex 61 G2
Bardfield Saling Essex 61 G3
Bardney Lincs 117 J7
Bardon Leics 86 F2
Bardon Mill Nthumb 149 K3
Bardowie E Duns 175 G4
Bardrainney Inver 174 C4
Bardsea Cumb 129 G5
Bardsey Leeds 124 B2
Bardsey Island Gwynd 94 B7
Bardwell Suffk 91 L8
Bare Lancs 129 K6
Barfad D & G 145 G2
Barford Norfk 92 D3
Barford Warwks 72 C3
Barford St John Oxon 57 H2
Barford St Martin Wilts 28 B5
Barford St Michael Oxon 57 H2
Barfrestone Kent 35 H5
Bargeddie N Lans 175 J5
Bargoed Caerph 53 J7
Bargrennan D & G 153 H6
Barham Cambs 89 G7
Barham Kent 35 G5
Barham Suffk 78 D4
Barham Crematorium Kent 35 G5
Bar Hill Cambs 75 L2
Barholm Lincs 88 F2
Barkby Leics 87 J2
Barkby Thorpe Leics 87 J2
Barkestone-le-Vale Leics 102 C5
Barkham Wokham 42 C6
Barking Gt Lon 45 H3
Barking Suffk 78 C4
Barkingside Gt Lon 45 H3
Barking Tye Suffk 78 C4
Barkisland Calder 122 F6
Barkla Shop Cnwll 3 J2
Barkston Lincs 102 F4
Barkston Ash N York 124 D4
Barkway Herts 75 L7
Barlanark C Glas 175 H5
Barlaston Staffs 99 K5
Barlavington W Susx 18 C3
Barlborough Derbys 115 J6
Barlby N York 124 F4
Barlestone Leics 86 E3
Barley Herts 76 B6
Barley Lancs 122 B3
Barleythorpe Rutlnd 88 B2
Barling Essex 46 F3
Barlings Lincs 117 H6
Barlochan D & G 146 E4
Barlow Derbys 115 G6
Barlow Gatesd 150 E3
Barlow N York 124 F5
Barmby Moor E R Yk 125 J2
Barmby on the Marsh E R Yk 125 G5
Barmollack Ag & B 161 K1
Barmouth Gwynd 80 E1
Barmpton Darltn 141 H4
Barmston E R Yk 135 J7
Barnacarry Ag & B 182 E8
Barnack C Pete 88 F3
Barnard Castle Dur 140 D4
Barnard Gate Oxon 57 H6
Barnardiston Suffk 77 G5
Barnbarroch D & G 146 E4
Barnburgh Donc 115 J2
Barnby Suffk 93 K5
Barnby Dun Donc 124 F8
Barnby in the Willows Notts 102 E3
Barnby Moor Notts 116 A5
Barncorkrie D & G 144 D7
Barnes Gt Lon 44 E5
Barnes Street Kent 33 H4
Barnet Gt Lon 44 E2
Barnetby le Wold N Linc 126 C8
Barney Norfk 106 B6
Barnham Suffk 91 K7
Barnham W Susx 18 C5
Barnham Broom Norfk 92 C3
Barnhead Angus 197 G5
Barnhill C Dund 187 H2
Barnhill Moray 214 E3
Barnhills D & G 152 B7
Barningham Dur 140 D5
Barningham Suffk 91 L7
Barnoldby le Beck NE Lin 118 C2
Barnoldswick Lancs 122 C2
Barns Green W Susx 31 J6
Barnsley Barns 115 G1
Barnsley Gloucs 56 B6
Barnsley Crematorium Barns 115 G1
Barnstaple Devon 23 J5
Barnston Essex 61 G4
Barnston Wirral 111 J5
Barnstone Notts 102 B5
Barnt Green Worcs 85 H8
Barnton C Edin 177 G4
Barnton Ches W 112 F6
Barnwell All Saints Nhants 88 F6
Barnwell St Andrew Nhants 88 F6
Barnwood Gloucs 55 K4
Barr S Ayrs 153 G4
Barra W Isls 233 b9
*Barra Airport* W Isls 233 b9
Barrachan D & G 145 H5
Barraigh W Isls 233 b9
Barrananaoil Ag & B 182 B6
Barrapoll Ag & B 188 B7
Barrasford Nthumb 158 A7
Barrhead E Rens 174 F6
Barrhill S Ayrs 152 F5
Barrington Cambs 76 B5
Barrington Somset 26 B7
Barripper Cnwll 3 H4
Barrmill N Ayrs 174 C7
Barrock Highld 231 J2
Barrow Gloucs 55 K3
Barrow Lancs 121 L3
Barrow Rutlnd 88 C1
Barrow Somset 27 G5
Barrow Suffk 77 H2
Barrowby Lincs 102 E5
Barrowden Rutlnd 88 D4
Barrowford Lancs 122 C3
Barrow Gurney N Som 38 D6
Barrow Haven N Linc 126 D6
Barrow-in-Furness Cumb 128 E5
Barrow Island Cumb 128 E5
Barrow-upon-Humber N Linc 126 D6
Barrow upon Soar Leics 101 L8
Barrow upon Trent Derbys 101 G6
Barry Angus 187 J1
Barry V Glam 37 H6
Barry Island V Glam 37 H6
Barsby Leics 87 K2
Barsham Suffk 93 H5
Barston Solhll 86 B7
Bartestree Herefs 69 L6
Barthol Chapel Abers 216 F7
Bartholomew Green Essex 61 H4
Barthomley Ches E 99 H3
Bartley Hants 28 F8
Bartley Green Birm 85 H6
Bartlow Cambs 76 E5
Barton Cambs 76 B4
Barton Ches W 98 C2
Barton Gloucs 56 C3
Barton Lancs 120 E8
Barton Lancs 121 G3
Barton N York 141 G5
Barton Oxon 57 K6
Barton Torbay 7 K3
Barton Bendish Norfk 91 G3
Barton End Gloucs 39 J2
Barton Hartshorn Bucks 57 M2
Barton in Fabis Notts 101 K6
Barton in the Beans Leics 86 E3
Barton-le-Clay C Beds 59 H2
Barton-le-Street N York 133 L5
Barton-le-Willows N York 133 L6
Barton Mills Suffk 91 G8
Barton-on-Sea Hants 16 B4
Barton-on-the-Heath Warwks 56 E2
Barton Park Services N York 140 F5
Barton St David Somset 26 D5
Barton Seagrave Nhants 88 C7
Barton Stacey Hants 29 H3
Barton Town Devon 23 L4
Barton Turf Norfk 107 H7
Barton-under-Needwood Staffs 100 D8
Barton-upon-Humber N Linc 126 C6
Barton Waterside N Linc 126 C6
Barvas W Isls 232 f1
Barway Cambs 90 D7
Barwell Leics 86 F4
Barwick Devon 10 E4
Barwick Somset 26 E8
Barwick in Elmet Leeds 124 B3
Baschurch Shrops 98 B7
Bascote Warwks 72 E2
Bashall Eaves Lancs 121 K2
Basildon Essex 46 B3
Basildon & District Crematorium Essex 46 C3
Basingstoke Hants 29 M2
Basingstoke Crematorium Hants 29 K3
Baslow Derbys 114 E6
Bason Bridge Somset 25 M3
Bassaleg Newpt 37 L3
Bassendean Border 167 K1
Bassenthwaite Cumb 137 H2
Bassett C Sotn 29 H7
Bassingbourn-cum-Kneesworth Cambs 75 L5
Bassingham Lincs 102 E1
Bassingthorpe Lincs 102 F6
Bassus Green Herts 60 A3
Baston Lincs 89 G2
Bastwick Norfk 107 J8

**Batchworth** Herts 43 H2
**Batcombe** Dorset 14 C2
**Batcombe** Somset 27 G4
**Batford** Herts 59 J5
**Bath** BaNES 39 H7
**Bathampton** BaNES 39 H7
**Bath, City of** BaNES 39 H7
**Bathealton** Somset 25 G6
**Batheaston** BaNES 39 H6
**Bathford** BaNES 39 H6
**Bathgate** W Loth 176 D5
**Bathley** Notts 102 C2
**Bathpool** Cnwll 5 L2
**Bathpool** Somset 25 K6
**Bath Side** Essex 62 F2
**Bathville** W Loth 176 C5
**Bathway** Somset 26 E2
**Batley** Kirk 123 J5
**Batsford** Gloucs 71 L7
**Battersby** N York 142 D5
**Battersea** Gt Lon 44 F5
**Battisford Tye** Suffk 78 B4
**Battle** E Susx 20 F3
**Battle** Powys 52 F2
**Battledykes** Angus 196 D5
**Battlesbridge** Essex 46 C2
**Battleton** Somset 24 E6
**Baughton** Worcs 70 F6
**Baughurst** Hants 41 L7
**Baulds** Abers 206 B6
**Baulking** Oxon 40 F3
**Baumber** Lincs 117 L6
**Baunton** Gloucs 56 A6
**Baverstock** Wilts 28 B5
**Bawburgh** Norfk 92 D2
**Bawdeswell** Norfk 106 C7
**Bawdrip** Somset 25 M4
**Bawdsey** Suffk 79 H6
**Bawtry** Donc 115 M3
**Baxenden** Lancs 122 B5
**Baxterley** Warwks 86 C4
**Bay** Highld 208 D4
**Bayble** W Isls 232 g2
**Baybridge** Hants 29 K6
**Baycliff** Cumb 129 G5
**Baydon** Wilts 40 F5
**Bayford** Herts 60 A6
**Bayford** Somset 27 G5
**Bayhead** W Isls 233 b6
**Baylham** Suffk 78 D4
**Baysham** Herefs 54 E3
**Bayston Hill** Shrops 83 J2
**Baythorne End** Essex 77 G6
**Bayton** Worcs 84 C8
**Bayworth** Oxon 57 J7
**Beachampton** Bucks 73 L6
**Beachamwell** Norfk 91 H3
**Beachy Head** E Susx 20 C6
**Beacon** Devon 12 F2
**Beacon End** Essex 62 A3
**Beacon Hill** Notts 102 D2
**Beacon Hill** Surrey 30 E4
**Beacon's Bottom** Bucks 42 C2
**Beaconsfield** Bucks 42 F3
**Beaconsfield Services** Bucks 42 F3
**Beadlam** N York 133 K3
**Beadlow** C Beds 75 G6
**Beadnell** Nthumb 169 J4
**Beaford** Devon 10 E2
**Beal** N York 124 E5
**Beal** Nthumb 169 G2
**Bealsmill** Cnwll 6 A1
**Beaminster** Dorset 13 L3
**Beamish** Dur 150 F4
**Beamish Museum** Dur 150 F4
**Beamsley** N York 131 K8
**Beanacre** Wilts 39 K7
**Beanley** Nthumb 169 G5
**Beardon** Devon 10 D7
**Beare Green** Surrey 31 K3
**Bearley** Warwks 71 L3
**Bearpark** Dur 151 G6
**Bearsden** E Duns 174 F4
**Bearsted** Kent 33 K3
**Bearstone** Shrops 99 G5
**Bearwood** Birm 85 H6
**Bearwood** Herefs 69 H4
**Bearwood** Poole 15 K3
**Beattock** D & G 155 J2
**Beauchamp Roding** Essex 60 F6
**Beaufort** Blae G 53 J5
**Beaulieu** Hants 16 E3
**Beauly** Highld 212 E5
**Beaumaris** IoA 109 H6
**Beaumaris Castle** IoA 109 J6
**Beaumont** Cumb 148 C3
**Beaumont** Essex 62 E3
**Beaumont** Jersey 236 c7
**Beaumont Leys** C Leic 87 H2
**Beausale** Warwks 72 B1
**Beauworth** Hants 29 L6
**Beaworthy** Devon 10 C5
**Beazley End** Essex 61 H3
**Bebington** Wirral 111 K5
**Beccles** Suffk 93 J5
**Becconsall** Lancs 120 F6
**Beckbury** Shrops 84 D3
**Beckenham** Gt Lon 45 G6
**Beckenham Crematorium** Gt Lon 45 G6
**Beckermet** Cumb 136 E6
**Beckfoot** Cumb 147 J5
**Beckford** Worcs 71 H7
**Beckhampton** Wilts 40 C6
**Beckingham** Lincs 102 E2
**Beckingham** Notts 116 C4
**Beckington** Somset 27 J2
**Beckjay** Shrops 83 H7
**Beckley** E Susx 21 G2
**Beckley** Oxon 57 K5
**Beck Row** Suffk 91 G7
**Beck Side** Cumb 128 F3
**Beckton** Gt Lon 45 H4
**Beckwithshaw** N York 132 D8
**Becontree** Gt Lon 45 J3
**Becquet Vincent** Jersey 236 c6
**Bedale** N York 132 D2
**Bedchester** Dorset 27 J7
**Beddau** Rhondd 37 G4
**Beddgelert** Gwynd 95 K3
**Beddingham** E Susx 19 L4
**Beddington** Gt Lon 44 F6
**Beddington Corner** Gt Lon 44 F6
**Bedfield** Suffk 78 F2
**Bedford** Bed 74 F5
**Bedford Crematorium** Bed 75 G4
**Bedhampton** Hants 17 K2
**Bedingfield** Suffk 78 E2
**Bedlam** N York 132 D7
**Bedlington** Nthumb 159 G5
**Bedlinog** Myr Td 53 H7
**Bedminster** Bristl 38 E6
**Bedminster Down** Bristl 38 E6
**Bedmond** Herts 59 J7
**Bednall** Staffs 99 L8
**Bedrule** Border 167 J5
**Bedstone** Shrops 83 G7
**Bedwas** Caerph 37 J3
**Bedwellty** Caerph 53 J7
**Bedworth** Warwks 86 D6
**Beeby** Leics 87 J2
**Beech** Hants 30 B4
**Beech** Staffs 99 J5
**Beech Hill** W Berk 42 B7
**Beechingstoke** Wilts 40 C8
**Beedon** W Berk 41 J5
**Beeford** E R Yk 135 H8
**Beeley** Derbys 114 E7
**Beelsby** NE Lin 117 K2
**Beenham** W Berk 41 L6
**Beer** Devon 13 G5
**Beer** Somset 26 B5
**Beercrocombe** Somset 25 L7
**Beer Hackett** Dorset 14 B1
**Beesands** Devon 7 J7
**Beesby** Lincs 118 F5
**Beeson** Devon 7 J7
**Beeston** C Beds 75 H5
**Beeston** Ches W 98 D2
**Beeston** Leeds 123 K4
**Beeston** Norfk 91 K1
**Beeston** Notts 101 K5
**Beeston Regis** Norfk 106 E4
**Beeswing** D & G 146 F2
**Beetham** Cumb 129 K4
**Beetham** Somset 25 L8
**Beetley** Norfk 106 A8
**Begbroke** Oxon 57 J5
**Begelly** Pembks 49 J6
**Beguildy** Powys 82 D7
**Beighton** Norfk 93 H2
**Beighton** Sheff 115 H5
**Beinn Na Faoghla** W Isls 233 c7
**Beith** N Ayrs 174 C7
**Bekesbourne** Kent 35 G4
**Belaugh** Norfk 107 G8
**Belbroughton** Worcs 85 G7
**Belchalwell** Dorset 14 E1
**Belchamp Otten** Essex 77 J6
**Belchamp St Paul** Essex 77 H6
**Belchamp Walter** Essex 77 J6
**Belchford** Lincs 118 D6
**Belford** Nthumb 169 G3
**Belgrave** C Leic 87 H3
**Belhaven** E Loth 178 E3
**Belhelvie** Abers 207 H2
**Belhinnie** Abers 215 K8
**Bellabeg** Abers 205 H3
**Bellanoch** Ag & B 182 A8
**Bellaty** Angus 195 K4
**Bell Busk** N York 131 G7
**Belleau** Lincs 118 E5
**Bell End** Worcs 85 G7
**Bellerby** N York 131 L2
**Belle Vue** Cumb 148 C4
**Belle Vue** Wakefd 123 L6
**Bellfield** S Lans 164 F3
**Bellingdon** Bucks 58 F6
**Bellingham** Nthumb 157 L5
**Belloch** Ag & B 161 H2
**Bellochantuy** Ag & B 161 H3
**Bell o' th' Hill** Ches W 98 D4
**Bellshill** N Lans 175 J6
**Bellside** N Lans 175 L6
**Bellsquarry** W Loth 176 E5
**Bells Yew Green** E Susx 33 G6
**Belluton** BaNES 38 E7
**Belmaduthy** Highld 213 G3
**Belmont** Bl w D 121 K7
**Belmont** Gt Lon 44 E7
**Belmont** S Ayrs 163 J5
**Belmont** Shet 235 d2
**Belnacraig** Abers 205 J3
**Belper** Derbys 101 G3
**Belsay** Nthumb 158 D6
**Belses** Border 167 J4
**Belsford** Devon 7 H4
**Belsize** Herts 59 G7
**Belstead** Suffk 78 D6
**Belstone** Devon 10 F6
**Belthorn** Lancs 121 L5
**Beltinge** Kent 47 K6
**Beltingham** Nthumb 149 K3
**Beltoft** N Linc 116 D1
**Belton** Leics 101 H7
**Belton** Lincs 102 F4
**Belton** N Linc 116 C1
**Belton** Norfk 93 K3
**Belton** Rutlnd 88 B3
**Belton House** Lincs 102 F5
**Belvedere** Gt Lon 45 J4
**Belvoir** Leics 102 D5
**Bembridge** IoW 17 J5
**Bemerton** Wilts 28 C5
**Bempton** E R Yk 135 J5
**Benacre** Suffk 93 K6
**Benbecula** W Isls 233 c7
*Benbecula Airport* W Isls 233 c6
**Benbuie** D & G 154 C3
**Benderloch** Ag & B 191 H8
**Benenden** Kent 33 K6
**Benfieldside** Dur 150 D4
**Bengeo** Herts 60 A5
**Bengeworth** Worcs 71 J5
**Benhall Green** Suffk 79 H3
**Benhall Street** Suffk 79 H3
**Benholm** Abers 197 K3
**Beningbrough** N York 133 H7
**Benington** Herts 59 M4
**Benington** Lincs 104 C3
**Benllech** IoA 109 G5
**Benmore** Ag & B 173 K2
**Bennan** N Ayrs 162 C5
**Ben Nevis** Highld 192 B3
**Benniworth** Lincs 117 K5
**Benover** Kent 33 J4
**Ben Rhydding** C Brad 123 H2
**Benslie** N Ayrs 163 J2
**Benson** Oxon 41 L3
**Benthoul** C Aber 206 F5
**Bentley** Donc 115 K1
**Bentley** E R Yk 126 C4
**Bentley** Hants 30 C3
**Bentley** Suffk 78 D6
**Bentley** Warwks 86 C4
**Bentley Crematorium** Essex 45 L2
**Bentpath** D & G 156 B4
**Bentwichen** Devon 24 B5
**Bentworth** Hants 30 A4
**Benvie** Angus 186 E2
**Benville** Dorset 14 A2
**Benwick** Cambs 89 L5
**Beoley** Worcs 71 J1
**Beoraidbeg** Highld 199 L6
**Bepton** W Susx 18 B3
**Berden** Essex 60 D3
**Berea** Pembks 48 D2
**Bere Alston** Devon 6 C3
**Bere Ferrers** Devon 6 C3
**Bere Regis** Dorset 14 F4
**Bergh Apton** Norfk 93 G4
**Berinsfield** Oxon 41 L2
**Berkeley** Gloucs 55 G7
**Berkhamsted** Herts 59 G6
**Berkley** Somset 27 J2
**Berkswell** Solhll 86 B7
**Bermondsey** Gt Lon 45 G4
**Bernera** Highld 200 C2
**Bernisdale** Highld 208 F4
**Berrick Prior** Oxon 41 L2
**Berrick Salome** Oxon 41 L2
**Berriedale** Highld 227 K4
**Berrier** Cumb 137 L2
**Berriew** Powys 82 D4
**Berrington** Shrops 83 K3
**Berrington** Worcs 69 L2
**Berrington Green** Worcs 69 L2
**Berrow** Somset 25 L2
**Berrow Green** Worcs 70 D3
**Berryfields** Bucks 58 C5
**Berryhillock** Moray 215 L3
**Berryhillock** Moray 215 L4
**Berrynarbor** Devon 23 J3
**Berry Pomeroy** Devon 7 J4
**Bersham** Wrexhm 97 L3
**Bersted** W Susx 18 C5
**Berwick** E Susx 20 B5
**Berwick Bassett** Wilts 40 C5
**Berwick Hill** Nthumb 158 F6
**Berwick St James** Wilts 28 B4
**Berwick St John** Wilts 27 L6
**Berwick St Leonard** Wilts 27 L5
**Berwick-upon-Tweed** Nthumb 179 K7
**Bescar** Lancs 120 E7
**Besford** Worcs 71 G5

**Bessacarr** Donc 115 L2
**Bessingby** E R Yk 135 J6
**Bessingham** Norfk 106 E5
**Besthorpe** Norfk 92 C4
**Besthorpe** Notts 116 D8
**Bestwood Village** Notts 101 K3
**Beswick** E R Yk 126 C2
**Betchworth** Surrey 31 K2
**Bethel** Gwynd 109 G7
**Bethel** IoA 108 E7
**Bethersden** Kent 34 C6
**Bethesda** Gwynd 109 J7
**Bethesda** Pembks 49 J4
**Bethlehem** Carmth 51 K1
**Bethnal Green** Gt Lon 45 G4
**Betley** Staffs 99 H3
**Betsham** Kent 45 L5
**Betteshanger** Kent 35 J4
**Bettiscombe** Dorset 13 K3
**Bettisfield** Wrexhm 98 C5
**Bettws** Newpt 37 L3
**Bettws Cedewain** Powys 82 C4
**Bettws Ifan** Cerdgn 65 J5
**Bettws-Newydd** Mons 54 A6
**Bettyhill** Highld 229 L3
**Betws** Brdgnd 36 D3
**Betws** Carmth 51 J3
**Betws Bledrws** Cerdgn 66 D4
**Betws Gwerfil Goch** Denbgs 97 G3
**Betws-y-Coed** Conwy 96 C2
**Betws-yn-Rhos** Conwy 110 C6
**Beulah** Cerdgn 65 J5
**Beulah** Powys 67 K4
**Bevercotes** Notts 116 B6
**Beverley** E R Yk 126 C3
**Beverston** Gloucs 39 K2
**Bewcastle** Cumb 156 F7
**Bewdley** Worcs 84 D7
**Bewerley** N York 132 B6
**Bewholme** E R Yk 126 E1
**Bexhill** E Susx 20 E4
**Bexley** Gt Lon 45 J5
**Bexleyheath** Gt Lon 45 J5
**Bexwell** Norfk 90 F3
**Beyton** Suffk 77 L2
**Beyton Green** Suffk 77 L2
**Bhaltos** W Isls 232 d2
**Bhatarsaigh** W Isls 233 b10
**Bibury** Gloucs 56 C6
**Bicester** Oxon 57 L4
**Bickenhill** Solhll 85 L6
**Bicker** Lincs 103 L5
**Bickerstaffe** Lancs 112 C2
**Bickerton** N York 124 C1
**Bickford** Staffs 84 F2
**Bickington** Devon 7 J2
**Bickington** Devon 23 H5
**Bickleigh** Devon 6 D4
**Bickleigh** Devon 12 B2
**Bickley** Ches W 98 D3
**Bickley** Gt Lon 45 H6
**Bickley** N York 134 E2
**Bicknacre** Essex 61 J7
**Bicknoller** Somset 25 H4
**Bicknor** Kent 33 L2
**Bicton** Shrops 82 F6
**Bicton** Shrops 83 J1
**Bidborough** Kent 32 F5
**Biddenden** Kent 33 L5
**Biddenham** Bed 74 E4
**Biddestone** Wilts 39 K5
**Biddisham** Somset 26 B2
**Biddlesden** Bucks 73 J6
**Biddulph** Staffs 99 K2
**Biddulph Moor** Staffs 99 K2
**Bideford** Devon 23 G6
**Bidford-on-Avon** Warwks 71 K4
**Bielby** E R Yk 125 J2
**Bieldside** C Aber 207 G5
**Bierley** IoW 17 G6
**Bierton** Bucks 58 D5
**Big Balcraig** D & G 145 H6
**Bigbury** Devon 6 F6
**Bigbury-on-Sea** Devon 6 F6
**Bigby** Lincs 117 H1
**Biggar** S Lans 165 K2
**Biggin** Derbys 100 D2
**Biggin Hill** Gt Lon 32 D2
**Biggleswade** C Beds 75 H5
**Bigholms** D & G 156 B6
**Bighouse** Highld 230 C3
**Bighton** Hants 29 L4
**Biglands** Cumb 148 A4
**Bignor** W Susx 18 D3
**Bigrigg** Cumb 136 D5
**Big Sand** Highld 219 H5
**Bigton** Shet 235 c7
**Bilborough** C Nott 101 K4
**Bilbrook** Somset 25 G3
**Bilbrough** N York 124 E2
**Bilbster** Highld 231 K5
**Bildershaw** Dur 140 F3
**Bildeston** Suffk 78 B5
**Billericay** Essex 46 B2
**Billesdon** Leics 87 K3
**Billesley** Warwks 71 K3
**Billingborough** Lincs 103 J5
**Billinge** St Hel 112 D2
**Billingford** Norfk 92 E7
**Billingford** Norfk 106 B7
**Billingham** S on T 141 K3
**Billinghay** Lincs 103 J2
**Billingley** Barns 115 H1
**Billingshurst** W Susx 31 H6
**Billingsley** Shrops 84 C6
**Billington** C Beds 58 F4
**Billington** Lancs 121 L4
**Billockby** Norfk 93 J2
**Billy Row** Dur 150 E7
**Bilsborrow** Lancs 121 G3
**Bilsby** Lincs 119 G6
**Bilsham** W Susx 18 D5
**Bilsington** Kent 34 D7
**Bilsthorpe** Notts 101 M1
**Bilston** Mdloth 177 H5
**Bilston** Wolves 85 G4
**Bilstone** Leics 86 D3
**Bilton** E R Yk 126 E4
**Bilton** N York 132 D7
**Bilton** Warwks 86 F8
**Bilton-in-Ainsty** N York 124 D1
**Binbrook** Lincs 117 K3
**Bincombe** Dorset 14 D5
**Binegar** Somset 26 E2
**Binfield** Br For 42 D6
**Binfield Heath** Oxon 42 C5
**Bingfield** Nthumb 158 B7
**Bingham** Notts 102 B4
**Bingley** C Brad 123 G3
**Binham** Norfk 106 B5
**Binley** Covtry 86 E7
**Binley** Hants 29 H2
**Binley Woods** Warwks 86 E7
**Binnegar** Dorset 15 G5
**Binniehill** Falk 176 B4
**Binscombe** Surrey 30 F3
**Binstead** IoW 17 H4
**Binsted** Hants 30 C3
**Binsted** W Susx 18 D4
**Binton** Warwks 71 K4
**Bintree** Norfk 106 B7
**Birch** Essex 61 M4
**Bircham Newton** Norfk 105 J5
**Bircham Tofts** Norfk 105 J6
**Birchanger** Essex 60 E4
**Birchanger Green Services** Essex 60 E4
**Birch Cross** Staffs 100 C6
**Bircher** Herefs 69 J2
**Birchfield** Birm 85 J5
**Birch Green** Essex 61 M4
**Birchgrove** Cardif 37 J4
**Birchgrove** Swans 51 K5
**Birchgrove** W Susx 32 D7
**Birchington** Kent 35 J2
**Birchley Heath** Warwks 86 C5
**Birchover** Derbys 100 E1
**Birch Services** Rochdl 122 C8
**Birch Vale** Derbys 114 A4
**Birchwood** Lincs 116 F7
**Birch Wood** Somset 25 K8
**Birchwood** Warrtn 112 F4
**Bircotes** Notts 115 M3
**Birdbrook** Essex 77 G6
**Birdforth** N York 133 G4
**Birdham** W Susx 17 M3
**Birdingbury** Warwks 72 E2
**Birdlip** Gloucs 55 L5
**Birdsall** N York 134 C6
**Birds Edge** Kirk 123 J8
**Birds Green** Essex 60 F6
**Birdsgreen** Shrops 84 D6
**Birdsmoorgate** Dorset 13 K3
**Birdwell** Barns 115 G2
**Birgham** Border 168 B2
**Birichin** Highld 223 G3
**Birkby** N York 141 H6
**Birkdale** Sefton 120 D7
**Birkenbog** Abers 215 L2
**Birkenhead** Wirral 111 K4
**Birkenhead (Queensway) Tunnel** Lpool 111 K4
**Birkenhills** Abers 216 E5
**Birkenshaw** Kirk 123 J5
**Birkhall** Abers 205 H6
**Birkhill** Angus 186 F1
**Birkhill** D & G 166 B6
**Birkin** N York 124 E5
**Birley** Herefs 69 J4
**Birley Carr** Sheff 115 G3
**Birling** Kent 46 B7
**Birlingham** Worcs 71 G5
**Birmingham** Birm 85 J6
*Birmingham Airport* Solhll 85 L6
**Birnam** P & K 195 G7
**Birness** Abers 217 J7
**Birse** Abers 206 B6
**Birsemore** Abers 205 L5
**Birstall** Kirk 123 J5
**Birstall** Leics 87 H2
**Birstwith** N York 132 C7
**Birtley** Gatesd 151 G4
**Birtley** Herefs 69 G2
**Birtley** Nthumb 157 L6
**Birtley Crematorium** Gatesd 151 G4
**Birts Street** Worcs 70 D7
**Bisbrooke** Rutlnd 88 C4
**Biscathorpe** Lincs 118 C5
**Bisham** W & M 42 D4
**Bishampton** Worcs 71 H4
**Bish Mill** Devon 24 B6
**Bishop Auckland** Dur 140 F2
**Bishopbridge** Lincs 117 G4
**Bishopbriggs** E Duns 175 G4
**Bishop Burton** E R Yk 126 B3
**Bishop Middleham** Dur 141 H2
**Bishopmill** Moray 214 F2
**Bishop Monkton** N York 132 E6
**Bishop Norton** Lincs 117 G3
**Bishopsbourne** Kent 35 G4
**Bishops Cannings** Wilts 40 B7
**Bishop's Castle** Shrops 83 G5
**Bishop's Caundle** Dorset 27 G8
**Bishop's Cleeve** Gloucs 55 L3
**Bishop's Frome** Herefs 70 B5
**Bishop's Green** Essex 61 G4
**Bishop's Hull** Somset 25 J6
**Bishop's Itchington** Warwks 72 E3
**Bishops Lydeard** Somset 25 J5
**Bishop's Norton** Gloucs 55 J3
**Bishop's Nympton** Devon 24 B6
**Bishop's Offley** Staffs 99 H6
**Bishop's Stortford** Herts 60 D4
**Bishop's Sutton** Hants 29 L5
**Bishop's Tachbrook** Warwks 72 C3
**Bishop's Tawton** Devon 23 J5
**Bishopsteignton** Devon 7 K2
**Bishopstoke** Hants 29 J7
**Bishopston** Swans 51 H7
**Bishopstone** Bucks 58 D6
**Bishopstone** E Susx 19 M5
**Bishopstone** Herefs 69 H5
**Bishopstone** Kent 47 K6
**Bishopstone** Swindn 40 E4
**Bishopstone** Wilts 28 B6
**Bishopstrow** Wilts 27 K3
**Bishop Sutton** BaNES 38 E7
**Bishop's Waltham** Hants 29 K7
**Bishopswood** Somset 25 K8
**Bishop's Wood** Staffs 84 E2
**Bishopsworth** Bristl 38 E6
**Bishop Thornton** N York 132 D6
**Bishopthorpe** C York 124 F2
**Bishopton** Darltn 141 J3
**Bishopton** Rens 174 E4
**Bishop Wilton** E R Yk 134 C7
**Bishton** Newpt 38 B3
**Bishton** Staffs 100 A7
**Bisley** Gloucs 55 K6
**Bisley** Surrey 42 F8
**Bissoe** Cnwll 3 K3
**Bisterne** Hants 15 L3
**Bitchfield** Lincs 103 G6
**Bittadon** Devon 23 J3
**Bittaford** Devon 6 F4
**Bitterley** Shrops 83 L7
**Bitterne** C Sotn 29 J8
**Bitteswell** Leics 87 G6
**Bitton** S Glos 39 G6
**Bix** Oxon 42 B4
**Bixter** Shet 235 c5
**Blaby** Leics 87 H4
**Blackadder** Border 179 H7
**Blackawton** Devon 7 J5
**Blackborough** Devon 12 E1
**Blackborough End** Norfk 90 F1
**Black Bourton** Oxon 56 F6
**Blackboys** E Susx 20 B2
**Blackbrook** Derbys 101 G3
**Blackbrook** St Hel 112 D3
**Blackbrook** Staffs 99 H5
**Blackburn** Abers 206 F3
**Blackburn** Bl w D 121 K5
**Blackburn** W Loth 176 D5
**Blackburn with Darwen Services** Bl w D 121 K5
**Blackcraig** E Ayrs 164 C7
**Black Crofts** Ag & B 182 D1
**Blackdog** Abers 207 H3
**Black Dog** Devon 11 J3
**Blackdown** Dorset 13 K2
**Blacker Hill** Barns 115 G2
**Blackfen** Gt Lon 45 J5
**Blackfield** Hants 16 E3
**Blackford** P & K 185 J5
**Blackford** Somset 26 B2
**Blackford** Somset 26 F6
**Blackfordby** Leics 101 G8
**Blackhall** C Edin 177 H4
**Blackhall Colliery** Dur 151 K6
**Blackhall Mill** Gatesd 150 E4
**Blackhaugh** Border 166 F2
**Blackheath** Gt Lon 45 G5

**Blackheath** Sandw 85 H6
**Blackheath** Suffk 93 J8
**Blackheath** Surrey 31 G3
**Blackhill** Abers 217 K3
**Blackhill** Abers 217 K5
**Blackhill** Dur 150 D5
**Blackhill of Clackriach** Abers 217 H5
**Blackhorse** Devon 12 C4
**Blacklaw** D & G 165 K7
**Blackley** Manch 113 J2
**Blackley Crematorium** Manch 113 J2
**Blacklunans** P & K 195 J4
**Blackmarstone** Herefs 69 K6
**Blackmill** Brdgnd 36 E3
**Blackmoor** Hants 30 C5
**Blackmoor** N Som 38 C7
**Blackmoorfoot** Kirk 123 G7
**Blackmore** Essex 60 F7
**Blackmore End** Essex 61 H2
**Black Mountains** 53 K3
**Blackness** Falk 176 E3
**Blacknest** Hants 30 D3
**Black Notley** Essex 61 J4
**Blacko** Lancs 122 C3
**Black Pill** Swans 51 J7
**Blackpool** Bpool 120 D4
**Blackpool** Devon 7 K6
**Blackpool Zoo** Bpool 120 D4
**Blackridge** W Loth 176 B5
**Blackrod** Bolton 121 J7
**Blacksboat** Moray 214 E6
**Blackshaw** D & G 147 J2
**Blackshaw Head** Calder 122 E5
**Blackstone** W Susx 19 H3
**Black Street** Suffk 93 K6
**Blackthorn** Oxon 57 L4
**Blackthorpe** Suffk 77 K2
**Blacktoft** E R Yk 125 J5
**Blacktop** C Aber 207 G4
**Black Torrington** Devon 10 C4
**Blackwall** Derbys 100 E3
**Blackwall Tunnel** Gt Lon 45 H4
**Blackwater** Cnwll 3 J3
**Blackwater** Hants 42 D7
**Blackwater** IoW 17 G5
**Blackwater** Somset 25 K7
**Blackwaterfoot** N Ayrs 162 A4
**Blackwell** Cumb 148 D4
**Blackwell** Derbys 101 H2
**Blackwell** Derbys 114 C6
**Blackwell** Warwks 72 B5
**Blackwell** Worcs 71 H1
**Blackwood** Caerph 37 J2
**Blackwood** D & G 154 F5
**Blackwood** S Lans 164 F1
**Blacon** Ches W 111 L7
**Bladnoch** D & G 145 J4
**Bladon** Oxon 57 J5
**Blaenannerch** Cerdgn 65 H5
**Blaenau Ffestiniog** Gwynd 96 A4
**Blaenavon** Torfn 53 K6
**Blaenavon Industrial Landscape** Torfn 53 K6
**Blaenffos** Pembks 65 H6
**Blaengarw** Brdgnd 36 D2
**Blaengwrach** Neath 52 D6
**Blaengwynfi** Neath 36 D2
**Blaenpennal** Cerdgn 66 E2
**Blaenplwyf** Cerdgn 80 D7
**Blaenporth** Cerdgn 65 J5
**Blaenrhondda** Rhondd 52 E7
**Blaenwaun** Carmth 50 B1
**Blaen-y-coed** Carmth 65 K8
**Blaen-y-cwm** Rhondd 52 E7
**Blagdon** N Som 38 D8
**Blagdon** Somset 25 K7
**Blagdon** Torbay 7 K4
**Blagdon Hill** Somset 25 K7
**Blaich** Highld 191 K2
**Blain** Highld 190 D3
**Blaina** Blae G 53 J6
**Blair Atholl** P & K 194 D4
**Blair Drummond** Stirlg 184 F7
**Blairgowrie** P & K 195 J7
**Blairhall** Fife 176 D2
**Blairingone** P & K 185 K7
**Blairlogie** Stirlg 185 H7
**Blairmore** Ag & B 173 L2
**Blairmore** Highld 228 C4
**Blair's Ferry** Ag & B 173 G4
**Blaisdon** Gloucs 55 G5
**Blakebrook** Worcs 84 E7
**Blakedown** Worcs 84 F7
**Blake End** Essex 61 H4
**Blakemere** Ches W 112 D7
**Blakemere** Herefs 69 G6
**Blakenall Heath** Wsall 85 H3
**Blakeney** Gloucs 54 F6
**Blakeney** Norfk 106 B4
**Blakenhall** Ches E 99 G3
**Blakenhall** Wolves 85 G4
**Blakesley** Nhants 73 J4
**Blanchland** Nthumb 150 B5
**Blandford Forum** Dorset 15 G2
**Blandford St Mary** Dorset 15 G2
**Blanefield** Stirlg 174 F3
**Blankney** Lincs 103 H1
**Blantyre** S Lans 175 J6
**Blàr a' Chaorainn** Highld 191 L3
**Blargie** Highld 202 F6
**Blarmachfoldach** Highld 191 L3
**Blaston** Leics 88 B4
**Blatherwycke** Nhants 88 D4
**Blawith** Cumb 129 G2
**Blawquhairn** D & G 154 B5
**Blaxhall** Suffk 79 H3
**Blaxton** Donc 116 A2
**Blaydon** Gatesd 150 F3
**Bleadney** Somset 26 C3
**Bleadon** N Som 25 M1
**Blean** Kent 34 F3
**Bleasby** Notts 102 B3
**Blebocraigs** Fife 187 G4
**Bleddfa** Powys 68 E2
**Bledington** Gloucs 56 E4
**Bledlow** Bucks 58 C7
**Bledlow Ridge** Bucks 42 D2
**Blegbie** E Loth 178 B6
**Blencarn** Cumb 138 F2
**Blencogo** Cumb 147 L5
**Blendworth** Hants 30 B8
**Blenheim Palace** Oxon 57 H5
**Blennerhasset** Cumb 147 L6
**Bletchingdon** Oxon 57 J4
**Bletchingley** Surrey 32 B3
**Bletchley** M Keyn 58 E2
**Bletchley** Shrops 98 F5
**Bletchley Park Museum** M Keyn 74 C7
**Bletherston** Pembks 49 H4
**Bletsoe** Bed 74 E3
**Blewbury** Oxon 41 K4
**Blickling** Norfk 106 E6
**Blidworth** Notts 101 L2
**Blidworth Bottoms** Notts 101 L2
**Blindcrake** Cumb 147 K7
**Blindley Heath** Surrey 32 C4
**Blisland** Cnwll 5 H2
**Blissford** Hants 28 D8
**Bliss Gate** Worcs 84 D8
**Blisworth** Nhants 73 K4
**Blithbury** Staffs 100 B8
**Blockley** Gloucs 71 L7
**Blofield** Norfk 93 G2
**Blofield Heath** Norfk 93 G2
**Blo Norton** Norfk 92 B7
**Bloomfield** Border 167 J4
**Blore** Staffs 100 C3
**Bloxham** Oxon 72 E7
**Bloxholm** Lincs 103 H2
**Bloxwich** Wsall 85 H3
**Bloxworth** Dorset 15 G4
**Blubberhouses** N York 132 B7
**Blue Anchor** Somset 24 F3
**Blue Bell Hill** Kent 46 C7
**Blue John Cavern** Derbys 114 C5
**Blundellsands** Sefton 111 J2
**Blundeston** Suffk 93 L4
**Blunham** C Beds 75 H4
**Blunsdon St Andrew** Swindn 40 C3
**Bluntington** Worcs 84 F8
**Bluntisham** Cambs 89 L8
**Blurton** C Stke 99 K4
**Blyborough** Lincs 116 F3
**Blyford** Suffk 93 J7
**Blymhill** Staffs 84 E2
**Blyth** Notts 115 L4
**Blyth** Nthumb 159 H5
**Blyth Bridge** Border 165 M1
**Blythburgh** Suffk 93 J7
**Blyth Crematorium** Nthumb 159 H5
**Blythe** Border 178 D7
**Blythe Bridge** Staffs 99 L4
**Blyth Services** Notts 115 L4
**Blyton** Lincs 116 D3
**Boarhills** Fife 187 J5
**Boarhunt** Hants 17 H2
**Boarstall** Bucks 57 L5
**Boath** Highld 222 D6
**Boat of Garten** Highld 203 L2
**Bobbing** Kent 46 E6
**Bobbington** Staffs 84 E5
**Bocking** Essex 61 J4
**Bocking Churchstreet** Essex 61 J3
**Boddam** Abers 217 L6
**Boddam** Shet 235 c7
**Boddington** Gloucs 55 K3
**Bodedern** IoA 108 D5
**Bodelwyddan** Denbgs 110 D6
**Bodenham** Herefs 69 K4
**Bodenham** Wilts 28 D6
**Bodenham Moor** Herefs 69 K4
**Bodewryd** IoA 108 E4
**Bodfari** Denbgs 110 F7
**Bodffordd** IoA 108 F6
**Bodfuan** Gwynd 94 F5
**Bodham** Norfk 106 D4
**Bodiam** E Susx 33 K7
**Bodicote** Oxon 72 F6
**Bodinnick** Cnwll 5 H5
**Bodle Street Green** E Susx 20 D3
**Bodmin** Cnwll 5 G3
**Bodmin Moor** Cnwll 5 J1
**Bodsham** Kent 34 E5
**Bodwen** Cnwll 5 G4
**Bogallan** Highld 212 F4
**Bogbrae** Abers 217 J7
**Bogend** S Ayrs 163 K3
**Boggs Holdings** E Loth 177 L4
**Boghall** Mdloth 177 H5
**Boghall** W Loth 176 D5
**Boghead** S Lans 164 F2
**Bogmoor** Moray 215 H2
**Bogmuir** Abers 197 G3
**Bogniebrae** Abers 216 B5
**Bognor Regis** W Susx 18 C6
**Bogroy** Highld 203 L2
**Bogue** D & G 154 B6
**Bohortha** Cnwll 3 L5
**Bohuntine** Highld 201 L8
**Bolam** Dur 140 F3
**Bolberry** Devon 7 G7
**Boldmere** Birm 85 K5
**Boldre** Hants 16 C3
**Boldron** Dur 140 C4
**Bole** Notts 116 C4
**Bolehill** Derbys 100 F2
**Bolham** Devon 24 E7
**Bolham Water** Devon 25 J8
**Bolingey** Cnwll 3 K1
**Bollington** Ches E 113 L6
**Bolney** W Susx 31 L6
**Bolnhurst** Bed 74 F3
**Bolnore** W Susx 19 J2
**Bolshan** Angus 197 G6
**Bolsover** Derbys 115 J7
**Bolsterstone** Sheff 114 F3
**Boltby** N York 133 G3
**Boltenstone** Abers 205 J3
**Bolton** Bolton 121 L8
**Bolton** Cumb 138 F3
**Bolton** E Loth 178 B4
**Bolton** E R Yk 125 J1
**Bolton** Nthumb 169 G6
**Bolton Abbey** N York 131 K8
**Bolton-by-Bowland** Lancs 122 B1
**Boltonfellend** Cumb 148 E2
**Boltongate** Cumb 147 M6
**Bolton-le-Sands** Lancs 129 K6
**Bolton Low Houses** Cumb 147 M6
**Bolton-on-Swale** N York 141 G7
**Bolton Percy** N York 124 E3
**Bolton upon Dearne** Barns 115 J2
**Bolventor** Cnwll 5 J1
**Bomere Heath** Shrops 98 C8
**Bonar Bridge** Highld 222 E3
**Bonawe** Ag & B 182 E2
**Bonby** N Linc 126 C7
**Boncath** Pembks 65 H6
**Bonchester Bridge** Border 167 J6
**Bondleigh** Devon 10 F4
**Bonds** Lancs 121 G2
**Bo'ness** Falk 176 D3
**Boney Hay** Staffs 85 J2
**Bonhill** W Duns 174 D3
**Boningale** Shrops 84 E3
**Bonjedward** Border 167 K5
**Bonkle** N Lans 175 L6
**Bonnington** Angus 196 F7
**Bonnington** Kent 34 E7
**Bonnybank** Fife 186 F6
**Bonnybridge** Falk 175 L3
**Bonnykelly** Abers 217 G4
**Bonnyrigg** Mdloth 177 J5
**Bonnyton** Angus 196 B8
**Bonsall** Derbys 100 F2
**Bonshaw Tower** D & G 155 M7
**Bont-Dolgadfan** Powys 81 J4
**Bont-goch** Cerdgn 80 F6
**Bontnewydd** Cerdgn 66 E2
**Bontnewydd** Gwynd 95 H1
**Bontuchel** Denbgs 97 G2
**Bonvilston** V Glam 37 G5
**Boode** Devon 23 H4
**Booker** Bucks 42 D3
**Boon** Border 167 J1
**Boosbeck** R & Cl 142 E4
**Boose's Green** Essex 61 K2
**Boot** Cumb 137 G6
**Booth** Calder 122 F5
**Boothby Graffoe** Lincs 103 G2
**Boothby Pagnell** Lincs 102 F6
**Boothferry** E R Yk 125 H5
**Boothstown** Salfd 113 G2
**Bootle** Cumb 128 D2
**Bootle** Sefton 111 K3
**Boraston** Shrops 70 B1
**Bordeaux** Guern 236 e2
**Borden** Kent 34 B3

**Borders Crematorium** Border 167 H3
**Boreham** Essex 61 J6
**Boreham Street** E Susx 20 D4
**Borehamwood** Herts 44 D2
**Boreland** D & G 155 L4
**Boreraig** Highld 208 C4
**Borgh** W Isls 232 f1
**Borgh** W Isls 233 b9
**Borgie** Highld 229 K4
**Borgue** D & G 146 B5
**Borgue** Highld 227 K4
**Borley** Essex 77 J6
**Borneskitaig** Highld 218 B7
**Borness** D & G 146 A5
**Boroughbridge** N York 132 F6
**Borough Green** Kent 33 G2
**Borrowash** Derbys 101 H5
**Borrowby** N York 132 F2
**Borrowstoun** Falk 176 D3
**Borstal** Medway 46 B6
**Borth** Cerdgn 80 E5
**Borthwickbrae** Border 166 F6
**Borthwickshiels** Border 166 F6
**Borth-y-Gest** Gwynd 95 K5
**Borve** Highld 209 G5
**Borve** W Isls 232 d4
**Borve** W Isls 232 f1
**Borve** W Isls 233 b9
**Borwick** Lancs 129 L5
**Bosbury** Herefs 70 C5
**Boscastle** Cnwll 8 E6
**Boscombe** Bmouth 15 L4
**Boscombe** Wilts 28 D4
**Bosham** W Susx 17 L2
**Bosherston** Pembks 49 G8
**Bosley** Ches E 113 K7
**Bossall** N York 133 L7
**Bossiney** Cnwll 8 E6
**Bossingham** Kent 34 F5
**Bossington** Somset 24 D2
**Bostock Green** Ches W 112 F7
**Boston** Lincs 104 B4
**Boston Crematorium** Lincs 104 A4
**Boston Spa** Leeds 124 C2
**Boswinger** Cnwll 4 F7
**Botallack** Cnwll 2 C5
**Botany Bay** Gt Lon 59 M7
**Botesdale** Suffk 92 C7
**Bothal** Nthumb 159 G5
**Bothamsall** Notts 116 A6
**Bothel** Cumb 147 L6
**Bothenhampton** Dorset 13 L4
**Bothwell** S Lans 175 J6
**Bothwell Services** S Lans 175 J6
**Botley** Bucks 59 G7
**Botley** Hants 29 K8
**Botley** Oxon 57 J6
**Botolph Claydon** Bucks 58 B3
**Botolphs** W Susx 19 G4
**Bottesford** Leics 102 D5
**Bottesford** N Linc 125 L8
**Bottisham** Cambs 76 D3
**Bottomcraig** Fife 186 F3
**Bottoms** Calder 122 D6
**Botusfleming** Cnwll 6 B4
**Botwnnog** Gwynd 94 E6
**Bough Beech** Kent 32 E4
**Boughrood** Powys 68 C6
**Boughton** Nhants 73 L2
**Boughton** Norfk 91 G3
**Boughton** Notts 116 B7
**Boughton Aluph** Kent 34 D5
**Boughton Green** Kent 33 K3
**Boughton Monchelsea** Kent 33 K3
**Boughton Street** Kent 34 E3
**Bouldon** Shrops 83 K6
**Boulmer** Nthumb 169 K6
**Boultham** Lincs 116 F7
**Bourn** Cambs 75 K3
**Bourne** Lincs 103 H7
**Bournebridge** Essex 45 J2
**Bournebrook** Birm 85 J6
**Bourne End** Bucks 42 E3
**Bourne End** C Beds 74 D5
**Bourne End** Herts 59 G6
**Bournemouth** Bmouth 15 K4
*Bournemouth Airport* Dorset 15 L3
**Bournemouth Crematorium** Bmouth 15 L4
**Bournes Green** Sthend 46 E3
**Bournheath** Worcs 85 G8
**Bournmoor** Dur 151 H5
**Bournville** Birm 85 J7
**Bourton** Dorset 27 H5
**Bourton** Oxon 40 E3
**Bourton** Shrops 83 L4
**Bourton** Wilts 40 B7
**Bourton on Dunsmore** Warwks 72 E1
**Bourton-on-the-Hill** Gloucs 56 D2
**Bourton-on-the-Water** Gloucs 56 D4
**Bousd** Ag & B 189 G4
**Bouth** Cumb 129 H3
**Bouthwaite** N York 131 L5
**Boveridge** Dorset 28 B7
**Bovey Tracey** Devon 7 J1
**Bovingdon** Herts 59 G7
**Bow** Devon 11 G4
**Bow** Gt Lon 45 G4
**Bow** Ork 234 b7
**Bow Brickhill** M Keyn 74 C7
**Bowbridge** Gloucs 55 J6
**Bowburn** Dur 151 H7
**Bowcombe** IoW 16 F5
**Bowd** Devon 12 E4
**Bowden** Border 167 H4
**Bowden Hill** Wilts 39 L6
**Bowdon** Traffd 113 H4
**Bower** Highld 231 J3
**Bowerchalke** Wilts 28 A6
**Bowermadden** Highld 231 J3
**Bowers** Staffs 99 J5
**Bowers Gifford** Essex 46 C3
**Bowershall** Fife 176 F1
**Bower's Row** Leeds 124 B5
**Bowes** Dur 140 C4
**Bowgreave** Lancs 121 G2
**Bowhouse** D & G 147 H2
**Bowland** Border 167 G2
**Bowley** Herefs 69 K4
**Bowlhead Green** Surrey 30 E4
**Bowling** C Brad 123 H4
**Bowling** W Duns 174 E4
**Bowmanstead** Cumb 137 J7
**Bowmore** Ag & B 170 F6
**Bowness-on-Solway** Cumb 147 L3
**Bowness-on-Windermere** Cumb 137 L7
**Bow of Fife** Fife 186 E5
**Bowriefauld** Angus 196 E6
**Bowsden** Nthumb 168 E2
**Bow Street** Cerdgn 80 E6
**Bowthorpe** Norfk 92 E2
**Box** Gloucs 55 K7
**Box** Wilts 39 J6
**Boxford** Suffk 77 L6
**Boxford** W Berk 41 H6
**Boxgrove** W Susx 18 B4
**Boxley** Kent 33 K2
**Boxmoor** Herts 59 H6
**Boxted** Essex 62 B2
**Boxted** Essex 62 B2
**Boxted** Suffk 77 J4
**Boxted Cross** Essex 62 B2
**Boxworth** Cambs 75 L2
**Boyden Gate** Kent 47 L6
**Boylestone** Derbys 100 D5
**Boyndie** Abers 216 C2
**Boyndlie** Abers 217 G2
**Boynton** E R Yk 135 H6
**Boysack** Angus 197 G6
**Boyton** Cnwll 9 J6
**Boyton** Suffk 79 H5
**Boyton** Wilts 27 L4
**Boyton Cross** Essex 61 G6
**Boyton End** Suffk 77 G5
**Bozeat** Nhants 74 C3
**Brabourne** Kent 34 E6
**Brabourne Lees** Kent 34 E6
**Brabstermire** Highld 231 K2
**Bracadale** Highld 208 E6
**Braceborough** Lincs 88 F2
**Bracebridge Heath** Lincs 117 G7
**Bracebridge Low Fields** Lincs 116 F7
**Braceby** Lincs 103 G5
**Bracewell** Lancs 122 C2
**Brackenfield** Derbys 101 G2
**Brackenhirst** N Lans 175 K5
**Brackla** Brdgnd 36 E4
**Bracklesham** W Susx 17 L3
**Brackletter** Highld 201 J8
**Brackley** Nhants 73 H6
**Bracknell** Br For 42 E6
**Braco** P & K 185 H5
**Bracobrae** Moray 215 L4
**Bracon Ash** Norfk 92 E4
**Bracora** Highld 199 L6
**Bracorina** Highld 199 L6
**Bradbourne** Derbys 100 D3
**Bradbury** Dur 141 H2
**Bradden** Nhants 73 J5
**Bradeley** C Stke 99 K3
**Bradenham** Bucks 42 D2
**Bradenstoke** Wilts 39 M4
**Bradfield** Devon 12 D1
**Bradfield** Essex 62 D2
**Bradfield** Norfk 106 F5
**Bradfield** Sheff 114 F3
**Bradfield** W Berk 41 L6
**Bradfield Combust** Suffk 77 K3
**Bradfield Green** Ches E 99 G2
**Bradfield Heath** Essex 62 D3
**Bradfield St Clare** Suffk 77 K3
**Bradfield St George** Suffk 77 K3
**Bradford** C Brad 123 H4
**Bradford** Devon 9 L4
**Bradford Abbas** Dorset 26 E8
**Bradford Leigh** Wilts 39 J7
**Bradford-on-Avon** Wilts 39 J7
**Bradford-on-Tone** Somset 25 J6
**Bradford Peverell** Dorset 14 C4
**Bradiford** Devon 23 J5
**Brading** IoW 17 H5
**Bradley** Derbys 100 E4
**Bradley** Hants 29 M3
**Bradley** NE Lin 118 C1
**Bradley** Staffs 99 K8
**Bradley** Wolves 85 G4
**Bradley** Worcs 71 H3
**Bradley Green** Worcs 71 H3
**Bradley in the Moors** Staffs 100 B4
**Bradley Stoke** S Glos 38 E4
**Bradmore** Notts 101 L6
**Bradninch** Devon 12 C2
**Bradnop** Staffs 100 A2
**Bradpole** Dorset 13 L4
**Bradshaw** Calder 123 G4
**Bradstone** Devon 9 K8
**Bradwall Green** Ches E 113 H8
**Bradwell** Derbys 114 D5
**Bradwell** Essex 61 J4
**Bradwell** M Keyn 74 B6
**Bradwell** Norfk 93 K3
**Bradwell Crematorium** Staffs 99 J3
**Bradwell-on-Sea** Essex 62 B6
**Bradwell Waterside** Essex 62 B6
**Bradworthy** Devon 9 J3
**Brae** Highld 213 G2
**Brae** Shet 235 c4
**Braeface** Falk 175 K3
**Braehead** Angus 197 H5
**Braehead** D & G 145 J4
**Braehead** S Lans 176 C7
**Braeintra** Highld 210 D7
**Braemar** Abers 204 E6
**Braemore** Highld 221 G5
**Braemore** Highld 227 J3
**Brae Roy Lodge** Highld 201 L6
**Braeside** Inver 173 L4
**Braes of Coul** Angus 195 L5
**Braes of Enzie** Moray 215 J3
**Braeswick** Ork 234 d4
**Braevallich** Ag & B 182 D6
**Brafferton** Darltn 141 H3
**Brafferton** N York 132 F5
**Brafield-on-the-Green** Nhants 74 B3
**Bragar** W Isls 232 f2
**Bragbury End** Herts 59 L4
**Braidwood** S Lans 175 L8
**Brailsford** Derbys 100 E4
**Braintree** Essex 61 J4
**Braiseworth** Suffk 78 D1
**Braishfield** Hants 29 G6
**Braithwaite** Cumb 137 H3
**Braithwell** Donc 115 K3
**Bramber** W Susx 19 G4
**Bramcote** Warwks 86 E5
**Bramcote Crematorium** Notts 101 J5
**Bramdean** Hants 29 L5
**Bramerton** Norfk 93 G3
**Bramfield** Herts 59 M5
**Bramfield** Suffk 93 H8
**Bramford** Suffk 78 D5
**Bramhall** Stockp 113 K5
**Bramham** Leeds 124 C2
**Bramhope** Leeds 123 K2
**Bramley** Hants 41 M8
**Bramley** Leeds 123 K4
**Bramley** Rothm 115 J3
**Bramley** Surrey 31 G3
**Bramley Corner** Hants 41 M8
**Bramling** Kent 35 G4
**Brampford Speke** Devon 11 L5
**Brampton** Cambs 75 J1
**Brampton** Cumb 138 F3
**Brampton** Cumb 148 F3
**Brampton** Lincs 116 D5
**Brampton** Norfk 106 F7
**Brampton** Rothm 115 H2
**Brampton** Suffk 93 J6
**Brampton Abbotts** Herefs 54 E3
**Brampton Ash** Nhants 87 L6
**Brampton Bryan** Herefs 83 G8
**Brampton-en-le-Morthen** Rothm 115 J4
**Bramshall** Staffs 100 B6
**Bramshaw** Hants 28 F7
**Bramshott** Hants 30 D5
**Bramwell** Somset 26 B5
**Branault** Highld 190 B3

**Brancaster** Norfk 105 J4
**Brancaster Staithe** Norfk 105 J4
**Brancepeth** Dur 150 F7
**Branchill** Moray 214 D4
**Branderburgh** Moray 214 F1
**Brandesburton** E R Yk 126 E2
**Brandeston** Suffk 78 F3
**Brandiston** Norfk 106 D7
**Brandon** Dur 151 G6
**Brandon** Lincs 102 E3
**Brandon** Suffk 91 H6
**Brandon** Warwks 86 E7
**Brandon Parva** Norfk 92 C2
**Brandsby** N York 133 J5
**Brandy Wharf** Lincs 117 G3
**Bran End** Essex 61 G3
**Branksome** Poole 15 K4
**Branksome Park** Poole 15 K4
**Bransbury** Hants 29 H3
**Bransby** Lincs 116 E5
**Branscombe** Devon 12 F5
**Bransford** Worcs 70 E4
**Bransgore** Hants 16 A3
**Bransholme** C KuH 126 D4
**Bransley** Shrops 84 B7
**Branston** Leics 102 D6
**Branston** Lincs 117 G7
**Branston** Staffs 100 E7
**Branston Booths** Lincs 117 H7
**Branstone** IoW 17 G5
**Brant Broughton** Lincs 102 E2
**Brantham** Suffk 78 D7
**Branthwaite** Cumb 136 E3
**Branthwaite** Cumb 148 B7
**Brantingham** E R Yk 125 L5
**Branton** Donc 115 M2
**Branton** Nthumb 168 F6
**Branton Green** N York 132 F6
**Branxton** Nthumb 168 D2
**Brassington** Derbys 100 E2
**Brasted** Kent 32 E3
**Brasted Chart** Kent 32 E3
**Brathens** Abers 206 D5
**Bratoft** Lincs 119 G8
**Brattleby** Lincs 116 F5
**Bratton** Wilts 27 K2
**Bratton** Wrekin 84 B2
**Bratton Clovelly** Devon 10 C6
**Bratton Fleming** Devon 23 K4
**Bratton Seymour** Somset 26 F5
**Braughing** Herts 60 C3
**Braunston** Nhants 73 G2
**Braunston** Rutlnd 88 B3
**Braunton** Devon 23 H4
**Brawby** N York 134 B4
**Brawl** Highld 230 B3
**Bray** W & M 42 E4
**Braybrooke** Nhants 87 L6
**Brayford** Devon 23 L4
**Bray Shop** Cnwll 5 M2
**Brayton** N York 124 F4
**Braywick** W & M 42 E4
**Breachwood Green** Herts 59 J4
**Breadsall** Derbys 101 G5
**Breadstone** Gloucs 55 G7
**Breage** Cnwll 3 G5
**Breakachy** Highld 212 D5
**Breakish** Highld 199 L2
**Breakspear Crematorium** Gt Lon 43 H3
**Brealangwell Lodge** Highld 222 C3
**Bream** Gloucs 54 E6
**Breamore** Hants 28 D7
**Brean** Somset 25 L1
**Breanais** W Isls 232 d3
**Brearton** N York 132 E7
**Breascleit** W Isls 232 e2
**Breasclete** W Isls 232 e2
**Breaston** Derbys 101 J5
**Brechfa** Carmth 66 C7
**Brechin** Angus 196 F4
**Breckles** Norfk 91 L5
**Brecon** Powys 53 G3
*Brecon Beacons National Park* 52 F3
**Bredbury** Stockp 113 L3
**Brede** E Susx 21 G3
**Bredenbury** Herefs 69 L3
**Bredfield** Suffk 78 F4
**Bredgar** Kent 34 B3
**Bredhurst** Kent 46 D7
**Bredon** Worcs 71 G6
**Bredon's Hardwick** Worcs 71 G7
**Bredon's Norton** Worcs 71 G6
**Bredwardine** Herefs 69 G5
**Breedon on the Hill** Leics 101 H7
**Breich** W Loth 176 C6
**Breightmet** Bolton 121 L8
**Breighton** E R Yk 125 G4
**Breinton** Herefs 69 J6
**Bremhill** Wilts 39 L5
**Brenchley** Kent 33 H5
**Brendon** Devon 24 B2
**Brenfield** Ag & B 172 E2
**Brenish** W Isls 232 d3
**Brent Cross** Gt Lon 44 E3
**Brent Eleigh** Suffk 77 L5
**Brentford** Gt Lon 44 D5
**Brentingby** Leics 102 C8
**Brent Knoll** Somset 25 M2
**Brent Mill** Devon 7 G4
**Brent Pelham** Herts 60 C2
**Brentwood** Essex 45 L2
**Brenzett** Kent 21 K1
**Brenzett Green** Kent 34 D8
**Brereton** Staffs 85 J1
**Brereton Green** Ches E 113 H8
**Bressay** Shet 235 d6
**Bressingham** Norfk 92 C7
**Bretby** Derbys 100 F7
**Bretby Crematorium** Derbys 100 F7
**Bretford** Warwks 86 E7
**Bretforton** Worcs 71 K5
**Bretherton** Lancs 121 G6
**Breton** C Pete 89 H4
**Brettabister** Shet 235 d5
**Brettenham** Norfk 91 L6
**Brettenham** Suffk 77 L4
**Bretton** Flints 111 K8
**Brewood** Staffs 84 F2
**Briantspuddle** Dorset 14 F4
**Brickendon** Herts 60 A6
**Bricket Wood** Herts 59 J7
**Brick Houses** Sheff 114 F5
**Bricklehampton** Worcs 71 H6
**Bride** IoM 237 e2
**Bridekirk** Cumb 147 K7
**Bridestowe** Devon 10 D6
**Brideswell** Abers 216 B6
**Bridford** Devon 11 J7
**Bridge** Kent 35 G4
**Bridgefoot** Angus 186 F1
**Bridgehampton** Somset 26 E6
**Bridge Hewick** N York 132 E5
**Bridgehill** Dur 150 D5
**Bridgemary** Hants 17 H2
**Bridgend** Abers 215 L7
**Bridgend** Ag & B 161 K2
**Bridgend** Ag & B 171 G6
**Bridgend** Angus 196 E3
**Bridgend** Brdgnd 36 E4
**Bridgend** Cerdgn 65 G5
**Bridgend** D & G 165 L7
**Bridgend** Devon 6 E6
**Bridgend** Fife 186 F5
**Bridgend** Moray 215 J7
**Bridgend** P & K 186 B3
**Bridgend** W Loth 176 E3
**Bridgend of Lintrathen** Angus 195 L5
**Bridge of Alford** Abers 206 B2
**Bridge of Allan** Stirlg 185 G7
**Bridge of Avon** Moray 204 E2
**Bridge of Avon** Moray 214 E7
**Bridge of Balgie** P & K 193 J6
**Bridge of Brewlands** Angus 195 J4
**Bridge of Brown** Highld 204 D2
**Bridge of Cally** P & K 195 J6
**Bridge of Canny** Abers 206 C6
**Bridge of Craigisla** Angus 195 K5
**Bridge of Dee** D & G 146 C3
**Bridge of Don** C Aber 207 H4
**Bridge of Dye** Abers 206 C7
**Bridge of Earn** P & K 186 B4
**Bridge of Ericht** P & K 193 H5
**Bridge of Feugh** Abers 206 D6
**Bridge of Gairn** Abers 205 H6
**Bridge of Gaur** P & K 193 H5
**Bridge of Marnoch** Abers 216 B4
**Bridge of Muchalls** Abers 207 G6
**Bridge of Orchy** Ag & B 192 E7
**Bridge of Tilt** P & K 194 D4
**Bridge of Tynet** Moray 215 J3
**Bridge of Walls** Shet 235 b5
**Bridge of Weir** Rens 174 D5
**Bridgerule** Devon 9 H4
**Bridge Sollers** Herefs 69 H6
**Bridge Street** Suffk 77 K5
**Bridgetown** Somset 24 E5
**Bridge Trafford** Ches W 112 C7
**Bridgham** Norfk 91 L6
**Bridgnorth** Shrops 84 C5
**Bridgwater** Somset 25 L4
**Bridgwater Services** Somset 25 L4
**Bridlington** E R Yk 135 J6
**Bridport** Dorset 13 L4
**Bridstow** Herefs 54 E3
**Brierfield** Lancs 122 C3
**Brierley** Barns 124 C7
**Brierley** Gloucs 54 F5
**Brierley Hill** Dudley 85 G6
**Brigg** N Linc 117 G1
**Briggate** Norfk 107 G6
**Briggswath** N York 143 H5
**Brigham** Cumb 136 F2
**Brigham** E R Yk 135 G8
**Brighouse** Calder 123 H6
**Brighstone** IoW 16 E5
**Brighthampton** Oxon 57 G7
**Brightley** Devon 10 E5
**Brightling** E Susx 20 D2
**Brightlingsea** Essex 62 C5
**Brighton** Br & H 19 J5
*Brighton City Airport* W Susx 19 G5
**Brighton le Sands** Sefton 111 J2
**Brightons** Falk 176 C3
**Brightwalton** W Berk 41 H5
**Brightwell** Suffk 78 F5
**Brightwell Baldwin** Oxon 41 M2
**Brightwell-cum-Sotwell** Oxon 41 L3
**Brightwell Upperton** Oxon 42 A2
**Brignall** Dur 140 D5
**Brig o'Turk** Stirlg 184 C6
**Brigsley** NE Lin 118 C2
**Brigsteer** Cumb 129 K2
**Brigstock** Nhants 88 D6
**Brill** Bucks 58 A5
**Brill** Cnwll 3 J5
**Brilley** Herefs 68 F5
**Brimfield** Herefs 69 K2
**Brimfield Cross** Herefs 69 K2
**Brimington** Derbys 115 H6
**Brimley** Devon 7 J1
**Brimpsfield** Gloucs 55 L5
**Brimpton** W Berk 41 K7
**Brimscombe** Gloucs 55 K7
**Brimstage** Wirral 111 J5
**Brincliffe** Sheff 115 F4
**Brind** E R Yk 125 H4
**Brindister** Shet 235 c5
**Brindle** Lancs 121 J5
**Brineton** Staffs 84 E2
**Bringhurst** Leics 88 B5
**Bringsty Common** Herefs 70 C4
**Brington** Cambs 88 F7
**Brininghan** Norfk 106 C5
**Brinkhill** Lincs 118 E6
**Brinkley** Cambs 76 F4
**Brinklow** Warwks 86 E7
**Brinkworth** Wilts 40 A4
**Brinscall** Lancs 121 J6
**Brinsley** Notts 101 J3
**Brinsworth** Rothm 115 H4
**Brinton** Norfk 106 C5
**Brinyan** Ork 234 c5
**Brisley** Norfk 105 M7
**Brislington** Bristl 38 F6
**Brissenden Green** Kent 34 C6
**Bristol** Bristl 38 E5
*Bristol Airport* N Som 38 D7
**Bristol Zoo Gardens** Bristl 38 E5
**Briston** Norfk 106 C6
**Britford** Wilts 28 D5
**Brithdir** Caerph 53 J7
**Brithdir** Gwynd 96 B8
**British Legion Village** Kent 33 J2
**Briton Ferry** Neath 51 L6
**Britwell Salome** Oxon 42 A2
**Brixham** Torbay 7 L5
**Brixton** Devon 6 E5
**Brixton** Gt Lon 44 F5
**Brixton Deverill** Wilts 27 K4
**Brixworth** Nhants 73 L1
**Brize Norton** Oxon 56 F6
*Brize Norton Airport* Oxon 56 F6
**Broad Alley** Worcs 70 F2
**Broad Blunsdon** Swindn 40 D3
**Broadbottom** Tamesd 113 M3
**Broadbridge** W Susx 17 M2
**Broadbridge Heath** W Susx 31 J5
**Broad Campden** Gloucs 71 L6
**Broad Carr** Calder 123 G6
**Broad Chalke** Wilts 28 B6
**Broadclyst** Devon 12 C3
**Broadfield** Inver 174 C4
**Broadford** Highld 199 K2
**Broadford Bridge** W Susx 31 H6
**Broadgairhill** Border 166 C7
**Broad Green** Worcs 70 D4
**Broadhaugh** Border 179 H7
**Broad Haven** Pembks 48 E5
**Broadheath** Traffd 113 H4
**Broadhembury** Devon 12 E2
**Broadhempston** Devon 7 J3
**Broad Hinton** Wilts 40 C5
**Broadland Row** E Susx 21 G2
**Broadley** Moray 215 J3
**Broad Marston** Worcs 71 K5
**Broadmayne** Dorset 14 D5
**Broad Meadow** Staffs 99 J3

**Broadmoor** Pembks ...... 49 J6
**Broadoak** Dorset ...... 13 K3
**Broad Oak** E Susx ...... 20 C2
**Broad Oak** E Susx ...... 21 G2
**Broad Oak** Herefs ...... 54 C4
**Broad Oak** Kent ...... 35 G3
**Broad Oak** St Hel ...... 112 D3
**Broadsands** Torbay ...... 7 K4
**Broad's Green** Essex ...... 61 H5
**Broadstairs** Kent ...... 35 K2
**Broadstone** Poole ...... 15 J4
**Broadstone** Shrops ...... 83 K5
**Broad Street** E Susx ...... 21 H3
**Broad Street** Kent ...... 33 L2
**Broad Town** Wilts ...... 40 C5
**Broadwas** Worcs ...... 70 D4
**Broadwater** Herts ...... 59 L4
**Broadwater** W Susx ...... 18 F5
**Broadwaters** Worcs ...... 84 E7
**Broadway** Pembks ...... 48 E5
**Broadway** Somset ...... 25 L7
**Broadway** Worcs ...... 71 K6
**Broadwell** Gloucs ...... 54 E5
**Broadwell** Gloucs ...... 56 D3
**Broadwell** Oxon ...... 56 E6
**Broadwell** Warwks ...... 72 F2
**Broadwindsor** Dorset ...... 13 K2
**Broadwood Kelly** Devon ...... 10 F4
**Broadwoodwidger** Devon ...... 9 K6
**Brochel** Highld ...... 209 J5
**Brochroy** Ag & B ...... 182 E2
**Brockamin** Worcs ...... 70 D4
**Brockbridge** Hants ...... 29 L7
**Brockdish** Norfk ...... 92 E7
**Brockenhurst** Hants ...... 16 C3
**Brocketsbrae** S Lans ...... 164 F2
**Brockford Street** Suffk ...... 78 D2
**Brockhall** Nhants ...... 73 J2
**Brockham** Surrey ...... 31 K2
**Brockhampton** Gloucs ...... 56 B4
**Brockhampton** Hants ...... 17 K2
**Brockhampton** Herefs ...... 54 E2
**Brockholes** Kirk ...... 123 H7
**Brocklesby** Lincs ...... 126 E7
**Brockley** N Som ...... 38 C6
**Brockley** Suffk ...... 77 J1
**Brockley Green** Suffk ...... 77 G5
**Brockley Green** Suffk ...... 77 J4
**Brockmoor** Dudley ...... 84 F5
**Brockton** Shrops ...... 83 G3
**Brockton** Shrops ...... 83 G6
**Brockton** Shrops ...... 83 L5
**Brockweir** Gloucs ...... 54 D7
**Brockworth** Gloucs ...... 55 K5
**Brocton** Staffs ...... 99 L8
**Brodick** N Ayrs ...... 162 C3
**Brodie** Moray ...... 214 B3
**Brodsworth** Donc ...... 115 J1
**Brogaig** Highld ...... 218 C7
**Brokenborough** Wilts ...... 39 K3
**Broken Cross** Ches E ...... 113 K6
**Brokerswood** Wilts ...... 27 J2
**Bromborough** Wirral ...... 111 K5
**Brome** Suffk ...... 92 D7
**Brome Street** Suffk ...... 92 D7
**Bromeswell** Suffk ...... 79 G4
**Bromfield** Cumb ...... 147 L5
**Bromfield** Shrops ...... 83 J7
**Bromham** Bed ...... 74 E4
**Bromham** Wilts ...... 39 L7
**Bromley** Dudley ...... 85 G6
**Bromley** Gt Lon ...... 45 H6
**Bromley** Shrops ...... 84 D4
**Bromley Cross** Bolton ...... 121 L7
**Brompton** Medway ...... 46 C6
**Brompton** N York ...... 141 J7
**Brompton-by-Sawdon** N York ...... 134 E3
**Brompton-on-Swale** N York ...... 140 F7
**Brompton Ralph** Somset ...... 25 G5
**Brompton Regis** Somset ...... 24 E5
**Bromsberrow** Gloucs ...... 70 D7
**Bromsberrow Heath** Gloucs ...... 55 G2
**Bromsgrove** Worcs ...... 71 G1
**Bromyard** Herefs ...... 70 B4
**Bronant** Cerdgn ...... 66 E2
**Brongest** Cerdgn ...... 65 K5
**Bronington** Wrexhm ...... 98 C4
**Bronllys** Powys ...... 68 D7
**Bronwydd** Carmth ...... 50 E2
**Bronygarth** Shrops ...... 97 K5
**Brook** Hants ...... 28 F8
**Brook** IoW ...... 16 E5
**Brook** Kent ...... 34 E6
**Brook** Surrey ...... 30 F4
**Brooke** Norfk ...... 93 G4
**Brooke** Rutlnd ...... 88 B3
**Brookenby** Lincs ...... 117 K3
**Brookfield** Rens ...... 174 D5
**Brookhampton** Somset ...... 26 F5
**Brook Hill** Hants ...... 28 F8
**Brookhouse** Lancs ...... 129 L6
**Brookhouse** Rothm ...... 115 K4
**Brookhouse Green** Ches E ...... 99 J1
**Brookhouses** Derbys ...... 114 B4
**Brookland** Kent ...... 21 K1
**Brooklands** Traffd ...... 113 H4
**Brookmans Park** Herts ...... 59 L7
**Brook Street** Essex ...... 45 L2
**Brook Street** Kent ...... 34 C7
**Brookthorpe** Gloucs ...... 55 J5
**Brookwood** Surrey ...... 42 F8
**Broom** C Beds ...... 75 H6
**Broom** Rothm ...... 115 H3
**Broom** Warwks ...... 71 K4
**Broome** Norfk ...... 93 H5
**Broome** Shrops ...... 83 H7
**Broome** Worcs ...... 84 F7
**Broomedge** Warrtn ...... 113 G4
**Broomfield** Essex ...... 61 H5
**Broomfield** Kent ...... 33 L3
**Broomfield** Kent ...... 47 K6
**Broomfield** Somset ...... 25 K5
**Broomfleet** E R Yk ...... 125 K5
**Broomhaugh** Nthumb ...... 150 C3
**Broom Hill** Barns ...... 115 H2
**Broom Hill** Notts ...... 101 K3
**Broomhill** Nthumb ...... 159 G3
**Broompark** Dur ...... 151 G6
**Brora** Highld ...... 226 F7
**Broseley** Shrops ...... 84 C3
**Brotherlee** Dur ...... 150 A7
**Brotherton** N York ...... 124 D5
**Brotton** R & Cl ...... 142 E4
**Broubster** Highld ...... 230 F4
**Brough** Cumb ...... 139 H4
**Brough** E R Yk ...... 125 L5
**Brough** Highld ...... 231 J2
**Brough** Notts ...... 102 D2
**Brough** Shet ...... 235 d4
**Broughall** Shrops ...... 98 E4
**Brough Lodge** Shet ...... 235 d2
**Brough Sowerby** Cumb ...... 139 H5
**Broughton** Border ...... 165 L3
**Broughton** Cambs ...... 89 K7
**Broughton** Flints ...... 111 K8
**Broughton** Hants ...... 28 F5
**Broughton** Lancs ...... 121 G4
**Broughton** M Keyn ...... 74 C6
**Broughton** N Linc ...... 126 B8
**Broughton** N York ...... 122 D1
**Broughton** N York ...... 134 B5
**Broughton** Nhants ...... 88 B7
**Broughton** Oxon ...... 72 E6
**Broughton** Salfd ...... 113 J2
**Broughton** V Glam ...... 36 E6
**Broughton Astley** Leics ...... 87 G5
**Broughton Gifford** Wilts ...... 39 K7
**Broughton Green** Worcs ...... 71 G3
**Broughton Hackett** Worcs ...... 71 G4
**Broughton-in-Furness** Cumb ...... 128 F3
**Broughton Mains** D & G ...... 145 J6
**Broughton Mills** Cumb ...... 128 F2
**Broughton Moor** Cumb ...... 147 J7
**Broughton Poggs** Oxon ...... 56 E7
**Broughty Ferry** C Dund ...... 187 H2
**Brown Candover** Hants ...... 29 L4
**Brown Edge** Staffs ...... 99 K2
**Brownhill** Abers ...... 217 G6
**Brownhills** Fife ...... 187 H4
**Brownhills** Wsall ...... 85 J3
**Browninghill Green** Hants ...... 41 L7
**Brown Lees** Staffs ...... 99 K2
**Brownsea Island** Dorset ...... 15 J5
**Brown's Green** Birm ...... 85 J5
**Browns Hill** Gloucs ...... 55 K7
**Brownston** Devon ...... 7 G5
**Broxa** N York ...... 134 E2
**Broxbourne** Herts ...... 60 B6
**Broxburn** E Loth ...... 178 E3
**Broxburn** W Loth ...... 176 E4
**Broxted** Essex ...... 60 F3
**Bruan** Highld ...... 231 K7
**Bruar** P & K ...... 194 C3
**Bruchag** Ag & B ...... 173 J6
**Bruichladdich** Ag & B ...... 170 E6
**Bruisyard** Suffk ...... 79 G2
**Bruisyard Street** Suffk ...... 79 G2
**Brumby** N Linc ...... 125 K8
**Brund** Staffs ...... 100 C1
**Brundall** Norfk ...... 93 G2
**Brundish** Suffk ...... 78 F1
**Brundish Street** Suffk ...... 78 F1
**Brunery** Highld ...... 190 E3
**Brunswick Village** N u Ty ...... 159 G7
**Brunthwaite** C Brad ...... 122 F2
**Bruntingthorpe** Leics ...... 87 H5
**Brunton** Fife ...... 186 E3
**Brunton** Wilts ...... 28 E1
**Brushford** Devon ...... 11 G4
**Brushford** Somset ...... 24 E6
**Bruton** Somset ...... 27 G4
**Bryan's Green** Worcs ...... 70 F2
**Bryanston** Dorset ...... 15 G2
**Brydekirk** D & G ...... 155 L7
**Bryher** IoS ...... 2 a1
**Brympton** Somset ...... 26 D7
**Bryn** Carmth ...... 51 G5
**Bryn** Neath ...... 36 C3
**Bryn** Wigan ...... 112 E2
**Brynamman** Carmth ...... 51 K3
**Brynberian** Pembks ...... 64 F7
**Bryncir** Gwynd ...... 95 H4
**Bryn-côch** Neath ...... 51 L5
**Bryncroes** Gwynd ...... 94 D6
**Bryncrug** Gwynd ...... 80 E3
**Bryneglwys** Denbgs ...... 97 H3
**Brynford** Flints ...... 111 G6
**Bryn Gates** Wigan ...... 112 E2
**Bryngwran** IoA ...... 108 D6
**Bryngwyn** Mons ...... 54 B6
**Bryngwyn** Powys ...... 68 D5
**Bryn-Henllan** Pembks ...... 64 E6
**Brynhoffnant** Cerdgn ...... 65 K4
**Brynmawr** Blae G ...... 53 J5
**Bryn-mawr** Gwynd ...... 94 D5
**Brynmenyn** Brdgnd ...... 36 D4
**Brynmill** Swans ...... 51 J6
**Brynna** Rhondd ...... 36 F4
**Brynrefail** Gwynd ...... 109 H8
**Brynsadler** Rhondd ...... 37 G4
**Bryn Saith Marchog** Denbgs ...... 97 G3
**Brynsiencyn** IoA ...... 108 F7
**Brynteg** IoA ...... 109 G5
**Bryn-y-Maen** Conwy ...... 110 B6
**Bualintur** Highld ...... 198 F2
**Bubbenhall** Warwks ...... 86 D8
**Bubwith** E R Yk ...... 125 H4
**Buccleuch** Border ...... 166 E6
**Buchanan Smithy** Stirlg ...... 174 E1
**Buchanhaven** Abers ...... 217 L5
**Buchanty** P & K ...... 185 J2
**Buchany** Stirlg ...... 184 F6
**Buchlyvie** Stirlg ...... 184 C8
**Buckabank** Cumb ...... 148 C5
**Buckden** Cambs ...... 75 H2
**Buckden** N York ...... 131 H4
**Buckenham** Norfk ...... 93 H3
**Buckerell** Devon ...... 12 E3
**Buckfast** Devon ...... 7 H3
**Buckfastleigh** Devon ...... 7 H3
**Buckhaven** Fife ...... 186 F7
**Buckholt** Mons ...... 54 D5
**Buckhorn Weston** Dorset ...... 27 H6
**Buckhurst Hill** Essex ...... 45 H2
**Buckie** Moray ...... 215 J2
**Buckingham** Bucks ...... 73 K7
**Buckland** Bucks ...... 58 E5
**Buckland** Devon ...... 7 G6
**Buckland** Gloucs ...... 71 J7
**Buckland** Herts ...... 75 L7
**Buckland** Kent ...... 35 J6
**Buckland** Oxon ...... 41 G2
**Buckland** Surrey ...... 31 K2
**Buckland Brewer** Devon ...... 22 F7
**Buckland Common** Bucks ...... 58 F6
**Buckland Dinham** Somset ...... 27 H2
**Buckland Filleigh** Devon ...... 10 C3
**Buckland in the Moor** Devon ...... 7 G2
**Buckland Monachorum** Devon ...... 6 D3
**Buckland Newton** Dorset ...... 14 D2
**Buckland Ripers** Dorset ...... 14 C6
**Buckland St Mary** Somset ...... 25 L8
**Buckland-Tout-Saints** Devon ...... 7 H6
**Bucklebury** W Berk ...... 41 K6
**Bucklers Hard** Hants ...... 16 E3
**Bucklesham** Suffk ...... 78 F6
**Buckley** Flints ...... 111 J8
**Bucklow Hill** Ches E ...... 113 G5
**Buckminster** Leics ...... 102 E7
**Bucknall** C Stke ...... 99 K3
**Bucknall** Lincs ...... 117 K7
**Bucknell** Oxon ...... 57 K3
**Bucknell** Shrops ...... 83 G8
**Buckpool** Moray ...... 215 J2
**Bucksburn** C Aber ...... 207 G4
**Buck's Cross** Devon ...... 22 E6
**Bucks Green** W Susx ...... 31 H5
**Buckshaw Village** Lancs ...... 121 H6
**Bucks Horn Oak** Hants ...... 30 D3
**Buck's Mills** Devon ...... 22 E6
**Buckton** E R Yk ...... 135 J5
**Buckton** Nthumb ...... 169 G2
**Buckworth** Cambs ...... 89 G7
**Budby** Notts ...... 115 L7
**Bude** Cnwll ...... 9 G4
**Budge's Shop** Cnwll ...... 5 M4
**Budleigh Salterton** Devon ...... 12 D6
**Budock Water** Cnwll ...... 3 K5
**Buerton** Ches E ...... 99 G4
**Bugbrooke** Nhants ...... 73 J3

**Bugle** Cnwll 4 F4
**Bugley** Dorset 27 H6
**Bugthorpe** E R Yk 134 B7
**Buildwas** Shrops 84 B3
**Builth Wells** Powys 68 B4
**Bulbridge** Wilts 28 C5
**Bulford** Wilts 28 D3
**Bulkeley** Ches E 98 D2
**Bulkington** Warwks 86 E6
**Bulkington** Wilts 39 L8
**Bulkworthy** Devon 9 K3
**Bullbrook** Br For 42 E6
**Bullington** Hants 29 J3
**Bullington** Lincs 117 H6
**Bulmer** Essex 77 J6
**Bulmer** N York 133 L6
**Bulmer Tye** Essex 77 J6
**Bulphan** Thurr 45 M3
**Bulwark** Abers 217 H5
**Bulwell** C Nott 101 K4
**Bulwick** Nhants 88 D5
**Bumble's Green** Essex 60 C6
**Bunacaimb** Highld 199 K7
**Bunarkaig** Highld 201 J7
**Bunbury** Ches E 98 E2
**Bunchrew** Highld 212 F5
**Bundalloch** Highld 210 D8
**Bunessan** Ag & B 180 E3
**Bungay** Suffk 93 G5
**Bunnahabhain** Ag & B 171 H4
**Bunny** Notts 101 L6
**Buntait** Highld 212 C7
**Buntingford** Herts 60 B3
**Bunwell** Norfk 92 D5
**Burbage** Leics 86 F5
**Burbage** Wilts 40 E7
**Burchett's Green** W & M 42 D4
**Burcombe** Wilts 28 B5
**Burcott** Bucks 58 E4
**Bures** Essex 77 K7
**Burford** Oxon 56 E5
**Burford** Shrops 69 L2
**Burg** Ag & B 189 J7
**Burgates** Hants 30 C5
**Burgess Hill** W Susx 19 J2
**Burgh** Suffk 78 F4
**Burgh by Sands** Cumb 148 B3
**Burgh Castle** Norfk 93 K3
**Burghclere** Hants 41 J7
**Burghead** Moray 214 D1
**Burghfield** W Berk 42 A6
**Burghfield Common** W Berk 42 A6
**Burgh Heath** Surrey 44 E7
**Burghill** Herefs 69 J5
**Burgh Island** Devon 6 F6
**Burgh le Marsh** Lincs 119 G7
**Burgh next Aylsham** Norfk 106 F7
**Burgh on Bain** Lincs 117 L4
**Burgh St Margaret** Norfk 93 J2
**Burgh St Peter** Norfk 93 K5
**Burghwallis** Donc 124 E7
**Burham** Kent 46 B7
**Buriton** Hants 30 C7
**Burland** Ches E 98 E2
**Burlawn** Cnwll 4 F2
**Burleigh** Gloucs 55 K7
**Burlescombe** Devon 25 G7
**Burleston** Dorset 14 E4
**Burley** Hants 16 B2
**Burley** Rutlnd 88 C2
**Burleydam** Ches E 98 E4
**Burley Gate** Herefs 69 L5
**Burley in Wharfedale** C Brad 123 H2
**Burley Street** Hants 16 B2
**Burley Wood Head** C Brad 123 H2
**Burlton** Shrops 98 C7
**Burmarsh** Kent 34 E7
**Burmington** Warwks 72 C6
**Burn** N York 124 F5
**Burnage** Manch 113 K3
**Burnaston** Derbys 100 F6
**Burnbrae** N Lans 176 B6
**Burnby** E R Yk 125 K2
**Burneside** Cumb 138 D7
**Burneston** N York 132 D3
**Burnett** BaNES 38 F7
**Burnfoot** Border 166 F6
**Burnfoot** Border 167 H6
**Burnfoot** D & G 155 G4
**Burnfoot** D & G 156 C3
**Burnfoot** D & G 156 C4
**Burnfoot** P & K 185 K6
**Burnham** Bucks 42 F4
**Burnham Deepdale** Norfk 105 J4
**Burnham Market** Norfk 105 K4
**Burnham Norton** Norfk 105 K4
**Burnham-on-Crouch** Essex 46 F2
**Burnham-on-Sea** Somset 25 L2
**Burnham Overy** Norfk 105 K4
**Burnham Overy Staithe** Norfk 105 K4
**Burnham Thorpe** Norfk 105 K4
**Burnhead** D & G 154 E3
**Burnhervie** Abers 206 D2
**Burnhill Green** Staffs 84 E4
**Burnhope** Dur 150 F5
**Burnhouse** N Ayrs 174 D7
**Burniston** N York 134 F2
**Burnley** Lancs 122 C4
**Burnley Crematorium** Lancs 122 B4
**Burnmouth** Border 179 K6
**Burn of Cambus** Stirlg 184 F6
**Burnopfield** Dur 150 F4
**Burnsall** N York 131 J7
**Burnside** Angus 196 C4
**Burnside** Angus 196 E6
**Burnside** Fife 186 B5
**Burnside** Moray 214 E1
**Burnside** W Loth 176 E3
**Burnside of Duntrune** Angus 187 G1
**Burntisland** Fife 177 H2
**Burnton** E Ayrs 163 L7
**Burntwood** Staffs 85 J2
**Burntwood Green** Staffs 85 J2
**Burnt Yates** N York 132 C7
**Burnworthy** Somset 25 J7
**Burpham** Surrey 31 G2
**Burpham** W Susx 18 E4
**Burradon** Nthumb 168 E7
**Burrafirth** Shet 235 e1
**Burravoe** Shet 235 d3
**Burrells** Cumb 138 F4
**Burrelton** P & K 195 K8
**Burridge** Devon 13 H2
**Burridge** Hants 17 G1
**Burrill** N York 132 C3
**Burringham** N Linc 125 K8
**Burrington** Devon 10 F2
**Burrington** Herefs 69 J1
**Burrington** N Som 38 C8
**Burrough Green** Cambs 76 F4
**Burrough on the Hill** Leics 87 L2
**Burrow** Lancs 130 C4
**Burrow** Somset 24 E3
**Burrow Bridge** Somset 25 M5
**Burrowhill** Surrey 42 F7
**Burry Green** Swans 50 F7
**Burry Port** Carmth 50 F5
**Burscough** Lancs 120 F7
**Burscough Bridge** Lancs 120 F7
**Bursea** E R Yk 125 J4
**Bursledon** Hants 16 F1
**Burstall** Suffk 78 D5
**Burstock** Dorset 13 K2
**Burston** Norfk 92 D6
**Burstow** Surrey 32 B5
**Burstwick** E R Yk 126 F5
**Burtersett** N York 131 G2
**Burtholme** Cumb 148 F3
**Burthorpe Green** Suffk 77 H2
**Burtoft** Lincs 103 L5
**Burton** Ches W 111 K6
**Burton** Ches W 112 D8
**Burton** Dorset 15 M4
**Burton** Pembks 49 G6
**Burton** Somset 25 J3
**Burton** Wilts 39 J4
**Burton Agnes** E R Yk 135 H6
**Burton Bradstock** Dorset 13 L4
**Burton-by-Lincoln** Lincs 116 F6
**Burton Coggles** Lincs 103 G7
**Burton End** Essex 60 E4
**Burton Fleming** E R Yk 135 G5
**Burton Hastings** Warwks 86 E5
**Burton-in-Kendal** Cumb 129 L4
**Burton-in-Kendal Services** Cumb 129 L4
**Burton in Lonsdale** N York 130 C5
**Burton Joyce** Notts 101 M4
**Burton Latimer** Nhants 88 C8
**Burton Lazars** Leics 87 L1
**Burton Leonard** N York 132 E6
**Burton on the Wolds** Leics 101 L7
**Burton Overy** Leics 87 J4
**Burton Pedwardine** Lincs 103 J4
**Burton Pidsea** E R Yk 127 G4
**Burton Salmon** N York 124 D5
**Burton's Green** Essex 61 K3
**Burton upon Stather** N Linc 125 K6
**Burton upon Trent** Staffs 100 E7
**Burton Waters** Lincs 116 F6
**Burtonwood** Warrtn 112 E3
**Burtonwood Services** Warrtn 112 E4
**Burwardsley** Ches W 98 D2
**Burwarton** Shrops 84 B6
**Burwash** E Susx 33 H7
**Burwash Common** E Susx 20 D2
**Burwash Weald** E Susx 20 D2
**Burwell** Cambs 76 E2
**Burwell** Lincs 118 E5
**Burwen** IoA 108 E3
**Burwick** Ork 234 c8
**Bury** Bury 122 B7
**Bury** Cambs 89 K6
**Bury** Somset 24 E6
**Bury** W Susx 18 D3
**Bury Green** Herts 60 D4
**Bury St Edmunds** Suffk 77 J2
**Burythorpe** N York 134 C6
**Busby** E Rens 175 G6
**Buscot** Oxon 40 E2
**Bush** Abers 197 J4
**Bush Bank** Herefs 69 J4
**Bushbury** Wolves 85 G3
**Bushbury Crematorium** Wolves 85 G3
**Bushey** Herts 43 J2
**Bushey Heath** Herts 43 J2
**Bush Hill Park** Gt Lon 45 G2
**Bushley** Worcs 70 F7
**Bushmoor** Shrops 83 J6
**Bushton** Wilts 40 B5
**Bussage** Gloucs 55 K7
**Bussex** Somset 26 A4
**Butcombe** N Som 38 D7
**Bute** Ag & B 173 H4
**Butleigh** Somset 26 D5
**Butleigh Wootton** Somset 26 D4
**Butlers Marston** Warwks 72 D4
**Butley** Suffk 79 H4
**Buttercrambe** N York 133 L7
**Butterdean** Border 179 G5
**Butterknowle** Dur 140 E3
**Butterleigh** Devon 12 C2
**Buttermere** Cumb 137 G4
**Buttershaw** C Brad 123 H5
**Butterstone** P & K 195 G7
**Butterton** Staffs 99 J4
**Butterton** Staffs 100 B2
**Butterwick** Lincs 104 C4
**Butterwick** N York 133 L4
**Butterwick** N York 134 F5
**Buttington** Powys 82 E2
**Buttonoak** Shrops 84 D7
**Buxhall** Suffk 78 B3
**Buxted** E Susx 20 A2
**Buxton** Derbys 114 B6
**Buxton** Norfk 106 F7
**Buxton Heath** Norfk 106 E7
**Bwlch** Powys 53 J4
**Bwlchgwyn** Wrexhm 97 K2
**Bwlchllan** Cerdgn 66 D3
**Bwlchtocyn** Gwynd 94 E7
**Bwlch-y-cibau** Powys 97 J8
**Bwlch-y-ffridd** Powys 82 B4
**Bwlch-y-groes** Pembks 65 H7
**Bwlch-y-sarnau** Powys 82 B8
**Byers Green** Dur 150 F7
**Byfield** Nhants 73 G4
**Byfleet** Surrey 43 H7
**Byford** Herefs 69 H6
**Byker** N u Ty 151 G3
**Bylchau** Conwy 110 D8
**Byley** Ches W 113 G7
**Byrness** Nthumb 157 K2
**Bystock** Devon 12 D5
**Bythorn** Cambs 88 F7
**Byton** Herefs 69 G2
**Bywell** Nthumb 150 D3
**Byworth** W Susx 31 G7

## C

**Cabourne** Lincs 117 J2
**Cabrach** Ag & B 171 J5
**Cabrach** Moray 215 J8
**Cabus** Lancs 121 G2
**Cadbury** Devon 11 L4
**Cadbury World** Birm 85 J7
**Cadder** E Duns 175 G4
**Caddington** C Beds 59 H4
**Caddonfoot** Border 167 G3
**Cadeby** Donc 115 K2
**Cadeby** Leics 86 E3
**Cadeleigh** Devon 11 L4
**Cade Street** E Susx 20 C2
**Cadgwith** Cnwll 3 J7
**Cadham** Fife 186 D6
**Cadishead** Salfd 113 G3
**Cadle** Swans 51 J6
**Cadley** Lancs 121 G4
**Cadley** Wilts 28 E2
**Cadley** Wilts 40 E6
**Cadmore End** Bucks 42 C3
**Cadnam** Hants 28 F8
**Cadney** N Linc 117 G2
**Cadoxton** V Glam 37 H6
**Cadoxton Juxta-Neath** Neath 51 L5
**Caeathro** Gwynd 95 J1

**Caenby** Lincs 117 G4
**Caeo** Carmth 66 F6
**Caerau** Brdgnd 36 D2
**Caerau** Cardif 37 H5
**Caer Farchell** Pembks 48 D3
**Caergeiliog** IoA 108 D5
**Caergwrle** Flints 97 L2
**Caerlanrig** Border 156 D2
**Caerleon** Newpt 37 M3
**Caernarfon** Gwynd 108 F8
**Caernarfon Castle** Gwynd 108 F8
**Caerphilly** Caerph 37 J3
**Caersws** Powys 82 B5
**Caerwedros** Cerdgn 65 L4
**Caerwent** Mons 38 C3
**Caerwys** Flints 110 F6
**Cairinis** W Isls 233 c6
**Cairnbaan** Ag & B 172 E1
**Cairnbulg** Abers 217 J2
**Cairncross** Border 179 J5
**Cairncurran** Inver 174 C4
**Cairndow** Ag & B 183 H5
**Cairneyhill** Fife 176 E2
**Cairngarroch** D & G 144 C5
*Cairngorms National Park* 204 C5
**Cairnie** Abers 215 K5
**Cairnorrie** Abers 217 G6
**Cairnryan** D & G 144 C2
**Cairnty** Moray 215 H4
**Caister-on-Sea** Norfk 93 L2
**Caistor** Lincs 117 J2
**Caistor St Edmund** Norfk 92 F3
**Calanais** W Isls 232 e2
**Calbourne** IoW 16 E5
**Calcot** Flints 111 G6
**Calcot** Gloucs 56 C6
**Calcot Row** W Berk 42 A6
**Calcots** Moray 215 G2
**Caldbeck** Cumb 148 B6
**Caldecote** Cambs 75 L3
**Caldecote** Cambs 89 G5
**Caldecote Highfields** Cambs 75 L3
**Caldecott** Nhants 74 E2
**Caldecott** Oxon 41 J2
**Caldecott** Rutlnd 88 C5
**Calderbank** N Lans 175 K5
**Calder Bridge** Cumb 136 E6
**Caldercruix** N Lans 175 L5
**Calder Grove** Wakefd 123 L6
**Caldermill** S Lans 164 D2
**Calder Vale** Lancs 121 G2
**Calderwood** S Lans 175 H7
**Caldey Island** Pembks 49 K7
**Caldicot** Mons 38 C3
**Caldmore** Wsall 85 H4
**Caldwell** N York 140 E5
**Calf of Man** IoM 237 a7
**Calfsound** Ork 234 d4
**Calgary** Ag & B 189 J6
**Califer** Moray 214 D3
**California** Falk 176 B3
**California** Norfk 93 K1
**Calke** Derbys 101 G7
**Calke Abbey** Derbys 101 G7
**Callakille** Highld 209 L4
**Callander** Stirlg 184 D5
**Callanish** W Isls 232 e2
**Callestick** Cnwll 3 K2
**Calligarry** Highld 199 K5
**Callington** Cnwll 6 A3
**Callow** Herefs 69 J7
**Callow End** Worcs 70 E4
**Callow Hill** Wilts 40 B4
**Calmore** Hants 29 G7
**Calmsden** Gloucs 56 B6
**Calne** Wilts 39 M6
**Calshot** Hants 16 F3
**Calstock** Cnwll 6 C3
**Calstone Wellington** Wilts 40 B6
**Calthorpe** Norfk 106 E6
**Calthorpe Street** Norfk 107 J7
**Calthwaite** Cumb 148 E6
**Calton** Staffs 100 C3
**Calveley** Ches E 98 E2
**Calver** Derbys 114 E6
**Calverhall** Shrops 98 E5
**Calverleigh** Devon 11 L3
**Calverton** M Keyn 73 L6
**Calverton** Notts 101 L3
**Calvine** P & K 194 C3
**Calzeat** Border 165 L3
**Cam** Gloucs 55 H7
**Camasachoirce** Highld 190 F4
**Camasine** Highld 190 F4
**Camas Luinie** Highld 210 E8
**Camastianavaig** Highld 209 H6
**Camault Muir** Highld 212 D6
**Camber** E Susx 21 J2
**Camberley** Surrey 42 E7
**Camberwell** Gt Lon 44 F5
**Camblesforth** N York 124 F5
**Cambo** Nthumb 158 C5
**Camborne** Cnwll 3 H4
**Camborne & Redruth Mining District** Cnwll 3 H4
**Cambourne** Cambs 75 K3
**Cambridge** Cambs 76 C3
**Cambridge** Gloucs 55 H7
*Cambridge Airport* Cambs 76 C3
**Cambridge City Crematorium** Cambs 76 B3
**Cambrose** Cnwll 3 H3
**Cambus** Clacks 185 H8
**Cambusavie Platform** Highld 223 G3
**Cambusbarron** Stirlg 185 G8
**Cambuskenneth** Stirlg 185 G8
**Cambuslang** S Lans 175 H6
**Cambus o' May** Abers 205 J5
**Cambuswallace** S Lans 165 K2
**Camden Town** Gt Lon 44 F4
**Cameley** BaNES 38 E8
**Camelford** Cnwll 8 E7
**Camelon** Falk 176 B3
**Camerory** Highld 214 C7
**Camerton** BaNES 39 G8
**Camerton** Cumb 136 E2
**Camghouran** P & K 193 J5
**Camieston** Border 167 J4
**Cammachmore** Abers 207 G6
**Cammeringham** Lincs 116 F5
**Camore** Highld 223 G4
**Campbeltown** Ag & B 161 J5
*Campbeltown Airport* Ag & B 161 H5
**Cample** D & G 154 F4
**Campmuir** P & K 195 K8
**Camps** W Loth 176 E5
**Campsall** Donc 124 E7
**Campsea Ash** Suffk 79 G4
**Campton** C Beds 75 G6
**Camptown** Border 167 K6
**Camrose** Pembks 48 F4
**Camserney** P & K 194 C6
**Camusnagaul** Highld 191 L2
**Camusnagaul** Highld 220 D4
**Camusteel** Highld 209 L6
**Camusterrach** Highld 209 L6
**Canada** Hants 28 F7
**Candacraig** Abers 205 H5
**Candlesby** Lincs 118 F7
**Candy Mill** Border 165 L2
**Cane End** Oxon 42 B4
**Canewdon** Essex 46 E2
**Canford Cliffs** Poole 15 K5
**Canford Crematorium** Bristl 38 E5
**Canford Heath** Poole 15 J4
**Canisbay** Highld 231 L2
**Canley** Covtry 86 C7
**Canley Crematorium** Covtry 86 C7
**Cann** Dorset 27 K7
**Canna** Highld 198 C4
**Cann Common** Dorset 27 K7
**Cannich** Highld 211 L7
**Cannington** Somset 25 K4
**Canning Town** Gt Lon 45 H4
**Cannock** Staffs 85 H2
**Cannock Chase** Staffs 99 M8
**Cannon Bridge** Herefs 69 H6
**Canonbie** D & G 156 C6
**Canon Frome** Herefs 70 B5
**Canon Pyon** Herefs 69 J5
**Canons Ashby** Nhants 73 H4
**Canonstown** Cnwll 2 F4
**Canterbury** Kent 34 F3
**Canterbury Cathedral** Kent 34 F3
**Cantley** Norfk 93 H3
**Canton** Cardif 37 J5
**Cantraywood** Highld 213 J5
**Cantsfield** Lancs 130 C5
**Canvey Island** Essex 46 D4
**Canwick** Lincs 117 G7
**Canworthy Water** Cnwll 9 G6
**Caol** Highld 191 L2
**Caolas Scalpaigh** W Isls 232 e4
**Caoles** Ag & B 188 D6
**Caonich** Highld 201 G6
**Capel** Kent 33 H4
**Capel** Surrey 31 K4
**Capel Bangor** Cerdgn 80 E7
**Capel Coch** IoA 108 F5
**Capel Curig** Conwy 96 A2
**Capel Dewi** Carmth 50 F2
**Capel Dewi** Cerdgn 66 B6
**Capel-Dewi** Cerdgn 80 E6
**Capel Garmon** Conwy 96 C2
**Capel Hendre** Carmth 51 H4
**Capel Iwan** Carmth 65 J7
**Capel-le-Ferne** Kent 35 H6
**Capelles** Guern 236 d2
**Capel Parc** IoA 108 F4
**Capel St Andrew** Suffk 79 H5
**Capel St Mary** Suffk 78 C6
**Capel Seion** Cerdgn 80 E7
**Capelulo** Conwy 109 L6
**Capenhurst** Ches W 111 K6
**Cape Wrath** Highld 228 D1
**Capheaton** Nthumb 158 C6
**Caplaw** E Rens 174 E6
**Cappercleuch** Border 166 C5
**Capstone** Medway 46 C6
**Capton** Devon 7 J5
**Caputh** P & K 195 H7
**Caradon Mining District** Cnwll 5 L2
**Carbeth Inn** Stirlg 174 F3
**Carbis Bay** Cnwll 2 F4
**Carbost** Highld 208 F5
**Carbost** Highld 208 F7
**Carbrook** Sheff 115 G4
**Carbrooke** Norfk 91 L3
**Car Colston** Notts 102 B4
**Carcroft** Donc 124 E8
**Cardenden** Fife 186 C7
**Cardhu** Moray 214 F5
**Cardiff** Cardif 37 J5
*Cardiff Airport* V Glam 37 G6
**Cardiff & Glamorgan Crematorium** Cardif 37 J4
**Cardiff Gate Services** Cardif 37 K4
**Cardiff West Services** Cardif 37 H4
**Cardigan** Cerdgn 65 G5
**Cardington** Bed 74 F5
**Cardington** Shrops 83 K4
**Cardinham** Cnwll 5 H3
**Cardrain** D & G 144 D8
**Cardrona** Border 166 D2
**Cardross** Ag & B 174 C3
**Cardross Crematorium** Ag & B 174 C3
**Cardryne** D & G 144 D7
**Cardurnock** Cumb 147 L3
**Careby** Lincs 88 E1
**Careston** Angus 196 E4
**Carew** Pembks 49 H6
**Carew Cheriton** Pembks 49 H6
**Carew Newton** Pembks 49 H6
**Carey** Herefs 54 E2
**Carfin** N Lans 175 K6
**Carfraemill** Border 178 B7
**Cargate Green** Norfk 93 H2
**Cargenbridge** D & G 155 G7
**Cargill** P & K 195 J8
**Cargo** Cumb 148 C3
**Cargreen** Cnwll 6 C4
**Carham** Nthumb 168 B2
**Carhampton** Somset 24 F3
**Carharrack** Cnwll 3 J3
**Carie** P & K 193 K5
**Carinish** W Isls 233 c6
**Carisbrooke** IoW 16 F5
**Cark** Cumb 129 H4
**Carkeel** Cnwll 6 B4
**Càrlabhagh** W Isls 232 e2
**Carlbury** Darltn 140 F4
**Carlby** Lincs 88 F2
**Carleen** Cnwll 3 G5
**Carleton Crematorium** Bpool 120 D3
**Carleton Forehoe** Norfk 92 C3
**Carleton-in-Craven** N York 122 E1
**Carleton Rode** Norfk 92 D5
**Carleton St Peter** Norfk 93 H3
**Carlincraig** Abers 216 D5
**Carlingcott** BaNES 39 G8
**Carlisle** Cumb 148 D4
*Carlisle Airport* Cumb 148 E3
**Carlisle Crematorium** Cumb 148 C4
**Carlops** Border 177 G6
**Carloway** W Isls 232 e2
**Carlton** Barns 124 B7
**Carlton** Bed 74 D4
**Carlton** Cambs 76 F4
**Carlton** Leeds 123 L5
**Carlton** Leics 86 E3
**Carlton** N York 124 F5
**Carlton** N York 131 K3
**Carlton** N York 133 J3
**Carlton** Notts 101 L4
**Carlton** S on T 141 J3
**Carlton** Suffk 79 H2
**Carlton Colville** Suffk 93 K5
**Carlton Curlieu** Leics 87 K4
**Carlton Green** Cambs 76 F4
**Carlton Husthwaite** N York 133 G4
**Carlton-in-Cleveland** N York 142 B6
**Carlton in Lindrick** Notts 115 L5
**Carlton-le-Moorland** Lincs 102 E2
**Carlton Miniott** N York 132 F4
**Carlton-on-Trent** Notts 116 D8
**Carlton Scroop** Lincs 102 F4
**Carluke** S Lans 175 L7
**Carmacoup** S Lans 164 F4
**Carmarthen** Carmth 50 E2
**Carmel** Carmth 51 H3
**Carmel** Flints 111 G6
**Carmel** Gwynd 95 H2
**Carmichael** S Lans 165 H2
**Carmountside Crematorium** C Stke 99 K3

**Carmunnock** C Glas......175 G6
**Carmyle** C Glas......175 H6
**Carmyllie** Angus......196 E7
**Carnaby** E R Yk......135 H6
**Carnbee** Fife......187 J6
**Carnbo** P & K......185 L6
**Carn Brea** Cnwll......3 H3
**Carnbrogie** Abers......216 F8
**Carndu** Highld......210 D8
**Carnduff** S Lans......164 D1
**Carnell** E Ayrs......163 L3
**Carnforth** Lancs......129 K5
**Carn-gorm** Highld......200 E2
**Carnhell Green** Cnwll......3 G4
**Carnie** Abers......206 F4
**Carnkie** Cnwll......3 H4
**Carnkie** Cnwll......3 J4
**Carno** Powys......81 K4
**Carnock** Fife......176 E1
**Carnon Downs** Cnwll......4 C7
**Carnousie** Abers......216 C4
**Carnoustie** Angus......187 J1
**Carnwath** S Lans......176 D8
**Carol Green** Solhll......86 C7
**Carperby** N York......131 J2
**Carradale** Ag & B......161 K2
**Carrbridge** Highld......203 L2
**Carrefour** Jersey......236 c6
**Carreglefn** IoA......108 E4
**Carr Gate** Wakefd......123 L5
**Carrhouse** N Linc......116 C1
**Carrick** Ag & B......172 F2
**Carrick Castle** Ag & B......183 H8
**Carriden** Falk......176 D3
**Carrington** Mdloth......177 J6
**Carrington** Traffd......113 H3
**Carrog** Denbgs......97 H4
**Carron** Falk......176 B2
**Carron** Moray......214 F6
**Carronbridge** D & G......154 F3
**Carron Bridge** Stirlg......175 K2
**Carronshore** Falk......176 B2
**Carr Shield** Nthumb......149 K5
**Carrutherstown** D & G......155 J7
**Carruth House** Inver......174 C5
**Carrville** Dur......151 H6
**Carsaig** Ag & B......181 H3
**Carseriggan** D & G......145 G2
**Carsethorn** D & G......147 H3
**Carshalton** Gt Lon......44 F6
**Carsington** Derbys......100 E2
**Carskey** Ag & B......161 H7
**Carsluith** D & G......145 K4
**Carsphairn** D & G......153 L4
**Carstairs** S Lans......165 H1
**Carstairs Junction** S Lans......165 J1
**Carterton** Oxon......56 F6
**Carthew** Cnwll......4 F5
**Carthorpe** N York......132 D3
**Cartland** S Lans......165 G1
**Cartmel** Cumb......129 H4
**Carway** Carmth......50 F4
**Cashe's Green** Gloucs......55 J6
**Cassington** Oxon......57 J5
**Cassop** Dur......151 J7
**Castel** Guern......236 c3
**Casterton** Cumb......130 C4
**Castle Acre** Norfk......91 J1
**Castle Ashby** Nhants......74 C3
**Castlebay** W Isls......233 b9
**Castle Bolton** N York......131 J2
**Castle Bromwich** Solhll......85 K5
**Castle Bytham** Lincs......103 G8
**Castlebythe** Pembks......49 H2
**Castle Caereinion** Powys......82 D3
**Castle Camps** Cambs......76 F6
**Castle Carrock** Cumb......148 F4
**Castlecary** Falk......175 K3
**Castle Cary** Somset......26 F5
**Castle Combe** Wilts......39 J5
**Castle Donington** Leics......101 H6
**Castle Douglas** D & G......146 D3
**Castle Eaton** Swindn......40 C2
**Castle Eden** Dur......151 K7
**Castleford** Wakefd......124 C5
**Castle Frome** Herefs......70 C5
**Castle Gresley** Derbys......100 F8
**Castle Hedingham** Essex......77 H7
**Castlehill** Border......166 C3
**Castlehill** Highld......231 H2
**Castle Hill** Suffk......78 D5
**Castlehill** W Duns......174 D3
**Castle Howard** N York......133 L5
**Castle Kennedy** D & G......144 D3
**Castle Lachlan** Ag & B......182 E7
**Castlemartin** Pembks......48 F7
**Castlemilk** C Glas......175 G6
**Castlemorton** Worcs......70 E6
**Castlemorton Common** Worcs......70 E6
**Castle O'er** D & G......156 A4
**Castle Rising** Norfk......105 G7
**Castleside** Dur......150 D5
**Castle Stuart** Highld......213 H4
**Castlethorpe** M Keyn......74 B5
**Castleton** Border......156 E4
**Castleton** Derbys......114 D5
**Castleton** N York......142 E5
**Castleton** Newpt......37 K4
**Castleton** Rochdl......122 D7
**Castletown** Highld......231 H3
**Castletown** IoM......237 b7
**Castletown** Sundld......151 J4
**Castley** N York......123 K2
**Caston** Norfk......91 L4
**Castor** C Pete......89 G4
**Catacol** N Ayrs......172 F7
**Catcliffe** Rothm......115 H4
**Catcomb** Wilts......39 M5
**Catcott** Somset......26 B4
**Catcott Burtle** Somset......26 B3
**Caterham** Surrey......32 C3
**Catfield** Norfk......107 H7
**Catford** Gt Lon......45 G5
**Catforth** Lancs......121 G4
**Cathcart** C Glas......175 G6
**Cathedine** Powys......53 H3
**Catherington** Hants......30 B8
**Catherston Leweston** Dorset......13 J4
**Catisfield** Hants......17 G2
**Catlodge** Highld......202 F6
**Catmere End** Essex......76 C6
**Catmore** W Berk......41 J4
**Caton** Lancs......129 L6
**Caton Green** Lancs......129 L6
**Catrine** E Ayrs......164 B4
**Catsfield** E Susx......20 E3
**Catsgore** Somset......26 D6
**Catshill** Worcs......85 G8
**Cattadale** Ag & B......161 H7
**Cattal** N York......133 G8
**Cattawade** Suffk......62 D2
**Catterall** Lancs......121 G3
**Catterick** N York......141 G7
**Catterick Bridge** N York......141 G7
**Catterlen** Cumb......148 E7
**Catterline** Abers......197 L2
**Catterton** N York......124 D2
**Catteshall** Surrey......31 G3
**Catthorpe** Leics......87 G7
**Cattistock** Dorset......14 B3
**Catton** N York......132 E4
**Catton** Nthumb......149 L4
**Catwick** E R Yk......126 E2
**Catworth** Cambs......88 F8
**Caudle Green** Gloucs......55 L6
**Caulcott** Oxon......57 K3
**Cauldcots** Angus......197 G6
**Cauldhame** Stirlg......184 E8
**Cauldmill** Border......167 H6
**Cauldon** Staffs......100 B3
**Cauldwell** Derbys......86 B1
**Caulkerbush** D & G......147 G4
**Caulside** D & G......156 D6
**Caundle Marsh** Dorset......27 G8
**Caunton** Notts......102 C1
**Causeway End** D & G......145 J3
**Causeway End** Essex......61 G4
**Causewayend** S Lans......165 K3
**Causewayhead** Stirlg......185 G7
**Causeyend** Abers......207 H2
**Causey Park Bridge** Nthumb......158 F3
**Cavendish** Suffk......77 J5
**Cavenham** Suffk......77 H1
**Caversfield** Oxon......57 L3
**Caversham** Readg......42 B5
**Caverswall** Staffs......99 L4
**Caverton Mill** Border......167 M4
**Cawdor** Highld......213 K4
**Cawood** N York......124 E3
**Cawsand** Cnwll......6 C5
**Cawston** Norfk......106 D7
**Cawthorne** Barns......123 K8
**Caxton** Cambs......75 K3
**Caynham** Shrops......83 K8
**Caythorpe** Lincs......102 F3
**Caythorpe** Notts......102 B4
**Cayton** N York......135 G3
**Ceann a Bhaigh** W Isls......233 b6
**Ceannacroc Lodge** Highld......201 K3
**Cearsiadar** W Isls......232 f3
**Cefn** Newpt......37 L3
**Cefn-brîth** Conwy......96 E3
**Cefn-bryn-brain** Carmth......51 L3
**Cefn Cribwr** Brdgnd......36 D4
**Cefneithin** Carmth......51 G3
**Cefngorwydd** Powys......67 J5
**Cefn-mawr** Wrexhm......97 L4
**Cefn-y-pant** Carmth......49 K3
**Cellardyke** Fife......187 J6
**Cellarhead** Staffs......99 L3
**Cemaes** IoA......108 E3
**Cemmaes** Powys......81 H3
**Cemmaes Road** Powys......81 H3
**Cenarth** Cerdgn......65 J6
**Ceres** Fife......186 F5
**Cerne Abbas** Dorset......14 C3
**Cerney Wick** Gloucs......40 B2
**Cerrigydrudion** Conwy......96 E3
**Ceunant** Gwynd......95 J1
**Chaceley** Gloucs......55 J2
**Chacewater** Cnwll......3 K3
**Chackmore** Bucks......73 K7
**Chacombe** Nhants......72 F5
**Chadbury** Worcs......71 H5
**Chadderton** Oldham......113 K1
**Chaddesden** C Derb......101 G5
**Chaddesley Corbett** Worcs......84 F8
**Chaddlehanger** Devon......6 C1
**Chaddleworth** W Berk......41 H5
**Chadlington** Oxon......57 G4
**Chadshunt** Warwks......72 D4
**Chadwell** Leics......102 C7
**Chadwell Heath** Gt Lon......45 J3
**Chadwell St Mary** Thurr......45 M4
**Chadwick** Worcs......70 E2
**Chadwick End** Solhll......86 B8
**Chaffcombe** Somset......13 J1
**Chafford Hundred** Thurr......45 L4
**Chagford** Devon......11 G7
**Chailey** E Susx......19 K2
**Chainhurst** Kent......33 J4
**Chaldon** Surrey......32 B3
**Chaldon Herring** Dorset......14 E5
**Chale** IoW......16 F6
**Chale Green** IoW......16 F6
**Chalfont Common** Bucks......43 G3
**Chalfont St Giles** Bucks......43 G2
**Chalfont St Peter** Bucks......43 G3
**Chalford** Gloucs......55 K7
**Chalford** Wilts......27 K2
**Chalgrove** Oxon......41 M2
**Chalk** Kent......46 A5
**Chalkwell** Kent......34 B2
**Challacombe** Devon......23 L3
**Challoch** D & G......145 H2
**Challock** Kent......34 D5
**Chalton** C Beds......59 G3
**Chalton** Hants......30 B7
**Chalvey** Slough......42 F4
**Chalvington** E Susx......20 B4
**Chandler's Cross** Herts......43 H2
**Chandler's Ford** Hants......29 H7
**Channel Tunnel Terminal** Kent......35 G6
**Chanterlands Crematorium** C KuH......126 D4
**Chantry** Somset......27 G3
**Chantry** Suffk......78 D5
**Chapel** Fife......186 D8
**Chapel Allerton** Leeds......123 L3
**Chapel Allerton** Somset......26 B2
**Chapel Amble** Cnwll......4 F2
**Chapel Brampton** Nhants......73 K2
**Chapel Chorlton** Staffs......99 J5
**Chapelend Way** Essex......77 G6
**Chapel-en-le-Frith** Derbys......114 B5
**Chapel Green** Warwks......72 F3
**Chapel Haddlesey** N York......124 E5
**Chapelhall** N Lans......175 K5
**Chapel Hill** Abers......217 K7
**Chapel Hill** Lincs......103 K2
**Chapel Hill** N York......123 L2
**Chapelhope** Border......166 C5
**Chapelknowe** D & G......156 B7
**Chapel Lawn** Shrops......82 F7
**Chapel-le-Dale** N York......130 E4
**Chapel Leigh** Somset......25 H5
**Chapel of Garioch** Abers......206 D1
**Chapel Rossan** D & G......144 D6
**Chapel Row** W Berk......41 L6
**Chapel St Leonards** Lincs......119 H6
**Chapel Stile** Cumb......137 K6
**Chapelton** Abers......207 G6
**Chapelton** Angus......197 G6
**Chapelton** Devon......23 J6
**Chapelton** S Lans......175 J8
**Chapeltown** Bl w D......121 L7
**Chapeltown** Moray......204 F2
**Chapeltown** Sheff......115 G3
**Chapmanslade** Wilts......27 J2
**Chapmans Well** Devon......9 J6
**Chapmore End** Herts......60 B5
**Chappel** Essex......61 L3
**Chard** Somset......13 H2
**Chard Junction** Somset......13 J2
**Chardleigh Green** Somset......13 H1
**Chardstock** Devon......13 H2
**Charfield** S Glos......39 G3
**Charing** Kent......34 C5
**Charing Crematorium** Kent......34 C5
**Charingworth** Gloucs......71 L6
**Charlbury** Oxon......57 G4
**Charlcombe** BaNES......39 H6
**Charlcutt** Wilts......39 M5
**Charlecote** Warwks......72 C3
**Charlemont** Sandw......85 H5

**Charles** Devon 23 L5
**Charleston** Angus 196 C7
**Charlestown** C Aber 207 H5
**Charlestown** C Brad 123 H3
**Charlestown** Calder 122 E5
**Charlestown** Cnwll 5 G5
Charlestown Cnwll 5 G5
**Charlestown** Fife 176 E2
**Charlestown** Highld 213 G5
**Charlestown** Highld 219 J6
**Charlestown** Salfd 113 J2
**Charlestown of Aberlour** Moray 215 G5
**Charles Tye** Suffk 78 B4
**Charlesworth** Derbys 114 A3
**Charlinch** Somset 25 K4
**Charlottetown** Fife 186 E5
**Charlton** Gt Lon 45 H4
**Charlton** Nhants 73 G7
**Charlton** Nthumb 157 K5
**Charlton** Oxon 41 H3
**Charlton** Somset 25 L6
**Charlton** Somset 27 G2
**Charlton** W Susx 18 B3
**Charlton** Wilts 27 K6
**Charlton** Wilts 39 L3
**Charlton** Worcs 71 H5
**Charlton** Wrekin 83 L2
**Charlton Abbots** Gloucs 56 B3
**Charlton Adam** Somset 26 D5
**Charlton All Saints** Wilts 28 D6
**Charlton Down** Dorset 14 D4
**Charlton Horethorne** Somset 26 F6
**Charlton Kings** Gloucs 55 L4
**Charlton Mackrell** Somset 26 D5
**Charlton Marshall** Dorset 15 G2
**Charlton Musgrove** Somset 27 G5
**Charlton-on-Otmoor** Oxon 57 K5
**Charlton on the Hill** Dorset 15 G2
**Charlton St Peter** Wilts 28 C1
**Charlwood** Hants 30 A5
**Charlwood** Surrey 31 L3
**Charminster** Dorset 14 D4
**Charmouth** Dorset 13 J4
**Charndon** Bucks 58 A3
**Charney Bassett** Oxon 41 G2
**Charnock Richard** Lancs 121 H7
**Charnock Richard Crematorium** Lancs 121 H6
Charnock Richard Services Lancs 121 H7
**Charsfield** Suffk 78 F3
**Charter Alley** Hants 41 L8
**Charterhall** Border 179 G8
**Charterhouse** Somset 26 D1
**Chartershall** Stirlg 175 K1
**Chartham** Kent 34 E4
**Chartham Hatch** Kent 34 E4
**Chartridge** Bucks 58 F7
**Chart Sutton** Kent 33 K4
**Charvil** Wokham 42 C5
**Charwelton** Nhants 73 G4
**Chase Terrace** Staffs 85 J2
**Chasetown** Staffs 85 J2
**Chastleton** Oxon 56 E3
**Chasty** Devon 9 J4
**Chatburn** Lancs 121 L2
**Chatcull** Staffs 99 H5
**Chatham** Medway 46 C6
**Chatham Green** Essex 61 H5
**Chathill** Nthumb 169 J4
Chatsworth House Derbys 114 E7
**Chattenden** Medway 46 C5
**Chatteris** Cambs 90 B6
**Chatterton** Lancs 122 B6
**Chattisham** Suffk 78 C6
**Chatto** Border 168 B5
**Chatton** Nthumb 168 F4
**Chawleigh** Devon 11 G3
**Chawton** Hants 30 B4
**Cheadle** Staffs 100 A4
**Cheadle** Stockp 113 K4
**Cheadle Hulme** Stockp 113 K4
**Cheam** Gt Lon 44 E7
**Chearsley** Bucks 58 B6
**Chebsey** Staffs 99 J6
**Checkendon** Oxon 41 M4
**Checkley** Ches E 99 G4
**Checkley** Staffs 100 B5
**Chedburgh** Suffk 77 H3
**Cheddar** Somset 26 C2
**Cheddington** Bucks 58 F4
**Cheddleton** Staffs 99 L3
**Cheddon Fitzpaine** Somset 25 K6
**Chedgrave** Norfk 93 H4
**Chedington** Dorset 13 L2
**Chediston** Suffk 93 H7
**Chedworth** Gloucs 56 B5
**Chedzoy** Somset 25 M4
**Cheetham Hill** Manch 113 J2
**Cheldon** Devon 11 H3
**Chelford** Ches E 113 J6
**Chellaston** C Derb 101 G6
**Chellington** Bed 74 D4
**Chelmarsh** Shrops 84 C5
**Chelmondiston** Suffk 78 E6
**Chelmorton** Derbys 114 C7
**Chelmsford** Essex 61 H6
**Chelmsford Crematorium** Essex 61 H6
**Chelmsley Wood** Solhll 85 L6
**Chelsea** Gt Lon 44 F4
**Chelsfield** Gt Lon 45 J7
**Chelsworth** Suffk 77 L5
**Cheltenham** Gloucs 55 L4
**Cheltenham Crematorium** Gloucs 55 L4
**Chelveston** Nhants 74 E1
**Chelvey** N Som 38 C6
**Chelwood** BaNES 38 F7
**Chelwood Gate** E Susx 32 D6
**Cheney Longville** Shrops 83 H6
**Chenies** Bucks 43 G2
**Chepstow** Mons 38 D2
**Cherhill** Wilts 40 B6
**Cherington** Gloucs 55 K7
**Cherington** Warwks 72 C6
**Cheriton** Hants 29 L5
**Cheriton** Kent 35 G7
**Cheriton** Pembks 49 G7
**Cheriton** Swans 50 F6
**Cheriton Bishop** Devon 11 H6
**Cheriton Fitzpaine** Devon 11 K4
**Cherrington** Wrekin 98 F8
**Cherry Burton** E R Yk 126 B3
**Cherry Hinton** Cambs 76 C3
**Cherry Orchard** Worcs 70 F4
**Cherry Willingham** Lincs 117 G6
**Chertsey** Surrey 43 H6
Cherwell Valley Services Oxon 57 K3
**Cheselbourne** Dorset 14 E3
**Chesham** Bucks 58 F7
**Chesham** Bury 122 B7
**Chesham Bois** Bucks 58 F7
**Cheshunt** Herts 60 B7
**Chesil Beach** Dorset 14 B6
**Cheslyn Hay** Staffs 85 H3
**Chessetts Wood** Warwks 85 L8
**Chessington** Gt Lon 44 D7
Chessington World of Adventures Gt Lon 44 D7
**Chester** Ches W 112 B7
**Chesterblade** Somset 26 F3
**Chester Crematorium** Ches W 111 L7
**Chesterfield** Derbys 115 G7
**Chesterfield** Staffs 85 K3
**Chesterfield Crematorium** Derbys 115 H6
**Chesterhill** Mdloth 177 K5
**Chester-le-Street** Dur 151 G5
**Chester Moor** Dur 151 G5
**Chesters** Border 167 J5
**Chesters** Border 167 K7
Chester Services Ches W 112 C6
**Chesterton** Cambs 76 C3
**Chesterton** Cambs 89 G4
**Chesterton** Gloucs 56 A7
**Chesterton** Oxon 57 K4
**Chesterton** Shrops 84 D4
**Chesterton** Staffs 99 J3
**Chesterton Green** Warwks 72 D3
**Chesterwood** Nthumb 149 L2
Chester Zoo Ches W 112 B7
**Chestfield** Kent 47 J6
**Cheston** Devon 7 G4
**Cheswardine** Shrops 99 G6
**Cheswick** Nthumb 168 F1
**Chetnole** Dorset 14 B2
**Chettisham** Cambs 90 D6
**Chettle** Dorset 27 L8
**Chetton** Shrops 84 B5
**Chetwynd** Wrekin 99 G7
**Chetwynd Aston** Wrekin 99 H8
**Cheveley** Cambs 76 F3
**Chevening** Kent 32 E2
**Chevington** Suffk 77 H3
**Cheviot Hills** 168 A7
**Chevithorne** Devon 24 F7
**Chew Magna** BaNES 38 E7
**Chew Stoke** BaNES 38 E7
**Chewton Keynsham** BaNES 38 F6
**Chewton Mendip** Somset 26 E2
**Chicheley** M Keyn 74 C5
**Chichester** W Susx 18 B5
**Chichester Crematorium** W Susx 18 B4
**Chickerell** Dorset 14 C6
**Chicklade** Wilts 27 K4
**Chidden** Hants 30 A7
**Chiddingfold** Surrey 30 F4
**Chiddingly** E Susx 20 B3
**Chiddingstone** Kent 32 E4
**Chiddingstone Causeway** Kent 32 F4
**Chideock** Dorset 13 K4
**Chidham** W Susx 17 L2
**Chidswell** Kirk 123 K6
**Chieveley** W Berk 41 J5
Chieveley Services W Berk 41 J6
**Chignall St James** Essex 61 G6
**Chignall Smealy** Essex 61 G5
**Chigwell** Essex 45 H2
**Chigwell Row** Essex 45 J2
**Chilbolton** Hants 29 H4
**Chilcomb** Hants 29 J5
**Chilcombe** Dorset 13 M4
**Chilcompton** Somset 26 F2
**Chilcote** Leics 86 C2
**Childer Thornton** Ches W 111 K6
**Child Okeford** Dorset 27 J8
**Childrey** Oxon 41 G3
**Child's Ercall** Shrops 98 F7
**Childswickham** Worcs 71 J6
**Childwall** Lpool 112 B4
**Chilfrome** Dorset 14 B3
**Chilgrove** W Susx 18 A3
**Chilham** Kent 34 E4
**Chillaton** Devon 10 C8
**Chillenden** Kent 35 H4
**Chillerton** IoW 16 F5
**Chillesford** Suffk 79 H4
**Chillington** Devon 7 J7
**Chillington** Somset 13 K1
**Chilmark** Wilts 27 L5
**Chilmington Green** Kent 34 C6
**Chilson** Oxon 56 F4
**Chilsworthy** Cnwll 6 B2
**Chilsworthy** Devon 9 J4
**Chiltern Hills** 42 C2
**Chilterns Crematorium** Bucks 42 F2
**Chilthorne Domer** Somset 26 D7
**Chilton** Bucks 58 B5
**Chilton** Dur 141 H2
**Chilton** Oxon 41 J4
**Chilton Candover** Hants 29 L4
**Chilton Cantelo** Somset 26 E6
**Chilton Foliat** Wilts 40 F6
**Chilton Polden** Somset 26 B4
**Chilton Street** Suffk 77 H5
**Chilton Trinity** Somset 25 L4
**Chilwell** Notts 101 K5
**Chilworth** Hants 29 H7
**Chilworth** Surrey 31 G3
**Chimney** Oxon 57 G7
**Chineham** Hants 30 A1
**Chingford** Gt Lon 45 G2
**Chinley** Derbys 114 B5
**Chinnor** Oxon 58 C7
**Chipnall** Shrops 99 G6
**Chippenham** Cambs 76 F1
**Chippenham** Wilts 39 L5
**Chipperfield** Herts 59 H7
**Chipping** Herts 60 B2
**Chipping** Lancs 121 J2
**Chipping Campden** Gloucs 71 L6
**Chipping Norton** Oxon 56 F3
**Chipping Ongar** Essex 60 E7
**Chipping Sodbury** S Glos 39 G4
**Chipping Warden** Nhants 72 F5
**Chipstable** Somset 25 G6
**Chipstead** Kent 32 E3
**Chipstead** Surrey 32 B2
**Chirbury** Shrops 82 F4
**Chirk** Wrexhm 97 L5
**Chirnside** Border 179 H6
**Chirnsidebridge** Border 179 H7
**Chirton** Wilts 40 B8
**Chisbury** Wilts 40 F6
**Chiselborough** Somset 26 C8
**Chiseldon** Swindn 40 D4
**Chiselhampton** Oxon 57 L7
**Chisholme** Border 166 F6
**Chislehurst** Gt Lon 45 H6
**Chislet** Kent 47 L6
**Chisley** Calder 122 F5
**Chiswell Green** Herts 59 J6
**Chiswick** Gt Lon 44 E4
**Chisworth** Derbys 113 M3
**Chithurst** W Susx 30 D6
**Chittering** Cambs 76 C1
**Chitterne** Wilts 27 M3

**Chittlehamholt** Devon 23 K7
**Chittlehampton** Devon 23 K6
**Chittoe** Wilts 39 L6
**Chivelstone** Devon 7 H7
**Chivenor** Devon 23 H4
**Chlenry** D & G 144 D3
**Chobham** Surrey 42 F7
**Cholderton** Wilts 28 E3
**Cholesbury** Bucks 58 F6
**Chollerton** Nthumb 158 B7
**Cholsey** Oxon 41 L3
**Cholstrey** Herefs 69 J3
**Chop Gate** N York 142 C7
**Choppington** Nthumb 159 G5
**Chopwell** Gatesd 150 E4
**Chorley** Ches E 98 E3
**Chorley** Lancs 121 H6
**Chorley** Shrops 84 C6
**Chorleywood** Herts 43 H2
**Chorleywood West** Herts 43 G2
**Chorlton** Ches E 99 G3
**Chorlton-cum-Hardy** Manch 113 J3
**Chorlton Lane** Ches W 98 C3
**Choulton** Shrops 83 H5
**Chrishall** Essex 76 C6
**Chrisswell** Inver 173 L4
**Christchurch** Cambs 90 C4
**Christchurch** Dorset 15 M4
**Christchurch** Newpt 37 M3
**Christian Malford** Wilts 39 L5
**Christon** N Som 38 B8
**Christon Bank** Nthumb 169 J5
**Christow** Devon 11 J7
**Chudleigh** Devon 11 K8
**Chudleigh Knighton** Devon 7 J1
**Chulmleigh** Devon 11 G3
**Church** Lancs 121 L5
**Churcham** Gloucs 55 H4
**Church Aston** Wrekin 99 H8
**Church Brampton** Nhants 73 K2
**Church Broughton** Derbys 100 D5
**Church Cove** Cnwll 3 J8
**Church Crookham** Hants 30 D2
**Churchdown** Gloucs 55 K4
**Church Eaton** Staffs 99 J8
**Church End** C Beds 75 H6
**Churchend** Essex 47 G2
**Church End** Essex 61 H3
**Church End** Gt Lon 44 E3
**Church Enstone** Oxon 57 G3
**Church Fenton** N York 124 D3
**Churchfield** Sandw 85 H5
**Church Green** Devon 12 F3
**Church Hanborough** Oxon 57 H5
**Church Houses** N York 142 E7
**Churchill** Devon 13 H3
**Churchill** N Som 38 C7
**Churchill** Oxon 56 F3
**Churchill** Worcs 71 G4
**Churchill** Worcs 84 F7
**Churchinford** Somset 25 K8
**Church Knowle** Dorset 15 H6
**Church Langton** Leics 87 K5
**Church Lawford** Warwks 86 F7
**Church Leigh** Staffs 100 A5
**Church Lench** Worcs 71 H4
**Church Mayfield** Staffs 100 D4
**Church Minshull** Ches E 98 F1
**Church Norton** W Susx 18 B6
**Churchover** Warwks 87 G7
**Church Preen** Shrops 83 K4
**Church Pulverbatch** Shrops 83 H3
**Churchstanton** Somset 25 J8
**Churchstoke** Powys 82 F5
**Churchstow** Devon 7 G6
**Church Stowe** Nhants 73 J3
**Church Street** Kent 46 B5
**Church Stretton** Shrops 83 J5
**Churchtown** Cnwll 5 H1
**Churchtown** Derbys 114 E8
**Churchtown** IoM 237 d3
**Churchtown** Lancs 121 G2
**Church Village** Rhondd 37 H3
**Church Warsop** Notts 115 K7
**Churston Ferrers** Torbay 7 K5
**Churt** Surrey 30 D4
**Churton** Ches W 98 B2
**Churwell** Leeds 123 K5
**Chwilog** Gwynd 95 G5
**Chyandour** Cnwll 2 E5
**Cilcain** Flints 111 G7
**Cilcennin** Cerdgn 66 C3
**Cilfrew** Neath 52 B7
**Cilfynydd** Rhondd 37 G3
**Cilgerran** Pembks 65 H6
**Cilmaengwyn** Neath 51 L4
**Cilmery** Powys 67 L4
**Cilsan** Carmth 51 H2
**Ciltalgarth** Gwynd 96 D4
**Cilycwm** Carmth 67 G6
**Cimla** Neath 36 B2
**Cinderford** Gloucs 54 F5
**Cinder Hill** Wolves 85 G5
**Cippenham** Slough 42 F4
**Cirencester** Gloucs 56 A7
**City** Gt Lon 45 G4
*City Airport Gt Lon 45 H4*
**City of London Crematorium** Gt Lon 45 H3
**Clabhach** Ag & B 188 F5
**Clachaig** Ag & B 173 J3
**Clachan** Ag & B 172 C6
**Clachan** Ag & B 182 A4
**Clachan** Ag & B 182 F6
**Clachan** Ag & B 191 G7
**Clachan** Highld 209 H6
**Clachan-a-Luib** W Isls 233 c6
**Clachan Mor** Ag & B 188 C6
**Clachan na Luib** W Isls 233 c6
**Clachan of Campsie** E Duns 175 G3
**Clachan-Seil** Ag & B 181 M4
**Clachnaharry** Highld 213 G5
**Clachtoll** Highld 224 C3
**Clackavoid** P & K 195 J4
Clacket Lane Services Surrey 32 D3
**Clackmannan** Clacks 185 J8
**Clackmannanshire Bridge** Fife 176 C2
**Clackmarras** Moray 214 F3
**Clacton-on-Sea** Essex 62 E5
**Cladich** Ag & B 182 F3
**Cladswell** Worcs 71 J3
**Claggan** Highld 190 E6
**Claigan** Highld 208 C4
**Clanfield** Hants 30 B7
**Clanfield** Oxon 56 F7
**Clanville** Hants 28 F2
**Clanville** Somset 26 F5
**Claonaig** Ag & B 172 E6
**Clapgate** Herts 60 C3
**Clapham** Bed 74 F4
**Clapham** Gt Lon 44 F5
**Clapham** N York 130 E5
**Clapham** W Susx 18 F4
**Clapton** Somset 13 K2
**Clapton** Somset 26 F2
**Clapton-in-Gordano** N Som 38 C5
**Clapton-on-the-Hill** Gloucs 56 D4
**Claravale** Gatesd 150 E3
**Clarbeston** Pembks 49 H3
**Clarbeston Road** Pembks 49 H4
**Clarborough** Notts 116 B5
**Clare** Suffk 77 H5
**Clarebrand** D & G 146 D2
**Clarencefield** D & G 147 J2
**Clarilaw** Border 167 H5
**Clarkston** E Rens 175 G6
**Clashmore** Highld 223 G4
**Clashmore** Highld 224 C3
**Clashnessie** Highld 224 C3
**Clashnoir** Moray 204 F2
**Clathy** P & K 185 K4
**Clathymore** P & K 185 L3
**Clatt** Abers 205 L1
**Clatter** Powys 81 L5
**Clatworthy** Somset 25 G5
**Claughton** Lancs 121 G3
**Claughton** Lancs 130 B6
**Claughton** Wirral 111 J4
**Claverdon** Warwks 71 L2
**Claverham** N Som 38 C6
**Clavering** Essex 60 D2
**Claverley** Shrops 84 E5
**Claverton** BaNES 39 H7
**Clawdd-coch** V Glam 37 G5
**Clawdd-newydd** Denbgs 97 G3
**Clawton** Devon 9 J5
**Claxby** Lincs 117 J3
**Claxton** N York 133 L7
**Claxton** Norfk 93 H3
**Claybrooke Magna** Leics 86 F5
**Clay Coton** Nhants 87 H7
**Clay Cross** Derbys 115 H8
**Claydon** Oxon 72 F4
**Claydon** Suffk 78 D5
**Claygate** D & G 156 D6
**Claygate** Kent 33 J4
**Claygate** Surrey 44 D7
**Clayhall** Gt Lon 45 H3
**Clayhanger** Devon 24 F6
**Clayhidon** Devon 25 J7
**Clayhill** E Susx 21 G2
**Clayock** Highld 231 H4
**Claypits** Gloucs 55 H6
**Claypole** Lincs 102 D3
**Clayton** C Brad 123 G4
**Clayton** Donc 124 C8
**Clayton** W Susx 19 J3
**Clayton-le-Moors** Lancs 121 L4
**Clayton-le-Woods** Lancs 121 H6
**Clayton West** Kirk 123 K7
**Clayworth** Notts 116 B4
**Cleadale** Highld 199 G7
**Cleadon** S Tyne 151 J3
**Clearbrook** Devon 6 D3
**Clearwell** Gloucs 54 E6
**Cleasby** N York 141 G5
**Cleat** Ork 234 c8
**Cleatlam** Dur 140 E4
**Cleator** Cumb 136 D4
**Cleator Moor** Cumb 136 E4
**Cleckheaton** Kirk 123 J5
**Cleehill** Shrops 83 L7
**Cleekhimin** N Lans 175 K6
**Clee St Margaret** Shrops 83 L6
**Cleethorpes** NE Lin 127 H8
**Cleeton St Mary** Shrops 84 B7
**Cleeve** N Som 38 C7
**Cleeve** Oxon 41 L4
**Cleeve Hill** Gloucs 55 M3
**Cleeve Prior** Worcs 71 J5
**Cleghornie** E Loth 178 D2
**Clehonger** Herefs 69 J6
**Cleish** P & K 186 A7
**Cleland** N Lans 175 L6
**Clenamacrie** Ag & B 182 C2
**Clenchwarton** Norfk 104 F7
**Clenerty** Abers 216 E3
**Clent** Worcs 85 G7
**Cleobury Mortimer** Shrops 84 C7
**Cleobury North** Shrops 84 B6
**Cleongart** Ag & B 161 H3
**Clephanton** Highld 213 J4
**Clerkhill** D & G 156 A3
**Cleuch-head** D & G 154 E3
**Clevancy** Wilts 40 B5
**Clevedon** N Som 38 B6
**Cleveleys** Lancs 120 D2
**Cleverton** Wilts 39 L4
**Clewer** Somset 26 C2
**Cley next the Sea** Norfk 106 C4
**Cliburn** Cumb 138 E3
**Cliddesden** Hants 29 M2
**Cliffe** Medway 46 C5
**Cliffe** N York 125 G4
**Cliff End** E Susx 21 H3
**Cliffe Woods** Medway 46 C5
**Clifford** Herefs 68 E5
**Clifford** Leeds 124 C2
**Clifford Chambers** Warwks 71 L4
**Clifford's Mesne** Gloucs 55 G4
**Clifton** Bristl 38 E5
**Clifton** C Beds 75 H6
**Clifton** C Nott 101 K5
**Clifton** C York 133 J8
**Clifton** Calder 123 H6
**Clifton** Cumb 138 D2
**Clifton** Derbys 100 D4
**Clifton** Devon 23 J3
**Clifton** Donc 115 K3
**Clifton** Lancs 120 F4
**Clifton** N York 123 J2
**Clifton** Oxon 57 J2
**Clifton** Worcs 70 F5
**Clifton Campville** Staffs 86 B2
**Clifton Hampden** Oxon 41 K2
**Clifton Reynes** M Keyn 74 C4
**Clifton upon Dunsmore** Warwks 87 G7
**Clifton upon Teme** Worcs 70 C3
**Cliftonville** Kent 35 K1
**Climping** W Susx 18 D5
**Clink** Somset 27 H2
**Clint** N York 132 D7
**Clinterty** C Aber 206 F3
**Clint Green** Norfk 92 B2
**Clintmains** Border 167 J3
**Clippesby** Norfk 93 J2
**Clipsham** Rutlnd 88 D1
**Clipston** Nhants 87 K7
**Clipston** Notts 101 M5
**Clipstone** C Beds 58 F3
**Clipstone** Notts 115 L8
**Clitheroe** Lancs 121 L3
**Clive** Shrops 98 D7
Cliveden Bucks 42 E4
**Clixby** Lincs 117 J2
**Cloatley** Wilts 39 M3
**Clocaenog** Denbgs 97 G2
**Clochan** Moray 215 J3
**Clodock** Herefs 53 L3
**Clola** Abers 217 J5
**Clophill** C Beds 74 F6
**Clopton** Nhants 88 F7
**Clopton** Suffk 78 F4
**Clopton Corner** Suffk 78 F4
**Clos du Valle** Guern 236 d2
**Closeburn** D & G 154 F4
**Closeburnmill** D & G 154 F3
**Closworth** Somset 14 B1
**Clothall** Herts 59 L2
**Clotton** Ches W 112 D8

Clough Foot Calder 122 D5
Clough Head Calder 123 G6
Cloughton N York 143 K7
Clousta Shet 235 c5
Clova Angus 196 B2
Clovelly Devon 22 E6
Clovenfords Border 167 G3
Clovulin Highld 191 K4
Clowne Derbys 115 J6
Clows Top Worcs 70 C1
Cluanie Inn Highld 201 G3
Cluanie Lodge Highld 201 G3
Clugston D & G 145 H4
Clun Shrops 82 F7
Clunas Highld 213 K5
Clunbury Shrops 83 G7
Clunderwen Carmth 49 J4
Clune Highld 203 J1
Clunes Highld 201 J7
Clungunford Shrops 83 H7
Clunie P & K 195 H7
Clunton Shrops 83 G7
Cluny Fife 186 D7
Clutton BaNES 38 F8
Clutton Ches W 98 C2
Clutton Hill BaNES 38 F8
Clydach Mons 53 K5
Clydach Swans 51 K5
Clydach Vale Rhondd 36 F2
Clydebank W Duns 174 F4
Clydebank Crematorium W Duns 174 E4
Clyffe Pypard Wilts 40 B5
Clynder Ag & B 174 A2
Clyne Neath 52 C7
Clynnog-fawr Gwynd 95 G3
Clyro Powys 68 E5
Clyst Honiton Devon 12 C4
Clyst Hydon Devon 12 D3
Clyst St George Devon 12 C5
Clyst St Lawrence Devon 12 D3
Clyst St Mary Devon 12 C4
Cnoc W Isls 232 g2
Cnwch Coch Cerdgn 80 F8
Coad's Green Cnwll 5 L1
Coalburn S Lans 164 F3
Coalburns Gatesd 150 E3
Coaley Gloucs 55 H7
Coalhill Essex 61 J7
Coalpit Heath S Glos 38 F4
Coal Pool Wsall 85 H4
Coalport Wrekin 84 C3
Coalsnaughton Clacks 185 J7
Coaltown of Balgonie Fife 186 E7
Coaltown of Wemyss Fife 186 E7
Coalville Leics 86 E2
Coanwood Nthumb 149 H3
Coat Somset 26 C7
Coatbridge N Lans 175 J5
Coatdyke N Lans 175 K5
Coate Swindn 40 D4
Coate Wilts 40 B7
Coates Cambs 89 K4
Coates Gloucs 55 L7
Coates Lincs 116 E5
Coates W Susx 18 D3
Cobbaton Devon 23 K6
Coberley Gloucs 55 L5
Cobham Kent 46 A6
Cobham Surrey 43 J7
Cobham Services Surrey 43 J8
Cobnash Herefs 69 J3
Cobo Guern 236 c2
Cobridge C Stke 99 K3
Coburby Abers 217 H2
Cockayne Hatley C Beds 75 J5
Cock Bridge Abers 205 G4
Cockburnspath Border 179 G4
Cock Clarks Essex 61 K7
Cockenzie and Port Seton E Loth 177 L4
Cockerham Lancs 120 F1
Cockermouth Cumb 136 F2
Cockernhoe Herts 59 J4
Cockett Swans 51 J6
Cockfield Dur 140 E3
Cockfield Suffk 77 K4
Cockfosters Gt Lon 44 F2
Cock Green Essex 61 H4
Cocking W Susx 18 B3
Cocking Causeway W Susx 18 B2
Cockington Torbay 7 K3
Cocklake Somset 26 C2
Cockley Cley Norfk 91 H3
Cock Marling E Susx 21 H2
Cockpole Green Wokham 42 D4
Cockshutt Shrops 98 B6
Cockthorpe Norfk 106 B4
Cockwood Devon 12 C6
Cockyard Derbys 114 B5
Coddenham Suffk 78 D4
Coddington Herefs 70 C6
Coddington Notts 102 D2
Codford St Mary Wilts 27 L4
Codford St Peter Wilts 27 L4
Codicote Herts 59 K4
Codmore Hill W Susx 31 H7
Codnor Derbys 101 H3
Codrington S Glos 39 G5
Codsall Staffs 84 F3
Codsall Wood Staffs 84 F3
Coedpoeth Wrexhm 97 L3
Coed Talon Flints 97 L2
Coed-y-paen Mons 53 M7
Coffinswell Devon 7 K3
Cofton Devon 12 C6
Cofton Hackett Worcs 85 H7
Cogan V Glam 37 J6
Cogenhoe Nhants 74 B3
Cogges Oxon 57 G6
Coggeshall Essex 61 K4
Coignafearn Highld 203 H2
Coilacriech Abers 205 H6
Coilantogle Stirlg 184 D6
Coillore Highld 208 E6
Coity Brdgnd 36 E4
Col W Isls 232 g2
Colaboll Highld 225 L6
Colan Cnwll 4 D4
Colaton Raleigh Devon 12 D5
Colbost Highld 208 C5
Colburn N York 140 F7
Colby Cumb 138 F3
Colby IoM 237 b6
Colchester Essex 62 B3
Colchester Crematorium Essex 62 B4
Colchester Zoo Essex 62 A4
Cold Ash W Berk 41 K6
Cold Ashby Nhants 87 J7
Cold Ashton S Glos 39 H6
Cold Aston Gloucs 56 C4
Coldbackie Highld 229 J4
Cold Brayfield M Keyn 74 D4
Coldean Br & H 19 J4
Coldeast Devon 7 J2
Colden Calder 122 E5
Colden Common Hants 29 J6
Cold Hanworth Lincs 117 G5
Coldharbour Surrey 31 J3
Cold Higham Nhants 73 J4
Coldingham Border 179 J5
Cold Kirby N York 133 H3
Coldmeece Staffs 99 J6
Cold Norton Essex 61 K7
Cold Overton Leics 88 B2
Coldred Kent 35 H5
Coldridge Devon 11 G4
Coldstream Border 168 C2
Coldwaltham W Susx 18 D3
Coldwells Abers 217 H6
Cole Somset 26 F5
Colebatch Shrops 83 G6
Colebrook Devon 12 C2
Colebrooke Devon 11 H5
Coleby Lincs 102 F1
Coleby N Linc 125 L6
Coleford Devon 11 H5
Coleford Gloucs 54 E6
Coleford Somset 27 G2
Colegate End Norfk 92 E6
Colehill Dorset 15 J3
Coleman's Hatch E Susx 32 D6
Colemere Shrops 98 B6
Colemore Hants 30 B5
Colenden P & K 186 B2
Colerne Wilts 39 J6
Colesbourne Gloucs 56 A5
Coleshill Bucks 42 F2
Coleshill Oxon 40 E2
Coleshill Warwks 85 L5
Coley BaNES 26 E1
Colgate W Susx 31 L5
Colinsburgh Fife 187 H6
Colinton C Edin 177 H5
Colintraive Ag & B 173 H4
Colkirk Norfk 105 L7
Coll Ag & B 189 G5
Coll W Isls 232 g2
Collace P & K 186 C2
Collafirth Shet 235 c3
Coll Airport Ag & B 188 F5
Collaton Devon 7 G7
Collaton St Mary Torbay 7 K4
College of Roseisle Moray 214 E2
College Town Br For 42 D7
Collessie Fife 186 E5
Collier Row Gt Lon 45 J2
Collier's End Herts 60 B4
Collier Street Kent 33 J4
Collieston Abers 217 K8
Collin D & G 155 H6
Collingbourne Ducis Wilts 28 E2
Collingbourne Kingston Wilts 28 E1
Collingham Leeds 124 B2
Collingham Notts 102 D1
Collington Herefs 70 B3
Collingtree Nhants 73 L4
Collins Green Warrtn 112 E3
Colliston Angus 196 F7
Colliton Devon 12 E2
Collyweston Nhants 88 E3
Colmonell S Ayrs 152 D5
Colmworth Bed 75 G3
Colnabaichin Abers 205 G4
Colnbrook Slough 43 G5
Colne Cambs 89 L7
Colne Lancs 122 D3
Colne Engaine Essex 61 K3
Colney Norfk 92 E3
Colney Heath Herts 59 K6
Coln Rogers Gloucs 56 B6
Coln St Aldwyns Gloucs 56 C6
Coln St Dennis Gloucs 56 B5
Colonsay Ag & B 180 E7
Colonsay Airport Ag & B 180 E8
Colpy Abers 216 C7
Colquhar Border 166 E2
Colsterworth Lincs 102 F7
Colston Bassett Notts 102 B5
Coltfield Moray 214 D2
Coltishall Norfk 106 F8
Colton Cumb 129 G3
Colton Leeds 124 B4
Colton N York 124 E2
Colton Norfk 92 D2
Colton Staffs 100 B7
Colt's Hill Kent 33 H4
Colvend D & G 146 F4
Colwall Herefs 70 D6
Colwell Nthumb 158 B6
Colwich Staffs 100 A7
Colwinston V Glam 36 E5
Colworth W Susx 18 C5
Colwyn Bay Conwy 110 B5
Colwyn Bay Crematorium Conwy 110 A5
Colyford Devon 13 G4
Colyton Devon 13 G4
Combe Oxon 57 H5
Combe W Berk 41 G7
Combe Down BaNES 39 H7
Combe Fishacre Devon 7 J3
Combe Florey Somset 25 J5
Combe Hay BaNES 39 G7
Combeinteignhead Devon 7 K2
Combe Martin Devon 23 J3
Combe Raleigh Devon 12 F3
Comberbach Ches W 112 F6
Comberford Staffs 85 L3
Comberton Cambs 75 L4
Comberton Herefs 69 K2
Combe St Nicholas Somset 13 H1
Combrook Warwks 72 C4
Combs Derbys 114 B6
Combs Suffk 78 C3
Combs Ford Suffk 78 C3
Combwich Somset 25 K3
Comers Abers 206 D4
Comhampton Worcs 70 E2
Commins Coch Powys 81 J3
Commondale N York 142 E5
Common End Cumb 136 D3
Common Moor Cnwll 5 K2
Compstall Stockp 113 L4
Compstonend D & G 146 B4
Compton Devon 7 K3
Compton Hants 29 J6
Compton Staffs 84 E6
Compton Surrey 30 F3
Compton W Berk 41 K4
Compton W Susx 30 C7
Compton Wilts 28 C2
Compton Abbas Dorset 27 K7
Compton Abdale Gloucs 56 B5
Compton Bassett Wilts 40 B6
Compton Beauchamp Oxon 40 F3
Compton Bishop Somset 26 B1
Compton Chamberlayne Wilts 28 B5
Compton Dando BaNES 38 F7
Compton Dundon Somset 26 C5
Compton Durville Somset 26 B7
Compton Greenfield S Glos 38 E4
Compton Martin BaNES 38 D8
Compton Pauncefoot Somset 26 F6
Compton Valence Dorset 14 B4
Comrie Fife 176 D1
Comrie P & K 185 G3
Conaglen House Highld 191 K3
Conchra Highld 210 D8
Concraigie P & K 195 H7
Conderton Worcs 71 G6
Condicote Gloucs 56 D3
Condorrat N Lans 175 K4
Condover Shrops 83 J3

Coney Hill Gloucs 55 J4
Coneyhurst Common W Susx 31 J6
Coneysthorpe N York 133 L5
Coney Weston Suffk 91 L7
Congerstone Leics 86 D3
Congham Norfk 105 H7
Congleton Ches E 113 J8
Congresbury N Som 38 C7
Conheath D & G 147 H2
Conicavel Moray 214 B4
Coningsby Lincs 103 L2
Conington Cambs 75 K2
Conington Cambs 89 H6
Conisbrough Donc 115 K2
Conisholme Lincs 118 E3
Coniston Cumb 137 J7
Coniston E R Yk 126 E4
Coniston Cold N York 131 G8
Conistone N York 131 J6
Connah's Quay Flints 111 J7
Connel Ag & B 182 C1
Connel Park E Ayrs 164 C6
Connor Downs Cnwll 3 G4
Conon Bridge Highld 212 E4
Cononley N York 122 E2
Consall Staffs 99 M3
Consett Dur 150 E5
Constable Burton N York 132 B2
Constable Lee Lancs 122 B5
Constantine Cnwll 3 J5
Constantine Bay Cnwll 4 D2
Contin Highld 212 C3
Conwy Conwy 109 L6
Conwy Castle Conwy 109 L6
Conyer's Green Suffk 77 K2
Cooden E Susx 20 E4
Cookbury Devon 9 K4
Cookham W & M 42 E4
Cookham Dean W & M 42 E4
Cookham Rise W & M 42 E4
Cookhill Worcs 71 J3
Cookley Suffk 93 H7
Cookley Worcs 84 E7
Cookley Green Oxon 42 B3
Cookney Abers 207 G6
Cook's Green Essex 62 E4
Cooks Green Suffk 77 L4
Cooksmill Green Essex 61 G6
Coolham W Susx 31 J6
Cooling Medway 46 C5
Coombe Cnwll 4 E5
Coombe Devon 7 L2
Coombe Devon 12 E4
Coombe Gloucs 39 H2
Coombe Hants 30 A7
Coombe Abbey Warwks 86 E7
Coombe Bissett Wilts 28 C6
Coombe Cellars Devon 7 K2
Coombe Hill Gloucs 55 K3
Coombe Keynes Dorset 14 F5
Coombe Pafford Torbay 7 L3
Coombes W Susx 19 G4
Coombes-Moor Herefs 69 G2
Coombeswood Dudley 85 H6
Coopersale Common Essex 60 D7
Copdock Suffk 78 D6
Copford Green Essex 61 L4
Copgrove N York 132 E6
Copister Shet 235 d3
Cople Bed 75 G5
Copley Dur 140 D3
Copmanthorpe C York 124 E2
Copmere End Staffs 99 J6
Copp Lancs 120 F3
Coppenhall Staffs 99 K8
Copperhouse Cnwll 2 F4
Coppingford Cambs 89 H7
Copplestone Devon 11 H4
Coppull Lancs 121 H7
Copsale W Susx 31 K6
Copster Green Lancs 121 K4
Copston Magna Warwks 86 F5
Cop Street Kent 35 J3
Copt Hewick N York 132 E5
Copthorne W Susx 32 B5
Copt Oak Leics 86 F2
Copythorne Hants 28 F8
Corbets Tey Gt Lon 45 K3
Corbière Jersey 236 a7
Corbridge Nthumb 150 C3
Corby Nhants 88 C5
Corby Glen Lincs 103 G7
Cordon N Ayrs 162 D4
Coreley Shrops 84 B8
Corfe Somset 25 K7
Corfe Castle Dorset 15 H6
Corfe Mullen Dorset 15 J3
Corfton Shrops 83 J6
Corgarff Abers 205 G4
Corhampton Hants 29 L7
Corlae D & G 154 B3
Corley Warwks 86 C6
Corley Services Warwks 86 C6
Cormuir Angus 195 L3
Cornard Tye Suffk 77 K6
Cornforth Dur 151 H7
Cornhill Abers 216 B3
Cornhill-on-Tweed Nthumb 168 C2
Cornholme Calder 122 D5
Cornoigmore Ag & B 188 C6
Cornsay Dur 150 E6
Cornsay Colliery Dur 150 F6
Corntown Highld 212 E3
Corntown V Glam 36 E5
Cornwall Airport Newquay Cnwll 4 D3
Cornwell Oxon 56 F3
Cornwood Devon 6 E4
Cornworthy Devon 7 J5
Corpach Highld 191 L2
Corpusty Norfk 106 D6
Corrachree Abers 205 K4
Corran Highld 191 K4
Corran Highld 200 C4
Corrie D & G 155 L5
Corrie N Ayrs 162 C2
Corriecravie N Ayrs 162 B5
Corriegills N Ayrs 162 D3
Corriegour Lodge Hotel Highld 201 K6
Corriemoille Highld 212 B2
Corrimony Highld 212 B7
Corringham Lincs 116 E4
Corringham Thurr 46 B4
Corris Gwynd 81 G2
Corris Uchaf Gwynd 81 G2
Corrow Ag & B 183 H7
Corry Highld 199 K1
Corscombe Devon 10 F5
Corscombe Dorset 13 M2
Corse Gloucs 55 H3
Corse Lawn Gloucs 55 J2
Corsham Wilts 39 K6
Corsindae Abers 206 D4
Corsley Wilts 27 J3
Corsley Heath Wilts 27 J3
Corsock D & G 154 D6
Corston BaNES 39 G7
Corston Wilts 39 L4
Corstorphine C Edin 177 G4
Cortachy Angus 196 C4
Corton Suffk 93 L4
Corton Wilts 27 L4
Corton Denham Somset 26 F6
Coruanan Highld 191 L3
Corwen Denbgs 97 G4
Coryton Devon 10 C7
Coryton Thurr 46 C4
Cosby Leics 87 G4
Coseley Dudley 85 G5
Cosgrove Nhants 73 L6
Cosham C Port 17 J2
Cosheston Pembks 49 G6
Coshieville P & K 194 C6
Cossall Notts 101 J4
Cossington Leics 87 H2
Cossington Somset 26 A4
Costessey Norfk 92 E2
Costock Notts 101 L7
Coston Leics 102 D7
Coston Norfk 92 C3
Cote Oxon 57 G7
Cotebrook Ches W 112 E7
Cotehill Cumb 148 E5
Cotes Leics 101 K7
Cotesbach Leics 87 G6
Cotford St Luke Somset 25 J6
Cotgrave Notts 101 M5
Cothal Abers 207 G3
Cotham Notts 102 C3
Cotherstone Dur 140 C4
Cothill Oxon 57 J7
Cotleigh Devon 13 G3
Cotmanhay Derbys 101 J4
Coton Cambs 76 B3
Coton Nhants 73 J1
Coton Staffs 99 J7
Coton Clanford Staffs 99 K7
Coton Hill Shrops 83 J2
Coton in the Elms Derbys 86 B1
Cotswolds 55 M6
Cotswold Wildlife Park & Gardens Oxon 56 E6
Cott Devon 7 H4
Cottam Lancs 121 G4
Cottam Notts 116 D5
Cottenham Cambs 76 C2
Cottered Herts 60 A3
Cotteridge Birm 85 J7
Cotterstock Nhants 88 F5
Cottesbrooke Nhants 87 K8
Cottesmore Rutlnd 88 C2
Cottingham E R Yk 126 C4
Cottingham Nhants 88 B5
Cottingley C Brad 123 G3
Cottingley Hall Crematorium Leeds 123 K4
Cottisford Oxon 57 L2
Cotton Suffk 78 C2
Cottown Abers 206 E3
Cottown Abers 215 L8
Cottown of Gight Abers 216 F6
Cotts Devon 6 C3
Coughton Warwks 71 J3
Coulaghailtro Ag & B 172 C5
Coulags Highld 210 E5
Coull Abers 205 L5
Coulport Ag & B 173 L2
Coulsdon Gt Lon 32 B2
Coulston Wilts 27 L2
Coulter S Lans 165 K3
Coulton N York 133 K5
Coultra Fife 186 F3
Cound Shrops 83 L3
Coundon Dur 141 G2
Countersett N York 131 H2
Countess Wear Devon 12 B4
Countesthorpe Leics 87 H4
Counties Crematorium Nhants 73 K3
Countisbury Devon 24 B2
Coupar Angus P & K 195 K7
Coupland Nthumb 168 D3
Cour Ag & B 172 D8
Courteachan Highld 199 L6
Courteenhall Nhants 73 L4
Court Henry Carmth 51 H2
Courtsend Essex 47 G2
Courtway Somset 25 J5
Cousland Mdloth 177 K5
Cousley Wood E Susx 33 H6
Cove Ag & B 173 L2
Cove Border 179 G4
Cove Devon 24 E7
Cove Hants 30 E1
Cove Highld 219 J3
Cove Bay C Aber 207 H5
Covehithe Suffk 93 L6
Coven Staffs 85 G3
Coveney Cambs 90 C6
Covenham St Bartholomew Lincs 118 D3
Covenham St Mary Lincs 118 D3
Coventry Covtry 86 D7
Coverack Cnwll 3 K7
Coverack Bridges Cnwll 3 H5
Coverham N York 131 L3
Covington Cambs 74 F1
Covington S Lans 165 J2
Cowan Bridge Lancs 130 C4
Cowbeech E Susx 20 C3
Cowbit Lincs 103 L8
Cowbridge V Glam 36 F5
Cowden Kent 32 E5
Cowdenbeath Fife 177 G1
Cowers Lane Derbys 100 F3
Cowes IoW 16 F3
Cowesby N York 133 G2
Cowfold W Susx 31 K6
Cowhill S Glos 38 E3
Cowie Stirlg 175 L1
Cowley Devon 11 K5
Cowley Gloucs 55 L5
Cowley Gt Lon 43 H4
Cowley Oxon 57 K7
Cowling Lancs 121 H6
Cowling N York 122 E2
Cowling N York 132 C3
Cowlinge Suffk 77 G4
Cowpen Nthumb 159 H5
Cowplain Hants 17 K1
Cowshill Dur 149 L6
Cowslip Green N Som 38 C7
Cowthorpe N York 132 F8
Coxbank Ches E 98 F4
Coxbench Derbys 101 G4
Coxford Cnwll 8 F5
Coxford Norfk 105 K6
Coxheath Kent 33 J3
Coxhoe Dur 151 H7
Coxley Somset 26 D3
Coxley Wick Somset 26 D3
Coxtie Green Essex 45 K2
Coxwold N York 133 H4
Coychurch Brdgnd 36 E4
Coychurch Crematorium Brdgnd 36 E4
Coylton S Ayrs 163 K5
Coylumbridge Highld 203 L3
Coytrahen Brdgnd 36 D4
Crabbs Cross Worcs 71 J2
Crabtree W Susx 31 K6
Crackenthorpe Cumb 138 F3
Crackington Haven Cnwll 8 F5
Crackley Staffs 99 J3
Crackleybank Shrops 84 D2
Cracoe N York 131 J7
Craddock Devon 25 G8
Cradley Dudley 85 G6
Cradley Herefs 70 D5
Cradley Heath Sandw 85 G6
Cradoc Powys 52 F2
Crafthole Cnwll 6 B5
Craggan Highld 204 C1
Cragganmore Moray 214 E6
Craghead Dur 150 F5
Cragside House & Garden Nthumb 158 D2
Crai Powys 52 D3

**Craibstone** Moray 215 L3
**Craichie** Angus 196 E6
**Craig** Angus 197 H5
**Craig** Highld 211 G4
**Craigbank** E Ayrs 164 C6
**Craigburn** Border 177 H7
**Craigcleuch** D & G 156 C5
**Craigdam** Abers 216 F7
**Craigdhu** Ag & B 182 B6
**Craigearn** Abers 206 D3
**Craigellachie** Moray 215 G5
**Craigend** P & K 186 B4
**Craigend** Rens 174 E4
**Craigendoran** Ag & B 174 C3
**Craigends** Rens 174 D5
**Craighlaw** D & G 145 G3
**Craighouse** Ag & B 171 K5
**Craigie** P & K 195 H7
**Craigie** S Ayrs 163 K3
**Craigiefold** Abers 217 H2
**Craigley** D & G 146 D4
**Craig Llangiwg** Neath 51 K4
**Craiglockhart** C Edin 177 H4
**Craigmillar** C Edin 177 J4
**Craigneston** D & G 154 D5
**Craigneuk** N Lans 175 K5
**Craigneuk** N Lans 175 K6
**Craignure** Ag & B 190 E8
**Craigo** Angus 197 H4
**Craigrothie** Fife 186 F5
**Craigruie** Stirlg 184 B4
**Craigton** Angus 196 E8
**Craigton** C Aber 206 F5
**Craigton** E Rens 174 F7
**Craigton Crematorium** C Glas 174 F5
**Craigton of Airlie** Angus 196 B6
**Craik** Border 166 E7
**Crail** Fife 187 K5
**Crailing** Border 167 L4
**Craiselound** N Linc 116 C2
**Crakehall** N York 132 C2
**Crambe** N York 133 L6
**Cramlington** Nthumb 159 G6
**Cramond** C Edin 177 G3
**Cramond Bridge** C Edin 177 G4
**Cranage** Ches E 113 H7
**Cranberry** Staffs 99 J5
**Cranborne** Dorset 28 B8
**Cranbourne** Br For 42 F5
**Cranbrook** Devon 12 C4
**Cranbrook** Kent 33 K6
**Cranfield** C Beds 74 D6
**Cranford** Gt Lon 43 J5
**Cranford St Andrew** Nhants 88 D7
**Cranford St John** Nhants 88 D7
**Cranham** Gloucs 55 K5
**Crank** St Hel 112 D2
**Cranleigh** Surrey 31 H4
**Cranmore** Somset 26 F3
**Cranoe** Leics 87 L4
**Cransford** Suffk 79 G2
**Cranshaws** Border 178 E6
**Crantock** Cnwll 4 C4
**Cranwell** Lincs 103 G3
**Cranwich** Norfk 91 H4
**Cranworth** Norfk 92 B3
**Craobh Haven** Ag & B 182 A6
**Crarae** Ag & B 182 E7
**Crask Inn** Highld 225 L4
**Crask of Aigas** Highld 212 D6
**Craster** Nthumb 169 K5
**Cratfield** Suffk 93 G7
**Crathes** Abers 206 E6
**Crathes Crematorium** Abers 206 E6
**Crathie** Abers 205 G6
**Crathie** Highld 202 E6
**Crathorne** N York 141 K5
**Craven Arms** Shrops 83 H6
**Crawcrook** Gatesd 150 E3
**Crawford** S Lans 165 J5
**Crawfordjohn** S Lans 165 G5
**Crawley** Hants 29 H4
**Crawley** Oxon 57 G5
**Crawley** W Susx 31 L4
**Crawley Down** W Susx 32 C5
**Crawton** Abers 197 L1
**Cray** N York 131 H4
**Crayford** Gt Lon 45 K5
**Crayke** N York 133 H5
**Crays Hill** Essex 46 B2
**Creacombe** Devon 24 C7
**Creagan Inn** Ag & B 191 J7
**Creag Ghoraidh** W Isls 233 c7
**Creagorry** W Isls 233 c7
**Creaguaineach Lodge** Highld 192 E3
**Creaton** Nhants 73 K1
**Creca** D & G 155 M7
**Credenhill** Herefs 69 J5
**Crediton** Devon 11 J5
**Creebank** D & G 153 H6
**Creebridge** D & G 145 J2
**Creech Heathfield** Somset 25 L6
**Creech St Michael** Somset 25 L6
**Creed** Cnwll 4 E6
**Creekmouth** Gt Lon 45 J4
**Creeting St Mary** Suffk 78 D3
**Creeton** Lincs 103 G8
**Creetown** D & G 145 K3
**Cregneash** IoM 237 a7
**Creich** Fife 186 E3
**Creigiau** Cardif 37 G4
**Cremyll** Cnwll 6 C5
**Cressage** Shrops 83 L3
**Cressbrook** Derbys 114 D6
**Cresselly** Pembks 49 H6
**Cressex** Bucks 42 D3
**Cressing** Essex 61 J4
**Cresswell** Nthumb 159 H4
**Cresswell** Pembks 49 H6
**Cresswell** Staffs 99 L5
**Creswell** Derbys 115 K6
**Cretingham** Suffk 78 F3
**Cretshengan** Ag & B 172 C5
**Crewe** Ches E 99 G2
**Crewe-by-Farndon** Ches W 98 B2
**Crewe Crematorium** Ches E 99 G2
**Crewe Green** Ches E 99 G2
**Crew Green** Powys 83 G1
**Crewkerne** Somset 13 K1
**Crewton** C Derb 101 G5
**Crianlarich** Stirlg 183 L3
**Cribyn** Cerdgn 66 C4
**Criccieth** Gwynd 95 J5
**Crich** Derbys 101 G2
**Crichton** Mdloth 177 K6
**Crick** Nhants 87 H8
**Crickadarn** Powys 68 C6
**Cricket St Thomas** Somset 13 J2
**Crickhowell** Powys 53 K4
**Cricklade** Wilts 40 C2
**Cricklewood** Gt Lon 44 E3
**Crieff** P & K 185 H3
**Criggion** Powys 82 F1
**Crigglestone** Wakefd 123 L7
**Crimond** Abers 217 K3
**Crimplesham** Norfk 90 F3
**Crimscote** Warwks 72 B5
**Crinaglack** Highld 212 C6
**Crinan** Ag & B 182 A8
**Crindledyke** N Lans 175 L6
**Cringleford** Norfk 92 E3
**Crinow** Pembks 49 J5
**Croachy** Highld 213 G8
**Crockenhill** Kent 45 J6
**Crocker End** Oxon 42 B3
**Crockernwell** Devon 11 H6
**Crockerton** Wilts 27 K3
**Crocketford** D & G 154 E7
**Crockham Hill** Kent 32 D3
**Croeserw** Neath 36 D2
**Croes-goch** Pembks 48 D2
**Croes-lan** Cerdgn 65 L5
**Croesor** Gwynd 95 L4
**Croesyceiliog** Carmth 50 E3
**Croesyceiliog** Torfn 37 L2
**Croft** Leics 87 G4
**Croft** Lincs 104 E1
**Croft** Warrtn 112 F3
**Croftamie** Stirlg 174 E2
**Crofton** Wakefd 124 B6
**Croft-on-Tees** N York 141 H5
**Croftown** Highld 220 F5
**Crofts** Moray 215 G4
**Crofts Bank** Traffd 113 H3
**Crofts of Dipple** Moray 215 H3
**Crofts of Savoch** Abers 217 K3
**Crofty** Swans 51 G6
**Croggan** Ag & B 181 L3
**Croglin** Cumb 148 F5
**Croick** Highld 222 B3
**Cromarty** Highld 223 H7
**Crombie** Fife 176 E2
**Cromdale** Highld 214 D8
**Cromer** Herts 59 M3
**Cromer** Norfk 106 F4
**Cromford** Derbys 100 F2
**Cromhall** S Glos 39 G3
**Cromor** W Isls 232 f3
**Cromwell** Notts 102 D1
**Cronberry** E Ayrs 164 C5
**Crondall** Hants 30 C2
**Cronton** Knows 112 C4
**Crook** Cumb 138 C7
**Crook** Dur 150 E7
**Crookedholm** E Ayrs 163 L3
**Crookes** Sheff 114 F4
**Crookham** Nthumb 168 D2
**Crookham** W Berk 41 K7
**Crookham Village** Hants 30 C2
**Crook Inn** Border 165 L4
**Crooklands** Cumb 129 L3
**Crook of Devon** P & K 185 L7
**Cropredy** Oxon 72 F5
**Cropston** Leics 87 G2
**Cropthorne** Worcs 71 H5
**Cropton** N York 134 B2
**Cropwell Bishop** Notts 102 B5
**Cropwell Butler** Notts 102 B5
**Cros** W Isls 232 g1
**Crosbost** W Isls 232 f3
**Crosby** Cumb 147 J7
**Crosby** IoM 237 c5
**Crosby** N Linc 125 K7
**Crosby** Sefton 111 J2
**Crosby Garret** Cumb 139 G5
**Crosby Ravensworth** Cumb 138 F4
**Croscombe** Somset 26 E3
**Cross** Somset 26 B1
**Crossaig** Ag & B 172 E7
**Crossapol** Ag & B 188 C7
**Cross Ash** Mons 54 B4
**Cross-at-Hand** Kent 33 K4
**Crossbost** W Isls 232 f3
**Crosscanonby** Cumb 147 J6
**Crossdale Street** Norfk 106 F5
**Cross Flatts** C Brad 123 G3
**Crossford** Fife 176 E2
**Crossford** S Lans 175 L8
**Crossgatehall** E Loth 177 K5
**Crossgates** E Ayrs 163 J1
**Crossgates** Fife 176 F1
**Cross Gates** Leeds 124 B4
**Crossgates** N York 134 F3
**Crossgill** Lancs 129 L6
**Cross Green** Leeds 123 L4
**Cross Green** Suffk 77 K4
**Cross Green** Suffk 78 B4
**Cross Hands** Carmth 51 H3
**Crosshands** E Ayrs 163 L4
**Crosshill** Fife 186 C7
**Crosshill** S Ayrs 163 J7
**Crosshouse** E Ayrs 163 K2
**Cross Houses** Shrops 83 K3
**Cross in Hand** E Susx 20 B2
**Cross Inn** Cerdgn 65 L3
**Cross Keys** Ag & B 174 C2
**Crosskeys** Caerph 37 K3
**Crosskirk** Highld 230 F2
**Cross Lane** IoW 17 G4
**Cross Lane Head** Shrops 84 C4
**Crosslee** Rens 174 D5
**Crossmichael** D & G 146 C2
**Cross of Jackston** Abers 216 E7
**Cross o' th' hands** Derbys 100 F4
**Crossroads** Abers 206 B4
**Crossroads** Abers 206 E6
**Cross Street** Suffk 92 E7
**Crosston** Angus 196 E5
**Cross Town** Ches E 113 H5
**Crossway Green** Worcs 70 E2
**Crossways** Dorset 14 E5
**Crosswell** Pembks 64 F6
**Crosthwaite** Cumb 129 J2
**Croston** Lancs 121 G6
**Crostwick** Norfk 92 F1
**Crouch End** Gt Lon 44 F3
**Croucheston** Wilts 28 B6
**Crouch Hill** Dorset 14 D1
**Croughton** Nhants 73 G7
**Crovie** Abers 216 F2
**Crowan** Cnwll 3 H4
**Crowborough** E Susx 32 F6
**Crowborough Warren** E Susx 32 E6
**Crowcombe** Somset 25 H4
**Crowdecote** Derbys 114 C7
**Crowden** Derbys 114 B2
**Crow Edge** Barns 114 D2
**Crowell** Oxon 58 C7
**Crowfield** Suffk 78 D3
**Crowhill** E Loth 178 F4
**Crow Hill** Herefs 54 F3
**Crowhurst** E Susx 20 F3
**Crowhurst** Surrey 32 D4
**Crowland** Lincs 89 J2
**Crowland** Suffk 78 B1
**Crowlas** Cnwll 2 F5
**Crowle** N Linc 125 J7
**Crowle** Worcs 71 G4
**Crowle Green** Worcs 71 G3
**Crowmarsh Gifford** Oxon 41 L3
**Crown Corner** Suffk 78 F1
**Crownhill** C Plym 6 C4
**Crownhill Crematorium** M Keyn 74 B6
**Crownthorpe** Norfk 92 C3
**Crowntown** Cnwll 3 H5
**Crows-an-Wra** Cnwll 2 D5
**Crowthorne** Wokham 42 D7
**Crowton** Ches W 112 E6
**Croxdale** Dur 151 G7
**Croxden** Staffs 100 B5
**Croxley Green** Herts 43 H2
**Croxteth** Lpool 111 L3
**Croxton** Cambs 75 J3
**Croxton** N Linc 126 D7
**Croxton** Norfk 91 K6
**Croxton** Norfk 106 B6
**Croxton** Staffs 99 H6
**Croxton Kerrial** Leics 102 D6
**Croy** Highld 213 J4
**Croy** N Lans 175 J3
**Croyde** Devon 23 G4
**Croydon** Cambs 75 K5
**Croydon** Gt Lon 44 F6
**Croydon Crematorium** Gt Lon 44 F6
**Crubenmore** Highld 203 G7
**Cruckmeole** Shrops 83 H2

**Cruckton** Shrops 83 H2
**Cruden Bay** Abers 217 K6
**Crudgington** Wrekin 98 F8
**Crudie** Abers 216 E3
**Crudwell** Wilts 39 L2
**Crumlin** Caerph 37 K2
**Crumplehorn** Cnwll 5 K5
**Crumpsall** Manch 113 J2
**Crundale** Kent 34 E5
**Crunwear** Pembks 49 K5
**Crux Easton** Hants 29 H1
**Crwbin** Carmth 50 F3
**Cryers Hill** Bucks 42 E2
**Crymych** Pembks 65 G7
**Crynant** Neath 52 C6
**Crystal Palace** Gt Lon 45 G5
**Cuaig** Highld 209 L3
**Cuan** Ag & B 181 L4
**Cubert** Cnwll 4 C4
**Cublington** Bucks 58 D4
**Cublington** Herefs 69 H6
**Cuckfield** W Susx 32 B7
**Cucklington** Somset 27 H6
**Cuckney** Notts 115 K7
**Cuddesdon** Oxon 57 L7
**Cuddington** Bucks 58 C5
**Cuddington** Ches W 112 E7
**Cuddington Heath** Ches W 98 C3
**Cudham** Gt Lon 32 D2
**Cudliptown** Devon 6 D1
**Cudnell** Bmouth 15 K3
**Cudworth** Barns 124 B8
**Cudworth** Somset 13 J1
**Cuffley** Herts 59 M7
**Cuil** Highld 191 J5
**Culbokie** Highld 212 F3
**Culburnie** Highld 212 D6
**Culcabock** Highld 213 G5
**Culcharry** Highld 213 K4
**Culcheth** Warrtn 112 F3
**Culdrain** Abers 215 L7
**Culduie** Highld 209 L6
**Culford** Suffk 77 J1
**Culgaith** Cumb 138 E2
**Culham** Oxon 41 J2
**Culkein** Highld 224 C2
**Culkein Drumbeg** Highld 224 D2
**Culkerton** Gloucs 39 L2
**Cullen** Moray 215 L2
**Cullercoats** N Tyne 159 J7
**Cullerlie** Abers 206 E5
**Cullicudden** Highld 213 G2
**Cullingworth** C Brad 123 G3
**Cuillin Hills** Highld 199 G2
**Cullipool** Ag & B 181 L5
**Cullivoe** Shet 235 d2
**Culloden** Highld 213 H5
**Cullompton** Devon 12 C2
**Cullompton Services** Devon 12 D2
**Culm Davy** Devon 25 H7
**Culmington** Shrops 83 J6
**Culmstock** Devon 25 H8
**Culnacraig** Highld 224 C7
**Culnaightrie** D & G 146 D5
**Culnaknock** Highld 209 H2
**Culrain** Highld 222 D3
**Culross** Fife 176 D2
**Culroy** S Ayrs 163 H6
**Culsalmond** Abers 216 C7
**Culscadden** D & G 145 K5
**Culshabbin** D & G 145 G5
**Culswick** Shet 235 b6
**Cultercullen** Abers 207 H1
**Cults** C Aber 207 G5
**Culverstone Green** Kent 45 M7
**Culverthorpe** Lincs 103 G4
**Culworth** Nhants 73 G5
**Culzean Castle & Country Park** S Ayrs 163 G7
**Cumbernauld** N Lans 175 K4
**Cumbernauld Village** N Lans 175 K3
**Cumberworth** Lincs 119 G6
**Cuminestown** Abers 216 F4
**Cumledge** Border 179 G6
**Cummersdale** Cumb 148 D4
**Cummertrees** D & G 147 K2
**Cummingston** Moray 214 E1
**Cumnock** E Ayrs 164 B5
**Cumnor** Oxon 57 J7
**Cumrew** Cumb 148 F5
**Cumrue** D & G 155 J5
**Cumwhinton** Cumb 148 D4
**Cumwhitton** Cumb 148 E4
**Cundall** N York 132 F5
**Cunninghamhead** N Ayrs 163 J2
**Cunningsburgh** Shet 235 c7
**Cupar** Fife 186 F4
**Cupar Muir** Fife 186 F5
**Curbar** Derbys 114 E6
**Curbridge** Hants 17 G1
**Curbridge** Oxon 57 G6
**Curdridge** Hants 29 K8
**Curdworth** Warwks 85 L5
**Curland** Somset 25 L7
**Curridge** W Berk 41 J6
**Currie** C Edin 177 G5
**Curry Mallet** Somset 25 L6
**Curry Rivel** Somset 26 B6
**Curtisden Green** Kent 33 J5
**Curtisknowle** Devon 7 H5
**Cury** Cnwll 3 H6
**Cushnie** Abers 205 L3
**Cusworth** Donc 115 K2
**Cutcloy** D & G 145 J7
**Cutcombe** Somset 24 E4
**Cuthill** Highld 223 G4
**Cutnall Green** Worcs 70 F2
**Cutsdean** Gloucs 56 C3
**Cutthorpe** Derbys 115 G6
**Cuxham** Oxon 42 A2
**Cuxton** Medway 46 B6
**Cuxwold** Lincs 117 K2
**Cwm** Denbgs 110 E6
**Cwmafan** Neath 36 B3
**Cwmaman** Rhondd 52 F7
**Cwmbach** Carmth 50 B1
**Cwmbâch** Powys 68 D6
**Cwmbach** Rhondd 52 F7
**Cwmbach Llechrhyd** Powys 68 B4
**Cwmbran** Torfn 37 L2
**Cwmcarn** Caerph 37 K2
**Cwmcarvan** Mons 54 C6
**Cwm-cou** Cerdgn 65 J6
**Cwm Crawnon** Powys 53 H4
**Cwmdare** Rhondd 52 F7
**Cwmdu** Powys 53 J4
**Cwmdu** Swans 51 J6
**Cwmduad** Carmth 65 L7
**Cwmfelin** Brdgnd 36 D3
**Cwmfelin** Myr Td 53 H7
**Cwmfelin Boeth** Carmth 49 K4
**Cwmfelinfach** Caerph 37 J3
**Cwmffrwd** Carmth 50 E3
**Cwmgiedd** Powys 52 C5
**Cwmgorse** Carmth 51 K4
**Cwmgwili** Carmth 51 H4
**Cwmhiraeth** Carmth 65 K6
**Cwm Llinau** Powys 81 J2
**Cwmllynfell** Neath 51 L3
**Cwmmawr** Carmth 51 G3
**Cwmparc** Rhondd 36 E2
**Cwmpengraig** Carmth 65 K7
**Cwmtillery** Blae G 53 K6
**Cwm-twrch Isaf** Powys 52 B6
**Cwm-twrch Uchaf** Powys 51 L4
**Cwm-y-glo** Gwynd 109 H8
**Cwmystwyth** Cerdgn 81 H8
**Cwrt-newydd** Cerdgn 66 C5
**Cyfarthfa Castle Museum** Myr Td 53 G6
**Cylibebyll** Neath 51 L5
**Cymer** Neath 36 D2
**Cymmer** Rhondd 36 F3
**Cynghordy** Carmth 67 H6
**Cynonville** Neath 36 C2
**Cynwyd** Denbgs 97 G4
**Cynwyl Elfed** Carmth 65 L8

## D

**Daccombe** Devon 7 K3
**Dacre** Cumb 138 C2
**Dacre** N York 132 B7
**Dacre Banks** N York 132 B6
**Daddry Shield** Dur 149 M7
**Dadford** Bucks 73 J6
**Dadlington** Leics 86 E4
**Dafen** Carmth 51 G5
**Dagenham** Gt Lon 45 J3
**Daglingworth** Gloucs 55 M6
**Dagnall** Bucks 59 G5
**Dail bho Dheas** W Isls 232 g1
**Dailly** S Ayrs 152 F2
**Dairsie** Fife 187 G4
**Dalabrog** W Isls 233 b8
**Dalavich** Ag & B 182 D5
**Dalbeattie** D & G 146 E3
**Dalby** IoM 237 b5
**Dalby** N York 133 K5
**Dalcapon** P & K 194 F5
**Dalchalm** Highld 226 F7
**Dalchreichart** Highld 201 L3
**Dalchruin** P & K 184 F4
**Dalcrue** P & K 185 L2
**Dalditch** Devon 12 D5
**Daldowie Crematorium** C Glas 175 J6
**Dale** Derbys 101 H5
**Dale** Pembks 48 D6
**Dalelia** Highld 190 E3
**Dalgarven** N Ayrs 163 H1
**Dalgety Bay** Fife 177 G2
**Dalgig** E Ayrs 164 B6
**Dalginross** P & K 185 G3
**Dalguise** P & K 194 F6
**Dalhalvaig** Highld 230 C5
**Dalham** Suffk 77 G3
**Daliburgh** W Isls 233 b8
**Dalkeith** Mdloth 177 K5
**Dallas** Moray 214 D4
**Dallinghoo** Suffk 78 F4
**Dallington** E Susx 20 D2
**Dallington** Nhants 73 K3
**Dalmally** Ag & B 183 H3
**Dalmary** Stirlg 184 C7
**Dalmellington** E Ayrs 153 K2
**Dalmeny** C Edin 176 F3
**Dalmore** Highld 222 F7
**Dalmuir** W Duns 174 E4
**Dalnabreck** Highld 190 E3
**Dalnacardoch** P & K 194 B3
**Dalnahaitnach** Highld 203 K2
**Dalnaspidal** P & K 193 K2
**Dalnawillan Lodge** Highld 230 F7
**Daloist** P & K 194 C5
**Dalqueich** P & K 185 M6
**Dalquhairn** S Ayrs 153 G3
**Dalreavoch** Highld 226 D6
**Dalry** N Ayrs 174 B7
**Dalrymple** E Ayrs 163 J6
**Dalserf** S Lans 175 L7
**Dalsmeran** Ag & B 161 G6
**Dalston** Cumb 148 C5
**Dalston** Gt Lon 45 G3
**Dalswinton** D & G 155 G5
**Dalton** D & G 155 K7
**Dalton** N York 132 F4
**Dalton** N York 140 E5
**Dalton** Nthumb 158 E7
**Dalton-in-Furness** Cumb 128 F5
**Dalton-le-Dale** Dur 151 K5
**Dalton-on-Tees** N York 141 H5
**Dalton Piercy** Hartpl 141 L2
**Dalveich** Stirlg 184 D3
**Dalwhinnie** Highld 202 F7
**Dalwood** Devon 13 G3
**Damerham** Hants 28 C7
**Damgate** Norfk 93 J2
**Damnaglaur** D & G 144 D7
**Danbury** Essex 61 J6
**Danby** N York 142 F5
**Danby Wiske** N York 141 H7
**Dandaleith** Moray 215 G5
**Danderhall** Mdloth 177 J4
**Danebridge** Ches E 113 L7
**Dane End** Herts 60 B4
**Danehill** E Susx 32 D7
**Dane Hills** C Leic 87 H3
**Dane Street** Kent 34 E4
**Danshillock** Abers 216 D3
**Danskine** E Loth 178 C5
**Darenth** Kent 45 K5
**Daresbury** Halton 112 E5
**Darfield** Barns 115 H1
**Dargate** Kent 34 E3
**Dargavel** Rens 174 E4
**Darite** Cnwll 5 K3
**Darland** Medway 46 C6
**Darlaston** Wsall 85 H4
**Darlaston Green** Wsall 85 H4
**Darley** N York 132 C7
**Darley Abbey** C Derb 101 G5
**Darley Bridge** Derbys 100 E1
**Darley Dale** Derbys 114 F8
**Darley Green** Solhll 85 L8
**Darleyhall** Herts 59 J4
**Darley Head** N York 132 B7
**Darlingscott** Warwks 72 B6
**Darlington** Darltn 141 H4
**Darlington Crematorium** Darltn 141 G4
**Darlton** Notts 116 C6
**Darnick** Border 167 H3
**Darowen** Powys 81 H3
**Darra** Abers 216 E5
**Darracott** Devon 9 G2
**Darracott** Devon 23 G4
**Darras Hall** Nthumb 158 E7
**Darrington** Wakefd 124 D6
**Darsham** Suffk 79 J1
**Darshill** Somset 26 E3
**Dartford** Kent 45 K5
**Dartford Crossing** Kent 45 K5
**Dartington** Devon 7 H4
**Dartmoor National Park** Devon 10 F7
**Dartmouth** Devon 7 K5
**Darton** Barns 123 L7
**Darvel** E Ayrs 164 B2
**Darwen** Bl w D 121 K6
**Datchet** W & M 43 G5
**Datchworth** Herts 59 L4
**Daubhill** Bolton 121 K8
**Daugh of Kinermony** Moray 214 F6
**Dauntsey** Wilts 39 M4
**Dava** Highld 214 C6
**Davenham** Ches W 112 F7
**Daventry** Nhants 73 H3
**Davidson's Mains** C Edin 177 G4
**Davidstow** Cnwll 8 F7
**Davington** D & G 155 M2
**Davington Hill** Kent 34 D3
**Daviot** Abers 216 E8
**Daviot** Highld 213 H6
**Daviot House** Highld 213 H6
**Davoch of Grange** Moray 215 K4
**Davyhulme** Traffd 113 H3
**Daw End** Wsall 85 J4
**Dawesgreen** Surrey 31 K3
**Dawley** Wrekin 84 C2
**Dawlish** Devon 12 B6
**Dawlish Warren** Devon 12 C6
**Daybrook** Notts 101 L4
**Daylesford** Gloucs 56 E3

**Deal** Kent 35 K4
**Dean** Cumb 136 E3
**Dean** Devon 7 H3
**Dean** Devon 23 L2
**Dean** Hants 29 K7
**Dean** Oxon 57 G4
**Dean** Somset 26 F3
**Dean Bottom** Kent 45 L6
**Deanburnhaugh** Border 166 F6
**Deancombe** Devon 7 G3
**Dean Court** Oxon 57 J6
**Deane** Bolton 121 K8
**Deane** Hants 29 K2
**Deanhead** Kirk 122 F7
**Deanland** Dorset 27 M7
**Dean Prior** Devon 7 H3
**Deanraw** Nthumb 149 L3
**Deans** W Loth 176 D5
**Deanscales** Cumb 136 F2
**Deanshanger** Nhants 73 L6
**Deanshaugh** Moray 215 H4
**Deanston** Stirlg 184 F6
**Dearham** Cumb 147 J7
**Debach** Suffk 78 F4
**Debden** Essex 45 H2
**Debden** Essex 60 E2
**Debenham** Suffk 78 E2
**Deblin's Green** Worcs 70 E5
**Dechmont** W Loth 176 E4
**Dechmont Road** W Loth 176 D4
**Deddington** Oxon 57 J2
**Dedham** Essex 62 C2
**Dedworth** W & M 42 F5
**Deene** Nhants 88 D5
**Deenethorpe** Nhants 88 D5
**Deepcar** Sheff 114 F3
**Deeping Gate** C Pete 89 G2
**Deeping St James** Lincs 89 H2
**Deeping St Nicholas** Lincs 89 J1
**Deerhurst** Gloucs 55 K3
**Defford** Worcs 71 G5
**Defynnog** Powys 52 E3
**Deganwy** Conwy 109 L5
**Degnish** Ag & B 182 A5
**Deighton** C York 124 F2
**Deighton** N York 141 J6
**Deiniolen** Gwynd 109 H8
**Delabole** Cnwll 8 E7
**Delamere** Ches W 112 E7
**Delfrigs** Abers 207 H2
**Delliefure** Highld 214 D7
**Dell Quay** W Susx 18 A5
**Delnabo** Moray 204 E3
**Delny** Highld 223 G6
**Delph** Oldham 122 E8
**Delves** Dur 150 E5
**Dembleby** Lincs 103 H5
**Denaby** Donc 115 J2
**Denbigh** Denbgs 110 E7
**Denbighshire Crematorium** Denbgs 110 E6
**Denbrae** Fife 186 F4
**Denbury** Devon 7 J3
**Denby** Derbys 101 H4
**Denby Dale** Kirk 123 J8
**Denchworth** Oxon 41 G3
**Dendron** Cumb 128 F5
**Denfield** P & K 185 K4
**Denford** Nhants 88 E7
**Dengie** Essex 62 B7
**Denham** Bucks 43 H3
**Denham** Suffk 77 H3
**Denham** Suffk 92 E8
**Denham Green** Bucks 43 H3
**Denhead** Abers 217 J4
**Denhead** Fife 187 G5
**Denhead of Gray** C Dund 186 F2
**Denholm** Border 167 J5
**Denholme** C Brad 123 G4
**Denmead** Hants 30 A8
**Denmore** C Aber 207 H3
**Dennington** Suffk 79 G2
**Denny** Falk 175 L2
**Dennyloanhead** Falk 175 L3
**Den of Lindores** Fife 186 D4
**Denshaw** Oldham 122 E7
**Denside** Abers 206 F6
**Densole** Kent 35 G6
**Denston** Suffk 77 H4
**Denstone** Staffs 100 C4
**Denstroude** Kent 34 E3
**Dent** Cumb 130 D3
**Denton** Cambs 89 G6
**Denton** Darltn 140 F4
**Denton** E Susx 19 L5
**Denton** Kent 35 G5
**Denton** Lincs 102 E6
**Denton** N York 123 H2
**Denton** Nhants 74 B3
**Denton** Norfk 93 G5
**Denton** Tamesd 113 L3
**Denver** Norfk 90 E3
**Denwick** Nthumb 169 J6
**Deopham** Norfk 92 C4
**Deopham Green** Norfk 92 C4
**Depden** Suffk 77 H3
**Deptford** Gt Lon 45 G4
**Deptford** Wilts 28 A4
**Derby** C Derb 101 G5
**Derby** Devon 23 J5
**Derbyhaven** IoM 237 b7
**Derculich** P & K 194 D5
**Dereham** Norfk 92 B2
**Deri** Caerph 53 H7
**Derringstone** Kent 35 G5
**Derrington** Staffs 99 K7
**Derry Hill** Wilts 39 L6
**Derrythorpe** N Linc 125 J8
**Dersingham** Norfk 105 H6
**Dervaig** Ag & B 189 K6
**Derwen** Denbgs 97 G3
**Derwenlas** Powys 80 F4
**Derwent Valley Mills** Derbys 100 F2
**Derwent Water** Cumb 137 J3
**Desborough** Nhants 88 B6
**Desford** Leics 86 F3
**Deskford** Moray 215 L3
**Detling** Kent 33 K2
**Devauden** Mons 54 C7
**Devil's Bridge** Cerdgn 81 G7
**Devizes** Wilts 40 A7
**Devonport** C Plym 6 C5
**Devonside** Clacks 185 J7
**Devoran** Cnwll 4 C7
**Devoran & Perran** Cnwll 3 K4
**Dewarton** Mdloth 177 K5
**Dewlish** Dorset 14 E3
**Dewsbury** Kirk 123 K6
**Dewsbury Moor** Kirk 123 J6
**Dewsbury Moor Crematorium** Kirk 123 J6
**Deytheur** Powys 97 K8
**Dibden** Hants 16 E2
**Dibden Purlieu** Hants 16 E2
**Dickleburgh** Norfk 92 E6
**Didbrook** Gloucs 56 B2
**Didcot** Oxon 41 K3
**Diddington** Cambs 75 H2
**Diddlebury** Shrops 83 K6
**Didling** W Susx 18 A3
**Didmarton** Gloucs 39 J3
**Didsbury** Manch 113 J3
**Digby** Lincs 103 H2
**Digg** Highld 218 C7
**Diggle** Oldham 122 F8
**Digmoor** Lancs 112 C1
**Dihewyd** Cerdgn 66 C4
**Dilham** Norfk 107 G7
**Dilhorne** Staffs 99 L4
**Dill Hall** Lancs 121 L4
**Dillington** Cambs 75 G2
**Dilston** Nthumb 150 B3
**Dilton** Wilts 27 K2
**Dilton Marsh** Wilts 27 J2
**Dilwyn** Herefs 69 H4
**Dinas** Gwynd 94 E5
**Dinas** Pembks 64 E6
**Dinas-Mawddwy** Gwynd 81 J1
**Dinas Powys** V Glam 37 J6
**Dinder** Somset 26 E3
**Dinedor** Herefs 69 K6
**Dingestow** Mons 54 C6
**Dingle** Lpool 111 K4
**Dingley** Nhants 87 L6
**Dingwall** Highld 212 E3
**Dinnet** Abers 205 K5
**Dinnington** N u Ty 158 F7
**Dinnington** Rothm 115 K4
**Dinnington** Somset 26 B8
**Dinorwic** Gwynd 95 K1
**Dinton** Bucks 58 C5
**Dinton** Wilts 28 A5
**Dinwoodie** D & G 155 K4
**Dinworthy** Devon 9 J2
**Dipford** Somset 25 J6
**Dippen** Ag & B 161 K2
**Dippen** N Ayrs 162 D5
**Dippertown** Devon 10 C7
**Dipple** Moray 215 H3
**Dipple** S Ayrs 152 E2
**Diptford** Devon 7 G4
**Dipton** Dur 150 E4
**Dirleton** E Loth 178 B2
**Dirt Pot** Nthumb 149 L5
**Diseworth** Leics 101 J7
**Dishforth** N York 132 F5
**Disley** Ches E 113 L5
**Diss** Norfk 92 D7
**Distington** Cumb 136 D3
**Distington Hall Crematorium** Cumb 136 E3
**Ditchampton** Wilts 28 C5
**Ditcheat** Somset 26 F4
**Ditchingham** Norfk 93 G5
**Ditchling** E Susx 19 J3
**Ditherington** Shrops 83 K2
**Ditteridge** Wilts 39 J6
**Dittisham** Devon 7 K5
**Ditton** Kent 33 J2
**Ditton Green** Cambs 76 F3
**Ditton Priors** Shrops 83 L5
**Dixton** Mons 54 D5
**Dobcross** Oldham 113 M1
**Dobwalls** Cnwll 5 K3
**Doccombe** Devon 11 H7
**Dochgarroch** Highld 212 F6
**Docking** Norfk 105 J5
**Docklow** Herefs 69 L3
**Dockray** Cumb 137 L3
**Doddinghurst** Essex 60 F7
**Doddington** Cambs 90 B5
**Doddington** Kent 34 C4
**Doddington** Lincs 116 E7
**Doddington** Nthumb 168 E3
**Doddington** Shrops 84 B7
**Doddiscombsleigh** Devon 11 K7
**Dodd's Green** Ches E 98 E4
**Dodford** Nhants 73 H3
**Dodford** Worcs 85 G8
**Dodington** S Glos 39 H4
**Dodington** Somset 25 J4
**Dodleston** Ches W 98 A1
**Dodside** E Rens 174 F7
**Dod's Leigh** Staffs 100 A5
**Dodworth** Barns 114 F1
**Doe Bank** Birm 85 K4
**Dogdyke** Lincs 103 K2
**Dogmersfield** Hants 30 C2
**Dogsthorpe** C Pete 89 H4
**Dolanog** Powys 82 B2
**Dolbenmaen** Gwynd 95 J4
**Dolfach** Powys 81 K3
**Dolfor** Powys 82 C6
**Dolgarrog** Conwy 109 L7
**Dolgellau** Gwynd 96 B8
**Doll** Highld 226 F7
**Dollar** Clacks 185 K7
**Dollarfield** Clacks 185 K7
**Dolphin** Flints 111 H6
**Dolphinholme** Lancs 129 L8
**Dolphinton** S Lans 176 F8
**Dolton** Devon 10 E3
**Dolwen** Conwy 110 B6
**Dolwyddelan** Conwy 96 B3
**Domgay** Powys 97 L8
**Doncaster** Donc 115 L2
**Doncaster North Services** Donc 125 G7
*Doncaster Sheffield Airport* Donc 115 M2
**Donhead St Andrew** Wilts 27 K6
**Donhead St Mary** Wilts 27 K6
**Donibristle** Fife 177 G2
**Doniford** Somset 25 G3
**Donington** Lincs 103 K5
**Donington on Bain** Lincs 118 C5
**Donington Park Services** Leics 101 J7
**Donisthorpe** Leics 86 C2
**Donnington** Gloucs 56 D3
**Donnington** Shrops 83 L2
**Donnington** W Berk 41 J6
**Donnington** W Susx 18 B5
**Donnington** Wrekin 84 C2
**Donnington Wood** Wrekin 84 C2
**Donyatt** Somset 25 M8
**Doonfoot** S Ayrs 163 H5
**Dorback Lodge** Highld 204 D3
**Dorchester** Dorset 14 D4
**Dorchester-on-Thames** Oxon 41 L2
**Dordon** Warwks 86 C4
**Dore** Sheff 114 F5
**Dores** Highld 212 F7
**Dorking** Surrey 31 K2
**Dormansland** Surrey 32 D5
**Dormington** Herefs 69 L6
**Dormston** Worcs 71 H3
**Dorney** Bucks 42 F5
**Dornie** Highld 200 D1
**Dornoch** Highld 223 H4
**Dornock** D & G 147 M2
**Dorrery** Highld 230 F5
**Dorridge** Solhll 85 L8
**Dorrington** Lincs 103 H2
**Dorrington** Shrops 83 J3
**Dorrington** Shrops 99 G4
**Dorsington** Warwks 71 K4
**Dorstone** Herefs 69 G6
**Dorton** Bucks 58 B5
**Douglas** IoM 237 d6
**Douglas** S Lans 165 G4
**Douglas and Angus** C Dund 187 G2
**Douglas Crematorium** IoM 237 d5
**Douglas Pier** Ag & B 183 H7
**Douglastown** Angus 196 C6
**Douglas Water** S Lans 165 G3
**Douglas West** S Lans 164 F3
**Doulting** Somset 26 F3
**Dounby** Ork 234 b5
**Doune** Highld 221 L2
**Doune** Stirlg 184 F6
**Dounepark** S Ayrs 152 E3
**Dounie** Highld 222 D4
**Dousland** Devon 6 D3
**Dove Dale** Derbys 100 D3
**Dove Holes** Derbys 114 B6
**Dovenby** Cumb 147 J7
**Dover** Kent 35 J6
**Dover Castle** Kent 35 J6
**Dovercourt** Essex 62 F2
**Doverdale** Worcs 70 F2
**Doveridge** Derbys 100 C5
**Doversgreen** Surrey 31 L2
**Dowally** P & K 194 F6
**Dowdeswell** Gloucs 55 M4
**Dowlais** Myr Td 53 G6

**Dowland** Devon 10 E3
**Dowlish Wake** Somset 26 A8
**Down Ampney** Gloucs 40 C2
**Downderry** Cnwll 5 L5
**Downe** Gt Lon 45 H7
**Downend** Gloucs 39 J2
**Downend** S Glos 38 F5
**Downfield** C Dund 186 F2
**Downgate** Cnwll 6 A2
**Downham** Essex 46 B2
**Downham** Gt Lon 45 H5
**Downham** Lancs 122 B2
**Downham Market** Norfk 90 E3
**Down Hatherley** Gloucs 55 K4
**Downhead** Somset 26 E6
**Downhead** Somset 27 G3
**Downhill** P & K 186 A2
**Downholme** N York 140 E7
**Downies** Abers 207 H6
**Downley** Bucks 42 D2
**Down St Mary** Devon 11 H4
**Downs Crematorium** Br & H 19 J4
**Downs Crematorium** Br & H 19 J4
**Downside** Surrey 43 J8
**Down Thomas** Devon 6 D6
**Downton** Wilts 28 D6
**Dowsby** Lincs 103 J6
**Doynton** S Glos 39 G5
**Draethen** Caerph 37 K3
**Draffan** S Lans 164 F1
**Drakeholes** Notts 116 B4
**Drakemyre** N Ayrs 174 B7
**Drakes Broughton** Worcs 71 G5
**Draughton** N York 131 K8
**Draughton** Nhants 87 L7
**Drax** N York 125 G5
**Draycote** Warwks 72 F1
**Draycott** Derbys 101 H6
**Draycott** Gloucs 71 L7
**Draycott** Somset 26 C2
**Draycott in the Clay** Staffs 100 D6
**Draycott in the Moors** Staffs 99 M4
**Drayton** C Port 17 J2
**Drayton** Leics 88 B5
**Drayton** Norfk 92 E2
**Drayton** Oxon 41 J2
**Drayton** Oxon 72 E6
**Drayton** Somset 26 B6
**Drayton** Worcs 85 G7
**Drayton Bassett** Staffs 85 L4
**Drayton Beauchamp** Bucks 58 E5
**Drayton Manor Park** Staffs 85 L4
**Drayton Parslow** Bucks 58 D3
**Drayton St Leonard** Oxon 41 L2
**Dreen Hill** Pembks 48 F5
**Drefach** Carmth 51 G3
**Drefach** Carmth 65 K6
**Drefach** Cerdgn 66 C5
**Dreghorn** N Ayrs 163 J2
**Drellingore** Kent 35 H6
**Drem** E Loth 178 B3
**Dresden** C Stke 99 K4
**Drewsteignton** Devon 11 H6
**Driffield** E R Yk 134 F7
**Driffield** Gloucs 56 B7
**Drift** Cnwll 2 D5
**Drigg** Cumb 136 E7
**Drighlington** Leeds 123 J5
**Drimnin** Highld 190 B5
**Drimpton** Dorset 13 K2
**Drimsallie** Highld 191 J1
**Dringhouses** C York 124 E2
**Drinkstone** Suffk 77 L3
**Drinkstone Green** Suffk 77 L3
**Drointon** Staffs 100 A6
**Droitwich Spa** Worcs 70 F2
**Dron** P & K 186 B4
**Dronfield** Derbys 115 G5
**Drongan** E Ayrs 163 K5
**Dronley** Angus 186 E1
**Droop** Dorset 14 E2
**Droxford** Hants 29 L7
**Droylsden** Tamesd 113 K2
**Druid** Denbgs 97 G4
**Druidston** Pembks 48 E4
**Druimarbin** Highld 191 L3
**Druimavuic** Ag & B 191 K7
**Druimdrishaig** Ag & B 172 C4
**Druimindarroch** Highld 199 L7
**Drum** Ag & B 172 F3
**Drum** P & K 185 L7
**Drumalbin** S Lans 165 H2
**Drumbeg** Highld 224 D3
**Drumblade** Abers 216 B6
**Drumbreddon** D & G 144 C6
**Drumbuie** Highld 210 B7
**Drumburgh** Cumb 148 A3
**Drumburn** D & G 146 F4
**Drumburn** D & G 147 G3
**Drumchapel** C Glas 174 F4
**Drumchastle** P & K 193 L5
**Drumclog** S Lans 164 C2
**Drumeldrie** Fife 187 G6
**Drumelzier** Border 165 M3
**Drumfearn** Highld 199 L3
**Drumfrennie** Abers 206 D5
**Drumgley** Angus 196 C6
**Drumguish** Highld 203 J5
**Drumin** Moray 214 E7
**Drumjohn** D & G 153 L3
**Drumlamford** S Ayrs 153 G6
**Drumlasie** Abers 206 C4
**Drumleaning** Cumb 148 A5
**Drumlemble** Ag & B 161 H5
**Drumlithie** Abers 197 J1
**Drummoddie** D & G 145 H6
**Drummore** D & G 144 D7
**Drummuir** Moray 215 J5
**Drumnadrochit** Highld 212 D7
**Drumnagorrach** Moray 215 L4
**Drumpark** D & G 154 F6
**Drumrunie Lodge** Highld 224 E7
**Drumshang** S Ayrs 163 G6
**Drumuie** Highld 209 G5
**Drumuillie** Highld 204 B2
**Drumvaich** Stirlg 184 E6
**Drunzie** P & K 186 B5
**Drybeck** Cumb 138 F4
**Drybridge** Moray 215 K2
**Drybridge** N Ayrs 163 J3
**Drybrook** Gloucs 54 F4
**Dryburgh** Border 167 J3
**Dry Doddington** Lincs 102 D3
**Dry Drayton** Cambs 75 L3
**Drymen** Stirlg 174 E2
**Drymuir** Abers 217 G5
**Drynoch** Highld 208 F7
**Dubford** Abers 216 F2
**Duchally** Highld 225 J5
**Ducklington** Oxon 57 G6
**Duddenhoe End** Essex 76 C7
**Duddingston** C Edin 177 J4
**Duddington** Nhants 88 E4
**Duddlestone** Somset 25 K7
**Duddo** Nthumb 168 D2
**Duddon** Ches W 112 D8
**Dudleston** Shrops 97 M5
**Dudleston Heath** Shrops 98 A5
**Dudley** Dudley 85 G5
**Dudley** N Tyne 159 G7
**Dudley Port** Sandw 85 G5
**Dudsbury** Dorset 15 K3
**Duffield** Derbys 101 G4
**Duffryn** Neath 36 C2
**Dufftown** Moray 215 H6
**Duffus** Moray 214 E2
**Dufton** Cumb 139 G3
**Duggleby** N York 134 D6
**Duirinish** Highld 210 B7
**Duisdalemore** Highld 199 L3
**Duisky** Highld 191 K2
**Dukestown** Blae G 53 H6
**Duke Street** Suffk 78 C6
**Dukinfield** Tamesd 113 L2
**Dukinfield Crematorium** Tamesd 113 L2
**Dulcote** Somset 26 E3
**Dulford** Devon 12 D2
**Dull** P & K 194 C6
**Dullatur** N Lans 175 K3
**Dullingham** Cambs 76 F3
**Dulnain Bridge** Highld 204 B1
**Duloe** Bed 75 H3
**Duloe** Cnwll 5 K4
**Dulsie Bridge** Highld 213 L6
**Dulverton** Somset 24 E5
**Dulwich** Gt Lon 45 G5
**Dumbarton** W Duns 174 D4
**Dumbleton** Gloucs 71 H7
**Dumfries** D & G 155 G6
**Dumgoyne** Stirlg 174 F2
**Dummer** Hants 29 L3
**Dumpton** Kent 35 K2
**Dun** Angus 197 G4
**Dunalastair** P & K 193 L5
**Dunan** Ag & B 173 K4
**Dunan** Highld 209 J8
**Dunan** P & K 193 G5
**Dunaverty** Ag & B 161 H7
**Dunball** Somset 25 L3
**Dunbar** E Loth 178 E3
**Dunbeath** Highld 227 L3
**Dunbeg** Ag & B 182 C2
**Dunblane** Stirlg 185 G6
**Dunbog** Fife 186 E4
**Duncanston** Highld 212 F3
**Duncanstone** Abers 206 B1
**Dunchideock** Devon 11 K7
**Dunchurch** Warwks 72 F1
**Duncow** D & G 155 G5
**Duncrievie** P & K 186 B5
**Duncton** W Susx 18 C3
**Dundee** C Dund 186 F2
*Dundee Airport* C Dund 186 F2
**Dundee Crematorium** C Dund 186 F2
**Dundon** Somset 26 C5
**Dundonald** S Ayrs 163 J3
**Dundonnell** Highld 220 E4
**Dundraw** Cumb 147 L5
**Dundreggan** Highld 201 L3
**Dundrennan** D & G 146 D5
**Dundry** N Som 38 E6
**Dunecht** Abers 206 E4
**Dunfermline** Fife 176 F2
**Dunfermline Crematorium** Fife 176 F2
**Dunfield** Gloucs 40 C2
**Dungavel** S Lans 164 D3
**Dungeness** Kent 21 L3
**Dunham Massey** Traffd 113 H4
**Dunham-on-the-Hill** Ches W 112 C6
**Dunham-on-Trent** Notts 116 D6
**Dunhampton** Worcs 70 F2
**Dunham Town** Traffd 113 H4
**Dunham Woodhouses** Traffd 113 G4
**Dunholme** Lincs 117 G5
**Dunino** Fife 187 J5
**Dunipace** Falk 175 L2
**Dunkeld** P & K 195 G7
**Dunkerton** BaNES 39 G8
**Dunkeswell** Devon 12 E2
**Dunkeswick** N York 123 L2
**Dunkirk** Kent 34 E3
**Dunkirk** S Glos 39 H4
**Dunk's Green** Kent 33 G3
**Dunlappie** Angus 196 F3
**Dunley** Worcs 70 E2
**Dunlop** E Ayrs 174 D8
**Dunmaglass** Highld 202 F2
**Dunmore** Falk 176 B1
**Dunnet** Highld 231 J2
**Dunnichen** Angus 196 E6
**Dunning** P & K 185 L4
**Dunnington** C York 133 K8
**Dunnington** E R Yk 126 E1
**Dunnington** Warwks 71 J4
**Dunoon** Ag & B 173 K3
**Dunphail** Moray 214 C5
**Dunragit** D & G 144 E4
**Duns** Border 179 G7
**Dunsby** Lincs 103 J6
**Dunscore** D & G 154 F5
**Dunscroft** Donc 124 F8
**Dunsdale** R & Cl 142 D4
**Dunsden Green** Oxon 42 C5
**Dunsdon** Devon 9 J3
**Dunsfold** Surrey 31 G4
**Dunsford** Devon 11 J6
**Dunshalt** Fife 186 D5
**Dunshillock** Abers 217 J5
**Dunsill** Notts 101 J1
**Dunsley** N York 143 H5
**Dunsley** Staffs 84 F6
**Dunsmore** Bucks 58 E6
**Dunsop Bridge** Lancs 121 K1
**Dunstable** C Beds 59 G4
**Dunstall** Staffs 100 D7
**Dunstan** Nthumb 169 K5
**Dunster** Somset 24 F3
**Duns Tew** Oxon 57 J3
**Dunston** Gatesd 151 G3
**Dunston** Lincs 117 H8
**Dunston** Norfk 92 F3
**Dunston** Staffs 99 L8
**Dunstone** Devon 6 E5
**Dunstone** Devon 7 G2
**Dunsville** Donc 124 F8
**Dunswell** E R Yk 126 D4
**Dunsyre** S Lans 176 E8
**Dunterton** Devon 6 B1
**Duntisbourne Abbots** Gloucs 55 L6
**Duntisbourne Rouse** Gloucs 55 M6
**Duntish** Dorset 14 D2
**Duntocher** W Duns 174 E4
**Dunton** Bucks 58 D3
**Dunton** C Beds 75 J5
**Dunton** Norfk 105 L6
**Dunton Bassett** Leics 87 G5
**Dunton Green** Kent 32 F2
**Duntulm** Highld 218 C6
**Dunure** S Ayrs 163 G6
**Dunvant** Swans 51 H6
**Dunvegan** Highld 208 D5
**Dunwich** Suffk 79 K1
**Durgan** Cnwll 3 K5
**Durham** Dur 151 G6
**Durham Cathedral** Dur 151 G6
**Durham Crematorium** Dur 151 G6
**Durham Services** Dur 151 H7
*Durham Tees Valley Airport* S on T 141 J5
**Durisdeer** D & G 154 F2
**Durisdeermill** D & G 154 F2
**Durleigh** Somset 25 L4
**Durley** Hants 29 K7
**Durley** Wilts 40 E7
**Durley Street** Hants 29 K7
**Durlock** Kent 35 H3
**Durlock** Kent 35 J2
**Durness** Highld 228 F3
**Durno** Abers 216 D8
**Duror** Highld 191 K5
**Durran** Ag & B 182 D5
**Durrington** W Susx 18 F5

**Durrington** Wilts 28 D3
**Durris** Abers 206 E6
**Dursley** Gloucs 39 H2
**Dursley Cross** Gloucs 55 G4
**Durston** Somset 25 L5
**Durweston** Dorset 15 G2
**Duston** Nhants 73 K3
**Duthil** Highld 203 L1
**Dutton** Ches W 112 E5
**Duxford** Cambs 76 C5
**Duxford** Oxon 57 G7
Duxford IWM Cambs 76 C5
**Dwygyfylchi** Conwy 109 L6
**Dwyran** IoA 108 F7
**Dyce** C Aber 207 G3
**Dyffryn Ardudwy** Gwynd 95 K7
**Dyffryn Cellwen** Neath 52 D6
**Dyke** Lincs 103 J7
**Dyke** Moray 214 B3
**Dykehead** Angus 195 K5
**Dykehead** Angus 196 C4
**Dykehead** N Lans 176 B6
**Dykehead** Stirlg 184 D7
**Dykelands** Abers 197 H3
**Dykends** Angus 195 K5
**Dykeside** Abers 216 D5
**Dymchurch** Kent 34 E8
**Dymock** Gloucs 55 G2
**Dyrham** S Glos 39 H5
**Dysart** Fife 186 E8
**Dyserth** Denbgs 110 E5

## E

**Eagland Hill** Lancs 120 F2
**Eagle** Lincs 116 E7
**Eaglesfield** Cumb 136 F2
**Eaglesfield** D & G 155 M7
**Eaglesham** E Rens 175 G7
**Eagley** Bolton 121 L7
**Eakring** Notts 102 A1
**Ealand** N Linc 125 J7
**Ealing** Gt Lon 44 D4
**Eals** Nthumb 149 H4
**Eamont Bridge** Cumb 138 D2
**Earby** Lancs 122 D2
**Earcroft** Bl w D 121 K5
**Eardington** Shrops 84 C5
**Eardisland** Herefs 69 H3
**Eardisley** Herefs 68 F5
**Eardiston** Shrops 98 A7
**Eardiston** Worcs 70 C2
**Earith** Cambs 89 L8
**Earlestown** St Hel 112 E3
**Earley** Wokham 42 C6
**Earlham** Norfk 92 E2
**Earlham Crematorium** Norfk 92 E2
**Earlish** Highld 208 F3
**Earls Barton** Nhants 74 C2
**Earls Colne** Essex 61 K3
**Earls Common** Worcs 71 G3
**Earl's Croome** Worcs 70 F6
**Earlsdon** Covtry 86 D7
**Earlsferry** Fife 187 H7
**Earlsfield** Gt Lon 44 E5
**Earlsford** Abers 216 F7
**Earlsheaton** Kirk 123 K6
**Earl Shilton** Leics 86 F4
**Earl Soham** Suffk 78 F2
**Earl Sterndale** Derbys 114 C7
**Earlston** Border 167 J2
**Earlston** E Ayrs 163 K3
**Earlswood** Surrey 32 B4
**Earlswood** Warwks 85 K8
**Earnley** W Susx 17 M3
**Earsdon** N Tyne 159 H7
**Earsham** Norfk 93 G5
**Eartham** W Susx 18 C4
**Easby** N York 142 C5
**Easdale** Ag & B 181 L4
**Easebourne** W Susx 30 E6
**Easenhall** Warwks 86 F7
**Eashing** Surrey 30 F3
**Easington** Bucks 58 B6
**Easington** Dur 151 K6
**Easington** E R Yk 127 J6
**Easington** R & Cl 142 F4
**Easington Colliery** Dur 151 K6
**Easington Lane** Sundld 151 J5
**Easingwold** N York 133 H5
**Eassie and Nevay** Angus 196 B7
**East Aberthaw** V Glam 37 G6
**East Allington** Devon 7 H6
**East Anstey** Devon 24 D6
**East Ashey** IoW 17 H5
**East Ashling** W Susx 17 M2
**East Ayton** N York 134 F3
**East Barkwith** Lincs 117 K5
**East Barming** Kent 33 J3
**East Barnby** N York 143 G5
**East Barnet** Gt Lon 44 F2
**East Barns** E Loth 178 F3
**East Barsham** Norfk 105 L5
**East Beckham** Norfk 106 E4
**East Bedfont** Gt Lon 43 H5
**East Bergholt** Suffk 78 C7
**East Bilney** Norfk 106 A8
**East Blatchington** E Susx 20 A5
**East Boldon** S Tyne 151 J3
**East Boldre** Hants 16 D3
**Eastbourne** Darltn 141 H4
**Eastbourne** E Susx 20 C5
**Eastbourne Crematorium** E Susx 20 D5
**East Bradenham** Norfk 91 L2
**East Brent** Somset 25 M2
**Eastbridge** Suffk 79 J2
**East Bridgford** Notts 102 B4
**East Buckland** Devon 23 L5
**East Budleigh** Devon 12 D5
**Eastburn** C Brad 122 F2
**Eastbury** Herts 43 J2
**Eastbury** W Berk 41 G5
**East Butterwick** N Linc 116 D1
**Eastby** N York 131 J8
**East Calder** W Loth 176 E5
**East Carleton** Norfk 92 E3
**East Carlton** Leeds 123 J2
**East Carlton** Nhants 88 B5
**East Chaldon** Dorset 14 E5
**East Challow** Oxon 41 G3
**East Charleton** Devon 7 H7
**East Chelborough** Dorset 14 A2
**East Chiltington** E Susx 19 K3
**East Chinnock** Somset 26 C8
**East Chisenbury** Wilts 28 C2
**Eastchurch** Kent 47 G5
**East Clandon** Surrey 31 H2
**East Claydon** Bucks 58 C3
**East Coker** Somset 26 D8
**Eastcombe** Gloucs 55 K6
**East Compton** Somset 26 E3
**East Cornworthy** Devon 7 J5
**Eastcote** Gt Lon 43 J3
**Eastcote** Nhants 73 K4
**Eastcote** Solhll 85 L7
**Eastcott** Wilts 28 A1
**East Cottingwith** E R Yk 125 G3
**Eastcourt** Wilts 40 E7
**East Cowes** IoW 16 F4
**East Cowick** E R Yk 125 G6
**East Cowton** N York 141 H6
**East Cranmore** Somset 27 G3
**East Dean** E Susx 20 B6
**East Dean** Gloucs 54 F4
**East Dean** Hants 28 F6
**East Dean** W Susx 18 B3
**East Devon Crematorium** Devon 12 D4
**East Drayton** Notts 116 C6
**East Dulwich** Gt Lon 45 G5
**East Dundry** N Som 38 E7
**East Ella** C KuH 126 C5
**Eastend** Essex 46 F2
**East End** Hants 16 D3
**East End** Hants 41 H7
**East End** Kent 33 L6
**East End** Oxon 57 H5
**East End** Somset 26 F3
**Easter Balmoral** Abers 205 G6
**Easter Compton** S Glos 38 E4
**Easter Dalziel** Highld 213 H4
**Eastergate** W Susx 18 C5
**Easterhouse** C Glas 175 J5
**Easter Howgate** Mdloth 177 H5
**Easter Kinkell** Highld 212 E4
**Easter Moniack** Highld 212 E5
**Eastern Green** Covtry 86 C7
**Easter Ord** Abers 206 F4
**Easter Pitkierie** Fife 187 J6
**Easter Skeld** Shet 235 c6
**Easter Softlaw** Border 168 A3
**Easterton** Wilts 28 A1
**East Everleigh** Wilts 28 D2
**East Farleigh** Kent 33 J3
**East Farndon** Nhants 87 K6
**East Ferry** Lincs 116 D2
**Eastfield** N Lans 176 B5
**Eastfield** N York 135 G3
**East Fortune** E Loth 178 C3
**East Garston** W Berk 41 G5
**Eastgate** Dur 150 B7
**Eastgate** Norfk 106 D7
**East Goscote** Leics 87 J2
**East Grafton** Wilts 40 E7
**East Grimstead** Wilts 28 E5
**East Grinstead** W Susx 32 D5
**East Guldeford** E Susx 21 J2
**East Haddon** Nhants 73 J2
**East Hagbourne** Oxon 41 K3
**East Halton** N Linc 126 E6
**East Ham** Gt Lon 45 H4
**Easthampstead Park Crematorium** Br For 42 D6
**Easthampton** Herefs 69 H2
**East Hanney** Oxon 41 H2
**East Hanningfield** Essex 61 J7
**East Hardwick** Wakefd 124 C6
**East Harling** Norfk 92 B6
**East Harlsey** N York 141 K7
**East Harnham** Wilts 28 C5
**East Harptree** BaNES 26 E1
**East Harting** W Susx 30 D7
**East Hatch** Wilts 27 L5
**East Hatley** Cambs 75 K4
**East Hauxwell** N York 132 B2
**East Haven** Angus 187 J1
**East Heckington** Lincs 103 K4
**East Hedleyhope** Dur 150 E6
**East Helmsdale** Highld 227 H5
**East Hendred** Oxon 41 J3
**East Heslerton** N York 134 E4
**East Hoathly** E Susx 20 B3
**East Holme** Dorset 15 G5
**Easthope** Shrops 83 L4
**Easthorpe** Essex 61 L4
**East Horrington** Somset 26 E3
**East Horsley** Surrey 31 H2
**East Howe** Bmouth 15 K4
**East Huntington** C York 133 J7
**East Huntspill** Somset 26 A3
**East Ilsley** W Berk 41 J4
**Eastington** Devon 11 H3
**Eastington** Gloucs 55 H6
**Eastington** Gloucs 56 C5
**East Keal** Lincs 118 E8
**East Kennett** Wilts 40 C6
**East Keswick** Leeds 124 B2
**East Kilbride** S Lans 175 H7
**East Kirkby** Lincs 118 D8
**East Knighton** Dorset 14 F5
**East Knoyle** Wilts 27 K5
**East Lambrook** Somset 26 B7
**East Lancashire Crematorium** Bury 122 B8
**Eastlands** D & G 154 E7
**East Langdon** Kent 35 J5
**East Langton** Leics 87 K5
**East Lavant** W Susx 18 B4
**East Lavington** W Susx 18 C3
**East Layton** N York 140 E5
**Eastleach Martin** Gloucs 56 D6
**Eastleach Turville** Gloucs 56 D6
**East Leake** Notts 101 K7
**Eastleigh** Devon 23 H5
**Eastleigh** Hants 29 J7
**East Lexham** Norfk 105 K8
**Eastling** Kent 34 C4
**East Linton** E Loth 178 D3
**East Lockinge** Oxon 41 H3
**East London Crematorium** Gt Lon 45 H4
**East Lound** N Linc 116 C2
**East Lulworth** Dorset 15 G6
**East Lutton** N York 134 E5
**East Lydford** Somset 26 E5
**East Malling** Kent 33 J2
**East Marden** W Susx 30 D8
**East Markham** Notts 116 C6
**East Martin** Hants 28 B7
**East Marton** N York 122 D1
**East Meon** Hants 30 B6
**East Mersea** Essex 62 C5
*East Midlands Airport* Leics 101 J7
**East Molesey** Surrey 43 J6
**East Morden** Dorset 15 G4
**East Morton** C Brad 123 G3
**East Morton** D & G 154 F3
**East Ness** N York 133 L4
**Eastney** C Port 17 J3
**Eastnor** Herefs 70 D6
**East Norton** Leics 87 L4
**Eastoft** N Linc 125 J7
**East Ogwell** Devon 7 J2
**Easton** Cambs 75 G1
**Easton** Devon 11 G6
**Easton** Dorset 14 D7
**Easton** Hants 29 K5
**Easton** Lincs 102 F6
**Easton** Norfk 92 D2
**Easton** Somset 26 D3
**Easton** Suffk 79 G3
**Easton** Wilts 39 K6
**Easton Grey** Wilts 39 K3
**Easton-in-Gordano** N Som 38 D5
**Easton Maudit** Nhants 74 C3
**Easton-on-the-Hill** Nhants 88 E3
**Easton Royal** Wilts 40 D7
**East Orchard** Dorset 27 J7
**East Peckham** Kent 33 H4
**East Pennar** Pembks 49 G6

**East Pennard** Somset 26 E4
**East Perry** Cambs 75 G2
**East Portlemouth** Devon 7 H7
**East Prawle** Devon 7 H8
**East Preston** W Susx 18 E5
**East Putford** Devon 9 K2
**East Quantoxhead** Somset 25 H3
**East Rainton** Sundld 151 H5
**East Ravendale** NE Lin 118 C2
**East Raynham** Norfk 105 L7
**Eastrea** Cambs 89 K4
**East Riding Crematorium** E R Yk 134 F5
**Eastriggs** D & G 147 M2
**East Rigton** Leeds 124 B2
**Eastrington** E R Yk 125 J4
**Eastrop** Swindn 40 D2
**East Rounton** N York 141 K6
**East Rudham** Norfk 105 K6
**East Runton** Norfk 106 E4
**East Ruston** Norfk 107 H6
**Eastry** Kent 35 J4
**East Saltoun** E Loth 178 B5
**East Sheen** Gt Lon 44 D5
**East Shefford** W Berk 41 H5
**East Stockwith** Lincs 116 C3
**East Stoke** Dorset 15 G5
**East Stoke** Notts 102 C3
**East Stour** Dorset 27 J6
**East Stourmouth** Kent 35 H3
**East Stowford** Devon 23 K6
**East Stratton** Hants 29 K4
**East Studdal** Kent 35 J5
**East Taphouse** Cnwll 5 J3
**East-the-Water** Devon 23 G6
**East Thirston** Nthumb 158 F3
**East Tilbury** Thurr 46 B5
**East Tisted** Hants 30 B5
**East Torrington** Lincs 117 J5
**East Tuddenham** Norfk 92 C2
**East Tytherley** Hants 28 F5
**East Tytherton** Wilts 39 L5
**East Village** Devon 11 J4
**Eastville** Bristl 38 E5
**Eastville** Lincs 104 C2
**East Walton** Norfk 91 G1
**East Week** Devon 10 F6
**Eastwell** Leics 102 C6
**East Wellow** Hants 28 F7
**East Wemyss** Fife 186 E7
**East Whitburn** W Loth 176 C5
**Eastwick** Herts 60 C5
**East Wickham** Gt Lon 45 J5
**East Williamston** Pembks 49 J6
**East Winch** Norfk 91 G1
**East Winterslow** Wilts 28 E5
**East Wittering** W Susx 17 L3
**East Witton** N York 131 L3
**Eastwood** Notts 101 J3
**Eastwood** Sthend 46 D3
**East Woodburn** Nthumb 158 A5
**East Woodhay** Hants 41 H7
**East Worldham** Hants 30 C4
**East Wretham** Norfk 91 K5
**Eathorpe** Warwks 72 E2
**Eaton** Ches E 113 K7
**Eaton** Ches W 112 E8
**Eaton** Leics 102 D6
**Eaton** Norfk 92 E3
**Eaton** Notts 116 B6
**Eaton** Oxon 57 H7
**Eaton** Shrops 83 K5
**Eaton Bray** C Beds 58 F4
**Eaton Constantine** Shrops 83 L3
**Eaton Green** C Beds 58 F4
**Eaton Hastings** Oxon 56 E7
**Eaton Mascott** Shrops 83 K3
**Eaton Socon** Cambs 75 H3
**Eaton upon Tern** Shrops 98 F7
**Ebberston** N York 134 D3
**Ebbesborne Wake** Wilts 27 M6
**Ebbw Vale** Blae G 53 J6
**Ebchester** Dur 150 D4
**Ebford** Devon 12 C5
**Ebley** Gloucs 55 J6
**Ebnal** Ches W 98 C3
**Ebrington** Gloucs 71 L6
**Ecchinswell** Hants 41 J8
**Ecclaw** Border 178 F5
**Ecclefechan** D & G 155 L7
**Eccles** Border 168 A2
**Eccles** Kent 46 B7
**Eccles** Salfd 113 H2
**Ecclesall** Sheff 114 F5
**Ecclesfield** Sheff 115 G3
**Eccleshall** Staffs 99 J6
**Eccleshill** C Brad 123 H4
**Ecclesmachan** W Loth 176 E4
**Eccles Road** Norfk 92 B5
**Eccleston** Ches W 112 B8
**Eccleston** Lancs 121 G6
**Eccleston** St Hel 112 C3
**Echt** Abers 206 E4
**Eckford** Border 167 L4
**Eckington** Derbys 115 H5
**Eckington** Worcs 71 G6
**Ecton** Nhants 74 B2
**Edale** Derbys 114 C4
**Eday** Ork 234 d4
*Eday Airport* Ork 234 d4
**Edburton** W Susx 19 H4
**Edderton** Highld 222 F4
**Eddleston** Border 177 H8
**Eddlewood** S Lans 175 J7
**Edenbridge** Kent 32 D4
**Edenfield** Lancs 122 B6
**Edenhall** Cumb 138 E2
**Edenham** Lincs 103 H7
**Eden Park** Gt Lon 45 G6
*Eden Project* Cnwll 5 G5
**Edensor** Derbys 114 E7
**Edentaggart** Ag & B 183 K8
**Edenthorpe** Donc 115 L1
**Edern** Gwynd 94 E5
**Edgbaston** Birm 85 J6
**Edgcott** Bucks 58 B4
**Edgcott** Somset 24 D4
**Edge** Gloucs 55 J6
**Edgefield** Norfk 106 C5
**Edgefield Green** Norfk 106 D5
**Edgerton** Kirk 123 H6
**Edgeworth** Gloucs 55 L6
**Edgmond** Wrekin 99 G8
**Edgton** Shrops 83 H6
**Edgware** Gt Lon 44 D2
**Edgworth** Bl w D 121 L6
**Edinbane** Highld 208 E4
**Edinburgh** C Edin 177 H4
*Edinburgh Airport* C Edin 176 F4
*Edinburgh Castle* C Edin 177 H4
*Edinburgh Old & New Town* C Edin 177 H4
*Edinburgh Royal Botanic Gardens* C Edin 177 H4
*Edinburgh Zoo RZSS* C Edin 177 G4
**Edingale** Staffs 86 B2
**Edingham** D & G 146 E3
**Edingley** Notts 102 A2
**Edingthorpe** Norfk 107 G6
**Edingthorpe Green** Norfk 107 G6
**Edington** Border 179 J7
**Edington** Nthumb 158 E5
**Edington** Somset 26 B4
**Edington** Wilts 27 L2
**Edington Burtle** Somset 26 B3
**Edingworth** Somset 26 A2
**Edithmead** Somset 25 L2
**Edith Weston** Rutlnd 88 D3
**Edlesborough** Bucks 58 F4
**Edlingham** Nthumb 169 G7
**Edlington** Lincs 118 C7
**Edmondsham** Dorset 15 K1
**Edmondsley** Dur 151 G5
**Edmondthorpe** Leics 88 C1
**Edmonton** Gt Lon 45 G2
**Edmundbyers** Dur 150 C5
**Ednam** Border 167 L2
**Edradynate** P & K 194 D6
**Edrom** Border 179 H7
**Edstaston** Shrops 98 D6
**Edstone** Warwks 71 L3
**Edwalton** Notts 101 L5
**Edwinstowe** Notts 115 L7
**Edworth** C Beds 75 J6
**Edwyn Ralph** Herefs 70 B3
**Edzell** Angus 196 F3
**Edzell Woods** Abers 197 G3
**Efail-fach** Neath 36 B2
**Efail Isaf** Rhondd 37 G4
**Efailnewydd** Gwynd 94 F5
**Efailwen** Carmth 49 K3
**Efenechtyd** Denbgs 97 H2
**Effgill** D & G 156 B4
**Effingham** Surrey 31 J2
**Efford Crematorium** C Plym 6 D4
**Egerton** Bolton 121 K7
**Egerton** Kent 34 B5
**Eggborough** N York 124 E5
**Eggbuckland** C Plym 6 D4
**Eggesford** Devon 11 G3
**Eggington** C Beds 58 F3
**Egginton** Derbys 100 E6
**Eggleston** Dur 140 C3
**Egham** Surrey 43 G6
**Egleton** Rutlnd 88 C3
**Eglingham** Nthumb 169 G5
**Egloshayle** Cnwll 4 F2
**Egloskerry** Cnwll 9 H7
**Eglwysbach** Conwy 109 M7
**Eglwys Cross** Wrexhm 98 C4
**Eglwyswrw** Pembks 65 G6
**Egmanton** Notts 116 B7
**Egremont** Cumb 136 D5
**Egremont** Wirral 111 K3
**Egton** N York 143 G6
**Egton Bridge** N York 143 G6
**Egypt** Bucks 42 F3
**Eigg** Highld 199 G7
**Eight Ash Green** Essex 61 M3
**Eilanreach** Highld 200 C2
*Eilean Donan Castle* Highld 200 D1
**Elan Valley** Powys 67 J2
**Elan Village** Powys 67 K2
**Elberton** S Glos 38 E3
**Elburton** C Plym 6 D5
**Elcombe** Swindn 40 C4
**Eldersfield** Worcs 55 H2
**Elderslie** Rens 174 E5
**Eldon** Dur 141 G2
**Elerch** Cerdgn 80 F6
**Elfhill** Abers 206 F7
**Elford** Staffs 85 L2
**Elgin** Moray 214 F2
**Elgol** Highld 199 H3
**Elham** Kent 35 G6
**Elie** Fife 187 H7
**Elim** IoA 108 D4
**Eling** Hants 29 G8
**Elkesley** Notts 116 B6
**Elkstone** Gloucs 55 L5
**Ella** Abers 216 C3
**Ellacombe** Torbay 7 L3
**Elland** Calder 123 G6
**Ellary** Ag & B 172 C3
**Ellastone** Staffs 100 C4
**Ellel** Lancs 129 K7
**Ellemford** Border 178 F6
**Ellenabeich** Ag & B 181 L4
**Ellenhall** Staffs 99 J7
**Ellen's Green** Surrey 31 H4
**Ellerbeck** N York 141 K7
**Ellerby** N York 143 G4
**Ellerdine Heath** Wrekin 98 F7
**Elleric** Ag & B 191 K6
**Ellerker** E R Yk 125 L5
**Ellerton** E R Yk 125 G3
**Ellerton** N York 141 G7
**Ellesborough** Bucks 58 D6
**Ellesmere** Shrops 98 B5
**Ellesmere Port** Ches W 111 L6
**Ellingham** Norfk 93 H5
**Ellingham** Nthumb 169 H4
**Ellingstring** N York 132 B3
**Ellington** Cambs 75 H1
**Ellington** Nthumb 159 G4
**Elliots Green** Somset 27 J3
**Ellisfield** Hants 29 M3
**Ellishader** Highld 209 H2
**Ellistown** Leics 86 E2
**Ellon** Abers 217 H7
**Ellonby** Cumb 148 D7
**Elloughton** E R Yk 126 B5
**Ellwood** Gloucs 54 E6
**Elm** Cambs 90 C3
**Elmbridge** Worcs 70 F2
**Elmdon** Essex 76 C6
**Elmdon** Solhll 85 L6
**Elmer** W Susx 18 D5
**Elmers End** Gt Lon 45 G6
**Elmer's Green** Lancs 112 D1
**Elmesthorpe** Leics 86 F4
**Elmhurst** Staffs 85 K2
**Elmley Castle** Worcs 71 H6
**Elmley Lovett** Worcs 70 F1
**Elmore** Gloucs 55 H5
**Elmore Back** Gloucs 55 H5
**Elm Park** Gt Lon 45 K3
**Elmsett** Suffk 78 C5
**Elmstead Market** Essex 62 C3
**Elmsted** Kent 34 F5
**Elmstone** Kent 35 H3
**Elmstone Hardwicke** Gloucs 55 K3
**Elmswell** E R Yk 134 F7
**Elmswell** Suffk 78 B2
**Elmton** Derbys 115 J6
**Elphin** Highld 224 F6
**Elphinstone** E Loth 177 K4
**Elrick** Abers 206 F4
**Elrig** D & G 145 G5
**Elrington** Nthumb 149 L3
**Elsdon** Nthumb 158 B4
**Elsenham** Essex 60 E3
**Elsfield** Oxon 57 K6
**Elsham** N Linc 126 C7
**Elsing** Norfk 92 C1
**Elslack** N York 122 D2
**Elson** Hants 17 H3
**Elsrickle** S Lans 165 K2
**Elstead** Surrey 30 E3
**Elsted** W Susx 30 D7
**Elsthorpe** Lincs 103 H7
**Elston** Notts 102 C3
**Elstow** Bed 74 F5
**Elstree** Herts 44 D2
**Elstronwick** E R Yk 126 F4
**Elswick** Lancs 120 F3
**Elswick** N u Ty 151 G3
**Elsworth** Cambs 75 K2
**Elterwater** Cumb 137 K6
**Eltham** Gt Lon 45 H5
**Eltham Crematorium** Gt Lon 45 J5
**Eltisley** Cambs 75 J3
**Elton** Cambs 88 F5
**Elton** Ches W 112 C6
**Elton** Derbys 100 E1
**Elton** Herefs 69 J1
**Elton** Notts 102 C5
**Elton** S on T 141 J4
**Eltringham** Nthumb 150 D3

**Elvanfoot** S Lans 165 J6
**Elvaston** Derbys 101 H6
**Elveden** Suffk 91 J7
**Elvetham Heath** Hants 30 D1
**Elvingston** E Loth 178 A4
**Elvington** C York 125 G2
**Elvington** Kent 35 H5
**Elwick** Hartpl 141 K2
**Elworth** Ches E 99 H1
**Elworthy** Somset 25 G4
**Ely** Cambs 90 D7
**Ely** Cardif 37 H5
**Emberton** M Keyn 74 C5
**Embleton** Cumb 137 G2
**Embleton** Nthumb 169 J5
**Embo** Highld 223 H3
**Emborough** Somset 26 E2
**Embo Street** Highld 223 H3
**Embsay** N York 131 J8
**Emery Down** Hants 16 C2
**Emley** Kirk 123 K7
**Emmington** Oxon 58 C7
**Emneth** Norfk 90 C3
**Emneth Hungate** Norfk 90 D3
**Empingham** Rutlnd 88 D2
**Empshott** Hants 30 C5
**Emstrey Crematorium** Shrops 83 K2
**Emsworth** Hants 17 K2
**Enborne** W Berk 41 H7
**Enborne Row** W Berk 41 H7
**Enderby** Leics 87 G4
**Endmoor** Cumb 129 L3
**Endon** Staffs 99 L2
**Endon Bank** Staffs 99 L2
**Enfield** Gt Lon 60 B7
**Enfield Crematorium** Gt Lon 60 B7
**Enfield Lock** Gt Lon 60 B7
**Enfield Wash** Gt Lon 60 B7
**Enford** Wilts 28 C2
**Engine Common** S Glos 39 G4
**Englefield** W Berk 41 L6
**Englefield Green** Surrey 43 G6
**English Bicknor** Gloucs 54 E5
**Englishcombe** BaNES 39 G7
**English Frankton** Shrops 98 C6
**Enham-Alamein** Hants 29 G2
**Enmore** Somset 25 K4
**Enmore Green** Dorset 27 J6
**Ennerdale Bridge** Cumb 136 E4
**Enochdhu** P & K 195 G4
**Ensay** Ag & B 189 J6
**Ensbury** Bmouth 15 K3
**Ensdon** Shrops 83 H1
**Enstone** Oxon 57 G3
**Enterkinfoot** D & G 154 E2
**Enville** Staffs 84 E6
**Eòlaigearraidh** W Isls 233 b9
**Eoligarry** W Isls 233 b9
**Epney** Gloucs 55 H5
**Epperstone** Notts 102 A3
**Epping** Essex 60 D7
**Epping Green** Essex 60 C6
**Epping Upland** Essex 60 C6
**Eppleby** N York 140 F5
**Epsom** Surrey 44 E7
**Epwell** Oxon 72 D6
**Epworth** N Linc 116 C2
**Erbistock** Wrexhm 97 M4
**Erdington** Birm 85 K5
**Eridge Green** E Susx 32 F6
**Erines** Ag & B 172 E4
**Eriska** Ag & B 191 H7
**Eriskay** W Isls 233 c9
**Eriswell** Suffk 91 G7
**Erith** Gt Lon 45 K4
**Erlestoke** Wilts 27 L2
**Ermington** Devon 6 F5
**Erpingham** Norfk 106 E6
**Errogie** Highld 202 E2
**Errol** P & K 186 D3
**Erskine** Rens 174 E4
**Erskine Bridge** Rens 174 E4
**Ervie** D & G 144 B2
**Erwarton** Suffk 78 F7
**Erwood** Powys 68 C6
**Eryholme** N York 141 H5
**Eryrys** Denbgs 97 J2
**Escomb** Dur 140 F2
**Escrick** N York 124 F2
**Esgairgeiliog** Powys 81 G3
**Esh** Dur 150 F6
**Esher** Surrey 43 J7
**Eshott** Nthumb 158 F3
**Esh Winning** Dur 150 F6
**Eskadale** Highld 212 C6
**Eskbank** Mdloth 177 J5
**Eskdale Green** Cumb 137 G6
**Eskdalemuir** D & G 155 M3
**Esprick** Lancs 120 E3
**Essendine** Rutlnd 88 F2
**Essendon** Herts 59 L6
**Essich** Highld 213 G6
**Essington** Staffs 85 G3
**Esslemont** Abers 217 H7
**Eston** R & Cl 142 C4
**Etal** Nthumb 168 D2
**Etchilhampton** Wilts 40 B7
**Etchingham** E Susx 33 J7
**Etchinghill** Kent 34 F6
**Etchinghill** Staffs 100 B8
**Eton** W & M 42 F5
**Eton Wick** W & M 42 F5
**Etruria** C Stke 99 K3
**Etteridge** Highld 203 G6
**Ettersgill** Dur 139 K2
**Ettiley Heath** Ches E 99 G1
**Ettingshall** Wolves 85 G4
**Ettington** Warwks 72 C5
**Etton** C Pete 89 G3
**Etton** E R Yk 126 B2
**Ettrick** Border 166 D6
**Ettrickbridge** Border 166 F4
**Ettrickhill** Border 166 C6
**Etwall** Derbys 100 F6
**Euston** Suffk 91 K7
**Euxton** Lancs 121 H6
**Evanton** Highld 212 F2
**Evedon** Lincs 103 H3
**Evelix** Highld 223 G4
**Evenjobb** Powys 68 F3
**Evenley** Nhants 73 H7
**Evenlode** Gloucs 56 E3
**Evenwood** Dur 140 E3
**Evercreech** Somset 26 F4
**Everingham** E R Yk 125 J3
**Everleigh** Wilts 28 D2
**Eversholt** C Beds 59 G2
**Evershot** Dorset 14 B2
**Eversley** Hants 42 C7
**Eversley Cross** Hants 42 C7
**Everthorpe** E R Yk 125 L4
**Everton** C Beds 75 H4
**Everton** Hants 16 C4
**Everton** Lpool 111 K3
**Everton** Notts 116 B4
**Evertown** D & G 156 C6
**Evesbatch** Herefs 70 C5
**Evesham** Worcs 71 J5
**Evington** C Leic 87 J3
**Ewden Village** Sheff 114 F3
**Ewell** Surrey 44 E7
**Ewell Minnis** Kent 35 H6
**Ewelme** Oxon 41 M3
**Ewen** Gloucs 40 A2
**Ewenny** V Glam 36 D5
**Ewerby** Lincs 103 J3
**Ewhurst** Surrey 31 H4
**Ewhurst Green** E Susx 20 F2
**Ewhurst Green** Surrey 31 H4
**Ewloe** Flints 111 J7
**Ewood** Bl w D 121 K5
**Eworthy** Devon 10 C6
**Ewshot** Hants 30 D2
**Ewyas Harold** Herefs 54 B3
**Exbourne** Devon 10 E4
**Exbury** Hants 16 E3
**Exebridge** Somset 24 E6
**Exelby** N York 132 D3
**Exeter** Devon 11 L6
*Exeter Airport* Devon 12 C4
**Exeter & Devon Crematorium** Devon 12 B4
**Exeter Services** Devon 12 C4
**Exford** Somset 24 D4
**Exfordsgreen** Shrops 83 J3
**Exhall** Warwks 71 K4
**Exhall** Warwks 86 D6
**Exlade Street** Oxon 42 A4
**Exminster** Devon 12 B5
*Exmoor National Park* 24 D4
**Exmouth** Devon 12 C6
**Exning** Suffk 76 E2
**Exton** Devon 12 C5
**Exton** Hants 29 L7
**Exton** Rutlnd 88 D2
**Exton** Somset 24 E5
**Exwick** Devon 11 K6
**Eyam** Derbys 114 E6
**Eydon** Nhants 73 G4
**Eye** C Pete 89 J3
**Eye** Herefs 69 J2
**Eye** Suffk 92 D8
**Eyemouth** Border 179 K5
**Eyeworth** C Beds 75 J5
**Eyhorne Street** Kent 33 L3
**Eyke** Suffk 79 G4
**Eynesbury** Cambs 75 H3
**Eynsford** Kent 45 K6
**Eynsham** Oxon 57 H6
**Eype** Dorset 13 L4
**Eyre** Highld 208 F4
**Eythorne** Kent 35 H5
**Eyton** Herefs 69 J3
**Eyton** Shrops 98 C7
**Eyton on Severn** Shrops 83 L3
**Eyton upon the Weald Moors** Wrekin 84 B1

## F

**Faccombe** Hants 41 H8
**Faceby** N York 141 L6
**Fachwen** Powys 82 B1
**Faddiley** Ches E 98 E3
**Fadmoor** N York 133 K2
**Faerdre** Swans 51 K5
**Faifley** W Duns 174 F4
**Failand** N Som 38 D6
**Failford** S Ayrs 163 L4
**Failsworth** Oldham 113 K2
**Fairbourne** Gwynd 80 E2
**Fairburn** N York 124 D5
**Fairfield** Derbys 114 B6
**Fairfield** Worcs 85 G7
**Fairford** Gloucs 56 D7
**Fairgirth** D & G 146 F4
**Fair Green** Norfk 90 F1
**Fairhaven** Lancs 120 D5
**Fair Isle** Shet 235 e7
*Fair Isle Airport* Shet 235 e7
**Fairlands** Surrey 30 F2
**Fairlie** N Ayrs 173 L7
**Fairlight** E Susx 21 G4
**Fairmile** Devon 12 E3
**Fairmile** Surrey 43 J7
**Fairnilee** Border 167 G3
**Fair Oak** Hants 29 J7
**Fairoak** Staffs 99 H6
**Fair Oak Green** Hants 42 A7
**Fairseat** Kent 45 L7
**Fairstead** Essex 61 J5
**Fairstead** Norfk 105 G8
**Fairwarp** E Susx 32 E7
**Fairwater** Cardif 37 H5
**Fairy Cross** Devon 22 F6
**Fakenham** Norfk 105 L6
**Fakenham Magna** Suffk 91 K7
**Fala** Mdloth 177 L6
**Fala Dam** Mdloth 177 L6
**Faldingworth** Lincs 117 H5
**Faldouët** Jersey 236 e7
**Falfield** S Glos 39 G2
**Falkenham** Suffk 79 G6
**Falkirk** Falk 176 B3
**Falkirk Crematorium** Falk 176 B3
**Falkirk Wheel** Falk 176 A3
**Falkland** Fife 186 D6
**Fallburn** S Lans 165 J2
**Fallin** Stirlg 175 L1
**Fallodon** Nthumb 169 J5
**Fallowfield** Manch 113 J3
**Fallowfield** Nthumb 150 B2
**Falls of Blarghour** Ag & B 182 E5
**Falmer** E Susx 19 K4
**Falmouth** Cnwll 3 K5
**Falnash** Border 156 D2
**Falsgrave** N York 134 F2
**Falstone** Nthumb 157 J5
**Fanagmore** Highld 228 B5
**Fancott** C Beds 59 G3
**Fanellan** Highld 212 D5
**Fangdale Beck** N York 142 C7
**Fangfoss** E R Yk 134 B8
**Fanmore** Ag & B 189 K7
**Fannich Lodge** Highld 211 K2
**Fans** Border 167 J2
**Far Bletchley** M Keyn 74 C7
**Farcet** Cambs 89 H5
**Far Cotton** Nhants 73 L3
**Fareham** Hants 17 H2
**Farewell** Staffs 85 J2
**Faringdon** Oxon 40 F2
**Farington** Lancs 121 H5
**Farlam** Cumb 148 F3
**Farleigh** N Som 38 D6
**Farleigh** Surrey 32 C2
**Farleigh Hungerford** Somset 39 J8
**Farleigh Wallop** Hants 29 L3
**Farlesthorpe** Lincs 119 G6
**Farleton** Cumb 129 L4
**Farleton** Lancs 130 B6
**Farley** Staffs 100 B4
**Farley** Wilts 28 E5
**Farley Green** Surrey 31 H3
**Farley Hill** Wokham 42 C7
**Farleys End** Gloucs 55 H5
**Farlington** C Port 17 J2
**Farlington** N York 133 J6
**Farlow** Shrops 84 B7
**Farmborough** BaNES 38 F7
**Farmcote** Gloucs 56 B3
**Farmers** Carmth 66 E5
**Farmington** Gloucs 56 C5
**Farmoor** Oxon 57 J6
**Far Moor** Wigan 112 D2
**Farmtown** Moray 215 L4
**Farnborough** Gt Lon 45 H7
**Farnborough** Hants 30 E2
**Farnborough** W Berk 41 H4
**Farnborough** Warwks 72 E5
**Farnborough Park** Hants 30 E1
**Farncombe** Surrey 31 G3
**Farndish** Bed 74 D2
**Farndon** Ches W 98 B2
**Farndon** Notts 102 C3
**Farne Islands** Nthumb 169 J2
**Farnell** Angus 197 G5
**Farnham** Dorset 27 L7
**Farnham** Essex 60 D3
**Farnham** N York 132 E7
**Farnham** Suffk 79 H3
**Farnham** Surrey 30 D3

**Farnham Common** Bucks 42 F4
**Farnham Royal** Bucks 42 F4
**Farningham** Kent 45 K6
**Farnley** Leeds 123 K4
**Farnley** N York 123 J2
**Farnley Tyas** Kirk 123 H7
**Farnsfield** Notts 102 A2
**Farnworth** Bolton 113 G1
**Farnworth** Halton 112 D4
**Far Oakridge** Gloucs 55 L7
**Farr** Highld 203 K5
**Farr** Highld 213 G7
**Farr** Highld 229 L3
**Farraline** Highld 202 E2
**Farringdon** Devon 12 C4
**Farrington Gurney** BaNES 26 F1
**Far Sawrey** Cumb 137 K7
**Farthinghoe** Nhants 73 G6
**Farthingstone** Nhants 73 H4
**Fartown** Kirk 123 H6
**Fasnacloich** Ag & B 191 K6
**Fasnakyle** Highld 211 L8
**Fassfern** Highld 191 K2
**Fatfield** Sundld 151 H4
**Fauldhouse** W Loth 176 C6
**Faulkbourne** Essex 61 J5
**Faulkland** Somset 27 H1
**Fauls** Shrops 98 E6
**Faversham** Kent 34 D3
**Fawdington** N York 132 F5
**Fawdon** N u Ty 151 G2
**Fawkham Green** Kent 45 L6
**Fawler** Oxon 57 G4
**Fawley** Bucks 42 C3
**Fawley** Hants 16 F2
**Fawley** W Berk 41 H4
**Faxfleet** E R Yk 125 K5
**Faygate** W Susx 31 K5
**Fazakerley** Lpool 111 K3
**Fazeley** Staffs 85 L3
**Fearby** N York 132 B4
**Fearn** Highld 223 H6
**Fearnan** P & K 194 B7
**Fearnbeg** Highld 210 B3
**Fearnmore** Highld 209 L3
**Fearnoch** Ag & B 172 F3
**Featherstone** Staffs 85 G3
**Featherstone** Wakefd 124 C6
**Feckenham** Worcs 71 H3
**Feering** Essex 61 L4
**Feetham** N York 140 C7
**Felbridge** Surrey 32 C5
**Felbrigg** Norfk 106 E5
**Felcourt** Surrey 32 C5
**Felindre** Carmth 51 G2
**Felindre** Carmth 65 K6
**Felindre** Powys 82 D7
**Felindre** Swans 51 J5
**Felindre Farchog** Pembks 64 F6
**Felingwm Isaf** Carmth 51 G2
**Felingwm Uchaf** Carmth 51 G1
**Felixkirk** N York 133 G3
**Felixstowe** Suffk 79 G7
**Felling** Gatesd 151 G3
**Felmersham** Bed 74 E3
**Felmingham** Norfk 106 F6
**Felpham** W Susx 18 C5
**Felsham** Suffk 77 L3
**Felsted** Essex 61 G4
**Feltham** Gt Lon 43 J5
**Felthamhill** Surrey 43 H6
**Felthorpe** Norfk 106 E8
**Felton** Herefs 69 L5
**Felton** N Som 38 D7
**Felton** Nthumb 158 F3
**Felton Butler** Shrops 98 B8
**Feltwell** Norfk 91 G5
**Fence** Lancs 122 C3
**Fence** Rothm 115 H4
**Fencott** Oxon 57 L5
**Fendike Corner** Lincs 104 D1
**Fen Ditton** Cambs 76 C3
**Fen Drayton** Cambs 75 L2
**Feniscliffe** Bl w D 121 K5
**Feniscowles** Bl w D 121 J5
**Feniton** Devon 12 E3
**Fenland Crematorium** Cambs 90 B5
**Fenn Green** Shrops 84 D6
**Fenn Street** Medway 46 D5
**Fenny Bentley** Derbys 100 D3
**Fenny Bridges** Devon 12 E3
**Fenny Compton** Warwks 72 E4
**Fenny Drayton** Leics 86 D4
**Fenstanton** Cambs 75 K2
**Fen Street** Norfk 92 B4
**Fenton** Cambs 89 K7
**Fenton** Cumb 148 E4
**Fenton** Lincs 102 E3
**Fenton** Lincs 116 D6
**Fenton** Notts 116 C5
**Fenton** Nthumb 168 E3
**Fenton Barns** E Loth 178 B3
**Fenwick** Donc 124 F7
**Fenwick** E Ayrs 163 L2
**Fenwick** Nthumb 158 D7
**Fenwick** Nthumb 169 G2
**Feock** Cnwll 4 C7
**Feolin Ferry** Ag & B 171 H4
**Fergushill** N Ayrs 163 J2
**Feriniquarrie** Highld 208 B4
**Fermain Bay** Guern 236 d3
**Fern** Angus 196 D4
**Ferndale** Rhondd 36 F2
**Ferndown** Dorset 15 K3
**Ferness** Highld 214 B5
**Fernham** Oxon 40 F3
**Fernhill Heath** Worcs 70 F3
**Fernhurst** W Susx 30 E5
**Fernie** Fife 186 E4
**Ferniegair** S Lans 175 K7
**Fernilea** Highld 208 F7
**Fernilee** Derbys 114 A5
**Fernwood** Notts 102 D3
**Ferrensby** N York 132 E7
**Ferrindonald** Highld 199 K4
**Ferring** W Susx 18 F5
**Ferrybridge Services** Wakefd 124 D6
**Ferryden** Angus 197 H5
**Ferryhill** Dur 141 H2
**Ferryhill Station** Dur 141 H2
**Ferry Point** Highld 223 G4
**Ferryside** Carmth 50 D4
**Ferrytown** Highld 223 G4
**Fersfield** Norfk 92 C6
**Fersit** Highld 192 F2
**Feshiebridge** Highld 203 K4
**Fetcham** Surrey 31 J1
**Fetlar** Shet 235 e2
**Fetterangus** Abers 217 J4
**Fettercairn** Abers 197 G2
**Fewston** N York 132 B8
**Ffairfach** Carmth 51 J2
**Ffair Rhos** Cerdgn 67 G2
**Ffestiniog** Gwynd 96 A4
**Ffestiniog Railway** Gwynd 95 L4
**Fforest** Carmth 51 H5
**Fforest Fach** Swans 51 J6
**Ffostrasol** Cerdgn 65 L5
**Ffrith** Flints 97 L2
**Ffynnongroyw** Flints 111 G5
**Fickleshole** Surrey 32 C2
**Fiddington** Somset 25 K4
**Fiddleford** Dorset 27 J8
**Fiddlers Green** Cnwll 4 C5
**Field** Staffs 100 A5
**Field Dalling** Norfk 106 B5
**Field Head** Leics 86 F2
**Fifehead Magdalen** Dorset 27 H6
**Fifehead Neville** Dorset 14 E1
**Fifehead St Quintin** Dorset 14 E1
**Fife Keith** Moray 215 J4
**Fifield** Oxon 56 E4
**Fifield** W & M 42 E5
**Figheldean** Wilts 28 D3
**Filby** Norfk 93 K2
**Filey** N York 135 H4
**Filgrave** M Keyn 74 C5
**Filkins** Oxon 56 E6
**Filleigh** Devon 23 K5
**Fillingham** Lincs 116 F4
**Fillongley** Warwks 86 C6
**Filton** S Glos 38 E5
**Fimber** E R Yk 134 D7
**Finavon** Angus 196 D5
**Fincham** Norfk 91 G3
**Finchampstead** Wokham 42 D7
**Fincharn** Ag & B 182 C6
**Finchdean** Hants 30 C8
**Finchingfield** Essex 61 G2
**Finchley** Gt Lon 44 F2
**Findern** Derbys 100 F6
**Findhorn** Moray 214 C2
**Findhorn Bridge** Highld 213 J8
**Findochty** Moray 215 K2
**Findo Gask** P & K 185 L4
**Findon** Abers 207 H6
**Findon** W Susx 18 F4
**Findon Mains** Highld 212 F3
**Findrack House** Abers 206 B4
**Finedon** Nhants 88 D8
**Fingask** P & K 186 C4
**Fingest** Bucks 42 C3
**Finghall** N York 132 B2
**Fingland** D & G 164 E6
**Finglesham** Kent 35 J4
**Fingringhoe** Essex 62 B4
**Finlarig** Stirlg 184 C1
**Finmere** Oxon 57 M2
**Finnart** P & K 193 H5
**Finningham** Suffk 78 C1
**Finningley** Donc 116 A2
**Finsbay** W Isls 232 d5
**Finstall** Worcs 71 H1
**Finsthwaite** Cumb 129 H2
**Finstock** Oxon 57 G5
**Finstown** Ork 234 b6
**Fintry** Abers 216 E4
**Fintry** Stirlg 175 H2
**Finzean** Abers 206 B6
**Fionnphort** Ag & B 180 D3
**Fionnsbhagh** W Isls 232 d5
**Firbank** Cumb 130 C2
**Firbeck** Rothm 115 K4
**Firby** N York 132 D3
**Firby** N York 134 B6
**Firle** E Susx 19 M4
**Firsby** Lincs 118 F8
**Fir Tree** Dur 150 E7
**Fishbourne** IoW 17 G4
**Fishbourne** W Susx 18 A5
**Fishbourne Roman Palace** W Susx 18 A5
**Fishburn** Dur 141 J2
**Fishcross** Clacks 185 J7
**Fisherford** Abers 216 C7
**Fisherrow** E Loth 177 K4
**Fisher's Pond** Hants 29 J7
**Fisherton** Highld 213 H4
**Fisherton** S Ayrs 163 H6
**Fisherton de la Mere** Wilts 27 M4
**Fishery Estate** W & M 42 E4
**Fishguard** Pembks 64 D6
**Fishlake** Donc 125 G7
**Fishnish Pier** Ag & B 190 D7
**Fishponds** Bristl 38 F5
**Fishtoft** Lincs 104 B4
**Fishtoft Drove** Lincs 104 A3
**Fiskavaig** Highld 208 E7
**Fiskerton** Lincs 117 H6
**Fiskerton** Notts 102 C3
**Fittleton** Wilts 28 D2
**Fittleworth** W Susx 18 D2
**Fitz** Shrops 98 C8
**Fitzhead** Somset 25 H5
**Fitzwilliam** Wakefd 124 C7
**Five Ash Down** E Susx 19 M2
**Five Ashes** E Susx 32 F7
**Fivehead** Somset 26 A6
**Fivelanes** Cnwll 9 G8
**Five Oak Green** Kent 33 H4
**Five Oaks** Jersey 236 d7
**Five Oaks** W Susx 31 H5
**Five Roads** Carmth 50 F4
**Flackwell Heath** Bucks 42 E3
**Fladbury** Worcs 71 H5
**Fladdabister** Shet 235 c6
**Flagg** Derbys 114 C7
**Flamborough** E R Yk 135 K5
**Flamborough Head** E R Yk 135 K5
**Flamingo Land Theme Park** N York 134 B4
**Flamstead** Herts 59 H5
**Flamstead End** Herts 60 B7
**Flansham** W Susx 18 C5
**Flanshaw** Wakefd 123 L6
**Flasby** N York 131 H7
**Flash** Staffs 114 A7
**Flashader** Highld 208 E4
**Flaunden** Herts 59 G7
**Flawborough** Notts 102 C4
**Flawith** N York 133 G6
**Flax Bourton** N Som 38 D6
**Flaxby** N York 132 F7
**Flaxley** Gloucs 55 G5
**Flaxpool** Somset 25 H4
**Flaxton** N York 133 K6
**Fleckney** Leics 87 J5
**Flecknoe** Warwks 73 G2
**Fledborough** Notts 116 D6
**Fleet** Dorset 14 C6
**Fleet** Hants 30 D2
**Fleet** Lincs 104 C7
**Fleet Hargate** Lincs 104 C7
**Fleet Services** Hants 30 D1
**Fleetwood** Lancs 120 D2
**Fleggburgh** Norfk 93 J2
**Flemingston** V Glam 36 F6
**Flemington** S Lans 175 H6
**Flempton** Suffk 77 J1
**Fletchertown** Cumb 147 L6
**Fletching** E Susx 19 L2
**Flexbury** Cnwll 9 G4
**Flexford** Surrey 30 F2
**Flimby** Cumb 147 H7
**Flimwell** E Susx 33 J6
**Flint** Flints 111 H6
**Flintham** Notts 102 C4
**Flinton** E R Yk 126 F4
**Flitcham** Norfk 105 H6
**Flitton** C Beds 74 F7
**Flitwick** C Beds 74 F7
**Flixborough** N Linc 125 K7
**Flixborough Stather** N Linc 125 K7
**Flixton** N York 135 G4
**Flixton** Suffk 93 G6
**Flixton** Traffd 113 H3
**Flockton** Kirk 123 J7
**Flockton Green** Kirk 123 K7
**Flodigarry** Highld 218 C6
**Flookburgh** Cumb 129 H4
**Flordon** Norfk 92 E4
**Flore** Nhants 73 J3
**Flowton** Suffk 78 C5
**Flushing** Cnwll 3 L4
**Fluxton** Devon 12 E4
**Flyford Flavell** Worcs 71 H4
**Fobbing** Thurr 46 B4
**Fochabers** Moray 215 H3
**Fochriw** Caerph 53 H6
**Fockerby** N Linc 125 K6
**Foddington** Somset 26 E5
**Foel** Powys 81 L2
**Foggathorpe** E R Yk 125 H3
**Fogo** Border 179 G8
**Fogwatt** Moray 214 F3
**Foindle** Highld 228 B5
**Folda** Angus 195 J4

Fole Staffs 100 B5
Foleshill Covtry 86 D6
Folke Dorset 26 F8
Folkestone Kent 35 H7
Folkingham Lincs 103 H5
Folkington E Susx 20 B5
Folksworth Cambs 89 G5
Folkton N York 135 G4
Folla Rule Abers 216 D7
Follifoot N York 124 A1
Folly Gate Devon 10 E5
Fonthill Bishop Wilts 27 L5
Fonthill Gifford Wilts 27 L5
Fontmell Magna Dorset 27 K7
Fontmell Parva Dorset 27 J8
Fontwell W Susx 18 C4
Foolow Derbys 114 D6
Forbestown Abers 205 H3
Forcett N York 140 F5
Ford Ag & B 182 C6
Ford Bucks 58 C6
Ford Derbys 115 H5
Ford Devon 22 F6
Ford Gloucs 56 C3
Ford Nthumb 168 E2
Ford Somset 25 H5
Ford Staffs 100 B2
Ford W Susx 18 D5
Ford Wilts 39 J5
Fordcombe Kent 32 F5
Fordell Fife 177 G2
Forden Powys 82 E4
Ford End Essex 61 G5
Forder Green Devon 7 H3
Fordham Cambs 76 F1
Fordham Essex 61 L3
Fordham Norfk 90 E4
Fordingbridge Hants 28 D8
Fordon E R Yk 135 G4
Fordoun Abers 197 J2
Fordstreet Essex 61 L3
Ford Street Somset 25 J7
Fordwich Kent 35 G3
Fordyce Abers 216 B2
Forebridge Staffs 99 L7
Forest Guern 236 c4
Forest Chapel Ches E 113 L6
Forest Gate Gt Lon 45 H3
Forest Green Surrey 31 J3
Forest Hall N Tyne 151 G2
Forest Hill Gt Lon 45 G5
Forest Hill Oxon 57 L6
Forest Lane Head N York 132 E7
Forest Mill Clacks 185 K8
Forest of Bowland Lancs 130 C8
Forest of Dean Gloucs 54 F5
Forest of Dean Crematorium Gloucs 54 F5
Forest Park Crematorium Gt Lon 45 J2
Forest Row E Susx 32 D6
Forestside W Susx 30 C8
Forfar Angus 196 D6
Forgandenny P & K 186 A4
Forge Hammer Torfn 37 L2
Forgie Moray 215 J4
Forgieside Moray 215 J4
Forgue Abers 216 B5
Formby Sefton 111 J1
Forncett End Norfk 92 D5
Forncett St Mary Norfk 92 E5
Forncett St Peter Norfk 92 E5
Fornham All Saints Suffk 77 J2
Fornham St Martin Suffk 77 J2
Fornighty Highld 213 L4
Forres Moray 214 C3
Forsbrook Staffs 99 L4
Forse Highld 227 M2
Forsinard Highld 230 C6
Forss Highld 230 F2
Fort Augustus Highld 202 B4
Forteviot P & K 185 L4
Forth S Lans 176 C7
Forthampton Gloucs 55 K2
Fort Hommet Guern 236 c2
Forth Rail Bridge C Edin 176 F3
Forth Road Bridge Fife 176 F3
Fortingall P & K 194 B6
Fort le Marchant Guern 236 d1
Forton Hants 29 H3
Forton Lancs 121 G1
Forton Shrops 83 H1
Forton Somset 13 J2
Forton Staffs 99 H7
Fortrie Abers 216 C5
Fortrose Highld 213 H3
Fortuneswell Dorset 14 D7
Fort William Highld 191 L2
Forty Hill Gt Lon 60 B7
Fosbury Wilts 40 F8
Foscot Oxon 56 E4
Fosdyke Lincs 104 A5
Foss P & K 194 C5
Fossebridge Gloucs 56 B5
Foster Street Essex 60 D6
Foston Derbys 100 D6
Foston Leics 87 H4
Foston Lincs 102 E4
Foston N York 133 L6
Foston on the Wolds E R Yk 135 H7
Fotherby Lincs 118 D3
Fotheringhay Nhants 88 F5
Foula Shet 235 a6
Foula Airport Shet 235 a6
Foulden Border 179 J7
Foulden Norfk 91 H4
Foul End Warwks 86 B4
Foulness Island Essex 47 G2
Foulon Vale Crematorium Guern 236 d3
Foulridge Lancs 122 D3
Foulsham Norfk 106 B7
Fountainhall Border 177 L8
Four Ashes Suffk 78 B1
Four Cabots Guern 236 c3
Four Crosses Powys 97 K8
Four Elms Kent 32 E4
Four Forks Somset 25 K4
Four Gotes Cambs 90 C1
Four Lanes Cnwll 3 J4
Four Marks Hants 30 A4
Four Mile Bridge IoA 108 C5
Four Oaks Birm 85 K4
Four Oaks Solhll 86 B7
Fourpenny Highld 223 H3
Four Roads Carmth 50 F4
Fourstones Nthumb 149 M2
Four Throws Kent 33 K7
Fovant Wilts 28 A5
Foveran Abers 207 H2
Fowey Cnwll 5 H5
Fowlhall Kent 33 J4
Fowlis Angus 186 E2
Fowlis Wester P & K 185 J3
Fowlmere Cambs 76 B5
Fownhope Herefs 69 L7
Foxbar Rens 174 E6
Foxcote Somset 27 G1
Foxdale IoM 237 b5
Foxearth Essex 77 J5
Foxfield Cumb 128 F3
Foxhole Cnwll 4 F5
Foxholes N York 134 F5
Foxley Norfk 106 C7
Foxt Staffs 100 B3
Foxton Cambs 76 B5
Foxton Leics 87 K5
Foxton N York 141 K7
Foxwood Shrops 84 B7
Foy Herefs 54 E3
Foyers Highld 202 D2
Foynesfield Highld 213 L4
Fraddon Cnwll 4 E4
Fradley Staffs 85 L2
Fradswell Staffs 99 M6
Fraisthorpe E R Yk 135 J7
Framfield E Susx 20 A2
Framingham Earl Norfk 92 F3
Framingham Pigot Norfk 92 F3
Framlingham Suffk 79 G2
Frampton Dorset 14 C4
Frampton Lincs 104 B5
Frampton Cotterell S Glos 38 F4
Frampton Mansell Gloucs 55 L7
Frampton-on-Severn Gloucs 55 H6
Framsden Suffk 78 E3
Framwellgate Moor Dur 151 G6
Franche Worcs 84 E7
Frankby Wirral 111 H4
Frankley Worcs 85 H7
Frankley Services Worcs 85 H7
Frankton Warwks 72 E1
Frant E Susx 33 G6
Fraserburgh Abers 217 J2
Frating Essex 62 C4
Frating Green Essex 62 C4
Fratton C Port 17 J3
Freathy Cnwll 6 B5
Freckenham Suffk 76 F1
Freckleton Lancs 120 F5
Freeby Leics 102 D7
Freefolk Hants 29 J2
Freeland Oxon 57 H5
Freethorpe Norfk 93 J3
Freethorpe Common Norfk 93 J3
Freiston Lincs 104 B4
Fremington Devon 23 H5
Fremington N York 140 D7
Frenchay S Glos 38 F5
Frenich P & K 194 C5
Frensham Surrey 30 D3
Freshfield Sefton 120 C8
Freshford Wilts 39 H7
Freshwater IoW 16 D5
Fressingfield Suffk 92 F7
Freston Suffk 78 E6
Freswick Highld 231 L3
Fretherne Gloucs 55 G6
Frettenham Norfk 106 F8
Freuchie Fife 186 E6
Freystrop Pembks 49 G5
Friar Park Sandw 85 H4
Friday Bridge Cambs 90 C3
Friday Street Suffk 79 H3
Fridaythorpe E R Yk 134 D7
Friern Barnet Gt Lon 44 F2
Friesthorpe Lincs 117 H5
Frieston Lincs 102 F3
Frieth Bucks 42 D3
Frilford Oxon 41 H2
Frilsham W Berk 41 K5
Frimley Surrey 42 E8
Frindsbury Medway 46 C6
Fring Norfk 105 H5
Fringford Oxon 57 L3
Frinsted Kent 34 B4
Frinton-on-Sea Essex 62 F4
Friockheim Angus 196 F6
Frisby on the Wreake Leics 102 B8
Friskney Lincs 104 D2
Friston E Susx 20 B6
Friston Suffk 79 J3
Fritchley Derbys 101 G3
Fritham Hants 28 E8
Frithelstock Devon 23 G7
Frithelstock Stone Devon 23 G7
Frithville Lincs 104 A3
Frittenden Kent 33 K5
Frittiscombe Devon 7 J6
Fritton Norfk 92 F5
Fritton Norfk 93 K4
Fritwell Oxon 57 K3
Frizinghall C Brad 123 H4
Frizington Cumb 136 E4
Frocester Gloucs 55 H7
Frodesley Shrops 83 K3
Frodsham Ches W 112 D6
Frogden Border 168 B4
Frog End Cambs 76 B5
Froggatt Derbys 114 E6
Froghall Staffs 100 A3
Frogmore Devon 7 H7
Frognall Lincs 89 H2
Frog Pool Worcs 70 E2
Frogwell Cnwll 6 A3
Frolesworth Leics 87 G5
Frome Somset 27 H2
Frome St Quintin Dorset 14 B2
Fromes Hill Herefs 70 C5
Froncysyllte Denbgs 97 K4
Fron-goch Gwynd 96 D5
Fron Isaf Wrexhm 97 L4
Frosterley Dur 150 C7
Froxfield Wilts 40 F6
Froxfield Green Hants 30 B6
Fryern Hill Hants 29 H7
Fryerning Essex 61 G7
Fuinary Highld 190 C6
Fulbeck Lincs 102 F3
Fulbourn Cambs 76 D4
Fulbrook Oxon 56 E5
Fulflood Hants 29 J5
Fulford C York 124 F2
Fulford Somset 25 K5
Fulford Staffs 99 L5
Fulham Gt Lon 44 E5
Fulking W Susx 19 H4
Fullarton N Ayrs 163 H2
Fuller Street Essex 61 H5
Fullerton Hants 29 G4
Fulletby Lincs 118 D6
Fullready Warwks 72 C5
Full Sutton E R Yk 134 B7
Fullwood E Ayrs 174 E7
Fulmer Bucks 43 G4
Fulmodeston Norfk 106 B6
Fulnetby Lincs 117 H5
Fulney Lincs 103 L7
Fulstow Lincs 118 D3
Fulwell Sundld 151 J3
Fulwood Lancs 121 H4
Fulwood Sheff 114 F4
Fundenhall Norfk 92 D4
Funtington W Susx 17 L2
Funtullich P & K 184 F3
Furley Devon 13 H2
Furnace Ag & B 182 E7
Furnace Carmth 51 G5
Furness Vale Derbys 114 A5
Furneux Pelham Herts 60 C3
Furzley Hants 28 F7
Fyfield Essex 60 F6
Fyfield Hants 28 F3
Fyfield Oxon 57 H7
Fyfield Wilts 40 C6
Fyfield Wilts 40 D7
Fylingthorpe N York 143 J6
Fyning W Susx 30 D6
Fyvie Abers 216 E6

G

Gabroc Hill E Ayrs 174 E7
Gaddesby Leics 87 K2
Gaddesden Row Herts 59 H5
Gadgirth S Ayrs 163 K5

**Gaerllwyd** Mons 38 C2
**Gaerwen** IoA 108 F7
**Gailes** N Ayrs 163 H3
**Gailey** Staffs 85 G2
**Gainford** Dur 140 F4
**Gainsborough** Lincs 116 D4
**Gainsford End** Essex 77 G7
**Gairloch** Highld 219 J6
**Gairlochy** Highld 201 J8
**Gairneybridge** P & K 186 B7
**Gaitsgill** Cumb 148 C5
**Galashiels** Border 167 G3
**Galgate** Lancs 129 K7
**Galhampton** Somset 26 F5
**Gallanachbeg** Ag & B 182 B2
**Gallanachmore** Ag & B 182 B3
**Gallatown** Fife 186 E8
**Galleywood** Essex 61 H7
**Gallovie** Highld 202 E7
**Galloway Forest Park** 153 J5
**Gallowfauld** Angus 196 D7
**Gallowhill** P & K 186 B1
**Galltair** Highld 200 C2
**Galmisdale** Highld 199 G8
**Galmpton** Devon 7 G7
**Galmpton** Torbay 7 K5
**Galphay** N York 132 C5
**Galston** E Ayrs 163 L3
**Gamblesby** Cumb 149 G6
**Gamlingay** Cambs 75 J4
**Gamlingay Great Heath** Cambs 75 J4
**Gamrie** Abers 216 F2
**Gamston** Notts 101 L5
**Gamston** Notts 116 B6
**Ganavan Bay** Ag & B 182 B2
**Ganllwyd** Gwynd 96 B7
**Gannachy** Angus 196 F3
**Ganstead** E R Yk 126 E4
**Ganthorpe** N York 133 L5
**Ganton** N York 134 F4
**Garbity** Moray 215 H4
**Garboldisham** Norfk 92 B7
**Garbole** Highld 203 H1
**Garchory** Abers 205 G4
**Gardeners Green** Wokham 42 D6
**Garden of England Crematorium** Kent 46 E6
**Gardenstown** Abers 216 F2
**Garden Village** Sheff 114 E2
**Garderhouse** Shet 235 c5
**Gare Hill** Somset 27 H4
**Garelochhead** Ag & B 173 L1
**Garford** Oxon 41 H2
**Garforth** Leeds 124 B4
**Gargrave** N York 131 H8
**Gargunnock** Stirlg 184 F8
**Garlic Street** Norfk 92 E6
**Garlieston** D & G 145 K5
**Garlinge** Kent 35 J2
**Garlinge Green** Kent 34 F4
**Garlogie** Abers 206 E4
**Garmond** Abers 216 F4
**Garmouth** Moray 215 H2
**Garmston** Shrops 83 L3
**Garn-Dolbenmaen** Gwynd 95 J4
**Garrabost** W Isls 232 g2
**Garrallan** E Ayrs 164 B5
**Garras** Cnwll 3 J6
**Garreg** Gwynd 95 K4
**Garrigill** Cumb 149 J6
**Garroch** D & G 153 M6
**Garrochtrie** D & G 144 D7
**Garrochty** Ag & B 173 J7
**Garros** Highld 209 H2
**Garsdale Head** Cumb 130 E2
**Garsdon** Wilts 39 L3
**Garshall Green** Staffs 99 L5
**Garsington** Oxon 57 L7
**Garstang** Lancs 121 G2
**Garston** Herts 59 J7
**Garston** Lpool 112 B5
**Gartachossan** Ag & B 171 G6
**Gartcosh** N Lans 175 J5
**Garth** Powys 67 K5
**Garth** Wrexhm 97 K4
**Garthamlock** C Glas 175 H5
**Garthmyl** Powys 82 E4
**Garthorpe** Leics 102 D7
**Garthorpe** N Linc 125 K6
**Garth Row** Cumb 138 D7
**Gartly** Abers 215 L7
**Gartmore** Stirlg 184 C7
**Gartness** N Lans 175 K5
**Gartness** Stirlg 174 F2
**Gartocharn** W Duns 174 D2
**Garton-on-the-Wolds** E R Yk 134 F7
**Gartymore** Highld 227 H5
**Garva Bridge** Highld 202 E6
**Garvald** E Loth 178 D4
**Garvan** Highld 191 J2
**Garvard** Ag & B 171 G1
**Garve** Highld 212 B3
**Garvellachs** Ag & B 181 K5
**Garvestone** Norfk 92 B3
**Garvock** Inver 174 B4
**Garway** Herefs 54 C4
**Garyvard** W Isls 232 f3
**Gasper** Wilts 27 H5
**Gastard** Wilts 39 K6
**Gasthorpe** Norfk 91 L7
**Gaston Green** Essex 60 D5
**Gatcombe** IoW 16 F5
**Gate Burton** Lincs 116 D5
**Gateforth** N York 124 E5
**Gatehead** E Ayrs 163 K3
**Gate Helmsley** N York 133 L7
**Gatehouse** Nthumb 157 K4
**Gatehouse of Fleet** D & G 146 A4
**Gateley** Norfk 106 A7
**Gatenby** N York 132 E3
**Gateshaw** Border 168 B5
**Gateshead** Gatesd 151 G3
**Gateside** Angus 196 D7
**Gateside** E Rens 174 E6
**Gateside** Fife 186 C5
**Gateside** N Ayrs 174 C7
**Gateslack** D & G 154 F2
**Gatley** Stockp 113 J4
**Gattonside** Border 167 H3
*Gatwick Airport* W Susx 32 B5
**Gaulby** Leics 87 K4
**Gauldry** Fife 186 F3
**Gauldswell** P & K 195 K6
**Gautby** Lincs 117 K6
**Gavinton** Border 179 G7
**Gawcott** Bucks 58 B2
**Gawsworth** Ches E 113 K7
**Gawthrop** Cumb 130 D3
**Gawthwaite** Cumb 129 G3
**Gaydon** Warwks 72 D4
**Gayhurst** M Keyn 74 B5
**Gayle** N York 131 G2
**Gayles** N York 140 E5
**Gayton** Nhants 73 K4
**Gayton** Norfk 105 H8
**Gayton** Staffs 99 M6
**Gayton le Marsh** Lincs 118 F5
**Gayton Thorpe** Norfk 105 H8
**Gaywood** Norfk 105 G7
**Gazeley** Suffk 77 G2
**Gearraidh Bhaird** W Isls 232 f3
**Geary** Highld 208 D3
**Gedding** Suffk 77 L3
**Geddington** Nhants 88 C6
**Gedling** Notts 101 L4
**Gedney** Lincs 104 C7
**Gedney Broadgate** Lincs 104 C7
**Gedney Drove End** Lincs 104 D6
**Gedney Dyke** Lincs 104 C7
**Gedney Hill** Lincs 89 L2
**Geeston** Rutlnd 88 E3
**Geldeston** Norfk 93 H5
**Gellifor** Denbgs 110 F8
**Gelligaer** Caerph 37 H2
**Gellilydan** Gwynd 95 M4
**Gellinudd** Neath 51 K5
**Gellyburn** P & K 195 H8
**Gellywen** Carmth 50 C2
**Gelston** D & G 146 D3
**Gelston** Lincs 102 E4
**Gembling** E R Yk 135 H7
**Gentleshaw** Staffs 85 J2
**Georgefield** D & G 156 B4
**George Green** Bucks 43 G4
**Georgeham** Devon 23 G4
**Georgemas Junction Station** Highld 231 H4
**George Nympton** Devon 23 L6
**Georth** Ork 234 b5
**Germansweek** Devon 10 C6
**Gerrans** Cnwll 4 D8
**Gerrards Cross** Bucks 43 G3
**Gerrick** R & Cl 142 E5
**Gestingthorpe** Essex 77 J6
**Geuffordd** Powys 82 E2
**Gidea Park** Gt Lon 45 K3
**Giffnock** E Rens 175 G6
**Gifford** E Loth 178 C5
**Giffordtown** Fife 186 E5
**Giggleswick** N York 130 F6
**Gigha** Ag & B 171 L7
**Gilberdyke** E R Yk 125 K5
**Gilchriston** E Loth 178 B5
**Gilcrux** Cumb 147 K7
**Gildersome** Leeds 123 K5
**Gildingwells** Rothm 115 K4
**Gilesgate Moor** Dur 151 H6
**Gileston** V Glam 36 F6
**Gilfach** Caerph 53 J7
**Gilfach Goch** Brdgnd 36 F3
**Gilfachrheda** Cerdgn 65 L3
**Gilgarran** Cumb 136 E3
**Gillamoor** N York 133 K2
**Gillen** Highld 208 D3
**Gillesbie** D & G 155 K4
**Gilling East** N York 133 J4
**Gillingham** Dorset 27 J6
**Gillingham** Medway 46 C6
**Gillingham** Norfk 93 J5
**Gilling West** N York 140 F6
**Gillock** Highld 231 J4
**Gills** Highld 231 K2
**Gilmanscleuch** Border 166 E5
**Gilmerton** C Edin 177 J5
**Gilmerton** P & K 185 J3
**Gilmonby** Dur 140 C5
**Gilmorton** Leics 87 H6
**Gilroes Crematorium** C Leic 87 H3
**Gilsland** Nthumb 149 G2
**Gilston** Border 177 L6
**Gilston** Herts 60 D5
**Gilwern** Mons 53 K5
**Gimingham** Norfk 107 G5
**Gipping** Suffk 78 C2
**Gipsey Bridge** Lincs 103 M3
**Girdle Toll** N Ayrs 163 J2
**Girlsta** Shet 235 c5
**Girsby** N York 141 J5
**Girthon** D & G 146 A4
**Girton** Cambs 76 B3
**Girton** Notts 116 D7
**Girvan** S Ayrs 152 E3
**Gisburn** Lancs 122 C2
**Gisleham** Suffk 93 K5
**Gislingham** Suffk 78 C1
**Gissing** Norfk 92 D6
**Gittisham** Devon 12 E3
**Gladestry** Powys 68 E4
**Gladsmuir** E Loth 177 M4
**Glais** Swans 51 K5
**Glaisdale** N York 143 G6
**Glamis** Angus 196 C6
**Glanaman** Carmth 51 J3
**Glandford** Norfk 106 C4
**Glandwr** Pembks 49 K2
**Glandyfi** Cerdgn 80 F4
**Glanllynfi** Brdgnd 36 D3
**Glan-rhyd** Powys 52 B6
**Glanton** Nthumb 169 G6
**Glanvilles Wootton** Dorset 14 D2
**Glan-y-don** Flints 111 G5
**Glapthorn** Nhants 88 E5
**Glapwell** Derbys 115 J7
**Glasbury** Powys 68 D6
**Glascote** Staffs 86 B3
**Glascwm** Powys 68 D4
**Glasfryn** Conwy 96 E3
**Glasgow** C Glas 175 G5
*Glasgow Airport* Rens 174 E5
*Glasgow Prestwick Airport* S Ayrs 163 J4
**Glasgow Science Centre** C Glas 175 G5
**Glasinfryn** Gwynd 109 H7
**Glasnacardoch Bay** Highld 199 L6
**Glasnakille** Highld 199 H3
**Glassford** S Lans 175 J8
**Glasshouse** Gloucs 55 G4
**Glasshouses** N York 132 B6
**Glasslaw** Abers 216 F3
**Glasson** Cumb 148 A3
**Glasson** Lancs 129 K7
**Glassonby** Cumb 149 G7
**Glasterlaw** Angus 196 F6
**Glaston** Rutlnd 88 C4
**Glastonbury** Somset 26 D4
**Glatton** Cambs 89 H6
**Glazebrook** Warrtn 113 G3
**Glazebury** Warrtn 112 F3
**Glazeley** Shrops 84 C5
**Gleaston** Cumb 128 F5
**Glebe** Highld 202 D2
**Gledhow** Leeds 123 L3
**Gledpark** D & G 146 B5
**Gledrid** Shrops 97 L5
**Glemsford** Suffk 77 J5
**Glenallachie** Moray 215 G6
**Glenancross** Highld 199 K6
**Glenaros House** Ag & B 190 B7
**Glen Auldyn** IoM 237 d3
**Glenbarr** Ag & B 161 H3
**Glenbarry** Abers 216 B4
**Glenbeg** Highld 190 C4
**Glenbervie** Abers 197 J1
**Glenboig** N Lans 175 J5
**Glenborrodale** Highld 190 C4
**Glenbranter** Ag & B 183 G7
**Glenbreck** Border 165 K5
**Glenbrittle** Highld 198 F2
**Glenbuck** E Ayrs 164 E4
**Glencally** Angus 196 B4
**Glencaple** D & G 147 H2
**Glencarse** P & K 186 C3
**Glencoe** Highld 191 L5
**Glencothe** Border 165 L4
**Glencraig** Fife 186 C7
**Glencrosh** D & G 154 D4
**Glendale** Highld 208 B4
**Glendaruel** Ag & B 173 G2
**Glendevon** P & K 185 K6
**Glendoe Lodge** Highld 202 C4
**Glendoick** P & K 186 C3
**Glenduckie** Fife 186 D4
**Glenegedale** Ag & B 170 F7
**Glenelg** Highld 200 C2
**Glenerney** Moray 214 C5
**Glenfarg** P & K 186 B5
**Glenfield** Leics 87 G3
**Glenfinnan** Highld 191 H1
**Glenfintaig Lodge** Highld 201 K7
**Glenfoot** P & K 186 C4
**Glenfyne Lodge** Ag & B 183 H4
**Glengarnock** N Ayrs 174 C7
**Glengolly** Highld 231 G3
**Glengorm Castle** Ag & B 189 K5
**Glengrasco** Highld 209 G5
**Glenholm** Border 165 L3
**Glenhoul** D & G 154 A5

**Glenisla** Angus 195 K4
**Glenkin** Ag & B 173 K3
**Glenkindie** Abers 205 K3
**Glenlivet** Moray 214 F8
**Glenlochar** D & G 146 C3
**Glenlomond** P & K 186 C6
**Glenluce** D & G 144 E4
**Glenmassen** Ag & B 173 J2
**Glenmavis** N Lans 175 K5
**Glen Maye** IoM 237 b5
**Glenmore** Highld 209 G6
**Glenmore Lodge** Highld 204 B4
**Glen Nevis House** Highld 192 B3
**Glenochil** Clacks 185 H7
**Glen Parva** Leics 87 H4
**Glenquiech** Angus 196 C4
**Glenralloch** Ag & B 172 E5
**Glenridding** Cumb 137 L4
**Glenrothes** Fife 186 D7
**Glenshero Lodge** Highld 202 E6
**Glenstriven** Ag & B 173 J3
**Glentham** Lincs 117 G4
**Glentrool** D & G 153 H6
**Glen Trool Lodge** D & G 153 J6
**Glentruim** Highld 203 G6
**Glentworth** Lincs 116 F4
**Glenuig** Highld 190 D2
**Glenvarragill** Highld 209 G6
**Glen Vine** IoM 237 c5
**Glenwhilly** D & G 152 E7
**Glespin** S Lans 164 F4
**Glewstone** Herefs 54 E4
**Glinton** C Pete 89 H3
**Glooston** Leics 87 L4
**Glossop** Derbys 114 B3
**Gloster Hill** Nthumb 159 G2
**Gloucester** Gloucs 55 J4
**Gloucester Crematorium** Gloucs 55 J5
**Gloucester Services** Gloucs 55 J5
*Gloucestershire Airport* Gloucs 55 K4
**Glusburn** N York 122 F2
**Glutt Lodge** Highld 227 H2
**Glympton** Oxon 57 H4
**Glynarthen** Cerdgn 65 K5
**Glyn Ceiriog** Wrexhm 97 J5
**Glyncorrwg** Neath 52 D7
**Glynde** E Susx 19 L4
**Glyndyfrdwy** Denbgs 97 J4
**Glynneath** Neath 52 D6
**Glynn Valley Crematorium** Cnwll 5 H3
**Glyntaff Crematorium** Rhondd 37 H3
**Glyntawe** Powys 52 D5
**Glynteg** Carmth 65 K6
**Gnosall** Staffs 99 J7
**Gnosall Heath** Staffs 99 J7
**Goadby** Leics 87 L4
**Goadby Marwood** Leics 102 C7
**Goatacre** Wilts 40 A5
**Goathill** Dorset 26 F7
**Goathland** N York 143 H6
**Goathurst** Somset 25 K5
**Gobowen** Shrops 97 L5
**Godalming** Surrey 30 F3
**Goddard's Green** Kent 33 L6
**Godmanchester** Cambs 75 J1
**Godmanstone** Dorset 14 C3
**Godmersham** Kent 34 E5
**Godney** Somset 26 C3
**Godolphin Cross** Cnwll 3 G5
**Godre'r-graig** Neath 51 L4
**Godshill** IoW 17 G6
**Godstone** Surrey 32 C3
**Goetre** Mons 53 L6
**Goff's Oak** Herts 60 B7
**Gogar** C Edin 177 G4
**Goginan** Cerdgn 80 F7
**Golan** Gwynd 95 J4
**Golant** Cnwll 5 H5
**Golberdon** Cnwll 5 M2
**Golborne** Wigan 112 E3
**Golcar** Kirk 123 G7
**Goldcliff** Newpt 38 A4
**Golden Green** Kent 33 H4
**Goldenhill** C Stke 99 J2
**Golden Pot** Hants 30 B3
**Golders Green** Gt Lon 44 E3
**Golders Green Crematorium** Gt Lon 44 E3
**Goldhanger** Essex 61 L6
**Goldington** Bed 74 F4
**Goldsborough** N York 132 F7
**Goldsborough** N York 143 H4
**Golds Green** Sandw 85 H5
**Goldsithney** Cnwll 2 F5
**Goldsworth Park** Surrey 43 G8
**Goldthorpe** Barns 115 J2
**Goldworthy** Devon 22 F6
**Gollanfield** Highld 213 J4
**Golspie** Highld 223 H2
**Gomeldon** Wilts 28 D4
**Gomshall** Surrey 31 H2
**Gonalston** Notts 102 B3
**Gonerby Hill Foot** Lincs 102 E5
**Gonfirth** Shet 235 c4
**Good Easter** Essex 60 F5
**Gooderstone** Norfk 91 H3
**Goodleigh** Devon 23 J5
**Goodmanham** E R Yk 125 K2
**Goodmayes** Gt Lon 45 J3
**Goodnestone** Kent 34 D3
**Goodnestone** Kent 35 H4
**Goodrich** Herefs 54 E4
**Goodrington** Torbay 7 K4
**Goodshaw** Lancs 122 B5
**Goodwick** Pembks 64 C6
**Goodworth Clatford** Hants 29 G3
**Goole** E R Yk 125 H5
**Goom's Hill** Worcs 71 H4
**Goonbell** Cnwll 3 J2
**Goonhavern** Cnwll 3 K1
**Goonvrea** Cnwll 3 J2
**Goosecruives** Abers 206 E8
**Gooseford** Devon 11 G6
**Goose Green** Essex 62 D3
**Goose Green** S Glos 38 F5
**Gooseham** Cnwll 9 G2
**Goosey** Oxon 41 G3
**Goosnargh** Lancs 121 H3
**Goostrey** Ches E 113 H7
**Gordano Services** N Som 38 D5
**Gordon** Border 167 K2
**Gordon Arms Hotel** Border 166 D4
**Gordonstown** Abers 216 B3
**Gordonstown** Abers 216 D6
**Gorebridge** Mdloth 177 K6
**Gorefield** Cambs 90 B2
**Gores** Wilts 40 C8
**Gorey** Jersey 236 e7
**Goring** Oxon 41 L4
**Goring-by-Sea** W Susx 18 F5
**Gorleston on Sea** Norfk 93 L3
**Gornal Wood Crematorium** Dudley 85 G5
**Gorrachie** Abers 216 E3
**Gorran Churchtown** Cnwll 4 F7
**Gorran Haven** Cnwll 4 F7
**Gorsedd** Flints 111 G6
**Gorse Hill** Swindn 40 D3
**Gorseinon** Swans 51 H5
**Gorsgoch** Cerdgn 66 C4
**Gorslas** Carmth 51 H3
**Gorsley** Gloucs 55 G3
**Gorsley Common** Herefs 54 F3
**Gorstan** Highld 212 B2
**Gorsten** Ag & B 181 L2
**Gorsty Hill** Staffs 100 C6
**Gorthleck** Highld 202 E2
**Gorton** Manch 113 K3
**Gosbeck** Suffk 78 D4
**Gosberton** Lincs 103 L6
**Gosfield** Essex 61 J3
**Gosforth** Cumb 136 E6
**Gosforth** N u Ty 151 G2
**Gosport** Hants 17 H3
**Gossington** Gloucs 55 H7
**Gotham** Notts 101 K6
**Gotherington** Gloucs 55 L3
**Gotton** Somset 25 K5
**Goudhurst** Kent 33 J5
**Goulceby** Lincs 118 C5
**Gourdas** Abers 216 E6
**Gourdie** C Dund 186 F2
**Gourdon** Abers 197 K3
**Gourock** Inver 173 L3
**Govan** C Glas 174 F5
**Goveton** Devon 7 H6
**Govilon** Mons 53 K5
**Gowdall** E R Yk 124 F6
**Gower** Highld 212 D3
**Gower** Swans 51 G7
**Gowerton** Swans 51 H6
**Gowkhall** Fife 176 E1
**Goxhill** E R Yk 126 F2
**Goxhill** N Linc 126 D6
**Grabhair** W Isls 232 f3
**Graffham** W Susx 18 C3
**Grafham** Cambs 75 H2
**Grafham** Surrey 31 G3
**Grafton** N York 132 F6
**Grafton** Oxon 56 F7
**Grafton** Shrops 98 B8
**Grafton** Worcs 71 H6
**Grafton Flyford** Worcs 71 G4
**Grafton Regis** Nhants 73 L5
**Grafton Underwood** Nhants 88 D7
**Grafty Green** Kent 34 B5
**Graig** Conwy 109 M6
**Graigfechan** Denbgs 97 J2
**Grain** Medway 46 E5
**Grainsby** Lincs 118 C2
**Grainthorpe** Lincs 118 E3
**Grampound** Cnwll 4 E6
**Grampound Road** Cnwll 4 E5
**Gramsdal** W Isls 233 c6
**Gramsdale** W Isls 233 c6
**Granborough** Bucks 58 C3
**Granby** Notts 102 C5
**Grandborough** Warwks 72 F2
**Grand Chemins** Jersey 236 d7
**Grandes Rocques** Guern 236 c2
**Grandtully** P & K 194 E5
**Grange** Cumb 137 H4
**Grange** Medway 46 D6
**Grange** P & K 186 D3
**Grange Crossroads** Moray 215 K4
**Grange Hall** Moray 214 C3
**Grangehall** S Lans 165 J2
**Grange Hill** Essex 45 H2
**Grangemill** Derbys 100 E2
**Grange Moor** Kirk 123 J7
**Grangemouth** Falk 176 C3
**Grange of Lindores** Fife 186 D4
**Grange-over-Sands** Cumb 129 J4
**Grangepans** Falk 176 D3
**Grange Park** Nhants 73 L4
**Grangetown** R & Cl 142 C3
**Grangetown** Sundld 151 K4
**Grange Villa** Dur 151 G4
**Gransmoor** E R Yk 135 H7
**Granston** Pembks 64 C7
**Grantchester** Cambs 76 B4
**Grantham** Lincs 102 E5
**Grantham Crematorium** Lincs 102 F5
**Granton** C Edin 177 H3
**Grantown-on-Spey** Highld 214 C8
**Grantshouse** Border 179 G5
**Grasby** Lincs 117 H1
**Grasmere** Cumb 137 K5
**Grasscroft** Oldham 113 L1
**Grassendale** Lpool 111 L4
**Grassington** N York 131 J6
**Grassmoor** Derbys 115 H7
**Grassthorpe** Notts 116 C7
**Grateley** Hants 28 F3
**Graveley** Cambs 75 J2
**Graveley** Herts 59 L3
**Gravelly Hill** Birm 85 K5
**Graveney** Kent 34 E3
**Gravesend** Kent 46 A5
**Gravir** W Isls 232 f3
**Grayingham** Lincs 116 F3
**Grayrigg** Cumb 138 E7
**Grays** Thurr 45 L4
**Grayshott** Hants 30 E4
**Grayswood** Surrey 30 E4
**Greasbrough** Rothm 115 H3
**Greasby** Wirral 111 H4
**Great Abington** Cambs 76 D5
**Great Addington** Nhants 88 D7
**Great Alne** Warwks 71 K3
**Great Altcar** Lancs 111 K1
**Great Amwell** Herts 60 B5
**Great Asby** Cumb 138 F5
**Great Ashfield** Suffk 78 B2
**Great Ayton** N York 142 C5
**Great Baddow** Essex 61 H6
**Great Badminton** S Glos 39 J4
**Great Bardfield** Essex 61 G2
**Great Barford** Bed 75 G4
**Great Barr** Sandw 85 J4
**Great Barrington** Gloucs 56 E5
**Great Barrow** Ches W 112 C7
**Great Barton** Suffk 77 K2
**Great Barugh** N York 134 B4
**Great Bavington** Nthumb 158 C6
**Great Bealings** Suffk 78 F5
**Great Bedwyn** Wilts 40 F7
**Great Bentley** Essex 62 D4
**Great Billing** Nhants 74 B3
**Great Bircham** Norfk 105 J6
**Great Blakenham** Suffk 78 D4
**Great Blencow** Cumb 138 C2
**Great Bolas** Wrekin 98 F7
**Great Bookham** Surrey 31 J1
**Great Bourton** Oxon 72 F5
**Great Bowden** Leics 87 L5
**Great Bradley** Suffk 76 F4
**Great Braxted** Essex 61 K5
**Great Bricett** Suffk 78 C4
**Great Brickhill** Bucks 58 E3
**Great Bridgeford** Staffs 99 K6
**Great Brington** Nhants 73 J2
**Great Bromley** Essex 62 C3
**Great Broughton** Cumb 136 E2
**Great Broughton** N York 142 C6
**Great Budworth** Ches W 112 F6
**Great Burdon** Darltn 141 H4
**Great Burstead** Essex 46 B2

**Great Busby** N York 142 B6
**Great Carlton** Lincs 118 E4
**Great Casterton** Rutlnd 88 E2
**Great Chalfield** Wilts 39 K7
**Great Chart** Kent 34 C6
**Great Chatwell** Staffs 84 E1
**Great Chell** C Stke 99 K3
**Great Chesterford** Essex 76 D6
**Great Cheverell** Wilts 27 M1
**Great Chishill** Cambs 76 B6
**Great Clacton** Essex 62 E5
**Great Clifton** Cumb 136 E2
**Great Coates** NE Lin 126 F8
**Great Comberton** Worcs 71 G6
**Great Corby** Cumb 148 E4
**Great Cornard** Suffk 77 K6
**Great Cowden** E R Yk 126 F3
**Great Coxwell** Oxon 40 F2
**Great Cransley** Nhants 88 B7
**Great Cressingham** Norfk 91 J3
**Great Crosthwaite** Cumb 137 J3
**Great Cubley** Derbys 100 D5
**Great Cumbrae Island** N Ayrs 173 K6
**Great Dalby** Leics 87 L2
**Great Denham** Bed 74 E5
**Great Doddington** Nhants 74 C2
**Great Dunham** Norfk 91 K1
**Great Dunmow** Essex 61 G4
**Great Durnford** Wilts 28 C4
**Great Easton** Essex 60 F3
**Great Easton** Leics 88 B5
**Great Eccleston** Lancs 120 F3
**Great Ellingham** Norfk 92 B4
**Great Elm** Somset 27 H2
**Great Everdon** Nhants 73 H3
**Great Eversden** Cambs 75 L4
**Great Fencote** N York 132 D2
**Great Finborough** Suffk 78 B3
**Greatford** Lincs 88 F2
**Great Fransham** Norfk 91 K2
**Great Gaddesden** Herts 59 G5
**Greatgate** Staffs 100 B4
**Great Gidding** Cambs 89 G6
**Great Givendale** E R Yk 134 C8
**Great Glemham** Suffk 79 H3
**Great Glen** Leics 87 J4
**Great Gonerby** Lincs 102 E5
**Great Gransden** Cambs 75 J4
**Great Green** Cambs 75 K5
**Great Green** Suffk 77 K4
**Great Habton** N York 134 B4
**Great Hale** Lincs 103 J4
**Great Hallingbury** Essex 60 E4
**Greatham** Hants 30 C5
**Greatham** Hartpl 141 L2
**Greatham** W Susx 18 E3
**Great Hampden** Bucks 58 D7
**Great Harrowden** Nhants 74 C1
**Great Harwood** Lancs 121 L4
**Great Haseley** Oxon 57 M7
**Great Hatfield** E R Yk 126 F3
**Great Haywood** Staffs 100 A7
**Great Heck** N York 124 E6
**Great Henny** Essex 77 K6
**Great Hinton** Wilts 39 K8
**Great Hockham** Norfk 91 L5
**Great Holland** Essex 62 E4
**Great Hollands** Br For 42 E6
**Great Horkesley** Essex 62 B2
**Great Hormead** Herts 60 C3
**Great Horton** C Brad 123 H4
**Great Horwood** Bucks 58 C2
**Great Houghton** Barns 115 H1
**Great Houghton** Nhants 73 L3
**Great Hucklow** Derbys 114 D6
**Great Kelk** E R Yk 135 H7
**Great Kimble** Bucks 58 D6
**Great Kingshill** Bucks 42 E2
**Great Langdale** Cumb 137 J6
**Great Langton** N York 141 H7
**Great Leighs** Essex 61 H4
**Great Limber** Lincs 126 E8
**Great Linford** M Keyn 74 C6
**Great Livermere** Suffk 77 K1
**Great Longstone** Derbys 114 D6
**Great Lumley** Dur 151 H5
**Great Malvern** Worcs 70 D5
**Great Maplestead** Essex 77 J7
**Great Marton** Bpool 120 D4
**Great Massingham** Norfk 105 J7
**Great Milton** Oxon 57 L7
**Great Missenden** Bucks 58 E7
**Great Mitton** Lancs 121 K3
**Great Mongeham** Kent 35 K4
**Great Moulton** Norfk 92 E5
**Great Musgrave** Cumb 139 H4
**Great Ness** Shrops 98 B8
**Great Notley** Essex 61 H4
**Great Oak** Mons 54 B6
**Great Oakley** Essex 62 E3
**Great Oakley** Nhants 88 C6
**Great Offley** Herts 59 J3
**Great Ormside** Cumb 139 G4
**Great Orton** Cumb 148 B4
**Great Ouseburn** N York 133 G6
**Great Oxendon** Nhants 87 K6
**Great Park** N u Ty 158 F7
**Great Parndon** Essex 60 C6
**Great Paxton** Cambs 75 H2
**Great Plumpton** Lancs 120 E4
**Great Plumstead** Norfk 93 G2
**Great Ponton** Lincs 102 F6
**Great Preston** Leeds 124 B5
**Great Raveley** Cambs 89 J7
**Great Rissington** Gloucs 56 D5
**Great Rollright** Oxon 56 F2
**Great Ryburgh** Norfk 106 A6
**Great Ryton** Shrops 83 J3
**Great Saling** Essex 61 H3
**Great Salkeld** Cumb 148 F7
**Great Sampford** Essex 76 F7
**Great Saughall** Ches W 111 K7
**Great Shefford** W Berk 41 G5
**Great Shelford** Cambs 76 C4
**Great Smeaton** N York 141 H6
**Great Snoring** Norfk 105 M5
**Great Somerford** Wilts 39 L4
**Great Soudley** Shrops 99 G6
**Great Stainton** Darltn 141 H3
**Great Stambridge** Essex 46 E2
**Great Staughton** Cambs 75 G2
**Great Steeping** Lincs 118 F8
**Great Stoke** S Glos 38 F4
**Greatstone-on-Sea** Kent 21 L2
**Great Strickland** Cumb 138 D3
**Great Stukeley** Cambs 89 J8
**Great Sturton** Lincs 117 K6
**Great Swinburne** Nthumb 158 B6
**Great Tew** Oxon 57 H3
**Great Tey** Essex 61 L3
**Great Thurlow** Suffk 76 F4
**Great Torrington** Devon 23 H7
**Great Tosson** Nthumb 158 C3
**Great Totham** Essex 61 K5
**Great Totham** Essex 61 L5
**Great Urswick** Cumb 129 G5
**Great Wakering** Essex 46 F3
**Great Waldingfield** Suffk 77 K5
**Great Walsingham** Norfk 105 M5
**Great Waltham** Essex 61 H5
**Great Warley** Essex 45 L2
**Great Washbourne** Gloucs 71 H7
**Great Weeke** Devon 11 G7
**Great Wenham** Suffk 78 C6
**Great Whittington** Nthumb 158 C7
**Great Wigborough** Essex 62 A5
**Great Wilbraham** Cambs 76 D3
**Great Wishford** Wilts 28 B4
**Great Witcombe** Gloucs 55 K5
**Great Witley** Worcs 70 D2
**Great Wolford** Warwks 72 B7
**Greatworth** Nhants 73 G6
**Great Wratting** Suffk 77 G5
**Great Wymondley** Herts 59 K3
**Great Wyrley** Staffs 85 H3
**Great Yarmouth** Norfk 93 L3
**Great Yarmouth Crematorium** Norfk 93 K3
**Great Yeldham** Essex 77 H6
**Greenburn** W Loth 176 C6
**Green End** Herts 60 B2
**Green End** Herts 60 B4
**Greenfield** Ag & B 173 M1
**Greenfield** C Beds 74 F7
**Greenfield** Flints 111 H6
**Greenfield** Highld 201 J5
**Greenfield** Oldham 113 M2
**Greenford** Gt Lon 43 J4
**Greengairs** N Lans 175 K4
**Greengates** C Brad 123 J3
**Greenham** Somset 25 G7
**Green Hammerton** N York 133 G7
**Greenhaugh** Nthumb 157 K5
**Greenhead** Nthumb 149 H3
**Green Heath** Staffs 85 H2
**Greenhill** D & G 155 J6
**Greenhill** Falk 175 L3
**Greenhill** Kent 47 K6
**Greenhill** S Lans 165 H3
**Greenhills** S Lans 175 H7
**Greenhithe** Kent 45 L5
**Greenholm** E Ayrs 164 B3
**Greenhouse** Border 167 H5
**Greenhow Hill** N York 131 L6
**Greenland** Highld 231 J3
**Greenland** Sheff 115 H4
**Greenlaw** Border 167 L1
**Greenlea** D & G 155 H6
**Greenloaning** P & K 185 H6
**Greenmount** Bury 122 B7
**Greenock** Inver 174 B3
**Greenodd** Cumb 129 G3
**Green Ore** Somset 26 E2
**Green Quarter** Cumb 138 C6
**Greenshields** S Lans 165 K2
**Greenside** Gatesd 150 E3
**Greenside** Kirk 123 H7
**Greens Norton** Nhants 73 J4
**Greenstead Green** Essex 61 K3
**Green Street** Herts 59 K7
**Green Street** Herts 60 D4
**Green Tye** Herts 60 C4
**Greenway** Somset 25 L6
**Greenwich** Gt Lon 45 G4
**Greenwich Maritime** Gt Lon 45 H4
**Greet** Gloucs 56 B3
**Greete** Shrops 69 L1
**Greetham** Lincs 118 D7
**Greetham** Rutlnd 88 D2
**Greetland** Calder 123 G6
**Greinton** Somset 26 B4
**Grenaby** IoM 237 b6
**Grendon** Nhants 74 C3
**Grendon** Warwks 86 C4
**Grendon Underwood** Bucks 58 B4
**Grenoside** Sheff 115 G3
**Grenoside Crematorium** Sheff 114 F3
**Greosabhagh** W Isls 232 e4
**Gresford** Wrexhm 97 M2
**Gresham** Norfk 106 E5
**Greshornish** Highld 208 E4
**Gressenhall** Norfk 91 L1
**Gressenhall Green** Norfk 91 L1
**Gressingham** Lancs 130 B5
**Greta Bridge** Dur 140 D5
**Gretna** D & G 148 B2
**Gretna Green** D & G 148 B2
**Gretna Services** D & G 148 B2
**Gretton** Gloucs 56 A2
**Gretton** Nhants 88 C5
**Gretton** Shrops 83 K4
**Grewelthorpe** N York 132 C4
**Greyrigg** D & G 155 J4
**Greys Green** Oxon 42 B4
**Greysouthen** Cumb 136 E2
**Greystoke** Cumb 138 B2
**Greystone** Angus 196 E7
**Greywell** Hants 30 B2
**Griff** Warwks 86 D5
**Griffithstown** Torfn 53 L7
**Grimeford Village** Lancs 121 J7
**Grimesthorpe** Sheff 115 G4
**Grimethorpe** Barns 124 C8
**Grimley** Worcs 70 E3
**Grimmet** S Ayrs 163 H7
**Grimoldby** Lincs 118 E4
**Grimpo** Shrops 98 A7
**Grimsargh** Lancs 121 H4
**Grimsby** NE Lin 127 G7
**Grimsby Crematorium** NE Lin 118 C1
**Grimscote** Nhants 73 J4
**Grimscott** Cnwll 9 H4
**Grimshader** W Isls 232 f3
**Grimsthorpe** Lincs 103 H7
**Grimston** Leics 102 B7
**Grimston** Norfk 105 H7
**Grimstone** Dorset 14 C4
**Grimstone End** Suffk 77 L2
**Grindale** E R Yk 135 H5
**Grindleford** Derbys 114 E6
**Grindleton** Lancs 121 L2
**Grindley Brook** Shrops 98 D4
**Grindlow** Derbys 114 D6
**Grindon** Staffs 100 B2
**Gringley on the Hill** Notts 116 C4
**Grinsdale** Cumb 148 C4
**Grinshill** Shrops 98 D7
**Grinton** N York 140 D7

**Griomaisiader** W Isls 232 f3
**Grishipoll** Ag & B 188 F4
**Gristhorpe** N York 135 H3
**Griston** Norfk 91 L4
**Gritley** Ork 234 d6
**Grittenham** Wilts 40 B4
**Grittleton** Wilts 39 K4
**Grizebeck** Cumb 128 F3
**Grizedale** Cumb 137 K7
**Groby** Leics 87 G3
**Groes** Conwy 110 D8
**Groes-faen** Rhondd 37 G4
**Groeslon** Gwynd 95 H2
**Groes-Wen** Caerph 37 H3
**Grogarry** W Isls 233 b7
**Grogport** Ag & B 161 K1
**Groigearraidh** W Isls 233 b7
**Gronant** Flints 110 F5
**Groombridge** E Susx 32 F5
**Grosebay** W Isls 232 e4
**Grosmont** Mons 54 B3
**Grosmont** N York 143 H6
**Groton** Suffk 77 L6
**Grouville** Jersey 236 e7
**Grove** Notts 116 C5
**Grove** Oxon 41 H3
**Grove Green** Kent 33 K3
**Grove Park** Gt Lon 45 H5
**Grovesend** Swans 51 H5
**Gruinard** Highld 219 L4
**Gruinart** Ag & B 170 F5
**Grula** Highld 208 F8
**Gruline** Ag & B 190 B7
**Grundisburgh** Suffk 78 F4
**Gruting** Shet 235 c5
**Grutness** Shet 235 c8
**Gualachulain** Highld 192 B7
**Guardbridge** Fife 187 G4
**Guarlford** Worcs 70 E5
**Guay** P & K 194 F6
**Guernsey** Guern 236 c3
*Guernsey Airport* Guern 236 c3
**Guestling Green** E Susx 21 G3
**Guestling Thorn** E Susx 21 G3
**Guestwick** Norfk 106 C6
**Guide Bridge** Tamesd 113 L3
**Guilden Morden** Cambs 75 K5
**Guilden Sutton** Ches W 112 C7
**Guildford** Surrey 31 G2
**Guildford Crematorium** Surrey 31 G3
**Guildtown** P & K 186 B2
**Guilsborough** Nhants 87 J8
**Guilsfield** Powys 82 E2
**Guiltreehill** S Ayrs 163 J7
**Guineaford** Devon 23 J4
**Guisborough** R & Cl 142 D4
**Guiseley** Leeds 123 J3
**Guist** Norfk 106 B7
**Guiting Power** Gloucs 56 C3
**Gullane** E Loth 178 B2
**Gulval** Cnwll 2 E5
**Gulworthy** Devon 6 C2
**Gumfreston** Pembks 49 J7
**Gumley** Leics 87 K5
**Gunby** Lincs 102 E7
**Gunby** Lincs 118 F7
**Gundleton** Hants 29 L5
**Gun Hill** E Susx 20 C3
**Gunn** Devon 23 K5
**Gunnerside** N York 139 L7
**Gunnerton** Nthumb 158 A7
**Gunness** N Linc 125 K7
**Gunnislake** Cnwll 6 C2
**Gunnista** Shet 235 d6
**Gunthorpe** C Pete 89 H3
**Gunthorpe** N Linc 116 D3
**Gunthorpe** Norfk 106 B5
**Gunthorpe** Notts 102 B4
**Gunwalloe** Cnwll 3 H6
**Gurnard** IoW 16 F4
**Gurney Slade** Somset 26 F2
**Gurnos** Powys 52 B6
**Gussage All Saints** Dorset 15 J1
**Gussage St Andrew** Dorset 27 L8
**Gussage St Michael** Dorset 15 J1
**Guston** Kent 35 J5
**Gutcher** Shet 235 d2
**Guthrie** Angus 196 F6
**Guyhirn** Cambs 90 B3
**Guyzance** Nthumb 158 F2
**Gwaenysgor** Flints 110 F5
**Gwalchmai** IoA 108 E6
**Gwaun-Cae-Gurwen** Carmth 51 K3
**Gweek** Cnwll 3 J6
**Gwenddwr** Powys 68 B6
**Gwennap** Cnwll 3 J4
Gwennap Mining District Cnwll 3 K3
**Gwent Crematorium** Mons 37 L2
**Gwernaffield** Flints 111 H7
**Gwernesney** Mons 54 B7
**Gwernogle** Carmth 66 C7
**Gwernymynydd** Flints 97 J1
**Gwespyr** Flints 110 F5
**Gwinear** Cnwll 3 G4
**Gwithian** Cnwll 3 G3
**Gwyddelwern** Denbgs 97 G3
**Gwyddgrug** Carmth 66 B7
**Gwytherin** Conwy 96 D1

## H

**Habberley** Shrops 83 H3
**Habberley** Worcs 84 E7
**Habergham** Lancs 122 B4
**Habertoft** Lincs 119 G7
**Habrough** NE Lin 126 E7
**Hacconby** Lincs 103 J7
**Haceby** Lincs 103 G5
**Hacheston** Suffk 79 G3
**Hackbridge** Gt Lon 44 F6
**Hackenthorpe** Sheff 115 H5
**Hackford** Norfk 92 C3
**Hackforth** N York 132 C2
**Hackland** Ork 234 c5
**Hackleton** Nhants 74 B4
**Hacklinge** Kent 35 J4
**Hackness** N York 134 F2
**Hackney** Gt Lon 45 G3
**Hackthorn** Lincs 117 G5
**Hackthorpe** Cumb 138 D3
**Hadden** Border 168 B3
**Haddenham** Bucks 58 C6
**Haddenham** Cambs 90 C7
**Haddington** E Loth 178 B4
**Haddington** Lincs 116 E8
**Haddiscoe** Norfk 93 J4
**Haddo** Abers 216 F6
**Haddon** Cambs 89 G5
**Hadfield** Derbys 114 A3
**Hadham Ford** Herts 60 C4
**Hadleigh** Essex 46 D3
**Hadleigh** Suffk 78 B6
**Hadley** Worcs 70 F2
**Hadley** Wrekin 84 C2
**Hadley End** Staffs 100 C7
**Hadley Wood** Gt Lon 44 E1
**Hadlow** Kent 33 H3
**Hadlow Down** E Susx 20 B2
**Hadnall** Shrops 98 D7
Hadrian's Wall 150 B2
**Hadstock** Essex 76 D5
**Hadzor** Worcs 71 G3
**Haggersta** Shet 235 c5
**Haggerston** Nthumb 168 F2
**Haggs** Falk 175 L3
**Hagley** Herefs 69 L6
**Hagley** Worcs 85 G7
**Hagworthingham** Lincs 118 D7
**Haile** Cumb 136 E5
**Hailey** Oxon 57 G5
**Hailsham** E Susx 20 C4
**Hail Weston** Cambs 75 H3
**Hainault** Gt Lon 45 J2
**Hainford** Norfk 106 F8
**Hainton** Lincs 117 K5
**Haisthorpe** E R Yk 135 H6
**Hakin** Pembks 48 F6
**Halam** Notts 102 B2
**Halbeath** Fife 176 F1
**Halberton** Devon 24 F8
**Halcro** Highld 231 J4
**Hale** Cumb 129 K4
**Hale** Halton 112 C5
**Hale** Hants 28 D7
**Hale** Surrey 30 D2
**Hale** Traffd 113 H4
**Halebarns** Traffd 113 H4
**Hales** Norfk 93 H4
**Hales** Staffs 99 G5
**Halesowen** Dudley 85 G6
**Hales Place** Kent 34 F3
**Hale Street** Kent 33 H4
**Halesworth** Suffk 93 H7
**Halewood** Knows 112 C4
**Halford** Devon 7 J2
**Halford** Warwks 72 C5
**Halfpenny Green** Staffs 84 E5
**Halfway House** Shrops 83 G2
**Halfway Houses** Kent 46 F5
**Halifax** Calder 123 G5
**Halket** E Ayrs 174 D7
**Halkirk** Highld 231 G4
**Halkyn** Flints 111 H7
**Hall** E Rens 174 D7
**Halland** E Susx 20 A3
**Hallaton** Leics 87 L4
**Hallatrow** BaNES 38 F8
**Hallbankgate** Cumb 149 G3
**Hall Dunnerdale** Cumb 137 H7
**Hallen** S Glos 38 D4
**Hallgarth** Dur 151 H6
**Hallglen** Falk 176 B3
**Hall Green** Birm 85 K7
**Hallin** Highld 208 D3
**Halling** Medway 46 B7
**Hallington** Lincs 118 D4
**Hallington** Nthumb 158 C6
**Halliwell** Bolton 121 K7
**Halloughton** Notts 102 B3
**Hallow** Worcs 70 E3
**Hall's Green** Herts 59 L3
**Hallyne** Border 166 B2
**Halmore** Gloucs 55 G7
**Halnaker** W Susx 18 B4
**Halsall** Lancs 120 E7
**Halse** Nhants 73 H6
**Halse** Somset 25 H5
**Halsetown** Cnwll 2 E4
**Halsham** E R Yk 127 G5
**Halstead** Essex 61 K2
**Halstead** Kent 45 J7
**Halstead** Leics 87 L3
**Halstock** Dorset 14 A2
**Haltemprice Crematorium** E R Yk 126 C4
**Haltham** Lincs 118 C8
**Halton** Bucks 58 E6
**Halton** Halton 112 D5
**Halton** Lancs 129 K6
**Halton** Leeds 123 L4
**Halton** Nthumb 150 C2
**Halton** Wrexhm 97 L4
**Halton East** N York 131 K8
**Halton Gill** N York 131 G4
**Halton Holegate** Lincs 118 F7
**Halton Lea Gate** Nthumb 149 H4
**Halton Shields** Nthumb 150 C2
**Halton West** N York 130 F8
**Haltwhistle** Nthumb 149 J3
**Halvergate** Norfk 93 J3
**Halwell** Devon 7 H5
**Halwill** Devon 10 C5
**Halwill Junction** Devon 10 C5
**Ham** Devon 13 G3
**Ham** Gloucs 55 G7
**Ham** Gt Lon 44 D5
**Ham** Kent 35 J4
**Ham** Somset 25 L6
**Ham** Wilts 41 G7
**Hambleden** Bucks 42 C3
**Hambledon** Hants 29 M7
**Hambledon** Surrey 30 F4
**Hamble-le-Rice** Hants 16 F2
**Hambleton** Lancs 120 E3
**Hambleton** N York 124 E4
**Hambridge** Somset 26 B6
**Hambrook** W Susx 17 L2
**Hameringham** Lincs 118 D7
**Hamerton** Cambs 89 G7
**Ham Green** Worcs 71 H2
**Hamilton** S Lans 175 J7
Hamilton Services S Lans 175 J6
**Hamlet** Dorset 14 B2
**Hammersmith** Gt Lon 44 E4
**Hammerwich** Staffs 85 J3
**Hammoon** Dorset 27 J8
**Hamnavoe** Shet 235 c6
**Hampden Park** E Susx 20 C5
**Hampnett** Gloucs 56 C5
**Hampole** Donc 124 D7
**Hampreston** Dorset 15 K3
**Hampstead** Gt Lon 44 E3
**Hampstead Norreys** W Berk 41 K5
**Hampsthwaite** N York 132 C7
**Hampton** C Pete 89 H5
**Hampton** Gt Lon 43 J6
**Hampton** Kent 47 K6
**Hampton** Shrops 84 D6
**Hampton** Swindn 40 D3
**Hampton** Worcs 71 H5
**Hampton Bishop** Herefs 69 L6
Hampton Court Palace Gt Lon 44 D6
**Hampton Heath** Ches W 98 D3
**Hampton-in-Arden** Solhll 86 B7
**Hampton Lovett** Worcs 70 F2
**Hampton Lucy** Warwks 72 B3
**Hampton Magna** Warwks 72 C2
**Hampton Poyle** Oxon 57 J5
**Hampton Wick** Gt Lon 44 D6
**Hamptworth** Wilts 28 E7
**Hamsey** E Susx 19 L3
**Hamstall Ridware** Staffs 100 C8
**Hamstead** Birm 85 J5
**Hamstead Marshall** W Berk 41 H7
**Hamsterley** Dur 140 E2
**Hamsterley** Dur 150 E4
**Hamstreet** Kent 34 D7
**Ham Street** Somset 26 D4
**Hamworthy** Poole 15 J4
**Hanbury** Staffs 100 D6
**Hanbury** Worcs 71 G2
**Hanchurch** Staffs 99 J4
**Handa Island** Highld 228 A6
**Hand and Pen** Devon 12 D4
**Handbridge** Ches W 112 B7
**Handcross** W Susx 31 L5
**Handforth** Ches E 113 J5
**Handley** Ches W 98 C2
**Handley** Derbys 101 G1
**Handsworth** Birm 85 J5
**Handsworth** Sheff 115 H4
**Hanford** C Stke 99 K4

**Hanging Heaton** Kirk....123 K6
**Hanging Houghton** Nhants....87 L8
**Hanging Langford** Wilts....28 B4
**Hangleton** Br & H....19 H4
**Hanham** S Glos....38 F6
**Hankelow** Ches E....98 F4
**Hankerton** Wilts....39 L3
**Hanley** C Stke....99 K3
**Hanley Castle** Worcs....70 E6
**Hanley Child** Worcs....70 B2
**Hanley Swan** Worcs....70 E6
**Hanley William** Worcs....70 C2
**Hanlith** N York....131 G7
**Hanmer** Wrexhm....98 C4
**Hannaford** Devon....23 J5
**Hannington** Hants....29 K1
**Hannington** Nhants....74 B1
**Hannington** Swindn....40 D2
**Hannington Wick** Swindn....40 D2
**Hanslope** M Keyn....74 B5
**Hanthorpe** Lincs....103 H7
**Hanwell** Gt Lon....44 D4
**Hanwell** Oxon....72 E5
**Hanwood** Shrops....83 J2
**Hanworth** Gt Lon....43 J6
**Hanworth** Norfk....106 E5
**Happendon** S Lans....165 G3
Happendon Services S Lans....165 G3
**Happisburgh** Norfk....107 H6
**Happisburgh Common** Norfk....107 H6
**Hapsford** Ches W....112 C6
**Hapton** Lancs....122 B4
**Hapton** Norfk....92 E4
**Harberton** Devon....7 H4
**Harbertonford** Devon....7 H5
**Harbledown** Kent....34 F3
**Harborne** Birm....85 H6
**Harborough Magna** Warwks....86 F7
**Harbottle** Nthumb....158 B2
**Harbourneford** Devon....7 G4
**Harbury** Warwks....72 D3
**Harby** Leics....102 C6
**Harby** Notts....116 E7
**Harcombe** Devon....11 K8
**Harcombe** Devon....12 F4
**Harcombe Bottom** Devon....13 J4
**Harden** C Brad....123 G3
**Harden** Wsall....85 H4
**Hardenhuish** Wilts....39 K5
**Hardgate** Abers....206 E5
**Hardgate** D & G....146 E2
**Hardgate** W Duns....174 F4
**Hardham** W Susx....18 E3
**Hardingham** Norfk....92 C3
**Hardingstone** Nhants....73 L3
**Hardington** Somset....27 H2
**Hardington Mandeville** Somset....13 M1
**Hardington Marsh** Somset....13 M1
**Hardington Moor** Somset....26 D8
**Hardisworthy** Devon....22 C7
**Hardley** Hants....16 E2
**Hardley Street** Norfk....93 H4
**Hardraw** N York....131 G2
**Hardstoft** Derbys....115 H8
**Hardway** Hants....17 H3
**Hardway** Somset....27 G5
**Hardwick** Bucks....58 D4
**Hardwick** Cambs....75 L3
**Hardwick** Nhants....74 B1
**Hardwick** Norfk....92 F5
**Hardwick** Oxon....57 G6
**Hardwick** Oxon....57 L3
**Hardwick** Wsall....85 J4
**Hardwicke** Gloucs....55 H5
**Hardwicke** Gloucs....55 K3
Hardwick Hall Derbys....115 J8
**Hardy's Green** Essex....61 M4
**Hare Croft** C Brad....123 G4
**Harefield** Gt Lon....43 H3
**Hare Green** Essex....62 D3
**Hare Hatch** Wokham....42 D5
**Harehill** Derbys....100 D5
**Harehills** Leeds....123 L4
**Harelaw** Border....167 H5
**Harelaw** D & G....156 D6
**Harescombe** Gloucs....55 J6
**Haresfield** Gloucs....55 J6
**Harestock** Hants....29 J5
**Hare Street** Essex....60 C6
**Hare Street** Herts....60 C3
**Harewood** Leeds....123 L2
**Harewood End** Herefs....54 D3
**Harford** Devon....6 F4
**Hargrave** Ches W....98 C1
**Hargrave** Nhants....74 F1
**Hargrave** Suffk....77 H3
**Harkstead** Suffk....78 E7
**Harlaston** Staffs....86 B2
**Harlaxton** Lincs....102 E6
**Harlech** Gwynd....95 K6
Harlech Castle Gwynd....95 K6
**Harlescott** Shrops....83 K1
**Harlesden** Gt Lon....44 E4
**Harlesthorpe** Derbys....115 J6
**Harleston** Devon....7 J6
**Harleston** Norfk....92 F6
**Harleston** Suffk....78 B3
**Harlestone** Nhants....73 K2
**Harle Syke** Lancs....122 C4
**Harley** Rothm....115 G2
**Harley** Shrops....83 L3
**Harlington** C Beds....59 G2
**Harlington** Donc....115 J2
**Harlington** Gt Lon....43 H5
**Harlosh** Highld....208 D6
**Harlow** Essex....60 D6
Harlow Carr RHS N York....132 D8
**Harlow Hill** Nthumb....150 D2
**Harlthorpe** E R Yk....125 H3
**Harlton** Cambs....75 L4
**Harlyn** Cnwll....4 D2
**Harman's Cross** Dorset....15 J6
**Harmby** N York....131 L2
**Harmer Green** Herts....59 L5
**Harmer Hill** Shrops....98 C7
**Harmston** Lincs....116 F8
**Harnage** Shrops....83 L3
**Harnhill** Gloucs....56 B7
**Harold Hill** Gt Lon....45 K2
**Haroldston West** Pembks....48 E4
**Haroldswick** Shet....235 e1
**Harold Wood** Gt Lon....45 K3
**Harome** N York....133 K3
**Harpenden** Herts....59 J5
**Harpford** Devon....12 E4
**Harpham** E R Yk....135 H7
**Harpley** Norfk....105 J7
**Harpley** Worcs....70 C3
**Harpole** Nhants....73 K3
**Harpsdale** Highld....231 G4
**Harpswell** Lincs....116 F4
**Harpurhey** Manch....113 K2
**Harraby** Cumb....148 D4
**Harracott** Devon....23 J6
**Harrapool** Highld....199 K2
**Harrietfield** P & K....185 K2
**Harrietsham** Kent....33 L3
**Harringay** Gt Lon....44 F3
**Harrington** Cumb....136 D3
**Harrington** Lincs....118 E6
**Harrington** Nhants....87 L7
**Harringworth** Nhants....88 D4
**Harris** W Isls....232 d4
**Harrogate** N York....132 D7
**Harrogate Crematorium** N York....132 E8
**Harrold** Bed....74 D3
**Harrow** Gt Lon....44 D3
**Harrowbarrow** Cnwll....6 B2
**Harrowgate Village** Darltn....141 H4
**Harrow Green** Suffk....77 J4
**Harrow on the Hill** Gt Lon....44 D3
**Harrow Weald** Gt Lon....44 D2
**Harston** Cambs....76 B4
**Harston** Leics....102 D6
**Harswell** E R Yk....125 J3
**Hart** Hartpl....151 L7
**Hartburn** Nthumb....158 D5
**Hartburn** S on T....141 K4
**Hartest** Suffk....77 J4
**Hartfield** E Susx....32 E6
**Hartford** Cambs....89 J8
**Hartford** Ches W....112 F6
**Hartfordbridge** Hants....42 C8
**Hartford End** Essex....61 G4
**Hartforth** N York....140 F6
**Hartgrove** Dorset....27 J7
**Harthill** Ches W....98 D2
**Harthill** N Lans....176 B5
**Harthill** Rothm....115 J5
**Hartington** Derbys....100 C1
**Hartland** Devon....22 D6
**Hartland Quay** Devon....22 C6
**Hartlebury** Worcs....70 E1
**Hartlepool** Hartpl....151 L7
**Hartlepool Crematorium** Hartpl....142 B2
**Hartley** Cumb....139 H5
**Hartley** Kent....33 K6
**Hartley** Kent....45 L6
**Hartley Wespall** Hants....42 B8
**Hartley Wintney** Hants....30 C1
**Hartlip** Kent....46 D7
**Harton** N York....133 L6
**Harton** S Tyne....151 J2
**Hartpury** Gloucs....55 J3
**Hartshead** Kirk....123 J6
Hartshead Moor Services Calder....123 H5
**Hartshill** C Stke....99 K4
**Hartshill** Warwks....86 D5
**Hartshorne** Derbys....100 F7
**Hartwell** Nhants....73 L4
**Hartwith** N York....132 C6
**Hartwood** N Lans....175 L6
**Hartwoodmyres** Border....166 F4
**Harvel** Kent....46 A7
**Harvington** Worcs....71 J5
**Harvington** Worcs....84 F8
**Harwell** Notts....116 B3
**Harwell** Oxon....41 J3
**Harwich** Essex....62 F2
**Harwood Dale** N York....143 K7
**Harwood Park Crematorium** Herts....59 L4
**Harworth** Notts....115 L3
**Hasbury** Dudley....85 G6
**Hascombe** Surrey....31 G4
**Haselbech** Nhants....87 K7
**Haselbury Plucknett** Somset....13 L1
**Haseley** Warwks....72 B2
**Haselor** Warwks....71 K3
**Hasfield** Gloucs....55 J3
**Haskayne** Lancs....120 E8
**Hasketon** Suffk....78 F4
**Haslemere** Surrey....30 E5
**Haslingden** Lancs....122 B6
**Haslingfield** Cambs....76 B4
**Haslington** Ches E....99 G2
**Hassingham** Norfk....93 H3
**Hassocks** W Susx....19 J3
**Hassop** Derbys....114 E6
**Haster** Highld....231 K5
**Hastingleigh** Kent....34 E5
**Hastings** E Susx....21 G4
**Hastings Crematorium** E Susx....21 G3
**Hastingwood** Essex....60 D6
**Hastoe** Herts....58 F6
**Haswell** Dur....151 J6
**Haswell Plough** Dur....151 J6
**Hatch Beauchamp** Somset....25 L7
**Hatch End** Gt Lon....43 J3
**Hatchmere** Ches W....112 D6
**Hatcliffe** NE Lin....117 K2
**Hatfield** Donc....125 G8
**Hatfield** Herefs....69 L3
**Hatfield** Herts....59 L6
**Hatfield Broad Oak** Essex....60 E5
**Hatfield Heath** Essex....60 E5
**Hatfield Peverel** Essex....61 J5
**Hatfield Woodhouse** Donc....125 G8
**Hatford** Oxon....41 G2
**Hatherden** Hants....29 G2
**Hatherleigh** Devon....10 D4
**Hathern** Leics....101 J7
**Hatherop** Gloucs....56 D6
**Hathersage** Derbys....114 E5
**Hathersage Booths** Derbys....114 E5
**Hatherton** Ches E....99 G3
**Hatherton** Staffs....85 G2
**Hatley St George** Cambs....75 K4
**Hatt** Cnwll....6 B4
**Hattersley** Tamesd....113 M3
**Hatton** Abers....217 K6
**Hatton** Angus....196 D7
**Hatton** Derbys....100 E6
**Hatton** Gt Lon....43 J5
**Hatton** Lincs....117 K6
**Hatton** Shrops....83 J5
**Hatton** Warrtn....112 E5
**Hatton** Warwks....72 B2
**Hatton of Fintray** Abers....206 F3
**Haugh** E Ayrs....163 L4
**Haugham** Lincs....118 D5
**Haughhead** E Duns....175 G3
**Haughley** Suffk....78 B3
**Haughley Green** Suffk....78 B2
**Haugh of Glass** Moray....215 J6
**Haugh of Urr** D & G....146 E2
**Haughs of Kinnaird** Angus....197 G5
**Haughton** Ches E....98 E2
**Haughton** Shrops....98 B6
**Haughton** Staffs....99 K7
**Haughton le Skerne** Darltn....141 H4
**Haultwick** Herts....60 B4
**Haunton** Staffs....86 B2
**Hautes Croix** Jersey....236 c6
**Hauxton** Cambs....76 B4
**Havant** Hants....17 K2
**Havant Crematorium** Hants....17 K2
**Havenstreet** IoW....17 G4
**Havercroft** Wakefd....124 B7
**Haverfordwest** Pembks....48 F4
**Haverhill** Suffk....76 F5
**Haverigg** Cumb....128 E4
**Havering-atte-Bower** Gt Lon....45 K2
**Haversham** M Keyn....74 B6
**Haverthwaite** Cumb....129 H3
**Havyatt** N Som....38 C7
**Hawarden** Flints....111 J7
**Hawbush Green** Essex....61 J4
**Hawen** Cerdgn....65 K5
**Hawes** N York....131 G2
**Hawe's Green** Norfk....92 F4
**Hawford** Worcs....70 E3
**Hawick** Border....167 G6
**Hawkchurch** Devon....13 J3

Hawkedon Suffk 77 H4
Hawkeridge Wilts 27 K2
Hawkesbury S Glos 39 H3
Hawkesbury Upton S Glos 39 H3
Hawkhurst Kent 33 K6
Hawkinge Kent 35 G6
Hawkinge Crematorium Kent 35 G6
Hawkley Hants 30 C5
Hawkridge Somset 24 D5
Hawkshead Cumb 137 K7
Hawkshead Hill Cumb 137 K7
Hawksland S Lans 165 G2
Hawkstone Shrops 98 E6
Hawkswick N York 131 H5
Hawksworth Leeds 123 H3
Hawksworth Notts 102 C4
Hawkwell Essex 46 E2
Hawley Hants 42 E8
Hawling Gloucs 56 B4
Hawnby N York 133 H2
Haworth C Brad 122 F3
Hawstead Suffk 77 J3
Hawthorn Dur 151 K5
Hawthorn Hill Lincs 103 K2
Hawton Notts 102 C3
Haxby C York 133 J7
Haxey N Linc 116 C2
Haycombe Crematorium BaNES 39 G7
Haydock St Hel 112 E3
Haydon Bridge Nthumb 149 L3
Haydon Wick Swindn 40 C3
Hayes Gt Lon 43 J4
Hayes Gt Lon 45 H6
Hayes End Gt Lon 43 H4
Hayfield Ag & B 182 F3
Hayfield Derbys 114 B4
Hayhillock Angus 196 E7
Hayle Cnwll 2 F4
Hayle Port Cnwll 2 F4
Hayley Green Dudley 85 G6
Hayling Island Hants 17 K3
Hayne Devon 11 H7
Haynes (Church End) C Beds 74 F6
Haynes (Northwood End) C Beds 75 G6
Haynes (Silver End) C Beds 75 G6
Haynes (West End) C Beds 74 F6
Hay-on-Wye Powys 68 E6
Hayscastle Pembks 48 F3
Hayscastle Cross Pembks 48 F3
Hay Street Herts 60 C3
Hayton Cumb 147 K6
Hayton Cumb 148 E4
Hayton E R Yk 125 J2
Hayton Notts 116 B5
Haytor Vale Devon 7 H1
Haytown Devon 9 K3
Haywards Heath W Susx 19 J2
Haywood Donc 124 E7
Hazelbank S Lans 165 G1
Hazelbury Bryan Dorset 14 E2
Hazeleigh Essex 61 K7
Hazel Grove Stockp 113 L4
Hazelton Walls Fife 186 E3
Hazelwood Derbys 101 G4
Hazlemere Bucks 42 E2
Hazlerigg N u Ty 159 G7
Hazleton Gloucs 56 B4
Heacham Norfk 105 G5
Headbourne Worthy Hants 29 J5
Headcorn Kent 33 L4
Headingley Leeds 123 K4
Headington Oxon 57 K6
Headlam Dur 140 F4
Headlesscross N Lans 176 B6
Headless Cross Worcs 71 J2
Headley Hants 30 D4
Headley Hants 41 K7
Headley Surrey 31 K1
Headley Down Hants 30 D4
Headon Notts 116 C6
Heads Nook Cumb 148 E4
Heage Derbys 101 G3
Healaugh N York 124 D2
Healaugh N York 140 C7
Heald Green Stockp 113 J4
Heale Somset 25 K7
Heale Somset 26 B6
Healey N York 132 B4
Healeyfield Dur 150 D5
Healing NE Lin 126 F7
Heamoor Cnwll 2 E5
Heanor Derbys 101 H3
Heanton Punchardon Devon 23 H4
Heapham Lincs 116 E4
Heart of England Crematorium Warwks 86 E5
Heart of Scotland Services N Lans 176 B5
Heasley Mill Devon 24 B5
Heaste Highld 199 K2
Heath Derbys 115 J7
Heath Wakefd 123 L6
Heath and Reach C Beds 58 F3
Heathcote Derbys 100 D1
Heather Leics 86 E2
Heathfield E Susx 20 C2
Heathfield Somset 25 J6
Heath Green Worcs 71 J1
Heath Hall D & G 155 H6
Heath Hayes & Wimblebury Staffs 85 H2
Heath Hill Shrops 84 D2
Heathrow Airport Gt Lon 43 H5
Heathton Shrops 84 E5
Heath Town Wolves 85 G4
Heatley Warrtn 113 G4
Heaton C Brad 123 H4
Heaton N u Ty 151 G2
Heaton Staffs 113 L8
Heaton Chapel Stockp 113 K3
Heaton Mersey Stockp 113 K4
Heaton Norris Stockp 113 K4
Heaton's Bridge Lancs 120 E7
Heaverham Kent 33 G2
Heavitree Devon 12 B4
Hebburn S Tyne 151 H3
Hebden N York 131 J6
Hebden Bridge Calder 122 E5
Hebing End Herts 60 A4
Hebron Carmth 49 K3
Hebron Nthumb 158 F4
Heckfield Hants 42 B7
Heckfield Green Suffk 92 E7
Heckfordbridge Essex 61 M4
Heckington Lincs 103 J4
Heckmondwike Kirk 123 J5
Heddington Wilts 39 M6
Heddon-on-the-Wall Nthumb 150 E2
Hedenham Norfk 93 G5
Hedge End Hants 29 J8
Hedgerley Bucks 42 F3
Hedging Somset 25 L5
Hedley on the Hill Nthumb 150 D3
Hednesford Staffs 85 H2
Hedon E R Yk 126 F5
Hedsor Bucks 42 E3
Heeley Sheff 115 G5
Heglibister Shet 235 c5
Heighington Darltn 141 G3
Heighington Lincs 117 G7
Heightington Worcs 70 D1
Heiton Border 167 L4
Hele Devon 12 C2
Hele Devon 23 H3
Helensburgh Ag & B 174 B2
Helenton S Ayrs 163 K3
Helford Cnwll 3 K6
Helford Passage Cnwll 3 K6
Helhoughton Norfk 105 K7
Helions Bumpstead Essex 76 F6
Helland Cnwll 5 G2
Hellescott Cnwll 9 H6
Hellesdon Norfk 92 E2
Hellidon Nhants 73 G3
Hellifield N York 131 G7
Hellingly E Susx 20 C4
Helmdon Nhants 73 H5
Helme Kirk 123 G7
Helmingham Suffk 78 E3
Helmsdale Highld 227 H5
Helmshore Lancs 122 B6
Helmsley N York 133 J3
Helperby N York 133 G5
Helperthorpe N York 134 E5
Helpringham Lincs 103 J4
Helpston C Pete 89 G3
Helsby Ches W 112 C6
Helston Cnwll 3 H5
Helstone Cnwll 8 E8
Helton Cumb 138 D3
Hemel Hempstead Herts 59 H6
Hemerdon Devon 6 E4
Hemingbrough N York 125 G4
Hemingby Lincs 118 C6
Hemingford Abbots Cambs 75 K1
Hemingford Grey Cambs 75 K1
Hemingstone Suffk 78 D4
Hemington Leics 101 J6
Hemington Nhants 88 F6
Hemington Somset 27 G2
Hemley Suffk 79 G6
Hemlington Middsb 142 B4
Hempnall Norfk 92 F5
Hempnall Green Norfk 92 F5
Hempriggs Moray 214 D2
Hempstead Essex 76 F6
Hempstead Medway 46 C6
Hempstead Norfk 106 D5
Hempstead Norfk 107 J6
Hempton Norfk 105 L6
Hempton Oxon 57 H2
Hemsby Norfk 107 K8
Hemswell Lincs 116 F4
Hemswell Cliff Lincs 116 F4
Hemsworth Wakefd 124 C7
Hemyock Devon 25 H8
Henbury Bristl 38 E5
Hendon Gt Lon 44 E3
Hendon Sundld 151 K4
Hendon Crematorium Gt Lon 44 E2
Hendy Carmth 51 H5
Henfield W Susx 19 G3
Hengoed Caerph 37 J2
Hengoed Powys 68 E4
Hengrave Suffk 77 J2
Henham Essex 60 E3
Heniarth Powys 82 C2
Henlade Somset 25 L6
Henley Dorset 14 D2
Henley Somset 26 B5
Henley Suffk 78 E4
Henley W Susx 30 E6
Henley Green Covtry 86 D6
Henley-in-Arden Warwks 71 L2
Henley-on-Thames Oxon 42 C4
Henley's Down E Susx 20 E3
Henllan Cerdgn 65 K6
Henllan Denbgs 110 E7
Henllys Torfn 37 K3
Henlow C Beds 75 H6
Hennock Devon 11 J8
Henny Street Essex 77 K6
Henryd Conwy 109 L6
Henry's Moat (Castell Hendre) Pembks 49 H3
Hensall N York 124 F5
Henshaw Nthumb 149 J3
Hensingham Cumb 136 D4
Henstead Suffk 93 K6
Hensting Hants 29 J6
Henstridge Somset 27 G7
Henstridge Ash Somset 27 G7
Henton Oxon 58 C7
Henton Somset 26 C3
Henwick Worcs 70 E4
Henwood Cnwll 5 L2
Heol-y-Cyw Brdgnd 36 E4
Hepple Nthumb 158 C2
Hepscott Nthumb 158 F5
Heptonstall Calder 122 E5
Hepworth Kirk 114 D1
Hepworth Suffk 92 B8
Herbrandston Pembks 48 E6
Hereford Herefs 69 K6
Hereford Crematorium Herefs 69 J6
Hereson Kent 35 K2
Heribusta Highld 218 B7
Heriot Border 177 L7
Hermiston C Edin 177 G4
Hermitage Border 156 E3
Hermitage Dorset 14 C2
Hermitage W Berk 41 J5
Hermon Carmth 65 K7
Hermon Pembks 49 L2
Herne Kent 47 K6
Herne Bay Kent 47 K6
Herne Hill Gt Lon 44 F5
Herne Pound Kent 33 H3
Hernhill Kent 34 E3
Herodsfoot Cnwll 5 K4
Heronsford S Ayrs 152 D5
Herriard Hants 30 A3
Herringfleet Suffk 93 K4
Herringswell Suffk 77 G1
Herringthorpe Rothm 115 J3
Herrington Sundld 151 J4
Hersden Kent 35 G3
Hersham Surrey 43 J7
Herstmonceux E Susx 20 D3
Herston Ork 234 c7
Hertford Herts 60 B5
Hertford Heath Herts 60 B5
Hertingfordbury Herts 60 A5
Hesketh Bank Lancs 120 F5
Hesketh Lane Lancs 121 J3
Hesket Newmarket Cumb 148 C7
Hesleden Dur 151 K7
Heslington C York 124 F1
Hessay C York 133 H8
Hessenford Cnwll 5 L4
Hessett Suffk 77 L3
Hessle E R Yk 126 C5
Hessle Wakefd 124 C6
Hest Bank Lancs 129 K6
Heston Gt Lon 43 J5
Heston Services Gt Lon 43 J5
Hestwall Ork 234 b5
Heswall Wirral 111 J5
Hethe Oxon 57 L3
Hethersett Norfk 92 D3
Hethersgill Cumb 148 E2
Hett Dur 151 G7
Hetton N York 131 H7

**Hetton-le-Hole** Sundld 151 J5
**Heugh** Nthumb 158 D7
**Heughhead** Abers 205 J3
**Heugh Head** Border 179 H6
**Heveningham** Suffk 93 G8
**Hever** Kent 32 E4
**Heversham** Cumb 129 K3
**Hevingham** Norfk 106 E7
**Hewas Water** Cnwll 4 F6
**Hewelsfield** Gloucs 54 E7
**Hewish** Somset 13 K2
**Hewood** Dorset 13 J2
**Hexham** Nthumb 150 B3
**Hextable** Kent 45 K6
**Hexthorpe** Donc 115 K2
**Hexton** Herts 59 J2
**Hexworthy** Cnwll 9 K8
**Hexworthy** Devon 6 F2
**Heybridge** Essex 61 G7
**Heybridge** Essex 61 K6
**Heybrook Bay** Devon 6 D6
**Heydon** Cambs 76 B6
**Heydon** Norfk 106 D6
**Heydour** Lincs 103 G5
**Heylipoll** Ag & B 188 C7
**Heylor** Shet 235 c3
**Heysham** Lancs 129 J7
**Heyshott** W Susx 18 B3
**Heytesbury** Wilts 27 L3
**Heythrop** Oxon 57 G3
**Heywood** Rochdl 122 C7
**Heywood** Wilts 27 K2
**Hibaldstow** N Linc 116 F2
**Hickleton** Donc 115 J1
**Hickling** Norfk 107 J7
**Hickling** Notts 102 B6
**Hickling Green** Norfk 107 J7
**Hickstead** W Susx 31 L7
**Hidcote Bartrim** Gloucs 71 L6
**Hidcote Boyce** Gloucs 71 L6
**High Ackworth** Wakefd 124 C6
**Higham** Barns 114 F1
**Higham** Derbys 101 H2
**Higham** Kent 33 G4
**Higham** Kent 46 B5
**Higham** Lancs 122 B3
**Higham** Suffk 77 H2
**Higham** Suffk 78 B7
**Higham Ferrers** Nhants 74 D2
**Higham Gobion** C Beds 59 J2
**Higham Hill** Gt Lon 45 G3
**Higham on the Hill** Leics 86 E4
**Highampton** Devon 10 C4
**Highams Park** Gt Lon 45 H2
**High Ardwell** D & G 144 C6
**High Auldgirth** D & G 154 F5
**High Bankhill** Cumb 148 F6
**High Beach** Essex 60 C7
**High Bentham** N York 130 C5
**High Bickington** Devon 23 J7
**High Biggins** Cumb 130 B4
**High Blantyre** S Lans 175 J6
**High Bonnybridge** Falk 175 L3
**High Bray** Devon 23 L5
**Highbridge** Somset 25 L3
**Highbrook** W Susx 32 C7
**High Brooms** Kent 33 G5
**Highburton** Kirk 123 J7
**Highbury** Gt Lon 44 F3
**Highbury** Somset 27 G2
**High Catton** E R Yk 133 L8
**Highclere** Hants 41 H8
**Highcliffe** Dorset 16 B4
**High Coniscliffe** Darltn 141 G4
**High Crosby** Cumb 148 E3
**High Cross** E Ayrs 163 K1
**High Cross** Hants 30 B6
**High Cross** Herts 60 B4
**High Cross** Warwks 71 L2
**High Drummore** D & G 144 D7
**High Easter** Essex 60 F5
**High Ellington** N York 132 B3
**Higher Ansty** Dorset 14 E2
**Higher Bartle** Lancs 121 G4
**Higher Bockhampton** Dorset 14 D4
**Higher Brixham** Torbay 7 L5
**High Ercall** Wrekin 98 E8
**Higher Chillington** Somset 13 K1
**Higher Folds** Wigan 113 G2
**Higher Gabwell** Devon 7 L3
**Higher Heysham** Lancs 129 J7
**Higher Irlam** Salfd 113 G3
**Higher Kinnerton** Flints 97 L1
**Higher Muddiford** Devon 23 J4
**Higher Penwortham** Lancs 121 G5
**Higher Prestacott** Devon 9 K5
**Higher Town** Cnwll 4 C6
**Higher Town** Cnwll 4 F4
**Higher Town** IoS 2 b1
**Higher Walton** Lancs 121 H5
**Higher Walton** Warrtn 112 E4
**Higher Wambrook** Somset 13 H2
**Higher Waterston** Dorset 14 D4
**Higher Wheelton** Lancs 121 J6
**Higher Whitley** Ches W 112 F5
**Higher Wincham** Ches W 113 G6
**Higher Wraxhall** Dorset 14 B3
**Higher Wych** Ches W 98 C4
**High Etherley** Dur 140 F2
**Highfield** Gatesd 150 E3
**Highfield** N Ayrs 174 C7
**High Garrett** Essex 61 J3
**Highgate** Gt Lon 44 F3
**Highgate** Kent 33 K6
**High Grantley** N York 132 C5
**High Green** Norfk 92 D3
**High Green** Norfk 92 E5
**High Green** Sheff 115 G3
**High Halden** Kent 34 B7
**High Halstow** Medway 46 C5
**High Ham** Somset 26 B5
**High Harrington** Cumb 136 D3
**High Harrogate** N York 132 D7
**High Hatton** Shrops 98 E7
**High Hauxley** Nthumb 159 G2
**High Hawsker** N York 143 J5
**High Hesket** Cumb 148 E6
**High Hoyland** Barns 123 K8
**High Hurstwood** E Susx 32 E7
**High Hutton** N York 134 B5
**High Ireby** Cumb 147 M7
**High Kilburn** N York 133 H4
**High Lands** Dur 140 E3
**Highlane** Derbys 115 H5
**High Lane** Stockp 113 L4
**High Lanes** Cnwll 3 G4
**Highleadon** Gloucs 55 H4
**High Legh** Ches E 113 G5
**Highleigh** W Susx 18 A6
**High Leven** S on T 141 K5
**Highley** Shrops 84 D6
**High Littleton** BaNES 38 F8
**High Lorton** Cumb 137 G3
**High Marnham** Notts 116 D7
**High Melton** Donc 115 K2
**High Mickley** Nthumb 150 D3
**Highmoor** Oxon 42 B4
**Highmoor Cross** Oxon 42 B4
**Highnam** Gloucs 55 H4
**High Newport** Sundld 151 J4
**High Newton** Cumb 129 J3
**High Nibthwaite** Cumb 129 G2
**High Offley** Staffs 99 H7
**High Ongar** Essex 60 E7
**High Onn** Staffs 84 E1
**High Park Corner** Essex 62 C4
**High Pennyvenie** E Ayrs 163 L7
**High Roding** Essex 60 F4
**High Salvington** W Susx 18 F4
**High Spen** Gatesd 150 E3
**Highsted** Kent 34 B3
**High Street** Cnwll 4 F5
**Highstreet** Kent 34 E3
**Highstreet Green** Surrey 31 G4
**Hightae** D & G 155 J6
**Highter's Heath** Birm 85 J7
**Hightown** Sefton 111 J2
**Hightown Green** Suffk 77 L4
**High Toynton** Lincs 118 C7
**High Valleyfield** Fife 176 D2
**Highweek** Devon 7 J2
**Highwood** Essex 61 G7
**Highwood Hill** Gt Lon 44 E2
**Highworth** Swindn 40 D2
**High Wray** Cumb 137 K7
**High Wych** Herts 60 D5
**High Wycombe** Bucks 42 E2
**Hilborough** Norfk 91 J4
**Hilcott** Wilts 40 C8
**Hildenborough** Kent 32 F4
**Hilden Park** Kent 33 G4
**Hildersham** Cambs 76 D5
**Hilderstone** Staffs 99 L5
**Hilderthorpe** E R Yk 135 J6
**Hilgay** Norfk 90 E4
**Hill** S Glos 38 F2
**Hill** Warwks 72 F2
**Hillam** N York 124 D5
**Hill Brow** Hants 30 C6
**Hillbutts** Dorset 15 J3
**Hill Chorlton** Staffs 99 H5
**Hillcliffane** Derbys 100 F3
**Hill Common** Somset 25 H6
**Hilldyke** Lincs 104 B3
**Hillend** Fife 176 F2
**Hill End** Fife 185 L7
**Hill End** Gloucs 70 F6
**Hillend** Mdloth 177 H5
**Hillend** N Lans 175 L5
**Hillesden** Bucks 58 B3
**Hillesley** Gloucs 39 H3
**Hillfarrance** Somset 25 J6
**Hill Green** Kent 46 D7
**Hillhead** Abers 216 B7
**Hill Head** Hants 17 G2
**Hillhead** S Lans 165 J2
**Hillhead of Cocklaw** Abers 217 K5
**Hilliclay** Highld 231 H3
**Hillingdon** Gt Lon 43 H4
**Hillington** C Glas 174 F5
**Hillington** Norfk 105 H7
**Hillmorton** Warwks 87 G8
**Hill of Beath** Fife 176 F1
**Hill of Fearn** Highld 223 H5
**Hillowton** D & G 146 D3
**Hill Ridware** Staffs 100 B8
**Hillside** Abers 207 H5
**Hillside** Angus 197 H4
**Hill Side** Kirk 123 H6
**Hills Town** Derbys 115 J7
**Hillstreet** Hants 29 G7
**Hillswick** Shet 235 c3
**Hill Top** Sandw 85 H5
**Hill Top** Wakefd 123 L7
**Hillwell** Shet 235 c8
**Hilmarton** Wilts 40 A5
**Hilperton** Wilts 39 K8
**Hilsea** C Port 17 J2
**Hilston** E R Yk 127 G4
**Hilton** Border 179 H7
**Hilton** Cambs 75 K2
**Hilton** Cumb 139 G3
**Hilton** Derbys 100 E6
**Hilton** Dorset 14 E2
**Hilton** Dur 140 F3
**Hilton** Highld 223 J6
**Hilton** S on T 141 K5
**Hilton** Shrops 84 D4
**Hilton Park Services** Staffs 85 G3
**Himbleton** Worcs 71 G3
**Himley** Staffs 84 F5
**Hincaster** Cumb 129 L3
**Hinchley Wood** Surrey 44 D6
**Hinckley** Leics 86 E5
**Hinderclay** Suffk 92 B7
**Hinderwell** N York 143 G4
**Hindhead** Surrey 30 E4
**Hindhead Tunnel** Surrey 30 E4
**Hindley** Wigan 112 F1
**Hindlip** Worcs 70 F3
**Hindolveston** Norfk 106 C6
**Hindon** Wilts 27 K5
**Hindringham** Norfk 106 B5
**Hingham** Norfk 92 B3
**Hinstock** Shrops 99 G7
**Hintlesham** Suffk 78 C5
**Hinton** Herefs 69 G6
**Hinton** S Glos 39 G5
**Hinton** Shrops 83 H2
**Hinton Ampner** Hants 29 L6
**Hinton Blewett** BaNES 26 E1
**Hinton Charterhouse** BaNES 39 H8
**Hinton-in-the-Hedges** Nhants 73 H6
**Hinton Martell** Dorset 15 J2
**Hinton on the Green** Worcs 71 H6
**Hinton Parva** Swindn 40 E4
**Hinton St George** Somset 26 B8
**Hinton St Mary** Dorset 27 H7
**Hinton Waldrist** Oxon 57 G7
**Hints** Staffs 85 L3
**Hinwick** Bed 74 D3
**Hinxhill** Kent 34 D6
**Hinxton** Cambs 76 C5
**Hinxworth** Herts 75 J6
**Hipperholme** Calder 123 H5
**Hipswell** N York 140 F7
**Hirn** Abers 206 D5
**Hirnant** Powys 97 G7
**Hirst** Nthumb 159 G5
**Hirst Courtney** N York 124 F5
**Hirwaun** Rhondd 52 E6
**Hiscott** Devon 23 J6
**Histon** Cambs 76 B2
**Hitcham** Suffk 78 B4
**Hitcham Causeway** Suffk 78 B4
**Hitcham Street** Suffk 78 B4
**Hitchin** Herts 59 K3
**Hither Green** Gt Lon 45 H5
**Hittisleigh** Devon 11 H5
**Hive** E R Yk 125 J4
**Hixon** Staffs 100 A7
**Hoaden** Kent 35 H3
**Hoar Cross** Staffs 100 C7
**Hoarwithy** Herefs 54 D3
**Hoath** Kent 47 K7
**Hobarris** Shrops 82 F7
**Hobkirk** Border 167 J7
**Hobson** Dur 150 F4
**Hoby** Leics 102 A8
**Hockering** Norfk 92 C2

**Hockerton** Notts 102 B2
**Hockley** Essex 46 D2
**Hockley Heath** Solhll 85 L8
**Hockliffe** C Beds 58 F3
**Hockwold cum Wilton** Norfk 91 G6
**Hockworthy** Devon 25 G7
**Hoddesdon** Herts 60 B6
**Hoddlesden** Bl w D 121 L6
**Hoddom Cross** D & G 155 L7
**Hoddom Mains** D & G 155 K7
**Hodgeston** Pembks 49 H7
**Hodnet** Shrops 98 E6
**Hodsock** Notts 115 L4
**Hodsoll Street** Kent 45 M7
**Hodson** Swindn 40 D4
**Hodthorpe** Derbys 115 K6
**Hoe** Norfk 92 B1
**Hogben's Hill** Kent 34 D4
**Hoggeston** Bucks 58 D3
**Hoggrill's End** Warwks 86 B5
**Hoghton** Lancs 121 J5
**Hognaston** Derbys 100 E3
**Hogsthorpe** Lincs 119 H6
**Holbeach** Lincs 104 B7
**Holbeach Bank** Lincs 104 B6
**Holbeach Clough** Lincs 104 B6
**Holbeach Drove** Lincs 89 K2
**Holbeach Hurn** Lincs 104 C6
**Holbeach St Johns** Lincs 104 B8
**Holbeach St Mark's** Lincs 104 B6
**Holbeach St Matthew** Lincs 104 C6
**Holbeck** Notts 115 K6
**Holberrow Green** Worcs 71 H3
**Holbeton** Devon 6 F5
**Holborn** Gt Lon 44 F4
**Holbrook** Derbys 101 G4
**Holbrook** Suffk 78 E6
**Holbrooks** Covtry 86 D6
**Holbury** Hants 16 E2
**Holcombe** Devon 12 B7
**Holcombe** Somset 26 F2
**Holcombe Rogus** Devon 25 G7
**Holcot** Nhants 73 L1
**Holden** Lancs 122 B1
**Holdenby** Nhants 73 K2
**Holder's Green** Essex 61 G3
**Holdgate** Shrops 83 L5
**Holdingham** Lincs 103 H3
**Holditch** Dorset 13 J2
**Holemoor** Devon 10 B4
**Holford** Somset 25 J3
**Holgate** C York 124 E1
**Holker** Cumb 129 H4
**Holkham** Norfk 105 L4
**Hollacombe** Devon 9 K4
**Holland Fen** Lincs 103 L3
**Holland-on-Sea** Essex 62 E5
**Hollandstoun** Ork 234 e3
**Hollee** D & G 148 A2
**Hollesley** Suffk 79 H5
**Hollicombe** Torbay 7 K4
**Hollingbourne** Kent 33 L3
**Hollingbury** Br & H 19 J4
**Hollingdon** Bucks 58 E3
**Hollington** Derbys 100 E5
**Hollington** Staffs 100 B5
**Hollingworth** Tamesd 114 A3
**Hollinsclough** Staffs 114 B7
**Hollins End** Sheff 115 G5
**Hollins Green** Warrtn 113 G4
**Hollinswood** Wrekin 84 C2
**Hollocombe** Devon 10 F3
**Holloway** Derbys 100 F2
**Holloway** Gt Lon 44 F3
**Hollowell** Nhants 73 K1
**Hollowmoor Heath** Ches W 112 C7
**Hollows** D & G 156 C6
**Hollybush** Caerph 53 J7
**Hollybush** E Ayrs 163 K6
**Hollybush** Herefs 70 D6
**Hollym** E R Yk 127 H5
**Holmbridge** Kirk 114 C1
**Holmbury St Mary** Surrey 31 J3
**Holmbush** Cnwll 5 G5
**Holmcroft** Staffs 99 K7
**Holme** Cambs 89 H6
**Holme** Cumb 129 L4
**Holme** Kirk 114 C1
**Holme** N York 132 E3
**Holme** Notts 102 D2
**Holme Chapel** Lancs 122 C5
**Holme Hale** Norfk 91 K3
**Holme Lacy** Herefs 69 L7
**Holme Marsh** Herefs 69 G4
**Holme next the Sea** Norfk 105 H4
**Holme on the Wolds** E R Yk 126 B2
**Holme Pierrepont** Notts 101 L5
**Holmer** Herefs 69 K6
**Holmer Green** Bucks 42 E2
**Holme St Cuthbert** Cumb 147 J5
**Holmes Chapel** Ches E 113 H7
**Holmesfield** Derbys 114 F6
**Holmeswood** Lancs 120 F6
**Holmethorpe** Surrey 32 B3
**Holme upon Spalding Moor** E R Yk 125 J3
**Holmewood** Derbys 115 H7
**Holmfirth** Kirk 123 H8
**Holmhead** E Ayrs 164 B5
**Holmpton** E R Yk 127 J5
**Holmrook** Cumb 136 E7
**Holmsford Bridge Crematorium** N Ayrs 163 J2
**Holmside** Dur 150 F5
**Holne** Devon 7 G3
**Holnicote** Somset 24 E3
**Holsworthy** Devon 9 J4
**Holsworthy Beacon** Devon 9 K3
**Holt** Dorset 15 J2
**Holt** Norfk 106 C5
**Holt** Wilts 39 K7
**Holt** Worcs 70 E3
**Holt** Wrexhm 98 B2
**Holtby** C York 133 K8
**Holt End** Worcs 71 J1
**Holt Heath** Worcs 70 E2
**Holton** Oxon 57 L6
**Holton** Somset 27 G6
**Holton** Suffk 93 J7
**Holton cum Beckering** Lincs 117 J5
**Holton le Clay** Lincs 118 C2
**Holton le Moor** Lincs 117 H3
**Holton St Mary** Suffk 78 C6
**Holwell** Dorset 14 D1
**Holwell** Herts 59 K2
**Holwell** Leics 102 B7
**Holwell** Oxon 56 E6
**Holwick** Dur 139 K2
**Holybourne** Hants 30 B4
**Holyhead** IoA 108 C5
**Holy Island** IoA 108 C5
**Holy Island** Nthumb 169 H2
**Holy Island** Nthumb 169 H2
**Holymoorside** Derbys 115 G7
**Holyport** W & M 42 E5
**Holystone** Nthumb 158 B2
**Holytown** N Lans 175 K6
**Holytown Crematorium** N Lans 175 K6
**Holywell** C Beds 59 G5
**Holywell** Cambs 75 L1
**Holywell** Cnwll 4 B4
**Holywell** Dorset 14 B2
**Holywell** Flints 111 G6
**Holywell Green** Calder 123 G6
**Holywell Lake** Somset 25 H7
**Holywell Row** Suffk 91 G7
**Holywood** D & G 155 G6
**Holywood Village** D & G 155 G6
**Homer** Shrops 84 B3
**Homer Green** Sefton 111 K2
**Homersfield** Suffk 93 G6
**Homington** Wilts 28 C6
**Honeybourne** Worcs 71 K5
**Honeychurch** Devon 10 F4
**Honeystreet** Wilts 40 C7
**Honey Tye** Suffk 77 L7
**Honiley** Warwks 86 B8
**Honing** Norfk 107 G6
**Honingham** Norfk 92 D2
**Honington** Lincs 102 F4
**Honington** Suffk 91 K8
**Honington** Warwks 72 C6
**Honiton** Devon 12 F3
**Honley** Kirk 123 H7
**Honor Oak Crematorium** Gt Lon 45 G5
**Hooe** C Plym 6 D5
**Hooe** E Susx 20 E4
**Hoo Green** Ches E 113 G5
**Hoohill** Bpool 120 D3
**Hook** E R Yk 125 H5
**Hook** Gt Lon 44 D7
**Hook** Hants 30 B1
**Hook** Pembks 49 G5
**Hook** Wilts 40 B4
**Hooke** Dorset 14 A3
**Hook Green** Kent 33 H6
**Hook Norton** Oxon 57 G2
**Hookway** Devon 11 K5
**Hooley** Surrey 32 B3
**Hoo St Werburgh** Medway 46 C5
**Hooton Levitt** Rothm 115 K3
**Hooton Pagnell** Donc 124 D8
**Hooton Roberts** Rothm 115 J3
**Hope** Derbys 114 D5
**Hope** Devon 7 G7
**Hope** Flints 97 L2
**Hope** Staffs 100 C2
**Hope Bagot** Shrops 83 L8
**Hope Bowdler** Shrops 83 J5
**Hopehouse** Border 166 D6
**Hopeman** Moray 214 E1
**Hope Mansell** Herefs 54 F4
**Hopesay** Shrops 83 H6
**Hope under Dinmore** Herefs 69 K4
**Hopgrove** C York 133 K8
**Hopperton** N York 132 F7
**Hopstone** Shrops 84 D5
**Hopton** Derbys 100 E2
**Hopton** Staffs 99 L7
**Hopton** Suffk 92 B7
**Hopton Cangeford** Shrops 83 K7
**Hopton Castle** Shrops 83 G7
**Hoptonheath** Shrops 83 H7
**Hopton on Sea** Norfk 93 L4
**Hopton Wafers** Shrops 84 B7
**Hopwas** Staffs 85 L3
**Hopwood** Worcs 85 J7
**Hopwood Park Services** Worcs 85 J8
**Horam** E Susx 20 C3
**Horbling** Lincs 103 J5
**Horbury** Wakefd 123 K6
**Horden** Dur 151 K6
**Hordle** Hants 16 C4
**Hordley** Shrops 98 B6
**Horfield** Bristl 38 E5
**Horham** Suffk 92 E8
**Horkesley Heath** Essex 62 B3
**Horkstow** N Linc 126 B6
**Horley** Oxon 72 E5
**Horley** Surrey 32 B5
**Hornblotton Green** Somset 26 E5
**Hornby** Lancs 130 B5
**Hornby** N York 132 C2
**Hornby** N York 141 J6
**Horncastle** Lincs 118 C7
**Hornchurch** Gt Lon 45 K3
**Horncliffe** Nthumb 179 J7
**Horndean** Border 179 J8
**Horndean** Hants 30 B8
**Horndon** Devon 10 D8
**Horndon on the Hill** Thurr 46 A4
**Horne** Surrey 32 C4
**Horner** Somset 24 D3
**Horning** Norfk 107 H8
**Horninghold** Leics 88 B4
**Horninglow** Staffs 100 E7
**Horningsea** Cambs 76 C3
**Horningsham** Wilts 27 J3
**Horningtoft** Norfk 105 M7
**Horns Cross** Devon 22 F6
**Hornsea** E R Yk 126 F2
**Hornsey** Gt Lon 44 F3
**Hornton** Oxon 72 E5
**Horra** Shet 235 d2
**Horrabridge** Devon 6 D2
**Horringer** Suffk 77 J3
**Horrocksford** Lancs 121 L2
**Horsebridge** Devon 6 B2
**Horsebridge** E Susx 20 C4
**Horsebridge** Hants 29 G5
**Horsehay** Wrekin 84 C3
**Horseheath** Cambs 76 E5
**Horsehouse** N York 131 K4
**Horsell** Surrey 43 G8
**Horseman's Green** Wrexhm 98 C4
**Horsey** Norfk 107 K7
**Horsey** Somset 25 L4
**Horsford** Norfk 92 E1
**Horsforth** Leeds 123 J3
**Horsham** W Susx 31 K5
**Horsham** Worcs 70 D3
**Horsham St Faith** Norfk 92 E1
**Horsington** Lincs 117 K7
**Horsington** Somset 27 G6
**Horsley** Derbys 101 G4
**Horsley** Gloucs 39 J2
**Horsley** Nthumb 150 D2
**Horsley** Nthumb 157 L3
**Horsleycross Street** Essex 62 D3
**Horsleyhill** Border 167 H5
**Horsley Woodhouse** Derbys 101 H4
**Horsmonden** Kent 33 J5
**Horspath** Oxon 57 L6
**Horstead** Norfk 106 F8
**Horsted Keynes** W Susx 32 C7
**Horton** Bucks 58 F4
**Horton** Dorset 15 J2
**Horton** Lancs 122 C1
**Horton** Nhants 74 B4
**Horton** S Glos 39 H4
**Horton** Somset 25 L7
**Horton** Staffs 99 L2
**Horton** Swans 50 F7
**Horton** W & M 43 G5
**Horton** Wilts 40 B7
**Horton** Wrekin 84 C1
**Horton-cum-Studley** Oxon 57 L5
**Horton Green** Ches W 98 C3
**Horton-in-Ribblesdale** N York 130 F5
**Horton Kirby** Kent 45 K6
**Horwich** Bolton 121 J7
**Horwood** Devon 23 H6
**Hoscote** Border 166 F6
**Hose** Leics 102 B6
**Hosh** P & K 185 H3
**Hoswick** Shet 235 c7

**Hotham** E R Yk 125 L4
**Hothfield** Kent 34 C5
**Hoton** Leics 101 L7
**Hough** Ches E 99 G3
**Hougham** Lincs 102 E4
**Hough Green** Halton 112 C4
**Hough-on-the-Hill** Lincs 102 F3
**Houghton** Cambs 75 K1
**Houghton** Hants 29 G5
**Houghton** Pembks 49 G6
**Houghton** W Susx 18 D4
**Houghton Conquest** C Beds 74 F6
**Houghton Green** E Susx 21 H2
**Houghton-le-Spring** Sundld 151 H5
**Houghton on the Hill** Leics 87 J3
**Houghton Regis** C Beds 59 G4
**Houghton St Giles** Norfk 105 L5
**Hound Green** Hants 42 B8
**Houndslow** Border 178 D8
**Houndwood** Border 179 H5
**Hounslow** Gt Lon 43 J5
**Househill** Highld 213 L4
**Houses Hill** Kirk 123 J6
**Housieside** Abers 207 G1
**Houston** Rens 174 D5
**Houstry** Highld 227 K2
**Houton** Ork 234 b6
**Hove** Br & H 19 J5
**Hoveringham** Notts 102 B3
**Hoveton** Norfk 107 G8
**Hovingham** N York 133 K4
**How Caple** Herefs 54 E3
**Howden** E R Yk 125 H5
**Howden-le-Wear** Dur 150 E7
**Howe** Highld 231 K3
**Howe** N York 132 E4
**Howe** Norfk 92 F4
**Howe Bridge Crematorium** Wigan 112 F2
**Howe Green** Essex 61 J7
**Howegreen** Essex 61 K7
**Howell** Lincs 103 J4
**Howe of Teuchar** Abers 216 E5
**Howes** D & G 147 L2
**Howe Street** Essex 61 H5
**Howe Street** Essex 77 G7
**Howey** Powys 68 B3
**Howgate** Cumb 136 D3
**Howgate** Mdloth 177 H6
**Howick** Nthumb 169 K5
**Howlett End** Essex 76 E7
**Howley** Somset 13 H1
**How Mill** Cumb 148 E4
**Howmore** W Isls 233 b7
**Hownam** Border 168 B5
**Howsham** N Linc 117 H2
**Howsham** N York 133 L6
**Howtel** Nthumb 168 D3
**How Wood** Herts 59 J7
**Howwood** Rens 174 D6
**Hoxa** Ork 234 c7
**Hoxne** Suffk 92 E7
**Hoy** Ork 234 b7
**Hoylake** Wirral 111 H4
**Hoyland** Barns 115 G2
**Hoylandswaine** Barns 114 E1
**Hubberston** Pembks 48 E6
**Huby** N York 123 K2
**Huby** N York 133 J6
**Hucclecote** Gloucs 55 K4
**Hucking** Kent 33 L2
**Hucknall** Notts 101 K3
**Huddersfield** Kirk 123 H7
**Huddersfield Crematorium** Kirk 123 H6
**Huddington** Worcs 71 G3
**Hudswell** N York 140 E7
**Huggate** E R Yk 134 D7
**Hughenden Valley** Bucks 42 E2
**Hughley** Shrops 83 L4
**Hugh Town** IoS 2 b2
**Huish** Devon 10 D3
**Huish** Wilts 40 C7
**Huish Champflower** Somset 25 G5
**Huish Episcopi** Somset 26 B6
**Hùisinis** W Isls 232 d3
**Huisinish** W Isls 232 d3
**Hulcott** Bucks 58 D5
**Hulham** Devon 12 C5
**Hulland** Derbys 100 E3
**Hulland Ward** Derbys 100 E3
**Hullavington** Wilts 39 K4
**Hullbridge** Essex 46 D2
**Hull, Kingston upon** C KuH 126 D5
**Hulme** Manch 113 J3
**Hulme** Staffs 99 L4
**Hulme** Warrtn 112 E4
**Hulme End** Staffs 100 C2
**Hulme Walfield** Ches E 113 J7
**Hulverstone** IoW 16 E5
**Hulver Street** Suffk 93 K6
**Humber Bridge** N Linc 126 C5
*Humberside Airport* N Linc 126 D7
**Humberston** NE Lin 118 D1
**Humberstone** C Leic 87 J3
**Humbie** E Loth 178 B5
**Humbleton** E R Yk 126 F4
**Humby** Lincs 103 G6
**Hume** Border 167 L2
**Humshaugh** Nthumb 158 A7
**Huna** Highld 231 L2
**Huncote** Leics 87 G4
**Hundalee** Border 167 K5
**Hunderthwaite** Dur 140 C3
**Hundleby** Lincs 118 E7
**Hundleton** Pembks 49 G7
**Hundon** Suffk 77 G5
**Hundred House** Powys 68 C4
**Hungarton** Leics 87 K3
**Hungerford** Somset 25 G4
**Hungerford** W Berk 41 G6
**Hungerford Newtown** W Berk 41 G6
**Hungerstone** Herefs 69 J7
**Hunmanby** N York 135 H4
**Hunningham** Warwks 72 D2
**Hunsbury Hill** Nhants 73 K3
**Hunsdon** Herts 60 C5
**Hunsingore** N York 132 F8
**Hunslet** Leeds 123 L4
**Hunsonby** Cumb 149 G7
**Hunstanton** Norfk 105 G4
**Hunstanworth** Dur 150 B5
**Hunsterson** Ches E 99 G4
**Hunston** Suffk 77 L2
**Hunston** W Susx 18 B5
**Hunstrete** BaNES 38 F7
**Hunsworth** Kirk 123 J5
**Hunter's Quay** Ag & B 173 K3
**Huntham** Somset 25 M6
**Hunthill Lodge** Angus 196 D3
**Huntingdon** Cambs 89 J8
**Huntingfield** Suffk 93 G8
**Huntington** C York 133 J7
**Huntington** Ches W 112 B8
**Huntington** E Loth 178 B4
**Huntington** Herefs 68 E4
**Huntington** Staffs 85 H2
**Huntingtowerfield** P & K 185 M3
**Huntley** Gloucs 55 G4
**Huntly** Abers 215 L6
**Hunton** Kent 33 J4
**Hunton** N York 132 B2
**Huntscott** Somset 24 E3
**Huntsham** Devon 24 F7
**Huntshaw** Devon 23 H6
**Huntspill** Somset 25 L3
**Huntstile** Somset 25 K5
**Huntworth** Somset 25 L4
**Hunwick** Dur 140 F2
**Hunworth** Norfk 106 C5
**Hurdcott** Wilts 28 D5
**Hurdsfield** Ches E 113 L6
**Hurley** W & M 42 D4
**Hurley** Warwks 86 B4
**Hurley Common** Warwks 86 B4
**Hurlford** E Ayrs 163 L3
**Hurn** Dorset 15 L3
**Hursley** Hants 29 H6
**Hurst** Wokham 42 C5
**Hurstbourne Priors** Hants 29 H3
**Hurstbourne Tarrant** Hants 29 G2
**Hurst Green** E Susx 33 J7
**Hurst Green** Essex 62 C5
**Hurst Green** Lancs 121 K3
**Hurst Green** Surrey 32 D3
**Hurst Hill** Dudley 85 G5
**Hurstpierpoint** W Susx 19 J3
**Hurstwood** Lancs 122 C4
**Hurtiso** Ork 234 c6
**Hurworth-on-Tees** Darltn 141 H5
**Hurworth Place** Darltn 141 H5
**Husbands Bosworth** Leics 87 J6
**Husborne Crawley** C Beds 74 D7
**Husthwaite** N York 133 H4
**Hutcliffe Wood Crematorium** Sheff 115 G5
**Huthwaite** Notts 101 J2
**Huttoft** Lincs 119 G6
**Hutton** Border 179 J7
**Hutton** E R Yk 134 F8
**Hutton** Essex 45 M2
**Hutton** Lancs 121 G5
**Hutton** N Som 37 M8
**Hutton Buscel** N York 134 F3
**Hutton Conyers** N York 132 E5
**Hutton Cranswick** E R Yk 126 C1
**Hutton End** Cumb 148 D7
**Hutton Henry** Dur 151 K7
**Hutton-le-Hole** N York 133 L2
**Hutton Lowcross** R & Cl 142 D4
**Hutton Magna** Dur 140 E5
**Hutton Roof** Cumb 130 B4
**Hutton Roof** Cumb 148 C7
**Hutton Rudby** N York 141 K6
**Hutton Sessay** N York 133 G4
**Hutton Wandesley** N York 124 D1
**Huxham** Devon 12 B3
**Huxley** Ches W 98 D1
**Huyton** Knows 112 C4
**Hycemoor** Cumb 128 D2
**Hyde** Tamesd 113 L3
**Hyde Heath** Bucks 58 F7
**Hyde Lea** Staffs 99 K8
*Hylands House & Park* Essex 61 G7
**Hyndford Bridge** S Lans 165 H2
**Hynish** Ag & B 188 C8
**Hyssington** Powys 82 F5
**Hythe** Essex 62 B3
**Hythe** Hants 16 E2
**Hythe** Kent 34 F7
**Hythe End** W & M 43 G6

## I

**Ibberton** Dorset 14 E2
**Ible** Derbys 100 E2
**Ibsley** Hants 15 L1
**Ibstock** Leics 86 E2
**Ibstone** Bucks 42 C2
**Ibthorpe** Hants 29 G2
**Iburndale** N York 143 H5
**Ibworth** Hants 29 K1
**Ichrachan** Ag & B 182 E2
**Ickburgh** Norfk 91 J4
**Ickenham** Gt Lon 43 H3
**Ickford** Bucks 57 M6
**Ickham** Kent 35 G3
**Ickleford** Herts 59 K2
**Icklesham** E Susx 21 H3
**Ickleton** Cambs 76 C5
**Icklingham** Suffk 91 H8
**Ickornshaw** N York 122 E2
**Ickwell Green** C Beds 75 G5
**Icomb** Gloucs 56 E4
**Idbury** Oxon 56 E4
**Iddesleigh** Devon 10 E3
**Ide** Devon 11 K6
**Ideford** Devon 7 K1
**Ide Hill** Kent 32 E3
**Iden** E Susx 21 H2
**Iden Green** Kent 33 J5
**Iden Green** Kent 33 K6
**Idle** C Brad 123 H3
**Idless** Cnwll 4 C6
**Idlicote** Warwks 72 C5
**Idmiston** Wilts 28 D4
**Idole** Carmth 50 E3
**Idridgehay** Derbys 100 F3
**Idrigill** Highld 208 F2
**Idstone** Oxon 40 E4
**Iffley** Oxon 57 K7
**Ifield** W Susx 31 L4
**Ifold** W Susx 31 G5
**Iford** Bmouth 15 L4
**Iford** E Susx 19 L4
**Ifton** Mons 38 C3
**Ightfield** Shrops 98 E5
**Ightham** Kent 33 G2
**Ilam** Staffs 100 C3
**Ilchester** Somset 26 D6
**Ilderton** Nthumb 168 F5
**Ilford** Gt Lon 45 H3
**Ilford** Somset 26 A7
**Ilfracombe** Devon 23 H2
**Ilkeston** Derbys 101 J4
**Ilketshall St Andrew** Suffk 93 H6
**Ilketshall St Margaret** Suffk 93 H6
**Ilkley** C Brad 123 G2
**Illand** Cnwll 5 L1
**Illey** Dudley 85 H7
**Illogan** Cnwll 3 H3
**Illston on the Hill** Leics 87 K4
**Ilmer** Bucks 58 C6
**Ilmington** Warwks 72 B5
**Ilminster** Somset 26 A8
**Ilsington** Devon 7 H2
**Ilston** Swans 51 H7
**Ilton** N York 132 B4
**Ilton** Somset 25 M7
**Imachar** N Ayrs 161 L2
**Immingham** NE Lin 126 F7
**Immingham Dock** NE Lin 126 F7
**Impington** Cambs 76 C2
**Ince** Ches W 112 C6
**Ince Blundell** Sefton 111 K2
**Ince-in-Makerfield** Wigan 112 E1
**Inchbae Lodge Hotel** Highld 221 K7
**Inchbare** Angus 196 F4
**Inchberry** Moray 215 G4
**Incheril** Highld 211 G3
**Inchinnan** Rens 174 E5
**Inchlaggan** Highld 201 J5
**Inchmichael** P & K 186 D3
**Inchmore** Highld 212 E5
**Inchnacardoch Hotel** Highld 202 B3
**Inchnadamph** Highld 224 F4
**Inchture** P & K 186 D2

Inchvuilt Highld 211 K6
Inchyra P & K 186 C4
Indian Queens Cnwll 4 E4
Ingatestone Essex 61 G7
Ingbirchworth Barns 114 E1
Ingestre Staffs 99 L7
Ingham Lincs 116 F5
Ingham Norfk 107 H7
Ingham Suffk 77 J1
Ingham Corner Norfk 107 H6
Ingleby Derbys 101 G6
Ingleby Arncliffe N York 141 K6
Ingleby Barwick S on T 141 K4
Ingleby Greenhow N York 142 C6
Ingleigh Green Devon 10 E4
Inglesbatch BaNES 39 G7
Inglesham Swindn 56 D7
Ingleston D & G 147 G2
Ingleton Dur 140 F3
Ingleton N York 130 D5
Inglewhite Lancs 121 H3
Ingoe Nthumb 158 C7
Ingol Lancs 121 G4
Ingoldisthorpe Norfk 105 G6
Ingoldmells Lincs 119 H7
Ingoldsby Lincs 103 G6
Ingram Nthumb 168 F6
Ingrave Essex 45 M2
Ingrow C Brad 122 F3
Ings Cumb 138 C7
Ingst S Glos 38 E3
Ingthorpe Rutlnd 88 E2
Ingworth Norfk 106 E6
Inkberrow Worcs 71 H3
Inkhorn Abers 217 H6
Inkpen W Berk 41 G7
Inkstack Highld 231 J2
Innellan Ag & B 173 K4
Innerleithen Border 166 E3
Innerleven Fife 186 F7
Innermessan D & G 144 C3
Innerwick E Loth 178 F4
Innesmill Moray 215 G2
Insch Abers 216 C8
Insh Highld 203 J5
Inskip Lancs 120 F3
Instow Devon 23 G5
Intake Sheff 115 H5
Inver Abers 204 F6
Inver Highld 223 J5
Inver P & K 194 F7
Inverailort Highld 190 F1
Inveralligin Highld 210 C3
Inverallochy Abers 217 K2
Inveran Highld 222 D2
Inveraray Ag & B 182 F5
Inverarish Highld 209 J7
Inverarity Angus 196 D7
Inverarnan Stirlg 183 K4
Inverasdale Highld 219 J4
Inverbeg Ag & B 183 K7
Inverbervie Abers 197 K2
Inverboyndie Abers 216 C2
Invercreran House Hotel Ag & B 191 K6
Inverdruie Highld 203 L3
Inveresk E Loth 177 K4
Inveresragan Ag & B 182 E1
Inverey Abers 204 D7
Inverfarigaig Highld 202 D2
Inverfolla Ag & B 191 J7
Invergarry Highld 201 L5
Invergeldie P & K 184 F2
Invergloy Highld 201 K7
Invergordon Highld 222 F7
Invergowrie P & K 186 F2
Inverguseran Highld 200 B4
Inverhadden P & K 193 L5
Inverherive Hotel Stirlg 183 L3
Inverie Highld 200 B5
Inverinan Ag & B 182 E4
Inverinate Highld 200 E2
Inverkeilor Angus 197 G6
Inverkeithing Fife 176 F2
Inverkeithny Abers 216 C5
Inverkip Inver 173 L4
Inverkirkaig Highld 224 C4
Inverlael Highld 220 F4
Inverlair Highld 192 E1
Inverliever Lodge Ag & B 182 C6
Inverlochy Ag & B 183 H2
Invermark Angus 196 D1
Invermoriston Highld 202 C3
Invernaver Highld 229 L4
Inverneill Ag & B 172 E3
Inverness Highld 213 G5
*Inverness Airport Highld 213 J4*
Inverness Crematorium Highld 212 F5
Invernettie Abers 217 L5
Invernoaden Ag & B 183 G7
Inveroran Hotel Ag & B 192 D7
Inverquharity Angus 196 C5
Inverquhomery Abers 217 J5
Inverroy Highld 201 K8
Inversanda Highld 191 J4
Invershiel Highld 200 E2
Invershin Highld 222 D3
Invershore Highld 231 J8
Inversnaid Hotel Stirlg 183 K5
Inverugie Abers 217 L5
Inveruglas Ag & B 183 K5
Inveruglass Highld 203 J5
Inverurie Abers 206 E2
Inwardleigh Devon 10 E5
Inworth Essex 61 L4
Iochdar W Isls 233 b7
Iona Ag & B 180 D3
Iping W Susx 30 D6
iPort Logistics Park Donc 115 L2
Ipplepen Devon 7 J3
Ipsden Oxon 41 M4
Ipstones Staffs 100 A3
Ipswich Suffk 78 E5
Ipswich Crematorium Suffk 78 E5
Irby Wirral 111 J5
Irby in the Marsh Lincs 118 F8
Irby upon Humber NE Lin 117 K1
Irchester Nhants 74 D2
Ireby Cumb 147 M7
Ireby Lancs 130 C4
Ireleth Cumb 128 F4
Ireshopeburn Dur 149 L7
Irlam Salfd 113 G3
Irnham Lincs 103 G7
Iron Acton S Glos 39 G4
Ironbridge Wrekin 84 C3
*Ironbridge Gorge Wrekin 84 C3*
Ironmacannie D & G 154 B6
Ironville Derbys 101 H3
Irstead Norfk 107 H7
Irthington Cumb 148 E3
Irthlingborough Nhants 74 D1
Irton N York 134 F3
Irvine N Ayrs 163 H2
Isauld Highld 230 E3
Isbister Shet 235 c2
Isbister Shet 235 d4
Isfield E Susx 19 L3
Isham Nhants 88 C8
Isington Hants 30 C3
Islay Ag & B 171 G4
*Islay Airport Ag & B 170 F7*
Isle Abbotts Somset 26 A7
Isle Brewers Somset 26 A7
Isleham Cambs 90 F8
Isle of Dogs Gt Lon 45 G4
Isle of Grain Medway 46 E5
Isle of Lewis W Isls 232 f2
Isle of Man IoM 237 c4
*Isle of Man Ronaldsway Airport IoM 237 b7*
Isle of Mull Ag & B 181 J1
Isle of Purbeck Dorset 15 J5
Isle of Sheppey Kent 46 F6
Isle of Skye Highld 208 F6
Isle of Thanet Kent 35 J2
Isle of Walney Cumb 128 E6
Isle of Whithorn D & G 145 K7
Isle of Wight IoW 17 G5
Isle of Wight Crematorium IoW 17 G4
Isleornsay Highld 199 L3
Isles of Scilly IoS 2 b1
*Isles of Scilly St Mary's Airport IoS 2 b2*
Islesteps D & G 155 G7
Islet Village Guern 236 d2
Isleworth Gt Lon 44 D5
Isley Walton Leics 101 H7
Islibhig W Isls 232 d3
Islington Gt Lon 44 F3
Islington Crematorium Gt Lon 44 F3
Islip Nhants 88 E7
Islip Oxon 57 K5
Islivig W Isls 232 d3
Isombridge Wrekin 83 L2
Istead Rise Kent 45 M6
Itchen Abbas Hants 29 K5
Itchen Stoke Hants 29 K5
Itchingfield W Susx 31 J5
Itteringham Norfk 106 D6
Itton Mons 38 C2
Itton Common Mons 38 C2
Ivegill Cumb 148 D6
Iver Bucks 43 G4
Iver Heath Bucks 43 G4
Iveston Dur 150 E5
Ivinghoe Bucks 58 F5
Ivinghoe Aston Bucks 58 F4
Ivington Herefs 69 J3
Ivybridge Devon 6 F5
Ivychurch Kent 21 K1
Ivy Hatch Kent 33 G3
Iwade Kent 46 E6
Iwerne Courtney Dorset 27 K8
Iwerne Minster Dorset 27 K8
Ixworth Suffk 77 L1
Ixworth Thorpe Suffk 91 K8

## J

Jack-in-the-Green Devon 12 C4
Jackton S Lans 175 G7
Jacobstow Cnwll 9 G5
Jacobstowe Devon 10 E4
Jameston Pembks 49 H7
Jamestown Highld 212 D3
Jamestown W Duns 174 D3
Janetstown Highld 227 L3
Janetstown Highld 231 L5
Jardine Hall D & G 155 J5
Jarrow S Tyne 151 H3
Jasper's Green Essex 61 H3
Jawcraig Falk 175 L4
Jaywick Essex 62 D5
Jedburgh Border 167 K5
Jeffreyston Pembks 49 J6
Jemimaville Highld 213 H2
Jerbourg Guern 236 d4
Jersey Jersey 236 c6
*Jersey Airport Jersey 236 b7*
Jersey Crematorium Jersey 236 c7
Jesmond N u Ty 151 G2
Jevington E Susx 20 B5
Jockey End Herts 59 H5
Johnby Cumb 148 D7
*John Lennon Airport Lpool 112 B5*
John o' Groats Highld 231 L2
Johnshaven Abers 197 J3
Johnston Pembks 48 F5
Johnstone D & G 155 M3
Johnstone Rens 174 D5
Johnstonebridge D & G 155 J4
Johnstown Carmth 50 E2
Johnstown Wrexhm 97 L4
Joppa C Edin 177 J4
Joppa Cerdgn 66 D2
Joppa S Ayrs 163 K5
Jordanston Pembks 64 C7
Joyden's Wood Kent 45 K5
Juniper Nthumb 150 B3
Juniper Green C Edin 177 G5
Jura Ag & B 171 J2
Jurassic Coast Devon 13 H4
Jurby IoM 237 c2

## K

Kaber Cumb 139 H5
Kaimend S Lans 165 J1
Kames Ag & B 173 G4
Kames E Ayrs 164 D4
Kea Cnwll 4 C7
Keadby N Linc 125 K7
Keal Cotes Lincs 104 B1
Kearsley Bolton 113 H1
Kearsney Kent 35 H6
Kearstwick Cumb 130 B4
Kedington Suffk 77 G5
Kedleston Derbys 100 F4
Keelby Lincs 126 E8
Keele Staffs 99 J4
*Keele Services Staffs 99 J4*
Keelham C Brad 123 G4
Keeston Pembks 48 F4
Keevil Wilts 39 L8
Kegworth Leics 101 J7
Kehelland Cnwll 3 G3
Keig Abers 206 B2
Keighley C Brad 122 F3
Keighley Crematorium C Brad 122 F3
Keilarsbrae Clacks 185 J8
Keillour P & K 185 K3
Keiloch Abers 204 E6
Keils Ag & B 171 K5
Keinton Mandeville Somset 26 D5
Keir Mill D & G 154 E4
Keisley Cumb 139 G3
Keiss Highld 231 L4
Keith Moray 215 J4
Keithick P & K 195 K8
Keithock Angus 196 F4
Keithtown Highld 212 E3
Kelbrook Lancs 122 D2
Kelby Lincs 103 G4
Keld N York 139 K6
Kelfield N York 124 F3
Kelham Notts 102 C2
Kelhead D & G 147 K2
Kellamergh Lancs 120 E5
Kellas Angus 187 G1
Kellas Moray 214 E4
Kellaton Devon 7 J7
Kelling Norfk 106 C4
Kellington N York 124 E5
Kelloe Dur 151 J7
Kelloholm D & G 164 E6
Kelly Devon 9 K8
Kelmarsh Nhants 87 K7
Kelmscott Oxon 56 E7
Kelsale Suffk 79 H2
Kelsall Ches W 112 D7

**Kelshall** Herts 75 K7
**Kelsick** Cumb 147 L5
**Kelso** Border 167 L3
**Kelstedge** Derbys 115 G8
**Kelstern** Lincs 118 C4
**Kelston** BaNES 39 G6
**Keltneyburn** P & K 194 B6
**Kelton** D & G 155 H7
**Kelty** Fife 186 B8
**Kelvedon** Essex 61 K4
**Kelvedon Hatch** Essex 60 F7
**Kelynack** Cnwll 2 C5
**Kemback** Fife 187 G4
**Kemberton** Shrops 84 D3
**Kemble** Gloucs 39 M2
**Kemerton** Worcs 71 G6
**Kemeys Commander** Mons 53 M6
**Kemnay** Abers 206 E3
**Kempley** Gloucs 54 F3
**Kempley Green** Gloucs 55 G3
**Kempsey** Worcs 70 F5
**Kempsford** Gloucs 40 D2
**Kempshott** Hants 29 L2
**Kempston** Bed 74 F5
**Kempton** Shrops 83 G6
**Kemp Town** Br & H 19 J5
**Kemsing** Kent 32 F2
**Kenardington** Kent 34 C7
**Kenchester** Herefs 69 J6
**Kencot** Oxon 56 E6
**Kendal** Cumb 129 L2
**Kenfig** Brdgnd 36 C4
**Kenilworth** Warwks 72 C1
**Kenley** Gt Lon 32 B2
**Kenley** Shrops 83 L4
**Kenmore** Highld 210 B3
**Kenmore** P & K 194 B7
**Kenn** Devon 11 L7
**Kenn** N Som 38 B6
**Kennacraig** Ag & B 172 D5
**Kennall Vale** Cnwll 3 J4
**Kennerleigh** Devon 11 J4
**Kennessee Green** Sefton 111 L2
**Kennet** Clacks 176 C1
**Kennethmont** Abers 215 L8
**Kennett** Cambs 77 G2
**Kennford** Devon 11 L7
**Kenninghall** Norfk 92 C6
**Kennington** Kent 34 D5
**Kennington** Oxon 57 K7
**Kennoway** Fife 186 F6
**Kenny** Somset 25 L7
**Kenny Hill** Suffk 90 F7
**Kennythorpe** N York 134 C6
**Kenovay** Ag & B 188 C6
**Kensaleyre** Highld 208 F4
**Kensington** Gt Lon 44 E4
**Kensington Palace** Gt Lon 44 E4
**Kensworth Common** C Beds 59 G4
**Kentallen** Highld 191 K5
**Kent and Sussex Crematorium** Kent 33 G5
**Kentchurch** Herefs 54 B3
**Kentford** Suffk 77 G2
**Kentisbeare** Devon 12 D2
**Kentisbury** Devon 23 K3
**Kentish Town** Gt Lon 44 F3
**Kentmere** Cumb 138 C6
**Kenton** Devon 12 B5
**Kenton** Gt Lon 44 D3
**Kenton** N u Ty 150 F2
**Kenton** Suffk 78 E2
**Kenton Bankfoot** N u Ty 150 F2
**Kentra** Highld 190 D3
**Kent's Green** Gloucs 55 H4
**Kent's Oak** Hants 28 F6
**Kenwyn** Cnwll 4 C6
**Keoldale** Highld 228 F3
**Keppoch** Highld 200 D1
**Kepwick** N York 133 G2
**Keresley** Covtry 86 D6
**Kerrera** Ag & B 182 B2
**Kerris** Cnwll 2 D5
**Kerry** Powys 82 D5
**Kerrycroy** Ag & B 173 J6
**Kersall** Notts 116 B8
**Kersbrook** Devon 12 D5
**Kersey** Suffk 78 B5
**Kershader** W Isls 232 f3
**Kerswell** Devon 12 D2
**Kerswell Green** Worcs 70 F5
**Kesgrave** Suffk 78 F5
**Kessingland** Suffk 93 L6
**Kestle** Cnwll 4 F6
**Kestle Mill** Cnwll 4 D4
**Keston** Gt Lon 45 H7
**Keswick** Cumb 137 J3
**Keswick** Norfk 92 E3
**Kettering** Nhants 88 C7
**Kettering Crematorium** Nhants 88 C7
**Ketteringham** Norfk 92 E3
**Kettins** P & K 195 K8
**Kettlebaston** Suffk 77 L4
**Kettlebridge** Fife 186 E6
**Kettlebrook** Staffs 86 B3
**Kettleburgh** Suffk 78 F3
**Kettleholm** D & G 155 K6
**Kettleshulme** Ches E 113 M5
**Kettlesing** N York 132 C7
**Kettlesing Bottom** N York 132 C7
**Kettlestone** Norfk 106 A6
**Kettlethorpe** Lincs 116 D6
**Kettletoft** Ork 234 d4
**Kettlewell** N York 131 H5
**Ketton** Rutlnd 88 E3
**Kew** Gt Lon 44 D5
**Kew Royal Botanic Gardens** Gt Lon 44 D5
**Kewstoke** N Som 37 M7
**Kexby** C York 125 G1
**Kexby** Lincs 116 E4
**Key Green** Ches E 113 K8
**Keyham** Leics 87 J3
**Keyhaven** Hants 16 C4
**Keyingham** E R Yk 127 G5
**Keymer** W Susx 19 J3
**Keynsham** BaNES 38 F6
**Keysoe** Bed 74 F3
**Keysoe Row** Bed 74 F3
**Keyston** Cambs 88 F7
**Keyworth** Notts 101 L6
**Kibblesworth** Gatesd 151 G4
**Kibworth Beauchamp** Leics 87 K5
**Kibworth Harcourt** Leics 87 K5
**Kidbrooke** Gt Lon 45 H5
**Kidderminster** Worcs 84 E7
**Kidlington** Oxon 57 J5
**Kidmore End** Oxon 42 B5
**Kidsdale** D & G 145 J7
**Kidsgrove** Staffs 99 J2
**Kidwelly** Carmth 50 E4
**Kiel Crofts** Ag & B 191 H8
**Kielder** Nthumb 157 G4
**Kielder Forest** 157 G5
**Kiells** Ag & B 171 H5
**Kilbarchan** Rens 174 D5
**Kilbeg** Highld 199 K4
**Kilberry** Ag & B 172 C5
**Kilbirnie** N Ayrs 174 C7
**Kilbride** Ag & B 172 C3
**Kilbride** Ag & B 173 H5
**Kilbuiack** Moray 214 D3
**Kilburn** Derbys 101 G4
**Kilburn** Gt Lon 44 E4
**Kilburn** N York 133 H4
**Kilby** Leics 87 J4
**Kilchamaig** Ag & B 172 D6
**Kilchattan** Ag & B 173 J7
**Kilchattan** Ag & B 180 E7
**Kilcheran** Ag & B 191 G8
**Kilchoan** Highld 189 L4
**Kilchoman** Ag & B 170 D5
**Kilchrenan** Ag & B 182 E3
**Kilconquhar** Fife 187 H6
**Kilcot** Gloucs 55 G3
**Kilcoy** Highld 212 E4
**Kilcreggan** Ag & B 173 L3
**Kildale** N York 142 D5
**Kildalloig** Ag & B 161 J5
**Kildary** Highld 223 G6
**Kildavaig** Ag & B 173 G5
**Kildavanan** Ag & B 173 H5
**Kildonan** Highld 227 G4
**Kildonan** N Ayrs 162 D5
**Kildonan Lodge** Highld 226 F4
**Kildonnan** Highld 199 G7
**Kildrochet House** D & G 144 C4
**Kildrummy** Abers 205 K2
**Kildwick** N York 122 F2
**Kilfinan** Ag & B 172 F3
**Kilfinnan** Highld 201 K6
**Kilgetty** Pembks 49 J6
**Kilgrammie** S Ayrs 152 F2
**Kilgwrrwg Common** Mons 38 C2
**Kilham** E R Yk 135 G6
**Kilkenneth** Ag & B 188 B7
**Kilkenzie** Ag & B 161 H4
**Kilkerran** Ag & B 161 J5
**Kilkhampton** Cnwll 9 H3
**Killamarsh** Derbys 115 J5
**Killay** Swans 51 H6
**Killearn** Stirlg 174 F2
**Killen** Highld 213 G3
**Killerby** Darltn 140 F3
**Killerton** Devon 12 C3
**Killichonan** P & K 193 J5
**Killiechonate** Highld 192 D1
**Killiechronan** Ag & B 190 B7
**Killiecrankie** P & K 194 E4
**Killilan** Highld 210 E7
**Killimster** Highld 231 K4
**Killin** Stirlg 184 C2
**Killinghall** N York 132 D7
**Killington** Cumb 130 C2
**Killington Lake Services** Cumb 130 B2
**Killingworth** N Tyne 159 G7
**Killochyett** Border 167 G1
**Kilmacolm** Inver 174 C4
**Kilmahog** Stirlg 184 D5
**Kilmahumaig** Ag & B 182 A8
**Kilmaluag** Highld 218 C6
**Kilmany** Fife 186 F3
**Kilmarnock** E Ayrs 163 K2
**Kilmartin** Ag & B 182 B7
**Kilmaurs** E Ayrs 163 K2
**Kilmelford** Ag & B 182 B5
**Kilmersdon** Somset 27 G2
**Kilmeston** Hants 29 L6
**Kilmichael** Ag & B 161 H5
**Kilmichael Glassary** Ag & B 182 B8
**Kilmichael of Inverlussa** Ag & B 172 D2
**Kilmington** Devon 13 H3
**Kilmington** Wilts 27 H4
**Kilmington Common** Wilts 27 H4
**Kilmington Street** Wilts 27 H4
**Kilmorack** Highld 212 D5
**Kilmore** Ag & B 182 C3
**Kilmore** Highld 199 K4
**Kilmory** Ag & B 172 C4
**Kilmory** Highld 190 B3
**Kilmory** N Ayrs 162 B5
**Kilmuir** Highld 208 D5
**Kilmuir** Highld 213 G4
**Kilmuir** Highld 218 B7
**Kilmuir** Highld 223 G6
**Kilmun** Ag & B 173 K3
**Kilnave** Ag & B 170 F4
**Kilncadzow** S Lans 176 B8
**Kilndown** Kent 33 J6
**Kilninver** Ag & B 182 B3
**Kilnsea** E R Yk 127 J7
**Kilnsey** N York 131 H6
**Kilnwick** E R Yk 126 C1
**Kiloran** Ag & B 180 E7
**Kilpatrick** N Ayrs 162 A4
**Kilpeck** Herefs 54 C3
**Kilpin** E R Yk 125 J5
**Kilrenny** Fife 187 J6
**Kilsby** Nhants 73 H1
**Kilspindie** P & K 186 C3
**Kilstay** D & G 144 D7
**Kilsyth** N Lans 175 J3
**Kiltarlity** Highld 212 D6
**Kilton** R & Cl 142 E4
**Kilton Thorpe** R & Cl 142 E4
**Kilvaxter** Highld 218 B7
**Kilve** Somset 25 H3
**Kilvington** Notts 102 D4
**Kilwinning** N Ayrs 163 H2
**Kimberley** Norfk 92 C3
**Kimberley** Notts 101 J4
**Kimberworth** Rothm 115 H3
**Kimblesworth** Dur 151 G5
**Kimbolton** Cambs 75 G2
**Kimbolton** Herefs 69 K3
**Kimcote** Leics 87 H6
**Kimmeridge** Dorset 15 H6
**Kimpton** Hants 28 F3
**Kimpton** Herts 59 K4
**Kinbrace** Highld 226 F3
**Kinbuck** Stirlg 185 G6
**Kincaple** Fife 187 G4
**Kincardine** Fife 176 C2
**Kincardine** Highld 222 E4
**Kincardine Bridge** Fife 176 C2
**Kincardine O'Neil** Abers 206 B5
**Kinclaven** P & K 195 J8
**Kincorth** C Aber 207 H5
**Kincorth House** Moray 214 C3
**Kincraig** Highld 203 K4
**Kincraigie** P & K 194 F6
**Kindallachan** P & K 194 F6
**Kinerarach** Ag & B 172 B7
**Kineton** Gloucs 56 C3
**Kineton** Warwks 72 D4
**Kinfauns** P & K 186 C3
**Kingarth** Ag & B 173 J6
**Kingcausie** Abers 207 G5
**Kingcoed** Mons 54 B6
**Kingerby** Lincs 117 H3
**Kingham** Oxon 56 E3
**Kingholm Quay** D & G 155 G7
**Kinghorn** Fife 177 H2
**Kinglassie** Fife 186 D7
**Kingoodie** P & K 186 E2
**Kingsand** Cnwll 6 C5
**Kingsbarns** Fife 187 K5
**Kingsbridge** Devon 7 H6
**Kingsbridge** Somset 24 F4
**King's Bromley** Staffs 85 K1
**Kingsburgh** Highld 208 F4
**Kingsbury** Gt Lon 44 D3
**Kingsbury** Warwks 86 B4
**Kingsbury Episcopi** Somset 26 B7
**King's Caple** Herefs 54 E3
**Kingsclere** Hants 41 K8
**King's Cliffe** Nhants 88 E4
**Kings Clipstone** Notts 115 L8
**Kingscote** Gloucs 39 J2
**Kingscott** Devon 23 H7
**King's Coughton** Warwks 71 J3
**Kingscross** N Ayrs 162 D4
**Kingsdon** Somset 26 D6
**Kingsdown** Kent 35 K5
**Kingsdown** Swindn 40 D3
**Kingsdown** Wilts 39 J6
**Kingsdown Crematorium** Swindn 40 D3
**Kingseat** Abers 207 G2
**Kingseat** Fife 176 F1
**Kingsey** Bucks 58 C6

**Kingsfold** W Susx.......31 K4
**Kingsford** C Aber.......206 F4
**Kingsford** E Ayrs.......174 E8
**Kingsgate** Kent.......35 K1
**Kingshall Street** Suffk....77 K3
**King's Heath** Birm.......85 J7
**Kings Hill** Kent.......33 H3
**King's Hill** Wsall.......85 H4
**Kings House Hotel** Highld.......192 D5
**Kingshouse Hotel** Stirlg.......184 C4
**Kingshurst** Solhll.......85 L6
**Kingskerswell** Devon.......7 K3
**Kingskettle** Fife.......186 E5
**Kingsland** Herefs.......69 J3
**Kingsland** IoA.......108 C5
**Kings Langley** Herts.......59 H7
**Kingsley** Ches W.......112 D6
**Kingsley** Hants.......30 C4
**Kingsley** Staffs.......100 A3
**Kingsley Green** W Susx.......30 E5
**Kingsley Park** Nhants.....73 L3
**King's Lynn** Norfk.......104 F8
**Kings Meaburn** Cumb..138 E3
**King's Mills** Guern.......236 c3
**Kingsmuir** Angus.......196 D6
**Kings Muir** Border.......166 C2
**Kingsmuir** Fife.......187 J5
**Kingsnorth** Kent.......34 D6
**King's Norton** Birm.......85 J7
**King's Norton** Leics.......87 K4
**Kings Nympton** Devon.......23 L7
**King's Pyon** Herefs.......69 J4
**Kings Ripton** Cambs.......89 J7
**King's Somborne** Hants.......29 G5
**King's Stag** Dorset.......14 D1
**King's Stanley** Gloucs.....55 J7
**King's Sutton** Nhants.....72 F7
**Kingstanding** Birm.......85 J4
**Kingsteignton** Devon.......7 K2
**Kingsthorne** Herefs.......54 D2
**Kingsthorpe** Nhants.......73 L2
**Kingston** Cambs.......75 L4
**Kingston** Cnwll.......6 A2
**Kingston** Devon.......6 F6
**Kingston** Dorset.......14 E1
**Kingston** Dorset.......15 H6
**Kingston** E Loth.......178 C3
**Kingston** IoW.......16 F6
**Kingston** Kent.......35 G4
**Kingston Bagpuize** Oxon.......57 H7
**Kingston Blount** Oxon.......58 C7
**Kingston Deverill** Wilts.......27 J4
**Kingstone** Herefs.......69 H7
**Kingstone** Somset.......26 B8
**Kingstone** Staffs.......100 B6
Kingston Lacy House & Gardens Dorset.......15 J3
**Kingston Lisle** Oxon.......40 F3
**Kingston near Lewes** E Susx.......19 K4
**Kingston on Soar** Notts.......101 J6
**Kingston on Spey** Moray.......215 H2
**Kingston Russell** Dorset.......14 B4
**Kingston St Mary** Somset.......25 K5
**Kingston Seymour** N Som.......38 B6
**Kingston upon Hull** C KuH.......126 D5
**Kingston upon Thames** Gt Lon.......44 D6
**Kingston upon Thames Crematorium** Gt Lon.......44 D6
**King's Walden** Herts.......59 K4
**Kingswear** Devon.......7 K5
**Kingswells** C Aber.......207 G4
**Kings Weston** Bristl.......38 D5
**Kingswinford** Dudley.....84 F5
**Kingswood** Bucks.......58 B4
**Kingswood** Gloucs.......39 H3
**Kingswood** S Glos.......38 F5
**Kingswood** Somset.......25 H4
**Kingswood** Surrey.......31 L1
**Kingswood** Warwks.......71 L1
**Kingswood Common** Staffs.......84 E3
**Kings Worthy** Hants.......29 J5
**Kingthorpe** Lincs.......117 J6
**Kington** Herefs.......68 F3
**Kington** S Glos.......38 F3
**Kington** Worcs.......71 H4
**Kington Langley** Wilts....39 L5
**Kington Magna** Dorset.......27 H6
**Kington St Michael** Wilts.......39 K5
**Kingussie** Highld.......203 H5
**Kingweston** Somset.......26 D5
**Kinharrachie** Abers.......217 H7
**Kinharvie** D & G.......147 G2
**Kinkell Bridge** P & K.......185 J4
**Kinknockie** Abers.......217 J6
**Kinleith** C Edin.......177 G5
**Kinlet** Shrops.......84 C7
**Kinloch** Highld.......198 F5
**Kinloch** Highld.......225 H2
**Kinloch** Highld.......229 H5
**Kinloch** P & K.......195 J7
**Kinlochard** Stirlg.......184 B6
**Kinlochbervie** Highld....228 C4
**Kinlocheil** Highld.......191 J1
**Kinlochewe** Highld.......210 F3
**Kinloch Hourn** Highld...200 E4
**Kinlochlaggan** Highld...202 E7
**Kinlochleven** Highld.....192 C4
**Kinlochmoidart** Highld.......190 E2
**Kinlochnanuagh** Highld.......200 B8
**Kinloch Rannoch** P & K.......193 L5
**Kinloss** Moray.......214 C3
**Kinmel Bay** Conwy.......110 D5
**Kinmuck** Abers.......206 F2
**Kinmundy** Abers.......207 G2
**Kinnabus** Ag & B.......160 B2
**Kinnadie** Abers.......217 H5
**Kinnaird** P & K.......194 F5
**Kinneff** Abers.......197 K2
**Kinnelhead** D & G.......155 H2
**Kinnell** Angus.......196 F6
**Kinnerley** Shrops.......97 M7
**Kinnersley** Herefs.......69 G5
**Kinnersley** Worcs.......70 F5
**Kinnerton** Powys.......68 E2
**Kinnesswood** P & K.......186 C6
**Kinnordy** Angus.......196 B5
**Kinoulton** Notts.......102 B6
**Kinross** P & K.......186 B6
**Kinrossie** P & K.......186 C2
Kinross Services P & K.......186 B6
**Kinsham** Herefs.......69 G2
**Kinsham** Worcs.......71 G7
**Kinsley** Wakefd.......124 C7
**Kinson** Bmouth.......15 K3
**Kintail** Highld.......200 F2
**Kintbury** W Berk.......41 G6
**Kintessack** Moray.......214 B3
**Kintillo** P & K.......186 B4
**Kinton** Herefs.......83 H8
**Kinton** Shrops.......98 A8
**Kintore** Abers.......206 E3
**Kintour** Ag & B.......171 H7
**Kintra** Ag & B.......170 F8
**Kintra** Ag & B.......180 D3
**Kintraw** Ag & B.......182 B6
**Kintyre** Ag & B.......161 J2
**Kinveachy** Highld.......203 L2
**Kinver** Staffs.......84 E6
**Kippax** Leeds.......124 C4
**Kippen** Stirlg.......184 E7
**Kippford** D & G.......146 E4
**Kipping's Cross** Kent.....33 H5
**Kirbister** Ork.......234 b6
**Kirby Bedon** Norfk.......93 G3
**Kirby Bellars** Leics.......102 B8
**Kirby Cane** Norfk.......93 H5
**Kirby Cross** Essex.......62 E4
**Kirby Grindalythe** N York.......134 D6
**Kirby Hill** N York.......132 F5
**Kirby Hill** N York.......140 E6
**Kirby Knowle** N York.....133 G3
**Kirby-le-Soken** Essex.....62 F4
**Kirby Misperton** N York.......134 B4
**Kirby Muxloe** Leics.......87 G3
**Kirby Underdale** E R Yk.......134 C7
**Kirby Wiske** N York.......132 E3
**Kirdford** W Susx.......31 G6
**Kirk** Highld.......231 K4
**Kirkabister** Shet.......235 d6
**Kirkandrews** D & G.......146 A5
**Kirkandrews upon Eden** Cumb.......148 C4
**Kirkbampton** Cumb.......148 B4
**Kirkbean** D & G.......147 G3
**Kirk Bramwith** Donc.......124 F7
**Kirkbride** Cumb.......147 M4
**Kirkbuddo** Angus.......196 E7
**Kirkburn** Border.......166 D2
**Kirkburn** E R Yk.......134 F7
**Kirkburton** Kirk.......123 J7
**Kirkby** Knows.......111 L2
**Kirkby** Lincs.......117 H3
**Kirkby** N York.......142 C6
**Kirkby Fleetham** N York.......141 G7
**Kirkby Green** Lincs.......103 H2
**Kirkby-in-Ashfield** Notts.......101 J2
**Kirkby-in-Furness** Cumb.......128 F3
**Kirkby la Thorpe** Lincs.......103 J4
**Kirkby Lonsdale** Cumb.......130 B4
**Kirkby Malham** N York.......131 G7
**Kirkby Mallory** Leics.......86 F4
**Kirkby Malzeard** N York.......132 C5
**Kirkbymoorside** N York.......133 L3
**Kirkby on Bain** Lincs.....118 C8
**Kirkby Overblow** N York.......123 L2
**Kirkby Stephen** Cumb.......139 H5
**Kirkby Thore** Cumb.......138 F3
**Kirkby Underwood** Lincs.......103 H6
**Kirkby Wharf** N York.....124 D3
**Kirkcaldy** Fife.......186 D8
**Kirkcaldy Crematorium** Fife...186 D8
**Kirkcambeck** Cumb.......148 F2
**Kirkchrist** D & G.......146 B5
**Kirkcolm** D & G.......144 B2
**Kirkconnel** D & G.......164 E6
**Kirkconnell** D & G.......147 G2
**Kirkcowan** D & G.......145 G3
**Kirkcudbright** D & G.......146 B5
**Kirkdale** Lpool.......111 K3
**Kirk Deighton** N York.....124 B1
**Kirk Ella** E R Yk.......126 C5
**Kirkfieldbank** S Lans.....165 G2
**Kirkgunzeon** D & G.......146 F2
**Kirk Hallam** Derbys.......101 J4
**Kirkham** Lancs.......120 F4
**Kirkham** N York.......134 B6
**Kirkhamgate** Wakefd.....123 K6
**Kirk Hammerton** N York.......133 G7
**Kirkhaugh** Nthumb.......149 H5
**Kirkheaton** Kirk.......123 H6
**Kirkheaton** Nthumb.......158 C6
**Kirkhill** Highld.......212 E5
**Kirkhope** S Lans.......165 J7
**Kirkibost** Highld.......199 H2
**Kirkinch** P & K.......195 L7
**Kirkinner** D & G.......145 J5
**Kirkintilloch** E Duns.......175 H4
**Kirk Ireton** Derbys.......100 E3
**Kirkland** Cumb.......136 E4
**Kirkland** D & G.......154 E4
**Kirkland** D & G.......155 H4
**Kirkland** D & G.......164 E6
**Kirk Langley** Derbys.......100 F5
**Kirkleatham** R & Cl.......142 D3
**Kirkleatham Crematorium** R & Cl.......142 D3
**Kirklevington** S on T.....141 K5
**Kirkley** Suffk.......93 L5
**Kirklington** N York.......132 D4
**Kirklington** Notts.......102 B2
**Kirklinton** Cumb.......148 D2
**Kirkliston** C Edin.......176 F4
**Kirkmabreck** D & G.......145 K4
**Kirkmaiden** D & G.......144 D7
**Kirk Merrington** Dur.....141 G2
**Kirk Michael** IoM.......237 c4
**Kirkmichael** P & K.......195 H4
**Kirkmichael** S Ayrs.......163 J7
**Kirkmuirhill** S Lans.......164 F2
**Kirknewton** Nthumb.....168 D4
**Kirknewton** W Loth.......176 F5
**Kirkney** Abers.......215 L7
**Kirk of Shotts** N Lans....175 L5
**Kirkoswald** Cumb.......148 F6
**Kirkoswald** S Ayrs.......163 G7
**Kirkpatrick** D & G.......154 F4
**Kirkpatrick Durham** D & G.......154 D7
**Kirkpatrick-Fleming** D & G.......156 B7
**Kirk Sandall** Donc.......124 F8
**Kirksanton** Cumb.......128 D4
**Kirk Smeaton** N York....124 D7
**Kirkstall** Leeds.......123 K4
**Kirkstead** Lincs.......103 K1
**Kirkstile** Abers.......215 L7
**Kirkstile** D & G.......156 C4
**Kirkstyle** Highld.......231 L2
**Kirkthorpe** Wakefd.......124 B6
**Kirkton** Abers.......206 C1
**Kirkton** D & G.......155 G6
**Kirkton** Fife.......186 F3
**Kirkton** Highld.......210 C8
**Kirkton** Highld.......210 D6
**Kirkton** P & K.......185 K4
**Kirkton Manor** Border..166 C2
**Kirkton of Airlie** Angus.......195 L6
**Kirkton of Auchterhouse** Angus.......196 B8
**Kirkton of Barevan** Highld.......213 K5
**Kirkton of Collace** P & K.......186 C2
**Kirkton of Glenbuchat** Abers...205 J3
**Kirkton of Kingoldrum** Angus.......196 B5
**Kirkton of Logie Buchan** Abers.......217 J7
**Kirkton of Maryculter** Abers.....207 G5
**Kirkton of Menmuir** Angus.......196 E4
**Kirkton of Monikie** Angus.......196 E8
**Kirkton of Rayne** Abers.......216 D7
**Kirkton of Skene** Abers.......206 F4
**Kirkton of Tealing** Angus.......196 C8
**Kirkton of Tough** Abers.......206 C3

**Kirktown** Abers 217 J2
**Kirktown** Abers 217 K4
**Kirktown of Alvah** Abers 216 D3
**Kirktown of Bourtie** Abers 206 F1
**Kirktown of Fetteresso** Abers 206 F7
**Kirktown of Mortlach** Moray 215 H6
**Kirktown of Slains** Abers 217 K8
**Kirkurd** Border 165 M1
**Kirkwall** Ork 234 c6
*Kirkwall Airport* Ork 234 c6
**Kirkwhelpington** Nthumb 158 C5
**Kirk Yetholm** Border 168 C4
**Kirmington** N Linc 126 D7
**Kirmond le Mire** Lincs 117 K3
**Kirn** Ag & B 173 K3
**Kirriemuir** Angus 196 C5
**Kirstead Green** Norfk 93 G4
**Kirtlebridge** D & G 155 M7
**Kirtling** Cambs 77 G3
**Kirtling Green** Cambs 76 F4
**Kirtlington** Oxon 57 J4
**Kirtomy** Highld 229 M3
**Kirton** Lincs 104 A5
**Kirton** Notts 116 B7
**Kirton** Suffk 78 F6
**Kirtonhill** W Duns 174 D4
**Kirton in Lindsey** N Linc 116 F2
**Kirwaugh** D & G 145 J4
**Kishorn** Highld 210 C6
**Kislingbury** Nhants 73 K3
**Kittisford** Somset 25 G6
**Kitt's Green** Birm 85 L6
**Kittybrewster** C Aber 207 H4
**Kivernoll** Herefs 54 C2
**Kiveton Park** Rothm 115 J5
**Knaith** Lincs 116 D5
**Knap Corner** Dorset 27 J6
**Knaphill** Surrey 42 F8
**Knapp** Somset 25 L6
**Knapton** C York 124 E1
**Knapton** N York 134 D4
**Knapton** Norfk 107 G5
**Knapwell** Cambs 75 K2
**Knaresborough** N York 132 E7
**Knarsdale** Nthumb 149 H4
**Knaven** Abers 217 G5
**Knayton** N York 132 F2
**Knebworth** Herts 59 L4
**Knedlington** E R Yk 125 H5
**Kneesall** Notts 116 B8
**Kneeton** Notts 102 B4
**Knelston** Swans 50 F7
**Knenhall** Staffs 99 L5
**Knightcote** Warwks 72 E4
**Knightley** Staffs 99 J7
**Knighton** C Leic 87 H4
**Knighton** Dorset 14 C1
**Knighton** Powys 68 F1
**Knighton** Somset 25 J3
**Knighton** Staffs 99 G4
**Knighton** Staffs 99 H6
**Knighton on Teme** Worcs 70 B1
**Knightwick** Worcs 70 D4
**Knill** Herefs 68 F3
**Knipoch** Ag & B 182 B3
**Knipton** Leics 102 D6
**Kniveton** Derbys 100 E3
**Knock** Cumb 138 F2
**Knock** Highld 199 K4
**Knock** Moray 215 L4
**Knock** W Isls 232 g2
**Knockally** Highld 227 K3
**Knockan** Highld 224 F6
**Knockando** Moray 214 F6
**Knockbain** Highld 212 E5
**Knockbain** Highld 212 F3
**Knock Castle** N Ayrs 173 L5
**Knockdee** Highld 231 H4
**Knockdow** Ag & B 173 J4
**Knockdown** Wilts 39 J3
**Knockeen** S Ayrs 153 G3
**Knockenkelly** N Ayrs 162 D4
**Knockentiber** E Ayrs 163 K2
**Knockholt** Kent 32 E2
**Knockholt Pound** Kent 32 E2
**Knockin** Shrops 97 M7
**Knockinlaw** E Ayrs 163 K2
**Knocknain** D & G 144 B3
**Knockrome** Ag & B 171 K4
**Knocksharry** IoM 237 b4
**Knocksheen** D & G 153 M5
**Knockvennie Smithy** D & G 154 D7
**Knodishall** Suffk 79 J3
**Knodishall Common** Suffk 79 J3
**Knole** Somset 26 C6
**Knolls Green** Ches E 113 J5
**Knolton** Wrexhm 98 B5
**Knook** Wilts 27 L3
**Knossington** Leics 88 B2
**Knott End-on-Sea** Lancs 120 E2
**Knotting** Bed 74 E2
**Knotting Green** Bed 74 E3
**Knottingley** Wakefd 124 D5
**Knotty Ash** Lpool 112 B3
**Knowbury** Shrops 83 L7
**Knowe** D & G 153 G7
**Knowehead** D & G 154 A4
**Knoweside** S Ayrs 163 G6
**Knowle** Bristl 38 E6
**Knowle** Devon 11 H5
**Knowle** Devon 12 C2
**Knowle** Devon 12 D6
**Knowle** Devon 23 H4
**Knowle** Shrops 83 L8
**Knowle** Solhll 85 L7
**Knowle** Somset 24 E3
**Knowlefield** Cumb 148 D4
**Knowle Green** Lancs 121 J3
**Knowle St Giles** Somset 13 J1
**Knowl Hill** W & M 42 D4
**Knowsley** Knows 112 C3
**Knowsley Safari Park** Knows 112 C3
**Knowstone** Devon 24 C6
**Knox Bridge** Kent 33 K5
**Knoydart** Highld 200 C5
**Knucklas** Powys 82 F8
**Knuston** Nhants 74 D2
**Knutsford** Ches E 113 H5
**Knutsford Services** Ches E 113 G6
**Krumlin** Calder 122 F6
**Kuggar** Cnwll 3 J7
**Kyleakin** Highld 200 B1
**Kyle of Lochalsh** Highld 210 B8
**Kylerhea** Highld 200 B2
**Kylesku** Highld 224 F2
**Kylesmorar** Highld 200 C6
**Kyles Scalpay** W Isls 232 e4
**Kylestrome** Highld 224 F2
**Kynnersley** Wrekin 84 C1
**Kyrewood** Worcs 69 L2

## L

**La Bellieuse** Guern 236 d3
**Lacasaigh** W Isls 232 f3
**Lacasdal** W Isls 232 f2
**Laceby** NE Lin 117 K1
**Lacey Green** Bucks 58 D7
**Lach Dennis** Ches W 113 G6
**Lackford** Suffk 77 H1
**Lackford Green** Suffk 77 H1
**Lacock** Wilts 39 K6
**Ladbroke** Warwks 72 E3
**Laddingford** Kent 33 J4
**Ladock** Cnwll 4 D5
**Lady** Ork 234 d4
**Ladybank** Fife 186 E5
**Ladygill** S Lans 165 H4
**Lady Hall** Cumb 128 E3
**Ladykirk** Border 179 J8
**Ladywood** Birm 85 J6
**Ladywood** Worcs 70 F3
**La Fontenelle** Guern 236 e1
**La Fosse** Guern 236 d4
**Lag** D & G 154 F5
**Laga** Highld 190 D4
**Lagavulin** Ag & B 160 C1
**Lagg** N Ayrs 162 B5
**Laggan** Highld 201 L6
**Laggan** Highld 202 F6
**Lagganlia** Highld 203 K5
**La Greve** Guern 236 d2
**La Grève de Lecq** Jersey 236 b5
**La Hougue Bie** Jersey 236 d7
**La Houguette** Guern 236 b3
**Laid** Highld 228 F4
**Laide** Highld 219 L3
**Laig** Highld 199 G7
**Laigh Clunch** E Ayrs 174 E8
**Laigh Fenwick** E Ayrs 163 L2
**Laigh Glenmuir** E Ayrs 164 C5
**Laighstonehall** S Lans 175 J7
**Laindon** Essex 46 B3
**Lairg** Highld 225 M7
**Laisterdyke** C Brad 123 J4
**Lake** IoW 17 H5
**Lake** Wilts 28 C4
**Lake District** Cumb 137 H5
*Lake District National Park* Cumb 137 H5
**Lakenheath** Suffk 91 G6
**Lakesend** Norfk 90 D4
**Laleston** Brdgnd 36 D4
**Lamarsh** Essex 77 K7
**Lamas** Norfk 106 F7
**Lambden** Border 167 L2
**Lamberhurst** Kent 33 H6
**Lamberhurst Down** Kent 33 H6
**Lamberton** Border 179 K6
**Lambeth** Gt Lon 44 F4
**Lambeth Crematorium** Gt Lon 44 F5
**Lambfair Green** Suffk 77 G4
**Lambley** Notts 101 M4
**Lambley** Nthumb 149 H4
**Lambourn** W Berk 40 F5
**Lambourne End** Essex 45 J2
**Lambs Green** W Susx 31 L4
**Lamerton** Devon 6 C1
**Lamesley** Gatesd 151 G4
**Lamington** S Lans 165 J3
**Lamlash** N Ayrs 162 C3
**Lamonby** Cumb 148 D7
**Lamorna** Cnwll 2 E6
**Lamorran** Cnwll 4 D7
**Lampeter** Cerdgn 66 D5
**Lampeter Velfrey** Pembks 49 K5
**Lamphey** Pembks 49 H7
**Lamplugh** Cumb 136 F3
**Lamport** Nhants 87 L8
**Lamyatt** Somset 26 F4
**Lanark** S Lans 165 G2
**Lancaster** Lancs 129 K7
**Lancaster & Morecambe Crematorium** Lancs 129 K6
**Lancaster Services** Lancs 121 G1
**Lanchester** Dur 150 F5
**Lancing** W Susx 19 G5
**L'Ancresse** Guern 236 d1
**Landbeach** Cambs 76 C2
**Landcross** Devon 23 G6
**Landerberry** Abers 206 E4
**Landford** Wilts 28 E7
**Land-hallow** Highld 227 L2
**Landican Crematorium** Wirral 111 J4
**Landimore** Swans 50 F6
**Landkey** Devon 23 J5
**Landore** Swans 51 J6
**Landrake** Cnwll 6 B4
*Land's End Airport* Cnwll 2 C5
**Landulph** Cnwll 6 C4
**Lane** Cnwll 4 C4
**Laneast** Cnwll 9 G7
**Lane End** Bucks 42 D3
**Lane End** Wilts 27 J3
**Lane Ends** Derbys 100 E5
**Laneham** Notts 116 D6
**Lane Head** Dur 140 E5
**Lanehead** Dur 149 L6
**Lane Head** Wsall 85 H4
**Lane Side** Lancs 122 B6
**Langal** Highld 190 E3
**Langaller** Somset 25 K6
**Langar** Notts 102 B5
**Langbank** Rens 174 D4
**Langbar** N York 123 G1
**Langcliffe** N York 130 F6
**Langdale End** N York 134 E2
**Langdown** Hants 16 E2
**Langdyke** Fife 186 E6
**Langenhoe** Essex 62 B4
**Langford** C Beds 75 H6
**Langford** Devon 12 D2
**Langford** Essex 61 K6
**Langford** Notts 102 D2
**Langford** Oxon 56 E7
**Langford Budville** Somset 25 H6
**Langham** Essex 62 B2
**Langham** Norfk 106 B4
**Langham** Rutlnd 88 B2
**Langham** Suffk 77 L1
**Langho** Lancs 121 K4
**Langholm** D & G 156 C5
**Langland** Swans 51 H7
**Langlee** Border 167 H3
**Langley** Hants 16 F3
**Langley** Herts 59 K4
**Langley** Kent 33 K3
**Langley** Nthumb 149 L3
**Langley** Slough 43 G5
**Langley** Somset 25 G5
**Langley** W Susx 30 D5
**Langley** Warwks 71 L3
**Langley Burrell** Wilts 39 L5
**Langley Green** Essex 61 L4
**Langley Marsh** Somset 25 G5
**Langley Park** Dur 150 F6
**Langley Street** Norfk 93 H3
**Langley Upper Green** Essex 76 C7
**Langney** E Susx 20 D5
**Langold** Notts 115 L4
**Langore** Cnwll 9 J7
**Langport** Somset 26 B6
**Langrick** Lincs 103 L3
**Langridge** BaNES 39 H6
**Langrigg** Cumb 147 K5
**Langrish** Hants 30 B6
**Langsett** Barns 114 E2
**Langside** P & K 185 G5
**Langstone** Hants 17 K2
**Langthorne** N York 132 C2
**Langthorpe** N York 132 F6
**Langthwaite** N York 140 C6
**Langtoft** E R Yk 134 F6
**Langtoft** Lincs 89 G2
**Langton** Dur 140 F4
**Langton** Lincs 118 C7
**Langton** Lincs 118 E7
**Langton** N York 134 C6
**Langton by Wragby** Lincs 117 J6
**Langton Green** Kent 32 F5
**Langton Herring** Dorset 14 C6

**Langton Matravers** Dorset 15 J6
**Langtree** Devon 10 C2
**Langwathby** Cumb 148 F7
**Langwell House** Highld 227 K4
**Langwith** Derbys 115 K7
**Langwith Junction** Derbys 115 K7
**Langworth** Lincs 117 H6
**Lanhydrock House & Gardens** Cnwll 5 H3
**Lanivet** Cnwll 5 G3
**Lanlivery** Cnwll 5 G4
**Lanner** Cnwll 3 J4
**Lanreath** Cnwll 5 J4
**Lansallos** Cnwll 5 J5
**Lanteglos** Cnwll 8 E7
**Lanteglos Highway** Cnwll 5 J5
**Lanton** Border 167 J5
**Lanton** Nthumb 168 D3
**La Passee** Guern 236 d2
**Lapford** Devon 11 H3
**Laphroaig** Ag & B 160 C1
**Lapley** Staffs 84 F2
**La Pulente** Jersey 236 a7
**Lapworth** Warwks 71 L1
**Larachbeg** Highld 190 E6
**Larbert** Falk 176 B3
**Largie** Abers 216 B7
**Largiemore** Ag & B 172 F2
**Largoward** Fife 187 H5
**Largs** N Ayrs 173 L6
**Largybeg** N Ayrs 162 D5
**Largymore** N Ayrs 162 D4
**Larkfield** Inver 173 L4
**Larkfield** Kent 33 J2
**Larkhall** S Lans 175 K7
**Larkhill** Wilts 28 C3
**Larling** Norfk 92 B5
**La Rocque** Jersey 236 e8
**La Rousaillerie** Guern 236 d2
**Lartington** Dur 140 C4
**Lasham** Hants 30 A3
**Lasswade** Mdloth 177 J5
**Lastingham** N York 133 L2
**Latchford** Warrtn 112 F4
**Latchingdon** Essex 61 L7
**Latchley** Cnwll 6 B2
**Lathbury** M Keyn 74 C5
**Latheron** Highld 227 L2
**Latheronwheel** Highld 227 L3
**Lathones** Fife 187 H5
**Latimer** Bucks 59 G7
**Latteridge** S Glos 38 F4
**Lattiford** Somset 27 G6
**Latton** Wilts 40 C2
**Lauder** Border 178 C8
**Laugharne** Carmth 50 C4
**Laughterton** Lincs 116 D6
**Laughton** E Susx 20 A3
**Laughton** Leics 87 J5
**Laughton** Lincs 103 H6
**Laughton** Lincs 116 D3
**Laughton-en-le-Morthen** Rothm 115 K4
**Launceston** Cnwll 9 J7
**Launton** Oxon 57 L4
**Laurencekirk** Abers 197 H3
**Laurieston** D & G 146 B3
**Laurieston** Falk 176 B3
**Lavendon** M Keyn 74 D4
**Lavenham** Suffk 77 K5
**Lavernock** V Glam 37 J6
**Laversdale** Cumb 148 E3
**Laverstock** Wilts 28 D5
**Laverstoke** Hants 29 J2
**Laverton** Gloucs 71 J7
**Laverton** N York 132 C5
**Laverton** Somset 27 H2
**La Villette** Guern 236 d4
**Lavister** Wrexhm 98 A2
**Law** S Lans 175 L7
**Lawers** P & K 193 L7
**Lawford** Essex 62 C2
**Lawford** Somset 25 H4
**Law Hill** S Lans 175 L7
**Lawhitton** Cnwll 9 J7
**Lawkland** N York 130 E6
**Lawns Wood Crematorium** Leeds 123 K3
**Lawrenny** Pembks 49 H6
**Lawshall** Suffk 77 K4
**Laxay** W Isls 232 f3
**Laxdale** W Isls 232 f2
**Laxey** IoM 237 d4
**Laxfield** Suffk 93 G8
**Laxford Bridge** Highld 228 C6
**Laxo** Shet 235 d4
**Laxton** E R Yk 125 J5
**Laxton** Nhants 88 D4
**Laxton** Notts 116 B7
**Laycock** C Brad 122 F3
**Layer Breton** Essex 61 M4
**Layer-de-la-Haye** Essex 62 A4
**Layer Marney** Essex 61 L4
**Layham** Suffk 78 B6
**Laymore** Dorset 13 K2
**Laytham** E R Yk 125 H3
**Lazonby** Cumb 148 F6
**Lea** Derbys 101 G2
**Lea** Herefs 54 F4
**Lea** Lincs 116 D4
**Lea** Shrops 83 G5
**Lea** Wilts 39 L3
**Leachkin** Highld 212 F5
**Leadburn** Border 177 H7
**Leadenham** Lincs 102 F3
**Leaden Roding** Essex 60 F5
**Leadgate** Dur 150 E5
**Leadhills** S Lans 165 G6
**Leafield** Oxon 56 F5
**Leagrave** Luton 59 H4
**Leake Common Side** Lincs 104 C3
**Lealholm** N York 142 F5
**Lealt** Highld 209 H3
**Lea Marston** Warwks 86 B5
**Leamington Hastings** Warwks 72 F2
**Leamington Spa** Warwks 72 D2
**Leap Cross** E Susx 20 C4
**Leasgill** Cumb 129 K3
**Leasingham** Lincs 103 H3
**Leasingthorne** Dur 141 G2
**Leatherhead** Surrey 31 K1
**Leathley** N York 123 J2
**Leaton** Shrops 98 C8
**Leaveland** Kent 34 D4
**Leavenheath** Suffk 77 L6
**Leavening** N York 134 C6
**Leaves Green** Gt Lon 45 H7
**Lebberston** N York 135 G3
**Le Bigard** Guern 236 c4
**Le Bourg** Guern 236 c4
**Le Bourg** Jersey 236 e8
**Lechlade on Thames** Gloucs 56 E7
**Lecht Gruinart** Ag & B 170 E5
**Leck** Lancs 130 C4
**Leckbuie** P & K 193 L7
**Leckford** Hants 29 G4
**Leckhampstead** Bucks 73 K6
**Leckhampstead** W Berk 41 H5
**Leckhampstead Thicket** W Berk 41 H5
**Leckhampton** Gloucs 55 L4
**Leckmelm** Highld 220 F4
**Leconfield** E R Yk 126 C2
**Ledaig** Ag & B 191 H8
**Ledburn** Bucks 58 E4
**Ledbury** Herefs 70 C6
**Ledgemoor** Herefs 69 H4
**Ledmore Junction** Highld 224 F6
**Ledsham** Leeds 124 C4
**Ledston** Leeds 124 C5
**Ledwell** Oxon 57 H3
**Lee** Devon 23 H3
**Lee** Gt Lon 45 H5
**Leebotwood** Shrops 83 J4
**Lee Brockhurst** Shrops 98 D6
**Leece** Cumb 128 F5
**Lee Chapel** Essex 46 B3
**Lee Clump** Bucks 58 E6
**Leeds** Kent 33 L3
**Leeds** Leeds 123 K4
*Leeds Bradford Airport* Leeds 123 J3
**Leeds Castle** Kent 33 L3
**Leedstown** Cnwll 3 G4
**Leek** Staffs 99 M2
**Leek Wootton** Warwks 72 C2
**Lee Mill** Devon 6 E5
**Leeming** N York 132 D2
**Leeming Bar** N York 132 D2
**Lee-on-the-Solent** Hants 17 G3
**Lees** Derbys 100 E5
**Lees** Oldham 113 L2
**Lees Green** Derbys 100 E5
**Leesthorpe** Leics 87 L2
**Leeswood** Flints 97 K1
**Leetown** P & K 186 C3
**Leftwich** Ches W 112 F6
**Legbourne** Lincs 118 E5
**Legerwood** Border 167 J2
**Legoland** W & M 42 F5
**Le Gron** Guern 236 c3
**Legsby** Lincs 117 J4
**Le Haguais** Jersey 236 d8
**Le Hocq** Jersey 236 d8
**Leicester** C Leic 87 H3
**Leicester Forest East Services** Leics 87 G3
**Leigh** Dorset 14 C2
**Leigh** Gloucs 55 K3
**Leigh** Kent 32 F4
**Leigh** Surrey 31 L3
**Leigh** Wigan 112 F2
**Leigh** Wilts 40 B3
**Leigh** Worcs 70 D4
**Leigh Beck** Essex 46 D4
**Leigh Delamere** Wilts 39 K5
**Leigh Delamere Services** Wilts 39 K5
**Leigh Green** Kent 34 B7
**Leigh Knoweglass** S Lans 175 H7
**Leigh-on-Sea** Sthend 46 D3
**Leigh Park** Dorset 15 J3
**Leigh Park** Hants 17 K2
**Leigh Sinton** Worcs 70 D4
**Leighswood** Wsall 85 J3
**Leighterton** Gloucs 39 J3
**Leighton** Powys 82 E3
**Leighton** Shrops 84 B3
**Leighton Bromswold** Cambs 89 G7
**Leighton Buzzard** C Beds 58 F3
**Leigh upon Mendip** Somset 27 G3
**Leigh Woods** N Som 38 E6
**Leinthall Earls** Herefs 69 J2
**Leinthall Starkes** Herefs 69 J1
**Leintwardine** Herefs 83 H8
**Leire** Leics 87 G5
**Leiston** Suffk 79 J3
**Leith** C Edin 177 H3
**Leitholm** Border 168 B1
**Lelant** Cnwll 2 F4
**Lelley** E R Yk 126 F4
**Lempitlaw** Border 168 B3
**Lemreway** W Isls 232 f3
**Lemsford** Herts 59 L5
**Lenchwick** Worcs 71 J5
**Lendalfoot** S Ayrs 152 D4
**Lendrick** Stirlg 184 C6
**Lendrum Terrace** Abers 217 L6
**Lenham** Kent 34 B4
**Lenham Heath** Kent 34 B5
**Lenie** Highld 202 D1
**Lennel** Border 168 C2
**Lennox Plunton** D & G 146 A5
**Lennoxtown** E Duns 175 H3
**Lenton** C Nott 101 K5
**Lenton** Lincs 103 G6
**Lenwade** Norfk 106 D8
**Lenzie** E Duns 175 H4
**Leochel-Cushnie** Abers 205 L4
**Leominster** Herefs 69 K3
**Leonard Stanley** Gloucs 55 J7
**Leoville** Jersey 236 b6
**Lephin** Highld 208 B4
**Leppington** N York 134 B7
**Lepton** Kirk 123 J7
**Lerags** Ag & B 182 B3
**L'Erée** Guern 236 b3
**Lerryn** Cnwll 5 J4
**Lerwick** Shet 235 d6
**Les Arquets** Guern 236 b3
**Lesbury** Nthumb 169 J6
**Les Hubits** Guern 236 d3
**Leslie** Abers 206 B1
**Leslie** Fife 186 D6
**Les Lohiers** Guern 236 c3
**Lesmahagow** S Lans 164 F2
**Les Murchez** Guern 236 c4
**Lesnewth** Cnwll 8 F6
**Les Nicolles** Guern 236 c4
**Les Quartiers** Guern 236 d2
**Les Quennevais** Jersey 236 b7
**Les Sages** Guern 236 b3
**Lessingham** Norfk 107 H6
**Lessonhall** Cumb 147 L5
**Les Villets** Guern 236 c4
**Leswalt** D & G 144 B3
**L'Etacq** Jersey 236 a6
**Letchmore Heath** Herts 43 J2
**Letchworth Garden City** Herts 59 L2
**Letcombe Bassett** Oxon 41 G4
**Letcombe Regis** Oxon 41 G3
**Letham** Angus 196 E6
**Letham** Border 167 K7
**Letham** Falk 176 B2
**Letham** Fife 186 E4
**Letham Grange** Angus 197 G7
**Lethendy** P & K 195 H7
**Lethenty** Abers 206 B2
**Lethenty** Abers 216 F6
**Letheringham** Suffk 78 F3
**Letheringsett** Norfk 106 C5
**Letterewe** Highld 219 L7
**Letterfearn** Highld 200 D2
**Letterfinlay Lodge Hotel** Highld 201 K6
**Lettermorar** Highld 199 M7
**Letters** Highld 220 F4
**Lettershaw** S Lans 165 H5
**Letterston** Pembks 48 F2
**Lettoch** Highld 204 C2
**Lettoch** Highld 214 D7
**Letton** Herefs 69 G5
**Letty Green** Herts 59 M5
**Letwell** Rothm 115 K4
**Leuchars** Fife 187 G3
**Leumrabhagh** W Isls 232 f3
**Leurbost** W Isls 232 f3
**Levedale** Staffs 84 F1
**Leven** E R Yk 126 D2
**Leven** Fife 186 F7
**Levens** Cumb 129 K3
**Levens Green** Herts 60 B4
**Levenshulme** Manch 113 K3
**Levenwick** Shet 235 c7
**Leverburgh** W Isls 232 d5
**Leverington** Cambs 90 C2

**Leverstock Green** Herts 59 H6
**Leverton** Lincs 104 C3
**Le Villocq** Guern 236 c2
**Levington** Suffk 78 F6
**Levisham** N York 134 C2
**Lew** Oxon 56 F6
**Lewannick** Cnwll 9 H8
**Lewdown** Devon 10 C7
**Lewes** E Susx 19 L4
**Leweston** Pembks 48 F3
**Lewisham** Gt Lon 45 G5
**Lewisham Crematorium** Gt Lon 45 H5
**Lewiston** Highld 212 D8
**Lewistown** Brdgnd 36 E3
**Lewknor** Oxon 42 B2
**Lewson Street** Kent 34 C3
**Lewtrenchard** Devon 10 C7
**Lexden** Essex 62 A3
**Lexworthy** Somset 25 K4
**Leybourne** Kent 33 H2
**Leyburn** N York 131 L2
**Leygreen** Herts 59 K3
**Ley Hill** Bucks 59 G7
**Leyland** Lancs 121 H6
**Leylodge** Abers 206 E3
**Leys** Abers 217 J4
**Leys** P & K 195 K8
**Leysdown-on-Sea** Kent 47 G6
**Leysmill** Angus 196 F6
**Leys of Cossans** Angus 196 C6
**Leysters** Herefs 69 L2
**Leyton** Gt Lon 45 G3
**Leytonstone** Gt Lon 45 H3
**Lezant** Cnwll 5 M1
**Lhanbryde** Moray 215 G3
**Libanus** Powys 52 F3
**Libberton** S Lans 165 J2
**Liberton** C Edin 177 J4
**Lichfield** Staffs 85 K2
**Lichfield & District Crematorium** Staffs 85 L2
**Lickey** Worcs 85 H7
**Lickey End** Worcs 85 H8
**Lickfold** W Susx 30 F6
**Liddesdale** Highld 190 F4
**Liddington** Swindn 40 E4
**Lidgate** Suffk 77 G3
**Lidlington** C Beds 74 E6
**Liff** Angus 186 E2
**Lifford** Birm 85 J7
**Lifton** Devon 9 K7
**Liftondown** Devon 9 K7
**Lighthorne** Warwks 72 D4
**Lighthorne Heath** Warwks 72 D4
**Lightwater** Surrey 42 F7
**Lightwater Valley Theme Park** N York 132 D4
**Lightwood** C Stke 99 L4
**Lilbourne** Nhants 87 H7
**Lilleshall** Wrekin 84 D1
**Lilley** Herts 59 J3
**Lilliesleaf** Border 167 H4
**Lillingstone Dayrell** Bucks 73 K6
**Lillingstone Lovell** Bucks 73 K6
**Lillington** Dorset 26 F8
**Lilliput** Poole 15 K4
**Lilstock** Somset 25 J3
**Limbury** Luton 59 H3
**Limekilnburn** S Lans 175 J7
**Limekilns** Fife 176 E2
**Limerigg** Falk 176 B4
**Limerstone** IoW 16 E6
**Lime Street** Worcs 55 J2
**Limington** Somset 26 D6
**Limmerhaugh** E Ayrs 164 C4
**Limpenhoe** Norfk 93 H3
**Limpley Stoke** Wilts 39 H7
**Limpsfield** Surrey 32 D3
**Limpsfield Chart** Surrey 32 D3
**Linby** Notts 101 K3
**Linchmere** W Susx 30 E5
**Lincluden** D & G 155 G6
**Lincoln** Lincs 116 F7
**Lincoln Crematorium** Lincs 117 G7
**Lincomb** Worcs 70 E2
**Lindale** Cumb 129 J4
**Lindal in Furness** Cumb 128 F4
**Lindfield** W Susx 32 C7
**Lindford** Hants 30 D4
**Lindley** Kirk 123 G6
**Lindores** Fife 186 D4
**Lindridge** Worcs 70 C2
**Lindsell** Essex 61 G3
**Lindsey** Suffk 77 L5
**Lindsey Tye** Suffk 78 B5
**Lingdale** R & Cl 142 E4
**Lingen** Herefs 69 G2
**Lingfield** Surrey 32 C4
**Lingwood** Norfk 93 H2
**Liniclate** W Isls 233 b7
**Linicro** Highld 218 B7
**Linkend** Worcs 55 J2
**Linkenholt** Hants 41 G8
**Linkinhorne** Cnwll 5 L2
**Linktown** Fife 177 J1
**Linkwood** Moray 214 F3
**Linley** Shrops 83 G5
**Linley Green** Herefs 70 C4
**Linlithgow** W Loth 176 D3
**Linn Crematorium** E Rens 175 G6
**Linsidemore** Highld 222 D2
**Linslade** C Beds 58 E3
**Linstead Parva** Suffk 93 G7
**Linstock** Cumb 148 D4
**Linthurst** Worcs 85 H8
**Linthwaite** Kirk 123 G7
**Lintlaw** Border 179 H6
**Lintmill** Moray 215 L2
**Linton** Border 168 B4
**Linton** Cambs 76 E5
**Linton** Derbys 86 C1
**Linton** Herefs 54 F3
**Linton** Kent 33 K3
**Linton** Leeds 124 B2
**Linton** N York 131 J6
**Linton Hill** Herefs 54 F3
**Linton-on-Ouse** N York 133 G7
**Linwood** Lincs 117 J4
**Linwood** Rens 174 E5
**Lionacleit** W Isls 233 b7
**Lional** W Isls 232 g1
**Liphook** Hants 30 D5
**Liscard** Wirral 111 J3
**Liscombe** Somset 24 D5
**Liskeard** Cnwll 5 K3
**Lismore** Ag & B 191 G7
**Liss** Hants 30 C5
**Lissett** E R Yk 135 H7
**Lissington** Lincs 117 J5
**Lisvane** Cardif 37 J4
**Liswerry** Newpt 37 M3
**Litcham** Norfk 105 L8
**Litchborough** Nhants 73 J4
**Litchfield** Hants 29 J2
**Litherland** Sefton 111 K2
**Litlington** Cambs 75 K6
**Litlington** E Susx 20 B5
**Little Abington** Cambs 76 D5
**Little Addington** Nhants 88 D8
**Little Airies** D & G 145 J5
**Little Alne** Warwks 71 K3
**Little Altcar** Sefton 111 J1
**Little Amwell** Herts 60 B5
**Little Aston** Staffs 85 K4
**Little Ayton** N York 142 C5
**Little Baddow** Essex 61 J6
**Little Badminton** S Glos 39 J4
**Little Bampton** Cumb 148 A4
**Little Bardfield** Essex 61 G2
**Little Barford** Bed 75 H3
**Little Barningham** Norfk 106 D5
**Little Barrington** Gloucs 56 D5
**Little Barrow** Ches W 112 C7
**Little Bavington** Nthumb 158 C6
**Little Bedwyn** Wilts 40 F7
**Little Bentley** Essex 62 D3
**Little Berkhamsted** Herts 59 M6
**Little Billing** Nhants 74 B3
**Little Billington** C Beds 58 F4
**Little Birch** Herefs 54 D2
**Little Blakenham** Suffk 78 D5
**Little Blencow** Cumb 148 E7
**Little Bognor** W Susx 31 G7
**Little Bollington** Ches E 113 G4
**Little Bookham** Surrey 31 J1
**Littleborough** Notts 116 D5
**Littleborough** Rochdl 122 D7
**Littlebourne** Kent 35 G3
**Little Bourton** Oxon 72 F5
**Little Braxted** Essex 61 K5
**Little Brechin** Angus 196 F4
**Littlebredy** Dorset 14 B5
**Little Brickhill** M Keyn 58 E2
**Little Brington** Nhants 73 J2
**Little Bromley** Essex 62 C3
**Little Budworth** Ches W 112 E7
**Littleburn** Highld 212 F4
**Little Burstead** Essex 46 A2
**Littlebury** Essex 76 D6
**Littlebury Green** Essex 76 C6
**Little Bytham** Lincs 103 G8
**Little Carlton** Lincs 118 E4
**Little Casterton** Rutlnd 88 E2
**Little Cawthorpe** Lincs 118 E5
**Little Chalfont** Bucks 43 G2
**Little Chart** Kent 34 C5
**Little Chesterford** Essex 76 D6
**Little Cheverell** Wilts 27 M2
**Little Chishill** Cambs 76 B6
**Little Clacton** Essex 62 E4
**Little Clifton** Cumb 136 E2
**Little Coates** NE Lin 127 G8
**Little Comberton** Worcs 71 G5
**Little Common** E Susx 20 E4
**Little Compton** Warwks 56 E3
**Little Cornard** Suffk 77 K6
**Little Cowarne** Herefs 69 L4
**Little Coxwell** Oxon 40 F2
**Little Crakehall** N York 132 C2
**Little Cressingham** Norfk 91 K4
**Little Crosby** Sefton 111 K2
**Little Cubley** Derbys 100 D5
**Little Dalby** Leics 87 L2
**Littledean** Gloucs 54 F5
**Little Dewchurch** Herefs 54 D2
**Little Ditton** Cambs 76 F3
**Little Downham** Cambs 90 D6
**Little Driffield** E R Yk 134 F7
**Little Dunham** Norfk 91 K2
**Little Dunkeld** P & K 195 G7
**Little Dunmow** Essex 61 G4
**Little Durnford** Wilts 28 C5
**Little Easton** Essex 60 F3
**Little Eaton** Derbys 101 G4
**Little Ellingham** Norfk 92 B4
**Little Everdon** Nhants 73 H3
**Little Eversden** Cambs 75 L4
**Little Faringdon** Oxon 56 E7
**Little Fencote** N York 132 D2
**Little Fenton** N York 124 D4
**Little Fransham** Norfk 91 K2
**Little Gaddesden** Herts 59 G5
**Little Glemham** Suffk 79 H3
**Little Gorsley** Herefs 55 G3
**Little Gransden** Cambs 75 J4
**Little Green** Somset 27 G2
**Little Hadham** Herts 60 C4
**Little Hale** Lincs 103 J4
**Little Hallam** Derbys 101 J4
**Little Hallingbury** Essex 60 D4
**Littleham** Devon 12 D6
**Littleham** Devon 23 G6
**Littlehampton** W Susx 18 D5
**Little Harrowden** Nhants 74 C1
**Little Haseley** Oxon 57 M7
**Little Haven** Pembks 48 E5
**Littlehaven** W Susx 31 K5
**Little Hay** Staffs 85 K3
**Little Haywood** Staffs 100 A7
**Littlehempston** Devon 7 J4
**Little Hereford** Herefs 69 K2
**Little Horkesley** Essex 62 A2
**Little Hormead** Herts 60 C3
**Little Horsted** E Susx 19 M3
**Little Horton** C Brad 123 H4
**Little Horwood** Bucks 58 C2
**Little Houghton** Barns 115 H1
**Little Houghton** Nhants 74 B3
**Little Hucklow** Derbys 114 D5
**Little Hutton** N York 133 G4
**Little Irchester** Nhants 74 C2
**Little Keyford** Somset 27 H3
**Little Kimble** Bucks 58 D6
**Little Kineton** Warwks 72 D4
**Little Kingshill** Bucks 58 E7
**Little Knox** D & G 146 E3
**Little Langdale** Cumb 137 J6
**Little Langford** Wilts 28 B4
**Little Leigh** Ches W 112 F6
**Little Leighs** Essex 61 H5
**Little Lever** Bolton 121 L8
**Little Linford** M Keyn 74 B5
**Little Load** Somset 26 C6
**Little London** Cambs 90 B4
**Little London** E Susx 20 C2
**Little London** Hants 29 G2
**Little London** Hants 41 L8
**Little Longstone** Derbys 114 D6
**Little Maplestead** Essex 77 J7
**Little Marcle** Herefs 70 C7
**Little Marlow** Bucks 42 E3
**Little Massingham** Norfk 105 J7
**Little Melton** Norfk 92 E3
**Littlemill** Abers 205 H6
**Littlemill** Highld 213 L4
**Little Mill** Mons 53 L7
**Little Milton** Oxon 57 L7
**Little Missenden** Bucks 58 F7
**Littlemore** Oxon 57 K7
**Little Musgrave** Cumb 139 H5
**Little Ness** Shrops 98 B8
**Little Newcastle** Pembks 49 G2
**Little Newsham** Dur 140 E4

**Little Norton** Somset 26 C7
**Little Oakley** Essex 62 F3
**Little Oakley** Nhants 88 C6
**Little Orton** Cumb 148 C4
**Littleover** C Derb 101 G5
**Little Packington** Warwks 86 B6
**Little Paxton** Cambs 75 H3
**Little Petherick** Cnwll 4 E2
**Little Plumstead** Norfk 93 G2
**Little Ponton** Lincs 102 F6
**Littleport** Cambs 90 E6
**Little Preston** Nhants 73 H4
**Little Raveley** Cambs 89 J7
**Little Reedness** E R Yk 125 J6
**Little Ribston** N York 132 F8
**Little Rissington** Gloucs 56 D4
**Little Rollright** Oxon 56 F3
**Little Ryburgh** Norfk 106 A6
**Little Salkeld** Cumb 148 F7
**Little Sampford** Essex 76 F7
**Little Saughall** Ches W 111 K7
**Little Saxham** Suffk 77 H2
**Little Scatwell** Highld 212 B3
**Little Shelford** Cambs 76 C4
**Little Singleton** Lancs 120 E3
**Little Skipwith** N York 125 G3
**Little Smeaton** N York 124 D6
**Little Snoring** Norfk 106 A6
**Little Sodbury** S Glos 39 H4
**Little Somborne** Hants 29 G5
**Little Somerford** Wilts 39 L4
**Little Soudley** Shrops 99 G6
**Little Stainton** Darltn 141 J3
**Little Stanney** Ches W 112 B6
**Little Staughton** Bed 75 G3
**Little Steeping** Lincs 118 F8
**Little Stoke** Staffs 99 K6
**Littlestone-on-Sea** Kent 21 L2
**Little Stonham** Suffk 78 D3
**Little Stretton** Leics 87 J4
**Little Stretton** Shrops 83 J5
**Little Strickland** Cumb 138 E4
**Little Stukeley** Cambs 89 H7
**Little Sugnall** Staffs 99 J6
**Little Swinburne** Nthumb 158 B6
**Little Sypland** D & G 146 C4
**Little Tew** Oxon 57 G3
**Little Tey** Essex 61 L4
**Little Thetford** Cambs 90 D7
**Little Thorpe** Dur 151 K6
**Littlethorpe** Leics 87 G4
**Littlethorpe** N York 132 E5
**Little Thurlow** Suffk 76 F4
**Little Thurrock** Thurr 45 L4
**Littleton** Angus 196 B6
**Littleton** Ches W 112 C7
**Littleton** D & G 146 B4
**Littleton** Hants 29 J5
**Littleton** Somset 26 C5
**Littleton** Surrey 43 H6
**Littleton Drew** Wilts 39 J4
**Littleton-on-Severn** S Glos 38 E3
**Littleton Pannell** Wilts 27 M2
**Little Torrington** Devon 10 D2
**Littletown** Dur 151 H6
**Little Town** Lancs 121 K4
**Little Urswick** Cumb 128 F5
**Little Wakering** Essex 46 F3
**Little Walden** Essex 76 D6
**Little Waldingfield** Suffk 77 K5
**Little Walsingham** Norfk 105 M5
**Little Waltham** Essex 61 H5
**Little Weighton** E R Yk 126 B4
**Little Wenlock** Wrekin 84 B3
**Little Weston** Somset 26 F6
**Little Whitefield** IoW 17 H4
**Littlewick Green** W & M 42 D4
**Little Wilbraham** Cambs 76 D3
**Little Witcombe** Gloucs 55 K5
**Little Witley** Worcs 70 D2
**Little Wittenham** Oxon 41 K2
**Little Wolford** Warwks 72 C7
**Little Woodcote** Gt Lon 44 F7
**Littleworth** Oxon 40 F2
**Littleworth** Staffs 99 L7
**Littleworth** Worcs 70 F4
**Little Wymington** Bed 74 D2
**Little Wymondley** Herts 59 K3
**Little Wyrley** Staffs 85 H3
**Little Yeldham** Essex 77 H6
**Littley Green** Essex 61 H4
**Litton** Derbys 114 D6
**Litton** N York 131 G5
**Litton** Somset 26 E1
**Litton Cheney** Dorset 14 A4
**Liurbost** W Isls 232 f3
**Liverpool** Lpool 111 K4
**Liverpool Maritime Mercantile City** Lpool 111 K4
**Liversedge** Kirk 123 J5
**Liverton** Devon 7 J2
**Liverton** R & Cl 142 F4
**Livingston** W Loth 176 E5
**Livingston Village** W Loth 176 E5
**Lixwm** Flints 111 G7
**Lizard** Cnwll 3 J8
**Llanaelhaearn** Gwynd 95 G4
**Llanafan** Cerdgn 80 F8
**Llanafan-Fawr** Powys 67 L4
**Llanallgo** IoA 109 G4
**Llanarmon Dyffryn Ceiriog** Wrexhm 97 J6
**Llanarmon-yn-Ial** Denbgs 97 J2
**Llanarth** Cerdgn 65 L3
**Llanarth** Mons 54 B5
**Llanarthne** Carmth 51 G2
**Llanasa** Flints 110 F5
**Llanbadarn Fawr** Cerdgn 80 E7
**Llanbadarn Fynydd** Powys 82 C7
**Llanbadoc** Mons 54 B7
**Llanbeder** Newpt 38 B3
**Llanbedr** Gwynd 95 K7
**Llanbedr** Powys 53 K4
**Llanbedr-Dyffryn-Clwyd** Denbgs 97 H2
**Llanbedrgoch** IoA 109 G5
**Llanbedrog** Gwynd 94 F6
**Llanbedr-y-Cennin** Conwy 109 L7
**Llanberis** Gwynd 95 K1
**Llanbethêry** V Glam 37 G6
**Llanbister** Powys 82 C8
**Llanblethian** V Glam 36 F5
**Llanboidy** Carmth 49 L3
**Llanbradach** Caerph 37 J3
**Llanbrynmair** Powys 81 J3
**Llancadle** V Glam 37 G6
**Llancarfan** V Glam 37 G6
**Llancloudy** Herefs 54 D4
**Llandaff** Cardif 37 J5
**Llandanwg** Gwynd 95 K6
**Llanddaniel Fab** IoA 109 G7
**Llanddarog** Carmth 51 G3
**Llanddeiniol** Cerdgn 66 D1
**Llanddeiniolen** Gwynd 109 H7
**Llandderfel** Gwynd 96 F5
**Llanddeusant** IoA 108 D4
**Llanddew** Powys 53 G2
**Llanddewi** Swans 50 F7
**Llanddewi Brefi** Cerdgn 66 F4
**Llanddewi Rhydderch** Mons 53 M5
**Llanddewi Velfrey** Pembks 49 K4
**Llanddewi Ystradenni** Powys 68 C2
**Llanddoget** Conwy 109 M8
**Llanddona** IoA 109 H5
**Llanddowror** Carmth 50 B3
**Llanddulas** Conwy 110 C6
**Llanddwywe** Gwynd 95 K7
**Llanddyfnan** IoA 109 G5
**Llandefaelog-Tre'r-Graig** Powys 53 H3
**Llandefalle** Powys 68 C7
**Llandegfan** IoA 109 H6
**Llandegla** Denbgs 97 J3
**Llandegley** Powys 68 D2
**Llandegveth** Mons 37 M2
**Llandeilo** Carmth 51 J2
**Llandeilo Graban** Powys 68 C5
**Llandeloy** Pembks 48 E3
**Llandenny** Mons 54 B7
**Llandevaud** Newpt 38 B3
**Llandevenny** Mons 38 B3
**Llandinam** Powys 82 B5
**Llandissilio** Pembks 49 J3
**Llandogo** Mons 54 D7
**Llandough** V Glam 36 F6
**Llandough** V Glam 37 J5
**Llandovery** Carmth 67 G7
**Llandow** V Glam 36 E5
**Llandre** Carmth 66 F6
**Llandre** Cerdgn 80 E6
**Llandre Isaf** Pembks 49 J2
**Llandrillo** Denbgs 97 G5
**Llandrillo-yn-Rhos** Conwy 110 B5
**Llandrindod Wells** Powys 68 B3
**Llandrinio** Powys 97 L8
**Llandudno** Conwy 109 L5
**Llandudno Junction** Conwy 109 M6
**Llandulas** Powys 67 J6
**Llandwrog** Gwynd 95 H2
**Llandybie** Carmth 51 J3
**Llandyfaelog** Carmth 50 E3
**Llandyfriog** Cerdgn 65 K6
**Llandygai** Gwynd 109 H7
**Llandygwydd** Cerdgn 65 H5
**Llandyrnog** Denbgs 110 F8
**Llandyssil** Powys 82 E4
**Llandysul** Cerdgn 65 L6
**Llanedeyrn** Cardif 37 K4
**Llaneglwys** Powys 68 B6
**Llanegryn** Gwynd 80 D3
**Llanegwad** Carmth 51 G2
**Llaneilian** IoA 108 F3
**Llanelian-yn-Rhôs** Conwy 110 B6
**Llanelidan** Denbgs 97 H3
**Llanelieu** Powys 68 D7
**Llanellen** Mons 53 L5
**Llanelli** Carmth 51 G5
**Llanelli Crematorium** Carmth 51 G5
**Llanelltyd** Gwynd 96 A8
**Llanelwedd** Powys 68 B4
**Llanenddwyn** Gwynd 95 K7
**Llanengan** Gwynd 94 E6
**Llanerchymedd** IoA 108 E5
**Llanerfyl** Powys 82 B2
**Llanfachraeth** IoA 108 D5
**Llanfachreth** Gwynd 96 B7
**Llanfaelog** IoA 108 D6
**Llanfaelrhys** Gwynd 94 D6
**Llanfaethlu** IoA 108 D4
**Llanfair** Gwynd 95 K6
**Llanfair Caereinion** Powys 82 C3
**Llanfair Clydogau** Cerdgn 66 E4
**Llanfair Dyffryn Clwyd** Denbgs 97 H2
**Llanfairfechan** Conwy 109 K6
**Llanfairpwllgwyngyll** IoA 109 G6
**Llanfair Talhaiarn** Conwy 110 C7
**Llanfair Waterdine** Shrops 82 E7
**Llanfairynghornwy** IoA 108 D4
**Llanfair-yn-Neubwll** IoA 108 C6
**Llanfallteg** Carmth 49 K4
**Llanfallteg West** Carmth 49 K4
**Llanfarian** Cerdgn 80 D7
**Llanfechain** Powys 97 J7
**Llanfechell** IoA 108 E3
**Llanferres** Denbgs 97 J1
**Llanfihangel-ar-arth** Carmth 66 B6
**Llanfihangel Glyn Myfyr** Conwy 96 F3
**Llanfihangel Nant Bran** Powys 67 K7
**Llanfihangel Rhydithon** Powys 68 D2
**Llanfihangel Rogiet** Mons 38 C3
**Llanfihangel-y-Creuddyn** Cerdgn 80 F7
**Llanfihangel-yng-Ngwynfa** Powys 82 C1
**Llanfihangel yn Nhowyn** IoA 108 D6
**Llanfihangel-y-traethau** Gwynd 95 K5
**Llanfilo** Powys 53 H2
**Llanfoist** Mons 53 L5
**Llanfor** Gwynd 96 E5
**Llanfrechfa** Torfn 37 L2
**Llanfrynach** Powys 53 G3
**Llanfwrog** Denbgs 97 H2
**Llanfwrog** IoA 108 C5
**Llanfyllin** Powys 97 H8
**Llanfynydd** Carmth 66 D8
**Llanfynydd** Flints 97 L2
**Llanfyrnach** Pembks 49 L2
**Llangadfan** Powys 81 L2
**Llangadog** Carmth 66 F8
**Llangadwaladr** IoA 108 E7
**Llangaffo** IoA 108 F7
**Llangammarch Wells** Powys 67 K5
**Llangan** V Glam 36 E5
**Llangarron** Herefs 54 D4
**Llangathen** Carmth 51 H2
**Llangattock** Powys 53 K4
**Llangattock Lingoed** Mons 54 A4
**Llangedwyn** Powys 97 J7
**Llangefni** IoA 108 F6
**Llangeinor** Brdgnd 36 E3
**Llangeitho** Cerdgn 66 E3
**Llangeler** Carmth 65 L6
**Llangelynin** Gwynd 80 D3
**Llangendeirne** Carmth 50 F3
**Llangennech** Carmth 51 H5
**Llangennith** Swans 50 E7
**Llangernyw** Conwy 110 B7
**Llangian** Gwynd 94 E6
**Llangloffan** Pembks 64 C7
**Llanglydwen** Carmth 49 K3
**Llangoed** IoA 109 J5
**Llangollen** Denbgs 97 K4
**Llangolman** Pembks 49 J3
**Llangors** Powys 53 H3
**Llangower** Gwynd 96 D6
**Llangrannog** Cerdgn 65 K4
**Llangristiolus** IoA 108 F6
**Llangrove** Herefs 54 D4
**Llangunllo** Powys 68 E1
**Llangunnor** Carmth 50 E2

**Llangurig** Powys 81 K7
**Llangwm** Conwy 96 F4
**Llangwm** Mons 54 B7
**Llangwm** Pembks 49 G5
**Llangwnnadl** Gwynd 94 D6
**Llangwyryfon** Cerdgn 66 D1
**Llangybi** Cerdgn 66 E4
**Llangybi** Gwynd 95 G4
**Llangybi** Mons 38 A2
**Llangynhafal** Denbgs 110 F8
**Llangynidr** Powys 53 J4
**Llangynin** Carmth 50 B2
**Llangynog** Carmth 50 D3
**Llangynog** Powys 97 G7
**Llangynwyd** Brdgnd 36 D3
**Llanhamlach** Powys 53 H3
**Llanharan** Rhondd 36 F4
**Llanharry** Rhondd 36 F4
**Llanhennock** Mons 38 A2
**Llanhilleth** Blae G 53 K7
**Llanidloes** Powys 81 K6
**Llaniestyn** Gwynd 94 E5
**Llanigon** Powys 68 E6
**Llanilar** Cerdgn 80 E8
**Llanilid** Rhondd 36 F4
**Llanina** Cerdgn 65 L3
**Llanishen** Cardif 37 J4
**Llanishen** Mons 54 C7
**Llanllechid** Gwynd 109 J7
**Llanllowell** Mons 54 B7
**Llanllugan** Powys 82 B3
**Llanllwch** Carmth 50 E2
**Llanllwchaiarn** Powys 82 C5
**Llanllwni** Carmth 66 C6
**Llanllyfni** Gwynd 95 H3
**Llanmadoc** Swans 50 F6
**Llanmaes** V Glam 36 F6
**Llanmartin** Newpt 38 B3
**Llanmiloe** Carmth 50 B4
**Llannefydd** Conwy 110 D7
**Llannon** Carmth 51 G4
**Llannor** Gwynd 94 F5
**Llanon** Cerdgn 66 C2
**Llanover** Mons 53 L6
**Llanpumsaint** Carmth 65 L8
**Llanrhaeadr-ym-Mochnant** Powys 97 H7
**Llanrhian** Pembks 48 D2
**Llanrhidian** Swans 50 F6
**Llanrhychwyn** Conwy 96 B1
**Llanrhyddlad** IoA 108 D4
**Llanrhystud** Cerdgn 66 C1
**Llanrug** Gwynd 109 G8
**Llanrumney** Cardif 37 K4
**Llanrwst** Conwy 96 C1
**Llansadurnen** Carmth 50 C4
**Llansadwrn** Carmth 66 F7
**Llansadwrn** IoA 109 H6
**Llansaint** Carmth 50 E4
**Llansamlet** Swans 51 K6
**Llansanffraid Glan Conwy** Conwy 110 A6
**Llansannan** Conwy 110 C7
**Llansantffraed** Powys 53 H4
**Llansantffraed-Cwmdeuddwr** Powys 67 L2
**Llansantffraed-in-Elvel** Powys 68 C4
**Llansantffraid** Cerdgn 66 C2
**Llansantffraid-ym-Mechain** Powys 97 K7
**Llansawel** Carmth 66 E7
**Llansilin** Powys 97 K6
**Llansoy** Mons 54 C7
**Llanspyddid** Powys 52 F3
**Llanstadwell** Pembks 48 F6
**Llansteffan** Carmth 50 D4
**Llantarnam** Torfn 37 L2
**Llanteg** Pembks 49 K5
**Llanthewy Skirrid** Mons 53 M5
**Llanthony** Mons 53 L3
**Llantilio-Crossenny** Mons 54 B5
**Llantilio Pertholey** Mons 53 L5
**Llantrisant** Mons 38 B2
**Llantrisant** Rhondd 37 G4
**Llantrithyd** V Glam 37 G6
**Llantwit Fardre** Rhondd 37 G3
**Llantwit Major** V Glam 36 F6
**Llanuwchllyn** Gwynd 96 D6
**Llanvaches** Newpt 38 B3
**Llanvair Discoed** Mons 38 C3
**Llanvapley** Mons 54 A5
**Llanvetherine** Mons 54 A5
**Llanvihangel Crucorney** Mons 53 L4
**Llanwddyn** Powys 96 F8
**Llanwenog** Cerdgn 66 C5
**Llanwern** Newpt 38 A3
**Llanwinio** Carmth 50 C1
**Llanwnda** Gwynd 95 H2
**Llanwnda** Pembks 64 C6
**Llanwnnen** Cerdgn 66 C5
**Llanwnog** Powys 82 B5
**Llanwrda** Carmth 66 F7
**Llanwrin** Powys 81 H3
**Llanwrthwl** Powys 67 L2
**Llanwrtyd Wells** Powys 67 J5
**Llanwyddelan** Powys 82 C4
**Llanyblodwel** Shrops 97 K7
**Llanybri** Carmth 50 D3
**Llanybydder** Carmth 66 C5
**Llanycefn** Pembks 49 J3
**Llanychaer** Pembks 64 D7
**Llanymawddwy** Gwynd 96 D8
**Llanymynech** Powys 97 K7
**Llanynghenedl** IoA 108 D5
**Llanynys** Denbgs 110 F8
**Llanyre** Powys 68 B3
**Llanystumdwy** Gwynd 95 H5
**Llanywern** Powys 53 H3
**Llawhaden** Pembks 49 H4
**Llawryglyn** Powys 81 K5
**Llay** Wrexhm 97 M2
**Llechrhyd** Caerph 53 H6
**Llechryd** Cerdgn 65 H5
**Lledrod** Cerdgn 66 E1
**Lleyn Peninsula** Gwynd 94 E5
**Llithfaen** Gwynd 94 F4
**Lloc** Flints 111 G6
**Llowes** Powys 68 D6
**Llwydcoed** Rhondd 52 F6
**Llwydcoed Crematorium** Rhondd 52 F6
**Llwydiarth** Powys 82 B1
**Llwyncelyn** Cerdgn 66 B3
**Llwyndafydd** Cerdgn 65 K4
**Llwyngwril** Gwynd 80 D2
**Llwynmawr** Wrexhm 97 K5
**Llwynypia** Rhondd 36 F2
**Llynclys** Shrops 97 L7
**Llynfaes** IoA 108 E5
**Llysfaen** Conwy 110 B6
**Llyswen** Powys 68 C6
**Llysworney** V Glam 36 E5
**Llys-y-frân** Pembks 49 H3
**Llywel** Powys 52 D3
**Loan** Falk 176 C3
**Loanhead** Mdloth 177 J5
**Loaningfoot** D & G 147 G4
**Loans** S Ayrs 163 J3
**Lobhillcross** Devon 10 C7
**Lochailort** Highld 200 B8
**Lochaline** Highld 190 D7
**Lochans** D & G 144 C4
**Locharbriggs** D & G 155 H6
**Lochavich** Ag & B 182 D4
**Lochawe** Ag & B 183 G2
**Loch Baghasdail** W Isls 233 c8
**Lochboisdale** W Isls 233 c8
**Lochbuie** Ag & B 181 J3
**Lochcarron** Highld 210 D6
**Lochdon** Ag & B 181 L2
**Lochdonhead** Ag & B 181 L2
**Lochead** Ag & B 172 D3
**Lochearnhead** Stirlg 184 D3
**Lochee** C Dund 186 F2
**Locheilside Station** Highld 191 K1
**Lochend** Highld 212 F6
**Locheport** W Isls 233 c6
**Loch Euphoirt** W Isls 233 c6
**Lochfoot** D & G 154 F7
**Lochgair** Ag & B 172 F1
**Lochgelly** Fife 186 C8
**Lochgilphead** Ag & B 172 E2
**Lochgoilhead** Ag & B 183 H6
**Lochieheads** Fife 186 D5
**Lochill** Moray 215 G2
**Lochindorb Lodge** Highld 214 B7
**Lochinver** Highld 224 D4
*Loch Lomond and The Trossachs National Park* 184 A5
**Loch Loyal Lodge** Highld 229 J6
**Lochluichart** Highld 211 L2
**Lochmaben** D & G 155 J5
**Lochmaddy** W Isls 233 c6
**Loch nam Madadh** W Isls 233 c6
**Loch Ness** Highld 202 E1
**Lochore** Fife 186 C7
**Lochranza** N Ayrs 172 F7
**Loch Sgioport** W Isls 233 c7
**Lochside** Abers 197 H4
**Lochside** D & G 155 G6
**Lochside** Highld 213 J4
**Lochskipport** W Isls 233 c7
**Lochslin** Highld 223 J5
**Lochton** S Ayrs 152 F6
**Lochty** Angus 196 E4
**Lochty** Fife 187 H5
**Lochuisge** Highld 190 F5
**Lochwinnoch** Rens 174 C6
**Lochwood** D & G 155 J3
**Lockengate** Cnwll 5 G4
**Lockerbie** D & G 155 K5
**Lockeridge** Wilts 40 C6
**Lockerley** Hants 28 F6
**Locking** N Som 38 A8
**Locking Stumps** Warrtn 112 F3
**Lockington** E R Yk 126 B2
**Lockleywood** Shrops 99 G6
**Locksbottom** Gt Lon 45 H6
**Locks Heath** Hants 17 G2
**Lockton** N York 134 C2
**Loddington** Leics 87 L3
**Loddington** Nhants 88 B7
**Loddiswell** Devon 7 G6
**Loddon** Norfk 93 H4
**Lode** Cambs 76 D3
**Lode Heath** Solhll 85 L7
**Loders** Dorset 13 L4
**Lodge Hill Crematorium** Birm 85 H6
**Lodsworth** W Susx 30 F6
**Lofthouse** Leeds 123 L5
**Lofthouse** N York 131 L5
**Lofthouse Gate** Wakefd 123 L5
**Loftus** R & Cl 142 F4
**Logan** E Ayrs 164 C5
**Loganlea** W Loth 176 C6
**Loggerheads** Staffs 99 G5
**Logie** Angus 197 H4
**Logie** Fife 186 F4
**Logie** Moray 214 C4
**Logie Coldstone** Abers 205 K4
**Logie Newton** Abers 216 C6
**Logie Pert** Angus 197 G4
**Logierait** P & K 194 F6
**Logierieve** Abers 217 H8
**Login** Carmth 49 K3
**Lolworth** Cambs 75 L2
**Lonbain** Highld 209 L4
**Londesborough** E R Yk 125 K2
**London** Gt Lon 45 G4
**London Apprentice** Cnwll 4 F6
**London Colney** Herts 59 K7
**Londonderry** N York 132 D2
**London Gateway Services** Gt Lon 44 D2
*London Gatwick Airport* W Susx 32 B5
*London Heathrow Airport* Gt Lon 43 H5
*London Luton Airport* Luton 59 J4
*London Oxford Airport* Oxon 57 J5
*London Southend Airport* Essex 46 E3
*London Stansted Airport* Essex 60 E4
**Londonthorpe** Lincs 102 F5
**London Zoo ZSL** Gt Lon 44 F4
**Londubh** Highld 219 K5
**Lonemore** Highld 219 J6
**Long Ashton** N Som 38 D6
**Long Bank** Worcs 84 D8
**Long Bennington** Lincs 102 D4
**Longbenton** N Tyne 151 G2
**Longborough** Gloucs 56 D3
**Long Bredy** Dorset 14 B4
**Longbridge** Birm 85 H7
**Longbridge Deverill** Wilts 27 K4
**Long Buckby** Nhants 73 J2
**Longburton** Dorset 26 F8
**Long Clawson** Leics 102 B6
**Longcliffe** Derbys 100 E2
**Longcombe** Devon 7 J4
**Long Compton** Staffs 99 J7
**Long Compton** Warwks 56 F2
**Longcot** Oxon 40 F3
**Long Crendon** Bucks 58 B6
**Long Crichel** Dorset 15 J1
**Longden** Shrops 83 J3
**Long Ditton** Surrey 44 D6
**Longdon** Staffs 85 J2
**Longdon** Worcs 70 E7
**Longdon Green** Staffs 85 J2
**Longdon upon Tern** Wrekin 84 B1
**Longdown** Devon 11 K6
**Longdowns** Cnwll 3 J4
**Long Duckmanton** Derbys 115 H7
**Long Eaton** Derbys 101 J5
**Longfield** Kent 45 L6
**Longford** Covtry 86 D6
**Longford** Derbys 100 E5
**Longford** Gloucs 55 J4
**Longford** Shrops 98 F5
**Longford** Wrekin 99 G8
**Longforgan** P & K 186 E2
**Longformacus** Border 178 E6
**Longframlington** Nthumb 158 E3
**Long Green** Ches W 112 C7
**Longham** Dorset 15 K3
**Longham** Norfk 91 L1
**Long Hanborough** Oxon 57 H5
**Longhaven** Abers 217 L6
**Longhirst** Nthumb 158 F4
**Longhope** Gloucs 55 G4
**Longhope** Ork 234 b7
**Longhorsley** Nthumb 158 E4
**Longhoughton** Nthumb 169 J6
**Long Itchington** Warwks 72 E2
**Longlane** Derbys 100 E5

**Long Lawford** Warwks 86 F7
**Longleat Safari & Adventure Park** Wilts 27 J3
**Longlevens** Gloucs 55 J4
**Longleys** P & K 195 L7
**Long Load** Somset 26 C6
**Longmanhill** Abers 216 E2
**Long Marston** Herts 58 E5
**Long Marston** N York 124 D1
**Long Marston** Warwks 71 L5
**Long Marton** Cumb 138 F3
**Long Melford** Suffk 77 J5
**Longmoor Camp** Hants 30 C5
**Longmorn** Moray 214 F3
**Longmoss** Ches E 113 K6
**Long Newnton** Gloucs 39 K3
**Longnewton** Border 167 J4
**Long Newton** E Loth 178 B5
**Longnewton** S on T 141 J4
**Longney** Gloucs 55 H5
**Longniddry** E Loth 177 L3
**Longnor** Shrops 83 J4
**Longnor** Staffs 114 C8
**Longparish** Hants 29 H3
**Long Preston** N York 130 F7
**Longridge** Lancs 121 J3
**Longridge** W Loth 176 C5
**Longriggend** N Lans 175 L4
**Long Riston** E R Yk 126 E3
**Longrock** Cnwll 2 E5
**Longsdon** Staffs 99 L2
**Longside** Abers 217 K5
**Longstanton** Cambs 76 B2
**Longstock** Hants 29 G4
**Longstowe** Cambs 75 K4
**Long Stratton** Norfk 92 E5
**Long Street** M Keyn 74 B5
**Longstreet** Wilts 28 C2
**Long Sutton** Hants 30 C3
**Long Sutton** Lincs 104 C7
**Long Sutton** Somset 26 C6
**Longthorpe** C Pete 89 H4
**Long Thurlow** Suffk 78 B2
**Longthwaite** Cumb 138 B3
**Longton** Lancs 121 G5
**Longtown** Cumb 148 C2
**Longtown** Herefs 53 L3
**Longueville** Jersey 236 d7
**Longville in the Dale** Shrops 83 K5
**Long Waste** Wrekin 84 B1
**Long Whatton** Leics 101 J7
**Longwick** Bucks 58 C6
**Long Wittenham** Oxon 41 K2
**Longwitton** Nthumb 158 D4
**Longwood** D & G 146 C3
**Longworth** Oxon 57 G7
**Longyester** E Loth 178 C5
**Lonmay** Abers 217 J3
**Lonmore** Highld 208 D5
**Looe** Cnwll 5 K5
**Loose** Kent 33 K3
**Loosley Row** Bucks 58 D7
**Lootcherbrae** Abers 216 B4
**Lopen** Somset 26 B8
**Loppington** Shrops 98 C6
**Lordshill** C Sotn 29 H7
**Lords Wood** Medway 46 C7
**Lornty** P & K 195 J6
**Loscoe** Derbys 101 H3
**Losgaintir** W Isls 232 d4
**Lossiemouth** Moray 214 F1
**Lostock Gralam** Ches W 113 G6
**Lostock Green** Ches W 113 G6
**Lostwithiel** Cnwll 5 H4
**Lothbeg** Highld 227 G6
**Lothersdale** N York 122 E2
**Lothmore** Highld 227 G6
**Loudwater** Bucks 42 E3
**Loughborough** Leics 101 K8
**Loughborough Crematorium** Leics 101 K8
**Loughor** Swans 51 H6
**Loughton** Essex 45 H2
**Loughton** M Keyn 74 B6
**Lound** Lincs 103 H8
**Lound** Notts 116 B4
**Lound** Suffk 93 K4
**Lount** Leics 101 G8
**Louth** Lincs 118 D4
**Lover** Wilts 28 E7
**Loversall** Donc 115 L2
**Loveston** Pembks 49 J5
**Lovington** Somset 26 E5
**Low Ackworth** Wakefd 124 C6
**Low Barbeth** D & G 144 B2
**Low Bentham** N York 130 C5
**Low Biggins** Cumb 130 B4
**Low Borrowbridge** Cumb 138 E6
**Low Bradfield** Sheff 114 E3
**Low Bradley** N York 122 F2
**Low Burnham** N Linc 116 C2
**Lowca** Cumb 136 D3
**Low Catton** E R Yk 133 L8
**Low Crosby** Cumb 148 D3
**Lowdham** Notts 102 A3
**Low Dinsdale** Darltn 141 J5
**Lower Aisholt** Somset 25 J4
**Lower Ansty** Dorset 14 E2
**Lower Apperley** Gloucs 55 J3
**Lower Ashton** Devon 11 J7
**Lower Assendon** Oxon 42 C4
**Lower Bartle** Lancs 121 G4
**Lower Basildon** W Berk 41 L5
**Lower Beeding** W Susx 31 L6
**Lower Benefield** Nhants 88 E5
**Lower Bentley** Worcs 71 H2
**Lower Boddington** Nhants 72 F4
**Lower Bourne** Surrey 30 D3
**Lower Brailes** Warwks 72 C6
**Lower Breakish** Highld 199 L2
**Lower Broadheath** Worcs 70 E3
**Lower Broxwood** Herefs 69 G4
**Lower Bullingham** Herefs 69 K6
**Lower Burgate** Hants 28 D7
**Lower Caldecote** C Beds 75 H5
**Lower Chapel** Powys 68 B7
**Lower Chicksgrove** Wilts 27 L5
**Lower Chute** Wilts 28 F2
**Lower Clapton** Gt Lon 45 G3
**Lower Clent** Worcs 85 G7
**Lower Cumberworth** Kirk 123 J8
**Lower Darwen** Bl w D 121 K5
**Lower Dean** Bed 74 F2
**Lower Diabaig** Highld 210 C3
**Lower Dicker** E Susx 20 B4
**Lower Down** Shrops 83 G6
**Lower Dunsforth** N York 133 G6
**Lower Egleton** Herefs 70 B5
**Lower End** M Keyn 74 D6
**Lower Eythorne** Kent 35 H5
**Lower Failand** N Som 38 D5
**Lower Farringdon** Hants 30 B4
**Lower Feltham** Gt Lon 43 H6
**Lower Froyle** Hants 30 C3
**Lower Gabwell** Devon 7 L2
**Lower Gledfield** Highld 222 D4
**Lower Godney** Somset 26 C3
**Lower Gornal** Dudley 85 G5
**Lower Gravenhurst** C Beds 75 G7
**Lower Green** Kent 32 F5
**Lower Green** Kent 33 G5
**Lower Halliford** Surrey 43 H6
**Lower Halstow** Kent 46 E6
**Lower Hamworthy** Poole 15 J4
**Lower Hardres** Kent 34 F4
**Lower Hartwell** Bucks 58 C5
**Lower Hergest** Herefs 68 F4
**Lower Heyford** Oxon 57 J3
**Lower Heysham** Lancs 129 J7
**Lower Houses** Kirk 123 H7
**Lower Irlam** Salfd 113 G3
**Lower Killeyan** Ag & B 160 A2
**Lower Langford** N Som 38 C7
**Lower Largo** Fife 187 G6
**Lower Leigh** Staffs 100 A5
**Lower Loxhore** Devon 23 K4
**Lower Lydbrook** Gloucs 54 E5
**Lower Lye** Herefs 69 H2
**Lower Machen** Newpt 37 K3
**Lower Merridge** Somset 25 J4
**Lower Middleton Cheney** Nhants 73 G6
**Lower Moor** Worcs 71 H5
**Lower Morton** S Glos 38 F3
**Lower Nazeing** Essex 60 C6
**Lower Penarth** V Glam 37 J6
**Lower Penn** Staffs 84 F4
**Lower Peover** Ches E 113 H6
**Lower Place** Rochdl 122 D7
**Lower Quinton** Warwks 71 L5
**Lower Raydon** Suffk 78 C6
**Lower Roadwater** Somset 25 G4
**Lower Seagry** Wilts 39 L4
**Lower Shelton** C Beds 74 E6
**Lower Shiplake** Oxon 42 C4
**Lower Shuckburgh** Warwks 72 F3
**Lower Slaughter** Gloucs 56 D4
**Lower Standen** Kent 35 H6
**Lower Stanton St Quintin** Wilts 39 L4
**Lower Stoke** Medway 46 D5
**Lower Stone** Gloucs 38 F2
**Lower Stow Bedon** Norfk 91 L5
**Lower Street** Norfk 106 F5
**Lower Street** Suffk 78 D4
**Lower Swanwick** Hants 16 F1
**Lower Swell** Gloucs 56 D3
**Lower Tean** Staffs 100 A5
**Lower Town** Devon 7 G2
**Lower Town** Pembks 64 D6
**Lower Upham** Hants 29 K7
**Lower Weare** Somset 26 B2
**Lower Welson** Herefs 68 F4
**Lower Westmancote** Worcs 71 G6
**Lower Whatley** Somset 27 H3
**Lower Whitley** Ches W 112 E5
**Lower Wield** Hants 29 M4
**Lower Willingdon** E Susx 20 C5
**Lower Withington** Ches E 113 J7
**Lower Woodford** Wilts 28 C4
**Lower Wraxhall** Dorset 14 B3
**Lowesby** Leics 87 K3
**Lowestoft** Suffk 93 L5
**Loweswater** Cumb 137 G3
**Low Fell** Gatesd 151 G3
**Lowfield Heath** W Susx 31 L4
**Low Gartachorrans** Stirlg 174 E2
**Low Grantley** N York 132 C5
**Low Ham** Somset 26 B5
**Low Harrogate** N York 132 D7
**Low Hesket** Cumb 148 E5
**Low Hutton** N York 134 B6
**Lowick** Nhants 88 E7
**Lowick** Nthumb 168 F2
**Lowick Green** Cumb 129 G3
**Low Lorton** Cumb 137 G3
**Low Marnham** Notts 116 D7
**Low Mill** N York 142 E7
**Low Moorsley** Sundld 151 H5
**Low Moresby** Cumb 136 D3
**Low Newton** Cumb 129 J3
**Low Row** Cumb 149 G3
**Low Row** N York 140 B7
**Low Salchrie** D & G 144 B2
**Low Santon** N Linc 125 L7
**Lowsonford** Warwks 71 L2
**Low Tharston** Norfk 92 E4
**Lowther** Cumb 138 D3
**Lowthorpe** E R Yk 135 G7
**Lowton** Somset 25 J7
**Low Torry** Fife 176 D2
**Low Worsall** N York 141 J5
**Low Wray** Cumb 137 K6
**Loxbeare** Devon 11 L2
**Loxhill** Surrey 31 G4
**Loxhore** Devon 23 K4
**Loxley** Warwks 72 C4
**Loxton** N Som 26 A1
**Loxwood** W Susx 31 H5
**Lubenham** Leics 87 K6
**Luccombe** Somset 24 E3
**Luccombe Village** IoW 17 H6
**Lucker** Nthumb 169 H4
**Luckett** Cnwll 6 B2
**Lucking Street** Essex 77 J7
**Luckington** Wilts 39 J4
**Lucklawhill** Fife 187 G3
**Luckwell Bridge** Somset 24 E4
**Lucton** Herefs 69 J2
**Ludag** W Isls 233 b9
**Ludborough** Lincs 118 D3
**Ludbrook** Devon 6 F5
**Ludchurch** Pembks 49 K5
**Luddenden** Calder 122 F5
**Luddenden Foot** Calder 122 F5
**Luddesdown** Kent 46 A6
**Luddington** N Linc 125 J7
**Luddington** Warwks 71 L4
**Luddington in the Brook** Nhants 89 G6
**Ludford** Lincs 117 K4
**Ludford** Shrops 83 K8
**Ludgershall** Bucks 58 A4
**Ludgershall** Wilts 28 E2
**Ludgvan** Cnwll 2 E5
**Ludham** Norfk 107 H8
**Ludlow** Shrops 83 K7
**Ludney** Somset 26 B8
**Ludwell** Wilts 27 K6
**Ludworth** Dur 151 J6
**Luffness** E Loth 178 B3
**Lugar** E Ayrs 164 C5
**Luggate Burn** E Loth 178 D4
**Luggiebank** N Lans 175 K4
**Lugton** E Ayrs 174 D7
**Lugwardine** Herefs 69 K6
**Luib** Highld 209 J8
**Luing** Ag & B 181 L5
**Lulham** Herefs 69 H6
**Lullington** Derbys 86 B2

**Lullington** Somset 27 H2
**Lulsgate Bottom** N Som 38 D7
**Lulsley** Worcs 70 D4
**Lumb** Calder 122 F6
**Lumby** N York 124 D4
**Lumphanan** Abers 206 B4
**Lumphinnans** Fife 186 C8
**Lumsden** Abers 205 K2
**Lunan** Angus 197 H6
**Lunanhead** Angus 196 D6
**Luncarty** P & K 186 A2
**Lund** E R Yk 126 B2
**Lund** N York 125 G4
**Lundie** Angus 186 E1
**Lundin Links** Fife 187 G6
**Lundin Mill** Fife 187 G6
**Lundy** Devon 22 B3
**Lunga** Ag & B 181 L5
**Lunna** Shet 235 d4
**Lunsford** Kent 33 J2
**Lunsford's Cross** E Susx 20 E4
**Lunt** Sefton 111 K2
**Luppitt** Devon 12 F2
**Lupset** Wakefd 123 L6
**Lupton** Cumb 129 L4
**Lurgashall** W Susx 30 F6
**Lurley** Devon 11 L2
**Luscombe** Devon 7 J4
**Luss** Ag & B 183 L8
**Lussagiven** Ag & B 171 L2
**Lusta** Highld 208 D3
**Lustleigh** Devon 11 H8
**Luston** Herefs 69 J2
**Luthermuir** Abers 197 G3
**Luthrie** Fife 186 E4
**Luton** Devon 7 K1
**Luton** Devon 12 D2
**Luton** Luton 59 H4
**Luton** Medway 46 C6
*Luton Airport* Luton 59 J4
**Lutterworth** Leics 87 G6
**Lutton** Devon 6 E4
**Lutton** Devon 7 G4
**Lutton** Lincs 104 C7
**Lutton** Nhants 89 G6
**Luxborough** Somset 24 F4
**Luxulyan** Cnwll 5 G4
**Luxulyan Valley** Cnwll 5 G4
**Lybster** Highld 231 J7
**Lydbury North** Shrops 83 G6
**Lydd** Kent 21 K2
*Lydd Airport* Kent 21 L2
**Lydden** Kent 35 H5
**Lydden** Kent 35 K2
**Lyddington** Rutlnd 88 C4
**Lydeard St Lawrence** Somset 25 H5
**Lydford** Devon 10 D7
**Lydford on Fosse** Somset 26 E5
**Lydgate** Calder 122 D5
**Lydham** Shrops 83 G5
**Lydiard Millicent** Wilts 40 C3
**Lydiard Tregoze** Swindn 40 C4
**Lydiate** Sefton 111 K2
**Lydiate Ash** Worcs 85 H7
**Lydlinch** Dorset 27 H8
**Lydney** Gloucs 54 F7
**Lydstep** Pembks 49 J7
**Lye** Dudley 85 G6
**Lye Green** E Susx 32 F6
**Lye Green** Warwks 71 L2
**Lye's Green** Wilts 27 J3
**Lyford** Oxon 41 H2
**Lymbridge Green** Kent 34 F6
**Lyme Regis** Dorset 13 J4
**Lyminge** Kent 34 F6
**Lymington** Hants 16 C4
**Lyminster** W Susx 18 D5
**Lymm** Warrtn 113 G4
**Lymm Services** Warrtn 112 F4
**Lympne** Kent 34 F7
**Lympsham** Somset 25 M1
**Lympstone** Devon 12 C5
**Lynchat** Highld 203 J5
**Lynch Green** Norfk 92 D3
**Lyndhurst** Hants 16 C2
**Lyndon** Rutlnd 88 C3
**Lyndon Green** Birm 85 K6
**Lyne** Border 166 B2
**Lyne** Surrey 43 G7
**Lyneal** Shrops 98 C6
**Lyneham** Oxon 56 F4
**Lyneham** Wilts 40 A5
**Lynemouth** Nthumb 159 H4
**Lyne of Skene** Abers 206 E4
**Lyness** Ork 234 b7
**Lyng** Norfk 106 C8
**Lyng** Somset 25 M5
**Lynmouth** Devon 23 L2
**Lynsted** Kent 34 C3
**Lynton** Devon 23 L2
**Lyon's Gate** Dorset 14 C2
**Lyonshall** Herefs 69 G4
**Lytchett Matravers** Dorset 15 H4
**Lytchett Minster** Dorset 15 H4
**Lyth** Highld 231 K3
**Lytham** Lancs 120 E5
**Lytham St Anne's** Lancs 120 D5
**Lythe** N York 143 H5
**Lythmore** Highld 230 F3

## M

**Mabe Burnthouse** Cnwll 3 K4
**Mablethorpe** Lincs 119 G4
**Macclesfield** Ches E 113 K6
**Macclesfield Crematorium** Ches E 113 K6
**Macduff** Abers 216 D2
**Macharioch** Ag & B 161 J7
**Machen** Caerph 37 K3
**Machrie** N Ayrs 162 A3
**Machrihanish** Ag & B 161 G5
**Machrins** Ag & B 180 E8
**Machynlleth** Powys 81 G4
**Machynys** Carmth 51 G5
**Mackworth** Derbys 100 F5
**Macmerry** E Loth 177 L4
**Madderty** P & K 185 K3
**Maddiston** Falk 176 C3
**Madeley** Staffs 99 H4
**Madeley** Wrekin 84 C3
**Madingley** Cambs 76 B3
**Madley** Herefs 69 H6
**Madresfield** Worcs 70 E5
**Madron** Cnwll 2 E5
**Maenclochog** Pembks 49 J3
**Maendy** V Glam 36 F5
**Maentwrog** Gwynd 95 L4
**Maen-y-groes** Cerdgn 65 L3
**Maer** Staffs 99 H5
**Maerdy** Rhondd 36 F2
**Maesbrook** Shrops 97 L7
**Maesbury** Shrops 97 L7
**Maesbury Marsh** Shrops 97 L7
**Maesllyn** Cerdgn 65 K5
**Maesteg** Brdgnd 36 D3
**Maesybont** Carmth 51 H3
**Maesycwmmer** Caerph 37 J2
**Maggieknockater** Moray 215 H5
**Magham Down** E Susx 20 C4
**Maghull** Sefton 111 K2
**Magna Park** Leics 87 G6
**Magor** Mons 38 B3
**Magor Services** Mons 38 B3
**Maidenbower** W Susx 32 B6
**Maiden Bradley** Wilts 27 J4
**Maidencombe** Torbay 7 L3
**Maidenhayne** Devon 13 H4
**Maiden Head** N Som 38 E6
**Maidenhead** W & M 42 E4
**Maiden Newton** Dorset 14 B3
**Maidens** S Ayrs 163 G7
**Maiden's Green** Br For 42 E5
**Maiden Wells** Pembks 49 G7
**Maidford** Nhants 73 H4
**Maids Moreton** Bucks 73 K7
**Maidstone** Kent 33 K3
**Maidstone Services** Kent 33 L3
**Maidwell** Nhants 87 L7
**Mail** Shet 235 d6
**Maindee** Newpt 37 L3
**Mainland** Ork 234 c6
**Mainland** Shet 235 c5
**Mainsforth** Dur 141 H2
**Mains of Balhall** Angus 196 E4
**Mains of Balnakettle** Abers 197 G2
**Mains of Dalvey** Highld 214 D7
**Mains of Haulkerton** Abers 197 H2
**Mains of Lesmoir** Abers 215 K8
**Mains of Melgunds** Angus 196 E5
**Mainsriddle** D & G 147 G4
**Mainstone** Shrops 82 F6
**Maisemore** Gloucs 55 J4
**Major's Green** Worcs 85 K7
**Malborough** Devon 7 G7
**Maldon** Essex 61 K6
**Malham** N York 131 G6
**Maligar** Highld 209 G2
**Mallaig** Highld 199 L6
**Mallaigvaig** Highld 199 L5
**Malleny Mills** C Edin 177 G5
**Malltraeth** IoA 108 E7
**Mallwyd** Gwynd 81 J2
**Malmesbury** Wilts 39 L3
**Malmsmead** Devon 24 C2
**Malpas** Ches W 98 C3
**Malpas** Cnwll 4 D7
**Malpas** Newpt 37 L3
**Maltby** Rothm 115 K3
**Maltby** S on T 141 L5
**Maltby le Marsh** Lincs 118 F5
**Maltman's Hill** Kent 34 B6
**Malton** N York 134 C5
**Malvern** Worcs 70 D5
**Malvern Hills** 70 D5
**Malvern Link** Worcs 70 E5
**Malvern Wells** Worcs 70 D6
**Mamble** Worcs 70 C1
**Mamhilad** Mons 53 L7
**Manaccan** Cnwll 3 K6
**Manafon** Powys 82 C3
**Manais** W Isls 232 d5
**Manaton** Devon 11 H8
**Manby** Lincs 118 E4
**Mancetter** Warwks 86 D4
**Manchester** Manch 113 J3
*Manchester Airport* Manch 113 J5
**Manchester Crematorium** Manch 113 J3
**Mancot** Flints 111 K7
**Mandally** Highld 201 L5
**Manea** Cambs 90 C5
**Maney** Birm 85 K4
**Manfield** N York 140 F4
**Mangotsfield** S Glos 38 F5
**Manish** W Isls 232 d5
**Manley** Ches W 112 D7
**Manmoel** Caerph 53 J7
**Mannal** Ag & B 188 C7
**Manningford Bohune** Wilts 40 C8
**Manningford Bruce** Wilts 40 C8
**Manningham** C Brad 123 H4
**Mannings Heath** W Susx 31 K5
**Mannington** Dorset 15 K2
**Manningtree** Essex 62 D2
**Mannofield** C Aber 207 H4
**Manorbier** Pembks 49 H7
**Manorbier Newton** Pembks 49 H7
**Manorhill** Border 167 K3
**Manorowen** Pembks 64 C7
**Manor Park** Gt Lon 45 H3
**Manor Park Crematorium** Gt Lon 45 H3
**Mansell Gamage** Herefs 69 H5
**Mansell Lacy** Herefs 69 H5
**Mansfield** E Ayrs 164 C6
**Mansfield** Notts 101 K1
**Mansfield & District Crematorium** Notts 101 K2
**Mansfield Woodhouse** Notts 115 K8
**Manston** Dorset 27 J7
**Manston** Kent 35 J2
**Manston** Leeds 124 B4
**Manswood** Dorset 15 J2
**Manthorpe** Lincs 88 F1
**Manton** N Linc 116 F2
**Manton** Rutlnd 88 C3
**Manton** Wilts 40 D6
**Manuden** Essex 60 D3
**Maperton** Somset 26 F6
**Maplebeck** Notts 102 B1
**Mapledurham** Oxon 42 A5
**Mapledurwell** Hants 30 B2
**Maplehurst** W Susx 31 K6
**Maplescombe** Kent 45 K7
**Mapleton** Derbys 100 D3
**Mapperley** Derbys 101 H4
**Mapperley Park** C Nott 101 L4
**Mapperton** Dorset 13 L3
**Mappleborough Green** Warwks 71 J2
**Mappleton** E R Yk 126 F2
**Mapplewell** Barns 123 L7
**Mappowder** Dorset 14 E2
**Marazion** Cnwll 2 F5
**Marbury** Ches E 98 E4
**March** Cambs 90 B4
**March** S Lans 165 J6
**Marcham** Oxon 41 J2
**Marchamley** Shrops 98 E6
**Marchington** Staffs 100 C6
**Marchros** Gwynd 94 F7
**Marchwiel** Wrexhm 98 A3
**Marchwood** Hants 16 D1
**Marcross** V Glam 36 E6
**Marden** Herefs 69 K5
**Marden** Kent 33 J4
**Marden** Wilts 40 C8
**Marden Thorn** Kent 33 K5
**Mardy** Mons 53 L5
**Mareham le Fen** Lincs 103 L1
**Mareham on the Hill** Lincs 118 C7
**Marehill** W Susx 18 E3
**Maresfield** E Susx 19 M2
**Marfleet** C KuH 126 E5
**Marford** Wrexhm 98 A2
**Margam** Neath 36 B3
**Margam Crematorium** Neath 36 C4
**Margaret Marsh** Dorset 27 J7
**Margaretting** Essex 61 G7
**Margaretting Tye** Essex 61 G7
**Margate** Kent 35 K1
**Margnaheglish** N Ayrs 162 D3

Margrie D & G 145 M5
Margrove Park R & Cl 142 E4
Marham Norfk 91 G2
Marhamchurch Cnwll 9 G4
Marholm C Pete 89 G3
Mariansleigh Devon 24 B6
Marine Town Kent 46 F5
Marionburgh Abers 206 D4
Marishader Highld 209 H2
Maristow Devon 6 C3
Marjoriebanks D & G 155 J5
Mark Somset 26 B2
Markbeech Kent 32 E5
Markby Lincs 119 G5
Mark Cross E Susx 33 G6
Markeaton Crematorium C Derb 100 F5
Market Bosworth Leics 86 E3
Market Deeping Lincs 89 G2
Market Drayton Shrops 98 F5
Market Harborough Leics 87 K6
Market Lavington Wilts 28 A1
Market Overton Rutlnd 88 C1
Market Rasen Lincs 117 J4
Market Stainton Lincs 118 C5
Market Warsop Notts 115 K7
Market Weighton E R Yk 125 K3
Market Weston Suffk 92 B7
Markfield Leics 86 F2
Markham Caerph 53 J7
Markham Moor Notts 116 B6
Markinch Fife 186 E6
Markington N York 132 D6
Markle E Loth 178 C3
Marksbury BaNES 38 F7
Marks Tey Essex 61 L4
Markyate Herts 59 H5
Marlborough Wilts 40 D6
Marlcliff Warwks 71 K4
Marldon Devon 7 K3
Marlesford Suffk 79 G3
Marlingford Norfk 92 D2
Marloes Pembks 48 D5
Marlow Bucks 42 D3
Marlow Bottom Bucks 42 D3
Marlpit Hill Kent 32 D4
Marnhull Dorset 27 H7
Marple Stockp 113 L4
Marr Donc 115 K1
Marrick N York 140 D7
Marsden Kirk 122 F7
Marsden S Tyne 151 J3
Marshalswick Herts 59 K6
Marsham Norfk 106 E7
Marsh Baldon Oxon 57 K7
Marshborough Kent 35 J3
Marshbrook Shrops 83 J5
Marshchapel Lincs 118 E2
Marsh Farm Luton 59 H3
Marshfield Newpt 37 K4
Marshfield S Glos 39 H5
Marshgate Cnwll 8 F6
Marsh Gibbon Bucks 57 M4
Marsh Green Devon 12 D4
Marsh Green Kent 32 D4
Marshland St James Norfk 90 D2
Marsh Lane Derbys 115 H5
Marsh Street Somset 24 F3
Marshwood Dorset 13 J3
Marske N York 140 D6
Marske-by-the-Sea R & Cl 142 D3
Marston Herefs 69 G3
Marston Lincs 102 E4
Marston Oxon 57 K6
Marston Staffs 99 L6
Marston Wilts 27 L1
Marston Green Solhll 85 L6
Marston Magna Somset 26 E6
Marston Meysey Wilts 40 C2
Marston Montgomery Derbys 100 C5
Marston Moretaine C Beds 74 E6
Marston on Dove Derbys 100 E6
Marston St Lawrence Nhants 73 G6
Marston Trussell Nhants 87 K6
Marstow Herefs 54 D4
Marsworth Bucks 58 F5
Marten Wilts 40 F7
Martham Norfk 107 J8
Martin Hants 28 B7
Martin Kent 35 J5
Martin Lincs 103 J1
Martinhoe Devon 23 L2
Martin Hussingtree Worcs 70 F3
Martinstown Dorset 14 C5
Martlesham Suffk 78 F5
Martlesham Heath Suffk 78 F5
Martletwy Pembks 49 H5
Martley Worcs 70 D3
Martock Somset 26 C7
Marton Ches E 113 J7
Marton E R Yk 126 F3
Marton Lincs 116 D5
Marton Middsb 142 B4
Marton N York 132 F6
Marton N York 134 B3
Marton Shrops 82 F3
Marton Warwks 72 E2
Marton-le-Moor N York 132 E5
Martyr Worthy Hants 29 K5
Marwell Wildlife Hants 29 J6
Marwick Ork 234 b5
Marwood Devon 23 H4
Marybank Highld 212 D4
Maryburgh Highld 212 E3
Marygold Border 179 G6
Maryhill C Glas 175 G4
Maryhill Crematorium C Glas 175 G4
Marykirk Abers 197 H3
Marylebone Gt Lon 44 F4
Marylebone Wigan 121 H8
Marypark Moray 214 F6
Maryport Cumb 147 H7
Maryport D & G 144 D7
Marystow Devon 10 C7
Mary Tavy Devon 6 D1
Maryton Angus 197 H5
Marywell Abers 206 B6
Marywell Abers 207 H5
Marywell Angus 197 G7
Masham N York 132 C4
Masongill N York 130 C4
Masonhill Crematorium S Ayrs 163 J5
Mastin Moor Derbys 115 J6
Matching Green Essex 60 E5
Matching Tye Essex 60 E5
Matfen Nthumb 158 C7
Matfield Kent 33 H5
Mathern Mons 38 D3
Mathon Herefs 70 D5
Mathry Pembks 48 E2
Matlask Norfk 106 D5
Matlock Derbys 100 F1
Matlock Bath Derbys 100 F2
Matson Gloucs 55 J5
Mattersey Notts 116 B4
Mattingley Hants 42 B8
Mattishall Norfk 92 C2
Mattishall Burgh Norfk 92 C2
Mauchline E Ayrs 163 L4
Maud Abers 217 H5
Maufant Jersey 236 d6
Maugersbury Gloucs 56 D3
Maughold IoM 237 e3
Mauld Highld 212 C6
Maulden C Beds 74 F6
Maulds Meaburn Cumb 138 F4
Maunby N York 132 E3
Maundown Somset 25 G5
Mautby Norfk 93 K2
Mavesyn Ridware Staffs 85 J1
Mavis Enderby Lincs 118 E7
Mawbray Cumb 147 J5
Mawdesley Lancs 121 G7
Mawdlam Brdgnd 36 C4
Mawgan Cnwll 3 J6
Mawgan Porth Cnwll 4 D3
Mawla Cnwll 3 J3
Mawnan Cnwll 3 K5
Mawnan Smith Cnwll 3 K5
Mawsley Nhants 88 B7
Maxey C Pete 89 G2
Maxstoke Warwks 86 B6
Maxton Border 167 J4
Maxton Kent 35 J6
Maxwelltown D & G 155 G6
Maxworthy Cnwll 9 H6
May Bank Staffs 99 J3
Maybole S Ayrs 163 H7
Maybury Surrey 43 G8
Mayfield E Susx 33 G7
Mayfield Mdloth 177 K5
Mayfield Staffs 100 D4
Mayford Surrey 31 G1
May Hill Gloucs 55 G4
Mayland Essex 61 L7
Maylandsea Essex 61 L7
Maynard's Green E Susx 20 C3
Maypole Birm 85 J7
Maypole Green Norfk 93 J4
Maypole Green Suffk 77 K3
Meadgate BaNES 39 G8
Meadle Bucks 58 D6
Meadowfield Dur 151 G6
Meadwell Devon 9 K8
Meanwood Leeds 123 K3
Meare Somset 26 C3
Meare Green Somset 25 L6
Meare Green Somset 25 M6
Mearns E Rens 174 F7
Mears Ashby Nhants 74 B2
Measham Leics 86 D2
Meath Green Surrey 32 B4
Meathop Cumb 129 J4
Meavaig W Isls 232 d2
Meavy Devon 6 D3
Medbourne Leics 88 B5
Meddon Devon 9 H2
Meden Vale Notts 115 L7
Medmenham Bucks 42 D4
Medomsley Dur 150 E4
Medstead Hants 30 A4
Medway Crematorium Kent 46 C7
Medway Services Medway 46 D7
Meerbrook Staffs 99 M1
Meesden Herts 60 C2
Meeth Devon 10 E3
Meeting House Hill Norfk 107 G6
Meidrim Carmth 50 C2
Meifod Powys 82 D2
Meigle P & K 195 L7
Meikle Carco D & G 164 F6
Meikle Earnock S Lans 175 J7
Meikle Kilmory Ag & B 173 H6
Meikle Obney P & K 195 G8
Meikleour P & K 195 J7
Meikle Wartle Abers 216 D7
Meinciau Carmth 50 F4
Meir C Stke 99 L4
Melbourn Cambs 75 L5
Melbourne Derbys 101 G7
Melbourne E R Yk 125 H2
Melbury Abbas Dorset 27 K7
Melbury Bubb Dorset 14 B2
Melbury Osmond Dorset 14 B2
Melchbourne Bed 74 E2
Melcombe Bingham Dorset 14 E2
Meldon Devon 10 E6
Meldon Nthumb 158 E5
Meldreth Cambs 75 L5
Meldrum Stirlg 184 F7
Melfort Ag & B 182 B5
Meliden Denbgs 110 E5
Melin-y-wig Denbgs 97 G3
Melkinthorpe Cumb 138 D3
Melkridge Nthumb 149 J3
Melksham Wilts 39 K7
Melling Lancs 130 B5
Melling Sefton 111 L2
Mellis Suffk 92 C8
Mellon Charles Highld 219 K3
Mellon Udrigle Highld 219 K3
Mellor Lancs 121 J4
Mellor Stockp 113 M4
Mellor Brook Lancs 121 J4
Mells Somset 27 G2
Melmerby Cumb 149 G7
Melmerby N York 131 K3
Melmerby N York 132 E4
Melness Highld 229 J3
Melplash Dorset 13 L3
Melrose Border 167 H3
Melsetter Ork 234 b7
Melsonby N York 140 F5
Meltham Kirk 123 G7
Melton E R Yk 126 B5
Melton Suffk 79 G4
Melton Constable Norfk 106 C6
Melton Mowbray Leics 102 C8
Melton Ross N Linc 126 D7
Melvaig Highld 219 H4
Melverley Shrops 83 G1
Melvich Highld 230 C3
Membury Devon 13 H2
Membury Services W Berk 40 F5
Memsie Abers 217 H2
Memus Angus 196 C5
Menai Bridge IoA 109 H6
Mendham Suffk 92 F6
Mendip Crematorium Somset 26 E3
Mendip Hills 26 D2
Mendlesham Suffk 78 D2
Mendlesham Green Suffk 78 D2
Menheniot Cnwll 5 L4
Mennock D & G 164 F7
Menston C Brad 123 H2
Menstrie Clacks 185 H7
Mentmore Bucks 58 E4
Meoble Highld 200 C7
Meole Brace Shrops 83 J2
Meonstoke Hants 29 L7
Meopham Kent 45 M6
Mepal Cambs 90 B7
Meppershall C Beds 75 G7
Mere Ches E 113 G5
Mere Wilts 27 J5
Mere Brow Lancs 120 F6
Mereclough Lancs 122 C4
Mere Green Birm 85 K4
Mereworth Kent 33 H3
Meriden Solhll 86 B6
Merkadale Highld 208 F7
Merley Poole 15 J3
Merrion Pembks 48 F7
Merriott Somset 26 C8

**Merrow** Surrey 31 G2
**Merry Hill** Herts 43 J2
**Merryhill** Wolves 84 F4
**Merrymeet** Cnwll 5 L3
**Mersea Island** Essex 62 B5
**Mersey Crossing** Halton 112 D5
**Mersham** Kent 34 E6
**Merstham** Surrey 32 B3
**Merston** W Susx 18 B5
**Merstone** IoW 17 G5
**Merthyr Cynog** Powys 67 L6
**Merthyr Mawr** Brdgnd 36 D5
**Merthyr Tydfil** Myr Td 53 G6
**Merthyr Vale** Myr Td 53 G7
**Merton** Devon 10 D3
**Merton** Gt Lon 44 E6
**Merton** Norfk 91 K4
**Merton** Oxon 57 L4
**Meshaw** Devon 24 B7
**Messing** Essex 61 L4
**Messingham** N Linc 116 E2
**Metfield** Suffk 93 G7
**Metherell** Cnwll 6 B3
**Metheringham** Lincs 103 H1
**Methil** Fife 186 F7
**Methilhill** Fife 186 F7
**Methlick** Abers 217 G6
**Methven** P & K 185 L3
**Methwold** Norfk 91 G4
**Methwold Hythe** Norfk 91 G4
**Mettingham** Suffk 93 H5
**Metton** Norfk 106 E5
**Mevagissey** Cnwll 4 F6
**Mexborough** Donc 115 J2
**Mey** Highld 231 K2
**Meysey Hampton** Gloucs 56 C7
**Miabhaig** W Isls 232 d2
**Michaelchurch** Herefs 54 D3
**Michaelchurch Escley** Herefs 69 G7
**Michaelstone-y-Fedw** Newpt 37 K4
**Michaelston-le-Pit** V Glam 37 J5
**Michaelstow** Cnwll 5 G1
**Michaelwood Services** Gloucs 39 G2
**Micheldever** Hants 29 K4
**Micheldever Station** Hants 29 K3
**Michelmersh** Hants 29 G6
**Mickfield** Suffk 78 D3
**Micklebring** Donc 115 K3
**Mickleby** N York 143 G5
**Micklefield** Leeds 124 C4
**Mickleham** Surrey 31 K2
**Mickleover** C Derb 100 F5
**Mickleton** Dur 140 B3
**Mickleton** Gloucs 71 L5
**Mickletown** Leeds 124 B5
**Mickle Trafford** Ches W 112 C7
**Mickley** N York 132 C4
**Mickley Square** Nthumb 150 D3
**Mid Ardlaw** Abers 217 H2
**Midbea** Ork 234 c4
**Mid Beltie** Abers 206 C5
**Mid Calder** W Loth 176 E5
**Mid Clyth** Highld 231 K7
**Mid Culbeuchly** Abers 216 C3
**Middle Aston** Oxon 57 J3
**Middle Barton** Oxon 57 H3
**Middlebie** D & G 155 L6
**Middlebridge** P & K 194 D3
**Middle Chinnock** Somset 26 C8
**Middle Claydon** Bucks 58 B3
**Middleham** N York 131 L3
**Middle Handley** Derbys 115 H6
**Middlehill** Wilts 39 J6
**Middlehope** Shrops 83 K5
**Middle Kames** Ag & B 172 F1
**Middle Littleton** Worcs 71 J5
**Middlemarsh** Dorset 14 C2
**Middle Mayfield** Staffs 100 C4
**Middle Rasen** Lincs 117 H4
**Middle Rocombe** Devon 7 K2
**Middlesbrough** Middsb 141 L4
**Middleshaw** Cumb 129 L2
**Middlesmoor** N York 131 K5
**Middle Stoke** Medway 46 D5
**Middlestone** Dur 141 G2
**Middlestown** Wakefd 123 K6
**Middlethird** Border 167 K2
**Middleton** Ag & B 188 B7
**Middleton** Derbys 100 F2
**Middleton** Derbys 114 D8
**Middleton** Essex 77 K6
**Middleton** Hants 29 H3
**Middleton** Herefs 69 K1
**Middleton** Leeds 123 L5
**Middleton** N York 123 G2
**Middleton** N York 134 B3
**Middleton** Nhants 88 B5
**Middleton** Norfk 90 F1
**Middleton** Nthumb 158 D5
**Middleton** P & K 186 B6
**Middleton** Rochdl 113 K1
**Middleton** Shrops 83 K7
**Middleton** Suffk 79 J2
**Middleton** Swans 50 E7
**Middleton** Warwks 85 L4
**Middleton Cheney** Nhants 73 G6
**Middleton Crematorium** Rochdl 113 K1
**Middleton-in-Teesdale** Dur 139 L3
**Middleton Moor** Suffk 79 J2
**Middleton One Row** Darltn 141 J5
**Middleton-on-Sea** W Susx 18 C5
**Middleton on the Hill** Herefs 69 K2
**Middleton on the Wolds** E R Yk 125 L2
**Middleton Park** C Aber 207 H3
**Middleton Quernhow** N York 132 E4
**Middleton St George** Darltn 141 J5
**Middleton Scriven** Shrops 84 C6
**Middleton Stoney** Oxon 57 K4
**Middleton Tyas** N York 141 G6
**Middle Town** IoS 2 a2
**Middletown** Powys 82 F2
**Middle Tysoe** Warwks 72 D5
**Middle Wallop** Hants 28 F4
**Middlewich** Ches E 113 G7
**Middle Winterslow** Wilts 28 E5
**Middlewood** Cnwll 5 L2
**Middle Woodford** Wilts 28 C4
**Middlewood Green** Suffk 78 D3
**Middleyard** E Ayrs 163 M3
**Middlezoy** Somset 26 B5
**Midford** BaNES 39 H7
**Midgham** W Berk 41 K6
**Midgley** Calder 122 F5
**Midgley** Wakefd 123 K7
**Midhopestones** Sheff 114 E2
**Midhurst** W Susx 30 E6
**Mid Lavant** W Susx 18 B4
**Midlem** Border 167 H4
**Mid Mains** Highld 212 C6
**Midpark** Ag & B 173 H6
**Midsomer Norton** BaNES 26 F1
**Midtown** Highld 229 J4
**Mid Warwickshire Crematorium** Warwks 72 C3
**Mid Yell** Shet 235 d3
**Migvie** Abers 205 K4
**Milborne Port** Somset 26 F7
**Milborne St Andrew** Dorset 14 F3
**Milborne Wick** Somset 26 F7
**Milbourne** Nthumb 158 E6
**Milbourne** Wilts 39 L3
**Milburn** Cumb 138 F2
**Milbury Heath** S Glos 38 F3
**Milby** N York 132 F6
**Milcombe** Oxon 72 E7
**Milden** Suffk 77 L5
**Mildenhall** Suffk 91 G8
**Mildenhall** Wilts 40 E6
**Mileham** Norfk 105 L8
**Mile Oak** Br & H 19 H4
**Milesmark** Fife 176 E2
**Miles Platting** Manch 113 J2
**Mile Town** Kent 46 F5
**Milfield** Nthumb 168 D3
**Milford** Derbys 101 G4
**Milford** Devon 22 C6
**Milford** Staffs 99 L7
**Milford** Surrey 30 F3
**Milford Haven** Pembks 48 F6
**Milford on Sea** Hants 16 C4
**Milkwall** Gloucs 54 E6
**Millais** Jersey 236 a5
**Milland** W Susx 30 D5
**Mill Bank** Calder 122 F6
**Millbreck** Abers 217 J5
**Millbridge** Surrey 30 D3
**Millbrook** C Beds 74 E6
**Millbrook** C Sotn 29 G8
**Millbrook** Cnwll 6 B5
**Millbrook** Jersey 236 c7
**Mill Brow** Stockp 113 L4
**Millbuie** Abers 206 F4
**Millbuie** Highld 212 E4
**Millcorner** E Susx 21 G2
**Millcraig** Highld 222 E7
**Milldale** Staffs 100 C2
**Mill End** Bucks 42 C4
**Mill End** Herts 60 B2
**Millerhill** Mdloth 177 J4
**Miller's Dale** Derbys 114 C6
**Millerston** C Glas 175 H5
**Mill Green** Cambs 76 F5
**Mill Green** Essex 61 G7
**Mill Green** Lincs 103 L7
**Mill Green** Suffk 77 L6
**Mill Green** Suffk 78 B3
**Mill Green** Suffk 78 D3
**Millhalf** Herefs 68 F5
**Millheugh** S Lans 175 K7
**Mill Hill** Gt Lon 44 E2
**Millhouse** Ag & B 173 G4
**Millhousebridge** D & G 155 K5
**Millhouse Green** Barns 114 E2
**Millhouses** Sheff 115 G5
**Milliken Park** Rens 174 D6
**Millington** E R Yk 125 J1
**Millmeece** Staffs 99 J5
**Mill of Drummond** P & K 185 H4
**Mill of Haldane** W Duns 174 D2
**Millom** Cumb 128 E4
**Millport** N Ayrs 173 K7
**Mill Street** Suffk 78 C1
**Millthrop** Cumb 130 C2
**Milltimber** C Aber 207 G5
**Milltown** Abers 205 G4
**Milltown** Abers 205 K3
**Milltown** D & G 156 C6
**Milltown** Devon 23 J4
**Milltown of Auchindoun** Moray 215 H6
**Milltown of Campfield** Abers 206 C5
**Milltown of Edinvillie** Moray 215 G6
**Milltown of Learney** Abers 206 C5
**Milltown of Rothiemay** Moray 215 M5
**Milnathort** P & K 186 B6
**Milngavie** E Duns 175 G4
**Milnrow** Rochdl 122 D7
**Milnthorpe** Cumb 129 K3
**Milovaig** Highld 208 B4
**Milson** Shrops 84 B8
**Milstead** Kent 34 B3
**Milston** Wilts 28 D3
**Milthorpe** Nhants 73 H5
**Milton** C Stke 99 K3
**Milton** Cambs 76 C2
**Milton** Cumb 148 F3
**Milton** D & G 144 F4
**Milton** D & G 154 E7
**Milton** Derbys 100 F7
**Milton** Highld 209 L5
**Milton** Highld 212 D7
**Milton** Highld 212 E4
**Milton** Highld 223 G6
**Milton** Highld 231 L5
**Milton** Inver 174 C5
**Milton** Kent 46 A5
**Milton** Moray 204 E2
**Milton** Moray 215 L2
**Milton** N Som 37 M7
**Milton** Notts 116 B6
**Milton** Oxon 41 J3
**Milton** Oxon 72 F7
**Milton** P & K 195 G4
**Milton** Pembks 49 H6
**Milton** Somset 26 C6
**Milton** Stirlg 184 B6
**Milton** W Duns 174 D4
**Milton Abbas** Dorset 14 F3
**Milton Abbot** Devon 9 K8
**Milton Bridge** Mdloth 177 H5
**Milton Bryan** C Beds 58 F3
**Milton Clevedon** Somset 26 F4
**Milton Combe** Devon 6 D3
**Milton Damerel** Devon 9 K3
**Milton Ernest** Bed 74 E4
**Milton Green** Ches W 98 C2
**Milton Hill** Oxon 41 J3
**Milton Keynes** M Keyn 74 C6
**Milton Lilbourne** Wilts 40 D7
**Milton Malsor** Nhants 73 K4
**Milton Morenish** P & K 193 K8
**Milton of Auchinhove** Abers 206 B5
**Milton of Balgonie** Fife 186 E7
**Milton of Buchanan** Stirlg 174 E1
**Milton of Campsie** E Duns 175 H3
**Milton of Finavon** Angus 196 D5
**Milton of Leys** Highld 213 G6
**Milton of Murtle** C Aber 207 G5
**Milton on Stour** Dorset 27 J5
**Milton Regis** Kent 46 E6
**Milton-under-Wychwood** Oxon 56 E4
**Milverton** Somset 25 H6
**Milverton** Warwks 72 C2
**Milwich** Staffs 99 L6
**Minard** Ag & B 182 D7
**Minchinhampton** Gloucs 55 K7
**Minehead** Somset 24 F3

**Minera** Wrexhm 97 L3
**Minety** Wilts 40 A3
**Minffordd** Gwynd 95 K5
**Mingarrypark** Highld 190 D3
**Miningsby** Lincs 118 D8
**Minions** Cnwll 5 L2
**Minishant** S Ayrs 163 J6
**Minllyn** Gwynd 81 J2
**Minnigaff** D & G 145 J2
**Minnonie** Abers 216 E3
**Minskip** N York 132 F6
**Minstead** Hants 16 C1
**Minsted** W Susx 30 D7
**Minster** Kent 35 J2
**Minsterley** Shrops 83 G3
**Minster Lovell** Oxon 56 F5
**Minster-on-Sea** Kent 46 F5
**Minsterworth** Gloucs 55 H5
**Minterne Magna** Dorset 14 C2
**Minting** Lincs 117 K6
**Mintlaw** Abers 217 J5
**Mintlyn Crematorium** Norfk 105 G8
**Minto** Border 167 H5
**Minton** Shrops 83 H5
**Mirehouse** Cumb 136 D4
**Mireland** Highld 231 K4
**Mirfield** Kirk 123 J6
**Miserden** Gloucs 55 L6
**Miskin** Rhondd 37 G4
**Misson** Notts 116 B3
**Misterton** Notts 116 C3
**Misterton** Somset 13 L2
**Mistley** Essex 62 D2
**Mitcham** Gt Lon 44 F6
**Mitcheldean** Gloucs 54 F4
**Mitchell** Cnwll 4 D5
**Mitchellslacks** D & G 155 G3
**Mitchel Troy** Mons 54 C6
**Mitford** Nthumb 158 F5
**Mithian** Cnwll 3 J2
**Mixbury** Oxon 73 H7
**Mobberley** Ches E 113 H5
**Mobberley** Staffs 100 A4
**Mochdre** Powys 82 B5
**Mochrum** D & G 145 H5
**Mockbeggar** Kent 33 J4
**Mockerkin** Cumb 136 F3
**Modbury** Devon 6 F5
**Moddershall** Staffs 99 L5
**Moelfre** IoA 109 G4
**Moelfre** Powys 97 J6
**Moffat** D & G 155 J2
**Moggerhanger** C Beds 75 G5
**Moira** Leics 86 C1
**Molash** Kent 34 D4
**Mol-chlach** Highld 199 G3
**Mold** Flints 111 H8
**Moldgreen** Kirk 123 H7
**Molehill Green** Essex 60 E3
**Molescroft** E R Yk 126 C3
**Molesworth** Cambs 88 F7
**Moll** Highld 209 J7
**Molland** Devon 24 C5
**Mollington** Ches W 111 L7
**Mollington** Oxon 72 F5
**Mollinsburn** N Lans 175 J4
**Mondynes** Abers 197 J1
**Monewden** Suffk 78 F3
**Moneydie** P & K 185 M2
**Moniaive** D & G 154 D4
**Monifieth** Angus 187 H2
**Monikie** Angus 196 E8
**Monimail** Fife 186 E5
**Monken Hadley** Gt Lon 44 E1
**Monk Fryston** N York 124 D5
**Monkhide** Herefs 70 B5
**Monkhill** Cumb 148 C3
**Monkhopton** Shrops 84 B5
**Monkland** Herefs 69 J3
**Monkleigh** Devon 23 G7
**Monknash** V Glam 36 E6
**Monkokehampton** Devon 10 E4
**Monkseaton** N Tyne 159 H7
**Monks Eleigh** Suffk 77 L5
**Monk's Gate** W Susx 31 K6
**Monks Heath** Ches E 113 J6
**Monk Sherborne** Hants 29 L1
**Monksilver** Somset 25 G4
**Monks Kirby** Warwks 86 F6
**Monk Soham** Suffk 78 E2
**Monks Risborough** Bucks 58 D6
**Monksthorpe** Lincs 118 F7
**Monk Street** Essex 60 F3
**Monkswood** Mons 53 M7
**Monkton** Devon 12 F2
**Monkton** Kent 47 M6
**Monkton** S Ayrs 163 J4
**Monkton** S Tyne 151 H3
**Monkton Combe** BaNES 39 H7
**Monkton Deverill** Wilts 27 J4
**Monkton Farleigh** Wilts 39 J7
**Monkton Heathfield** Somset 25 K6
**Monkton Wyld** Dorset 13 J3
**Monkwearmouth** Sundld 151 J4
**Monkwood** Hants 29 M5
**Monmore Green** Wolves 85 G4
**Monmouth** Mons 54 D5
**Monnington on Wye** Herefs 69 G5
**Monreith** D & G 145 H6
**Montacute** Somset 26 D7
**Montford** Shrops 83 H1
**Montford Bridge** Shrops 83 H1
**Montgarrie** Abers 206 B2
**Montgomery** Powys 82 E4
**Montrose** Angus 197 H5
**Mont Saint** Guern 236 b3
**Monxton** Hants 28 F3
**Monyash** Derbys 114 D7
**Monymusk** Abers 206 D3
**Monzie** P & K 185 H3
**Moodiesburn** N Lans 175 J4
**Moonzie** Fife 186 E4
**Moor Allerton** Leeds 123 L3
**Moorby** Lincs 118 D8
**Moor Crichel** Dorset 15 J2
**Moordown** Bmouth 15 K4
**Moore** Halton 112 E5
**Moor End** Calder 122 F5
**Moorends** Donc 125 G7
**Moorhead** C Brad 123 H3
**Moorhouse** Cumb 148 B4
**Moorhouse** Notts 116 C7
**Moorhouse Bank** Surrey 32 D3
**Moorlinch** Somset 26 B4
**Moor Monkton** N York 133 H7
**Moorsholm** R & Cl 142 E4
**Moorside** Dorset 27 H7
**Moor Street** Birm 85 H6
**Moorswater** Cnwll 5 K3
**Moorthorpe** Wakefd 124 C7
**Moortown** Leeds 123 K3
**Moortown** Lincs 117 H2
**Morangie** Highld 223 G5
**Morar** Highld 199 L6
**Moray Crematorium** Moray 215 J3
**Morborne** Cambs 89 G5
**Morchard Bishop** Devon 11 H4
**Morcombelake** Dorset 13 K4
**Morcott** Rutlnd 88 D4
**Morda** Shrops 97 L6
**Morden** Dorset 15 H4
**Morden** Gt Lon 44 E6
**Mordiford** Herefs 69 L6
**Mordon** Dur 141 H2
**More** Shrops 83 G5
**Morebath** Devon 24 E6
**Morebattle** Border 168 B4
**Morecambe** Lancs 129 J6
**Moredon** Swindn 40 C3
**Morefield** Highld 220 E3
**Morehall** Kent 35 G7
**Moreleigh** Devon 7 H5
**Morenish** P & K 184 D1
**Morestead** Hants 29 K6
**Moreton** Dorset 14 F4
**Moreton** Essex 60 E6
**Moreton** Herefs 69 K2
**Moreton** Oxon 58 B6
**Moreton** Wirral 111 J4
**Moreton Corbet** Shrops 98 E7
**Moretonhampstead** Devon 11 H7
**Moreton-in-Marsh** Gloucs 56 D2
**Moreton Jeffries** Herefs 69 L5
**Moreton Morrell** Warwks 72 C4
**Moreton on Lugg** Herefs 69 K5
**Moreton Pinkney** Nhants 73 H5
**Moreton Say** Shrops 98 F5
**Moreton Valence** Gloucs 55 H6
**Morfa Nefyn** Gwynd 94 E4
**Morham** E Loth 178 C4
**Morland** Cumb 138 E3
**Morley** Ches E 113 J5
**Morley** Derbys 101 H4
**Morley** Leeds 123 K5
**Morley Green** Ches E 113 J5
**Morley St Botolph** Norfk 92 C4
**Morningside** C Edin 177 H4
**Morningside** N Lans 175 L7
**Morningthorpe** Norfk 92 F5
**Morpeth** Nthumb 158 F5
**Morphie** Abers 197 H4
**Morrey** Staffs 100 C8
**Morriston** Swans 51 J6
**Morston** Norfk 106 B4
**Mortehoe** Devon 23 G3
**Morthen** Rothm 115 J4
**Mortimer** W Berk 41 M7
**Mortimer West End** Hants 41 M7
**Mortlake** Gt Lon 44 E5
**Mortlake Crematorium** Gt Lon 44 D5
**Morton** Cumb 148 C4
**Morton** Derbys 101 H1
**Morton** Lincs 103 H7
**Morton** Lincs 116 D3
**Morton** Notts 102 B3
**Morton** Shrops 97 L7
**Mortonhall Crematorium** C Edin 177 H5
**Morton-on-Swale** N York 132 E2
**Morton on the Hill** Norfk 92 D1
**Morvah** Cnwll 2 D4
**Morvich** Highld 200 E2
**Morville** Shrops 84 C5
**Morwenstow** Cnwll 9 G2
**Mosborough** Sheff 115 H5
**Moscow** E Ayrs 163 L2
**Moseley** Birm 85 J6
**Moseley** Wolves 85 G4
**Moseley** Worcs 70 E3
**Moss** Ag & B 188 B7
**Moss** Donc 124 F7
**Mossat** Abers 205 K2
**Mossbank** Shet 235 d4
**Moss Bank** St Hel 112 D3
**Mossbay** Cumb 136 D2
**Mossblown** S Ayrs 163 K4
**Mossburnford** Border 167 K6
**Mossdale** D & G 154 B7
**Mossdale** E Ayrs 153 K2
**Moss Edge** Lancs 120 F2
**Mossend** N Lans 175 K6
**Mossley** Tamesd 113 L2
**Mosspaul Hotel** Border 156 D3
**Moss-side** Highld 213 K4
**Mosstodloch** Moray 215 H3
**Mossyard** D & G 145 L5
**Mossy Lea** Lancs 121 H7
**Mosterton** Dorset 13 L2
**Moston** Manch 113 K2
**Mostyn** Flints 111 G5
**Motcombe** Dorset 27 J6
**Mothecombe** Devon 6 F6
**Motherby** Cumb 138 B2
**Motherwell** N Lans 175 K6
**Motspur Park** Gt Lon 44 E6
**Mottingham** Gt Lon 45 H5
**Mottisfont** Hants 28 F6
**Mottisfont** Hants 28 F6
**Mottistone** IoW 16 E5
**Mottram in Longdendale** Tamesd 113 M3
**Mottram St Andrew** Ches E 113 K5
**Mouilpied** Guern 236 c3
**Mouldsworth** Ches W 112 D7
**Moulin** P & K 194 E4
**Moulsecoomb** Br & H 19 J4
**Moulsford** Oxon 41 L4
**Moulsoe** M Keyn 74 C6
**Moultavie** Highld 222 E7
**Moulton** Ches W 112 F7
**Moulton** Lincs 104 A7
**Moulton** N York 141 G6
**Moulton** Nhants 73 L2
**Moulton** Suffk 77 G2
**Moulton** V Glam 37 G6
**Moulton Chapel** Lincs 103 M8
**Moulton St Mary** Norfk 93 H3
**Moulton Seas End** Lincs 104 A6
**Mount** Cnwll 5 J3
**Mountain** C Brad 123 G4
**Mountain Ash** Rhondd 53 G7
**Mountain Cross** Border 176 F8
**Mount Ambrose** Cnwll 3 J3
**Mount Bures** Essex 61 L2
**Mountfield** E Susx 20 E2
**Mountgerald** Highld 212 E3
**Mount Hawke** Cnwll 3 J2
**Mountjoy** Cnwll 4 D4
**Mount Lothian** Mdloth 177 H6
**Mountnessing** Essex 60 F8
**Mounton** Mons 38 D2
**Mount Pleasant** Derbys 101 G3
**Mount Pleasant** Suffk 77 G5
**Mountsett Crematorium** Dur 150 E4
**Mountsorrel** Leics 87 H2
**Mount Tabor** Calder 122 F5
**Mousehole** Cnwll 2 E6
**Mouswald** D & G 155 J7
**Mow Cop** Ches E 99 J2
**Mowhaugh** Border 168 B5
**Mowmacre Hill** C Leic 87 H3
**Mowsley** Leics 87 J5
**Moy** Highld 202 C8
**Moy** Highld 213 J7
**Moyle** Highld 200 D2
**Moylegrove** Pembks 64 F5
**Muasdale** Ag & B 161 H2
**Muchalls** Abers 207 G6
**Much Birch** Herefs 54 D3

**Much Cowarne** Herefs....70 B5
**Much Dewchurch** Herefs....54 C2
**Muchelney** Somset....26 B6
**Muchelney Ham** Somset....26 C6
**Much Hadham** Herts....60 C4
**Much Hoole** Lancs....120 F6
**Muchlarnick** Cnwll....5 K5
**Much Marcle** Herefs....54 F2
**Much Wenlock** Shrops....84 B4
**Muck** Highld....189 K1
**Muckleburgh Collection** Norfk....106 D4
**Mucklestone** Staffs....99 G5
**Muckton** Lincs....118 E5
**Muddiford** Devon....23 J4
**Muddles Green** E Susx....20 B3
**Mudeford** Dorset....16 A4
**Mudford** Somset....26 E7
**Mudford Sock** Somset....26 E7
**Mugdock** Stirlg....175 G3
**Mugeary** Highld....209 G6
**Mugginton** Derbys....100 F4
**Muirden** Abers....216 D4
**Muirdrum** Angus....196 F8
**Muiresk** Abers....216 D5
**Muirhead** Angus....186 E1
**Muirhead** Fife....186 E6
**Muirhead** N Lans....175 J4
**Muirkirk** E Ayrs....164 D4
**Muirmill** Stirlg....175 J2
**Muir of Fowlis** Abers....206 B3
**Muir of Miltonduff** Moray....214 E3
**Muir of Ord** Highld....212 E4
**Muirshearlich** Highld....192 B1
**Muirtack** Abers....217 J6
**Muirton** P & K....185 J5
**Muirton Mains** Highld....212 C4
**Muirton of Ardblair** P & K....195 J7
**Muker** N York....139 K7
**Mulbarton** Norfk....92 E4
**Mulben** Moray....215 H4
**Mull** Ag & B....181 J1
**Mullion** Cnwll....3 H7
**Mullion Cove** Cnwll....3 H7
**Mumby** Lincs....119 G6
**Munderfield Row** Herefs....70 B4
**Munderfield Stocks** Herefs....70 B4
**Mundesley** Norfk....107 G5
**Mundford** Norfk....91 H5
**Mundham** Norfk....93 G4
**Mundon Hill** Essex....61 K7
**Mungrisdale** Cumb....137 K2
**Munlochy** Highld....213 G4
**Munnoch** N Ayrs....174 B8
**Munsley** Herefs....70 B6
**Munslow** Shrops....83 K6
**Murchington** Devon....11 G7
**Murcott** Oxon....57 L5
**Murkle** Highld....231 H2
**Murlaggan** Highld....200 F6
**Murroes** Angus....187 G1
**Murrow** Cambs....89 L3
**Mursley** Bucks....58 D3
**Murthill** Angus....196 D5
**Murthly** P & K....195 H8
**Murton** C York....133 K8
**Murton** Cumb....139 G3
**Murton** Dur....151 J5
**Murton** Nthumb....179 K8
**Musbury** Devon....13 H4
**Musselburgh** E Loth....177 K4
**Muston** Leics....102 D5
**Muston** N York....135 H4
**Muswell Hill** Gt Lon....44 F3
**Mutehill** D & G....146 C5
**Mutford** Suffk....93 K6
**Muthill** P & K....185 H4
**Mybster** Highld....231 H5
**Myddfai** Carmth....52 B3
**Myddle** Shrops....98 C7
**Mydroilyn** Cerdgn....66 B4
**Mylor** Cnwll....4 C8
**Mylor Bridge** Cnwll....4 C8
**Mynachlog ddu** Pembks....49 K2
**Mynydd-bach** Mons....38 C2
**Mynydd-Bach** Swans....51 J6
**Mynyddgarreg** Carmth....50 E4
**Mynydd Isa** Flints....111 J8
**Myrebird** Abers....206 E5
**Myredykes** Border....157 G3
**Mytchett** Surrey....30 E1
**Mytholm** Calder....122 E5
**Mytholmroyd** Calder....122 F5
**Myton-on-Swale** N York....132 F6

## N

**Naast** Highld....219 J5
**Na Buirgh** W Isls....232 d4
**Naburn** C York....124 F2
**Nab Wood Crematorium** C Brad....123 H3
**Nackington** Kent....34 F4
**Nacton** Suffk....78 F6
**Nafferton** E R Yk....135 G7
**Nailsbourne** Somset....25 K5
**Nailsea** N Som....38 C6
**Nailstone** Leics....86 E3
**Nailsworth** Gloucs....55 J7
**Nairn** Highld....213 K3
**Nannerch** Flints....111 G7
**Nanpantan** Leics....101 K8
**Nanpean** Cnwll....4 F5
**Nanstallon** Cnwll....5 G3
**Nanternis** Cerdgn....65 L3
**Nantgaredig** Carmth....50 F2
**Nantglyn** Denbgs....96 F1
**Nantmel** Powys....68 B2
**Nantmor** Gwynd....95 K4
**Nant Peris** Gwynd....95 K2
**Nantwich** Ches E....98 F3
**Nantyglo** Blae G....53 J6
**Nant-y-moel** Brdgnd....36 E2
**Naphill** Bucks....42 D2
**Napton on the Hill** Warwks....72 F3
**Narberth** Pembks....49 J4
**Narborough** Leics....87 G4
**Narborough** Norfk....91 H2
**Nasareth** Gwynd....95 H3
**Naseby** Nhants....87 K7
**Nash** Bucks....73 L7
**Nash** Newpt....37 M4
**Nash** Shrops....69 L1
**Nassington** Nhants....88 F4
**Nateby** Cumb....139 H6
**Nateby** Lancs....120 F2
**National Memorial Arboretum** Staffs....85 L1
**National Motor Museum (Beaulieu)** Hants....16 E2
**National Space Centre** C Leic....87 H3
**Natland** Cumb....129 L2
**Naughton** Suffk....78 B5
**Naunton** Gloucs....56 C4
**Naunton** Worcs....70 F6
**Naunton Beauchamp** Worcs....71 G4
**Navenby** Lincs....103 G2
**Navestock** Essex....45 K1
**Navestock Side** Essex....60 E8
**Navidale** Highld....227 J5
**Navity** Highld....213 J2
**Nawton** N York....133 K3
**Nayland** Suffk....77 L7
**Nazeing** Essex....60 C6
**Neap** Shet....235 d5
**Near Cotton** Staffs....100 B4
**Near Sawrey** Cumb....137 K7
**Neasden** Gt Lon....44 E3
**Neasham** Darltn....141 H5
**Neath** Neath....51 L6
**Neatham** Hants....30 C4
**Neatishead** Norfk....107 H7
**Nebo** Cerdgn....66 D2
**Nebo** Conwy....96 C2
**Nebo** Gwynd....95 H3
**Nebo** IoA....108 F4
**Necton** Norfk....91 K2
**Nedd** Highld....224 D3
**Nedging** Suffk....78 B5
**Nedging Tye** Suffk....78 B4
**Needham** Norfk....92 F6
**Needham Market** Suffk....78 C4
**Needingworth** Cambs....75 L1
**Neen Savage** Shrops....84 C7
**Neen Sollars** Shrops....84 B8
**Neenton** Shrops....84 B6
**Nefyn** Gwynd....94 E4
**Neilston** E Rens....174 E6
**Nelson** Caerph....37 H2
**Nelson** Lancs....122 C3
**Nemphlar** S Lans....165 G1
**Nempnett Thrubwell** BaNES....38 D7
**Nenthead** Cumb....149 K6
**Nenthorn** Border....167 K2
**Nercwys** Flints....97 K1
**Nereabolls** Ag & B....170 E7
**Nerston** S Lans....175 H6
**Nesbit** Nthumb....168 E3
**Nesfield** N York....123 G1
**Nesscliffe** Shrops....98 B8
**Neston** Ches W....111 J6
**Neston** Wilts....39 K6
**Netchwood** Shrops....84 B5
**Nether Alderley** Ches E....113 J6
**Netheravon** Wilts....28 D2
**Nether Blainslie** Border....167 H2
**Netherbrae** Abers....216 F3
**Nether Broughton** Leics....102 B7
**Netherburn** S Lans....175 L8
**Netherbury** Dorset....13 L3
**Netherby** N York....123 L2
**Nether Cerne** Dorset....14 C3
**Nethercleuch** D & G....155 K5
**Nether Compton** Dorset....26 E7
**Nether Crimond** Abers....206 F2
**Nether Dallachy** Moray....215 H2
**Netherend** Gloucs....54 E7
**Netherfield** E Susx....20 E2
**Netherfield** Notts....101 L4
**Nether Fingland** S Lans....165 H7
**Netherhampton** Wilts....28 C5
**Nether Handwick** Angus....196 B7
**Nether Haugh** Rothm....115 H3
**Netherhay** Dorset....13 K2
**Nether Headon** Notts....116 C6
**Nether Heage** Derbys....101 G3
**Nether Heyford** Nhants....73 J3
**Nether Howcleugh** S Lans....165 K6
**Nether Kellet** Lancs....129 K6
**Nether Kinmundy** Abers....217 K5
**Nether Langwith** Notts....115 K7
**Netherlaw** D & G....146 C6
**Netherley** Abers....207 G6
**Nethermill** D & G....155 H5
**Nethermuir** Abers....217 G5
**Netherne-on-the-Hill** Surrey....32 B3
**Netheroyd Hill** Kirk....123 H6
**Nether Padley** Derbys....114 E6
**Nether Poppleton** C York....133 J8
**Netherseal** Derbys....86 C2
**Nether Silton** N York....133 G2
**Nether Stowey** Somset....25 J4
**Netherthong** Kirk....123 H8
**Netherton** Angus....196 E5
**Netherton** Devon....7 K2
**Netherton** Dudley....85 G6
**Netherton** Kirk....123 H7
**Netherton** N Lans....175 K7
**Netherton** Nthumb....168 E7
**Netherton** P & K....195 J6
**Netherton** Sefton....111 K2
**Netherton** Stirlg....175 G3
**Netherton** Wakefd....123 K6
**Nethertown** Cumb....136 D5
**Nethertown** Highld....231 L1
**Nethertown** Staffs....100 C8
**Netherurd** Border....165 L1
**Nether Wallop** Hants....28 F4
**Nether Wasdale** Cumb....136 F6
**Nether Westcote** Gloucs....56 E4
**Nether Whitacre** Warwks....86 B5
**Nether Whitecleuch** S Lans....165 G5
**Nether Winchendon** Bucks....58 B5
**Netherwitton** Nthumb....158 D4
**Nethy Bridge** Highld....204 B2
**Netley** Hants....16 F2
**Netley Marsh** Hants....29 G8
**Nettlebed** Oxon....42 B3
**Nettlebridge** Somset....26 F2
**Nettlecombe** Dorset....13 M4
**Nettleden** Herts....59 G6
**Nettleham** Lincs....117 G6
**Nettlestead** Kent....33 H3
**Nettlestead Green** Kent....33 H3
**Nettlestone** IoW....17 H4
**Nettlesworth** Dur....151 G5
**Nettleton** Lincs....117 J2
**Nettleton** Wilts....39 J5
**Netton** Wilts....28 C4
**Nevern** Pembks....64 F6
**Nevill Holt** Leics....88 B5
**New Abbey** D & G....147 G2
**New Aberdour** Abers....217 G2
**New Addington** Gt Lon....45 G7
**Newall** Leeds....123 J2
**New Alresford** Hants....29 L5
**New Alyth** P & K....195 K6
**Newark** C Pete....89 H4
**Newark** Ork....234 e4
**Newark-on-Trent** Notts....102 D2
**Newarthill** N Lans....175 K6
**New Ash Green** Kent....45 L6
**New Balderton** Notts....102 D3
**New Barn** Kent....45 L6
**New Barnet** Gt Lon....44 F2
**Newbattle** Mdloth....177 J5
**New Bewick** Nthumb....169 G5
**Newbie** D & G....147 L3
**Newbiggin** Cumb....138 C2
**Newbiggin** Cumb....138 F2
**Newbiggin** Cumb....148 F5
**Newbiggin** Dur....139 K2
**Newbiggin** N York....131 J3
**Newbiggin-by-the-Sea** Nthumb....159 H5
**Newbigging** Angus....187 H1
**Newbigging** Angus....195 L7
**Newbigging** Angus....196 C8
**Newbigging** S Lans....165 K1
**Newbiggin-on-Lune** Cumb....139 G6
**New Bilton** Warwks....86 F7
**Newbold** Derbys....115 G6

**Newbold on Avon** Warwks 86 F7
**Newbold on Stour** Warwks 72 B5
**Newbold Pacey** Warwks 72 C3
**Newbold Verdon** Leics 86 F3
**New Bolingbroke** Lincs 104 A2
**Newborough** C Pete 89 H3
**Newborough** IoA 108 E7
**Newborough** Staffs 100 C7
**New Boultham** Lincs 116 F7
**Newbourne** Suffk 78 F6
**New Bradwell** M Keyn 74 B6
**New Brampton** Derbys 115 G7
**New Brancepeth** Dur 151 G6
**Newbridge** C Edin 176 F4
**Newbridge** Caerph 37 K2
**Newbridge** Cnwll 2 D5
**Newbridge** D & G 155 G6
**Newbridge** Hants 28 F7
**Newbridge** IoW 16 E5
**Newbridge Green** Worcs 70 E6
**Newbridge-on-Wye** Powys 67 L3
**New Brighton** Wirral 111 J3
**Newbrough** Nthumb 149 L2
**New Buckenham** Norfk 92 C5
**Newbuildings** Devon 11 J4
**Newburgh** Abers 207 J1
**Newburgh** Abers 217 H3
**Newburgh** Fife 186 D4
**Newburgh** Lancs 121 G7
**Newburgh Priory** N York 133 H4
**Newburn** N u Ty 150 F2
**Newbury** Somset 27 G2
**Newbury** W Berk 41 J6
**Newbury Park** Gt Lon 45 J3
**Newby** Cumb 138 E3
**Newby** Lancs 122 B2
**Newby** N York 130 D5
**Newby** N York 142 B5
**Newby Bridge** Cumb 129 H3
**Newby East** Cumb 148 E4
**New Byth** Abers 216 F4
**Newby West** Cumb 148 C4
**Newcastle** Mons 54 C5
**Newcastle** Shrops 82 E6
*Newcastle Airport* Nthumb 158 F7
**Newcastle Emlyn** Carmth 65 J6
**Newcastleton** Border 156 E5
**Newcastle-under-Lyme** Staffs 99 J4
**Newcastle upon Tyne** N u Ty 151 G3
**Newchapel** Pembks 65 H6
**Newchapel** Surrey 32 C5
**Newchurch** IoW 17 G5
**Newchurch** Kent 34 E7
**Newchurch** Mons 38 C2
**Newchurch** Powys 68 E4
**Newchurch** Staffs 100 D7
**New Costessey** Norfk 92 E2
**Newcraighall** C Edin 177 J4
**New Crofton** Wakefd 124 B6
**New Cross** Gt Lon 45 G5
**New Cross** Somset 26 B7
**New Cumnock** E Ayrs 164 C6
**New Deer** Abers 217 G5
**New Denham** Bucks 43 H4
**Newdigate** Surrey 31 K3
**New Duston** Nhants 73 K3
**New Earswick** C York 133 J7
**New Edlington** Donc 115 K2
**New Elgin** Moray 214 F3
**New Ellerby** E R Yk 126 E3
**Newell Green** Br For 42 E6
**New Eltham** Gt Lon 45 H5
**New End** Worcs 71 J3
**Newenden** Kent 33 L7
**New England** C Pete 89 H4
**Newent** Gloucs 55 G3
**New Ferry** Wirral 111 K4
**Newfield** Dur 150 F7
**Newfield** Highld 223 H6
**New Fletton** C Pete 89 H4
*New Forest National Park* 16 C2
**Newgale** Pembks 48 E3
**New Galloway** D & G 154 B6
**Newgate Street** Herts 59 M6
**New Gilston** Fife 187 G5
**New Grimsby** IoS 2 a1
**Newhall** Ches E 98 E4
**New Hartley** Nthumb 159 H6
**Newhaven** C Edin 177 H3
**Newhaven** E Susx 19 L5
**New Haw** Surrey 43 H7
**New Hedges** Pembks 49 J6
**New Holland** N Linc 126 D5
**Newholm** N York 143 H5
**New Houghton** Derbys 115 J7
**New Houghton** Norfk 105 J6
**Newhouse** N Lans 175 L6
**New Hutton** Cumb 130 B2
**Newick** E Susx 19 L2
**Newington** Kent 35 G6
**Newington** Kent 46 E6
**Newington** Oxon 41 L2
**New Inn** Carmth 66 B6
**New Inn** Torfn 53 L7
**New Invention** Shrops 82 F7
**New Lakenham** Norfk 92 F3
**New Lanark** S Lans 165 G2
*New Lanark Village* S Lans 165 G2
**Newland** C KuH 126 D4
**Newland** Gloucs 54 D6
**Newland** N York 125 G5
**Newland** Somset 24 C4
**Newland** Worcs 70 E5
**Newlandrig** Mdloth 177 K6
**Newlands** Border 156 E4
**Newlands** Nthumb 150 D4
**Newlands of Dundurcas** Moray 215 G4
**New Langholm** D & G 156 C5
**New Leake** Lincs 104 C2
**New Leeds** Abers 217 J4
**New Lodge** Barns 123 L8
**New Longton** Lancs 121 G5
**New Luce** D & G 144 E3
**Newlyn** Cnwll 2 E5
**Newmachar** Abers 207 G2
**Newmains** N Lans 175 L6
**New Malden** Gt Lon 44 E6
**Newman's Green** Suffk 77 K5
**Newmarket** Suffk 76 F2
**Newmarket** W Isls 232 f2
**New Marske** R & Cl 142 D3
**New Marston** Oxon 57 K6
**New Mill** Abers 206 E8
**Newmill** Border 167 G7
**New Mill** Cnwll 2 E4
**New Mill** Kirk 123 H8
**Newmill** Moray 215 K4
**Newmillerdam** Wakefd 123 L7
**Newmill of Inshewan** Angus 196 C4
**Newmills** C Edin 177 G5
**New Mills** Derbys 113 M4
**Newmills** Fife 176 D2
**Newmills** Mons 54 D6
**New Mills** Powys 82 C4
**Newmiln** P & K 186 B2
**Newmilns** E Ayrs 164 B2
**New Milton** Hants 16 B4
**New Mistley** Essex 62 D2
**New Moat** Pembks 49 H3
**Newney Green** Essex 61 G6
**Newnham** Hants 30 B2
**Newnham** Herts 75 J6
**Newnham** Kent 34 C3
**Newnham** Nhants 73 H3
**Newnham Bridge** Worcs 70 B2
**Newnham on Severn** Gloucs 55 G5
**New Ollerton** Notts 116 A7
**New Oscott** Birm 85 K5
**New Pitsligo** Abers 217 G3
**Newport** Cnwll 9 J7
**Newport** E R Yk 125 K4
**Newport** Essex 76 D7
**Newport** Gloucs 39 G2
**Newport** Highld 227 K4
**Newport** IoW 16 F5
**Newport** Newpt 37 L3
**Newport** Pembks 64 E6
**Newport** Wrekin 99 H8
**Newport-on-Tay** Fife 187 G2
**Newport Pagnell** M Keyn 74 C5
Newport Pagnell Services M Keyn 74 C5
**New Prestwick** S Ayrs 163 J4
**New Quay** Cerdgn 65 L3
**Newquay** Cnwll 4 C4
Newquay Zoo Cnwll 4 C4
**New Rackheath** Norfk 93 G2
**New Radnor** Powys 68 E3
**New Ridley** Nthumb 150 D3
**New Romney** Kent 21 L2
**New Rossington** Donc 115 L2
**New Sauchie** Clacks 185 J7
**Newseat** Abers 216 D7
**Newsham** Lancs 121 G4
**Newsham** N York 132 E3
**Newsham** N York 140 E5
**Newsham** Nthumb 159 H6
**New Sharlston** Wakefd 124 B6
**Newsholme** E R Yk 125 H5
**New Silksworth** Sundld 151 J4
**Newsome** Kirk 123 H7
**New Somerby** Lincs 102 F5
**New Southgate Crematorium** Gt Lon 44 F2
**Newstead** Border 167 H3
**Newstead** Notts 101 K3
**Newstead** Nthumb 169 H4
**New Stevenston** N Lans 175 K6
**Newthorpe** Notts 101 J4
**New Thundersley** Essex 46 C3
**Newton** Ag & B 182 F7
**Newton** Border 167 J5
**Newton** Brdgnd 36 C5
**Newton** C Beds 75 J5
**Newton** Cambs 76 B5
**Newton** Cambs 90 B1
**Newton** Ches W 98 D1
**Newton** Ches W 112 B7
**Newton** Cumb 128 F5
**Newton** Derbys 101 H2
**Newton** Herefs 53 M2
**Newton** Herefs 69 K4
**Newton** Highld 212 F4
**Newton** Highld 213 H5
**Newton** Highld 213 J2
**Newton** Highld 231 L5
**Newton** Lincs 103 H5
**Newton** Mdloth 177 J4
**Newton** Moray 214 E2
**Newton** Moray 215 H2
**Newton** Nhants 88 C6
**Newton** Norfk 91 J1
**Newton** Notts 102 B4
**Newton** Nthumb 150 C3
**Newton** S Lans 165 H3
**Newton** S Lans 175 H6
**Newton** Sandw 85 J5
**Newton** Staffs 100 B7
**Newton** Suffk 77 K6
**Newton** W Loth 176 E3
**Newton** Warwks 87 G7
**Newton Abbot** Devon 7 K2
**Newton Arlosh** Cumb 147 L4
**Newton Aycliffe** Dur 141 G3
**Newton Bewley** Hartpl 141 K2
**Newton Blossomville** M Keyn 74 D4
**Newton Bromswold** Nhants 74 E2
**Newton Burgoland** Leics 86 D2
**Newton-by-the-Sea** Nthumb 169 J4
**Newton by Toft** Lincs 117 H4
**Newton Ferrers** Devon 6 E6
**Newton Ferry** W Isls 232 c5
**Newton Flotman** Norfk 92 E4
**Newtongrange** Mdloth 177 J5
**Newton Green** Mons 38 D3
**Newton Harcourt** Leics 87 J4
**Newton Heath** Manch 113 K2
**Newtonhill** Abers 207 G6
**Newton-in-Bowland** Lancs 121 K1
**Newton Kyme** N York 124 C2
**Newton-le-Willows** N York 132 C2
**Newton-le-Willows** St Hel 112 E3
**Newtonloan** Mdloth 177 J5
**Newton Longville** Bucks 58 D2
**Newton Mearns** E Rens 174 F7
**Newtonmill** Angus 196 F4
**Newtonmore** Highld 203 H5
**Newton Morrell** N York 141 G5
**Newton of Balcanquhal** P & K 186 B5
**Newton of Balcormo** Fife 187 H6
**Newton-on-Ouse** N York 133 H7
**Newton-on-Rawcliffe** N York 134 C2
**Newton-on-the-Moor** Nthumb 158 F2
**Newton on Trent** Lincs 116 D6
**Newton Poppleford** Devon 12 E4
**Newton Purcell** Oxon 57 L3
**Newton Regis** Warwks 86 C3
**Newton Reigny** Cumb 138 C2
**Newton St Cyres** Devon 11 K5
**Newton St Faith** Norfk 92 F1
**Newton St Loe** BaNES 39 G7
**Newton St Petrock** Devon 9 K3
**Newton Solney** Derbys 100 F7
**Newton Stacey** Hants 29 H4
**Newton Stewart** D & G 145 J3
**Newton Tony** Wilts 28 E4
**Newton Tracey** Devon 23 H6
**Newton under Roseberry** R & Cl 142 C5
**Newton upon Derwent** E R Yk 125 H2
**Newton Valence** Hants 30 B5
**Newton Wamphray** D & G 155 K3

**Newton with Scales** Lancs 120 F4
**Newtown** Cumb 147 J5
**Newtown** Cumb 148 E3
**Newtown** D & G 164 F7
**Newtown** Devon 12 D3
**Newtown** Devon 24 B6
**New Town** E Susx 19 M2
**Newtown** Gloucs 54 F7
**Newtown** Hants 29 L8
**Newtown** Herefs 70 B5
**Newtown** Highld 202 B4
**Newtown** IoW 16 E4
**Newtown** Nthumb 168 F4
**Newtown** Poole 15 K4
**Newtown** Powys 82 C5
**Newtown** Shrops 98 C6
**Newtown** Somset 25 L8
**Newtown** Staffs 99 K1
**Newtown** Wigan 112 E1
**Newtown** Worcs 70 F4
**Newtown Linford** Leics 87 G2
**Newtown of Beltrees** Rens 174 D6
**Newtown St Boswells** Border 167 J3
**New Tredegar** Caerph 53 H7
**New Trows** S Lans 164 F2
**Newtyle** Angus 195 L7
**New Walsoken** Cambs 90 C2
**New Waltham** NE Lin 118 C1
**New Winton** E Loth 177 L4
**Newyork** Ag & B 182 D5
**New York** Lincs 103 L2
**New York** N Tyne 159 H7
**Neyland** Pembks 49 G6
**Nicholashayne** Devon 25 H7
**Nicholaston** Swans 51 G7
**Nidd** N York 132 D7
**Nigg** C Aber 207 H5
**Nigg** Highld 223 H6
**Nigg Ferry** Highld 223 H7
**Ninebanks** Nthumb 149 K4
**Nine Elms** Swindn 40 C3
**Ninfield** E Susx 20 E3
**Ningwood** IoW 16 E5
**Nisbet** Border 167 K4
**Nisbet Hill** Border 179 G7
**Niton** IoW 17 F6
**Nitshill** C Glas 174 F6
**Nocton** Lincs 117 H8
**Noke** Oxon 57 K5
**Nolton** Pembks 48 E4
**Nolton Haven** Pembks 48 E4
**No Man's Heath** Ches W 98 D3
**No Man's Heath** Warwks 86 C2
**Nomansland** Devon 11 J3
**Nomansland** Wilts 28 E7
**Noneley** Shrops 98 C6
**Nonington** Kent 35 H4
**Nook** Cumb 129 L3
**Norbiton** Gt Lon 44 D6
**Norbury** Ches E 98 E3
**Norbury** Derbys 100 C4
**Norbury** Gt Lon 44 F6
**Norbury** Shrops 83 G5
**Norbury** Staffs 99 H7
**Norchard** Worcs 70 F2
**Nordelph** Norfk 90 D4
**Nordley** Shrops 84 C4
*Norfolk Broads* Norfk 93 K2
**Norham** Nthumb 179 J8
**Norley** Ches W 112 E6
**Norleywood** Hants 16 D3
**Normanby** Lincs 117 G4
**Normanby** N Linc 125 K7
**Normanby** N York 134 B3
**Normanby** R & Cl 142 C4
**Normanby le Wold** Lincs 117 J3
**Normandy** Surrey 30 F2
**Norman's Green** Devon 12 D2
**Normanton** C Derb 101 G5
**Normanton** Leics 102 D4
**Normanton** Notts 102 B2
**Normanton** Wakefd 124 B6
**Normanton le Heath** Leics 86 D2
**Normanton on Cliffe** Lincs 102 F4
**Normanton on Soar** Notts 101 K7
**Normanton on the Wolds** Notts 101 L6
**Normanton on Trent** Notts 116 C7
**Norris Green** Lpool 111 L3
**Norris Hill** Leics 86 D1
**Norristhorpe** Kirk 123 J6
**Northall** Bucks 58 F4
**Northallerton** N York 141 J7
**Northam** C Sotn 29 H8
**Northam** Devon 23 G5
**Northampton** Nhants 73 L3
**Northampton** Worcs 70 E2
*Northampton Services* Nhants 73 K3
**North Anston** Rothm 115 K5
**North Ascot** Br For 42 E6
**North Aston** Oxon 57 J3
**Northaw** Herts 59 L7
**Northay** Somset 13 H1
**North Baddesley** Hants 29 H7
**North Ballachulish** Highld 191 L4
**North Barrow** Somset 26 E5
**North Barsham** Norfk 105 L5
**Northbay** W Isls 233 b9
**North Benfleet** Essex 46 C3
**North Berwick** E Loth 178 C2
**North Boarhunt** Hants 17 H1
**Northborough** C Pete 89 H3
**Northbourne** Kent 35 J4
**North Bovey** Devon 11 H7
**North Bradley** Wilts 27 J1
**North Brentor** Devon 10 C8
**North Brewham** Somset 27 G4
**Northbrook** Hants 29 K4
**North Buckland** Devon 23 G4
**North Burlingham** Norfk 93 H2
**North Cadbury** Somset 26 F6
**North Carlton** Lincs 116 F6
**North Carlton** Notts 115 L4
**North Cave** E R Yk 125 K4
**North Cerney** Gloucs 56 A6
**North Chailey** E Susx 19 K2
**Northchapel** W Susx 30 F5
**North Charford** Hants 28 D7
**North Charlton** Nthumb 169 H5
**North Cheam** Gt Lon 44 E6
**North Cheriton** Somset 27 G6
**North Chideock** Dorset 13 K4
**Northchurch** Herts 58 F6
**North Cliffe** E R Yk 125 K3
**North Clifton** Notts 116 D6
**North Cockerington** Lincs 118 E4
**North Connel** Ag & B 182 C1
**North Cornelly** Brdgnd 36 C4
**North Cotes** Lincs 118 E2
**Northcott** Devon 9 J6
**Northcourt** Oxon 57 J7
**North Cove** Suffk 93 K5
**North Cowton** N York 141 G6
**North Crawley** M Keyn 74 D5
**North Creake** Norfk 105 K5
**North Curry** Somset 25 L6
**North Dalton** E R Yk 125 L1
**North Deighton** N York 124 B1
**North Devon Crematorium** Devon 23 H5
**Northdown** Kent 35 K2
**North Downs** 34 B4
**North Duffield** N York 125 G3
**North East Surrey Crematorium** Gt Lon 44 E6
**North Elmham** Norfk 106 B7
**North Elmsall** Wakefd 124 D7
**North End** C Port 17 J3
**North End** Essex 61 G4
**North End** Hants 28 C7
**North End** Nhants 74 D2
**North End** W Susx 18 D5
**Northend** Warwks 72 E4
**Northenden** Manch 113 J4
**North Erradale** Highld 219 H5
**North Evington** C Leic 87 J3
**North Fambridge** Essex 61 K7
**North Ferriby** E R Yk 126 B5
**Northfield** Birm 85 H7
**Northfield** C Aber 207 G4
**Northfield** E R Yk 126 C5
**Northfields** Lincs 88 E2
**Northfleet** Kent 45 M5
**North Frodingham** E R Yk 135 H8
**North Gorley** Hants 15 M1
**North Green** Suffk 79 G3
**North Greetwell** Lincs 117 G6
**North Grimston** N York 134 C6
**North Haven** Shet 235 e7
**North Hayling** Hants 17 K2
**North Hertfordshire Memorial Park & Crematorium** Herts 59 K2
**North Hill** Cnwll 5 L1
**North Hillingdon** Gt Lon 43 H4
**North Hinksey Village** Oxon 57 J6
**North Holmwood** Surrey 31 K3
**North Huish** Devon 7 G5
**North Hykeham** Lincs 116 F7
**Northiam** E Susx 21 G2
**Northill** C Beds 75 G5
**Northington** Hants 29 K4
**North Kelsey** Lincs 117 H2
**North Kessock** Highld 213 G5
**North Killingholme** N Linc 126 E6
**North Kilvington** N York 132 F3
**North Kilworth** Leics 87 H6
**North Kyme** Lincs 103 J3
**North Landing** E R Yk 135 K5
**Northlands** Lincs 104 B2
**Northleach** Gloucs 56 C5
**North Lee** Bucks 58 D6
**Northleigh** Devon 12 F3
**North Leigh** Oxon 57 H5
**North Leverton with Habblesthorpe** Notts 116 C5
**Northlew** Devon 10 D5
**North Littleton** Worcs 71 J5
**North Lopham** Norfk 92 C6
**North Luffenham** Rutlnd 88 D3
**North Marden** W Susx 30 D7
**North Marston** Bucks 58 C4
**North Middleton** Mdloth 177 K6
**North Millbrex** Abers 216 F5
**North Milmain** D & G 144 C4
**North Molton** Devon 24 B5
**Northmoor** Oxon 57 H7
**North Moreton** Oxon 41 K3
**Northmuir** Angus 196 C5
**North Mundham** W Susx 18 B5
**North Muskham** Notts 102 D2
**North Newbald** E R Yk 125 L3
**North Newington** Oxon 72 E6
**North Newnton** Wilts 40 C8
**North Newton** Somset 25 L5
**Northney** Hants 17 K2
**North Nibley** Gloucs 39 H2
**Northolt** Gt Lon 43 J4
*Northolt Airport* Gt Lon 43 H4
**Northop** Flints 111 H7
**Northop Hall** Flints 111 J7
**North Ormesby** Middsb 142 B4
**North Ormsby** Lincs 118 C3
**Northorpe** Kirk 123 J6
**Northorpe** Lincs 103 K5
**Northorpe** Lincs 116 E3
**North Otterington** N York 132 E2
**North Owersby** Lincs 117 H3
**Northowram** Calder 123 G5
**North Perrott** Somset 13 L1
**North Petherton** Somset 25 L5
**North Petherwin** Cnwll 9 H6
**North Pickenham** Norfk 91 J3
**North Piddle** Worcs 71 G4
**North Poorton** Dorset 13 M3
**Northport** Dorset 15 H5
**North Queensferry** Fife 176 F3
**North Rauceby** Lincs 103 G3
**Northrepps** Norfk 106 F5
**North Reston** Lincs 118 E5
**North Rigton** N York 123 K1
**North Rode** Ches E 113 K7
**North Ronaldsay** Ork 234 e3
*North Ronaldsay Airport* Ork 234 e3
**North Runcton** Norfk 90 F1
**North Scarle** Lincs 116 D7
**North Shian** Ag & B 191 H7
**North Shields** N Tyne 151 J2
**North Shoebury** Sthend 46 F3
**North Shore** Bpool 120 D3
**North Side** C Pete 89 K4
**North Somercotes** Lincs 118 F3
**North Stainley** N York 132 D4
**North Stifford** Thurr 45 L4
**North Stoke** BaNES 39 G6
**North Stoke** Oxon 41 L3
**North Stoke** W Susx 18 D4
**North Street** Kent 34 D3
**North Street** W Berk 41 M6
**North Sunderland** Nthumb 169 J3
**North Tamerton** Cnwll 9 J5
**North Tawton** Devon 10 F4
**North Third** Stirlg 175 K1
**North Thoresby** Lincs 118 D2
**North Tolsta** W Isls 232 g2
**Northton** W Isls 232 d5
**North Town** Devon 10 D3
**North Town** Somset 26 E3
**North Town** W & M 42 E4
**North Tuddenham** Norfk 92 C2
**North Uist** W Isls 233 b6
*Northumberland National Park* Nthumb 157 L3
**North Walsham** Norfk 107 G6
**North Waltham** Hants 29 K3

**North Warnborough** Hants 30 B2
**North Weald Bassett** Essex 60 D7
**North Wheatley** Notts 116 C4
**Northwich** Ches W 112 F6
**Northwick** Worcs 70 E3
**North Widcombe** BaNES 38 E8
**North Willingham** Lincs 117 K4
**North Wingfield** Derbys 115 H8
**North Witham** Lincs 102 F7
**Northwold** Norfk 91 H4
**Northwood** C Stke 99 K3
**Northwood** Gt Lon 43 H3
**Northwood** IoW 16 F4
**Northwood** Shrops 98 C6
**Northwood Green** Gloucs 55 G5
**North Wootton** Dorset 26 F8
**North Wootton** Norfk 105 G7
**North Wootton** Somset 26 E3
**North Wraxall** Wilts 39 J5
*North York Moors National Park* 142 F6
**Norton** Donc 124 E7
**Norton** E Susx 19 M5
**Norton** Gloucs 55 J3
**Norton** Halton 112 D5
**Norton** Nhants 73 H2
**Norton** Notts 115 L6
**Norton** Powys 68 F2
**Norton** S on T 141 K3
**Norton** Shrops 84 D4
**Norton** Suffk 77 L2
**Norton** Swans 51 H7
**Norton** W Susx 18 C4
**Norton** Wilts 39 K4
**Norton** Worcs 70 F4
**Norton** Worcs 71 J5
**Norton Bavant** Wilts 27 K3
**Norton Canes** Staffs 85 H2
Norton Canes Services Staffs 85 H3
**Norton Canon** Herefs 69 H5
**Norton Disney** Lincs 102 E2
**Norton Fitzwarren** Somset 25 J6
**Norton Green** IoW 16 D5
**Norton Hawkfield** BaNES 38 E7
**Norton Heath** Essex 60 F6
**Norton in Hales** Shrops 99 G5
**Norton-Juxta-Twycross** Leics 86 D3
**Norton-le-Clay** N York 132 F5
**Norton-le-Moors** C Stke 99 K3
**Norton Lindsey** Warwks 72 B2
**Norton Little Green** Suffk 77 L2
**Norton Malreward** BaNES 38 E7
**Norton-on-Derwent** N York 134 C5
**Norton St Philip** Somset 27 H1
**Norton Subcourse** Norfk 93 J4
**Norton sub Hamdon** Somset 26 C7
**Norwell** Notts 102 C1
**Norwell Woodhouse** Notts 116 B8
**Norwich** Norfk 92 F2
*Norwich Airport* Norfk 92 E2
**Norwich (St Faith) Crematorium** Norfk 92 F1
**Norwick** Shet 235 e1
**Norwood** Clacks 185 J8
**Norwood Green** Gt Lon 43 J5
**Norwood Hill** Surrey 31 L3
**Norwoodside** Cambs 90 B4
**Noss Mayo** Devon 6 E6
**Nosterfield** N York 132 D4
**Nostie** Highld 210 D8
**Notgrove** Gloucs 56 C4
**Nottage** Brdgnd 36 C5
**Nottingham** C Nott 101 L5
**Notton** Wakefd 123 L7
**Notton** Wilts 39 K6
**Noutard's Green** Worcs 70 E2
**Nuffield** Oxon 42 A3
**Nunburnholme** E R Yk 125 K2
**Nuneaton** Warwks 86 D5
**Nunhead** Gt Lon 45 G5
**Nun Monkton** N York 133 H7
**Nunney** Somset 27 G3
**Nunnington** N York 133 K4
**Nunsthorpe** NE Lin 127 G8
**Nunthorpe** C York 124 F1
**Nunthorpe** Middsb 142 C4
**Nunthorpe Village** Middsb 142 C5
**Nunton** Wilts 28 D6
**Nunwick** N York 132 E5
**Nursling** Hants 29 G7
**Nutbourne** W Susx 17 L2
**Nutbourne** W Susx 18 E3
**Nutfield** Surrey 32 B3
**Nuthall** Notts 101 K4
**Nuthampstead** Herts 76 B7
**Nuthurst** W Susx 31 K6
**Nutley** E Susx 32 D7
**Nuttall** Bury 122 B7
**Nybster** Highld 231 L3
**Nyetimber** W Susx 18 B6
**Nyewood** W Susx 30 D6
Nymans W Susx 31 L5
**Nymet Rowland** Devon 11 G4
**Nymet Tracey** Devon 11 G5
**Nympsfield** Gloucs 55 J7
**Nynehead** Somset 25 H6
**Nyton** W Susx 18 C5

## O

**Oadby** Leics 87 J4
**Oad Street** Kent 34 B3
**Oakamoor** Staffs 100 B4
**Oakbank** W Loth 176 E5
**Oak Cross** Devon 10 D5
**Oakdale** Caerph 37 J2
**Oake** Somset 25 J6
**Oaken** Staffs 84 F3
**Oakenclough** Lancs 121 H2
**Oakengates** Wrekin 84 C2
**Oakenshaw** Dur 150 F7
**Oakenshaw** Kirk 123 H5
**Oakford** Cerdgn 66 B3
**Oakford** Devon 24 E6
**Oakham** RutInd 88 C2
**Oakhanger** Hants 30 C4
**Oakhill** Somset 26 F3
**Oakington** Cambs 76 B2
**Oakle Street** Gloucs 55 H4
**Oakley** Bed 74 E4
**Oakley** Bucks 57 M5
**Oakley** Fife 176 D1
**Oakley** Hants 29 K2
**Oakley** Suffk 92 E7
**Oakridge Lynch** Gloucs 55 K7
**Oaksey** Wilts 39 M2
**Oakthorpe** Leics 86 D2
**Oakwood** C Derb 101 G5
**Oakworth** C Brad 122 F3
**Oare** Kent 34 D3
**Oare** Somset 24 C3
**Oare** Wilts 40 D7
**Oasby** Lincs 103 G5
**Oath** Somset 26 B6
**Oathlaw** Angus 196 D5
**Oatlands Park** Surrey 43 H7
**Oban** Ag & B 182 B2
*Oban Airport* Ag & B 182 C1
**Obley** Shrops 83 G7
**Obney** P & K 195 G8
**Oborne** Dorset 26 F7
**Occold** Suffk 78 D1
**Occumster** Highld 231 J7
**Ochiltree** E Ayrs 163 L5
**Ockbrook** Derbys 101 H5
**Ocker Hill** Sandw 85 H5
**Ockham** Surrey 31 H1
**Ockle** Highld 190 B3
**Ockley** Surrey 31 J4
**Ocle Pychard** Herefs 69 L5
**Odcombe** Somset 26 D7
**Odd Down** BaNES 39 H7
**Oddingley** Worcs 71 G3
**Oddington** Gloucs 56 E3
**Oddington** Oxon 57 K5
**Odell** Bed 74 D3
**Odiham** Hants 30 C2
**Odsal** C Brad 123 H5
**Odsey** Cambs 75 K6
**Odstock** Wilts 28 D6
**Odstone** Leics 86 E3
**Offchurch** Warwks 72 D2
**Offenham** Worcs 71 J5
**Offerton** Stockp 113 K4
**Offham** E Susx 19 L3
**Offham** Kent 33 H2
**Offham** W Susx 18 D4
**Offord Cluny** Cambs 75 J2
**Offord D'Arcy** Cambs 75 J2
**Offton** Suffk 78 C5
**Offwell** Devon 12 F3
**Ogbourne Maizey** Wilts 40 D6
**Ogbourne St Andrew** Wilts 40 D6
**Ogbourne St George** Wilts 40 D5
**Ogle** Nthumb 158 E6
**Oglet** Lpool 112 C5
**Ogmore** V Glam 36 D5
**Ogmore-by-Sea** V Glam 36 D5
**Ogmore Vale** Brdgnd 36 E3
**Okeford Fitzpaine** Dorset 14 F1
**Okehampton** Devon 10 E5
**Oker Side** Derbys 100 F1
**Okewood Hill** Surrey 31 J4
**Old** Nhants 87 L8
**Old Aberdeen** C Aber 207 H4
**Old Alresford** Hants 29 L5
**Oldany** Highld 224 D2
**Old Auchenbrack** D & G 154 D3
**Old Basford** C Nott 101 K4
**Old Basing** Hants 30 A2
**Old Beetley** Norfk 106 A8
**Oldberrow** Warwks 71 K2
**Old Bewick** Nthumb 169 G5
**Old Bolingbroke** Lincs 118 E8
**Old Bramhope** Leeds 123 J2
**Old Brampton** Derbys 115 G6
**Old Bridge of Urr** D & G 146 D2
**Old Buckenham** Norfk 92 C5
**Old Burghclere** Hants 41 J8
**Oldbury** Sandw 85 H5
**Oldbury** Shrops 84 C5
**Oldbury** Warwks 86 C5
**Oldbury-on-Severn** S Glos 38 E2
**Oldbury on the Hill** Gloucs 39 J3
**Old Byland** N York 133 H3
**Old Cantley** Donc 115 L2
**Oldcastle** Mons 53 L3
**Old Catton** Norfk 92 F2
**Old Clee** NE Lin 127 G8
**Old Cleeve** Somset 25 G3
**Old Colwyn** Conwy 110 B6
**Oldcotes** Notts 115 L4
**Old Coulsdon** Gt Lon 32 B2
**Old Dailly** S Ayrs 152 F3
**Old Dalby** Leics 102 A7
**Old Deer** Abers 217 J5
**Old Edlington** Donc 115 K3
**Old Ellerby** E R Yk 126 E3
**Old Felixstowe** Suffk 79 G7
**Oldfield** Worcs 70 E2
**Old Fletton** C Pete 89 H4
**Oldford** Somset 27 H2
**Old Forge** Herefs 54 E4
**Old Grimsby** IoS 2 a1
**Old Hall Green** Herts 60 B4
**Oldham** Oldham 113 L1
**Oldham Crematorium** Oldham 113 K2
**Oldhamstocks** E Loth 178 F4
**Old Harlow** Essex 60 D5
**Old Hunstanton** Norfk 105 G4
**Old Hurst** Cambs 89 K7
**Old Hutton** Cumb 130 B2
Old Inns Services N Lans 175 K3
**Old Kilpatrick** W Duns 174 E4
**Old Knebworth** Herts 59 L4
**Old Lakenham** Norfk 92 F3
**Oldland** S Glos 38 F6
**Old Langho** Lancs 121 K4
**Old Leake** Lincs 104 C3
**Old Malton** N York 134 C5
**Oldmeldrum** Abers 216 F8
**Oldmill** Cnwll 6 B2
**Old Milverton** Warwks 72 C2
**Oldmixon** N Som 37 M8
**Old Newton** Suffk 78 C3
**Old Portlethen** Abers 207 H6
**Old Radford** C Nott 101 K4
**Old Radnor** Powys 68 E3
**Old Rayne** Abers 216 D8
**Old Romney** Kent 21 K2
**Old Shoreham** W Susx 19 G4
**Oldshoremore** Highld 228 C4
**Old Sodbury** S Glos 39 H4
**Old Somerby** Lincs 102 F5
**Oldstead** N York 133 H4
**Old Stratford** Nhants 73 L6
**Old Struan** P & K 194 C4
**Old Swinford** Dudley 84 F6
**Old Thirsk** N York 132 F3
**Old Town** Cumb 130 B3
**Old Town** E Susx 20 C5
**Old Town** IoS 2 b2
**Old Trafford** Traffd 113 J3
**Oldwall** Cumb 148 E3
**Oldwalls** Swans 50 F6
**Old Warden** C Beds 75 G5
**Old Weston** Cambs 89 G7
**Old Wick** Highld 231 L5
**Old Windsor** W & M 43 G5
**Old Wives Lees** Kent 34 E4
**Old Woking** Surrey 31 G1
**Olgrinmore** Highld 231 G5
**Olive Green** Staffs 100 C8
**Oliver's Battery** Hants 29 J6
**Ollaberry** Shet 235 c3
**Ollach** Highld 209 H6
**Ollerton** Ches E 113 H6
**Ollerton** Notts 116 A7
**Ollerton** Shrops 98 F7
**Olney** M Keyn 74 C4
**Olrig House** Highld 231 H3
**Olton** Solhll 85 K6
**Olveston** S Glos 38 E3
**Ombersley** Worcs 70 E2
**Ompton** Notts 116 B7
**Onchan** IoM 237 d5
**Onecote** Staffs 100 B2
**Onibury** Shrops 83 J7
**Onich** Highld 191 K4
**Onllwyn** Neath 52 C6
**Onneley** Staffs 99 H4
**Onslow Green** Essex 61 G4

**Onslow Village** Surrey....31 G2
**Onston** Ches W.............112 E6
**Opinan** Highld..............219 H6
**Orbliston** Moray............215 G3
**Orbost** Highld...............208 D5
**Orby** Lincs......................119 G7
**Orchard Portman** Somset......................25 K6
**Orcheston** Wilts.............28 B3
**Orcop** Herefs...................54 C3
**Orcop Hill** Herefs............54 C3
**Ord** Abers.......................216 C3
**Ordhead** Abers...............206 C3
**Ordie** Abers....................205 K5
**Ordiequish** Moray..........215 H3
**Ordsall** Notts..................116 B5
**Ore** E Susx........................21 G4
**Orford** Suffk......................79 J4
**Orford** Warrtn.................112 E4
**Organford** Dorset............15 H4
**Orkney Islands** Ork........234 c6
**Orkney Neolithic** Ork....234 b6
**Orlestone** Kent.................34 D7
**Orleton** Herefs.................69 J2
**Orleton** Worcs.................70 C2
**Orlingbury** Nhants..........74 C1
**Ormesby** R & Cl..............142 C4
**Ormesby St Margaret** Norfk.........93 K1
**Ormesby St Michael** Norfk...........................93 K1
**Ormiscaig** Highld...........219 K4
**Ormiston** E Loth.............177 L4
**Ormsaigmore** Highld....189 L4
**Ormsary** Ag & B.............172 C4
**Ormskirk** Lancs..............120 F8
**Oronsay** Ag & B..............171 G2
**Orphir** Ork.......................234 b6
**Orpington** Gt Lon.............45 J6
**Orrell** Sefton...................111 K3
**Orrell** Wigan....................112 D2
**Orroland** D & G...............146 D5
**Orsett** Thurr........................45 M4
**Orslow** Staffs.....................84 E1
**Orston** Notts...................102 C4
**Orton** Cumb....................138 F5
**Orton** Nhants....................88 B7
**Orton** Staffs......................84 F4
**Orton Longueville** C Pete.........................89 H4
**Orton-on-the-Hill** Leics.............................86 C3
**Orton Waterville** C Pete.........................89 H4
**Orwell** Cambs....................75 L4
**Osbaldeston** Lancs........121 J4
**Osbaldwick** C York........124 F1
**Osbaston** Leics..................86 E3
**Osbaston** Shrops...............97 L7
**Osborne House** IoW........17 G4
**Osbournby** Lincs............103 H5
**Oscroft** Ches W...............112 D7
**Ose** Highld.......................208 E6
**Osgathorpe** Leics...........101 H8
**Osgodby** Lincs................117 H3
**Osgodby** N York..............124 F4
**Osgodby** N York..............135 G3
**Oskaig** Highld.................209 H6
**Oskamull** Ag & B.............189 L7
**Osmaston** Derbys...........100 D4
**Osmington** Dorset............14 D5
**Osmington Mills** Dorset...........................14 E6
**Osmondthorpe** Leeds..123 L4
**Osmotherley** N York.....141 K7
**Osney** Oxon........................57 J6
**Ospringe** Kent....................34 D3
**Ossett** Wakefd.................123 K6
**Ossington** Notts.............116 C8
**Osterley** Gt Lon.................44 D5
**Oswaldkirk** N York.........133 K4
**Oswaldtwistle** Lancs.....121 L5
**Oswestry** Shrops...............97 L6
**Otford** Kent........................32 F2
**Otham** Kent........................33 K3
**Othery** Somset....................26 B5
**Otley** Leeds......................123 J2
**Otley** Suffk.........................78 E4
**Otterbourne** Hants.........29 J6
**Otterburn** N York...........131 G7
**Otterburn** Nthumb.......157 M4
**Otter Ferry** Ag & B.........172 F2
**Otterham** Cnwll...................8 F6
**Otterhampton** Somset...........................25 K3
**Otternish** W Isls.............232 c5
**Ottershaw** Surrey............43 G7
**Otterswick** Shet............235 d3
**Otterton** Devon..................12 E5
**Ottery St Mary** Devon....12 E4
**Ottinge** Kent.......................34 F6
**Ottringham** E R Yk........127 G5
**Oughterside** Cumb.......147 K6
**Oughtibridge** Sheff.......114 F3
**Oughtrington** Warrtn...113 G4
**Oulston** N York...............133 H5
**Oulton** Cumb..................147 M5
**Oulton** Norfk...................106 D6
**Oulton** Staffs......................99 K5
**Oulton** Suffk.......................93 L5
**Oulton Broad** Suffk.........93 L5
**Oulton Street** Norfk......106 D6
**Oundle** Nhants..................88 F6
**Ounsdale** Staffs.................84 F5
**Our Dynamic Earth** C Edin............................177 H4
**Ousby** Cumb...................149 G7
**Ousden** Suffk......................77 G3
**Ousefleet** E R Yk.............125 K6
**Ouston** Dur......................151 G4
**Outgate** Cumb................137 K7
**Outhgill** Cumb................139 H6
**Outhill** Warwks..................71 K2
**Outlane** Kirk....................123 G6
**Out Rawcliffe** Lancs......120 E3
**Outwell** Norfk.....................90 D3
**Outwood** Surrey.................32 B4
**Outwoods** Staffs................99 H8
**Ouzlewell Green** Leeds..........................123 L5
**Over** Cambs........................75 L1
**Overbury** Worcs.................71 G6
**Overcombe** Dorset.............14 D6
**Over Compton** Dorset....26 E7
**Overdale Crematorium** Bolton..........................121 K8
**Over Haddon** Derbys....114 D7
**Over Kellet** Lancs...........129 L5
**Over Kiddington** Oxon..............................57 H4
**Overleigh** Somset...........26 C4
**Over Norton** Oxon............56 F3
**Over Peover** Ches E......113 H6
**Overpool** Ches W...........111 L6
**Overscaig** Highld...........225 J4
**Overseal** Derbys................86 C1
**Over Silton** N York.........133 G2
**Oversland** Kent..................34 E3
**Overstone** Nhants............74 B2
**Over Stowey** Somset.......25 J4
**Overstrand** Norfk...........106 F4
**Over Stratton** Somset....26 B7
**Overthorpe** Nhants..........72 F6
**Overton** C Aber...............207 G3
**Overton** Hants....................29 K2
**Overton** Lancs..................129 J7
**Overton** N York................133 H7
**Overton** Shrops..................69 K1
**Overton** Swans...................50 F7
**Overton** Wakefd..............123 K7
**Overton** Wrexhm................98 A4
**Overtown** N Lans............175 L7
**Over Wallop** Hants...........28 F4
**Over Whitacre** Warwks..........................86 B5
**Over Worton** Oxon...........57 H3
**Oving** Bucks........................58 C4
**Oving** W Susx......................18 B5
**Ovingdean** Br & H.............19 K5
**Ovingham** Nthumb.......150 D3
**Ovington** Dur...................140 E4
**Ovington** Essex..................77 H6
**Ovington** Hants...................29 K5
**Ovington** Norfk...................91 K3
**Ovington** Nthumb.........150 D3
**Ower** Hants..........................28 F7
**Owermoigne** Dorset.........14 E5
**Owlerton** Sheff................115 G4
**Owlsmoor** Br For..............42 D7
**Owlswick** Bucks.................58 C6
**Owmby** Lincs....................117 G4
**Owmby** Lincs....................117 H1
**Owslebury** Hants...............29 K6
**Owston** Donc...................124 E7
**Owston** Leics.......................87 L3
**Owston Ferry** N Linc.....116 D2
**Owstwick** E R Yk.............127 G4
**Owthorne** E R Yk............127 H5
**Owthorpe** Notts..............102 A5
**Owton Manor** Hartpl....141 L2
**Oxborough** Norfk..............91 G3
**Oxcombe** Lincs................118 D6
**Oxenholme** Cumb..........129 L2
**Oxenhope** C Brad...........122 F4
**Oxen Park** Cumb.............129 G3
**Oxenpill** Somset.................26 C3
**Oxenton** Gloucs..................55 L2
**Oxenwood** Wilts.................40 F8
**Oxford** Oxon........................57 K6
*Oxford Airport* Oxon.......57 J5
**Oxford Crematorium** Oxon..............................57 K6
**Oxford Services** Oxon.....57 L6
**Oxhey** Herts........................43 J2
**Oxhill** Warwks....................72 C5
**Oxley** Wolves......................84 F3
**Oxley Green** Essex............61 L5
**Oxlode** Cambs....................90 C6
**Oxnam** Border..................167 L5
**Oxnead** Norfk...................106 F7
**Oxshott** Surrey...................43 J7
**Oxspring** Barns................114 F2
**Oxted** Surrey.......................32 D3
**Oxton** Border....................178 B7
**Oxton** N York...................124 D2
**Oxton** Notts......................101 M3
**Oxton** Wirral.....................111 J4
**Oxwich** Swans....................51 G7
**Oxwich Green** Swans.......50 F7
**Oykel Bridge** Highld.......221 K2
**Oyne** Abers.......................206 D1
**Oystermouth** Swans........51 H7

## P

**Pabail** W Isls...................232 g2
**Packington** Leics...............86 D1
**Packmoor** C Stke...............99 K2
**Padanaram** Angus..........196 C6
**Padbury** Bucks...................58 B2
**Paddington** Gt Lon............44 F4
**Paddlesworth** Kent..........35 G6
**Paddlesworth** Kent..........46 B7
**Paddock Wood** Kent.........33 H4
**Padiham** Lancs.................122 B4
**Padside** N York.................132 B7
**Padstow** Cnwll.....................4 E2
**Padworth** W Berk...............41 L7
**Pagham** W Susx..................18 B6
**Paglesham** Essex................46 F2
**Paignton** Torbay...................7 K4
**Pailton** Warwks....................86 F6
**Painscastle** Powys.............68 D5
**Painshawfield** Nthumb...........................150 D3
**Painsthorpe** E R Yk.........134 C7
**Painswick** Gloucs...............55 K6
**Painter's Forstal** Kent....34 D3
**Paisley** Rens......................174 E5
**Paisley Woodside Crematorium** Rens..............................174 E5
**Pakefield** Suffk....................93 L5
**Pakenham** Suffk..................77 L2
**Paley Street** W & M..........42 E5
**Palfrey** Wsall.......................85 H4
**Palgrave** Suffk.....................92 D7
**Pallington** Dorset...............14 E4
**Palmerston** E Ayrs..........163 L5
**Palnackie** D & G...............146 E4
**Palnure** D & G...................145 J3
**Palterton** Derbys..............115 J7
**Pamber End** Hants.............41 L8
**Pamber Green** Hants.........41 L8
**Pamber Heath** Hants.........41 L7
**Pamington** Gloucs..............55 L2
**Pamphill** Dorset..................15 J3
**Pampisford** Cambs.............76 C5
**Panbride** Angus................187 J1
**Pancrasweek** Devon............9 H4
**Pandy** Mons.........................53 M4
**Pandy Tudur** Conwy.......110 B8
**Panfield** Essex.....................61 H3
**Pangbourne** W Berk..........41 M5
**Pangdean** W Susx...............19 J4
**Pannal** N York...................123 L1
**Pannal Ash** N York...........132 D8
**Pant** Shrops..........................97 L7
**Pantasaph** Flints...............111 G6
**Pant-ffrwyth** Brdgnd.......36 E4
**Pant Glas** Gwynd.................95 H3
**Pantglas** Powys...................81 G4
**Panton** Lincs......................117 K5
**Pant-y-dwr** Powys..............81 L8
**Pant-y-mwyn** Flints.......111 H8
**Panxworth** Norfk................93 H2
*Papa Stour Airport* Shet..............................235 b5
*Papa Westray Airport* Ork..............................234 c3
**Papcastle** Cumb................136 F2
**Papigoe** Highld.................231 L5
**Papple** E Loth....................178 D4
**Papplewick** Notts............101 K3
**Papworth Everard** Cambs...........................75 K3
**Papworth St Agnes** Cambs...........................75 J2
**Par** Cnwll................................5 G5
**Parbold** Lancs...................121 G7
**Parbrook** Somset................26 E4
**Parc** Gwynd..........................96 D5
**Parc Gwyn Crematorium** Pembks.........................49 K5
**Parc Seymour** Newpt.......38 B3
**Pardshaw** Cumb...............136 F3
**Parham** Suffk.......................79 G3
**Park** D & G.........................154 F4
**Park** Nthumb......................149 H3
**Park Corner** Oxon...............42 B3
**Park Crematorium** Hants..............................30 E2
**Park Crematorium** Lancs............................120 E5
**Parkend** Gloucs...................54 E6
**Parker's Green** Kent.........33 G4
**Park Farm** Kent...................34 D6
**Parkgate** Ches W...............111 J6
**Parkgate** D & G.................155 H4
**Park Gate** Hants..................17 G2
**Park Gate** Leeds................123 J3
**Parkgate** Surrey..................31 K3
**Parkgrove Crematorium** Angus..........................196 F6
**Parkhall** W Duns...............174 E4
**Parkham** Devon...................22 F6
**Parkmill** Swans....................51 G7
**Park Royal** Gt Lon..............44 D4
**Parkside** Dur.....................151 K5
**Parkside** N Lans................175 L6
**Parkstone** Poole..................15 J4
**Park Street** Herts...............59 J6
**Park Wood Crematorium** Calder..........................123 G6
**Parndon Wood Crematorium** Essex..............................60 C6
**Parracombe** Devon............23 L3
**Parson Drove** Cambs.........89 L2
**Parson's Heath** Essex.......62 B3
**Partick** C Glas....................174 F5
**Partington** Traffd.............113 G3

Partney Lincs 118 F7
Parton Cumb 136 D3
Partridge Green W Susx 19 G2
Parwich Derbys 100 D2
Passenham Nhants 73 L6
Paston C Pete 89 H3
Paston Norfk 107 G5
Patcham Br & H 19 J4
Patching W Susx 18 E4
Patchway S Glos 38 E4
Pateley Bridge N York 132 B6
Pathhead Fife 186 E8
Pathhead Mdloth 177 K5
Path of Condie P & K 185 M5
Patna E Ayrs 163 K7
Patney Wilts 40 B8
Patrick IoM 237 b5
Patrick Brompton N York 132 C2
Patricroft Salfd 113 H2
Patrington E R Yk 127 H6
Patrington Haven E R Yk 127 H6
Patrixbourne Kent 35 G4
Patterdale Cumb 137 L4
Pattingham Staffs 84 E4
Pattishall Nhants 73 J4
Pattiswick Green Essex 61 K3
Paul Cnwll 2 E5
Paulerspury Nhants 73 K5
Paull E R Yk 126 E5
Paulton BaNES 26 F1
Pauperhaugh Nthumb 158 D3
Pavenham Bed 74 E4
Pawlett Somset 25 L3
Paxford Gloucs 71 L6
Paxton Border 179 J7
Payhembury Devon 12 E3
Paythorne Lancs 122 C1
Peacehaven E Susx 19 L5
*Peak District National Park* 114 D3
Peak Forest Derbys 114 C5
Peakirk C Pete 89 H3
Peasedown St John BaNES 39 G8
Peasemore W Berk 41 J5
Peasenhall Suffk 79 H2
Pease Pottage W Susx 31 L5
Pease Pottage Services W Susx 31 L5
Peaslake Surrey 31 H3
Peasley Cross St Hel 112 D3
Peasmarsh E Susx 21 H2
Peathill Abers 217 H2
Peat Inn Fife 187 G5
Peatling Magna Leics 87 H5
Peatling Parva Leics 87 H5
Pebmarsh Essex 77 J7
Pebsham E Susx 20 F4
Pebworth Worcs 71 K5
Pecket Well Calder 122 E5
Peckforton Ches E 98 D2
Peckham Gt Lon 45 G5
Peckleton Leics 86 F4
Pedlinge Kent 34 F7
Pedmore Dudley 85 G6
Pedwell Somset 26 B4
Peebles Border 166 C2
Peel IoM 237 b4
Peel Green Crematorium Salfd 113 H3
Peene Kent 35 G6
Pegsdon C Beds 59 J2
Pegswood Nthumb 159 G5
Pegwell Kent 35 K2
Peinchorran Highld 209 H7
Peinlich Highld 208 F3
Peldon Essex 62 B5
Pelsall Wsall 85 H3
Pelton Dur 151 G4
Pelynt Cnwll 5 K5
Pemberton Carmth 51 G5
Pemberton Wigan 112 D2
Pembrey Carmth 50 E5
Pembridge Herefs 69 H3
Pembroke Pembks 49 G7
Pembroke Dock Pembks 49 G6
*Pembrokeshire Coast National Park Pembks* 48 E4
Pembury Kent 33 G5
Pen-allt Herefs 54 E3
Penallt Mons 54 D6
Penally Pembks 49 J7
Penarth V Glam 37 J6
Pen-bont Rhydybeddau Cerdgn 80 F6
Penbryn Cerdgn 65 J4
Pencader Carmth 66 B7
Pencaitland E Loth 177 L5
Pencarnisiog IoA 108 D6
Pencarreg Carmth 66 C5
Pencelli Powys 53 H3
Penclawdd Swans 51 G6
Pencoed Brdgnd 36 E4
Pencombe Herefs 69 L4
Pencraig Herefs 54 E4
Pencraig Powys 97 G6
Pendeen Cnwll 2 C4
Penderyn Rhondd 52 E6
Pendine Carmth 50 B4
Pendlebury Salfd 113 H2
Pendleton Lancs 121 L3
Pendock Worcs 55 H2
Pendoggett Cnwll 8 D8
Pendomer Somset 13 M1
Pendoylan V Glam 37 G5
Penegoes Powys 81 G4
Pen-ffordd Pembks 49 J3
Pengam Caerph 37 J2
Pengam Cardif 37 K5
Penge Gt Lon 45 G6
Pengelly Cnwll 8 E7
Penhallow Cnwll 3 K2
Penhalvean Cnwll 3 J4
Penhill Swindn 40 D3
Penhow Newpt 38 B3
Penicuik Mdloth 177 H6
Penifiler Highld 209 G6
Peninver Ag & B 161 J4
Penistone Barns 114 E2
Penkill S Ayrs 152 F3
Penkridge Staffs 85 G2
Penley Wrexhm 98 B4
Penllyn V Glam 36 F5
Penmachno Conwy 96 C3
Penmaen Caerph 37 J2
Penmaen Swans 51 G7
Penmaenmawr Conwy 109 K6
Penmaenpool Gwynd 95 M8
Penmark V Glam 37 G6
Penmount Crematorium Cnwll 4 C6
Penmynydd IoA 109 G6
Pennal Gwynd 80 F4
Pennan Abers 216 F2
Pennant Powys 81 J4
Pennerley Shrops 83 G4
Pennines 122 E4
Pennington Cumb 128 F4
Pennorth Powys 53 H3
Penn Street Bucks 42 F2
Penny Bridge Cumb 129 G3
Pennycross Ag & B 181 G3
Pennyghael Ag & B 181 H3
Pennyglen S Ayrs 163 H7
Pennymoor Devon 11 K3
Pennywell Sundld 151 J4
Penparc Cerdgn 65 H5
Penperlleni Mons 53 L6
Penpoll Cnwll 5 J5
Penponds Cnwll 3 H4
Penpont D & G 154 E4
Pen-rhiw Pembks 65 H6
Penrhiwceiber Rhondd 37 G2
Pen Rhiwfawr Neath 51 L4
Penrhiwllan Cerdgn 65 K6
Penrhiw-pal Cerdgn 65 K5
Penrhos Gwynd 94 F5
Penrhos Mons 54 B5
Penrhyn Bay Conwy 110 A5
Penrhyn-coch Cerdgn 80 E6
Penrhyndeudraeth Gwynd 95 K5
Penrice Swans 50 F7
Penrioch N Ayrs 161 L1
Penrith Cumb 138 D2
Penrose Cnwll 4 D2
Penruddock Cumb 138 B2
Penryn Cnwll 3 K4
Pensarn Conwy 110 C5
Pensax Worcs 70 C2
Penselwood Somset 27 H5
Pensford BaNES 38 F7
Pensham Worcs 71 G5
Penshaw Sundld 151 H4
Penshurst Kent 32 F4
Pensilva Cnwll 5 L2
Pensnett Dudley 85 G5
Pentewan Cnwll 4 F6
Pentir Gwynd 109 H7
Pentire Cnwll 4 C4
Pentlow Essex 77 J5
Pentney Norfk 91 G2
Pentonbridge Cumb 156 D6
Penton Mewsey Hants 29 G3
Pentraeth IoA 109 G5
Pentre Mons 54 B7
Pentre Rhondd 36 F2
Pentre Shrops 98 A8
Pentrebach Myr Td 53 G7
Pentre-bach Powys 52 E2
Pentre Berw IoA 108 F6
Pentrebychan Crematorium Wrexhm 97 L3
Pentrecelyn Denbgs 97 J2
Pentre-celyn Powys 81 J3
Pentre-chwyth Swans 51 J6
Pentre-cwrt Carmth 65 L6
Pentredwr Denbgs 97 J3
Pentrefelin Gwynd 95 J5
Pentrefoelas Conwy 96 D3
Pentregat Cerdgn 65 K4
Pentre-Gwenlais Carmth 51 H3
Pentre Hodrey Shrops 83 G7
Pentre Llanrhaeadr Denbgs 110 F8
Pentre Meyrick V Glam 36 E5
Pentre-tafarn-y-fedw Conwy 96 C1
Pentrich Derbys 101 G3
Pentridge Dorset 28 B7
Pen-twyn Mons 54 D6
Pentwynmaur Caerph 37 J2
Pentyrch Cardif 37 H4
Penwithick Cnwll 5 G5
Penybanc Carmth 51 H2
Penybont Powys 68 C2
Pen-y-bont Powys 97 K7
Pen-y-bont-fawr Powys 97 G7
Pen-y-bryn Pembks 65 G6
Penycae Wrexhm 97 L4
Pen-y-clawdd Mons 54 C6
Pen-y-coedcae Rhondd 37 G3
Penycwn Pembks 48 E3
Pen-y-felin Flints 111 G7
Penyffordd Flints 97 L1
Pen-y-Garnedd Powys 97 H7
Pen-y-graig Gwynd 94 D5
Penygraig Rhondd 36 F3
Penygroes Carmth 51 H3
Penygroes Gwynd 95 H2
Pen-y-Mynydd Carmth 50 F5
Penymynydd Flints 97 L1
Penysarn IoA 108 F4
Pen-y-stryt Denbgs 97 J3
Penywaun Rhondd 52 F6
Penzance Cnwll 2 E5
Peopleton Worcs 71 G4
Peplow Shrops 98 F7
Perceton N Ayrs 163 J2
Percyhorner Abers 217 H2
Perelle Guern 236 b3
Perham Down Wilts 28 E2
Periton Somset 24 E3
Perivale Gt Lon 44 D4
Perkins Village Devon 12 D4
Perlethorpe Notts 115 M7
Perranarworthal Cnwll 3 K4
Perranporth Cnwll 3 K1
Perranuthnoe Cnwll 2 F5
Perranwell Cnwll 3 K4
Perranzabuloe Cnwll 3 K2
Perry Birm 85 J5
Perry Barr Birm 85 J5
Perry Barr Crematorium Birm 85 J5
Perry Green Wilts 39 L3
Pershall Staffs 99 J6
Pershore Worcs 71 G5
Pertenhall Bed 74 F2
Perth P & K 186 B3
Perth Crematorium P & K 186 A3
Perthy Shrops 98 A5
Perton Herefs 69 L6
Perton Staffs 84 F4
Peterborough C Pete 89 H4
Peterborough Crematorium C Pete 89 H3
Peterborough Services Cambs 89 G5
Peterchurch Herefs 69 G6
Peterculter C Aber 206 F5
Peterhead Abers 217 L5
Peterlee Dur 151 K6
Petersfield Hants 30 C6
Peter's Green Herts 59 J4
Petersham Gt Lon 44 D5
Peters Marland Devon 10 C3
Peterstone Wentlooge Newpt 37 K4
Peterston-super-Ely V Glam 37 G5
Peterstow Herefs 54 E3
Peter Tavy Devon 6 D1
Petham Kent 34 F4
Petherwin Gate Cnwll 9 H6
Petrockstow Devon 10 D3
Pett E Susx 21 H3
Pettaugh Suffk 78 E3
Petterden Angus 196 C7
Pettinain S Lans 165 J2
Pettistree Suffk 79 G4
Petton Devon 24 F6
Petts Wood Gt Lon 45 J6
Pettycur Fife 177 H2
Pettymuk Abers 207 G1
Petworth W Susx 31 G6
Pevensey E Susx 20 D5
Pevensey Bay E Susx 20 D5
Pewsey Wilts 40 D7
Phepson Worcs 71 G3
Philham Devon 22 D6
Philiphaugh Border 166 F4
Phillack Cnwll 2 F4
Philleigh Cnwll 4 D7
Philpstoun W Loth 176 E3
Phoenix Green Hants 30 C1
Pibsbury Somset 26 C6
Pickburn Donc 115 K1

Pickering N York 134 C3
Pickford Covtry 86 C6
Pickhill N York 132 E3
Picklescott Shrops 83 J4
Pickmere Ches E 113 G6
Pickney Somset 25 J5
Pickwell Leics 87 L2
Pickworth Lincs 103 H5
Pickworth Rutlnd 88 E2
Picton Ches W 112 B7
Picton N York 141 K5
Piddinghoe E Susx 19 L5
Piddington Nhants 74 B4
Piddington Oxon 57 M5
Piddlehinton Dorset 14 D3
Piddletrenthide Dorset 14 D3
Pidley Cambs 89 K7
Piercebridge Darltn 140 F4
Pierowall Ork 234 c3
Pilgrims Hatch Essex 45 L2
Pilham Lincs 116 E3
Pillaton Cnwll 6 A3
Pillerton Hersey Warwks 72 C5
Pillerton Priors Warwks 72 C5
Pilley Barns 115 G2
Pilley Hants 16 D3
Pillgwenlly Newpt 37 L3
Pilling Lancs 120 E2
Pilning S Glos 38 D4
Pilsbury Derbys 114 C8
Pilsdon Dorset 13 K3
Pilsley Derbys 101 H1
Pilsley Derbys 114 E7
Pilson Green Norfk 93 H2
Piltdown E Susx 19 L2
Pilton Devon 23 J5
Pilton Nhants 88 E6
Pilton Rutlnd 88 D3
Pilton Somset 26 E3
Pimlico Herts 59 H6
Pimperne Dorset 15 G1
Pinchbeck Lincs 103 L7
Pin Green Herts 59 L3
Pinhoe Devon 12 C4
Pinley Green Warwks 72 B2
Pinminnoch S Ayrs 152 E4
Pinmore S Ayrs 152 E4
Pinn Devon 12 E5
Pinner Gt Lon 43 J3
Pinner Green Gt Lon 43 J3
Pinvin Worcs 71 G5
Pinwherry S Ayrs 152 E5
Pinxton Derbys 101 J2
Pipe and Lyde Herefs 69 K5
Pipe Aston Herefs 69 J1
Pipe Gate Shrops 99 G4
Piperhill Highld 213 K4
Pipewell Nhants 88 B6
Pirbright Surrey 30 F1
Pirnie Border 167 K4
Pirnmill N Ayrs 161 L1
Pirton Herts 59 J2
Pishill Oxon 42 B3
Pistyll Gwynd 94 F4
Pitblae Abers 217 J2
Pitcairngreen P & K 185 M3
Pitcalnie Highld 223 H6
Pitcaple Abers 206 D1
Pitcarity Angus 196 B4
Pitchcombe Gloucs 55 J6
Pitchcott Bucks 58 C4
Pitchford Shrops 83 K3
Pitch Green Bucks 58 C7
Pitchroy Moray 214 E6
Pitcombe Somset 26 F5
Pitcox E Loth 178 E4
Pitfichie Abers 206 D3
Pitglassie Abers 216 D5
Pitgrudy Highld 223 H3
Pitlessie Fife 186 E5
Pitlochry P & K 194 E5
Pitmachie Abers 216 C8
Pitmain Highld 203 H5
Pitmedden Abers 217 G8
Pitmedden Garden Abers 217 G8
Pitminster Somset 25 K7
Pitmuies Angus 196 F6
Pitmunie Abers 206 C3
Pitney Somset 26 C5
Pitroddie P & K 186 C3
Pitscottie Fife 187 G5
Pitsea Essex 46 C3
Pitsford Nhants 73 L2
Pitstone Bucks 58 F5
Pittarrow Abers 197 H2
Pittenweem Fife 187 J6
Pitteuchar Fife 186 D7
Pittington Dur 151 H6
Pittodrie House Hotel Abers 206 D1
Pitton Wilts 28 E5
Pittulie Abers 217 H2
Pity Me Dur 151 G5
Pixham Surrey 31 K2
Plains N Lans 175 L5
Plaish Shrops 83 K4
Plaistow Gt Lon 45 H4
Plaistow W Susx 31 G5
Plaitford Hants 28 F7
Plawsworth Dur 151 G5
Plaxtol Kent 33 G3
Playden E Susx 21 H2
Playford Suffk 78 F5
Play Hatch Oxon 42 C5
Playing Place Cnwll 4 C7
Playley Green Gloucs 55 H2
Plealey Shrops 83 H3
Plean Stirlg 175 L2
Pleasance Fife 186 D5
Pleasington Bl w D 121 J5
Pleasington Crematorium Bl w D 121 J5
Pleasley Derbys 115 J8
Pleasurewood Hills Suffk 93 L4
Pleinheaume Guern 236 d2
Plemont Jersey 236 a5
Plemstall Ches W 112 C7
Pleshey Essex 61 G5
Plockton Highld 210 C7
Plowden Shrops 83 H6
Pluckley Kent 34 B5
Pluckley Thorne Kent 34 B5
Plumbland Cumb 147 K6
Plumley Ches E 113 G6
Plumpton Cumb 148 E7
Plumpton E Susx 19 K3
Plumpton Nhants 73 H5
Plumpton Green E Susx 19 K3
Plumstead Gt Lon 45 J4
Plumstead Norfk 106 D5
Plumtree Notts 101 L6
Plungar Leics 102 C5
Plurenden Kent 34 C7
Plush Dorset 14 D3
Plwmp Cerdgn 65 K4
Plymouth C Plym 6 C5
Plympton C Plym 6 D5
Plymstock C Plym 6 D5
Plymtree Devon 12 D2
Pockley N York 133 K3
Pocklington E R Yk 125 J2
Podimore Somset 26 D6
Podington Bed 74 D3
Podmore Staffs 99 H5
Pointon Lincs 103 J6
Pokesdown Bmouth 15 L4
Polbain Highld 224 B6
Polbathic Cnwll 6 A4
Polbeth W Loth 176 D5
Poldark Mine Cnwll 3 H5
Polebrook Nhants 88 F6
Polegate E Susx 20 C5
Polesden Lacey Surrey 31 J2
Polesworth Warwks 86 C3
Polglass Highld 224 C6
Polgooth Cnwll 4 F5
Polgown D & G 154 C2
Poling W Susx 18 E5
Poling Corner W Susx 18 E5
Polkerris Cnwll 5 H5
Pollington E R Yk 124 F6
Polloch Highld 190 F3
Pollokshaws C Glas 175 G6
Pollokshields C Glas 175 G5
Polmassick Cnwll 4 F6
Polmont Falk 176 C3
Polnish Highld 200 B8
Polperro Cnwll 5 K5
Polruan Cnwll 5 H5
Polstead Suffk 78 B6
Poltalloch Ag & B 182 B7
Poltimore Devon 12 C3
Polton Mdloth 177 J5
Polwarth Border 178 F7
Polyphant Cnwll 9 H7
Polzeath Cnwll 4 E1
Pomathorn Mdloth 177 H6
Pondersbridge Cambs 89 J5
Ponders End Gt Lon 45 G2
Ponsanooth Cnwll 3 K4
Ponsworthy Devon 7 G2
Pont Abraham Services Carmth 51 H4
Pontac Jersey 236 e8
Pontantwn Carmth 50 F3
Pontardawe Neath 51 K5
Pontarddulais Swans 51 H5
Pont-ar-gothi Carmth 51 G2
Pontarsais Carmth 66 B8
Pontblyddyn Flints 97 L1
Pontcysyllte Aqueduct Wrexhm 97 L4
Pontefract Wakefd 124 C6
Pontefract Crematorium Wakefd 124 C6
Ponteland Nthumb 158 F7
Ponterwyd Cerdgn 81 G7
Pontesbury Shrops 83 H3
Pontesford Shrops 83 H3
Pontfadog Wrexhm 97 K5
Pontfaen Pembks 64 E7
Pont-faen Powys 67 L7
Pontgarreg Cerdgn 65 K4
Ponthenri Carmth 50 F4
Ponthir Torfn 37 M2
Ponthirwaun Cerdgn 65 J5
Pontllanfraith Caerph 37 J2
Pontlliw Swans 51 H5
Pontlottyn Caerph 53 H6
Pontlyfni Gwynd 95 G3
Pontnêddféchan Neath 52 D6
Pontnewydd Torfn 37 L2
Pontrhydfendigaid Cerdgn 67 G2
Pont-rhyd-y-fen Neath 36 C2
Pontrhydygroes Cerdgn 81 G8
Pontrilas Herefs 54 B3
Pont Robert Powys 82 C2
Pontshaen Cerdgn 66 B5
Pontsticill Myr Td 53 G5
Pontwelly Carmth 65 L6
Pontyates Carmth 50 F4
Pontyberem Carmth 51 G4
Pontybodkin Flints 97 L2
Pontyclun Rhondd 37 G4
Pontycymer Brdgnd 36 D3
Pont-y-pant Conwy 96 B2
Pontypool Torfn 53 L7
Pontypridd Rhondd 37 G3
Pontywaun Caerph 37 K2
Pool Cnwll 3 H3
Poole Poole 15 J4
Poole Crematorium Poole 15 J3
Poole Keynes Gloucs 39 M2
Poolewe Highld 219 K5
Pooley Bridge Cumb 138 C3
Poolfold Staffs 99 K1
Poolhill Gloucs 55 G3
Pool in Wharfedale Leeds 123 J2
Pool of Muckhart Clacks 185 L7
Pool Street Essex 77 H6
Poplar Gt Lon 45 G4
Porchfield IoW 16 F4
Poringland Norfk 92 F3
Porkellis Cnwll 3 J5
Porlock Somset 24 D3
Porlock Weir Somset 24 D2
Portachoillan Ag & B 172 C6
Port-an-Eorna Highld 210 B7
Port Appin Ag & B 191 H7
Port Askaig Ag & B 171 H5
Portavadie Ag & B 172 F4
Port Bannatyne Ag & B 173 J5
Portbury N Som 38 D5
Port Carlisle Cumb 147 M3
Port Charlotte Ag & B 170 E6
Portchester Hants 17 H2
Portchester Crematorium Hants 17 H2
Port Driseach Ag & B 173 G4
Port Ellen Ag & B 160 C1
Port Elphinstone Abers 206 E2
Portencalzie D & G 152 B7
Portencross N Ayrs 173 K8
Port Erin IoM 237 a6
Portesham Dorset 14 B5
Portessie Moray 215 K2
Port Eynon Swans 50 F7
Portfield Gate Pembks 48 F4
Portgate Devon 10 B7
Port Gaverne Cnwll 8 D8
Port Glasgow Inver 174 C4
Portgordon Moray 215 J2
Portgower Highld 227 H5
Porth Cnwll 4 C4
Porth Rhondd 36 F3
Porthallow Cnwll 3 K6
Porthallow Cnwll 5 K5
Porthcawl Brdgnd 36 C5
Porthcothan Cnwll 4 D2
Porthcurno Cnwll 2 C6
Port Henderson Highld 219 H6
Porthgain Pembks 64 A7
Porthgwarra Cnwll 2 C6
Porthill Staffs 99 J3
Porthkerry V Glam 37 G6
Porthleven Cnwll 3 H6
Porthmadog Gwynd 95 K5
Porth Navas Cnwll 3 K5
Porthoustock Cnwll 3 K6
Porthpean Cnwll 5 G5
Porthtowan Cnwll 3 J2
Porthyrhyd Carmth 51 G3
Portincaple Ag & B 183 J8
Portinfer Jersey 236 a5
Portington E R Yk 125 J4
Portinnisherrich Ag & B 182 D5
Portinscale Cumb 137 H3
Port Isaac Cnwll 8 D8
Portishead N Som 38 C5
Portknockie Moray 215 K2
Portland Dorset 14 D7
Portlethen Abers 207 H6
Portling D & G 146 F4
Portloe Cnwll 4 E7
Port Logan D & G 144 D6
Portmahomack Highld 223 K5
Portmeirion Gwynd 95 K5
Portmellon Cnwll 4 F6
Port Mòr Highld 189 K1
Portnacroish Ag & B 191 H6
Portnaguran W Isls 232 g2
Portnahaven Ag & B 170 D7
Portnalong Highld 208 E7

**Port nan Giuran** W Isls 232 g2
**Port nan Long** W Isls 232 c5
**Port Nis** W Isls 232 g1
**Portobello** C Edin 177 J4
**Portobello** Wolves 85 G4
**Port of Menteith** Stirlg 184 D6
**Port of Ness** W Isls 232 g1
**Porton** Wilts 28 D4
**Portpatrick** D & G 144 B4
**Port Quin** Cnwll 8 C8
**Port Ramsay** Ag & B 191 H7
**Portreath** Cnwll 3 H3
**Portreath Harbour** Cnwll 3 H3
**Portree** Highld 209 G5
**Port Righ** Ag & B 161 K2
**Port St Mary** IoM 237 b7
**Portscatho** Cnwll 4 D8
**Portsea** C Port 17 J3
**Portskerra** Highld 230 C3
**Portskewett** Mons 38 D3
**Portslade** Br & H 19 H4
**Portslade-by-Sea** Br & H 19 H5
**Portslogan** D & G 144 B3
**Portsmouth** C Port 17 J3
**Portsmouth** Calder 122 D5
**Portsmouth Dockyard** C Port 17 J3
**Port Soderick** IoM 237 c6
**Portsonachan Hotel** Ag & B 182 F3
**Portsoy** Abers 216 B2
**Port Sunlight** Wirral 111 K5
**Portswood** C Sotn 29 H8
**Port Talbot** Neath 36 B3
**Port Tennant** Swans 51 K6
**Portuairk** Highld 189 K3
**Portway** Sandw 85 H6
**Portway** Worcs 85 J8
**Port Wemyss** Ag & B 170 D7
**Port William** D & G 145 H6
**Portwrinkle** Cnwll 6 A5
**Portyerrock** D & G 145 K7
**Poslingford** Suffk 77 H5
**Posso** Border 166 B3
**Postbridge** Devon 10 F8
**Postcombe** Oxon 58 B7
**Postling** Kent 34 F6
**Postwick** Norfk 93 G2
**Potarch** Abers 206 B6
**Potten End** Herts 59 G6
**Potter Brompton** N York 134 F4
**Potterhanworth** Lincs 117 H7
**Potterhanworth Booths** Lincs 117 H7
**Potter Heigham** Norfk 107 J8
**Potterne** Wilts 39 M8
**Potterne Wick** Wilts 39 M8
**Potters Bar** Herts 59 L7
**Potters Crouch** Herts 59 J6
**Potters Green** Covtry 86 D6
**Potters Marston** Leics 87 G4
**Potterspury** Nhants 73 L6
**Potter Street** Essex 60 D6
**Potterton** Abers 207 H3
**Potto** N York 141 L6
**Potton** C Beds 75 J5
**Pott Shrigley** Ches E 113 L5
**Poughill** Cnwll 9 G4
**Poughill** Devon 11 K3
**Poulner** Hants 15 M2
**Poulshot** Wilts 39 L7
**Poulton** Gloucs 56 C7
**Poulton** Wirral 111 J4
**Poulton-le-Fylde** Lancs 120 D3
**Poundbury** Dorset 14 D4
**Poundffald** Swans 51 H6
**Pound Green** E Susx 20 B2
**Pound Green** Suffk 77 G4
**Pound Hill** W Susx 32 B5
**Poundon** Bucks 57 M3
**Poundsgate** Devon 7 G2
**Poundstock** Cnwll 9 G5
**Pouton** D & G 145 K5
**Povey Cross** Surrey 31 L3
**Powburn** Nthumb 168 F6
**Powderham** Devon 12 C5
**Powerstock** Dorset 13 M3
**Powfoot** D & G 147 K2
**Powick** Worcs 70 E4
**Powmill** P & K 185 L7
**Poxwell** Dorset 14 E5
**Poyle** Slough 43 G5
**Poynings** W Susx 19 H4
**Poyntington** Dorset 26 F7
**Poynton** Ches E 113 L5
**Poynton Green** Wrekin 98 E8
**Praa Sands** Cnwll 3 G5
**Praze-an-Beeble** Cnwll 3 H4
**Prees** Shrops 98 D5
**Preesall** Lancs 120 E2
**Prees Green** Shrops 98 E6
**Prees Heath** Shrops 98 E5
**Prees Higher Heath** Shrops 98 E5
**Pren-gwyn** Cerdgn 65 L5
**Prenteg** Gwynd 95 K4
**Prescot** Knows 112 C3
**Prescott** Devon 25 H8
**Presnerb** Angus 195 J3
**Prestatyn** Denbgs 110 E5
**Prestbury** Ches E 113 K6
**Prestbury** Gloucs 55 L4
**Presteigne** Powys 69 G2
**Prestleigh** Somset 26 F4
**Preston** Border 179 G6
**Preston** Br & H 19 J4
**Preston** Devon 7 K2
**Preston** Dorset 14 D5
**Preston** E R Yk 126 F4
**Preston** Gloucs 56 B7
**Preston** Herts 59 K3
**Preston** Kent 34 D3
**Preston** Kent 35 H3
**Preston** Lancs 121 H4
**Preston** Nthumb 169 H4
**Preston** Rutlnd 88 C3
**Preston** Somset 25 H4
**Preston** Torbay 7 K4
**Preston** Wilts 40 B5
**Preston Bagot** Warwks 71 L2
**Preston Bissett** Bucks 58 A3
**Preston Bowyer** Somset 25 H6
**Preston Brockhurst** Shrops 98 D7
**Preston Brook** Halton 112 E5
**Preston Candover** Hants 29 L3
**Preston Capes** Nhants 73 H4
**Preston Crematorium** Lancs 121 H4
**Preston Green** Warwks 71 L2
**Preston Gubbals** Shrops 98 C8
**Preston on Stour** Warwks 72 B4
**Preston on the Hill** Halton 112 E5
**Preston on Wye** Herefs 69 H6
**Prestonpans** E Loth 177 K4
**Preston Patrick** Cumb 129 L3
**Preston Plucknett** Somset 26 D7
**Preston St Mary** Suffk 77 L4
**Preston-under-Scar** N York 131 K2
**Preston upon the Weald Moors** Wrekin 84 C1
**Preston Wynne** Herefs 69 L5
**Prestwich** Bury 113 J1
**Prestwick** S Ayrs 163 J4
*Prestwick Airport* S Ayrs 163 J4
**Prestwood** Bucks 58 E7
**Prickwillow** Cambs 90 E6
**Priddy** Somset 26 D2
**Priest Hutton** Lancs 129 L5
**Priestland** E Ayrs 164 B2
**Priest Weston** Shrops 82 F4
**Primrosehill** Border 179 G6
**Primrose Hill** Dudley 85 G6
**Primsidemill** Border 168 B4
**Princes Risborough** Bucks 58 D7
**Princethorpe** Warwks 72 E1
**Princetown** Devon 6 E2
**Priors Hardwick** Warwks 72 F4
**Priorslee** Wrekin 84 C2
**Priors Marston** Warwks 72 F3
**Priors Norton** Gloucs 55 K3
**Priston** BaNES 39 G7
**Prittlewell** Sthend 46 E3
**Privett** Hants 30 B6
**Prixford** Devon 23 J4
**Probus** Cnwll 4 E6
**Prora** E Loth 178 C3
**Prospect** Cumb 147 K6
**Prospidnick** Cnwll 3 H5
**Protstonhill** Abers 216 F2
**Prudhoe** Nthumb 150 D3
**Publow** BaNES 38 F7
**Puckeridge** Herts 60 C4
**Puckington** Somset 26 B7
**Pucklechurch** S Glos 39 G5
**Puddington** Ches W 111 K6
**Puddington** Devon 11 J3
**Puddletown** Dorset 14 E4
**Pudsey** Leeds 123 J4
**Pulborough** W Susx 18 E3
**Pulford** Ches W 98 A2
**Pulham** Dorset 14 D2
**Pulham Market** Norfk 92 E6
**Pulham St Mary** Norfk 92 E6
**Pulloxhill** C Beds 74 F7
**Pulverbatch** Shrops 83 H3
**Pumpherston** W Loth 176 E4
**Pumsaint** Carmth 66 E6
**Puncheston** Pembks 49 G2
**Puncknowle** Dorset 14 A5
**Punnett's Town** E Susx 20 C2
**Purbrook** Hants 17 J2
**Purfleet** Thurr 45 K4
**Puriton** Somset 25 L3
**Purleigh** Essex 61 K7
**Purley** Gt Lon 44 F7
**Purley** W Berk 42 A5
**Purse Caundle** Dorset 27 G7
**Purtington** Somset 13 K2
**Purton** Gloucs 54 F6
**Purton** Gloucs 55 G7
**Purton** Wilts 40 C3
**Purton Stoke** Wilts 40 C3
**Pury End** Nhants 73 K5
**Pusey** Oxon 41 G2
**Putley** Herefs 70 B6
**Putley Green** Herefs 70 B6
**Putney** Gt Lon 44 E5
**Putney Vale Crematorium** Gt Lon 44 E5
**Puttenham** Surrey 30 F2
**Puxley** Nhants 73 L6
**Puxton** N Som 38 B7
**Pwll** Carmth 50 F5
**Pwll-glâs** Denbgs 97 H2
**Pwllgloyw** Powys 68 B7
**Pwllheli** Gwynd 94 F5
**Pwllmeyric** Mons 38 D2
**Pwll-trap** Carmth 50 C3
**Pwll-y-glaw** Neath 36 C2
**Pye Bridge** Derbys 101 H3
**Pyecombe** W Susx 19 J3
**Pyle** Brdgnd 36 C4
**Pyleigh** Somset 25 H5
**Pylle** Somset 26 E4
**Pymoor** Cambs 90 C6
**Pymore** Dorset 13 L4
**Pyrford** Surrey 43 H8
**Pyrton** Oxon 42 B2
**Pytchley** Nhants 88 C8
**Pyworthy** Devon 9 J4

## Q

**Quadring** Lincs 103 L6
**Quadring Eaudike** Lincs 103 L5
**Quainton** Bucks 58 C4
**Quantock Hills** Somset 25 J4
**Quarff** Shet 235 c6
**Quarley** Hants 28 F3
**Quarndon** Derbys 101 G4
**Quarrier's Village** Inver 174 C5
**Quarrington** Lincs 103 H4
**Quarrington Hill** Dur 151 H7
**Quarry Bank** Dudley 85 G6
**Quarrywood** Moray 214 E2
**Quarter** N Ayrs 173 L6
**Quarter** S Lans 175 J7
**Quatford** Shrops 84 D5
**Quatt** Shrops 84 D6
**Quebec** Dur 150 F6
**Quedgeley** Gloucs 55 J5
**Queen Adelaide** Cambs 90 E7
**Queen Camel** Somset 26 E6
**Queen Charlton** BaNES 38 F6
**Queen Elizabeth Forest Park** Stirlg 184 B6
**Queenhill** Worcs 70 F6
**Queen Oak** Dorset 27 H5
**Queen's Bower** IoW 17 H5
**Queensbury** C Brad 123 G4
**Queensferry** Flints 111 K7
**Queensferry Crossing** Fife 176 F3
**Queenslie** C Glas 175 H5
**Queen's Park** Bed 74 F4
**Queenzieburn** N Lans 175 J3
**Quendon** Essex 60 E3
**Queniborough** Leics 87 J2
**Quenington** Gloucs 56 C7
**Queslett** Birm 85 J4
**Quethiock** Cnwll 5 L3
**Quidenham** Norfk 92 B6
**Quidhampton** Wilts 28 C5
**Quinton** Nhants 73 L4
**Quintrell Downs** Cnwll 4 D4
**Quixwood** Border 179 G5
**Quoig** P & K 185 H3
**Quorn** Leics 87 H1
**Quothquan** S Lans 165 J2
**Quoyburray** Ork 234 c6
**Quoyloo** Ork 234 b5

## R

**Raasay** Highld 209 J5
**Rachan Mill** Border 165 L3
**Rachub** Gwynd 109 J7
**Rackenford** Devon 24 D7
**Rackham** W Susx 18 E3
**Rackheath** Norfk 93 G1
**Racks** D & G 155 H7
**Rackwick** Ork 234 a7
**Radbourne** Derbys 100 F5

**Radcliffe** Bury 113 H1
**Radcliffe on Trent** Notts 101 M5
**Radclive** Bucks 73 J7
**Raddery** Highld 213 H3
**Radernie** Fife 187 G5
**Radford** Covtry 86 D7
**Radford Semele** Warwks 72 D2
**Radlett** Herts 59 K7
**Radley** Oxon 57 K7
**Radley Green** Essex 60 F6
**Radnage** Bucks 42 C2
**Radstock** BaNES 27 G1
**Radstone** Nhants 73 H6
**Radway** Warwks 72 D5
**Radwell** Bed 74 E3
**Radwell** Herts 75 J7
**Radwinter** Essex 76 E6
**Radyr** Cardif 37 H4
**Rafford** Moray 214 C3
**RAF Museum Cosford** Shrops 84 E3
**RAF Museum Hendon** Gt Lon 44 E3
**Ragdale** Leics 102 A8
**Raglan** Mons 54 B6
**Ragnall** Notts 116 D6
**Raigbeg** Highld 213 J8
**Rainbow Hill** Worcs 70 F4
**Rainford** St Hel 112 C2
**Rainham** Gt Lon 45 K4
**Rainham** Medway 46 D6
**Rainhill** St Hel 112 C4
**Rainhill Stoops** St Hel 112 D4
**Rainow** Ches E 113 L6
**Rainsbrook Crematorium** Warwks 87 G8
**Rainton** N York 132 E4
**Rainworth** Notts 101 L2
**Rait** P & K 186 D3
**Raithby** Lincs 118 D5
**Raithby** Lincs 118 E7
**Rake** Hants 30 D5
**Ralia** Highld 203 H5
**Ramasaig** Highld 208 B5
**Rame** Cnwll 3 J4
**Rame** Cnwll 6 B6
**Rampisham** Dorset 14 B3
**Rampside** Cumb 128 F6
**Rampton** Cambs 76 B2
**Rampton** Notts 116 D5
**Ramsbottom** Bury 122 B6
**Ramsbury** Wilts 40 F6
**Ramscraigs** Highld 227 K3
**Ramsdean** Hants 30 B6
**Ramsdell** Hants 41 L8
**Ramsden** Oxon 57 G5
**Ramsden Bellhouse** Essex 46 B2
**Ramsey** Cambs 89 K6
**Ramsey** Essex 62 E2
**Ramsey** IoM 237 e3
**Ramsey Forty Foot** Cambs 89 K6
**Ramsey Heights** Cambs 89 J6
**Ramsey Island** Essex 61 M6
**Ramsey Island** Pembks 48 B3
**Ramsey Mereside** Cambs 89 K5
**Ramsey St Mary's** Cambs 89 J6
**Ramsgate** Kent 35 K2
**Ramsgill** N York 131 L5
**Ramshope** Nthumb 157 J2
**Ramshorn** Staffs 100 B4
**Ramsnest Common** Surrey 30 F5
**Ranby** Lincs 118 B5
**Ranby** Notts 116 A5
**Rand** Lincs 117 J5
**Randalls Park Crematorium** Surrey 44 D8
**Randwick** Gloucs 55 J6
**Ranfurly** Rens 174 D5
**Rangemore** Staffs 100 D7
**Rangeworthy** S Glos 39 G3
**Rankinston** E Ayrs 163 L6
**Rannoch Station** P & K 193 G5
**Ranscombe** Somset 24 E3
**Ranskill** Notts 116 A4
**Ranton** Staffs 99 J7
**Ranton Green** Staffs 99 J7
**Ranworth** Norfk 93 H1
**Raploch** Stirlg 185 G7
**Rapness** Ork 234 c4
**Rascarrel** D & G 146 D5
**Rashfield** Ag & B 173 K2
**Rashwood** Worcs 71 G2
**Raskelf** N York 133 G5
**Rastrick** Calder 123 H6
**Ratagan** Highld 200 E2
**Ratby** Leics 87 G3
**Ratcliffe Culey** Leics 86 D4
**Ratcliffe on Soar** Notts 101 J6
**Ratcliffe on the Wreake** Leics 87 J1
**Rathen** Abers 217 J3
**Rathillet** Fife 186 F3
**Rathmell** N York 130 F7
**Ratho** C Edin 176 F4
**Ratho Station** C Edin 176 F4
**Rathven** Moray 215 K2
**Ratley** Warwks 72 E5
**Ratling** Kent 35 H4
**Ratlinghope** Shrops 83 H4
**Rattar** Highld 231 J2
**Rattery** Devon 7 H4
**Rattlesden** Suffk 77 L3
**Ratton Village** E Susx 20 C5
**Rattray** P & K 195 J7
**Raunds** Nhants 88 E8
**Ravenfield** Rothm 115 J3
**Ravenglass** Cumb 136 F7
**Raveningham** Norfk 93 H4
**Ravenscar** N York 143 K6
**Ravenscraig** N Lans 175 K6
**Ravensden** Bed 74 F4
**Ravenshead** Notts 101 K2
**Ravensthorpe** Kirk 123 J6
**Ravensthorpe** Nhants 73 J1
**Ravenstone** Leics 86 E2
**Ravenstone** M Keyn 74 B4
**Ravenstonedale** Cumb 139 G6
**Ravenstruther** S Lans 165 H1
**Ravensworth** N York 140 E5
**Rawcliffe** C York 133 J8
**Rawcliffe** E R Yk 125 G6
**Rawdon** Leeds 123 J3
**Rawdon Crematorium** Leeds 123 J3
**Rawling Street** Kent 34 B3
**Rawmarsh** Rothm 115 H3
**Rawreth** Essex 46 C2
**Rawridge** Devon 12 F2
**Rawtenstall** Lancs 122 B6
**Raydon** Suffk 78 C6
**Rayleigh** Essex 46 D2
**Rayne** Essex 61 H4
**Raynes Park** Gt Lon 44 E6
**Reach** Cambs 76 E2
**Read** Lancs 122 B4
**Reading** Readg 42 B5
**Reading Crematorium** Readg 42 B5
**Reading Services** W Berk 42 A6
**Reading Street** Kent 34 B8
**Reading Street** Kent 35 K2
**Reagill** Cumb 138 E4
**Realwa** Cnwll 3 G4
**Rearquhar** Highld 223 G3
**Rearsby** Leics 87 J2
**Reay** Highld 230 D3
**Reculver** Kent 47 L6
**Red Ball** Devon 25 H7
**Redberth** Pembks 49 J6
**Redbourn** Herts 59 J5
**Redbourne** N Linc 116 F2
**Redbrook** Gloucs 54 D6
**Redbrook** Wrexhm 98 D4
**Redbrook Street** Kent 34 C7
**Redburn** Highld 213 L5
**Redcar** R & Cl 142 D3
**Redcastle** D & G 146 E2
**Redcastle** Highld 212 E4
**Redding** Falk 176 C3
**Reddingmuirhead** Falk 176 C3
**Reddish** Stockp 113 K3
**Redditch** Worcs 71 J2
**Redditch Crematorium** Worcs 71 J2
**Rede** Suffk 77 J4
**Redenhall** Norfk 92 F6
**Redesmouth** Nthumb 157 L5
**Redford** Abers 197 J3
**Redford** Angus 196 F7
**Redford** W Susx 30 E6
**Redfordgreen** Border 166 E6
**Redgorton** P & K 186 A2
**Redgrave** Suffk 92 C7
**Redhill** Abers 206 E4
**Red Hill** Bmouth 15 K4
**Redhill** Herts 59 M2
**Redhill** N Som 38 D7
**Redhill** Surrey 32 B3
**Redisham** Suffk 93 J6
**Redland** Bristl 38 E5
**Redland** Ork 234 b5
**Redlingfield** Suffk 78 E1
**Redlingfield Green** Suffk 78 E1
**Red Lodge** Suffk 77 G1
**Redlynch** Somset 27 G5
**Redlynch** Wilts 28 D7
**Redmarley** Worcs 70 D2
**Redmarley D'Abitot** Gloucs 55 H2
**Redmarshall** S on T 141 J3
**Redmile** Leics 102 D5
**Redmire** N York 131 K2
**Redmyre** Abers 197 J2
**Rednal** Shrops 98 A6
**Redpath** Border 167 J3
**Redpoint** Highld 219 H7
**Red Roses** Carmth 49 L5
**Red Row** Nthumb 159 G3
**Redruth** Cnwll 3 J3
**Redstone** P & K 186 C1
**Red Street** Staffs 99 J3
**Red Wharf Bay** IoA 109 G5
**Redwick** Newpt 38 B4
**Redwick** S Glos 38 D3
**Redworth** Darltn 141 G3
**Reed** Herts 75 L7
**Reedham** Norfk 93 J3
**Reedness** E R Yk 125 J6
**Reeds Holme** Lancs 122 B5
**Reepham** Lincs 117 H6
**Reepham** Norfk 106 D7
**Reeth** N York 140 C7
**Reeves Green** Solhll 86 C7
**Regil** N Som 38 D7
**Reiff** Highld 224 B5
**Reigate** Surrey 31 L2
**Reighton** N York 135 H4
**Reisque** Abers 207 G2
**Reiss** Highld 231 L5
**Relubbus** Cnwll 2 F5
**Relugas** Moray 214 B5
**Remenham** Wokham 42 C4
**Remenham Hill** Wokham 42 C4
**Rempstone** Notts 101 L7
**Rendcomb** Gloucs 56 A6
**Rendham** Suffk 79 H2
**Rendlesham** Suffk 79 H4
**Renfrew** Rens 174 F5
**Renhold** Bed 74 F4
**Renishaw** Derbys 115 J6
**Rennington** Nthumb 169 J5
**Renton** W Duns 174 D3
**Renwick** Cumb 149 G6
**Repps** Norfk 93 J1
**Repton** Derbys 100 F6
**Reraig** Highld 210 C8
**Resaurie** Highld 213 H5
**Resipole Burn** Highld 190 E4
**Reskadinnick** Cnwll 3 H3
**Resolis** Highld 213 G2
**Resolven** Neath 52 C7
**Rest and be thankful** Ag & B 183 J6
**Reston** Border 179 H6
**Reswallie** Angus 196 E6
**Retford** Notts 116 B5
**Rettendon** Essex 61 J7
**Revesby** Lincs 103 M1
**Rewe** Devon 12 B3
**Rew Street** IoW 16 F4
**Reymerston** Norfk 92 B3
**Reynalton** Pembks 49 J5
**Reynoldston** Swans 50 F7
**Rezare** Cnwll 6 A1
**Rhandirmwyn** Carmth 67 H5
**Rhayader** Powys 67 L2
**Rheindown** Highld 212 D5
**Rhes-y-cae** Flints 111 G7
**Rhewl** Denbgs 97 H1
**Rhewl** Denbgs 97 J4
**Rhicarn** Highld 224 D4
**Rhiconich** Highld 228 C5
**Rhicullen** Highld 222 F6
**Rhigos** Rhondd 52 E6
**Rhireavach** Highld 220 D3
**Rhives** Highld 223 H2
**Rhiwbina** Cardif 37 J4
**Rhiwderyn** Newpt 37 K3
**Rhiwlas** Gwynd 109 H7
**Rhoden Green** Kent 33 H4
**Rhodes Minnis** Kent 34 F6
**Rhodiad-y-brenin** Pembks 48 C3
**Rhonehouse** D & G 146 C3
**Rhoose** V Glam 37 G6
**Rhos** Carmth 65 L7
**Rhos** Neath 51 L5
**Rhoscolyn** IoA 108 C6
**Rhoscrowther** Pembks 48 F6
**Rhosesmor** Flints 111 H7
**Rhosgoch** Powys 68 D5
**Rhoshill** Pembks 65 H6
**Rhoshirwaun** Gwynd 94 D6
**Rhoslefain** Gwynd 80 D3
**Rhosllanerchrugog** Wrexhm 97 L3
**Rhosmeirch** IoA 108 F6
**Rhosneigr** IoA 108 D6
**Rhosnesni** Wrexhm 97 M3
**Rhôs-on-Sea** Conwy 110 B5
**Rhossili** Swans 50 E7
**Rhostryfan** Gwynd 95 H2
**Rhostyllen** Wrexhm 97 L3
**Rhosybol** IoA 108 F4
**Rhos-y-gwaliau** Gwynd 96 E5
**Rhosymedre** Wrexhm 97 L4
**Rhu** Ag & B 174 B2
**Rhuallt** Denbgs 110 F6
**Rhubodach** Ag & B 173 H4
**Rhuddlan** Denbgs 110 E6
**Rhunahaorine** Ag & B 172 C8
**Rhyd** Gwynd 95 L4
**Rhydargaeau** Carmth 50 F1
**Rhydcymerau** Carmth 66 D6
**Rhyd-Ddu** Gwynd 95 K3
**Rhydlewis** Cerdgn 65 K5
**Rhydowen** Cerdgn 66 B5
**Rhyd-uchaf** Gwynd 96 D5
**Rhyd-y-clafdy** Gwynd 94 F5
**Rhyd-y-foel** Conwy 110 C6
**Rhydyfro** Neath 51 K4
**Rhyd-y-groes** Gwynd 109 H7

**Rhyd-y-pennau** Cerdgn 80 E6
**Rhyl** Denbgs 110 D5
**Rhymney** Caerph 53 H6
**Rhynd** P & K 186 B4
**Rhynie** Abers 215 L8
**Rhynie** Highld 223 J5
**Ribbesford** Worcs 84 D8
**Ribbleton** Lancs 121 H4
**Ribchester** Lancs 121 J4
**Riby** Lincs 126 F8
**Riccall** N York 124 F3
**Riccarton** Border 156 F3
**Riccarton** E Ayrs 163 K3
**Richards Castle** Herefs 69 J1
**Richmond** Gt Lon 44 D5
**Richmond** N York 140 F6
**Richmond** Sheff 115 H4
**Richmond Fort** Guern 236 b3
**Rickerscote** Staffs 99 L7
**Rickford** N Som 38 C8
**Rickham** Devon 7 H7
**Rickinghall** Suffk 92 C7
**Rickling Green** Essex 60 E3
**Rickmansworth** Herts 43 H2
**Riddell** Border 167 H4
**Riddlecombe** Devon 10 F3
**Riddlesden** C Brad 123 G3
**Ridge** Dorset 15 H5
**Ridge** Herts 59 K7
**Ridge** Wilts 27 L5
**Ridge Lane** Warwks 86 C4
**Ridgeway** Derbys 115 H5
**Ridgewell** Essex 77 G6
**Ridgewood** E Susx 19 M2
**Ridgmont** C Beds 74 E7
**Riding Mill** Nthumb 150 C3
**Ridlington** Norfk 107 H6
**Ridlington** Rutlnd 88 B3
**Ridsdale** Nthumb 158 A5
**Rievaulx** N York 133 J3
**Rigg** D & G 148 B2
**Riggend** N Lans 175 K4
**Righoul** Highld 213 K4
**Rigsby** Lincs 118 F6
**Rigside** S Lans 165 G3
**Riley Green** Lancs 121 J5
**Rilla Mill** Cnwll 5 L2
**Rillington** N York 134 D5
**Rimington** Lancs 122 B2
**Rimpton** Somset 26 E6
**Rimswell** E R Yk 127 H5
**Rinaston** Pembks 49 G3
**Rindleford** Shrops 84 D4
**Ringford** D & G 146 C4
**Ringland** Norfk 92 D2
**Ringmer** E Susx 19 L3
**Ringmore** Devon 6 F6
**Ringmore** Devon 7 L2
**Ringorm** Moray 215 G5
**Ringsfield** Suffk 93 J5
**Ringsfield Corner** Suffk 93 J6
**Ringshall** Herts 59 G5
**Ringshall** Suffk 78 C4
**Ringshall Stocks** Suffk 78 C4
**Ringstead** Nhants 88 E7
**Ringstead** Norfk 105 H4
**Ringwood** Hants 15 L2
**Ringwould** Kent 35 K5
**Rinmore** Abers 205 J3
**Ripe** E Susx 20 B4
**Ripley** Derbys 101 H3
**Ripley** Hants 15 M3
**Ripley** N York 132 D7
**Ripley** Surrey 31 H1
**Riplington** Hants 30 A6
**Ripon** N York 132 D5
**Rippingale** Lincs 103 H6
**Ripple** Kent 35 J5
**Ripple** Worcs 70 F6
**Ripponden** Calder 122 F6
**Risabus** Ag & B 160 B2
**Risbury** Herefs 69 K4
**Risby** Suffk 77 H2
**Risca** Caerph 37 K3
**Rise** E R Yk 126 E3
**Risegate** Lincs 103 K6
**Riseley** Bed 74 F3
**Riseley** Wokham 42 B7
**Rishangles** Suffk 78 E2
**Rishton** Lancs 121 L4
**Rishworth** Calder 122 F6
**Risley** Derbys 101 J5
**Risley** Warrtn 112 F3
**Risplith** N York 132 C5
**River** Kent 35 J6
**River** W Susx 30 F6
**Riverford** Highld 212 E4
**Riverhead** Kent 32 F3
**Rivington** Lancs 121 J7
**Rivington Services** Lancs 121 J7
**Roade** Nhants 73 L4
**Roadmeetings** S Lans 176 B7
**Roadside** E Ayrs 164 B5
**Roadside** Highld 231 H4
**Roadwater** Somset 25 G4
**Roag** Highld 208 D5
**Roan of Craigoch** S Ayrs 153 G2
**Roath** Cardif 37 J5
**Roberton** Border 166 F6
**Roberton** S Lans 165 H4
**Robertsbridge** E Susx 20 E2
**Roberttown** Kirk 123 J6
**Robeston Wathen** Pembks 49 J4
**Robgill Tower** D & G 155 M7
**Robin Hood Crematorium** Solhll 85 K7
**Robin Hood's Bay** N York 143 K6
**Roborough** Devon 6 D4
**Roborough** Devon 10 E2
**Robroyston** C Glas 175 H5
**Roby** Knows 112 B4
**Rocester** Staffs 100 C5
**Roch** Pembks 48 E3
**Rochdale** Rochdl 122 D7
**Rochdale Crematorium** Rochdl 122 C7
**Roche** Cnwll 4 F4
**Rochester** Medway 46 C6
**Rochester** Nthumb 157 L3
**Rochford** Essex 46 E3
**Rochford** Worcs 70 B2
**Rock** Cnwll 4 E2
**Rock** Nthumb 169 J5
**Rock** Worcs 70 D1
**Rockbeare** Devon 12 C4
**Rockbourne** Hants 28 C7
**Rockcliffe** Cumb 148 C3
**Rockcliffe** D & G 146 E4
**Rockend** Torbay 7 L4
**Rock Ferry** Wirral 111 K4
**Rockfield** Highld 223 K5
**Rockfield** Mons 54 C5
**Rockford** Devon 24 B2
**Rockhampton** S Glos 38 F2
**Rockhill** Shrops 82 F7
**Rockingham** Nhants 88 C5
**Rockland All Saints** Norfk 92 B4
**Rockland St Mary** Norfk 93 G3
**Rockland St Peter** Norfk 92 B4
**Rockley** Notts 116 B6
**Rockville** Ag & B 173 L1
**Rockwell End** Bucks 42 D3
**Rodborough** Gloucs 55 J6
**Rodbourne** Swindn 40 C4
**Rodbourne** Wilts 39 L4
**Rodden** Dorset 14 B5
**Rode** Somset 27 J2
**Rode Heath** Ches E 99 J2
**Rodel** W Isls 232 d5
**Roden** Wrekin 83 L1
**Rodhuish** Somset 24 F4
**Rodington** Wrekin 83 L1
**Rodington Heath** Wrekin 83 L1
**Rodley** Gloucs 55 H5
**Rodmarton** Gloucs 39 L2
**Rodmell** E Susx 19 L4
**Rodmersham** Kent 34 B3
**Rodmersham Green** Kent 34 B3
**Rodney Stoke** Somset 26 C2
**Rodsley** Derbys 100 D4
**Roecliffe** N York 132 E6
**Roe Green** Herts 59 K6
**Roe Green** Herts 75 K7
**Roehampton** Gt Lon 44 E5
**Roffey** W Susx 31 K5
**Rogart** Highld 226 C7
**Rogate** W Susx 30 D6
**Rogerstone** Newpt 37 L3
**Roghadal** W Isls 232 d5
**Rogiet** Mons 38 C3
**Roke** Oxon 41 L2
**Roker** Sundld 151 J3
**Rollesby** Norfk 93 J1
**Rolleston** Leics 87 K4
**Rolleston** Notts 102 C3
**Rolleston on Dove** Staffs 100 E6
**Rolston** E R Yk 126 F2
**Rolvenden** Kent 33 L6
**Rolvenden Layne** Kent 33 L7
**Romaldkirk** Dur 140 C3
**Romanby** N York 132 E2
**Romanno Bridge** Border 177 G8
**Romansleigh** Devon 24 B7
**Romesdal** Highld 208 F4
**Romford** Dorset 15 K1
**Romford** Gt Lon 45 K3
**Romiley** Stockp 113 L4
**Romsey** Cambs 76 C3
**Romsey** Hants 29 G6
**Romsley** Shrops 84 D6
**Romsley** Worcs 85 G7
**Rona** Highld 209 K3
**Ronachan** Ag & B 172 C7
**Rookhope** Dur 150 B6
**Rookley** IoW 17 G5
**Rooks Bridge** Somset 26 A2
**Rooks Nest** Somset 25 H5
**Rookwith** N York 132 C3
**Roos** E R Yk 127 G4
**Roothams Green** Bed 75 G3
**Ropley** Hants 29 M5
**Ropley Dean** Hants 29 L5
**Ropsley** Lincs 103 G5
**Rora** Abers 217 K4
**Rorrington** Shrops 82 F4
**Rosarie** Moray 215 J4
**Rose** Cnwll 3 K1
**Rose Ash** Devon 24 C6
**Rosebank** S Lans 175 L7
**Rosebush** Pembks 49 J2
**Rosedale Abbey** N York 142 F7
**Rose Green** Essex 61 L3
**Rose Green** Suffk 77 L5
**Rose Green** Suffk 77 L6
**Rose Green** W Susx 18 B5
**Rosehall** Highld 225 K7
**Rosehearty** Abers 217 H2
**Rose Hill** Lancs 122 C4
**Rose Hill Crematorium** Donc 115 L2
**Roseisle** Moray 214 E2
**Roselands** E Susx 20 C5
**Rosemarket** Pembks 49 G5
**Rosemarkie** Highld 213 H3
**Rosemary Lane** Devon 25 J7
**Rosemount** P & K 195 J7
**Rosenannon** Cnwll 4 E3
**Rosewell** Mdloth 177 J6
**Roseworth** S on T 141 K3
**Rosgill** Cumb 138 D4
**Roskhill** Highld 208 D5
**Rosley** Cumb 148 B6
**Roslin** Mdloth 177 H5
**Rosliston** Derbys 86 B1
**Rosneath** Ag & B 174 B2
**Ross** D & G 146 B6
**Rossett** Wrexhm 98 A2
**Rossett Green** N York 132 D8
**Rossington** Donc 115 L2
**Ross-on-Wye** Herefs 54 E4
**Roster** Highld 231 J7
**Rostherne** Ches E 113 H5
**Rosthwaite** Cumb 137 H4
**Roston** Derbys 100 C4
**Rosyth** Fife 176 F2
**Rothbury** Nthumb 158 D2
**Rotherby** Leics 87 J1
**Rotherfield** E Susx 32 F7
**Rotherfield Greys** Oxon 42 B4
**Rotherfield Peppard** Oxon 42 B4
**Rotherham** Rothm 115 H3
**Rotherham Crematorium** Rothm 115 J3
**Rothersthorpe** Nhants 73 K3
**Rotherwick** Hants 30 B1
**Rothes** Moray 215 G4
**Rothesay** Ag & B 173 J5
**Rothiebrisbane** Abers 216 E6
**Rothiemurchus Lodge** Highld 204 B4
**Rothienorman** Abers 216 D7
**Rothley** Leics 87 H2
**Rothmaise** Abers 216 D7
**Rothwell** Leeds 123 L5
**Rothwell** Lincs 117 J2
**Rothwell** Nhants 88 B7
**Rottal Lodge** Angus 196 B3
**Rottingdean** Br & H 19 K5
**Rottington** Cumb 136 D5
**Roucan** D & G 155 H6
**Roucan Loch Crematorium** D & G 155 H6
**Rougham** Norfk 105 K7
**Rougham** Suffk 77 K3
**Rough Common** Kent 34 F3
**Roughpark** Abers 205 H3
**Roughton** Lincs 118 C8
**Roughton** Norfk 106 F5
**Roughton** Shrops 84 D5
**Roundbush Green** Essex 60 F5
**Round Green** Luton 59 J4
**Roundham** Somset 13 K1
**Roundhay** Leeds 123 L3
**Rounds Green** Sandw 85 H5
**Roundswell** Devon 23 H5
**Roundway** Wilts 40 A7
**Roundyhill** Angus 196 C6
**Rousay** Ork 234 c4
**Rousdon** Devon 13 H4
**Rousham** Oxon 57 J3
**Rous Lench** Worcs 71 H4
**Routenburn** N Ayrs 173 L6
**Routh** E R Yk 126 D3
**Row** Cumb 129 K2
**Rowanburn** D & G 156 D6
**Rowardennan** Stirlg 183 L7
**Rowarth** Derbys 114 A4
**Rowberrow** Somset 38 C8
**Rowde** Wilts 39 L7
**Rowen** Conwy 109 L6
**Rowfoot** Nthumb 149 H3
**Rowhedge** Essex 62 B4
**Rowington** Warwks 72 B2
**Rowland** Derbys 114 E6
**Rowland's Castle** Hants 17 K1
**Rowlands Gill** Gatesd 150 E4
**Rowledge** Surrey 30 D3
**Rowley** Dur 150 D5
**Rowley Regis** Sandw 85 H6

Rowley Regis Crematorium Sandw 85 G6
Rowlstone Herefs 54 A3
Rowly Surrey 31 H4
Rowner Hants 17 H3
Rowney Green Worcs 71 J1
Rownhams Hants 29 G7
Rownhams Services Hants 29 H7
Rowrah Cumb 136 E4
Rowsham Bucks 58 D4
Rowsley Derbys 114 E7
Rowston Lincs 103 H2
Rowton Ches W 112 C8
Rowton Wrekin 98 E8
Roxburgh Border 167 L4
Roxby N Linc 125 L6
Roxton Bed 75 G4
Roxwell Essex 61 G6
Royal Leamington Spa Warwks 72 D2
Royal Sutton Coldfield Birm 85 K4
Royal Tunbridge Wells Kent 33 G5
Royal Wootton Bassett Wilts 40 B4
Royal Yacht Britannia C Edin 177 H3
Roy Bridge Highld 192 D1
Roydon Essex 60 C6
Roydon Norfk 92 D7
Roydon Norfk 105 H7
Roydon Hamlet Essex 60 C6
Royston Barns 124 B7
Royston Herts 75 L6
Royton Oldham 122 D8
Rozel Jersey 236 e6
Ruabon Wrexhm 97 L4
Ruaig Ag & B 188 D6
Ruan Lanihorne Cnwll 4 D7
Ruan Major Cnwll 3 J7
Ruan Minor Cnwll 3 J7
Ruardean Gloucs 54 F4
Ruardean Hill Gloucs 54 F5
Ruardean Woodside Gloucs 54 F5
Rubery Birm 85 H7
Rubha Ban W Isls 233 c9
Ruckhall Herefs 69 J6
Ruckinge Kent 34 D7
Ruckley Shrops 83 K4
Rudby N York 141 L6
Rudchester Nthumb 150 E2
Ruddington Notts 101 L6
Rudge Somset 27 J2
Rudgeway S Glos 38 F3
Rudgwick W Susx 31 H5
Rudheath Ches W 112 F6
Rudley Green Essex 61 K7
Rudloe Wilts 39 J6
Rudry Caerph 37 J3
Rudston E R Yk 135 H6
Rudyard Staffs 99 L2
Ruecastle Border 167 J5
Rufford Lancs 120 F7
Rufford Abbey Notts 115 M8
Rufforth C York 124 D1
Rugby Warwks 87 G7
Rugeley Staffs 100 B8
Ruishton Somset 25 K6
Ruislip Gt Lon 43 H3
Rùm Highld 198 F5
Rumbach Moray 215 J4
Rumbling Bridge P & K 185 L7
Rumburgh Suffk 93 H7
Rumford Cnwll 4 D2
Rumford Falk 176 C3
Rumney Cardif 37 K5
Runcorn Halton 112 D5
Runcton W Susx 18 B5
Runcton Holme Norfk 90 E2
Runfold Surrey 30 E3
Runhall Norfk 92 C3
Runham Norfk 93 K2
Runnington Somset 25 H6
Runswick N York 143 G4
Runtaleave Angus 195 L3
Runwell Essex 46 C2
Ruscombe Wokham 42 D5
Rushall Herefs 70 B7
Rushall Norfk 92 E6
Rushall Wilts 28 C1
Rushall Wsall 85 H4
Rushbrooke Suffk 77 K3
Rushbury Shrops 83 K5
Rushden Herts 60 A2
Rushden Nhants 74 D2
Rushenden Kent 46 E5
Rushford Norfk 91 K7
Rush Green Essex 62 E5
Rush Green Gt Lon 45 K3
Rush Green Warrtn 113 G4
Rushlake Green E Susx 20 D3
Rushmere Suffk 93 K6
Rushmoor Surrey 30 E4
Rushock Worcs 70 F1
Rusholme Manch 113 J3
Rushton Nhants 88 B6
Rushton Spencer Staffs 113 L8
Rushwick Worcs 70 E4
Rushyford Dur 141 G2
Ruskie Stirlg 184 D7
Ruskington Lincs 103 H3
Rusland Cross Cumb 129 H2
Rusper W Susx 31 K4
Ruspidge Gloucs 54 F5
Russell's Water Oxon 42 B3
Russ Hill Surrey 31 L4
Rusthall Kent 32 F5
Rustington W Susx 18 E5
Ruston N York 134 E3
Ruston Parva E R Yk 135 G6
Ruswarp N York 143 H5
Rutherford Border 167 K4
Rutherglen S Lans 175 H6
Ruthernbridge Cnwll 4 F3
Ruthin Denbgs 97 H2
Ruthrieston C Aber 207 H4
Ruthven Abers 215 L5
Ruthven Angus 195 L6
Ruthven Highld 203 H5
Ruthven Highld 213 J7
Ruthvoes Cnwll 4 E4
Ruthwell D & G 147 J2
Ruyton-XI-Towns Shrops 98 B7
Ryal Nthumb 158 C7
Ryall Dorset 13 K4
Ryall Worcs 70 F6
Ryarsh Kent 33 H2
Rydal Cumb 137 K6
Ryde IoW 17 H4
Rye E Susx 21 H2
Rye Foreign E Susx 21 H2
Rye Street Worcs 70 D7
Ryhall Rutlnd 88 F2
Ryhill Wakefd 124 B7
Ryhope Sundld 151 K4
Ryland Lincs 117 G5
Rylands Notts 101 K5
Rylstone N York 131 H7
Ryme Intrinseca Dorset 14 B1
Ryther N York 124 E3
Ryton Gatesd 150 E3
Ryton Shrops 84 D3
Ryton-on-Dunsmore Warwks 86 E8
RZSS Edinburgh Zoo C Edin 177 G4

## S

Sabden Lancs 122 B3
Sacombe Herts 60 B4
Sacriston Dur 151 G5
Sadberge Darltn 141 H4
Saddell Ag & B 161 K3
Saddington Leics 87 J5
Saddlebow Norfk 90 E1
Saddlescombe W Susx 19 H4
Saffron Walden Essex 76 D6
Sageston Pembks 49 H6
Saham Hills Norfk 91 K3
Saham Toney Norfk 91 K3
Saighton Ches W 98 C1
St Abbs Border 179 J5
St Agnes Border 178 E5
St Agnes Cnwll 3 J2
St Agnes IoS 2 a2
St Agnes Mining District Cnwll 3 J2
St Albans Herts 59 J6
St Allen Cnwll 4 C5
St Andrew Guern 236 c3
St Andrews Fife 187 H4
St Andrews Botanic Garden Fife 187 H4
St Andrews Major V Glam 37 H6
St Andrews Well Dorset 13 L4
St Anne's Lancs 120 D5
St Ann's D & G 155 J4
St Ann's Chapel Cnwll 6 B2
St Ann's Chapel Devon 6 F6
St Anthony-in-Meneage Cnwll 3 K6
St Anthony's Hill E Susx 20 D5
St Arvans Mons 38 D2
St Asaph Denbgs 110 E6
St Athan V Glam 36 F6
St Aubin Jersey 236 b7
St Austell Cnwll 4 F5
St Bees Cumb 136 D5
St Blazey Cnwll 5 G5
St Boswells Border 167 J3
St Brelade Jersey 236 b7
St Brelade's Bay Jersey 236 b7
St Breock Cnwll 4 F2
St Breward Cnwll 5 H1
St Briavels Gloucs 54 E6
St Bride's Major V Glam 36 D5
St Brides-super-Ely V Glam 37 H5
St Brides Wentlooge Newpt 37 L4
St Budeaux C Plym 6 C4
Saintbury Gloucs 71 K6
St Buryan Cnwll 2 D6
St Catherines Ag & B 183 G6
St Chloe Gloucs 55 J7
St Clears Carmth 50 C3
St Cleer Cnwll 5 K3
St Clement Cnwll 4 D6
St Clement Jersey 236 e8
St Clether Cnwll 9 G7
St Colmac Ag & B 173 H5
St Columb Major Cnwll 4 E3
St Columb Minor Cnwll 4 D4
St Columb Road Cnwll 4 E4
St Combs Abers 217 K2
St Cross South Elmham Suffk 93 G6
St Cyrus Abers 197 J4
St David's P & K 185 K4
St Davids Pembks 48 C3
St Davids Cathedral Pembks 48 C3
St Day Cnwll 3 J3
St Dennis Cnwll 4 E4
St Dogmaels Pembks 65 G5
St Dominick Cnwll 6 B3
St Donats V Glam 36 E6
St Endellion Cnwll 4 F1
St Enoder Cnwll 4 D4
St Erme Cnwll 4 D6
St Erney Cnwll 6 B4
St Erth Cnwll 2 F4
St Erth Praze Cnwll 3 G4
St Ervan Cnwll 4 D2
St Eval Cnwll 4 D3
St Ewe Cnwll 4 F6
St Fagans Cardif 37 H5
St Fagans: National History Museum Cardif 37 H5
St Fergus Abers 217 K4
St Fillans P & K 184 F3
St Florence Pembks 49 J7
St Gennys Cnwll 8 F5
St George Conwy 110 D6
St Georges N Som 38 B7
St George's V Glam 37 H5
St Germans Cnwll 6 A4
St Giles in the Wood Devon 23 H7
St Giles-on-the-Heath Devon 9 K6
St Harmon Powys 81 L8
St Helen Auckland Dur 140 F2
St Helen's E Susx 21 G4
St Helens IoW 17 J5
St Helens St Hel 112 D3
St Helens Crematorium St Hel 112 C3
St Helier Gt Lon 44 E6
St Helier Jersey 236 d7
St Hilary Cnwll 2 F5
St Hilary V Glam 36 F5
St Ippollitts Herts 59 K3
St Ishmael's Pembks 48 E6
St Issey Cnwll 4 E2
St Ive Cnwll 5 L3
St Ives Cambs 75 K1
St Ives Cnwll 2 F3
St James's End Nhants 73 L3
St James South Elmham Suffk 93 G7
St Jidgey Cnwll 4 E3
St John Cnwll 6 B5
St John Jersey 236 c5
St John's E Susx 32 E6
St John's IoM 237 b5
St John's Kent 32 F3
St Johns Surrey 43 G8
St Johns Worcs 70 E4
St John's Chapel Devon 23 H5
St John's Chapel Dur 149 M7
St John's Fen End Norfk 90 D2
St John's Kirk S Lans 165 J3
St John's Town of Dalry D & G 154 B6
St John's Wood Gt Lon 44 F4
St Judes IoM 237 d3
St Just Cnwll 2 C5
St Just-in-Roseland Cnwll 4 D8
St Just Mining District Cnwll 2 D5
St Katherines Abers 216 E7
St Keverne Cnwll 3 K6
St Kew Cnwll 5 G1
St Kew Highway Cnwll 5 G2
St Keyne Cnwll 5 K4
St Lawrence Essex 62 A6
St Lawrence IoW 17 G6
St Lawrence Jersey 236 c6
St Lawrence Kent 35 K2
St Leonards Bucks 58 E6
St Leonards Dorset 15 L2
St Leonards E Susx 20 F4
St Levan Cnwll 2 C6
St Lythans V Glam 37 H6
St Mabyn Cnwll 5 G2
St Madoes P & K 186 C3
St Margarets Herefs 69 G7

St Margarets Herts 60 B5
St Margaret's at Cliffe Kent 35 K5
St Margaret's Hope Ork 234 c7
St Margaret South Elmham Suffk 93 G6
St Marks IoM 237 c6
St Martin Cnwll 3 J6
St Martin Cnwll 5 K5
St Martin Guern 236 d3
St Martin Jersey 236 e6
St Martin's IoS 2 b1
St Martin's P & K 186 B2
St Martin's Shrops 97 L5
St Mary Jersey 236 b6
St Mary Bourne Hants 29 H2
St Marychurch Torbay 7 L3
St Mary Church V Glam 36 F6
St Mary Cray Gt Lon 45 J6
St Mary in the Marsh Kent 34 E8
St Marylebone Crematorium Gt Lon 44 E3
St Mary's IoS 2 b1
St Mary's Ork 234 c6
St Mary's Bay Kent 21 L1
St Mary's Hoo Medway 46 D5
St Mary's Platt Kent 33 G2
St Maughans Green Mons 54 C5
St Mawes Cnwll 3 L5
St Mawgan Cnwll 4 D3
St Mellion Cnwll 6 B3
St Mellons Cardif 37 K4
St Merryn Cnwll 4 D2
St Michael Caerhays Cnwll 4 F7
St Michael Church Somset 25 L5
St Michael Penkevil Cnwll 4 D7
St Michaels Kent 34 B7
St Michaels Worcs 69 L2
St Michael's Mount Cnwll 2 F5
St Michael's on Wyre Lancs 120 F3
St Minver Cnwll 4 F1
St Monans Fife 187 H6
St Neot Cnwll 5 J3
St Neots Cambs 75 H3
St Newlyn East Cnwll 4 C5
St Nicholas Pembks 64 C7
St Nicholas V Glam 37 H5
St Nicholas-at-Wade Kent 47 L6
St Ninians Stirlg 185 G8
St Olaves Norfk 93 J4
St Osyth Essex 62 D5
St Ouen Jersey 236 b6
St Owen's Cross Herefs 54 D3
St Paul's Cray Gt Lon 45 J6
St Paul's Walden Herts 59 K4
St Peter Jersey 236 b6
St Peter Port Guern 236 d3
St Peter's Guern 236 b3
St Peter's Kent 35 K2
St Peter's Hill Cambs 89 J8
St Pinnock Cnwll 5 J3
St Quivox S Ayrs 163 J5
St Sampson Guern 236 d2
St Saviour Guern 236 c3
St Saviour Jersey 236 d7
St Stephen Cnwll 4 E5
St Stephens Cnwll 6 B4
St Stephens Cnwll 9 J7
St Teath Cnwll 8 E8
St Thomas Devon 11 K6
St Tudy Cnwll 5 G1
St Twynnells Pembks 48 F7
St Veep Cnwll 5 J5
St Vigeans Angus 197 G7
St Wenn Cnwll 4 F3
St Weonards Herefs 54 D3
Salcombe Devon 7 H7
Salcombe Regis Devon 12 F5
Salcott-cum-Virley Essex 61 M5
Sale Traffd 113 H3
Saleby Lincs 118 F5
Sale Green Worcs 71 G3
Salehurst E Susx 20 F2
Salem Cerdgn 80 F6
Salen Ag & B 190 C7
Salen Highld 190 D4
Salford C Beds 74 D6
Salford Oxon 56 F3
Salford Salfd 113 J3
Salford Priors Warwks 71 J4
Salfords Surrey 32 B4
Salhouse Norfk 93 G1
Saline Fife 185 L8
Salisbury Wilts 28 C5
Salisbury Crematorium Wilts 28 D5
Salisbury Plain Wilts 28 B3
Salkeld Dykes Cumb 148 F7
Salle Norfk 106 D7
Salmonby Lincs 118 D6
Salperton Gloucs 56 B4
Salsburgh N Lans 175 L5
Salt Staffs 99 L6
Saltaire C Brad 123 H3
Saltaire C Brad 123 H3
Saltash Cnwll 6 B4
Saltburn Highld 223 G7
Saltburn-by-the-Sea R & Cl 142 E3
Saltby Leics 102 D7
Saltcoats N Ayrs 163 G2
Saltdean Br & H 19 K5
Salterbeck Cumb 136 D3
Salterforth Lancs 122 D2
Salterton Wilts 28 C4
Saltfleet Lincs 118 F3
Saltfleetby All Saints Lincs 118 F4
Saltfleetby St Clement Lincs 118 F3
Saltfleetby St Peter Lincs 118 F4
Saltford BaNES 39 G6
Salthouse Norfk 106 C4
Saltley Birm 85 K6
Saltmarshe E R Yk 125 J5
Saltney Flints 111 L8
Salton N York 133 L4
Saltrens Devon 23 G6
Saltwell Crematorium Gatesd 151 G3
Saltwood Kent 34 F7
Salvington W Susx 18 F5
Salwarpe Worcs 70 F3
Salway Ash Dorset 13 L3
Sambourne Warwks 71 J3
Sambrook Wrekin 99 G7
Sampford Arundel Somset 25 H7
Sampford Brett Somset 25 H4
Sampford Courtenay Devon 10 F5
Sampford Moor Somset 25 H7
Sampford Peverell Devon 25 G8
Sampford Spiney Devon 6 D2
Samsonlane Ork 234 d5
Samuelston E Loth 178 B4
Sanaigmore Ag & B 170 E4
Sancreed Cnwll 2 D5
Sancton E R Yk 125 L3
Sandaig Highld 199 L5
Sandal Magna Wakefd 123 L6
Sanday Ork 234 d4
Sanday Airport Ork 234 d4
Sandbach Ches E 99 H1
Sandbach Services Ches E 99 H1
Sandbank Ag & B 173 K3
Sandbanks Poole 15 K5
Sandend Abers 216 B2
Sanderstead Gt Lon 45 G7
Sandford Cumb 139 G4
Sandford Devon 11 J4
Sandford Dorset 15 H5
Sandford Hants 15 M3
Sandford IoW 17 G6
Sandford N Som 38 B8
Sandford S Lans 164 E2
Sandford-on-Thames Oxon 57 K7
Sandford Orcas Dorset 26 F7
Sandford St Martin Oxon 57 H3
Sandgate Kent 35 G7
Sandhaven Abers 217 H2
Sandhead D & G 144 D5
Sand Hills Leeds 124 B3
Sandhills Oxon 57 K6
Sandhills Surrey 30 F4
Sandhoe Nthumb 150 B2
Sandhole Ag & B 182 E7
Sand Hole E R Yk 125 J3
Sandholme E R Yk 125 J4
Sandhurst Br For 42 D7
Sandhurst Gloucs 55 J4
Sandhurst Kent 33 K7
Sandhutton N York 132 F3
Sand Hutton N York 133 L7
Sandiacre Derbys 101 J5
Sandilands Lincs 119 G5
Sandleheath Hants 28 C7
Sandleigh Oxon 57 J7
Sandley Dorset 27 H6
Sandness Shet 235 b5
Sandon Essex 61 H6
Sandon Herts 75 K7
Sandon Staffs 99 L6
Sandon Bank Staffs 99 L6
Sandown IoW 17 H5
Sandplace Cnwll 5 K4
Sandridge Herts 59 K6
Sandringham Norfk 105 H6
Sandsend N York 143 H5
Sandtoft N Linc 125 H8
Sandway Kent 34 B5
Sandwell Valley Crematorium Sandw 85 H5
Sandwich Kent 35 J3
Sandwick Shet 235 c7
Sandwick W Isls 232 g2
Sandwith Cumb 136 D4
Sandy C Beds 75 H5
Sandyford D & G 155 L4
Sandygate Devon 7 K2
Sandygate IoM 237 d3
Sandyhills D & G 146 F4
Sandylands Lancs 129 J6
Sandy Lane Wilts 39 L6
Sandy Park Devon 11 G6
Sangobeg Highld 228 F3
Sangomore Highld 228 F3
Sankyn's Green Worcs 70 E2
Sanna Highld 189 K3
Sanndabhaig W Isls 232 g2
Sannox N Ayrs 162 C1
Sanquhar D & G 164 F7
Santon Bridge Cumb 136 F6
Santon Downham Suffk 91 J6
Sapcote Leics 86 F5
Sapey Common Herefs 70 C2
Sapiston Suffk 91 K7
Sapperton Gloucs 55 L7
Sapperton Lincs 103 G5
Saracen's Head Lincs 104 B6
Sarclet Highld 231 L6
Sarisbury Hants 17 G2
Sarn Powys 81 K4
Sarn Powys 82 E5
Sarnau Cerdgn 65 K4
Sarnau Powys 82 E1
Sarn Meyllteyrn Gwynd 94 D6
Sarn Park Services Brdgnd 36 D4
Saron Carmth 51 H3
Saron Gwynd 109 G7
Sarratt Herts 59 H7
Sarre Kent 47 L6
Sarsden Oxon 56 F4
Satley Dur 150 E6
Satterleigh Devon 23 L6
Satterthwaite Cumb 129 H2
Sauchen Abers 206 D3
Saucher P & K 186 C2
Sauchieburn Abers 197 G3
Saul Gloucs 55 H6
Saundby Notts 116 C4
Saundersfoot Pembks 49 K6
Saunderton Bucks 58 C7
Saunton Devon 23 G4
Sausthorpe Lincs 118 E7
Savile Town Kirk 123 K6
Sawbridge Warwks 73 G2
Sawbridgeworth Herts 60 D5
Sawdon N York 134 E3
Sawley Lancs 122 B2
Sawley N York 132 C6
Sawston Cambs 76 C5
Sawtry Cambs 89 H6
Saxby Leics 102 D8
Saxby Lincs 117 G4
Saxby All Saints N Linc 126 B7
Saxelbye Leics 102 B7
Saxham Street Suffk 78 C3
Saxilby Lincs 116 E6
Saxlingham Norfk 106 B5
Saxlingham Green Norfk 92 F4
Saxlingham Nethergate Norfk 92 F4
Saxlingham Thorpe Norfk 92 E4
Saxmundham Suffk 79 H2
Saxondale Notts 102 B4
Saxon Street Cambs 76 F3
Saxtead Suffk 78 F2
Saxtead Green Suffk 78 F2
Saxtead Little Green Suffk 78 F2
Saxthorpe Norfk 106 D6
Saxton N York 124 D3
Sayers Common W Susx 19 H3
Scackleton N York 133 K5
Scafell Pike Cumb 137 H5
Scaftworth Notts 116 A3
Scagglethorpe N York 134 C5
Scalasaig Ag & B 180 E8
Scalby E R Yk 125 K5
Scalby N York 134 F2
Scaldwell Nhants 73 L1
Scaleby Cumb 148 D3
Scalebyhill Cumb 148 D3
Scales Cumb 129 G5
Scales Cumb 137 K2
Scalford Leics 102 C7
Scaling N York 142 F4
Scalloway Shet 235 c6
Scalpay Highld 209 J7
Scamblesby Lincs 118 C5
Scamodale Highld 191 G2
Scampston N York 134 D4
Scampton Lincs 116 F5
Scaniport Highld 212 F6
Scapegoat Hill Kirk 123 G7
Scarba Ag & B 181 K6

**Scarborough** N York 135 G2
**Scarcewater** Cnwll 4 E5
**Scarcliffe** Derbys 115 J7
**Scarcroft** Leeds 124 B3
**Scarfskerry** Highld 231 J2
**Scarinish** Ag & B 188 D7
**Scarisbrick** Lancs 120 E7
**Scarning** Norfk 91 L2
**Scarrington** Notts 102 B4
**Scartho** NE Lin 118 C1
*Scatsta Airport* Shet 235 c4
**Scaur** D & G 146 E4
**Scawby** N Linc 116 F1
**Scawsby** Donc 115 K1
**Scawthorpe** Donc 115 K1
**Scawton** N York 133 H3
**Scayne's Hill** W Susx 19 K2
**Scethrog** Powys 53 H3
**Scholar Green** Ches E 99 J2
**Scholemoor Crematorium** C Brad 123 H4
**Scholes** Kirk 123 H8
**Scholes** Leeds 124 B3
**Scholes** Rothm 115 H3
**Scholes** Wigan 112 E1
**Scissett** Kirk 123 K7
**Scleddau** Pembks 64 C7
**Scofton** Notts 115 M5
**Scole** Norfk 92 D7
**Scone** P & K 186 B3
**Sconser** Highld 209 H7
**Scoonie** Fife 186 F6
**Scopwick** Lincs 103 H2
**Scoraig** Highld 220 C3
**Scorborough** E R Yk 126 C2
**Scorrier** Cnwll 3 J3
**Scorton** Lancs 121 G2
**Scorton** N York 141 G7
**Scotby** Cumb 148 D4
**Scotch Corner** N York 140 F6
Scotch Corner Rest Area N York 140 F6
**Scotforth** Lancs 129 K7
**Scothern** Lincs 117 G6
**Scotlandwell** P & K 186 C6
**Scotscalder Station** Highld 231 G4
**Scot's Gap** Nthumb 158 C5
**Scotsmill** Abers 206 B2
**Scotstoun** C Glas 174 F5
**Scotswood** N u Ty 150 F3
**Scotter** Lincs 116 E2
**Scotterthorpe** Lincs 116 E2
Scottish Seabird Centre E Loth 178 C2
Scottish Wool Centre Stirlg 184 C7
**Scotton** Lincs 116 E2
**Scotton** N York 132 E7
**Scotton** N York 140 F7
**Scoulton** Norfk 92 B4
**Scourie** Highld 228 B6
**Scourie More** Highld 228 B6
**Scousburgh** Shet 235 c7
**Scrabster** Highld 231 G2
**Scraesburgh** Border 167 K5
**Scrane End** Lincs 104 C4
**Scraptoft** Leics 87 J3
**Scratby** Norfk 93 K1
**Scrayingham** N York 133 L7
**Scredington** Lincs 103 H4
**Scremby** Lincs 118 F7
**Scremerston** Nthumb 179 L8
**Screveton** Notts 102 B4
**Scriven** N York 132 E7
**Scrooby** Notts 115 M4
**Scropton** Derbys 100 D6
**Scrub Hill** Lincs 103 L2
**Scruton** N York 132 D2
**Scullomie** Highld 229 J4
**Sculthorpe** Norfk 105 L6
**Scunthorpe** N Linc 125 K7
**Seaborough** Dorset 13 K2
**Seabridge** Staffs 99 J4
**Seabrook** Kent 35 G7
**Seaburn** Sundld 151 J3
**Seacombe** Wirral 111 K4
**Seacroft** Leeds 123 L4
**Seafield** W Loth 176 D5
**Seafield Crematorium** C Edin 177 J4
**Seaford** E Susx 20 A6
**Seaforth** Sefton 111 K3
**Seagrave** Leics 101 L8
**Seaham** Dur 151 K5
**Seahouses** Nthumb 169 J3
**Seal** Kent 32 F2
**Sealand** Flints 111 K7
**Seale** Surrey 30 E2
**Seamer** N York 134 F3
**Seamer** N York 142 B5
**Seamill** N Ayrs 173 L8
**Sea Palling** Norfk 107 J6
**Searby** Lincs 117 H1
**Seasalter** Kent 47 H6
**Seascale** Cumb 136 E6
**Seathwaite** Cumb 137 H7
**Seatoller** Cumb 137 H4
**Seaton** Cnwll 5 L5
**Seaton** Cumb 136 E2
**Seaton** Devon 13 G4
**Seaton** E R Yk 126 E2
**Seaton** Kent 35 G3
**Seaton** Nthumb 159 H6
**Seaton** Rutlnd 88 C4
**Seaton Carew** Hartpl 142 B2
**Seaton Delaval** Nthumb 159 H6
**Seaton Ross** E R Yk 125 J3
**Seaton Sluice** Nthumb 159 H6
**Seatown** Dorset 13 K4
**Seave Green** N York 142 C7
**Seaview** IoW 17 J4
**Seaville** Cumb 147 K4
**Seavington St Mary** Somset 26 B7
**Seavington St Michael** Somset 26 B7
**Sebergham** Cumb 148 C6
**Seckington** Warwks 86 C3
**Second Severn Crossing** Mons 38 D3
**Sedbergh** Cumb 130 C2
**Sedbury** Gloucs 38 D2
**Sedbusk** N York 131 G2
**Sedgeberrow** Worcs 71 H6
**Sedgebrook** Lincs 102 D5
**Sedgefield** Dur 141 J2
**Sedgeford** Norfk 105 H5
**Sedgehill** Wilts 27 K5
**Sedgemoor Crematorium** Somset 25 L3
Sedgemoor Services Somset 26 A2
**Sedgley** Dudley 85 G5
**Sedgley Park** Bury 113 J2
**Sedgwick** Cumb 129 L3
**Sedlescombe** E Susx 20 F3
**Sedrup** Bucks 58 D5
**Seend** Wilts 39 L7
**Seend Cleeve** Wilts 39 L7
**Seer Green** Bucks 42 F3
**Seething** Norfk 93 G4
**Sefton** Sefton 111 K2
**Seighford** Staffs 99 K7
**Seion** Gwynd 109 H7
**Seisdon** Staffs 84 E4
**Selattyn** Shrops 97 K5
**Selborne** Hants 30 C5
**Selby** N York 124 F4
**Selham** W Susx 30 F7
**Selhurst** Gt Lon 45 G6
**Selkirk** Border 167 G4
**Sellack** Herefs 54 E3
**Sellafield Station** Cumb 136 E6
**Sellafirth** Shet 235 d2
**Sellindge** Kent 34 E6
**Selling** Kent 34 D4
**Sells Green** Wilts 39 L7
**Selly Oak** Birm 85 J6
**Selmeston** E Susx 20 B4
**Selsdon** Gt Lon 45 G7
**Selsey** W Susx 18 B6
**Selside** N York 130 E4
**Selsley** Gloucs 55 J7
**Selsted** Kent 35 G5
**Selston** Notts 101 J2
**Selworthy** Somset 24 E3
**Semer** Suffk 78 B5
**Semington** Wilts 39 K7
**Semley** Wilts 27 K6
**Send** Surrey 31 G1
**Senghenydd** Caerph 37 H3
**Sennen** Cnwll 2 C6
**Sennen Cove** Cnwll 2 C6
**Sennybridge** Powys 52 E3
**Sessay** N York 133 G4
**Setchey** Norfk 90 F2
**Seton Mains** E Loth 177 L4
**Settle** N York 130 F6
**Settrington** N York 134 C5
**Sevenhampton** Gloucs 56 B4
**Sevenhampton** Swindn 40 E3
**Seven Hills Crematorium** Suffk 78 F6
**Seven Kings** Gt Lon 45 J3
**Sevenoaks** Kent 32 F3
**Sevenoaks Weald** Kent 32 F3
**Seven Sisters** Neath 52 C6
**Seven Star Green** Essex 61 M3
**Severn Beach** S Glos 38 D4
**Severn Bridge** S Glos 38 E3
**Severn Stoke** Worcs 70 F5
Severn View Services S Glos 38 E3
**Sevington** Kent 34 D6
**Sewards End** Essex 76 E6
**Sewell** C Beds 59 G4
**Sewerby** E R Yk 135 J5
**Seworgan** Cnwll 3 J5
**Sewstern** Leics 102 E7
**Sgiogarstaigh** W Isls 232 g1
**Shabbington** Bucks 58 A6
**Shackerstone** Leics 86 D3
**Shackleford** Surrey 30 F3
**Shader** W Isls 232 f1
**Shadforth** Dur 151 H6
**Shadingfield** Suffk 93 J6
**Shadoxhurst** Kent 34 C7
**Shadwell** Leeds 123 L3
**Shadwell** Norfk 91 L6
**Shaftenhoe End** Herts 76 B6
**Shaftesbury** Dorset 27 K6
**Shafton** Barns 124 B7
**Shakerley** Wigan 113 G2
**Shalbourne** Wilts 40 F7
**Shalden** Hants 30 B3
**Shaldon** Devon 7 L2
**Shalfleet** IoW 16 E5
**Shalford** Essex 61 H3
**Shalford** Surrey 31 G3
**Shalford Green** Essex 61 H3
**Shalmsford Street** Kent 34 E4
**Shalstone** Bucks 73 J7
**Shamley Green** Surrey 31 G3
**Shandford** Angus 196 D4
**Shandon** Ag & B 174 B2
**Shandwick** Highld 223 J6
**Shangton** Leics 87 K4
**Shanklin** IoW 17 H6
**Shantron** Ag & B 174 C2
**Shap** Cumb 138 E4
**Shapinsay** Ork 234 c5
**Shapwick** Dorset 15 H3
**Shapwick** Somset 26 B4
**Shard End** Birm 85 L5
**Shardlow** Derbys 101 H6
**Shareshill** Staffs 85 G3
**Sharlston** Wakefd 124 B6
**Sharman's Cross** Solhll 85 K7
**Sharnbrook** Bed 74 E3
**Sharnford** Leics 86 F5
**Sharoe Green** Lancs 121 G4
**Sharow** N York 132 E5
**Sharpenhoe** C Beds 59 H2
**Sharperton** Nthumb 158 B2
**Sharpness** Gloucs 54 F7
**Sharrington** Norfk 106 C5
**Shatterford** Worcs 84 E7
**Shaugh Prior** Devon 6 D3
**Shavington** Ches E 99 G3
**Shaw** Oldham 122 D8
**Shaw** Swindn 40 C4
**Shaw** W Berk 41 J6
**Shaw** Wilts 39 K7
**Shawbirch** Wrekin 84 B2
**Shawbost** W Isls 232 e2
**Shawbury** Shrops 98 E7
**Shawell** Leics 87 G7
**Shawford** Hants 29 J6
**Shawhead** D & G 154 F6
**Shaw Mills** N York 132 C6
**Shawsburn** S Lans 175 K7
**Shearington** D & G 147 H2
**Shearsby** Leics 87 J5
**Shearston** Somset 25 L5
**Shebbear** Devon 10 C3
**Shebdon** Staffs 99 H7
**Shebster** Highld 230 E3
**Sheddens** E Rens 175 G6
**Shedfield** Hants 29 K8
**Sheen** Staffs 100 C1
**Sheepridge** Kirk 123 H6
**Sheepscar** Leeds 123 L4
**Sheepscombe** Gloucs 55 K6
**Sheepstor** Devon 6 E3
**Sheepwash** Devon 10 C4
**Sheepy Magna** Leics 86 D3
**Sheepy Parva** Leics 86 D3
**Sheering** Essex 60 E5
**Sheerness** Kent 46 F5
**Sheerwater** Surrey 43 H7
**Sheet** Hants 30 C6
**Sheffield** Sheff 115 G4
**Sheffield City Road Crematorium** Sheff 115 G4
Sheffield Park E Susx 19 L2
**Shefford** C Beds 75 G6
**Sheigra** Highld 228 B4
**Sheinton** Shrops 83 L3
**Shelderton** Shrops 83 H7
**Sheldon** Birm 85 L6
**Sheldon** Derbys 114 D7
**Sheldon** Devon 12 E2
**Sheldwich** Kent 34 D4
**Shelfanger** Norfk 92 D6
**Shelford** Notts 102 A4
**Shelley** Kirk 123 J7
**Shelley** Suffk 78 B6
**Shellingford** Oxon 40 F2
**Shellow Bowells** Essex 60 F6
**Shelsley Beauchamp** Worcs 70 D2
**Shelsley Walsh** Worcs 70 C2
**Shelton** Bed 74 F2
**Shelton** Norfk 92 F5
**Shelton** Notts 102 C4
**Shelton Lock** C Derb 101 G6
**Shelton Under Harley** Staffs 99 J5
**Shelve** Shrops 83 G4
**Shelwick** Herefs 69 K6
**Shenfield** Essex 45 L2
**Shenington** Oxon 72 D6
**Shenley** Herts 59 K7
**Shenley Brook End** M Keyn 74 B7
**Shenley Church End** M Keyn 74 B7
**Shenmore** Herefs 69 H6
**Shennanton** D & G 145 H3
**Shenstone** Staffs 85 K3

**Shenstone** Worcs 84 F8
**Shenton** Leics 86 E4
**Shenval** Moray 214 F7
**Shephall** Herts 59 L4
**Shepherd's Bush** Gt Lon 44 E4
**Shepherdswell** Kent 35 H5
**Shepley** Kirk 123 J8
**Shepperton** Surrey 43 H6
**Shepreth** Cambs 76 B5
**Shepshed** Leics 101 J8
**Shepton Beauchamp** Somset 26 B7
**Shepton Mallet** Somset 26 F3
**Shepton Montague** Somset 27 G5
**Shepway** Kent 33 K3
**Sheraton** Dur 151 K7
**Sherborne** Dorset 26 F7
**Sherborne** Gloucs 56 D5
**Sherborne** Somset 26 E1
**Sherborne St John** Hants 29 L1
**Sherbourne** Warwks 72 C3
**Sherburn** Dur 151 H6
**Sherburn** N York 134 E4
**Sherburn Hill** Dur 151 H6
**Sherburn in Elmet** N York 124 D4
**Shere** Surrey 31 H2
**Shereford** Norfk 105 L6
**Sherfield English** Hants 28 F6
**Sherfield on Loddon** Hants 42 B8
**Sherford** Devon 7 H6
**Sheriffhales** Shrops 84 D2
**Sheriff Hutton** N York 133 K6
**Sheringham** Norfk 106 E4
**Sherington** M Keyn 74 C5
**Shernborne** Norfk 105 H6
**Sherrington** Wilts 27 L4
**Sherston** Wilts 39 J3
**Sherwood** C Nott 101 K4
**Sherwood Forest** Notts 101 L1
**Sherwood Forest Crematorium** Notts 116 A7
**Shetland Islands** Shet 235 c5
**Shettleston** C Glas 175 H5
**Shevington** Wigan 121 H8
**Sheviock** Cnwll 6 B5
**Shibden Head** C Brad 123 G5
**Shide** IoW 16 F5
**Shidlaw** Nthumb 168 B2
**Shiel Bridge** Highld 200 E2
**Shieldaig** Highld 210 C4
**Shieldhill** D & G 155 H5
**Shieldhill** Falk 176 B3
**Shieldhill House Hotel** S Lans 165 J2
**Shields** N Lans 175 K7
**Shielfoot** Highld 190 D3
**Shielhill** Angus 196 C5
**Shielhill** Inver 173 L4
**Shifnal** Shrops 84 D2
**Shilbottle** Nthumb 169 J7
**Shildon** Dur 141 G3
**Shillford** E Rens 174 E6
**Shillingford** Devon 24 F6
**Shillingford** Oxon 41 L2
**Shillingford Abbot** Devon 11 K6
**Shillingford St George** Devon 11 K7
**Shillingstone** Dorset 14 F1
**Shillington** C Beds 75 G7
**Shilton** Oxon 56 E6
**Shilton** Warwks 86 E6
**Shimpling** Norfk 92 D6
**Shimpling** Suffk 77 J4
**Shimpling Street** Suffk 77 K4
**Shincliffe** Dur 151 H6
**Shiney Row** Sundld 151 H4
**Shinfield** Wokham 42 B6
**Shinness** Highld 225 L5
**Shipbourne** Kent 33 G3
**Shipdham** Norfk 91 L3
**Shipham** Somset 38 C8
**Shiphay** Torbay 7 K3
**Shiplake** Oxon 42 C5
**Shipley** C Brad 123 H3
**Shipley** W Susx 31 J6
**Shipley Bridge** Surrey 32 B5
**Shipmeadow** Suffk 93 H5
**Shippon** Oxon 41 J2
**Shipston-on-Stour** Warwks 72 B6
**Shipton** Gloucs 56 B4
**Shipton** N York 133 H7
**Shipton** Shrops 83 L5
**Shipton Bellinger** Hants 28 E3
**Shipton Gorge** Dorset 13 L4
**Shipton Green** W Susx 17 L3
**Shipton Moyne** Gloucs 39 K3
**Shipton-on-Cherwell** Oxon 57 J5
**Shiptonthorpe** E R Yk 125 K2
**Shipton-under-Wychwood** Oxon 56 F4
**Shirburn** Oxon 42 B2
**Shirdley Hill** Lancs 120 E7
**Shirebrook** Derbys 115 K7
**Shiregreen** Sheff 115 G3
**Shirehampton** Bristl 38 D5
**Shiremoor** N Tyne 159 H7
**Shirenewton** Mons 38 C2
**Shireoaks** Notts 115 K5
**Shirland** Derbys 101 H2
**Shirley** C Sotn 29 H8
**Shirley** Derbys 100 E4
**Shirley** Gt Lon 45 G6
**Shirley** Solhll 85 K7
**Shirrell Heath** Hants 29 L8
**Shirvan** Ag & B 172 E2
**Shirwell** Devon 23 J4
**Shiskine** N Ayrs 162 B4
**Shobdon** Herefs 69 H3
**Shobrooke** Devon 11 K5
**Shoby** Leics 102 B7
**Shocklach** Ches W 98 C3
**Shoeburyness** Sthend 46 F3
**Sholden** Kent 35 K4
**Sholing** C Sotn 16 F1
**Shop** Cnwll 9 G2
**Shoreditch** Gt Lon 45 G4
**Shoreditch** Somset 25 K6
**Shoreham** Kent 45 K7
**Shoreham-by-Sea** W Susx 19 H5
**Shorley** Hants 29 L6
**Shorne** Kent 46 B6
**Shortgate** E Susx 20 A3
**Short Heath** Birm 85 K5
**Short Heath** Wsall 85 H4
**Shortlanesend** Cnwll 4 C6
**Shortlees** E Ayrs 163 K3
**Shorwell** IoW 16 F5
**Shoscombe** BaNES 27 G1
**Shotesham** Norfk 92 F4
**Shotgate** Essex 46 C2
**Shotley** Suffk 78 F7
**Shotley Bridge** Dur 150 D4
**Shotley Gate** Suffk 78 F7
**Shotley Street** Suffk 78 F7
**Shottenden** Kent 34 D4
**Shottery** Warwks 71 L4
**Shotteswell** Warwks 72 E5
**Shottisham** Suffk 79 G5
**Shottlegate** Derbys 100 F3
**Shotton** Dur 151 K6
**Shotton** Flints 111 J7
**Shotton Colliery** Dur 151 J6
**Shotts** N Lans 176 B6
**Shotwick** Ches W 111 K6
**Shougle** Moray 214 F4
**Shouldham** Norfk 90 F2
**Shouldham Thorpe** Norfk 90 F2
**Shoulton** Worcs 70 E3
**Shrawardine** Shrops 83 H1
**Shrawley** Worcs 70 E2
**Shrewley** Warwks 72 B2
**Shrewsbury** Shrops 83 J2
**Shrewton** Wilts 28 B3
**Shripney** W Susx 18 C5
**Shrivenham** Oxon 40 E3
**Shropham** Norfk 92 B5
**Shroton** Dorset 27 K8
**Shucknall** Herefs 69 L6
**Shudy Camps** Cambs 76 E5
**Shuna** Ag & B 181 M5
**Shurdington** Gloucs 55 L4
**Shurlock Row** W & M 42 D5
**Shurrery** Highld 230 F4
**Shurrery Lodge** Highld 230 F4
**Shurton** Somset 25 J3
**Shustoke** Warwks 86 B5
**Shute** Devon 11 K5
**Shute** Devon 13 G3
**Shutford** Oxon 72 E6
**Shut Heath** Staffs 99 K7
**Shuthonger** Gloucs 70 F7
**Shutlanger** Nhants 73 K4
**Shuttington** Warwks 86 B3
**Shuttlewood** Derbys 115 J6
**Shuttleworth** Bury 122 B6
**Siabost** W Isls 232 e2
**Siadar** W Isls 232 f1
**Sibbertoft** Nhants 87 K6
**Sibford Ferris** Oxon 72 D6
**Sibford Gower** Oxon 72 D6
**Sible Hedingham** Essex 77 H7
**Sibley's Green** Essex 60 F3
**Sibsey** Lincs 104 B3
**Sibson** Cambs 89 G4
**Sibson** Leics 86 D4
**Sibster** Highld 231 K5
**Sibthorpe** Notts 102 C4
**Sibthorpe** Notts 116 B6
**Sibton** Suffk 79 H1
**Sicklesmere** Suffk 77 K3
**Sicklinghall** N York 124 B2
**Sidbury** Devon 12 E4
**Sidbury** Shrops 84 C6
**Sidcot** N Som 38 B8
**Sidcup** Gt Lon 45 J5
**Siddington** Ches E 113 J7
**Siddington** Gloucs 56 B7
**Sidestrand** Norfk 106 F4
**Sidford** Devon 12 E4
**Sidlesham** W Susx 18 B6
**Sidley** E Susx 20 E4
**Sidmouth** Devon 12 E5
**Sigglesthorne** E R Yk 126 E2
**Sigingstone** V Glam 36 F6
**Silchester** Hants 41 L7
**Sileby** Leics 87 H1
**Silecroft** Cumb 128 D3
**Silfield** Norfk 92 D4
**Silkstone** Barns 114 F1
**Silkstone Common** Barns 114 F1
**Silk Willoughby** Lincs 103 H4
**Silloth** Cumb 147 K4
**Silpho** N York 134 E2
**Silsden** C Brad 122 F2
**Silsoe** C Beds 74 F7
**Silton** Dorset 27 H5
**Silverburn** Mdloth 177 G6
**Silverdale** Lancs 129 K4
**Silverdale** Staffs 99 J3
**Silver End** Essex 61 K4
**Silverford** Abers 216 E2
**Silverstone** Nhants 73 J5
**Silverton** Devon 12 B2
**Silvington** Shrops 84 B7
**Simonburn** Nthumb 157 L7
**Simonsbath** Somset 24 B4
**Simonstone** Lancs 122 B4
**Simprim** Border 168 C1
**Simpson** M Keyn 74 C7
**Simpson Cross** Pembks 48 F4
**Sinclair's Hill** Border 179 G7
**Sinclairston** E Ayrs 163 L6
**Sinderby** N York 132 E3
**Sinderland Green** Traffd 113 G4
**Sindlesham** Wokham 42 C6
**Sinfin** C Derb 101 G6
**Singleton** Kent 34 D6
**Singleton** Lancs 120 E3
**Singleton** W Susx 18 B3
**Singlewell** Kent 46 A6
**Sinnarhard** Abers 205 K3
**Sinnington** N York 134 B3
**Sinton** Worcs 70 E3
**Sinton** Worcs 70 F2
**Sinton Green** Worcs 70 E3
**Sissinghurst** Kent 33 K5
**Siston** S Glos 39 G5
**Sithney** Cnwll 3 H5
**Sittingbourne** Kent 34 B3
**Six Ashes** Shrops 84 E5
**Sixhills** Lincs 117 K4
**Six Mile Bottom** Cambs 76 E3
**Sixpenny Handley** Dorset 27 M7
**Six Rues** Jersey 236 c6
**Skaill** Ork 234 d6
**Skara Brae** Ork 234 b5
**Skares** E Ayrs 164 B6
**Skateraw** Abers 207 G6
**Skateraw** E Loth 178 F4
**Skeabost** Highld 208 F5
**Skeeby** N York 140 F6
**Skeffington** Leics 87 L3
**Skeffling** E R Yk 127 J6
**Skegby** Notts 101 J1
**Skegby** Notts 116 C7
**Skegness** Lincs 119 H8
**Skelbo** Highld 223 H3
**Skelbo Street** Highld 223 H3
**Skelbrooke** Donc 124 D7
**Skeldyke** Lincs 104 B5
**Skellingthorpe** Lincs 116 F6
**Skellow** Donc 124 E7
**Skelmanthorpe** Kirk 123 J7
**Skelmersdale** Lancs 112 C1
**Skelmorlie** N Ayrs 173 L5
**Skelpick** Highld 229 L4
**Skelston** D & G 154 E5
**Skelton** C York 133 J7
**Skelton** Cumb 148 D7
**Skelton** E R Yk 125 H5
**Skelton** R & Cl 142 E4
**Skelton on Ure** N York 132 E5
**Skelwith Bridge** Cumb 137 K6
**Skendleby** Lincs 118 F7
**Skene House** Abers 206 E4
**Skenfrith** Mons 54 C4
**Skerne** E R Yk 135 G7
**Skerray** Highld 229 K3
**Skerricha** Highld 228 C5
*Skerries Airport* Shet 235 e4
**Skerton** Lancs 129 K6
**Sketchley** Leics 86 E5
**Sketty** Swans 51 J6
**Skewsby** N York 133 K5
**Skiall** Highld 230 E3
**Skidby** E R Yk 126 C4
**Skigersta** W Isls 232 g1
**Skilgate** Somset 24 F6
**Skillington** Lincs 102 E7
**Skinburness** Cumb 147 K4
**Skinflats** Falk 176 B2
**Skinidin** Highld 208 C5
**Skipness** Ag & B 172 F6
**Skipper's Bridge** D & G 156 C5
**Skipsea** E R Yk 135 J8
**Skipton** N York 122 E1
**Skipton-on-Swale** N York 132 E4
**Skipwith** N York 125 G3
**Skirlaugh** E R Yk 126 E3
**Skirling** Border 165 L2
**Skirmett** Bucks 42 C3

**Skirpenbeck** E R Yk 134 B7
**Skirwith** Cumb 149 G7
**Skirza** Highld 231 L2
**Skokholm Island** Pembks 48 C6
**Skomer Island** Pembks 48 C5
**Skulamus** Highld 199 K2
**Skye Green** Essex 61 L4
**Skye of Curr** Highld 204 B1
**Slack** Calder 122 E5
**Slacks of Cairnbanno** Abers 216 F5
**Slad** Gloucs 55 K6
**Slade** Devon 23 H3
**Slade Green** Gt Lon 45 K5
**Slade Hooton** Rothm 115 K4
**Slaggyford** Nthumb 149 H4
**Slaidburn** Lancs 130 D8
**Slaithwaite** Kirk 123 G7
**Slaley** Nthumb 150 B4
**Slamannan** Falk 176 B4
**Slapton** Bucks 58 F4
**Slapton** Devon 7 J6
**Slapton** Nhants 73 J5
**Slaugham** W Susx 31 L5
**Slaughterford** Wilts 39 J5
**Slawston** Leics 87 L5
**Sleaford** Hants 30 D4
**Sleaford** Lincs 103 H4
**Sleagill** Cumb 138 E4
**Sleapford** Wrekin 84 B1
**Sleasdairidh** Highld 222 E3
**Sledmere** E R Yk 134 E6
**Sleetbeck** Cumb 156 E6
**Sleights** N York 143 H5
**Slickly** Highld 231 K3
**Sliddery** N Ayrs 162 B5
**Sligachan** Highld 209 G7
**Sligrachan** Ag & B 173 K1
**Slimbridge** Gloucs 55 H7
**Slindon** Staffs 99 J6
**Slindon** W Susx 18 C4
**Slinfold** W Susx 31 J5
**Slingsby** N York 133 L4
**Slip End** C Beds 59 H4
**Slip End** Herts 75 K6
**Slipton** Nhants 88 D7
**Slitting Mill** Staffs 100 B8
**Slockavullin** Ag & B 182 B7
**Sloncombe** Devon 11 H7
**Sloothby** Lincs 119 G7
**Slough** Slough 43 G4
**Slough Crematorium** Bucks 43 G4
**Slough Green** Somset 25 L7
**Slumbay** Highld 210 D6
**Slyne** Lancs 129 K6
**Smailholm** Border 167 K3
**Smallburgh** Norfk 107 G7
**Small Dole** W Susx 19 G3
**Smalley** Derbys 101 H4
**Smallfield** Surrey 32 B5
**Small Heath** Birm 85 K6
**Small Hythe** Kent 34 B8
**Smallridge** Devon 13 H3
**Smallthorne** C Stke 99 K3
**Smallworth** Norfk 92 B7
**Smannell** Hants 29 G2
**Smarden** Kent 34 B6
**Smarden Bell** Kent 34 B6
**Smart's Hill** Kent 32 F5
**Smearisary** Highld 190 D2
**Smeatharpe** Devon 12 F1
**Smeeth** Kent 34 E6
**Smeeton Westerby** Leics 87 K5
**Smerral** Highld 227 L2
**Smestow** Staffs 84 F5
**Smethwick** Sandw 85 H6
**Smisby** Derbys 101 G8
**Smithfield** Cumb 148 D3
**Smith's Green** Essex 76 F6
**Smithstown** Highld 219 J6
**Smithton** Highld 213 H5
**Smoo** Highld 228 F3
**Smythe's Green** Essex 61 L4
**Snade** D & G 154 E5
**Snailbeach** Shrops 83 G3
**Snailwell** Cambs 76 F2
**Snainton** N York 134 E3
**Snaith** E R Yk 124 F6
**Snape** N York 132 D3
**Snape** Suffk 79 H3
**Snape Street** Suffk 79 H3
**Snaresbrook** Gt Lon 45 H3
**Snarestone** Leics 86 D2
**Snarford** Lincs 117 H5
**Snargate** Kent 34 D8
**Snave** Kent 34 D8
**Sneaton** N York 143 J5
**Snelland** Lincs 117 H5
**Snelston** Derbys 100 D4
**Snetterton** Norfk 92 B5
**Snettisham** Norfk 105 G5
**Snitter** Nthumb 158 C2
**Snitterby** Lincs 117 G3
**Snitterfield** Warwks 72 B3
**Snitton** Shrops 83 L7
**Snodland** Kent 46 B7
**Snowdon** Gwynd 95 K2
*Snowdonia National Park* 96 C6
**Snow End** Herts 60 C2
**Snowshill** Gloucs 71 K7
**Soake** Hants 17 J1
**Soay** Highld 199 G3
**Soberton** Hants 29 L7
**Soberton Heath** Hants 29 L8
**Sockburn** Darltn 141 J6
**Soham** Cambs 90 E8
**Solas** W Isls 232 c5
**Soldridge** Hants 29 M4
**Sole Street** Kent 34 E5
**Sole Street** Kent 46 A6
**Solihull** Solhll 85 L7
**Sollers Dilwyn** Herefs 69 H4
**Sollers Hope** Herefs 54 E2
**Solva** Pembks 48 D3
**Solwaybank** D & G 156 B6
**Somerby** Leics 87 L2
**Somerby** Lincs 117 H1
**Somercotes** Derbys 101 H2
**Somerford** Dorset 15 M4
**Somerford Keynes** Gloucs 40 A2
**Somerley** W Susx 17 M3
**Somerleyton** Suffk 93 K4
**Somersal Herbert** Derbys 100 C5
**Somersby** Lincs 118 D6
**Somersham** Cambs 89 L7
**Somersham** Suffk 78 C5
**Somerton** Oxon 57 J3
**Somerton** Somset 26 C5
**Somerton** Suffk 77 J4
**Sompting** W Susx 19 G5
**Sonning** Wokham 42 C5
**Sonning Common** Oxon 42 B4
**Sopley** Hants 15 M3
**Sopwell** Herts 59 J6
**Sopworth** Wilts 39 J3
**Sorbie** D & G 145 J5
**Sordale** Highld 231 G3
**Sorisdale** Ag & B 189 H4
**Sorn** E Ayrs 164 B4
**Sortat** Highld 231 K3
**Sotby** Lincs 117 K5
**Sotterley** Suffk 93 J6
**Soughton** Flints 111 H7
**Soulbury** Bucks 58 E3
**Soulby** Cumb 139 H5
**Souldern** Oxon 57 K2
**Souldrop** Bed 74 E3
**Sound** Ches E 98 F3
**Sound Muir** Moray 215 H4
**Soundwell** S Glos 38 F5
**Sourton** Devon 10 D6
**Soutergate** Cumb 128 F3
**South Acre** Norfk 91 J2
**South Alkham** Kent 35 H6
**Southall** Gt Lon 43 J4
**South Allington** Devon 7 J7
**South Alloa** Falk 185 J8
**Southam** Gloucs 55 L3
**Southam** Warwks 72 E3
**South Ambersham** W Susx 30 E7
**Southampton** C Sotn 29 H8
*Southampton Airport* Hants 29 J7
**Southampton Crematorium** Hants 29 H7
**South Anston** Rothm 115 K5
**South Ashford** Kent 34 D6
**South Baddesley** Hants 16 D3
**South Ballachulish** Highld 191 K5
**South Bank** C York 124 F1
**South Barrow** Somset 26 E5
**South Beddington** Gt Lon 44 F7
**South Benfleet** Essex 46 C3
**Southborough** Gt Lon 45 H6
**Southborough** Kent 33 G5
**Southbourne** Bmouth 15 L4
**Southbourne** W Susx 17 L2
**South Bramwith** Donc 124 F7
**South Brent** Devon 7 G4
**South Brewham** Somset 27 G4
**South Bristol Crematorium** Bristl 38 E6
**South Broomhill** Nthumb 159 G3
**Southburgh** Norfk 92 B3
**South Burlingham** Norfk 93 H3
**Southburn** E R Yk 134 F8
**South Cadbury** Somset 26 F6
**South Carlton** Lincs 116 F6
**South Carlton** Notts 115 L5
**South Cave** E R Yk 125 L4
**South Cerney** Gloucs 40 B2
**South Chailey** E Susx 19 K3
**South Charlton** Nthumb 169 H5
**South Cheriton** Somset 27 G6
**South Church** Dur 140 F2
**Southchurch** Sthend 46 E3
**South Cliffe** E R Yk 125 K4
**South Clifton** Notts 116 D7
**South Cockerington** Lincs 118 E4
**South Cornelly** Brdgnd 36 C4
**Southcott** Cnwll 9 G5
**Southcott** Devon 11 H8
**Southcourt** Bucks 58 D5
**South Cove** Suffk 93 K7
**South Creake** Norfk 105 K5
**South Croxton** Leics 87 K2
**South Dalton** E R Yk 126 B2
**South Darenth** Kent 45 K6
**South Dell** W Isls 232 g1
*South Downs National Park* 19 K4
**South Duffield** N York 125 G4
**South Earlswood** Surrey 32 B4
**Southease** E Susx 19 L5
**South Elkington** Lincs 118 D4
**South Elmsall** Wakefd 124 D7
**Southend** Ag & B 161 H7
*Southend Airport* Essex 46 E3
**Southend Crematorium** Sthend 46 E3
**Southend-on-Sea** Sthend 46 E3
**Southerndown** V Glam 36 D5
**Southerness** D & G 147 G4
**South Erradale** Highld 219 H7
**Southerton** Devon 12 D4
**Southery** Norfk 90 E5
**South Essex Crematorium** Gt Lon 45 L3
**South Fambridge** Essex 46 E2
**South Ferriby** N Linc 126 B6
**South Field** E R Yk 126 C5
**Southfield** Falk 175 L4
**Southfleet** Kent 45 L5
**Southgate** Gt Lon 44 F2
**Southgate** Swans 51 G7
**South Gorley** Hants 15 M1
**South Gosforth** N u Ty 151 G2
**South Green** Essex 46 B2
**South Green** Kent 33 L2
**South Green** Norfk 92 C2
**South Gyle** C Edin 177 G4
**South Hanningfield** Essex 61 H8
**South Harting** W Susx 30 C7
**South Hayling** Hants 17 K3
**South Heath** Bucks 58 E7
**South Heighton** E Susx 19 L5
**South Hetton** Dur 151 J6
**South Hiendley** Wakefd 124 B7
**South Hill** Cnwll 5 M2
**South Hinksey** Oxon 57 K7
**South Holmwood** Surrey 31 K3
**South Hornchurch** Gt Lon 45 K4
**South Huish** Devon 7 G7
**South Hykeham** Lincs 116 F8
**South Hylton** Sundld 151 J4
**Southill** C Beds 75 H6
**Southington** Hants 29 J2
**South Kelsey** Lincs 117 H2
**South Kessock** Highld 213 G5
**South Killingholme** N Linc 126 E7
**South Kilvington** N York 132 F3
**South Kilworth** Leics 87 H6
**South Kirkby** Wakefd 124 C7
**South Kyme** Lincs 103 K3
**South Lanarkshire Crematorium** S Lans 175 J7
**South Leicestershire Crematorium** Leics 87 H4
**Southleigh** Devon 12 F4
**South Leigh** Oxon 57 H6
**South Leverton** Notts 116 C5
**South Lincolnshire Crematorium** Lincs 103 L6
**South Littleton** Worcs 71 J5
**South London Crematorium** Gt Lon 44 F6
**South Lopham** Norfk 92 C7
**South Luffenham** Rutlnd 88 D3
**South Lynn** Norfk 104 F8
**South Malling** E Susx 19 L4
**South Marston** Swindn 40 D3
**South Merstham** Surrey 32 B3
**South Milford** N York 124 D4
**South Milton** Devon 7 G7
**South Mimms** Herts 59 L7
**South Mimms Services** Herts 59 L7
**Southminster** Essex 62 A7
**South Molton** Devon 23 L6
**South Moor** Dur 150 F5

Southmoor Oxon 41 H2
South Moreton Oxon 41 K3
Southmuir Angus 196 C5
South Mundham W Susx 18 B5
South Newbald E R Yk 125 L4
South Newington Oxon 57 H2
South Newton Wilts 28 C4
South Normanton Derbys 101 H2
South Norwood Gt Lon 45 G6
South Ockendon Thurr 45 L4
Southoe Cambs 75 H2
Southolt Suffk 78 E2
South Ormsby Lincs 118 E6
Southorpe C Pete 88 F3
South Otterington N York 132 E3
Southover Dorset 14 C4
South Owersby Lincs 117 H3
Southowram Calder 123 G5
South Oxfordshire Crematorium Oxon 41 H2
South Park Surrey 31 L2
South Perrott Dorset 13 L2
South Petherton Somset 26 B7
South Petherwin Cnwll 9 J8
South Pickenham Norfk 91 J3
South Pill Cnwll 6 B4
South Pool Devon 7 H7
South Poorton Dorset 13 M3
Southport Sefton 120 D6
Southport Crematorium Lancs 120 E7
South Queensferry C Edin 176 F3
South Rauceby Lincs 103 G4
South Raynham Norfk 105 L7
South Reddish Stockp 113 K3
Southrepps Norfk 106 F5
South Reston Lincs 118 E5
Southrey Lincs 117 J7
South Ronaldsay Ork 234 c7
Southrop Gloucs 56 D7
Southrope Hants 30 A3
South Runcton Norfk 90 F2
South Scarle Notts 116 D8
Southsea C Port 17 J3
South Shian Ag & B 191 H7
South Shields S Tyne 151 J2
South Shields Crematorium S Tyne 151 J3
South Shore Bpool 120 D4
Southside Dur 140 E2
South Stainley N York 132 D6
South Stifford Thurr 45 L4
South Stoke BaNES 39 H7
South Stoke Oxon 41 L4
South Stoke W Susx 18 D4
South Street Kent 34 E3
South Street Kent 47 J6
South Tarbrax S Lans 176 D7
South Tawton Devon 10 F6
South Tehidy Cnwll 3 H3
South Thoresby Lincs 118 E6
Southtown Norfk 93 L3
South Uist W Isls 233 c8
Southwaite Cumb 148 D6
Southwaite Services Cumb 148 D6
South Walsham Norfk 93 H2
Southwark Gt Lon 44 F4
South Warnborough Hants 30 B3
Southwater W Susx 31 J6
South Weald Essex 45 L2
Southwell Notts 102 B2
South West Middlesex Crematorium Gt Lon 43 J5
South Weston Oxon 42 B2
South Wheatley Notts 116 C4
Southwick Hants 17 J2
Southwick Nhants 88 E5
Southwick Sundld 151 J4
Southwick W Susx 19 H5
Southwick Wilts 27 J1
South Widcombe BaNES 38 E8
South Wigston Leics 87 H4
South Willesborough Kent 34 D6
South Willingham Lincs 117 K5
South Wingfield Derbys 101 G2
South Witham Lincs 102 F8
Southwold Suffk 93 K7
South Woodham Ferrers Essex 61 J7
South Wootton Norfk 105 G7
South Wraxall Wilts 39 J7
South Zeal Devon 10 F6
Sovereign Harbour E Susx 20 D5
Sowerby Calder 122 F6
Sowerby N York 132 F4
Sowerby Bridge Calder 122 F5
Sowood Calder 123 G6
Sowton Devon 6 D3
Sowton Devon 12 C4
Soyland Town Calder 122 F6
Spain's End Essex 76 F6
Spalding Lincs 103 L7
Spaldington E R Yk 125 H4
Spaldwick Cambs 89 G8
Spalford Notts 116 D7
Spanby Lincs 103 H5
Sparham Norfk 106 C8
Spark Bridge Cumb 129 G3
Sparkford Somset 26 E6
Sparkhill Birm 85 K6
Sparkwell Devon 6 E4
Sparrowpit Derbys 114 C5
Sparrows Green E Susx 33 H6
Sparsholt Hants 29 H5
Sparsholt Oxon 41 G3
Spaunton N York 133 L2
Spaxton Somset 25 K4
Spean Bridge Highld 201 K8
Spearywell Hants 28 F6
Speen Bucks 58 D7
Speen W Berk 41 J6
Speeton N York 135 J5
Speke Lpool 112 C5
Speldhurst Kent 32 F5
Spellbrook Herts 60 D4
Spencers Wood Wokham 42 B6
Spen Green Ches E 99 J1
Spennithorne N York 131 L2
Spennymoor Dur 151 G7
Spetchley Worcs 70 F4
Spetisbury Dorset 15 G3
Spexhall Suffk 93 H7
Spey Bay Moray 215 H2
Speybridge Highld 204 C1
Speyview Moray 215 G6
Spilsby Lincs 118 E7
Spinkhill Derbys 115 J5
Spinningdale Highld 222 F4
Spital Wirral 111 K5
Spital Hill Donc 115 L3
Spittal E Loth 178 B3
Spittal Highld 231 H5
Spittal Nthumb 179 L7
Spittal Pembks 49 G3
Spittalfield P & K 195 H7
Spittal of Glenmuick Abers 205 G7
Spittal of Glenshee P & K 195 H3
Spittal-on-Rule Border 167 J5
Spixworth Norfk 92 F1
Splatt Devon 10 E4
Splayne's Green E Susx 19 L2
Splottlands Cardif 37 K5
Spofforth N York 124 B1
Spondon C Derb 101 H5
Spooner Row Norfk 92 D4
Sporle Norfk 91 J2
Spott E Loth 178 E4
Spottiswoode Border 178 D7
Spratton Nhants 73 K1
Spreakley Surrey 30 D3
Spreyton Devon 11 G5
Spriddlestone Devon 6 D5
Spridlington Lincs 117 G5
Springburn C Glas 175 G5
Springfield D & G 148 B2
Springfield Essex 61 H6
Springfield Fife 186 E5
Springholm D & G 154 E7
Springside N Ayrs 163 J2
Springthorpe Lincs 116 E4
Springwell Sundld 151 H4
Springwood Crematorium Lpool 112 B4
Sproatley E R Yk 126 F4
Sproston Green Ches W 113 G7
Sprotbrough Donc 115 K2
Sproughton Suffk 78 D5
Sprouston Border 168 A3
Sprowston Norfk 92 F2
Sproxton Leics 102 D7
Sproxton N York 133 J3
Spurstow Ches E 98 D2
Spyway Dorset 14 A4
Stableford Shrops 84 D4
Stacey Bank Sheff 114 F4
Stackhouse N York 130 F6
Stackpole Pembks 49 G7
Stackpole Elidor Pembks 49 G7
Staddiscombe C Plym 6 D5
Stadhampton Oxon 57 L7
Stadhlaigearraidh W Isls 233 b7
Staffield Cumb 148 F6
Staffin Highld 218 D7
Stafford Staffs 99 L7
Stafford Crematorium Staffs 99 L7
Stafford Services (northbound) Staffs 99 K6
Stafford Services (southbound) Staffs 99 K6
Stagsden Bed 74 E5
Stainburn Cumb 136 E2
Stainby Lincs 102 E7
Staincross Barns 123 L7
Staindrop Dur 140 E3
Staines-upon-Thames Surrey 43 G6
Stainforth Donc 124 F7
Stainforth N York 130 F6
Staining Lancs 120 D4
Stainland Calder 123 G6
Stainsacre N York 143 J5
Stainton Cumb 129 L3
Stainton Cumb 138 C2
Stainton Donc 115 K3
Stainton Dur 140 D4
Stainton Middsb 141 L4
Stainton by Langworth Lincs 117 H6
Staintondale N York 143 K7
Stainton le Vale Lincs 117 K3
Stainton with Adgarley Cumb 128 F5
Stair E Ayrs 163 K5
Stairhaven D & G 144 E4
Staithes N York 143 G4
Stakes Hants 17 K2
Stalbridge Dorset 27 G7
Stalbridge Weston Dorset 27 G7
Stalham Norfk 107 H7
Stalisfield Green Kent 34 C4
Stallen Dorset 26 E7
Stallingborough NE Lin 126 F7
Stalmine Lancs 120 E2
Stalybridge Tamesd 113 L2
Stambourne Essex 77 G6
Stambourne Green Essex 77 G6
Stamford Lincs 88 E3
Stamford Nthumb 169 J5
Stamford Bridge Ches W 112 C7
Stamford Bridge E R Yk 133 L7
Stamfordham Nthumb 158 D7
Stamford Hill Gt Lon 45 G3
Stanbridge C Beds 58 F3
Stanbury C Brad 122 F3
Stand N Lans 175 K5
Standburn Falk 176 C4
Standeford Staffs 85 G3
Standen Kent 33 L5
Standerwick Somset 27 J2
Standford Hants 30 D4
Standingstone Cumb 147 J7
Standish Wigan 121 H7
Standlake Oxon 57 H7
Standon Hants 29 H6
Standon Herts 60 C4
Standon Staffs 99 J5
Stane N Lans 176 B6
Stanfield Norfk 105 M7
Stanford C Beds 75 H6
Stanford Kent 34 F6
Stanford Bishop Herefs 70 C4
Stanford Bridge Worcs 70 C2
Stanford Dingley W Berk 41 L6
Stanford in the Vale Oxon 41 G2
Stanford le Hope Thurr 46 B4
Stanford on Avon Nhants 87 H7
Stanford on Soar Notts 101 K7
Stanford on Teme Worcs 70 C2
Stanfree Derbys 115 J6
Stanghow R & Cl 142 E4
Stanground C Pete 89 H4
Stanhoe Norfk 105 J5
Stanhope Border 165 L4
Stanhope Dur 150 C6
Stanhope Kent 34 D6
Stanion Nhants 88 D6
Stanley Derbys 101 H4
Stanley Dur 150 F4
Stanley P & K 186 B2
Stanley Staffs 99 L3
Stanley Crook Dur 150 E7
Stanley Pontlarge Gloucs 55 M3
Stanmer Br & H 19 K4
Stanmore Gt Lon 44 D2
Stanmore Hants 29 J5
Stannersburn Nthumb 157 J5
Stanningfield Suffk 77 K3
Stannington Nthumb 158 F6
Stannington Sheff 114 F4

**Stannington Station** Nthumb 158 F5
**Stansbatch** Herefs 69 G3
**Stansfield** Suffk 77 H4
**Stanstead** Suffk 77 J5
**Stanstead Abbotts** Herts 60 C5
**Stansted** Kent 45 L7
*Stansted Airport* Essex 60 E4
**Stansted Mountfitchet** Essex 60 E3
**Stanton** Gloucs 71 J7
**Stanton** Nthumb 158 E4
**Stanton** Staffs 100 C4
**Stanton** Suffk 91 L8
**Stanton by Bridge** Derbys 101 G6
**Stanton by Dale** Derbys 101 J5
**Stanton Drew** BaNES 38 E7
**Stanton Fitzwarren** Swindn 40 D3
**Stanton Harcourt** Oxon 57 H6
**Stanton in Peak** Derbys 114 E8
**Stanton Lacy** Shrops 83 K7
**Stanton Lees** Derbys 114 E8
**Stanton Long** Shrops 83 L5
**Stanton-on-the-Wolds** Notts 101 M6
**Stanton Prior** BaNES 39 G7
**Stanton St Bernard** Wilts 40 C7
**Stanton St John** Oxon 57 L6
**Stanton St Quintin** Wilts 39 K4
**Stanton Street** Suffk 77 L2
**Stanton under Bardon** Leics 86 F2
**Stanton upon Hine Heath** Shrops 98 E7
**Stanton Wick** BaNES 38 E7
**Stanway** Essex 61 M3
**Stanway** Gloucs 56 B2
**Stanwell** Surrey 43 H5
**Stanwick** Nhants 74 E1
**Stanwix** Cumb 148 D4
**Staoinebrig** W Isls 233 b8
**Stape** N York 143 G7
**Stapeley** Ches E 99 G3
**Stapenhill** Staffs 100 E7
**Staple** Kent 35 H4
**Staple Cross** Devon 25 G7
**Staplecross** E Susx 20 F2
**Staplefield** W Susx 32 B7
**Staple Fitzpaine** Somset 25 K7
**Stapleford** Cambs 76 C4
**Stapleford** Herts 60 A5
**Stapleford** Leics 102 D8
**Stapleford** Lincs 102 E2
**Stapleford** Notts 101 J5
**Stapleford** Wilts 28 B4
**Stapleford Abbotts** Essex 45 K2
**Staplegrove** Somset 25 K6
**Staplehay** Somset 25 K6
**Staplehurst** Kent 33 K5
**Staplers** IoW 17 G5
**Staplestreet** Kent 34 E3
**Stapleton** Herefs 69 G2
**Stapleton** Leics 86 E4
**Stapleton** N York 141 G5
**Stapleton** Shrops 83 J3
**Stapleton** Somset 26 C7
**Stapley** Somset 25 J8
**Staploe** Bed 75 G3
**Staplow** Herefs 70 C6
**Star** Fife 186 E6
**Star** Pembks 65 H7
**Star** Somset 38 C8
**Starbeck** N York 132 E7
**Starbotton** N York 131 H5
**Starcross** Devon 12 C6
**Stareton** Warwks 72 D1
**Starlings Green** Essex 60 D2
**Starston** Norfk 92 F6
**Startforth** Dur 140 D4
**Startley** Wilts 39 L4
**Statenborough** Kent 35 J4
**Statham** Warrtn 112 F4
**Stathe** Somset 26 A5
**Stathern** Leics 102 C6
**Staughton Green** Cambs 75 G2
**Staunton** Gloucs 54 D5
**Staunton** Gloucs 55 H3
**Staunton on Arrow** Herefs 69 G3
**Staunton on Wye** Herefs 69 G5
**Staveley** Cumb 138 C7
**Staveley** Derbys 115 H6
**Staveley** N York 132 E6
**Staveley-in-Cartmel** Cumb 129 H3
**Staverton** Devon 7 J3
**Staverton** Gloucs 55 K4
**Staverton** Nhants 73 G3
**Staverton** Wilts 39 J7
**Stawell** Somset 26 A4
**Stawley** Somset 25 G6
**Staxigoe** Highld 231 L5
**Staxton** N York 134 F4
**Staynall** Lancs 120 E2
**Stean** N York 131 K5
**Stearsby** N York 133 J5
**Steart** Somset 25 L3
**Stebbing** Essex 61 G3
**Stechford** Birm 85 K6
**Stedham** W Susx 30 E6
**Steelend** Fife 185 L8
**Steele Road** Border 156 F4
**Steen's Bridge** Herefs 69 K3
**Steep** Hants 30 C6
**Steep Lane** Calder 122 F5
**Steeple** Essex 61 M7
**Steeple Ashton** Wilts 27 K1
**Steeple Aston** Oxon 57 J3
**Steeple Bumpstead** Essex 76 F6
**Steeple Claydon** Bucks 58 B3
**Steeple Gidding** Cambs 89 G7
**Steeple Langford** Wilts 28 B4
**Steeple Morden** Cambs 75 K6
**Steeton** C Brad 122 F2
**Stein** Highld 208 D3
**Stelling Minnis** Kent 34 F5
**Stembridge** Somset 26 B7
**Stenalees** Cnwll 4 F4
**Stenhouse** D & G 154 D4
**Stenhousemuir** Falk 176 B2
**Stenscholl** Highld 218 D7
**Stenson Fields** Derbys 101 G6
**Stenton** E Loth 178 D4
**Steornabhagh** W Isls 232 f2
**Stepaside** Pembks 49 K6
**Stepford** D & G 154 E5
**Stepney** Gt Lon 45 G4
**Steppingley** C Beds 74 E7
**Stepps** N Lans 175 H5
**Sternfield** Suffk 79 H3
**Stert** Wilts 40 B8
**Stetchworth** Cambs 76 F3
**Stevenage** Herts 59 L3
**Stevenston** N Ayrs 163 H2
**Steventon** Hants 29 K2
**Steventon** Oxon 41 J3
**Steventon End** Essex 76 E6
**Stevington** Bed 74 E4
**Stewartby** Bed 74 E6
**Stewartfield** S Lans 175 H7
**Stewarton** Ag & B 161 H5
**Stewarton** E Ayrs 163 K1
**Stewkley** Bucks 58 D3
**Stewley** Somset 25 L7
**Steyning** W Susx 19 G4
**Steynton** Pembks 48 F6
**Stibb** Cnwll 9 G3
**Stibbard** Norfk 106 B6
**Stibb Cross** Devon 10 C2
**Stibb Green** Wilts 40 E7
**Stibbington** Cambs 88 F4
**Stichill** Border 167 L2
**Sticker** Cnwll 4 F5
**Stickford** Lincs 104 B1
**Sticklepath** Devon 10 F6
**Stickney** Lincs 104 B2
**Stiffkey** Norfk 106 A4
**Stifford Clays** Thurr 45 L4
**Stilligarry** W Isls 233 b7
**Stillingfleet** N York 124 F3
**Stillington** N York 133 J6
**Stillington** S on T 141 J3
**Stilton** Cambs 89 H5
**Stinchcombe** Gloucs 55 G7
**Stinsford** Dorset 14 D4
**Stiperstones** Shrops 83 G4
**Stirchley** Wrekin 84 C3
**Stirling** Abers 217 L6
**Stirling** Stirlg 185 G8
**Stirling Castle** Stirlg 185 G8
**Stirling Services** Stirlg 175 L2
**Stirtloe** Cambs 75 H2
**Stirton** N York 131 H8
**Stisted** Essex 61 J3
**Stithians** Cnwll 3 J4
**Stivichall** Covtry 86 D7
**Stixwould** Lincs 117 K7
**St Michaels** Fife 187 G3
**Stoak** Ches W 112 B6
**Stobo** Border 166 B2
**Stoborough** Dorset 15 H5
**Stobs Castle** Border 167 G7
**Stobswood** Nthumb 158 F3
**Stock** Essex 61 H7
**Stock** N Som 38 C7
**Stockbridge** Hants 29 G4
**Stockbriggs** S Lans 164 F3
**Stockbury** Kent 46 D7
**Stockcross** W Berk 41 H6
**Stockerston** Leics 88 B4
**Stock Green** Worcs 71 H3
**Stocking** Herefs 54 F2
**Stockingford** Warwks 86 D5
**Stocking Pelham** Herts 60 D3
**Stockland** Devon 13 G2
**Stockland Bristol** Somset 25 K3
**Stockleigh English** Devon 11 K4
**Stockleigh Pomeroy** Devon 11 K4
**Stockley** Wilts 39 M6
**Stocklinch** Somset 26 B7
**Stockport** Stockp 113 K4
**Stockport Crematorium** Stockp 113 K4
**Stocksbridge** Sheff 114 E2
**Stocksfield** Nthumb 150 D3
**Stockton** Herefs 69 K3
**Stockton** Norfk 93 H5
**Stockton** Shrops 84 C4
**Stockton** Warwks 72 E2
**Stockton** Wilts 27 M4
**Stockton** Wrekin 84 D1
**Stockton Brook** Staffs 99 K3
**Stockton Heath** Warrtn 112 E4
**Stockton-on-Tees** S on T 141 K4
**Stockton on Teme** Worcs 70 C2
**Stockton on the Forest** C York 133 K7
**Stockwell End** Wolves 84 F4
**Stockwood** Bristl 38 F6
**Stockwood** Dorset 14 B2
**Stock Wood** Worcs 71 H3
**Stodmarsh** Kent 35 G3
**Stody** Norfk 106 C5
**Stoer** Highld 224 C3
**Stoford** Somset 26 E8
**Stoford** Wilts 28 B4
**Stogumber** Somset 25 H4
**Stogursey** Somset 25 J3
**Stoke** Covtry 86 D7
**Stoke** Devon 22 C6
**Stoke** Hants 17 K3
**Stoke** Hants 29 H2
**Stoke** Medway 46 D5
**Stoke Abbott** Dorset 13 L3
**Stoke Albany** Nhants 88 B5
**Stoke Ash** Suffk 78 D1
**Stoke Bardolph** Notts 101 M4
**Stoke Bliss** Worcs 70 B2
**Stoke Bruerne** Nhants 73 L4
**Stoke-by-Clare** Suffk 77 G5
**Stoke-by-Nayland** Suffk 78 B7
**Stoke Canon** Devon 12 B3
**Stoke Charity** Hants 29 J4
**Stoke Climsland** Cnwll 6 A2
**Stoke Cross** Herefs 70 B4
**Stoke D'Abernon** Surrey 43 J8
**Stoke Doyle** Nhants 88 E6
**Stoke Dry** Rutlnd 88 C4
**Stoke Edith** Herefs 69 L6
**Stoke Farthing** Wilts 28 B6
**Stoke Ferry** Norfk 91 G4
**Stoke Fleming** Devon 7 K6
**Stokeford** Dorset 15 G5
**Stoke Gabriel** Devon 7 J4
**Stoke Gifford** S Glos 38 F4
**Stoke Golding** Leics 86 E4
**Stoke Goldington** M Keyn 74 B5
**Stokeham** Notts 116 C6
**Stoke Hammond** Bucks 58 E3
**Stoke Holy Cross** Norfk 92 F3
**Stokeinteignhead** Devon 7 L2
**Stoke Lacy** Herefs 70 B5
**Stoke Lyne** Oxon 57 K3
**Stoke Mandeville** Bucks 58 D6
**Stokenchurch** Bucks 42 C2
**Stoke Newington** Gt Lon 45 G3
**Stokenham** Devon 7 J7
**Stoke-on-Trent** C Stke 99 K3
**Stoke Orchard** Gloucs 55 K3
**Stoke Poges** Bucks 42 F4
**Stoke Prior** Herefs 69 K3
**Stoke Prior** Worcs 71 G2
**Stoke Rivers** Devon 23 K4
**Stoke Rochford** Lincs 102 F6
**Stoke Row** Oxon 42 B4
**Stoke St Gregory** Somset 25 M6
**Stoke St Mary** Somset 25 K6
**Stoke St Michael** Somset 26 F3
**Stoke St Milborough** Shrops 83 L6
**Stokesby** Norfk 93 J2
**Stokesley** N York 142 B5
**Stoke sub Hamdon** Somset 26 C7
**Stoke Talmage** Oxon 58 B7
**Stoke Trister** Somset 27 H5
**Stoke upon Tern** Shrops 98 F6
**Stolford** Somset 25 K3
**Stondon Massey** Essex 60 F7
**Stone** Bucks 58 C5
**Stone** Gloucs 39 G2
**Stone** Rothm 115 K4
**Stone** Staffs 99 K5
**Stone** Worcs 84 F7
**Stone Allerton** Somset 26 B2
**Ston Easton** Somset 26 F2
**Stonebridge** N Som 38 B7

**Stonebridge** Warwks 86 B6
**Stonebroom** Derbys 101 H2
**Stone Cross** Kent 35 J4
**Stonecrouch** Kent 33 J6
**Stoneferry** C KuH 126 D4
**Stonefield Castle Hotel** Ag & B 172 E4
**Stonegate** E Susx 33 H7
**Stonegrave** N York 133 K4
**Stonehaven** Abers 207 G7
**Stonehenge** Wilts 28 C3
**Stonehouse** C Plym 6 C5
**Stonehouse** Gloucs 55 J6
**Stonehouse** S Lans 164 E1
**Stone in Oxney** Kent 21 J1
**Stoneleigh** Warwks 86 D8
**Stonesby** Leics 102 D7
**Stonesfield** Oxon 57 H4
**Stones Green** Essex 62 E3
**Stone Street** Kent 33 G3
**Stone Street** Suffk 93 H6
**Stonewells** Moray 215 G2
**Stoneybridge** W Isls 233 b8
**Stoneyburn** W Loth 176 D5
**Stoneygate** C Leic 87 H3
**Stoneykirk** D & G 144 C4
**Stoney Middleton** Derbys 114 E6
**Stoney Stanton** Leics 86 F4
**Stoney Stoke** Somset 27 G5
**Stoney Stratton** Somset 26 F4
**Stoneywood** C Aber 207 G3
**Stoneywood** Falk 175 L2
**Stonham Aspal** Suffk 78 D3
**Stonnall** Staffs 85 J3
**Stonor** Oxon 42 B3
**Stonton Wyville** Leics 87 K4
**Stony Houghton** Derbys 115 J7
**Stony Stratford** M Keyn 73 L6
**Stoodleigh** Devon 23 K5
**Stoodleigh** Devon 24 E7
**Stop 24 Services** Kent 34 F7
**Stopham** W Susx 18 D2
**Stopsley** Luton 59 J3
**Stornoway** W Isls 232 f2
*Stornoway Airport* W Isls 232 g2
**Storrington** W Susx 18 E3
**Storth** Cumb 129 K4
**Storwood** E R Yk 125 H2
**Stotfield** Moray 214 F1
**Stotfold** C Beds 75 J7
**Stottesdon** Shrops 84 C6
**Stoughton** Leics 87 J3
**Stoughton** Surrey 31 G2
**Stoughton** W Susx 17 L1
**Stoulton** Worcs 70 F4
**Stourbridge** Dudley 84 F6
**Stourbridge Crematorium** Dudley 84 F6
**Stourhead** Wilts 27 H5
**Stourpaine** Dorset 15 G1
**Stourport-on-Severn** Worcs 70 E1
**Stour Provost** Dorset 27 H6
**Stour Row** Dorset 27 J7
**Stourton** Staffs 84 F6
**Stourton** Warwks 72 C6
**Stourton** Wilts 27 H5
**Stourton Caundle** Dorset 27 G7
**Stove** Shet 235 c7
**Stoven** Suffk 93 J6
**Stow** Border 167 G1
**Stow** Lincs 116 E5
**Stow Bardolph** Norfk 90 F3
**Stow Bedon** Norfk 91 L4
**Stowbridge** Norfk 90 E3
**Stow-cum-Quy** Cambs 76 D3
**Stowe** Shrops 82 F8
**Stowe by Chartley** Staffs 100 A6
**Stowell** Somset 27 G6
**Stowey** BaNES 38 E7
**Stowford** Devon 10 C7
**Stowlangtoft** Suffk 77 L2
**Stow Longa** Cambs 75 G1
**Stow Maries** Essex 61 K7
**Stowmarket** Suffk 78 C3
**Stow-on-the-Wold** Gloucs 56 D3
**Stowting** Kent 34 F6
**Stowupland** Suffk 78 C3
**Straanruie** Highld 204 B3
**Strachan** Abers 206 D6
**Strachur** Ag & B 182 F6
**Stradbroke** Suffk 92 F8
**Stradishall** Suffk 77 H4
**Stradsett** Norfk 90 F3
**Stragglethorpe** Lincs 102 E3
**Straiton** Mdloth 177 H5
**Straiton** S Ayrs 153 H2
**Straloch** Abers 207 G2
**Straloch** P & K 195 G4
**Stramshall** Staffs 100 B5
**Strang** IoM 237 c5
**Strangeways** Salfd 113 J2
**Strangford** Herefs 54 E3
**Stranraer** D & G 144 C3
**Stratfield Mortimer** W Berk 42 A7
**Stratfield Saye** Hants 42 B7
**Stratfield Turgis** Hants 42 B7
**Stratford** Gt Lon 45 H3
**Stratford St Andrew** Suffk 79 H3
**Stratford St Mary** Suffk 78 C7
**Stratford sub Castle** Wilts 28 C5
**Stratford Tony** Wilts 28 C6
**Stratford-upon-Avon** Warwks 72 B4
**Strath** Highld 219 J5
**Strathan** Highld 224 D4
**Strathan** Highld 229 J3
**Strathaven** S Lans 164 D1
**Strathblane** Stirlg 175 G3
**Strathcanaird** Highld 220 F2
**Strathcarron** Highld 210 E6
**Strathcoil** Ag & B 181 K2
**Strathdon** Abers 205 H3
**Strathkinness** Fife 187 G4
**Strathloanhead** W Loth 176 C4
**Strathmashie House** Highld 202 F6
**Strathmiglo** Fife 186 C5
**Strathpeffer** Highld 212 D3
**Strathtay** P & K 194 E5
**Strathwhillan** N Ayrs 162 D3
**Strathy** Highld 230 B3
**Strathy Inn** Highld 230 B3
**Strathyre** Stirlg 184 C4
**Stratton** Cnwll 9 G4
**Stratton** Dorset 14 C4
**Stratton** Gloucs 56 A7
**Stratton Audley** Oxon 57 L3
**Stratton-on-the-Fosse** Somset 26 F2
**Stratton St Margaret** Swindn 40 D3
**Stratton St Michael** Norfk 92 E5
**Stratton Strawless** Norfk 106 F7
**Streat** E Susx 19 K3
**Streatham** Gt Lon 44 F5
**Streatley** C Beds 59 H3
**Streatley** W Berk 41 L4
**Street** Devon 12 F5
**Street** Somset 26 C4
**Street Ashton** Warwks 86 F6
**Street Dinas** Shrops 97 M5
**Street End** Kent 34 F4
**Street End** W Susx 18 A5
**Streethay** Staffs 85 K2
**Streetlam** N York 141 H7
**Streetly Crematorium** Wsall 85 J4
**Streetly End** Cambs 76 E5
**Street on the Fosse** Somset 26 F4
**Strelitz** P & K 186 C1
**Strelley** Notts 101 K4
**Strensall** C York 133 K7
**Strensham Services (northbound)** Worcs 70 F6
**Strensham Services (southbound)** Worcs 70 F6
**Stretcholt** Somset 25 L3
**Strete** Devon 7 J6
**Stretford** Traffd 113 H3
**Strethall** Essex 76 C6
**Stretham** Cambs 90 D8
**Strettington** W Susx 18 B4
**Stretton** Derbys 101 H1
**Stretton** Rutlnd 88 D1
**Stretton** Staffs 84 F2
**Stretton** Staffs 100 E7
**Stretton** Warrtn 112 F5
**Stretton Grandison** Herefs 70 B5
**Stretton-on-Dunsmore** Warwks 86 E8
**Stretton on Fosse** Warwks 72 B6
**Stretton Sugwas** Herefs 69 J6
**Stretton under Fosse** Warwks 86 F7
**Stretton Westwood** Shrops 83 L4
**Strichen** Abers 217 H4
**Stringston** Somset 25 J3
**Strixton** Nhants 74 C3
**Stroat** Gloucs 38 E2
**Strollamus** Highld 209 J8
**Stroma** Highld 231 L1
**Stromeferry** Highld 210 D7
**Stromness** Ork 234 b6
**Stronaba** Highld 201 J8
**Stronachlachar** Stirlg 183 L5
**Stronafian** Ag & B 173 H3
**Stronchrubie** Highld 224 F5
**Strone** Ag & B 173 L3
**Strone** Highld 192 B1
**Strone** Highld 212 E8
**Stronmilchan** Ag & B 183 G2
**Stronsay** Ork 234 d5
*Stronsay Airport* Ork 234 d5
**Strontian** Highld 191 G4
**Strood** Medway 46 B6
**Stroud** Gloucs 55 J6
**Stroud** Hants 30 B6
**Stroud Green** Gloucs 55 J6
**Stroxton** Lincs 102 E6
**Struan** Highld 208 E6
**Struan** P & K 194 C4
**Strumpshaw** Norfk 93 H3
**Strutherhill** S Lans 175 K7
**Struthers** Fife 186 F5
**Struy** Highld 212 B6
**Stuartfield** Abers 217 H5
**Stubbers Green** Wsall 85 J3
**Stubbington** Hants 17 G2
**Stubbins** Lancs 122 B6
**Stubton** Lincs 102 E3
**Stuckton** Hants 28 D8
**Studham** C Beds 59 G5
**Studland** Dorset 15 J6
**Studley** Warwks 71 J2
**Studley** Wilts 39 L6
**Studley Roger** N York 132 D5
**Studley Royal** N York 132 D5
**Studley Royal Park & Fountains Abbey** N York 132 D5
**Stuntney** Cambs 90 D7
**Sturmer** Essex 77 G5
**Sturminster Common** Dorset 27 H8
**Sturminster Marshall** Dorset 15 H3
**Sturminster Newton** Dorset 27 H8
**Sturry** Kent 35 G3
**Sturton** N Linc 116 F2
**Sturton by Stow** Lincs 116 E5
**Sturton le Steeple** Notts 116 C5
**Stuston** Suffk 92 D7
**Stutton** N York 124 D3
**Stutton** Suffk 78 D7
**Styal** Ches E 113 J5
**Stynie** Moray 215 H3
**Styrrup** Notts 115 L4
**Succoth** Ag & B 183 K6
**Suckley** Worcs 70 C4
**Sudborough** Nhants 88 D6
**Sudbourne** Suffk 79 J4
**Sudbrook** Lincs 102 F4
**Sudbrook** Mons 38 D3
**Sudbrooke** Lincs 117 G6
**Sudbury** Derbys 100 D6
**Sudbury** Gt Lon 44 D3
**Sudbury** Suffk 77 K6
**Suffield** N York 134 F2
**Suffield** Norfk 106 F6
**Sugnall** Staffs 99 H6
**Sugwas Pool** Herefs 69 J6
**Suisnish** Highld 199 J3
**Sulby** IoM 237 d3
**Sulgrave** Nhants 73 G5
**Sulham** W Berk 41 M5
**Sulhamstead** W Berk 41 M6
**Sullom** Shet 235 c4
**Sullom Voe** Shet 235 c4
**Sully** V Glam 37 J6
*Sumburgh Airport* Shet 235 c8
**Summerbridge** N York 132 C6
**Summercourt** Cnwll 4 D5
**Summerfield** Norfk 105 J5
**Summerhill** Pembks 49 K6
**Summerhouse** Darltn 140 F4
**Summersdale** W Susx 18 B4
**Summerseat** Bury 122 B7
**Summertown** Oxon 57 K6
**Sunbury-on-Thames** Surrey 43 J6
**Sundaywell** D & G 154 E5
**Sunderland** Ag & B 170 E5
**Sunderland** Cumb 147 L7
**Sunderland** Lancs 129 J7
**Sunderland** Sundld 151 J4
**Sunderland Bridge** Dur 151 G7
**Sunderland Crematorium** Sundld 151 J4
**Sundhope** Border 166 E4
**Sundon Park** Luton 59 H3
**Sundridge** Kent 32 E3
**Sunningdale** W & M 42 F6
**Sunninghill** W & M 42 F6
**Sunningwell** Oxon 57 J7
**Sunniside** Dur 150 E7
**Sunniside** Gatesd 150 F3
**Sunnyhill** C Derb 101 G6
**Sunnyhurst** Bl w D 121 K6
**Sunnylaw** Stirlg 185 G7
**Sunnymead** Oxon 57 J6
**Surbiton** Gt Lon 44 D6
**Surfleet** Lincs 103 L6
**Surlingham** Norfk 93 G3
**Surrex** Essex 61 L4
**Surrey & Sussex Crematorium** W Susx 32 B5
**Sustead** Norfk 106 E5
**Susworth** Lincs 116 D2
**Sutcombe** Devon 9 J3
**Sutcombemill** Devon 9 J3
**Sutterby** Lincs 118 E6
**Sutterton** Lincs 103 M5
**Sutton** C Beds 75 J5

**Sutton** C Pete 89 G4
**Sutton** Cambs 90 C7
**Sutton** Devon 7 G7
**Sutton** E Susx 20 A5
**Sutton** Gt Lon 44 E7
**Sutton** Kent 35 J5
**Sutton** N York 124 D5
**Sutton** Norfk 107 H7
**Sutton** Notts 102 C5
**Sutton** Oxon 57 H6
**Sutton** Shrops 83 K2
**Sutton** Shrops 84 D6
**Sutton** Staffs 99 H7
**Sutton** Suffk 79 G5
**Sutton** W Susx 18 D3
**Sutton-at-Hone** Kent 45 K6
**Sutton Bassett** Nhants 87 L5
**Sutton Benger** Wilts 39 L5
**Sutton Bonington** Notts 101 K7
**Sutton Bridge** Lincs 104 D7
**Sutton Cheney** Leics 86 E4
**Sutton Coldfield** Birm 85 K4
**Sutton Coldfield Crematorium** Birm 85 K4
**Sutton Courtenay** Oxon 41 J2
**Sutton cum Lound** Notts 116 B5
**Sutton Green** Surrey 31 G1
**Sutton Howgrave** N York 132 D4
**Sutton-in-Ashfield** Notts 101 J1
**Sutton-in-Craven** N York 122 F2
**Sutton Maddock** Shrops 84 C3
**Sutton Mallet** Somset 26 A4
**Sutton Mandeville** Wilts 27 M5
**Sutton Montis** Somset 26 F6
**Sutton-on-Hull** C KuH 126 E4
**Sutton on Sea** Lincs 119 G5
**Sutton-on-the-Forest** N York 133 J6
**Sutton on the Hill** Derbys 100 E5
**Sutton on Trent** Notts 116 D7
**Sutton St Edmund** Lincs 89 L2
**Sutton St James** Lincs 104 C8
**Sutton St Nicholas** Herefs 69 K5
**Sutton Scotney** Hants 29 J4
**Sutton-under-Brailes** Warwks 72 C6
**Sutton-under-Whitestonecliffe** N York 133 G3
**Sutton upon Derwent** E R Yk 125 G2
**Sutton Valence** Kent 33 L4
**Sutton Veny** Wilts 27 K3
**Sutton Waldron** Dorset 27 K7
**Sutton Weaver** Ches W 112 D5
**Sutton Wick** BaNES 38 E8
**Sutton Wick** Oxon 41 J2
**Swaby** Lincs 118 E6
**Swadlincote** Derbys 100 F8
**Swaffham** Norfk 91 J2
**Swaffham Bulbeck** Cambs 76 D3
**Swaffham Prior** Cambs 76 E2
**Swafield** Norfk 107 G6
**Swainby** N York 141 L6
**Swainsthorpe** Norfk 92 F4
**Swainswick** BaNES 39 H6
**Swalcliffe** Oxon 72 E6
**Swalecliffe** Kent 47 J6
**Swallow** Lincs 117 K2
**Swallow Beck** Lincs 116 F7
**Swallowcliffe** Wilts 27 L6
**Swallowfield** Wokham 42 B7
**Swanage** Dorset 15 J6
**Swanbourne** Bucks 58 D3
**Swan Green** Ches W 113 G6
**Swanland** E R Yk 126 B5
**Swanley** Kent 45 K6
**Swanley Village** Kent 45 K6
**Swanmore** Hants 29 L7
**Swannington** Leics 86 E1
**Swannington** Norfk 106 D8
**Swanpool** Lincs 116 F7
**Swanscombe** Kent 45 L5
**Swansea** Swans 51 J6
*Swansea Airport* Swans 51 H7
**Swansea Crematorium** Swans 51 J5
**Swansea West Services** Swans 51 J5
**Swanton Abbot** Norfk 106 F7
**Swanton Morley** Norfk 106 B8
**Swanton Novers** Norfk 106 B6
**Swan Village** Sandw 85 H5
**Swanwick** Derbys 101 H2
**Swanwick** Hants 17 G1
**Swarby** Lincs 103 H4
**Swardeston** Norfk 92 E3
**Swarkestone** Derbys 101 G6
**Swarland** Nthumb 158 F2
**Swarraton** Hants 29 K4
**Swarthmoor** Cumb 129 G4
**Swaton** Lincs 103 J5
**Swavesey** Cambs 75 L2
**Sway** Hants 16 C3
**Swayfield** Lincs 103 G7
**Swaythling** C Sotn 29 H7
**Sweetham** Devon 11 K5
**Sweethaws** E Susx 32 E7
**Sweets** Cnwll 8 F5
**Sweetshouse** Cnwll 5 H4
**Swefling** Suffk 79 H2
**Swepstone** Leics 86 D2
**Swerford** Oxon 57 G2
**Swettenham** Ches E 113 J7
**Swilland** Suffk 78 E4
**Swillington** Leeds 124 B4
**Swimbridge** Devon 23 K5
**Swimbridge Newland** Devon 23 J5
**Swinbrook** Oxon 56 F5
**Swincliffe** N York 132 C7
**Swinderby** Lincs 116 E8
**Swindon** Gloucs 55 L3
**Swindon** Staffs 84 F5
**Swindon** Swindn 40 D4
**Swine** E R Yk 126 E4
**Swinefleet** E R Yk 125 H6
**Swineshead** Bed 74 F2
**Swineshead** Lincs 103 L4
**Swiney** Highld 227 M2
**Swinford** Leics 87 H7
**Swingfield Minnis** Kent 35 G6
**Swingfield Street** Kent 35 H6
**Swingleton Green** Suffk 77 L5
**Swinhoe** Nthumb 169 J4
**Swinithwaite** N York 131 K2
**Swinside** Cumb 137 H3
**Swinstead** Lincs 103 G7
**Swinton** Border 179 H8
**Swinton** N York 132 C4
**Swinton** N York 134 B5
**Swinton** Rothm 115 J2
**Swinton** Salfd 113 H2
**Swithland** Leics 87 G2
**Swordale** Highld 212 E2
**Swordland** Highld 200 B6
**Swordly** Highld 229 M3
**Swynnerton** Staffs 99 J5
**Swyre** Dorset 13 M5
**Sychtyn** Powys 81 L3
**Syde** Gloucs 55 L5
**Sydenham** Gt Lon 45 G5
**Sydenham** Oxon 58 B7
**Sydenham Damerel** Devon 6 B2
**Syderstone** Norfk 105 K6
**Sydling St Nicholas** Dorset 14 C3
**Sydmonton** Hants 41 J8
**Syerston** Notts 102 C3
**Sykehouse** Donc 124 F6
**Symbister** Shet 235 d4
**Symington** S Ayrs 163 J3
**Symington** S Lans 165 J3
**Symondsbury** Dorset 13 K4
**Symonds Yat (West)** Herefs 54 E5
**Syre** Highld 229 L6
**Syreford** Gloucs 56 B4
**Syresham** Nhants 73 J6
**Syston** Leics 87 J2
**Syston** Lincs 102 F4
**Sytchampton** Worcs 70 E2
**Sywell** Nhants 74 B2

## T

**Tackley** Oxon 57 J4
**Tacolneston** Norfk 92 D4
**Tadcaster** N York 124 D2
**Taddington** Derbys 114 C7
**Tadley** Hants 41 L7
**Tadlow** Cambs 75 K5
**Tadmarton** Oxon 72 E6
**Tadworth** Surrey 44 E8
**Taff's Well** Rhondd 37 H4
**Taibach** Neath 36 B3
**Tain** Highld 223 G5
**Tain** Highld 231 J3
**Tairbeart** W Isls 232 e4
**Takeley** Essex 60 F4
**Takeley Street** Essex 60 E4
**Talaton** Devon 12 D3
**Talbenny** Pembks 48 E5
**Talbot Village** Bmouth 15 K4
**Taleford** Devon 12 E3
**Talerddig** Powys 81 K4
**Talgarreg** Cerdgn 65 L4
**Talgarth** Powys 68 D7
**Talisker** Highld 208 E7
**Talke** Staffs 99 J2
**Talke Pits** Staffs 99 J3
**Talkin** Cumb 148 F4
**Talladale** Highld 219 L7
**Talla Linnfoots** Border 165 M5
**Tallaminnock** S Ayrs 153 J3
**Tallarn Green** Wrexhm 98 C4
**Tallentire** Cumb 147 K7
**Talley** Carmth 66 E7
**Tallington** Lincs 88 F2
**Talmine** Highld 229 J3
**Talog** Carmth 50 D1
**Talsarn** Cerdgn 66 D4
**Talsarnau** Gwynd 95 K5
**Talskiddy** Cnwll 4 E3
**Talwrn** IoA 109 G6
**Tal-y-bont** Cerdgn 80 E5
**Tal-y-Bont** Conwy 109 L7
**Tal-y-bont** Gwynd 95 K7
**Tal-y-bont** Gwynd 109 J7
**Talybont-on-Usk** Powys 53 H4
**Tal-y-Cafn** Conwy 109 M7
**Tal-y-coed** Mons 54 B5
**Talysarn** Gwynd 95 H2
**Tamar Valley Mining District** Devon 6 C3
**Tamerton Foliot** C Plym 6 C4
**Tamworth** Staffs 86 B3
**Tamworth Services** Warwks 86 B4
**Tandridge** Surrey 32 C3
**Tanfield** Dur 150 F4
**Tanfield Lea** Dur 150 F4
**Tangasdale** W Isls 233 b9
**Tangley** Hants 28 F2
**Tangmere** W Susx 18 B4
**Tankerness** Ork 234 c6
**Tankersley** Barns 115 G2
**Tankerton** Kent 47 J6
**Tannach** Highld 231 K6
**Tannachie** Abers 206 E8
**Tannadice** Angus 196 D5
**Tanner's Green** Worcs 85 J8
**Tannington** Suffk 78 F2
**Tannochside** N Lans 175 J6
**Tansley** Derbys 100 F1
**Tansor** Nhants 88 F5
**Tantobie** Dur 150 F4
**Tanworth in Arden** Warwks 71 K1
**Tan-y-groes** Cerdgn 65 J5
**Taobh Tuath** W Isls 232 d5
**Taplow** Bucks 42 E4
**Tarbert** Ag & B 172 B7
**Tarbert** Ag & B 172 E5
**Tarbert** W Isls 232 e4
**Tarbet** Ag & B 183 K6
**Tarbet** Highld 200 B6
**Tarbet** Highld 228 B5
**Tarbolton** S Ayrs 163 K4
**Tarbrax** S Lans 176 D7
**Tardebigge** Worcs 71 H2
**Tarfside** Angus 196 D1
**Tarland** Abers 205 K4
**Tarleton** Lancs 120 F6
**Tarlton** Gloucs 55 L7
**Tarnock** Somset 26 B2
**Tarporley** Ches W 112 D8
**Tarrant Crawford** Dorset 15 H2
**Tarrant Gunville** Dorset 27 L8
**Tarrant Hinton** Dorset 15 H1
**Tarrant Keyneston** Dorset 15 H2
**Tarrant Launceston** Dorset 15 H1
**Tarrant Monkton** Dorset 15 H2
**Tarrant Rawston** Dorset 15 H2
**Tarrant Rushton** Dorset 15 H2
**Tarring Neville** E Susx 19 L5
**Tarrington** Herefs 70 B6
**Tarskavaig** Highld 199 J4
**Tarves** Abers 217 G7
**Tarvin** Ches W 112 C7
**Tasburgh** Norfk 92 E4
**Tatenhill** Staffs 100 D7
**Tathwell** Lincs 118 D5
**Tatsfield** Surrey 32 D2
**Tattenhall** Ches W 98 C2
**Tatterford** Norfk 105 K6
**Tattersett** Norfk 105 K6
**Tattershall** Lincs 103 K2
**Tattershall Thorpe** Lincs 103 L1
**Tattingstone** Suffk 78 D6
**Tattingstone White Horse** Suffk 78 D6
**Tatton Park** Ches E 113 H5
**Tatworth** Somset 13 J2
**Tauchers** Moray 215 J4
**Taunton** Somset 25 K6
**Taunton Deane Crematorium** Somset 25 J6
**Taunton Deane Services** Somset 25 J7
**Taverham** Norfk 92 E2
**Tavernspite** Pembks 49 K5

**Tavistock** Devon 6 C2
**Tavistock** Devon 6 C2
**Taw Green** Devon 10 F5
**Tawstock** Devon 23 J5
**Taxal** Derbys 114 A5
**Tay Bridge** C Dund 187 G2
**Taychreggan Hotel** Ag & B 182 F3
**Tay Forest Park** P & K 194 C4
**Tayinloan** Ag & B 161 H1
**Taynton** Gloucs 55 G4
**Taynton** Oxon 56 E5
**Taynuilt** Ag & B 182 E2
**Tayport** Fife 187 G2
**Tayvallich** Ag & B 172 C2
**Tealby** Lincs 117 J4
**Tealing** Angus 196 C8
**Team Valley** Gatesd 151 G3
**Teangue** Highld 199 K4
**Teanord** Highld 212 F2
**Tebay** Cumb 138 E6
**Tebay Services** Cumb 138 E6
**Tebworth** C Beds 59 G3
**Tedburn St Mary** Devon 11 J6
**Teddington** Gloucs 55 L2
**Teddington** Gt Lon 44 D6
**Tedstone Delamere** Herefs 70 C3
**Tedstone Wafer** Herefs 70 C3
**Teesside Crematorium** Middsb 141 L4
**Teeton** Nhants 73 K1
**Teffont Evias** Wilts 27 M5
**Teffont Magna** Wilts 27 M5
**Tegryn** Pembks 65 H7
**Teigh** Rutlnd 88 C1
**Teigngrace** Devon 7 K2
**Teignmouth** Devon 12 B7
**Teindside** Border 166 F7
**Telford** Wrekin 84 C2
**Telford Crematorium** Wrekin 84 D2
**Telford Services** Shrops 84 D2
**Tellisford** Somset 27 J1
**Telscombe** E Susx 19 L5
**Tempar** P & K 193 L5
**Templand** D & G 155 J5
**Temple** Cnwll 5 J2
**Temple** Mdloth 177 J6
**Temple Bar** Cerdgn 66 C4
**Temple Cloud** BaNES 38 F8
**Templecombe** Somset 27 G6
**Temple Grafton** Warwks 71 K4
**Temple Guiting** Gloucs 56 C3
**Temple Hirst** N York 124 F5
**Temple Normanton** Derbys 115 H7
**Temple of Fiddes** Abers 206 F8
**Temple Sowerby** Cumb 138 E2
**Templeton** Devon 11 K3
**Templeton** Pembks 49 J5
**Templetown** Dur 150 E5
**Tempsford** C Beds 75 H4
**Tenbury Wells** Worcs 69 L2
**Tenby** Pembks 49 J7
**Tendring** Essex 62 D3
**Tendring Green** Essex 62 D3
**Tendring Heath** Essex 62 D3
**Ten Mile Bank** Norfk 90 E4
**Tenterden** Kent 34 B7
**Terling** Essex 61 J5
**Ternhill** Shrops 98 F6
**Terregles** D & G 155 G6
**Terrington** N York 133 K5
**Terrington St Clement** Norfk 104 E7
**Terrington St John** Norfk 90 D2
**Teston** Kent 33 J3
**Testwood** Hants 29 G8
**Tetbury** Gloucs 39 K2
**Tetchill** Shrops 98 B6
**Tetcott** Devon 9 J5
**Tetford** Lincs 118 D6
**Tetney** Lincs 118 D2
**Tetsworth** Oxon 58 B7
**Tettenhall** Wolves 84 F4
**Tettenhall Wood** Wolves 84 F4
**Teversal** Notts 101 J1
**Teversham** Cambs 76 C3
**Teviothead** Border 156 D2
**Tewin** Herts 59 L5
**Tewkesbury** Gloucs 55 K2
**Teynham** Kent 34 C3
**Thackley** C Brad 123 H3
**Thainstone** Abers 206 E2
**Thakeham** W Susx 18 F3
**Thame** Oxon 58 B6
**Thames Ditton** Surrey 44 D6
**Thamesmead** Gt Lon 45 J4
**Thamesport** Medway 46 E5
**Thanet Crematorium** Kent 35 K2
**Thanington** Kent 34 F4
**Thankerton** S Lans 165 J2
**Tharston** Norfk 92 E5
**Thatcham** W Berk 41 K6
**Thaxted** Essex 60 F2
**Theakston** N York 132 D3
**Thealby** N Linc 125 K6
**Theale** Somset 26 C3
**Theale** W Berk 41 M6
**Thearne** E R Yk 126 D3
**The Beeches** Gloucs 56 B7
**Theberton** Suffk 79 J2
**The Braes** Highld 209 H7
*The Broads* 93 K2
**The Brunt** E Loth 178 E4
**The Bungalow** IoM 237 d4
**The Burf** Worcs 70 E2
**The City** Bucks 42 C2
**The Common** Wilts 28 E5
**Theddingworth** Leics 87 J6
**Theddlethorpe All Saints** Lincs 118 F4
**Theddlethorpe St Helen** Lincs 119 G4
**The Deep** C KuH 126 D5
**The Den** N Ayrs 174 C7
**The Forstal** Kent 34 D6
**The Green** Cumb 128 E3
**The Green** Essex 61 J4
**The Green** N York 143 G6
**The Green** Wilts 27 K5
**The Headland** Hartpl 151 M7
**The Hill** Cumb 128 E3
**The Lee** Bucks 58 E6
**The Lhen** IoM 237 d2
**Thelnetham** Suffk 92 B7
**The Lochs** Moray 215 G2
**Thelveton** Norfk 92 E7
**Thelwall** Warrtn 112 F4
**Themelthorpe** Norfk 106 C7
**The Middles** Dur 150 F5
**The Moor** Kent 33 K7
**The Mumbles** Swans 51 J7
**The Murray** S Lans 175 H7
**The Neuk** Abers 206 D5
**Thenford** Nhants 73 G6
**The Reddings** Gloucs 55 K4
**Therfield** Herts 75 L6
**The Ross** P & K 185 G3
**The Spring** Warwks 86 C8
**The Stocks** Kent 21 H1
**The Strand** Wilts 39 L8
**Thetford** Norfk 91 K6
**Thetford Forest Park** 91 J5
**Theydon Bois** Essex 60 D7
**Thickwood** Wilts 39 J5
**Thimbleby** Lincs 118 C7
**Thimbleby** N York 141 K7
**Thingwall** Wirral 111 J5
**Thirkleby** N York 133 G4
**Thirlby** N York 133 G3
**Thirlestane** Border 178 C8
**Thirn** N York 132 C3
**Thirsk** N York 132 F3
**Thistleton** Lancs 120 E3
**Thistleton** Rutlnd 102 E8
**Thistley Green** Suffk 90 F7
**Thixendale** N York 134 C7
**Thockrington** Nthumb 158 B6
**Tholomas Drove** Cambs 90 B3
**Tholthorpe** N York 133 G6
**Thomastown** Abers 216 B6
**Thompson** Norfk 91 K4
**Thongsbridge** Kirk 123 H8
**Thoralby** N York 131 J3
**Thoresway** Lincs 117 K3
**Thorganby** Lincs 117 K3
**Thorganby** N York 125 G3
**Thorgill** N York 142 E7
**Thorington** Suffk 93 J8
**Thorington Street** Suffk 78 B7
**Thorlby** N York 131 H8
**Thorley** Herts 60 D4
**Thorley Street** IoW 16 D5
**Thormanby** N York 133 G5
**Thornaby-on-Tees** S on T 141 K4
**Thornage** Norfk 106 C5
**Thornborough** Bucks 73 L7
**Thornborough** N York 132 D4
**Thornbury** C Brad 123 J4
**Thornbury** Devon 9 K3
**Thornbury** Herefs 70 B3
**Thornbury** S Glos 38 F3
**Thornby** Nhants 87 J7
**Thorncliff** Staffs 100 A2
**Thorncliffe Crematorium** Cumb 128 E5
**Thorncombe** Dorset 13 J2
**Thorndon** Suffk 78 D1
**Thorndon Cross** Devon 10 D6
**Thorne** Donc 125 G7
**Thorner** Leeds 124 B3
**Thorne St Margaret** Somset 25 H7
**Thorney** C Pete 89 K3
**Thorney** Notts 116 E6
**Thorney** Somset 26 B6
**Thorney Hill** Hants 16 A3
**Thorney Island** W Susx 17 L2
**Thornfalcon** Somset 25 L6
**Thornford** Dorset 26 E8
**Thorngrafton** Nthumb 149 K2
**Thorngumbald** E R Yk 126 F5
**Thornham** Norfk 105 H4
**Thornham Magna** Suffk 78 D1
**Thornham Parva** Suffk 92 D8
**Thornhaugh** C Pete 88 F4
**Thornhill** C Sotn 29 J8
**Thornhill** Cumb 136 D5
**Thornhill** D & G 154 F3
**Thornhill** Derbys 114 D5
**Thornhill** Kirk 123 K6
**Thornhill** Stirlg 184 E7
**Thornholme** E R Yk 135 H6
**Thornicombe** Dorset 15 G2
**Thornington** Nthumb 168 D3
**Thornley** Dur 150 E7
**Thornley** Dur 151 J6
**Thornliebank** E Rens 174 F6
**Thorns** Suffk 77 G4
**Thornsett** Derbys 114 A4
**Thornthwaite** Cumb 137 H3
**Thornthwaite** N York 132 B7
**Thornton** Angus 196 C6
**Thornton** Bucks 73 L7
**Thornton** C Brad 123 G4
**Thornton** E R Yk 125 H2
**Thornton** Fife 186 E7
**Thornton** Lancs 120 D3
**Thornton** Leics 86 F3
**Thornton** Middsb 141 L4
**Thornton** Nthumb 179 K8
**Thornton Curtis** N Linc 126 D6
**Thornton Garden of Rest Crematorium** Sefton 111 K2
**Thorntonhall** S Lans 175 G7
**Thornton Heath** Gt Lon 44 F6
**Thornton Hough** Wirral 111 J5
**Thornton-in-Craven** N York 122 D2
**Thornton in Lonsdale** N York 130 D5
**Thornton-le-Beans** N York 132 F2
**Thornton-le-Clay** N York 133 L6
**Thornton-le-Dale** N York 134 C3
**Thornton le Moor** Lincs 117 H3
**Thornton-le-Moor** N York 132 F2
**Thornton-le-Moors** Ches W 112 C6
**Thornton-le-Street** N York 132 F3
**Thorntonloch** E Loth 178 F4
**Thornton Rust** N York 131 H2
**Thornton Steward** N York 132 B3
**Thornton Watlass** N York 132 C3
**Thornydykes** Border 178 D8
**Thornythwaite** Cumb 137 L3
**Thoroton** Notts 102 C4
**Thorp Arch** Leeds 124 C2
**Thorpe** Derbys 100 D3
**Thorpe** E R Yk 126 B2
**Thorpe** N York 131 J6
**Thorpe** Notts 102 C3
**Thorpe** Surrey 43 G6
**Thorpe Abbotts** Norfk 92 E7
**Thorpe Arnold** Leics 102 C7
**Thorpe Audlin** Wakefd 124 D7
**Thorpe Bassett** N York 134 D5
**Thorpe Bay** Sthend 46 E3
**Thorpe by Water** Rutlnd 88 C4
**Thorpe Constantine** Staffs 86 C2
**Thorpe End** Norfk 93 G2
**Thorpe Green** Essex 62 E4
**Thorpe Green** Suffk 77 L4
**Thorpe Hesley** Rothm 115 G3
**Thorpe in Balne** Donc 124 F7
**Thorpe Langton** Leics 87 L5
**Thorpe Lea** Surrey 43 G6
**Thorpe-le-Soken** Essex 62 E4
**Thorpe le Street** E R Yk 125 K2
**Thorpe Malsor** Nhants 88 B7
**Thorpe Mandeville** Nhants 73 G5
**Thorpe Market** Norfk 106 F5
**Thorpe Marriot** Norfk 92 E1
**Thorpe Morieux** Suffk 77 L4
**Thorpeness** Suffk 79 K3
**Thorpe on the Hill** Lincs 116 E7
**Thorpe Park** Surrey 43 G6
**Thorpe St Andrew** Norfk 92 F2
**Thorpe St Peter** Lincs 104 D1
**Thorpe Salvin** Rothm 115 K5

**Thorpe Satchville** Leics 87 K2
**Thorpe Thewles** S on T 141 J3
**Thorpe Tilney** Lincs 103 J2
**Thorpe Underwood** N York 133 G7
**Thorpe Waterville** Nhants 88 E7
**Thorpe Willoughby** N York 124 E4
**Thorrington** Essex 62 C4
**Thorverton** Devon 11 L4
**Thrandeston** Suffk 92 D7
**Thrapston** Nhants 88 E7
**Threapwood** Ches W 98 C4
**Threapwood** Staffs 100 B4
**Threave** S Ayrs 163 J7
**Three Bridges** W Susx 32 B5
**Three Chimneys** Kent 33 L5
**Three Cocks** Powys 68 D6
**Three Counties Crematorium** Essex 61 J3
**Three Crosses** Swans 51 H6
**Three Cups Corner** E Susx 20 D2
**Threekingham** Lincs 103 H5
**Three Leg Cross** E Susx 33 H6
**Three Legged Cross** Dorset 15 K2
**Three Mile Cross** Wokham 42 B6
**Threemilestone** Cnwll 3 K3
**Threemiletown** W Loth 176 E3
**Three Oaks** E Susx 21 G3
**Threlkeld** Cumb 137 J3
**Threshers Bush** Essex 60 D6
**Threshfield** N York 131 J6
**Thrigby** Norfk 93 K2
**Thrintoft** N York 132 D2
**Thriplow** Cambs 76 B5
**Throcking** Herts 60 B3
**Throckley** N u Ty 150 E2
**Throckmorton** Worcs 71 H4
**Throop** Bmouth 15 L4
**Thropton** Nthumb 158 C2
**Throsk** Stirlg 176 B1
**Throughgate** D & G 154 F5
**Throwleigh** Devon 11 G6
**Throwley Forstal** Kent 34 C4
**Thrumpton** Notts 101 J6
**Thrumster** Highld 231 L6
**Thrunscoe** NE Lin 127 H8
**Thrupp** Gloucs 55 K7
**Thrussington** Leics 87 J1
**Thruxton** Hants 28 F3
**Thruxton** Herefs 69 J7
**Thrybergh** Rothm 115 J3
**Thulston** Derbys 101 H6
**Thundersley** Essex 46 C3
**Thurcaston** Leics 87 H2
**Thurcroft** Rothm 115 J4
**Thurgarton** Norfk 106 E5
**Thurgarton** Notts 102 B3
**Thurgoland** Barns 114 F2
**Thurlaston** Leics 87 G4
**Thurlaston** Warwks 72 F1
**Thurlbear** Somset 25 K7
**Thurlby** Lincs 89 G1
**Thurlby** Lincs 102 E1
**Thurlby** Lincs 119 G6
**Thurleigh** Bed 74 F3
**Thurlestone** Devon 7 G7
**Thurloxton** Somset 25 L5
**Thurlstone** Barns 114 E2
**Thurlton** Norfk 93 J4
**Thurmaston** Leics 87 H2
**Thurnby** Leics 87 J3
**Thurne** Norfk 93 J1
**Thurnham** Kent 33 K2
**Thurning** Nhants 88 F6
**Thurning** Norfk 106 C6
**Thurnscoe** Barns 115 J1
*Thurrock Services* Thurr 45 L4
**Thursby** Cumb 148 B5
**Thursford** Norfk 106 B5
**Thursley** Surrey 30 E4
**Thurso** Highld 231 G2
**Thurstaston** Wirral 111 H5
**Thurston** Suffk 77 L2
**Thurstonfield** Cumb 148 B4
**Thurstonland** Kirk 123 H7
**Thurton** Norfk 93 G4
**Thurvaston** Derbys 100 E5
**Thuxton** Norfk 92 B3
**Thwaite** N York 139 K7
**Thwaite** Suffk 78 D2
**Thwaite Head** Cumb 129 H2
**Thwaite St Mary** Norfk 93 G4
**Thwing** E R Yk 135 G5
**Tibbermore** P & K 185 L3
**Tibbers** D & G 154 E3
**Tibberton** Gloucs 55 H4
**Tibberton** Worcs 70 F3
**Tibberton** Wrekin 99 G7
**Tibbie Shiels Inn** Border 166 C5
**Tibenham** Norfk 92 D5
**Tibshelf** Derbys 101 H1
*Tibshelf Services* Derbys 101 H1
**Tibthorpe** E R Yk 134 E7
**Ticehurst** E Susx 33 H7
**Tichborne** Hants 29 L5
**Tickencote** Rutlnd 88 E2
**Tickenham** N Som 38 C6
**Tickhill** Donc 115 L3
**Ticklerton** Shrops 83 J5
**Ticknall** Derbys 101 G7
**Tickton** E R Yk 126 D3
**Tidcombe** Wilts 40 F8
**Tiddington** Oxon 57 M6
**Tiddington** Warwks 72 B4
**Tidebrook** E Susx 33 G7
**Tideford** Cnwll 6 A4
**Tidenham** Gloucs 38 E2
**Tideswell** Derbys 114 D6
**Tidmarsh** W Berk 41 M5
**Tidmington** Warwks 72 C6
**Tidworth** Wilts 28 E2
**Tiers Cross** Pembks 48 F5
**Tiffield** Nhants 73 K4
**Tigerton** Angus 196 E4
**Tigh a' Ghearraidh** W Isls 233 b6
**Tigharry** W Isls 233 b6
**Tighnabruaich** Ag & B 173 G4
**Tigley** Devon 7 H4
**Tilbrook** Cambs 74 F2
**Tilbury** Thurr 45 M5
**Tile Cross** Birm 85 L6
**Tile Hill** Covtry 86 C7
**Tilehurst** Readg 42 A5
**Tilford** Surrey 30 E3
**Tilgate** W Susx 31 L4
**Tilham Street** Somset 26 E4
**Tillicoultry** Clacks 185 J7
**Tillietudlem** S Lans 164 F1
**Tillingham** Essex 62 B7
**Tillington** Herefs 69 J5
**Tillington** W Susx 30 F6
**Tillington Common** Herefs 69 J5
**Tillybirloch** Abers 206 D4
**Tillyfourie** Abers 206 C3
**Tillygreig** Abers 207 G2
**Tillyrie** P & K 186 B6
**Tilmanstone** Kent 35 J4
**Tilney All Saints** Norfk 104 F8
**Tilney High End** Norfk 104 E8
**Tilney St Lawrence** Norfk 90 D2
**Tilshead** Wilts 28 B2
**Tilstock** Shrops 98 D5
**Tilston** Ches W 98 C3
**Tilstone Fearnall** Ches W 98 E1
**Tilsworth** C Beds 59 G3
**Tilton on the Hill** Leics 87 L3
**Tiltups End** Gloucs 39 J2
**Timberland** Lincs 103 J2
**Timbersbrook** Ches E 113 K8
**Timberscombe** Somset 24 E3
**Timble** N York 132 B8
**Timpanheck** D & G 156 B7
**Timperley** Traffd 113 H4
**Timsbury** BaNES 38 F8
**Timsbury** Hants 29 G6
**Timsgarry** W Isls 232 d2
**Timsgearraidh** W Isls 232 d2
**Timworth** Suffk 77 J2
**Timworth Green** Suffk 77 J2
**Tincleton** Dorset 14 E4
**Tindale** Cumb 149 G3
**Tingewick** Bucks 58 A2
**Tingrith** C Beds 59 G2
*Tingwall Airport* Shet 235 c6
**Tingwell** Ork 234 c5
**Tinhay** Devon 9 K7
**Tinsley** Sheff 115 H4
**Tinsley Green** W Susx 32 B5
**Tintagel** Cnwll 8 E7
**Tintern** Mons 54 D7
**Tintinhull** Somset 26 D7
**Tintwistle** Derbys 114 A3
**Tinwald** D & G 155 H5
**Tinwell** Rutlnd 88 E3
**Tipton** Sandw 85 G5
**Tipton Green** Sandw 85 G5
**Tipton St John** Devon 12 E4
**Tiptree** Essex 61 L5
**Tiptree Heath** Essex 61 L5
**Tirabad** Powys 67 J6
**Tiree** Ag & B 188 D7
*Tiree Airport* Ag & B 188 C7
**Tiretigan** Ag & B 172 C6
**Tirley** Gloucs 55 J3
**Tiroran** Ag & B 181 G2
**Tirphil** Caerph 53 H7
**Tirril** Cumb 138 D2
**Tisbury** Wilts 27 L5
**Tissington** Derbys 100 D3
**Titchberry** Devon 22 C6
**Titchfield** Hants 17 G2
**Titchmarsh** Nhants 88 E7
**Titchwell** Norfk 105 J4
**Tithby** Notts 102 B5
**Titley** Herefs 69 G3
**Titsey** Surrey 32 D3
**Titson** Cnwll 9 H5
**Tittensor** Staffs 99 K5
**Tittleshall** Norfk 105 L7
**Titton** Worcs 70 E1
**Tiverton** Ches W 98 D1
**Tiverton** Devon 24 E8
**Tivetshall St Margaret** Norfk 92 E6
**Tivetshall St Mary** Norfk 92 E6
**Tixall** Staffs 99 L7
**Tixover** Rutlnd 88 E4
**Toab** Shet 235 c8
**Tobermory** Ag & B 189 L5
**Toberonochy** Ag & B 181 L5
**Tobha Mòr** W Isls 233 b7
**Tocher** Abers 216 D7
**Tochieneal** Moray 215 L2
**Tockenham** Wilts 40 B4
**Tockholes** Bl w D 121 K6
**Tockington** S Glos 38 E3
**Tockwith** N York 133 G8
**Todber** Dorset 27 J7
**Toddington** C Beds 59 G3
**Toddington** Gloucs 56 B2
*Toddington Services* C Beds 59 G3
**Todenham** Gloucs 72 B7
**Todhills** Angus 196 C8
*Todhills Rest Area* Cumb 148 C3
**Todmorden** Calder 122 D5
**Todwick** Rothm 115 J5
**Toft** Cambs 75 L4
**Toft** Lincs 88 F1
**Toft** Shet 235 c3
**Toft Hill** Dur 140 E2
**Toft Monks** Norfk 93 J4
**Toft next Newton** Lincs 117 H4
**Toftrees** Norfk 105 L6
**Togston** Nthumb 159 G2
**Tokavaig** Highld 199 J3
**Tokers Green** Oxon 42 B5
**Tolastadh bho Thuath** W Isls 232 g2
**Tolland** Somset 25 H5
**Tollard Royal** Wilts 27 L7
**Toll Bar** Donc 124 E8
**Toller Fratrum** Dorset 14 B3
**Toller Porcorum** Dorset 14 B3
**Tollerton** N York 133 H6
**Tollerton** Notts 101 L5
**Tollesbury** Essex 62 A6
**Tolleshunt D'Arcy** Essex 61 L5
**Tolleshunt Knights** Essex 61 L5
**Tolleshunt Major** Essex 61 L5
**Toll of Birness** Abers 217 J7
**Tolpuddle** Dorset 14 E4
**Tolworth** Gt Lon 44 D6
**Tomatin** Highld 213 J8
**Tomchrasky** Highld 201 K3
**Tomdoun** Highld 201 H5
**Tomich** Highld 211 L8
**Tomich** Highld 212 E5
**Tomich** Highld 222 F7
**Tomich** Highld 226 A7
**Tomintoul** Moray 204 E2
**Tomnacross** Highld 212 D6
**Tomnavoulin** Moray 204 F1
**Tonbridge** Kent 33 G4
**Tondu** Brdgnd 36 D4
**Tonedale** Somset 25 H6
**Tong** C Brad 123 J4
**Tong** Kent 34 C4
**Tong** Shrops 84 E3
**Tong** W Isls 232 g2
**Tonge** Leics 101 H7
**Tongham** Surrey 30 E2
**Tongland** D & G 146 C4
**Tong Norton** Shrops 84 E2
**Tongue** Highld 229 J4
**Tongwynlais** Cardif 37 H4
**Tonmawr** Neath 36 C2
**Tonna** Neath 52 B7
**Tonwell** Herts 60 B5
**Tonypandy** Rhondd 36 F3
**Tonyrefail** Rhondd 36 F3
**Toot Baldon** Oxon 57 K7
**Toot Hill** Essex 60 E7
**Toothill** Swindn 40 C4
**Tooting** Gt Lon 44 F5
**Tooting Bec** Gt Lon 44 F5
**Topcliffe** N York 132 F4
**Topcroft** Norfk 92 F5
**Topcroft Street** Norfk 92 F5
**Toppesfield** Essex 77 G6
**Toprow** Norfk 92 E4
**Topsham** Devon 12 C5
**Torbeg** N Ayrs 162 A4
**Torboll** Highld 223 G2
**Torbreck** Highld 213 G6
**Torbryan** Devon 7 J3
**Torcastle** Highld 192 B2
**Torcross** Devon 7 J7
**Tore** Highld 212 F4
**Torinturk** Ag & B 172 D5
**Torksey** Lincs 116 D5
**Torlundy** Highld 192 B2
**Tormarton** S Glos 39 H5
**Tormore** N Ayrs 161 M3
**Tornagrain** Highld 213 J4
**Tornaveen** Abers 206 C4
**Torness** Highld 212 E8
**Toronto** Dur 140 F2
**Torpenhow** Cumb 147 L6
**Torphichen** W Loth 176 C4

Torphins Abers 206 C5
Torpoint Cnwll 6 C5
Torquay Torbay 7 L3
Torquay Crematorium Torbay 7 K3
Torquhan Border 177 L8
Torran Highld 209 J5
Torrance E Duns 175 H4
Torranyard N Ayrs 163 J1
Torridon Highld 210 D3
Torridon House Highld 210 D3
Torrin Highld 199 J2
Torrisdale Ag & B 161 K3
Torrisdale Highld 229 K3
Torrish Highld 227 G5
Torrisholme Lancs 129 K6
Torrobull Highld 226 A7
Torry C Aber 207 H4
Torryburn Fife 176 D2
Torteval Guern 236 b4
Torthorwald D & G 155 H6
Tortington W Susx 18 D5
Torton Worcs 84 E8
Tortworth S Glos 39 G2
Torvaig Highld 209 H5
Torver Cumb 137 J7
Torwood Falk 175 L2
Torwoodlee Border 167 G2
Torworth Notts 116 A4
Toscaig Highld 209 L6
Toseland Cambs 75 J3
Tosside Lancs 130 E7
Tostock Suffk 77 L2
Totaig Highld 208 C4
Tote Highld 208 F5
Tote Highld 209 H3
Totland IoW 16 D5
Totley Sheff 114 F5
Totnes Devon 7 J4
Toton Notts 101 J5
Totronald Ag & B 188 F5
Totscore Highld 208 F2
Tottenham Gt Lon 45 G3
Tottenhill Norfk 90 F2
Totteridge Gt Lon 44 E2
Totternhoe C Beds 59 G4
Tottington Bury 122 B7
Totton Hants 29 G8
Toulton Somset 25 J5
Toulvaddie Highld 223 J5
Tovil Kent 33 K3
Toward Ag & B 173 K5
Toward Quay Ag & B 173 J5
Towcester Nhants 73 K5
Towednack Cnwll 2 E4
Tower of London Gt Lon 45 G4
Towersey Oxon 58 B6
Towie Abers 205 K3
Tow Law Dur 150 E6
Town End Cambs 90 B4
Townend W Duns 174 D3
Townhead Barns 114 D2
Townhead D & G 155 H4
Townhead of Greenlaw D & G 146 C3
Townhill Fife 176 F1
Town Littleworth E Susx 19 L3
Towns End Hants 41 K8
Townshend Cnwll 3 G5
Town Street Suffk 91 H6
Town Yetholm Border 168 B4
Towthorpe C York 133 K7
Towton N York 124 D3
Towyn Conwy 110 D5
Toxteth Lpool 111 K4
Toynton All Saints Lincs 118 E8
Toy's Hill Kent 32 E3
Trabboch E Ayrs 163 K5
Trabbochburn E Ayrs 163 L5
Tradespark Highld 213 K3
Trafford Park Traffd 113 H3
Trallong Powys 52 E3
Tranent E Loth 177 L4
Tranmere Wirral 111 J4
Trantelbeg Highld 230 C5
Trantlemore Highld 230 C5
Trap Carmth 51 J2
Traprain E Loth 178 D4
Traquair Border 166 E3
Trawden Lancs 122 D3
Trawsfynydd Gwynd 96 A5
Trealaw Rhondd 36 F3
Treales Lancs 120 F4
Trearddur Bay IoA 108 C5
Treaslane Highld 208 F4
Trebetherick Cnwll 4 E1
Treborough Somset 24 F4
Trebullett Cnwll 5 M1
Treburley Cnwll 6 A1
Trecastle Powys 52 D3
Trecwn Pembks 64 D7
Trecynon Rhondd 52 F7
Tredegar Blae G 53 H6
Tredington Gloucs 55 K3
Tredington Warwks 72 C5
Tredunnock Mons 38 B2
Treen Cnwll 2 D6
Treeton Rothm 115 H4
Trefasser Pembks 64 C6
Trefecca Powys 53 H2
Trefeglwys Powys 81 L5
Treffgarne Pembks 49 G3
Treffgarne Owen Pembks 48 E3
Trefforest Rhondd 37 G3
Trefilan Cerdgn 66 D3
Trefin Pembks 64 B7
Trefnant Denbgs 110 E7
Trefonen Shrops 97 K6
Trefor Gwynd 94 F4
Trefriw Conwy 109 L8
Tregadillett Cnwll 9 H7
Tregare Mons 54 B6
Tregaron Cerdgn 66 F3
Tregarth Gwynd 109 H7
Tregeare Cnwll 9 H7
Tregeiriog Wrexhm 97 J5
Tregele IoA 108 D3
Treglemais Pembks 48 D2
Tregonetha Cnwll 4 E3
Tregonning & Gwinear Mining District Cnwll 3 G5
Tregony Cnwll 4 E6
Tregorrick Cnwll 4 F5
Tregoyd Powys 68 E6
Tre-groes Cerdgn 65 L5
Tregynon Powys 82 C4
Tre-gynwr Carmth 50 E2
Trehafod Rhondd 37 G3
Trehan Cnwll 6 B4
Treharris Myr Td 37 H2
Treherbert Rhondd 52 E7
Trekenner Cnwll 6 A1
Treknow Cnwll 8 D7
Trelawnyd Flints 110 F5
Trelech Carmth 65 J7
Treleddyd-fawr Pembks 48 C2
Trelewis Myr Td 37 H2
Trelights Cnwll 8 C8
Trelill Cnwll 5 G1
Trellech Mons 54 D6
Trelogan Flints 110 F5
Tremadog Gwynd 95 K4
Tremail Cnwll 8 F7
Tremain Cerdgn 65 H5
Tremaine Cnwll 9 G6
Tremar Cnwll 5 K3
Trematon Cnwll 6 B4
Tremeirchion Denbgs 110 F6
Trenance Cnwll 4 D3
Trenance Cnwll 4 E2
Trench Wrekin 84 C2
Trenear Cnwll 3 H5
Treneglos Cnwll 9 G7
Trent Dorset 26 E7
Trentham C Stke 99 K4
Trentishoe Devon 23 K2
Trent Vale C Stke 99 K4
Treoes V Glam 36 E5
Treorchy Rhondd 36 E2
Trequite Cnwll 5 G1
Trerhyngyll V Glam 36 F5
Trerulefoot Cnwll 5 M4
Tresaith Cerdgn 65 J4
Tresco IoS 2 a1
Trescowe Cnwll 3 G5
Tresean Cnwll 4 C4
Tresham Gloucs 39 H3
Treshnish Isles Ag & B 189 G7
Tresillian Cnwll 4 D6
Treskinnick Cross Cnwll 9 G5
Tresmeer Cnwll 9 G7
Tresparrett Cnwll 8 F6
Tressait P & K 194 C4
Tresta Shet 235 c5
Tresta Shet 235 e3
Treswell Notts 116 C5
Treswithian Downs Crematorium Cnwll 3 H3
Tre Taliesin Cerdgn 80 E5
Trethevey Cnwll 8 E6
Trethewey Cnwll 2 C6
Trethurgy Cnwll 5 G5
Tretire Herefs 54 D4
Tretower Powys 53 J4
Treuddyn Flints 97 K2
Trevalga Cnwll 8 E6
Trevalyn Wrexhm 98 B2
Trevarrian Cnwll 4 D3
Treveal Cnwll 4 C4
Treveighan Cnwll 8 E8
Trevellas Downs Cnwll 3 J2
Trevelmond Cnwll 5 K3
Treverva Cnwll 3 K5
Trevescan Cnwll 2 C6
Treviscoe Cnwll 4 E5
Trevone Cnwll 4 D2
Trevor Wrexhm 97 L4
Trewalder Cnwll 8 E7
Trewarmett Cnwll 8 E7
Trewavas Mining District Cnwll 3 G6
Trewen Cnwll 9 H7
Trewint Cnwll 9 G8
Trewithian Cnwll 4 D7
Trewoon Cnwll 4 F5
Treyford W Susx 30 D7
Trimdon Dur 151 J7
Trimdon Colliery Dur 151 J7
Trimdon Grange Dur 151 J7
Trimingham Norfk 107 G5
Trimley St Martin Suffk 78 F6
Trimley St Mary Suffk 79 G7
Trimsaran Carmth 50 F5
Trimstone Devon 23 H3
Trinafour P & K 194 B4
Tring Herts 58 F5
Trinity Angus 196 F4
Trinity Jersey 236 d6
Trinity Gask P & K 185 K4
Triscombe Somset 25 J4
Trislaig Highld 191 L2
Trispen Cnwll 4 D5
Tritlington Nthumb 158 F4
Trochry P & K 194 F7
Troedyraur Cerdgn 65 K5
Troedyrhiw Myr Td 53 G7
Trois Bois Jersey 236 c6
Troon Cnwll 3 H4
Troon S Ayrs 163 H3
Tropical World Roundhay Park Leeds 123 L3
Trossachs Stirlg 184 B5
Trossachs Pier Stirlg 184 B6
Troston Suffk 91 K8
Trotshill Worcs 70 F4
Trottiscliffe Kent 33 H2
Trotton W Susx 30 D6
Troutbeck Cumb 137 L6
Troutbeck Bridge Cumb 137 L7
Troway Derbys 115 H5
Trowbridge Wilts 39 J8
Trowell Notts 101 J4
Trowell Services Notts 101 J4
Trowse Newton Norfk 92 F3
Trudoxhill Somset 27 H3
Trull Somset 25 K6
Trumpan Highld 208 C3
Trumpet Herefs 70 B6
Trumpington Cambs 76 C4
Trunch Norfk 107 G5
Truro Cnwll 4 C6
Trusham Devon 11 K7
Trusley Derbys 100 E5
Trusthorpe Lincs 119 G5
Trysull Staffs 84 F5
Tubney Oxon 57 H7
Tuckenhay Devon 7 J5
Tuckhill Shrops 84 E6
Tuckingmill Cnwll 3 H3
Tuckingmill Wilts 27 L5
Tuckton Bmouth 15 L4
Tuddenham Suffk 77 G1
Tuddenham Suffk 78 E5
Tudeley Kent 33 G4
Tudhoe Dur 151 G7
Tudweiliog Gwynd 94 D5
Tuffley Gloucs 55 J5
Tufton Hants 29 J3
Tufton Pembks 49 H2
Tugby Leics 87 L4
Tugford Shrops 83 L6
Tughall Nthumb 169 J4
Tullibody Clacks 185 H7
Tullich Abers 205 J6
Tullich Highld 212 F8
Tullich Highld 223 J6
Tulliemet P & K 194 F5
Tulloch Abers 216 F7
Tullochgorm Ag & B 182 D7
Tulloch Station Highld 192 F1
Tullymurdoch P & K 195 J5
Tullynessle Abers 206 B2
Tulse Hill Gt Lon 44 F5
Tumble Carmth 51 G3
Tumby Lincs 103 L1
Tumby Woodside Lincs 103 L2
Tummel Bridge P & K 194 B5
Tunbridge Wells Kent 33 G5
Tundergarth D & G 155 L6
Tunga W Isls 232 g2
Tunley BaNES 39 G8
Tunstall E R Yk 127 H4
Tunstall Kent 34 B3
Tunstall Lancs 130 B5
Tunstall N York 140 F7
Tunstall Norfk 93 J2
Tunstall Staffs 99 H6
Tunstall Suffk 79 H4
Tunstall Sundld 151 J4
Tunstead Derbys 114 C6
Tunstead Norfk 107 G7
Tunstead Milton Derbys 114 B5
Tupsley Herefs 69 K6
Turgis Green Hants 42 B8
Turkdean Gloucs 56 C4
Tur Langton Leics 87 K5
Turleigh Wilts 39 J7
Turnastone Herefs 69 G7
Turnberry S Ayrs 152 E2
Turnditch Derbys 100 F3
Turner's Hill W Susx 32 C6
Turnhouse C Edin 177 G4
Turnworth Dorset 14 F2
Turriff Abers 216 D4
Turton Bottoms Bl w D 121 L7
Turves Cambs 89 L4
Turvey Bed 74 D4
Turville Bucks 42 C3

**Turweston** Bucks 73 H6
**Tushielaw Inn** Border 166 D5
**Tutbury** Staffs 100 E6
**Tutshill** Gloucs 38 D2
**Tuttington** Norfk 106 F6
**Tuxford** Notts 116 C7
**Twatt** Ork 234 b5
**Twatt** Shet 235 c5
**Twechar** E Duns 175 J3
**Tweedbank** Border 167 H3
**Tweedmouth** Nthumb 179 K7
**Tweedsmuir** Border 165 L4
**Twelveheads** Cnwll 3 K3
**Twemlow Green** Ches E 113 H7
**Twenty** Lincs 103 J7
**Twerton** BaNES 39 G7
**Twickenham** Gt Lon 44 D5
**Twigworth** Gloucs 55 J4
**Twineham** W Susx 19 H2
**Twinstead** Essex 77 J6
**Twitchen** Devon 24 C5
**Two Dales** Derbys 114 F8
**Two Gates** Staffs 86 B4
**Two Waters** Herts 59 H6
**Twycross** Leics 86 D3
Twycross Zoo Leics 86 C3
**Twyford** Bucks 58 A3
**Twyford** Hants 29 J6
**Twyford** Leics 87 K2
**Twyford** Norfk 106 B7
**Twyford** Wokham 42 C5
**Twynholm** D & G 146 B4
**Twyning Green** Gloucs 70 F6
**Twynllanan** Carmth 51 L2
**Twywell** Nhants 88 D7
**Tyberton** Herefs 69 H6
**Tyburn** Birm 85 K5
**Tycroes** Carmth 51 H4
**Tycrwyn** Powys 97 H8
**Tydd Gote** Lincs 104 D8
**Tydd St Giles** Cambs 90 B1
**Tydd St Mary** Lincs 104 C8
**Tye Green** Essex 76 E7
**Tyldesley** Wigan 113 G2
**Tyler Hill** Kent 34 F3
**Tylorstown** Rhondd 36 F2
**Ty-nant** Conwy 96 F4
**Tyndrum** Stirlg 183 K2
**Ty'n-dwr** Denbgs 97 K4
**Tynemouth** N Tyne 151 J2
**Tynemouth Crematorium** N Tyne 151 J2
**Tyne Tunnel** S Tyne 151 H2
**Tyninghame** E Loth 178 D3
**Tynron** D & G 154 E4
**Tynygraig** Cerdgn 66 F1
**Ty'n-y-Groes** Conwy 109 L7
**Tyn-y-nant** Rhondd 37 G4
**Tyrie** Abers 217 H2
**Tyringham** M Keyn 74 C5
**Tyseley** Birm 85 K6
**Tythegston** Brdgnd 36 D5
**Tytherington** Ches E 113 K6
**Tytherington** S Glos 38 F3
**Tytherington** Wilts 27 K3
**Tytherleigh** Devon 13 H2
**Tytherton Lucas** Wilts 39 L5
**Tywardreath** Cnwll 5 H5
**Tywyn** Gwynd 80 D4

## U

**Ubbeston Green** Suffk 79 G1
**Ubley** BaNES 38 D8
**Uckfield** E Susx 19 M2
**Uckinghall** Worcs 70 F6
**Uckington** Gloucs 55 K3
**Uddingston** S Lans 175 J6
**Uddington** S Lans 165 G3
**Udimore** E Susx 21 H2
**Udny Green** Abers 207 G1
**Udny Station** Abers 207 G1
**Uffculme** Devon 25 G8
**Uffington** Lincs 88 F3
**Uffington** Oxon 40 F3
**Uffington** Shrops 83 K2
**Ufford** C Pete 89 G3
**Ufford** Suffk 79 G4
**Ufton** Warwks 72 E3
**Ufton Nervet** W Berk 41 M6
**Ugadale** Ag & B 161 K4
**Ugborough** Devon 7 G5
**Uggeshall** Suffk 93 J7
**Ugglebarnby** N York 143 H5
**Ughill** Sheff 114 E4
**Ugley** Essex 60 E3
**Ugley Green** Essex 60 E3
**Ugthorpe** N York 143 G5
**Uibhist A Deas** W Isls 233 c8
**Uibhist A Tuath** W Isls 233 b6
**Uig** Ag & B 188 F5
**Uig** Highld 208 C4
**Uig** Highld 208 F2
**Uig** W Isls 232 d2
**Uigshader** Highld 209 G5
**Uisken** Ag & B 180 E4
**Ulbster** Highld 231 K7
**Ulceby** Lincs 118 F6
**Ulceby** N Linc 126 D7
**Ulceby Skitter** N Linc 126 E7
**Ulcombe** Kent 33 L4
**Uldale** Cumb 147 M7
**Uley** Gloucs 55 H7
**Ulgham** Nthumb 159 G4
**Ullapool** Highld 220 E3
**Ullenhall** Warwks 71 K2
**Ulleskelf** N York 124 D3
**Ullesthorpe** Leics 87 G6
**Ulley** Rothm 115 J4
**Ullingswick** Herefs 69 L4
**Ullinish Lodge Hotel** Highld 208 E6
**Ullock** Cumb 136 E3
**Ullswater** Cumb 138 B3
Ullswater Steamers Cumb 137 L4
**Ulpha** Cumb 128 E2
**Ulrome** E R Yk 135 J7
**Ulsta** Shet 235 d3
**Ulva** Ag & B 189 K7
**Ulverley Green** Solhll 85 K6
**Ulverston** Cumb 129 G4
**Ulwell** Dorset 15 J6
**Ulzieside** D & G 164 F7
**Umberleigh** Devon 23 J6
**Unapool** Highld 224 F2
**Underbarrow** Cumb 129 K2
**Under Burnmouth** Border 156 E5
**Undercliffe** C Brad 123 J4
**Underdale** Shrops 83 K2
**Underriver** Kent 32 F3
**Underwood** Notts 101 J3
**Undy** Mons 38 C3
**Union Mills** IoM 237 c5
**Unst** Shet 235 d1
**Unstone** Derbys 115 G6
**Upavon** Wilts 28 C1
**Upchurch** Kent 46 D6
**Upcott** Devon 24 B5
**Up Exe** Devon 12 B2
**Upgate** Norfk 106 D8
**Uphall** Dorset 14 B2
**Uphall** W Loth 176 E4
**Upham** Devon 11 K3
**Upham** Hants 29 K7
**Uphampton** Herefs 69 H2
**Uphampton** Worcs 70 E2
**Uphill** N Som 37 L8
**Up Holland** Lancs 112 D1
**Uplawmoor** E Rens 174 E7
**Upleadon** Gloucs 55 H3
**Upleatham** R & Cl 142 D4
**Uploders** Dorset 13 L4
**Uplowman** Devon 24 F7
**Uplyme** Devon 13 H4
**Up Marden** W Susx 30 D8
**Upminster** Gt Lon 45 K3
**Up Mudford** Somset 26 E7
**Up Nately** Hants 30 B2
**Upottery** Devon 12 F2
**Upper Affcot** Shrops 83 J6
**Upper Ardchronie** Highld 222 E4
**Upper Arley** Worcs 84 D7
**Upper Basildon** W Berk 41 L5
**Upper Beeding** W Susx 19 G4
**Upper Benefield** Nhants 88 E5
**Upper Bentley** Worcs 71 H2
**Upper Bighouse** Highld 230 C4
**Upper Boddington** Nhants 72 F4
**Upper Brailes** Warwks 72 C6
**Upper Broadheath** Worcs 70 E4
**Upper Broughton** Notts 102 B7
**Upper Bucklebury** W Berk 41 K6
**Upper Burgate** Hants 28 D7
**Upperby** Cumb 148 D4
**Upper Caldecote** C Beds 75 H5
**Upper Chapel** Powys 67 L6
**Upper Chicksgrove** Wilts 27 L5
**Upper Chute** Wilts 28 F2
**Upper Clapton** Gt Lon 45 G3
**Upper Clatford** Hants 29 G3
**Upper Cound** Shrops 83 K3
**Upper Cumberworth** Kirk 123 J8
**Upper Dallachy** Moray 215 H2
**Upper Deal** Kent 35 K4
**Upper Dean** Bed 74 F2
**Upper Denby** Kirk 114 E1
**Upper Dicker** E Susx 20 B4
**Upper Dounreay** Highld 230 E3
**Upper Dovercourt** Essex 62 F2
**Upper Drumbane** Stirlg 184 E6
**Upper Dunsforth** N York 133 G6
**Upper Eashing** Surrey 30 F3
**Upper Eathie** Highld 213 J2
**Upper Egleton** Herefs 70 B5
**Upper Elkstone** Staffs 100 B2
**Upper Ellastone** Staffs 100 C4
**Upper Farringdon** Hants 30 B4
**Upper Framilode** Gloucs 55 H6
**Upper Froyle** Hants 30 C3
**Upperglen** Highld 208 E4
**Upper Godney** Somset 26 C3
**Upper Gravenhurst** C Beds 75 G7
**Upper Green** W Berk 41 G7
**Upper Grove Common** Herefs 54 E3
**Upper Hale** Surrey 30 D2
**Upper Halliford** Surrey 43 H6
**Upper Hambleton** Rutlnd 88 C3
**Upper Harbledown** Kent 34 F3
**Upper Hartfield** E Susx 32 E6
**Upper Hatherley** Gloucs 55 L4
**Upper Heaton** Kirk 123 H6
**Upper Helmsley** N York 133 L7
**Upper Hergest** Herefs 68 F4
**Upper Heyford** Nhants 73 J3
**Upper Heyford** Oxon 57 J3
**Upper Hill** Herefs 69 J4
**Upper Hopton** Kirk 123 J6
**Upper Hulme** Staffs 100 A1
**Upper Inglesham** Swindn 40 D2
**Upper Killay** Swans 51 H6
**Upper Kinchrackine** Ag & B 183 G2
**Upper Knockando** Moray 214 E5
**Upper Lambourn** W Berk 40 F4
**Upper Landywood** Staffs 85 H3
**Upper Langford** N Som 38 C7
**Upper Langwith** Derbys 115 K7
**Upper Largo** Fife 187 G6
**Upper Leigh** Staffs 100 A5
**Upper Lochton** Abers 206 D6
**Upper Longdon** Staffs 85 J2
**Upper & Lower Stondon** C Beds 75 H7
**Upper Lybster** Highld 231 J7
**Upper Lydbrook** Gloucs 54 E5
**Upper Lye** Herefs 69 H2
**Uppermill** Oldham 113 M1
**Upper Milton** Worcs 84 E8
**Upper Minety** Wilts 40 A3
**Upper Mulben** Moray 215 H4
**Upper Netchwood** Shrops 83 L5
**Upper Nobut** Staffs 100 B5
**Upper Norwood** W Susx 18 C3
**Upper Poppleton** C York 133 H8
**Upper Ratley** Hants 28 F6
**Upper Rissington** Gloucs 56 D4
**Upper Rochford** Worcs 70 B2
**Upper Ruscoe** D & G 145 L3
**Upper Sapey** Herefs 70 C2
**Upper Seagry** Wilts 39 L4
**Upper Shelton** C Beds 74 E5
**Upper Sheringham** Norfk 106 D4
**Upper Skelmorlie** N Ayrs 173 L5
**Upper Slaughter** Gloucs 56 D4
**Upper Soudley** Gloucs 54 F6
**Upper Standen** Kent 35 H6
**Upper Stoke** Norfk 92 F3
**Upper Stowe** Nhants 73 J3
**Upper Street** Hants 28 D7
**Upper Street** Norfk 93 H1
**Upper Street** Norfk 107 G8
**Upper Street** Suffk 77 H4
**Upper Street** Suffk 78 D4
**Upper Sundon** C Beds 59 H3
**Upper Swell** Gloucs 56 D3
**Upper Tasburgh** Norfk 92 E4
**Upper Tean** Staffs 100 A5
**Upperthong** Kirk 123 H8
**Upperton** W Susx 30 F6
**Upper Town** Herefs 69 L5
**Uppertown** Highld 231 L1
**Upper Town** N Som 38 D7
**Upper Town** Suffk 77 K2
**Upper Tumble** Carmth 51 G3
**Upper Tysoe** Warwks 72 D5
**Upper Victoria** Angus 187 J1
**Upper Wardington** Oxon 72 F5
**Upper Welland** Worcs 70 D6
**Upper Wellingham** E Susx 19 L3

**Upper Weybread** Suffk 92 F7
**Upper Wield** Hants 29 L4
**Upper Winchendon** Bucks 58 C5
**Upper Woodford** Wilts 28 C4
**Upper Wraxall** Wilts 39 J5
**Uppingham** Rutlnd 88 C4
**Uppington** Shrops 83 L2
**Upsall** N York 133 G3
**Upsettlington** Border 168 C1
**Upshire** Essex 60 C7
**Up Somborne** Hants 29 H5
**Upstreet** Kent 35 G3
**Upton** Bucks 58 C5
**Upton** C Pete 89 G4
**Upton** Cambs 89 H7
**Upton** Ches W 112 B7
**Upton** Cnwll 5 L2
**Upton** Devon 7 G7
**Upton** Devon 12 E2
**Upton** Dorset 14 E5
**Upton** Dorset 15 J4
**Upton** Halton 112 C4
**Upton** Hants 29 G1
**Upton** Hants 29 G7
**Upton** Leics 86 D4
**Upton** Lincs 116 E4
**Upton** Norfk 93 H2
**Upton** Notts 102 B2
**Upton** Notts 116 C6
**Upton** Oxon 41 K3
**Upton** Slough 43 G5
**Upton** Somset 24 F5
**Upton** Somset 26 C6
**Upton** Wakefd 124 D7
**Upton** Wirral 111 J4
**Upton Bishop** Herefs 54 F3
**Upton Cheyney** S Glos 39 G6
**Upton Cressett** Shrops 84 B5
**Upton Grey** Hants 30 B2
**Upton Hellions** Devon 11 J4
**Upton Lovell** Wilts 27 L4
**Upton Magna** Shrops 83 K2
**Upton Noble** Somset 27 G4
**Upton Pyne** Devon 11 L5
**Upton St Leonards** Gloucs 55 K5
**Upton Scudamore** Wilts 27 K2
**Upton Snodsbury** Worcs 71 G4
**Upton-upon-Severn** Worcs 70 F6
**Upton Warren** Worcs 71 G2
**Upwaltham** W Susx 18 C3
**Upwell** Norfk 90 C3
**Upwood** Cambs 89 J6
**Urchfont** Wilts 40 B8
**Urmston** Traffd 113 H3
**Urquhart** Moray 215 G2
**Urquhart Castle** Highld 212 E8
**Urra** N York 142 C6
**Urray** Highld 212 D4
**Usan** Angus 197 H5
**Ushaw Moor** Dur 151 G6
**Usk** Mons 54 B7
**Usselby** Lincs 117 H3
**Usworth** Sundld 151 H4
**Utkinton** Ches W 112 D7
**Utley** C Brad 122 F3
**Uton** Devon 11 J5
**Utterby** Lincs 118 D3
**Uttoxeter** Staffs 100 C5
**Uxbridge** Gt Lon 43 H4
**Uyeasound** Shet 235 d2
**Uzmaston** Pembks 49 G5

## V

**Vale** Guern 236 d2
**Vale Crematorium** Luton 59 J3
**Vale of Glamorgan Crematorium** V Glam 37 H6
**Valley** IoA 108 C5
**Valtos** Highld 209 H2
**Valtos** W Isls 232 d2
**Vange** Essex 46 B3
**Vatsetter** Shet 235 d3
**Vatten** Highld 208 D5
**Vaynor** Myr Td 53 G6
**Veensgarth** Shet 235 c6
**Velindre** Powys 68 D7
**Venngreen** Devon 9 K3
**Venn Ottery** Devon 12 D4
**Ventnor** IoW 17 G6
**Venton** Devon 6 E4
**Vernham Dean** Hants 29 G1
**Vernham Street** Hants 41 G8
**Verwood** Dorset 15 K2
**Veryan** Cnwll 4 E7
**Vickerstown** Cumb 128 E5
**Victoria** Cnwll 4 F4
**Vidlin** Shet 235 d4
**Viewfield** Moray 215 G2
**Viewpark** N Lans 175 J6
**Vigo** Kent 45 M7
**Village de Putron** Guern 236 d3
**Ville la Bas** Jersey 236 a5
**Villiaze** Guern 236 c3
**Vines Cross** E Susx 20 C3
**Vinters Park Crematorium** Kent 33 K2
**Virginia Water** Surrey 43 G6
**Virginstow** Devon 9 K6
**Vobster** Somset 27 G2
**Voe** Shet 235 c4
**Vowchurch** Herefs 69 G7

## W

**Waberthwaite** Cumb 128 D2
**Wackerfield** Dur 140 E3
**Wacton** Norfk 92 E5
**Wadborough** Worcs 70 F5
**Waddesdon** Bucks 58 C5
**Waddesdon Manor** Bucks 58 B5
**Waddeton** Devon 7 K4
**Waddingham** Lincs 117 G3
**Waddington** Lancs 121 L2
**Waddington** Lincs 116 F8
**Waddon** Gt Lon 44 F7
**Wadebridge** Cnwll 4 F2
**Wadeford** Somset 13 H1
**Wadenhoe** Nhants 88 E6
**Wadesmill** Herts 60 B4
**Wadhurst** E Susx 33 H6
**Wadshelf** Derbys 114 F7
**Wadworth** Donc 115 K3
**Wainfleet All Saints** Lincs 104 D2
**Wainfleet St Mary** Lincs 104 D2
**Wainhouse Corner** Cnwll 9 G5
**Wainscott** Medway 46 C6
**Wainstalls** Calder 122 F5
**Waitby** Cumb 139 H5
**Waithe** Lincs 118 C2
**Wakefield** Wakefd 123 L6
**Wakefield Crematorium** Wakefd 123 L7
**Wake Green** Birm 85 K6
**Wakehurst Place** W Susx 32 C6
**Wakerley** Nhants 88 D4
**Wakes Colne** Essex 61 L3
**Walberswick** Suffk 93 K8
**Walberton** W Susx 18 C4
**Walbutt** D & G 146 D2
**Walcombe** Somset 26 D3
**Walcot** Lincs 103 H5
**Walcot** Shrops 83 L2
**Walcot** Swindn 40 D4
**Walcote** Leics 87 H6
**Walcot Green** Norfk 92 D7
**Walcott** Lincs 103 J2
**Walcott** Norfk 107 H6
**Walden Stubbs** N York 124 E6
**Walderslade** Medway 46 C7
**Walderton** W Susx 17 L1
**Walditch** Dorset 13 L4
**Waldridge** Dur 151 G5
**Waldringfield** Suffk 79 G5
**Waldron** E Susx 20 B2
**Wales** Rothm 115 J5
**Wales** Somset 26 E6
**Walesby** Lincs 117 J3
**Walesby** Notts 116 B7
**Walford** Herefs 54 E4
**Walford** Herefs 83 H8
**Walford Heath** Shrops 98 C8
**Walgherton** Ches E 99 G3
**Walgrave** Nhants 74 B1
**Walkden** Salfd 113 G2
**Walker** N u Ty 151 H3
**Walkerburn** Border 166 E3
**Walkeringham** Notts 116 C3
**Walkerith** Lincs 116 C3
**Walkern** Herts 59 M3
**Walker's Heath** Birm 85 J7
**Walkerton** Fife 186 D6
**Walkford** Dorset 16 B4
**Walkhampton** Devon 6 D2
**Walkington** E R Yk 126 B3
**Walkley** Sheff 115 G4
**Walk Mill** Lancs 122 C5
**Walkwood** Worcs 71 J2
**Wall** Nthumb 150 A2
**Wall** Staffs 85 K3
**Wallacetown** S Ayrs 153 G2
**Wallacetown** S Ayrs 163 J5
**Wallands Park** E Susx 19 L4
**Wallasey** Wirral 111 J3
**Wallasey (Kingsway) Tunnel** Wirral 111 K4
**Wall Heath** Dudley 84 F5
**Wallingford** Oxon 41 L3
**Wallington** Gt Lon 44 F6
**Wallington** Hants 17 H2
**Wallington** Herts 75 K7
**Wallisdown** Poole 15 K4
**Walliswood** Surrey 31 J4
**Walls** Shet 235 b5
**Wallsend** N Tyne 151 H2
**Wallyford** E Loth 177 K4
**Walmer** Kent 35 K5
**Walmer Bridge** Lancs 121 G5
**Walmley** Birm 85 K5
**Walmley Ash** Birm 85 K5
**Walpole** Suffk 93 H8
**Walpole Cross Keys** Norfk 104 E8
**Walpole Highway** Norfk 90 D2
**Walpole St Andrew** Norfk 104 D8
**Walpole St Peter** Norfk 90 C1
**Walsall** Wsall 85 H4
**Walsden** Calder 122 D6
**Walsgrave on Sowe** Covtry 86 E7
**Walsham le Willows** Suffk 78 B1
**Walshford** N York 132 F8
**Walsoken** Norfk 90 C2
**Walston** S Lans 165 K1
**Walsworth** Herts 59 K3
**Walter's Ash** Bucks 42 D2
**Waltham** Kent 34 E5
**Waltham** NE Lin 118 C2
**Waltham Abbey** Essex 60 C7
**Waltham Chase** Hants 29 K7
**Waltham Cross** Herts 60 B7
**Waltham on the Wolds** Leics 102 D7
**Waltham St Lawrence** W & M 42 D5
**Walthamstow** Gt Lon 45 G3
**Walton** C Pete 89 H3
**Walton** Cumb 148 F3
**Walton** Derbys 115 G7
**Walton** Leeds 124 C2
**Walton** Leics 87 H6
**Walton** M Keyn 74 C7
**Walton** Powys 68 F3
**Walton** Somset 26 C4
**Walton** Suffk 79 G7
**Walton** W Susx 17 M2
**Walton** Wakefd 123 L6
**Walton** Wrekin 98 E8
**Walton Cardiff** Gloucs 55 K2
**Walton East** Pembks 49 H3
**Walton Highway** Norfk 90 C2
**Walton-in-Gordano** N Som 38 B5
**Walton Lea Crematorium** Warrtn 112 E4
**Walton-le-Dale** Lancs 121 H5
**Walton-on-Thames** Surrey 43 J6
**Walton-on-the-Hill** Staffs 99 L7
**Walton on the Hill** Surrey 31 L1
**Walton-on-the-Naze** Essex 62 F4
**Walton on the Wolds** Leics 101 L8
**Walton-on-Trent** Derbys 100 E8
**Walton Park** N Som 38 B6
**Walton West** Pembks 48 E5
**Waltonwrays Crematorium** N York 122 E1
**Walworth** Darltn 141 G4
**Walworth** Gt Lon 45 G4
**Walwyn's Castle** Pembks 48 E5
**Wambrook** Somset 13 H2
**Wanborough** Surrey 30 F2
**Wanborough** Swindn 40 E4
**Wandsworth** Gt Lon 44 E5
**Wangford** Suffk 93 K7
**Wanlip** Leics 87 H2
**Wanlockhead** D & G 165 G6
**Wannock** E Susx 20 C5
**Wansford** C Pete 88 F4
**Wansford** E R Yk 135 G7
**Wanshurst Green** Kent 33 K4
**Wanstead** Gt Lon 45 H3
**Wanstrow** Somset 27 G3
**Wanswell** Gloucs 55 G7
**Wantage** Oxon 41 H3
**Wappenbury** Warwks 72 E2
**Wappenham** Nhants 73 J5
**Warbleton** E Susx 20 C3
**Warborough** Oxon 41 L2
**Warboys** Cambs 89 K7
**Warbreck** Bpool 120 D3
**Warbstow** Cnwll 9 G6
**Warburton** Traffd 113 G4
**Warcop** Cumb 139 H4
**Warden** Nthumb 150 A2
**Ward End** Birm 85 K5
**Wardington** Oxon 72 F5
**Wardle** Ches E 98 E2
**Wardle** Rochdl 122 D6
**Wardley** Gatesd 151 H3
**Wardley** Rutlnd 88 B4
**Wardlow** Derbys 114 D6
**Wardy Hill** Cambs 90 C6
**Ware** Herts 60 B5
**Wareham** Dorset 15 H5
**Warehorne** Kent 34 D7
**Warenford** Nthumb 169 H4
**Wareside** Herts 60 C5

**Waresley** Cambs 75 J4
**Warfield** Br For 42 E6
**Warfleet** Devon 7 K6
**Wargrave** Wokham 42 C5
**Warham** Norfk 105 M4
**Wark** Nthumb 157 L6
**Wark** Nthumb 168 C2
**Warkleigh** Devon 23 K6
**Warkton** Nhants 88 C7
**Warkworth** Nhants 72 F6
**Warkworth** Nthumb 159 G2
**Warlaby** N York 132 E2
**Warleggan** Cnwll 5 J3
**Warley Town** Calder 122 F5
**Warlingham** Surrey 32 C2
**Warmfield** Wakefd 124 B6
**Warmingham** Ches E 99 G1
**Warmington** Nhants 88 F5
**Warmington** Warwks 72 E5
**Warminster** Wilts 27 K3
**Warmley** S Glos 38 F5
**Warmsworth** Donc 115 K2
**Warmwell** Dorset 14 E5
**Warner Bros. Studio Tour** Herts 59 H7
**Warnford** Hants 29 L6
**Warnham** W Susx 31 J5
**Warningcamp** W Susx 18 D4
**Warninglid** W Susx 31 L6
**Warren** Ches E 113 K7
**Warren** Pembks 48 F7
**Warrenhill** S Lans 165 J2
**Warren Row** W & M 42 D4
**Warren Street** Kent 34 C4
**Warrington** M Keyn 74 C4
**Warrington** Warrtn 112 E4
**Warriston** C Edin 177 H4
**Warriston Crematorium** C Edin 177 H3
**Warsash** Hants 16 F2
**Warslow** Staffs 100 C2
**Warter** E R Yk 125 K1
**Warthermaske** N York 132 C4
**Warthill** N York 133 K7
**Wartling** E Susx 20 D4
**Wartnaby** Leics 102 B7
**Warton** Lancs 120 E5
**Warton** Lancs 129 K5
**Warton** Warwks 86 C3
**Warwick** Warwks 72 C2
**Warwick Bridge** Cumb 148 E4
**Warwick Castle** Warwks 72 C2
**Warwick Services** Warwks 72 D3
**Wasbister** Ork 234 c4
**Wasdale Head** Cumb 137 G5
**Washaway** Cnwll 5 G2
**Washbourne** Devon 7 J5
**Washbrook** Suffk 78 D6
**Washfield** Devon 11 L2
**Washford** Somset 25 G3
**Washford Pyne** Devon 11 J3
**Washingborough** Lincs 117 G7
**Washington** Sundld 151 H4
**Washington** W Susx 18 F3
**Washington Services** Gatesd 151 G4
**Washwood Heath** Birm 85 K5
**Wasperton** Warwks 72 C3
**Wass** N York 133 H4
**Wast Water** Cumb 137 G6
**Watchet** Somset 25 G3
**Watchfield** Oxon 40 E3
**Watchgate** Cumb 138 D7
**Water** Devon 11 H8
**Waterbeach** Cambs 76 C2
**Waterbeach** W Susx 18 B4
**Waterbeck** D & G 155 M6
**Water End** E R Yk 125 J3
**Waterfall** Staffs 100 B3
**Waterfoot** Ag & B 161 K3
**Waterfoot** E Rens 175 G7
**Waterford** Herts 60 A5
**Waterheads** Border 177 H7
**Waterhouses** Staffs 100 B3
**Wateringbury** Kent 33 H3
**Waterloo** Highld 199 K2
**Waterloo** N Lans 175 L7
**Waterloo** P & K 195 G8
**Waterloo** Pembks 49 G6
**Waterloo** Sefton 111 K2
**Waterlooville** Hants 17 J1
**Watermead** Bucks 58 D5
**Watermillock** Cumb 138 C3
**Water Newton** Cambs 89 G4
**Water Orton** Warwks 85 L5
**Waterperry** Oxon 57 L6
**Waterrow** Somset 25 G6
**Watersfield** W Susx 18 D3
**Waterside** Bl w D 121 K5
**Waterside** E Ayrs 163 K7
**Waterside** E Ayrs 163 L2
**Waterside** E Duns 175 J4
**Waterstein** Highld 208 B5
**Waterstock** Oxon 57 M6
**Waterston** Pembks 48 F6
**Water Stratford** Bucks 73 J7
**Waters Upton** Wrekin 98 F8
**Watford** Herts 43 J2
**Watford** Nhants 73 H2
**Watford Gap Services** Nhants 73 H2
**Wath** N York 132 B6
**Wath** N York 132 E4
**Wath upon Dearne** Rothm 115 H2
**Watlington** Norfk 90 E2
**Watlington** Oxon 42 B2
**Watten** Highld 231 J5
**Wattisfield** Suffk 92 B8
**Wattisham** Suffk 78 B4
**Watton** Dorset 13 L4
**Watton** E R Yk 126 C1
**Watton** Norfk 91 K4
**Watton-at-Stone** Herts 60 A4
**Wattston** N Lans 175 K4
**Wattsville** Caerph 37 J3
**Waulkmill** Abers 206 C6
**Waunarlwydd** Swans 51 H6
**Waunfawr** Cerdgn 80 E6
**Waunfawr** Gwynd 95 J2
**Wavendon** M Keyn 74 C6
**Waveney Crematorium** Suffk 93 J6
**Waverbridge** Cumb 147 L5
**Waverton** Ches W 112 C8
**Waverton** Cumb 147 L5
**Wawne** E R Yk 126 D3
**Waxham** Norfk 107 J7
**Wayford** Somset 13 K2
**Waytown** Dorset 13 L3
**Way Village** Devon 11 K3
**Weacombe** Somset 25 H4
**Weald** Oxon 56 F7
**Wealdstone** Gt Lon 44 D3
**Weardley** Leeds 123 K2
**Weare** Somset 26 B2
**Weare Giffard** Devon 23 G6
**Wearhead** Dur 149 L6
**Wearne** Somset 26 B5
**Wear Valley Crematorium** Dur 141 G2
**Weasenham All Saints** Norfk 105 K7
**Weasenham St Peter** Norfk 105 K7
**Weaste** Salfd 113 J2
**Weaverham** Ches W 112 E6
**Weaverthorpe** N York 134 E5
**Webheath** Worcs 71 H2
**Wedderlairs** Abers 216 F7
**Weddington** Warwks 86 D5
**Wedhampton** Wilts 40 B8
**Wedmore** Somset 26 C2
**Wednesbury** Sandw 85 H4
**Wednesfield** Wolves 85 G4
**Weedon** Bucks 58 D4
**Weedon Bec** Nhants 73 J3
**Weedon Lois** Nhants 73 H5
**Weeford** Staffs 85 K3
**Weeke** Hants 29 J5
**Weekley** Nhants 88 C7
**Week St Mary** Cnwll 9 H5
**Weel** E R Yk 126 D3
**Weeley** Essex 62 D4
**Weeley Crematorium** Essex 62 D4
**Weeley Heath** Essex 62 D4
**Weem** P & K 194 D6
**Weethley** Warwks 71 J4
**Weeting** Norfk 91 H5
**Weeton** E R Yk 127 H6
**Weeton** Lancs 120 E4
**Weeton** N York 123 K2
**Weetwood** Leeds 123 K3
**Weir** Lancs 122 C5
**Weir Quay** Devon 6 C3
**Weisdale** Shet 235 c5
**Welborne** Norfk 92 C2
**Welbourn** Lincs 102 F2
**Welburn** N York 133 L6
**Welbury** N York 141 J6
**Welby** Lincs 102 F5
**Welcombe** Devon 22 C7
**Weldon** Nhants 88 D5
**Welford** Nhants 87 J7
**Welford** W Berk 41 H5
**Welford-on-Avon** Warwks 71 K4
**Welham** Leics 87 L5
**Welham** Notts 116 B5
**Welham Green** Herts 59 L6
**Well** Hants 30 C3
**Well** Lincs 118 F6
**Well** N York 132 D3
**Welland** Worcs 70 E6
**Wellbank** Angus 196 D8
**Wellesbourne** Warwks 72 C4
**Well Head** Herts 59 K3
**Welling** Gt Lon 45 J5
**Wellingborough** Nhants 74 C2
**Wellingham** Norfk 105 L7
**Wellingore** Lincs 103 G2
**Wellington** Cumb 136 F6
**Wellington** Herefs 69 K5
**Wellington** Somset 25 H7
**Wellington** Wrekin 84 B2
**Wellington Heath** Herefs 70 C6
**Wellow** BaNES 39 H8
**Wellow** IoW 16 E5
**Wellow** Notts 116 A7
**Wells** Somset 26 D3
**Wells-next-the-Sea** Norfk 105 L4
**Wellstye Green** Essex 61 G4
**Welltree** P & K 185 K3
**Wellwood** Fife 176 E2
**Welney** Norfk 90 D5
**Welshampton** Shrops 98 C5
**Welsh Frankton** Shrops 98 A6
**Welsh Newton** Herefs 54 D4
**Welshpool** Powys 82 E3
**Welsh St Donats** V Glam 36 F5
**Welton** Cumb 148 C6
**Welton** E R Yk 126 B5
**Welton** Lincs 117 G5
**Welton** Nhants 73 H2
**Welton le Marsh** Lincs 119 G7
**Welton le Wold** Lincs 118 C4
**Welwick** E R Yk 127 H6
**Welwyn** Herts 59 L5
**Welwyn Garden City** Herts 59 L5
**Wem** Shrops 98 D6
**Wembdon** Somset 25 L4
**Wembley** Gt Lon 44 D3
**Wembury** Devon 6 D6
**Wembworthy** Devon 10 F3
**Wemyss Bay** Inver 173 L4
**Wendens Ambo** Essex 76 D7
**Wendlebury** Oxon 57 K4
**Wendling** Norfk 91 L2
**Wendover** Bucks 58 E6
**Wendron** Cnwll 3 H5
**Wendron Mining District** Cnwll 3 J5
**Wendy** Cambs 75 K5
**Wenhaston** Suffk 93 J7
**Wennington** Cambs 89 J7
**Wennington** Gt Lon 45 K4
**Wennington** Lancs 130 C5
**Wensley** Derbys 100 E1
**Wensley** N York 131 K2
**Wentbridge** Wakefd 124 D6
**Wentnor** Shrops 83 H5
**Wentworth** Cambs 90 C7
**Wentworth** Rothm 115 G2
**Wenvoe** V Glam 37 H6
**Weobley** Herefs 69 H4
**Wepham** W Susx 18 E4
**Wereham** Norfk 90 F3
**Werrington** C Pete 89 H3
**Werrington** Cnwll 9 J7
**Wervin** Ches W 112 B6
**Wesham** Lancs 120 F4
**Wessex Vale Crematorium** Hants 29 J7
**Wessington** Derbys 101 G2
**West Acre** Norfk 91 H1
**West Alvington** Devon 7 G6
**West Anstey** Devon 24 D6
**West Ashby** Lincs 118 C6
**West Ashling** W Susx 17 M2
**West Ashton** Wilts 27 K1
**West Auckland** Dur 140 F3
**West Ayton** N York 134 F3
**West Bagborough** Somset 25 J5
**West Bank** Halton 112 D5
**West Barkwith** Lincs 117 K5
**West Barnby** N York 143 G5
**West Barns** E Loth 178 E3
**West Barsham** Norfk 105 L5
**West Bay** Dorset 13 L4
**West Beckham** Norfk 106 D5
**West Bedfont** Surrey 43 H5
**Westbere** Kent 35 G3
**West Bergholt** Essex 62 A3
**West Berkshire Crematorium** W Berk 41 K6
**West Bexington** Dorset 13 M5
**West Bilney** Norfk 91 G1
**West Blatchington** Br & H 19 J4
**West Boldon** S Tyne 151 J3
**Westborough** Lincs 102 D4
**Westbourne** Bmouth 15 K4
**Westbourne** W Susx 17 L2
**West Bowling** C Brad 123 H4
**West Bradenham** Norfk 91 K2
**West Bradford** Lancs 121 L2
**West Bradley** Somset 26 E4
**West Bretton** Wakefd 123 K7
**West Bridgford** Notts 101 L5
**West Bromwich** Sandw 85 H5
**Westbrook** Kent 35 J2
**Westbrook** W Berk 41 H6
**West Buckland** Devon 23 K5
**West Buckland** Somset 25 J7
**West Burrafirth** Shet 235 b5
**West Burton** N York 131 J3
**Westbury** Bucks 73 J7
**Westbury** Shrops 83 G2
**Westbury** Wilts 27 K2
**Westbury Leigh** Wilts 27 K2
**Westbury-on-Severn** Gloucs 55 G5

**Westbury-on-Trym** Bristl 38 E5
**Westbury-sub-Mendip** Somset 26 D2
**West Butterwick** N Linc 116 D1
**Westby** Lancs 120 E4
**West Byfleet** Surrey 43 H7
**West Cairngaan** D & G 144 D8
**West Caister** Norfk 93 K2
**West Calder** W Loth 176 D5
**West Camel** Somset 26 E6
**West Chaldon** Dorset 14 E5
**West Challow** Oxon 41 G3
**West Charleton** Devon 7 H7
**West Chiltington** W Susx 18 E3
**West Chinnock** Somset 26 C8
**West Clandon** Surrey 31 H2
**West Cliffe** Kent 35 J5
**Westcliff-on-Sea** Sthend 46 E3
**West Coker** Somset 26 D8
**Westcombe** Somset 27 G4
**West Compton** Somset 26 E3
**West Compton Abbas** Dorset 14 B4
**Westcote** Gloucs 56 E4
**Westcote Barton** Oxon 57 H3
**Westcott** Bucks 58 B5
**Westcott** Devon 12 C2
**Westcott** Surrey 31 J2
**West Cottingwith** N York 125 G3
**Westcourt** Wilts 40 E7
**West Cowick** E R Yk 124 F6
**West Cross** Swans 51 H7
**West Curthwaite** Cumb 148 B5
**Westdean** E Susx 20 B5
**West Dean** W Susx 18 B3
**West Dean** Wilts 28 E6
**West Deeping** Lincs 89 G2
**West Derby** Lpool 111 L3
**West Dereham** Norfk 90 F4
**West Down** Devon 23 H3
**Westdowns** Cnwll 8 E7
**West Drayton** Gt Lon 43 H4
**West Drayton** Notts 116 B6
**West Dunnet** Highld 231 J2
**West Ella** E R Yk 126 C5
**West End** Bed 74 E4
**West End** Hants 29 J8
**West End** N Som 38 C6
**West End** Norfk 93 K2
**West End** Surrey 42 F7
**West End** Surrey 43 J7
**West End** Wilts 27 M6
**West End Green** Hants 42 A7
**Wester Aberchalder** Highld 202 E2
**Westerdale** Highld 231 G5
**Westerdale** N York 142 E6
**Westerfield** Suffk 78 E5
**Westergate** W Susx 18 C5
**Westerham** Kent 32 D3
**Westerhope** N u Ty 150 F2
**Westerland** Devon 7 K4
**Westerleigh** S Glos 39 G4
**Westerleigh Crematorium** S Glos 39 G5
**Western Isles** W Isls 232 d5
**Wester Ochiltree** W Loth 176 D4
**Wester Pitkierie** Fife 187 J6
**Wester Ross** Highld 220 C5
**Westerton of Rossie** Angus 197 G5
**Westerwick** Shet 235 c6
**West Farleigh** Kent 33 J3
**West Farndon** Nhants 73 G4
**West Felton** Shrops 97 M7
**Westfield** BaNES 26 F2
**Westfield** Cumb 136 D2
**Westfield** E Susx 21 G3
**Westfield** Highld 230 F3
**Westfield** N Lans 175 J4
**Westfield** Norfk 92 B2
**Westfield** W Loth 176 C4
**Westfields** Herefs 69 K6
**Westfields of Rattray** P & K 195 J6
**Westgate** Dur 150 A7
**Westgate** N Linc 125 J8
**Westgate-on-Sea** Kent 35 J2
**West Grafton** Wilts 40 E7
**West Green** Hants 30 C1
**West Grimstead** Wilts 28 E6
**West Grinstead** W Susx 31 K6
**West Haddlesey** N York 124 E5
**West Haddon** Nhants 73 J1
**West Hagbourne** Oxon 41 K3
**West Hagley** Worcs 84 F7
**Westhall** Suffk 93 J7
**West Hallam** Derbys 101 H4
**West Halton** N Linc 125 L6
**Westham** Dorset 14 C6
**Westham** E Susx 20 D5
**West Ham** Gt Lon 45 H4
**Westham** Somset 26 B3
**Westhampnett** W Susx 18 B4
**West Handley** Derbys 115 H6
**West Hanney** Oxon 41 H2
**West Hanningfield** Essex 61 H7
**West Harnham** Wilts 28 C5
**West Harptree** BaNES 38 E8
**West Harting** W Susx 30 C7
**West Hatch** Somset 25 L7
**West Hatch** Wilts 27 L5
**West Haven** Angus 187 J1
**Westhay** Somset 26 C3
**West Heath** Birm 85 J7
**West Helmsdale** Highld 227 H5
**West Hendred** Oxon 41 H3
**West Hertfordshire Crematorium** Herts 59 J7
**West Heslerton** N York 134 E4
**West Hewish** N Som 38 B7
**Westhide** Herefs 69 L5
**Westhill** Abers 206 F4
**West Hill** Devon 12 D4
**West Hoathly** W Susx 32 C6
**West Holme** Dorset 15 G5
**Westhope** Herefs 69 J4
**Westhope** Shrops 83 J6
**West Horndon** Essex 45 M3
**Westhorpe** Lincs 103 L6
**Westhorpe** Suffk 78 C2
**West Horrington** Somset 26 E3
**West Horsley** Surrey 31 H2
**West Hougham** Kent 35 H6
**Westhoughton** Bolton 112 F1
**Westhouse** N York 130 D5
**Westhouses** Derbys 101 H2
**West Howe** Bmouth 15 K4
**Westhumble** Surrey 31 K2
**West Huntingtower** P & K 185 M3
**West Huntspill** Somset 25 L3
**West Hythe** Kent 34 F7
**West Ilsley** W Berk 41 J4
**West Itchenor** W Susx 17 L3
**West Kennett** Wilts 40 C6
**West Kilbride** N Ayrs 173 L8
**West Kingsdown** Kent 45 L7
**West Kington** Wilts 39 J5
**West Kirby** Wirral 111 H4
**West Knapton** N York 134 D4
**West Knighton** Dorset 14 D5
**West Knoyle** Wilts 27 K5
**Westlake** Devon 6 F5
**West Lambrook** Somset 26 B7
**West Lancashire Crematorium** Lancs 120 F7
**West Langdon** Kent 35 J5
**West Lavington** W Susx 30 E7
**West Lavington** Wilts 28 A2
**West Layton** N York 140 E5
**West Leake** Notts 101 K7
**Westleigh** Devon 23 G5
**Westleigh** Devon 25 G7
**West Leigh** Somset 25 H5
**Westleton** Suffk 79 J2
**West Lexham** Norfk 91 J1
**Westley** Suffk 77 J2
**Westley Waterless** Cambs 76 E3
**West Lilling** N York 133 K6
**Westlington** Bucks 58 C6
**West Linton** Border 176 F7
**Westlinton** Cumb 148 D3
**West Littleton** S Glos 39 H5
**West Lockinge** Oxon 41 H3
**West London Crematorium** Gt Lon 44 E4
**West Lothian Crematorium** W Loth 176 D5
**West Lulworth** Dorset 14 F6
**West Lutton** N York 134 E5
**West Lydford** Somset 26 E5
**West Lyng** Somset 25 L5
**West Lynn** Norfk 104 F7
**West Malling** Kent 33 H2
**West Malvern** Worcs 70 D5
**West Marden** W Susx 30 C8
**West Markham** Notts 116 B6
**Westmarsh** Kent 35 H3
**West Marsh** NE Lin 127 G8
**West Marton** N York 122 D1
**West Melbury** Dorset 27 K7
**West Meon** Hants 29 M6
**West Mersea** Essex 62 B5
**Westmeston** E Susx 19 K3
**West Midland Safari Park** Worcs 84 E7
**Westmill** Herts 60 B3
**West Milton** Dorset 13 L3
**Westminster** Gt Lon 44 F4
**Westminster Abbey & Palace** Gt Lon 44 F4
**West Molesey** Surrey 43 J6
**West Monkton** Somset 25 K5
**West Moors** Dorset 15 K2
**West Morden** Dorset 15 G4
**West Morriston** Border 167 J2
**West Mudford** Somset 26 E7
**Westmuir** Angus 196 B5
**West Ness** N York 133 L4
**Westnewton** Cumb 147 K6
**West Newton** E R Yk 126 F3
**West Newton** Norfk 105 H6
**West Newton** Somset 25 L5
**West Norwood** Gt Lon 44 F5
**West Norwood Crematorium** Gt Lon 44 F5
**Westoe** S Tyne 151 J2
**West Ogwell** Devon 7 J2
**Weston** BaNES 39 G6
**Weston** Ches E 99 G3
**Weston** Devon 12 E3
**Weston** Devon 12 F5
**Weston** Hants 30 B6
**Weston** Herts 59 L3
**Weston** Lincs 103 M7
**Weston** N York 123 H2
**Weston** Nhants 73 H5
**Weston** Notts 116 C7
**Weston** Shrops 83 L5
**Weston** Shrops 97 L6
**Weston** Staffs 99 L6
**Weston** W Berk 41 H5
**Weston Beggard** Herefs 69 L6
**Westonbirt** Gloucs 39 J3
**Weston by Welland** Nhants 87 L5
**Weston Colville** Cambs 76 E4
**Weston Corbett** Hants 30 B3
**Weston Coyney** C Stke 99 L4
**Weston Favell** Nhants 73 L3
**Weston Green** Cambs 76 F4
**Weston Heath** Shrops 84 D2
**Westoning** C Beds 59 G2
**Weston-in-Gordano** N Som 38 C5
**Weston Jones** Staffs 99 H7
**Weston Longville** Norfk 92 D1
**Weston Lullingfields** Shrops 98 B7
**Weston Mill Crematorium** C Plym 6 C4
**Weston-on-the-Green** Oxon 57 K4
**Weston Park** Staffs 84 E2
**Weston Patrick** Hants 30 B3
**Weston Rhyn** Shrops 97 L5
**Weston-sub-Edge** Gloucs 71 K6
**Weston-super-Mare** N Som 37 L7
**Weston-super-Mare Crematorium** N Som 38 A7
**Weston Turville** Bucks 58 D6
**Weston-under-Lizard** Staffs 84 E2
**Weston under Penyard** Herefs 54 F4
**Weston-under-Redcastle** Shrops 98 E6
**Weston under Wetherley** Warwks 72 D1
**Weston Underwood** Derbys 100 F4
**Weston Underwood** M Keyn 74 C4
**Weston-upon-Trent** Derbys 101 H6
**Westonzoyland** Somset 25 M4
**West Orchard** Dorset 27 J7
**West Overton** Wilts 40 C6
**Westow** N York 134 B6
**West Park** Abers 206 E5
**West Parley** Dorset 15 K3
**West Peckham** Kent 33 H3
**West Pelton** Dur 151 G4
**West Pennard** Somset 26 D4
**West Pentire** Cnwll 4 B4
**West Perry** Cambs 75 G2
**West Porlock** Somset 24 D3
**Westport** Somset 26 B7
**West Putford** Devon 9 K2
**West Quantoxhead** Somset 25 H3
**Westquarter** Falk 176 B3
**West Rainton** Dur 151 H5
**West Rasen** Lincs 117 H4
**Westray** Ork 234 c3
*Westray Airport Ork 234 c3*
**West Raynham** Norfk 105 L7
**Westrigg** W Loth 176 B5

**West Road Crematorium** N u Ty 150 F2
**Westrop** Swindn 40 D2
**West Rounton** N York 141 K6
**West Row** Suffk 90 F7
**West Rudham** Norfk 105 K6
**West Runton** Norfk 106 E4
**Westruther** Border 178 D7
**Westry** Cambs 90 B4
**West Saltoun** E Loth 178 B5
**West Sandford** Devon 11 J4
**West Sandwick** Shet 235 d3
**West Scrafton** N York 131 K3
**West Stafford** Dorset 14 D4
**West Stockwith** Notts 116 C3
**West Stoke** W Susx 17 M2
**West Stour** Dorset 27 H6
**West Stourmouth** Kent 35 H3
**West Stow** Suffk 77 J1
**West Stowell** Wilts 40 C7
**West Street** Suffk 78 B1
**West Suffolk Crematorium** Suffk 77 J2
**West Tanfield** N York 132 D4
**West Taphouse** Cnwll 5 J3
**West Tarbert** Ag & B 172 E5
**West Tarring** W Susx 18 F5
**West Thirston** Nthumb 158 F3
**West Thorney** W Susx 17 L3
**West Thorpe** Notts 101 L7
**West Thurrock** Thurr 45 L4
**West Tilbury** Thurr 46 A4
**West Tisted** Hants 29 M5
**West Torrington** Lincs 117 J5
**West Town** Hants 17 K3
**West Town** N Som 38 C6
**West Tytherley** Hants 28 F5
**West Walton** Norfk 90 C2
**Westward** Cumb 148 B6
**Westward Ho!** Devon 23 G5
**Westwell** Kent 34 D5
**Westwell** Oxon 56 E6
**Westwell Leacon** Kent 34 C5
**West Wellow** Hants 28 F7
**West Wembury** Devon 6 D6
**West Wemyss** Fife 186 E7
**Westwick** Cambs 76 B2
**West Wickham** Cambs 76 E5
**West Wickham** Gt Lon 45 G6
**West Williamston** Pembks 49 H6
**West Wiltshire Crematorium** Wilts 39 K7
**West Winch** Norfk 90 F1
**West Winterslow** Wilts 28 E5
**West Wittering** W Susx 17 L3
**West Witton** N York 131 K2
**Westwood** Devon 12 C3
**Westwood** Kent 35 K2
**Westwood** Wilts 39 J8
**West Woodburn** Nthumb 157 M5
**West Woodhay** W Berk 41 H7
**Westwoodside** N Linc 116 C2
**West Worldham** Hants 30 C4
**West Worthing** W Susx 18 F5
**West Wratting** Cambs 76 E4
**West Wylam** Nthumb 150 E3
**Wetheral** Cumb 148 E4
**Wetherby** Leeds 124 B2
**Wetherby Services** N York 124 C1
**Wetherden** Suffk 78 B3
**Wetheringsett** Suffk 78 D2
**Wethersfield** Essex 61 H2
**Wetherup Street** Suffk 78 D2
**Wetley Rocks** Staffs 99 L3
**Wettenhall** Ches E 98 F1
**Wetton** Staffs 100 C2
**Wetwang** E R Yk 134 E7
**Wetwood** Staffs 99 H5
**Wexcombe** Wilts 40 F8
**Weybourne** Norfk 106 D4
**Weybourne** Surrey 30 D2
**Weybread** Suffk 92 F7
**Weybread Street** Suffk 92 F7
**Weybridge** Surrey 43 H7
**Weycroft** Devon 13 H3
**Weydale** Highld 231 H3
**Weyhill** Hants 28 F3
**Weymouth** Dorset 14 D6
**Weymouth Crematorium** Dorset 14 C6
**Whaddon** Bucks 74 B7
**Whaddon** Cambs 75 L5
**Whaddon** Gloucs 55 J5
**Whaddon** Wilts 28 D6
**Whaddon** Wilts 39 K7
**Whaley** Derbys 115 K7
**Whaley Bridge** Derbys 113 M5
**Whaley Thorns** Derbys 115 K7
**Whaligoe** Highld 231 K7
**Whalley** Lancs 121 L4
**Whalsay** Shet 235 d4
**Whalton** Nthumb 158 E6
**Whaplode** Lincs 104 A7
**Whaplode Drove** Lincs 89 K2
**Wharf** Warwks 72 E4
**Wharfe** N York 130 E5
**Wharles** Lancs 120 F4
**Wharley End** C Beds 74 D5
**Wharncliffe Side** Sheff 114 F3
**Wharram-le-Street** N York 134 D6
**Wharton** Herefs 69 K4
**Whashton** N York 140 E6
**Whasset** Cumb 129 L4
**Whatcote** Warwks 72 C5
**Whateley** Warwks 86 B4
**Whatfield** Suffk 78 B5
**Whatley** Somset 13 J2
**Whatley** Somset 27 G3
**Whatlington** E Susx 20 F3
**Whatton** Notts 102 C5
**Whauphill** D & G 145 J5
**Wheal Peevor** Cnwll 3 J3
**Wheatacre** Norfk 93 K5
**Wheathampstead** Herts 59 K5
**Wheatley** Hants 30 C4
**Wheatley** Oxon 57 L6
**Wheatley Hill** Dur 151 J6
**Wheatley Hills** Donc 115 L1
**Wheaton Aston** Staffs 84 F2
**Wheddon Cross** Somset 24 E4
**Wheelock** Ches E 99 H2
**Wheelton** Lancs 121 J6
**Wheldrake** C York 125 G2
**Whelford** Gloucs 56 D7
**Whelpley Hill** Bucks 59 G6
**Whempstead** Herts 60 A4
**Whenby** N York 133 K5
**Whepstead** Suffk 77 J3
**Wherstead** Suffk 78 E6
**Wherwell** Hants 29 H3
**Wheston** Derbys 114 C6
**Whetsted** Kent 33 H4
**Whetstone** Leics 87 G4
**Whicham** Cumb 128 D3
**Whichford** Warwks 72 C7
**Whickham** Gatesd 150 F3
**Whiddon Down** Devon 11 G6
**Whigstreet** Angus 196 D7
**Whilton** Nhants 73 J2
**Whimple** Devon 12 D3
**Whimpwell Green** Norfk 107 H6
**Whinburgh** Norfk 92 B2
**Whinnieliggate** D & G 146 C4
**Whinnyfold** Abers 217 K7
**Whippingham** IoW 17 G4
**Whipsnade** C Beds 59 G4
**Whipsnade Zoo ZSL** C Beds 59 G4
**Whipton** Devon 12 B4
**Whisby** Lincs 116 E7
**Whissendine** RutInd 88 B2
**Whissonsett** Norfk 105 L7
**Whistlefield** Ag & B 183 J8
**Whistlefield Inn** Ag & B 183 G8
**Whistley Green** Wokham 42 C5
**Whiston** Knows 112 C3
**Whiston** Nhants 74 B3
**Whiston** Rothm 115 H4
**Whiston** Staffs 84 F2
**Whiston** Staffs 100 B3
**Whitbeck** Cumb 128 D3
**Whitbourne** Herefs 70 D3
**Whitburn** S Tyne 151 J3
**Whitburn** W Loth 176 C5
**Whitby** N York 143 J5
**Whitchester** Border 178 F6
**Whitchurch** BaNES 38 F6
**Whitchurch** Bucks 58 D4
**Whitchurch** Cardif 37 J4
**Whitchurch** Devon 6 D2
**Whitchurch** Hants 29 J2
**Whitchurch** Herefs 54 D4
**Whitchurch** Oxon 41 M5
**Whitchurch** Pembks 48 D3
**Whitchurch** Shrops 98 D4
**Whitchurch Canonicorum** Dorset 13 K4
**Whitchurch Hill** Oxon 41 M5
**Whitcombe** Dorset 14 D5
**Whitcot** Shrops 83 H5
**Whitcott Keysett** Shrops 82 F6
**Whiteacre Heath** Warwks 86 B5
**White Ball** Somset 25 H7
**Whitebridge** Highld 202 D3
**Whitebrook** Mons 54 D6
**Whitebushes** Surrey 32 B4
**Whitecairns** Abers 207 H2
**Whitechapel** Gt Lon 45 G4
**White Chapel** Lancs 121 H3
**Whitecliffe** Gloucs 54 E6
**White Colne** Essex 61 L3
**Whitecraig** E Loth 177 K4
**Whitecrook** D & G 144 E4
**White Cross** Cnwll 3 H6
**Whitecross** Falk 176 C3
**Whiteface** Highld 222 F4
**Whitefarland** N Ayrs 161 L2
**Whitefaulds** S Ayrs 163 H7
**Whitefield** Bury 113 J1
**Whitefield** Somset 25 G5
**Whiteford** Abers 206 D1
**Whitegate** Ches W 112 F7
**Whitehall** Ork 234 d5
**Whitehaven** Cumb 136 D4
**Whitehill and Bordon** Hants 30 C5
**Whitehills** Abers 216 C2
**Whitehouse** Abers 206 C3
**Whitehouse** Ag & B 172 D6
**Whitehouse Common** Birm 85 K4
**Whitekirk** E Loth 178 D3
**White Lackington** Dorset 14 D3
**Whitelackington** Somset 26 B7
**White Ladies Aston** Worcs 71 G4
**Whiteleaf** Bucks 58 D6
**Whiteley** Hants 17 G1
**Whiteley Bank** IoW 17 G6
**Whitemire** Moray 214 B4
**Whitemoor** C Nott 101 K4
**Whitemoor** Cnwll 4 F4
**Whiteness** Shet 235 c6
**White Notley** Essex 61 J4
**Whiteparish** Wilts 28 E6
**White Pit** Lincs 118 E6
**Whiterashes** Abers 206 F2
**White Roding** Essex 60 E5
**Whiterow** Highld 231 L5
**Whiterow** Moray 214 C3
**Whiteshill** Gloucs 55 J6
**Whitesmith** E Susx 20 B3
**Whitestaunton** Somset 13 H1
**Whitestone Cross** Devon 11 K6
**White Waltham** W & M 42 D5
**Whitewell** Lancs 121 K2
**Whitfield** C Dund 187 G2
**Whitfield** Kent 35 J5
**Whitfield** Nhants 73 H6
**Whitfield** Nthumb 149 K4
**Whitfield** S Glos 38 F3
**Whitford** Devon 13 G4
**Whitford** Flints 111 G5
**Whitgift** E R Yk 125 J6
**Whitgreave** Staffs 99 K6
**Whithorn** D & G 145 J6
**Whiting Bay** N Ayrs 162 D4
**Whitkirk** Leeds 124 B4
**Whitland** Carmth 49 L4
**Whitlaw** Border 167 G6
**Whitletts** S Ayrs 163 J5
**Whitley** N York 124 E6
**Whitley** Readg 42 B6
**Whitley** Sheff 115 G3
**Whitley** Wilts 39 K6
**Whitley Bay** N Tyne 159 J7
**Whitley Bay Crematorium** N Tyne 159 H7
**Whitley Chapel** Nthumb 150 B4
**Whitley Lower** Kirk 123 J6
**Whitminster** Gloucs 55 H6
**Whitmore** Staffs 99 J4
**Whitnage** Devon 25 G7
**Whitnash** Warwks 72 D2
**Whitney-on-Wye** Herefs 68 F5
**Whitsbury** Hants 28 C7
**Whitsome** Border 179 H7
**Whitson** Newpt 38 B4
**Whitstable** Kent 47 J6
**Whitstone** Cnwll 9 H5
**Whittingham** Nthumb 168 F6
**Whittingslow** Shrops 83 H5
**Whittington** Derbys 115 G6
**Whittington** Gloucs 55 M4
**Whittington** Lancs 130 B4
**Whittington** Norfk 91 G4
**Whittington** Shrops 97 L6
**Whittington** Staffs 84 F6
**Whittington** Staffs 85 L2
**Whittington** Warwks 86 C4
**Whittington** Worcs 70 F4
**Whittlebury** Nhants 73 K5
**Whittle-le-Woods** Lancs 121 H6
**Whittlesey** Cambs 89 J4
**Whittlesford** Cambs 76 C5
**Whitton** N Linc 125 L5
**Whitton** Nthumb 158 D3
**Whitton** Powys 68 F2
**Whitton** S on T 141 J3
**Whitton** Shrops 83 L8
**Whittonstall** Nthumb 150 D4
**Whitway** Hants 41 J8
**Whitwell** Derbys 115 K6

**Whitwell** Herts 59 K4
**Whitwell** IoW 17 G6
**Whitwell** N York 141 G7
**Whitwell** Rutlnd 88 D2
**Whitwell-on-the-Hill** N York 133 L6
**Whitwell Street** Norfk 106 D7
**Whitwick** Leics 86 E1
**Whitworth** Lancs 122 D6
**Whixall** Shrops 98 D5
**Whixley** N York 133 G7
**Whorlton** Dur 140 E4
**Whyle** Herefs 69 L3
**Whyteleafe** Surrey 32 C2
**Wibsey** C Brad 123 H4
**Wibtoft** Warwks 86 F6
**Wichenford** Worcs 70 D3
**Wichling** Kent 34 B4
**Wick** Bmouth 15 L4
**Wick** Highld 231 L5
**Wick** S Glos 39 G5
**Wick** V Glam 36 E6
**Wick** W Susx 18 D5
**Wick** Worcs 71 G5
**Wicken** Cambs 76 E1
**Wicken** Nhants 73 L6
**Wicken Bonhunt** Essex 60 D2
**Wickenby** Lincs 117 H5
**Wicken Green Village** Norfk 105 K6
**Wickersley** Rothm 115 J3
**Wicker Street Green** Suffk 77 L6
**Wickford** Essex 46 C2
**Wickham** Hants 17 H1
**Wickham** W Berk 41 H6
**Wickham Bishops** Essex 61 K5
**Wickhambreaux** Kent 35 G3
**Wickhambrook** Suffk 77 H4
**Wickhamford** Worcs 71 J6
**Wickham Green** Suffk 78 D2
**Wickham Market** Suffk 79 G4
**Wickhampton** Norfk 93 J3
**Wickham St Paul** Essex 77 J7
**Wickham Skeith** Suffk 78 C2
**Wickham Street** Suffk 78 C1
*Wick John o' Groats Airport* Highld 231 L5
**Wicklewood** Norfk 92 C3
**Wickmere** Norfk 106 E5
**Wick St Lawrence** N Som 38 A7
**Wicksteed Park** Nhants 88 C7
**Wickwar** S Glos 39 G3
**Widdington** Essex 60 E2
**Widdrington** Nthumb 159 G3
**Widdrington Station** Nthumb 159 G4
**Widecombe in the Moor** Devon 7 G1
**Widegates** Cnwll 5 L4
**Widemouth Bay** Cnwll 9 G4
**Wide Open** N Tyne 159 G7
**Widford** Essex 61 H6
**Widford** Herts 60 C5
**Widmer End** Bucks 42 E2
**Widmerpool** Notts 101 M6
**Widmore** Gt Lon 45 H6
**Widnes** Halton 112 D4
**Widnes Crematorium** Halton 112 D4
**Widworthy** Devon 13 G3
**Wigan** Wigan 112 E1
**Wigan Crematorium** Wigan 112 E2
**Wigborough** Somset 26 C7
**Wiggaton** Devon 12 E4
**Wiggenhall St Germans** Norfk 90 E2
**Wiggenhall St Mary Magdalen** Norfk 90 E2
**Wiggenhall St Mary the Virgin** Norfk 90 E2
**Wigginton** C York 133 J7
**Wigginton** Herts 58 F6
**Wigginton** Oxon 57 H2
**Wigginton** Staffs 86 B3
**Wigglesworth** N York 130 F7
**Wiggonby** Cumb 148 B4
**Wighill** N York 124 D2
**Wighton** Norfk 105 M4
**Wightwick** Wolves 84 F4
**Wigley** Hants 29 G7
**Wigmore** Herefs 69 H2
**Wigmore** Medway 46 D6
**Wigsley** Notts 116 E7
**Wigsthorpe** Nhants 88 F6
**Wigston** Leics 87 H4
**Wigston Fields** Leics 87 H4
**Wigston Parva** Leics 86 F5
**Wigthorpe** Notts 115 L5
**Wigtoft** Lincs 103 L5
**Wigton** Cumb 148 A5
**Wigtown** D & G 145 J4
**Wike** Leeds 123 L3
**Wilbarston** Nhants 88 B5
**Wilberfoss** E R Yk 125 H1
**Wilburton** Cambs 90 C7
**Wilby** Nhants 74 C2
**Wilby** Norfk 92 B5
**Wilby** Suffk 78 F1
**Wilcot** Wilts 40 C7
**Wilcott** Shrops 98 B8
**Wildboarclough** Ches E 113 M7
**Wilden** Bed 75 G4
**Wilden** Worcs 84 E8
**Wildmanbridge** S Lans 175 L7
**Wildmoor** Worcs 85 G7
**Wildsworth** Lincs 116 D3
**Wilford** C Nott 101 K5
**Wilford Hill Crematorium** Notts 101 L5
**Wilkesley** Ches E 98 F4
**Wilkhaven** Highld 223 K4
**Wilkieston** W Loth 176 F5
**Willand** Devon 12 D1
**Willaston** Ches E 99 G3
**Willaston** Ches W 111 K6
**Willen** M Keyn 74 C6
**Willenhall** Covtry 86 D7
**Willenhall** Wsall 85 H4
**Willerby** E R Yk 126 C4
**Willerby** N York 134 F4
**Willersey** Gloucs 71 K6
**Willersley** Herefs 68 F5
**Willesborough** Kent 34 D6
**Willesborough Lees** Kent 34 D6
**Willesden** Gt Lon 44 E3
**Willesley** Wilts 39 J3
**Willett** Somset 25 H5
**Willey** Shrops 84 C4
**Willey** Warwks 86 F6
**Willey Green** Surrey 30 F2
**Williamscot** Oxon 72 F5
**Willian** Herts 59 L2
**Willingale** Essex 60 F6
**Willingdon** E Susx 20 C5
**Willingham** Cambs 76 B1
**Willingham by Stow** Lincs 116 E5
**Willington** Bed 75 G4
**Willington** Derbys 100 F6
**Willington** Dur 150 F7
**Willington** Kent 33 K3
**Willington** N Tyne 151 H2
**Willington** Warwks 72 C6
**Willitoft** E R Yk 125 H4
**Williton** Somset 25 G3
**Willoughby** Lincs 119 G6
**Willoughby** Warwks 73 G2
**Willoughby-on-the-Wolds** Notts 101 M7
**Willoughby Waterleys** Leics 87 H5
**Willoughton** Lincs 116 F3
**Willows Green** Essex 61 H4
**Willtown** Somset 26 B6
**Wilmcote** Warwks 71 L3
**Wilmington** Devon 13 G3
**Wilmington** E Susx 20 B5
**Wilmington** Kent 45 K5
**Wilmslow** Ches E 113 J5
**Wilpshire** Lancs 121 K4
**Wilsden** C Brad 123 G3
**Wilsford** Lincs 103 G4
**Wilsford** Wilts 28 C4
**Wilsford** Wilts 40 C8
**Wilshaw** Kirk 123 G8
**Wilsill** N York 132 B6
**Wilson** Leics 101 H7
**Wilsontown** S Lans 176 C7
**Wilstead** Bed 74 F5
**Wilsthorpe** Lincs 88 F2
**Wilstone** Herts 58 E5
**Wilton** Herefs 54 E3
**Wilton** N York 134 D3
**Wilton** R & Cl 142 C4
**Wilton** Wilts 28 C5
**Wilton** Wilts 40 E7
**Wilton Dean** Border 167 G6
**Wimbish Green** Essex 76 E7
**Wimbledon** Gt Lon 44 E6
**Wimblington** Cambs 90 B5
**Wimboldsley** Ches W 113 G8
**Wimborne Minster** Dorset 15 J3
**Wimborne St Giles** Dorset 28 B8
**Wimbotsham** Norfk 90 E3
**Wimpole** Cambs 75 L4
**Wimpstone** Warwks 72 B5
**Wincanton** Somset 27 G5
**Winchburgh** W Loth 176 E4
**Winchcombe** Gloucs 56 A3
**Winchelsea** E Susx 21 H3
**Winchester** Hants 29 J5
**Winchester Services** Hants 29 K4
**Winchet Hill** Kent 33 J5
**Winchfield** Hants 30 C1
**Winchmore Hill** Bucks 42 F2
**Winchmore Hill** Gt Lon 44 F2
**Wincle** Ches E 113 L7
**Wincobank** Sheff 115 G3
**Windermere** Cumb 137 L7
**Windermere Steamboats & Museum** Cumb 137 L7
**Winderton** Warwks 72 D6
**Windhill** Highld 212 E5
**Windlesham** Surrey 42 F7
**Windmill** Cnwll 4 D2
**Windmill Hill** E Susx 20 D4
**Windmill Hill** Somset 25 L7
**Windrush** Gloucs 56 D5
**Windsole** Abers 216 B3
**Windsor** W & M 42 F5
**Windsor Castle** W & M 42 F5
**Windsoredge** Gloucs 55 J7
**Windsor Green** Suffk 77 K4
**Windygates** Fife 186 E7
**Wineham** W Susx 31 L7
**Winestead** E R Yk 127 G5
**Winfarthing** Norfk 92 D6
**Winford** IoW 17 G5
**Winford** N Som 38 D7
**Winforton** Herefs 68 F5
**Winfrith Newburgh** Dorset 14 F5
**Wing** Bucks 58 E4
**Wing** Rutlnd 88 C3
**Wingate** Dur 151 J7
**Wingerworth** Derbys 115 G7
**Wingfield** C Beds 59 G3
**Wingfield** Suffk 92 F7
**Wingfield** Wilts 27 J1
**Wingham** Kent 35 H3
**Wingrave** Bucks 58 E4
**Winkburn** Notts 102 B2
**Winkfield** Br For 42 E6
**Winkfield Row** Br For 42 E6
**Winkhill** Staffs 100 B3
**Winkleigh** Devon 10 F4
**Winksley** N York 132 C5
**Winlaton** Gatesd 150 F3
**Winless** Highld 231 K5
**Winmarleigh** Lancs 120 F2
**Winnall** Hants 29 J5
**Winnersh** Wokham 42 C6
**Winnington** Ches W 112 F6
**Winscombe** N Som 38 B8
**Winsford** Ches W 112 F7
**Winsford** Somset 24 E4
**Winsham** Somset 13 J2
**Winshill** Staffs 100 F7
**Winshwen** Swans 51 K6
**Winskill** Cumb 149 G7
**Winsley** Wilts 39 J7
**Winslow** Bucks 58 C3
**Winson** Gloucs 56 C6
**Winsor** Hants 28 F8
**Winster** Cumb 129 J2
**Winster** Derbys 100 E1
**Winston** Dur 140 E4
**Winston** Suffk 78 E3
**Winstone** Gloucs 55 L6
**Winswell** Devon 10 D3
**Winterborne Came** Dorset 14 D5
**Winterborne Clenston** Dorset 14 F2
**Winterborne Houghton** Dorset 14 F2
**Winterborne Kingston** Dorset 15 G3
**Winterborne Monkton** Dorset 14 D5
**Winterborne Stickland** Dorset 14 F2
**Winterborne Whitechurch** Dorset 14 F3
**Winterborne Zelston** Dorset 15 G3
**Winterbourne** S Glos 38 F4
**Winterbourne** W Berk 41 J6
**Winterbourne Abbas** Dorset 14 C4
**Winterbourne Bassett** Wilts 40 C5
**Winterbourne Dauntsey** Wilts 28 D4
**Winterbourne Earls** Wilts 28 D5
**Winterbourne Gunner** Wilts 28 D4
**Winterbourne Monkton** Wilts 40 C6
**Winterbourne Steepleton** Dorset 14 C4
**Winterbourne Stoke** Wilts 28 B3
**Winterburn** N York 131 H7
**Winteringham** N Linc 125 L6
**Winterley** Ches E 99 H2
**Winterslow** Wilts 28 E5
**Winterton** N Linc 125 L6
**Winterton-on-Sea** Norfk 107 K8
**Winthorpe** Notts 102 D2
**Winton** Bmouth 15 K4
**Winton** Cumb 139 H5
**Wintringham** N York 134 D5
**Winwick** Cambs 89 G7
**Winwick** Nhants 87 J8
**Winwick** Warrtn 112 E3
**Wirksworth** Derbys 100 F2
**Wirral** 111 J4
**Wirswall** Ches E 98 D4
**Wisbech** Cambs 90 C2
**Wisbech St Mary** Cambs 90 B2
**Wisborough Green** W Susx 31 H6
**Wiseman's Bridge** Pembks 49 K6
**Wiseton** Notts 116 B4

Wishaw N Lans 175 L7
Wisley Garden RHS Surrey 43 H8
Wispington Lincs 117 K6
Wissett Suffk 93 H7
Wissington Suffk 61 M2
Wistanstow Shrops 83 H6
Wistanswick Shrops 98 F6
Wistaston Ches E 99 G2
Wistaston Green Ches E 99 G2
Wiston Pembks 49 H4
Wiston S Lans 165 J3
Wiston W Susx 18 F3
Wistow Cambs 89 K7
Wistow N York 124 F4
Wiswell Lancs 121 L3
Witcham Cambs 90 C7
Witchampton Dorset 15 J2
Witchford Cambs 90 C7
Witcombe Somset 26 C6
Witham Essex 61 K5
Witham Friary Somset 27 H3
Witham on the Hill Lincs 103 H8
Withcall Lincs 118 C5
Withdean Br & H 19 J4
Witherenden Hill E Susx 33 H7
Witheridge Devon 11 J3
Witherley Leics 86 D4
Withern Lincs 118 F5
Withernsea E R Yk 127 H5
Withernwick E R Yk 126 F3
Withersdale Street Suffk 92 F7
Withersfield Suffk 76 F5
Witherslack Cumb 129 J3
Withiel Cnwll 4 F3
Withiel Florey Somset 24 F5
Withington Gloucs 56 B5
Withington Herefs 69 L5
Withington Manch 113 J3
Withington Shrops 83 L2
Withington Staffs 100 B5
Withleigh Devon 11 K3
Withnell Lancs 121 J6
Withybed Green Worcs 85 H8
Withybrook Warwks 86 E6
Withycombe Somset 24 F3
Withyham E Susx 32 E6
Withypool Somset 24 D4
Withywood Bristl 38 E6
Witley Surrey 30 F4
Witnesham Suffk 78 E4
Witney Oxon 57 G6
Wittering C Pete 88 F3
Wittersham Kent 21 H1
Witton Birm 85 J5
Witton Norfk 93 G2
Witton Norfk 107 H6
Witton Gilbert Dur 151 G5
Witton le Wear Dur 140 E2
Witton Park Dur 140 F2
Wiveliscombe Somset 25 G5
Wivelrod Hants 30 A4
Wivelsfield E Susx 19 K2
Wivelsfield Green E Susx 19 K2
Wivenhoe Essex 62 C4
Wiveton Norfk 106 C4
Wix Essex 62 E3
Wixams Bed 74 F5
Wixford Warwks 71 K4
Wixoe Suffk 77 G6
Woburn C Beds 58 F2
Woburn Safari Park C Beds 74 D7
Woburn Sands M Keyn 74 D7
Woking Surrey 43 G8
Woking Crematorium Surrey 42 F8
Wokingham Wokham 42 D6
Woldingham Surrey 32 C3
Wold Newton E R Yk 135 G5
Wold Newton NE Lin 118 C3
Wolfclyde S Lans 165 K3
Wolferton Norfk 105 G6
Wolfhill P & K 186 B2
Wolf's Castle Pembks 49 G3
Wolfsdale Pembks 48 F3
Wollaston Dudley 84 F6
Wollaston Nhants 74 C2
Wollaston Shrops 83 G2
Wollaton C Nott 101 K4
Wollaton Hall & Park C Nott 101 K5
Wollerton Shrops 98 F6
Wollescote Dudley 85 G6
Wolseley Bridge Staffs 100 A7
Wolsingham Dur 150 D7
Wolstanton Staffs 99 J3
Wolston Warwks 86 E7
Wolvercote Oxon 57 J6
Wolverhampton Wolves 85 G4
*Wolverhampton Halfpenny Green Airport* Staffs 84 E5
Wolverley Worcs 84 E7
Wolverton Hants 41 K8
Wolverton M Keyn 74 B6
Wolverton Warwks 72 B3
Wolverton Wilts 27 H5
Wolvesnewton Mons 54 C7
Wolvey Warwks 86 E6
Wolvey Heath Warwks 86 E5
Wolviston S on T 141 K3
Wombleton N York 133 K3
Wombourne Staffs 84 F5
Wombwell Barns 115 H2
Womenswold Kent 35 G5
Womersley N York 124 E6
Wonersh Surrey 31 G3
Wonford Devon 12 B4
Wonston Dorset 14 E2
Wonston Hants 29 J4
Wooburn Green Bucks 42 E3
Woodacott Devon 9 K4
Woodall Rothm 115 J5
Woodall Services Rothm 115 J5
Woodbastwick Norfk 93 G1
Wood Bevington Warwks 71 J4
Woodborough Notts 101 M3
Woodborough Wilts 40 C7
Woodbridge Suffk 78 F5
Woodbury Devon 12 C5
Woodbury Salterton Devon 12 C5
Woodchester Gloucs 55 J7
Woodchurch Kent 34 C7
Woodcombe Somset 24 E3
Woodcote Gt Lon 44 F7
Woodcote Oxon 41 M4
Woodcote Wrekin 84 D1
Woodcroft Gloucs 38 D2
Wood Dalling Norfk 106 C6
Woodditton Cambs 76 F3
Woodeaton Oxon 57 K5
Wood End Gt Lon 43 J4
Wood End Herts 60 B3
Woodend Highld 190 F4
Woodend Nhants 73 H5
Woodend W Loth 176 C4
Woodend W Susx 17 M2
Wood End Warwks 71 K1
Wood End Wolves 85 G4
Wood Enderby Lincs 118 C8
Woodfalls Wilts 28 D7
Woodford Cnwll 9 G3
Woodford Gloucs 39 G2
Woodford Gt Lon 45 H2
Woodford Nhants 88 D7
Woodford Stockp 113 K5
Woodford Bridge Gt Lon 45 H2
Woodford Green Gt Lon 45 H2
Woodford Halse Nhants 73 G4
Woodford Wells Gt Lon 45 H2
Woodgate Birm 85 H6
Woodgate Devon 25 H7
Woodgate W Susx 18 C5
Woodgate Worcs 71 H2
Wood Green Gt Lon 44 F2
Woodgreen Hants 28 D7
Woodhall N York 131 J2
Woodhall Spa Lincs 117 K8
Woodham Bucks 58 B4
Woodham Surrey 43 H7
Woodham Ferrers Essex 61 J7
Woodham Mortimer Essex 61 K6
Woodham Walter Essex 61 K6
Wood Hayes Wolves 85 G3
Woodhead Abers 216 E6
Woodhill Shrops 84 D6
Woodhill Somset 26 A6
Woodhorn Nthumb 159 H4
Woodhouse Leeds 123 K4
Woodhouse Leics 87 G1
Woodhouse Sheff 115 H4
Woodhouse Wakefd 124 B6
Woodhouse Eaves Leics 87 G2
Woodhouselee Mdloth 177 H5
Woodhouselees D & G 156 D6
Woodhouses Oldham 113 K2
Woodhouses Staffs 100 D8
Woodhurst Cambs 89 K7
Woodingdean Br & H 19 K5
Woodkirk Leeds 123 K5
Woodland Abers 207 G2
Woodland Devon 6 F5
Woodland Devon 7 J3
Woodland Dur 140 D2
Woodland S Ayrs 152 E3
Woodlands Abers 206 E6
Woodlands Donc 124 E8
Woodlands Dorset 15 K2
Woodlands Hants 16 C1
Woodlands N York 132 E8
Woodlands (Coleshill) Crematorium Warwks 85 L5
Woodlands Park W & M 42 E5
Woodlands (Scarborough) Crematorium N York 134 F3
Woodlands (Scunthorpe) Crematorium N Linc 125 K7
Woodleigh Devon 7 H6
Woodley Wokham 42 C5
Woodmancote Gloucs 39 H2
Woodmancote Gloucs 55 L3
Woodmancote Gloucs 56 A6
Woodmancote W Susx 17 L2
Woodmancote W Susx 19 H3
Woodmancott Hants 29 K3
Woodmansey E R Yk 126 C3
Woodmansgreen W Susx 30 E6
Woodmansterne Surrey 32 B2
Woodmanton Devon 12 C5
Woodnesborough Kent 35 J4
Woodnewton Nhants 88 F5
Wood Norton Norfk 106 B6
Woodplumpton Lancs 121 G4
Woodrising Norfk 92 B3
Wood's Corner E Susx 20 D2
Woodseaves Staffs 99 H7
Woodsetts Rothm 115 K5
Woodsford Dorset 14 E4
Wood's Green E Susx 33 H6
Woodside Br For 42 F6
Woodside Fife 187 G5
Woodside Gt Lon 45 G6
Woodside P & K 195 K8
Woodside Crematorium Inver 174 B3
Woodstock Oxon 57 H5
Woodston C Pete 89 H4
Wood Street Norfk 107 H7
Wood Street Village Surrey 30 F2
Woodton Norfk 93 G5
Woodtown Devon 22 F6
Woodvale Crematorium Br & H 19 J4
Woodville Derbys 100 F8
Wood Walton Cambs 89 J7
Woofferton Shrops 69 K2
Wookey Somset 26 D3
Wookey Hole Somset 26 D2
Wool Dorset 14 F5
Woolacombe Devon 23 G3
Woolage Green Kent 35 H5
Woolaston Gloucs 54 E7
Woolaston Common Gloucs 54 E7
Woolavington Somset 25 M3
Woolbeding W Susx 30 E6
Woolbrook Devon 12 E5
Wooler Nthumb 168 E4
Woolfardisworthy Devon 11 J3
Woolfardisworthy Devon 22 E7
Woolfords S Lans 176 D6
Woolhampton W Berk 41 L6
Woolhope Herefs 69 L7
Woolland Dorset 14 E2
Woolley BaNES 39 H6
Woolley Cambs 89 G8
Woolley Wakefd 123 L7
Woolley Edge Services Wakefd 123 K7
Woolmere Green Worcs 71 G2
Woolmer Green Herts 59 L4
Woolminstone Somset 13 K2
Woolpit Suffk 77 L3
Woolstaston Shrops 83 J4
Woolsthorpe Lincs 102 D5
Woolsthorpe-by-Colsterworth Lincs 102 F7
Woolston C Sotn 16 E1
Woolston Shrops 97 L7
Woolston Somset 25 H4
Woolston Somset 26 F5
Woolston Warrtn 112 F4
Woolstone Gloucs 55 L3
Woolstone M Keyn 74 C6
Woolstone Oxon 40 F3
Woolston Green Devon 7 H3
Woolton Lpool 112 B4
Woolton Hill Hants 41 H7
Woolverstone Suffk 78 E6
Woolverton Somset 27 H2
Woolwich Gt Lon 45 H4
Woonton Herefs 69 G4
Woore Shrops 99 G4

**Wootten Green** Suffk ..... 92 F8
**Wootton** Bed ..... 74 E5
**Wootton** Kent ..... 35 G5
**Wootton** N Linc ..... 126 D7
**Wootton** Nhants ..... 73 L3
**Wootton** Oxon ..... 57 H4
**Wootton** Oxon ..... 57 J7
**Wootton** Staffs ..... 100 C4
**Wootton Bassett** Wilts ..... 40 B4
**Wootton Bridge** IoW ..... 17 G4
**Wootton Courtenay** Somset ..... 24 E3
**Wootton Fitzpaine** Dorset ..... 13 J4
**Wootton Rivers** Wilts ..... 40 D7
**Wootton St Lawrence** Hants ..... 29 L2
**Wootton Wawen** Warwks ..... 71 L2
**Worcester** Worcs ..... 70 F4
**Worcester Crematorium** Worcs ..... 70 F3
**Worcester Park** Gt Lon ..... 44 E6
**Wordsley** Dudley ..... 84 F6
**Worfield** Shrops ..... 84 D4
**Workington** Cumb ..... 136 D2
**Worksop** Notts ..... 115 L5
**Worlaby** N Linc ..... 126 C7
**Worlds End** Hants ..... 29 M8
**Worlds End** W Susx ..... 19 J2
**Worle** N Som ..... 38 A7
**Worleston** Ches E ..... 98 F2
**Worlingham** Suffk ..... 93 J5
**Worlington** Devon ..... 11 H3
**Worlington** Suffk ..... 91 G8
**Worlingworth** Suffk ..... 78 F2
**Wormbridge** Herefs ..... 54 B2
**Wormegay** Norfk ..... 90 F2
**Wormelow Tump** Herefs ..... 54 C3
**Wormhill** Derbys ..... 114 C6
**Wormingford** Essex ..... 61 M2
**Worminghall** Bucks ..... 57 M6
**Wormington** Gloucs ..... 71 J7
**Wormit** Fife ..... 186 F3
**Wormleighton** Warwks ..... 72 F4
**Wormley** Herts ..... 60 B6
**Wormley** Surrey ..... 30 F4
**Wormshill** Kent ..... 34 B3
**Wormsley** Herefs ..... 69 H5
**Worplesdon** Surrey ..... 30 F2
**Worrall** Sheff ..... 114 F3
**Worsbrough** Barns ..... 115 G2
**Worsbrough Bridge** Barns ..... 115 G2
**Worsbrough Dale** Barns ..... 115 G2
**Worsley** Salfd ..... 113 H2
**Worstead** Norfk ..... 107 G7
**Worsthorne** Lancs ..... 122 C4
**Worston** Devon ..... 6 E5
**Worston** Lancs ..... 122 B3
**Worth** Kent ..... 35 J4
**Wortham** Suffk ..... 92 C7
**Worthen** Shrops ..... 83 G3
**Worthenbury** Wrexhm ..... 98 B4
**Worthing** Norfk ..... 106 B8
**Worthing** W Susx ..... 18 F5
**Worthing Crematorium** W Susx ..... 18 F4
**Worthington** Leics ..... 101 H7
**Worth Matravers** Dorset ..... 15 H6
**Wortley** Barns ..... 114 F2
**Wortley** Leeds ..... 123 K4
**Worton** N York ..... 131 H2
**Worton** Wilts ..... 39 L8
**Wortwell** Norfk ..... 92 F6
**Wotton-under-Edge** Gloucs ..... 39 H2
**Wotton Underwood** Bucks ..... 58 B5
**Woughton on the Green** M Keyn ..... 74 C6
**Wouldham** Kent ..... 46 B7
**Wrabness** Essex ..... 62 E2
**Wrafton** Devon ..... 23 H4
**Wragby** Lincs ..... 117 J6
**Wragby** Wakefd ..... 124 C6
**Wrangaton** Devon ..... 7 G4
**Wrangle** Lincs ..... 104 C3
**Wrangway** Somset ..... 25 H7
**Wrantage** Somset ..... 25 L6
**Wrawby** N Linc ..... 126 C8
**Wraxall** N Som ..... 38 C6
**Wraxall** Somset ..... 26 E4
**Wray** Lancs ..... 130 B6
**Wraysbury** W & M ..... 43 G5
**Wrayton** Lancs ..... 130 C5
**Wrea Green** Lancs ..... 120 E4
**Wreay** Cumb ..... 148 D5
**Wrecclesham** Surrey ..... 30 D3
**Wrekenton** Gatesd ..... 151 G3
**Wrelton** N York ..... 134 B3
**Wrenbury** Ches E ..... 98 E3
**Wreningham** Norfk ..... 92 E4
**Wrentham** Suffk ..... 93 K6
**Wrentnall** Shrops ..... 83 H3
**Wressle** E R Yk ..... 125 G4
**Wressle** N Linc ..... 126 B8
**Wrestlingworth** C Beds ..... 75 J5
**Wretton** Norfk ..... 91 G4
**Wrexham** Wrexhm ..... 97 M3
**Wrexham Industrial Estate** Wrexhm ..... 98 B3
**Wribbenhall** Worcs ..... 84 E7
**Wrinehill** Staffs ..... 99 H3
**Wrington** N Som ..... 38 C7
**Writhlington** BaNES ..... 27 G1
**Writtle** Essex ..... 61 G6
**Wrockwardine** Wrekin ..... 84 B2
**Wroot** N Linc ..... 116 B2
**Wrose** C Brad ..... 123 H3
**Wrotham** Kent ..... 33 G2
**Wroughton** Swindn ..... 40 C4
**Wroxall** IoW ..... 17 G6
**Wroxall** Warwks ..... 72 B1
**Wroxeter** Shrops ..... 83 L2
**Wroxham** Norfk ..... 107 G8
**Wroxton** Oxon ..... 72 E6
**Wyaston** Derbys ..... 100 D4
**Wyberton East** Lincs ..... 104 B4
**Wyboston** Bed ..... 75 H3
**Wybunbury** Ches E ..... 99 G3
**Wychbold** Worcs ..... 71 G2
**Wychnor** Staffs ..... 85 L1
**Wyck Rissington** Gloucs ..... 56 D4
**Wycliffe** Dur ..... 140 E4
**Wycoller** Lancs ..... 122 D3
**Wycomb** Leics ..... 102 C7
**Wycombe Marsh** Bucks ..... 42 E3
**Wyddial** Herts ..... 60 B2
**Wye** Kent ..... 34 E5
**Wyke** C Brad ..... 123 H5
**Wyke** Dorset ..... 27 H6
**Wyke Champflower** Somset ..... 26 F4
**Wykeham** N York ..... 134 E3
**Wyken** Covtry ..... 86 D7
**Wyken** Shrops ..... 84 D4
**Wyke Regis** Dorset ..... 14 C6
**Wykey** Shrops ..... 98 B7
**Wylam** Nthumb ..... 150 E3
**Wylde Green** Birm ..... 85 K5
**Wylye** Wilts ..... 28 A4
**Wymeswold** Leics ..... 101 L7
**Wymington** Bed ..... 74 D2
**Wymondham** Leics ..... 102 D8
**Wymondham** Norfk ..... 92 D3
**Wynford Eagle** Dorset ..... 14 B3
**Wyre Forest Crematorium** Worcs ..... 84 E8
**Wyre Piddle** Worcs ..... 71 G5
**Wysall** Notts ..... 101 L6
**Wythall** Worcs ..... 85 J7
**Wytham** Oxon ..... 57 J6
**Wythenshawe** Manch ..... 113 J4
**Wyton** Cambs ..... 89 K8
**Wyton** E R Yk ..... 126 E4
**Wyverstone** Suffk ..... 78 C2
**Wyverstone Street** Suffk ..... 78 B2

## Y

**Yaddlethorpe** N Linc ..... 116 E1
**Yafforth** N York ..... 141 H7
**Yalberton** Torbay ..... 7 K4
**Yalding** Kent ..... 33 J3
**Yanwath** Cumb ..... 138 D2
**Yanworth** Gloucs ..... 56 B5
**Yapham** E R Yk ..... 125 J1
**Yapton** W Susx ..... 18 D5
**Yarborough** N Som ..... 38 B8
**Yarburgh** Lincs ..... 118 E3
**Yarcombe** Devon ..... 13 G2
**Yard** Devon ..... 24 B6
**Yardley** Birm ..... 85 K6
**Yardley Crematorium** Birm ..... 85 K6
**Yardley Gobion** Nhants ..... 73 L5
**Yardley Hastings** Nhants ..... 74 C3
**Yardley Wood** Birm ..... 85 K7
**Yarkhill** Herefs ..... 69 L6
**Yarley** Somset ..... 26 D3
**Yarlington** Somset ..... 26 F5
**Yarm** S on T ..... 141 K5
**Yarmouth** IoW ..... 16 D4
**Yarnbrook** Wilts ..... 27 K1
**Yarnfield** Staffs ..... 99 K6
**Yarnscombe** Devon ..... 23 J6
**Yarnton** Oxon ..... 57 J5
**Yarpole** Herefs ..... 69 J2
**Yarrow** Border ..... 166 E4
**Yarrow Feus** Border ..... 166 E4
**Yarrowford** Border ..... 166 F4
**Yarwell** Nhants ..... 88 F4
**Yate** S Glos ..... 39 G4
**Yateley** Hants ..... 42 D7
**Yatesbury** Wilts ..... 40 B6
**Yattendon** W Berk ..... 41 K5
**Yatton** Herefs ..... 69 H2
**Yatton** N Som ..... 38 B7
**Yatton Keynell** Wilts ..... 39 K5
**Yaverland** IoW ..... 17 H5
**Yaxham** Norfk ..... 92 B2
**Yaxley** Cambs ..... 89 H5
**Yaxley** Suffk ..... 92 D8
**Yazor** Herefs ..... 69 H5
**Yeading** Gt Lon ..... 43 J4
**Yeadon** Leeds ..... 123 J3
**Yealand Conyers** Lancs ..... 129 K5
**Yealand Redmayne** Lancs ..... 129 K4
**Yealmpton** Devon ..... 6 E5
**Yearsley** N York ..... 133 J5
**Yeaton** Shrops ..... 98 B8
**Yeaveley** Derbys ..... 100 D4
**Yeavering** Nthumb ..... 168 D4
**Yedingham** N York ..... 134 D4
**Yelford** Oxon ..... 57 G6
**Yell** Shet ..... 235 d3
**Yelling** Cambs ..... 75 J3
**Yelvertoft** Nhants ..... 87 H7
**Yelverton** Devon ..... 6 D3
**Yelverton** Norfk ..... 93 G3
**Yenston** Somset ..... 27 G7
**Yeoford** Devon ..... 11 H5
**Yeolmbridge** Cnwll ..... 9 J7
**Yeovil** Somset ..... 26 D7
**Yeovil Crematorium** Somset ..... 26 D7
**Yeovil Marsh** Somset ..... 26 D7
**Yeovilton** Somset ..... 26 D6
**Yesnaby** Ork ..... 234 b5
**Yetminster** Dorset ..... 14 B1
**Yettington** Devon ..... 12 D5
**Yetts o'Muckhart** Clacks ..... 185 L6
**Yew Tree** Sandw ..... 85 H4
**Y Felinheli** Gwynd ..... 109 G7
**Y Ferwig** Cerdgn ..... 65 G5
**Y Ffôr** Gwynd ..... 95 G5
**Y Gyffylliog** Denbgs ..... 97 G2
**Yielden** Bed ..... 74 E2
**Yieldshields** S Lans ..... 176 B7
**Yiewsley** Gt Lon ..... 43 H4
**Y Maerdy** Conwy ..... 96 F4
**Ynysboeth** Rhondd ..... 37 G2
**Ynysddu** Caerph ..... 37 J2
**Ynyshir** Rhondd ..... 36 F3
**Ynystawe** Swans ..... 51 K5
**Ynysybwl** Rhondd ..... 37 G2
**Yockleton** Shrops ..... 83 H2
**Yokefleet** E R Yk ..... 125 J5
**Yoker** C Glas ..... 174 F5
**York** C York ..... 124 F1
**York City Crematorium** C York ..... 124 F2
**Yorkletts** Kent ..... 34 E3
**Yorkley** Gloucs ..... 54 F6
*Yorkshire Dales National Park* ..... 131 G4
**York Town** Surrey ..... 42 E7
**Youlgreave** Derbys ..... 114 E8
**Youlthorpe** E R Yk ..... 134 B7
**Youlton** N York ..... 133 G6
**Yoxall** Staffs ..... 100 C8
**Yoxford** Suffk ..... 79 H2
**Y Rhiw** Gwynd ..... 94 D6
**Ysbyty Ifan** Conwy ..... 96 C3
**Ysbyty Ystwyth** Cerdgn ..... 67 G1
**Ysceifiog** Flints ..... 111 G7
**Ystalyfera** Neath ..... 52 B6
**Ystrad** Rhondd ..... 36 F2
**Ystrad Aeron** Cerdgn ..... 66 C4
**Ystradfellte** Powys ..... 52 E5
**Ystradgynlais** Powys ..... 52 C6
**Ystrad Meurig** Cerdgn ..... 66 F2
**Ystrad Mynach** Caerph ..... 37 H2
**Ystradowen** V Glam ..... 36 F5
**Ythanbank** Abers ..... 217 G7
**Ythanwells** Abers ..... 216 C6
**Ythsie** Abers ..... 217 G7

## Z

**Zeal Monachorum** Devon ..... 11 G4
**Zeals** Wilts ..... 27 H5
**Zelah** Cnwll ..... 4 C5
**Zennor** Cnwll ..... 2 E4
**Zouch** Notts ..... 101 J7
**ZSL London Zoo** Gt Lon ..... 44 F4
**ZSL Whipsnade Zoo** C Beds ..... 59 G4

# Ireland

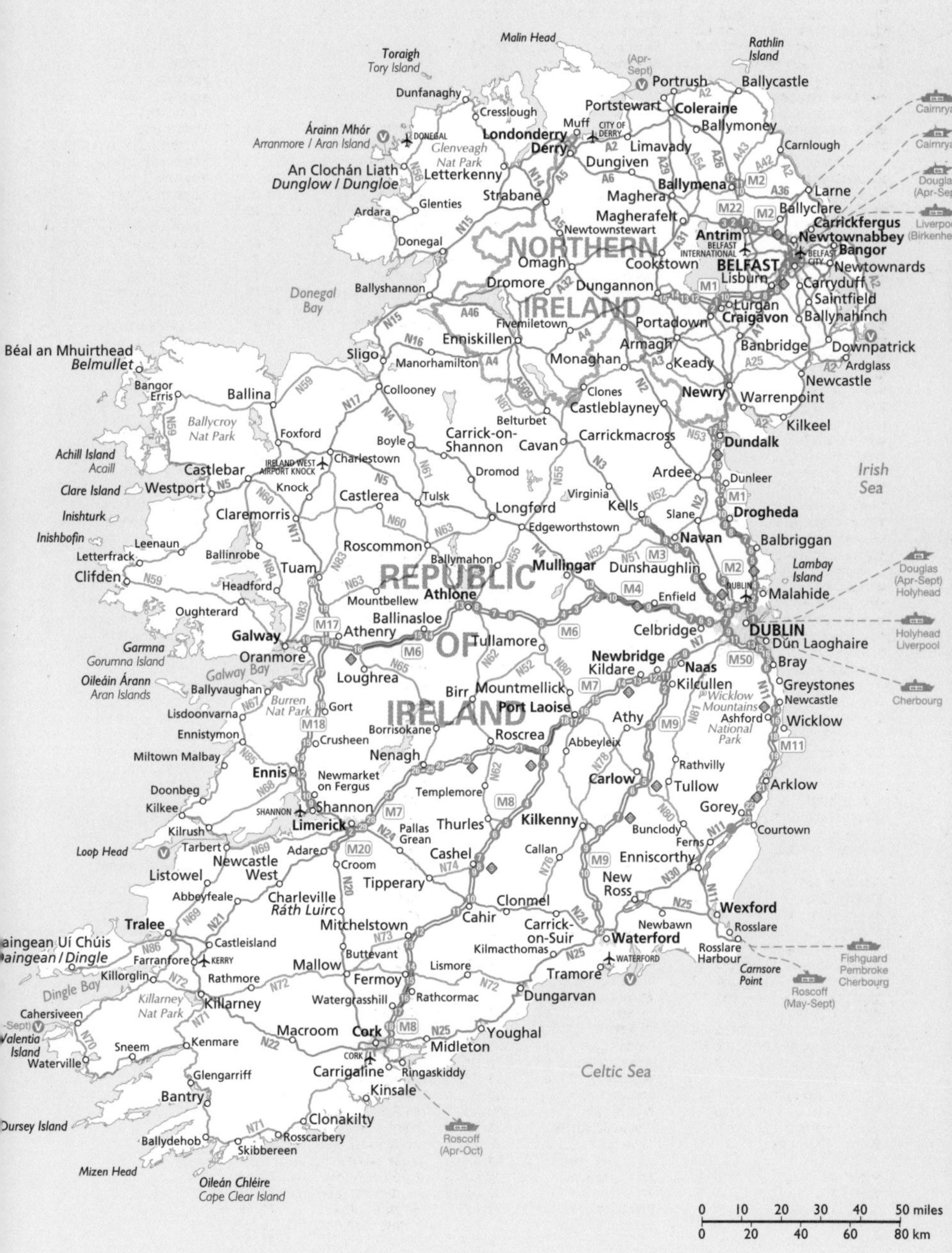

Malin Head
Toraigh
Tory Island
Rathlin
Island
(Apr-
Sept)
Portrush
Ballycastle
Dunfanaghy
Cresslough
Portstewart
Coleraine
Ballymoney
Cairnryan
Árainn Mhór
Arranmore / Aran Island
DONEGAL
Glenveagh
Nat Park
Muff
CITY OF
DERRY
Londonderry
Derry
Limavady
Carnlough
An Clochán Liath
Dunglow / Dungloe
Letterkenny
Dungiven
Douglas
(Apr-Sept)
Ballymena
Larne
Strabane
Maghera
Glenties
Ardara
Magherafelt
Ballyclare
Newtownstewart
Carrickfergus
Liverpool
(Birkenhead)
Antrim
BELFAST
INTERNATIONAL
Newtownabbey
Donegal
BELFAST
CITY
Bangor
NORTHERN
Omagh
Cookstown
BELFAST
Newtownards
Lisburn
Donegal
Bay
Ballyshannon
Dromore
Dungannon
Carryduff
IRELAND
Saintfield
Lurgan
Craigavon
Ballynahinch
Fivemiletown
Portadown
Enniskillen
Armagh
Banbridge
Downpatrick
Béal an Mhuirthead
Belmullet
Sligo
Manorhamilton
Monaghan
Keady
Ardglass
Newcastle
Bangor
Erris
Ballina
Collooney
Clones
Newry
Warrenpoint
Castleblayney
Ballycroy
Nat Park
Belturbet
Kilkeel
Foxford
Boyle
Carrick-on-
Shannon
Cavan
Carrickmacross
Dundalk
Achill Island
Acaill
Castlebar
IRELAND WEST
AIRPORT KNOCK
Charlestown
Dromod
Ardee
Irish
Sea
Dunleer
Clare Island
Westport
Knock
Virginia
Castlerea
Tulsk
Kells
Inishturk
Claremorris
Longford
Slane
Drogheda
Edgeworthstown
Inishbofin
Leenaun
Navan
Balbriggan
Letterfrack
Ballinrobe
Roscommon
Lambay
Island
Tuam
Ballymahon
Mullingar
Dunshaughlin
Clifden
Douglas
(Apr-Sept)
Holyhead
Headford
REPUBLIC
Mountbellew
Athlone
Enfield
Malahide
DUBLIN
Oughterard
Ballinasloe
Galway
Athenry
Celbridge
Holyhead
Liverpool
DUBLIN
Tullamore
Dún Laoghaire
Garmna
Gorumna Island
Oranmore
OF
Newbridge
Kildare
Naas
Bray
Galway Bay
Loughrea
Oileáin Árann
Aran Islands
Ballyvaughan
Mountmellick
Kilcullen
Greystones
Cherbourg
Birr
Wicklow
Mountains
Burren
Nat Park
Port Laoise
Newcastle
Lisdoonvarna
Gort
IRELAND
Athy
Ashford
Wicklow
National
Park
Ennistymon
Borrisokane
Roscrea
Crusheen
Abbeyleix
Miltown Malbay
Nenagh
Rathvilly
Ennis
Carlow
Arklow
Newmarket
on Fergus
Tullow
Doonbeg
Templemore
Kilkee
SHANNON
Shannon
Gorey
Kilkenny
Thurles
Limerick
Pallas
Grean
Bunclody
Courtown
Kilrush
Loop Head
Tarbert
Adare
Cashel
Callan
Ferns
Newcastle
West
Croom
Enniscorthy
Listowel
Tipperary
New
Ross
Abbeyfeale
Charleville
Ráth Luirc
Clonmel
Wexford
Tralee
Cahir
Mitchelstown
Carrick-
on-Suir
Newbawn
Rosslare
Waterford
Castleisland
Kilmacthomas
Rosslare
Harbour
Fishguard
Pembroke
Cherbourg
Farranfore
KERRY
Buttevant
WATERFORD
Carnsore
Point
Killorglin
Mallow
Lismore
Roscoff
(May-Sept)
Rathmore
Fermoy
Tramore
Dingle Bay
Killarney
Nat Park
Killarney
Watergrasshill
Rathcormac
Dungarvan
Cahersiveen
Macroom
Cork
Youghal
Kenmare
Midleton
Sneem
Waterville
CORK
Celtic Sea
Glengarriff
Carrigaline
Ringaskiddy
Bantry
Kinsale
Clonakilty
Roscoff
(Apr-Oct)
Ballydehob
Rosscarbery
Skibbereen
Mizen Head
Oileán Chléire
Cape Clear Island
0 10 20 30 40 50 miles
0 20 40 60 80 km

# Map pages north

Western Isles
Steornabhagh (Stornoway)
232
233
208
Portree
198
188
189
180
170
Islay